ANDREA BRANZI

$E = mc^2$ THE PROJECT IN THE AGE OF RELATIVITY

EDITED BY
ELISA C. CATTANEO

Editor:
Elisa C. Cattaneo

Editorial Coordination:
Elisa C. Cattaneo
Ricardo Devesa

Tailoring of Content:
Elisa C. Cattaneo

Layout:
Elisa C. Cattaneo
Actar Publisher

Translation:
Elisa C. Cattaneo
Stephanie Carwin

Proofreading:
Elisa C. Cattaneo
Pietro Servalli
Debora Vermi

Archive work:
Elisa C. Cattaneo
with:
Studio Andrea Branzi
Francesca Bovalino
Daniele Macchi
and with
Francesca Balena Arista
Marco de Santi
Chiara Fauda Pichet

Funding:
Graham Foundation Grant Program

The completion of this project could not have been possible without the participation and contributions of right owners and without the support of Graham Foundation.

I express my deep sense of gratitude to Francesca Bovalino, Daniele Macchi and Francesca Balena Arista, whose help have contributed immensely to the development on the project.

Contents

Foreword
by Charles Waldheim

> "[...] è il territorio a divenire protagonista privilegiato dell'economia postindustriale, come luogo di elaborazione delle energie deboli e diffuse di una produttività pulviscolare, che bene risponde alla realtà pulviscolare e cangiante dei mercati."
>
> Andrea Branzi, 2006[1]

Andrea Branzi is among the most provocative and prescient urbanists of our era. His work offers a rare line of continuity from the 1960s neo-avant gardes to our contemporary concerns for ecological urbanism and planetary urbanization. Branzi's projects and texts offer fecund forecasts, anticipating the debates of the day in design discourse on the city. Over the past five decades Branzi has consistently authored timely projects that seem to sum up, in one or two images, or a few hundred words, the potential and parameters describing our current cultural predicaments vis a vis the city.

Branzi anticipated our present preoccupations with ecology, geography, territory, and countryside. In his 2006 publication *Modernità debole e diffusa*, Branzi's precise prose describes how the logic of post-industrial capital renders the formerly marginal agricultural hinterland as the central venue, the "privileged protagonist" of the postindustrial era. Branzi's account of the pulverized production of postindustrial economy spread across fertile fields builds upon his longstanding interest in a "weak" urbanization. Branzi articulated the potential for a weak urbanization through projects, photographs, and texts over the past quarter century, based in part on Gianni Vattimo's concept of il pensiero debole, and its reading of postmodern political economy.[2]

1. Andrea Branzi, *Modernità debole e diffusa. Il mondo del progetto all'inizio del XXI secolo*, Milan Skira, 2006; 114. The English language translation of the same year (2006), reads: "It is the territory that becomes the privileged protagonist of the post-industrial economy, acting as a place for working out the weak and diffuse energies of a powder-fine productivity, which perfectly matches the powder-fine and ever-changing reality of the market." Andrea Branzi, *Weak and Diffuse Modernity: The World of Projects at the beginning of the 21st Century*, Milan, Skira, 2006; 114.
2. Gianni Vattimo, P. A. Rovatti. *Il Pensiero Debole*, Milan, Feltrinelli, 1983.

Over the past half century, Branzi has been remarkably consistent in his commitment to the autonomy of the urban project in support of a radically "non-figurative" urbanism. This stance has rendered itself through various media and modes of project-making, yet has remained indelibly legible. Branzi's commitment to a non-figurative urban project links him with a longstanding tradition of progressive urbanists whose alternative urban projects occupied a position of cultural autonomy as a form of resistance to the social conditions and political economy of the contemporary city. This longstanding mode of urban work extends from Ludwig Hilberseimer on the one hand, through Branzi, and more recently to the work of Pier Vittorio Aureli, on the other. Aureli's excellent essay in this volume expands on this minor genealogy, and offers significant insight into Branzi's various formats for work over the past half century.

Born and educated in Florence, Branzi's intellectual formation emerged from within the political and cultural contexts of the 1960s, and a concern for questions of labor and class. Branzi's architectural education was informed by the cultural milieu of student strikes and occupations in support of workers movement "Operaismo." His early projects in this context contributed to the formulation of the Florentine "architettura radicale." His work has consistently described the contemporary mechanisms of urbanization, and reproduced their dominant modes and methods, ad absurdum. Branzi's *progetti urbani* occupy the cultural status of architecture, presuming the autonomy of the project as a medium of cultural and political critique.

Beginning with his contribution to the canonical collaborative *No-Stop City* (1968-71) a half century ago, and continuing through his development of *Agronica* (1993-94) a quarter century ago, Branzi has consistently articulated the underlying conditions shaping processes of urbanization. This line of thought has signified a rhetorical shift from factory to farm as a metaphor for the mechanisms underpinning contemporary political economy and its patterns of urbanization. In this regard, Branzi's projects effectively presaged architectural discourse's transit from architecture to environment and from figure to field. Given this historic trajectory, and its ongoing relevance for contemporary culture, we can expect that this publication will contribute to our understanding of the project of the city, and to Branzi's formulation of it.

THE GRIN WITHOUT A CAT

By Elisa C. Cattaneo

Within international architectural culture, Andrea Branzi is the personality who more than others has been able to generate continuous short-circuits of meaning, and therefore of form, in the world of design.

By continually regenerating the meaning of the discipline, and therefore of the things of the discipline, his output could be defined as an operation of continual re-founding, in which the projects are all prototypes, experiments, and genetic objects with the power of prefiguring and anticipation.

As a theoretical physicist, Branzi produces architectural theorems whose cognitive value comes before that of the discipline and which are configured as explorations rather than speculative operations. As experiments before applied resolutions.

The specificity of his language, which reflects both the dissolution of the well-known discipline and its re-founding, always eludes the direct representation of the subject of the project. In the city, architecture dissolves, and in design it avoids function: it is therefore a kind of research that is deliberately without a center, such as that inaugurated by Ilya Prigogine on the peripheral systems of theoretical physics.

Far from the exhibitionist triumphalism of contemporary architecture, for Branzi the correspondence between the real and the thinking about the real is absolute, and design thought is design in itself, so that every design step becomes a formulation of a theory.
A practice that is exercised by producing, in parallel, writings and works, theoretical equations and drawings, like inseparable elements in the formulation of its poetics.

The investigative spirit that characterizes him founds within the aesthetic a cognitive practice that, by way of theory, leads it to slide from art to gneoseology, toward a theory of authentic knowledge in which design is always proceeding in the search for its task, according to a method that is able to survive even in the absence of the practice of architecture and of architecture in itself, understood in the communal and construction sense.

The continuous search for new foundations will lead him to the definition of universal theories, but not according to a method of only re-founding the discipline, rather a continuous *anthropological re-founding.* A re-founding that advances by rigorously asking questions about the problems of knowing, and that transforms design into a cognitive practice.

This way of proceeding does not have as a method the conceptual and nominal continuity of the things of architecture, but rather, approaching Bachelard's epistemological rupture, inserts itself into conceptual discontinuities, which do not see the project as a corrective, fundamentalist, or perpetualizing instrument in relation to history and to the discipline itself, and from which does it not try to survive. Instead, his method sees in the sense of the problem the true scientific spirit, centering itself on the epistemological limits of the interpretation of the real, and not on factual limits. Eliminating the apodictic character of each a priori concept.

It is in this light that his "theory of the negative" is reinforced, which, as in the case of the ruptures made in the transition toward a non-Newtonian physics, or toward a non-Euclidean geometry, leads to an architecture that negates itself as form and in its foundational presuppositions, redefining itself as a process of imagination of the spatially unexpected: by calling into question the anteriority of architecture, its genesis and its origins, he necessarily recaptures even the endogenous characteristics, which find their own point of reference on the re-founding of their own imaginative origins. But there is no paradigm in Branzi, rather a way of proceeding according to that particular deleuzian "surface effect" that can generate new momentary anthropological realities through form.

This sensibility of his in universal terms, connects him on a level that relativizes the historical-contextual conditions in which he works and that leads him to play in anticipation of them: the de-territorializing process of the image indeed acquires in his work a universal force, so as to shake off the reasons determining the project toward a new non-iconography (*anicografia*).

That is why it is possible to talk about his work as tautologically imaginative.

The research undertaken in this book deals exclusively with the production of Branzi's territories and of his interpretation of the city, and necessarily intercepts several questions relative to the product of design, without the latter being thoroughly explored.

Territories that can not be understood elementally according to scalar conditions, but according to conceptual categories, that is, through spaces that are offered up by reality such that design can act and perform cognitively: in this sense, the city becomes a critical concept capable of overcoming its own image, scale and shape.

Each passage, which selects the main projects of a vast amount of both iconographic and textual output, presents a precise anthropological articulation: from the concept of commodity civilization to that of immateriality, from the concept of the metropolis to that of the anthropological territory, in which the infinitely small and the immensely large coincide, to the point of generating and passing beyond our commonly held concept of the city: objects become a concave, immersive, and extremely vast space, transporting us into the infinitely great. As a "thought of the universe," [1] they enter into the dark thickness of the world and, deciphering it, re-found it through the role of the conceptually and spatially unexpected.

The projects presented therefore include his research beginning from the early stages, based on the crisis of the unity of the discipline, on the breadth of the concept of design, on the rethinking of its categories, in which reality, freed from ideologies and symbols, in which every metaphysical and metaphorical connotation is removed, and is instead interpreted according to a principle of discontinuity as opposed to one of order, gives a glimpse of the negative thought of Cacciari in the first stage, and French post-structuralist philosophy (particularly that of Deleuze and Foucault) in the later one as philosophy intersects with his investigation.

In the first phase of his output, linked to the Archizoom Group, which he founded in 1966 with Gilberto Corretti, Paolo Deganello, and

Massimo Morozzi (the crucial movement of "Radical Design" as coined by Germano Celant in 1971), Branzi advances with the criticism of the precise systems of the Modern Movement and, incubated in the logic of Pop culture, his early works maintain in the background a critical view of systematizing ideologies.

With *No-Stop City*, he definitively negates architecture as crucial *medium* for the construction of urban space, and eliminates the figurative as necessary for the formulation of the project of architecture. By subverting the typical categories of the city, Branzi hypothesizes a space without any distinctive element, but rather as cybernetic and catatonic, totally different from the historical-geographical tradition of the European city, instead bringing it closer to a potential and serial space closely linked to Warhol's silkscreens.

Tending toward the zero degree of urban writing, he works on new formulations in the glossary of design, such as *neutral space, neutral surface*, or potential planes that are able to accommodate the new subjects appearing in consumer society: commodities.

By working continuously on the theme of the city, even in the theoretical metropolises developed in the eighties and nineties, such as *Agronica* and *The Commodity Metropolis*, rooted in the new fuzzy logic and Baumanian liquidity, Branzi represents the new state of a weak and diffuse metropolis: a reversible, evolving, provisional, unstable city that corresponds to a fluid and non-metaphysical society, of which the metropolis is a genetic field of information and objects.

It is only actually the objects that become the glue between the urban parts: representative of a weak metaphysics, his production of industrial design generates the paradox of building spaces without scalable consequentiality, moving from the XS scale of the object to the XL one of the territory, eliminating the historical role of architecture as mediator.

Already in the early collaborations with Memphis and Alchimia, in the works of industrial design he lends wholeness to their theoretical design by transforming the generic (commodity) into a sublime product, in which the hyper-connoted hyper-domesticated object will become the new subject of a city without architecture: the dissolution of disciplinary boundaries indeed leaves room for a design in which de-specialization involves an intentional hybridization of content, continuous etymological overlaps, producing a counter-design as a manifestation of another way of thinking about the end-use product and that finally de-legitimizes the relationship of form-function-ergonomics, freeing a new design force that represents the utmost expressionism of everyday life.

This work of subversion is also directed toward teaching: in 1982, he founds the Domus Academy, the first postgraduate school of design, which reformulates the concept of teaching through the liberation of the individual-student's creativity, thus defining a discipline of design that comes from mass production and creates a new idea of cultured and élite artisanship.

The subsequent phase of output, clearly intersecting with French post-structuralist philosophy (especially the Deleuzian and Foucauldian philosophy), ventures into hybridizations that introduce not only new relationships between opposites but also initiate a process of overlapping and contamination of times and forms. With *Grandi Legni* (2008), he changes the scale of the design object, which becomes an expansive and animistic installation like the anthropological and existential themes represented, accumulating the demons of antiquity and the myths of contemporaneity. The most oneiric and complex compositions appear in *Solid Dreams* (2014), in which objects become monumental iconographies that are put into relation with elements of quotidian banality, merging the sublime and the ordinary in a new idea of "sacralization" of design as a titulary deity, capable of re-founding our concept of the image.

This new expressionism finds itself at work in the current research, which refers to a new dramaturgy of the subject, in its battle between tragedy and normality.

Branzi's recent works, like Quintiliano playing with rhetoric and the constant slippage of meaning, allow for new figurations of the "negative catharsis" of contemporary man and his spaces in which the filter of architecture becomes, as in the case of the *Dolmen*, a transparent wall that only delineates an interior, understood as the interiority of thought coming before that of space. They are therefore new extremisms, fundamentalisms that generate, as Foucault had anticipated in the introduction to *The Order of Things*, or as Borges had made in *The Book of Imaginary Beings*, a new vocabulary to which taxonomy belongs to further future anteriors: events already realized in a time that has not happened yet.

Anticipated by *The Primitive Metropolis*, the heterogeneous and the impossible of Borges connect in Branzi, so that even time becomes elliptical and nonlinear, in which man lives in a single "integrated reality of nature, artifice, rites, myths, technologies, commodities, narratives." And, with time, our idea of image, form, and representation is dismantled.

Recently, Branzi has thus inaugurated a neo-primitive design through the production of newly archetypal *Places* in which design becomes supra-historical and accumulates time in all its canonical dimensions, realizing the Deleuzian Aion: endless and overlying itself, it completes the paradoxical phrase of Nabokov: "The future only makes sense in reverse."

His production, in a continuous short-circuit with respect to architectural research and that never represents anything but the object of design, thus fulfilling what Deleuze had always wanted in the *The Logic of Sense*: the need to eliminate the specifically designated object. And, as Deleuze explains through Carroll, Branzi realizes the cat-free grin in the field of architecture. The designated of another designation that does not make sense to represent through a transparent phenomenology. But only through the falsifying power of the mirror.

ARCHITECTURE AS THEORETICAL PHYSIS

By Elisa C. Cattaneo

PART ONE: RADICAL REALISM

1. Scenarios: Criticism of the Modern Movement

"There exists, then, the fundamental problem of man, which is the cognitive one, intending by a cognitive problem not so much that of the functional or scientific explanation of phenomena, but rather that of their placement within frameworks of meaning."
A. Branzi, Thesis Memorandum, 1966

Andrea Branzi's investigation develops by intertwining different crest points of the architectural discipline, which directly or indirectly determined the construction of the architectural space beginning from the crisis of the Modern.

In the genesis of the critique of the Modern, preceding the formation of the Radical Movement and traceable in the theoretical space belonging to Western culture in the brackets between the last CIAMs (marking the end of the heroic phase)[2] and the post-war phase, the Fifties in particular had already been marked by two distinct positions: on one side, the attempt to retrieve its statutes through a slippage from the concept of space to that of place (on the part of the masters of the Modern themselves and, subsequently, from the historicist position undertaken through its weakening in the Modernist sphere),[3] loosening up the most absolutizing content; on the other, its critical subversion generated by the European avant-garde of the Fifties first and then by the neo-avant-garde architecture of the Sixties, insinuating itself into the fractures of Modern itself, as already framed in that "sense of tension" indicated by Baudelaire and specified by Harvey,[4] by Berman,[5] and later in the Italian sphere by Tafuri.

Following these analytical pathways, the Modern Movement – which we use as a linguistic artifice without investigating the terminological specification of the Modern Movement, Modern Architecture, and Modern Design – is understood in the Sixties as a reference point for an epistemological rupture that brings a profound mutation in the problematic that is cognitive first then applicative of the discipline: in the first case, in the meaning of the *rational* term; In the second, through a critique of the *contextual* positions.[6]

Summarily investigating the crisis of the Modern Movement and its morphology, it could be summarized that it radicalized at the moment when the city becomes the central subject of the design debate. Always and above all oriented toward the object, of architecture or of design, the investigation into the Modern Movement shifts definitively in the 1950s from an architecture-object relationship to an architecture-city relationship.

In his revisiting of Italian criticism, if the positions of Tafuri and Argan[7] see its failure in light of the new class struggle in relation to capitalism, the concept of the Modern is filtered, however, before entering into the Italian debate as introduced by operaismo, through Habermas,[8] who sees it as a physiological transition in different ages; through Pevsner,[9] who with his history of 1936 introduces the concept of "sachlich" (suitable, practical, objective); through Giedion[10] who focuses on moral demands, on technological progress, and on the figurative avant-gardes; and through

Rogers, who by imposing the Italian and modernist necessities speaks of the flexibility of modernity.[11]

For Andrea Branzi, the Modern Movement is identified as a cognitive and interpretive space in addition to being a formal one, to which he responds with a new relationship between design and history, toward a definition of a new contemporaneity that foresees the transition from a clear and defined vision of the world and of the future to a "weak," diffuse, and creatively chaotic one; toward the dissolution of bourgeois culture through a counterculture of the masses and, understanding the Modern in its theoretical entirety, he implements his own cognitive antithesis: rebelling against imitation and against continuity with the models, he frees it from both the line of research that attempts to a *normalization* of tradition and from the historicist one that attempts instead a *localization*, formulating a new aesthetic conscience of design.

In parallel with other research outside of the discipline (one thinks of Joyce's research on language, on the change of the status of music with Glass), his declination of the discipline manifests itself through the research of a new urban form as a site of a new temporary resolution, going beyond the *flatus vocis*.

The antecedents – or the intellectual family to which Branzi indirectly refers to in his period of study – focus in particular on two positions rooted in the criticism of the Modern: the Situationalist movement and the Pop Art of Anglo-Saxon origin.

As signaled by Charles Waldheim,[12] in 1956 in particular, a convergence of facts arises that open a Pandora's box in research on the city in relation to the positions of the Modern: first, the Urban Design conference at Harvard[13] and the Hilberseimer projects for Detroit, to which are added the CIAM of Dubrovnik and radically subversive positions in Europe, such as the exhibition *This is Tomorrow* and the *Alba Congress*.

These analytical lines, one that branches off from the last CIAMs, and the other from the European neo-avant-gardes, mark a first step in the process of the deformation of the dominant systems activated in architecture from the beginning of the century.

Such congresses designate the end or suspension of universalizing theories, orienting toward a return to a less idealized reality – "from the history of the discipline to the history of the real"[14] – it is a new way of thinking about design in relation to the city that takes on a discriminating role, not intending to regain any predetermined genesis in either the stability of the past or in the absolute faith of modern syntheses, because it is no longer relevant to the conditions of contemporary society.

Although Branzi was not aware of the Situationist movement, nor did he come into contact with the protagonists of that movement, he does, nonetheless, intuit in parallel with the French movement that urban practices need a form of liberation that is first social and then spatial.

In parallel with the research of the Radical movement in fact, analyzing the more controversial of the 1956 Congresses, that of Alba, which formalizes the Situationist movement, it is evident that, in this, the critique of the Modern acquires an already radical value, so as to completely overthrow the theoretical foundations and strongly criticize the social and, therefore, the formal contents.

As evaluated by Emanuela Bandini,[15] Situationalist criticism of the modern urban model "found its true field of investigation in the disapproval of the evolution of the form of the city. The project of collective life introduced by rapid functionalist modernization – the economic-administrative reorganization of the city center and the 'deportation' of the inhabitants in those *grands ensembles* that were built on the logical-formal model of the Corbusian unité d'habitation – is the main charge that Letterist International levels against the existing order: the Theory of the Dérive (i.e., "the practice of emotional disorientation enacted through sudden changes in the environment and at the same time a means of study of situational psychology," defined by Debord in the famous 1958 work[16]) and Psychogeography (i.e., the "study of the exact laws and the precise effects of the geographic environment, consciously organized or not, on the emotions and behavior of individuals"[17]) are the practices by which they concretize this experimental criticism; Formulary for A New Urbanism (Pour un urbanisme nouveau[18]) by Ivan Chtcheglov (Gilles Ivain) is instead its theological manifesto."

Overcoming the original/mythical ambiguity between stationary and nomadic city, in fact, with Situationalism a wandering perspective of space is formulated, and the possibility of defining a system of non-structural relations and linking the parts according to new relations of meaning, allowing for a more radical questioning of the concept of urban space in the twentieth century, configured as the aesthetic/creative possibility of solving and changing the situation of the bourgeois and Corbusian cities.[19]

These relations define cities that are unstable and established on an intangible relationship between objects, places, and travelers and, through the theme of the path and the journey, begins a process of liberation of space that is no longer anchored on immutable components, places defined by morphogenetic works of architecture, but rather through multiple directions and vectors of which architectural objects become elements of a trajectory.

Inhabiting the city according to principles no longer of the cave but of the tent, the two original prototypes of the dwelling, thus corresponds initially to two different representations of the construction of space (the first physical, the second metaphorical or symbolic), but also to the possibility of recognizing it as a closed space (for the permanent bourgeois city) or open (for nomadism). No longer standing architecture, but rather a floating space that can free itself from urban morphology, reinterpreted through symbols, psychogeographies, and metaphors, reassignable to what Jammer identifies as primitive spatiality.[20]

This interpretation reveals methods of using of the city that are substantially different from the modern ones, and among these methods, even the perception of time understood as momentariness and circulation becomes dominant.

More precisely, the complex genesis of the Situationist International[21] and its intuitive coinciding with Branzi's spatial research could be identified in three steps: the interpretation of everyday life as ludic time (Lefebvre, Debord)[22]; the idea of design as an aesthetic experiment of permanent revolution (Bréton,[23] Constant); and the possibility of revealing the urban environment through a non-formal and unstructured process (Constant, Debord).

In fact, for both movements (the Radicals and Situationists), in the attempt to define an interrelationship between urban space and social behavior in the transition from *homo economicus* to *homo ludens*, the characteristics of this second principle become generative of new formal expressions: if they generate subversive urban maps for the Situationists, maps of a changing and non-fixative character, whose recognizable places appear to be the result of a "unity of the environment," they become for the Italian Radicals the opportunity to experiment with the first ludic projects that, nonetheless, will be linked to Pop expressionism.

In particular, Branzi also senses, like the Situationist environment, the challenge of canonical representations and, like Lettrism reduced poetry to letters, painting to "multiform painting, the story in a metagraphic fresco, cinema without the image,"[24] the iconographic reduction carries him toward a new concept of creation and interpretation of the real, understood as the fulfillment of all the phenomena of everyday life and that is rebuilt in its entirety through the non-iconographic (*anicografico*) artistic process.

However, if the Situationist research takes on art and politics by attempting a fusion "between Rimbaud's dream and Marx's abstract logic, according to the well-known Breton precept,"[25] and if the Breton example of social transformation through permanent revolution, in particularly from 1957 to 1961, acts on the aesthetic dimension of research, the Archizoom group will not bring themselves closer to the sociological approach of Henri Lefebvre, instead reversing the criticism of the capitalist path underway in modern consumer society.

The two objectives that Archizoom will pursue will be rather the desire to transform society through an aesthetics in which "the marvelous is united with the everyday, bringing art into life, giving it a revolutionary subject."[26]

Running its course in a limited time, beginning in 1962 the Situationist International dissolves with the great social and political crisis of the 1960s. The Radical Movement then begins when Situationism ceases to exist: that is, when it explicitly identifies its own limits, which is that of working in reality in ideological terms. The fundamental difference in the Radicals' research is in fact to be found precisely in the capacity for acceptance and transfiguration of reality as it presents itself, without a critical or value judgment, but as a pure element on which one can act with art.

But it is particularly in the figure of Constant that Branzi reveals a clear process of parallelism: "It is in absolute realism that classical modernity began to collapse, due to its inability to govern the complexity that it itself induced. Constant warns [...] that the relationship between city and architecture is entering into crisis, which is interrupting that organic continuity on which modern design was founded: the traditional relationships were about to explode and a state of fundamental incompatibility (or conflict) between a part and the whole was opening up [...]. The political thickness underpinning *New Babylon* constitutes, however, an element of absolute novelty with respect to the avant-garde of the post-WWII period, above all with respect to its Archigram peers, and introduces important elements not for the social solutions it proposes, but for the analysis that Constant formulates on urban phenomenon: he is the first to see the contemporary city as a completely original phenomenon, which no longer has any kind of either structural or functional continuity with the historic city. The city has become a totally ungovernable, formally dissociated, ever-evolving organism because of the unpredictable drives of what Constant calls mass creativity [...]. From this is derived the theoretical premises [...] of the Italian Radicals who, despite not fully knowing his work, will soon have come to the same theoretical conclusions. In Constant's proposals, elements of that radical realism that characterized a whole generation appear."[27]

It is therefore the interpretation of the urban phenomenon according to a radical realism that allows Constant to make the epistemological leap with respect to the reasoning of design, and will allow Branzi to pass over the local reasons and Italian politics toward a new non-iconography (anicografia).

As a result, Constant brings together both the undermining of the preceding conditions on the city (in its being conceived, interpreted, and designed) and a new language in urban design: its machines, moving steel ribs, ferrying toward the first megastructural hypotheses and toward the first projects of the Italian Radicals.

This clarifies Branzi's own position in relation to Constant's research and to the theme of the megastructure, reversing its common reading: "The megastructures present in Constant (and also present in the work of Yona Friedman soon thereafter, and in Archizoom's *No-Stop City*) are in fact a hybrid between a building and a neighborhood, that is, between a work of architecture and a piece of a city: as such, they do not correspond, as it is believed, to a hyperdimension of architecture, but exactly the opposite: and that is to say to an architecture that is progressively absorbed by the city, which loses its traditional dimension to become a sort of new urban tectonics. The utopia of *New Babylon*, precisely because it was never realized, it was placed at the origin of a wider movement that, beginning way back in the Sixties, was the most vital element in the renewal of European architecture. All of Constant's work was for a long time little known and appreciated perhaps because of its limited political objective, because he remained beyond the watershed of Pop Art. He remained thus external (and extraneous) at that overturning that Pop represented precisely with respect to Constant's hopes, because it proved that the revolution was not happening through socialism, but through its very opposite: the market."[28]

In the megastructural hypotheses of the avant-garde of the Sixties, in fact, precisely because they are contaminated by Pop's irruption, the theory and the city will be proposed as images, as a ruthless representation of the reality of consumption, far from any metaphysical symbolism or anything ideologically driven.

In fact, 1956 crosses over with another exhibition, *This is Tomorrow*, which allows the irruption of Pop Art[29] and its subsequent transfiguration into the architectural field.

Branzi confirms his position of radical realism even during his years of training, in particular from '64 to '67, with the interest for the diffusion on a vast scale of this new architectural avant-garde of Anglo-Saxon origin, together with that of experiments of the Austrian avant-garde. In particular, for the former, the "celebration of the present" becomes a lucid definition of a concept that will influence the first formation of Archizoom.

This is Tomorrow, the multi-faceted exhibition that opened on August 8, 1956,[30] at the Whitechapel Art Gallery in London, focused on Marshall McLuhan's theoretical positions on the link between means of communication and society and celebrating the Independent Group's research,[31] begins the clearance and acceptance of the consumer society as a state of fact, accepting its iconographic and theoretical form, and conveys, through the figure of Lawrence Alloway, a link between English and American Pop Art.[32]

As an art of rupture, paving the way to a new mass media-consumerism-iconography relationship, Pop Art has the merit of having played a part in Branzi's training not only as an iconographic device, but as an art of liberation from positivist ideologies and of importing irony as a critical category within design, without extrojecting it towards society, thus demystifying the project itself in the narrow sense and in a broader sense, endowing it with the ethical/ameliorative ideals linked to bourgeois culture.

In the first stage of production, Andrea Branzi and the Archizoom group are affected by at least three conditions in Pop culture: the first, British experiments on supergraphics and acknowledgment of reality as a non-ideological or non-ideologizable matter of fact (*Superarchitettura*); the second, in the relationship with the Archigram group and their self-deprecating humor as the critical criterion of positioning the architect as a figure within the bourgeois society – in a more general sense – and within the discipline (*Discorsi per Immagini*); the third, through the interpretation of American seriality as defined by Warhol's silkscreens (*No Stop-City*).

In particular, the first phase of the connection to Pop culture is influential because it gives rise to the formation of the Archizoom group both in terms of content and self-naming, in the use of the hard and the soft as design elements (where the former represents megastructures and the latter the interchangeability of the elements), Archigram and later Archizoom realize the happy utopia of facilities, of comfort, of mobile cells that offer maximum freedom to an individual immersed in media and colors. In the work on television images, on advertising signs, on a city that moves in a form that not utopian but ludic, they lose the Debordian *pathos*, emphasizing the ephemeral rather than social value. And with this begins the turn toward the possibility of developing an idea of a city that is neither alternative nor tautological with respect to the modern and bourgeois one.

Defining a glossary free from any scientific dogmatism in the magazine *Archigram* (founded in '61) and articles appearing in *Architectural Design* (Theo Crosby was its editor from 1953 to 1962), a cybernetic future appears, one that is able to be ironic and to expand an urban condition of colors and mutations, anti-ideological, and devoid of any reference to the consolidated city, which becomes an energetic charge for the functioning of a city that moves.

Intensifying the provocation aspect rather than that of necessity, as Banham said in his commentary in the text on Archigram: "Archigram is a sort of theory, long on draughtmanship and craftmanship [...]. They are in the image of business and they have been blessed with the power to create some of the most compelling images of our time,"[33] lending themselves to a new theoretical enunciation for the theme of the urban as well, for Archizoom this comes from the third issue of the magazine Archigram in 1963: "The logic of consumption and the prompting of the most advanced industrial technologies merge with the aesthetics of expendability to attempt yet another solution to the problems of the capitalist city at the level of organizing building and adaptation systems, more prophesied than actually studied, in the building sector of production and consumption of industrial neocapitalism."[34]

This new anthropology, represented by the Archigram group, will initially be taken up by Branzi as an attempt to render intelligible the reality of the new metropolitan condition: that of the object.

Among the first to intercept the figurative system of Pop in Italy was in fact Ettore Sottsass, Jr., who in an essay published in *Domus* in 1965,[35] conveys it as a new language anchored in the real, a counterpoint to modernist design and revival as expressed in Italian culture, importing "totally new possibilities" for the figurative system.

But it was Adolfo Natalini, a member of the Superstudio group, training as a painter beginning in 1958 and joining the School of Pistoia, as it was defined by Cesare Vivaldi, through the frequenting of Paolozzi in London in the 1960s, who imports both the content and the forms.

These first transitions of content from the world of architecture and art are united with the experimentation of Cedric Price between 1957 and 1961, the XIII Trienniale on Leisure Time directed by Eco and Gregotti,[36] the introduction of the First Italian Piper[37]: all of the experiments that attempt to make a clearing for a new cultural system alongside that of the youth, which will soon become a major reference point for generations of young Europeans and North Americans: that of the Beat Generation, which will convey American pop culture, imported into Italy via the Venice Biennale of 1964 and 1966,[38] which definitively shift the view on pictorial and artistic research from Europe to the United States, confirming the role of a "critical agent" within the production of iconography.

Yet the emergence of new figurative phenomena is not only intertwined with Pop culture: already beginning in the late Fifties, several operators in the art world can be found that expand the figurative role of the discipline towards a behavioral one, expressing the unease of design both in terms of the general social contexts and in relation to those directly formal ones.

In addition to the concomitant formation of Minimal Art, Pop Art, the Fluxus movement, and the Italian experimentation by Pino Pascali, Manzoni, etc....in the architectural field, in alignment with these theoretical and linguistic experiments, a proto-radical dimension, even if often of a visionary nature, could be intertwined in the utopia of Fuller's and Otto's megastructures, in the research by Christo and Oldenburg in New York from 1967 onward, in Japanese Metabolism, and in Yona Friedman.

However, it was Viennese culture in particular that influenced the formation of the Italian Radicals, which, although varied in its exponents (in particular Pichler, Hollein, Terzic, Lesak, Peinter, Missing Link, and Himmelblau), renews the distancing from the Modern Movement and the refusal of the discipline's orthodoxy, ideologically anchoring itself in Hollein's *Manifesto of Absolute Architecture* and in the Pichler's exhibition *Architektur* (especially with the *Compact City* of 1963), in 1962 and 1963,[39] respectively. For these leading exponents of the Viennese avant-garde in the Sixties, together with Hundertwasser, Kiesler and Sedlmayr, their research extends the transdisciplinary dimension of the project, demystifying it, portraying it through hybridized techniques: writings, performances, installations. But, going beyond the question of the synthesis of the arts, they re-examine design as the possibility of a significant change in reality and expand its field of action with respect to the traditional one.

As Hollein clarifies: "The limited and traditional definitions of architecture and its means have lost a great deal of their validity today. Our commitment is to the environment as a whole, and to all the means that determine it. On TV as in the art world, from the means of transport to clothing, the telephone as well as lodging. The expansion of the human environment and means of determining the environment far exceeds that of the built. Today, 'practically' everything can be architecture: 'Architecture' is one of these means."[40]

The archaic relationship between man and nature, which conceives design as a paradoxical archaeology, will lead this avant-garde to the definition of new archetypes interwoven with the oneiric, capable of pervading and introjecting both the materials of the present and the more mystery-based ones, for which "the present observed as probable future archeology acquires profound meanings: the tomb of the golf player, the necropolis, with a minuscule, maniacal graphic combines to form a counterposition to artificial natural chaos an apparent natural one."[41]

The Viennese proto-radicalism, however, remains an isolated experience until 1956, that is, until – through the dissemination of the magazines – the first details about the avant-garde phenomena of the 1950 begin to circulate.[42]

The experience of the colossal and irony-inflected projects such as those of Hollein, Oldenburg, and Vostell, will introduce an experimental phase for Archizoom as well, and even though Superstudio is the most indebted to this current from the other side of the Alps, in the photomontage phase even Branzi will momentarily take up the figurative charge.

2. Scenarios: *Operaismo* and the *Negative Thought*

The realistic approach is seen in Branzi's research by also re-reading his output in relation to the Italian contexts within which it is formed.
In addition to the international phenomena, which is actually phenomena of a more artistic-discipline nature, two typical Italian aspects can also be placed in this context: the first, the relationship between intellectuals and Operaismo (understood as a new class structure); the second, the School of Florence.

With regard to Operaismo,[43] its relationship with the crisis of unity of the (modern) project, and the identification of the city (and no longer of architecture) as a new urban subject, it is worth mentioning, as done in-depth by Pier Vittorio Aureli, that "the fundamental task of the intellectual groups of the left in the late Fifties and early Sixties had to confront was rebuilding a rigorous theoretical approach to the political reality of the class struggle and the workers' movement."[44]

This new political thought, "which introduces the proletarianization of the entire society, the rejection of social-democratic reformism, the weakening of Marxism and the positive and alternative utopias in favor of a realistic acceptance of a system that develops in solely quantitative terms, takes hold in Italy and France through the theoretical work of a number of magazines: *Socialisme ou Barbarie* (1948-67)[45] and *Quaderni Rossi* (1961-66),[46] founded and directed by Raniero Panzieri, around which the first nucleus of activists and operaismo intellectuals is formed."[47] To these can be added *Classe Operaia* (1964-68),[48] founded by Mario Tronti in 1964, and others of a more intellectual aspect, such as *Potere Operaio* (1969-1973)[49] and, above all, *Contropiano* (1968-1971),[50] directed by Massimo Cacciari, Asor Rosa and Toni Negri, and on which Mario Tronti, Nicola Licciardello and Francesco Dal Co will contribute to the conversation.

Most of the Italian neo-avant-gardes have shared, in different ways and levels of participation, the militant attitude of Operaismo as filtered through these channels of communication.

The adhesion and centrality of Tronti's position for left-wing intellectuals, and in particular for Archizoom, is two-fold: with respect to the position of Fortini or Panzieri, Tronti both focuses the attention on the real, that is, on the possibility of dissolving dialectics and the oppositions between Capital and Operaismo, implementing an "inside and against" strategy[51] so that the various subjects – such as intellectuals, workers, politicians – become part of the complexity of society, and liberates Operaismo and intellectual action from all ideology: his affirmation, "The Classe operaia [worker class], a pure pagan race, that only wants more money and less work,"[52] in fact frees Operaismo from any kind of ontological harassment or from any ontological shift or one in the permanence of values.

It will be above all this liberating nihilism that will loosen up the thought of intellectuals from a more orthodox Marxism, and that will manifest itself for Archizoom in a total emancipation from ideological thought. A position that will reflect the approach coined by Archizoom with the *No-Stop City*.

The question of the real, the abandonment of ideological and utopian ideologies,[53] the role of an active intellectual within the new society of capital but liberated from ideological legacies, the integration of the arts into the production cycle, become the central themes of the Italian debate: the resulting placement of design as a structure carries the intellectual work entirely into the capitalist cycle, so as to trigger the debate on the autonomy of the discipline with respect to its contingent co-participation. A line of thought that will involve both the Radical Movement and the research by Aldo Rossi.

As Asor Rosa describes: "On one side, against that architectural thought which, proposing itself as an ideology and instrument of civil coexistence, is in reality offered as a secular arm of the capitalist sphere; on the other, against that architectural thought which, starting from certain sectors of urban proletarian organization [...], elaborates an 'alternative ideology,' this as well wholly subordinated to the guiding principles of capitalist development."[54]

Branzi places himself in close proximity to the Marxian ideas of Tronti, as they are conveyed in *Contropiano* by Tafuri, and it is exactly within this cultural framework that the thinking on design is renewed, in particular by anchoring itself to the dialectics of the negative as defined by Cacciari and linked to the Trontian position both in action within Capital and in the destruction of the dialectical-metaphysical legacy typical of nineteenth-century and bourgeois culture.

The "school of suspicion,"[55] as defined by Ricœur and identifiable in the positions of Marx, Nietzsche, and Freud, "unmasking" the ideology underlying culture and consciousness, is specified in Cacciari not through a substitution of ideologies, but through the possibility of dissolving both the dialectical thought underlying them and the metaphysical ideology that structured Western philosophy.

Defining the concept of *Krisis* as an ineliminable condition of contemporaneity and as an anti-metaphysical category, this is indeed how he expresses it: "The crisis is not a moment, like it was for the neoclassicists. The crisis is constantly performing *Wille Zur Macht*, and to the extent that this is repeated, it will never reach, like the Schopenhauerian ascent, an endpoint, a perfect synthesis, the crisis will be the becoming itself, irremedially."[56]

If, in fact, dialectical thought "coincides with the historical forms of bourgeois political culture, rethought and reestablished in the light of idealism"[57] and crisis has become a permanent concept, the dialectics of the negative make possible a mode of action from within (like how Tronti operated in Capitalism), through the instrument of the creativity of the subject, no longer an external observer of reality, but confuting the "legitimacy of the deontological implication" of things.

Cacciari's position, defined as "creative Marxism," comes to be translated into the art world to the point that the Sixties were a decade of "announced deaths," not intended in a nihilist sense, but as a new way of thinking about art.

As Branzi points out: "The Gruppo 63 theorized the death of literature and the novel; Manfredo Tafuri spoke of the death of architecture; Carmelo Bene and the Living Theater worked toward the death of the theater; the anarchist movements claimed the death of politics [...]. These extreme end-of-life diagnoses did not correspond to the disappearance of art, literature, architecture, theater, or politics, but were rather signs of irreversible transformations between the old and the new [...]. In this framework of the liberation of institutional politics and specialized categories of culture, our 'exaggerated' generation proposed a design approach independent of any client and any social function, as an individual creative process, liberated from those behavioral frames [...]. A new common pantheism was generated, one that broke open the closed circles within which everything had so far been carried out. The destructive thrust of the new avant-gardes served as a liberating reestablishing of the way of understanding and developing the natural creative inclinations of each individual, outside the programmed productive function. This was thus not a utopia, but a presage of a profound change that the capitalist system was undergoing: transforming society into a multitude of free creative consumers, where the freedom of the individual was identified with the liberality of the entire system."[58]

Thus, Cacciari with Tronti together with the radical avant-gardes, through the definition of Crisis as a permanent state, the formation of a negative thinking capable of generating the dissolution of the legacies of metaphysical and bourgeois dialectical thinking, Marxist creativity as a possibility of action within the real, usher in a season of non-nihilistic deaths, reformulated by Branzi in his glossary of the period, focusing on a redefinition of elements without substitutions or reconstructions of the paradigms of the past (*Dissolution of objects, the city, labor*, etc....). The end of art, understood in this positive sense, is therefore one of the conditions in which Branzi's work will configure itself.

If philosophically such a death is defined in the transition in Nietzsche and before him, in Hegel and Heidegger, the death of art will completely come to fruition in the *Postmodern Condition*, as defined by Lyotard, and coinciding with the end of meta-narratives. In particular, "The aestheticization of contemporaneity aligns with that list of metaphors from the signification of the negative that seek to identify the ways in which art has attempted to redefine its mimetic state, "de-definition of art" (Harold Rosenberg), "the dematerialization of the art object" (Lucy Lippard), the "aesthetics of disappearance" (Paul Virilio), "the disappearance of art" (Jean Baudrillard), "art in a gaseous state" (Yves Michaud), "the philosophical disenfranchisement of art" (Arthur Danto). The internal unease in the arts, an all-around unease that permeates every dimension (mimetic and technical, social and political), is the reaching of a new awareness [...]: art problematically abdicates its exclusive role of producing the aesthetic or more precisely its role of narrating beauty through its own operating [...]. In the immense anthropomorphic projection of industrial modernity, art loses its epicenter: an ever-growing image among images, increasingly less 'beautiful' among the possible and accessible instances of 'beauty.'"[59]

It is in terms of the entirety of this debate that Tafuri's positions were further clarified in relation to the question of Operaismo/Capitalism, which shifts the general question of this relation onto the crisis of the Modern and onto the city as a new critical category for design.

In particular, Tafuri will express his views in three texts: "La città Territorio,"[60] "Per una Critica all'Ideologia architettonica,"[61] *Progetto e Utopia*.[62]

Contropiano hosts four essays, later conveyed and partially modified in *Progetto e Utopia*: "Per una critica dell'ideologia architettonica" in No. 1 of 1969; "Lavoro intellettuale e sviluppo capitalistico," in No. 2 of 1970; "Socialdemocrazia e città nella Repubblica di Weimar," in No. 1, 1971;"AustroMarxismo e città. Das Rote Wien," in No. 2, 1971.

Embracing the general themes of the end of the dialectics of 19th-century origin, of "destiny" as a bourgeois principle that gave a form to the "associative" life of the city, Tafuri already clarifies in "La Città Territorio" the breadth of the debate at stake for architecture: "Because it entails not simply an updating of the tools of intervention and investigation, but rather the identification of a whole series of new issues, and more than that, of the relationships between them: that assume the characteristics of a real structural plot, constituting the backbone of new realities."[63]

The relationship between history and capitalist development, as a criterion for judging the observing of reality in general and of the city specifically, in such a way to lead him to affirm: "Capitalist development is the condition in which the Western world has come to be shaped as it is: that is, not so much or only a mode of production in the hands of one social class (the bourgeoisie) at the expense of another (the proletariat) – and therefore not only the antagonist, the enemy of the latter – but also the formidable birthplace of everything that we know,"[64] produces first and foremost a precise position with respect to the critique of bourgeois ideology and, subsequently, to the role that the intellectual (Cacciari's creative subject) needs to play in this context.[65]

In this general framework, the critique by Tafuri takes shape, both toward the Modern, interpreted in terms of the discipline as a crisis of the architectural object, as well as toward the theme of the city in relation to the role of architecture, meaning the city as a determinative critical category of design understood as a political structure.[66]

In addition to the change in scale,[67] a delicate and poorly resolved issue in modern design, this transition involves changing the parameters that determine the city as a category within a structural vision.

Indeed, the convergence between architectural activity and the political dimension undoubtedly leads to the loss of a dual role for design with Tafuri: both the organizing agentive object within the city and in its development – concomitantly with its presumed tautology – and its autonomy, but it introduces the paradox of the Tafurian position itself: ideologically pushing architecture into the process of politics, thus into a new structural process.

Tafuri "deconstructs" architectural and design ideology, placing it in the contradiction of the metropolis and capital without it having a tautological, reformist, utopian, or dialectical value (and in this direction, the critique of architecture becomes a critique of ideology, "avoiding all the means of entering into progressive discussions with techniques of rationalization of the contradictions of capital"[68]); he eliminates the question of the form (and therefore of the superstructure and autonomy) of architecture in the narrow sense and within the city, which becomes a process of production (evident in his criticism of Austro-Marxist urbanism and the Hof as an absolute form, understood as "critical interruptions that never succeed in becoming a game of transformation of the real"); he puts the determinative issue of the designer as an active actor in reality backs into the center (implementing a battle in the images "exemplified in the critical examples of the Weimar Republic and in Red Vienna before the Anschluss, to the Karl Marx Hof by Karl Ehn," and in Italy in the positions of the Radicals); he eliminates the question of "language" in architectural practice for the benefit of a realistic dimension of the project[69]; but the rooting in politics will remain as a critical criterion for the value of architectural activity.

Despite the fact that the Tafuri-Dal Co thread finds that "the acquisition of contingency leads to the acceptance of the instruments and modes of operation of contingency itself," they will remain linked, paradoxically, to an ideological view of contingency that is understood in terms of political purpose, without being able to break the connection between the *reasons* for architecture and its *design*. And, above all, in the mistake of linking design back to a structure.

In this sense, this clarifies and sheds light on the diatribe with Archizoom[70]: the debate, all focused on the dialectic with the real, becomes a crucial dimension of the Italian exchange, but if the Tafurian thread is centered only on the political-social relationship, the Radical Movement leads it to a massive and effective epistemological leap. Acting within the dialectical, Archizoom finds in it a conceptual way to pierce it, dislodging design from the ideology in which Italian critics are still entangled, even though they might have understood the importance of the complexity and of the abandonment of the ideological approach.

The work of Archizoom and the Italian Radicals in fact not only speeds up the process of "aging" and sterilization of the Modern and of ideology in design, but also of the Italian debate *on* the Modern and the convergence between design and the political structure, of which the Modern, in a sense, became the specious subject.

On the international scene, the Modern was in fact already historicized, then analyzed as a deciphered phenomenon by a number of authors: Bruno Zevi with *A History of Modern Architecture* in 1950; Giedion is translated into Italian in 1954, Pevsner in 1959, Benevolo published in 1960.[71] The debate introduced by Tafuri at the end of the Sixties already sees a decade-long delay, and will drag along for the next decade. Tafuri, carrying and resolving the crisis of the Modern with the reasoning of the Italian historical epiphenomenon, hybridizes the times and terms of criticism, generating an Italian delay that is still active and agentive: actually shifting the value of design solely through the political question amplified the typical Italian training that has an analytical and intellectual basis in relation to design, thus voiding the role of design quality, hence superstructural, in the strict sense.

The intellectuals' responses to this debate, especially with respect to the subject of design, will usher in the two most interesting currents of the time, the Radical and Tendenza movements, that will respond in opposing ways and two-fold to the question of design itself in relation to the city, to reality, and to politics: if Archizoom will indeed connect design with the new urban subject, generating a city wholly centered on the reception of commodities, Rossi will reconsider architecture as an element that can respond to urban issues, through a reading of the identity of works of architecture that make up the city. The Rossian "monemes," stable and typologizable, counterbalance the punctual and variable ones of the *No-Stop City*, the non-figurative one that has made it possible to get out of the rhetoric of the renewal of tradition and of filiation as a useful and legitimate concept for design.

Yet, independent of the convergences and differences with Tafuri, the initial debate generated by *Contropiano* and in particular Tronti's thinking, will definitively influence the formation of the Florentine group, thanks above all to the figure of Claudio Greppi who, in his dissertation in 1965, began experimenting with the relationship between industrialized territory and design, taking a first step toward the idea of a powdery and a-hierarchical urbanization, in which reality and its autonomous transfiguration began to coincide with a free image.

3. Contexts: Florence/The Florentine School and the Thesis. Pop Hybridization

In addition to the assumptions that directly and indirectly influence the forming of Branzi's poetics in the landscape of international and national debate, a second genetic nucleus appears, more linked to the author' s biography, which explains his training, yet already coinciding with the production of works: the Florentine context.

Branzi expresses it thus: "Paradoxically, Florence has revealed itself over time to be a city capable of generating cultural movements that were fed from its own substantial extraneity from both the classical and modern traditions: a sort of neutral laboratory that made it possible to 'invent' both a new classicism and a new modernity."[72]

Despite a general conservative background of historical revivalism,[73] during the Fifties in Florence transdisciplinary relationships began to intertwine amid a political background of change, introduced by rather controversial figures, if viewed from an orthodox point of view, as much as they were interesting from the intellectual perspective: the mayor Mario Fabiani of the PC first of all and, above all, beginning in 1951, Giorgio La Pira who, as a Dominican Tertiary, professor of Roman Law and founder of the *Colloqui del Mediterraneo* (*Mediterranean Conversations*),[74] brings a figure of a nonconformist Catholic, realizing a first reformist desire within Italian religious culture.

Without going into the debate that would involve other figures of the reformulation of Catholic culture working in the Florentine area (such as Don Milani, Father Balducci, etc.), it is important to note that through these figures in Florence the conceptual freeze that characterized it is cleared out, so much so as to bring this desire for reform into confluence with the cultural actions such as the *Circolo della Cultura*[75] (reopened in 1945) through Tristano di Codignola's initiative, member of the Constituent Assembly and Socialist parliamentarian.

The cultural activism activated by La Pira also reactivates numerous publishing houses: Nuova Italia, Vallecchi, Sansoni, Le Monnier, and Branzi's father's Libreria Editrice Fiorentina.

Parallel to this early political and social activism, the arts see a new relationship with the international avant-garde movements: the *Arte Oggi*[76] movement dedicated to the ethical relationship between artist and society, the *Vita Musicale Contemporanea* Association will create a circulation of artists later merging in Fluxus[77], and the formation of the *Centro Proposte*, inaugurating a close avant-garde relationship between artists of various disciplines in an experimental and processual dimension of design.

To this transdisciplinary circulation, two exhibitions organized in the city can be added: the one never carried out on Wright in 1951 and the one on Le Corbusier at Palazzo Strozzi in 1952, conveying the contents of the Modern Masters.

In this context, the new Italian university occupations were also launched[78]: in 1963 at the Faculty of Sociology of the University of Trento, and later in Milan, Turin, and Rome. The same in Florence, where, however, a review of teaching theories and a new dialogue between students and faculty members was generated.[79]

Adopting from the Italian background the role of the political responsibility of artistic activity, the Lega Studenti Architetti (League of Student Architects) is formed in Florence, through the initiative of Claudio Greppi, Paola Jervis, Paolo Donati, and Giovanni Francovich, to which belong from the beginning, among others, Massimo Morozzi, Paolo Deganello, Gilberto Corretti, and Andrea Branzi,[80] imprinted politically on the first Quaderni Rossi and Classe Operaia at a later time.

This student activism leads to a rethinking, at least in Florence, of the teaching formulas (thanks to the presence of Leonardo Benevolo, Leonardo Ricci, and Leonardo Savioli, but also of Umberto Eco, Ludovico Quaroni, Adalberto Libera, and Giovanni Koenig), which changes direction both with respect to the general tendency of continuity with regard to the Modern and historicism, and with respect to the Tendenza movement that is being formed in Milanese-Venetian circles, focusing on experimentation as expressed by the European avant-gardes. Some of the young students will later, recomposed, form the Radicals.

Even if in substantially different terms, three professors will influence Branzi's education and, conversely, the young Branzi's output will be recognized by those instructors: Benevolo, fresh off the publication of the two volumes of *The History of Modern Architecture*, initiated a rethinking of the relationship between architecture and social evolution; Ricci, importing, thanks to his stay in the United States, an experimentation with the multidisciplinarity of design and its role as an agent of experiments; Savioli, a new transdisciplinary relationship between painting, sculpture, and architecture.

Changing the domination of the courses (Integrated Urbanism, Visual Design, and Theoretical Urbanism are a few of them), the academic content begins to hybridize with the new mass culture iconographies, as imported from England and Vienna in particular, definitively departing from the Croce-based aesthetics dominant within universities.

The enrollment of those making up the Radical movement at the faculty of Architecture of Florence occurs roughly in the same years: Andrea Branzi and Gilberto Corretti in 1960, Paolo Deganello, Massimo Morozzi, Adolfo Natalini and Toraldo di Francia, and Giampiero Frassinelli in 1959, Alessandro Magris in 1961, and Lucia Morozzi and Dario Bartolini in 1963. It is a period that also sees, within the Faculty, the presence of future founders of the 9999, UFO, and Zziggurat groups.

In this cultural environment, a critical review of design and of the city begins at the Faculty, initially interpreted in megastructural tones: Deganello, Chiappi, and Marliani propose, for the '62-'63 academic year, the project for an *Urban Structure for 70,000 Inhabitants* in Brozzi, or a *Città Operaia*.[81]

The first work to signal a marked distance from the functionalism of the Modern Movement is immediately followed the next academic year (1963-64) by another project that inaugurates a new design and teaching experiment: drafted by Branzi with Toraldo di Francia, Corretti, Morozzi, Navai, Pastorini, and Spagna, which encompasses various academic courses, such as the course of Architectural Composition I taught by Cardini, that of Urbanism II by Detti, that of the Art of Gardens by Savioli, and that of Interior Design by Ricci, the first group project preserved at the Centre Pompidou is born, called *La Città Estrusa* (*The Extruded City*).

The theme is that of the design of the new headquarters of the Faculty of Architecture in Florence, in the Sesto Fiorentino plain.

Still starting from the revisiting of predetermined plans, hybridizing formal interpretations with extra-disciplinary concepts, a macrostructure comes to be proposed.[82]

The subject of design[83] was in fact concerned with the placement of a machine containing services for industry, and already indicated a first intention of a figurative restitution of the socioeconomic conditions of the Florence-Pistoia area: literally extruding the elements of the mechanism of production by uniting in an urban macrostructure the idea of an industrial machine of Anglo-Saxon origin, the monumental historicism of Kahn, and the rhetoric of allegory or, as Gargiani explains, of "Architecture that speaks" from the Enlightenment mold, *La Città Estrusa* is represented and described in a theoretical text In the form of an epistle written by Branzi with the pseudonym Aulo Rufio, entitled *De re Geometrica* or *Libro degli Ambasciatori* (*The Book of Ambassadors*).[84]

Accompanied by Branzi's comic strips, *La Città Estrusa* was the first attempt made to reconcile what had always been irreconcilable: all of the characteristics of the productive city in a single urban phenomenon, in a language contaminated by megastructural monumentalism and by Pop Art as the chosen code for the representation of the real.

The megastructural idea is constantly interwoven with the design of the second half of the twentieth century: from Le Corbusier's *Plan Obus* (1931) to Hans Hollein's 1964 aircraft carrier, to the American brutalism of Paul Rudolph, to Price's technical expertise, to Japanese metabolism, up to the positions of Archigram. But to these interpretations can also be added the supra-historical dimension of Louis Kahn and the idea of monumentalism, which will become crucial to the design of Archizoom's *Discorsi per Immagini* and, in a permanent way, for the visions of Superstudio's *Monumento Continuo* that will continuously develop the theme of giganticism in their own research, making it absolute and carrying it out in the concept of *Supersuperficie*.

While remaining in the field of the imagination, *La Città Estrusa* demonstrates their knowledge of both the international and Italian debates, which are cited through the contamination with French Enlightenment thought, as will be continued by Rossi.

Prior to moving on to environmental projects such as those on the Pipers[85] and subsequently to the immersive space of exhibitions on *Superarchitettura*, the projects of the future Radicals are therefore monumental machines, which will have an impact up to the 1967 *Competition for the Fortezza da Basso* in Florence.

But if the academic experiments are still influenced by megastructures and by an emphatic formulation of the image, it is with his own Thesis[86] that Branzi definitively introduces the transition to Pop culture: permanently archiving the theme of the techno-morphism, he definitively orients himself towards leisure culture represented in an anti-ideological way.

The dissertation plan, which is structured as a "triptych" – with the parallel exhibitions of Paolo Deganello (*Osservatorio Astronomico. Attrezzatura Adatta a ricerche Solari, in Campo Ottico, Radioastronomia e Ricezione Satelliti*)[87] and Gilberto Corretti (*Parco pubblico Territoriale delle Cascine di Prato, con Individuazione e Progettazione di Unità Ricreative e Culturali*, then transformed into *Attrezzatura per il Tempo Libero alle Cascine di Poggio a Caiano*) – is intended to depict the plain of Prato, the central theme of several ongoing discussions given the advanced industrialization of the site.

The subject matter developed in the three theses deals with the theme of leisure time in relation to the city according to the phenomena of the city itself: "Three distinct moments have been roughly identified, the subject of three separate theses arising from a common cultural premise and need. 1: Leisure time in historic centers: as the utilization and recovery of old structures destined generically as urban monuments, through the introduction of autonomous internal organisms. 2: Leisure time in the countryside, such as placing a substantially useless object within a landscape; an object that would be, however, capable of giving the landscape itself a hierarchy of interpretation and a useful signification. 3: Leisure time on the periphery, the subject of this current investigation, in the sense of an urban intervention capable of placing itself as a unit in an unqualified fabric with the potential of restructuring it."[88]

Rooted in "bowellism" as studied by Banham and in Price's *Fun Palace*, and represented in line with Lichtenstein's graphics, the dissertation is used as a pretext for some more general considerations regarding the discipline and the city: distancing itself from the progressive considerations of time (more linked to a left-wing ideology that found its habitat in the social centers), it is in fact a primary method for reconfiguring a new prototype of the city and of design, of which leisure time is considered the ultimate goal.

This is how Branzi expresses himself in *Casabella* in "Tempo Morto" (Dead Time): "Before talking about structures for leisure time, let's analyze the idea of leisure time for society today, or what it should be, or whether it is having a certain special meaning, and therefore if leisure time ultimately needs to exist. The concept of leisure time was created as the negative of working: it is the time it advances [...]. Such a vision of time that flows that we occupy with work and freely at controlled intervals dates back to the idea of absolute time expressed by Newton [...]: an idea that has already been replaced by that of relative time [...]. This is what physics says [...]. The social forces in power draw broadly from scientific and philosophical thought to build their own infrastructures [...]. Its time, its availability for humans is quantified and divided into elementary units of measurement."[89]

Under the surface, Branzi seems to be comparing leisure time to an equation, one in which the relationship between leisure time and work comes to be reset. By refusing to work, one already sees the possibility of recovering individual creative productivity that can dissolve the cultural and binary dimension that had characterized and continued to characterize urban research.

The criticism underlying the XII Triennale di Milano (which takes on the same theme in 1964) thus begins with a relativization of the very concept of time, which is dissociated from Newtonian linearity in order to relativize itself in Einsteinian quantum theory (also included in the title), and from the relation connected to design emerge a series of considerations: first of all, the problem of leisure time is that of the consumption of the city: "Understanding leisure time as a moment of the overall form of the city [...]. At this point, however, the need to comprehensively introduce the problem of the city arises, going beyond the boundaries of historical criticism and sociology, and trying to understand it as the site of a particular kind of knowledge through practice."[90]

In search of a "comprehensive structural law" that makes it possible to address the irregular characteristics of the city in a single phenomenon, the components of the dissertation are quantum, exactly like in theoretical physics: they are conceptual "leaps" that do not allow for any dialectical principle within design, which replaces the thesis-antithesis-synthesis relationship with a practice of design through conceptual and methodological discontinuities that are capable of demystifying the city as a whole.

Getting away from the "syncretism and eclecticism" that would lead to a juxtapositional relationship of design with the historical dimensions of the city and the homogenization of the various components that belong to the contemporary city, it is the artificiality underlying the free market that solicits the artificiality of the designed product, bypassing architecture in the strict sense. Getting away from a typological or morphological response, Branzi makes architecture disappear into a "celibate mechanism" capable of resolving all the heterogeneous issues that besiege the city.

Its spatial configuration in fact represents the ludic functions that fill the general cubic prism from which both inflatable volumes and air ducts emerge, all to induce a behavior before a form: as an undifferentiated figure, the central volume allows absorption within it of all the other social components.

Juxtaposed in the form of a bricolage, and therefore free of a hierarchical definition of the parts, design avoids stylistic unity, amplifies randomness as a subjective design criterion, and the use of color, a component that recalls Anglo-Saxon Pop, allows the artificiality of the gesture to stand out, enhancing the role of architecture as an aestheticization of the everyday, that is, as an element that can only be understood within a defined cultural framework: in this sense, Branzi surpasses the purely aesthetic dimension, considering design as an art of consumption.

4. The Genesis of the Florentine Radicals

The genesis of the Florentine group of Radicals has a symbolic beginning date of November 4, 1966: the Arno flood triggers a new idea of the city – a vision of the land and the urban surface areas – that are capable of not only giving a new face to tragedy by transfiguring it, but also of producing a vision of the world that can be modified through new continuous and liquid forms: a neutral, superficial, and non-distinctive space.

As the first collective experience, in 1966, whithin Pop culture, although postponed by the same flood, the *Superarchitettura* exhibition at the Jolly Gallery in Pistoia[91] had its opening.

Focusing on the definition of a new theory of architecture (*Super*) and on the definition of a new language capable of totally dissolving every historical-formal reference from both a conceptual and an implementational standpoint, the prefix reappears in the output of the 1960s after Gio Ponti had created the *Superleggera* in 1957, Sottsass the *Superbo*, underlining the tendency of design to overcome its technical and formal limits. A prefix that already indicates the particular desire for "exaggeration" that Branzi identifies as the adjective-bearer of the Radical generation: an exaggeration of contents, an explosion of forms, a decisive critique of academic production. Exaggeration thus as a controlled willingness to overcome each and every cultural and formal construction in favor of a design that highlights the exasperated needs and features of consumer society.

Building upon the culture of North American production, the manifesto thus states: "Superarchitecture is the architecture of super-production, of super-consumption, of superconduction, of superconsumption, of the supermarket, of the superman, and of super-unleaded gasoline. It is an exhibition of 'Archizoom' and 'Superstudio.[92]' And, expressing its assumptions, Archizoom relates it in *Relazione Moda* this way: "The civilization of consumption' has changed the 'law of development' to the point that 'the product offering' precedes demand; it is now creating the 'figure of a super-consumer' thanks to the new industry of formal models."[93]

In Pistoia, in addition to the new design objects, the dissertations of Branzi and of Morozzi (the *Cultural Center in the Castello dell'Imperatore in Prato*) are shown, that of Corretti (*Teatro Serra in Poggio a Caiano*) and, immersed in the path of the wave, the visitor is not called on to use the products, but rather to dive into a space similar to the one experienced in the academic Pipers and in Branzi's dissertation, getting into the Pop machine designed during the same year.

Their anti-functional, non-ergonomic designs that are aesthetically bulky in form and color give rise to a decisive breakthrough for the history of industrial design, so much so as to be considered prototypes of a Counter-Design that will be more fully realized by Branzi in subsequent experiences.

In a setting similar to that of the Anglo-Saxon Pop rooms, Archizoom and Superstudio replicate the title of the Pistoia exhibition in the one in Modena, while differentiating the contents, from March 19 to April 12, 1967 in the gallery of the Town Hall's Cultural Hall where their academic projects are exhibited.

This is how they express themselves in the Manifesto: "The myths of society take shape in the images that society produces. The new objects are at once things and images of things: the dream-car is a car and the projection of a car. The new monument is the image of the monument. The accumulation of visual data conditions the new urban scene and through its shock power creates the consumer from it. The hidden persuader is the sorcerer apprentice: what do you know about the duplicator of images? The use of the familiar lexicon of popular-spectacular-industrial figures does not imply a new vocabulary but a critical consciousness and a state of receptivity capable of accommodating all the new demands. The overcoming of conventions and the creation of temporary patterns of behavior occur through the direct relationship with the totality of urban conditions, with current events and the news. A new set of implications that includes irony as a form of criticism is present in the proposed objects. Beyond an architecture of monuments, we invent mechanisms capable of producing images, we invent prototypes, we organize their production, consumption, and consumption inducement. Let's build a consumer. *Superarchitettura* accepts the logic of production and consumption and exerts a demystifying action upon it. It is an architecture of images with a strong charge of imageability, thus capable of evoking rigorous images and of inspiring behaviors, thus capable of inducing its own consumption. It is an architecture with the subversive charge of advertising, but even more effective because it inserts images charged with intentionality into a 'grand design' and into the reality of the city with all its permanence and its history [...]. The adherence to the world of images and the certainty of the ingeniousness of their communicative power through the 'grand design' form the basis of our present work and the overcoming of these limited positions."[94]

Thus begins some specific work on the image as an element of self-interest of both design and as a feature in the practice of a new intellectual.

Along these lines, the relationship with the European avant-gardes of that time is affirmed, among which, as anticipated, the Viennese proto-avant-gardes, the Situationists, but hybridized in sculpture, experimental photography, conceptual art, figurative arts, and, above all, in Pop iconography. All of it reinterpreted through the lens of "consumer goods": without having any final aim, spontaneous cultural phenomena are radicalized through images, closely in line with the expansion of culture and mass creativity as defined by Branzi as the ultimate goal of the research of the avant-garde.

Parallel to the principles of the Pistoia exhibition, the heterogeneous positions, named the Radical Movement, begin to evolve, as formulated by Germano Celant in *Casabella* in 1971: Ugo La Pietra in Milan; Archizoom Associati, Superstudio, UFO, 9999, Zziggurat, Remo Buti, Gianni Pettena, Ettore Sottsass Jr. in Florence; Almerico De Angelis and Riccardo Dalisi in Naples; the Cavart Group in Padua; Strum, Studio 65, and the Libidarch Group in Turin.

To which can also be added, successively and fitting within a post-Radical framework, the projects of Gaia Scienza, Creatività di Massa, Dressing Design, Design Primario, Progetto Decorativo, Design Banale, Nuova Scena Teatrale, Nuovo Artigianato, Nuove Arti Applicate, Anti Farm.

As Colomina explains,[95] the dissemination of their research and affiliations takes place primarily through magazines, or rather, through the publication of manifesto-texts in the principal magazines and the production of new ones expressive of the counterculture in progress: in Italy through *Domus* and *Casabella* (under Mendini's direction from 1970 to 1976), *IN* and *INpiù* (Ugo La Pietra, from 1971 to 1973 for the former, from 1973 to 1975 for the latter); *Marcatrè* by Gruppo 63 (1963–1970). At an international level, they are linked to the *Archigram* (1970–1975); *Utopie* by Jean Aubert and Paul Jungmann; *Bau: Schrift für Architektur und Städtebau* by Hans Hollein; *Architectural Design* by Robin Middleton.

Intersecting with the dissemination of the printed matter, the Radical groups will encounter one another, albeit in different groupings, at five main events: the first, *Utopia and/or Revolution*, in Turin in 1968; the second, in the XIV Triennale di Milano on the *Great Number* also in 1968 (where Archizoom will present the *Centro di Cospirazione Eclettica/Center for Eclectic Conspiracy*); the third, the MoMA exhibition, *Italy: The New Domestic Landscape*, in 1972; the fourth, with the experience of *Global Tools* in 1973; and the fifth, through the exhibition *Contemporanea* in Rome, in 1973.[96]

While working in distinct urban areas, everyone has the common desire to theorize a new design method that can surpass the efforts of the first avant-garde groups (accused of self-interest and unable to bring art and life together in the same alternative process to bourgeois culture), through a rethinking of the city as a privileged focus of experimentation: at the same time avoiding the resolution of its contradictions, the Italian avant-garde movement is posited as an interrogation and contradiction itself within the mutations of contemporary society.

The terms of the discourse are that of reestablishing architecture as a cognitive movement before being one of design, rooted in the criticism of the Modern and of the new formulation of a architect-subject far removed from any commonly held stereotype. And within this position, nullifying every reference to culture, to morality, to history, and to tradition as legitimizing phenomena of the process of thinking and therefore of form.

The goal is that of an extensive and individual creativity, in which all individuals are called upon to build another world of values, of perceptions, of figures, of ways of living, totally free from any social and cultural conditioning.

The principal common criteria can therefore be identified, in general terms, in the interpretation of architecture as a discipline of discontinuity with culture, which can be implemented through strategies for the dissolution of architecture itself and of the formulation of new interpretative categories of reality; the method is that of a new non-technical intellectual figure; the goal is one of liberating a society of individual creators.

The process generated is a complete short-circuit with respect to the confirmed paradigms of the discipline: eliminating architecture as a spatial mediator, eliminating its historical-geographic genesis, contextualism and, in their glossary, to point out the critical distance they effect, they work toward the destruction of the object (understood as the element that designates and solves the urban form) and they eliminate the city (understood in its morpho-typological, structural, and historical characteristics). Inaugurating a vocabulary whose lemma is found in *neutral surfaces*, *neutral spaces*, *gray environments*, etc., in which design is positioned as an instrument of experimentation and not of resolution.

Selecting among the ample experiences of the Radicals those of the greatest intensity and duration, in a literary text similar to a scientific autobiography, Andrea Branzi describes the Movement in his recent book, *Una Generazione Esagerata*[97]: "The Radical movement had an early common incubation period in Pop architecture and in Situationism, as the first phase of clearing out the official constraints of the Modern Movement. Right from our first works, there emerged two very different ways of interpreting the Pop situation: for Superstudio it was the occasion for neo-monumental architecture with a symmetrical structure, with pyramids and zigurats, that recall Joe Tilson's works, but especially those of Louis Kahn. For Archizoom, on the other hand, Oldenburg's urban mega-objects were interpreted in a political sense, as explicit images of a world devoid of values and profoundly 'materialistic.' Kitsch was seen as the result of popular demolition (without reconstruction) of bourgeois culture; indicating that under the apparent Pop carnival there was 'a marble chicken,' the imperialist boulder that does not move and does not eat [...]. Lapo Binazzi's UFOs interpreted the Pop universe as testifying to an urban disintegration that was already underway, which opened up unanticipated spaces to anarchist creativity, such as the ANAS buildings, the Giro d'Italia, and the narrative-sets in the boutiques of Florence. In Milan, Ugo La Pietra created his 'disequilibrating systems' by spreading false environmental information, macrostructures of information, and sociological surveys on the popular idea of the home: the city was just a flow of messages, of people, of events. This was no longer a material reality, but an 'experiential' territory, traversable, indefinite, lacking pre-established functions; a kind of gym where a restless society moved [...]. All this, in my opinion, was not yet Radical Architecture. That had its beginning in 1968, when the different groups were formed and consolidated, each one acquiring a clearer identity. That year, the competition for a seat at the Fiera dell'Artigianato (Artisan Fair) inside the Fortezza del Basso in Florence was launched. It was the occasion of a sort of derby among the Radicals [...]. The path of the two major Radical groups was now set: Archizoom toward *No Stop City*, Superstudio toward the *Monumento Continuo* [...]. What is called Radical Architecture was thus born when the phenomenon of 'radicalism' had already given its first signals in Europe and the United States: a spontaneous movement of a molecular nature, lacking (deliberately) a common programmatic manifesto, a recognizable code, and a possible operational perspective. Now it was necessary to take a step forward and start addressing the great theoretical and political issues in which the Modern Movement had become bogged down.
(...)
Despite the increasing rivalry, if we analyze the work of the Italian Radical group from 1968

onwards, we can see that, in different forms, they all worked around a central polarity. This polarity was made up of the intuition of 'the end of the strategic unity of the Modern Project' that was based on the presumption that there existed a sort of spontaneous harmony between the project and the city, architecture, the universe of objects [...]. In order to compare the divergent lines of work of the major Radical Italian groups, we can identify (by extrapolating from the multiple and contradictory projects) four fundamental polarities that emerged spontaneously from this new reality: the city without architecture (Archizoom); architecture without the city (Superstudio); objects without the city and without architecture (UFO); architects without architecture (Ugo La Pietra and the Situationists)."

The theme of the city, therefore, central as it was to the Italian debate, is still resolved in terms that are distant boundary-wise from each group, just as the deformation of the concept of architecture. Together, they come to be consumed exactly like the object of consumption of pop culture.

If the Radical experience is defined by Germano Celant in 1971,[98] in the attempt to gather these new anti-modern experiences into one phenomenon, Alessandro Mendini, director of *Casabella*, attempts a first historicization in the monographic issue of 1972, "Radical Architecture."[99] He describes it in this way: "When the projects and images, writings and objects of 'Radical Architecture' were being produced, Radical Architecture did not exist. Now that this label exists, Radical Architecture no longer exists; in other words, it was not just yet another movement or school with well-defined homogeneous characteristics, but a series of situations, intentions, and behaviors. The negation of the discipline and the destruction of its specificity were the liberating techniques: irony, provocation, paradox, false syllogism and logical extrapolation, terrorism, mysticism, humanism, and pathos were the categories used from time to time. Continuous shifts, discontinuity, and 'the knight's move' were the driving components."

Celant's "The spiral changes sign" instead identifies in the Radical movement a subversion determined by a cultural production linked to the ideology, myth, designative and "metaphorical-contemplative" will of the project as a step towards an "untitled" output: an output of primary goods because they "explode" all the way to a radical modification. An output in which, in fact, the intellectual does not allow for any distinction between art and life.[100]

But parallel to Celant's point of view, underlining the subversions carried out by Radical Architecture, starting with a two-fold interrogation, namely, what are the prospects of avant-garde architecture in relation to the traditional ones, Branzi responds with the centrality of the role of experimentation[101] rather than that of a solution: the question is always in the present, in the surrounding reality.

For this brief phenomenon – both Superstudio and Archizoom interrupt their collective activities and dissolve in the early 1970s (1978 and '72) – the common features seem to be the subversion of compositional rules in a narrow sense, a cynically positive and scientific vision of the world that is transfigured into urban visions, the elimination of the architectural object in its endogenous compositional features, criticism of the Modern, and the substitution of urban logics with the logic of consumer society.

In terms of its genesis, despite the fact that the date of its foundation is disputed,[102] the group Archizoom Associati forms in September 1966, when Andrea Branzi, Gilberto Corretti, Paolo Deganello, and Massimo Morozzi define themselves as an active collective in Florence (on Via Strozzi), naming themselves according to a visual prompt introduced by Archigram's publication No. 4 (also reproduced in Nos. 5 and 6), published in 1964, in which lightning becomes the symbol of rupturing the serene sky of the Modern city with the introduction of a new image-based culture and of sudden breakthroughs in the realm of architecture. To these will be added the designers Dario and Lucia Bartolini.

Aligning with the anti-modern avant-gardes and maintaining a critically ideological vision of society and the architectural system proposed by the masters of the Modern Movement in the background of their theoretical research, Archizoom reveals its operations in the discipline in the context of an "existential verism" that sets the conditions of development of the territorial model they advanced on the needs of the present.

A long way thus, like the majority of the avant-garde groups of the 1960s, from the attempt to hypothesize an ameliorative urban model, the underlying verism of Archizoom's projects reveals rather the determination to represent the present state of a homogeneous society, oriented by a relativization of epistemological layers of experience, rather close to a quantitative functionalism representative of the state of reality, far removed from the mythical one of the Masters of Modernity.

Reality, therefore, as the material of design, liberated from ideologies and symbols, in support of a theory that nullifies metaphysics and every utopian sublimation, refuses the discipline as the parenthesis of a verified study, which is not subject to the systematizing desires of the general systems, which responds with a spatiality devoid of quality and metaphors, but which corresponds to real-life conditions and synthesizes them in minimal and diagrammatical frameworks. Therefore, not a utopian model or one with a continuity of solutions, but another way of thinking about territory.

The cultural outcome is oriented towards a very high level of abstraction without the second term of the reference, that of the symbol, remaining a direct representation of a will that intellectually returns to an absolute objectivity in its own reading of the phenomena.

The result will manifest itself in a catatonic kind of architecture and territory and therefore correspondence, a correspondence that is real and channeled by the economic laws of the most epidermic layer of society, the layer of actual needs, primary functions, of commodities, of primary space, of diffuse quantity.

In this sense, Andrea Branzi states: "It is not utopia, at least in its classical sense, as it is not attempting to prefigure a better society or a more modern city, but on the contrary, the true utopian terms of reality itself are restored."[103]

But if we were to list the characteristics of action of the Archizoom group, we could identify them in:

1. The genesis of a counterculture,[104] or rather of the "liberation of man from culture,"[105] intending by liberation the removal of formal and moral parameters that act in an inhibitory manner on the subject. By removal of culture, what is meant is a process not of replacing culture itself,[106] with the aim of the removal of work[107] and creativity of the masses;[108]

2. The formation of a scientific discipline that emerges from the categories and paradigms of the city, which has the role of accelerating urban phenomena, and not of resolving them. In this sense, history is eliminated[109] as an acting phenomenon of transformation;

3. The connection between art and reality;[110]

4. The rejection of the established canons of design, through the reduction of the design processes to zero, refusing its objective and avoiding any kind of linguistic renewal (hence endogenous);

5. The removal of the concept of quality and aesthetics for the benefit of quantity and mode of use;[111]

6. The definition of a new figure of architect, who becomes a creator of images embracing the full role of intellectual and non-technical.

The transition is that from a Society to a Civilization, that is, the overcoming of ideology toward a complete cultural system with its own meanings and its own morphology. From which the new subjects are the objects, the only elements capable of working within the new social conditions without attempting a resolution, but rather by experiencing the crisis, without a conciliatory will, by "overturning their usual habits."[112]

5. Glossary. The Destruction of Architecture and the City: Neutral Surfaces and Gray Environments

The destruction of architecture and the city: neutral surfaces and gray environments.

The specification of the "formal" features of Archizoom are initially articulated in line with the idea of counterculture as a cognitive platform of reference, through a process of a conceptual reset in terms of the typical categories of design: the dissolution of architecture (1) the liquefaction of objects (2), the elimination of the city (3), and all of it aimed at the disappearance of the work.

The modes of implementation point toward the definition of the *Neutral Surface* (4) and of *Gray Environments* (5).

Each of these steps, always in light of the formation of another way of conceptualizing space that oversteps the knowledge of the discipline, means, respectively: upending the typical tools of architectural design and the value of architecture as a medium through a new mode of theoretical coding that passes, polemically and ironically, through the image; the dissolution of the typical categories of architectural practice, still linked to an idea of perfect synthesis and of *firmitas,* for which the semantic parceling of an unrecognizable object is substituted. At the same time, the formation of a neutral surface that nullifies any symbolic role of both the designer and the space, allowing the individual creativity of the inhabitants to act; the destruction of the synthetic-visual logic applied to the formation of the city, which is substituted by the idea of liberating urban space in a way that corresponds to the new logic that determines it: the commodity.

The disappearance of work as an end, as already formulated by the Situationists, allows a complete overturning of the system under way: that is, the non-identification between the worker and the production system, which leads to the simulation of the desires of the less well-off toward those of the bourgeoisie. By eliminating work, not only are social hierarchies eliminated, but, above all, the system's ideology is scrapped in its entirety.

With respect to these resets, through *I Discorsi per Immagini*, the dissolution of architecture is explained, centering the research around the urban planning debate in Italy.

Created in the form of photomontage (the Radicals' privileged medium of expression, because it produces reformulations of imagery not rooted in history and geography) in April 1969, and disseminated via *Domus* and *L'Architecture d'aujourd'hui*, I Discorsi per Immagini belongs to a collection of new design positions that Celant was implementing, particularly on American Land Art.[113]

Archizoom's Pop iconographic matrices in this case intertwine with the scalar contamination of Earth Work, whose logic is transported inside the city.[114] (For example, Archizoom's *Aerodynamic City*, which is in dialogue with the American spaces favored for the works of Land Art).

The relationship between the "backgrounds" and the images is paradoxical and deliberately excessive: in New York, a spectacular tower exemplary of its hyperconcentration is repositioned, in Berlin, the replication of the Wall, in Bologna, the center that was about to be emptied in Bologna of its marginal classes is gutted.

The key themes are those of representation of reality in which the noumene and phenomenon have now been identified; the impossibility of integrating architecture and its media value within design practice and within the city; the substitution of quantitative vs. qualitative and aesthetic parameters (architecture becomes larger, out of scale, it grows and shrinks arbitrarily); and a critique of the historical self-placement of architecture. Thus, the elaboration of a process of crafting images focused on the subject of the city and the territory begins, in which the term "discourse" replaces both the written rhetoric of Italian intellectuals and introduces a new way of thinking about narrative: having escaped from the conceptual and scalar scope of the city as traditionally understood, the new discourses are now introduced not only in new global spatialities, but also by using paradox as a privileged narrative tool and the image as a substitute for the text.

The paradox thus (and the game for Superstudio[115]) as the distancing from common sense and the ability to render the status of design dynamic and open to discussion.

For Archizoom, using paradox as a tool has the meaning of calling into question the principles of authority and identity that are defined and considered as eternally valid; of claiming new forms of "improper legitimization" for design; of increasing the level of heterogeneity in formal and cognitive systems, by keeping the field of research perpetually unstable and uncertain; of the branching out of the disjunction of the elements rather than their synthesis; of inserting transitional and unstable passages.

Paradox thus becomes a tool for rethinking, for opening up to a multiplicity of meanings, for defining and re-orienting design towards roads not yet taken, toward the infinite epistemological and formal possibilities that design possesses and foresees.

It is, thus, in a Deleuzian way,[116] "a tangled tale," where sense works with non-sense, capable of defining new degrees of freedom for design and its radical rethinking, where a form is one of the possible manifestations of sense that the rethinking foresees. In this direction, it acquires the meaning of a rethinking of defined identities, of contents believed to be accurate, of immediate, logical, clear steps.

And by overwhelming the dialectical context/project, Archizoom demonstrates how design dynamics and categories have now become disconnected from both a theoretical linear-synthetic method and from a historical-geographic methodology.

For the hypertelia of modern architecture, or the simultaneous relationship of contextualism, orders are substituted that are other than those of contingency. By eliminating the atony of architectural and territorial research, and with it the replicability of the Modern Movement, they reversed, rather, historical contingency in its exasperated and provocative formal outcome.

Radicalizing the transition from a qualitative-aesthetic vision to a quantitative one, architecture becomes in *Discorsi per Immagini* a "right to a service comparable to that which a refrigerator or electronic calculator provides us."[117]

Between 1971 and 1972, Archizoom edits two monographic issues of the magazine *IN*, devoted to the destruction of objects and to the demolition and construction of the city.

In the editorial to the first monograph, *The Destruction of Objects*, Pierpaolo Saporito, then director, invites Archizoom and Superstudio to coordinate "all of the alternative and socially and politically engaged cultural experiences: from the Radical architects to artists, from sociologists to semiologists and critics. Each issue investigated an area of research and decoding in the various systems."[118]

In particular, "*IN* intends to treat certain themes that are of vital importance to the evolution of environmental structures on a monographic level, in particular by investigating the aspects in which the most profound transformation is taking place, aimed at the destruction of existing power structures. These themes will be examined in three issues of the magazine. The topics discussed will be: 1) *The destruction of the object*; 2) *The elimination of the city*; 3) *The disappearance of the work*."

The hypothesis of eliminating formal canonical structures toward a state of design completely free from any conditioning focuses in the first issue – *The Destruction of Objects* – on the progressive criticism of a cultural system that based its identification on the object understood as the iconography of the bourgeois model and, in a sense more related to the discipline, as the precise and reproducible outcome of design in general.

Its liquefaction therefore indicates a criticism of a defined social model, together with the dissolution of the well-known discipline and the elimination of superstructural redundancy to which the object refers. All of this is aimed at making the design product a potential field in which processes of individual creation can flow together.

The transition is therefore that of the design product as an exact synthesis, the pinnacle of a design process that seeks in architecture the identification of a reproducible and global cultural system, to that of transforming the object itself into a neutral environment with variable objects, a space that can be made available to every cultural and formal variation.

Regarding this hypothesis, the following individuals and groups were asked to express their position: Raimund Abraham, Malcolm Allum, Archigram, Franco Basaglia, Jim Burns, Germano Celant, Jacques Famery, Heinz Frank, Haus-Rucker-co, Bau-cooperative Himmelblau, Ugo La Pietra, 9999, Max Peinter, Salz der Erde, Angelo Sordi, Ettore Sottsass Jr., George J. Sowden, and Tommaso Trini. But for Archizoom, this dissolution is doubly linked both to the reasons of the reset of the discipline already expressed in *Discorsi per Immagini* and to the ongoing Italian debate, particularly those focused on the more general crisis of the artistic object in relation to the formation of new lines of thought and experimentation, as suggested in the conference *The Crisis of the Object*, held on November 25, 1968 at the National Institute of Architecture in Rome.

The failure of proto-design, attributable to the logic of the system and attempting to solve design through a simplification of reproducible forms, carries the reasoning, under the surface, to two different definitions of the concept of the *rational*: if on one hand the modern object is reduced to the smallest possible terms because this is defensible through the process of production, that of Archizoom means instead the precise observation – and not design-directed – of the earlier logics preceding production, which do not foresee, because expressive of the social, any reductive or reproducible possibility, neither in terms of interpretation nor in aesthetic terms.

In this framework, the destruction of the object re-identifies the roles of all parties concerned: the designer's escape from his or her therapeutic role in relation to the consumer (thus eliminating the distinction between Culture and cultures), according to a more flexible relationship for which the purpose is that of "generating space," a neutral surface in which multiple and subjective processes of genesis are inserted: a surface capable of accommodating the differentiated, the heterogeneous, the multiple. In this sense, the destruction of objects is "an operation that tends to reduce to zero all of the symbolic communications through which objects are made. To free objects means to free man from significant formal structures that act with their interrelations as formative of his action, conditioning it and repressing it like all moral, cultural, and behavioral structures. Reducing to zero the communication through objects also signifies not intending design to be the supporting structure of the figuration, but only a neutral part, functionally accurate, which aims to clear itself out by providing as many services as possible."[119]

The living space thus becomes an "equipped empty space, that is, a neutral parking lot within which it is possible to operate freely outside of a pre-existing architectural and spatial figuration."[120]

Through images parallel to the text, those terms in the glossary that begin to "take shape" in the theoretical research of the Archizoom are explained: "neutral surface," "surface vs. space," "annulment," "reduction." The images indeed seem to be increasingly more specific in terms of their content, according to the pairs of parallel sequences: on one side, "objects with cuneiform feet and components anchored to walls and ceilings, such as a counter-relief by Tatlin or a Proun by El Lissitzky, and of a suprematist or Bauhaus geometry, at times similar to autism, to mechanical idols such as those of Depero or Oskar Schlemmer and his collaborators at the Bauhaus, or the Bizzarie di varie figure drawn by Gian Battista Bracelli; and those with the appearance of irregularly faceted and polychrome crystal-shaped agglomerations. The first objects invade the center of the rooms, the second ones being depicted in a film sequence showing the progressive liquefaction, on the example of Kaprow's happening, being dissolved into corpuscles and leaving the room empty. Both types of objects take the place of the bulky Trojan Horses, but their configurations have now definitively been freed from the conventional ones of furniture [...] and they allude to the generation of new spaces without specifying them, such as histograms, Planiti or Prouns projected in domestic interiors without a program and a function, without an indication of structure and materials."[121]

In those that follow (No. 8 images), the rooms become "installations," introducing a new way of thinking about the living space that replaces the canonical home. New metropolitan nomads (naked like Debord's *Naked City*) feature artisanal and primary objects by setting up their own spaces that react with the ancestral and the industrial, overlapping the new with the primitive.

The last "rooms" instead define habitats in which several multifunctional design objects can be recognized, always dislocated in space without this acquiring a common order.

The same *détournement* of design culture is specified in the second monographic theme of *IN: Destruction and Reappropriation of the City.*

Already in the titling, both the criticism of the contemporary city and the ongoing investigations into its rethinking are evident, as well as the fact that the second term "reappropriation" does not provide for reconstruction, but replaces the logic of rebuilding (in more of a cultural sense than a formal one) with that individual cultural reappropriation also seen in previous writings. The objective remains the collection of less established positions on the theme of the city, in line with the European avant-garde.[122]

In the first issue edited on the theme (No. 5), still experimenting by means of the paradox, what they propose "is an analytical criterion for the setting up of the city itself, and therefore of destroying the city, given that we remove its episodes from the context in which they are found in order to insert them into another. In fact, the installation must never be an interpretation or a dream, but firm reason that introduces a certain reality to consciousness [...]. The installation is a way of enumerating reality, freeing objects from viscous logic and placing them in a neutral field, according to a homogeneous grid capable of neutralizing any ultimate cultural significance of a material destined for scientific memory."[123]

The contestation of the formal figures that run parallel to the cultural ones already mentioned allows the city to no longer be a place but a "condition": the substitution of the concept of home with that of installation, already identified by the destruction of objects, and the definition of the neutral field come into play in parallel with the contemporary *No-Stop City*, out of which the first locations in the North American area seem to be conceptualized, the most suitable for the experiment of the factory city.

The images parallel to the text indeed seem to confirm their feasibility under specific and "typically" assigned conditions in the field of architecture, in order to underline the change of conceptual and spatial meaning: the more general visions of North America, to which infrastructures of the catatonic city are superimposed, are specified in "urban landscapes" depicting "the residential sector," "the agriculture sector," and the "industry sector." With these drawings, Archizoom seems to confirm the infinite potential of *No-Stop City*, capable of articulating itself in constant modifications and specifications, thanks precisely to the maximum potential of the invented diagram: its maximum synthesis in fact foresees not only the placement in every territorial sphere (and in this they do not voluntarily distinguish urban conditions, thus historically defined, from the natural, thus geographically defined), but also in the precise functional specification. In fact, the different *Paesaggi Urbani* (*Urban Landscapes*) require only primary structures as defined in the *No-Stop* manifesto, and can generate infinite formal variations without the latter being typologically defined. Thus, a variation of a diagram that makes it possible for them to play with continuous spatial configurations and dislocations without the *No-Stop City* feeling the effect of it on a general level.

In a certain sense, this freedom in the specification of architectural and functional "definitions" takes up precisely that aspect of liberation from culture and the new formation of free creation already sought for the individual. Since they were to live off the same process, the form and the subject freely define spatial variables, within a neutral structure, a neutral field, such as that of *No-Stop* could guarantee its effectiveness.

The second text, "La città Amorale" ("The Amoral City"), in *IN* n. 7, of 1972, instead refers back to the criticism occurring with the Tendenza and technological hyper-validation in place. A double controversy, therefore: one linked to the attempt to renew modern language in Italy, and the other to the confidence in the technical in Europe.

Now liberated, Archizoom link the failure of leftist ideology to the ineffectiveness of academic and historic positions that are above all Italian: "In reality the alleged overcoming from the left through an unattainable escape ends up becoming a vicious turn to the right of bourgeois ideology as the autonomy of 'artistic practice' with regard to the objectivity of the relations of production is again reiterated, cultivating in ever more inaccessible greenhouses the privileges of those born under Saturn."[124]

Amorality is thus twofold: on the one hand, an accusation (according to a more bourgeois and common idea of a judgment in terms of values and ideals), on the other is the desirable objective of design (and this is the true paradoxical sense of their text) so that that the quantitative city that could accelerate the use value for its inhabitants could be implemented.

It is also in the same essay in *IN* issue n. 5 that Archizoom recall the disappearance of the work as the aim of this new civilization, exactly as Branzi had evoked in his dissertation. In this sense, they both specify the Debordian debate on leisure time and re-activate the Trontian "refusal of work" theme, which allows the subject to liberate a specific creativity to be developed in a living space that is out of the control of the Existenzminimum.

In terms of general research, the hypothesis of the dissolution of work as the ultimate aim is proposed in three circumstances: at the Rotterdam Kunststichting exhibition, where they will exhibit *Unlimited (or Total) Refraction Boxes* (*Residential Parking, No-Stop Theater, Residential Wood, Living Free-Flat, Competition for the University of Florence*), and the inhabitable closet; at the Seventh Biennial of Paris,[125] they propose them again; at the competition *Intermediate Urban* for Graz, they present the city overlaid by geometric and quantitative coordinates, demonstrating the capacity of the *No-Stop* quantitative system to take in, reset, and re-signify each specific circumstance, by re-signifying the qualitative value for the benefit of a scientific entity, measurable by a "neutral surface," which has now become a specific term for Archizoom's research. This experiment, they write, "is a way of enumerating and cataloging episodes, always varied among them, of the bourgeois city by removing them from their natural localization of exceptions to insert them into a spatial catalogue where all the points are equal and all phenomena are homogeneous. It is a way of rendering the city continuous and no longer the sum total of different spaces and uses, but a neutral plane where events cease to be such so as to become the numbers of their coordinates."[126]

In all three experiences, architecture has disappeared as a medium and, having eliminated architecture, it has to focus on the other two themes: the object that will persist in its fruitful delineation, and the city, which will become the great neutral housing inhabited exclusively by objects.

The loss of architecture's credibility, exemplified by the "unmooring from traditional formal values"[127] that was being developed in the Radicals' research, is fully reflected in the 1972 exhibition, organized by Abet Print and curated by Guido Jannon, *Uso della superficie neutra* (*Use of the Neutral Surface*).

Conceived as a traveling event by Ettore Sottsass, Archizoom Associati, Superstudio, Goerge Sowden, and Clino Trini Castelli are called on to respond to the theme of the "Neutral Surface," thus liberated from any kind of cultural conditioning. The laminate, as it is devoid of traditions, is an experimental material suitable for the search for new perceptual stimuli.

Conceived as new environments, the neutral spaces of the project, meant as resetting both the concept of the modern imprint toward an idea of the surface and as a new zero degree of generic form, become a new theoretical formulation, as described in the publication dedicated to this operation[128]: "The discussion about the "neutral surface" does not contain any message, it does not propose a house of the future, it does not offer dwelling models, or projects. The surface is neutral in the sense that it is free from the historically determined conditioning of any material, which has no constraints or cultural implications, which is therefore fundamentally ahistorical [...]. It was plastic laminate that presented itself as a material and essential tool in this search for new perceptual stimuli capable of interrupting the past discourse of objects and furnishings, from which the user is by definition excluded. Why? Firstly because plastic laminate is an ahistorical material par excellence [...]. Plastic laminate appears here in contemporaneity: pure material, however, not only in the sense of its availability but also of its integrity."[129]

The proposals made by the Archizoom group (*Armadio Abitabile/Inhabitable Closet* and *Contenitore Multifunzionale/Multifunctional Container*) were, however, never realized,[130] but it remains a crucial step for their own definition of anti-industrial design.

As recounted by Castelli in his interview, the projects remained as such because all available funds were shifted to another event of that same year: the exhibition at MoMA in New York, *Italy: The New Domestic Landscape*, curated by Emilio Ambasz and inside of which Abet Laminati sponsored the proposal of Archizoom Associati and the intervention of Ugo La Pietra in the sections of *Macro-environments* and *Micro-environments*.

The occasion of the exhibition on the *Neutral Surface* nonetheless represents a starting point for a major collaboration, the one with Clino Trini Castelli, who writes in the catalogue: "With the development of solid state chemistry and physics, the most advanced technologies, such as microcircuitry, will tend to systematically recapture many objects and components of the environment in which we live into simple, primary – often two-dimensional – geometric configurations, whose formal structure will come to be recognized as basically neutral. These reactive surfaces, capable of reacting to different stimuli producing different effects, if inserted into the environment they will assume generic and undifferentiated formal characteristics. The new formal nature that these surfaces will assume, closely linked to their capacity to receive and emit, will no longer represent an anecdotal description of the environment in which they are placed, but will maintain with that space a new aesthetic relationship."

The text contains the meaning of the particular Primary Design that will then be at the center of Branzi's research.

The last definition in Archizoom's glossary definitively specifies the precedents, through the conception of the *Ambiente Grigio/ Gray Environment*, as proposed at the MoMA exhibition *Italy: The New Domestic Landscape*, from 1972, housed in the garden terrace and in the building's galleries.

Designed by Emilio Ambasz and exhibited from May 23 to September 11, 1972, and divided into three sections, two of which are dedicated to product design[131] with a collection of 180 objects in anthological form and in a bracket of the competition for "design of micro-environments and micro-events,"[132] Archizoom participate in the third session dedicated to the "house environments" of the future.

If, in the first session, a design approach can be distinguished as one producing problem-solving objects, that is capable of formulating solutions to problems of the language and composition of the themes, the second, identifiable and later defined as counter-design, chooses to emphasize the need for a renewal of the general discourse about design itself, just as it occurs for *No-Stop City* and for the Radicals' research on the theme of the city. New conceptual prototypes are therefore set up, in order to define new guidelines for industrial production.

Among the eleven installations exhibited, including those of Gae Aulenti, Mario Bellini, Joe Colombo, Ugo La Pietra, Gaetano Pesce, Alberto Rosselli, Richard Sapper, Ettore Sottsass, Jr., the Sturm Group, Superstudio, Marco Zanuso, and 9999, Ambasz' curatorial set-up defines macro-categories of self-positioning of the different design protagonists in three sessions: the "conformist," the "reformist," and the "contesting" position, in which Archizoom is placed.[133]

As revealed in the full press release of May 26, 1972, the critical position of the curatorial set-up reflects the role of Italian design in its two-fold dimension as a local representative but with an international scope and, in parallel, in relation to the micro-manufacturing industries: "Italy has become a micromodel in which a wide range of possibilities, limitations and critical issues of contemporary design are brought into sharp focus [...] the purpose of this exhibition is therefore not only to report on current developments in Italian design, but to use them as a concrete framework of reference for a number of issues of concern to designers all over the world."[134]

However, the expressions that MoMA uses lead to an under-the-surface reading that reflects on the same terms used by the curator: domestic landscape, environment, micro-landscape, etc. [...] that already constitute new oxymorons and the annulment of canonical categories for industrial production as well: the theme of the house, typically owing to Italy, is demythologized and demystified, for the benefit of objects that no longer need a pre-established and *a priori* system.

Considering that the theme of the home had been the subject of countless exhibitions – from Villa Olmo in 1957, or even before that the Triennales of the 1930s – in the MoMA exhibition the household object and domestic space are freed from their own environment, they self-manage and emancipate themselves from each relationship with their own "context": the home becomes an environment, losing, like architecture, its secular role.

The objects exhibited in the first session, including modular "vitrines"[135] that simulate both a museum display and a virtual store, also indicate their commercial and cultural value.

Archizoom realizes the perfect prototype of what has already been anticipated in the studies on the dissolution of objects and the destruction of the city: a *Ambiente Grigio* (*Gray Environment*) closely aligned with the research already carried out with *Le Stanze vuote e i Gazebo* (*The Empty Rooms and the Gazebos*) of 1968 but, in this case, the term "neutral" does not become a negation, but an active specification and a specific choice of one's own language.

Minimalist in appearance, the *Ambiente Grigio*, moving conceptually from the idea of the room to that of the environment, that is, from the concept of solidity to that of the void, becomes an environmental space in which the creativity of the inhabitant can generate new specific and individual relationships. The space as set up, which eliminates the specific connotations of the room, such as the door (one actually enters from a surface that opens up), highlights that there is not a search for other models or types, but instead the resetting of the type as a voluntary choice toward a surface without qualities but capable of accommodating all the variations of the multiple inhabitants and the multitude of objects that accompany them. In a sense, it is the same concept as the *No-Stop City* that is proposed in terms of a real prototype on a smaller scale: if we consider *No-Stop* as a continuous interior, MoMA's Gray Environment is the design of that interior.

As already mentioned in three texts, which will then be summarized in the catalogue, "Abitare è facile" (*Living is Easy*) "Africa è Vicina" (*Africa Is Close*) "La Gioconda sbarbata" (*The Shaven Gioconda*), written for *Casabella* before '72, with the subtitle "Il ruolo delle avanguardie" (*The Role of the Avant-Gardes*), in which Branzi elaborates on the discontinuity with bourgeois culture and the avant-garde role in, precisely, contemporary practice) the *Ambiente Grigio* approaches well in advance the "sensorial" vision of spaces (which later Branzi will develop as *Sensory Urbanism*): the only presence is a sound rather than music. Florentine musician Giuseppe Chiari, in accordance with a non-defined environment, will in fact replace the music initially requested by Archizoom with a text read by a little girl who describes with wonder the missing objects in the environment.[136]

The object-environment exhibited at MoMA will cause the interest in their production to explode in Europe. Indeed, a number of exhibitions will succeed one another from '72 to '73, such as the *Problèmes du Design Italien* (Maison de la Culture de Grenoble) and *Industrial Design aus Italien* (Museum of the Twentieth Century, Vienna[137]), an exhibition that is accompanied by the debate on "Anti-design" at the roundtable with Koenig, Gregotti, Sottsass, and Hollein.

But at the center of the MoMA exhibition, despite the heterogeneity of the projects, there is the critique of a model of living that will extend beyond the exhibition and that will influence a debate circulated in the magazines – in particular *Casabella* – in which the critical placement of Celant's thinking takes on particular importance (who promotes the Radical Movement from 1969 onward in *Casabella*'s pages), defining *New Design* as a "tautological medium" that can be understood as "an abstract-concrete sign without references to what is real or achievable, but that plays an important role in providing information about the nature and the future of architecture [...]."[138]

The value of the exhibition is indeed even more incisive if still in relation to the current debate in Italy, and it is directly ferried to an encounter with the Tendenza movement, which organizes in a cohesive manner the XV Triennale di Milano of 1973.[139]

The two sections, one led by Aldo Rossi (Architecture) and the second (Design) by Ettore Sottsass, Jr. with Andrea Branzi, show, on the one hand, the position of the Tendenza that is working on a transformation of bourgeois culture and, on the other, the irreversible revolution effected by the Radicals, which can be expressed above all in the realm of product design.

Marking its opening with an homage to Bottoni, Rogers and Schmidt, according to research that revisits the values of Rationalism and the Modern Movement (with works by Le Corbusier, Terragni, and Loos), Rossi's Architecture section is wholly summed up in Cantafora's *Analogue City*: a historical transfiguration characterized by the continuity that consecrates Tendenza as a mediator between Tafuri's guiding lines and the continuity of the Italian academy.

Confirming the crisis of the Triennale already underway starting from the occupation during the XIV edition on the *Great Number* (which involved the new generations in a political dimension but also simultaneous with respect to the coeval protests in the world) considering the Triennale as one of "contestation," for the XV Triennale, or of "Restoration," in relation to the Architecture section directed by Rossi, the radically dialectical positions on architecture or design are clarified, the "ideology of the permanent or temporary, disciplinary or multidisciplinary discourse."[140]

In fact, the Industrial Design section, by upending the criteria of the Architecture section, avoids the laying out of the production, and opens the debate to increasingly large social niches, staging unresolved ambiguities of reality: through a completely black, thus neutral, room, the videos projected by Branzi and Sottsass represent the crises of design, its problems and not its constructed solutions: crises without the possibility of resolution, and in which designers decide to persist. Thus, design also disappears and transforms into a conceptual relationship between environment and individuals.

From this moment on, Branzi will initiate a discussion published in *Casabella* directed by Mendini – the *Radical Notes* – radical positions with respect to the arguments of architecture and product design. Published from 1972 to 1976, like margin notes written in an unpublished text, these writings become programmatic notes both in relation to the contestation of the status of design in Italy and the guidelines regarding the hot issues of this never resolved Italian debate.

PART TWO: NO-STOP CITY. THE LOGICAL RIGORISM

Like the artistic culture of the 1960s, like the emblematic "Warhol silk-screens or the products of Arte Programmata, an infinite organism stretched horizontally, or like a Musilian city without qualities, without monuments, and without history,"[141] the *No-Stop City* is the formulation of elements that are always equal, non-hierarchical, without a center or boundaries, tending to the zero degree of form, which is expressed in the substitution of the built city with a continuous, unlimited, and indefinite plane as a neutral field.

Able to be considered as the first example of conceptual architecture, drawing the combinative possibilities of elements from conceptual art, as happened already in Le Witt, Bell, and Robert Morris, *No-Stop City* accentuates the importance of the category of design in itself, in which design is a critical concept, without function and without aesthetics: it is therefore a discourse on architecture for a "proletarianized society," that is, homogeneous.

Through a diagrammatic representation, which introduces an absolute degree of abstraction in the drawing and manifests the renunciation of any possibility of orientation, hierarchy, and differentiation, Archizoom infinitely extends a spatiality without obstacles, without points of tension.

It is precisely this continuity and homogeneity that define what is initially identified as a "neutral field" and subsequently as a "neutral surface," increasing the degree of the cancelling out of the composite space of architecture.

Calling to mind Barthes and the zero degree of writing, the desire to de-alkalize urban space has in effect the sense of a cancelling out of existing conditions as well as a neutralizing position for the new: "to the rationalism of alienation corresponds a maximum of freedom."[142]

The cancelling out and the distance from history, culture, previous forms, and conditions in the discipline affect the urban form that is neutralized by being defined as multidirectional, non-hierarchical, completely potential, without semantic signs capable of bringing the individual back to any degree of recognizability of the place or time.

Rather, according to an inversion of the parts, neutrality allows for a continuous mutation, a definition of a non-conditioning, but able to be conditioned space, not symbolic but to be brought back to the symbol even if domestic and individual, not marked by the strata of history but inclined to submit to a time that is flexible, changing, and open to continuous changes.[143]

Developed by Archizoom from 1968 to 1971, *No-Stop City* could be rooted in the following theoretical steps: the elimination of ideological ontologies that can be referred to the city (as expressed in the manifesto text in *Casabella*); the transliteration of social discourse into a pure aesthetic concept; the formulation of this aesthetic as a formal reduction (historical, geographical, symbolic) that tends to a zero degree in design writing; the definition of a new compositional synthesis that, through a method of "logical rigorism," leads to a new definition of artistic practice, which has a non-utopian theoretical/conceptual value; the resulting formulation of a meta-project as a new cognitive tool.[144]

Archizoom's city thus marks the ultimate state of a united and synthetic vision of the modern and historic city, replacing it with aseptic visions and cybernetic spaces where mass production logic assumes an iconic value that had neither historical nor cultural precedents.

But, as in conceptual art, the interpretation of reality draws attention instead to a question of method: that is, how the new consumer society can coincide with a new urban formulation that, by iconizing it, transfigures it into an absolute form, in which the unstable, the fast, progress, and the factory come into being as new conforming subjects and become the new reality on which new and other creative processes can be incorporated, but they dissolve, in representation, as pretexts for a discourse on architecture in itself.

If the design response to realism is achieved with the cancelling out of architecture in the city-artifact, starting from the finding that the urban condition is "dependent on the growing and unstoppable demand for habitable surface,"[145] implying "a totally homogeneous urban condition devoid of an overall image,"[146] the innovative nucleus of their intervention, it is not only the intuition of an infinite, continuous and homogeneous city that corresponds to it and is defined exclusively by basic punctiform technologies, but the suspension that the diagram possesses, which accentuates the characteristics of a quantitative universal territorial field.

Turning to the work of Mies,[147] they call on "the reduction of architecture [...] to its technological essence, of the irrepressible impulse toward simplification all the way to the zero-degree reduction of the artistic form, to the structure with a degree of abstraction such that it can contain every function with indifference,"[148] distancing itself from the traditional compositional situation. And, of Mies, they also reclaim the role of technique as a new device that generates continuous and indivisible spaces, with simplification as a point of arrival for the project of architecture.

And, with Mies, Hilberseimer[149]: the connection between design and theory, the formal reduction of architecture and its elimination as a generative fact, the transition from the cell (interior) to the city, will be all contents that Archizoom will carry with them in their city-prototype, in which urban artifacts become conceptual categories.

The breaking point with respect to the previous output and able to be considered as the first step towards *No-Stop City* took place with the *Fortezza da Basso Competition project*,[150] which was held in Florence in 1969, where, for the first time, the concept of neutral space is radicalized. The intransigent rationalism of Archizoom leads them to create an anonymous space quite similar to that of the undefined, anticompositional, amorphous factory, and placed above a historical artifact (signed by Antonio da Sangallo il Giovane), which, symbolically, represents both the entire city and History as an agent of the project. In this sense, besides the ancient-new relationship, the "fortress" is conceptually extensible to the concept of the formal resistance of the city, but also to the conceptually ideal one of historical Italian architecture.[151]

The non-figurative architecture defined through the neutral space will become from this point forward an indispensable term for their glossary: architecture without volume but made of interiors, achievable thanks to artificial technology, corresponding to the iconography of the factory, welcoming any formal or functional variation, and therefore representing the maximum formal flexibility.

Non-figurativity, which will enter into the architectural debate for the first time, thus overturns the canons of typical Western composition in its designative and expressive character, finding itself for the first time deprived of its codes up to the elimination of itself as a self-qualifying object/subject and qualifying urban space, becoming its paradoxical opposite: an inexpressive and anti-compositional space.

But the formal abstraction of the *Fortezza da Basso* and *No-Stop City* do not only represent the maximum potential of the space of production: through a de-territorializing transmigration effectuated with representation, this space coincides with a new idea of architecture and space in itself. The paradox of a commodity always in motion generates the opposite in its design: an abstract and potential city, capable of liberating through a continuous plane not only the entire movement necessary for the commodity to express itself, but to express everything else. Thus a matrix space, repeatable as a new rule without language and without figures, in which the abstraction of the factory type leads to the conception of a new spatial matrix without architecture, a-topical and a-scalar and, above all, universal.

These two seemingly opposed impulses (the hyper-connotation of the commodity as the genesis and generic matrix as an interpretation) lead the reasons that dictate its form to extreme dissolution and lead it to be the city of the utmost power of all the reasons determining a form. By nullifying figurativity, they indeed also nullify the determinant causes that, in a process of re-territorialization, could be transmuted and changed.

In this sense, *No-Stop* becomes not only a theoretical project, but the clearest, most potential and innovative urban prototype expressed in the last century and not yet surpassed, precisely because of the double passage of interpretation of their formal reasons until their nullification: a theoretical prototype that comes out of its own historical conditions to become the city that represents all the existing and potential cities, both contemporary and future. The counter-form becomes, paradoxically, the form of maximum formal freedom, of synthesis but also of every possible specification.[152]

The name, *Residential Park, a city, a social assembly chain*, appears for the first time in *Casabella* nos. 350-51 from 1970.

With Mann's opening in *Royal Highness* and with the quote by Gogol, Archizoom first analyzes the politics of equilibrium between the opposites with respect to Capital and outlines design as an element of action (like an "instrumental utopia," theoretical and not alternative) that is limited and partial, prefiguring the universal reality that loses through art any ideological condition, instead moving toward a theoretical one: interrupting the bond between the city and cultural actions that are upstream of form, freeing the debate on the city from its structures, they overcome the vicious circle that shifts the urban from the "objective" to the "formal" plane and vice versa.

Going beyond the relationship between city and capital, and the categories of the city toward those of art, and once the connection is affirmed between unity and contradiction, between order and chaos as genetic categories of a hybrid equilibrium, in the third part of the text, relating to the metropolis, they reiterate the value of a two-dimensional mesh in which all components are equilibrated with the same degree of freedom. Traffic, as a concept of universality, thus becomes the rational and objective framework of a general urban process, not as a structure of services, but as a figurative and logical framework of the urban phenomenon.

The logic of industrial production and its needs thus becomes universal law, in which the city becomes an assembly chain, or better yet a series, a matrix of social models: *the city as a social assembly chain.*

The city as a social assembly chain is therefore able to restore the greatest number of interconnections within the chain: it becomes the stable structure of social communications, the ensemble of distribution points for electronic information and consumption, in which every dichotomy disappears because the very idea of an ordered and hierarchical city disappears.

The reiteration at the end of the text that, "The aim of modern architecture is the elimination of architecture itself,"[153] refers to the role of typology, which leads one to believe that a synthetic visual relationship with the System is still possible, and is still believed to be functional in fight as an alternative model.

Branzi will take up this content again in the *Radical Notes* as well, especially in *Abitare è Facile*,[154] which will also reiterate the role of the designer as a transformative agent of productive needs in rational values; He will reduce the avant-garde to a language in which the destructive charge becomes an analytic form, rationally unusable and autonomous, where the universality of art becomes the universality of the product that the designer, positioned as an intermediary between the necessities of production and the physical reality of the commodity, tends to transform into elementary data, into simple geometric figures, in order to facilitate its introduction into the machine that must reproduce it.

The only possible re-founding for the designer is therefore placed in the home and the city, but not residing in formally renewed design operations, nor in the uncontrolled push towards a technological approach in the sector, but rather in the "modification of existing relationships between user and reality, between users and inhabitable structures [...]. The end of managed culture and the liberation of work mean exactly that. Recovering the right to the self-identification of one's habitat as a place without coded meanings."

In the text-manifesto published in *Domus* of 1971,[155] images appear less diagrammatic than those of *Casabella*, so as to represent the narrative premises outlined in the previous publication. The *Viewfinders* reveal, from a certain point of view, MoMA's projects: they allow you to "peek" into one of these.

In the thoughts that accompany the article, the first point that is clarified is the definition of the urban phenomenon as the most fragile part of the industrial system. Without being considered an unresolved issue, it is rather interpreted as a historical phenomenon to overcome: it is necessary, therefore, to understand if "capital still faces, like a century ago, the problem of managing its image and its functioning at the level of urban form or if the transformations that have taken place and under way have not transferred its reality to another scale, transforming the concept of the city."[156]

By thus demystifying resolute intentions with respect to the urban phenomenon in relation to the ideology of the city, Archizoom invert and downgrade Capital as an agent of urban form and with it also the naturalistic myth that, looking out, provided for a natural balance between opposites: the artificial is instead the interface, allowing for a deeper penetration into social reality.

Once again, traffic in this sense not only shapes a space without a terminus that corresponds to the new scalar availability of the metropolis, but it guarantees, through its two-dimensional grid, the dovetailing of all non-soluble urban elements: as the most general definition possible, it becomes the objective and figurative framework of urban operations.

By tilting the skyline of the city, from the vertical to the horizontal, Archizoom eliminates vision as a characteristic of bourgeois society and the bourgeois city itself, suppressing the distances between object and subject, where the city represents nothing but a programmed and isotropic plane, in order to represent both production and consumption, which have the same characteristics of continuity and undifferentiation.

The factory and the supermarket as a solution therefore, as new a-scalar models of the city that transforms into a fully equipped parking lot, that is, in the least common denominator in a space that seeks to provide the greatest degree of freedom to the user, inside a figuration with the most potential possible, in which architecture comes to recognize its new destiny.

Introducing the value of the individual, they also introduce the theme of the interior as the only characterizing element of space: an explosion of formal and expressive variables that we observe through windows/viewfinders, new tools of representation of the multiple and differentiated interiors.

Architecture thus becomes an open shell based on quantity and not on the definition of qualitative polarities, but it also envisages "alienation as liberation from every bourgeois tradition [as] a new existential condition that Richard Hamilton and pop culture had overturned as the mature fruit of a radical materialism."[157]

The problem is therefore not that of imagining a more humane and ordered metropolis, but rather that of truly understanding the objective laws that preside over the configuration of the urban-architectural phenomenon, demystifying the complex ideology that accompanies the debate around it and influences its form.

By also specifying the neutral term as that of the neutral surface, with the term surface defined in the *Città Non Discontinua Ed Omogenea* project (*Non-Discontinuous and Homogeneous City*), that is, a plane that loses all the features of architectural space, with these revealing the true meaning of the infinite continuity of the formulated urban territories. Such territories, imposing themselves as planes, thus eliminating any element that can be exceptional or discontinuous with respect to what surrounds it, amplify the concept of neutrality, in order to reveal the substantial nature of the future city: the infinite nature of space, as a representation of the society of now globalized consumption; non-discontinuity, capable of defining the equivalence between the parts and the negation of any compositional hierarchy; homogeneity, understood as quantitative parity and the privation of any objective quality of the elements.[158]

The proposed diagrammatric representation or the value of the prototype represented equally highlights the neutrality of a language that nullifies and resets any linguistic, representative, or subjective aspect of design.

No-Stop City, Diagramma Abitativo Omogeneo_ Ipotesi di un Linguaggio non Figurativo (Homogeneous Habitational Diagram_Hypothesis of Non-Figurative Language), thus radicalizes an idea of empty space without qualities that dominates and defines the urban, and which nullifies any possibility of the differentiation of space, either internal and external, at different scales. As Branzi specifies in *Una Generazione Esagerata* (*An Exaggerated Generation*): "In actuality, even *No-Stop City* was a mental project, a kind of theoretical diagram of an amoral city, of a city without qualities, as Hilberseimer said; yet it constituted an important radical analysis of architectural design and of design, in which we took precisely that rational design whose end we theorized to its extreme consequences, grasping through this the political inability to pursue that guiding thread that united its most radical experiences: 'a kind of architecture that is no longer architecture,' as Hannes Meyer said".

Branzi thus concludes in another way the abstraction process of the Modern Movement, bringing the representation of design – design itself – onto a plane of spatial, temporal, and subjective independence.

By shifting architectural work and avant-garde research toward the intellectual arena of art, *No-Stop City* is therefore a model of total urbanization. For this reason, it is not considered a utopia, but a critical utopia (it comes in fact after the failure of the *Utopia e/o Rivoluzione* (*Utopia and/or Revolution*) conference[159]). It is in fact an obvious manifestation of the crisis of utopia in conjunction with the urban crisis, according to that reversal of trend initiated in 1968 by Rossi.

Unlike other urbanization models (such as those of Soleri, Friedman, Architecture Principle, Metabolism, Hollein, Pichler, Abraham, Archigram, La Pietra), Archizoom's city does not attempt evasions but instead a conciliatory resolution of internal contradictions in the city, in the way that, in the same rootedness to reality, the Italian Radicals of Italy remain in general: Ugo La Pietra inaugurates situationism through disequilibrating systems, the Strum group (Pietro Derossi, Giorgio Ceretti, Carlo Giammarico, Riccardo Rosso, Maurizio Vogliazzo) focuses on the value of the class struggle with *La città intermedia* (*Intermediate City)*; the ZZiggurat group (Giuliano Fiorenzoli, Alberto Breschi, Roberto Pecchioni), with *La città lineare. Proposta di un corridoio urbano* (*Linear City, Proposal for an Urban Corridor*, 1969), seek strategies for a new tourist infrastructure development.[160]

However, only Archizoom and Superstudio will attempt a formulation of total urbanization alternative to the common concept of the city, a global vision and a critical interpretation of the city itself that goes beyond contingent problems toward a new theoretical-formal formulation, while elaborating positions that are far from being similar, indeed, they are opposing. The closeness between the two groups is in fact interrupted in the comparison between *No-Stop City* and the *Monumento Continuo*: where Archizoom uses reality and its structural data as a possibility for a non-representative, "tautologically neutral" city, Superstudio chooses hyper-representation and rhetoric as critical art of re-signification, through a process of elevated ready-mades, with fragments accumulated in mass culture. Precisely through a shift of meaning and through the exacerbation of these fragments, they propagate an attack on the discipline through the collapse of the imagination of the discipline itself.[161]

The two groups thus work in opposing terms: where Superstudio shift the tropes, Archizoom invent a new space. Where there is transliteration for Superstudio, for Archizoom there is the nullification of any known formal reference toward the spatial unknown. In Archizoom, there is also a voluntary de-humanization of architectural design: space resembles, for Branzi, an in vitro experiment of physical-theoretical space, underlining how the processes of the two groups work in opposing ways: Archizoom with invention, Superstudio with interpretation.

If the work of Archizoom, by Branzi in particular, has the power to be a prototype, that of Superstudio is instead that of revealing the maneuvers inherent in interpretation, and it can thus be expressed through *manifesto*, but it will not have the power of the prototype, understood as a new concept of the world and therefore as a new revelation of a new space for the world.

Branzi will also proceed afterward by perfecting the anti-compositive and anti-typological components of the city hypothesized by Archizoom. But as a signifying form, *No-Stop City* already presents Branzi's two design dynamics: the judgment on architecture and its proposition, both understood via the connection between analysis of the real and transfiguration of the real itself.

With *No-Stop City*, transforming the world of observation and knowledge, Branzi's work will proceed both toward the dissolution of the well-known discipline and toward the formulation of other territories.

But already with *No-Stop*, the meta-project that will mark and will be read under the surface in all of its research on territories up until the Nineties, we approach an idea that is able to collect the plankton of goods, meanings, information, and people, which have as an outcome a metropolis that is a large interior, a single air-conditioned and artificially illuminated space. A metropolis that then becomes its opposite: an introverted space, a continuous interior, a "high-tech Amazon."

PART THREE: THE WEAK AND DIFFUSE METROPOLISES OF THE SECOND MODERNITY

The third section of the book gathers together Branzi's territorial and theoretical work from the Eighties, identified as the temporal brackets of the transition from the first modernity to the second, expressed in the production a mass market, in the introduction of information technology and new communication media, in a new imperfect and incomplete post-industrial era, of which Branzi identifies:

1: General cultural settings;
2: Epistemological breaks with respect to the First Modernity;
3: New Conceptual Metropolises;
4: Prototypes, that is, specific Metropolises that can correspond to the general cultural settings, consistent with defined urban theories and within the descriptive frameworks of the conceptualized Metropolises.

The interpretation of the settings is affected, like in the first chapter, by a two-fold tendency: on one side, the more general one of global epistemological changes (*A Strong Century*, *Fuzzy Thinking*, *Liquid Modernity*, *The Man Without Quantities*, *Time and Network*)[162]; on the other, the Italian debate that becomes a specific picture of the phenomena in progress (*Modern, Post-Modern, Millenial*).[163]

The transition that needs to be pointed out is the one from a Mechanical Society to a more elastic one, *languinosa*, capable of interpreting the cultural dynamics in a new way: "If the era of mechanics was the era of noise, of friction, of violent rationality, the era of electronics is the era of silence that expresses an energy similar to that of the moon, which every night raises all the oceans of the world without making any noise."[164]

Analyzing the culture of design and more generally the ethical-political *débâcle* beginning with the French Revolution up until the end of the 20th century, Branzi highlights the crisis of contemporary ideologies and the concomitant entry into a positively post-ideological and post-industrial society, as modern ones have failed because of the complexity of the elements generated by it, dragging along with them the failure of an idea of progress constituted from industrial and subsequently social growth, the failure of the principle of order and the non-fulfillment of "purist prophecy." As a result, rationalism now appears like a rigid code in a fluid contemporaneity.

The observation of the fall of European ideologies from a critical distance inaugurates a season in which even secularism and theology, politics and culture, as disciplines and universal systems decay, and it leads Branzi to codify a transition from a mechanical era, including physical technology and metaphysics, as the perfect and controllable engine of history and the world, to a weak one, as the most effective response to the new virtual and sensorial systems introduced. Within this transitional period, even the avant-garde concept changes, having to confront the long time of an "Eternal Modernity,"[165] and reintroducing it as a permanent stance as opposed to the historical and conflictual one of the 1960s.

The core problematic of this research can be defined as *Theoretical Urbanism*, and it goes back to the reasons for the transformation of industrial society into a post-industrial one: "The factory, victorious, began a new era, tied to long time, to broader and more extended visions [...]. The factory today [Eighties] finds itself in a hyper-industrialized world: all of its ideological tensions, the whole radical burden of the heroic years, during which it claimed the role of a model of a future world, have been quelled. Today, it works not to operate itself and its quantitative logic, but to implement an incommunicable model of well-being, luxury, and new qualities of life. This incommunicable model (and for this reason even stronger) is formed by the Society of Leisure Time, with its artistic-liberating myths, or, from time to time, by the Society of Well-Being, of Consumption, of Services, of Electronics, of the Society Without Work, of Aesthetic Society. But these models are always too absolute and incomplete, uncertain or too specific; above all, these are models that only sociologists (and not all of them) define, while society and industry are completely unaware of them. It is now clear that this society, this system, no longer has any overall model, no developmental direction, no communicable myth to reach [...]. In this transition, from a political economy to a market economy, the project (of both design and architecture) is experiencing a profound transformation. It accepts that it must seek the motives of its existence from within itself [...]. During the years of the mutation (1968-88), of that long turn that has been the transition from industrial to post-industrial society, design has thus moved by searching for itself, its own language, and its role. It had to take a path within new technologies and within art, investigating neighboring territories, gathering the scraps useful to its own survival and regeneration."[166]

With regard to the design dynamics and the crisis of the concept of design as understood by the Modern and its traces, the supporting hypothesis to his research makes it possible to identify, under the surface, the problem of design in exalting the role of architectural object-project and its "fixity," understood as a synthesis of a designation process in which its conceptual methods and forms are absolved.

For Branzi, such a presupposition is not only indicative of a compositional argument, but carries with it broader considerations concerning the relationship between method and design, and is related to a cultural system that, in a bipolar way, on one side is increasingly oriented toward the exaltation of universal forms; on the other, toward a resistance to experimenting with other design processes far removed from the "vertical" and precise method of the idea of *composition*.

Relative to the exploration of the project's problematics, one can trace three main factors that become the prerequisites for his research: the first is the need for an approach that frees itself from the value of designation, synthesized by the architectural object and urban design as an expression of a overall order, considered ineffective for the city's problems. Branzi then breaks with the investigation and the identification of project and object (which also implies project=methodological synthesis, project=design, project=type). Thus, the reflection on the project as a self-referential monad, as "essence," is eliminated for the benefit of transformative scenarios that can proceed using instability as a method and form. He will thus propose a non-designative, potential, virtual, and genetic space that will acquire "relative" and "relational" characteristics, first in the methodological sense, then in ia formal one.

The second, consequential, core problematic is defined as the hypertelia of architecture: the impossibility of decoding the new immaterial realities has oriented design toward a solid hyper-reality that makes it the simulacrum of the real, leading it to produce resistant forms rather than newly interpretative/imaginative ones. The decision to eliminate the "invisible other" from the real, and the category of the virtual from design, but also, in a duplicate manner, from the imagination, compromises not only the transformative capacity of thinking about space, but a new "substance" through an order other than that of the mirroring of contingency onto its logic and its forms, going along with a "transparency" that reintroduces linear/positivist methodological processes.

The third core problematic, which descends from the preceding ones, can be defined as atony, that is, the expression of a monotonous, homogeneous, and mono-logical line that is unable to detect the differences of the events that concatenate in different cities and territories, to find common and shared paradigms. Architecture is therefore a place incapable of entertaining the possibility of configuring itself as a sequence of unstable, receptive, differentiated, and pulviscular conditions. In this sense, the atony is referable to two particular conditions: the first is the linguistic homogenization of modern architecture and its revisions, which is revealed in poles in both lexical and methodological equivalencies. The second, consequential, is the loss of experimentation as a possible strategy for a new epistemological leap in design.

The three summarized problematics indicated thus represent three meanings of a different and consequential reduction, which specify the hypervaluation of the designation as a design principle, where the first exemplifies the need for new methodological conditions that are ultimately freed from precise synthesis parameters; the second is the inability of the architectural object to renounce itself as a problem-solving space; the third, the incapacity to be thought of as a differential and dynamic moment in a new unstable process[167].

1. Scenarios of Weak Modernity

The texts selected in the scenarios section clearly describe the new conditions in place as generative of a global epistemological leap: the transition from a strong century to a weak one; fuzzy thought as genetic of a "languinoso" state; a liquid modernity that can adapt to the flexibility of the existing; the fall of the concept of quality as a category aimed at a universal good; the new conception of time as a virtual and non-linear variable.

The event triggering this process of global rethinking is identified in the fall of the Berlin Wall in 1989, which puts an end to definitive solutions, giving way to an era characterized by the absence of heroism towards a state of normality that is made up of exceptions, through the refusal of global models and of solid and unifying certainties. And that generates the transition, in the world of design, from the historical avant-gardes to the permanent ones.

The weak and diffuse energies of contemporaneity, energies of a political, natural, and computer-based nature, therefore lead to a new social and physical "sloth" in a positive sense, which no longer generates *strong cathedrals* of mechanical logic, but tenuous energies.

Modernity, therefore, first understood as Classical Modernity, becomes, as defined by Bauman, a *Liquid Modernity*,[168] where the adjectivification of liquid possesses a generative sense, as the state of a material without its own form but ductile with respect to the transformations in progress.

The concept of liquefaction is considered by Branzi to be a primitive process typical of the *Second Modernity*, a movement of liberation from the structural nodes of history that is able to dissolve the orthodoxy of the disciplines, breaking up the behavioral structures of repression (in this sense, he embraces the interpretation of William Reich).

Unlike the interpretation of the "liquefaction of solid bodies" of the Communist Party Manifesto,[169] which belongs to the First Modernity and which sought new solidities in an attempt to cope with the new logic of profit, Branzi's liquefaction generates an operational void that, like for Bauman, is filled with the spontaneity of individual behaviors and of local initiatives: "The flexibility of the system is the product and the sediment of the freedom expressed by human agents."[170]

This molecular freedom leads to a new understanding of entrepreneurship and society, conceived as a new spontaneity away from the Political Economy and from the structural vision of politics. It thus comes out of mega-container concepts, which also generated an opposing counterbalance in terms of "exaggeration."

As he describes in *Pomeriggi alla media industria*: "The social landscape that stretches out ahead of us (and of which design is a part) has changed: it is no longer society divided into horizontal bands, by income and class, like up until the Sixties. However, neither is it the lively and experimental society of the Seventies, divided into market segments and consisting of provisional minorities. European society at the threshold of the last decade of the century (and millennium) possesses instead the stable form of a chessboard. Or of a matrix, as the mathematicians would say. A society constituted by a set of stable differences, neither provisional nor experimental, attested to by formal and behavioral styles [...]. The interesting novelty of this 'identity matrix' resides not only in its stability, but in the fact that the individual who acts in this system is free to continuously choose a square, changing their lifestyle depending on the time of day, circumstances, inspiration, or age [...]. This system operates under two conditions: that adhesion to each matrix square does not require moral or ideological participation, and that each box constitutes a permanent, established and tested value. The provisional, the ephemeral, and the experimental are acceptable only if they are presented as an official category, that is, paradoxically stable. Here, then, the majority that is formed is colorful, takes on the characteristics of a sum of so many false minorities, adopts eccentricity as a new common norm. Abnormality is defined as a normal life technique [...]. In this matrix society, design finds a great many difficulties in imposing its historical theorems of great stylistic rigor and of absolute methodological coherence: it also makes it difficult to pass to an experimentalism often lacking in stability and weak in image."[171]

The multiplication and fragmentation of society into molecular positions, and of the economy into individual micro-productions, thus welcomes with them the shift from an idea of society to a polychrome, non-ideological, dimension, as Bauman states, "Ours is a type of individualized, privatized modernity, in which the burden of weaving the tapestry and the responsibility of failure primarily falls on the individual."[172]

It is therefore a new concept of individual freedom that involves the liquefaction of the system.

And, anthropologically, Branzi identifies the counterpart of this new global inhabitant in *The Man without Quantities*: that is, the man who acts and observes the world with the criteria of a past modernity, in dyschrony with a new world that has re-functionalized the city as an object-oriented universe and has generated a new mass entrepreneurship and created a new relational economy.

Man himself also becomes a quantitative process, a new physical, corporeal, and expressive reality capable of generating a mobile landscape of cells carrying diversity, like "horizontal plankton."[173] Branzi therefore begins to shift his attention to a new anthropology, suspended for the time being and then fully expressed with *The Primitive Metropolis*.

Along with the concept of space, contemporaneity also defines a new concept of time: the classical separation between space and time (*Time and Network*[174]) leads us to ask questions, transversally in the texts, on three issues: on the general characteristics of the concept of time in the contemporary world; on the value it assumes in relation to the debate on historical/contextual memory/identity; on the particular character that time assumes in creating a project.

As is the case with architecture that becomes non-figurative, Branzi also frees design from a chronological view, orienting it rather toward a variable of temporal *relativization*, aestheticizing it into a dynamic, ephemeral, mobile architecture.

But the question of this elusive and immaterial time is obviously also linked to web culture and the new power of information technology, which undermines the usual linear perception: web culture not only defines new urban spaces but it abolishes the functionality of history and geography as operating systems, and of time as a bipartite condition.

The issue of the network leads to a new vision of the world that has in cybernetics its disequilibrating discipline. Anchored to Norbert Wiener's 1947 definition, "working in the entropy of the world"[175] according to which "to live is to communicate," the telecommunication and communication processes derived from it, as developed in the United States in the research of computer systems, will influence the collective intelligence, introducing multiplicity into the concept of the True and Chaos Theory as counterbalancing that of the Cartesian order.[176]

As described, "introducing unexplored horizons, these developments in computer science and communication fascinated artists: among them, Jonas Mekas or Nam June Paik experimented with new media during the Sixties. At that time, no one was talking about cybernetics, but everyone, from Rauschenberg, Oldenburg, Fuller, to Cage had read MacLuhan and his thesis on the development of communication processes in relation to the impact of media. After a primitive stage, where hearing is crucial to perceiving words, following the civilization of the press, when the press took communication from listening to the eyes. MacLuhan described the third phase, the Digital Age, where audiovisual civilization reintroduces into communication the proximity that is present in oral society and especially the sense of touch."[177]

Along these lines, Branzi will increase the value of the sensorial and will also lose interest in design technique understood in the traditional and material sense, ferrying his experiments towards a digital and invisible technology, adapted to the formulation of a sensory space that goes beyond the concept of technique itself.

This is how he explains it in relation to the theme of the virtual, and his proposal of it as an anthropological *Second Nature*: "The idea has yet to be developed that matters of design constitute a core of autonomous reflection, not based on furnishings or industrial technologies, but on a much wider philosophical and physical territory that runs through the twentieth century and that, starting from the historical question of a new relationship between technological culture and humanistic culture, ends today with the investigation of the relationship of humanity with the present artificial universe [...].There are several new elements that characterize the difference of design today from the historical one: elements of a quantitative and qualitative nature. These elements were not produced by methodological changes internal to the discipline and to linguistics, but rather from a more global mutation of the artificial universe and of the behavioral culture that this mutation produces in history [...]. A technological, flexible, and articulated universe, which constitutes in fact our second nature. This second nature extends uninterruptedly from our private (even corporeal) habitat to the great metropolitan settings, to the point of creating a functional area of the entire land map. In this thick and varied artificial cosmos, the culture of design can no longer clearly distinguish the traditional hierarchical distinctions between urbanism, architecture, and design. Their sacred boundaries, based on the typological and dimensional differences (micro-objects in design, macro-objects in architecture, territorial structures in urbanism), are constantly overcome by the invasive processes of industrial multiplication on the territory, and by the qualitative verticalization of new environmental technologies [...]. Architecture, which is still largely organized around the theme of the unity, continuity, and specificity of the discipline, finds itself experiencing, in the great deposits of post-industrial metropolises, a condition of total schizophrenia between its inner space, its own external image, and the metropolitan setting [...]. In every case, design, architecture, and urbanism see their historic boundaries in the great artificial universe of the metropolis become fluid, in order to regenerate themselves in a new environmental tendency, where different dimensional parameters are co-present, but all aimed not at building the old categories of objects, architecture, or neighborhoods, but at relating in a new way to this universe-artifact and with this technological semisphere that surrounds us [...]. In this different environmental dimension, a great historical transformation of the disciplines of the project is realized: these are no longer definable typologically and dimensionally but operate globally in the great technological and semantic magma of post-industrial metropolises."[178]

The strategy is therefore transversal and is indicative of a wider humanist context, of a new cultural theorem, which repositions design as a general interpretative medium and not exclusively with a formal aim.

In this sense, Branzi also reverses the role of technique on theory: if the project is an act of humanistic/scientific re-founding, technique, understood as mechanics and the invasion of practice in theory, is downgraded for the benefit of new sciences more akin to this epistemological and anthropological refounding: For a long time, architecture was a plastic art,"[179] but now new technologies allow for a total liberation of the form-function-material relationship, which is able to represent the space of a metropolis that has seen the setting of physical bodies as determining their general form.

Branzi's approach is, rather, of a chemical type, that is, an invisible operation capable of generating and representing the complexities of a new sensorial world. In a certain sense, cybernetics and new technologies will make it possible to create a new concept of anthropology, capable of transforming design into a primary hybrid liquid between the natural and the artificial.

But the process of the weakening of modernity and its parameters comes to be further reinforced by *Fuzzy Logic*[180]: a logic that is etymologically *languinosa*, intermediate, heterogeneous, hazy.

Like that used for the first time by logician Lotfi Zadeh[181] and more recently by Bart Kosko,[182] "It belongs to that particular tradition of modern science that has propelled itself towards the unexplored border of overcoming rigid dual logic."[183]

In place of dual logic, Branzi substitutes a dialogical and relational logic, particularly focusing on the value of dialogue with respect to dialectics.

Inserted into Morin's principles of intelligibility (dialogical, recursive, hologrammatic)[184], the dialogical position expresses two principal conditions, both of which mean the elimination of binary thinking: the elimination of closed disciplinary systems and the overcoming of relations based on opposition or substitution.

Beyond to the distinctive polarities, he undertakes what Morin had already defined as the seventh path of complexity: "The path of the crisis of closed and clear concepts, that is, the crisis of clarity and of separation in the explanation [...]. We are witnessing the end of the dream of establishing a clear and distinct demarcation between science and non-science."[185] In the discipline, retroactive dichotomies such as architecture/city, city/country, etc., or Manichean oppositions, such as order/disorder, solid/void, are overcome in favor of the possibility of science working with open sets, transdisciplinary and dialogical among the parts, in which the co-production of multiples and opposites and the value of contradiction become central[186].

2. Theories of Weak Urbanization

The described scenarios lead him to the definition of new general principles that characterize society of design: the definition of a Second Modernity creates an opening for a *Dolce Stil Novo*[187] as a "stile languinoso" with the flexible thresholds characterized by a new "Natural Science."

Similar to how the fourteenth-century Italian poets Guido Cavalcanti, Guido Guinizzelli, Lapo Gianni, and Dante Alighieri gave the sweet signal that an era was over, for Branzi an expressive era is approaching, one that allows architecture to find new conditions outside of itself: the golden age in which plans, buildings, and chairs were designed passed to that of a visible/invisible plankton of technonatural technologies.

The solution is in environmental components, which can generate a new narrative that takes part in the artificial universe and which aims to produce spaces that decipher the functional dimension in a poetic sense. In a vision that goes beyond scalar coherence, his metropolis is recognized through its interiors, spaces that are simultaneously technological and immersive, domestic but global. This is how he describes it: "Our strategy is based on two different movements: on the one hand, we move in this vast horizon of environmental components (signs, sounds, lights, colors, information, structures, services, and functions) and through this dispersed supply we recompose a new narrative, an exciting fiction, a few dense environmental enclaves, even provisional (it's not important), which gains strength by the fact of being different from and an alternative to what surrounds it. An artificial environment, a sound on which an island of meaning rises in the middle of the background noise [...]. Let's take a segment of this universe of artificial detritus, and upon it let's create a powerful surge of design: almost a profound and unexpected cloning of ourselves; a strong and mysterious image, which is more important in terms of what it does not explain and what it hides, than what it clarifies and illuminates."[188]

Thus, *the Scenografie per il Prossimo Millennio* (*Scenographies for the Next Millennium*)[189] are introduced, capable of responding to the crises of complexity and of quality through new spatial holograms, which lead him to the formation of the theory of *Relational Space*[190].

Into this context of permanent reformism, the crisis of complexity, or rather, the resizing of programmed complexity, is inserted: "Western culture has found itself acting within a complex, contradictory, discontinuous system, but one that is mono-logical, that is, based only on the laws of the market. From this obsequious homogenization, the category of complexity that was our great discovery during the '70s and '80s today comes out of it heavily reduced and suffering from a serious crisis of credibility. Within a worldwide mono-logical system, inside the planetary markets of commodities and information, complexity is not a bearer of significant diversity, but rather indicates a sampling of possible variants, a catalogue of practicable exceptions, which in their entirety reconstruct a kind of gray sound, a kind of background noise in a setting where each component is different from the other; yet their mixture is no longer explosive, but in fact produces a kind of cold fusion that thus produces energy without adding to the deflagration of the whole."[191]

Therefore, going outside the brackets of the theory of complexity involves, in design, not the reduction of uncertainty, but an augmentation of it: impossible to approach through preliminary definitions, Branzi inserts the irruption of uncertainties and the definition of a pluralist epistemology.

Along these lines, beyond the *Principle of Simplification*,[192] or of variation, avoiding both holism and reductionism,[193] Branzi generates new meaningful units: namely, new types of processes and research based on molecular phenomena of self-organization, not yet properly verified or investigated in terms of the discipline, performing a narrowing of the boundaries between science and philosophy, between *ego cogitans* and *res extensa*, through the acceptance of a permanent disequilibrium.[194]

To the crisis of the concept of complexity, the crisis of quality is added, as a value never clearly defined and replaced with that of quantity.

This is how it is expressed in *La Crisi della Qualità* (*The Quality Crisis*): "The political turnaround that occurred at the end of the 1980s caused a leap forward even for the crisis of our concept of quality. A concept today that is completely devoid of communicable and recognizable reference elements. The lengthy debate that took place during the 1980s, when hope spread that it might be possible to replace the quantitative model of the system with a never well-identified model of qualitative development, proved to be a purely verbal hypothesis; in the sense that no one was able to give this quality a practical definition [...]. I therefore believe that the mistaken point is precisely the use (and abuse) of the term qualitative to indicate the new and the desirable, because this term never follows a more precise definition but instead a return to unknown categories [...]. Architectural composition, based on the formation of expressive organisms falls into crisis: the useless search for new languages, when the qualitative reference falls short, gives way to a defensive concept of design: a project where territory and structures (on the micro and macro scales) coincide, following a concept that we will call relational space."[195]

The outcome of the crisis of the concept of complexity and that of quality results in Relational Space, that is, a holistic postmodern narrative space "in which the dimensional categories of urban planning, architecture, and design are surpassed in the processes where the small and the large scale coincide without any more disciplinary distinctions [...]. It is not derived from a unitary project, but from a way of understanding reality, a way of assembling it and reassembling it, and from the consciousness of the definitive collapse of the figurative and narrative systems of architecture as such."[196]

This relational vision of design seems to relate to the idea of the relation undertaken during the same period by Umberto Eco, with the text *Opera Aperta* (*The Open Text*) as an epistemological metaphor,[197] and it involves a critique of the conception of matter as divided both into scalar measurements as well as composite bodies, pointing to the idea that relations between architecture and the world exclude the claim of the object to have a substantive and scalar value.

This is only, strictly speaking, carrying the ancient principle of interrelationship of things to its logical consequences. Already Leibniz had argued in *Monadology* that "tout corps se ressent de tout ce qui se fait dans l'univers."[198] But working in terms of relationships also makes it possible to multiply the characteristics of space so that it can shed any principle of homogenization and substantiality: "In relational space, the predominant issue is the relationship that it allows, the functionoids that can be implemented, the information and the filters that can be activated [...]. The characteristics of this space are therefore not of an aesthetic nature, nor compositional, nor narrative, but indeed performative: performativity does not mean functional according to the old definition of pragmatists, who carefully separated the aesthetic and functional issues. In the relational space, this distinction falls away: aesthetics is a functional part of design, as functional issues are part of the aesthetics of design [...]. Therefore, a space defined by a system of regional and local services corresponding to weak design fields of energy, capable of producing vast "sloths" and slow, tectonic micro-motions; metropolitan hypertensions within which single design episodes lose much of their identity, their perimeters, their rigidity [...]. A space in which the difference between design and non-design tends to disappear."[199]

In this work of breaking design boundaries, Branzi remembers, without skepticism, the vision of Goedel's meta-mathematics, of science as a discipline of inexactness and the anti-paradigmatic, beyond the descriptive control of phenomena, as also expressed by Kosko,[200] Mach, Heisenberg, Kuhn, Popper, and above all Feyerabend, who affirms its anarchist role in *Against Method*.[201]

Branzi thus introduces design to "possible but non-necessary events" (introduced from the world of quantum physics), whose purpose is to represent and be nurtured through the multiplicity of meanings, in action and potentially, of an inversion of subjects and of times, taking charge of "weaving together [...] different codes in a plural, multifaceted view of the world."[202]

And it is precisely this transition that leads him to outline a new fusion of Science and Nature as a characteristic of *Relational Space*, seeing science as no longer an isolated perceived perfection, but as a discipline capable of introducing and acting with the chaos and complexity of nature, understood as the place of the perfect union of the manifold.

This is a structural transition in his research, equally defining "a new scientific and technological Naturalism, which no longer considers Nature a primitive stage to modify, but rather as an evolutionary model to imitate in the constructive processes of the new,"[203] which will lead him to delineate a New Naturalism that can be put in proximity with the concept of Technonature (which we will take up again later), not in a Romantic-aesthetic sense, but in a newly and differently logical/scientific sense.

But the definition of *Relational Space*, as the theoretical space of the second modernity, is specified in Branzi in a first general theoretical model – *Elastic Classicism* – the conceptual and spatial meta-project of reference.

According to the tautologically creative mode that it is,[204] against the coeval contextual Italian logic or the American formalist one,[205] Branzi reawakens through *Elastic Classicism*[206] a universal reference for the contemporary metropolis: a territory in which the classical nature of agriculture and the agricultural nature of architecture is integrated and makes it possible to accommodate all the manifold of the real, in a vision of design that is continuously provisional.

The theoretical Roman territorial mesh, capable of generating conceptual structures, makes it possible, in fact, to maintain, without fixity, spatial and political conditions that are expandable, heterogeneous, deformable, accommodating, and hybrid, according to the premise of weak urbanization models.

"Rome was a polycentric system [...]. That territory was urbanized through a very simple architectural system, based only on columns and trabeations, where the stylistic elements corresponded entirely with the static elements [...]. Onto this uniform fabric were connected the building segments, up to the construction of the layout of the city, and around this the fields where the crops were equally arranged according to the same rules. The classical nature of agriculture (and the agricultural nature of architecture) have their origins in this process of the transformation of the territory, where individual constructions were placed as a visible intensification of a theoretical mesh.

This type of traversable, indifferent, extensive continuity that contained cities, cultivated fields, and streets corresponded to the Latin concept of a civilization not based on individual cities, but, as Cicero explains, on the principles of law and civil institutions [...]. An expandable structure where it was possible to contain all of the most contradictory cultures, cultivations, logics and religions [...]. Elastic classicism is the reference model of our elastic modernity as a deformable system [...] avoiding traumas and fractures and continuing to finely build the best conditions of freedom and knowledge."[207]

3. Prototypes of Weak Urbanization

The prototypes of weak urbanization therefore rely on this conceptual model and also play on a double binary: the elimination of architecture as something definitive and the formulation of a new design glossary that will lead to the early theoretical metropolises.

The term weak[208] has theoretical as well as methodological and spatial specifications, and is rooted in the debate instituted in those years from the publication of *Pensiero Debole* (*Weak Thought*),[209] edited by Gianni Vattimo and PierAldo Rovatti, to which Branzi refers back above all to weak ontology, which refocuses a hermeneutics without the 20th-century syntheses, without unitary systems in politics and design, typical of the "strong" and definitive models.[210]

Branzi acquires in this the value of relativization, in a positive and propositional sense, in order to experiment with a non-compositional, anti-fundamentalist architecture, thus interpreting weakness as the limit state of the discipline's thresholds, of their construction and their meaning. Moving away from precise theories, from equilibrium systems, he moves in the direction of the concept of the *oligopticon*, that is, a space through which the world and thought pass without stabilizing themselves, and in which the continuous levels of instability refer to the neutralization of all pretensions of being fixed, both ideological and formal.

As a premise, speculation about the weakness of design passes, via theory, through criticism of the Modern and to synthetic-precise processes; methodologically in the overcoming of dualistic/dialectical concepts in favor of dialogical ones, in minimizing the centrality of the value of architectural scale and architecture in general as a topic of interest for urban transformation. Operatively, privileging horizontal surfaces over vertical ones and over the skyline, reactivating, while not specifically naming it, the concept of field as a place of relations.

Without deepening the signified-signifier relationship, which would imply a resumption of by now exhausted contents (if not in citational terms) of the relationship between architecture and semiotics, Branzi seems to concentrate on the oxymoron of the etymology of the word weak,[211] namely, on its potential to define itself as *in-firmitas*: that is, as an attempt to dispose of the "solid" definitions of architecture from a spatial as well as a metaphysical/symbolic standpoint, re-enunciating (albeit momentarily) the categories of design.

Eliminating the substantiality and the figurativity of architecture and configuring itself as an oxymoronic and anti-classical word, it is understood not only as a process of destabilization, but also as a definition of architectonic space as *decoration*, understood as an information code that is an alternative to that of *composition*.

He describes it in this way: "Architecture has carried out a great battle to get rid of nineteenth-century decoration, but the new style has often become punitive, that is, reductive. We know very little about decoration, its nature, and its linguistic organization [...]. It should not be understood as a by-product of painting or fashion, but as a true information system: cultural information about the product, about its use, linguistic information, and visual information. The decorative sign represents the design of a virtually infinite system of signs, which thus presupposes that it develops in a homogeneous manner on a theoretically unlimited plane. This design hypothesis means that the decorative sign possesses its own somatic characteristics: unlike the frame, the decorative surface has in its smallest part the totality of the decorative system's information, since it contains the single sign that will be repeated on the entire surface."[213]

The decorative space harkens back to Deleuze's concept of smooth space and folded space, thus a horizontal space, which throws perspectival, compositional, geometric, and visual principles into crisis, overturning architecture, and the art of building.

Branzi therefore transports architecture toward a non-structural, but calligraphic, epidermal environment, a heterogeneous arabesque, deliberately non-decipherable only visually.

But, transversally, Branzi constructs his prototypes according to a concept of field.

As a concept coming from physics (from Faraday to Einstein), Branzi considers space and time as non-divisible, anti-material, and dynamic, and the mirror used in the models emphasizes the release from the three-dimensional perception of space: he eliminates the figure/background dichotomy (as in Rothko's paintings and the music of Glass) in favor of a background/background relationship intended as a performative and non-figurative pattern. Precisely in its being non-figurative, the field refuses to replicate the "synthetic" characteristics of both urban morphology and of diffuse typologies, generating the maximum formal and temporal flexibility; the non-figurativity of individual elements; continuity between interior and exterior in the enzymatic sense; and the provisional nature of the parts and of the whole.

Design therefore becomes anti-fundamentalist and sheds the conditions on which it has always worked: *Vitruvian commodatio*, *simmetria* (in the ancient sense of the term = correspondence between the parts), *allineamento discontinui*, and then he introduces a design future in which the logic of weakness as a positive category generates a new stylistic figure, a "stable state [that] foresees the collapse of meaning of the design gesture (as a gesture that serves to reform but not to give value to the system), and it consists precisely in the renunciation of a possible qualifying adjective of the metropolis and a global model of theoretical transformation."[214]

And if the city becomes "polychrome, relational, notational, molecular, reversible, and virtual,"[215] the weakness interacting with the *solid side*[216] of urban reality articulates architecture into a link, an interface reinforces the idea that architecture might have lost a formal and civil figurative code, its role as a metaphor of history and context, and he pulls it towards a new non-figurative configuration with technopoetic characteristics introduced by the virtual, as well as those that were typical of decoration, as an art of the surface. Making them lost their meaning as a corpus, in its extreme ephemeralization, bringing it closer to a cyberspace without depth[217].

The role that theory exercises on practice leads him to specify the characteristics of his theoretical metropolises, understood as synthetic conceptual models[218].

Theoretical metropolises are therefore for prototypes as theoretical physics is for physics: while they do not correspond to reality, they introduce it in a conceptual vision in which design simulates, in a certain sense, reality itself, of which the designed Metropolis is a partial and synthetic hologram.

The pre-prototypes or meta-theories that Branzi identifies are respectively:[219] the *Mechanical Metropolis* (as it belongs to the historical avant-garde, which divides reality into parts and is active from the beginning of the 20th century to the Twenties) and the *Homogeneous Metropolis* (realized between the two wars up to the Fifties, which has the assembly line as a territorial diagram and mirrors a phase of dramatic realism of design culture. Based on the stylistics of the Modern Movement, finding its utmost expression in the North American city hypothesized by Hilberseimer) relative to the First Modernity, and which is ferried to those representing the Second Modernity, that is, the *Hybrid Metropolis* and the *Cold Metropolis* (which, instead, manages, in opposition, a new normality made of official minorities. Design, in this case, becomes a producer of diverse and anthropological qualities, generating a "semiosphere of product categories and information that are only apparently contradictory, which are instead heterogeneous wealth").[220]

It is precisely in the concept of hybridization and in the *Hybrid Metropolis* that the transition is marked from *No-Stop City* toward the final outcome of what will become *The Primitive Metropolis*: Branzi initiates an approach toward anthropology by taking up anew the contents of an elastic classicism as already defined, capable of generating a flexible and weak spatiality.

In fact, the *Hybrid Metropolis*, typical of a mature post-industrial society, refocuses the design role on its ability not to generate new global visions of the world but to place itself alongside the city and existing reality via new narrative imaginaries: it gets rid of its characteristic of being a general category of critique (like in *No-Stop City*), and it becomes a fragmentary, discontinuous system that exalts the differences and exceptions instead of great ideological and spatial unities.

The prototypes presented in the text thus become specifications or visual metaphors of the previously defined categories, and in particular they represent seven specifications and alterations of the metropolis of the *Second Modernity*. Their taxonomy touches the principal nuclei of Branzi's theoretical work, and it reverses design's large-scale categories, focusing on continuous conceptual and spatial alterations, and ever farther from systemic visions.

These are divided into: *Genetic Metropolis*; *the Second Nature Metropolis*; *Reversible Metropolis*; *Sensorial Metropolis*; *Commodity Metropolis*; *Metropolis of Continuous Work*; and *Art Metropolis*.

The *Genetic Metropolis* (1988) is the metropolis where the biological energies of society are liberated and reach their maximum level of liquefaction. Echoing Kevin Kelly,[221] and the theory according to which the organization of intelligence is structured according to micro-components, a vision applicable to both man and to artificial intelligence, according to a relational system in which human beings and objects are connected, Branzi re-actualizes the synergy and the connection between subject and system, between individual and market, which produce a new definition of the metropolis (from here on out the term city is no longer used) as a large genetic field, in that aulic sense of imperial Rome, of present-day Mumbai or

Lagos, or like the textile fabric proposed by Gandhi, in which everything is interrelated with everything.

Urban reality, along these lines, becomes a vast bio-technological system, a vital system where the interests of the individual intertwine with the analogous and primordial interest of others. The city thus becomes an amniotic fluid that follows an evolutionary logic in which any paradigm or organizational model is always transitory and specifiable, in search of a higher level of environmental and social systems for the defense and consolidation of their own configuration.

This prospective union between computer science as an artificial intelligence system and genetics as a subjective patrimony (also exemplified in *Genetic Tales*, i.e. a manual for relations according to a human atlas, a Mendelssohnian process) leads to a vision of the city as anthropological stock, as a bio-technological environment close to agricultural systems.

And it is precisely the agricultural system that becomes crucial in Branzi's research that, completely, with *Agronica*, developed with Domus Academy for Philips Co. in 1995 and considerably the second model of his research, after *No-Stop City* and before the *Primitive Metropolis*, he realizes this new idea of natural science that he had already anticipated.

In fact, *The Second Nature Metropolis* (or technonatural[222]) leads to a new humanism, namely, that of an artificial nature created by the man of the Second Modernity: architecture and agriculture are but two different typologies of the universal logic of profit.

The Second Nature Metropolis is proposed as an experimental mode of interpretation/design of the contemporary landscape, according to a renewal of the very idea of nature that can overcome both dichotomous relationships linked to thinking about the artificiality, and every attempt at vernacularism, of immanent hibernation, or of conciliation, such as the aesthetics of disappearance, camouflage, metaphor, and, above all, of any deviance from sustainability or from environmentalism as repair systems.

Being an anti-dialectical perspective, it understands nature as a continuous renewal of its capacity for genesis, creation, and, above all, adaptation, "absorbing artificial matter as its component, clearing out the anemic categories of belonging and aspiring to that wonderful regenerative fluidity that eludes opposites and makes them its own," where "a paradigmatic nuance should be observed: what might seem to be the result of a hybridization between the natural and its opposite, artificial, is instead an alternating interpenetration that makes us comprehend the transformational reality of nature. It is, more simply, the very concept of nature that is being denatured from the secular fixity, producing one of the most revolutionary changes that has ever occurred in history."[223] Conceptually unfreezing itself, it finally "melts from the immanent hibernation that has always followed it."[224]

Nature is therefore proposed as a time of maximum productivity, of maximum potential in terms of its own modification/integration with culture, technology, and artificial knowledge.

Through this modification of itself, it renews its capacity for genesis, creation, and adaptation. As Pessoa had already stated, "Artificiality is a way of savoring naturalness [...]. Civilization is the education of nature. Artificiality is the pathway for approaching the natural."[225]

Branzi intends to develop and set as a condition of research, therefore, a new "natural" perspective, one that is able to combat the conditions in place not by retreating but from within, according to an anti-dialectical reconciliation between nature and artifice. Where the second meaning is completely incorporated into the first that, in the power of its rethinking, absorbs the genetic, productive and projective abilities into itself, to the point of approaching the concept of cyberspace in its maximum articulation. Indeed, as Nicolescu maintains, "Virtual reality has produced a veritable Technonature, which now coexists with cosmic processes that have been developing since the dawn of time, even before the appearance of humans. The latest result to emerge from techno nature is cyberspace, which has a unique role because it reaches a new barrier of human intelligence."[226]

Thus, a shift toward a new state of ambiguity, in a scientific bracket that sees new transdisciplinary paradigms based on mutable identities.

Shifting the classic paradigms to that of Second Nature, his definition in *Architecture/ Agriculture* becomes central, when he argues: "It is the territory that becomes the privileged protagonist of the post-industrial economy, as a place for developing the weak and diffuse energies of a productivity that is pulviscular and iridescent [...]. Natural technology is therefore becoming a more sophisticated construction model [...]. The world of the artificial, born to replace an inadequate nature, is rediscovering nature as a realm of unrivaled technology."[227]

In this sense, his weak city is oriented toward fragile urbanization models, which refer to "a concept of reversibility and traversability typical of agriculture, and indicate in fact a way of understanding structures as a temporary, lightweight, elastic reality, placed within a built territory, but integrated into agricultural production."[228]

Far from being an idea of nature as a Romantic narrative project, it structurally substitutes itself for the city as a new matrix, in which there is no longer division between ecosystems, all of which belong to a hybrid ecosystem recognized and investigated as such.

Operatively, it accompanies infra-free systems, that is, objects/devices ready for articulations of a function, of local environmental, energy-related, and performative needs. The infra-free systems allow for the regeneration of urban structures from the inside while keeping the idea of the field intact, becoming devices waiting to be able to fulfill their functions, even temporarily. Acquiring all the characteristics of a natural artifact (ecological, evolutionary, entropic, ephemeral), they transform them into artificial ones (performative, potential, undefined, removable, etc....).

Agronica, or *The Symbiotic Metropolis* (1994-95), returns and perfectly reflects this new concept of technonature.

Presented as an incomplete utopia, not as a comprehensive model, but as a partial model of the city that is approached through a conflicting juxtaposition that generates an unstable equilibrium in the already uncertain one, *Agronica* represents exactly the synthesis of the weak models and the theoretical metropolises presented.

The seven theses that accompany it (*Separation between technology and form*; *Separation between form and function*; *Weak urbanism*; *Living is a shopper*; *Virtual metropolis and natural metropolis*; *Weak urbanization*; *The vineyard is not wine*)[229] are all oriented to define a city that dislodges itself from the previous stylistic codes, a city without syntax that eliminates the concept of the Plan and of History, but collaborating with symbols and technologies without coinciding with the symbols it nonetheless represents.

Its variations can also be seen in subsequent processes: in the *Parco Virgiliano* Branzi seems to echo the *The Three Ecologies* of Guattari, through the three theorems proposed for "An Ecology of the Artificial World"[230] (*Ecology of Complexity*, *Ecology of Design*, and *Ecology of Relations*), toward the possibility of determining new interpersonal codes (thus genetic ones) for which ergonomics and proximity lose their meaning; in *Architecture/Agriculture* he again takes up the genetic variability of nature, which leads to the definition of a nature as the realm of "unrivaled technology"[231]; in *Residential Agriculture* he focuses on the new human/technology interfaces, in which the proposed natural architecture becomes a light and variable structure between man and instrument, where man overlaps with the electronic instrument; in the *Woods of Architecture*, the infra-free system generates functionoids, that is, organisms without a precise function or delimitation, which determine, through a low-resolution architecture, a new idea of protected space, without it being enclosed in perimeters and defined forms.

The indefiniteness of the forms and the idea of a *Weak and Reversible Urbanism* will lead him to the genesis of three other prototypes: *Light Streets*, *Heaven and Earth*, and *High-Tech Favelas* (Eindhoven), which in fact represent a different model than both the Western idea of the city and the elements that have always generated it.

We are, in this particular example, in Italy at the heart of the debate on design, to which a morphogenetic value is given: the street, the paths, the urban traces have always defined, in the culture of Italy in the Eighties, the first elements capable of "structuring" new neighborhoods and new portions of the city.

Eliminating the street, rendering ephemeral the paths in favor of a multidirectional and open space, Branzi not only criticizes the positions of contextualists and Italian structuralists but, at the same time, he negates the value of the morphogenetic components on which they base their criteria, defining them as "an acid social moralism that freezes every possible solution."[232]

In these projects of reversible urbanism, between criticism and proposal, one can thus see a counter-tendency to the ongoing research on the formation of new peripheries, on their presumed continuity with respect to the theme of urban identity, on the attempt to still see a city as a definitive physical and social structure.

With respect to this, Branzi shifts the axis towards a *Sensorial Urbanism* that disengages from the eye as a classical, positivist synthesis and process, towards an anti-analytical design definition that belongs to those *Born Under Saturn*.

The senses, as anti-modern tools, are reactivated as a cognitive tool of the reality and the formation of the individual, according to an idea of *surface reality for a surface knowledge*.

The dichotomy between modern sensibility – analytical, mechanical, and neoplastic – and the contemporary one – synthetic, electronic, sign-based – thus generates a genetic mutation that slowly shifts the codes of the *Mechanical Metropolis* toward those of the *Hybrid Metropolis*.

The Commodity Metropolis instead deforms the object of the commodity into an extreme city: the object becomes the synecdoche of the city, with which it has a quantitative and conceptual nature in common. It is in fact the commodity that creates the urban setting, transforming it into the commodity itself: architecture replaces objects in circulation, and the entire city takes the form of a large supermarket. Thus revisiting the value of the object within the urban system, Branzi downgrades and eliminates any meaning of the architectural body.

And, if the *Commodity Metropolis* deforms the object inhabiting the city – the commodity – in the city itself, the *Metropolis of Continuous Work* (generated by Vitra's *Citizen Office exhibition*[233]), demonstrates how the liquefaction of the forms of politics and business have led to the paradox of achieving the opposite of what was hoped for during the Radical period: society, in fact, because of the presence of the Buzz Economy (relational, non-productive economies) and of the Net Economy, instead of attaining the liberation from work for a diffuse leisure time, has generated diffuse work with a reduction in leisure time. The inversion of the prophecy will lead Branzi to define liquefied spaces, in which times and forms can overlap without finding resolution in continuity, with blurred perimeters like the time of subjective entrepreneurship.

Coming from the logic of the production of businesses, the individual-entrepreneur manages time and modes according to new and anti-Fordian fluidity, for which neutral and non-functionalized spaces are most suited. In this sense, even the code to identify spaces disappears in a metropolitan circuit with a low level of identity, in which transparent cells are the new germinal nuclei for a new form of immaterial production.

In the *Art Metropolises*, however, Branzi grants a two-fold meaning: on the one hand, he generates a sort of "family collage," invoking the authors to whom he feels close: "Biography [...] [e]veryone can interpret it, recount it or modify it at will. Truth is not an absolute category and will never be traceable."[234]

The whole value of the work shifts in these more real than real-life relations. Thus, nothing to do with the documentary-based history of architecture or with the endogenous categories of design, but rather with the private aspect of the author hybridized by his ability to render, by means of visual images, conceptual prototypes through which inner desire falsifies the historical and phenomenological aspect.

And the invention of these collaborations delineates not only a voluntary absence of objective information in the image, but also the implementation of the practice of the "deceptive *détournement*" as defined by Debord, or "re-use in a new unit of pre-existing artistic elements."[235]

Branzi purloins the works and, repeating or displacing them, implements the meaning of *Difference and Repetition*:[236] he raises their power to the nth degree by reproducing them and displacing them in time and space. Realizing the dream of Deleuze, he overthrows architectural Platonism, which must always go through a substitution and therefore a *composition* of the parts to reach the whole. And he realizes the Duchamp ready-made on a territorial scale.

The *collage* (which does not replace but *displaces*, which does not compose but *deviates*) is thus configured like a Deleuzian paradox, generating a series of spatial and temporal short-circuits of sense that find a solution solely in the continuous slippage of the tropes, with no mono-directional meaning.

The temporal paradox discharges *Kronos* (the author in the present, the works in the simple past and simultaneously in the time of the Myth, Hausmannian Paris in the remote past), and time is constituted by a material that bends, attracted by the mass of thought, as in the general theory of relativity.

The spatial paradox gives a glimpse of the repeatable matrix works, mythological devices that momentarily determine the infinite potential of the catatonic city elaborated by Branzi in '68 and that, precisely because of its maximum synthesis, allows for an limitless possibility of variations and punctuations in different formal and imaginative declinations.

The collage fills the void left by architecture, always listless in relation to the revolution of meaning, and realizes in the background the mirage of Deleuze: "Perhaps the highest end of art is to implement all of these things (or repetitions), with their difference in nature and rhythm, with their respective shifts and guises, with their divergences and decentralizations, to insert them into one another and, from one to another, to envelop them with 'illusions,' the effect of which varies from case to case. Art does not imitate because first it repeats, and repeats all repetitions on behalf of an inner power."[237]

But in this series, anti-monumental art becomes a "Monument to the Secularity of the Unexpected," presenting itself as dogma and as discontinuity within a city with which it breaks every relation of linearity and literal transparency.

The proposed metropolises all pursue, transversally, the problem of the crisis of the city and of architecture in its global epistemological role, and in its attempt for resistance through compositional processes.

Already clearly expressed in the introductory manifesto, *For a Non-Figurative Architecture*, the attempt is that of downgrading the canonical status of architectural practice, to get out of the metaphor of history (which was indeed experiencing a revival in the Italian postmodern), also carrying with it an non-compositional innovation that made it possible to compensate for the fact that architecture could no longer be understood as abstract and reconceptualizable thought, with an urban state that no longer posed formal and solid questions, but rather physiological and liquid ones.

Responding to urban weakness with weak models, again using paradox as a tool for interpreting design reasoning and solutions, Branzi continues in his own purposeful denunciation of the crisis of architecture as a crisis of the interpretation of reality.[238] A crisis that will be expressed in the Venice Biennale of 1980, with the extremism of *La Strada Nuovissima* (*The Presence of the Past*) and the Postmodern.

Branzi will continually speak out against the rhetorical dimension of architecture ("Eccettuato il puro deserto," 1973; "Un plastico d'oro," 1974; "Architettura e Modestia," 1974; "E se non ha stile si chiamerà post-moderna," 1980; "I post-Romani a Venezia," 1980; "Genius Loci," 1983; "Cose e Case," 1988; "Per un'architettura enzimatica," 2005; "Contro l'architettura," 2008), and he will again see in a new dimension of understanding object design a discipline capable of re-signifying the discourse on design.

PART FOUR: FOR A NEW URBAN DRAMATURGY. NEO-PRIMITIVISM AND POETIC REALISM

The melting of the rigidity of the mechanical metropolis, the relativization of technology as a new outlook for salvation, and the introduction of a weak and diffuse modernity leave room, in Branzi's more recent output, for a new outlook that can formalize an unstable equilibrium for a city that no longer needs conciliatory solutions, focusing instead on how to re-found the design processes of the new urban reality, in a post-technological, symbiotic world.

The post-industrial metropolis passes to the post-technological one, in which the supply of electronics has not been able to produce a society capable of completely dissolving the hardness of the mechanical through an "intelligent"[239] scenario.

To this new failure, Branzi adds on the historic event of the attack on the Twin Towers,[240] intended as a replicable spatial matrix of a globalized society, focusing, in this incident, on the cultural failure in Western ideologies, on the inability of the intellectuals to analyze the new "catastrophes" in progress and to explain the cultural reasons for them and, above all, he reconsiders the major themes forgotten by modernity, such as life and death.

The arrival in the world of new fundamentalisms will lead him to upend the concept of design, definitively removing it from any category that is naively ethical and spatially consequential, rather moving toward an interrogation of a new urban dramaturgy, based on anthropological platforms ignored by modernity.

His relationship with design changes, and he seems to want to achieve what Foucault said about Borges the introduction to *The Order of Things*:[241] the possibility of uniting a heterogeneity that changes the level of discourse, that enters into a new dimension that, for Branzi, can touch things "by organizing them into new relationships, not into new forms. So a project that perhaps tends toward the inexpressivity of the individual elements, but that creates different processes of aggregation, of juxtaposition: personally, I find it very exciting to think of categories as one thing over the other, or inside one another"[242], capable of reassembling existing things in order to create new worlds.

It is reassembly as a method that comes to be used, in recent works, again to undermine the roots of design in their genetic and expressive forms: the concept of image, of figure, of space, and their representations.

The first step of this research is filtered through the formulation of an imperfect metropolis, one capable of naming its own canons through new processes that decipher this new urban and anthropological reality.

I Dieci Modesti Consigli per una Nuova Carta d'Atene (*Ten Modest Advices for a New Athens Charter*) of 2009 are thus generated by this presumption: closing the circle of criticism of the Modern, Branzi starts anew from the cohesion of the multiple to upend the logic of the world: the high-tech favelas, the Global South, this becomes the prototype for a new form of temporary equilibrium for the global city of the present.

By generalizing the theories of weak urbanization, he takes up the theme of micro-actions and of the minority as a new agent for a complete revisiting of the contemporary self-reformist city, in which technological devices and sensory architecture coexist with a metropolis that has lost the features of solid form, to become rather the "Metropolis of Humans,"[243] that is, a dense ensemble of actions, techniques, myths, and genetics, capable of coexisting in a totally new landscape in which physical, corporeal, expressive, and imaginative realities coexist.

Disrupting the perspective of architecture, this metropolis is formed by subsystems intended as continuous interiors, for which design logic is no longer that of composition nor that of dissolution, but one of the "above and below": that is, of the union of a heterogeneity that can introduce new genetic options.

The new "mega-geographical" world defined in his *Athens Charter* thus becomes the first theoretical model of the spurious and post-technological society, like the Corbusian one was for modern and industrial society.

Branzi completely overturns the modern model: to the precise categorization of the 95 items of the *Charter* of 1933 (linked to the four human functions) he counterposes an elastic list of indications; to the structural observation (of the present) and the predictive reproduction (of the future), he reaffirms work in the present as already acting design, without ameliorative objectives; to the functional division of spaces, a commingling and densification of different elements; to the downgrading of the modern external space, a continuum between interior and exterior; to the anthropocentric *Modulor*, a non-anthropocentrism for an enlarged reality that sheds the connotations of ideologization to carry the project into a semiosphere inhabited by a multiplicity.

In addition, if the *Charter* of '33 tried to respond to the dynamics of the market by proposing a new relationship between city and society, it advanced a functionalism oriented toward a new idea of cosmopolitanism in which urban functionality, the replicability of the elements, and the disaggregation between the parts generated the identically repeatable, to which Branzi responds with a cosmopolitanism of the variable.

His proposal for the city thus becomes polychrome, canceling out the black and white of the modern that go back to a bi-chromaticity corresponding to solids and voids or to a selective reading of figures on a background, allowing for a replacement of terms, new possibilities of placing design in multiple hybrid and non-dualistic relationships, in which design becomes a molecular and notational condition.

As an oral phrasing, the notational system of his *Athens Charter* has a multiplicative and deviating capacity with respect to a place, a history, a form, to existence, to process, and it breaks the unitary tension of the grand narrative, which it no longer supports. This notational mode of accessing design is articulated according to anti-lyrical, anti-aesthetic, and anti-ideological variations, leading it to acquire the characteristics of a conceptually and formally minority architecture, an enunciative architecture that refers to the unorganized style of the Favelas.[244]

Where the Global South invokes the eternal New World, perpetual re-founding itself, and as an alternative to Western History.

This research into new genetic sites leads him to the definition of *New Fundamentalisms* for design, fundamentalisms that are, in fact, capable of mining design itself in its foundational expressions (image, figure, time, and space): he thus initiates work on neo-primitivism.

Again changing direction with respect to the verified, the contents in this session become the containers, holograms of both general territories and specific micro-environments, eliminating the first distinction between general and particular space, between city and interior, between thinking and design. The designed object, exploding conceptually, becomes the whole territory.

In his interpretation of primitivism, Branzi eliminates the external physical world as the sole referent, appealing also to his sensorial sentiment as a description of an anthropological condition. Describing this research as a neo-original radicalism, where advanced technology, nature, mass communications, and life become homogeneous materials and inaugurate a design in which codes of sensation replace the one-directional ones of reason.

And like the primitives generate hybrid archetypes, according to which "the primitive condition indicates the existential reality of contemporary man in the wild context of the present metropolis, where fragments of technology coexist with a reality in which dream, memory, and myth are intimately overlapping [...]. A condition that does not signify regression, but absolute freedom within a bio-technological environment from which one cannot escape [...]. *Primitivism* is therefore a new level of our normality."[245]

Primitivism is thus not a cultural movement or a cultural avant-garde, but the current reality of design, the unplanned result of contemporary society, the outcome – also formally – of an anthropological condition typical of man within post-technological and post-industrial metropolitan reality.

In the specific Branzian interpretation, *Neo-Primitivism* originates in the paradox of technology, which from a principle of order becomes an artificial expression of the maximum ungovernability of the devices that should have helped man live in the world. By again reversing the opposites and reconceptualizng them, the artificial for Branzi is exploded, becoming itself that disorder represented by the natural other. It is the crisis of the artificial that thus led to the definition of a second nature, generating a new cultural condition that no longer converges with the philosophy of cyberspace or the electronic age, but in a new poetics of the heterogeneous in which a non-monodirectional universal space can be rewritten.

Thus, a new concept of chaos is generated with respect to the one described above, closer to that of Hesiod, that is, a poetic and no longer exclusively rational expression of a universe linked to the world read with perceivable logics.[246]

For this reason, through this loss of technological and logical absoluteness, Branzi approaches anthropology.

Arising during in the second phase of historical colonialism in a mechanical Europe, precisely when the interest for primitivism surfaces through the discovery of the "Other," the discovery of psycho-sensory devices that go back to a primal state seems to be the way in which art finds or seeks a non-conciliatory position with Western history and, above all, with the non-universality of codes and languages. As Restany points out: "After centuries of the tyranny of the object as a synthetic element of consumer society, art has doubts about its material justification, is de-materialized, is conceptualized, [...] questions itself."[247]

In its own cultural origins, even the definition of *Primitivism* is formed concomitantly with the new anthropological science, particularly in Russia in 1912, with Alexander Shevchenko's *Neo-Primitivism Manifesto*,[248] linked to symbolism between 1904-8, and Russian art will develop it in the direction of abstraction, and not towards naturalism.[249]

Branzi moves toward Shevchenko's first definition: "The word neo-primitivism on the one hand testifies to our point of departure, and on the other – with its prefix, neo – also reminds us of its involvement in the painterly traditions of our age."[250] This is therefore a starting point, and not a resumption or reconciliation of forms and contents.

But from the dual nature of *Primitivism* (one that deviates from nature, the other toward reality), Branzi privileges the latter. Just as in the dual meaning of primitivism in art, he prefers expressionism over abstraction, demonstrated by the distancing from any attempt at formal simplification. What he seeks is, in fact, no longer a reduction of the form, but undermining the form itself through a new definition of the codes of art: taking up again neither primitive art (implying a return to the past or hybridization with respect to other local cultures) nor the exoticism typical of *Expressionism*, nor Cubist appropriation, nor Brancusi-style formal simplification, nor Russian *Symbolism*, eliminating any intellectual or ideological characteristic that *Primitivism* carries within itself.

He then moves away from the stance of reconstructing the *Other*, or of the contamination with the Other, instead moving closer to a non-systematic approach that traces in the behavioral attitudes of contemporary mankind a new and original universalization of perceptual sensoriality, in which imagination is encoded by sensitivity. The aim is the search for an "object's anthropological mutation,"[251] which must be able to convey human biology and human sensoriality with the artificiality of the surrounding environment in a new grammar of expression.

And the non-universality of language and logic leads him to identify other codes, "like animals in the forest": sensorial codes, smells, signs, and colors that still lead to a primordial and shared origin. Like expressive archetypes, Branzi therefore seeks the founding elements of art as anthropology.

The shift, even in the focus on the sensorial, from absolute values to more subjective but generalizable ones, is thus derived from the observation that even art no longer has a purpose or a unitary ideology, but orients itself toward magic, alchemy, the emotional, or, better, towards a *Logic of Sensation*,[252] which contemporary humanity uses to live in this technological Amazon that is the contemporary city. An Amazon that can never be perceived and understood from the outside or in its entirely, but which can only be resolved by generating micro-spaces and elective micro-systems in which the subject reconstructs its entirety from within. A sort of new intellectual "reserves" that can introduce and reconstruct, like holograms, the thinking about everything. Also about everything urban.

His models are exactly the representation of this interior, which represents a whole that is now no longer even definable exclusively as a city or as a concrete space.

In fact, at the center of this thinking lies the crisis of the city as a historical institution and as a body. As in Pierre Restany's *Manifesto of the Rio Negro*, but aimed at the contemporary city rather than at *Integral Naturalism*,[253] the urban environment is saturated not only with objects but with symbols, rites, techniques, heterogeneities, and hybridizations that, grouped together, form an infinite number of realities that no longer correspond to the capitalist and solid logics ("that do not develop but expand"[254]), but rather work in an imaginary depth rebuilt by sensorial superficiality.

The theme of the body as a subject also appears for the first time, understood through the body-animal relationship: "The ape is us," says Branzi, echoing the animalesque transformations of Bacon's subjects. Even in this sense, Darwinian regression that he theorizes about in *The Primitive Metropolis* has a meaning: man returns to his primordial lineage and his time becomes the time of art: absolute time, a neutral interval in which the present, past, and future are reconcilable thanks to a continuous present that still refers to the universality of the whole. And in which only the spatial and temporal unexpected can become a real experimentation of the territories of the imaginary.

Science is demystified along these lines, and the "wild horse" of Platonic irrationality becomes the instrument with which to survive and decipher an exploded world. "*Neo-Primitivism* – thus – can be much more than a mere transition. Because what strikes at the heart is not just the concept of the avant-garde, but the very limit of humankind. It is not about a grammar, but about functioning as replicants and taking possession of a memory that is not one's own, up until becoming more indigenous than the indigenous ones themselves, more mythical than mythologies, more human than the human."[255]

In this neo-primitive light, in *Solid Dreams* and in *Dolmen*, Branzi moves the barometers of art and begins to plumb the unconscious, avoiding the game of hermeneutics.

He thus undertakes research that again eliminates any structural codification, working towards new Kafkian mental and later spatial coordinates, capable of installing a creative process far removed from the common order of meanings.

In this dramaturgy, Branzi realizes a new anthropology of the imagination by researching *Fundamentalisms*, through a Lukácsian process of the "destruction of reason,"[256] as a form of anti-intellectualism that goes beyond the definitions, distinctions, and deductions they gave a clear and distinct vision of reality.

Almost in the form of an ontological irrationalism, the new research is based on a principle that is rational in a different way, in which the Dionysian and decadent aspect of the human being generates a new phenomenology of urban/universal reality, almost to the point of defining an apologetics of art.

After renouncing dialectical thinking, Branzi really looks for a radical surpassing of the previous dialogical positions, on the meaning of the image of art and its expression, almost to the point of paradoxically realizing the phrase of the later Heidegger: "Thinking begins only when we have come to know that reason, glorified for centuries, is the most stiff-necked adversary of thought."[257]

This rejection of the finalistic and ontological attributes given to the work carries with it first and foremost the rejection of the categories of the image, of the figure, and of vision as an aesthetic act. Rather than proceeding to their re-signification, Branzi resets them and goes back to find their foundations.

As expressed in French philosophy, in particular by Deleuze and Foucault, Branzi sees art as a logic and not as a language, and to create it he goes beyond Western metaphysics again, passing over the discipline of art and even that of the reasoning of art, entering a new design terrain, unexplorable within the discipline but also philosophically.

His way of proceeding thus becomes, leaping over the meta-design condition, a theoretical problem beyond the boundaries of language and science. Entering the territories of de-territorialization, he no longer needs a return to the real, because it has been eliminated from another level of reality, eluding the canonical conditions of the ability to think about space and its meaning as traditionally understood.

In the process of replacing the word civilization with that of dramaturgy, the *Decline of the West*,[258] the necessary re-founding of art as a new neo-primitive anthropology and based on neo-primitive codes, brings his research to inverse the process, putting the individual at the center, with his specificities and changing variations, as a motor that can trigger a new anthropology.

The individual as in instrument of the understanding of reality and the loss of confidence in positivism, thus definitively detaches him from any Marxist position, moving closer instead to those of William James, Wilhelm Dilthey, but above all Henri Bergson[259] and the role of intuition and time as a subjective element, ferrying it toward the interest in Einsteinian and Heisenbergian physics, particularly in the concept of relativity and indeterminacy.

The relativization of *exactitude* leads him toward a marked interest in Freud's theories, particularly in relation to the internal conflict of each individual, as well as to the renaming of the concept of normality and to the analysis of the unconscious and its forms of expression as central: in particular, the dream.

The problem of the genesis of dreams, or of the origin of dreamed subjects, in a moment when consciousness can no longer be the vigil element, puts the focus back on the role of *rêverie* as a place of primitive and unfathomable reality, on which thought has not still acted.

The primitivism in *Solid Dreams* is thus revealed both through the choice of dream as a privileged place for a resetting of consciousness (and thus of science), and as the maximum expression of the resetting of the concept of image in favor of a new anthropology based on the imagination.

If, in fact, in the same way that it is inherent in the concept of primitivism, Branzi re-formulates an alternative to the origin, and from this origin he will develop new aesthetic definitions.

The theme of rêverie in Branzi, close to Bachelard, is again indicative not only of an alternative to knowledge, but, according to his method of always seeking asymmetrical solutions, another way of accessing the Real. But, unlike Freud's position, for Branzi dreams are not revelatory of a psychic mechanism, nor of ideological or utopian images, but rather an anthropological re-founding guaranteed by the passage, via the artistic process, from intuition (or imaginative experience) of the One to that of the Many. It is therefore a typical dynamic of poetics.

Through the dream, Branzi traces his own *Porto Sepolto* (*Buried Port*) and finds in it the question of existence and rediscovers an general anthropology that passes through the dream as a poetic dimension: he recenters the value of oneiric experience as the primary imaginary of the poetic act.

He therefore does not intend for the dream to be a psychological deciphering (of which it is the basic grammar), thus also excluding the concept of "desire" or as subject that can be interpreted according to the criteria and the plots of the vigilant state of consciousness: this is rather a specific form of imaginative experience, which abandons psychological theory to enter a theory of knowledge. And, precisely because typical of the theory of knowledge, the dream is an experience, an oneiric experience that can reveal an "anthropological transcendence" that passes through the imagination.

In this sense, he reawakens his Jewish genes: indeed as evidenced in the Old Testament, Jews communicate through dreams: prophetic dreams and revelatory dreams, which are the concrete soul of Revelation.[260]

But if in biblical dreams, the content is related to fate, in Branzi's it is anthropological. In fact, he doesn't take up either a finalistic or a psychological reading, but deciphers them in relation to the world, as a new anthropology that is formed in the world.[261]

Therefore far from the hermeneutics of symbols and from the attempt at philosophical articulation, this originating moment reveals rather the desire to define a new anthropology of the imagination, which calls for new definitions of the concept of the image and of imagination itself, which manifests itself through worlds other than that of the vigilant mind.

The dream therefore is not a flight from the real, but an experience of art linked to the world of the image and its representation: "It is the image before poetry, and poetry is the primitive form of language, the mother tongue of humanity. The dream is thus at the very beginning of becoming and of objectivity." And in this sense it is not only a possibility of the imagination, but its privileged condition, its "objective transcendence."[262]

And passing from the One (the dreaming subject) to the Many, or from the subjective to the trans-subjective, Branzi reveals the universality of the dream, which reproduces the primal, or primitive, and irreducible elements of human history, manifesting, in the dream, the entire human condition.

Along these lines, "The theorization of a phenomenology of the imagination is the full expression of a transfiguring intention,"[263] and it makes it possible to consider the imagination itself – or rather its experience – as the original condition of knowledge.

As *a priori* knowledge of other disciplines (such as philosophy and psychology), he intends to affirm, through *Solid Dreams*, that imagination is the primitive and fundamental state with respect to its evolution in images, and that, through it, it is possible to rediscover a new anthropology.

Delving into the question of the *things* of the original, unlike the image, which blocks the imagination at a precise moment, and which refers to the cogito of being awake, the imagination, in a Foucauldian way, lives only iconoclastically with images that, paradoxically, represent its opposite: if imagination indeed involves a process of continuous transformation, the image fixes the canons of this process, thus belonging to a stage that is not primitive but historical, of which it is the crystallized expression.

Branzi therefore seeks a process at the origin of poetic production, beyond the contrivance of the image, in search of the origin of expression, and of how expression becomes the condition for an anthropological description, for a new definition of an aesthetics of the imagination *via* poetics. But this anticipates an emancipation of the role of the imagination into a downgrading of the role of the image, which represents a vigilant compromise with the rationality of the cogito, with history, with philosophy, or with all other cultural mediation processes.

The subject of *Solid Dreams*, therefore, before being crystallized into the various images proposed, is therefore the artistic imagination, it being the primitive state of a new anthropology based on the dramaturgy of the subject.

The represented dreams, as the early and primitive possibility of the genesis of the imagination, are articulated only later in images: as miniatures, they are later explained in the temporal contradictions and signs that make up and generate them. Space, in fact, makes the temporally distant simultaneous, the temporally ubiquitous, reconceptualizing the present objects, representing "the things" of an anthropology of art understood as a "revealed religion."

The archaism of the chosen images always suggests a voluminous iconoclastic approach, imposing that particular "realism of unreality" as already defined by Bachelard.[264] As anthropological foundations, images are re-positionings, such that the observer is dispersed in the face of the anti-lyricism of the subjects: Branzi radically dismantles our iconography of the image, our traditional knowledge, our symbolically placing of notable images into certain eras, and he repositions them not in a compositional way, but through juxtaposition, in a new time and in a new space that breaks with every iconographic surety of Western culture: like in *Dead Christ*, and like in the *Unité d'habitation* that, as a symbol of Western architectural culture of the 20th century, sees the housing of the sleeping Asian Buddha of the 5th century BC, where the pagan and the sacred coexist peacefully, "not so much as are areas of knowledge that would have already preliminarily covered what they want to talk about," but in how it reveals a deep and elliptical time that does not proceed linearly, a kind of time that reappears in the involuntary memory of the dream. A memory that does not recall the past, but that, through the domestic objects represented, reveals that "cosmic childhood" as defined by Bachelard: the kind of time that really marks out and contains the secret law of our time, of the inner life of a new anthropological subject.

As anthropological archetypes, Branzi re-proposes the three major themes of his experience of a young Florentine artist: late-Latin domesticity, Christian dramaturgy, Oriental culture.

As visual poems, the *Dolmen* instead become the physical manifestation of the analysis that Deleuze did of Beckett (in the theater) and Bacon (in painting): they express the transition from a concept of "digital" art to an "analogue" one, where if the former passes through an aesthetic and learnable code, one that can be expressed in an abstract work, the latter expresses paralinguistic signs, through the violent irruption of a presence, of a form that imposes itself immediately.[265]

Dolmen, prehistoric, megalithic, single-room tombs, evoke a neo-primitivism in which a new vision of a stone room comes to life, in which the contemporary subject experiences his or her own end concomitantly with the end of figuration. Like the exhausted of Beckett, the subjects of Branzi's *Dolmen* are exhausted (*épuisé*), and represent the concept not so much of death (thus of a decisive and final outcome), but rather to penultimate-ness, at one step away from an end that it is not represented in the image of the models, but presents itself, triggered by the image itself, in the thought of the observer.

In this passage between the penultimate and the last, it reveals not only an anthropological interplay, but also one between language and form, or rather, between formal and a-formal.

Branzi's exhausted one, which accompanies the parkour and new mystics of *The Primitive Metropolis*, and which represents *Le Grand Malade*, has exhausted with him/herself everything possible, according to a "relentless Spinozism"[266] that always compels him/her one step away from the end.

As opposed to birth, the *Dolmen* demonstrate how being is not a concept of superman (*übermensch*), but rather a "sordid and twilight"[267] experience, which takes place between sleep and wakefulness.

And from the Deleuzian exhausted, they seem to take up the posture as well: "The exhausted has a posture: it is seated [...]. For there is a difference between seated exhaustion and the tiredness that lies down, crawls or gets stuck. Tiredness affects action in all its states, whereas exhaustion only relates to the amnesic witness. The seated is the witness around which the other turns, while developing every degree of tiredness."[268]

If state of sitting in the Indo-European tradition is associated with the idea of inactivity, of the suspension of any activity, Branzi goes back to its Latin genesis, that of *desidiosus*, that of inertia, of ceasing to do.

But apart from representing the new contemporary subject, Branzi's exhausted ones, along with the damned of Beckett, Bacon, and Dante, represent an entire vision of artwork as an idea about the world, summing up an entire vision of art itself.

Touching on both the theme of the figure and that of the body, his damned ones are deprived of sublime content, and their representation through the body makes the meaning of that explicit: the problem of the body indeed acquires greater significance if one thinks of Branzi's work as an attempt at dissolution. If the *Dolmen* actually incarnate the desire to dissolve the figurativity of the work, they enact this through the body.

Becoming subject and object simultaneously, the body, not coinciding with its structure, is a form without organs, according to the expression borrowed from Artaud (with his "body without organs") that Deleuze with Guattari had adopted in *Anti-Oedipus*.

As in Bacon, it is slaughtered meat, that is, a contemporary state of life and death, of structure (bones), and of meat and, like slaughtered meat, it has retained within it all the suffering of death and the color of life.

But the canceling out of the figure does not pass through the dissolution of the ego and the body, but instead comes closer to Blanchot's position, that is, in the fusion of the highest presence and utmost dissolution, avoiding a new emancipatory perspective of the dissolution of the subject, according to a nihilistic way of thinking.

But the canceling out of the figure, which paradoxically passes through the body, occurs in the *Dolmen* also through other levels, and among those the first consists in positioning the isolated and decentralized bodies: in decentralization, Branzi nullifies its figurative, narrative character. Through the "purely figural," that is, through "extraction and isolation," the image breaks with representation, it does not lead to a narrative, it frees the figure in its being a fact in itself.

And by stripping the figure of the temptation of figuration, it frees them from any kind of code, and brings them to their own level of understanding, that is, that of sensation: "The Figure is the sensible form related to a sensation; it acts immediately upon the nervous system, which is of the flesh, whereas abstract form is addressed to the head, and acts through the intermediary of the brain, which is closer to the bone."[269]

Sensation, expressed through the body of the *Dolmen*, is immediately established relative to the observer, without going through the decoding of the work or its narration: "Violence of the represented is replaced by the violence of representation."[274] But this violence does not only represent an anthropological dimension, but also that of the artist in terms of the canonical data of representation, "to enter the very body of the visible."[270]

And secondarily, having the characteristic of moving from one threshold of reality to another, through a process of de-formation, Branzi's men also deform, despite being at rest: "The deformation of the bodies of the subjects is static, and the entire body is traversed by intense movement: a deformedly deformed movement, which at any moment goes back to the real image of the body."[271]

Entering the category of "monstrous" as an antinomy to the traditional one and that concretizes precisely in the body of the subjects, Branzi eliminates figuration also through the convulsive line painted on the twisted bodies, a "surface line, in service of the accident,"[272] and not a regular one at the service of the Spirit.

However, the body's chromaticity enters into opposition with the monochromatism of the space of the *Dolmen*, that is, of the room, which is simultaneously space and time.

In the time of insomnia, the neutrality of the space of the room precedes the action of the exhausted, and it is configured as a closed and defined space. As gray or homogenous zones of a same space, they are distinguished only by the sampling of transparent walls. Although it is a definite space, it is an anyspace, but its fragmentation carries out a first de-potentialization.

Fragmenting the walls and making them transparent, Branzi diminishes their formal qualification, to which the stones yet refer: like the weights of the outside world and at the same time the thought of the subject of the Dolmen, they float in the void so as to render unfathomable both their relationship with the subject, and the figurative value that belongs to the subject.

In this broken tale, of unexpressed language, even the repetition of the images in a combinatorics of twelve gives strength to the dissolution: in the force of repetition.

In addition to linguistic mediations, using the third language of sensation, Branzi also continues with the dissolution of the gaze: the hysteresis of the subject leads him to a new haptic definition of art, such that the tactile replaces the eye and sight, inaugurating a new dimension of sensoriality with respect to the first definition of weak and diffuse territories.

As an exhausted subject, Branzi's attendants therefore exhaust every possibility of form.

Neo-Prehistory also fits into this re-founding or neo-primitive dimension.

In the exhibition for the XXI Triennale di Milano, with Kenya Hara, Branzi returns to the relationship between *Words and Things*, generating a double taxonomy that interlaces discourse on language (the 100 verbs) and discourse on the visible (the 100 objects) and between the content (the objects and the verbs) and that which contains (mirrored space).

Simulating a metropolis of the imagination, which calls into question all of the fundamental canons of artistic practice, Branzi in this territory re-formulates the fundamental codes of the theory of representation and that of language prior to intervening in the discipline: the visible and the enunciable, "the discursive and non-discursive formations, the forms of expression, and those of content."[273]

Unlike Kosuth's research that finds in representation the concept of its relativization, or in relation to the distance that Magritte generates between representation and language, Branzi's operation does not attempt either a division between the word and the thing, or a link in the sole field of representation: he attempts, rather, the dissolution of both and a new reconciliation in the territory of the imagination, in which, however, words and things continue to be neither conformed, nor isomorphic, nor symbolized, but instead maintain, in continuous disjunction, the particular relationship with the heterogeneous as previously investigated by Foucault with Borges.[274]

In this non-relation, this disjunction between the visible and the enunciable, a distinction in nature is maintained, underlined by the fact that the words used are not the *Names* of the represented objects, but are *Verbs*.

Only in the scheme of the imagination do they unite, by an anthropological imagination that weaves them together in a dimension that is not that of the description of forms or the connection between form and word: a third informal dimension diagonally cuts the meaning of first two, eliminating not only the primacy of one over the other, but their plane of conciliation.

It is therefore once again the relationship of heterogeneity that generates a new axis of relations between the objects of the world and words and, in this new plane of thinking, Branzi does not only mine language in itself, but also the syntax of things and the modes with which they are interpreted and connected in the world itself.

Exchanging verbs and objects, and having them travel in parallel, ruptures the literal transparence that connects them, and the bond of representation that has always linked them in the common order.

Representing the dispersion of identity, the proliferation of verbs generates in this first sequence (language) a law independent even from the objects represented and, as with Humpty Dumpty, the verbs lead to the impenetrability of meaning:[275] the choice of verbs has in fact as a consequence the destitution of the identity of the object, the loss of its own name. According to Deleuze, "The singular proper name is guaranteed by the permanence of knowledge; such knowledge is embodied in the general names that designate pauses and states of rest, nouns and adjectives with which it maintains a constant relationship [...] But when nouns and adjectives begin to merge, when the names that designate pauses and rests are carried by the verbs of pure becoming and slipping into the language of events, every identity of the ego is lost [...]. As if the events enjoyed an unreality that is communicated to knowledge, and to people, through language."[276]

It is therefore the collapse in the proper name as the fixative and immobile principle of thought, as definitive naming, as achieved stability.

As derived from the subject and the object, without belonging to either one or the other, the verbs generate an always open proposition: if, as Mallarmé maintains, "nommer an objet c'est supprimer les trois quarts de la jouissance du poème," Branzi replaces the fixity of the naming and the direct relationship with things through an analogous attribution between the word and the object, in which the word, as verb, benefits new possible heterogeneous, non-immediate relationships.

The verb, elevated by the naming and belonging to an eternal and repeatable time, approaches only subsequent to the object, and removes it from its historical depth and from the common archaeological principle.

On the one hand, thus, the object with its own verticality and historical corporeality specifies precise temporal dating; on the other hand, the words that express some of the possible logical attributes that can be connected to the object itself and that diagonally traverse time.

The relationship between objects and verbs is therefore not by association, but through a relation between general and open actions and specific and historicizable objects. A relation that voluntarily always eludes and always in the field of the changeable and of non-reconcilable. Only in appearance do they connect back to each other.

And, in parallel with verbs, objects are also heteroclite subjects.

As anti-lyrical objects, each of them, in their being presented as small individual columns and not representing any linear category in their sequence, forms specific conceptual categories that refer back to a specific knowledge or a specific disciplinary model or, even, to a specific anthropology.

Their seemingly historical order and their intentionally heterogeneous nature generate that middle region that eludes every specific discipline and every specification.

As evidence, objects thus represent not only things but also the story of their relationship with the world to which they belong. Since they are all enunciations, the proposed order, which is neither philological nor taxonomic, rather reveals in the singularity of objects the epiphenomena that have made the development of a science possible, as if it were "the *a priori* historical and in the element of which positivity the ideas were able to appear, the sciences formed [...] knowledge is not thus described in its progress [...] but the field of epistemology, the episteme in which knowledge, considered apart from any reference criterion in terms of its rational value or its objective forms and immerging into its positivity in such a way manifests a history that does not coincide with that of its growing perfection, but is rather the history of its conditions of possibility [...]. The configurations that have given rise to the various forms of empirical knowledge. More than a history in the traditional sense, it is an *archaeology*."[277]

An archaeology that, as such, highlights the distance between contemporary thought and historical thought, but that, in this distance, enables the revealing of all historical specifics through a diagonal, heterogeneous, and, hence, contemporary representation. In this sense, Branzi's is a neo-prehistory: in the hybridization between method and object of observation, between a new way of reconciling the irreconcilable without arriving at a synthesis.

Representation, being the first principle of archaeological discovery, allows Branzi to generate that future anterior in which genesis and the future are accumulated in the use of the devices of the word and the thing.

And the object, in this double sequence of words and things, is relativized in favor of a new concept of representation that proves to be the only plane that is seemingly dialogical.

The mirroring space, in this sense, not only reaffirms the preceding contents, among which the limitation emerges of the lyricism of the objects and the destruction of their ordering principle, but adds a theoretical and falsifying plane in which language and objects interweave: the plane on which, because absolute and falsifying, the heterogeneous and the discordant can be represented together.

Definitively approaching Foucaultian positions, Branzi "therefore discovers an unknown land in which a literary form, a scientific proposition, or an everyday phrase are still enunciated, but without a common measure, without any reduction or discursive equivalence. Science and poetry are knowledge in the same way."[278]

This space could only be Borges' table: an unlikely three-dimensional space without time or place: a neutral space, but absolute, solemn, precisely because it is precisely this space that can generate the critical cut of the exhibition and the sense of the whole. It is the mirror surface of the median region and the plane of reconciliation.

Again, the envelope becomes the subject of an irreconcilable multiplicity and magnitude, which represents a new a priori of design, language, and representation.

NOTES

1. A. Branzi, "Gli oggetti come pensiero dell'universo," in *Modo* n. 94, November 1986;

2. In particular, since the CIAM VIII in Hoddesdon, on the Heart of the City, and that of Dubrovnik, in 1956;

3. E. C. Cattaneo, Introduction, *Loaded Void. City Theory since 1956*, Maggioli, Milan, 2015;

4. D. Harvey, *The Condition of Postmodernity. An Enquiry into the Origins of Cultural Change*, Blackwell Publisher, Cambridge, 1990;

5. M. Berman, *The Experience of the Modernity*, Penguin Books, NY, 1982;

6. Contextualism will develop widely in Italy, especially in Milan and Venice starting from the Rogers' school, *via* Gregotti, generating new cultural positions in the relationship between urban morphology, typology, and city, intended as a system of signs;

7. G. C. Argan, "Introduzione a Wright" in *Metron*, n. 18, 1947, and "Arte e rivoluzione," in *Superfici*, n. 6, September 1963;

8. J. Habermas, "Moderno, Postmoderno e Neoconservatorismo," in *Alfabeta*, March 1981;

9. N. Pevsner, *An Outline of European Architecture*, 1943, and *Pioneers of Modern Design*, 1949;

10. S. Giedion, *Space, Time and Architecture. The Growth of a new tradition*, Cambridge, 1941 and *Breviario di architettura*, Garzanti, Milan, 1961;

11. See E. N. Rogers, *Esperienza dell'Architettura*, edited by Luca Molinari, Skira publisher, Milan, 1997;

12. C. Waldheim, "The Other '56," in *Urban Design*, edited by Alex Krieger and William S. Saunders, University of Minnesota Press, 2009;

13. Organized by J.L. Sert; As expressed by Mumford in the text "The Emergence of Urban Design in the Breakup of the CIAM," in A. Krieger and W. Saunders, *Op. Cit.*:"The phrase Urban Design was introduced to Harvard and the general public by Sert and Giedion in the early 1950s. Sert seems to have first used it publicly in a 1953 lecture, 'Urban Design', given shortly after he was appointed dean at Harvard. The venue was the Regional Conference of the AIA—Middle Atlantic District in Washington, D.C., where Sert spoke in a series of AIA seminars, *The Architect and Urban Design and Urban Redevelopment*";

14. For a detailed study, see J. M. Montaner, *After the Modern Movement. Architecture in the Second Half of the Twentieth Century*, Laterza, Rome-Bari 2002;

15. M. Bandini, *L'estetico, il politico. Da Cobra all'Internazionale Situazionista, 1948-57*, Costa & Nolan Pub., Genoa, 1999;

16. G. Debord, "Definitions," in *Internationale Situationniste* #1, Paris, June 1958;

17. G. Debord, Ibidem;

18. Ivan Chtchglov, "Formulary for a New Urbanism," in *Internationale Situationniste* #1, Ibidem;

19. To demonstrate the summarized theses, Debord's psychogeographic plans are elaborated: *Fin de Copenhague*, *Guide Psychogéographique de Paris* e *The Naked City*. Published in J. Jorn *Pour La forme i détournement e la dérive*, 1958;

20. M. Jammer, *Concepts of Space. The History of Theories of Space in Physics*, Harvard University Press, Cambridge, 1954;

21. Debord, in *Report on the Construction of Situations*, 1957, summarizes the first conceptual nucleus of Situationism;

22. H. Lefebvre, *Critique de la vie quotidienne*, ed. Grasset, Paris, 1947 and G. Debord, *La Société du Spectacle*, Buchet/Chastel Publisher, Paris, 1967;

23. A. Breton, *Manifeste du surréalisme*, Éditions du Sagittaire, Paris, 1924;

24. M. Bandini, *Op. Cit.*;

25. M. Bandini, *Op. Cit.*;

26. Ettore Sottsass, at the Congress of Alba: "All the expressive possibilities of the plastic world must contribute to the creation of a new and ultimately true structure, which is no longer the set of pillars and beams holding up the construction, but the structure of an intense, modulated, open, and continuous space;"

27. A. Branzi, "Constant's Poetic Revolution," in *Domus* n. 880, 2003;

28. A. Branzi, "Constant's Poetic Revolution," *Op. Cit.*;

29. As described by Paola Navone in "Radical Architecture," by Paola Navone and Bruno Orlandoni, *Casabella*, Milan, 1974: "Among the fundamental dates that can be indicated for the origins of English Pop: the winter of 1952-53 with the foundation of the Independent Group by Reyner Banham, and 1953, the year of the exhibition *Parallel of Life and Art* at the ICA (Institute of Contemporary Art) in London; 1955, *Man, Machine and Motion* exhibition at the ICA; 1956, with the exhibition *This is Tomorrow* at the Whitechapel Art Gallery in London. The entire phenomenon is examined in the essay "The Development of British Pop," by Alloway, in Lucy R. Lippard, *Pop Art*, Praeger, 1967. The dates of American Pop are a little behind. The first "combines" by Robert Rauschenberg are from 1955. After three years of collaboration as the set daesigner for the Merce Cunningham Dance Company, in 1958 he performed the piece "Bizarre Encounter" with the same company and with the music of John Cage. In the same year, Rauschenberg and Jasper Johns held two personal exhibitions at the Leo Castelli Gallery in New York. Also in 1958, Allan Kaprow performed the first happening. 1959 sees the first solo exhibition of Oldenburg, and in 1960 the first of Jim Dine. Andy Warhol and Roy Lichtenstein began to exhibit Pop artists in 1963. In Italy, Pop became a commonly known phenomenon following the 32nd Venice Biennale of 1964 (within the US Pavilion, works by Rauschenberg, Johns, Dine, and Oldenburg were exhibited). Between 1963 and 1965, the first informal publications on Italian magazines started to be published (*Metro*, *Il Verri*, *La botte e il Violino*, but especially *Collage* and *Marcatrè*). With respect to the criticism written about Pop Art, the first attempts to historicize the phenomenon were in 1965: John Rublowsky, *Pop Art*, Basic Books Inc., New York, and Mario Amaya, *Pop As Art - a Survey of the New Super Realism*, Studio Vista, London. From 1966 is *Pop Art* by Lucy R. Lippard (Thames and Hudson), which would be released in Italy in 1967. Also in 1967, Pop Art will be released in the USA by Alberto Boatto (Lerici);"

30. The exhibition was divided into twelve sections each organized by a group of artists. Of particular note is Group 2, in which Richard Hamilton presented the collage *Just What Is It That Makes Today's Homes So Different, So Appealing?*;

31. The Independent Group (IG), formed within the Institute of Contemporary Arts (ICA) in London, and considered the forerunner of Pop Art, was operative from 1952 to 1955. Composed of artists of different disciplinary backgrounds, it was oriented toward criticism of the Modern, and it introduced the topic of mass culture into the elitist one;

32. See Bonito Oliva, *Il territorio magico. Comportamenti alternativi nell'arte*, Le Lettere, Florence, 2009;

33. R. Banham, Introduction, *Archigram*, by Peter Cook and Michael Webb, Princeton Architectural Press, 1973;

34. P. Navone, *Op. Cit.*;

35. This is how it is expressed: "All terms, reports, controls, and classical organizations crumbled, blew up, leaving space for the new

images that light up and go out here and there, provoked by vital explosions where there are, by sexual debauchery, heroic ambitions, frantic activity, repentance, egoism, terror, insolence, in a sort of chaotic, confused, overbearing, and overblown landscape as the landscape of medieval Europe, or the Middle Ages in the East, or the Middle Ages of Mexico, or whatever, could have been... What do my furnishings have to do with it? They are nothing, and they do not matter at all. But the idea would be to invent whole new possibilities, new forms, new symbols: to climb on things that are dying to see if it is possible to throw into people's lives other people's energy, other lives, and other dynamics." Ettore Sottsass, "Furniture 1965 for Poltronova," in *Domus* n. 433, 1965;

36. The Thirteenth Triennial of Milan in 1964, led by Vittorio Gregotti, was divided into four parts: the *Introductory Section* of an international character and with connecting spaces; *the Italian Section*; *the Foreign Sections*; *the Park and temporary exhibitions*. For further details, see the *Thirteenth Triennial of Milan, International Exhibition of Decorative and Industrial Modern Arts and of Modern Architecture*, June 12-September 27, 1964, Archive, of the Triennial of Milan;

37. The first Italian Piper was inaugurated on February 17, 1965 in Rome. Welcoming artists from all over Italy, it was understood as an icon of the Beat Generation, from which it took both social and graphic contents in furnishings;

38. From the site of the Venice Biennale about the Exhibition of 1964: "That of 1964 was the edition of the clamorous arrival of American Pop Art, which returned vitality to the Biennale. The prize reserved for a foreign artist was awarded to Robert Rauschenberg, shifting the balance of pictorial research from Europe to the United States. Pop Art in Venice was also represented by Jasper Johns, Jim Dine, and Claes Oldenburg. A parallel exhibition of pop artists was organized by Leo Castelli and Ileana Sonnabend, in the ex-US Consulate in San Gregorio. This additional exhibition showed that the United States was firmly oriented toward Pop Art.
The Grand Prize awarded to Rauschenberg caused many controversies, including within the international jury. Moreover, as the artist exhibited only four paintings in the official pavilion, as soon as he knew of the prize, some of the works exhibited at San Gregorio were quickly transferred to the Gardens. The clamor that Pop Art elicited in European criticism and the press cast a shadow over the other exhibitions of that year;"

39. Pichler e Hollein, in *Absolute Architecture*: "The shape of the building doesn't develop out of the material condition of its purpose. A building shall not show it s purpose. It is not an expression of structure and construction, it is not an enclosure or refuge. A building is itself. Architecture is without purpose," 1962;

40. H. Hollein, *Alles ist Architektur*, *Op. Cit.*;

41. F. Raggi, "Vienna Orchestra," in *Casabella* n. 392, 1974;

42. P. Navone, *Op. Cit.*;

43. Developed in Italy in the early 1960s, Operaismo reversed the roles of power between capitalism and the worker class, believing that the latter was the engine of economic progress, and not vice versa. In this light, the worker class became subject to a revolutionary process aimed at renouncing work, through a process of the "self-destruction" of the class necessary for the elimination of capital.
The main theorists of Italian Operaismo were Mario Tronti, Toni Negri, and Raniero Panzieri, who, through the foundation of *Quaderni Rossi*, gave a voice to the intellectuals who were detached from both the Communist Party and the Socialist Party. In particular, Michael Hardt and Toni Negri defined Operaismo as a current of anti-authoritarian Marxist thinking. Subsequently, with the foundation of *Classe Operaia*, Mario Tronti, Alberto Asor Rosa, Rita Di Leo, Romeno Alquati, Toni Negri, and Massimo Cacciari undertook a more transdisciplinary position, involving the theme of intellectuals and their role within the debate on class structure. At the end of the Sixties, Operaismo divided into Potere Operaio and Lotta Continua. Operaismo concluded in the mid-1970s, when a more complex political season began, occasionally intersecting with Italian terrorism. See: S. Mezzadra, "Operaismo," in R. Esposito, C. Galli, *Enciclopedia del pensiero politico. Autori, concetti, dottrine*, Laterza, Rome-Bari, 2000; G. Trotta and F. Milana, *L'operaismo degli anni Sessanta. Da "Quaderni rossi" a "Classe Operaia,"* DeriveApprodi publisher, Rome, 2008; M. Pasquinelli, "Italian Operaismo and the Information Machine," in *Theory, Culture & Society* n.2, 2014; S. Wright, *L'assalto al cielo. Per una storia dell'operaismo*, Edizioni Alegre, Rome, 2008; M. Filippini, *Mario Tronti e l'operaismo politico degli anni Sessanta*, EuroPhilosophie Publisher, 2011; F. Milanesi, *Nel Novecento. Storia, teoria, politica nel pensiero di Mario Tronti*, Mimesis, Milan, 2014;

44. P. V. Aureli, *Il progetto dell'autonomia. Politica e architettura dentro e contro il capitalismo*, Quodlibet, Macerata, 2016; English text: *Project of Autonomy: Politics and Architecture Within and Against Capitalism*, Princeton Architectural Press, 2012;

45. *Socialisme ou Barbarie* was a French organization founded in 1948 by Cornelius Castoriadis and Claude Lefort, characterized by a libertarian and anti-Leninist orientation. In particular, it approached an anti-dogmatic Marxism that was against Stalinism. Its theoretical position was expressed in the magazine with the same name, from 1949 to 1967. Guy Debord also joined the Movement for a short time (from 1960 to 1961). See: *Socialisme ou Barbarie, Chronique des grèves en France en 1953 et 1957*, Éditions Acratie, La Bussière, 1985; *Socialisme ou Barbarie, Anthologie*, Éditions Acratie, La Bussière, 2007; P. Gottraux, *"Socialisme ou Barbarie," un engagement politique et intellectuel dans la France de l'après-guerre*, Lausanne, Payot, 1997;

46. Operative from 1961 to 1966 and founded by Raniero Panzieri and Mario Tronti, it introduced a closer relationship between political interest and the role of the intellectual, deepening the themes of class struggle and the capitalist organization of labor, in which Operaismo became an active class. In 1963, Mario Tronti, Alberto Asor Rosa, and Massimo Cacciari abandoned it to found the *Classe Operaia*. See: R. Panzieri, *Spontaneità e organizzazione. Gli anni dei Quaderni rossi* (1959-1964), BFS Edizioni, 1994; G. Roggero, F. Pozzi, G. Borio, *Futuro anteriore. Dai Quaderni rossi al movimento globale. Ricchezze e limiti dell'operaismo italiano*, DeriveApprodi, Rome, 2002; G. Borio, F. Pozzi, G. Roggero, *Gli operaisti: Autobiografie dei cattivi maestri*, DeriveApprodi, Rome, 2005; G. Trotta, F. Milana, *L'operaismo degli anni Sessanta. Da Quaderni rossi a Classe operaia*, DeriveApprodi, Rome, 2008;

47. P.V. Aureli, *Il progetto dell'autonomia. Op. Cit;*

48. Historical magazine of the workerist Left, it was founded in 1964 to give a more concrete form to the themes of *Quaderni Rossi*. In addition to the founders, Toni Negri and Claudio Greppi took part in it;

49. *Potere Operaio* was published weekly beginning in September 1969 as an instrument of Antonio Negri's, Oreste Scalzone's and Franco Piperno's group. Beginning in March 1971, it was published biweekly until the summer of the same year. Beginning in the autumn of 1971, it became a monthly and was accompanied by a weekly magazine titled *Potere Operaio del lunedì*. The story of these two magazines followed the downward trend of political formation, ending in fact by the end of 1973;

50. From the editorial board of *Contropiano*: "The first issue of the four-monthly magazine directed by Alberto Asor Rosa and Massimo Cacciari came out in January 1968, few months after the end of the *Classe Operaia* experience. Toni Negri was also a member of the founders' group, but he left shortly thereafter because of a diverging opinion on the relationship with the PCI and the Worker Movement. Negri wrote two important essays ("La teoria capitalistica del '29: John M. Keynes" and "Marx sul ciclo e la crisi"). The magazine was composed of three sections (essays, materials, notes). It played an important political-cultural role, as Tronti himself points out, especially in the valorization (of which political Operaismo was a herald) of "that kind of culture that came from any other place, indeed from exactly opposite

places, because it was a culture of a great bourgeois decadence, with strong irrational ideas, but with a great attention to the entire phenomenon of artistic, historical avant-gardes in the figurative arts, in literature, in poetry, and in music." The last issue of the magazine was the September / December 1971 one;

51. M. Tronti, in *Operai e capitale*, addressing the theme of political autonomy. See M. Tronti, *Operai e capitale*, DeriveApprodi, Rome, 2006;

52. M. Tronti, Introduction, *Operai e capitale*, DeriveApprodi, Rome, 2006;

53.M. Tronti, *Op. Cit.*: "For a long time, rigorously and without fail, we must remained fixed on the object to look at: the present society, the society of capital, its two classes, the struggle between these classes, their history, their predictions on their development. To those who ask what will be next, we have to answer: we do not know yet. This problem has yet to come. One should not depart from this problem. We have not arrived at it. And that is one of the reasons why in all this talk that the future seems not to exist. Of all that exists today, in fact, nothing for us is the future. And anticipating the model of a society of the future in the analysis of the current one is a bourgeois ideological vice that only the oppressed working class and the avant-garde intellectuals could reasonably inherit: it is the fanfare before the procession, or a reward for cowardice with the promise that there is the world of the righteous. No worker fighting the owner asks you: and afterwards? The fight against the owner is all. The organization of this struggle is everything. But already all this is a world. Agreed. It's the old world that needs to be pulled down. But who tells you that, to overthrow it, this simple will to overthrow the power organized in the dominant class is enough? On one side the working class, on the other capitalist society: this is the modern scheme of class struggle. It's not true that in this way the relation of forces shifts in favor of capital. The opposite is true. The working class acquires and recognizes only its own strength, of the only living, active, productive element of society, of the hinge of social relations, - a fundamental link between economic development and hence potentially in its hands the political dominance over the present. The revolutionary process through which this dominance will become real could also see forced steps of progress, with the skipping of some phases. But at the height of development, the power wrested from the capitalists, a difficult period of political dictatorship of the workers across society – this, no, cannot be skipped. And that's the best of the future we are able to see, the furthest we want to see. As a goal of the struggle, that's enough. As an organization of the fight, we need it. More than that cannot be said. The prophecies about the new world, about the new man, about the new human community, they now seem to us like dirty things, like the justification of a shameful past. No, today's problem is not what needs to replace the old world. The problem today is still how to break it down. It is essential, therefore, to know what it is, where it is going and why, with what forces behind it and with what struggles";

54. A. Asor Rosa, "Critica dell'ideologia ed esercizio storico," in *Casabella* n. 619-620, 1995. See also M. Assennato "La domanda irrisolta di Manfredo Tafuri. Architettura e Operaismo," in *AURA*, 27 June 2016;

55. The School of Suspicion is a term used by Paul Ricœur and indicates the common feature of anti-ideological positions developed by Karl Marx, Friedrich Nietzsche, and Sigmund Freud, represented respectively by historical materialism, the genealogical method, and the psychoanalytic method. See P. Ricoeur, *Freud & Philosophy: An Essay on Interpretation* (1965) and *The Conflict of Interpretations* (1969);

56. M. Cacciari, *Pensiero negativo e razionalizzazione. Problemi e funzione della critica del sistema dialettico*, Marsilio, Padua, 1978;

57. M. Cacciari, *Op. Cit.*;

58. A. Branzi, *Una generazione esagerata. Dai Radical italiani alla crisi della globalizzazione*, ed.Baldini & Castoldi, Milan, 2014;

59. A. Mecacci, "La morte dell'Arte e l'ascesa della Merce design," in *Aisthesis*, anno II n. 2, 2009;

60. See M. Tafuri: "Studi e ipotesi di lavoro per il sistema direzionale di Rome," in *Casabella-Continuità*, n. 264, June 1962, pp. 27-36; "La città territorio: verso una nuova dimensione," with G. Piccinato and V. Quilici, in *Casabella-Continuità* n. 270, December 1962, pp. 16-25; "Un'ipotesi per la città-territorio di Rome – Strutture produttive e direzionali nel comprensorio pontino," with E. Fattinnanzi, in *Casabella-Continuità* n. 274, April 1963, pp. 26-3. At that time, *Casabella-Continuità* began a series of publications on the theme of the territory as the enlarged site of the project;

61 M. Tafuri, "Per una critica dell'ideologia architettonica," in *Contropiano Materiali marxisti* n. 1/1969;

62 M. Tafuri, *Progetto e utopia: architettura e sviluppo capitalistico*, Rome-Bari, Laterza, 1973;

63 M. Tafuri, "La città territorio: verso una nuova dimensione," in *Casabella-Continuità*, *Op. Cit.*;

64 M. Tafuri, "La città territorio: verso una nuova dimensione," in *Casabella-Continuità*, *Op. Cit.*;

65 See M. Tafuri, in *Per una Critica Ideologica*: "To dispel anxiety by understanding and internalizing its causes: this would seem to be one of the principal ethical imperatives of bourgeois art. It matters little whether the conflicts, contradictions and torments that create anxiety are absorbed into a comprehensive mechanism capable of reconciling those differences, or whether catharsis is achieved through contemplative sublimation. We recognize, in any case, the 'necessity' of the bourgeois intellectual in the imperative significance his "social" mission assumes: in other words, there exists, between the avant-gardes of capital and the intellectual avant-gardes, a kind of tacit understanding, so tacit indeed that any attempt to bring it into the light elicits a chorus of indignant protest. Culture, in its intermediary role, has so defined its distinguishing features in ideological terms that in its shrewdness it has reached the point — beyond all intellectual good faith — of imposing forms of contestation and protest upon its own products. And the higher the formal level of the sublimation of conflicts, the more the structures confirming and validating that sublimation remain hidden. If we are to confront the subject of the ideology of architecture from this perspective, we must attempt to shed light on how one of the most functional proposals for the reorganization of capital has come to suffer the most humiliating frustrations, to the point where it can be presented today as objective and transcending all connotations of class, or even as a question of alternatives, a terrain of direct confrontation between intellectuals and capital;"

66 By tracing the genesis of the architecture crisis already in the 18th century, which begins to "become aware of the problem of the city as an autonomous field of communicative experiences – and of the traditional concept of form," interpreting the anticipatory value of Piranesi's Campo Marzio, identified as a project of the crisis of universality and of totality, Tafuri begins to develop the concept of the decline of architecture, understood as the crisis of bourgeois ideology under the Modern Movement: "Uselessly anguished because it is useless to struggle when one is trapped inside a capsule with no exit. The crisis of modern architecture does not issue from 'weariness' or 'dissipation.' Rather, it is a crisis of the ideological function of architecture. The 'fall' of modern art is the ultimate testimony of bourgeois ambiguity, poised as it is between 'positive' goals—the reconciliation of contradictions—and the merciless exploration of its own objective commodification. There is no more 'salvation' to be found within it: neither by wandering restlessly through 'labyrinths' of images so polyvalent that they remain mute, nor by shutting oneself up in the sullen silence of geometries content with their own perfection. This is why there can be no proposals of architectural 'anti- spaces': any search for an alternative within the structures determining the mystification of planning is an obvious contradiction in terms. Reflection on architecture, as a critique of the concrete ideology 'realized' by architecture itself, can only push further, and strive for a specifically concrete dimension in which the systematic destruction of the mythologies sustaining its

development is only one of the objectives. But only the future conditions of the class struggle will tell us whether the task we are setting ourselves is that of an avant-garde or a rearguard." As underlined by Franco Purini in the introduction to *Project and Utopia*, Tafuri both implements an inversion and highlights the role of contradiction within the city's themes: the inversion and the replacement of architecture by the city, he returns "the problematic role of architecture," which oscillates between its active and "structural" dimension and the formal one, not allowing an escape from the complexity and contradiction inherent in the urban question. So, "For those who want to break with a traditional conception and link architecture to the destiny of the city, all that remains is to conceive the city itself as the specific place of technological production and the technological product itself, reducing architecture to just a moment in the chain of production." Along these lines, Dal Co, referring to the transition from architecture to the city: "Urbanism was the most pertinent response architecture could give at that moment [...]. The continuity of architectural design finds in urbanism its own point of arrival, the space that up to that point was the 'data' on which architecture intervened, in order to give it a new configuration. Now, it appears as the true end of architecture, whose task becomes to 'broadly define' the space, thus reaching the highest point of the whole process of rationalization within architecture itself [...]; the political mandate of architects, in the face of this irreversible situation, is realized outside of architecture itself: it is no longer sufficient to think and operate for the death of architecture, that death must become a political death"; F. Dal Co, "Note per una critica dell'ideologia," in Contropiano n.1, 1968;

67 M. Tafuri, *La città Territorio*: "At the roundtable of the Convegno di Lecce, also in 1959, between Giancarlo de Carlo, Piero Moroni, Eduardo Vittoria, and Ludovico Quaroni, it was said that, "The scale has changed in the urban scene like it has changed in life, in works, in physical and real space, as well as in the conception of these things [...]. The dilation, the fusion of cities in the city-region derives or can result from it, it results in a practical plurality of functions and aspects, and the physical and not just physical dimensions of the open city and the large spaces [...]. We are still on the level of intuitions and more than a little nebulous; however, the particular reasons that lead to a new integration of urbanism and architecture, combining expressive research on sociological and technological bases, are already indicated. At the same time, but with a more official tone, the *Code of Urbanism* was elaborated, which soon appeared as the concluding act of the entire political-cultural battle that the Istituto Nazionale di Urbanistica had been undertaking in those years [...] they attempted to include the various sectorial planning into a general programming framework;"

68 M. Tafuri, *Progetto e Utopia*, *Op. Cit.*, p. 73; See also M. Biraghi, *Progetto di crisi. Manfredo Tafuri e l'architettura contemporanea*, Marinotti, Milan, 2005;

69 In this way, Tafuri's interest in the pragmatic attitude of the American city is evident, in particular the position of Hilberseimer, who understands the city as a social machine and eliminates the question of architecture by eliminating architecture itself in favor of the cell-city relationship;

70 M. Tafuri, "Per una Critica ideologica dell'architettura," p. 73: "Pop Art, Op Art, analyses of the city's imageability, and esthetique prospective, all these things converge toward a single objective: that of dissimulating the contradictions of the contemporary city, resolving them in polyvalent images, figuratively glorifying that formal complexity which, when read with the proper parameters, proves to be nothing more than the explosion of the incurable conflicts that elude the plans of advanced capitalism (...). An art that refuses to place itself in the vanguard of the cycles of production, demonstrates, well beyond all verbal challenges, that the consumption process extends to infinity, and that even rubbish, when sublimated into useless or nihilistic objects, can assume a new use value, thus reentering, if only by the back door, the cycle of production and consumption. Yet this rear guard is also an indication of the capitalist plan's refusal—perhaps only temporary—to fully resolve the contradictions of the city and transform the city into a totally organized machine without archaic forms of waste or generalized dysfunctions;"

71 See *Op. Cit* n. 51, 1981;

72 A. Branzi, "Florence," unpublished text within the book;

73 C. Toraldo di Francia, in *Superstudio*, edited by G. Mastrigli, Quodlibet, Macerata, 2016: "In those years the atmosphere in Florence was conservative, reduced to cynically exploiting its historical heritage in a purely commercial and consumerist way. However, beginning in the early Sixties, some of us had already begun a first ideological revision of the history of architecture and the city: we reacted in this way to a climate of political indifference supported by a liberal and historicist kind of aesthetic reading, essentially related to Benedetto Croce's matrix, and we were trying to define our role as critical intellectuals and producers inside and outside of the system. But we were not the first: the city had on several occasions expressed critical and creative energies, often of a realistic and anti-academic nature;"

74 As quoted on Giorgio La Pira's official website: "La Pira began organizing *Colloqui Mediterranei* in 1958. Their 'official' purpose was to search for common cultural roots among the peoples of the Mediterranean. But the meetings were part of an informal diplomacy that in those years originated precisely in Florence [...]. The meetings in Florence indeed provided the occasion for influential but not official personalities of two conflicting parties (French and French Algerians, Israelis and Arabs, etc.) to establish informal contacts with the 'pretext' of an event of a cultural nature. 'The important moment – La Pira used to say – is the one in which work is interrupted for a coffee break.' [...] They had as a unifying point and purpose the dialogue between the three main religious groups (Jews, Christians, Muslims), seen as an essential contribution to world peace; they subsequently expanded the horizons to sub-Saharan Africa, attracting the countries that in the 1960s freed themselves from colonialism;"

75 C. Toraldo di Francia, *Op. Cit.*: "The *Il Circolo della Cultura* was important for introducing the city to an international debate and for the definition of a new political and cultural model, addressed to a society in rapid evolution [...]. It was a center of debate on political, economic, and social issues, expressed in the form of Liberal Socialism, after the Matteotti criminal case was closed;"

76 C. Toraldo di Francia, *Op. Cit.*: "(*the* movement) had seen its apex in the 1950s with the *Manifesto of Classical Abstractionism* drawn up by the philosopher Ermanno Migliorini. They expressed it in this way: 'The artist intervenes in reality, changes it, and he is responsible for this intervention';"

77 The multidisciplinary group that launched several artist figures, strongly influenced by John Cage because of the centrality of experimentation, was founded in 1961 by George Maciunas, concurrently with the magazine bearing the same name and disseminating its contents;

78 See *Casabella* n. 287, May 1964;

79 As Gilberto Corretti said: "The occupation lasted just over a week, the academic body immediately started a soft negotiation spread out over time. Classes were suspended, and a coordinating committee that included students and professors was activated. Study commissions were made. The meetings alternated with the assemblies, the days flowing like sand through the hourglass. It was a strategy, common under national skies, aimed at preserving the existing climate. The more the days passed, and the more one was covered with the dust of the 'revolution.' The June exams were quickly approaching, the risk of losing a term remaining empty-handed convinced even the most rebellious to give up, and everything went back to normal. Not really everything to be honest. Group examinations were allowed in design matters. The initiative, stemming from the ideological fury of the student assemblies and demagogically supported by the professors, introduced dangerous shortcuts for less equipped students. It happens in revolutions of every age. This concession strengthened the virtuous practice of studying together and favored the creation of affiliated design groups through elective affinities and not just to reduce the burden of exams";

80 C. Toraldo di Francia, *Op. Cit.*;

81 A project proposed for the Interior Architecture examination taught by Giuseppe Gori, together with that of Architectural Composition I, taught by Domenico Cardini and Rodolfo Raspollini;

82 As Corretti describes it in *The Extruded City. To the Roots of Radical Architecture*: "From this healthy bathing of ideas, provocations, and sudden insights in which the intellectual game earned its merit through the stimulating and fueling of our enthusiasm, came an ambitious prophetic vision of the possible future development of the entire area downstream of Florence condensed into about fifty tables designed in AO format, but some over two meters in length, and a huge plastic model depicting the *Città Estrusa*.
This definition appears in my agenda on September 4th and is accompanied by an explanatory note: 'extrusion = industrial production concept extending to everything pre-existing, including culture' [...]. The exam, at which we arrived with an indescribable amount of drawings, plastic models, photographs, and various documents, took place in the Minerva classroom, concluding an initiatory journey started the year before in that classroom on November 27, 1964. In front of us, seated and defended by a long series of drafting tables, there was a commission of about fifteen people, made up of professors and assistants. Behind us, a crowd of students gathered for the event. The farthest away were standing on the tables so as to not miss the show. In the middle, us, eight bewildered and dazed students because of the inevitable long nights. After an animated presentation, a true theatrical performance that was not once interrupted by anyone as if it were a concert of virtuoso soloists, the committee retired for some long hours, as if it were the jury of a political process in which, because of the nature of the offenses, it was almost impossible to find agreement.
In the end, we passed with top marks. For me and the others in the group, it was just the beginning of a trajectory that would later be called Radical Architecture;"

83 As related by Roberto Gargiani, *Dattiloscritto*, Bartolini Archive: "The theme of the project – we read in a document written by Archizoom – concerned the identification of an interesting urban macrostructure throughout the Florence-Pistoia district. Within this organization, services were provided for manufacturing, university equipment, and freight. The project sought to identify the economic and social tensions of the Florence-Pistoia hinterland, but above all it sought to identify an instrument of analysis and architectural restitution of the complex anthropological and civil content of the entire phenomenon of urbanization and industry;" See Roberto Gargiani, *Archizoom associati, 1966-1974: dall'onda pop alla superficie neutra*, Electa, Milan, 2007;

84 As it says in the description of the project, as related by Gargiani in reference to the document stored in the CSAC Archive,s of Parma (Andrea Branzi's documents): "To know itself, therefore, Society represents itself, and there are four moments of it watching itself, each of them being indispensable. The first moment is therefore democracy, where in an amphitheater enclosed within a sphere, the Senators speak verbally with each other defending infinite different interests, without any synthesis, but fulfilling a single representative mandate. The next two moments are those of social representation, parallel and complementary, but not yet united. They concern the Order of the World of Ideas and the Order of the World of Goods. The first is the Procession [...]. In it, men represent all hierarchies and communicate in a line in the same direction. The other moment is analogous to this, it is the Exhibition of Goods, in which all the individual works of the men is exhibited in the public square and blessed in front of the temple, and in this act they are given meaning in the Civilization of men beyond the envy of the merchants. The last and supreme moment of the Synthesis of representation takes place in the 'theater,' where the Ministers of Signs reside, in which arts, poetry, music, dance, potency, painting, and architecture all belong because they were largely lie with words, sounds, and figures, houses and cities, and help man recognize Chaos in Order";

85 Carried out in the course taught by Savioli;

86 Defended on July 21 1966;

87 Defended on March 9 marzo with Savioli as Supervisor;

88 A. Branzi, *Relazione alla Tesi di Laurea*, 1966;

89 A. Branzi, "Luna Park permanente a Prato," in *Casabella* n. 366, June 1972, p. 37;

90 A. Branzi, Ibidem;

91 Set in a basement, in two rooms;

92 Archizoom e Superstudio, *Manifesto Superarchitettura Exhibition*, 1966;

93 Archizoom, in *Relazione Moda*, 1967;

94 Archizoom and Superstudio, *Manifesto Modena Exhibition*, 1967;

95 B. Colomina and C. Buckley, *Clip Stamp Fold. The radical architecture of little magazines*, 196x-197x, Actar, Barcelona-New York, 2014;

96 For more information on this subject, see Emanuele Piccardo's research;

97 A. Branzi, *Una generazione esagerata*, *Op. Cit.*;

98 G. Celant, "Untitled," in *Domus* 496, 1971;

99 A. Mendini, "Radical Design," in *Casabella* 367, 1972;

100 G. Celant, "Senza Titolo," *Op. Cit.*;

101 A. Branzi, Introduction, "Architettura Radicale," *Op. Cit.*;

102 As stated in a handwritten note from the Deganello Archive,: "The date of the founding is controversial but it was located in September 1966. We have a phone beginning in March 1967. We have the kerosene stove as of November 10, 1967. The Archizoom studio has a large private and public clientele who are very satisfied. The studio is interested in design, architectural design, and urban planning [...]. No member of the studio has ever been enrolled in a political party;"

103 A. Branzi, *Una generazione esagerata*, *Op. Cit.*;

104 On coltroculture, see A. Branzi, *Radical Notes* n. 1, "Strategia dei tempi lunghi" ("A Long-Term Strategy,") in *Casabella* n. 370, 1972 and Radcal Notes n. 14, "Alpinismo" ("Mountain Climbing and Existenz Minimum,") in *Casabella* n. 388, 1974;

105 See A. Branzi, "La Gioconda Sbarbata" ("The Shaved Gioconda. The Role of the Avant-garde"), in *Casabella* n. 364, 1972, and A. Branzi, "Radical Architecture. Refusing the Disciplinary Role," in *Casabella* n. 386, 1974;

106 See A. Branzi, "The Shaved Gioconda," *Op. Cit.*;

107 A. Branzi, "The Shaved Gioconda," *Op. Cit.*;

108 See A. Branzi, *Radical Notes* n. 8: "Lite creativa e creatività di massa" ("The Elite and Mass Creativity,") in *Casabella* n. 378, 1973 and *Radical Notes* n. 13, "Tecnica povera" ("Minimal Technology,") in *Casabella* n. 385, 1974;

109 In "The Shaved Gioconda," Branzi resumes Gombrowicz's position, "For me the story is a black hole";

110 A. Branzi, "The Shaved Gioconda," *Op. Cit.*;

111 See A. Branzi, *Radical Notes* n. 12, "Si scoprono le tombe" ("Unsealing the Shrine,") in *Casabella* n. 383, 1973;

112 See Archizoom, "Architettonicamente," in *Casabella* n. 334, 1969;

113 We underline that *Earth Works* was the title of the exhibition organized by Robert Smithson in October 1968 at the Dwan Gallery in New York, which affirms the presence of Land Art in the international art scene;

114 Germano Celant was gathering images and information on the experience of American Land Art; see the text "Nature is Insurrected," in *Casabella* 33, 1969;

115 As Deleuze: "It is necessary to imagine other principles, even those which appear inapplicable, by means of which the game would become pure (...). this game is reserved then for thought and art. In it there is nothing but victories for those who know how to play, that is, how to affirm and ramify chance, instead of dividing it in order to dominate it, in order to wager, in order to win. This game, which can only exist in thought and which has no other result that the work of art, is also that by which thought and art are real and disturbing reality, morality, and the economy of the world." G. Deleuze, *Logique du sens*, Éditions de Minuit, Paris, 1969;

116 See G. Deleuze, *Op. Cit.*:"Sense is thus inseparable from a new kind of paradoxes which mark the presence of nonsense within signification;"

117 A. Branzi, *Radical Notes* n. 10, "Eccettuato il puro Deserto" ("Except for Pure Wasteland,") in *Casabella* n. 380-381, 1973;

118 *IN* n. 1, 1971;

119 *IN* n. 2-3, 1971;

120 *IN* n. 2-3, 1971;

121 R. Gargiani, *Archizoom Associati 1966-1974. Dall'onda pop alla superficie neutra*, Electa, Milan, 2007;

122 Andrea Branzi in speech with Pier Vittorio Aureli, 2014;

123 Archizoom Associati, *IN* n. 5, 1972;

124 Archizoom Associati, *IN* n. 7, 1972;

125 The Seventh Biennale of Paris, Italian Section curated by Achille Bonito Oliva, held on September 24 to November 1, 1971;

126 in *IN* n. 5;

127 in *IN* n. 2-3, May-June 1971;

128 A.A.V.V., *L'invenzione della superficie neutra*, Abet Print, Bra, 1973;

129 In the introduction it also states: "We decided to name this exhibition *The Use of the Neutral Surface*, precisely because in the formulation of the environment, we thought to develop a concept of space defined by neutral surfaces, to definitively cut off any linguistic conditioning connection. This makes it possible to create an undifferentiated relationship between the individual and the environment, in the direction that goes from the individual to the environment and not vice versa. This neutral membrane positioned between the subject and the objects serves to undo the different materialities, the different technologies, the different surface values, reducing all of them to an intermediate field without natural characteristics, a kind of neutral matter where everything at the limit resembles everything else. A materially homogeneous environment makes it possible to perceive as a single phenomenon its biological and electrical existence as the only force capable of defining time and habitat;"

130 Instead, Superstudio's "Quaderna" textures were realized;

131 In the first meeting of objects, selected for their technical and formal significance, were exhibited: Danilo and Corrado Airoldi, Roberto Arioli, Archizoom (*Mies, Supernova, Safari Sofa* by Poltronova and the *Dream Beds*), Sergio Asti, Gae Aulenti, Giampiero and Giovanni Bassi, Cini Boeri, Mario Bellini, Dario Bellini, Rodolfo Bonetto, Cesare Casati, Anna Castelli Ferrieri, Franco Catellan, Gianfranco Frattini, Anna Castelli with Ignazio Gardella, Achille e Pier Giacomo Castiglioni, Livio Castiglioni, Giorgio Ceretti, Joe Colombo, Silvio Coppola, Marcello Cuneo, Donato D'Urbino, Jonathan De Pas, Piero Gilardi, Giuliana Gramigna, Vittorio Gregotti, Group G 14, Gruppo Architetti and Urbanisti Città Nuova, Gruppo Strum, Angelo Jacober with Pierangela d'Aniello, Ugo La Pietra, Paolo Lamazzi, Cesare Leonardi and Franca Stagi, Roberto Lucci, Ennio Lucini, Antonio Macchi Cassia, Vico Magistretti, Angelo Mangiarotti, Roberto Mango, Pio Manzù, Enzo Mari, Gino Marotta, Giancarlo Mattioli, Giorgio Mazza with Giuliana Gramigna, Ludovico Meneghetti, Ettore and Peduzzi-Riva, Eleonore Peruzzi-Riva, Marcello Pietrantoni, Alfredo Pizzo Greco, Emanuele Ponzio, Gaetano Pesce, Giuseppe Raimondi, Richard Sapper, Marcello Siard, Ettore Sottsass Jr., Giorgio Soavi, Giotto Stoppino, Giancarlo Piretti, Alberto Rosselli, Roberto Sambonet, Gino Sarfatti, Afra and Tobia Scarpa, Studio TG, Studio OPI, Superstudio, Gino Valle, Nanda Vigo, Massimo Vignelli, Hans von Klier, Marco Zanuso; within the second session: Alessandro Becchi, Mario Bellini, Cini Boeri, Achille Castiglioni, Giacomo Castiglioni, Cesare Casati, Umberto Catalano, Joe Colombo, Jonathan De Pas, Donato D'Urbino, Piero Gatti, Giancarlo Iliprandi, Fabio Lenci, Paolo Lomazzi, Angelo Mangiarotti, Luigi Massoni, Gianfranco Masi, Sebastiano Matta, Giancarlo with Luigi and Roberto Monsani, Bruno Munari, Internotredici, Cesare Paolini, Emanuele Ponzio Rocchetto, Franco Teodoro, Alberto Salvati, Alberto Seassaro, Ufficio Tecnico Snaidero, Ambrogio Tresoldi;

132 See E. Ambaz, *Italy: The New Domestic Landscape*: "Both the commissioned designers and those entering the competition were requested to explore the domestic landscape with a sense for its 'places,' and to propose the spaces and artifacts that give them form, the ceremonies and behaviors that assign them meaning;" E. Ambaz, *Italy: The New Domestic Landscape: acheivements and problems of Italian design*, Museum of Modern Art in collaboration with Centro Di, Florence, 1972;

133 See E. Ambasz: "It is possible to differentiate in Italy today three prevalent attitudes toward design: the first is conformist, the second is reformist, and the third is, rather, one of contestation, attempting both inquiry and action. By the first, or conformist approach, we refer to the attitude of certain designers who conceive of their work as an autonomous activity responsible only to itself; they do not question the sociocultural context in which they work, but instead continue to refine already established forms and functions....that answer the traditional needs of domestic life; the second, or reformist attitude, is motivated by a profound concern of the designer's role in a society that fosters consumption as one means of inducing individual happiness, thereby insuring social stability. Torn by the dilemma of having been trained as creators of objects, and yet being incapable of controlling either the significantce or the ultimate uses of these objects, they find themselves unable or reconcile the conflicts between their social concerns and their professional practices. They have thus developed a rhetorical mode to cope with these contradictions. Convinced that there can be no renovation of design until structurel changes have occurred in society, but not attempting to bring these about themselves, they do not invent substantially new forms; instead, they engage in a rhetorical operation of redesigning conventional objects with new, ironic, and sometimes self-deprecatory sociocultural and aesthetic references. In their ambiguous attitude toward the object, these designers justify their activity by giving to their designs shapes that deliberately attempt a commentary upon the roles that these objects are normally expected to play in our society. The diversity of these rhetorical operations permits us to recognize at least half a dozen different procedures for recharging know forms with altered meanings....the third approach to design, which we have designated as one of contestation, attempts to deal with such a situation. This attitude reveals itself in two main trends in Italy today, each trying to get to the root in very different way. The first is by a commitment to a present socioindustrial system. Here, 'antiobject' literally means 'not making objects' and the designer's pursuits are either confined to political action and philosophical postulation, or else consist of total withdrawal. Those following the second tendency share with the preceding group the disbelief that an object can be designed as a single, isolated entity, without regard for its physical and sociocultural context. Their reaction to the problem, however, is not one of passive abstention but rather one of active critical participation. ...object of this sort are conceived as environmental ensembles and permit differentt modes of social interaction, while at the same time they allow the user to make his own statement about both privacy and communality. The products of this mode of Italian design do, in fact, seem to correspond to the preoccupations of a changing society. It has therefore been the environmental approach that the present exhibition has been particularly concerned with exploring". E. Ambaz, Introduction, *Italy: The New Domestic Landscape, Op. Cit.*;

134 E. Ambaz, Press release, May 26, 1972;

135 Ambaz himself handled the installation of the exhibition. See the catalogue, *Op.Cit.*;

136 Text within the book;

137 The Vienna exhibition was organized by Tommaso Ferraris and Dario Marchesoni and the exhibition design was by Piero de Amicis. After an introduction, which exhibited a series of objects from the 1930s, the exhibition focused on the design of the 1960s;

138 G. Celant, "Radical Architecture," in *Italy: The New Domestic Landscape*, *Op. Cit.*;

139 From the Triennale website: "1973. XV Triennial of Milan. International exhibition of modern decorative and industrial arts and modern architecture. [*The Living Space*]. The 15th Triennial opened in 1973 with a few years of delay compared to the expected opening date of 1971, due to the alternatives for the election of representatives of the various bodies within the Board of Directors and the political friction from the events concerning the 14th Triennial in '68. The theme of the exhibition is to find ways of living based on a better use of living space and on new structures capable of enriching the existence of contemporary man. Despite the political climate and the uncertainty of cultural debate, the exhibition is rich in both the Italian and international sections, as well as the temporary exhibitions. Aldo Rossi sets up the international architecture exhibition that highlights La Tendenza that brings Italian architects into the center of the international theoretical and design debate. Also interesting is the International Exhibition of Industrial Design, curated by Ettore Sottsass with Andrea Branzi, where audiovisual communication stands out, as there is no object;"

140 "15 Triennale," in *Casabella* 385, 1974;

141 P. Navone, *Op. Cit.*: "If by conceptual art we mean the reduction of artistic practice to the exclusive expression of tautological concepts relative to its own position in relation to reality, in the sense that it is meant by Kosuth and Art & Language, the only truly conceptual architecture remains the discourse on architecture;"

142 A. Branzi in speech with E. C. Cattaneo, 2016;

143 A. Branzi in speech with E. C. Cattaneo, 2016;

144 Paola Navone also writes along these lines. See P. Navone, *Op. Cit.*;

145 Archizoom Associati, *Casabella* n. 350-51, 1970;

146 Archizoom Associati, *Casabella*, *Op. Cit.*;

147 The work of Mies (in particular the Barcelona Pavilion) will also be transposed into the competition for the 1970 Osaka Universal Exposition, in which Archizoom participated in 1969, and in which architectural language is related to a primary plane (green meadow) and a primary crystal architecture, overcoming the meta-historical and spectacular role of technology;

148 R. Gargiani, *Op. Cit.*;

149 Interest in Hilberseimer in Italy is also confirmed by Tafuri and Rossi;

150 See *Casabella* n. 336, 1969;

151 An award-winning project, titled *New York 7000 Km*. The idea of global coverage is resolved primarily through a neo-Enlightenment citation, from which, however, Archizoom distances itself through an ironic attitude that moves them away from positivist contemporary positions. An extraordinary competition, which sees neo-plastic and avant-garde solutions proposed by major Italian intellectuals and designers (including Leonardo Ricci, Savioli, Mario Negri, Adolfo Natalini, and others), the extendibility of the Archizoom project matrix, altogether similar to the extendibility of the *No-Stop City*, speaks for the first time about a non-figurative architecture, a neutral space able to accommodate the uncontrollable dynamics of the commodity;

152 As they said: "We are not interested in elaborating a new theory of space, meaning with this term the materialization (by a culture capable of recording only endured phenomena) of an element that is part of a much more complex architectural phenomenon, and the result of compositional laws not usable spatially. But if we mean this term as a counter-form and negative, that is, everything that we are and that surrounds us, and which constitutes the basis on which our formal acts acquire significance and depth, we can only attack it, destroy it, and then replace it;

153 Archizoom Associati, "Città Catena di Montaggio del sociale, ideologia e teoria della metropoli," ("City, assembly line of the social") in *Casabella* n. 350-51, 1970;

154 A. Branzi, "Abitare è facile. Il ruolo dell'avanguardia" ("Inhabiting is Easy. The Role of the Avant-garde,") in *Casabella* n. 365, 1972;

155 Archizoom Associati, "No-Stop City Residential Parkings Climatic Universal Sistem," in *Domus* n.496, 1971;

156 Archizoom Associati, "No-Stop City Residential Parkings Climatic Universal Sistem," in *Domus*, *Op. Cit.*;

157 Andrea Branzi, "No-Stop City," in *No-Stop City*, Hyx, Orlean, 2006;

158 Branzi ne riprende i contenuti in particolare nel testo "Il sogno del villaggio" ("The Dream of the Village,") in *Casabella* n. 371, 1972: "Debates on town-planning are invariably bedevilled by the tacit belief that the city represents the highest and fullest expression of social culture (...). The new frontier, then, is the reformulation of the problem of the city in scientific terms: this radically new approach should guarantee not utopian but transferable solution; neutrality of form should guarantee not squalor but an advance beyond the aesthetic solution, the element now blocking the free and open use of structures;"

159 The 1969 *Progetto/Utopia* meeting/exhibition was promoted by the Turin research group U and/or R. Archizoom refused to participate in the debate, rather choosing the option of sending a report contesting the terms utopia and revolution. In this sense, they reiterate their position as non-utopian architects, but able to work "within and against" the system, without suggesting an escape or improvement, aligning and confirming their Trontian position of the non-ideologization of design. At the exhibition-meeting, however, other internationally important architects such as Archigram, Yona Friedman, and Paolo Soleri participated;

160 See E. Piccardo, *Radical City*, Exhibition, Archive, di Stato di Torino, 2012;

161 As indeed Mastrigli claims in the book *Superstudio*, *Op. Cit.*: "The work of Superstudio was an incessant process of collecting, selecting, and cataloging of the fragments of a collective memory, recognized in pop culture as in classical tradition, in the phenomenology of modernity as in the anthropological view, in the perspectives of scientific research as in marginal culture surveys. In this process, the finished product, the new 'order of things', to quote Foucault, is the unveiling of the possibility of things themselves, seemingly innocuous but not for this any less definitive: things begin to appear for what they can be, until they are dismantled, slowly, for what they are already. In the stories of Superstudio, what is prefigured is the fulfillment of their destiny;"

162 The texts are excerpted from Andrea Branzi's book, *Weak and Diffuse Modernity*, Skira, Milan, 2006;

163 A. Branzi, *Moderno, postmoderno, millenario: scritti teorici*, 1972-1980, Studio Forma, 1980;

164 A. Branzi in speech with Elisa C. Cattaneo, 2016;

165 A. Branzi, *Moderno, postmoderno...*, *Op. Cit.*;

166 A. Branzi, *Pomeriggi alla Media Industria. Design e seconda modernità*, Idea Books edizioni, Milan, 1988; English edition: A. Branzi, Learning from Milan, M.I.T. Press, Cambridge, 1988;

167 See A. Branzi, "I territori dell'immaginario," in A. Branzi, *Pomeriggi alla Media Industria. Design e seconda modernità*, Idea Books edizioni, Viareggio, 1988;

168 E. C. Cattaneo, *Weakcity. Notes on Landscape Urbanism*, List Publisher, Trento, 2015;

169 A. Branzi, *Pomeriggi alla media industria, Op. Cit.*:

170 A. Branzi, *Pomeriggi alla media industria, Op. Cit.*:

171 A. Branzi, *Pomeriggi alla media industria, Op. Cit.*:

172 Z. Bauman, *Liquid Modernity*, Polity Press, Cambridge, 2000;

173 A. Branzi, *Weak and Diffuse Modernity, Op. Cit.*:

174 A. Branzi, "Time and Network," in *Weak and Diffuse Modernity, Op. Cit.*;

175 A. Branzi, *Objects et Territoire*, Introduction, Alternatives Publisher, Paris, 2014;

176 Ibidem;

177 Ibidem;

178 A. Branzi, *Design e Universo Artificiale*, in *Pomeriggi alla Media Industria, Op. Cit.*;

179 A. Branzi, 1988;

180 A. Branzi, "Fuzzy Thinking," in *Weak and Diffuse Modernity*, Skira, Milan, 2006;

181 See: *Fuzzy sets. Information and Control*, 1965; "Fuzzy sets and systems" in, J. Fox, *System Theory*, Polytechnic Press, New York, 1965; "A fuzzy-set-theoretical interpretation of linguistic hedges," in *Journal of Cybernetics*, 1972; "Outline of a new approach to the analysis of complex systems and decision processes," in *IEEE Transformation, Systems, Man and Cybernetics*, 1973; "Fuzzy logic and its application to approximate reasoning" in *Information Processing* 74, 1974; "Fuzzy logic and approximate reasoning," in *Synthese*, 1975; "Calculus of fuzzy restrictions," in L.A. Zadeh, K.S. Fu, K. Tanaka, M. Shimura, *Fuzzy Sets and their Applications to Cognitive and Decision Processes*, Academic Press, New York, 1975;

182 See: *Neural Networks and Fuzzy Systems: A Dynamical Systems Approach to Machine Intelligence*, Prentice Hall, Upper Saddle River, 1991; *Fuzzy Thinking: The New Science of Fuzzy Logic*, Hyperion, New York, 1993; *Fuzzy Engineering*, Prentice Hall, Upper Saddle River, 1996; *The Fuzzy Future: From Society and Science to Heaven in a Chip*, Harmony Press, New york, 1999;

183 A. Branzi, "Fuzzy Thinking," in *Weak and Diffuse Modernity, Op. Cit.*;

184 cfr. E. Morin, *Introduction à la pensée complexe*, Seuil Publisher, Paris, 1990;

185 cfr. E. Morin, *Introduction à la pensée complexe,* 1990 and Stephen J. Gould, *Wonderful Life: The Burgess Shale and the Nature of History*, W.W. Norton, New York, 1989; and E. Morin, *La Methode*, t.1;

186 C. Cattaneo, *Weakcity. Notes on Landscape Urbanism, Op. Cit.*;

187 A. Branzi, *Terrazzo* n. 5;

188 A. Branzi in *The Fourth Metropolis. Design and Environmental Culture*, Domus Academy Edition, Milan, 1990;

189 A. Branzi, "Scenografie del prossimo millennio," in *Gap Casa* n. 54, February 1989;

190 A. Branzi, "Crisi della qualità, crisi della complessità e spazio relazionale," in A. Branzi, *La Crisi della qualità*, Edizioni Della Battaglia, Palermo, 1996;

191 A. Branzi, "Crisi della qualità, crisi della complessità e spazio relazionale," *Op. Cit.*;

192 E. Morin, *Op. Cit.*;

193 E. Morin, *Op. Cit.*;

194 I. Prigogine, I. Stengers, *The End of Certainty* and *La Nouvelle Alliance (Order out of Chaos)*, The Free Press, 1984;

195 A. Branzi, "Crisi della Qualità, Crisi della Complessità e Spazio Relazionale," *Op. Cit.*;

196 A. Branzi, "Crisi della Qualità, Crisi della Complessità e Spazio Relazionale," *Op. Cit.*;

197 U. Eco, in *Opera Aperta. Forma e indeterminazione nelle poetiche contemporanee*, Bompiani, Milan, 1962: "All this explains how contemporary art can be seen as an epistemological metaphor. The discontinuity of phenomena has called into question the possibility of a unified, definitive image of our universe; art suggests a way for us to see the world in which we live, and, by seeing it, to accept it and integrate it into our sensibility. The open work assumes the task of giving us an image of discontinuity. It does not narrate it; it is it. It takes on a mediating role between the abstract categories of science and the living matter of our sensibility; it almost becomes a sort of transcendental scheme which allows us to comprehend new aspects of the world."

198 G. Leibniz, *Monadologie*, 1714;

199 A. Branzi, "Crisi della Qualità...," *Op. Cit.*;

200 Branzi refers to A. Einstein: "...As far as the laws of mathematics refer to reality, they are not certain, and as far as they are certain, they do not refer to reality," in *Geometrie und Erfahrung*, Prussian Academy of Sciences, Berlin, January 27th 1921;

201 P. Feyerabend, *Against Method*, First Eidtion 1975:"Science is essentially an anarchic enterprise: theoretical anarchism is more humanitarian and more likely to encourage progress than its law-and-order alternatives;"

202 E. C. Cattaneo, *WeakCity. Notes on Landscape Urbanism*, List, Trento, 2015, cit. I. Calvino, *Relazione per il Convegno internazionale Livelli della realtà*, Palazzo Vecchio, Florence, September 9-13 1978;

203 A. Branzi, "Crisi della Qualità...," *Op. Cit.*;

204 A. Branzi, "Territori dell'Immaginazione," *Op. Cit.*;

205 The second meaning of the territories of the imaginary necessarily refers also to the Italian debate, which has been dragging on since the late 1960s: see A. Branzi, *Moderno, Postmoderno, Millenario, Op. Cit.*;

206 A. Branzi,"Elastic Classicity," in *Weak and Diffuse Modernity, Op. Cit.*;

207 A. Branzi, Ibidem.;

208 E. C. Cattaneo, *WeakCity..., Op. Cit.*;

209 P. A. Rovatti, G. Vattimo, *Il Pensiero Debole*, Feltrinelli, Milan, 1983;

210 P. A. Rovatti, G. Vattimo, *Il Pensiero Debole, Op. Cit.*;

211 See E. C. Cattaneo, *WeakCity...,Op. Cit.*;

212 A. Branzi, "The Symbiotic Metropolis. Agronica," in *The Solid Side*, edited by E. Manzini and M. Susani, V+K Publishing, Blaricum, 1995;

213 See E. C. Cattaneo, *WeakCity...,Op. Cit.*;

214 A. Branzi, "Architectural Link," in *Weak and Diffuse Modernity, Op. Cit.*;

215 See E. C. Cattaneo, *WeakCity...,Op. Cit.*;

216 A. Branzi, "Architectural Link," in *Weak and Diffuse Modernity, Op. Cit.*;

217 See E. C. Cattaneo, *WeakCity, Op. Cit.*; in particular Pierre Lévy *L'Intelligence collective. Pour une anthropologie du cyberespace*, La Découverte, Paris, 1994;

218 A. Branzi, *The Fourth Metropolis, Op. Cit.*;

219 A. Branzi, *The Fourth Metropolis*, *Op. Cit.*;

220 A. Branzi, *The Fourth Metropolis*, *Op. Cit.*;

221 K. Kelly, *Out of Control: The New Biology of Machines, Social Systems, and the Economic World*, Addison Wesley, Boston,1994: "There is only one epoch in the history of the planet, when every individual and every single thing are connected, and we are alive in that exact moment;"

222 On Technonature, see E. C. Cattaneo, *WeakCity*, *Op. Cit.*;

223 E. C. Cattaneo, *WeakCity*, *Op. Cit.*; quote: M. Ponty, *La nature. Notes de cours du Collège de France*, Éditions du Seuil, Paris, 1995;

224 E. C. Cattaneo, *WeakCity*, *Op. Cit.*; quote: M. M. Ponty, *Op. Cit.*;

225 F. Pessoa, *Livro do Desassossego: Composto por Bernardo Soares, ajudante de guardalivros na cidade de Lisboa*, 1984;

226 B. Nicolescu, *Manifesto of Transcidiplinarity*, State University of New York Press, 2002;

227 A. Branzi, "Architecture/Agriculture," in *Weak and Diffuse Modernity*, *Op. Cit.*;

228 A. Branzi, "Architecture/Agriculture," in *Weak and Diffuse Modernity*, *Op. Cit.*;

229A. Branzi, *The Fourth Metropolis*, *Op. Cit.*;

230 A. Branzi, Ibidem.;

231 A. Branzi, "Architecture/Agriculture," in *Weak and Diffuse Modernity*, *Op. Cit.*;

232 A. Branzi, unpublished, 2017;

233 *The Citizen Office Exhibition* began at the Vitra Museum in 1991;

234 A. Branzi, *Andrea Branzi's Probable Autobiography*, unpublished, 2013;

235 G. Debord, "Mode d'emploi du détournement," 1956;

236 G. Deleuze, *Difference and Repetition*, Columbia University Press, New York, 1994;

237 G. Deleuze, Ibidem.;

238 A. Branzi, in *Radical Notes*, *Op. Cit.*;

239 A. Branzi, "Dalla società post-industriale alla società post-tecnologica" ("From the post-industrial Society to the Post-Technological Society,") in *Interni* n. 453, 1995;

240 A. Branzi, "Per una modernità debole" ("Toward a weak Modernity,") in *Interni* 518, 2002;

241 M. Foucault, Introduction, *Les Mots et les Choses (Une archéologie des sciences humaines)*, Gallimard, Paris, 1966;

242 A. Branzi, "Sopra e sotto" ("Above and Below,") in *Interni* n.499, 1995;

243 A. Branzi, "La metropoli degli umani" ("The Metropolis of Human Being,") in *Interni* n. 551, 2005;

244 See E. C. Cattaneo, *WeakCity*, *Op. Cit.*;

245 A. Branzi, "La scimmia che è in noi" ("The Monkey in Us,") in *Abitare* n. 531, 2013;

246 M. Jammer, *Concepts of space. The history of theories of space in physics*, Harvard university press, Cambridge, 1954;

247 P. Restany, *Manifeste du Rio Negro du Naturalisme Intégral*, 1978;

248 A. Shevchenko, *Neo-Primitivism: Its Theory, Its Potentials, Its Achievements*, 1912;

249 For example, it is emblematic in the works of Malevich, Larionov, or Goncharova;

250 A. Shevchenko, *Op. Cit.*;

251 P. Restany, *Op. Cit.*;

252 G. Deleuze, *Francis Bacon: The Logic of Sensation*, Continuum publisher, London,2003;

253 P. Restany, *Op. Cit.*;

254 A. Branzi, Interview with Pierre Restany, in *Modo* n. 80, 1985;

255 "Braccio di Ferro tra Gianpaolo Fabris e Pierre Restany," in *Modo* n. 80, 1985;

256 G. Lukacs, *The Destruction of Reason*, Merlin Press, London, 1980;

257 M. Heidegger, in *Sentieri Interrotti*, La Nuova Italia, Venice, 1979;

258 O. Spengler, *The Decline of the West. Ed. Arthur Helps, and Helmut Werner*, Oxford UP, New York, 1991;

259 H. Bergson in *Time and Free Will: An Essay on the Immediate Data of Consciousness*, Dover Publications, New York, 2001;

260 See M. Foucault, *Dream and Existence*, 1954: "The theme [...] is not so much dreams and existence, but how existence appears to itself and how it can be deciphered in dreams: existence in the mode of being of the dream in which it announces itself in a meaningful way. The dream is proclaimed as the fundamental form of existence. This implies, in fact: 1) that dream analysis will not end at the level of a hermeneutics of symbols, but starting from an external interpretation, which is still in the order of decoding, it can reach an understanding of existential structures without having to take refuge in a philosophy. (which is in fact man, in its forms of existence, the only way to reach man). The meaning of the dream unfolds continually from the figure of appearance to the modes of existence. 2) an entire anthropology of the imagination; it demands a new definition of the relationship between meaning and symbol, image and expression: a new way of conceiving the manifestation of meanings;"

261 M. Foucault, *Op. Cit.*;

262 M. Foucault, *Op. Cit.*;

263 M. Foucault, *Op. Cit.*;

264 See G. Bachelard, *The Psychoanalysis of Fire*, first published 1937;

265 See G. Deleuze, *Francis Bacon*, *Op. Cit.*;

266 G. Deleuze, *The Exhausted*, in Sub Stance, Vol. 24, No. 3, Issue 78, 1995;

267 G. Agamben, Afterworld, Italian Edition of *The Exhausted*;

268 G. Deleuze, *The Exhausted*, *Op. Cit.*;

269 G. Deleuze, *Francis Bacon...*, *Op. Cit.*;

270 G. Deleuze, *Francis Bacon...*, *Op. Cit.*;

271 G. Deleuze, *Francis Bacon...*, *Op. Cit.*;

272 G. Deleuze, *Francis Bacon...*, *Op. Cit.*;

273 G. Deleuze, *Foucault* (1986), Italian edition, translated by Pier Aldo Rovatti and Federica Sossi, Feltrinelli, Milan, 1987;

274 M. Foucault, *Les Mots et les Choses. Une archéologie des sciences humaines*, Gallimard, Paris, 1966;

275 G. Deleuze, *The Logic of Sense*, *Op. Cit.*;

276 G. Deleuze, *The Logic of Sense*, *Op. Cit.*;

277 M. Foucault, *Les Mots et les Choses*, *Op. Cit.*

278 G. Deleuze, *Foucault*, *Op. Cit.*

$E = mc^2$

The Project in the Age of Relativity

This formula, developed by Albert Einstein in 1915, is, in the most simple and elegant manner, the definition of the General Theory of Relativity, a masterpiece that would forever change our understanding of the world.

Energy = mass times the speed of light (squared) exceeds the immobile conception of Newtonian space, replacing it with a dynamic vision of a space that flexes, bends, and distorts; and with it, light and time.

To those of us who are not scientists and do not study physics but the culture of the project, it is an opportunity to guide us toward some important considerations.

The first, and perhaps the most important, is that planning, architecture, and design are not separated and antagonistic disciplines, but the expression of a single dynamic force, constituted by the transformational energy of the world as it presents itself.

This means that the design of a household object is only the molecular dimension of this energy and as such contributes to change the space of the world.

The second consideration derives from the total absence of a unity of the trends and methods of the project; there is not "the theory of the" but an infinite number of theories, each of which has its own right to exist.

Physicist Carlo Rovelli provides, in this regard, a very fitting example: two Jews discuss a question and, not able to agree, decide to contact a rabbi.

The rabbi listens to the reasons of the first man and concludes, "You're right."

Then he listens the reasons of the second man and he concludes, “You’re right.”

The rabbi’s wife, in the kitchen listening to their conversation, intervenes, saying, “You cannot tell them they are both right.”

Rabbi concludes, “You’re right, too.”

Similarly, any theoretical position cannot exclude the other, because there is no single truth, but an infinite declination of different projects; for this reason, there are not two equal cities in the world, two equal works of architecture, two artifacts identical to each other.

The material world is thus made up of an infinite space, fluid, free from any perimeter because without any single foundation; time is no longer constituted by a present, a past, and a future, but from a material that flexes itself, attracted by the mass of thought.

Contrary to what Modernity and its dogmas taught us, the principle of General Relativity is no stranger to the world of design, but it is a clearer demonstration of it, an everyday derivative based on the infinite energy of transformation of the material universe.

We should consider the actions of the project all together, not one at a time, as a phenomenon linked to the theory of physics and not to formal composition, to a style or a technique; only then will we realize the relativity of our actions, our being part of the material world and not only of the discipline...

Andrea Branzi

SESSION 1

COMMODITY CIVILIZATION

THE RADICAL MOVEMENT AND THE SEASON OF THE ANNOUNCED DEATHS

A. Branzi, *Commodity Civilization*, 2016

#_scenarios:
The End of the Ideologies and the New Contemporary: The Criticism of the Modern Movement and the Italian Context

A. Branzi, *The Sunset of Gods: The Fracture with the Modern Movement*, 2014
A. Branzi, *The Negative Thought and the Announced Death*, 2014
A. Branzi, *The Existential Verism: Micro-catastrophes and Operaismo*, 2014
Archizoom Associati, *Declaration, XVII International Congress of Artists, Critics, Scholars of Art*, Rimini, 1968

#_contexts:
Florence and the Florentine School. Urban Megastructures and Pop Hybridizations

A. Branzi, *Florence*, 2014
A. Branzi, *The Florentine School*, 2014

#_background:
Identification of Quantum of Equipment for the Free-Time

A. Branzi, *An Everlastic Luna Park (within a Supermarket)*, 1966
A. Branzi, *Excerpt from the Thesis Report, Original Document*, 1966
A. Branzi, "Dead Time," in *Casabella* n. 366, 1972

1.1: SuperArchitecture: 1966. Pop Intrusions and the *New Design*

Archizoom Associati and Superstudio, *Superarchitettura/Superarchitecture*, 1966, Pistoia Exhibition
Archizoom Associati and Superstudio, *Superarchitettura/Superarchitecture*, 1967, Modena Exhibition
A. Branzi, *Superarchitecture*, 2014

1.2: The Radical Movement: an Exaggerated Generation

#_Definitions:
Essays on Radical Movement

G. Celant, "Untitled," in *Domus* n. 496, 1971
A. Mendini, "Radical Design," in *Casabella* n. 367, 1972
C. Jencks, "The Supersensualists," in *AD* n. 1, 1972
A. Isozaki, "The Hot House. Italian New Wave Design," 1984
"Archizoom," in *L'architecture d'aujourd'hui* n. 145, 1969
A. Branzi, *An Exaggerated Generation*, 2016

#_Theories:
Radical Essays

Archizoom Associati, "Architettonicamente," in *Casabella* n. 334, 1969
A. Branzi, Introduction, *Architettura Radicale*, edited by Paola Navone and Bruno Orlandoni, *Casabella*, 1974
A. Branzi, "Africa is nearby. The Role of the Avant-garde," in *Casabella* n. 362, 1972
A. Branzi, "The Shaved Gioconda. The Role of the Avant-garde," in *Casabella* n. 364, 1972
A. Branzi, "Inhabiting is Easy. The Role of the Avant-garde," in *Casabella* n. 365, 1972
A. Branzi, "Cultural Crisis and Protheses," in *Casabella* n. 385, 1984
A. Branzi, "Radical Architecture. Refusing the Disciplinary Role," in *Casabella* n. 386, 1974

#_Apparatus:
For a Diffuse Creativity

A. Branzi, "Technology or Euthanasia," Global Tools, in *Casabella* n. 397, 1976
A. Branzi, "Homework. Remember Pasolini," in *Casabella* n. 409, 1976

1.3: Prototypes of Dissolution. The Negative Thought

A: The Dissolution of Architecture. *Urban Photomontages* and *Speeches by Images*
B: The Liquefaction of the Object. Situationist Components
C: The Removal of the City. The Liberation of the Habitat
D: Neutral Field. Reactive Surfaces and Artificial Landscape
E: Grey Environments

1.4: Microenvironments and the *Nuovo Design*

Archizoom Associati, "The Empty Rooms and the Gazebos," in *Pianeta Fresco* n. 1, 1967
Archizoom Associati, "Impossible Theatre," in *Pianeta Fresco* n. 2-3, 1968
Archizoom Associati, "Centre of Eclectic Conspiracy," in *Domus* n. 466, 1968
Archizoom Associati, "Marble Chicken," in *Casabella* n. 325, 1968
E. Sottsass jr., "Archizoom," in *Domus* n. 455, 1967
Archizoom Associati, "Dressing is easy," in *Casabella* n. 384, 1973

#_Apparatus: Radical Vs Tendenza

Commodity Civilization was not a passing malformation, but the beginning of an entirely new era.

Commodity Civilization is in fact not the result of superficial phenomena, like consumerism, exhibitionism, the insatiable thirst for purchase and risk, the myth of a material wellbeing of the masses. It involves a mutation that not only concerns the relationship between man and merchandise, but the birth of a new economy and new human relations.

Urban territory can be identified in an ungovernable molecular flow, in a continuous transformation, hyper-expressive but not reducible to a single image, the origin of which was detectable in the urgency of the market to satisfy as quickly as possible the "right to happiness of the individual," without any kind of mediation or filter. It was a type of happiness that modernity had unsuccessfully tried to satisfy through "social justice." But "utility and justice" were categories that implied the "certainty and stability" of a framework of shared values, which no longer existed.

Commodity Civilization introduces elusive categories into society, ones that are provisional and continuously expanding, lacking a common horizon, based on unpredictable paradigms that had nothing in common with the old theologies of the twentieth century.

It is a manifold universe, which needs to be tested in real time, directly in the field.

Its happiness is the "instant gratification" through consumer goods: a strategy that aims to both save the "status quo and to saturate it as much as possible," risking, however, of shattering in the face of religious, spiritual, and anthropological questions, to which it is not possible to provide a commercial response.

Metaphysical necessities that divide the world into two opposing sides; between those who produce "innovation" and those who reject "innovation"; those looking for instant gratification and those who seek eternal happiness.

The first Trojan Horse of Commodity Civilization inside the European rationalist fortress came from England, apparently the most conservative nation, and coming out in pieces, despite the victory, from World War II.

Compared to the American model, which tended to flatten the individual in mass models, the British model included individual creativity.

Pragmatic London, Labour-leaning and snobbish, was the first to wonder how the new world was really functioning: the famous exhibition *This is Tomorrow* of 1956, organized by Alison and Peter Smithson, Eduardo Paolozzi, Richard Hamilton, and Theo Crosby, presented without pretense the world of the industrial suburbs, the working-class neighborhoods, and the relentless growth of consumerism.

Andrea Branzi, 2016

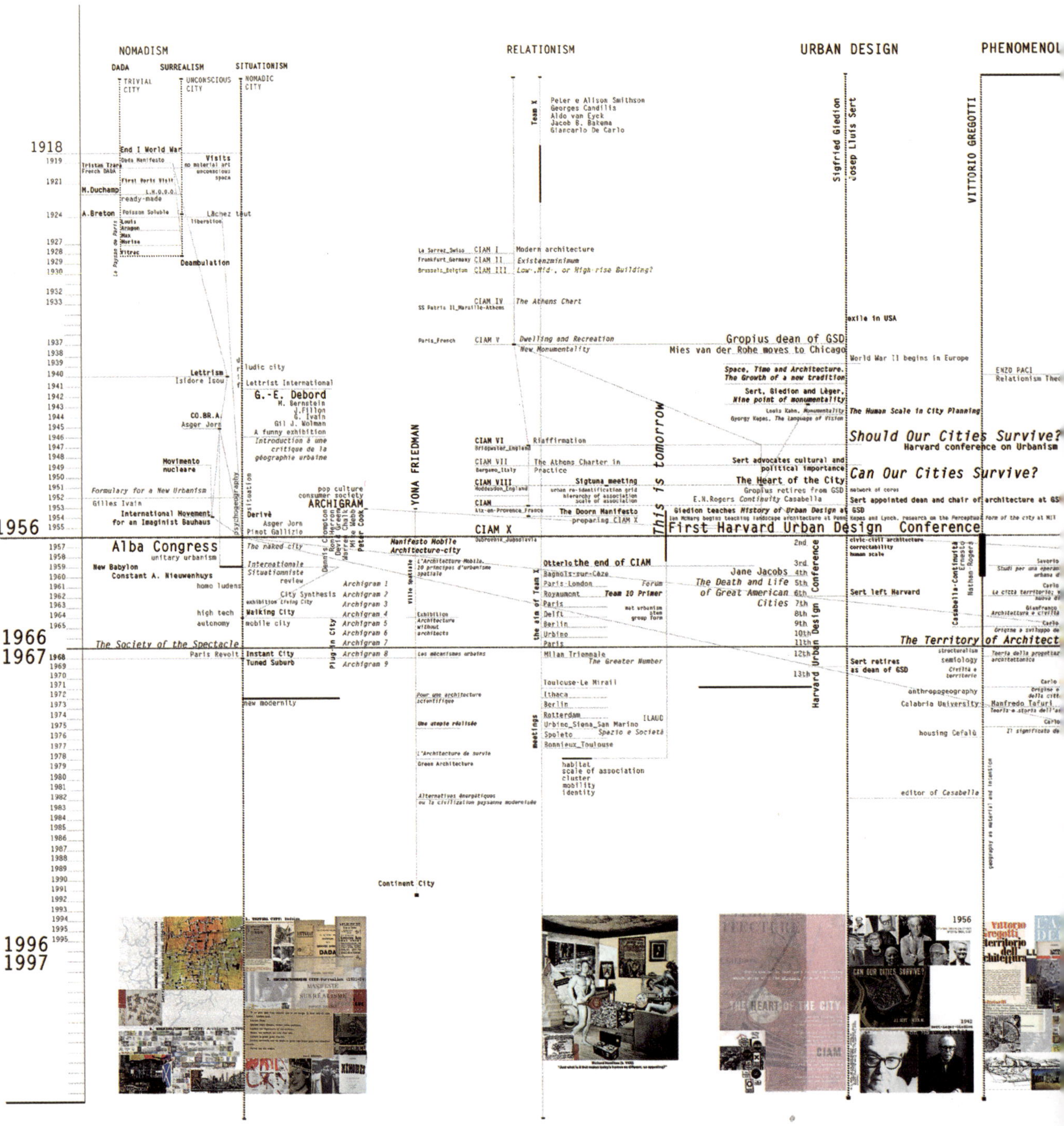
NOMADISM
DADA
SURREALISM
SITUATIONISM
TRIVIAL CITY
UNCONSCIOUS CITY
NOMADIC CITY
RELATIONISM
URBAN DESIGN
PHENOMENOL
Team X
Peter e Alison Smithson
Georges Candilis
Aldo van Eyck
Jacob B. Bakema
Giancarlo De Carlo
Sigfried Giedion
Josep Lluis Sert
VITTORIO GREGOTTI
1918
1919
1921
1924
1927
1928
1929
1930
1932
1933
1937
1938
1939
1940
1941
1942
1943
1944
1945
1946
1947
1948
1949
1950
1951
1952
1953
1954
1955
1956
1957
1958
1959
1960
1961
1962
1963
1964
1965
1966
1967
1968
1969
1970
1971
1972
1973
1974
1975
1976
1977
1978
1979
1980
1981
1982
1983
1984
1985
1986
1987
1988
1989
1990
1991
1992
1993
1994
1995
1996
1997
End I World War
Dada Manifesto
Tristan Tzara
French DADA
First Paris Visit
M.Duchamp
L.H.O.O.Q.
ready-made
A.Breton
Poisson Soluble
Louis Aragon
Max Morise
Vitrac
Le Paysan de Paris
Visits
no material art
unconscious space
Lâchez tout
liberation
Deambulation
La Sarraz_Swiss CIAM I Modern architecture
Frankfurt_Germany CIAM II Existenzminimum
Brussels_Belgium CIAM III Low-, Mid-, or High-rise Building?
CIAM IV The Athens Chart
Paris_French CIAM V Dwelling and Recreation
New Monumentality
exile in USA
Gropius dean of GSD
Mies van der Rohe moves to Chicago
World War II begins in Europe
ludic city
Lettrism
Isidore Isou
Lettrist International
G.-E. Debord
M. Bernstein
J.Fillon
G. Ivain
Gil J. Wolman
A funny exhibition
Introduction à une critique de la géographie urbaine
CO.BR.A.
Asger Jorn
Space, Time and Architecture.
The Growth of a new tradition
Sert, Giedion and Léger,
Nine point of monumentality
Louis Kahn, Monumentality
Gyorgy Kepes, The Language of Vision
The Human Scale in City Planning
ENZO PACI
Relationism Theo
This is tomorrow
YONA FRIEDMAN
CIAM VI Riaffirmation
Bridgwater_England
CIAM VII The Athens Charter in Practice
Bergamo_Italy
CIAM VIII
Hoddesdon_England
Sigtuna meeting
Movimento nucleare
Formulary for a New Urbanism
Gilles Ivain
International Movement for an Imaginist Bauhaus
Derivè
Asger Jorn
Pinot Gallizio
psychogeography
situation
pop culture
consumer society
ARCHIGRAM
Dennis Crompton
Ron Herron
David Greene
Warren Chalk
Mike Webb
Peter Cook
Should Our Cities Survive?
Harvard conference on Urbanism
Sert advocates cultural and political importance
The Heart of the City
Gropius retires from GSD
E.N.Rogers Continuity Casabella
Can Our Cities Survive?
Sert appointed dean and chair of architecture at GSD
CIAM
Aix-en-Provence_France
The Doorn Manifesto
preparing CIAM X
Giedion teaches History of Urban Design at GSD
First Harvard Urban Design Conference
Alba Congress
unitary urbanism
New Babylon
Constant A. Nieuwenhuys
homo ludens
The naked city
Internationale Situationniste review
City Synthesis
exhibition Living City
high tech
autonomy
Walking City
mobile city
The Society of the Spectacle
Paris Revolt
Instant City
Tuned Suburb
new modernity
Manifesto Mobile
Architecture-city
L'Architecture Mobile.
10 principes d'urbanisme spatiale
Ville Spatiale
Plug-in City
Archigram 1
Archigram 2
Archigram 3
Archigram 4
Archigram 5
Archigram 6
Archigram 7
Archigram 8
Archigram 9
Exhibition Architecture without architects
Les mécanismes urbains
Pour une architecture scientifique
Une utopie réalisée
L'Architecture de survie
Green Architecture
Alternatives énergétiques ou la civilisation paysanne modernisée
Continent City
CIAM X
Dubrovnik_Jugoslavia
Otterlo the end of CIAM
Bagnols-sur-Cèze
Paris London
Royaumont
Team 10 Primer
Forum
Paris
Delft
Berlin
Urbino
Paris
the aim of Team X
Milan Triennale
The Greater Number
Toulouse-Le Mirail
Ithaca
Berlin
Rotterdam
Urbino_Siena_San Marino
ILAUD
Spoleto
Spazio e Società
Bonnieux_Toulouse
meetings
habitat
scale of association
cluster
mobility
identity
Jane Jacobs
The Death and Life of Great American Cities
2nd
3rd
4th
5th
6th
7th
8th
9th
10th
11th
12th
13th
Harvard Urban Design Conference
civic-civil architecture
correctability
human scale
Sert left Harvard
Sert retires as dean of GSD
Casabella-Continuità
Ernesto Nathan-Rogers
The Territory of Architect
structuralism
semiology
anthropogeography
Calabria University
housing Cefalù
editor of Casabella
Saverio
Carlo
Manfredo Tafuri
Carlo
geography as material and intention
1956
1942
CAN OUR CITIES SURVIVE?
THE HEART OF THE CITY
CIAM
Vittorio Gregotti
territorio dell architettura

SCENARIOS

The End of the Ideologies and the New Contemporary: The Criticism of the Modern Movement and the Italian Context

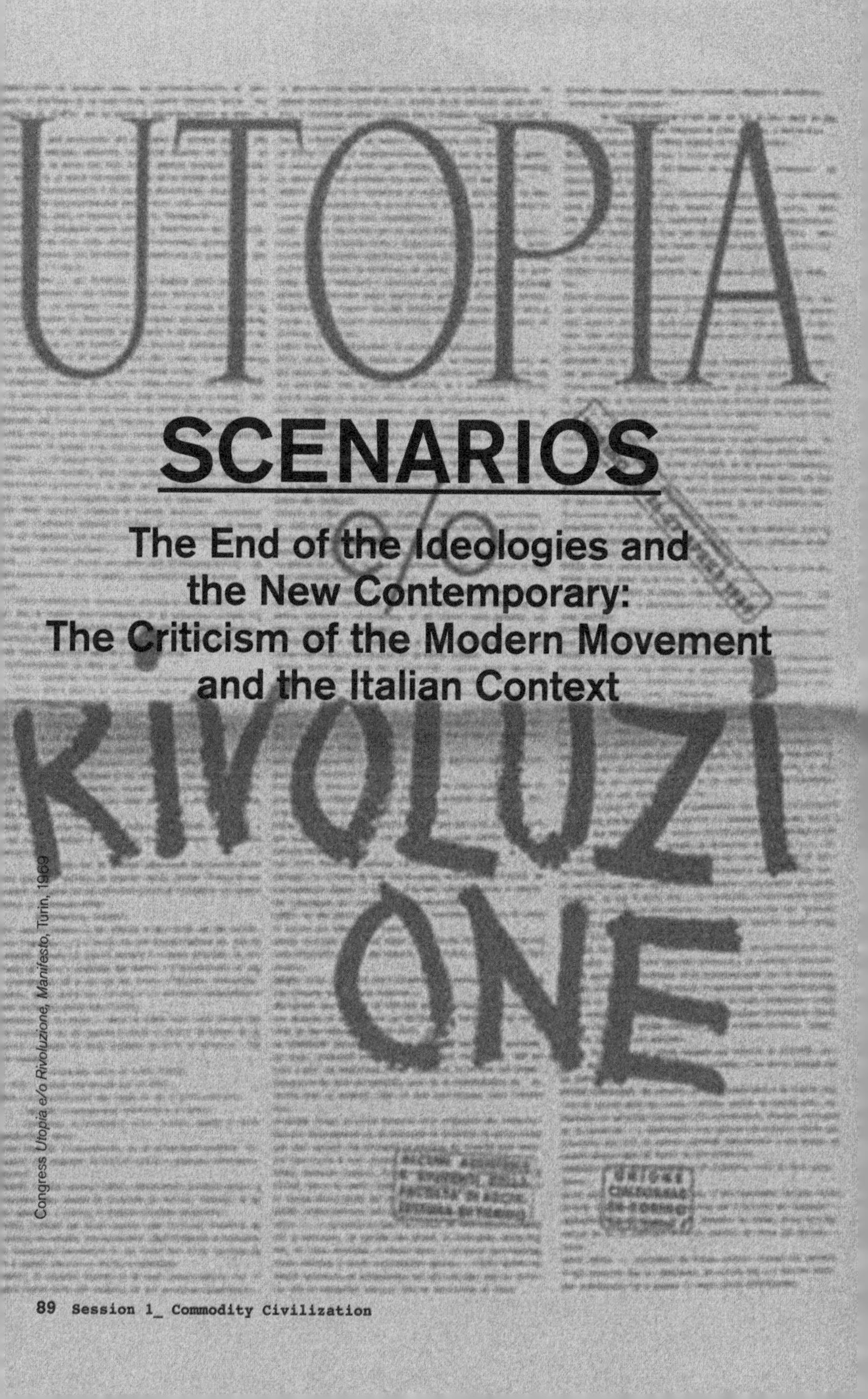

Congress *Utopia e/o Rivoluzione*, *Manifesto*, Turin, 1969

The Sunset of Gods: The Fracture with the Modern Movement

Andrea Branzi, 2014

//

The Sixties generation was thus a generation that revolutionized both the politics and the culture of the project, but warped them through deliberately exaggerated programs, often ironic but also prescient. A model of architecture, ours, more "moral" than practical, quite different from the possibilist "moralism" of the rationalists; a generation marked by the end of theological unity and the birth of a new polytheism. Outside of ideologies and indifference.

Then, the Radical Movement was a way to respond to the self-referentiality of the modern project, which continued to imitate itself, and unlike all other cultural practices (art, music, literature) had gone through two world wars, the nuclear conflict, racial extermination, the great dictatorships of the right and left, without its linguistic code experiencing the slightest disturbance. Sure of its own objective foundation, rationalism had always guaranteed a "happy ending" for industrial society, in a future predicated on order and social justice...

This indifference to the "real story" in favor of a "disciplinary history" had pushed architecture toward complete isolation, committed to saving itself from the tragedies of the century; in the certainty that its survival coincided with the salvation of all humanity.

We reacted to this isolation through an even more radical isolation: an aggressive autonomy from the prudence of the project.

This internal split in the modern project was one of the main insights of the Radical Movement, realistically antithetical to the rationalist utopia of a spontaneous harmony that, "from the spoon to the city," was heading toward a future situated in the order of Reason and that presupposed an objective difference between "city" and "spoon." Today we know that the city "is just a set of spoons" and that the uniqueness of the project is an impractical and dangerous rigidity, far away from the current multiplicity of the future.

That fracture foreshadowed a system of widespread futures, in the complexity and chaos of the world market. Because we were witnesses of a modernity that was losing control of the project, we had two options: to force the disintegration of the modern theorem toward a super-architecture made up of objects and immaterial goods, or to rebuild an architecture capable of restoring (also in a traumatic way) the social and formal order of the world. Within the Radical Movement all these different options (and many others) coexisted.

It was during this period that a new definition "of contemporary" began, one in which man lives in a conflictual way with his own time, always preserving "different critical gradients toward the contemporaneity itself": incomplete, imperfect, useless. This schizophrenia led man to place himself outside of history in order to belong to history; as in the law of perspective for which the observer must be "off the stage" in order to represent it in the form of theater. Thus, a new contract between design and history was established, which implied a critical alliance that concerned not only politics but the great epochal transformations that took place in the darkness of knowledge: the project criticized society, and society criticized the project. This distancing also traversed the Eighties, the Nineties, and the end of the century: for this reason, today the reality of the twenty-first century has not been adequately analyzed, because this conflict has not had (and perhaps it will never have) a solution.

If I consider the different seasons that I've gone through, I have to say that I always had the impression that they were placed into a momentary void, between two different eras. Between the end of classic modernity and the beginning of post-modernity; between the end of ideologies and the beginning of the free dispute.

The Negative Thought and the Announced Deaths
Andrea Branzi, 2014

//

The 60s were a decade of "announced deaths" that influenced our generation. The Conceptual Movement maintained the Death of Art and its sublimation, the Gruppo 63 theorized the Death of Literature and of the Novel, Tafuri and the Radicals asserted the Death of Architecture, Carmelo Bene attested the Death of the Theatre as Antonin Artaud had first prophesied, Anarchist Movements claimed the Death of Politics.

These extreme diagnoses of end of life did not lead at all to the disappearance of Art, Literature, Architecture and Politics, but rather to the reversal of the ancillary role of the "author" as to the "work" one.

In other words, artists, writers, architects and political activists do survive to the death of disciplines and play a central and independent role in the experience (and survival) of the cultural practices.

The historical context in which such phenomena took place was the progressive rejection of the work which did not correspond to the end of productivity, but rather to intellectual mass-production. Mass-production that, at the beginning of the following century in the context of globalization, took shape and found its theory in the expansion of post-Fordist work as global producer of innovation.

This clot of uncoordinated avant-gardes, which in the 60s worked for the disintegration of any form of disciplinary production by de-structuralising it from the inside, actually claimed a new and important principle: if creativity exists, then everybody can be creative. There is no longer a difference between culture professionals and their users: all children are creative, but only 1 per cent become art professionals because of life events.

The problem was not any longer the production of "more culture," but rather of "less culture," thereby allowing the removal of the pre-existing qualitative theorems in favor of a social expansion of mass-creativity.

Within this strategic framework of social and political liberation of the culture, the Radical Movement proposed a super-architecture independent of any client, corresponding to a free design process that had not to answer to anyone for its actions.

Likewise, poets, artists and political activists imagined behind the word "death" a sort of "super diffusion" of culture and politics, an uncontrollable expression of a new diffusive pantheism (if the sacred exists, then everything is sacred) that destroyed the closed circles where previously everything happened.

This destructive thrust of the new avant-gardes, then worked as a positive re-foundation of the way of understanding and practicing the free creative aptitude of each individual.

It was not a utopia, but the omen that the capitalist system was maturing: to transform society into a multitude of free creative consumers, where the freedom of the individual would identify with the generosity of the entire system.

A society where corrosive avant-gardes would serve as a solvent of the molecular system of a new social statute arranged by professional consumers.

The Existential Verism: Micro-catastrophes and Operaismo

Andrea Branzi, 2014

//

Italy is the only country that has never had a revolution. For this reason, it has developed great capabilities in the art of managing its own contradictions, without ever resolving them completely.

This is the reason why the category of "exaggeration" has become a useful strategy to expand, without ever arriving at the point of rupture, the conflictual coexistence between the social parts, between its history and its present, between its merits and its flaws. According to the wise flexible and Catholic tradition in which sin is always followed by forgiveness.

A country such as ours, which has been able, beginning with the Futurists, to imagine a different modernity because according to the facts real modernity was never achieved; capable of recuperating its delay relative to other countries by suddenly carrying itself ahead of them, without ever being like them.

I would not be able to identify what the micro-event was that triggered the catastrophe that involved that exaggerated generation of which I was a part, and which was formed during the sixties, when our world was compressed between the Cold War and the Economic Miracle.

To overcome this mammoth contrast, a small minority of us, who took the name Radicals, began to use political conflict not as an ideological category, but as a figurative theme, which also involved Pop culture and which was able to make visible the impossibility of the times together with their orgonic force, repressed by the threat of cosmic destruction, which everyone knew was impossible.

One of the most characteristic exaggerations of my generation was, however, the myth of Revolution. From Che Guevara to the Chinese Cultural Revolution, it seemed like the world was on the brink of a global mutation. But in Europe this hypothesis was never followed by an adequately structured political program: the Revolution that we were talking about corresponded more with a general aspiration, with occasional revolts, in a mediatic category or with a slogan aimed at emphasizing the range of ongoing problems, and along with that the inability to solve them.

In the vocabulary of the intellectuals and the students, the Revolution remained a conceptual and non-operational category, a symbolic fracture of the political climate but also an expression of a desire to become an official partner of that Political Power that they wanted to theoretically break down.

classe operaia

1

LENIN IN INGHILTERRA

"Sì" al centro-sinistra

No al riformismo

Classe Operaia n. 1, 1964, Cover

"The working class: a rude, pagan race without ideals, without faith, without morals: they want to earn more and work less"

M. Tronti, *Operai e Capitale,* 1966.

I partecipanti al XVII Convegno Internazionale Artisti Critici Studiosi d' arte riuniti a Rimini dal 21 al 24 Settembre 1968,

Visto l' andamento dei lavori del convegno stesso, lavori caratterizzati dalla continua pericolosa volontà di prevaricare individuando un sempre maggiore e libero spazio al potere della classe intellettuale,

Constata la volontà di coinvolgere l'ignara popolazione in un dibattito democratico al fine di giustificare presso il governo e le autorità tale tipo di richiesta,

constatata altresì l'estrema decisione dei designers di iniziare operazioni su scala urbana allo scopo di investire globalmente l'intero teatro della lotta di classe per rinviarne la deflagrazione,

consapevoli della natura dell'impegno culturale, come strumento in qualsiasi caso utilizzato dalla borghesia al fine di eliminare il negativo della propria idea di progresso, e di attenuare così gli effetti più molesti del proprio meccanismo di sfruttamento,

consapevoli altresì del fatto che oggi nessuna immagine di una società migliore riesce a mettere in crisi la borghesia, a meno che tale immagine non sia quella della dittatura del proletariato, cioè di un sistema che lede realmente i suoi interessi e pone sul tappeto i problemi in tutta la loro deflagrante dimensione,

auspicano che nel futuro la classe operaia possa più attentamente vigilare con opportuni strumenti di censura e di controllo su quanto gli intellettuali, o contestatori, privatamente o in consesso dicono, fanno, propongono,

decidono di rifiutare qualsiasi impegno sociale che lo Stato borghese riconosca loro, qualsiasi organizzazione metodologica e didattica del dissenso, di mantenersi calmi per non ingenerare ulteriore panico fra le classi lavoratrici, di ritirarsi nell'esercizio più stretto e rigoroso della loro professione, nell'attesa fiduciosa che venga altrove e nei modi opportuni deciso il loro destino di borghesi.

Andrea Branzi - Gilberto Corretti - Paolo Deganello - Massimo Morozzi

Archizoom Associati, *Declaration, XVII International Conference of Artists, Critics and Scholars of Art*, Rimini, 1968

DECLARATION

THE PARTICIPANTS IN THE 17TH INTERNATIONAL CONFERENCE OF ARTISTS, CRITICS, AND SCHOLARS OF ART Gathered in Rimini from September 21 to 24, 1968

The participants in the 17th International Conference of Artists, Critics, and Scholars of Art gathered in Rimini from September 21 to 24, 1968,

Given the direction of the works of the conference itself, works characterized by the continuous dangerous desire to abuse their power by individuating an increasingly greater and open space to the power of intellectual class,

Finding the desire to involve the unsuspecting population in a democratic debate in order to justify this type of demand among the government and authorities,

Having further noted the extreme decision of the designers to initiate operations on an urban scale aimed at comprehensively laying siege to the entire theatre of the class struggle in order to postpone its deflagration,

Aware of the nature of the cultural engagement, as an instrument utilized in each case by the bourgeoisie in order to eliminate the negative side of their own idea of progress, and thus mitigating the most disturbing effects of its mechanism of exploitation,

Further aware of the fact that today no image of a better society succeeds in undermining the bourgeoisie, unless the image is that of the dictatorship of the proletariat, that is, a system that actually harms its own interests, and puts the issues on the table in all their explosive dimension,

Hoping that in the future the working class can more attentively monitor, with appropriate tools of censure and control, how much the intellectuals, or objectors, privately or in the public arena say, do, propose,

Deciding to reject any social engagement that the bourgeois State recognizes as its own, any methodological and didactic organization of dissent, to keep calm so as to avoid causing further panic among the working classes, to retire into the more strict and rigorous exercise of their profession, in the confident anticipation that elsewhere and in opportune ways their fate as the bourgeoisie will be decided.

Andrea Branzi – Gilberto Corretti – Paolo Deganello – Massimo Morozzi

Quaderni
rossi

La fabbrica
e la società

2

Alla fine della Terza Sezione, quando è ormai compiuta la produzione del plusvalore assoluto, Marx torna a distinguere le due facce della produzione capitalistica e quindi i due punti di vista da cui si può considerare la forma capitalistica di produzione delle merci: processo lavorativo e processo di valorizzazione. Nel primo, l'operaio non tratta i mezzi di produzione come capitale, l'operaio *consuma* i mezzi di produzione come materiale della sua attività produttiva; nel secondo, « non è piú l'operaio che adopera i mezzi di produzione, ma sono i mezzi di produzione che adoperano l'operaio », è il capitale dunque che *consuma* la forza-lavoro. E' vero che già nel processo lavorativo il capitale si sviluppa in *comando sul lavoro*, sulla forza-lavoro e quindi

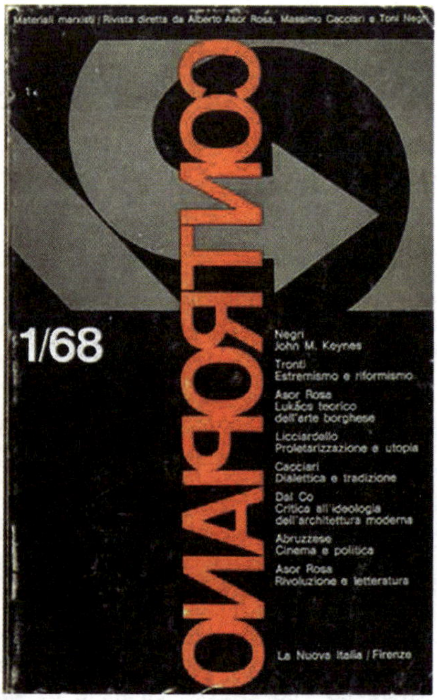

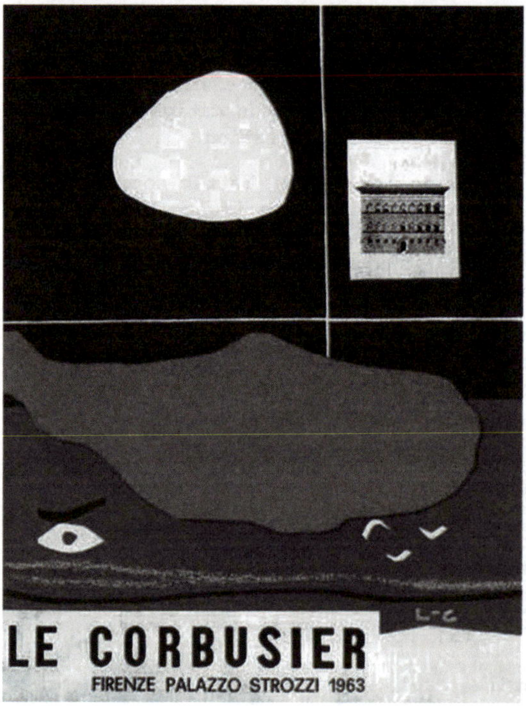

Quaderni Rossi n. 2, 1962, Cover

Contropiano n. 1, 1968, Cover

Manifesto, Le Corbusier Exhibition, Palazzo Strozzi, Florence, 1963

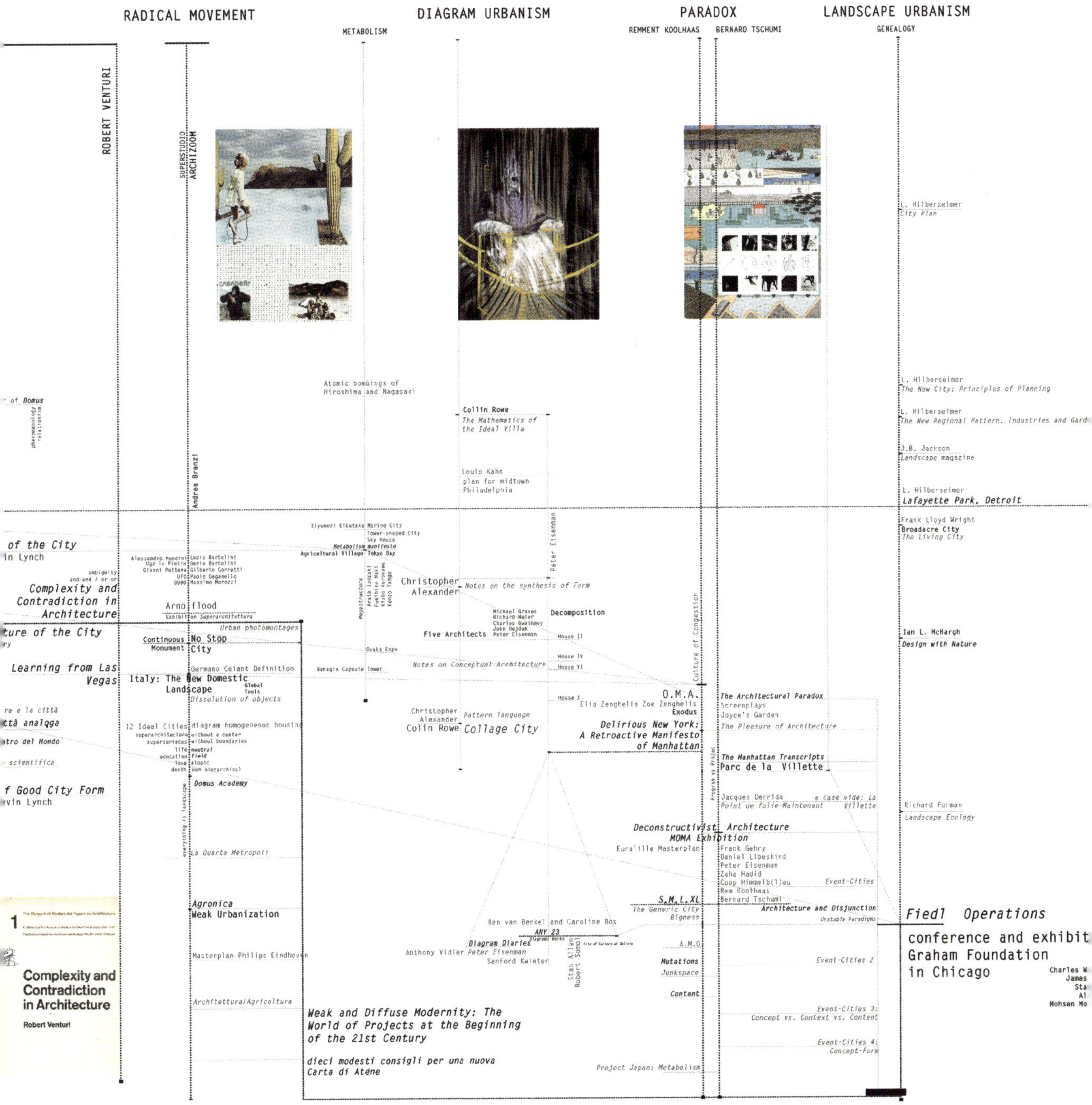
RADICAL MOVEMENT
DIAGRAM URBANISM
PARADOX
LANDSCAPE URBANISM
METABOLISM
REMMENT KOOLHAAS
BERNARD TSCHUMI
GENEALOGY
ROBERT VENTURI
SUPERSTUDIO
ARCHIZOOM
L. Hilberseimer
City Plan
Atomic bombings of Hiroshima and Nagasaki
Collin Rowe
The Mathematics of the Ideal Villa
Louis Kahn
plan for midtown Philadelphia
L. Hilberseimer
The New City: Principles of Planning
L. Hilberseimer
The New Regional Pattern, Industries and Gard
J.B. Jackson
Landscape magazine
L. Hilberseimer
Lafayette Park, Detroit
Andrea Branzi
Frank Lloyd Wright
Broadacre City
The Living City
of the City
in Lynch
Complexity and Contradiction in Architecture
Christopher Alexander
Notes on the synthesis of Form
Peter Eisenman
Arno flood
Decomposition
Five Architects
ture of the City
Continuous Monument
No Stop City
Urban photomontages
Ian L. McHargh
Design with Nature
Learning from Las Vegas
Italy: The New Domestic Landscape
Germano Celant Definition
Notes on Conceptual Architecture
Dissolution of objects
O.M.A.
Elia Zenghelis Zoe Zenghelis
Exodus
The Architectural Paradox
Screenplays
Joyce's Garden
The Pleasure of Architecture
Culture of Congestion
Christopher Alexander
Pattern language
Colin Rowe
Collage City
Delirious New York: A Retroactive Manifesto of Manhattan
12 Ideal Cities
diagram homogeneous housing
The Manhattan Transcripts
Parc de la Villette
f Good City Form
vin Lynch
Domus Academy
Jacques Derrida
Point de folie-Maintenant
a Case vide: La Villette
Richard Forman
Landscape Ecology
Deconstructivist Architecture
MOMA Exhibition
Euralille Masterplan
La Quarta Metropoli
Frank Gehry
Daniel Libeskind
Peter Eisenman
Zaha Hadid
Coop Himmelb(l)au
Rem Koolhaas
Bernard Tschumi
Event-Cities
S,M,L,XL
The Generic City
Bigness
Architecture and Disjunction
Agronica
Weak Urbanization
Fiedl Operations
conference and exhibit
Graham Foundation
in Chicago
Ben van Berkel and Caroline Bos
ANY 23
Diagram Diaries
Anthony Vidler
Peter Eisenman
Sanford Kwinter
Stan Allen
Robert Somol
A.M.O
Mutations
Junkspace
Event-Cities 2
Masterplan Philips Eindhoven
Content
Complexity and Contradiction in Architecture
Robert Venturi
Architettura Agricoltura
Event-Cities 3: Concept vs. Context vs. Content
Weak and Diffuse Modernity: The World of Projects at the Beginning of the 21st Century
Event-Cities 4: Concept-Form
dieci modesti consigli per una nuova Carta di Atene
Project Japan: Metabolism

CONTEXTS

Florence and the Florentine School: Urban Megastructures and Pop Hybridizations

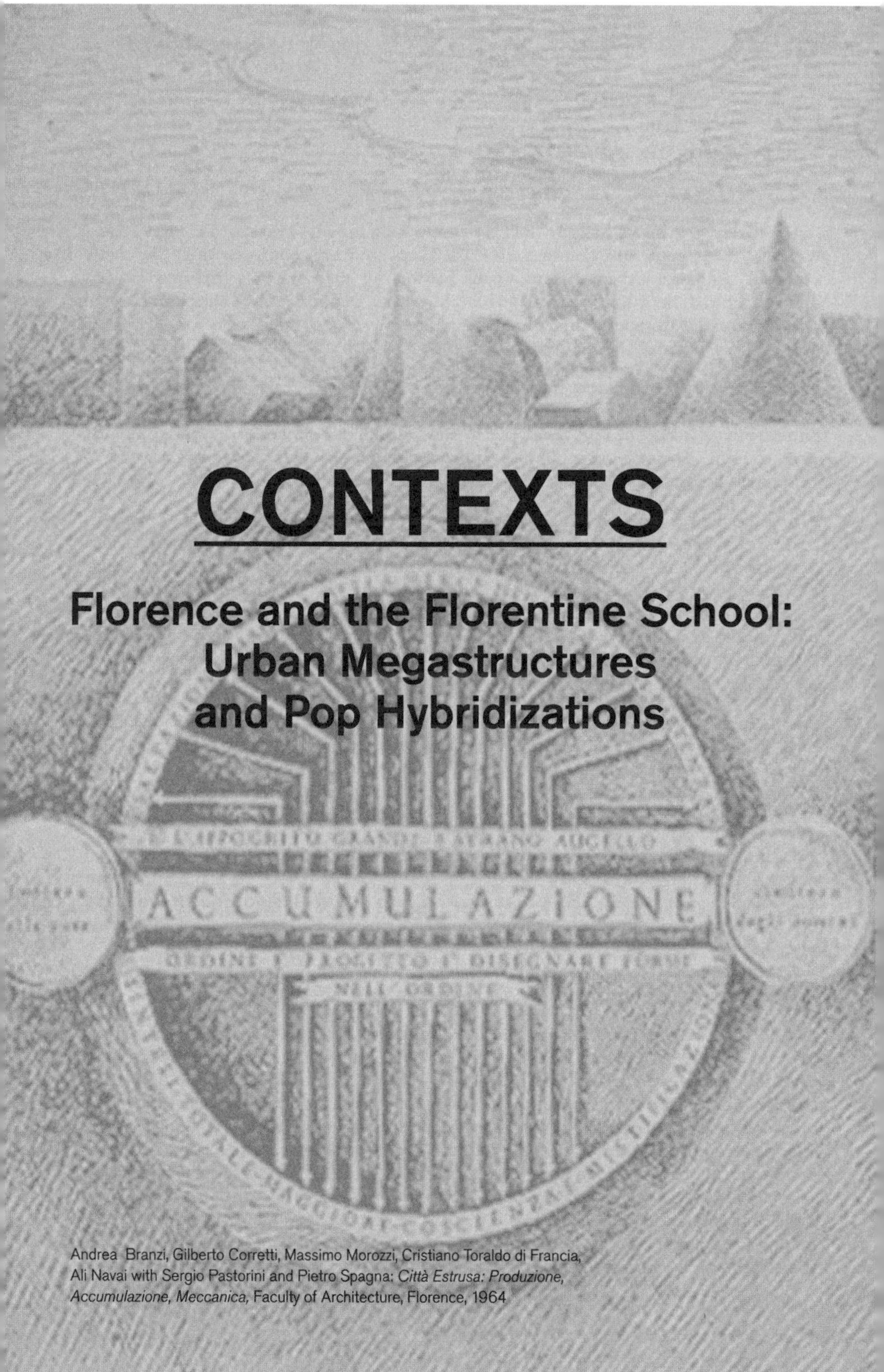

Andrea Branzi, Gilberto Corretti, Massimo Morozzi, Cristiano Toraldo di Francia, Ali Navai with Sergio Pastorini and Pietro Spagna: *Città Estrusa: Produzione, Accumulazione, Meccanica,* Faculty of Architecture, Florence, 1964

Florence

Andrea Branzi, 2014

//

Many times we have asked, and we have wondered, how is it that the Radical Movement originated in Florence, a city that is not particularly modern, instead of in Milan, recognized as the capital of design. The answer could be paradoxical: for the same reason that the Renaissance was born in Florence, a city of Etruscan origin, and not in Rome, the home of classical architecture.

Paradoxically, Florence has revealed itself over time to be a city capable of generating cultural movements that were fed from its own substantial extraneity from both the classical tradition and that of the modern. A sort of neutral laboratory that made it possible to "invent" both a new classicism and a new modernity.

Florence has always been a city of great contradictions and internal conflicts: the wars between Guelphs and Ghibellines, the revolt of the Ciompi, the Pazzi conspiracy, Savonarola against the Medici, the controversy between modernists and innovators, the clashes on the new Santa Maria Novella station, up through the Battle of Florence between partisans and fascists, and in the seventies the lettered mayors in the Palazzo Vecchio, and the "Monster of Florence" in the countryside.

Therefore, a city that has always made mediations of any kind difficult. This diversity has fueled not only its difficult approach to modernity, but has also made it difficult to be on good terms with its own history. The environmental difficulties that modern architecture has always met there have pushed it to try and break its isolation through a path made of formal exaggerations and exasperations.

For its historical precedents, the Florentine reality had been interpreted as "naturally modern," which could then do without modern materials, recycling the old ones, within a landscape indifferent to the seasons like a new Parthenon, made up of olive and cypress trees that never lose their leaves. This attitude is also the effect of Italian pessimism with regard to modernity and its ability to build new masterpieces, of which it feels nonetheless to be the heir.

In 1951, a major exhibition on the work of F. L. Wright was organized at the Palazzo Strozzi, that the host of the city hypothesized moving to Fiesole, where already in 1910 a villa had been designed on Via Verdi. However, this never came to pass. In the fifties, Jackson Pollock donated one of his paintings for an anticipated Museum of Modern Art (never completed), but his work, totally misunderstood, ended up in a nondescript city office and thus ruined. Even Le Corbusier, in 1962 on the occasion of an exhibition of his, was invited by Mayor La Pira to make a proposal for Florence, but his plan fell on deaf ears. The Faculty of Architecture, after a long period of reflection, decided not to confer him with an honorary degree, foreseen by the program...

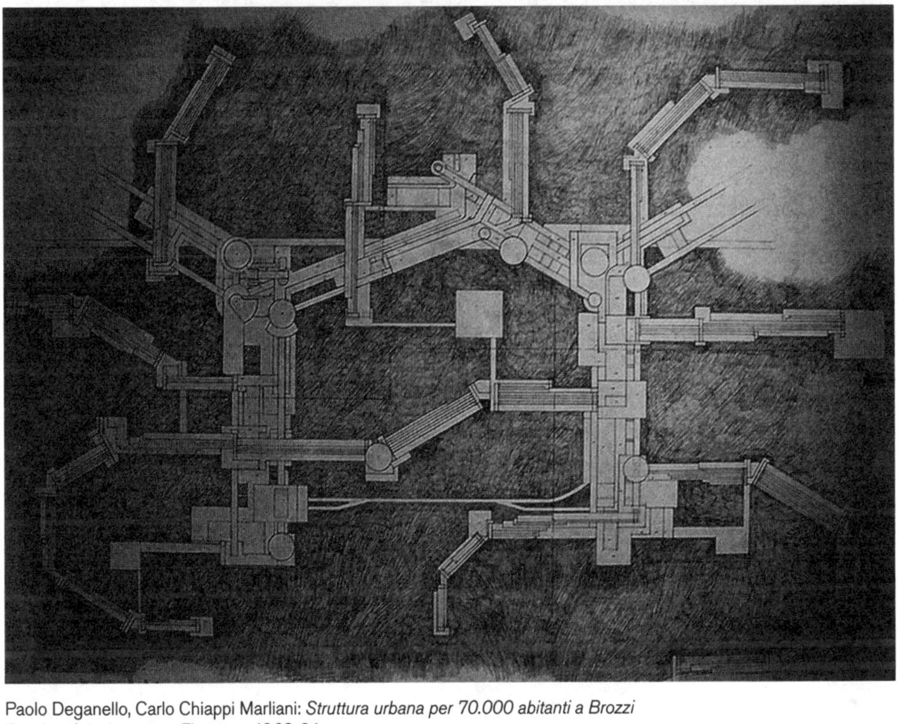

Paolo Deganello, Carlo Chiappi Marliani: *Struttura urbana per 70.000 abitanti a Brozzi*
Faculty of Architecture, Florence, 1963-64

Andrea Branzi, Gilberto Corretti, Massimo Morozzi, Cristiano Toraldo di Francia, Ali Navai with Sergio Pastorini and Pietro Spagna, *Città Estrusa: Allegoria morale della Città Estrusa,* and *Il nastro della produzione industriale,* Faculty of Architecture, Florence, 1964

Andrea Branzi, Gilberto Corretti, Massimo Morozzi, Cristiano Toraldo di Francia, Ali Navai with Sergio Pastorini and Pietro Spagna
Città Estrusa: Produzione, Accumulazione, Meccanica, Faculty of Architecture, Florence, 1964

The Florentine School

Andrea Branzi, 2014

//

The young Faculty of Architecture of Florence (orphan of Giovanni Michelucci who abandoned it in 1948) became a sort of Academy of "organic Florentine expressionism," represented above all by Leonardo Savioli and Leonardo Ricci.

As Paolo Portoghesi noted, the movement actually had no connection either with the work of Wright or with that of Alvar Aalto, but rather with the local confines of a Modern without modernity, where there existed neither a social context nor adequate technologies.

Thus, a way of designing schematically, based on the use of simple materials such as stone, brick, wrought iron, as if they were the origins of a self-sufficient modernity.

Many times I have been asked what the influence of Ricci and Savioli was with respect to the founding of the Radical Movement. Personally, I do not think they are the ones who had an influence on us, but perhaps we were the ones who influenced them.

Between 1962 and 1966, the Faculty of Architecture of Florence experienced a particularly fortuitous moment, because of the presence of many high-quality professors, like specifically Ludovico Quaroni and Adalberto Libera, Leonardo Benevolo, Gillo Dorfles, and Umberto Eco, and also because of the presence of a student movement that in 1965 organized the first occupation of the Rector's office in Italy.

Certainly a greater influence on our training were other professors, like Ludovico Quaroni, an intellectual architect and problematic urban planner, and also Adalberto Libera, a tough and rigorous designer of a great lucidity.

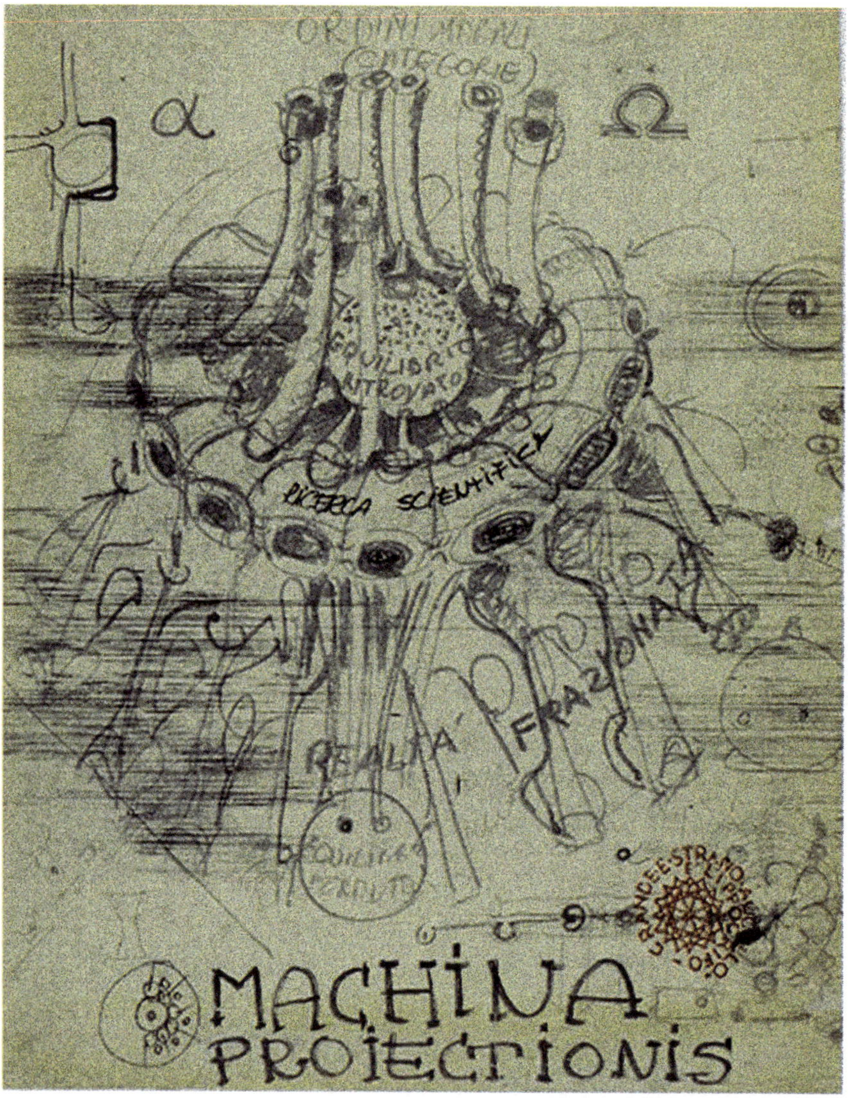

Andrea Branzi, Gilberto Corretti, Massimo Morozzi,
Cristiano Toraldo di Francia, Ali Navai with Sergio Pastorini
and Pietro Spagna
Città Estrusa: Machina Proiectionis
Faculty of Architecture, Florence, 1964

BACKGROUND

Identification of Quantum of Equipment for the Free-Time

An Everlasting Luna Park (within A Supermarket)

Andrea Branzi, Master Thesis, July, 1966
Supervisor Prof. Domenico Cardini

//

The theme is clearly Pop and refers to the growing society of leisure time and consumerism.

The traditional territorial functions, rigid and definitive, are gradually being replaced by new entities, endowed with a strong emotional charge.

The physical image of architecture is replaced by maxi-graphic curtains, inside of which the undulating course of the roller coasters penetrate and disappear.

The Enlightenment tenets of Le Corbusier are ignored, and the contemplative silence of modernity is replaced with the soundtrack of Jerry Lee Lewis's acrobatic piano.

Therefore, the references are entirely unrelated to the academic issues of that time (prefabrication, mass production, functionalism, organization) and are instead confronted with the modernity that has lost control of its own linked industry: it is the first step towards a Superarchitettura that adapts to super-consumption, supermen, and super-unleaded gas.

ESTRATTO DALLA RELAZIONE DI TESI. Firenze, 21 luglio 1966

PROBLEMA DEL TEMPO LIBERO COME PROBLEMA DEL VIVERE-CONSUMARE LA CITTA': CONOSCENZA ATTRAVERSO LA PRASSI, NECESSITA' DI UNA INDAGINE ANTROPOLOGICA DEL FENOMENO URBANO.

Capire il tempo libero non solo come tema capace di suggerire una serie di attrezzature - servizio da distribuire in maniera omogenea nel tessuto urbano, ma capire il tempo libero come momento della percezione della "forma globale" della città, cioè come tempo di recupero di una conoscenza dimensionalmente più civile del vivere urbano.

E' il momento in cui avviene l'acquisizione di quei miti e di quei comportamenti, di quelle"morfologie" sociali che caratterizzano i consorzi umani. Momento in cui avviene la conoscenza globale della realtà del sistema attraverso le forme da lui espresse e le realtà oggettive che lo sostanziano.

Tempo libero quindi come momento delle scelte. Nella civiltà dei consumi infatti esso ha esattamente il valore equivalente di acquisizione di ideologia che ha il "tempo di fabbrica" per i marxisti: acquisizione cioè di una coscienza globale e di adesione ad una ideologia, nel momento stesso del contatto con le strutture reali. Momento di tempo libero quindi come momento di conoscenza attraverso la prassi.

Andrea Branzi, *Master Thesis - Report,* original document, 1966.

2)

Tempo libero allora come tempo di vivere in città e di usarla. Si pone però a questo punto la necessità di impostare globalmente il problema della città superando i limiti della critica storica e della sociològia, e cercando di capirla come luogo di un particolare tipo di conoscenza attraverso la prassi.

Esiste oggi la necessità di studiare i fenomeni caratteristici di una comunità individuando una legge strutturale complessiva che permetta di raffrontarli in un unico sistema: gli studi fatti sulla linguistica sono rivelatori, però non sono sufficienti per definire tutte le manifestazioni umani come "linguaggio" perché rinviano il problema solo in parte risolto.

In realtà il linguaggio si muove all'interno di un complesso sistema di riferimenti formali, di una struttura cioè antropologica che è quella che poi permette la formazione da un semplice consorzio sociale impegnato a comunicare, in una civiltà capace di esprimere una cultura collettiva e una significazione totale.

Esiste cioè il problema fondamentale dell'uomo che è quello conoscitivo, intendendo per problema conoscitivo non tanto quello della spiegazione funzionale o scientifica dei fenomeni, ma semmai quello della loro collocazione all'interno di quadri significanti.

Organizzare cioè in "cultura" tutta una somma di fenomeni oggettivamente casuali, come ad esempio la natura, dandogli un valore quali momenti dimostrativi di una ideologia generale. Su questa capacità

37

dell'uomo di conoscere una realtà come cultura, e di emettere quindi un giudizio su di essa, risiede la legge e la potenzialità evolutiva dei sistemi.

Legge di evoluzione o di trasformazione che non è una legge dialettica: tesi,antitesi,sintesi, che lascerebbe intravedere sviluppi organici dei sistemi, come molta storia della cultura e come la teoria economico-liberale ha supposto. In realtà il ~~xxxxxxx~~ sistema segue una progressione di sviluppo che avviene per salti, cioè per assorbimento di modelli formali catalizzanti.

Esiste quindi una attrezzatura oggettiva che permette l'esistenza e il consumo di tutti gli stimoli capaci di sviluppare, di percepire, e di giudicare il sistema: la città è quindi un luogo di riferimenti in cui i modelli formali possono agire e si inseriscono restituendo ad un livello conoscitivo maggiore il sistema totale, agendo all'interno di un'area di demistificazione e di ambiguità totale.

La città è quindi un luogo in cui il sistema si rappresenta, si significa e si percepisce a sé medesimo.

CRISI DEL METODO STORICO ALL'INTERNO DI DUE GROSSI FENOMENI CULTURALI: ECLETTISMO E SINCRETISMO.

La crisi del metodo storico come strumento capace di restituirci i fenomeni ormai strutturali, nel senso antropologico, della città, è il prodotto in realtà di una serie di necessità maturate nel tempo, crisi che investe più generalmente il mondo culturale architettonico

4)

giustificando tutta una serie di polemiche parziali in questi ultimi anni esplose: crsi del funzionalismo, superamento del razionalismo, revivals, ecc.
Questi fatti possono essere ricondotti ad una più generale fase di sviluppo del sistema, ed in linea di massima possono essere inquadrati in due aspetti sintomatici del momento culturale che stiamo attraversando: essi sono l'<u>eclettismo</u> e il <u>sincretismo</u>.

ECLETTISMO

Due ne sono i motivi principali:
1) Il <u>momento di violento sviluppo del sistema</u> che necessariamente tende a far recuparare tutta una serie di passate esperienze sulla base di una disinvolta capacità di assorbimento e di accostamento.
2) <u>Crisi autonoma di maturazione del razionalismo</u> che demistificando ed accettando come convenzionale il linguaggio ne permette il suo uso metastorico.

Da questi duplici motivi ne consegue una <u>crisi oggetiva del metodo storico</u> come strumento incapace di controllare e giustificare un uso spregiudicato di linguaggi e forme sorte in determinati climi e all'interno di strutture storiche precise.
Eclettismo quindi come fenomeno temporaneo: assunzione eclettica del repertorio formale nel momento in cui vengono forzate le dimensioni dell'intervento.

57

Eclettismo però come indicativo sintomo della estraneità nella filosofia attuale della soluzione dello iato tra "conoscenza" e "azione operativa".

La libertà di decisione e di adesione a lotte e ideologie rimane al livello dell'individualismo più inesplorato. Ugualmente l'adesione della "forma" alla "funzione" è rimasto nonostante gli sforzi di sistemazione scientifica sul piano della scelta incontrollata, permettendo in un certo momento l'uso di soluzioni altrove ed in altri tempi sperimentate.

SINCRETISMO

Se l'eclettismo accetta su di una base di tardo razionalismo la presenza simultanea di due più linguaggi che presumono processi formativi diversi, il sincretismo accetta la presenza ed il recupero di più sistemi strutturali e ideologici diversi all'interno di un macro-organismo sociale.

La dilatazione del sistema capitalistico a livelli mondiali, presume l'uso puramente strumentale di forme di economia e di pensiero sorti in un determinato clima ideologico e che si prefiggevano contenuti anche totalmente diversi. (Pianificazione, programmazione, ecc., possono divenire strumenti di razionalizzazione della realtà al momento del suo assorbimento del sistema. I contenuti dimensionali della pacificazione delle chiese permette oggi la presenza simultanea di culture e di civiltà di pensiero un tempo escludentesi a vicenda.)

6)

La stessa civiltà del benessere impone l'individuazione all'interno di uno stesso organismo di strutture autonome a tempo di consumo diverso. Si pone quindi il problema di individuare una nuova prassi di progettazione più idonea ad agire ai livelli raggiunti ed alla luce di una situazione storica oggettivamente mutata.

CIVILTA' DI CONSUMI, INDUSTRIA DEL COMPORTAMENTO E IDEOLOGIA ARTIFICIALE.

L'avvento della civiltà dei consumi non è da considerarsi un semplice fenomeno di opulenza produttiva o di iper-disponibilità del mercato di assorbimento; esso è piuttosto la prima maturazione di un capovolgimento di struttura di un vecchio mercato basato sul sistema dialettico di domanda e offerta.
Mentre infatti, nell'ipotesi di una economia arcaico-capitalista, la legge di sviluppo giaceva nella libera richiesta e scelta del consumatore, oggi l'offerta del prodotto precede nello spazio e nel tempo la domanda e attraverso complessi canali di induzione riesce a sollecitarla.
Si è venuto così sostituendo al concetto naturalistico di libero mercato quello della sua completà artificialità: da qui la possibilità di dilatazione macroscopica della produzione attraverso la creazione del super consumatore.
Per ottenere un simile processo si è venuta creando ad un determina-

to livello del sistema una vera e propria industria dei modelli formali capaci di introdurre il comportamento completo nel consumatore. Tale comportamento ha la necessità di essere giustificato e qualificato da una ideologia globale, che determinati operatori culturali vengono elaborando in forma di arte, di mito, o di simbolo.
Tale settore del sistema, che elabora modelli formali di comportamento al consumo, ha una struttura unica e caratteristica che è quella di identificare completamente il resultato culturale in quello commerciale. Ciò significa che il criterio di valutazione di un determinato fatto culturale è la sua capacità di divenire costume e di interessare un mercato di consumatori.
Il comportamento è la disponibilità all'uso di un certo contesto di prodotti esprimenti una determinata ideologia, per cui il mercato complessivo per qualificarsi rimanda a determinati prodotti che per la loro capacità di violenta caratterizzazione riescono ad indurre un comportamento nel consumatore. L'ideologia che ne risulta può definirsi allora come ideologia artificiale, contro la definizione di ideologia spontanea o politica, generata cioè da determinate situazioni sociali, e diviene anch'essa un bene di consumo al pari di un qualsiasi prodotto imposto dal sistema.

I livelli di super produzione raggiunti oggi dal sistema richiedono l'individuazione di strumenti capaci di generalizzare il mercato: per far questo la distanza tra elaborazione culturale a livello ideologico

8)

ed elaborazione di modelli di consumo si è fortemente ridotta ~~in~~ fin quasi ad annullarsi.

Di questo fenomeno ne è oggi interessata la stessa architettura, come struttura fondamentale capace di inserirsi nel processo di induzione di tali modelli.

SOSTANZIALE AMBIGUITA' DEL FATTO ARCHITETTONICO COME SPARTIACQUE DECISIONALE.

L'architettura, la città, restituisce ad un livello maggiore la realtà, ma di per sé, proprio perché forma non può essere unidirezionale: non può cioè vincolare le decisioni imponendo un'unica interpretazione, prevaricando cioè il consumo ambiguo che di essa vien fatto. Adorazione, suicidio, rivoluzione.

Tutte le azioni che si svolgono ad un determinato livello sovrastrutturale (arte, letteratura, architettura) anche se storicamente condizionate possiedono una dimensione demistificatrice tale da costituire un vero e proprio spartiacque decisionale. Non esiste allora il problema di architettura integrata o di architettura di protesta, ma esiste piuttosto oggi il problema del recupero di una "dimensionalità operativa" capace di generare un risultato decisionale a livello omogeneo con il sistema.

IL TEMA DEL TEMPO LIBERO E DESCRIZIONE DELL'ORGANISMO PROGETTATO.

Il tema del "tempo libero" è stato affrontato nella maniera più organica possibile. Sono stati individuati grosso modo tre momenti distinti, tema di tre tesi di laurea separate, nascenti da una premessa e necessità culturale comune:

Il tempo libero nei centri storici, come utilizzazione e recupero di vecchie strutture destinate genericamente a monumenti urbani, attraverso l'introduzione di organismi interni autonomi.

Il tempo libero in campagna, come collocamento d'un oggetto sostanzialmente inutile all'interno d'un paesaggio; oggetto che fosse però capace di dare al paesaggio stesso una gerarchia di lettura ed un significato di uso.

Il tempo libero in periferia, oggetto del presente studio, nel senso di un intervento urbano capace di collocarsi unitariamente in un tessuto inqualificato con la potenzialità di ristrutturarlo. Prato, importante centro industriale di rigenerazione e produzione tessile, possiede una periferia tipica delle piccole cittadine che hanno subito il proprio sviluppo edilizio al seguito di uno industriale eccessivamente minuto.
Non esiste una vera e propria serie di quartieri operai, a causa del

fatto che l'industria acquisisce la propia mano d'opera attraverso i pendolari e attraverso il progressivo deterioramento dell'attività agricola nel territorio circostante.

La polverizzazione dell'attività imprenditoriale non ha permesso la formazione di una classe operaia sindacalmente forte, capace cioè d'imporre uno sviluppo per salti al sistema industriale.

Quello che ne risulta è una città in cui il livello medio di vita si presenta omogeneo senza zone cittadine eccessivamente inferiori, ma sostanzialmente risulta inutilizzata dal punto di vista dei consumi. Questa condizione di Prato, come città che produce e non consuma, è abbastanza tipica: si impone un intervento capace di sbloccare con l'urto una situazione di equilibrio protrattasi fin troppo.

Dalla constatazione di questa condizione eccessivamente omogenea ed inqualificata è sorta l'idea di un intervento unico, sul piano di una violenta figuralità, che fosse capace di assommare una xxxxx categoria i consumi che già oggi costituiscono la struttura da giudicare del sistema.

Il luogo per la costruzione è stato individuato in quella larga zona di verde agricolo rimasta circoscritta dalla periferia a causa del vincolo cimiteriale, e che sarà pensata trasformata in parco pubblico.

L'organismo è composto da: un grosso cinema per 1500 persone che con-

3)

tiene sul proprio tetto un piccolo cine-club per non più di 400 posti. Sulla testata del parco è prevista una palestra con un sistema di terme e bagni turchi che si snodano all'interno di una struttura a ponte che costituisce una sorta di passeggiata termica terminante in un bar vegetariano.

La spina principale è costituita da un organismi contenente gli uffici di amministrazione, un grande super-market, con sopra una pista da ballo, bar, boutique, night-club. Da questo nodo centrale che compone il grosso cubo si snoda un sistema di vendita automatica definito come tunnel dei distributori caratterizzato da colonne verticali contenenti distributori, luci, suoni, condizionatori d'aria, ecc. All'interno di questo tunnel è prevista x l'individuazione di spazi chiusi intorno a funzioni temporanee.

Tutta una serie di organismi fittizi in struttura gonfiabile o costituiti da gxx grosse immagini-oggetto, è infine inserita su di un percorso ondeggiante che termina nella grande ruota panoramica.

L'ottovolante percorre quasi tutto l'organismo penetrando nella pista da ballo, traversando il super-market, inserendosi come un'onda gigante dentro il tunnel dei distributori ed uscando poi, attraverso un tubo, nel parco circostante.

POLIFUNZIONALITA' COME MAGGIORE SUPERFICE DI CONTATTO.

La <u>polifunzionalità</u> dell'organismo progettato non significa la previsione di una esatta successione di usi nello spazio, ma piuttosto l'individuazione di certe gerarchie dimensionali e formali dix strutture singolarmente autonome, accostate con la disinvoltura del bricolage. Questo nel senso che il tutto non si identifica in una unità stilisticamente percepibile, ma semmai in un certo spirito che guida l'accostamento o l'ammucchiamento delle parti.

L'edificio non è generato da un unico atto progettuale, ma semmai costruito attraverso l'uso di parti già esistenti montate dentro e attorno ad una struttura metallica principale (sulla quale corre l'ottovolante) dalla quale si partono percorsi e accessi assolutamente casuali.

La polifunzionalità è intesa come una ricerca della maggiore possibilità di superficie di contatto tra edificio e utenti.

Nella prima fase di studio era presente l'intenzione di procedere all'individuazione dell'attrezzatura secondo una logica di montaggio prossima a quella dell'edilizia industriale, che segue cioè disinvoltamente la successione spaziale di funzioni diverse senza darne una sintesi progettuale o stilistica.

Il tutto veniva pensato per parti: percorsi in tubi, spazi individuati da necessità di cubaggio, treni di uffici che si infilavano all'int rno di una struttura maggiore che li conteneva senza giustificarli. Il progetto si muoveva secondo una logica stringente da "macchina per divertirsi" sulla quale montare e passare una giornata senza toccare il suolo, servendosi solo di gettoni.

In un momento successivo si è fatta largo la necessità di sperimentare una morfologia più eterogenea e più aderente, attraverso i simboli, al tipo di comportamento che si proponeva di indurre. L'uso del colore, di materiali più diversi, accostati secondo una gerarchia di tempi diversi di consumo, una chiassosità ed una freschezza maggiore capace di riscattare la macro-struttura. E' emersa così l'idea del cubo gigantesco, forma omogenea ed indifferenziata dal quale si riparte e si precipita tutta una serie di strutture minori, piazzato sordamente all'incrocio di due direttive principali, che sono quelle dell'ottovolante e del cinema-terme. Il cubo, come forma <u>non progettata</u> permette di relazionare ed esaltarne altre più complesse, determinando per il proprio peso volumetrico una lettura gerarchica ma simultanea delle altre parti.

L'<u>ottovolante</u> costituisce fin dalla prima parte di studio il filo conduttore capace di collegare e di dare un senso a presenze oggettivamente indifferenti, riconducendole ad un tempo di percezione e di consumo fulmineo. L'ottovolante permette di profanare la simultaneità degli avvenimenti passando dal chiuso all'aperto e viceversa, e venendo infine sparato al di fuori del sistema per immergersi nel parco circostante.

MOTIVI DI UNA SCELTA TECNOLOGICA: L'USO DELL'ACCIAIO COME NUOVA POSSIBILITA' LINGUISTICA.

La scelta dell'acciaio come materiale costruttivo è stata motivata da una serie di soluzioni che la tecnologia del metallo stesso permette di fare sul piano generale dell'architettura:

1) L'alta resistenza dell'acciaio allo sforzo permette l'adesione della struttura all'andamento reale delle forze, generando una **estrema leggibilità e fruibilità del fatto architettonico**, sul piano delle sue componenti e all'interno di un processo di estrema semplificazione. Non esistono più masse ma solo reticoli.
Quella che ne risulta è un'architettura nella quale la legge strutturale si riduce realmente ad un fatto tecnico-scientifico che arrichisce la logica interna e la potenzialità espressiva dell'organismo.

2) L'esistenza di un'esatta tecnica di carpenteria metallica permette l'introduzione di una serie di elementi non progettati: ne risulta una architettura in cui certe scale di disegno vengono rigorosamente bruciate, recuperando una tolleranza (nel senso di una progettazione non eccessivamente grafica) che l'uso del cemento aveva fortemente svirilizzato.

3) La mancanza di un colore naturale nell'acciaio come materiale da costruzione permette l'inserimento del colore artificiale nell'organismo architettonico.

Questo fatto apre un grosso discorso urbano inserendosi come una possibilità nuova nel problema attuale della sintesi delle arti, e della capacità figurale del fatto architettonico.
L'uso del colore permette di porre in risalto inoltre la completa "artificialità" del fatto architettonico: questo nel senso che la costruzione in legno, in cotto, in pietra, e in fondo anche in cemento, proprio per l'esistenza di un "colore naturale" di questi materiali, ha confermato una sorta di rapporto diretto tra natura e architettura. In realtà l'architettura, come arte, si sostituisce alla natura sovrapponendosi a questa e dandole un senso all'interno di un sistema di riferimenti culturali. Il colore più artificiale e autonomo, cioè progettato, permette oggi di spingere avanti questo aspetto costituzionale del fare architettonico, portandolo alle estreme conseguenze e lasciando intravedere una nuova e ricca serie di sviluppi.

4) L'acciaio, molto meglio del cemento armato, proprio per questa sua natura completamente controllata, ridotta cioè alla pura funzione strutturale, senza scarti o grosse tolleranze, permette l'accostamento con altre tecnologie di materiali completamente artificiali (plastica, gomma, carta, ecc.). Ne risulta una capacità enorme di arricchimento del fatto architettonico, specialmente quando l'individuazione di nuovi temi richiede l'esistenza di una nuova capacità espressiva e l'adesione a funzioni e tempi di consumo inusitati.

Excerpt from the thesis report

Andrea Branzi, Master Thesis, July 21, 1966
(Supervisor Prof. Renato Cardini)

//

The problem of leasure time as the problem of living-consuming in the city: Knowledge through praxis, the need for an anthropological investigation of the urban phenomenon

Understanding leisure time not only as a theme capable of suggesting a series of tools – services to distribute in a consistent manner in the urban fabric, but understanding free time as the moment of perception of the "global form" of the city, that is, as a time of recuperating an awareness that is dimensionally more civil in terms of urban living.

It is the moment in which the acquisition of those myths and those behaviors occurs, of those social "morphologies" that characterize human groups. The moment in which the overall knowledge of the reality of the system occurs through the forms that are expressed by it and the objective reality that substantiates it.

Leisure time thus a moment of decisions. In consumer society, in fact, it has exactly the equivalent value in terms of acquisition of ideology that the "time of the factory" has for Marxists: that is, the acquisition of a global consciousness and an adherence to an ideology, in the same exact moment of contact with the real structures. Leisure time thus as a moment of knowledge through practice.

Thus, free time as a time to live in the city and to use it. At this point, however, there is the need to tackle the problem of the city globally, overcoming the limits of historical criticism and sociology, and trying to understand the city itself as a place for a particular type of knowledge through practice.

There exists today the need to study the characteristic phenomena of a community by identifying an overall structural law that makes it possible to compare them in a single system: the studies done on linguistics are revealing, however, they are not sufficient to define all human manifestations as "language" because they render the problem only partly solved.

In reality, language moves within a complex system of formal references, within a therefore anthropological structure that is the one that then allows the formation of a simple social group committed to communicating, in a civilization capable of expressing a collective culture and an overall signification.

That is to say, there exists the fundamental problem of man, which is the cognitive one, meaning by a cognitive problem not so much that of a functional or scientific explanation of phenomena, but rather that of their placement within frameworks of meaning.

Therefore, a whole range of objectively random phenomena are organized in "culture," such as nature for example, giving these demonstrative moments the value of a general ideology. On this capability of man to know reality as culture, and thus make a judgment about it, rests the law and the evolutionary potential of the systems.

A law of evolution or of transformation that is not a dialectical law: thesis, antithesis, synthesis, which would allow for a glimpse of organic developments of the systems, like much of the history of culture and as assumed by liberal economic theory. In reality, the system follows a progression of development that occurs in jumps, that is, in the absorption of catalyzing formal models.

There is, therefore, an objective tool that allows for the existence and consumption of all the stimuli capable of developing, perceiving, and judging the system: the city is therefore a place of reference in which formal models can act and are inserted, reestablishing the total system on a higher cognitive level, acting within an area of demystification and total ambiguity.

The city is therefore a place in which the system represents, gives meaning to, and perceives itself.

Crisis of the historical method within two major cultural phenomena: eclecticism and syncretism

The crisis of the historical method as an instrument capable of restoring the now structural phenomena, in the anthropological sense, of the city is actually the product of a series of needs that developed over time, a crisis that attacks more generally the architectural cultural world, justifying a whole series of partial controversies that have exploded in recent years: the crisis of functionalism, the overcoming of rationalism, revivals, etc.

These facts may each be brought back to a more general phase of the system's development, and in principle can be framed within two symptomatic aspects of the cultural moment which we are traversing: they are eclecticism and syncretism.

Eclecticism

There are two principal reasons for this:

1) The moment of the violent development of the system that necessarily tends to recover a whole series of past experiences on the basis of an informal capacity of absorption and juxtaposition.

2) An autonomous crisis of the maturation of Rationalism that by demystifying and accepting language as conventional allows for its meta-historical use.

From these dual reasons follows an objective crisis of historical method as an instrument unable to control and justify an unscrupulous use of languages and forms that arose in certain climates and within specific historical structures.

Eclecticism thus as a temporary phenomenon: the eclectic assumption of the formal repertory at the moment in which the dimensions of the intervention are forced.

Eclecticism, though, as an indicative symptom of the extraneity in the philosophy of today of the solution for the gap between "knowledge" and "operational action."

The freedom of decision and of adherence to struggles and ideologies remains at the level of a mostly unexplored individualism. Equally, the adherence of the "form" to the "function" has remained, despite the efforts of scientific systematization in terms of uncontrolled choice, allowing at a certain time the use of solutions tried out elsewhere and in other times.

Syncretism

If eclecticism accepts, on a basis of late rationalism, the simultaneous presence of several languages that presume a diversity of formative processes, syncretism accepts the presence and recuperation of several different structural and ideological systems within a social macro-organism.

The expansion of the capitalist system on a worldwide level presumes the purely instrumental use of forms of economy and of thought that emerged in a certain ideological climate and that set their sights on contents that were also totally different. (Planning, programming, etc., can become instruments of rationalization of reality at the time of its absorption of the system. The dimensional content of the pacification of churches today allows for the simultaneous presence of cultures and civilizations of thought once exclusive of each other.)

The same affluent society imposes the identification within the same organism of autonomous structures in different consumption times. This thus raises the problem of identifying a new practice of design more appropriate for acting on the levels achieved and in light of an objectively changed historical situation.

Consumer society, the behavior industry, and artificial ideology

The advent of consumer society is not to be considered a simple phenomenon of productive opulence or of hyper-availability of the market of absorption; it is rather the first maturation of a structural reversal of an old market based on the dialectic system of supply and demand.

While in fact, in the hypothesis of an archaic-capitalist economy, the law of development resided in the free demand and choice of the consumer, today the product offering precedes the demand in space and time and through complex induction channels succeeds in soliciting it.

This is how the naturalistic concept of the free market has come to be replaced by that of its complete artificiality: from here the possibility of the macroscopic expansion of production through the creation of the super-consumer.

To obtain a similar process, a veritable industry of formal models capable of introducing a complete behavior in the consumer is currently emerging at a specific level of the system. Such behavior needs to be justified and qualified through a global ideology that certain cultural operators are developing in the form of art, myth, or symbol.

This sector of the system, which develops formal models of consumer behavior, has a unique and characteristic structure, which is that of completely identifying the cultural result within the commercial one. This means that the criterion of valuation of a particular cultural phenomenon is its ability to become a custom and to interest a consumer market.

Behavior is the availability for use of a certain context of products expressing a certain ideology, for which the overall market, in order to rank, refers to certain products which due to their capacity for extreme characterization are able to induce a behavior in the consumer. The ideology that results from this can then be defined as an artificial ideology, against the definition of spontaneous or political ideology, that is, generated by specific social situations, and this also becomes a commodity like any product imposed by the system.

The levels of super production achieved today by the system require the identification of tools capable of spreading the market: to do this, the distance between cultural elaboration on an ideological level and the elaboration of consumer models is greatly reduced, almost to the point of being erased.

This phenomenon is today interesting architecture itself, as a fundamental structure capable of entering into the induction process of such models.

The fundamental ambiguity of architectural reality as a decision-making divide

Architecture, the city, reestablishes reality at a higher level, but in and of itself, precisely because form cannot be unidirectional: that is, it cannot constrain decisions in imposing a single interpretation, thus taking advantage of the ambiguous consumption that has been done of it. Adoration, suicide, revolution.

All the actions that take place at a specific superstructural level (art, literature, architecture), even if historically conditioned, have a demystifying dimension such that it constitutes a real decision-making divide. There does not exist then the problem of integrated architecture or protest architecture, but rather there now exists the problem of the recuperation of a "operational dimensionality" capable of generating a decision-making result on a level consistent with the system.

The subject of leisure time and the description of the designed organism

The subject of "leisure time" has been addressed in the most organic way possible. Roughly three distinct moments have been identified, the subject of three separate theses, growing out of a common premise and a cultural need:

- Leisure time in the historical centers, like the utilization and recuperation of old structures generically intended to be urban monuments, through the introduction of autonomous internal organisms.

- Leisure time in the countryside, such as the placement of an essentially useless object within a landscape; an object that would be, however, capable of giving the landscape itself an interpretive hierarchy and a signification of use.

- Leisure time in the suburbs, the focus of the present study, in the sense of an urban intervention capable of uniformly placing itself into a fabric with the potential of restructuring it. Prato, an important industrial center of textile regeneration and production, has the typical suburbs of small towns that have suffered from their own building development in the wake of an excessively minute industry.

There does not exist a real series of working-class neighborhoods, due to the fact that the industry gets its workforce from commuters and through the progressive deterioration of agriculture in the surrounding territory.

The pulverization of business activity did not allow for the formation of a strong unionized working class, that is, one capable of imposing leaps in development on the industrial system.

What results is a city in which the average level of life presents itself as homogeneous without excessively inferior urban zones, but remains substantially unused from the point of view of consumers. This situation in Prato, as a city that produces and does not consume, is fairly typical: it requires an intervention that would unblock with a jolt a situation in equilibrium lasting all too long.

From the observation of this excessively homogeneous and unqualified condition arose the idea of a single intervention, on the plane of a violent figurality, which would be able to amount to a category of consumption that already today constitutes the judging structure of the system.

The site for construction was identified in that broad agricultural greenbelt remaining circumscribed by the periphery because of the limits of the cemetery, and that will be considered being transformed into a public park.

The organism is composed of: a large movie theater for 1500 people that holds on its roof a small cine-club with no more than 400 seats. At the wide end of the park, a gym with a system of spas and steam baths is planned, which wind around a bridge-like structure that constitutes a sort of thermal walkway terminating in a vegetarian bar.

The main spine is made up of a body containing the administrative offices, a large supermarket, with a dance floor, bar, boutique, and nightclub above. From this central node that makes up the large cube, winds an automatic vending system defined as a tunnel of distributors that are characterized by vertical columns containing distributors, lights, sound, air conditioners, etc. Within this tunnel, the individuation of closed spaces for temporary functions is planned.

A whole series of artificial bodies with inflatable structures or comprised of large object-images, is at the end inserted over an undulating path that terminates in the large Ferris wheel.

The roller coaster runs along almost the entire length of the organism penetrating the dance floor space, crossing the supermarket, inserting itself like a giant wave inside the tunnel of distributors and then exiting, through a tube, to the surrounding park.

Multifuncionality as more contact surface

The multifunctionality of the designed organism does not mean anticipating a precise succession of uses in space, but rather the identification of certain dimensional and formal hierarchies of individually independent structures, juxtaposed with the ease of bricolage. This in the sense that the whole is not identified in a stylistically perceptible unit, but rather in a certain spirit that guides the combination or the stacking of the parts.

The building is not generated by a single act of design, but rather constructed through the use of already existing parts mounted inside and around a principal metallic structure (on which the roller coaster runs) from which absolutely random paths and accessways depart.

Multifunctionality is understood as a search for the greatest potential contact area between the building and the users.

In the first phase of the study, the intention was to proceed to the identification of the apparatus according to a logic of assembly close to that of industrial building, that is, that follows with ease the spatial succession of different functions without giving it a design or stylistic synthesis.

The whole was conceived of in parts: paths in tubes, spaces identified by the need for cubing, trains of offices that are inserted within a larger structure that contained them without justifying them. The project proceeded according to a cogent logic of a "fun machine" on which to climb and spend a day without touching the ground, using only tokens.

The period that followed gave way to the need to experiment with a more heterogeneous morphology and one adhering more, through symbols, to the type of behavior that it was intended to induce. The use of color and the most diverse materials, juxtaposed according to a hierarchy of different times of consumption, a greater showiness and freshness capable of redeeming the macro-structure. Thus emerged the idea of the gigantic cube, a homogeneous, undifferentiated form from which a whole series of minor structures begin and proceed, placed quietly at the intersection of two main directions, which are those of the roller coaster and the movie theater-baths. The cube, as a non-designed form, makes it possible to relate and enhance other more complex ones, determining through their volumetric weight a hierarchical but simultaneous reading of the other parts.

The roller coaster constitutes, from the first part of the study, the guiding thread capable of connecting and giving a meaning to objectively indifferent presences, reducing them to a time of perception and instantaneous consumption. The roller coaster makes it possible to violate the simultaneity of events, going from indoors to outdoors and vice versa, and finally being shot out of the system to then plunge into the surrounding park.

Reasons for a technological choice: the use of steel as new linguistic possibility

The choice of steel as a construction material was motivated by a series of solutions that the technology of the metal itself makes possible to do on a general architectural level:

1) The high resistance of the steel to force allows it to adhere to the structure according to the real performance of forces, generating an extreme readability and usability of the architectural object, on the level of its components and within an process of extreme simplification. There are no longer masses but only grids.

What emerges is a work of architecture in which the structural law is actually reduced to a technical-scientific fact that enriches the internal logic and the expressive potential of the organism.

2) The existence of a precise technique of metal carpentry allows for the introduction of a series of non-designed elements: what results is a work of architecture in which certain drawing scales are rigorously abandoned, recuperating a sense of restraint (in the sense of a design that is not overly graphic) that the use of cement had greatly emasculated.

3) The lack of a natural color in steel as a construction material allows for the insertion of artificial color into the architectural body.

This introduces a major urban debate, being inserted as a new possibility in the current issue of the synthesis of the arts, and of the figural ability of the architectural object.

The use of color also makes it possible to emphasize the complete "artificiality" of the architectural object: this in this sense that construction in wood, brick, stone, and essentially in concrete as well, precisely because of the existence of a "natural color" of these materials, confirmed a kind of direct relationship between nature and architecture. In fact architecture, like art, substitutes itself for nature, superimposing itself over the latter and giving it a meaning within a system of cultural references. The most artificial and autonomous color, i.e. the designed one, today makes it possible to push ahead with this constitutional aspect of architectural practice, taking it to its extreme consequences and revealing a rich new series of developments.

4) Steel, much better than reinforced concrete, precisely because of this completely controlled nature, reduced therefore to pure structural function, without waste or large tolerances, allows for the combination with other technologies of completely artificial materials (plastic, rubber, paper, etc.). What results is an enormous capacity to enrich the architectural object, especially when the identification of new themes requires the existence of a new expressive capability and adherence to unusual functions and consumption times.

mente nell'intervento qui riportato del prof. Toraldo, che un sistema di tempo come quello che stiamo vivendo è, oltre che sbagliato, naturalmente vecchio: non siamo noi che ci incaselliamo nel tempo (che ci facciamo incasellare dagli altri) ma originiamo noi il tempo con il nostro agire; la libertà coincide con la disponibilità del nostro tempo.
Questo è quanto dice la fisica; non è in effetti dimostrato che un uomo debba comportarsi come un evento fisico (un atomo o una galassia ai confini dell'universo conosciuto) ma evidentemente interessano il contenuto e il significato. Tanto è che la definizione di Newton può avere avuto il suo peso nell'ordinamento sociale anche a secoli di distanza; ed allora possiamo essere ottimisti prevedendo che il pensiero di Einstein, maturato dalla storia, darà analogamente i suoi frutti. Ma non è per un facile ottimismo che diciamo queste cose, bensì per evidenziare una contraddizione di fatto nella quale stiamo vivendo. E aggiungiamo che non solo la fisica ha messo a punto un concetto di tempo alternativo a quello assoluto — capitalistico; la serie di brani e di stralci che proponiamo vuole dimostrare che ampi settori della cultura e del pensiero hanno già assunto il tempo come uno dei parametri fondamentali per la loro ristrutturazione: certe tendenze dell'architettura dove lo spazio è dato come "matrice neutra ed indifferenziata" (Archizoom) per definire il tempo come "spazio dello sviluppo umano"; così la musica — per eccellenza arte temporale — che ha superato le definizioni canoniche di contemporaneità e successione dei suoni (armonia e melodia), che è stata aiutata dai mezzi di diffusione (disco, registrazione e filodiffusione) ad annullare quell'unità intrinseca tempo di esecuzione-luogo-ascoltatore, che con le nuove esperienze elettroniche fa coincidere i tempi di creazione esecuzione ed ascolto (Grossi); così la critica che ha già tentato una lettura del nostro retaggio storico assumendo il tempo come qualità pura che coordina e dà significato alla creatività estetica (Bettini); così la biologia che assume il tempo come struttura essenziale, addirittura come "manifestazione" della vita (Jacob) — e che tramite comportamenti tecnici quali l'ibernazione e la fecondazione artificiale tende a rallentare il tempo o a rompere l'unità di spazio-tempo che è sempre stata all'origine della vita; per non parlare della letteratura: non esistono in effetti esempi più chiari di soggettivizzazione del tempo quali la « Recherche » di Proust (Fusco) o di annullamento del tempo come misura contingente quali l'« Ulisse » di Joyce (un migliaio di pagine per un volger di sole).
E l'elenco potrebbe comprendere l'antropologia, lo studio comparativo dell'idea di tempo tra oriente e occidente, l'esame del tempo finalizzato della cultura giudaico-cristiana eccetera.
Verificheremmo ulteriormente che tutto quanto l'industria del tempo libero oggi ci propina (dagli oggetti del design all'organizzazione del territorio) oltre ad essere violenza alla nostra libertà, finirà per scontrarsi di fatto con un nuovo modello culturale che l'integrazione di tutte le ricerche cui si è accennato non potrà non affermare (in questo senso si può accennare che le lotte sindacali per la riduzione degli orari di lavoro tendono ad una diminuzione del rapporto tempo occupato-tempo libero in chiave essenzialmente quantitativa: è necessario che si evolvano al più presto sul piano qualitativo e che nel discorso intervengano tutte le energie culturali della società).
Le immagini di architettura che pubblichiamo sono perciò necessariamente polemiche; le marine, i centri residenziali di collina e di montagna (le seconde case), troppe attività sportive e dello spettacolo nascono alienanti allo stesso livello del lavoro: la categoria del loro tempo è proprio uguale a quella del lavoro. La mobilità territoriale è poi un abile trucco per vendere il tutto; la crisi ecologica e la distruzione del territorio ne sono, in buona parte, inevitabile conseguenza. (E. D. B.)

TEMPO MORTO

Il materialismo storico-naturale, eredità del razionalismo illuminista, trova un terreno particolarmente fertile nella nascente società industriale del diciannovesimo secolo.
Le forze sociali al potere attingono largamente dal pensiero scientifico e filosofico per costruire le proprie infrastrutture; il risultato è una solida ed intima comunione fra ideologia e struttura di potere, tanto che più tardi nello stesso Freud la convinzione che tutta la realtà si fonda nella costrizione al lavoro e nella repressione degli istinti non gli impedisce di lasciare il campo alla rassegnazione ed alla pretesa correzione delle deviazioni "naturali" del nostro inconscio. Come è avvenuto tutto questo? In un modo molto semplice, spostando l'obiettivo dalla conquista della condizione umana nel sociale alla conquista e al dominio delle forze della Natura; in breve l'idea di progresso.
E' la scienza e non la religione a prestare l'ideologia per la costruzione della complessa macchina del capitalismo nascente; di qui la pretesa oggettività e ineluttabilità del nuovo ordine sociale.
La scienza garantisce un'unica cultura e l'uomo deve adeguarvisi.
L'uomo è forza lavoro e come tale suscettibile di essere sottoposto a valutazione e misura come qualsiasi forza e quantità fisica, la provata oggettività naturale dell'ordine in cui viene inserito gli garantisce l'uguaglianza.
Il suo tempo, la sua disponibilità umana è quantizzata e scissa in unità di misura elementari; a ciascuna di esse il sistema richiede un certo rendimento produttivo accertato da unità campioni ottimali. Dapprima si parla di efficienza fisica ottimale derivata da uno stato di sufficiente nutrizione e tale è all'inizio il livello di integrazione della classe operaia nella nascente società industriale, cioè quello della sopravvivenza.
Anche la missione di Taylor all'inizio del nostro secolo aveva come scopo la riorganizzazione del lavoro su base scientifica per renderlo più efficiente.
A questo scopo si analizza, si misura, si costruiscono parametri fisici e temporali con i quali sia possibile tabulare il ritmo produttivo di un operaio in perfette condizioni psichico-fisiche.
Nell'equazione "organizzazione del ritmo biologico umano = lavoro" si concede come unica variabile il livello ottimale di efficienza fisica. Lo stesso metodo scientifico ribaltato sulla condizione operaia ne traccia obiettivamente la disastrosa situazione.
Ancora la scienza è chiamata in causa e varie dottrine concorrono a tracciare la curva metabolica ideale per un buon lavoratore; più tardi ci si preoccuperà anche della sua salute psichica.
Una volta soddisfatte ed annullate a zero queste variabili rimane più lucida e splendente che mai l'equazione iniziale, anzi è divenuta una eguaglianza: TEMPO = LAVORO.
Esistono naturalmente delle perturbazioni, delle deviazioni dalla norma; le scienze sociali appositamente create hanno il delicato compito di studiare il fenomeno uomo e di rimuovere quelle sbavature che impediscono all'individuo di adattarsi al sistema o meglio di liberare la sua disponibilità al sistema sepolta in qualche strato del suo essere.
Il tempo dell'uomo scorre in quantità misurabili ed universalmente valide, l'ampiezza di queste quantità è dedotta facilmente dalla sua produttività teorica.
A queste quantità corrispondono naturalmente opportune misure di superficie e di volume riferite agli atti compiuti in quel determinato tempo. E gli atti non possono che essere sempre gli stessi perché unico è il loro fine: la produttività del lavoro. Ma l'uomo non basta contenerlo, ci si accorge che la sua produttività aumenta proporzionalmente al suo grado di conoscenza dell'ideologia del sistema; occorre anche educarlo.
A questo è chiamata la qualità dello spazio e degli oggetti di cui si circonda. Quantità e qualità: all'interno di questo campo si svolge la storia dell'architettura moderna tradotta in termini di equidistanza o di avvicinamento all'uno o all'altro polo.
Il Movimento Moderno stabilizza le forze in gioco: col design per gli oggetti d'uso, con l'Existenz-Minimum attribuisce all'abitare la funzione di fornire il mezzo per ottenere quell'identificazione necessaria allo sviluppo della società capitalista tra individuo e comunità realizzando la crescita sociale dello sfruttamento.
Ma come nelle scienze fisiche l'affinarsi degli strumenti di misura e dei mezzi di indagine pone sempre più in crisi la convinzione di restituire l'oggettività della realtà fisica, così nel sociale il perfezionamento del piano mina alla base l'oggettività della sua esistenza ponendo in luce la natura contingente e strumentale della sua costruzione.
Non esiste un Fenomeno restituibile ma esistono tante realtà quante sono le forme di conoscenza; non esiste una Cultura ma esistono infinite culture possibili e sperimentabili all'interno di un interno conoscitivo; non esiste la Libertà come adeguamento ad una struttura sociale fatta cor-

36

"Tempo morto", *Dead Time* in *Casabella* n. 366, 1972
Following page: Andrea Branzi, "Luna Park permanente a Prato"

(Tesi di laurea di Andrea Branzi, relatore prof. Domenico Cardini)

(Estratto dalla relazione)
... Capire il Tempo Libero non solo come tema di individuazione di una serie di attrezzature di servizio da distribuire in maniera omogenea sul territorio urbano, ma capire il Tempo Libero come momento di percezione della "forma globale" della città, cioè come tempo di recupero di una conoscenza più completa del vivere urbano.
Durante il Tempo Libero avviene l'acquisizione di quei comportamenti e di quei modelli sociali propri dei consorzi umani: momento in cui avviene la conoscenza globale della realtà del Sistema attraverso le forme da lui espresse e i sistemi di induzione al consumo.
Tempo Libero dunque come momento di integrazione ma an come momento di giudizio.
Se il Tempo di Lavoro infatti permette di conoscere in manie diretta la realtà produttiva, il Tempo Libero permette di conoscere e sperimentare la parte non contraddittoria dei Consumi...

rispondere al preteso equilibrio naturale dell'uomo ma esistono infinite libertà costruite all'interno della "quantità" della informazioni ricevute dai singoli individui.
Non si tratta di annunciare la caduta di un regno e di proclamarne un altro ma piuttosto di acquistare un grado di libertà in più restringendo il campo dell'assoluto a quello del possibile.
Il tempo è lo spazio dello sviluppo umano e lo spazio non è più il contenente di elementarità fisiche determinate ma può essere soltanto una matrice neutra e indifferenziata sulla quale ognuno ha il diritto di elaborare privatamente il proprio intorno intellettuale e fisico.
Il merito di una struttura sociale e fisica valida non sta tanto nella "qualità" del segnale trasmesso quanto nella capacità di trasmettere qualsiasi messaggio.
La produttività dell'individuo non ha più riferimenti oggettivi esterni ma si svolge nel campo della liberazione delle facoltà individuali e l'organizzazione del sociale si riproduce come produzione di energia sviluppata in base alle informazioni ricevute.
L'equazione tempo = lavoro è rovesciata: rifiutiamo il lavoro per recuperare la produttività personale.

Archizoom Associati

Dead Time

Andrea Branzi, *Casabella* n.366, 1972

//

Historical-natural materialism, legacy of Enlightenment rationalism, finds a particularly fertile ground in the nascent nineteenth-century industrial society.

The social forces in power largely derive from scientific and philosophical thought in order to construct their own infrastructures; the result is a solid and intimate communion between ideology and power structure, so much so that later Freud's own conviction that all reality is founded in the constraints of work and in the repression of instincts does not prevent him from opening the field to resignation and to the purported correction of the "natural" deviations of our unconscious. How did all this happen? In a very simple way, shifting the objective from the conquest of the human condition in the social to the conquest and domination of the forces of Nature: in short, the idea of progress.

It is science and not religion that provides the ideology for the construction of the complex machine of nascent capitalism; hence the alleged objectivity and ineluctability of the new social order.

Science guarantees a single culture, and man must adapt to it.

Man is a labor energy and, as such, subjected to evaluation and measurement as any force and physical quantity. The proven natural objectivity of the order in which he is placed guarantees him equality.

His time, his human availability is quantized and divided into elementary units of measurement; from each of them the system requires a certain productive efficiency determined by optimal sample units. First we speak of the optimal physical efficiency derived from a state of sufficient nutrition and such is at the beginning the level of integration of the working class in the nascent industrial society, that is, that of survival.

Even Taylor's mission at the beginning of this century was to reorganize scientific work to make it more efficient.

To this purpose, we analyze, measure, and build physical and temporal parameters with which it is possible to tabulate the productive rhythm of a worker in perfect psycho-physical conditions.

In the equation "organization of the human biological rhythm = work," the optimal level of physical efficiency is granted as the only variable. The same scientific method tilted toward the working condition objectively traces its disastrous situation.

Still science is called into question, and various doctrines contribute to tracing the ideal metabolic curve for a good worker; later we will also worry about his psychic health.

Once satisfied and canceled out to zero, these variables remains more lucid and shining than the initial equation ever was; indeed it has become one of equality: TIME = WORK.

Naturally, there are perturbations, deviations from the norm; the specially created social sciences have the delicate task of studying the phenomenon of man and of removing those imperfections that prevent the individual from adapting to the system, or rather freeing his availability to the system buried in some layer of his being.

Man's time flows in measurable and universally valid quantities, and the magnitude of these quantities is easily deduced from his theoretical productivity.

Naturally, these quantities correspond to appropriate surface and volume measurements referring to the acts carried out at that particular time. And the acts are always the same because their purpose is the same: the productivity of work.

Yet it is not enough to contain man; we realize that his productivity increases proportionally to his degree of knowledge of the ideology of the system: we must also educate him.

The quality of the space and the objects that surround him are called upon to answer this question. Quantity and quality: within this field there is the history of modern architecture, translated in terms of equidistance or approach to one or the other pole.

The Modern Movement stabilizes the forces in play: with the design for objects of use, with the Existenzminimum, it assigns to inhabiting the function of providing the tools for obtaining that identification necessary for the development of capitalist society, between individual and community, implementing social growth through exploitation.

But just as in the physical sciences, the refinement of the measuring instruments and the means of investigation increasingly generate a crisis in terms of the conviction of restoring the objectivity of physical reality; so in the social the perfection of the plan undermines the objectivity of its existence by highlighting the contingent and instrumental nature of its construction.

There is no recoverable phenomenon, but there are as many realities as there are forms of knowledge; there is no one Culture, but there are endless possible cultures capable of experimentation within a cognitive interior; freedom does not exist as an adaptation to a social structure that is made to correspond to the supposed natural equilibrium of man, but there are endless liberties built up within the "quantity" of information received from individuals.

It is not a matter of announcing the fall of a kingdom and of proclaiming another, but rather of acquiring a greater degree of liberty by restricting the field of the absolute to that of the possible.

Time is the space of human development, and space is no longer the container of determined physical elementariness but can only be a neutral and undifferentiated matrix on which everyone has the right to privately elaborate their own intellectual and physical surroundings.

The merit of a valid social and physical structure is not so much in the "quality" of the transmitted signal as in the ability to transmit any message.

The productivity of the individual no longer has objective external references but takes place in the realm of the liberation of individual faculties, and the organization of the social reproduces itself as the production of energy developed on the basis of the received information.

The equation "time = work" is reversed: we refuse work to recover personal productivity.

1.1

SUPER ARCHITECTURE 1966

POP INTRUSIONS AND THE NEW DESIGN

Archizoom Associati, *Logo*, 1966

Next page:
Archigram, Cover *Archigram* n. 4, 1964

AMAZING ARCHIGRAM 4
ZOOM
SCOTT BROWNRIGG
AND TURNER
Chartered Architects
and
Town Planning Consultants
7 Soho Square London W1
ARCHIGRAM
ZOOM
architectural books from the corners of the world
Tiranti art bookshop

Archizoom Associati and Superstudio, *Superarchitettura*, 1966, Pistoia Exhibition - recto

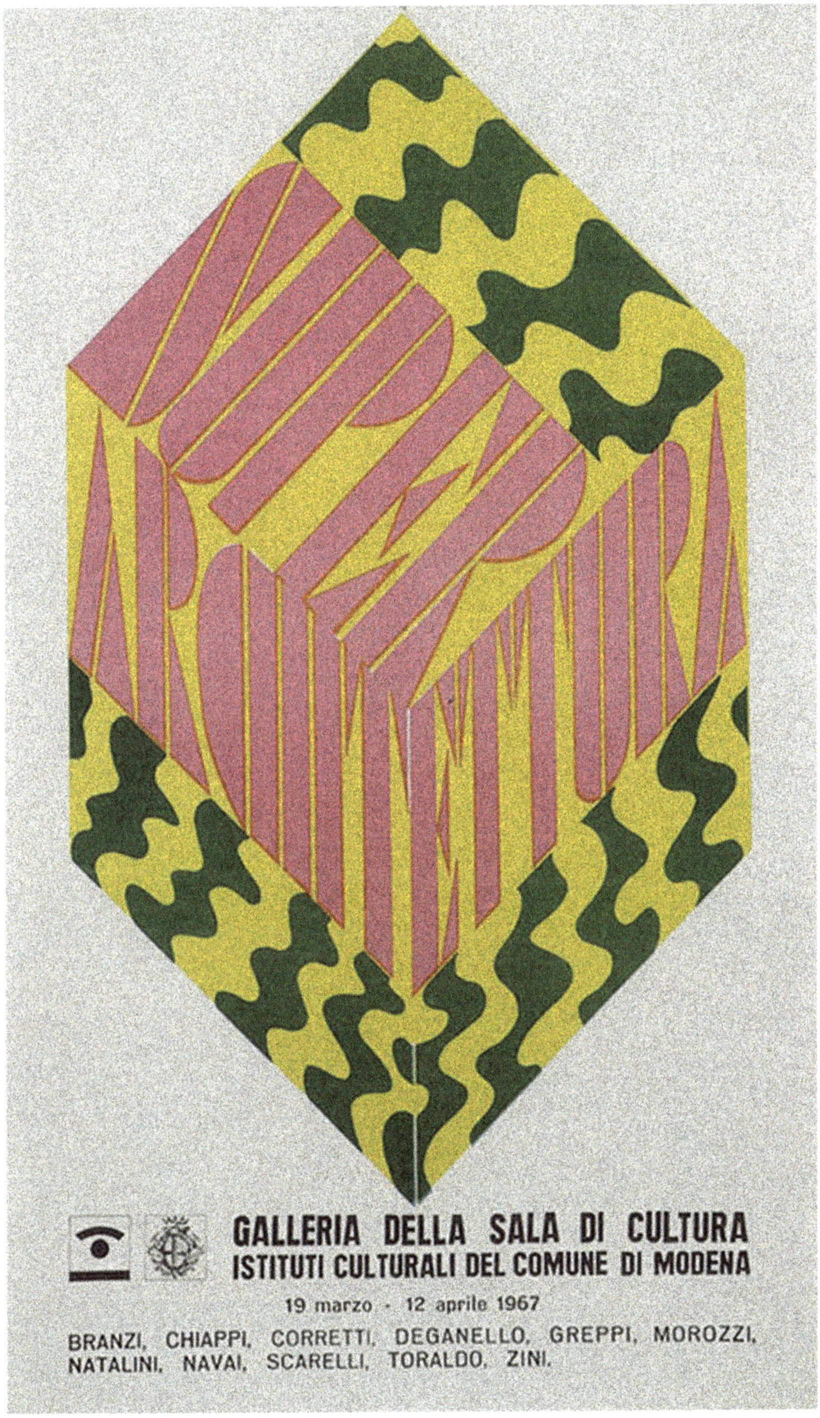

Archizoom Associati and Superstudio, *Superarchitettura*, 1967, Modena Exhibition - recto

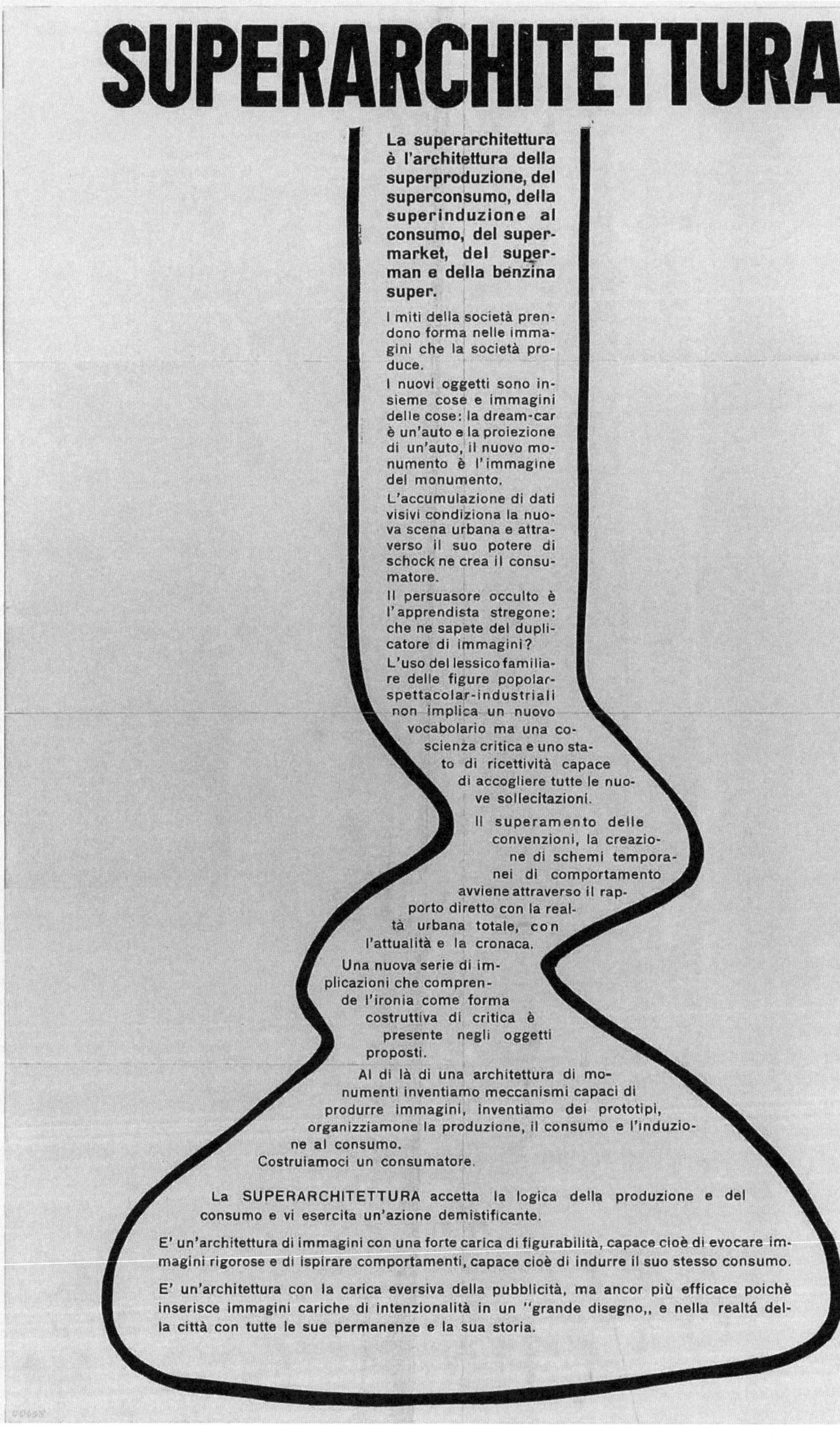

SUPERARCHITETTURA

La superarchitettura è l'architettura della superproduzione, del superconsumo, della superinduzione al consumo, del supermarket, del superman e della benzina super.

I miti della società prendono forma nelle immagini che la società produce.

I nuovi oggetti sono insieme cose e immagini delle cose: la dream-car è un'auto e la proiezione di un'auto, il nuovo monumento è l'immagine del monumento.

L'accumulazione di dati visivi condiziona la nuova scena urbana e attraverso il suo potere di schock ne crea il consumatore.

Il persuasore occulto è l'apprendista stregone: che ne sapete del duplicatore di immagini?

L'uso del lessico familiare delle figure popolar-spettacolar-industriali non implica un nuovo vocabolario ma una coscienza critica e uno stato di ricettività capace di accogliere tutte le nuove sollecitazioni.

Il superamento delle convenzioni, la creazione di schemi temporanei di comportamento avviene attraverso il rapporto diretto con la realtà urbana totale, con l'attualità e la cronaca.

Una nuova serie di implicazioni che comprende l'ironia come forma costruttiva di critica è presente negli oggetti proposti.

Al di là di una architettura di monumenti inventiamo meccanismi capaci di produrre immagini, inventiamo dei prototipi, organizziamone la produzione, il consumo e l'induzione al consumo.
Costruiamoci un consumatore.

La SUPERARCHITETTURA accetta la logica della produzione e del consumo e vi esercita un'azione demistificante.

E' un'architettura di immagini con una forte carica di figurabilità, capace cioè di evocare immagini rigorose e di ispirare comportamenti, capace cioè di indurre il suo stesso consumo.

E' un'architettura con la carica eversiva della pubblicità, ma ancor più efficace poichè inserisce immagini cariche di intenzionalità in un "grande disegno,, e nella realtá della città con tutte le sue permanenze e la sua storia.

Archizoom Associati and Superstudio, *Manifesto Superarchitettura*, 1967, Modena Exhibition, recto

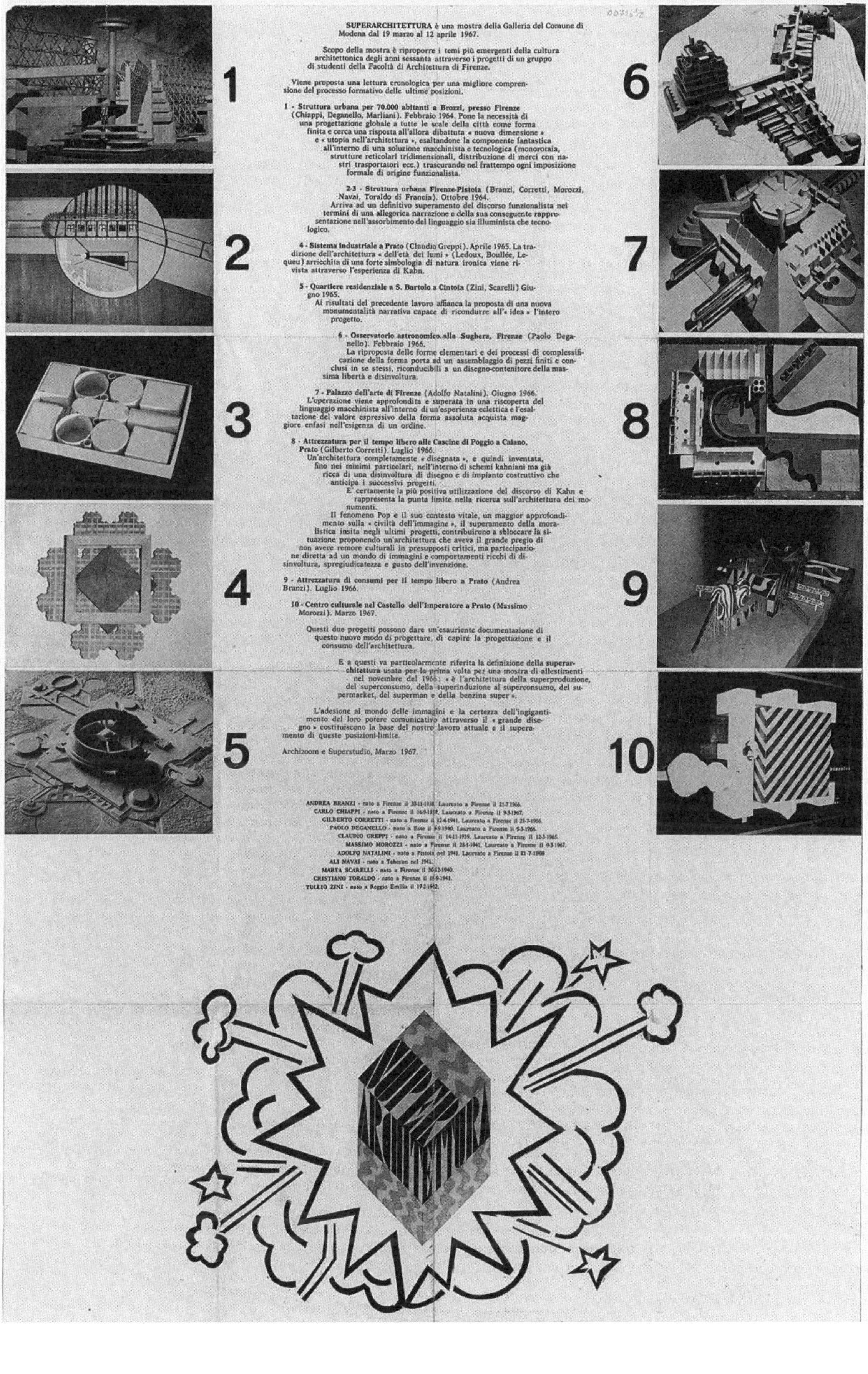

SUPERARCHITETTURA è una mostra della Galleria del Comune di Modena dal 19 marzo al 12 aprile 1967.

Scopo della mostra è riproporre i temi più emergenti della cultura architettonica degli anni sessanta attraverso i progetti di un gruppo di studenti della Facoltà di Architettura di Firenze.

Viene proposta una lettura cronologica per una migliore comprensione del processo formativo delle ultime posizioni.

1 - **Struttura urbana per 70.000 abitanti a Brozzi, presso Firenze** (Chiappi, Deganello, Marliani). Febbraio 1964. Pone la necessità di una progettazione globale a tutte le scale della città come forma finita e cerca una risposta all'allora dibattuta « nuova dimensione » e « utopia nell'architettura », esaltandone la componente fantastica all'interno di una soluzione macchinista e tecnologica (monorotaia, strutture reticolari tridimensionali, distribuzione di merci con nastri trasportatori ecc.) trascurando nel frattempo ogni imposizione formale di origine funzionalista.

2-3 - **Struttura urbana Firenze-Pistoia** (Branzi, Corretti, Morozzi, Navai, Toraldo di Francia). Ottobre 1964.
Arriva ad un definitivo superamento del discorso funzionalista nei termini di una allegorica narrazione e della sua conseguente rappresentazione nell'assorbimento del linguaggio sia illuminista che tecnologico.

4 - **Sistema industriale a Prato** (Claudio Greppi). Aprile 1965. La tradizione dell'architettura « dell'età dei lumi » (Ledoux, Boullée, Lequeu) arricchita di una forte simbologia di natura ironica viene rivista attraverso l'esperienza di Kahn.

5 - **Quartiere residenziale a S. Bartolo a Cintoia** (Zini, Scarelli) Giugno 1965.
Ai risultati del precedente lavoro affianca la proposta di una nuova monumentalità narrativa capace di ricondurre all'« idea » l'intero progetto.

6 - **Osservatorio astronomico alla Sughera, Firenze** (Paolo Deganello). Febbraio 1966.
La riproposta delle forme elementari e dei processi di complessificazione della forma porta ad un assemblaggio di pezzi finiti e conclusi in se stessi, riconducibili a un disegno-contenitore della massima libertà e disinvoltura.

7 - **Palazzo dell'arte di Firenze** (Adolfo Natalini). Giugno 1966.
L'operazione viene approfondita e superata in una riscoperta del linguaggio macchinista all'interno di un'esperienza eclettica e l'esaltazione del valore espressivo della forma assoluta acquista maggiore enfasi nell'esigenza di un ordine.

8 - **Attrezzatura per il tempo libero alle Cascine di Poggio a Caiano, Prato** (Gilberto Corretti). Luglio 1966.
Un'architettura completamente « disegnata », e quindi inventata, fino nei minimi particolari, nell'interno di schemi kahniani ma già ricca di una disinvoltura di disegno e di impianto costruttivo che anticipa i successivi progetti.
E' certamente la più positiva utilizzazione del discorso di Kahn e rappresenta la punta limite nella ricerca sull'architettura dei monumenti.
Il fenomeno Pop e il suo contesto vitale, un maggior approfondimento sulla « civiltà dell'immagine », il superamento della moralistica insita negli ultimi progetti, contribuirono a sbloccare la situazione proponendo un'architettura che aveva il grande pregio di non avere remore culturali in presupposti critici, ma partecipazione diretta ad un mondo di immagini e comportamenti ricchi di disinvoltura, spregiudicatezza e gusto dell'invenzione.

9 - **Attrezzatura di consumi per il tempo libero a Prato** (Andrea Branzi). Luglio 1966.

10 - **Centro culturale nel Castello dell'Imperatore a Prato** (Massimo Morozzi). Marzo 1967.

Questi due progetti possono dare un'esauriente documentazione di questo nuovo modo di progettare, di capire la progettazione e il consumo dell'architettura.

E a questi va particolarmente riferita la definizione della superarchitettura usata per la prima volta per una mostra di allestimenti nel novembre del 1966: « è l'architettura della superproduzione, del superconsumo, della superinduzione al superconsumo, del supermarket, del superman e della benzina super ».

L'adesione al mondo delle immagini e la certezza dell'ingigantimento del loro potere comunicativo attraverso il « grande disegno » costituiscono la base del nostro lavoro attuale e il superamento di queste posizioni-limite.

Archizoom e Superstudio, Marzo 1967.

ANDREA BRANZI - nato a Firenze il 30-11-1938. Laureato a Firenze il 21-7-1966.
CARLO CHIAPPI - nato a Firenze il 16-9-1939. Laureato a Firenze il 9-3-1967.
GILBERTO CORRETTI - nato a Firenze il 12-4-1941. Laureato a Firenze il 21-7-1966.
PAOLO DEGANELLO - nato a Este il 9-9-1940. Laureato a Firenze il 9-3-1966.
CLAUDIO GREPPI - nato a Firenze il 14-11-1939. Laureato a Firenze il 12-3-1965.
MASSIMO MOROZZI - nato a Firenze il 28-1-1941. Laureato a Firenze il 9-3-1967.
ADOLFO NATALINI - nato a Pistoia nel 1941. Laureato a Firenze il 21-7-1966.
ALI NAVAI - nato a Teheran nel 1941.
MARTA SCARELLI - nata a Firenze il 30-12-1940.
CRISTIANO TORALDO - nato a Firenze il 15-9-1941.
TULLIO ZINI - nato a Reggio Emilia il 19-2-1942.

Archizoom Associati and Superstudio, *Manifesto Superarchitettura*, 1967, Modena Exhibition, verso

Superarchitecture
Andrea Branzi, 2014

//

The Radical Movement began in a seemingly random manner, with the organization of the exhibition *Superarchitettura* in Pistoia in 1966 in an unlikely gallery "Jolly Due" in a warehouse of a fish wholesaler, with a Pop manifesto written by Paolo Deganello (for Archizoom) and Adolfo Natalini. The Manifesto said: "Superarchitecture is the architecture of superproduction, superconsumption, superinducement to superconsumption, of the supermarket, of the superman, of super gasoline." This exhibition improvised with our theses, a few colored objects and a multicolored entrance (reconstructed by the Pecci Centre in Prato in 1999), with the music of the Beatles, the Rolling Stones, and Jimi Hendrix blaring, explained our points of reference in a clearer manner, totally unrelated to issues of design.

***Superarchitettura* had the effect of a spark in an environment so dry that it produced a kind of spontaneous combustion. In a short time in Florence, in addition to Superstudio, UFO, Zziggurat, the 999, Remo Buti, Gianni Pettena, and from Milan Ugo La Pietra, all came into action.**

During the sixties, the West was transformed from an Architectural Civilization to a Commodity Civilization. While the former identified with the act of building, the solidity of structures, and the eternity of foundations and was highly symbolic, Commodity Civilization was by its nature a transferable reality; exportable, provisional, which could cross any boundary or border. It was therefore an anti-territorializing reality, molecular, which transformed the very definition of the city from the architectural aggregate to the free movement of goods, information, promotions, and mass communication. This transformation had taken place without design culture truly realizing it, limiting itself to rejecting consumerism without ever in fact elaborating a true alternative model, without realizing that the market was by then taking on a global dimension and that the free trade of goods was feeding the entire global economy.

The urgency of a new, harsh, and merciless realism that would make apparent how things really were thus traversed the West, taking hold of everything that orthodox modernity had excluded from its sacred precincts. The most obvious aspect of this new period was Pop Art culture, which was born of the exploration of the huge continent that was made up of the market, mass communication, and consumerist culture, in which American recognized itself, free from European critical moralism and the self-referential limits of abstraction.

In 1972, Robert Venturi, Denise Scott Brown, and Steven Izenour published a book that was destined to characterize an era: *Learning From Las Vegas*. In this famous essay, for the first time we looked outside of utopias, at what the world had become, and at Las Vegas with its ephemeral monuments that represented the real model of the urban future.

The origin of the Pop Movement, therefore, was not only artistic in nature but was a result of a new political world vision that sarcastically opposed the Manichean indifference of the official culture. This indifference had distant roots in something called Rationalism.

By the fifties, in a London still marked by Hitler's V2 missiles, there was a confrontation of two different paths: on one side that of Francis Bacon who testified to the impossibility for art to survive the mass exterminations; on the other side was Richard Hamilton who was tackling the world of mass communication, consumer models, and commercial messages and who, like Peter Sellers in *Being There*, accepted it without prejudice in a simple and naive manner like a new, two-dimensional human landscape. The deep roots of Pop culture can therefore be found in Anglo-Saxon pragmatism and in its distrust of ideological theorems.

Passing over the confines of theoretical modernity through real modernity. Definitively renouncing "qualitative utopias" in favor of only "quantitative utopias," which are the only ones capable of offering the true musical, wearable, edible, and danceable happiness of capitalism.

The Radical Movement was thus one of the first incubations in Pop and Situationist architecture, like the first phase of legitimization from the official ties of the Modern Movement.

From our earliest works, two very different modes of interpreting Pop reality emerged: for Superstudio it was the occasion for neo-monumental works of architecture with symmetrical structure, with pyramids and ziggurats, reminiscent of the works of Joe Tilson but above all of Louis Kahn.

For Archizoom, on the other hand, Oldenburg's large-scale urban objects were interpreted in a political sense, like explicit images of a deeply materialistic world devoid of values. Kitsch was seen as the result of the working-class demolition (without reconstruction) of bourgeois culture, signaling that beneath the ostensible pop masquerade there was a "marble chicken, the imperialist boulder that does not move or eat."

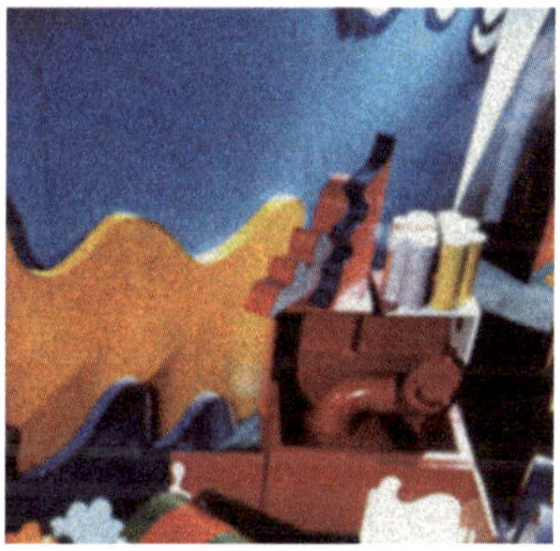

Superarchitettura Exhibition, Jolly Gallery, Pistoia, 1966

1.2

THE RADICAL MOVEMENT

AN EXAGGERATED GENERATION

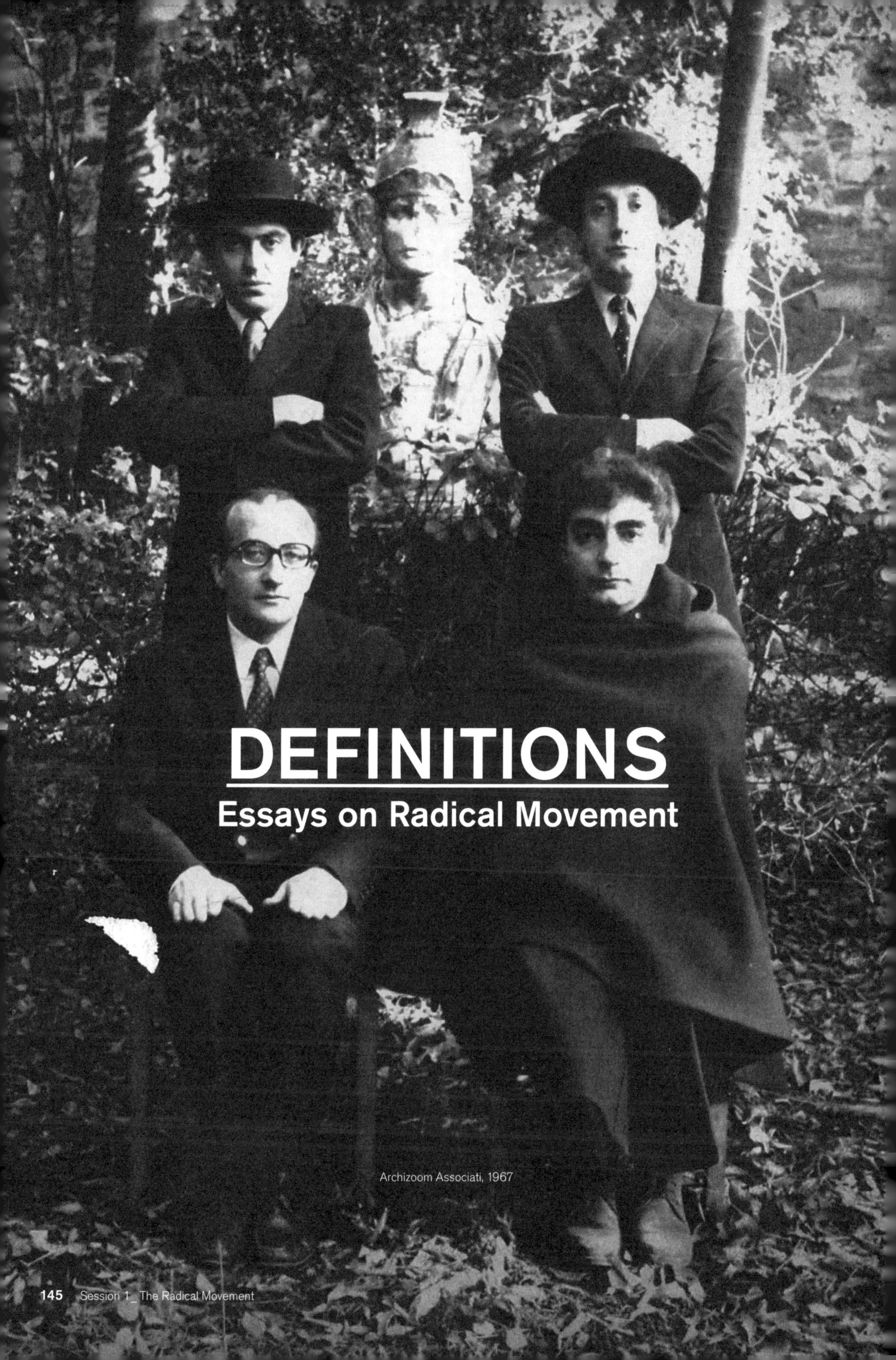

DEFINITIONS

Essays on Radical Movement

Archizoom Associati, 1967

information documentation archives

untitled

The spiral has snapped and gone off on its own. Radicalization of the relationship between art and life has halted and is in process of abolishing the negative pole — art — just when the structures of utility (markets, banks, big stores, economic trusts), posturing as progressive activists, are trying desperately to keep the artist on the leash and turn the inutilizable catharsis of art-in-life into yet another consumer product. Straining to substitute one product for another, they have replaced the theme of the mass-media, the consumer society, the existential gesture, gestalt, language and visuality with that of life, nature, the spontaneous, the nomadic event, improvisation the body, death, concept and imagination.

If, in fact, we analyze the present state of *arte povera* and Conceptual Art, and also of theatre-on-the-streets, the guerilla-warfare theatre, cinéma reportage, uncritical criticism, imaginary architecture, spontaneous politics and all the counter-cultural attitudes that aim at turning work into life or action, we observe that one episode (artistic, political, architectural, theatrical, cinematographic, philosophical, critical, etc.) has taken over from another, but the utilization has remained the same. The attempt to destroy, annull or dissolve the myth of culture as art, theatre, architecture, cinema, philosophy, science, law or history into everyday utility, has failed.

The structures of privilege have thus kept going, nomadism and politics have been turned into forms and images, art and the entire cultural or counter-cultural scene continue to serve contemplation and are exhausted in work dedicated exclusively to abstract knowledge that can never be translated into either action or stasis, intervention or immobilism, revolution or Nirvana, never become a physical method.

This attitude, typical of the climate of the years between 1966 and 1970, although it may appear to derive its activities from concepts and ideas, turns them into images and symbols, which are always individual and particular. Despite the attempt to express mental and physical facts objectively, ambiguous and equivocal terminology reduces them to metaphor, thus aiding and abetting the culture-consumption structures without modifying their utility. This sort of consumption, by exploiting the visual and objectual qualities of its products, encourages the myth of art and the heroic view of culture, thus perpetuating myth and heroism as the continuing appropriation of art and intellectual activity on the part of the Establishment and small-or large-scale consumer and market concerns. This leads to parallel expansion of the economic and polical power of both art and culture, of the Establishment and of the structures that control and exalt them.

Yet reality and life, which have primary goods of their own, need not myths or heroes but either the instruments of activity or an absolute stasis in order to become functional and established as procedures or rites. Either activism or total immobilism might thus achieve an objective transformation based not on secondary goods such as culture (art, cinema, theatre, philosophy, architecture, politics, etc.) but on the primary goods which are utility, consumption, exchange, mediation and services.

Instead of this, art, theatre, cinema, philosophy, criticism, architecture and politics continue to create myths and heroes for imitation, thus ensuring that the materials and outcome of culture and counter-culture do not become changes, contractions, utilizations and definitions of primary goods, but simply remain merchandise and power. The myth goes on creating superthings, though reality and life require not super-things, but obvious, banal, untitled things.

For this reason, radicalization of the attitude to art and cultural activity of all kinds has become absolute and gone off on its own. This seems to be demonstrated by the work of whole classes of intellectuals (1) who are busy shifting action from a metaphorical-contemplative state to a condition of utility or the annullment of utility in which every kind of work becomes a utensil (2) or else is dissolved in the everyday reality of primary goods, exploding, modifing or defining, annulling or revolutionizing them.

Thus the Weathermen Underground, the OHO Group, the N.E. Thing Co., Siegelaub, Godard, Long and Flanagan, Schechner, Information Documentation Archives, the underground press, Archizoom, the Descriptive Improvisation Group, Living Theatre and other intellectuals are changing direction in their work in order to get off the seesaw of inversions and substitutions of theme. They have gone over from a productive status which can be identified only with the finished product or object, to a status through which work is understood as definition, revolution, introduction or alteration of utility and utility itself. They act on the customs that permeate daily life and constitute primary goods, without adding super-things and no longer admitting any distinction between the artistic and cultural sphere and the extra-cultural and extra-artistic. Their work becomes actual, no longer having an aesthetic-formal dimension, but a practical-concrete one, fused with the reality of utilization, functionality and the services. They thus disappear into the shadows to work no longer on themes, which become systematically transformed into aesthetic forms or entities, symbols of power and exchange groups, functions or services (such as banks, markets, universities, big stores, museums, parties, institutes, theatres and producers), but, instead, to stir up and revolutionize the systems and standards of utility and of culture and counter-culture. This means blowing up the joints and structures of service and power, utilizing the same instruments of service and utility, countering the utility groups and bodies by altering their methods and procedures. They thus shift from work that is haphazard, vague and confused to needful and continuous work that is in a position to confront the procedures, regulations, rites, utilities and primary systems that surround and mould them.

It is these utility groups, bodies and structures that constitute the real obstacle to creating tangible utility attitudes. Thus work as utilization tends to derange, upset, deteriorate, transgress, counteract, aggrandize and bankrupt obvious and banal uses through use of them that is obvious and banal, but adulterated or differently styled.

That is the reason why all these intellectuals have gone beyond bounds in working on art, theatre, cinema, politics, information, criticism, architecture, to try to turn work into utility or the revolution of utility so that it may be committed totally (in space, time and utility) to the existing utility structures (TV, information services, banks, stores, airports, services, laws, newspapers, society, etc.).

In this sense work has not been translated afresh into objects and products, symbols of redemption and liberation from the « ills » of the world and society, but turned into negative opposition to present-day utilization of work which, as produce or objects in the hands of the utilization structures has remained mythical and metaphorical, existing according to the rules of representation. Work is thus translated into visual ideas or facts that, for the benefit of bourgeois aesthetes, can be assessed as to quantity and location and, on the contrary, as utilization or non-utilization, annulls and destroys the realm of art and culture with all its appendices.

If, in fact, we go into the merits of the work done by all these intellectuals we observe that it does not acquire or no longer preserves any typical or specifically linguistic characteristics. It is no longer just art, theatre, cinema, information, architecture or politics, but action and practical method, indefinable and untitled, relative to the world and no longer just to culture. This is proved by the diseappearance of the individual as hero to be replaced by a set of initials, a public or private body or a structure that can easily be integrated at an explosive and modifying level with the other sets of initials (IBM, DATAMATION, A.B. DICK COMPANY, KYBE, RCA, TAB, TV, PHI, BNL, etc.) which are the bricks and mortar of primary goods, and therefore culture. Like the N.E. Thing Co., founded in Vancouver by Iain Baxter in 1966 with its business address in Canada and consisting of eleven research departments: research, things, accounts, ACT, ART, photography, COP, films, projects and consultations. These departments carry out different functions within the company environment, which sees itself not so much as a producer of art works as an alternative instrument for the utilization of cultural knowledge. The N.E. Thing Co. does not produce objects or products for a specific circulation, but was founded as a consultant company for visual communications, sensorial information, imagination, ICOM, ideas and all kinds of qualitative and quantitative innovation. Aesthetic work has become utilization, function and services. It has gone so far into the shadows that it has become confused with all the other information and consultation services. Iain Baxter, President, General Manager, Employee, etc. now goes to all the big business exhibitions and trade fairs, with the American Telephone Punch Company, Boeing Computer Services Division, UNIVAC, Xerox Corporation, Data Processing and Tube Company. N.E. Thing Co. competes with the rest, Baxter has annulled himself as an artist, but acts as an intellectual on the utilization and information systems, using instruments such as telex, computers, TV, xerox, not technically or artistically but for operations designed to change their use or revolutionize their functions. On the same lines the OHO group, four Jugoslav intellectuals, are presently working to set up in a big consumer and recreation complex new practical methods of utilization, behaviour and selection of primary goods. The internal function of the complex, now under construction, is clearly not that of an artist, or group of artists, collaborating on the aesthetic structure of the building or group of buildings. The group works from inside, studying the utilization and overall direction of the complex. It works directly on the behaviour patterns of those responsible for practical functioning, on the selection of foods and consumer products, on viability, on internal procedures and regulations and all the primary utilization structures of the complex. Similarly the Weathermen Underground have adopted the same procedures for their destructive and revolutionary activities at airports, in skyscrapers, big stores, banks and markets in America. Weathermen Underground contract with and make use of the same utility services in America, the primary goods of Western society, to destroy or damage them. They place a time-bomb in a skyscraper and then inform the police that the bomb is due to explode in twenty minutes — just the time needed to empty a skyscraper, as tested by the police and the fire insurance companies. The destruction of the building is attained by making use, or counter-use, of the typical utilization systems themselves. Or else they use dynamite in the big stores, airports, banks and stations, making use of all the typical functioning and security systems tested and approved by the companies themselves, but conversely to blow them up and cause revolutions. In this way the very utilities and regulation systems, exalted and overpraised by the utilization structures, revolt against themselves in order to achieve a change of direction.

In the same way the underground press (Manifesto, Re Nudo, Realist, etc.) has ceased merely to mock the utilization structures and set out to provide an alternative information service and to use information differently. It is no longer underground, but makes a direct confrontation, like the N.E. Thing Co. This is tangible and physical information, outside cultural taboos and objective myths, independent and not susceptible to incor-

Germano Celant, "Untitled," in *Domus* n. 496, 1971

information documentation archives

poration by the utilization structures, which are clearly not going to tolerate competition aimed at rendering them inactive. It is information that deals with the facts and not their interpretation, going as far as to reveal the techniques of interpretation and the regulations for the utilization of information.

Work on the regulations and mechanism of interpretation is done by the « *Gruppo di improvvisazione descrittiva/descrizione/descrizione/descritto* », associate administrator Emilio Prini, which provides a continuous stream of data on the standards of registration, purchase and consumption. The group works systematically to provide concepts, actions and data on the theory of goods, the theory of values, the theory of communications, of information, of tautology, of utilization, on the theory of chance, the theory of things, of artistic language, of the dynamics of society, the theory of cause, of primary automatism (psychic-linguistic) and secondary (mechanical), on the theory of theory of utilization (as opposed to consumption). For the standards of consumption, the « gruppo di improvvisazione descrittiva » has presented the consumption, or utilization duration of a camera, a tape-recorder, a spotlight, a flat, a Fiat 500 car, things that carry out their normal functioning until they stop, without any aesthetic intervention. Registration of the (utilization) standards is a datum in itself, maintaining the original value and irremovable from its own context, therefore not material for insertion into the history of the aesthetic object, because the standard is an independent entity, anonymous and unrecognizable with respect to the other standards. Thus registration of sets of initials, letterheads, insignia and entries, and of all the utilization standards, which possess a meaning from the meaning of the initials or insignia themselves, becomes tangible in confirmations or participations, variants of diction, exposition, edition and position (3).

In the environment of the laws of utilization, Seth Siegelaub, having founded and organized International General, a production and distribution company, issued as an intellectual books and publications that carried on his previous occupation as a gallery owner, but with more emphasis on the capitalization of products and the accumulation of information as work. Recently he has been promoting and studying a series of norms or laws that can regulate and block the use of intellectual products, of whatever kind they may be. His action is directed at eliminating irregular and arbitrary utilization on the part of the economic powers-that-be of all work stored or storable by the consumer structures such as publishers, galleries, museums, industry banks, etc. This drawing up of rules for utilization teds towards the elimination of arbitrary possession or deceptive exploitation of information and of intellectual work, unhinging the tacit and Mafia-like rules of the market in intellectual and artistic goods, upsets the exploitation of artists and the manipulation of their ideas, and creates a law or norm, in a system that uses the norm only for economic repression, but refuses to accept the norm as a counter-attack aimed at anti-economic and anti-exploitation utilization. This attack on market laws and procedures is also being pressed by other artists and jurists such as Beuys, Heerich and Staeck, who are opposed not only to the art market and its utilization, but to the continued operation of the monopoly laws or deceptive and oppressive utilizations. In England, Long and Flanagan are presently campaigning for the introduction of a law that would place an intellectual in every factory or industry, not of course as a producer, but with the task of breaking up existing behaviour and procedural patterns. This change of indication of rules, norms and utilizations becomes, for I.D.A. (Information Documentation Archives) the annullment of the power or selection of information or documents, on the part of art critics. This is done by setting itself up as a service for the diffusion and distribution of information for every kind of intellectual entity. A service, with a utilization structure that emits continuously on all possible channels, both theoretical and practical, information and documentation, thus reversing the role of the critic, turning him into an instrument controlled by the intellectual. I.D.A. in fact makes use of all the information channels (newspapers, magazines, TV, posters, books, photographs and publications) and offers them to the workers, becoming a medium of information and denies its own power of selection or judgement or of acting repressively on things. It is structured to be able to work at three levels: a theoretical level tending towards the elaboration of operational and behavioural methods, studying and initiating research with the maximum economy of concepts and ideas; an information level that uses all the existing instruments for the propagation and diffusion of ideas, theories and utilization and behavioural methods worked out by intellectuals; and an operative-organizational level, tending to put into concrete use the operative methods and modifications in utilization proposed by the workers, taking over total responsibility for making use of all existing organizations and materials with relation to single and collective ideology.

It was the same sort of setting itself up as a service, distant yet active and in contact with everyday reality, that led the Living Theatre to emerge from the trap of the theatre in order to break down the barrier of art as a prison in the power of the Establishment and investigate the function and utilization of all kinds of action and inaction. Aware that in a spectacular society every product is a spectacle, and thus that the theatrical object only increased the merchandizing cycle, the Living Theatre went out of production and into analysis of violent and non-violent utilizations and procedures that may lead to the fall of the Bureaucratic-Military-Authoritarian-Police Combine. It worked, of course, in the shadows, in an unknown and non-linguistic environment, but a physical and practical one, in which utilization and functioning of action have a tautological meaning, not a symbolic and moral one. It takes up a position instead of describing, presents but does not represent, destroying and annulling the seen-but-not-expressed which serves the interests of the Upper Classes, exalting action and speech on utilization and consumption, the field of those who always tell us what we should do and how we ought to do it.

This work on the utilization of action and of the instruments of work are transformed by Schechner into information-divulging activity when he uses the communication media (newspapers, books and magazines), changing their sign and function to make them spectacular at the moment of publishing a series of events that everyone can use against the Establishment. These are events deprived of the protection of copyright, instituted as possible utilizations of the roads, spaces and services of the revolutionary structure, on the limits and procedures of urban guerrilla-warfare.

Of course, contraction, revolution, decyphering, interpretation, annullment and the reversal of utilization values cannot be achieved solely through the work of a small number of groups and bodies. That is why these, and many others, are uniting and forming bigger groups, recognizing each other and collaborating, to form a social power as a counter-society that can construct and invent, project or achieve or annull utilization instruments that have community aims, unitary aspirations and the will to work constructively, destructively or towards Nirvana.

Only the coming together and rendering concrete the forces operating on utilization and counter-utilization can, indeed, create and command a real, and not ephemeral, dimension in which to oppose actively through concrete action the existing utilization and consumption structures of the Establishment. These have, in fact, enabled us to become aware, tragically, of the vanity and uselessness of all isolated and imaginative gestures, which are ephemeral and incidental, bound to the gesture rather than to the procedure, justified by Freud but denied by Pavlov, in a society dedicated to utilization and recurrent and continuous exchange that is obvious and general. Thus only the setting up of a counter-society, or, rather the recognition that we belong to one, can show the way to delirium, imagination, fantasy and escaping from physical traps and from the mind (4) (« dementia », from « de mente ») becoming norms and procedures based not only on the present but on continuity (space, time and utility). This is an escape and a change of indication as to the utilization procedures that can be based on utilization structures and materials, on individual and collective work centres, on general and particular activities, on concrete realizations or non-realizations, on the discovery of areas of work and utilization, on the liberalization of working space, utilizing materials, of course, and existing or new organizations, the latter, though, on the user's total responsibility and for his own use.

This is therefore a step from work which so far, directed by the instruments of the Establishment, has aimed at the creation of totems and fashions for the upper or aestheticising classes, to work on utilizations and the modification of the use of means and instruments, with total integration of work into utility and the final abolition of art, theatre, cinema, architecture, criticism, politics, philosophy and all the institutions. *Germano Celant*

(1) The term « intellectual » is used with intent to abolish the specific and mythical nature of work and thus pass on from particular action to general. It is, admittedly, a generic and indicative term, but an insignificant one.

(2) The concept of culture as utility is altogether removed from that of applied culture (art, theatre, cinema, architecture, philosophy, criticism and politics) which is nothing more than another form of alienation from the product and merchandise.

(3) These positions include the work of « Fiat Sai Assicura », « Shell » and « Domus ». The first consists in placing in the city of Turin a single publicity hoarding for Fiat and Sai Insurance Co., just as it is, presented visually to consumers and clients. This hoarding adds nothing to the aesthetic dimension and disappears into the dimension of application, revealing its real utility. While the meaning of « Fiat-Sai-Assicura » is « Sia-Sai-Assicura ». The second is in the placing in Genoa of a neon-sign with the word « Shell », which acquires an advertising meaning different from the original shell. But, for Western onlookers there is a progression of language levels to Shell as an image-sign-symbol through which the sign Shell draws attention to itself as a linguistic symbol. The Descriptive Improvisation Group also gives the title «Domus» as an example of confirmation through participation, in all the subtitles appearing in the magazine, on the cover, in the synopses, monograms, etc. The title « Domus » is another utilization standard, a linguistic and advertising symbol like IBM, CGIL, UIL or RCA.

(4) Conceptual Art, imaginary architecture and all the activities that have apparently switched attention from the physical to the mental have, on the contrary, reduced the mental to an image, falling once again into the physical and visual. Therefore « demential » action, understood as a continuous free flux, unbindable and not to be rendered physical, may become a modification of the utilization of the mind and extremely logical.

Alessandro Mendini, "Radical Design," in *Casabella* n. 367, 1972

RADICAL DESIGN

Mentre il "controdesign" prepara la tournée alla Summer Session di Londra, a New York fa cantare al design di linea italiana l'ultima romanza*/While preparing the tour to the Summer Session in London, in New York "counter design" lets Italian design sing its last aria*

Arte di comportamento: Laszlo Toth a Roma martella la Pietà, De Dominicis alla biennale di Venezia espone un mongoloide, Rockefeller a New York — come Re Mida — trasforma in oro tutte le opere d'arte che accetta nel suo Museum of Modern Art. Il M.O.M.A. non è un edificio, è una enorme cassaforte di oggetti d'oro, molto ospitale con chi vuole visitarne la ricchezza. Il controdesign italiano è arrivato al M.O.M.A., ma forse Rockefeller non lo ha "toccato". E' stata l'occasione liberale per diffondere su larga scala un messaggio limitato finora agli addetti. I "non oggetti" presentati a New York dal controdesign parlano chiaro: come essere oggi così vacuamente ottimisti da puntare ancora sul criterio razionalista dell'architettura, sui miti della metodologia, della tipologia, del concetto di spazio minimo vivibile, di cellula abitativa? La tecnologia è cieca, il gioco formale della forma è reazionario: entrambi sono servili gregari del mondo produttivo.
Non si può disegnare cose congeniali solo allo spirito di sopraffazione, alla corsa pazza al consumo, all'intenzione di appropriarsi di cose a spese degli altri. Dove cercare sbocchi? Fuori o dentro alle discipline del design?
Le ipotesi dei gruppi avanzati sono molte e sottili: il nomadismo e la tribù quali alternative alle strettoie della proprietà e della famiglia minimum, la città istantanea, sotterranea o non-stop quale liberazione dall'architettura-accademia, l'innesto diretto fra alta tecnologia ed uomo nel suo senso primordiale per uscire dalla palude della burocrazia-dittatura, il rifiuto del lavoro come condizione necessaria al recupero di civiltà meditative, la distruzione della cultura se questa è il luogo della élite che trattiene in se stessa il diritto alla creatività. La tecnica povera in rivolta chiede la liberazione della esperienza esistenziale e della fantasia di ogni singolo contro la tirannide del metodo economico competitivo, che impone criteri produttivi massificati e asettici: il funzionalismo è un'arida strada che conduce diritta al semplicismo spirituale. Recupero poetico dell'oggetto, recupero dell'oggetto poetico. Sono queste alcune cose raccontate da quelli del controdesign a Topolino, che ci ha assicurato di tenerne conto. Quando il supersensualism — come lo chiamano a Londra — dice queste cose, evviva le sue tournées.

Alessandro Mendini

* Alcuni protagonisti del controdesign, Archizoom, La Pietra, Sottsass, gruppo Strum, Superstudio — collaboratori di Casabella — hanno partecipato alla mostra « Italy: the new domestic landscape », allestita da Emilio Ambasz presso il Museum of Modern Art in New York e recensita nel numero scorso da Franco Raggi. In particolare i tre fotoromanzi del gruppo Strum (libretto bianco « The struggle for housing », libretto rosso « The mediatory city », libretto verde « Utopia ») sono editi da Casabella in inglese, e verranno pubblicati in italiano nel numero doppio 368-369 della rivista. Gli stessi gruppi partecipano, assieme a Casabella, alla Summer Session che si terrà a Londra in agosto, sessione estiva di architettura e di design organizzata dall'Architectural Association, cui sono invitate ad esprimersi le avanguardie internazionali. Questi ed altri gruppi avanzati dei quali si occupa assiduamente la rivista sono stati chiamati di volta in volta: radical architecture, supersensualism, italian reinvolution, tecnica povera in rivolta, controdesign, new generation.

The art of behaviour: in Rome Laszlo Toth smashes the Pietà with a hammer; at the Venice Biennale de Dominicis puts a mongoloid idiot on exhibition; in New York Rockefeller — like King Midas — transforms into gold all the works he accepts in his Museum of Modern Art.
Italian counter-design arrived in the Museum of Modern Art, but perhaps Rockefeller did not "touch" it. It was a liberal occasion for speaking on a vast scale a message which hitherto had been reserved exclusively for the "ins". The meaning of these "non-objects" shown in New York by counter-design is clear enough: how can anyone go on believing in the rationalist way of architecture, in the myths of methodology and typology, the concept of minimum living space and the home as cell? Technology is blind, the formal play of form is reactionary: they are both servile followers of production. One cannot design things congenial only to the spirit of oppression, to the mad rush to consumption. Is there no way out — either in or out of design?
The suggestions of the avant-garde groups are numerous and subtle: nomadism and the tribe as alternatives to the difficulties of property and the minimum family, or the instant city, whether underground or non-stop as a liberation from academic architecture; the direct synthesis of advanced technology and man in his primordial sense as a way out of the morass of our bureaucracy-dictatorship; the rejection of work as a necessary condition to the recovery of a meditative civilization; the destruction of culture if this is to be regarded as the appanage of an élite with the right of creativity. Minimal technique in revolt calls for the liberation of the existential experience and imagination of every individual from the tyranny of the competitive economic method, which imposes the criterion of aseptic mass-production: functionalism is an arid road which leads directly to a simplistic spiritual outlook.
There must be a poetic recovery of the object and a recovery of the poetic object. These are some of the things that have been told by counter-designers to Mickey Mouse, who assures us that he will keep them in mind. And as long as supersensualism — as they call it in London — goes on saying them, three cheers for its tour!

A. M.

*** Some of the leading groups in counter-design — Archizoom, La Pietra, Sottsass, the Strum group, and Superstudio, all collaborators of Casabella — took part in the exhibit "Italy: the new domestic landscape", staged by Emilio Ambasz at the Museum of Modern Art of New York and reviewed in last month's Casabella by Franco Raggi.**
The three "picture-stories" of the Strum group — "The struggle for housing", "The mediatory city", and "Utopia" — have been published by Casabella in English and will be published in Italian in the double issue 368-369 (August-September) of our review. The same groups are taking part, along with Casabella, in the Summer Session of art and design organized by the Architectural Association to be held in London in August; it will be the opportunity for the international avant-garde to express themselves. These and other advanced groups, whose activities our review has followed assiduously, have been called: radical architecture supersensualism, Italian reinvolution, minimal technique in revolt, counter-design, and new generation.

the super

Charl

Every now and then one steps into an odd environment and has a sudden flash of insight. The mathematician Henri Poincaré stepped on to a bus in Coutances and suddenly solved the problem of Fuchsian functions. Reyner Banham stepped, with a movie camera, into a southern Illinoian swimming pool and saw the point of lightweight technology, cleanliness etc. St. Paul on the road to Damascus . . . When I walked into the *Cimitero Monumentale* in Milan I suddenly understood a whole area of architectural endeavour. I realized what motivated the ideal cities of the Renaissance, the Utopian plans of Le Corbusier, the beautiful elevations and perspectives which every architect aspires to build. Eternity. The idea that much architecture intends to be eternal occurred to me in the "Monumental Cemetery" of Milan and the thought that therefore this architecture had to be for the dead quickly followed. It was beautiful, more beautiful than a rendering, well-kept up and open on all sides so that one could study it like a jewel. Every style was represented from Lombardy Gothic to Saarinen orange-peel **1** from Art Deco **2** to Mussolini modern **3**. No living city had seen such a rich texture of perfected monuments. It took a cemetery to realize the age-old architectural dream of everything in its place and a place for everything, and the harmony and stillness, only broken by the occasional grave-keeper, whispered out the long suspected truth – "perfect architecture is only for the dead".

Back in the living, bungled centre of Milan, the architect Ettore Sottsass jr. spoke of the omnipresence of death. His friend, the designer Joe Colombo, had just died; a close relative had committed suicide; he had himself barely escaped death twice. First in a concentration camp, second in the early sixties when Adriano Olivetti had flown him to the States for treatment of an "incurable disease" (as far as the Italian doctors knew). "We flirt with death", Sottsass said of the Italian designers and one can find this

1 Cimitero Monumentale, Milan

3

4 Ettore Sottsass Jr. "White Vase – Yantra di Terracotta"

18

nsualists* Part II

*Part I, AD June, 1971 pp.345-7

2

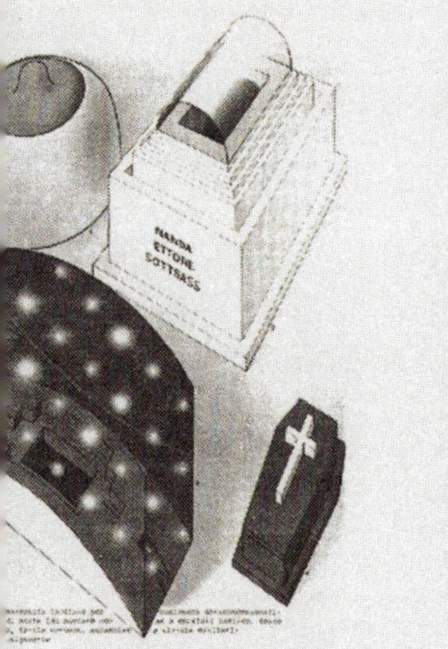

ottsass Jr.,' Destruction of the object' 1) Diagram of motherhood (box contraceptives). 2,3 Diagram of take with you to cocktail parties, fairs, conferences, assemblies and parades 4 cigarette box.

flirtation in his own ceramics and terracotta vases which are like so many superclean tombstones 4. Their high gloss finish and precision geometry make them final statements in the art of the reliquary even though they are intended as ash-trays, or fruit dishes or vases in the house. Their status as consumer objects to be worshipped, fondled, loved is beyond compare. Yet Sottsass was sceptical. "I can't get rid of the love of objects; I'm trying hard". He had just contributed to an edition of the Milanese magazine *IN*, edited by Superstudio and Archizoom, with the overall theme "The Destruction of the Object".5 I'm from the older generation and I find objects are very important for the control of our life, because they concentrate meanings. The problem is to make a new symbol or image with objects and transform their function."

The attempt to Destroy the Object is all the rage in Milan and Florence. The next two issues of *IN* will be titled "The Elimination of the City" and "The Disappearance of Work" following on from Superstudio and Archizoom's philosophy that the collapse of "formal structures" accompanies the liberation of men. They speak of the "elimination of fetishism and semantic redundancy". One is reminded of Le Corbusier's "vacuum-cleaning" period of modern architecture. All the results of this purgation, like Le Corbusier's, turn into new objects of worship: fantastically sensual pieces of metaphysical furniture sold to the *borghese* of Milan through one of the many outlets: Poltronova, Cassina, Knoll International etc. For instance the 'Mies' chair of Archizoom presents the metaphysical problem of sitting down with utmost elegant wit. One sees a flat, dark slab leaning down between two chromium triangles. With its head rest and position, one thinks its an operating table titled towards the end so as to more easily push off the recently departed. But then if one dares lie on this table, the dark slab of elastic suddenly gives way under the bottom and

Charles Jencks, "The Supersensualists," in *AD* n.1, 1972

the chrome bars turn into armrests.6 The overall triangular geometry is even more simplified than a chair by Mies. It is one of the strangest propositions in modern furniture having all sort of funereal overtones. In fact the metaphors of death pervade much of Archizoom's work from their "dreambeds" which resemble sacrificial alters 7 to their "gazebi" and enclosed "meditation centre" 8 which resemble areas set apart for mourning and remembrance. Behind these early works is perhaps the subconscious attempt to destroy fetishism for objects, by taking it to the ultimate limit. At any rate Archizoom speaks of creating a "closed basin", a semi-enclosed world, where the normal meanings of objects are either contradicted or pushed to absurdity.

More recently they have done the same with the whole city and once again the results resemble the static perfection of the graveyard.** They have evolved what they call the "No-Stop City, a climatic universal system" which can be spread homogeneously around the world resolving the contradictions between city and country in an even mixture of both 9. Elevators, beds, dining tables, rivers and trees are evenly distributed in a perfected plan that recalls the *Ville Radieuse.* As with Le Corbusier this ideal plan is the *termination* of a process, an industrial process most of all. Instead of taking the Futurist point that technology is in a constant state of compromising change – always scrapping, always innovating, never finished, never perfect – Archizoom freezes a certain stage of development and re-arranges the results in a radical way. All the elevators and spiral staircases are normal and standardised, without a history. The implication in "No-Stop City" is that technology stopped and was perfected about 1925. And yet like Le Corbusier, the philosophy which underlies this is not just the culmination of development (i.e. death), but the process itself. In their explanation, Archizoom justifies "No-Stop City" as a logical development of the urban and social process.

**Superstudio's twelve ideal cities are even more the *end* of a process – "the supreme achievement of twenty thousand years of civilisation, blood, sweat and tears; the final haven of Man in possession of Truth, free from contradictions, doubts, equivocations and indecision; totally and for ever replete with his own PERFECTION." *AD* 12/71, pp. 737-742

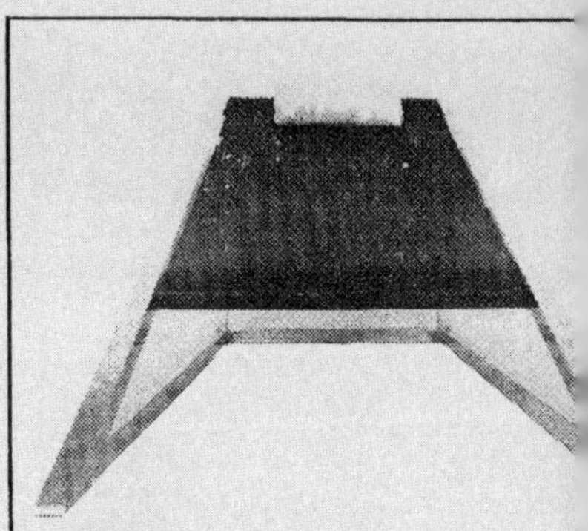

6 Archizoom, "Mies Chair", 1968.

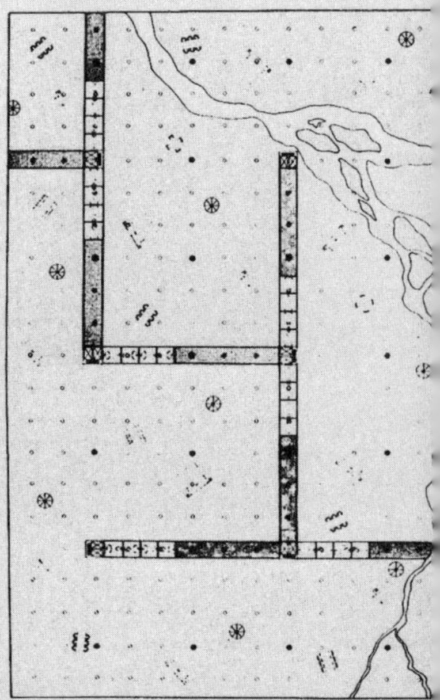

9 Archizoom, "No-Stop City – Resid

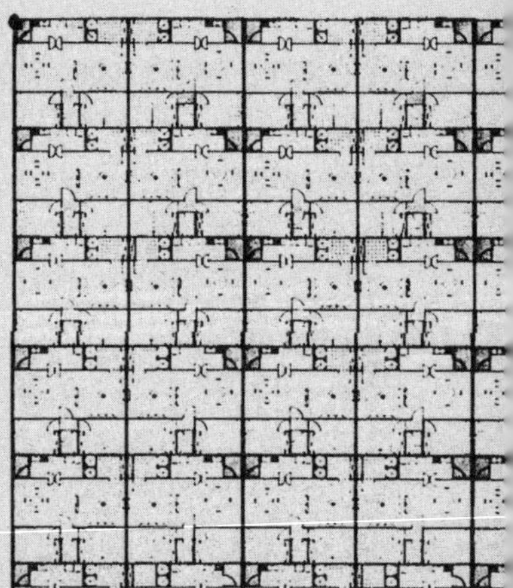

11(a) Archizoom, "Typological Plan"

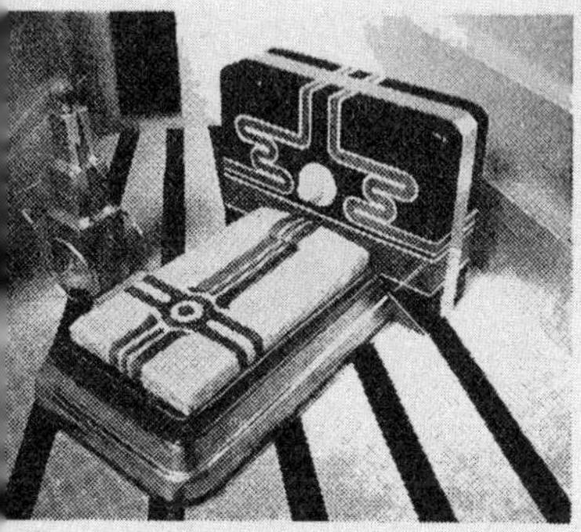

rchizoom, "Dream Bed, Rosa d'Arabia", 1968

8 Archizoom, "Gazebo-Meditation Centre", 1968

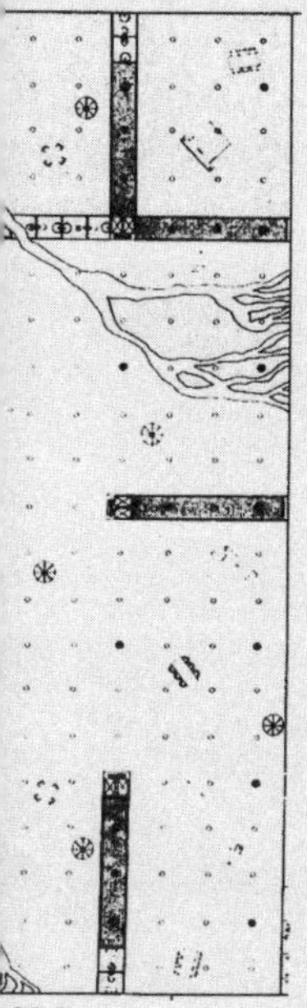

1970.

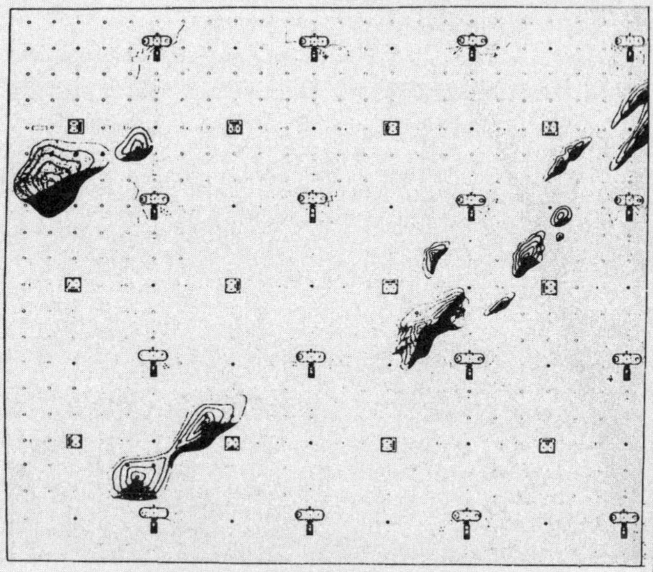

10 Archizoom, "No-Stop City – Residential Wood", 1970.

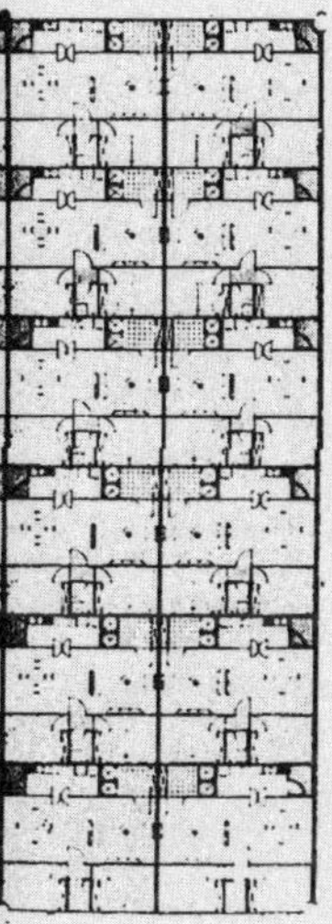

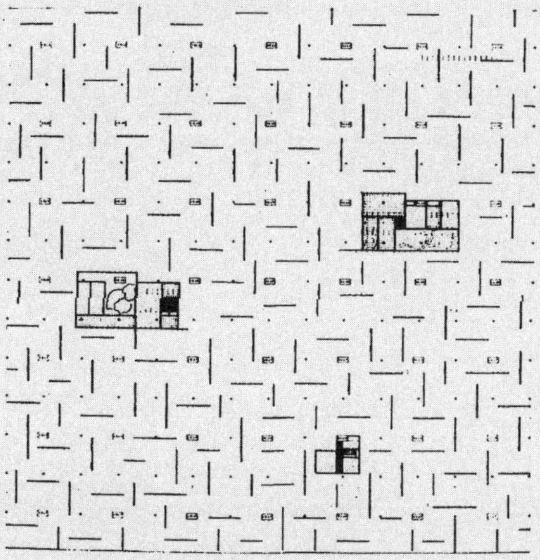

(b) "Homogeneous Living Diagram"

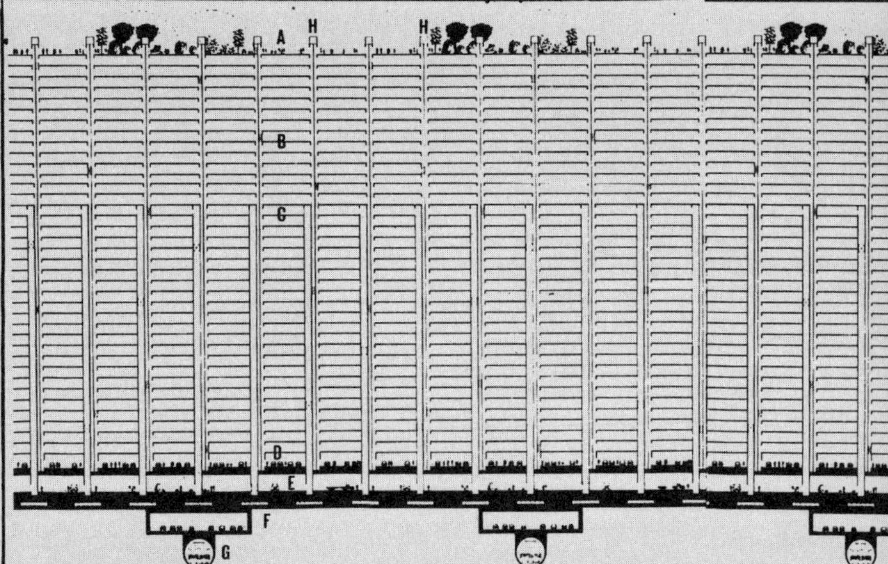

12 Archizoom, "No-Stop Section"; A – roof garden; B – Residencies; C – Services, D – tra
G – Underground.

12 (b) Archizoom, "Homogeneous residential structures".

13 Archizoom, "No-Stop Interior Landscape".

20

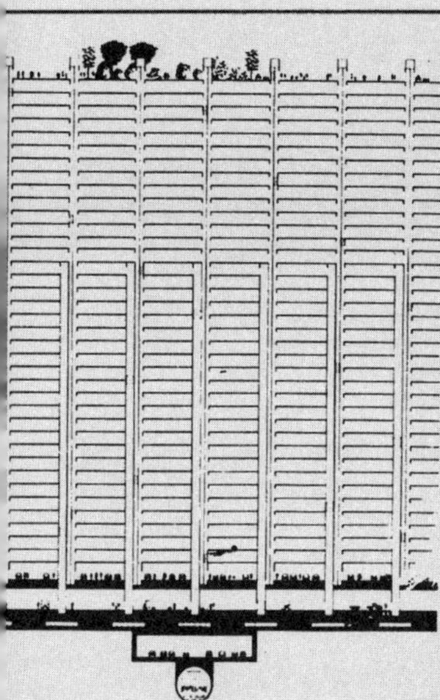

tranport; F – Highways;

Their ideas are partly based on the Marxist dialectic and current views of the post-industrial society. Hence they speak of the old bourgeois city, which is now superseded, as a collecting point of capital which reflects even in its pyramidal skyline the accumulation of wealth toward the centre. In opposition to this visual pyramid they place a "two-dimensional net" of services and communication **10** or a gigantic, homogeneous and endless structure **11,12** Their point is that the urban realm has become itself the market mechanism and this mechanism is now based on information technologies which decentralise and equalise the market in every point of the world.

. . . now the use of electronic media takes the place of the direct urban praxis: artificial inducements to consumption allow a much deeper infiltration into the social structure than did the (bourgeois) city's weak channels of information. The metropolis ceases to be a "place", to become a condition: in fact it is just this condition which is made to circulate uniformly, through Consumer Products, in the social phenomenon. The future dimension of the metropolis coincides with the market itself. 13.

Their view of the market mechanism can be termed idealistic, non-Marxist and based on the belief in the "managerial revolution", because they think that with the market's proper management all conflicts can be resolved.

Production and consumption possess one and the same ideology, which is that of programming. Both hypothesize a social and physical reality completely continuous and undifferentiated. No other realities exist. The factory and the supermarket became the specimen models of the future city . . . the house becomes a well-equipped parking lot . . . Thus (architecture) mediates between the contradictory forces of public and private: now however, this conflict is no longer left on the speculative level of existential consciousness.

Why not? Because now –

Economic Planning, by organizing the whole of society productively, eliminates the conflict, considers the contradiction fictitious and takes any strictly individual datum as experimental . . . Nowadays the only possible utopia is quantitative. Social conflict is no longer going through the phase of confrontation of alternative models, but is in that of dialectical negotiation between a balanced development of the system and the growing cost of the labour force . . . Quantitative language replaces qualitative, thus becoming the only scientific means of approach to the undifferentiated stratification of production and hence of reality.

Perhaps the nicest thing about these arguments and the "No-Stop City" is that they both take certain omnipresent truths to the extreme and thereby clarify their nature.

Of course no present post-industrial society resembles the ideal of scientific managers making just rational decisions which eliminate social conflicts, but this ideology pervades both Russian and American State capitalism and it is pleasant to see it laid bare in its pure, absurd form. This is the ideology of technocrats, planners, bureaucrats, social engineers, the men of "think tanks" and latter-day Saint Simonians such as Buckminster Fuller. Happily, Archizoom has pushed the assumptions to the point where one can see how they're both wrong and poetic at the same time. For if the market mechanism were perfectly regulated and "isotropic", then it might result in the "quantitative utopia" represented by No-Stop City. However, the obvious mistakes in the assumptions are 1: that the managerial revolution has occurred, 2: that any living city could result in the static, dead perfection which they represent, and 3: that a quantitative utopia could give any significance or meaning to life – or for that matter death.

The whole question of the significance of death has begun to preoccupy similar kinds of architects in different countries. Hans Hollein, a great influence on Archizoom, Superstudio and Sottsass, designed an exhibition "Death" in 1970 which developed a rather new attitude towards its significance. He constructed an archaelogical site and gave participants shovels to dig up the various remains of the present: smashed coke bottles, golf clubs and so on **14,15**. As well as this, he placed the accoutrements of dying near by – a sterile white hospital bed, screen, and garments to dress the corpse **16**. Part of the virtue of this approach is that it gets the living involved in a process with the dead; either discovering their remains or seeing how we treat people in their last moments. In a way this involvement is an alternative to the pathos connected with the usual forms of memorialisation.

It was a feeling of pathos which pervaded the gigantic mortuary of the *Cimitero Monumentale.* There, the remains of the deceased are packed in an endless grid-iron, or No-Stop Grave Yard **17**. Many of the memorial plaques have photos and small descriptions which are meant to remind close relatives and friends of the particular significance of the departed.

14 Hans Hollein, "Exhibition Death", 19

ns Hollein, "Exhibition Death", 1970.

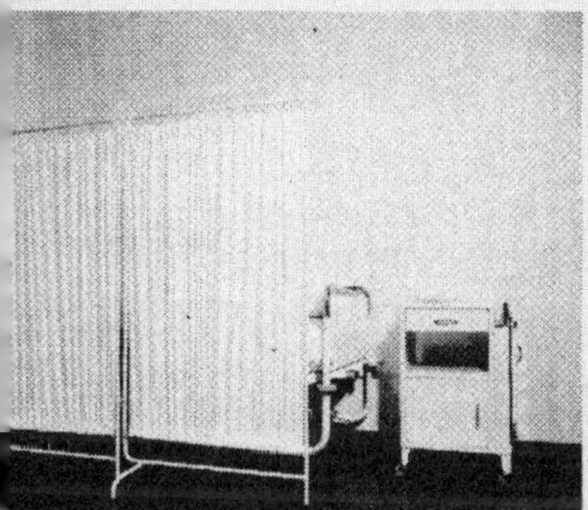

Hollein, "Death Bed in a corridor".

the mortuary. Each remembrance is private and hence doomed to extinction in a short time. Each grave is overwhelmed by the presence of too many others. Like a telephone book, or New York's vast slab-heap of memorials, the omnipresence of numbers robs the significance of any one. Sottsass commented on this irony: "People are buried in monuments to be remembered. A single monument is effective, but in a graveyard there are no memories, no people."

Perhaps a reason for this situation is the Christian idea of the individual soul inhabiting eternity. If one believes in an individual after-life, then it makes sense to memorialize every person, although presumably God, being infinitely non-forgetful, would not need to be reminded of each soul. Yet these beliefs in eternal after-life have eroded to the point where, most obviously, the individual graves have become kitsch reminders to and for the living. If this is true, it would seem inevitable that the pagan idea of immortality replace the Christian idea of eternity and that architecture, which crystallizes memory, would follow this change. Instead of representing a perfected process like No-Stop City, it would accentuate the individual act which stands out from this process. It would seek to memorialize that which is public and can be shared within society, giving to perishable human action that only kind of immortality open to it: the ability to be remembered by the living as a unique occurrence in a mass of expectedness.

Arata Isozaki
Introduction, "The Hot House. Italian New Wave Design"
MIT press, 1984

In the mid-1960s, it became apparent that the "avant-garde" in architecture and design was no longer functioning as it had in the early period of the Modern Movement. In the mid-1980s, it is clear that the avant-garde is no longer performing its role of instigating new movements in any cultural arena. Thus passed a mechanism contrived by modern society in order to perpetuate itself-a mechanism that was an integral component of our conception of progress.

(...) Andrea Branzi is testimony to the fact that the various experiments in design that have taken place over the last twenty years have contributed to the demise of the avant-garde. There is an insinuation of something catastrophic and traumatic as Branzi ventures into the boundless, unknown wilderness.

Modern architecture, since its beginnings, has sought to develop technology and attain utopia, and the avant-garde was given responsibility for steering its course. After the early 1960s, however, the avant-garde could no longer fulfill this responsibility. At that time, young architects from Tokyo, London, Vienna, and other centers were creating utopian technical proposals for the city of the future. My own career as an architect was launched via such proposals. But some of these architects had already become aware that the future would not be rosy, that technology could become destructive, and that the "utopian" residences they were planning were only congested places where people would swarm like ants or bees. It became apparent that serious questions had to be asked about the fundamental tenets of modern architecture. And so they were.

At that time I was caught between two forces. While in Japan I sympathized with the radical tendency that would culminate in the "abandonment of art;" on the other hand, I was making full use of technology in assembling a robot, to be displayed at the Milan Triennale of 1968, which abstracted the hidden violent character of technology. But despite its intent, my work was denied because I was associated with the regime of the established industrial society that ruled the production and distribution of design.

Borrowing a Zen term, this denial was a strong coup to me. In Zen training, the master imposes on his trainees various difficult questions to help them attain a new realization of the world. The purpose of the questions is to trap the trainees in paradox. In this way, the master asks the trainees to empty their minds. But in most cases, because candidates are limited by knowledge gained in the past, they cannot attain the real void. At such times, the master, sometimes through verbal means and sometimes through physical violence, delivers a strong blow, whereupon some trainees come to feel emptiness and to free their minds from knowledge based in the past. I received such a liberating coup in 1968.

I consider the course of modern architecture pioneered by the avant-garde to have been changed definitively and qualitatively by the confrontation resulting from the occupation of the Triennale exhibition building in 1968, which was in turn part of a cultural revolution whose origins were in Paris. I later came to regard the year of the Triennale as a cultural watershed, comparable to 1527 when the Sack of Rome helped to stimulate Renaissance architecture. At the time, however, I was too much a hostage to immediate events to have any perspective on the situation. Recovering from that coup, I signed the agreement for the occupation. I remember the name of Archizoom among the list of signatures, but I did not know at the time that Andrea Branzi was a member of this group.

After being struck by the coup of confrontation, I turned my attention to the work of architects who were actively engaged in destroying the canon that had supported modern architecture. Among such architects, I found two groups who, breaking off relations with former avant-garde thought, presented an attitude of extreme radicalism. Both groups were based in Florence: Superstudio and Archizoom.

What their work shared in common was a fundamental criticism of the established concept of architecture. Superstudio, to strip the designed object of its own immanent meaning, adopted the strategy of covering the object's entire surface with a continuous neutral grid. And then they extended this grid beyond the city, beyond the earth, even to cosmic space, calling the result a *Continuous Monument*.

Archizoom also developed a project of infinitely extended neutral architecture: this was the *No-Stop City*, where parking, residential space, and offices were arranged in layers of artificial space, strung out like groceries in a supermarket. Because it abandoned any dependence on natural light, *No-Stop City* went on growing into a strange assemblage beyond the usual limits of architecture. The composition of elements and the forms of production, conjunction, traffic, and distribution were to be the last direct product of the rationalism that had supported the development of modern architecture. The result was the terribly homogeneous city that would emerge when the naturalistic constraints that work to keep these elements in balance were removed.

Superstudio adopted the means of sanctifying an architectural object by eliminating its details. Their continuous architecture is very similar to the Nirvana sought by the Flower Children. Here architecture becomes united to nature and is submerged. Archizoom's *No-Stop City* presents the utmost extremity of modern rationalism, where any kind of fantasy is forbidden. Using a nasty trick, they turned our present situation inside out, a development driven by a rationalism that was now extended to the production system also. One must acknowledge a certain black humor in this.

The aspect of a city formulated according to these proposals, whether it reaches a saturated state or a state of super-homogeneity, is never the naturalistic utopia that modern architecture sought. Rather, such proposals should be perceived as fundamental criticisms of modern architecture through the presentation of an instantaneous glimpse of the nightmare of the future.

There is concealed in both the *Continuous Monument* and the *No-Stop City*, I believe, the memory and experience of the great flood that visited Florence in 1966, which must have had a profound effect on the members of Superstudio and Archizoom who were graduated from the University that year. During the flood, the center of Florence, a symbol of urban culture since the Renaissance, was submerged. This abrupt invasion by an alien substance buried the well-balanced city of beauty and elegance. Just as the flood was symbolic of the destruction that could level physical culture in an instant, the *Continuous Monument* and the *No-Stop City* are architectural concepts that might launch a destructive attack against the city; at the same time, both are endless objects that might plot a homogeneous, untamed, reckless invasion. Are they not analogous to the violent conditions of the flood in this sense? Indeed, both projects may well be regarded as metaphors of the flood, whose impact on the young designers was comparable to the coup of Zen.

Since the mid-1970s, Andrea Branzi has been involved in new design experiments with Ettore Sottsass Jr., Alessandro Mendini, and others. These experiments exhibit the same characteristics that were featured in *No-Stop City* - an endless expansion reaching toward insanity and meant as an offensive attack against established norms. Concretely, the products of their design encompass all the elements that compose the environment, such as technology, objects, surfaces, colors, materials, clothes, and furniture. They reduce each of these elements to its original state and then try to understand it from a new point of view. They adopt, as the most effective due, a critical method that I wish to call "constraint-free rationalism." As the concept of design was actually born in the Modern Movement of architecture, so it is deeply supported by rationalistic thought. Therefore, when we intend to criticize modern architecture or design, we cannot avoid the difficulty of having only the rationalist way of thought at our command. This is tantamount to the contradiction posed in another sphere of thought today, namely, that in order to criticize the compositional logic (*logos*) that supports language, we have no means of criticism other than the very language that is the subject of the critique. Andrea Branzi and his colleagues release the objects produced rationalistically from the frame that has confined their rationality, and extend this rationality to the furthest reaches and beyond. Here it is expected that the excess or the border incursion will occur. It is clear that the activities of Memphis and Alchimia have already been influential beyond the borders of Italy.

It seems to me that these movements have passed beyond the labels "avant-garde" and "radical." They have progressed to a stage that might be called "critical rationalism." My wish, however, is not to limit what they are doing to the parameters of this term, but rather to relate what issues from Andrea Branzi and others to the more eloquent, fluid, and fundamentally invasive idea of the flood.

ARCHIZOOM

Il est très caractéristique de constater que la classe intellectuelle, après une tentative longue et difficile entreprise au lendemain de la guerre, est arrivée actuellement au point où elle doit se poser la question fondamentale de savoir si ses rapports avec la classe ouvrière se soldent par une adoption ou ne constituent pas plutôt aujourd'hui l'acte officiel qui constate la mort par incapacité de survivre au contact d'une praxis exclusivement révolutionnaire.
En fait il faudrait savoir si par manque de tâches à accomplir on a licencié en bloc tous les Battista qui prêchaient dans le désert : « Préparez-vous à la révolution ! », ou si ceux-ci briguent un rôle important et d'une certaine représentativité à l'intérieur même du mouvement de lutte effective.
Avant de proposer une réponse à cette question, il serait bon de faire remarquer que ce type d'interrogation est caractéristique des années 60, il est, disons-nous, caractéristique, mais aussi très peu politique.
En effet, pour aborder un thème aussi général, il ne serait pas superflu d'analyser le stade de développement actuel du système et les formes sous lesquelles se manifeste l'opposition ouvrière. De façon immédiate, on en conclurait que les deux hypothèses : Utopie et Révolution et Utopie ou Révolution, sont bien mal posées.
1) Nous assistons actuellement à la disparition progressive et inéluctable de la distinction entre deux secteurs de ce système : la production et la circulation des biens de consommation. Distinction entre ce qui constitue le mécanisme de production, qui est traditionnellement limité et partiel par rapport à l'ensemble de la société et ce qui était une zone franche, indépendant de la production, dans laquelle le processus de l'échange instaurait la valeur marchande du produit.
Ce phénomène est survenu à la suite de la multiplication d'un certain type d'usines dans la société, ce qui détermine la mise en œuvre des possibilités sous-jacentes de raisonnement impliquées par le travail organisé qui, par l'entremise du Plan, est passé d'un secteur spatial limité à celui de la société tout entière. Cette société s'est ainsi transformée totalement en une force du travail qui se différencie par les organismes employeurs et les fonctions occupées.
Ce moment de crise où le système se réalise entièrement, c'est-à-dire où il assume ses propres contraintes éthiques dans une société qui n'était pas encore un système (mais seulement son espace et son hinterland improductif et informe) marque aussi l'aboutissement de la contradiction extrême du système même, sa contrepartie plus générale : la prolétarisation de toute la société.

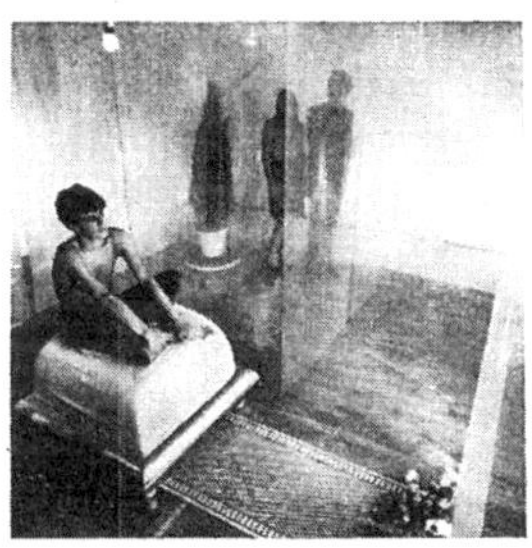

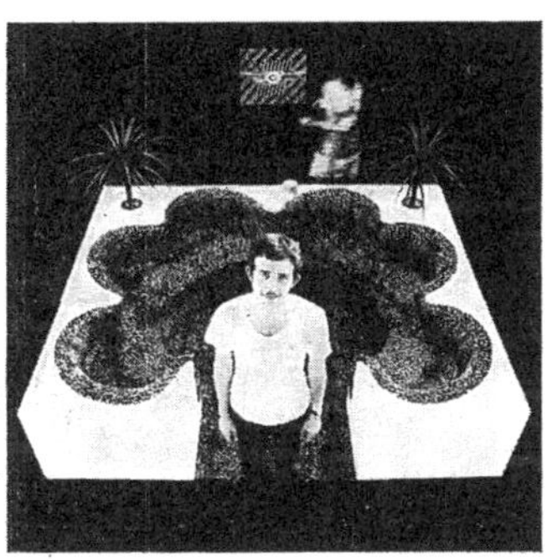

En effet, au moment même où la société tout entière devient, par le Plan, une force du travail, la barrière traditionnelle entre bourgeoisie improductive et force du travail salariée disparaît ; mais si cette barrière tombe, la société demeure toujours une société classique et le fait de se prolétarisar reste « honteux » (Licciardello). C'est l'origine des tourments qui agitent toute cette bourgeoisie qui n'accepte pas ce processus et qui s'y oppose avec force en faisant de la politique et en trouvant de nouveaux moyens d'opposition de masse au capital.
Au moment où cette angoisse de la prolétarisation devient conscience politique, le reflux d'une vieille idéologie de classe qui n'a pas encore atteint le stade de la théorie aborde l'hypothèse générale d'ensemble, thaumaturge et scatologique de la Révolution.
L'espoir messianique que représente cette Révolution en tant que sacrifice, autodestruction sexuelle, bain de sang purificateur, rejoint l'image chère à la classe ouvrière de l'agneau pur, qui n'a pas été contaminé par le bien-être et que l'on immolera pour le plus grand bien de tous.
Toutes les frustrations secrètes d'une classe intellectuelle humiliée par sa propre inutilité, dans le contexte d'un système qui se suffit entièrement à lui-même, viennent s'ajouter à la spontanéité de l'humanisme paysan que la classe ouvrière aurait conservé et qui constituerait même le ferment révolutionnaire susceptible d'instaurer une société dépositaire de ces valeurs humanistes qui sont aujourd'hui reniées de toutes parts. On assiste aux derniers soubresauts de la simplicité artisanale pré-industrielle perdue, qu'une technologie sans pitié a vaincue.
Ainsi, à la limite, on tend à nier au capital toute valeur d'instrument de civilisation et cela au nom même d'une pauvreté chrétienne des moyens. Mais la classe ouvrière a déjà effectué son propre choix indépendant et spontané, franchissant le pas qui la séparait du niveau de développement que le système avait atteint.
2) Ainsi que le dit Tronti, la petite larme humanitaire versée sur les conditions inhumaines du travail en usine a fait son temps. Depuis la crise économique des années 30, « la révolution des revenus » a été l'initiative économique la plus marquante du nouveau capital. Sur ce plan, le mot « salaire » prend pour les ouvriers une spécificité propre.
En effet, à l'intérieur d'une société qui possède un programme économique et qui tend à réaliser simultanément une « révolution permanente des revenus et un développement harmonieux du système », l'idéologie du salaire est la seule qui puisse déterminer des conditions de crise ca-

ANDREA BRANZI GILBERTO CORRETTI PAOLO DEGANELLO MASSIMO MOROZZI

"Archizoom", in *L'architecture d'aujourd'hui* n. 145, 1969

pables de dissocier le binôme : Grande Industrie-Etat et d'entraîner un changement de commande des leviers du pouvoir.
Cette quête du pouvoir se poursuit donc, non pas tellement pour essayer d'améliorer la société existante, mais plutôt comme le seul moyen de concrétiser la seule véritable impulsion révolutionnaire que la classe ouvrière connaisse et qui est aussi la seule chose qui maintienne sa cohésion et son adhésion au parti et aux syndicats : le désir intransigeant d'un salaire plus élevé pour un temps de travail réduit.
Il y a déjà longtemps que le prolétariat a découvert la gestion ouvrière du capital et il n'a pas l'intention d'y renoncer, expérimentant dans la lutte son degré extrême d'aliénation et d'intégration au mécanisme du système.
Comme les Noirs dans les pays colonisés, ce n'est pas pour un monde meilleur qu'il se bat, mais pour devenir le remplaçant des colonisateurs blancs (Fanon).
D'où la disparition immédiate du moment de création idéologique qu'une « théorie » concrète de classe vient remplacer.
Aussi le choix des armes ou de la démocratie comme moyen de conquérir le pouvoir pour la classe ouvrière n'a pas de valeur en soi : l'important est de ne croire à aucun d'eux, car là n'est pas le problème.
A ce stade de notre propos, le problème Utopie et/ou Révolution disparaît en tant que produit d'une mutation idéologique qui conduit à une conception erronée de la classe ouvrière, justement parce qu'elle s'identifie à l'inexistence de toute théorie de la classe ouvrière.
Mais il est vrai aussi que ces propos ne s'arrêtent pas là ; les deux hypothèses à peine écartées, voilà que surgit le danger d'une attente apocalyptique des événements.
En réalité la crise de la culture actuelle ne se présente pas tellement comme une crise politique, mais plutôt comme une crise historique authentique dont les termes ne coïncident pas de façon parfaite avec son contenu social.
A la lumière des considérations que nous venons rapidement d'évoquer, il est évident que la « tension sociale » de la culture du XXe siècle a pour origine une prise de conscience progressive de cette prolétarisation, d'abord dans ses rêves troublés d'une fin de siècle, puis dans l'angoisse de cet « engagement » (1), non pas tant comme conscience morale, mais de plus en plus comme fraction directement concernée.
Depuis un certain temps, en fait depuis le début de la révolution industrielle, le processus d'assimilation de la réalité globale à son modèle formel s'est amorcé de façon directe. C'est depuis ce moment-là que date la crise de la culture qui, peu à peu, a cédé le pas à la civilisation culturelle.
En effet, si la culture en tant qu'instrument agit par irradiation, c'est-à-dire par tension éthique d'un modèle formel vis-à-vis du tout, la civilisation culturelle agit par convention, elle agit directement sur la masse amorphe de « l'inconnu » en laquelle peu

(1) En français dans le texte.

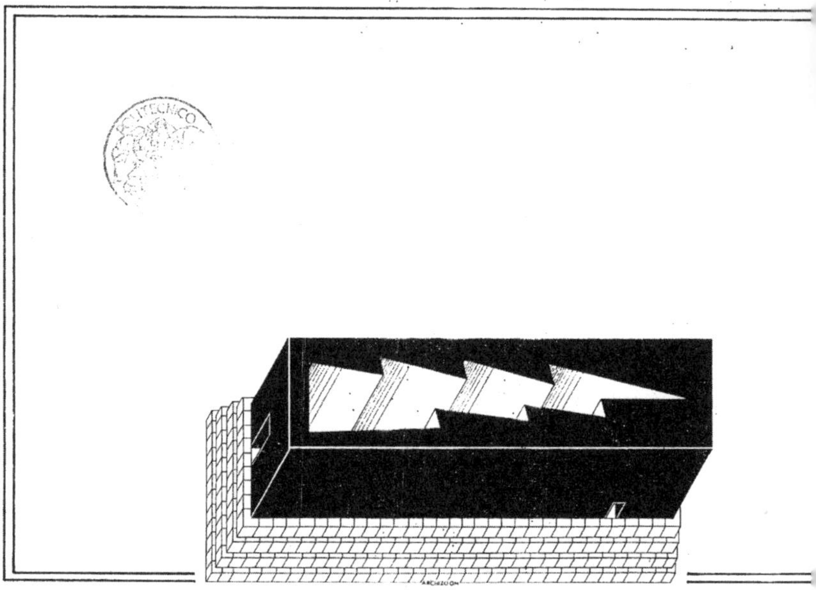

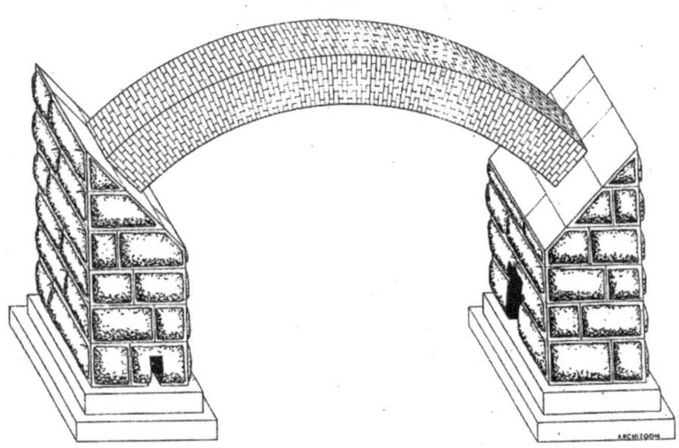

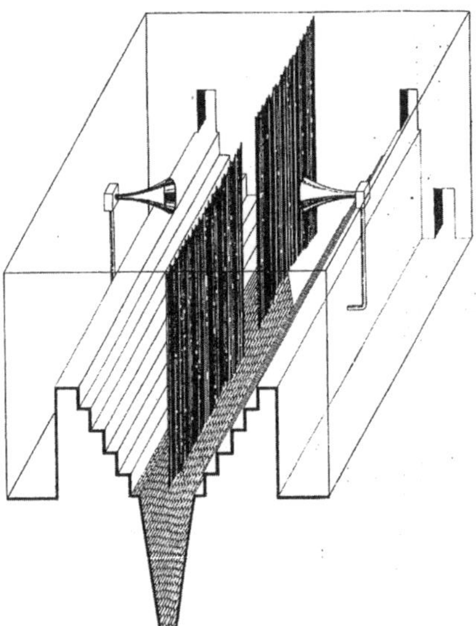

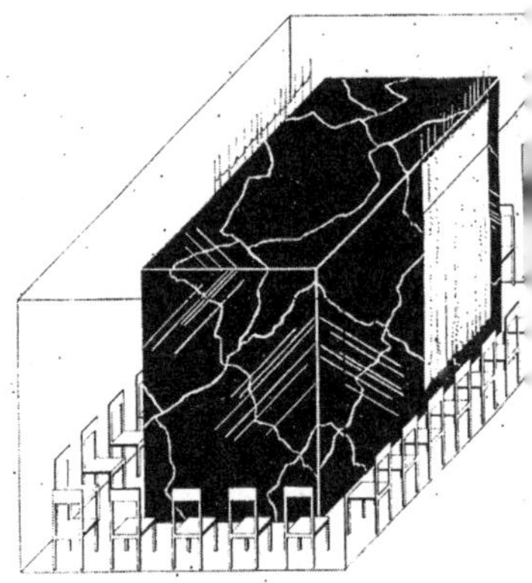

à peu le capital tend à s'incarner.
C'est ainsi que naît le personnage de l'intellectuel, c'est-à-dire de celui qui crée des problèmes, de celui qui n'agit plus sur la forme mais sur le climat qui l'entoure.
C'est déjà une condition de crise, car la culture au contact d'une réalité économique lancée à toute vitesse accentue sa propre nature de super-structure, elle perd son pouvoir de synthèse et commence à s'occuper de l'organisation d'un pays en négatif, de son exploitation plus ou moins consciente, et des comportements de l'individu, d'abord par le romantisme, puis par la psychanalyse, elle réussit ainsi à offrir au capital un terrain que l'analyse et les énigmes de l'individu ont dragué et qui a été débarrassé de tout secteur d'ombre.
C'est à ce moment-là que la culture a dû choisir entre l'esprit et la psychologie, entre l'architecture comme réalité physique reposant sur des principes logiques et le concept d'espace, c'est-à-dire entre la forme et l'exploitation.
La meilleure production de notre siècle (Mann, Picasso, Le Corbusier) est encore caractérisée par ce dualisme déchirant (Asor Rosa).
Mais le mode de réalisation, lorsque cette réalisation était possible, s'est par la suite éteint : le capital s'est incarné dans la différenciation sociale du travail et a ainsi assumé son propre devoir-être, franchissant d'un bond la dernière bande d'espace qui le séparait de la société, cet espace dans lequel la culture devait, par nature, évoluer.
Ou bien la culture devient, comme toutes les fractions du tout, un secteur productif avec ses valeurs et ses plus-values, ou alors elle cesse d'exister parce qu'elle ne peut satisfaire, dans son action créatrice, aux exigences d'une lutte politique qui tend à épuiser son propre contenu dans le concept de « salaire ».
Mais même si nous concluons à la non-existence d'une culture actuelle et à la disparition complète de toute forme d'action politique directe, il n'en est pas moins vrai que l'architecture continue d'exister et de se réaliser.
Au moment même où nous assistons à la mort progressive de toutes les autres catégories intellectuelles, l'architecture semble dans l'immédiat échapper à ce destin, peut-être en vertu d'un niveau d'intégration insuffisant qui semble encore nécessiter un certain nombre de pas en avant pour qu'elle devienne un secteur industriel organisé qui soit d'un bon rapport.
Cela nous ne pouvons pas le prévoir dans la mesure où les « grands courants » ont manqué à l'architecture. Nous voulons parler de ces courants de nature morale et sociale qui ont permis au mouvement moderne de se réaliser sur le plan formel : le fonctionnalisme, l'attitude rationaliste, l'optique structuraliste, mais aussi la verdure, le soleil, le bonheur de l'homme... tout ce qui était il y a encore quelques années le champ d'action de la création. A présent on ne peut plus y croire dans la mesure où toute force subversive a disparu, ainsi que les contenus sociaux autres que ceux de l'humanitarisme ambigu de la démocratie sociale.
En dehors de ces « courants », de

LXVII

cette foi en quelque chose qui n'était pas seulement l'architecture, mais grâce auxquels l'architecture réussissait à s'insérer, il se manifeste un désir de récupérer la réalité architecturale telle qu'elle existait auparavant. C'est un processus formel intransigeant reposant sur des principes logiques, qui ne se préoccupe absolument pas des questions d'utilisation et des contraintes sociales.
La vérité est qu'aujourd'hui le système peut très bien se passer d'une création qui le représente, car il est en mesure de se représenter très bien tout seul.
Le problème de la « forme de la ville » comme produit manufacturé unique est remplacé par celui d'une conception urbanistique totalement homogène, dépourvue de toute image d'ensemble comme élément catalyseur formel et structural, agissant sur ce qui n'est pas urbain.
En fait il n'existe aucune nécessité d'unité de la forme du moment que le capital s'est incarné en ce qui n'était pas le capital : les idéologies n'ont plus cours, les conceptions différentes du monde ne s'affrontent plus, les formes, de même que les comportements, ne s'opposent plus : l'unité s'est réalisée.
La façon dont les ouvriers utilisent la notion de salaire afin de déclencher cette « révolution permanente des revenus au sein d'une évolution dirigée par le système lui-même » démontre bien qu'il est possible d'utiliser de façon consciente l'instrument le plus simple et le plus immédiat, lui faisant acquérir ainsi, par la seule opération quantitative, une valeur politique générale qui est une menace de crise continuelle pour l'équilibre existant.
On peut déclencher une opération analogue en jouant sur une situation urbaine axée sur une demande croissante et inextinguible en superficie habitable.
Le fragile équilibre de fonctionnement de la ville qui en dépit de la démesure des développement horizontaux et verticaux s'est maintenu jusqu'à présent, par des normes quantitatives spécifiques, serait immédiatement rompu.
Jusqu'ici la hauteur des édifices et les diverses typologies se sont conformées aux limites imposées par des équilibres spontanés : luminosité, aération naturelle et espace avant tout, sont l'émanation d'une image des revenus et d'un mode de vie qui cadre avec les conditions générales d'une économie qu'il faut absolument renverser. Mais le problème n'est pas de prévoir de nouveaux quartiers ouvriers conçus suivant des typologias améliorées, il faut penser des structures a-formelles ou à une seule forme, dont le contenu utopique se traduit en termes quantitatifs. Il ne s'agit pas d'imaginer l'organisation d'une société différente, meilleure et plus équitable où les maisons seraient plus belles, la seule chose qui doit nous préoccuper pour le moment est que ces maisons soient spacieuses.
Ce n'est pas du ressort de l'architecture dans la mesure où les problèmes ne sont pas résolus si toutefois ils sont posés de nouveau et dans la mesure où l'on n'essaie pas de recréer l'unité de la forme mais bien l'homogénéité du tout.
Nous ajouterons toutefois, en ce qui nous concerne, que ce sont plutôt des problèmes de « styling » où en fait l'intervention sur le plan esthétique ne se réalise pas au moment méthodologique de la création, mais se borne tout au plus à poser sur le toit des palmes ou des plumes d'autruche !

Congrès de Turin,
25, 26, 27 avril 1969.

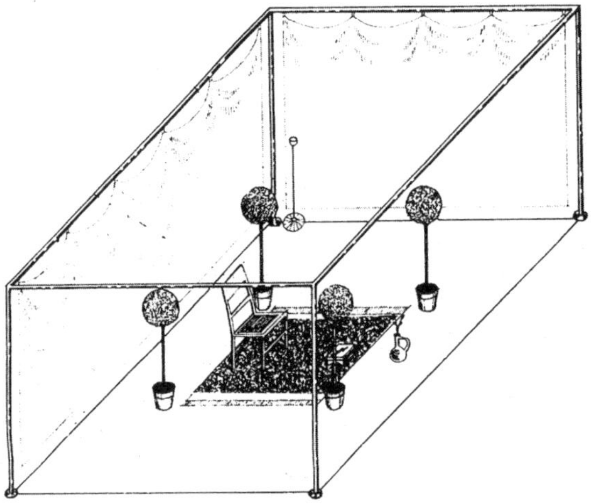

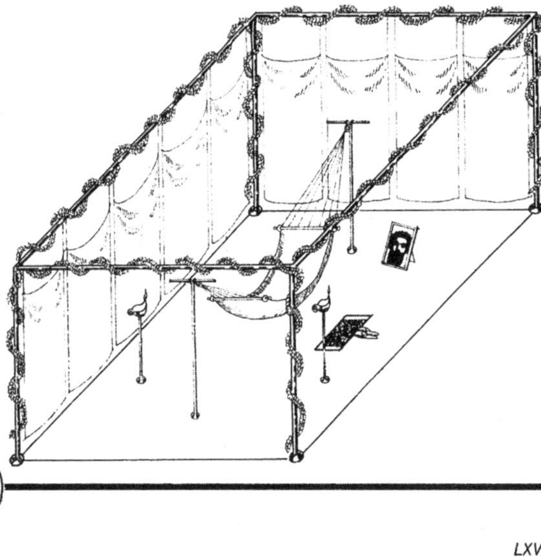

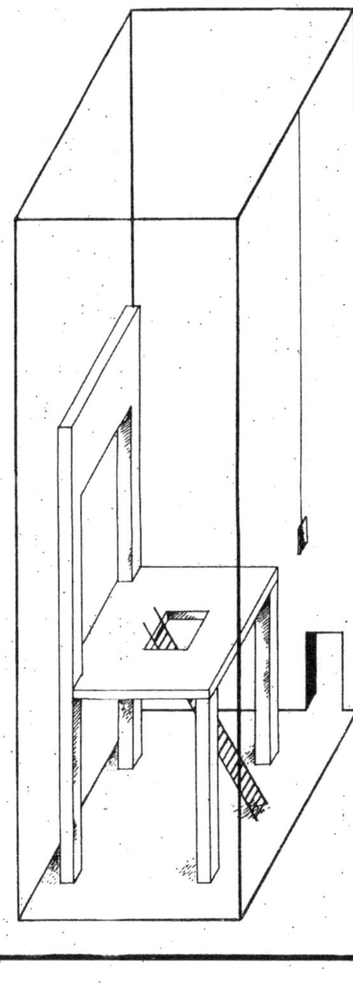

An Exaggerated Generation
Andrea Branzi, 2014

//

"Exaggeration" was a characteristic condition of the generation to which I belong, at least those born around the beginning of the forties; an exaggeration necessary to react to a modest bourgeoisie exaggerated in its moralism, in its cultural mediocrity, in respectability. Under this heavy burden everyone felt, in different forms, his or her own diversity and ambition, and the only way to react was with "exaggeration" to the surrounding "exaggerations"...

In different forms, my generation was beginning to feel quite different from the mediocrity of the surrounding world and began to declare itself entirely foreign to it; not in a hostile, violent way, but more in a wittier and more intelligent manner. If at one time to be normal was a social goal, the goal now was to overcome the gray normality of the next-door neighbor, of the condominiums, of the professional success, of the frustrated professors.

The seed of the "exaggerated generation" began to sprout in the early sixties to become a phenomenon that had its roots in the history of this country, where "exaggeration" has always been the only way to survive...

It's not easy to describe the Radical Movement and its effect on design culture, both contemporary and current, if not as a youthful, generational avant-garde movement that created an early imbalance in the certainties of classic Modernism, placing it in the forefront of a scenario already in action, but until then buried in the fog: a scenario that already beginning in 1964 materialized itself in the reality of the market, in society, in the failure of Rationalism, in the certainty of an ordered future and in the internal split of the modern project. In this sense, our position was "utopian" because radically "realist;" exaggerated because witness of a potentially exaggerated, but in fact inert, reality: we could speak of a "negative utopia" that was not concerned with a better future, but with the present, criticizing it through the paradox of radical narratives; no polemics against industry, against the bourgeoisie, against power, but accepting them as part of a present to discover outside the veil of distorting ideologies...

It was in that void that two fraternal twins were born, which were the last Italian movements that have had a wide international echo in the culture of the project: the Radical Movement and the Tendenza of Aldo Rossi. With one big difference: the Tendenza worked to build a new kind of architecture immediately, while the Radical Movement was primarily of an intellectual and iconic nature and did not build anything, a witness to the mediocrity of the times and following the noble and distant legacy of the Renaissance, for which architecture is primarily a reflection of a vision of the world, destined for the long duration of history.

In general, architects love architecture excessively (this is their greatest defect) for questioning its roots, to the point of considering it a discipline whose building material is architecture itself, as a tautological reality indifferent to history. Basically, architecture differs from the rest of the world because it is identical to itself.

This self-referentiality went through the fifties and the sixties, arriving at our times, marked by this pathological delay, this hyper-professionalism feeding off of brilliant solutions to false problems. We looked at the world through a distorting lens, like that of a telescope magnifying the monstrosity of the system in general and that of a microscope showing its molecular imperfections. By merging into a single framework the metropolis and the universe of objects, we warned that the world was changing from an "Architectural Civilization" to a "Civilization of Commodities," where traditional hierarchies between disciplines of the project were being overturned...

This state of "mobile threshold" deeply influenced the birth of the Radical Movement. A movement that has not yet been fully analyzed or historically contextualized, and the few critical contributions have often produced more confusion than clarity; especially in Italy, both for a lack of objective criticism of the local culture, then because the radical protagonists themselves, moving in a context of rapid evolution, have not been able to interpret and communicate their work with clarity.

To date, the movement has been considered a unitary phenomenon and as such indecipherable, because it consists of groups and designers with very different methods, "They constituted the first critical front with respect to the granite-hard certainties of classical modernity." This definition, even if correct, always involves two limitations: either it neglects to investigate in a comparative manner the different components of the movement, or it investigates the work of individual players, but does not elaborate on the overall nature of the phenomena.

In other words, we have not yet analyzed both the effect and the causes of the movement. Perhaps this long absence of attention from the official critics was lucky, because it gives us today an untouched historical phenomenon, yet to be interpreted…

The avant-gardes of the last century had been an expression of militant minorities that, through their actions, had renewed the cultural repertoire of bourgeois society. According to the intuition of the Radical Movement, normality became the exception; gray ignorance in a society entirely made of exceptions and diversity. So, what was waiting for us would be a future not ruled by order but by complexity, by discontinuity, by exceptions, where chaos became the new social order, the new physical law of an anarchic system "without an exterior."

In the world of the project, this transformation meant that the creative ways and the anarchy of the avant-garde had become the only usable instruments in the context of a globalized and saturated market, where in order for the industrial system to survive amid global competition it needs continuous inflows of unexpected and unforeseen innovation. Since that moment, the project has lost its methodological unity.

And it was in this perspective that the movement instinctively refused any linguistic and methodological unity, burning within it all traces of the old certainty and definitive solutions. Thus, a project that had lost its way and had become the result of a kind of design, an expression of the creative work of mass society…

The movement has marked (for better or worse) this generation who felt that the set of political and cultural values on which the world was rebuilt after the war was beginning to crack and could not be replaced by a more robust system, but rather by a weaker and more confused one, pushing to the extreme the paradoxical instances of the Modern Movement and foreshadowing the urgent need to "liberate man from architecture," but also "architecture from the presence of man."

It is important to point out that from these premises the Radical Movement never "built" anything, just models, drawings, prototypes, theoretical texts, icons, from the moment it rejected the assumption that architecture coincided solely with building practices, in favor of an idea of the project as a culturally complex reality that produces analyses of society, history, technology, and politics...

In this sense, it was a mediatic phenomenon above all, one that understood that the area of the project was not created only by the real market, but also by immense spaces of mass communication, producing "images that generate new images," in an era where ideas can be more important than material reality. Changing ideas means changing the world…

To make the divergent lines of work of the major groups of the Italian radical movement compatible with each other, we can identify (extrapolating from the multiple and contradictory projects) four fundamental polarities from which this new reality spontaneously emerged:

- The city without architecture (Archizoom);
- Architecture without the city (Superstudio);
- Objects with no city and no architecture (UFO);
- Architects without architecture (Ugo La Pietra and the Situationists);

Their specificity consists of the fact that all these have taken as first the concept of "deterritorialization" of the project; which is to say the overcoming of the "local limits" on which architecture has always been based, such as the segment rooted in the territory, built on rigid foundations and the sum of that which is called the "city" is born.

Both Archizoom and Superstudio, UFOs and Ugo La Pietra operated instead in a territorial (and mental) dimension that was unlimited, infinite, nebulous, planetary, that was used to conquer new dimensions of the project...

From this singular point of departure (or arrival) none of us ever came to either fantascientific or utopian conclusions, but rather the realistic representation of the worldwide dimension that the capitalist system and media had reached. A geo-political dimension that no longer provided the perimeters of architecture, regional mapping, urban diversity: everything is city, everything is market, everything is desert…

At the end of a long process, the Radical Movement has produced a kind of overall scenario, a unity for different parts much richer and more elaborate than the initial one. The common factor for the whole movement was the feeling of being at work in a "desert" of physical and cultural values: where "maximum alienation" matched "maximum freedom." Refoundings, dissolutions, chaos, and dematerialization were different categories only because of different narrative strategies with which to illustrate a world "that was no longer united," and for this reason they were introducing new knowledge and new freedoms on the Left, but also new cultures on the Right. Both groups of Right and Left in fact began to realize that they did not have a possible future in front of them, except through criminal and terrorist practices ("The comrades who make mistakes" as they were called in an ambiguous way by "Lotta Continua"), that in fact were not directed toward taking power but rather, much more modestly, to ensure the survival of groups despite their failure...

THEORIES

Radical Essays

Archizoom Associati, 1967

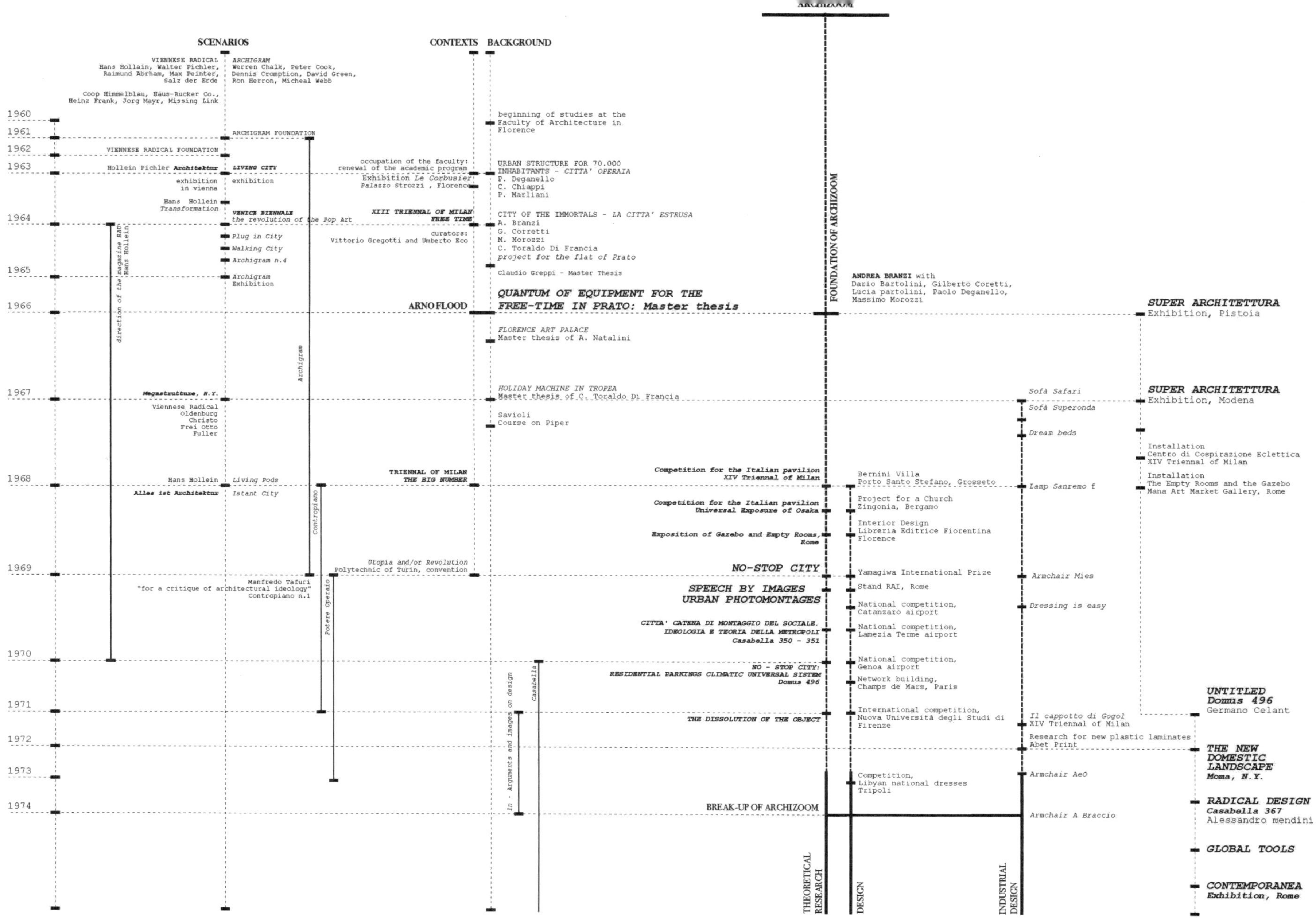
ARCHIZOOM
SCENARIOS
CONTEXTS
BACKGROUND
VIENNESE RADICAL
Hans Hollein, Walter Pichler, Raimund Abrham, Max Peinter, Salz der Erde
ARCHIGRAM
Werren Chalk, Peter Cook, Dennis Crompton, David Green, Ron Herron, Micheal Webb
Coop Himmelblau, Haus-Rucker Co., Heinz Frank, Jorg Mayr, Missing Link
1960
1961
1962
1963
1964
1965
1966
1967
1968
1969
1970
1971
1972
1973
1974
ARCHIGRAM FOUNDATION
VIENNESE RADICAL FOUNDATION
Hollein Pichler Architektur
LIVING CITY
exhibition
exhibition in vienna
Hans Hollein Transformation
VENICE BIENNALE
the revolution of the Pop Art
Plug in City
Walking City
Archigram n.4
Archigram Exhibition
direction of the magazine BAU Hans Hollein
Archigram
Megastrutture, N.Y.
Viennese Radical
Oldenburg
Christo
Frei otto
Fuller
Hans Hollein
Living Pods
Alles ist Architektur
Istant City
Contropiano
Manfredo Tafuri
"for a critique of architectural ideology"
Contropiano n.1
Potere Operaio
occupation of the faculty: renewal of the academic program
Exhibition Le Corbusier
Palazzo Strozzi , Florence
XIII TRIENNAL OF MILAN
FREE TIME
curators:
Vittorio Gregotti and Umberto Eco
ARNO FLOOD
TRIENNAL OF MILAN
THE BIG NUMBER
Utopia and/or Revolution
Polytechnic of Turin, convention
In - Arguments and images on design
Casabella
beginning of studies at the Faculty of Architecture in Florence
URBAN STRUCTURE FOR 70.000 INHABITANTS - CITTA' OPERAIA
P. Deganello
C. Chiappi
P. Marliani
CITY OF THE IMMORTALS - LA CITTA' ESTRUSA
A. Branzi
G. Corretti
M. Morozzi
C. Toraldo Di Francia
project for the flat of Prato
Claudio Greppi - Master Thesis
QUANTUM OF EQUIPMENT FOR THE FREE-TIME IN PRATO: Master thesis
FLORENCE ART PALACE
Master thesis of A. Natalini
HOLIDAY MACHINE IN TROPEA
Master thesis of C. Toraldo Di Francia
Savioli
Course on Piper
FOUNDATION OF ARCHIZOOM
ANDREA BRANZI with
Dario Bartolini, Gilberto Coretti, Lucia partolini, Paolo Deganello, Massimo Morozzi
Competition for the Italian pavilion
XIV Triennal of Milan
Competition for the Italian pavilion
Universal Exposure of Osaka
Exposition of Gazebo and Empty Rooms, Rome
NO-STOP CITY
SPEECH BY IMAGES
URBAN PHOTOMONTAGES
CITTA' CATENA DI MONTAGGIO DEL SOCIALE.
IDEOLOGIA E TEORIA DELLA METROPOLI
Casabella 350 - 351
NO - STOP CITY:
RESIDENTIAL PARKINGS CLIMATIC UNIVERSAL SISTEM
Domus 496
THE DISSOLUTION OF THE OBJECT
BREAK-UP OF ARCHIZOOM
Bernini Villa
Porto Santo Stefano, Grosseto
Project for a Church
Zingonia, Bergamo
Interior Design
Libreria Editrice Fiorentina
Florence
Yamagiwa International Prize
Stand RAI, Rome
National competition,
Catanzaro airport
National competition,
Lamezia Terme airport
National competition,
Genoa airport
Network building,
Champs de Mars, Paris
International competition,
Nuova Università degli Studi di Firenze
Competition,
Libyan national dresses
Tripoli
Sofà Safari
Sofà Superonda
Dream beds
Lamp Sanremo f
Armchair Mies
Dressing is easy
Il cappotto di Gogol
XIV Triennal of Milan
Research for new plastic laminates
Abet Print
Armchair AeO
Armchair A Braccio
THEORETICAL RESEARCH
DESIGN
INDUSTRIAL DESIGN
SUPER ARCHITETTURA
Exhibition, Pistoia
SUPER ARCHITETTURA
Exhibition, Modena
Installation
Centro di Cospirazione Eclettica
XIV Triennal of Milan
Installation
The Empty Rooms and the Gazebo
Mana Art Market Gallery, Rome
UNTITLED
Domus 496
Germano Celant
THE NEW DOMESTIC LANDSCAPE
Moma, N.Y.
RADICAL DESIGN
Casabella 367
Alessandro mendini
GLOBAL TOOLS
CONTEMPORANEA
Exhibition, Rome

Architettonicamente

Archizoom: Andrea Branzi, Gilberto Corretti, Paolo Deganello, Massimo Morozzi

On the side of architecture

by Archizoom: Andrea Branzi, Gilberto Corretti, Paolo Deganello, Massimo Morozzi

■ Although the phenomenon that we are witnessing today may be considered the natural effect of a mercantile civilization based on the mechanism of production and consumption, it reveals a truth which is both important and, in some respects, even new: the disappearance of a general law of development.

For, while in a hypothetically free market demand precedes supply, we now have the supply of a product preceding demand in both space and time, and soliciting it successfully through complex channels of « persuasion ». In such a case, we can speak of « artificially induced ideologies » — induced, that is, and not spontaneous.

Today we have a civilization which does not require the changeable products of so quick a consumption as to be instantaneous or even antecedent to production, but with the death of the scientific-entrepreneur phase a demand has grown for products as civilized and cultural values transcending the market situation.

What we are living in today is not a civilization of technology and science, but of trade and commerce.

While on the political plane any given level of power is met by a corresponding level of opposition, on the cultural plane things are much more complex: the dilemma of integration or no integration no longer exists; what exists is the dilemma of the will to change or not.

If this statement is to have any meaning, each one of us will have to start by accepting a particular title, that of « intellectual professional ». Accepting this title today means choosing one's specific rôle in the struggle now going on; it also means understanding and accepting a new range in the political struggle today: intellectual action, too, should have its own systematization, and this should start with the realization of one's own rôle and limits, so as to put them to use.

A badly interpreted tradition in planning led to the most committed forces in architecture being directed to the solution of problems in the application and modernization of technology, in the hope that a technically and functionally correct result would bear witness to a scientific and moral method of investigation which was valid in a general sense, and capable of constituting an aesthetically valid formal result in the finished product.

With the advent of mass-societies the design industry has become an industry producing formal models capable of influencing the consumer's behaviour, an industry with a structure aimed at identifying cultural and commercial results.

Our task is not to transform a particular kind of behaviour pattern into another, to modify the townscape into a homogeneous environment in which man happily recognizes a false image of himself by avoiding reality, but to accelerate that modification of that reality by rejecting the other.

It is not by commitment as an intellectual class that one can collaborate in a political struggle.

The political and revolutionary meaning of beauty today is to be found in its ability to avoid exhausting its raison d'être in use, and to constitute, within the channels of consumption, something which is not merely a vague extra which cannot be consumed. Clearly, this is not the way to a better world, but this is not a plan to act directly, but to discard the usual methods and restore the spoiled consumer's bad conscience and fright on discovering objects which cannot be consumed.

■ Il fenomeno a cui in questi anni ass
mo, anche se esso è il naturale effet
una civiltà mercantile (e non scientifica
sata sul fondamentale meccanismo del
sumare e del produrre, al fine di proc
un sempre maggiore profitto, è in grac
dimostrare una verità molto più import
e per certi aspetti nuova: la scompars
una legge di sviluppo generale.
Diremo brevemente che mentre nell'ip
di un libero mercato la domanda pre
l'offerta, oggi l'offerta del prodotto pre
nello spazio e nel tempo la domanda,
traverso complessi canali di induzione
sce a sollecitarla. Si è venuto così a s
tuire al concetto dialettico e naturali
del mercato, quello della sua completa
tificialità ». Tale constatazione non è im
tante soltanto nella sua implicazione
ceologica, ma tende ad investire alla
dice il meccanismo stesso di sviluppo
sistema socio-culturale.
Noi oggi infatti constatiamo come tal
stema, lungi dal seguire un continuu
libera concorrenza democratica, raggi
un determinato grado di maturazione
pie violenti « balzi », cioè assorbiment
o meno rivoluzionari di modelli forma
natura sociale, economica e politica,
volta a volta gli si pongono dinanzi,
matisi nella propria controforma, e che
so ingloba come momento di violento
in avanti nel processo del proprio svilu
Tali modelli o antitesi, qualora non si
nifestino spontaneamente, cioè qualora
si formino a causa di una opposizione
raia, ideologicamente e strutturalment
dicata a sviluppare opposizioni in se
al difuori del sistema, è la stessa cl
borghese al potere a generarli, al fin
accelerare processi di assestamento i
to o di unificazione al livello internazio
Questo è sempre possibile riportand
esempio il confronto rivoluzionario s
un piano generazionale, o sistemand
ideologia a copertura e individuazion
un mercato dei consumi specializzat
questo caso possiamo parlare di feno
di « ideologia artificiale », cioè indot
non spontanea.
Tralasciando per un attimo le implica
sociali, politiche, culturali, letterarie,
tiche, psicologiche..., riflesso dell'av
della civiltà dei consumi, cerchiamo c
dividuare un nocciolo più utilizzabile.
1. Anche la cultura tende ad uno svil
per salti, cioè per inglobamenti di r
nate e cresciute al di fuori di lei e
necessariamente deve, in determinati p
di storici (che corrispondono a forti
luzioni culturali) scontrare e scontare
noi guardiamo la storia del movimento
derno, possiamo capire come esso
fase della sua formazione più eroica s
trovato di fronte ad uno di questi « s
Il mondo architettonico che si pone
fronte alla generazione venuta fuori
cultura accademica dell'eclettismo ott
tesco, era costituito dalla presenza di
realtà svoltasi in maniera autonoma da
siasi cultura, già operante e presente,
ta di una propria logica e di una pr
morfologia. Essa era l'architettura
grandi fabbriche, dei silos, dei tralicci
le macchine: l'inserimento violento di
sti corpi inculturalizzati generò l'aspett
guisticamente più rivoluzionario della
tura architettonica in formazione, pe
tendo di guadagnare i termini reali d
stema nel quale bisognava agire. (« La
come macchina per abitare », gli o
trovati dei Dada.) Dopo cinquant'an
cultura, uscendo dall'impasse dell'
male, ha rivoluzionariamente adottato
flagrante incultura dei sistemi di comu
zione a lei esterni.
Cinquanta anni fa tale criterio risult

Archizoom Associati, "Architettonicamente," in *Casabella* n. 334, 1969 ito, in parte per la sopravvalutazione della capacità politica della cultura, e soprattutto per la fiducia tipica nella scienza e nella tecnologia come strumenti « naturali » di salvamento, senza considerare la loro presenza all'interno dei sistemi mercantili se non in senso accidentale.

Noi viviamo oggi, o siamo vissuti, all'interno delle grandi linee culturali e strategiche elaborate negli anni intorno al venti. Ma ciò di fronte a cui ci troviamo oggi non è più la proiezione direttamente proporzionale di ciò che avveniva sessanta anni fa. La seconda guerra mondiale non ha soltanto portato a maturazione la nascita della civiltà dei consumi: quella che era la « società » della macchina si è trasformata ed è divenuta una civiltà a cui il conflitto mondiale ha donato autocoscienza. Dire che da « società » essa si è trasformata in « civiltà » significa che essa ha superato la sua fase di significazione ideologica per divenire un sistema culturale completo e dotato di propri significati e di una propria morfologia.

Vuol dire che esiste oggi una civiltà che non richiede i labili prodotti del consumo più rapido fino a divenire istantaneo o addirittura antecedente alla produzione stessa (fatto questo che è del tutto marginale ed occasionale nella meccanica di sviluppo del sistema), ma con la morte della fase scientifico-imprenditoriale si è passati a richiedere prodotti come valori civili e culturali superiori all'occasione di mercato, prodotti metastorici ed assoluti, testimonianza di un regno escatologico.

Quella nella quale viviamo oggi non è la civiltà della tecnica e della scienza, ma dei traffici e del commercio: il turbine del consumismo e la rapidità di fagocitazione non devono trarci in inganno, perché dietro di essi vi è un « pollo di marmo » che non si mangia e non si sposta.

A questo livello del potere la risposta politica e culturale deve essere chiara: bisogna rendersi conto che oggi qualsiasi battaglia condotta per una maggiore democratizzazione, liberalizzazione e spartizione del potere tra generazioni, non riesce, neppure nelle sue forme più politicizzate e violente, a scuotere lo stato borghese, sia perché queste lotte fanno parte della sua tradizione eroica, sia perché non intaccano il meccanismo di produzione economica.

C'è una sola minaccia che ancora oggi riesce a terrorizzare la borghesia e a smascherare i suoi oppositori-parenti, ed è la immagine della dittatura. Perché questo? Perché soltanto attraverso l'abolizione del sistema parlamentare, partitico e classista essa riesce ad intravedere una immagine di società diversa dalla propria e nella quale non si riconosce. E' solo allora che la radiosa immagine di un avvenire sereno a cui tutte le forze contrastanti concorrono dialetticamente si frantuma e diviene relativa. L'immagine della dittatura oggi è un'unica che realmente lede i suoi interessi vitali e pone i problemi sul tappeto in tutta la loro dimensione deflagrante: un impero si sconfigge solo con un altro impero.

Questa affermazione, anche se ha un valore puramente terroristico, significa che a un determinato livello di potere corrisponde un livello analogo di opposizione.

Solo così il sogno borghese della scomparsa progressiva dell'Inferno, cioè della progressiva eliminazione del negativo al proprio concetto di progresso, avrà una risposta: a tanto bene tanto male. La posta in gioco è totale.

Naturalmente il discorso è più complesso. ...mo subito che il dilemma tra integrazione e non integrazione non sussiste più: sussiste tra volontà rivoluzionaria e non. ...rché tale affermazione abbia un signifi-

« Oh, voi che avete la passione delle belle arti! Abbandonatevi senza riserve a tutte le gioie che può procurare questa sublime passione. Niente è tanto puro. Sì, è questa passione che fa sorgere in noi l'amore per lo studio. Essa che trasforma le nostre pene in piaceri. Essa che, col suo fuoco divino, fa sì che il genio offra i suoi oracoli. È essa infine che vi chiama verso l'immortalità ».

(Etienne-Louis Boullee: « Architettura saggio sull'arte », edizioni Marsilio, Padova)

37

cato bisogna che ciascuno di noi parta dall'accettazione di una propria qualifica, che è quella di « intellettuali professionisti ».
Questa accettazione non significa tanto eludere una qualifica politica o un impegno sociale, ma serve semmai ad evitare troppo facili improvvisazioni o gratuite responsabilità, derivanti dal lungo complesso di colpa della classe intellettuale borghese, che quotidianamente rifiuta il proprio destino sovrastrutturale, cercando di nascondere la propria cattiva coscienza con alibi tecnologici o con la invenzione perenne di formule di non-integrazione culturale.
In realtà accettare questa qualifica oggi non ha tanto il valore di un mea-culpa, ma serve semmai ad individuare un proprio specifico ruolo all'interno di una lotta in atto, accettando uno schieramento storico di forze, senza che a questo vengano gratuitamente sostituiti ruoli strategici improvvisati e incontrollabili.
Significa inoltre capire ed accettare una dimensione nuova della lotta politica oggi: in un momento in cui l'« établissement » imperiale supera la stessa ristretta geografia partitica, nel momento in cui la dimensione del sistema all'interno del quale viviamo richiede la normalizzazione delle sue stesse opposizioni, anche l'azione intellettuale richiede una propria sistematizzazione, che parte dal prendere atto di propri ruoli e limiti, al fine di strumentalizzarli all'interno di una propria volontà e strategia di operazioni formali.
Per capire il significato di questo bisogna conoscere i legami logici ed intuitivi che l'architettura è in grado di mettere in movimento con un proprio atto di natura formale (o dimensionale), e d'uso. E cioè capire le capacità di un oggetto di p
all'interno di un ambiente preesistente
esso il territorio, la città o la casa), e
stabilire con questo un rapporto di c
tinuità o di crisi, ed il grado di tollera
con cui un oggetto esaurisce o no nell'
le ragioni della propria esistenza.
Una male interpretata tradizione prog
tuale, e più precisamente la codificazi
dell'indagine razionale della funzione,
fatto sì che gli sforzi culturali della p
gettazione più impegnata fossero dir
alla soluzione di problemi d'uso e di
giornamento tecnologico, nella tipica f
cia che un risultato tecnicamente e
zionalmente corretto testimoniasse di
metodo scientifico e morale di indag
valido in senso generale, e quindi di
se stesso in grado di educare ad un
monico sviluppo delle necessità individ

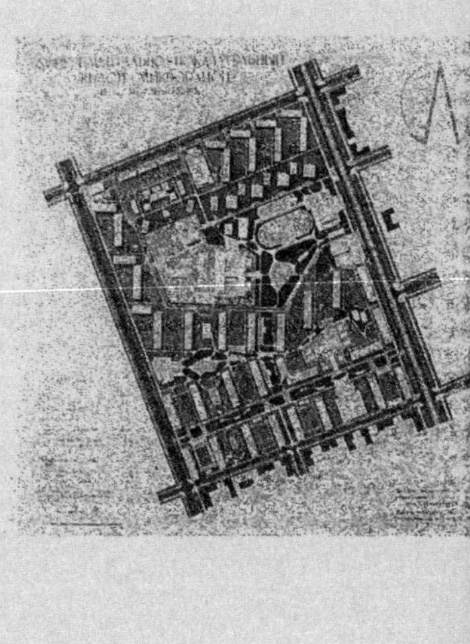

on quelle collettive, ed in grado di co-ire a prodotto finito un risultato for-a esteticamente valido. Il risultato lin-tico derivante da tale processo imper-o sul problema di metodo è stato quel-i esaurire completamente nell'atto pro-uale il valore dell'operazione, in manie-ale che, rimosse le premesse funzionali cnologiche, veniva a disgregarsi com-amente il sistema connettivo dell'og-o come prodotto fruibile esteticamente. sta adesione completa del linguaggio ccasione-oggetto entra in crisi nel mo-to in cui si introducono alcune con-razioni sulla natura sostanzialmente ttica dell'operazione culturale oggi. ttismo di cui sono motivi principali: momento di violento sviluppo del si-na che necessariamente tende a far perare una serie di esperienze avvenute in tempi e luoghi diversi, accostando disinvoltamente, su una base di latente sincretismo, fenomeni linguistici di natura e di epoche completamente eterogenee.

2) La crisi autonoma di maturazione del razionalismo che, demistificando ed accettando come convenzionale il linguaggio, ne permette il suo uso metastorico.

Questo significa che oggi è possibile riassumere la responsabilità completa del fenomeno estetico, organizzandolo all'interno di poetiche concluse in se stesse, in grado di contenere le singole occasioni entro un sistema di rappresentazione unitario, ad esse precedente e da esse estraibile, testimonianza di una posizione intellettuale precisa ed intransigente, non « accaduta » cioè, ma scelta.

Con l'avvento della civiltà di massa l'industria del design, insieme ad altre industrie, come quella della moda e della canzone ad esempio, è divenuta l'industria dei modelli formali capaci di introdurre al comportamento privato e urbano del consumatore, con una tipica struttura interna tesa ad identificare completamente il risultato culturale in quello commerciale. Si applica così su larga scala un metodo di progettazione, indagine e soluzione, che serve da modello nel quale l'utente riconosce direttamente i propri miti di intelligenza, buon gusto, bellezza, salute...

Intorno a questo supporto formale (ad una certa fenomenologia del comportamento indotta, nella tipica fiducia socialdemocratica che crede di poter ottenere attraverso la modificazione educativa di alcune abitudini di vita, di costume e di comportamento, risultati ottenibili soltanto attraverso profonde e spesso violente modificazio-

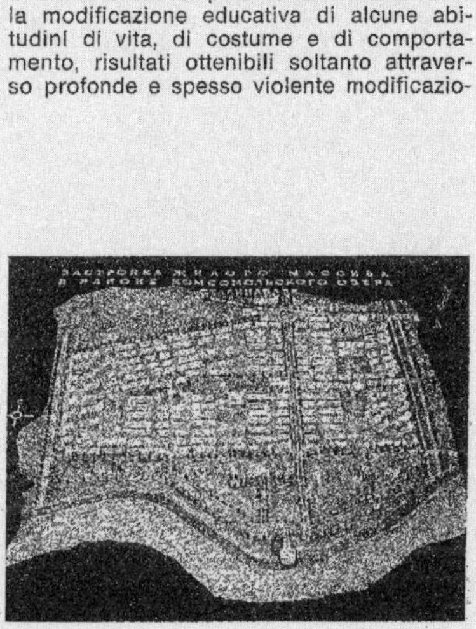

ni economiche), è abbastanza facile cedere alla tentazione di introdurre modificazioni che in qualche maniera rispecchino problemi sociologici, ottenendo però come unico risultato quello di sostituire polemicamente un comportamento ad un altro, un modo di vita troppo arido e chiuso con un altro nel quale vi sia più disinvoltura, più amore, più musica, più gioia, più vita. La casa diviene allora un limbo lontano dal frastuono del mondo, porto fidato nel quale trovare sempre una giustificazione ed una conferma della propria salvezza in uno stile inappuntabile di vita.

La città diviene un teatro armonico nel quale tutte le componenti confluiscono fino a raggiungere un equilibrio perfetto, al quale l'architettura dona quell'unità formale e funzionale inesistente sul piano politico.

In questa vocazione alla armonizzazione del rapporto tra individuo e collettività attraverso successive osmosi prive di scosse e contraccolpi, riconosciamo una caratteristica costante della cultura attuale. Dalla rivoluzione industriale in poi, da quando cioè una certa realtà sociale ed economica ha cominciato a realizzarsi e ad agire, la cultura ha sempre più perduto il suo controllo sui fenomeni in atto ed ha cominciato a subirli come clima nel quale muoversi. Essa ha cioè progressivamente caratterizzato il proprio ruolo sovrastrutturale al contatto di un meccanismo economico lanciato a pieno ritmo, cominciando ad operare sulla sistemazione del negativo di questo, cioè sulla sua fruizione più o meno consapevole e sul comportamento individuale, prima attraverso il romanticismo, poi attraverso la psicoanalisi, riuscendo a fornire alla borghesia il svolto utilizzabile di una situazione sto profondamente diversa. Questo tipo di voro, sull'impronta che il sistema lasc nella società, ha costituito la caratter ca critica registrativa e non creativa, cologica e non spirituale, della cul moderna: la letteratura dell'angoscia, l'a biografismo, la psicoanalisi, la sociolo l'estetica applicata.

Anche nella concezione architettonica venivano fenomeni analoghi, di cui il facilmente registrabile sul piano del co ne linguaggio critico fu l'apparizione « concetto di spazio », arrivando alla terializzazione di un dato che non es o se esiste è solo un elemento della zione del fatto architettonico, molto complesso e dotato di leggi composi non fruibili spazialmente.

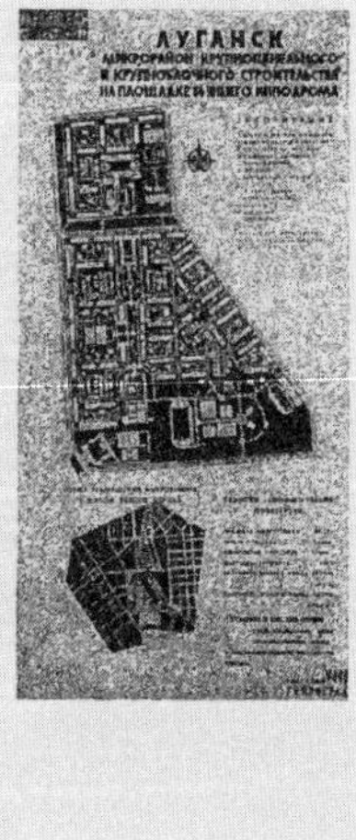

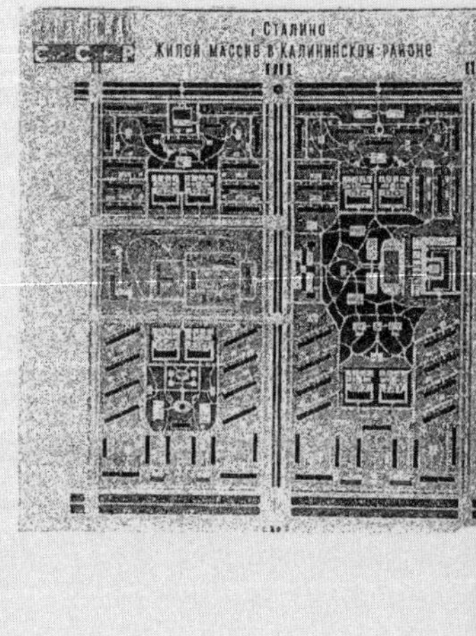

40

Si è portato così in primo piano l'effetto riflesso di quella che è la sostanziale natura formale dell'atto architettonico, cioè fisica, sistematizzando criticamente solo il campo della sua percezione e togliendo soprattutto all'intervento, come atto creativo-costruttivo, un valore in se stesso.
Si è così indagato il significato dell'atto estetico come atto allegorico, fino quasi a misurarne scientificamente la risonanza, ma tralasciando il significato politico-sociale dell'atto estetico in se stesso, non tanto come testimonianza esistenziale, ma come presenza-miracolo, cioè abnorme, all'interno dei circuiti logici esistenti.
Non a caso infatti siamo stati abituati ad indagare il miracolo come fatto simbolico, metaforico, mentre esso in realtà non ha nessun significato se non nella propria a-normalità, cioè se non come testimonianza di una volontà in grado di interrompere, secondo un criterio particolare (e non generale), il corso regolare di una determinata realtà.
Non è attraverso l'impegno come classe intellettuale che possiamo collaborare ad una lotta politica, ma è accettando un ruolo al livello individuale che possiamo evitare di coinvolgervi la classe borghese illuminata attraverso la sistemazione metodologica e la normalizzazione degli interventi.
Nostro compito non è quello della trasformazione di un determinato comportamento civile in un altro, della modificazione del paesaggio urbano in un ambiente omogeneo nel quale l'uomo riconosca felice una sua falsa immagine evitando la potenzialità deflagrante della realtà, ma semmai quello di accelerarla con il proprio rifiuto, con la violenza di una presenza assolutamente estranea che restituisca al cento per cento i dati della committenza e sposti la propria azione su un piano eversivo.
Il significato politico, rivoluzionario della bellezza oggi consiste proprio nella sua capacità di non esaurire in rapporti fruibili la propria ragione d'essere, ma di costituire all'interno dei canali di consumo qualcosa che non sia un ambiguo sovrappiù che non si riesce a consumare.
E' chiaro che non è attraverso questi attimiracolo che otterremo un mondo migliore; essi infatti non sono destinati ad agire direttamente, ma ad « interrompere », a denotare nelle cose una volontà che le prevarica, a ribaltare le consuete misure, restituendo al viziato consumatore la cattiva coscienza e lo spavento di oggetti che non si consumano.

Archizoom

Radical Architecture
Andrea Branzi, 1974

//

"The ultimate end of modern architecture is the elimination of architecture itself." _Archizoom Associati

We can ask ourselves (and in fact we ask all the time), what are the real prospects, or at least the political ones, of the experiments of avant-garde architecture? I think the answer can only be given if we broaden the question. And so: what are the real prospects, or at least the political ones, of traditional architecture? This question does not, at present, have a credible answer, and if anything, there is an indirect response to the role of experimentation.

Few people, and very few architects, still have the knowledge of how abstract and convoluted architecture is. By architecture, I mean all the formal, structural, functional, and design tools that actually constitute the final act of the profession of the architect, the urban planner, and the designer.

As long as that job was shifted to the technical and political specifications that are upstream of design, it managed to retrieve a new space and an original role, but when it reenters within the realm of institutional tools, in order to coherently complete its role, it experiences a contradiction generated not so much by the transition between different skills, but by the real backwardness of architecture itself. Just think of all the urban models in recent years everywhere in the world: Chandigarh, Brasilia, the New English Towns, the Unitè d'Abitation, the Swedish neighborhoods, the rationalist neighborhoods.

There is no model, urban shape, or prototypical district that has not failed or is not on the road to failure. The stock of models available today for a city planner has thinned or already disappeared. The punctual failure of all possible operative models begins to suggest the historical impossibility of finding new ones, functional even in the future. Now, planning is done through laws and perhaps before long will be done via machine guns. Among other things, the difficulties encountered in Italy for any kind of urban policy, and the battle that ensues, generate a further political-cultural misunderstanding.

The crisis of all urban models has complex origins, which are the objective limits of all architectural tools and the crisis of the relationship between architecture and society.

There is always, at the origin of the disaster of modern urban planning, a crisis between the quantitative judging criteria that shape the pre-urban project (number

of inhabitants, community services, types, connections, urban standards, etc. and the qualitative tool that presides over construction (architecture). If this last qualitative tool fails, as in general it fails, there is nothing correct on the sociological level about the planning assumption that enables us to say it is successful. The architectural quality is still tacit in any urban form, but it is not yet part of the scientific criteria already widely available for urban planning.
In fact, planning is accomplished through a proper territorial policy, but it must in fact leave itself, in its terminal phase, for instruments that are not political. So on one hand, we are witnessing a discipline that works toward the identification of a territorial structure and then introduces an improper system for the used method, asking architecture for a visual verification of the civic value of its operations.
On the other hand, we see an architecture that, using traditional and competitive instruments, seeks to return (allegorically), through the correct structural ratio, the final step of a political process to the citizen. Not only that, but in fact it is trying to make these "qualities" unitary, attributing to architecture a social value and to the political an aesthetic value (!).

In fact, within bourgeois ideology the city is the supreme body where there is the general mediation between private interests and interests of the community. That being the case, the urban plan becomes the instrument of mediation between culture and technology, engineering and nature, man and society, all within a functional and rigid system with its own scientific foundation not detached from a certain linguistic grace, inside a conscious civil testimony.

This balance has never existed, and even if for one day only it was realized in satire, that day has been gone for centuries.

In reality, urban planning and modern architecture act on a plane of total utopia: which is a permanent fact in the nature of design, but now limits its application, because it is an unconscious and non-strategic utopia.

The result of such a disciplinary crisis is seen in most cases as simple professional revenge against uncontrolled speculation or against the ignorance of politicians; just look at the projects presented in architectural or planning competitions to see how the solution is sought by the reduction in size of the design. The model replaces all verification processes: macro-regional ornaments, technological allegories, quotations from everyday objects... The model, as the most synthetic tool for communicating the project, has become the project; in its absurd perfection it placates neuroses and exorcises certain failure. The plastic effect that it represents will be perceptible in reality only if viewed from 1,000 meters above: the trend of roofs, being the main dimension in the model, has taken the role that at one time was that of the façade... In fact, architecture did not renew its tools of representation: it is still tied to the simulation and the miniaturization of reality, which affects only the virtual relationship with the design parameters.

These limits means that architecture tends to renew itself only linguistically: many avant-garde groups have also made this mistake (Archigram, Metabolism), accepting the tautology that architecture of a technological civilization must be technological, or that the architecture of an organic society must be organic.

We see the old allegorical relationship between architecture and society continuing, for which the city, before being a facility of use, is a great system of the figurative representation of the society.

The difficulty of overcoming its figurative limitations is the major handicap of all modern architecture.

The search for an alternative culture, a different relationship between man and the city, pushed the Modern Movement toward all forms of social struggle for possession or for political use of the city. It is thought that the set of proletarian social and urban claims constituted in fact the premise for the development of a new model of the city.

This error had already been pointed out by Engels in the *Question of housing*, where he clarified that for the working class it is not the problem of a different city; there is, if anything, the problem of ownership of the current city. Which means that there is no urban theory of class, but a criticism by the class of urban theory; and more generally, we say that the city is the scene of a political struggle, but this struggle does not generate an alternative model of the city, but rather its functional failure (barricades). There is no working-class metropolis.

This observation concerns the whole problem with the production of culture. The set of social and workerist demands does not constitute a working-class culture: they occur in terms of quantity and not of content. The cultural tools used by the working class are not original instruments; originality, if anything, is the final result. The revolutionary innovation is not in content but in usage. The worker uses, within his economic escalation, some bourgeois cultural models as goals of wealth; he does not plan new goals for his life that are not those that can quickly be seen in immediate reality.

The operation of imitation that he undertakes, however, determines in fact the destruction of all bourgeois models he proposes, because in reaching them he destroys all economic and social equilibrium on which the models are based.

Conscious of its own limitations to find working models of urbanization, urban planning in some cases has placed itself at the full disposal of sociology: it renounced the project alone in order to become the formal instrument of a larger sociological project. This is the case of the British New Towns. The result was that the urban tool, just by the fact of its existence, determined a new social reality, different from the one analyzed by sociological tools, with a new form of an "urban" crisis in social groups as a result, a crisis that can no longer be remedied if not precisely with "urban" instruments. At the end of this cycle, town planning found its autonomy, but already in terms of an unsolvable problem.

The speed of cultural consumption, the entropy of all urban models, actually creates a permanent crisis between architecture and society. By analyzing a particular social situation, we see that architecture tends to strike a balance between the immediate reality of this situation and the aspirations or directions of the development of this reality. The result is a compromise between present and future: but the very fact of formalizing this balance actually shifts it and creates new objectives, thus forming the basis for the crisis of the architectural solution proposed. The crisis in the relationship between architecture and society lies also in this factor: the impossibility today of finding a "permanent" social condition that is not immediately questioned due to the fact of it having been reached.

The Modern Movement stands to operate under different conditions: the social reality allowed it to design typologies that could assume the status of "permanent," since economic growth was not only controlled, but directed toward development models that then seemed sufficiently clear. The Existenzminimum was in this sense the utopia of a connection between the conditions of the working class and rational society, between development and natural limits. The myth collapsed, revealing that the condition of the workers was not a constitutive cultural parameter but a necessarily provisional social state.

For its part, the middle class is no longer able to offer a single model for the city, due to both its political and its cultural impossibility.

The crushing of its cultural structure, attacked by the escalation of the economically "uncultivated" classes and the cruel breeze of rationalism (the assembly line became the only way to understand reality), push it to a renunciation of any unified program.

Even Programming, the dream of one last beach on which finally to lie out, can only be the installation of a social world devoid of destiny, a bricolage of a thousand different utopias, as so many social functions are.

Thus, we see the rejection of all possible urban models towards a sort of primary archetype: the "dream of a village" of small and balanced communities in a valley, like the dream of a lost childhood (that we never had). The granite benches on Park Avenue... the flowerpots of Rockefeller Center...the electronic fountains in a square ...They put together so many little episodes, shattering the urban experiment into smaller dimensions, on details of scale, trying to simulate therein the existence of equilibria that are still ongoing. Because of this, we are not able to overcome the architectural limits of the metropolis; we are forced to create a network of minimum references through which an exercise of judgment is still permitted, even if only visually.

Architecture does not have the courage to jump into "non-quality," toward the suspension of its old systems of control by now dried up and without function. It remains locked in its concept of space, of limits and of judgment, within a mega-urban and social reality that burn, make dirty, waste, use up, but finally get free of all formal structures, until they become neutral tools of life.

Planning and traditional architecture act on a plane of absolute utopia. Unconsciously, through their own presence, they continue to repropose to the world an architectural order and values of a formal culture beyond simple housing functions. It is a terminal utopia, unconscious, but one that actually gives rise to a crisis within the social relations of architecture itself.

Radical Architecture reverses the process: it takes utopia as the initial data of the work, and develops it realistically. Once the process has concluded, nothing is excluded, everything is enacted, as an act perfectly realized in itself, as pure creative energy transformed, without losing anything, into constructive energy. Utopia is not the end but within the real. There is no moral motivation, but only a pure process of an immediate release. There is not allegory but a natural phenomenon...

It is in this act that the architecture of the avant-garde movements can recover its own absolute realism: it accepts the conditions of a discontinuous reality without speculating about a different one, it moves on the plane of a mediocre reality, rejecting a glorious destiny.

Its actions are always one-to-one and do not refer to further realization processes. It discovered "architectural practice," which does not mean only building houses, or in general building definitive things, but it means expressing itself, communicating, inventing through tools and architectural conditions: how to make love is not just about having children, but about how to communicate through sex.

The separation between creative activities within the discipline of architecture – and the traditional buildable activities of the same – allows us to explore the primary motivations that are upstream of architecture, even before it identifies itself with its building systems and compositional languages. It allows for the detection of elemental relationships between the human being and the physical environment, relationships that until today were mediated exclusively through architecture, understood both as a physical structure and as a designed cultural structure.

It is in this passage that the experience of the avant-garde sets in motion deadly phenomena and strategies for a very long time. In fact, it works toward "a new social use of culture," which is the total recovery on the part of the society of all the creative individual faculties, as a natural right and not as a coded message.

The avant-garde works toward the destruction of technical culture, delivering it into the hands of a society as free psychomotor activity, already totally deconstructed from a technical standpoint and fully adhering to reality.

Any culture is repressive because the repressive in itself is the social distinction on which it is based: a functional separation between producers and consumers of culture. If men are all equal, as they are, there exists only an improper distinction between artist and user, favored by the current division of labor.

The mechanism of the production of culture in fact ends with a user who receives, through the circulation of choices not his own, the simulation of a use of his own totally atrophied creative faculties. This atrophy is a social alienation, which prevents producing and consuming its own creative activity as a phenomenon of spontaneous communication.

"Artistic (and architectural) practice," as activities aimed to engage and to affirm the materiality of the course and the electricity of nervous systems, already possesses a completed sense within itself, as a kind of psychophysical therapy of liberation, without shifted meanings.

Art is no longer reality, but it totally coincides with it. Today, to do music, poetry, painting, dance, architecture, or any other physical activity, you need the technical knowledge of the different disciplines. The avant-garde destroyed these techniques: as the institutional counterpart of the intellectual class, the readers, the subscribers, the visitors, the consumers, the fans, the observers, and the voyeurs, become authors.

All the possible techniques of culture's liberation act as negative signs that cause a reduction in the distance between the operator and his or her own actions, between meaning and physical dimension, between game and masterpiece, stopping the continuous critical removal that morality makes of our acts.

The term "Radical Architecture" indicates more than a unified movement, a "cultural site," an energetic trend.

Among the many components of this movement, there has always been this effort to work on the identification of this "place," that is, the awareness of destiny and strategy of radical architecture.

....

You will understand at least the existence of an area of thought remaining outside of that great reactionary design that travels across the political management of ecology, a mechanism of blackmail and conservative international orthodoxy, run by ambiguous civic committees committed to teaching everyone how to live.

In effect, the cultural pollution that ecology is effecting among the young is ruining a large part of a generation that, born into the youth movements, finds itself today sending letters to provincial newspapers about pruning trees on an avenue, or to support the electoral campaign of some savior of sacred soil.

It will help to understand the existence of an era of thought remaining outside the other major reactionary operation that passes through the disciplinary re-foundation of Italian architecture, from neo-monumentalism to neo-Enlightenment and in general to all the operations which revived the historical quality of architecture as a revolutionary value.

The current crisis of culture, its segmentation, its impossibility in achieving universal and lasting values, the futility of its messages, the absence of a credible role, is in fact simulated by monumentalists who propose a totally artificial system of values, almost like a cultural prosthesis or an orthopedic culture, which if it isn't real is still useful to simulate a real culture. This simulation is neither suicide nor ironic: it is only reactionary because it does not accept the death of culture as a positive phenomenon, able to give man an extra freedom, but considers the death of culture as a shot in the dark, and it is afraid.

What initially held together different groups of the Italian avant-garde was the refusal of the teaching of a Social Democratic ideology, of reformism, of intimate mediocrity, which already in 1963-64 drove us toward a radical position in architecture, towards a political and cultural utopia as the first instance of a global commitment. It was the first negative push to ensure that the vast majority of this group was born in the faculty of Florence, where a mediocre and paternalistic pedagogy was accompanied, minus a few exceptions, by one of the most fearful and moralistic professional frameworks.

Today the term "Radical Architecture" brings together internationally all the eccentric experiments with respect to a straight professional line: controdesign, conceptual architecture, poor technology, eclecticism, iconoclasty, neo-dadaism, nomadism... What holds together all these phenomena today is no longer the battlefront against opponents who have already lost a lot of credibility, but the autonomous maturation of a movement and the acquisition of a directional identity.

This direction is constituted from the corrosive work "inside" the structures of architecture, inside the specifics of architecture: when the groups' experiments emerge from these conditions, they lose any chance of becoming gallery art.

The acceptance of a "disciplinary elite" has always been an important choice of the historical avant-garde, a choice which acted as a sign of the reducer of technological and professional structures. Kandinsky when he discovered that painting did not consist of representation but of creative energy, John Cage when he realized that music was just noise, they never ceased to declare themselves painters or musicians, because only in this way could they act in places, in conditions, in traditional communication systems in order to upset them. The damage they did to so-called painting or to so-called music was perhaps irreparable: perhaps even void, if they had not deduced from their discoveries a reason for "non-action," for an exit from the stage or for an ironic silence.

One of the accusations that we hear most often directed toward the avant-garde cultural groups is their isolation as élite.

We say that avant-garde culture today no longer seeks, as in the postwar years, the development of a model of values to propose to society (concerts for metal-workers), but aims on the contrary to not set any model to imitate, stating that the sole point of reference for society is the liberation of the creative faculties of the whole entire society in itself. Hence, the effort is no longer to match culture to a set of technical standards or languages (solely through which you can today reach the universal value of the aesthetic message), but trying to match culture with the very nature of man and with the spontaneous systems of communication. It is in this effort and in this framework that the experiences of the avant-garde can also be defined as hermetic, but in the sense that they work on the structures of culture and on its products; the contradiction is not between the liberating end and the elite circuit, but between a new experiment and a codified reality.

The new experiment is the condition of an alternative use of culture. The contradiction that architecture understood as a possible instrument without communication and self-definition, and the common concept of architecture as a formal framework of the history.

Let's say as Flaubert did: "Architecture is me."

Andrea Branzi, "Africa is Nearby. The Role of the Avant-garde," in *Casabella* n. 362, 1972

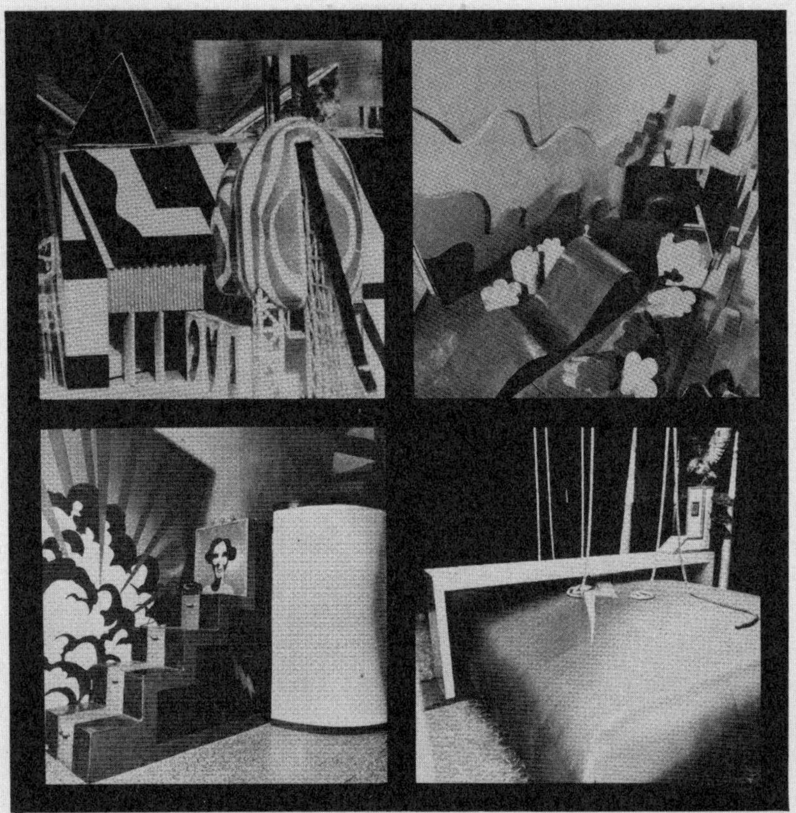

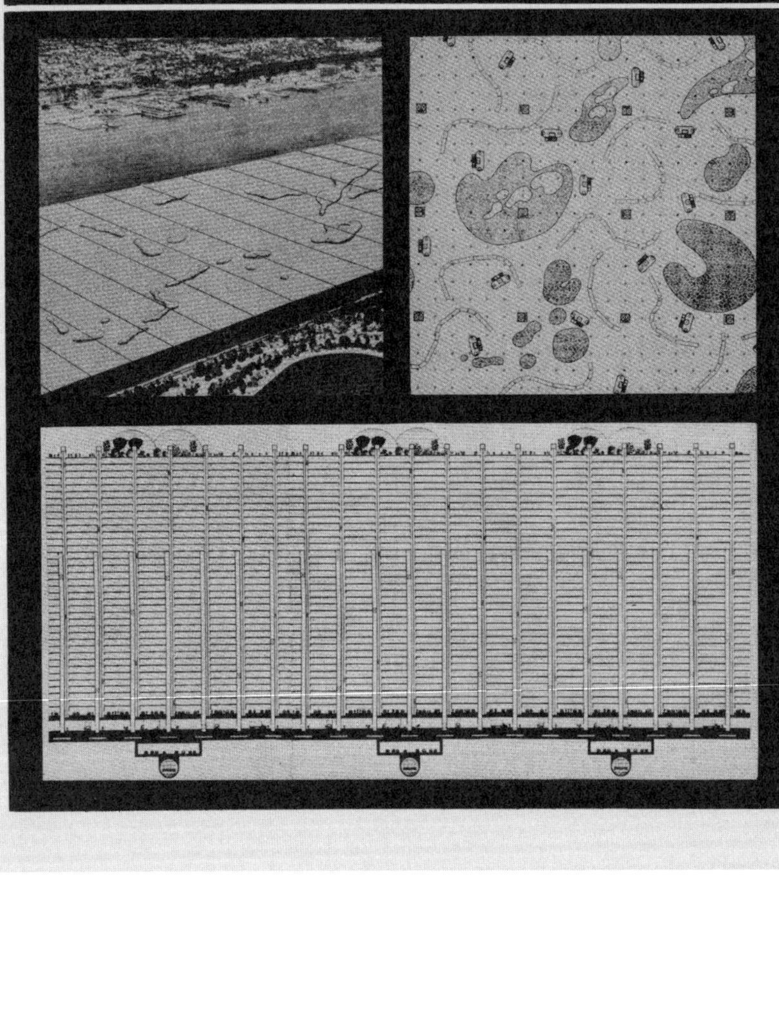

Nella città borghese, viene ricercata la non impossibile armonia tra l'uomo e la società e tra la società e la natura.
Secondo l'ideologia borghese questi due equilibri si devono verificare simultaneamente.
Nel piano urbanistico si incastrano componenti contraddittorie, accettate come tali, ma mescolate tra di loro fino a raggiungere una "successione armonica" che simula l'unità culturale: Pubblico, Privato, Costruzioni, Natura, ecc.
L'uomo, diventato "cittadino", gode di un equilibrio formalmente realizzato nel quale si nobilita la sua integrazione " naturale" con la società.
La città gli appare sempre come una realtà molto più complessa e molto più spirituale dell'uso che egli quotidianamente può farne: la città diventa un diaframma ideologico tra lui e le strutture gerarchiche della società.
La metropoli, nella sua articolazione di eventi urbani come momenti scenici diversi, mantiene con il proprio utente un rapporto visuale.
Tale genere di rapporto visuale costituisce per l'individuo la struttura fondamentale che organizza la sua esperienza e la sua memoria urbana. Lo strato di città che egli utilizza arriva fino alla quota di due metri da terra: come dice Kevin Lynch, egli costruisce dei tunnel-memoriali, strettamente privati, che gli permettono di organizzare un proprio sistema di immagini, che vanno dalle insegne luminose a singoli elementi di arredo urbano. La città come unità di immagine e di cultura non è più verificabile nella prassi.
L'architettura non è più uno strumento di rappresentazione del sistema, perché il sistema non ha più un'immagine fruibile.
Lo sforzo di far coincidere la logica "machiniste" della civiltà industriale con una architettura "machiniste" è un equivoco storico, generato da un semplice aggiornamento linguistico.
La logica della singola fabbrica infatti, o della singola macchina, non è rapportabile, come una parte al tutto, alla realtà della Programmazione: la legge del montaggio permette di assemblare parti diverse di un oggetto o di un edificio, ma l'ideologia della Programmazione permettere di assemblare le parti diverse della intera società, rendendola omogenea nella produzione.
La metropoli attuale, come concentrazione intensiva, trae origine nella distinzione del territorio in città e in campagna.
Il Capitalismo, nato nelle città, si identifica inizialmente nell'organizzazione urbana del suolo, ma attraverso la Programmazione estende il proprio raziocinante dominio su tutto il territorio, organizzandolo produttivamente.
La "condizione urbana", l'esser cittadino, non significa essere integrato più di un noncittadino, dal momento che non esiste zona territoriale non organizzata nel sistema. La metropoli cessa di essere allora un "luogo" per diventare una "condizione": è tale condizione che viene fatta circolare in maniera omogenea nel territorio e nella società attraverso i Consumi.
La città cioè coincide con la dimensione del mercato e non più con quella di un luogo determinato.

L'avanguardia d'architettura non si propone più di progettare una città "migliore" da contrapporre a quella attuale.
Essa compie un'altra operazione; contesta l'ideologia della metropoli borghese, denunciandone il ruolo mistificante, e rifonda l'urbanistica intesa come struttura disponibile ad un uso diverso, e non come strumento di figurazione sociale e di induzione di valori.
Del resto, come diceva Engels, da parte operaia il problema di una città diversa non si pone; si pone semmai quello di impossessarsi della città che già esiste.

Accostiamo il lavoro di diversi gruppi di avanguardia, gli Archigram, il Superstudio e gli Archizoom Associati, per verificarli sulla base di premesse generali e per constatare polemicamente le differenze.
Charles Jencks pubblicando recentemente su « Architectural Design » una serie di articoli sui gruppi italiani, li ha definiti: "The Supersensualists": una banda di febbricitanti filosofi impegnati a trovare relazioni tra « l'amore sensoriale, l'angoscia metafisica, la bellezza, la tecnologia avanzata e (forse) il Marxismo ».
Immersi in un cristianesimo socio-miracolistico oscillante tra Fellini e Pasolini, dice Jencks, sono capaci di « spingere un'idea bizzarra, o un paradosso, alle sue estreme conseguenze ».
« E' una totale inversione della scienza che noi siamo abituati a comprendere... Dove molta gente è abituata ad accettare la morte come una necessità razionale per l'evoluzione, l'amore come funzionalmente giustificato per la sopravvivenza della specie, e la guerra come il mezzo di trasformazione sociale, i Supersensualists prendono tutte queste forze cosmiche e invertono le loro basi unitarie e il loro significato. »
« Per un paese che ha appena sperimentato il miracolo economico ed è parzialmente saltato dall'economia paesana ad un avanzato stato di industrializzazione, ogni fatto di vita deve probabilmente essere considerato fantastico e miracoloso. »
Insomma, l'Africa è vicina.
Nel 1966, in occasione di una mostra a Pistoia, Archizoom e Superstudio definiscono la "Superarchitettura": « La superarchitettura è l'architettura della superproduzione, del superconsumo, della superinduzione al superconsumo, del supermarket, del superman e della benzina super. »
All'ondata di culturizzazione consumistica viene risposto con il terrorismo dogmatico: « Il turbine del consumismo e la rapidità di fagocitazione del Grande Numero non devono trarci in inganno, perché dietro di essi vi è un "Pollo di Marmo" che non si mangia e non si sposta » (Archizoom, 1968).
Tra il '67 e il '68 l'Archizoom Associati sviluppa una propria originale linea di accostamento a temi orientali: risponde al pacifismo indù con la guerra santa musulmana (Malcolm X) e gioca sulla contaminazione di culture diverse per ottenere effetti acidi (l'Afro-Tirolese del Centro di cospirazione eclettica alla Triennale di Milano).
Viene teorizzata l'accettazione strategica del proprio ruolo di intellettuali borghesi impegnati a produrre cultura (« una cultura dura e clandestina... inutile a tutti se non a coloro che rispecchiandovisi vi si riconoscono, una

cultura cioè da tenere nascosta nei soppalchi e nelle cantine come le armi o la farina buona per il Giorno della Grande Festa », Archizoom, 1968), ma respinge anche l'impegno umanitario in nome di un rigido stalinismo-ironico, e nello stesso anno al Convegno di Rimini l'Archizoom fa passare una mozione in cui si auspica la censura: « Visto l'andamento dei lavori del convegno... auspicano che nel futuro la classe operaia possa più attentamente vigilare con opportuni strumenti di censura e di controllo su quanto gli intellettuali, o contestatori, privatamente o in concesso dicono, fanno, propongono; decidono di rifiutare qualsiasi impegno sociale lo stato borghese riconosca loro, qualsiasi organizzazione metodologica e didattica del dissenso, di mantenersi calmi per non ingenerare ulteriore panico nelle classi lavoratrici, di ritirarsi nell'esercizio più stretto e rigoroso della propria professione nell'attesa fiduciosa che venga altrove e nei modi opportuni deciso il loro destino di borghesi ». (Approvato a maggioranza).

Fino a tutto il 1969 la strategia di non essere mai dove li cercano e di non accettare mai una definizione, garantisce agli Archizoom Associati un proprio spazio di manovra e una propria autonomia di sperimentazione.

Dal 1970 a oggi però la loro ricerca sulla città si precisa con una direzione e con una metodologia specifica.

Per gli Archizoom Associati i luoghi campione della città futura, cioè i luoghi dove il sistema ha realizzato compiutamente la propria ideologia della Programmazione, sono la Fabbrica e il Supermarket: i Consumi e la Produzione ipotizzano infatti una realtà sociale e fisica assolutamente continua e indifferenziata, e la Fabbrica e il Supermarket sono le strutture urbane ottimali, potenzialmente infinite, dove le funzioni produttive o le informazioni merceologiche si organizzano liberamente su di un piano continuo, reso omogeneo da un sistema di illuminazione e areazione artificiale senza interruzioni o interferenze. L'immagine esteriore di questi organismi non costituisce la struttura linguistica dell'organismo ma è semplicemente una superficie di contatto tra due situazioni a diverso grado di organizzazione. Se noi applichiamo il livello tecnologico e l'organizzazione funzionale, già raggiunti e utilizzati in questi settori della città, anche alle abitazioni, vediamo, dicono gli Archizoom, che si verifica una trasformazione totale della città. Infatti oggi la metropoli è basata sul rispetto di alcuni standards di illuminazione e areazione naturali: ogni corpo di fabbrica non può superare una determinata profondità per permettere l'infiltrazione al suo interno dell'aria e della luce. Questo fatto determina una continua "formazione" di blocchi architettonici, pieni di corti interne, di strade ecc. Introducendo la luce e l'areazione artificiale su scala urbana, vediamo che non è più necessario procedere al continuo spezzettamento immobiliare tipico della morfologia urbana: la città diviene una struttura residenziale continua, priva di vuoti e anche di immagini architettoniche.

La città, come manufatto artificiale, e la natura non scorrono più allora su di un unico piano: quello che ne risulta infatti è un

nuovo genere di rapporto tra di loro. Nella città borghese la natura simula al cittadino la perfetta armonizzazione del sistema con le leggi naturali, ed è utilizzata come strumento consolatorio.
Nella "No-Stop City" la natura non è più uno strumento di figurazione della città, non è più un episodio urbano, ma recupera una propria totale autonomia.
L'individuo non la riceve più contaminata da elementi architettonici che tendono a attribuire a questa un significato culturale: la natura rimane un campo neutro, privo di valori, disponibile ad una conoscenza tutta fisica e non mediata.
I grandi piani micro-climatizzati permettono di superare i limiti della attuale tipologia residenziale, e del concetto corrente di architettura.
« Cercando di fornire il maggior numero possibile di gradi di libertà all'utente, all'interno di una figurazione la più rigida possibile, l'architettura (attuale) si trova a riconoscere nel fenomeno urbano il suo vero destino, e nel privato la sua vera natura.
Così in maniera contraddittoria essa prefigura in ogni singola occasione un ordine generale delle cose, e contemporaneamente si pone a difesa della parzialità dell'esperienza individuale nei riguardi delle esperienze collettive. Essa media così in maniera figurale la contraddizione tra pubblico e privato. » (Archizoom, « No-Stop City », marzo 1971)
I limiti di questo ruolo non si riscattano, per l'Archizoom, attraverso operazioni di progettazione, ma attraverso una modificazione dell'uso stesso dell'architettura, intesa come struttura neutra, disponibile ad un uso indifferenziato, non strumento di organizzazione della società, ma libera area attrezzata in cui sia possibile compiere operazioni spontanee di sperimentazione di habitat individuali o collettivi.

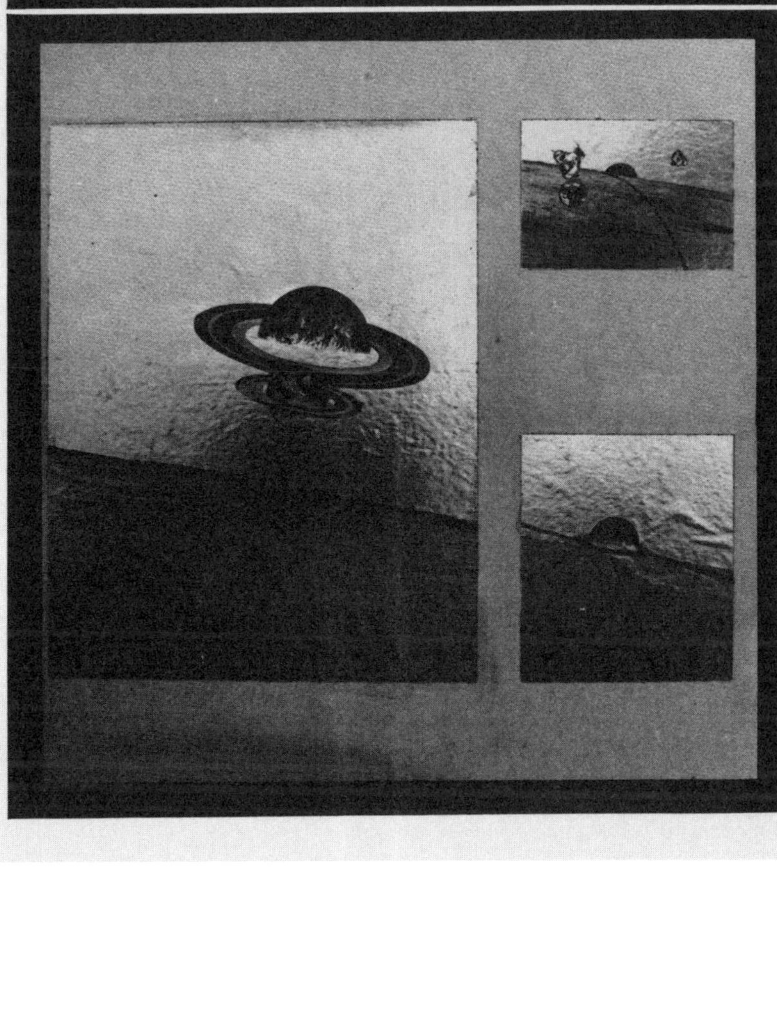

Il Superstudio porta avanti un proprio concetto del ruolo dell'architettura moderna. Essa non è, per il Superstudio, uno strumento tecnico che permette di progettare architetture libere da significati culturali, ma al contrario l'architettura del cosiddetto "razionalismo esaltato" (come direbbe Aldo Rossi), proprio perché dotata di fondazioni logiche autonome è lo strumento supremo di culturizzazione dell'intero universo. Nel 1969 il Superstudio mette a punto un manifesto programmatico sul significato della propria architettura, ipotizzando una struttura monumentale continua, una sorta di acquedotto romano, che attraversa tutto il pianeta: « Il Monumento Continuo è il polo estremo di una serie di operazioni progettuali incentrate sull'idea del "disegno unico", un disegno che si trasporta da un'area all'altra rimanendo immutato: un'immagine impassibile e inalterabile la cui statica perfezione muove il mondo attraverso l'amore che fa nascere per sé.
Attraverso una serie di operazioni mentali si può prender possesso della realtà e raggiungere la serenità: così l'architettura è comprensione del mondo e autocoscienza ».
Il fatto stesso di progettare, è ciò che interessa il Superstudio: l'atto progettuale è per loro un'operazione demiurgica, miracolistica e insieme capace di dare un ordine al mondo. Infatti il monumento di cui parlano è sempre un corpo estraneo alla real-

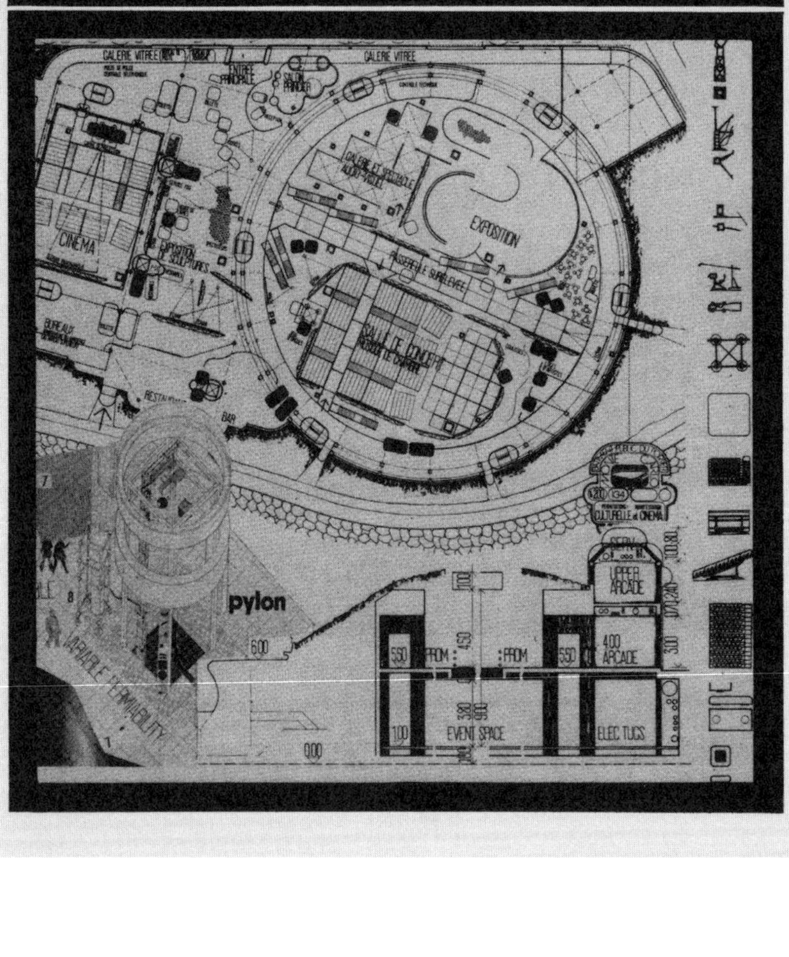

tà circostante, in quanto dotato di una logica autonoma, la quale però non agisce (come i Dream-Beds dell'Archizoom) come un cavallo di Troia in grado di sciogliere i circuiti logici della realtà circostante liberandola, ma al contrario agisce come induttore di valori e significati d'ordine sul caos della natura circostante.
La lettura che il Superstudio fa del mondo attuale è una lettura feticista e non strutturale: e dichiarano infatti: « L'autostrada è il parametro dimensionale, è il primo monumento continuo », e poi ancora: « La Kaaba e il Vertical Assembly Building sono due uguali cubiche pietre nere, ugualmente monumentali ».
L'architettura è per il Superstudio dunque una sorta di presenza metastorica sulla quale si depositano le diverse citazioni linguistiche: la levigatezza del Monumento Continuo non è che il piano neutro sul quale essi compiono le proprie operazioni di revivals, dallo stile italiano degli anni trenta a quello della secessione viennese (progetto per Modena, 1970).
In « Premonizioni della parusia urbanistica o Visioni di dodici città ideali » il Superstudio compie una lettura critica della città borghese, spingendo alle estreme conseguenze le diverse componenti di questa. Significativo è il linguaggio usato nelle descrizioni delle città, a cavallo tra la fantascienza e il Vangelo: significativo cioè del rapporto statico che essi hanno con la cultura e con la storia, per cui il futuro si realizza ma solo nella misura in cui somiglia al passato.
Il falso letterario, cioè il sogno, diventa il loro strumento di indagine.
Ma la fantasia non li conduce mai ad immaginare azioni dinamiche, e la soluzione che essi ci prospettano per liberarci dagli incubi urbani, è almeno idealistica: « Dall'orrore di ciascuno di noi e da ciò che ci circonda può nascere la "rivelazione". Salite allora al Vecchio della Montagna... e scendete quando sarete rinati... e potrete preparare le fondamenta della Nuova Città dalle Bianche Mura ».
La risposta infatti che il Superstudio dà alla città borghese è l'Architettura Interplanetaria « come presa di coscienza della frustrazione terrestre... » (1972).
Per il Superstudio dunque, non deve essere la società a modificare l'arte e la cultura, ma al contrario devono essere l'arte e la cultura (e insieme l'architettura) a modificare la società. L'architettura per loro è uno strumento sacrificale e punitivo proprio perché "illuminato".
Il suo tono carismatico, al di là dell'ironia, è l'estrema difesa dell'architetto che rifiuta la propria scomparsa divinizzando i computers, e ponendo tra sé e la realtà il diaframma dell'allegoria, sperando che questa lo preservi dai meccanismi della storia.

Gli Archigram sono stati i primi padri a rilanciare la problematica dell'avanguardia nel periodo buio dell'inizio degli anni '60. Il sobbalzo che hanno fatto fare ai cultori del vecchio svizzero, è stato un brutale aggiornamento tecnologico, in grado di bruciare tutte le confessioni intimiste martellate sul cemento armato.
L'operazione iniziale degli Archigram è ricorrente nella storia del Movimento Moderno: il recupero di una morfologia non cultu-

ralizzata nata al di fuori dell'architettura ufficiale fino a diventare alternativa a questa. L'atmosfera fantascientifica, l'utopia tecnologica che essi rilanciano come prospettiva più globale che non il dibattito sulle tipologie e sui quartieri svedesi, ha tutti i presupposti della rivoluzione disciplinare, limitata al rinnovamento di una problematica specifica. Non a caso gli anni della loro formazione sono ancora lontani dalla crisi politica, senza uscita, di tutte le scuole d'architettura ed essi conservano una fiducia tutta anglosassone negli strumenti tecnicamente ben fatti. La tecnica di presentazione dei progetti diventa con loro, per la prima volta, una tecnica specifica che niente ha a che vedere con il linguaggio architettonico: il disegno non è più una riduzione in scala della realtà, ma un prodotto finito in se stesso, che non deve necessariamente essere realizzato.

Però nella loro operazione di riduzione a zero di tutte le operazioni di progettazione tradizionale, ciò a cui gli Archigram non rinunciano, è nel credere che il risultato finale dell'architettura, o di ciò che la sostituisce, ha la capacità di rappresentare il sistema nel quale viviamo: il tubo percorribile, il traliccio, la valvola abitabile, i contenitori pneumatici, le strutture mobili ecc. sono per gli Archigram una sorta di grande allegoria del sistema, l'interno di quel motore gigante che ci fa tutti trottare. Il ritmo nevrotico dei loro montaggi, l'isteria del collage, denuncia un uso tutto narrativo e quindi statico del progetto.

Nel recente progetto per Montecarlo, gli Archigram hanno ripreso e sviluppato il tema del "heap", cioè del mucchio, dove affastellando liberamente i volumi architettonici e ricoprendoli di terra, si ottengono fenomeni geografici artificiali, come collinette o dune. Qui l'immagine architettonica è completamente scomparsa, e all'interno della caverna la diverse funzioni sono contenute liberamente, senza procedere ad una articolazione formale dell'organismo. Questo genere di proposta ha molti punti di contatto con la ricerca urbana degli Archizoom: in entrambi vi è il tentativo di svincolarsi dai limiti della leggibilità formale del progetto architettonico, ma mentre per gli Archizoom tale superamento si ottiene attraverso l'accumulazione meccanica e indifferenziata di piani liberi su cui scorrono funzioni e usi diversi, per gli Archigram è la stessa architettura che "modella" la forma della collina, come una stratificazione affiorante dal terreno.

Per gli Archizoom cioè la città sceglie la propria logica di manufatto artificiale, tutto da usare, autonomo da una natura anch'essa tutta da vivere e non da vedere, mentre per gli Archigram lo "heap" serve a « fondere la campagna con le costruzioni e con l'industria, e a fondere il porto con il mare ».

Diverso chiaramente è il radicalismo con cui i due gruppi utilizzano due soluzioni analoghe: per gli Archigram la distruzione dell'architettura è operata dalla beffa tecnologica e dall'invenzione, che essi manovrano spregiudicatamente, mentre per gli Archizoom tale distruzione avviene nel rifiuto del ruolo figurale dell'architettura e nella modificazione delle sue strutture d'uso.

A. Branzi

(2-continua. L'articolo precedente è stato pubblicato in Casabella 363.)

Because the bourgeois city is in itself an instrument of control, the not impossible harmony between man and society, and between society and nature, is sought. According to bourgeois ideology these two harmonies must take place simultaneously.
The Town Planning Scheme includes contradictory elements that are accepted as they are, but mixed together so as to achieve a "harmonic succession" simulating cultural unity — Public, Private, Building, Nature. Man has become a "citizen" and enjoys a balance, on the face of things, in which his "natural" integration with society is glorified. The city is always presented to him as a much more complex and spiritual reality than the use he can make of it each day. The city becomes an ideological diaphragm between him and the hierarchical structures of society.
In its articulation of urban events as different scenic moments, the metropolis maintains a visual relationship with its users. This kind of visual relationship constitutes the individual's fundamental structure, organizing his urban experience and memory. The layer of city which he utilizes reaches a height of two metres above ground level. As Kevin Lynch says, he builds strictly private memory tunnels that allow him to organize a system of images of his own, ranging from neon signs to individual items of urban decoration. The city as a unity of images and culture can no longer be verified in practice.
Architecture is no longer an instrument for representing the system, because the system no longer has a usable image.
Today's metropolis, as an intensive concentration, stems from a distinction made between town and country.
Capitalism was born in the town and was at first identified with the urban organization of the land, but through urban Planning, it extends its rationalizing rule over the whole territory and organizes it productively. "Urban status", or being a town-dweller, does not mean that one is more integrated than one who is not, since there is no territorial zone that is not organized within the system. The metropolis then ceases to be a "place" and becomes a "condition".
It is this condition which is circulated evenly throughout the territory and society through consumption. The city thus coincides with the dimension of the market and no longer with that of a particular place.
The architectural avant-garde is no longer concerned with designing a "better" city to contrast with today's in a keen cultural conflict. It is busy performing another operation — protesting against the ideology of the bourgeois city, denouncing its mystifying rôle and re-establishing urban planning as a structure available for a different use, and not as an instrument of social figuration and induction of values.
For that matter, as Engels said, as far as the workers are concerned the problem of a different city does not arise; if there is a problem, it is that of taking possession of the already existing city.

We shall be looking at the work of some different avant-garde groups in these pages — Archigram, Superstudio and Archizoom Associati — with the object of verifying them on the basis of general premises and controversially to note the differences, which may even be profound, that exist between them. First of all it will be noticed that the groups were born in two different national climates.
Charles Jencks, in a series of articles on Italian groups, recently published in « Architectural Design », defined them as "The Supersensualists". The term is a fairly good rendering of the image which the Italian architectural vanguard displays outside its own cultural area: a gang of feverish philosophers busy trying to find, as Jencks says, relations between « sensual love, metaphysical angst, beauty, advanced technology and (perhaps) Marxism ».
Up to their necks in a socio-miraculous Christianity oscillating between Fellini and Pasolini, Jencks remarks, they are capable of « pushing a bizarre proposition, or paradox, to its extreme conclusion ».
Passionateness and self-repression, imagination and an icy control of this imagination...
« It is a total inversion of the science we are used to comprehending... Whereas most people are habituated to accepting death as a rational necessity for evolution, love as functionally justified for the survival of the species and conflict as the engine of social change — the Supersensualists grasp all these cosmic forces and invert their utilitarian bases of explanations. After all, from an individual, human point of view they are gratuitous and absurd. No one really wants to die, even if it is in some large sense functionally necessary. For a country which has just experienced the "Economic Miracle", and partially jumped from a peasant economy to an advanced industrial state, every fact of life is likely to be just as fantastic and miraculous. »
In other words, it sounds a bit like Africa.
In 1966, at a Pistoia exhibition, Archizoom and Superstudio defined "Superarchitecture": « Superarchitecture is that of super-production, super-consumption, super-inducement to superconsumption, supermarkets, superman, super petrol ». The wave of consumer culture is countered by dogmatic terrorism: « The whirl of consumerism and the rapid phagocytosis of the Great Number must not deceive us, for behind it lies the "marble hen" which is not for eating and which does not shift » (Archizoom paper submitted to the competition for the Italian pavilion at the 14th Triennale, 1968).
Between 1967 and 1968 Archizoom Associati developed their own original line of approach to oriental themes; answering Hindu pacifism with the Moslem holy war (Malcolm X) and playing on the contamination of different cultures to achieve acid effects (the Afro-Tyrolese or the Egypto-American at the Center for Eclectic Conspiracy at the Milan Triennale).
Theories were put forward regarding their own role as intellectual middle class people engaged in the production of « a hard and clandestine culture... of no use to anyone except those who recognize their own reflections in it — a culture, in short, to be kept hidden in attics and cellars like arms or good flour for the Great Day of Rejoicing » (Archizoom, « Pianeta Fresco n. 2 », 1968), but they also reject any humanitarian commitment in the name of a rigid, ironic stalinism, and in the same year, at the Rimini Congress, Archizoom got a motion passed expressing

hope for censorship: « in view of the course taken by the congress and its proceedings... it is to be hoped that in future the working class may keep a more attentive watch with appropriate means of censorship and control, on what the intellectuals, or protesters, say, do or propose either privately or jointly; the motion being that of refusing any social commitment recognized by the bourgeois state, and any methodological and didactic organization of dissent, keeping calm so as not to stir up further panic among the working classes, retreating into the strictest and most rigorous practice of ones own profession pending suitable decisions elsewhere concerning their fate as bourgeois ». (Approved by majority vote).

Until the end of 1969 the strategy of never being where they are looked for and never accepting a definition, guaranteed Archizoom Associati a maneuvering space of their own and their own independence in the field of experimentation. Since 1970, however, their research on the city has taken a definite course and adopted a specific methodology. Archizoom Associati see the key points of the future city, places where the system will have fully realized its programming ideology, as the factory and the supermarket. Consumption and production in fact envisage an absolutely continuous and undifferentiated social and physical reality. The factory and the supermarket are optimal urban structures — potentially infinite — where productive functions or trade information are freely organized on a continous plane made homogeneous by a system of illumination and artificial ventilation, with no interruptions or interferences. The outward image of these units "does not exist", inasmuch as their front does not form the linguistic structure of the organism but simply a contact surface between two situations with different levels of organization. If we apply the technological level and functional organization, already reached and utilized in these sectors of the city, to residential housing also, we shall see, say Archizoom, that there will be a total transformation of the city. In fact, the metropolis today is based on the respect for certain standards of natural lighting and ventilation; no building block can go beyond a particular depth, in order that air and light may be allowed to infiltrate within. This fact gives rise to a continuous "formation" of architectonic blocks, full of inner courtyards, streets, etc. By introducing artificial lighting and ventilation on an urban scale, we find that it is no longer necessary to carry on with the fragmentary architecture typical of urban morphology today; the city thus becomes a continuous residential structure. The city, as an artificial product, and nature, no longer stick to a single plane; and the result is a new kind of relationship between them. In the bourgeois city nature simulates the perfect harmonization of the system in the eyes of the citizen, with natural laws, and is manipulated as a means of consolation.

In the "No-Stop City" nature is no longer an instrument for the figuration of the city, no longer an urban episode, but recovers a total autonomy of its own. The individual no longer receives it polluted by architectonic elements that tend to attribute a cultural meaning to this nature; instead nature remains a neutral field without values, available to a completely physical and not mediated knowledge. The big microclimatized plans and the « homogeneous dwelling diagrams », as Archizoom Associati define them, allow us to overcome the limits of the current residential typology and of today's concept of architecture.

« In an attempt to provide the highest possible number of degrees of freedom to the user, within a figuration as rigid as possible, architecture today recognizes its true destiny in the urban phenomenon, and its true nature in private architecture. Thus, in a contradictory way, on each single occasion it prefigures a general order of things and at the same time defends the partiality of individual experience in relation to collective experiments. In this way it mediates the contradiction between public and private » (Archizoom, « No-Stop City », March 1971).

The limits of this role cannot be redeemed, in Archizoom's view, through design operations, but through a change in the actual use that is made of architecture as a neutral structure, available for undifferentiated use and not as a tool for organizing society, but as a free area in which spontaneous experiments in private and collective living can be carried out.

Superstudio advances its own personal concept of the role of modern architecture. Superstudio believes that it is not a technical implement permitting the design of architecture free of cultural significance. On the contrary, the architecture of the so-called "exalted rationalism" (as Aldo Rossi would say), precisely because it is endowed with independent logical functions, which are therefore universally valid, is the supreme instrument of cultural education in the entire world. In 1969 Superstudio developed what might be described as a Programmatic Manifesto on the meaning of its architecture, envisaging a continuous monumental structure — a sort of Roman acqueduct — crossing the whole planet. « The Continuous Monument is the farthest pole in a series of architectural planning operations centered round the idea of "unique design": a design that is carried from one area to the next without alteration — an impassive and unalterable image whose static perfection moves the world through the love which it produces for itself. Through a series of mental operations it is possible to take possession of reality and attain peacefulness; thus architecture is an understanding of the world and self-conscience. »

The fact of designing itself is what interests Superstudio: the act of designing is for them a demiurgic, miraculous operation and at the same time one capable of bringing order to the world. In fact, the monument they mention, not just by chance, is always a body that is extraneous to the surrounding reality, inasmuch as it is equipped with an independent logic of its own, which, however, does not act (like Archizoom's Dream-Beds) like a Trojan horse capable of loosening the logical circuits of the surrounding reality by freeing it, but on the contrary, acts as an inductor of values and ordered meanings on the chaos of the surrounding nature.

Superstudio interprets the current world in a fetishistic and not in a structural way, and its members indeed declare: « the motorway is the dimensional parameter, the first continuous monument », and again, « the Kaaba and the Vertical Assembly Building are two identical black cubic stones, both equally monumental ».

Architecture is for Superstudio, therefore, a sort of metahistorical presence on which different linguistic quotations are deposited. The smoothness of the Continuous Monument is none other than the neutral plane on which they perform their revivals from the Italian style of the thirties to that of the Viennese secession (project for the Parco della Resistenza at Modena, 1970).

In « Premonitions of the mystical rebirth of urbanism or Twelve visions of ideal cities », Superstudio makes a critical appraisal of the bourgeois city, driving the different components of that city to its extreme logical consequences. The language used in the descriptions of these cities, half way between science fiction and the Gospel, is noteworthy: that is, it throws light on the static relationship they have with culture and with history, whereby the future is realized not just to the extent in which it resembles the past, and technological products resemble the Tibetan temples. The literary falsehood, namely the dream, becomes their implement of enquiry.

But their imagination never leads them to picture dynamic actions, and the solution we are offered to liberate ourselves from the nightmares is at least an idealistic one: « The horror of each one of us and our surroundings can produce the "revelation". Climb up, then, to the Old Man of the Mountain... and come down again when you are reborn... and you will be able to prepare the foundations of the New City with White Walls ».

The answer, in fact, which Superstudio gives to the bourgeois city is Interplanetary Architecture, namely a series of hypotheses for cosmic changes worked by manufactured products on a telluric scale: « A hypothesis of interplanetary architecture as a new awareness of the frustration of earthly architecture...» (1972). Superstudio, therefore, maintains that it is not society that must alter art and culture, but that on the contrary, art and culture (together with architecture) must alter society. They see architecture as a sacrifical and punitive tool precisely because it is "enlightened".

Its charismatic tone, beyond irony, is the extreme defence of the architect, who refuses to disappear in the worship of computers, and by placing between himself and reality the screen of allegory, in the hope that this will preserve him from the devices of history.

Archigram were the first fathers to relaunch the avant-garde issue in the dark days of the early sixties. They jerked the followers of the "old Swiss" into a brutal technological revision capable of burning all the innermost confessions hammered onto reinforced concrete. The beginning of Archigram's operation belongs to the story of the Modern Movement — the recovery of a non-culturalized morphology born outside official architecture, to the point of becoming an alternative to it.

The atmosphere of science fiction and technological idealism which they have relaunched as more of an overall prospect than a debate on Swedish typologies and housing estates, contains all the presuppositions of a disciplinary revolution limited to the renewal of a specific problem area. Significantly, their training took place in years that were still a long way from the political crisis and cul-de-sac that was to hit all the architectural schools later on. They have preserved a typically Anglo-Saxon faith in technically sound tools, and their closeness to London's urban reality is much greater than would appear at first sight.

For the first time the presentation technique has, in their hands, become a specific technique that has no connection with the architectonic idiom. The drawing is no longer a scaled reduction of reality, but a finished product in itself which need not necessarily be put into effect.

The impossibility of realization is accepted and becomes not a source of frustration, but one more degree of freedom. However, in their reducing to zero of all traditional architectural design, what the Archigrams do not renounce is their belief that the ultimate result of their architecture, or of what substitutes it, has the capacity to represent the system we live in. The moving tube, the trellis, the inhabitable valve, the pneumatic containers, the mobile structures, etc., are for Archigram a sort of vast allegory of the system — the inside of that giant engine that keeps us all trotting. The neurotic rhythm of their assemblies, the hysteria of their collages, reveals a fully narrative use of design.

The relation between user and architecture remains completely visual. In a recent design for Montecarlo, Archigram resumed and developed a theme that would seem to be a contradiction of what we have been saying here. This theme is the « heap », where, by bundling the architectonic volumes together and covering them up with earth, artificial geographical phenomena are obtained, such as hillocks or dunes. Here the architectonic image has completely disappeared, and inside the caves the various functions are freely contained, without proceeding with any formal articulation of the organism. This kind of proposal has many points of contact with the urban research conducted by Archizoom. In both instances there is an attempt to shake off the limits of formal readability of the architectonic design, but while in the case of Archizoom this limitation is overcome through the mechanical and undifferentiated accumulation of free planes on which different functions and uses occur, in the case of Archigram it is the architecture itself which "models" the shape of the hill, like a tectonic stratification flowering out of the ground.

In the Archizoom way of thinking the city chooses its own logic as an artificial product, all to be used, and which is independent from a nature that likewise is all to be experienced and not seen, while in the case of Archigram the heap serves to « merge the countryside with the constructions and with industry, and to merge the harbour with the sea ». Clearly the radicalism with which the two groups use two similar solutions is different. As far as Archigram is concerned the destruction of architecture is carried out by technological mockery and by invention, which this group maneuvers with great insouciance, whereas in the case of Archizoom this destruction takes place in the refusal of the figural role of architecture and in the modification of its use structures.

A. Branzi

(2-to be continued. The first part of the article has been published in Casabella N. 363.)

ANDREA BRANZI

LA GIOCONDA SBARBATA

IL RUOLO DELL'AVANGUARDIA

DUCHAMP. L.H.O.O.Q. (1919)

DUCHAMP. L.H.O.O.Q./SHAVED(1964)

Andrea Branzi, "The Shaved Gioconda. The Role of the Avant-garde," in *Casabella* n. 364, 1972

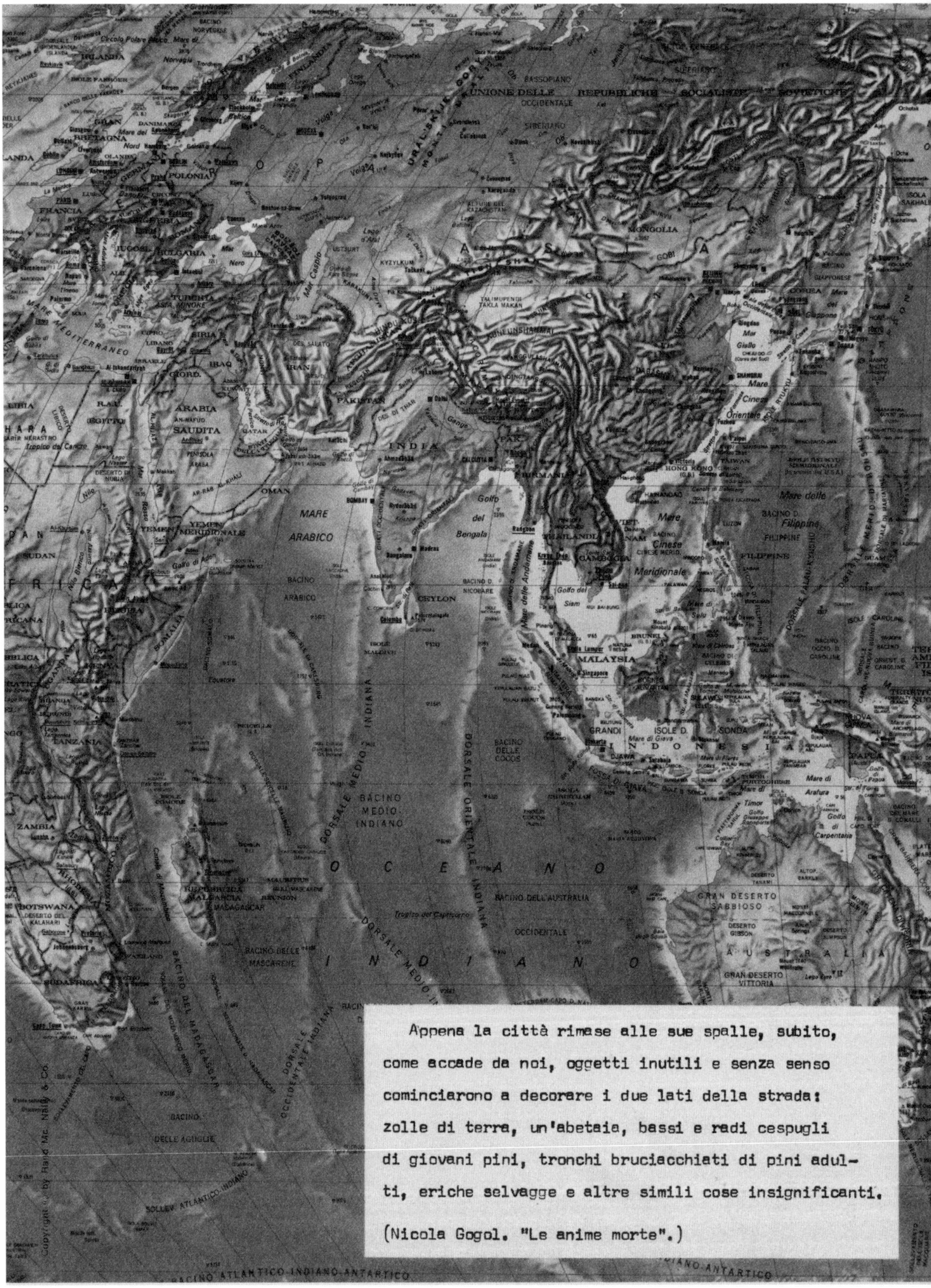

Appena la città rimase alle sue spalle, subito, come accade da noi, oggetti inutili e senza senso cominciarono a decorare i due lati della strada: zolle di terra, un'abetaia, bassi e radi cespugli di giovani pini, tronchi bruciacchiati di pini adulti, eriche selvagge e altre simili cose insignificanti.

(Nicola Gogol. "Le anime morte".)

Cercherò di essere chiarissimo: non farò una analisi oggettiva dei programmi e delle strategie dell'avanguardia attuale, ma verificherò questa sulla base di una tesi da me premessa. Il materiale storico serve solo come illustrazione di una ipotesi attuale. Nessuna eredità ci giunge infatti dal passato: come diceva Gombrowicz, « per me la storia è un buco nero ».

La premessa da dimostrare è questa: la avanguardia ha oggi un ruolo preciso, che consiste nella "distruzione tecnica della cultura".
Per cultura si intende tutti i valori e tutti i significati morali, religiosi, estetici della società nella quale viviamo.
Per distruzione si intende rimozione senza sostituzione di valori o significati nuovi. Storicamente tutte le volte che tale tentativo è stato compiuto, la cultura borghese ha recuperato brillantemente il terreno: la distruzione della cultura è diventata una cultura in più, e la distruzione del linguaggio un linguaggio in più.
Pur tuttavia le condizioni dimensionali di tale operazione oggi sono cambiate. E a favore del segno negativo.
E' aumentata soprattutto la "distruzione sociale" della cultura.

Esiste infatti una distruzione operata dal Capitale, il quale giunge a definire un processo di totale sostituzione di "valori", attraverso "altri valori", e rilancia l'azione spontanea come sola promotrice di modelli produttivi e di consumo, tutti vivibili.
Non sono più necessari cioè i modelli ottimali (che minacciano di radicalizzare le contraddizioni dello sviluppo) ma piuttosto un sistema dinamico di modelli, che si contestano reciprocamente e si sovrappongono.
Per il Capitale la cultura ha già perduto la sua unità, e al posto di una nascono mille e mille utopie, e nel momento in cui la Programmazione e la società si identificano, i contenuti del Piano coincidono con i contenuti spontanei della società stessa.
Una morale universale non è più funzionale: la sua morte testimonia anzi della scientificità del Piano stesso, come puro coordinamento tecnico.
E sono proprio i consumi a fornire il campo d'azione di questa spontaneità: essi non forniscono un modello unico, ma al limite tanti modelli quante sono le individualità in azione, e delimitano il perimetro dei processi liberatori.
Esiste un altro genere di distruzione sociale della cultura, che non avviene attraverso la contrapposizione di modelli alternativi (non in maniera dialettica cioè), ma in maniera meccanica: tale distruzione è generata dalla crescita economica del proletariato.
La classe operaia non produce infatti cultura alternativa, ma utilizza i modelli prodotti dalla classe borghese come tappe strategiche della propria escalation economica. Utilizza questi modelli e insieme li distrugge, proprio perché per raggiungerli distrugge gli equilibri economici sui quali tali modelli si basano.
I modelli borghesi vengono così accettati come puri riferimenti formali privi di contenuti, e ne viene logorata la capacità di comunicare lo status sociale nel quale sono nati. Il Kitsch diventa l'avanguardia culturale spontanea della società, proprio perché

non riconosce alla cultura consacrata un valore autonomo che non possa essere acquistato insieme al prodotto, né conosce una area culturale che non abbia un prezzo trattabile.

Non è dunque l'avanguardia culturale a elaborare i contenuti di una rivoluzione sociale. (E questo si sapeva.)

Ciò nonostante resta da spiegare la spesso miracolosa unità di direzione tra rivoluzione sociale e rivoluzione culturale.

Wilhelm Reich lo spiega molto bene quando si chiede se i programmi di una rivoluzione socialista coincidono con l'avvento di una società sessualmente permissiva. Egli risponde che questa coincidenza esiste, ma non tanto perché la classe operaia possiede un modello di società sessualmente più evoluto, ma perché nell'itinerario che la conduce al potere essa frantuma gli equilibri economici che utilizzano l'inibizione sessuale come strumento di difesa del potere costituito.

L'identità è dunque realizzata da processi tecnici analoghi, uno dentro al sistema che raggiunge un determinato risultato per via speculativa, l'altro esterno al sistema che raggiunge lo stesso risultato attraverso la prassi. Lo scambio non avviene necessariamente all'interno di un programma unico. Operando la distruzione di tutte le strutture culturali e morali si compie una operazione liberatoria che ha come fine la rimozione dei diaframmi che impediscono una conoscenza diretta della realtà. In questo senso l'avanguardia compie una operazione "indirettamente" politica, che modifica la disponibilità rivoluzionaria individuale e collettiva.

La realtà che ci circonda infatti è priva di valore perché generata da un sistema privo di destino; la cultura, l'estetica, la morale, attribuendo invece alle cose e alla storia "valori" e "significati", impediscono di agire liberamente verso di questa, dal momento che essa ci appare come proiezione di noi stessi, come una realtà naturale nella quale possiamo riconoscerci profondamente. La riduzione della realtà ai soli "parametri quantitativi" è la direzione (scientifica?) dell'avanguardia.

Distruggere la cultura come settore organizzabile di produzione di valori (riconoscere che il mare non vuol dire niente, come dice Alain Robbe-Grillet), non vuol dire immaginare un uomo tutto fredda razionalità (che sarebbe ancora proporre un modello), ma al contrario rinunciare a qualsiasi verifica formale sulla sua azione. Per fare questo bisogna modificare "l'uso sociale" della cultura stessa. Morton Feldman fa un paragone molto significativo tra Luigi Nono e John Cage: il primo, constatando che la società non funziona, vorrebbe che fosse l'arte a modificarla; il secondo, vedendo che l'arte non funziona, vorrebbe che fosse la società a modificarla. Nono ripropone l'arte come modello sociale, Cage prospetta una modificazione d'uso sociale dell'arte stessa, consegnandola in mano alla società come libera attività psico-motoria, già totalmente smontata dal punto di vista tecnico e completamente aderente alla realtà.

Il recupero totale di tutte le proprie facoltà creative come diritto naturale e non come messaggio in codice, è il "nuovo" uso sociale della cultura.

La cultura come produttrice di modelli di comportamento è un momento dell'organizzazione produttiva della società stessa.

Rifiutare la cultura vuol dire rifiutare il lavoro.

Tale rifiuto non è più il segreto sogno di qualche sbandato, o la profetica dottrina di gruppi sparsi: sarà la più grossa scoperta collettiva di questo secolo.

Il rifiuto del lavoro è la componente oggettiva, la legge di fondo di tutta la dinamica sociale: è la base che spinge ad una crescita vertiginosa il prezzo stesso della forza lavoro. La libertà come fine diventa subito strumento di lotta.

Lo slogan operaio « più soldi - meno lavoro » ribalta in termini quantitativi i "contenuti" di qualsiasi dibattito politico.

Qualsiasi cultura è "repressiva" perché repressiva è la distinzione sociale su cui si basa: separazione funzionale tra produttori e consumatori di cultura.

Se gli uomini sono tutti uguali, come lo sono, tra utente e artista non esiste che una distinzione impropria, favorita dalla attuale divisione del lavoro.

I bambini sono tutti artisti; gli adulti lo sono uno su mille.

Non basta quindi rifiutare il ruolo di produttore specializzato di cultura, ma bisogna rifiutare l'intero rapporto di produzione, che termina in un utente il quale riceve, attraverso la circolazione di scelte che non ha mai fatto, la simulazione dell'uso delle proprie facoltà creative totalmente atrofizzate.

Tale atrofizzazione è una alienazione sociale, che impedisce di auto-produrre e autoconsumare la propria attività creativa come un fenomeno di comunicazione spontanea.

Il "fare artistico", come attività tesa ad impegnare e ad affermare la materialità del corpo, o la elettricità dei sistemi nervosi, ha già un senso concluso in se stesso, come una sorta di terapia psico-fisica liberatoria priva di significati traslati.

L'arte non rappresenta più la realtà, ma coincide totalmente con questa.

Entro i prossimi anni la società si troverà in grado di recuperare tutti i processi creativi oggi demandati a pochi specialisti.

Il Capitale infatti sta rispondendo al rifiuto del lavoro "automatizzando" i propri cicli produttivi.

Liberandosi del lavoro umano (e insieme dello sciopero), sta programmando una società trasformata in pura "Forza di Consumo"; e per il Capitale consumare "è" una attività creativa perché produce valori e modelli. La libertà che ne risulta però è una libertà "modulare", di cui si conosce già il meccanismo di sviluppo e il parametro dimensionale.

Il Lavoro Morto non introduce quindi ad un'era metastorica, in cui i giuochi sono già fatti: il problema al contrario rimane proprio quello della "gestione" di questa automazione, da parte della società.

L'attuale concetto di Tempo Libero si basa sulla necessità di ristabilire un equilibrio momentaneo che permetta un rilancio delle possibilità produttive individuali.

La cultura attuale serve a concentrare in un prodotto un processo meditativo accelerato, funzione proporzionale dei tempi stessi del possibile consumo.

La necessità di fornire un messaggio in fra-

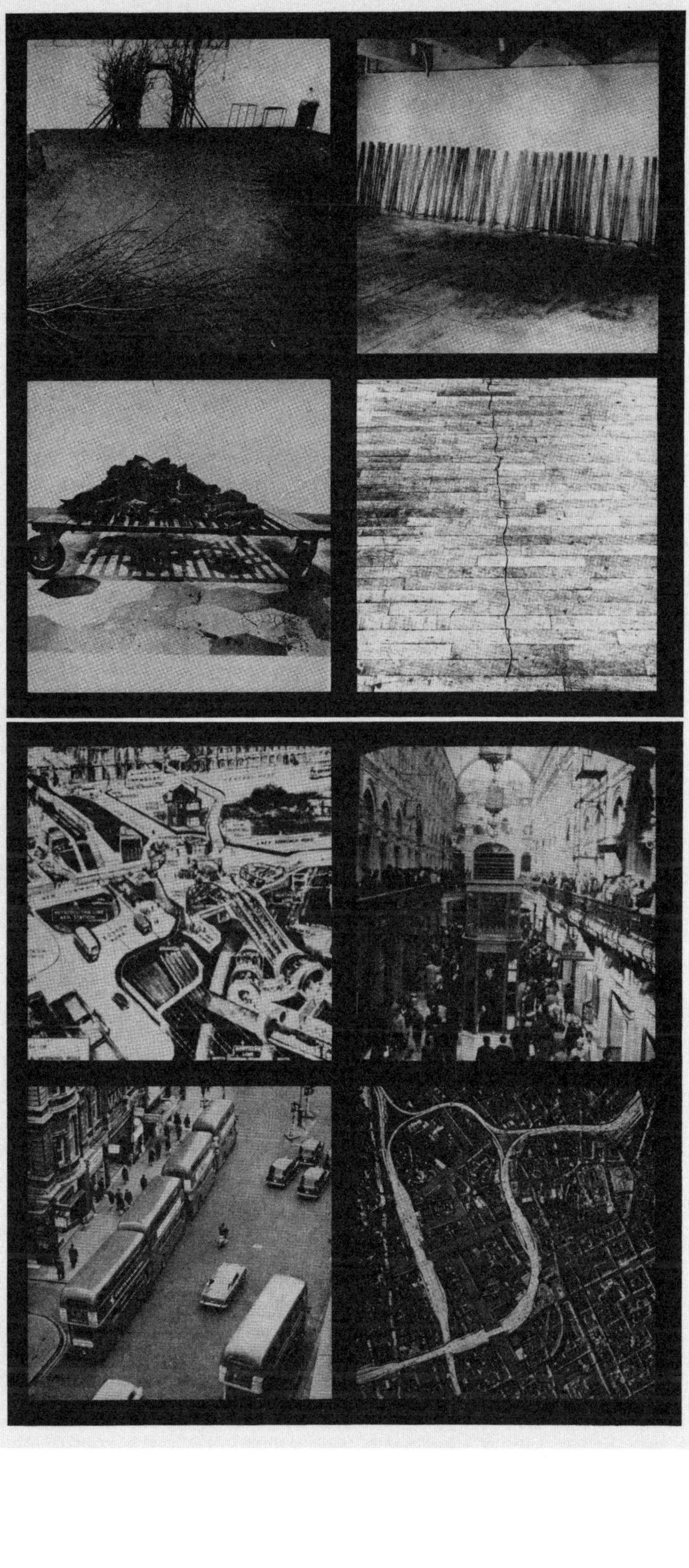

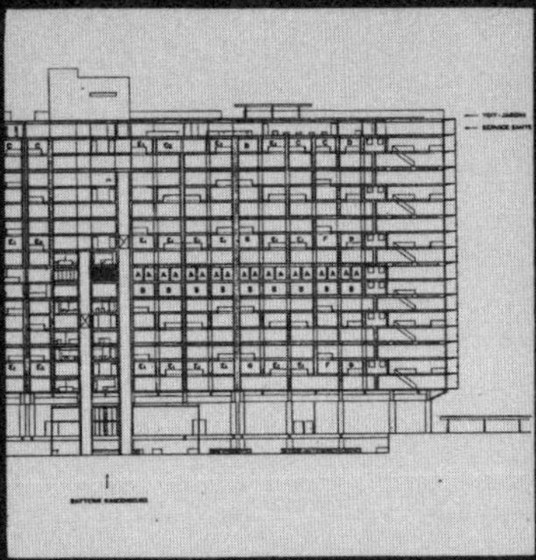

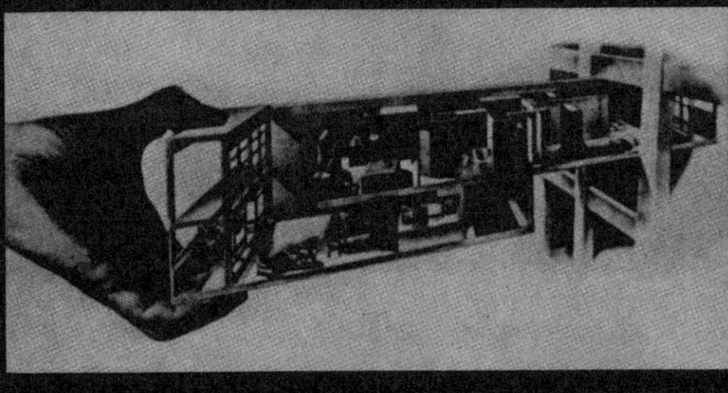

zioni di tempo ridotte, è la base di tutta la evoluzione tecnica della cultura moderna.
La diminuzione quantitativa dei tempi di lavoro sconvolgerà la struttura culturale odierna, distruggendola. I "tempi lunghi" di consumo rimuovono le premesse del giuoco sintetico del messaggio artistico; la controparte istituzionale della classe intellettuale, i lettori, gli abbonati, i visitatori, i consumatori, gli osservatori, i voyeurs, diventeranno i protagonisti.
Il messaggio del singolo artista alla società, forte della sua "diversità" (i « Nati sotto Saturno » di Wittkower), cederà il posto alla "Produzione Intellettuale di Massa".
A questo appuntamento storico bisogna giungere avendo già minato e distrutto tutte le strutture e tutte le tecnologie che fanno della cultura un prodotto di specialisti, non utilizzabile dalle masse.
Per fare oggi musica, poesia, pittura, scultura, danza, o qualsiasi altra attività fisica occorre la conoscenza tecnica delle diverse discipline. L'avanguardia distrugge queste tecniche, premettendo a qualsiasi operazione che compie il suo unico programma tecnico che è questo: L'ARTE E' FACILE.
Tutte le possibili tecniche di liberazione dall'arte agiscono come segni negativi che imprimono una riduzione della distanza tra l'operatore e la propria azione, tra produttore e merce, tra significato e dimensione fisica, fermando la continua asportazione critica che la morale fa dei nostri atti.
L' "avanguardia d'architettura" si colloca all'interno di questo contesto generale. Essa tende a ridurre a zero tutti i processi di progettazione, rifiutando il ruolo di settore disciplinare impegnato a prefigurare attraverso le strutture ambientali un futuro già scelto da altri.
L'avanguardia d'architettura rinuncia a ipotizzare la "forma della città futura"; essa stabilisce con la città un rapporto "scientifico", nel senso che rimuove dal dibattito urbano qualsiasi concetto di qualità, tipico dell'architettura, riportando il fenomeno ai soli "parametri quantitativi".
La metropoli infatti è un tessuto compatto di servizi, privo di una "immagine globale". Tra la casa e la città non esiste che un rapporto multiplo diverso; è possibile transitare dall'una all'altra come in un sistema di coordinate omogenee, senza introdurre variabili esterne.
Piazze, palazzi, boulevards, monumenti, strade, viali, case, chiese, uffici, teatri ecc. ecc. sono ancora momenti scenici di un vecchio concetto organico di città.
Non è più possibile invece stabilire con essa un "rapporto visuale", di controllo e di lettura. L'organizzazione dell'intera società nel Piano Produttivo ha definitivamente eliminato quello "spazio vuoto" nel quale il Capitale si espandeva nel proprio processo di crescita. Non esiste più una "realtà esterna" al sistema stesso.
La città non rappresenta più il sistema, ma "è" il sistema stesso.
L'ideologia della metropoli attuale nasce nell'idea settecentesca della "città come oggetto naturale" teso a realizzare il delicato equilibrio tra l'uomo e il suo ambiente naturale. Nella ideologia borghese infatti equilibrio ecologico e giustizia sociale sono parti di una stessa battaglia, e la città fornisce con la propria immagine la verifica formale di tale equilibrio raggiunto.

Nel Piano Urbanistico dunque viene ricercata la non impossibile armonia tra l'Interesse Generale e l'Interesse Particolare (tra Pubblico e Privato cioè): tali categorie vengono però sempre acquisite come fenomeni antitetici, contrastanti e non mediabili.

Il problema diventa allora quello di trovare una maglia bidimensionale che garantisca l'incastro di tali componenti non solubili.

Il "traffico" diventa il tramite più generale perché costituisce il tessuto degli scambi e della penetrazione urbana. La città diventa così una struttura di scorrimento e di distribuzione delle merci; la "strada" non solo serve la città, ma la "seziona" individuando i piani di facciata sui quali il linguaggio architettonico si colloca.

Pubblico, privato, strade, case, natura, edifici ecc., parti contrastanti di logiche diverse, nella città borghese cercano di trovare una possibile armonia, perché la città borghese è la città degli equilibri realizzati, dove non esistono contraddizioni insanabili.

Ogni città ha così apparentemente una propria pianta, una propria immagine, una propria storia che rende impossibile lo studio scientifico del fenomeno urbano e delle sue leggi di sviluppo generali. Le città invece, tutte le città, sono un cesso ogni 100 m^3 e basta.

Le più grandi invenzioni dell'Architettura Moderna sono state "invenzioni quantitative": il Grattacielo e L'Unità d'Abitazione. Ambedue hanno distrutto gli equilibri della città borghese.

Il Grattacielo compie una brutale operazione di accumulazione su di un piano urbanistico tradizionale: il rapporto tra pianta e alzato è completamente distrutto.

Il grattacielo ha quattro facciate solo perché è collocato su di un lotto di terreno molto piccolo: potenzialmente esso può sviluppare la dimensione che ha raggiunto verticalmente anche nelle altre quattro direzioni. Esso è ancora architettura a causa della propria eccezionalità rispetto al luogo dove si trova, che è ancora un luogo "urbano" nel senso che sottintende ancora qualcosa che non è città, e cioè la "campagna".

Così lo skyline della grande metropoli è ancora il diagramma della accumulazione spontanea del Capitale sul suolo.

L'Unità di Abitazione compie invece una altra operazione: prende una città, con tutte le sue componenti tradizionali e la colloca in verticale. Il risultato è sconvolgente. La differenza tra singolo edificio e città scompare.

Alle diverse funzioni della città non corrispondono più forme architettoniche diverse: i negozi, i teatri, le scuole ecc., non possiedono più una "forma" propria. Sono divenuti parti omogenee di un unico piano di servizi non distinguibile da quelli delle abitazioni.

La città e la natura non si incastrano più su di un unico piano bidimensionale di esperienze; la natura non disegna più la città, e la città non ritaglia più la natura; i "pilotis" permettono ai due fenomeni di scorrere separatamente. La città non giace più su di un territorio né vi identifica la sua storia, ma piuttosto vi si appoggia liberamente come un grande manufatto che possiede una logica propria, chiaramente artificiale.

A. Branzi

A pagina 27:
L'opera di Duchamp: L.H.O.O.Q. (1919-1964) riprodotta in alto appartiene alla collezione della Galleria Schwarz, Milano.

A pagina 28:
La carta riprodotta, tratta dall'« Atlante internazionale », è pubblicata per gentile concessione della Arnoldo Mondadori Editore.

I shall not make an objective analysis of the programs and strategy of the present avant-garde, but verify it on the premise of a thesis. Any historical material serves only to illustrate a present hypothesis. For we inherit nothing from the past.

The premise I shall demonstrate is this: the precise role of today's avant-garde is the « technical destruction of culture ».

By culture are meant all the values and meanings, moral, religious and aesthetic, of the society in which we find ourselves.

By destruction is meant the removal without substitution of new values or meanings.

Historically, every time such an attempt has been made, bourgeois culture has brilliantly regained its ground; the destruction of culture has become still another culture, the destruction of language still another language.

Yet the dimensional conditions of this operation have changed today. And in favor of the negative sign. Above all, the « social destruction » of culture has increased.

There is, in fact, a destruction worked by Capital which reaches the point of structuring a process of total substitution of « values » by means of « other values ».

There is another kind of social destruction of culture which occurs not through the opposition of alternative patterns (not in a dialectic manner, that is), but in a mechanical way. This destruction is generated by the economic growth of the proletariat. The working class, in fact, does not produce an alternative culture, but uses the patterns produced by the bourgeois class as strategic steps in its own economic escalation. It uses these patterns and at the same time destroys them, precisely because in order to reach them, it destroys the economic equilibrium on which they are based.

The destruction of all cultural and moral structures is an operation of release which has as its goal the removal of the diaphragms which prevent a direct knowledge of reality. In this sense, the operation of the avant-garde is « indirectly » political, modifying the revolutionary availability of the individual and the group.

The (scientific?) direction of the avant-garde is to reduce reality to simply « quantitative parameters ». To destroy culture as an organizable sector of the production of values does not mean we visualize man as all cold logic (which would be proposing a pattern), but that on the contrary we refuse any formal verification of his actions. In order to do this we must modify the « social use » of culture itself.

The total recovery of all of one's own creative faculties, considered a natural right and not a message in code — that is the « new » social use of culture.

Culture as producer of patterns of behavior is a moment of the productive organization of society.

« To reject culture is to reject work ». This rejection is no longer the secret dream of some derelict or the prophetic doctrine of scattered groups: it will be the biggest collective discovery of this century.

Any culture is « repressive » because the social distinction on which it stands, the functional separation between producers and consumers of culture, is repressive.

If all men are equal, and they are, the distinction between user and artist is false, favored by the present division of labor.

All children are artists; only one adult out of a thousand is.

Capital is, in fact, answering the rejection of labor with the « automation » of its productive cycles. Freeing itself of human labor (and strikes), it is programming a society transformed into pure « Consumer Force ». And Capital considers consumption a creative activity because it produces values and patterns. The freedom which results is, however, a patterned one of which the development mechanism and dimensional perimeter are already known.

Dead Work, then, does not introduce an era beyond history in which all the plays have been placed; quite the contrary, « how society will operate » this automation remains the problem to be solved.

The individual artist's message for society, strong with a sense of his « differentness » will cede its place to the « Intellectual Production of the Masses ».

We must arrive at this historical appointment with all the structures and technologies that render culture a product of specialists, unusable for the masses, already undermined and destroyed.

Today, creating music, poetry, painting, sculpture, dance, engaging in any other physical activity requires a technical knowledge of the particular subject matter. The avant-garde destroys these techniques, prefacing any operation it undertakes with this only program: « Art is easy ».

The avant-garde of architecture aims to reduce all processes of design to zero, refusing the role of disciplinary sector engaged in prefiguring with environmental structures a future already selected by others.

The avant-garde of architecture refuses to hypothesize on the « form of the city of the future ». It establishes a scientific rapport with the city, in the sense that it eliminates any concept of quality, typical of architecture, from urban debate, reducing the phenomenon to simply « quantitative parameters ».

The greatest inventions of Modern Architecture have been « quantitative inventions »: the Skyscraper and the Housing Unit.

Both have destroyed the equilibrium of the bourgeois city.

The Skyscraper effects a brutal accumulation upon a traditional city plan; the relation between plan and rise is completely destroyed.

The Housing Unit, instead, is different: is takes a city with all its traditional components and collocates them on a vertical plane. The results are shocking. The difference between the single building and the city disappears.

There are no longer different architectonic forms corresponding to the different functions of the city: stores, theatres, schools, etc. no longer have a « shape » of their own. They have become homogeneous parts of a single plane of services that cannot be distinguished from those of the dwellings. The city and the nature no longer fit in together on a single bidimensional plane of experience. Nature no longer designs the city and the city no longer outlines nature. The « pilotis » allow the two phenomena to flow separately. The city no longer lies upon the land, nor does it identify its history with it, but rather it is placed freely upon it like a great manufacture possessing a clearly artificial logic all its own. 33

ANDREA BRANZI

ABITARE È FACILE

IL RUOLO DELL'AVANGUARDIA

Andrea Branzi, "Inhabiting is Easy. The Role of the Avant-garde," in *Casabella* n. 365, 1972

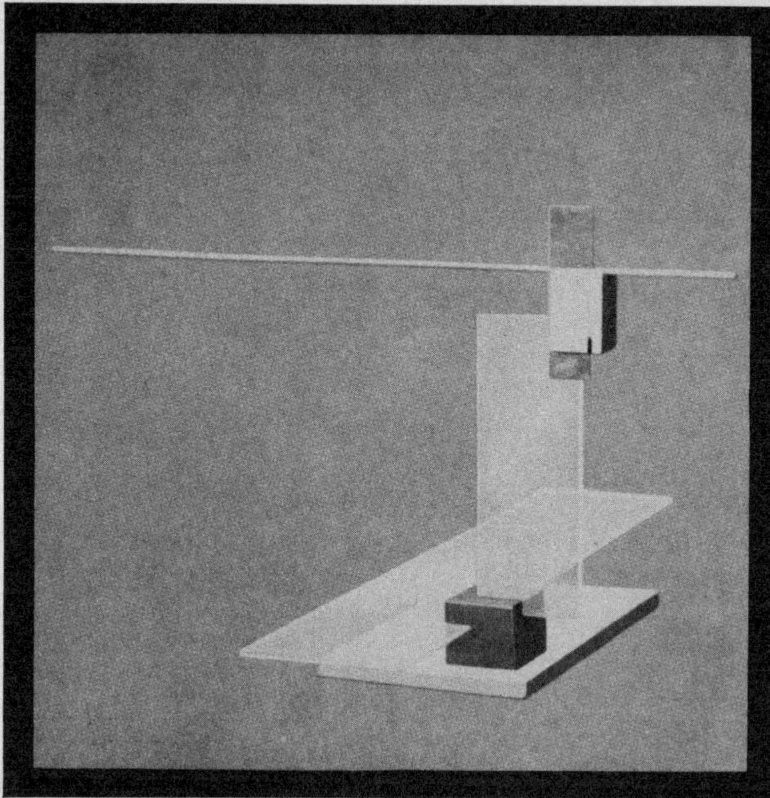

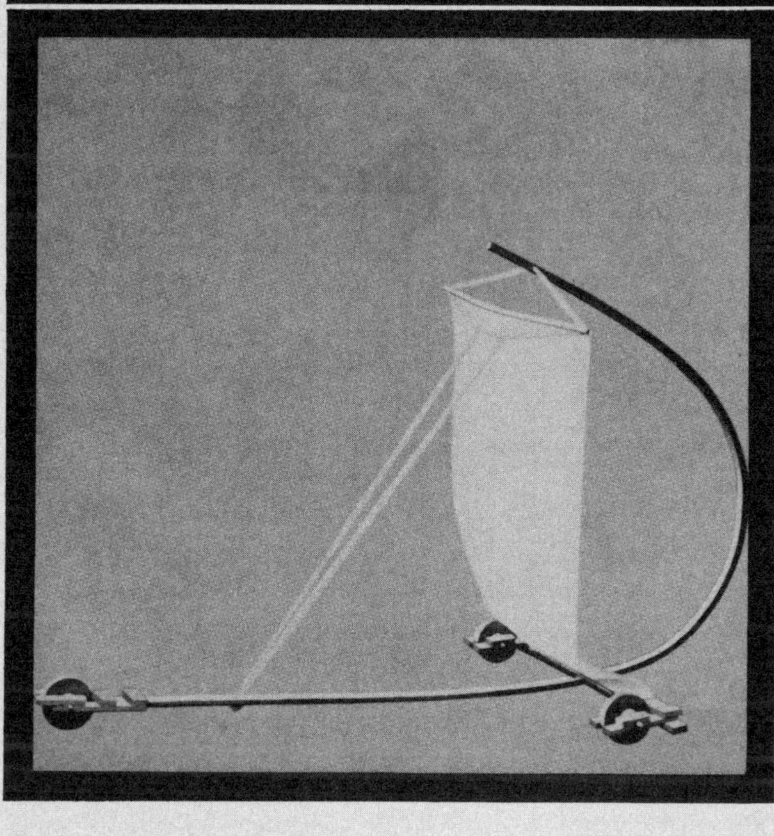

Sul finire del secolo scorso, il movimento spontaneo di liberazione dell'uomo dall'arte e dalla cultura sembrò aver trovato nella produzione industriale il grande strumento universale atto a favorire tale liberazione.
L'ondata di ribrezzo sollevata negli animi più avvertiti dalla merce esposta nelle grandi Esposizioni Universali sembrò generata più da un presentimento di morte che da un dissenso critico. Il Capitale, la produzione industriale, inizia la propria trasformazione sociale distruggendo i riferimenti della civiltà mercantile che la precede. La semplice produzione quantitativa si rivela lo strumento di scardinamento di un vecchio mondo e dei suoi valori.
La macchina infatti, riproducendo migliaia di volte oggetti nati in copia unica, non solo distrugge le loro capacità di comunicare lo status economico del luogo dove si trovano, ma rimuove il criterio di attribuzione di "valore oggettivo" della merce, che è costituito dalla quantità di lavoro manuale necessario alla sua realizzazione.
Il lavoro umano cessa di essere una struttura costitutiva degli oggetti e diventa pura energia produttiva: l'oggetto perde la sua connotazione culturale per acquistarne una esclusivamente tecnologica.
Trasformando l'artigianato in forza lavoro, viene tolta all'uomo la gestione delle proprie facoltà produttive ed il controllo sui modelli di produzione.
La realtà industriale comincia ad assumersi la gestione della società (attraverso il salario) e il compito di fornire i modelli a questa società. Tali modelli non devono più essere esterni al mondo del lavoro, ma piuttosto nella logica profonda che lo determina. La "fabbrica", anche se limitata e parziale rispetto ad un mondo ancora largamente mercantile e agricolo, rivendica una propria universalità, sia attraverso il proprio uso di una logica razionale, sia nella propria tensione ad integrare tutta intera la società, e ad organizzarla nel lavoro.
L'intellettuale non viene assunto come elaboratore esterno di utopie e morali, ma come operatore interno al ciclo, anzi mediatore diretto tra la produzione come fatto tecnologico e il fine sociale della produzione stessa: il suo ruolo diventa quello di scoprire la logica intrinseca alla natura dei processi produttivi.
E' qui che nasce il designer: egli assume il ruolo di trasformare le necessità produttive in valori razionali, e in tale direzione recupera tutte le esperienze più avanzate dell'avanguardia riducendola a semplici esperimenti di linguaggio e utilizzando la loro carica distruttiva come forza analitica, razionalmente utilizzabile.
In tale maniera viene simulata una coincidenza perfetta tra rivoluzione culturale e rivoluzione industriale. La carica liberatoria della prima, il suo tendere ad una nuova gestione dei modelli estetici e ad una relatività assoluta dei medesimi, viene utilizzata come dimostrazione di una forza contestativa trascinante propria della produzione industriale.
La distruzione della cultura diventa nel designer lo sforzo di rivelare alla produzione la sua stessa razionalità, fino al punto di renderla autonoma da lui: inoltre il suo sforzo per far raggiungere al prodotto il livello ottimale di identificazione tra qualità

tecniche e comunicative, pone le premesse affinché l'industria possa lanciarsi nella Serie Definitiva. L'universalità dell'arte diventa universalità del prodotto.
Il designer, ponendosi come intermediario tra le necessità produttive e la realtà fisica della merce, tende a trasformare la realtà in dati elementari, in figure geometriche semplici, al fine di facilitarne l'introduzione nella macchina che deve riprodurla.
Se lo smontaggio dell'oggetto facilita l'organizzazione del lavoro, l'identificazione tra la logica interna della forma e le necessità produttive diventa totale, e quindi la soluzione progettuale obbligata.
L'estetica della produzione diventa una categoria definitiva, frutto di una coincidenza tra formatività dell'oggetto e i processi produttivi di questo; ma così operando, la produzione sembra divenire una operazione a termine, un semplice riempimento del vuoto costituito dai bisogni, che una volta colmato non richiede altro se non una normale manutenzione.
L'uomo nuovo della "civilisation machiniste" è l'uomo che adotta le leggi produttive come propria intima natura, riconoscendo nella razionalità della produzione lo strumento scientifico di organizzazione della realtà (design), ma anche e soprattutto vi riconosce la propria più profonda formatività (cubismo).
Solo così il rapporto tra fabbrica e società diviene legge naturale.
L'uomo "tutta-produzione" sacrifica a questa tutto: egli sublima le proprie ambizioni borghesi in un Existenz-Minimum, circondato da oggetti utensili.
Il design sembra essere lo strumento di demistificazione proprio di quei processi di mercificazione indotti dalla produzione industriale: ma la liberazione che esso opera serve a riservare tutte le energie dell'individuo nella propria potenzialità produttiva. In questo senso profondo l'operazione del design risulta repressiva. Non solo: nell'integrazione totale viene simulata la liberazione dell'operaio dalla condizione borghese.
Il processo di smontaggio che il protodesign opera di tutte le superfetazioni culturali dell'oggetto, non serve tanto a garantire una maggiore autonomia dai miti, ma piuttosto a indurre alla rinuncia agli oggetti stessi.
Il Movimento Moderno sembra impegnarsi a definire la condizione operaia come "condizione primaria", priva di superfetazioni culturali, proprie della classe borghese, e tutta impregnata della logica di fabbrica, nella quale riconosce uno strumento di dura contestazione della morale dei padroni.
La classe operaia si riconosce dunque spontaneamente nella condizione di fabbrica, prefigurando in se stessa una civiltà futura tutta impegnata nell'efficienza produttiva, rifiutando i Consumi come momento improprio alla produzione.
Produrre e non consumare diventa la morale rivoluzionaria, in conflitto con la realtà borghese che al contrario consuma e non produce.
Ma tale ipotesi è rifiutata da ambedue le parti in conflitto.
La classe operaia riconosce nella fabbrica solo uno strumento di organizzazione della propria lotta, che è una lotta contro la con-

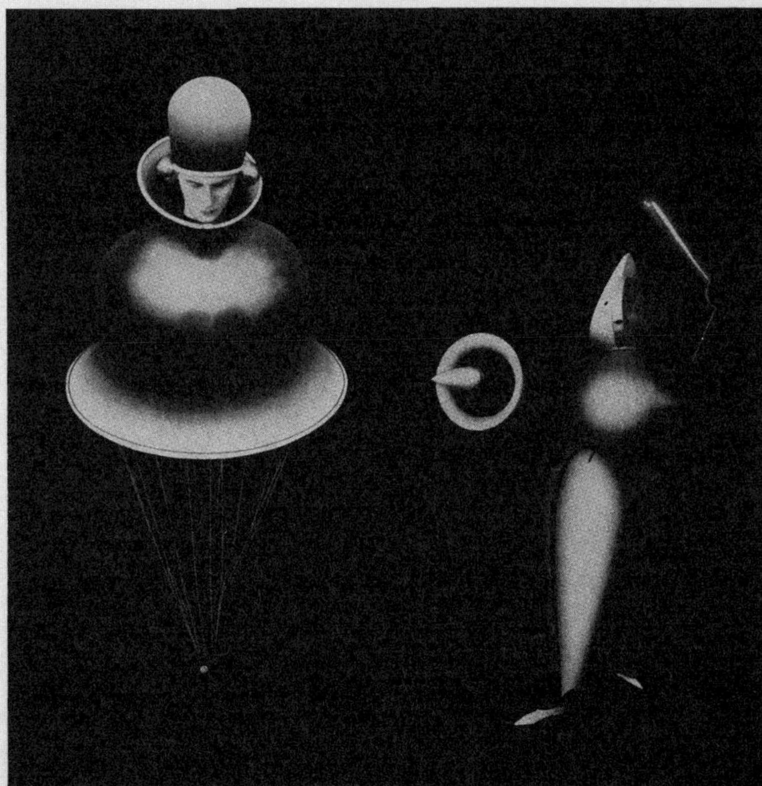

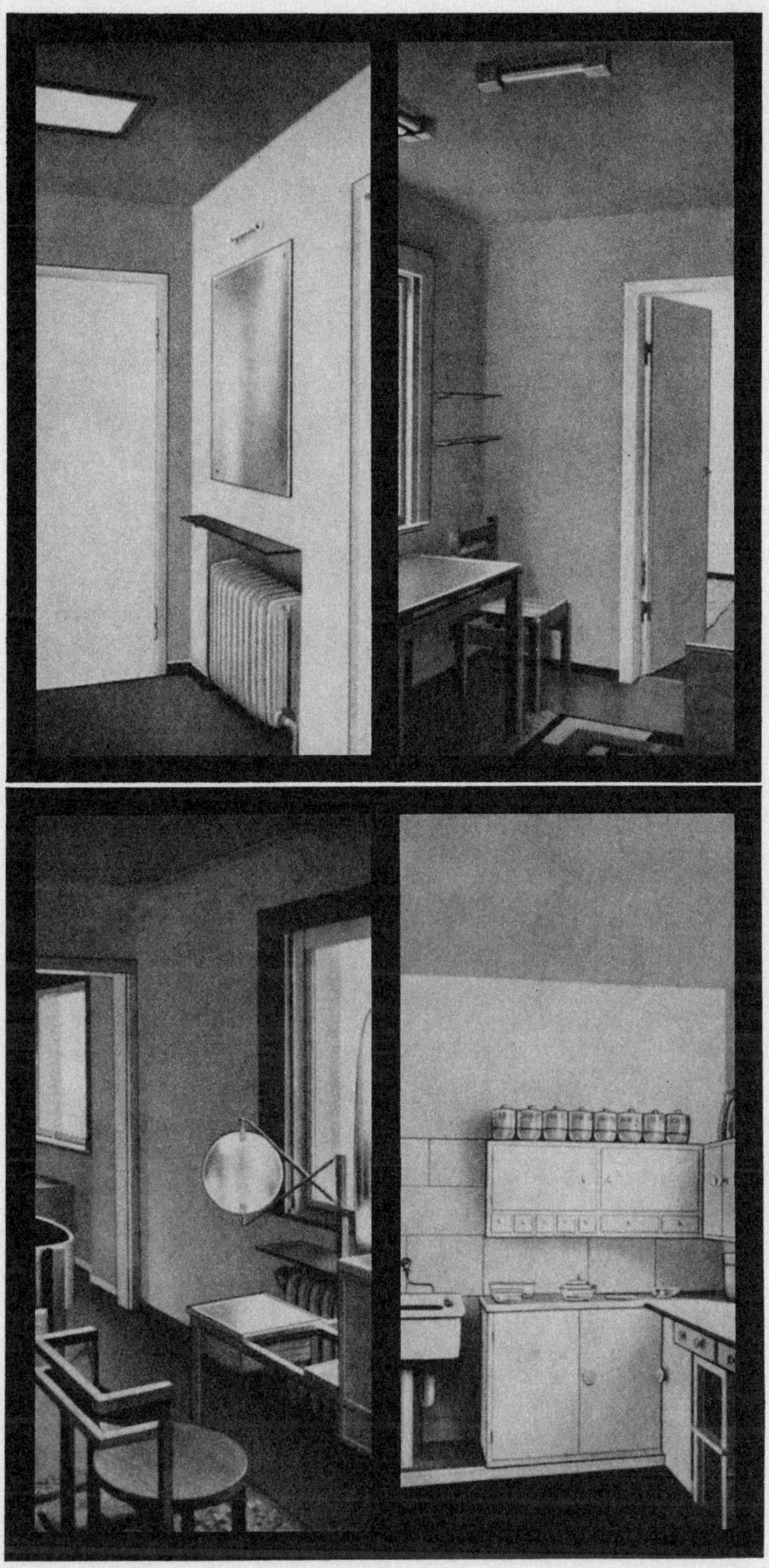

dizione operaia, che vuol dire miseria, e possibilmente contro il lavoro stesso.
Adotta il meccanismo dei consumi come verifica della propria escalation sociale e, strategicamente, per distruggere con metodo tutti gli equilibri raggiunti dallo sviluppo del sistema. Ha come modello la classe borghese, e sostituendola la distrugge, unitamente ai suoi modelli e ai suoi valori. Rifiuta il design come un modello culturale che inibisce e smorza la carica rivoluzionaria della classe, che è appunto basata su di una spinta imitativa, e non su una cultura alternativa.
Anche il Capitale rifiuta il modello di design: la produzione non può richiedere la scomparsa dei consumi, ma anzi il loro progressivo incremento. Un consumatore soddisfatto è anche un operaio migliore.
Anzi: la produzione, per la classe operaia e per la società integrata nel Piano Economico, deve restare un fatto marginale, un episodio secondario rispetto ai consumi, che danno significato e scopo al momento produttivo.
Non deve essere dunque la società a somigliare alla fabbrica, ma la fabbrica alla società. La cultura deve così valorizzare i consumi, creando un sistema di modelli transitori di comportamento. La cultura deve perdere la sua connotazione unitaria, e al posto di una nascono mille e mille utopie. Non la scientificità del Bauhaus, ma lo sperimentalismo di Picasso.
Se l'identificazione tra Piano Economico e Società è reale, al limite i contenuti del piano devono coincidere con i contenuti spontanei della società stessa.
I consumi forniscono il campo di azione di questa spontaneità: essi non forniscono un modello unico, ma al limite tanti modelli quante sono le individualità in azione.
Il campo dei consumi simula la contestazione al sistema e garantisce un falso recupero della propria individualità, alienata dalla realtà del lavoro.
Il design recupera un proprio ruolo ufficiale: prefigura la "casa del futuro" come astratta proiezione del presente, e simula all'utente una cultura che egli non possiede e un insieme di scelte che egli non ha mai fatto.
Stimola l'azione dell'utente all'interno di una libertà "modulare", cioè di un sistema di riferimento del quale è già garantita la verifica del processo creativo, che deve avvenire all'interno di un perimetro di combinazioni e all'interno di una figurazione predeterminata.
La maggior parte delle volte è proprio l'utente, sollecitato a modificare il proprio paesaggio domestico, che rifiuta tale stimolo, preferendo rendere permanenti una serie di riferimenti formali e funzionali che egli utilizza per recuperare nel più breve tempo possibile quel minimo di equilibrio psicofisico che gli permetta di rinnovare le proprie energie produttive.
Il design così si trova a compiere un'azione di prefigurazione e di stimolo che puntualmente viene rifiutata, o passa al di sopra delle possibilità di assimilazione dell'utente. Lo sforzo di individuare un possibile ruolo ad un ipotetico anti-design, destinato a fungere da stimolo ad una cultura di opposizione, o ricade nell'errore storico di conte-

stare i modelli culturali borghesi attraverso l'elaborazione di altri modelli, o corre il rischio di compiere una azione sostanzialmente reazionaria spingendo verso un rifiuto del benessere, coincidendo al limite con il disegno padronale.
L'unica rifondazione possibile del design, della casa e della città, non risiede in operazioni progettuali formalmente rinnovate, né tanto meno nella spinta incontrollata verso un aggiornamento tecnologico del settore, ma nella modificazione dei rapporti d'uso oggi esistenti tra utente e realtà, tra utente e strutture abitative.
Fino ad oggi il rapporto fondamentale che ha legato l'utente a tutte le strutture progettate, è stato un legame di natura visuale. La proprietà privata, in quanto tale, ha sempre distinto fermamente le due parti componenti la realtà: l'interno e l'esterno. L'esterno, in quanto superficie di contatto tra privato e collettività, restituisce uno schema di lettura convenzionale dell'oggetto, collocandolo senza contraddizioni alla "pubblica visione". Questa realtà discontinua, che non permette una continuità d'uso delle strutture, ma anzi le oggettivizza sempre e le auto-rappresenta, determina una sostanziale alienazione dell'individuo, relegandolo a voyeur di una realtà molto più ampia e molto più complessa dell'insieme delle strutture che egli può utilizzare.
E così la città: una realtà complessiva che l'utente recepisce solo come linguaggio formale, essendogliene impedito un uso totale. Questa realtà formale che egli consuma solo attraverso un rapporto visivo, ha la funzione di restituire la realtà come una struttura culturale, dotata di "valori" che egli recepisce come "naturali", essendo proiezioni della società civile di cui fa parte.
Tali valori preesistono e permangono alla sua esperienza, ed egli non può fare altro che accettarli o rifiutarli, subendo in ogni caso la suggestione dell'esistenza di un significato extra-fisico delle cose.
La gestione del processo formativo di tali valori culturali gli è completamente estranea: non solo, ma all'interno delle relazioni di significato della realtà che ci circonda, qualsiasi atto creativo dell'utente, o meglio qualsiasi attività psico-motoria che noi compiamo, acquista immediatamente un significato di relazione, diventa un'allegoria di se stessa, e sostanzialmente ce ne viene estraniato il significato culturale, come di un qualsiasi prodotto del quale ignoriamo il destino e lo scopo.
L'atto stesso di "abitare" diventa un fatto culturale, cioè di comunicazione con gli altri, ma non di comunicazione spontanea, bensì di comunicazione convenzionale che avviene secondo un codice del quale l'utente non possiede la chiave.
Da qui la necessità di utilizzare un insieme di oggetti già in grado di compiere tale genere di comunicazione.
Gli itinerari del comportamento domestico, tutto organizzato sui tempi di lavoro, ne risultano individuati come da trincee, al di fuori delle quali sembra non esista un significato allo stesso atto di vivere.
La fine della cultura "gestita" e la liberazione dal lavoro significano proprio questo: recuperare il diritto di auto-individuare il proprio habitat come un luogo privo di si-

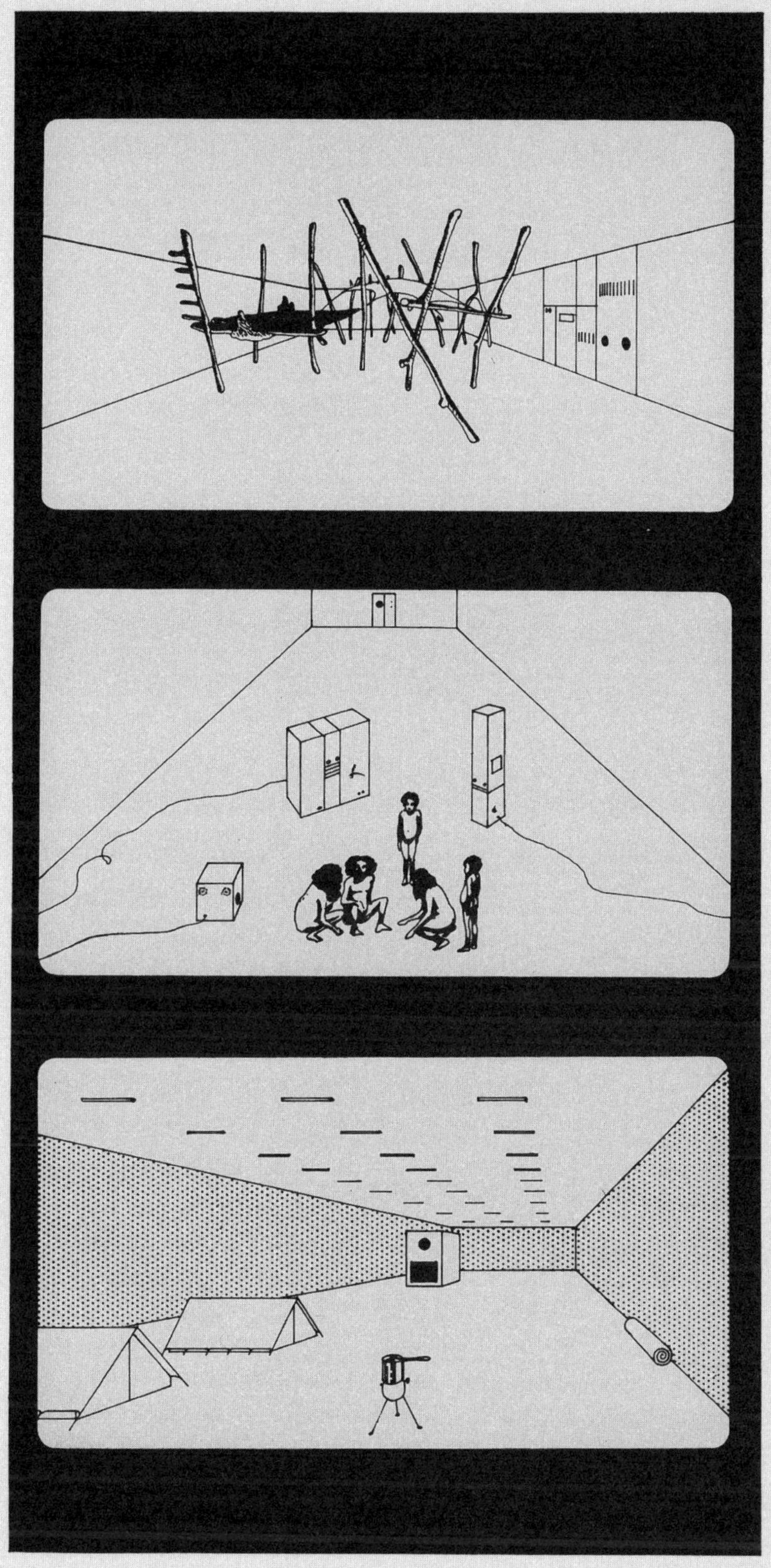

gnificati in codice, privo di una "immagine globale", struttura d'uso e non allegoria culturale.
La rifondazione del design, come di tutte le scienze umane, nasce da un modificato rapporto d'uso con le strutture portanti la società: il ruolo dell'industria cessa di essere quello di fornitrice di un mondo già confezionato, del quale non resta altro che reiventarne il consumo, per divenire quello di fornitrice di strumenti di servizio che individuano un vuoto abitare e non l'immagine della casa del futuro.
La casa come palestra, nella quale sperimentare le proprie facoltà creative atrofizzate da secoli di lavoro produttivo; la casa come parcheggio attrezzato, dentro la quale attuare direttamente lo stesso fenomeno di vivere.
In fondo l'unica buona novella che possiamo almeno annunciare a questo mondo di preoccupati visitatori di Saloni del Mobile è questa: state tranquilli, abitare è facile.

A. Branzi

(3 - fine. Gli articoli precedenti sono stati pubblicati in Casabella 363 e 364.)

Towards the end of the last century, the spontaneous movement to free man from art and culture seemed to have found the great universal instrument with which to achieve its goal in industrial production.
The wave of repugnance the merchandise exhibited in enormous Universal Expositions aroused in the more aware seemed generated rather by a premonition of death than by critical dissent.
Capital, industrial production, begins its social transformation by destroying the reference points of the mercantile civilization which preceeded it. Simply quantitative production proved to be the instrument that unseated the old world and its values.
In fact, the machine, reproducing thousands of times objects born in a single copy, not only destroys their capacity to communicate the economic status of the place they are found in, but removes the criteria for assigning the goods their "objective value", which is constituted by the quantity of labor necessary for their realization. Human labor ceases to be a basic structure of the object and becomes pure productive energy; the object loses its cultural connotation and acquires one that is exclusively technological.
With the transformation of handcraft into labor force, man is denied the management of his productive faculties and the control of production. Industrial reality begins to assume the management of society (through salary) and the task of supplying this society with its patterns. Such patterns are no longer to be external to the world of labor, but rather, in the profound logic which determines it. The factory, even if limited and partial compared with a world still largely mercantile and agricultural, claims its own universality, both through its use of a rational logic and through its efforts to integrate the whole of society and to organize it in labor.
The intellectual is no longer employed as an external elaborator of utopias and morals, but as an operator completely within the cycle and even, the direct mediator between production as a technological fact and its social goal. His role becomes that of discovering the intrinsic logic in the nature of productive processes.
It is here that the designer is born: his role is to transform productive necessities into rational values, and in this direction he salvages all the most advanced experiments of the avant-garde, reducing them to simple exercises in language and using their destructive power as an analytic force that can be utilized rationally.
In this way a perfect coincidence between cultural and industrial revolution is simulated. The force of the former, its tendency towards new management of aesthetic patterns and towards their absolute relativity, is employed as a demonstration of the overwhelming force for contestation inherent in industrial production itself.
(continued on page 74)

TRANSLATIONS

Inhabiting is easy

(continued from page 40)

In the designer, the destruction of culture becomes the effort to reveal to production its own rationality, up to the point of granting it autonomy. Moreover, his efforts to have the product reach the optimal level of identification of technical with communicative qualities lay the premises from which industry can launch itself in the Definitive Series. The universality of art becomes the universality of the product.

The designer, setting himself as intermediary between productive necessities and the physical reality of the goods, tends to transform reality into elementary data, into simple geometric figures, to facilitate their introduction into the machine that must reproduce them.

While disassembly of the object facilitates the organization of labor, identification between the internal logic of the form and productive necessities becomes total, restricting the solution of design.

Production aesthetics becomes a definitive category, fruit of the coincidence between the formativity of the object and its productive processes, but in this way production seems to become a time-operation, a simple filling in of the void formed by needs which once full requires only normal maintenance.

The new man of the "civilisation machiniste" is the one who adopts the laws of production as his own intimate nature, recognizing in the rationality of production, the scientific instrument for the organization of reality (design), but also and above all, his own most profound formativity (cubism).

Only in this way does the relation between factory and society become natural law.

The "all-production" man sacrifices everything to this; he sublimates his own bourgeois ambitions in an "Existenz-Minimum" surrounded by tools.

Design seems the natural debunking instrument of the goods-producing processes induced by industrialization, but the liberation it effects serves to turn all the individual's energy back into his productive potentials. In this profound sense, design operation is repressive. What's more, total integration simulates the liberation of the worker from the bourgeois condition.

The process which proto-design effects of disassembly of all the cultural accessories of the object, does not so much guarantee greater autonomy from myths, as induce rejection of the objects themselves.

The Modern Movement seems decided to define the condition of labor as a "primary condition", devoid of cultural accessories typical of the bourgeois class, pervaded with the logic of the factory which it sees as an instrument of unrelenting contestation of the ruling class's morals.

The working class, therefore, sees itself spontaneously in the factory condition, prefiguring in itself a future civilization wholly engaged in productive efficiency, refusing consumption as a moment extraneous to production.

Production without consumption becomes the revolutionary moral, in contrast with bourgeois reality which instead consumes and does not produce.

But such a hypothesis is rejected by both of the conflicting parties. The working class sees in the factory only an instrument of organization for its battle, which is a struggle against the working condition, meaning poverty, and, possibly, against work itself.

It adopts the mechanism of consumption to verify its own social escalation and, strategically, the methodic destruction of the equilibrium reached the development of the system. Its model is the bourgeois class; substituting for it, it destroys it, together with its patterns and its values. It rejects design as a cultural pattern inhibiting and blunting the revolutionary surge of the class, based upon an imitative thrust and not upon an alternate culture.

Capital also refuses the pattern of design; production cannot demand the disappearance of consumption, but, on the contrary, its progressive increase. A satisfied consumer is also a better worker.

Indeed, production for the working class and for all of society integrated into the Economic Plan must remain a marginal fact, a secondary episode with respect to consumption which gives significance and scope to the productive moment.

Thus, it must not be society that resembles the factory, but the factory, society.

Culture, then, must make the most of consumption, creating a system of transitory behavior patterns. It must lose its unitary connotation and then, instead of one, thousands and thousands of utopias will be born. Not the scientific ethos of the Bauhaus, but the experimentalism of Picasso. If the identification of the Economic plan with Society is real, then the contents of the Plan must coincide with the spontaneous contents of society.

Consumption supplies the field of action with this spontaneity; it does not supply just one pattern, but as many as there are individualities in action.

The field of consumption simulates the contestation of the system and guarantees a false recovery of its own individuality, alienated from the reality of labor.

Design recovers its official role: it prefigures the "house of the future" as an abstract projection of the present and simulates a culture for the consumer which the latter does not possess and an array of choices never made.

It stimulates the action of the consumer within a "modular" freedom, that is, within a system of reference, the verification of the creative process of which is already guaranteed, that must take place within a perimeter of combinations and within a predetermined scheme.

Most of the time it is the consumer himself, invited to modify his domestic landscape, who rejects such a stimulus, preferring to render permanent a series of formal and functional references he uses to recover in the briefest possible time that minimum of psycho-physical equilibrium which permits him to renew his own productive energy.

Design thus finds itself engaged in an action of prefiguration and stimulation which is then punctually rejected or which surpasses the consumer's possibilities of assimilation.

The effort to single out a possible role for a hypothetical "Anti-design", intended as a stimulus for a culture of opposition, either falls into the historic error of contesting bourgeois culture patterns with the elaboration of other patterns, or runs the risk of conducting an action substantially reactionary, pushing towards a rejection of well-being, coinciding at its worst with the plan of the ruling class.

The only possible refounding of design, of the house and city, does not lie in formally renewed projects, nor, even less, in the uncontrolled thrust towards a technological modernization of the sector, but in the modification of the customary relations existing today between consumer and reality, between consumer and habitation structures.

Up to now the fundamental relation binding the consumer to all projects has been a tie of a visual nature. Private property as such has always firmly distinguished between the two components of reality: the interior and the exterior.

The exterior as surface of contact between the private and the collective, gives back a conventional reading of the object, collocating, it without contradictions of the "public viewpoint". This discontinuous reality, which does not allow a continuity of use of the structures, but rather objectifies them and self-represents them, determines a substantial alienation of the individual, reducing him to an onlooker of a reality much greater and more complex than the group of structures he can utilize.

Thus the city: a complex reality the consumer perceives only as a formal language since he is prevented the full use of it.

This formal reality which he consumes only through a visual relationship, has the function of giving back reality as a cultural structure, equipped with "values" he perceives as "natural", since they are a projection of the civilized society of which he is a part.

Such values preexist and endure in his experience; he can only accept or reject them, receiving in either case the impression of the existence of an extra-physical significance of things. The management of the formative process of such cultural values is completely extraneous. Not only that: within the relationships of meaning of the reality which surrounds us, any creative act of the consumer, or, even any psycho-motory activity in which we engage immediately acquires the significance of a rapport, becomes an allegory of itself and, in substance, its cultural significance is estranged from us like that of any product of which we ignore the destiny and scope.

The very act of "inhabiting" becomes a cultural fact, of communication with others, that is, but not spontaneous, rather, conventional communication which takes place according to a code to which the user has no key. From this stems the necessity of employing a combination of objects that can already effect this kind of communication.

The itineraries of domestic behavior, organized completely on the basis of allowed time, stand out like trenches, outside of which it seems there exists no meaning in the very act of living.

The end of "managed" cultures and liberation from work mean exactly this: recovery of the right to the self-determination of one's own habitat as a place free of meanings in code, without a meaningful "global image", a structure to be used and not a cultural allegory.

The refounding of design, as of all human sciences, comes from a modified rapport with the structures bearing society: the role of industry ceases to be that of supplier of a ready-made world, for which nothing remains to be done except reinvent its consumption, to become that of supplier of instruments which serve to single out the habitational void and not the image of the house of the future.

The house as a gymnasium in which to experiment one's own creative faculties, atrophied by centuries of productive work; the house as an equipped parking lot where one can act out directly the very phenomenon of living. After all, the only good news we can at least announce to this world of worried visitors of Furniture Fairs is this: Stay calm, inhabiting is easy.

Le Mostre d'Architettura già nella loro definizione linguistica confermano un equivoco: l'equivoco consiste nel credere che l'architettura sia una cosa da mettere in "mostra", cioè da vedere.
In effetti l'architettura, così come ce la consegna la tradizione storica, è lo strumento più generale per "rappresentare" la città: la sua qualità formale coincide con l'impegno linguistico a figurare, quasi letterariamente, la città e gli insediamenti urbani.
Piante, sezioni, prospetti, assonometrie e prospettive sono passati da strumenti tecnici di controllo a operazioni culturali compiute in se stesse: l'architettura non riesce a superare il suo limite di "oggetto", non riesce a diventare sistema di strutture d'uso.
La città attuale non rappresenta più se stessa, non ha cioè una forma significativa, e questo non tanto perché la speculazione ha distrutto certi equilibri, ma perché storicamente il messaggio "visuale" è superato: la città possiede una forma, ma tale forma non ha significato alcuno. Sarebbe come cercare di attribuire un qualche valore estetico o allegorico alle coltivazioni agricole, considerando il loro margine come un "fronte", una "facciata", e non come un semplice passaggio tra due diverse coltivazioni del terreno.
Ciò che oggi "costituisce la città" non è più il "luogo architettonico", ma le informazioni, i costumi, le comunicazioni, i servizi. La qualità della vita si migliora attraverso altri parametri, non certo più attraverso il linguaggio architettonico.
La Sezione internazionale di Industrial Design che noi abbiamo organizzato non è una mostra di architettura o di design, ma è la registrazione di problemi, discorsi, idee, programmi, catastrofi e invenzioni: non abbiamo esposto neppure un oggetto.
Il fatto che risultasse impossibile al visitatore recepire tutti i messaggi che la Sezione presentava, è da considerarsi una condizione inevitabile, legata alla natura del design e alla reale molteplicità degli operatori. Esponendo oggetti, secondo una formula tradizionale, in realtà forniamo al visitatore ancora meno informazioni.
E' stato detto, e sono d'accordo, che questa XV Triennale ha avuto il merito di presentare un limpido diagramma delle diverse posizioni culturali all'interno dello schieramento architettonico italiano.
Non sono d'accordo quando si identifica questo schieramento in monumentalismo, product-design e contro-design. Le differenze non sono solo queste dal momento che il contro-design è anche monumentalismo, e il product-design è anche contro-design ecc. Le differenze non sono di questa natura infatti, ma di natura ideologica.
Diciamo che vi è un diverso atteggiamento verso la "libertà individuale": per i monumentalisti essa non esiste se non come qualità culturale e mai come libertà d'uso; per il product-design tradizionale la libertà è un fenomeno isterico legato solo al consumo differenziato a livello individuale; per il contro-design la libertà è prima di tutto libertà "dalla cultura", dalle sue strutture di valori e dai suoi sistemi estetici.
La crisi attuale della cultura, la sua segmentazione, la sua impossibilità a raggiungere valori universali e duraturi, l'inutilità dei suoi messaggi, l'assenza di un suo ruolo ecc. viene simulata dai monumentalisti, che giungono a proporre un sistema di valori totalmente artificiale, direi quasi una protesi culturale, o cultura ortopedica, che se non è reale serve a simulare una cultura reale. Tale simulazione non è né suicida né ironica: è soltanto reazionaria perché non accetta la morte della cultura come un fenomeno positivo, in grado di fornire all'uomo una libertà in più, ma considerano la morte della cultura come un salto nel buio, nel vuoto, e hanno paura.
Come i saggi di Salamanca che rifiutavano l'America...

Andrea Branzi

Crisi e protesi culturali
Cultural crises and prostheses

**By their very linguistic definition exhibitions of architecture give credence to a mistaken notion, the notion that architecture is something to put on exhibit, something to see.
Actually, architecture, as it has been handed down to us by tradition, is indeed the most general instrument for "representing" a city: its formal qualities coincide with the linguistic commitment to shape (almost literally shape) the city and all other urban settlements.
Plans, sections, perspectives, axonometry, and façades have become not only instruments of technical control but also cultural operations in themselves: architecture cannot get beyond its limit as an "object" to become a system of useful structures.
The city today no longer represents itself; it lacks, that is, a significant form, and not so much because speculation has destroyed certain balances, but because its "visual" message has been historically superseded: the city has a form, but that form has no significance whatsoever. It would be like attributing some aesthetic or allegorical value to crops, considering the divisions of the field to be "fronts" or "façades", and not simple passages from one type of cultivation to another. What "constitutes the city" today is no longer the "architectonic place", but its information, customs, communications, and services. The quality of life improves through other parameters and certainly no longer through architectonic idiom.
The International Section of Industrial Design that we have organized at the Triennale is not an exhibition of architecture or design, but a recording of problems, speeches, ideas, programmes, catastrophes, and inventions: we haven't exhibited a single object.
The fact that the visitor found it impossible to receive all the messages presented by the Section may be considered inevitable, part of the nature of design and the very real multiplicity of the operators.
By exhibiting objects in a traditional way we would only have provided even less information for the visitor.
It has been said, and I agree, that this XV Triennale may be credited with having presented a clear picture of the various cultural positions held on the Italian architectonic scene. But I cannot agree that this line-up is identical with monumentalism, product-design, and counter-design. These are not the only differences, since counter-design is also monumentalism, and product-design is also counter-design, etc. The differences are not of this nature in fact, but are ideological.
Let us say that there is a different attitude towards "individual freedom": for the monumentalist it does not exist except as a cultural quality and never as freedom of use; for traditional product-design freedom is an hysterical phenomenon exclusively bound up with differentiated individual consumption; for counter-design freedom is first of all freedom "from culture", from its structure of values and its aesthetic systems.
The current cultural crisis, its segmentation, its inability to achieve universal and lasting values, the uselessness of its messages, the lack of a rôle of its own, etc. — all this is simulated by the monumentalists, who offer nothing less than a system of completely artificial values, almost a cultural prosthesis or "orthopaedic culture" which, though not real, is useful in that it simulates real culture. This simulation is neither suicidal nor ironic: it is only reactionary, because it does not accept the death of culture as a positive phenomenon capable of providing man with one more freedom, but considers the death of culture as a leap into darkness and the void, and they are afraid.
Like the wise men of Salamanca who rejected America...**

36

"Cultural Crises and Protheses," in *Casabella* n. 385, 1984

Andrea Branzi, "Radical Architecture," in *Casabella* n. 386, 1974

Andrea Branzi (Archizoom Associati)

Radical architecture

Il rifiuto del ruolo disciplinare

La radical architecture si colloca all'interno del più generale movimento di liberazione dell'uomo dalla cultura, intendendo per liberazione individuale dalla cultura la rimozione di tutti i parametri formali e morali che agendo come strutture inibitorie (inibitorie in quanto non auto-progettate) impediscono all'individuo di realizzarsi compiutamente.
La radical architecture si colloca all'interno di questo movimento e tende a ridurre a zero tutti i processi di progettazione, rifiutando il ruolo di settore disciplinare impegnato a prefigurare attraverso le strutture ambientali un futuro già codificato.
La radical architecture rinuncia a ipotizzare la ' forma della città futura '; essa stabilisce con la città un rapporto scientifico, nel senso che rimuove dal dibattito urbano qualsiasi concetto di qualità tipico dell'architettura borghese, riportando il fenomeno ai soli parametri quantitativi.
Piazze, palazzi, boulevards, monumenti, strade, viali, case, chiese, uffici, teatri, ecc., sono momenti scenici di un vecchio concetto teatrale di città, città con la quale non è possibile stabilire se non un rapporto di natura ' visuale '. Il tentativo è quello di andare al di là di questo rapporto, per individuare strutture d'uso e non strutture estetiche.
Dicendo che il nostro tentativo è anche quello di rimuovere i parametri qualitativi o estetici dalle strutture abitative, intendiamo affermare una cosa di fondamentale importanza: il problema non è la forma della casa del futuro, ma ' l'uso futuro della casa '.
Una nuova architettura non può nascere da un semplice atto di progettazione, ma dalla modificazione dell'uso che l'individuo può fare del proprio ambiente. Più questo ambiente possiede connotazioni culturali e linguistiche proprie, più il suo libero uso ne resta impedito; più l'individuo è costretto a muoversi all'interno di un medium culturalmente già codificato e più egli rinuncerà all'uso delle proprie facoltà creative, già profondamente atrofizzate dal suo destino di produttore (e non di creatore).
La casa tradizionale, perfettamente funzionale all'interno dell'attuale società, dove la produzione di cultura come libera e spontanea forma di comunicazione è resa impossibile, agisce come comunicazione sociale codificata; tali codici non sono posseduti dall'utente ma dal progettista, il quale opera scelte culturali in sua vece.
Uscire fuori da questo circuito di rapporti produttore-utente significa lasciar cadere le connotazioni spaziali dell'ambiente per puntare all'individuazione di un vuoto vivibile; la casa non più come tipologia sociale, ma come palestra disponibile alla continua sperimentazione della creatività individuale, non la sua forma appunto è importante, ma il suo uso.
L'utopia che la radical architecture utilizza non rappresenta un modello migliore di società da proporre al mondo, ma rappresenta piuttosto uno strumento di accelerazione della realtà al fine di ottenerne una lettura migliore: essa utopia dichiara che fine ultimo della lotta sociale è la liberazione dell'uomo dal lavoro, e che fine ultimo dell'eliminazione della cultura è la produzione intellettuale di massa.
Non importa quale sarà il comportamento dell'uomo libero dal lavoro, né quale sarà il contenuto di una produzione intellettuale di massa; quello che è importante è l'uso diverso che ognuno potrà fare del proprio immaginario inespresso e quindi della propria vita.

Andrea Branzi (Archizoom Associati)

Radical architecture

Refusing the disciplinary rôle

Radical architecture may be considered part of the more general movement for the liberation of man from culture, meaning by individual liberation from culture the removal of all formal and moral parameters which create inhibitory structures (inhibitory because not self-engendered) and prevent the individual from fully realizing himself.
As part of this movement radical architecture tends to reduce all planning processes to zero, refusing to act as a disciplinary sector charged with prefiguring an already codified future through environmental structures.
Radical architecture no longer advances hypotheses regarding ' the form of the future city '. It establishes a scientific relationship with the city, in the sense that it removes from the discussion of urban problems any concept of quality typical of middle-class architecture, relating problems to quantitative parameters alone.
Squares, public-buildings, boulevards, monuments, streets, avenues, houses, churches, office-buildings, theatres, etc., are moments in the scenery of the old theatrical concept of the city, a city with which it is possible to establish only a ' scenic ' relationship. The aim is to go beyond this relationship in order to single out structures in which use rather than aesthetics is the main consideration.
In saying that it is also our intention to remove qualitative or aesthetic parameters from habitational structures, we mean to underscore a thing of the very greatest importance: that the problem is not the form of the future home but ' the future use ' of the home.
A new architecture cannot spring from a simple act of designing, but only from a modification in the use that an individual makes of his environment. The more this environment has cultural and linguistic qualities of its own, the more one is restricted in his use of this environment; the more the individual is compelled to move within the limits of a medium already conditioned culturally, the less he will use his own creative faculties, which have already atrophied considerably as a result of his work as a producer rather than a creator.
Perfectly functional within the context of present-day society, where the production of culture as a free and spontaneous form of communication has become impossible, the traditional home represents codified social communication; these codes are not owned by the householder but by the designer, who makes cultural choices in his stead.
If we are to escape from this circuit of producer-householder relationships we must abandon the spatial ' qualities ' of our architectural surroundings and concentrate on the definition of habitable empty space; the house, in other words, is no longer to be considered a social typology, but a kind of gymnasium available for the continuous experimentation of individual creativity; in other words, the important thing is not its form but its use.
The Utopia utilized by radical architecture represents not so much a better model of society to propose to the world, as an instrument for accelerating reality in order to make better use of it: this Utopia testifies that the end-purpose of the social struggle is the liberation of man from work, and that the end-purpose of the elimination of culture is intellectual production on the part of the masses.
It does not matter what man's behaviour will be once he is freed from work, nor what the content will be of intellectual production on the part of the masses; what is important is the use every man will make of his own untried imagination and therefore of his own life.

Andrea Branzi

Immagini da « The Last Whole Earth Catalog - access to tools «.

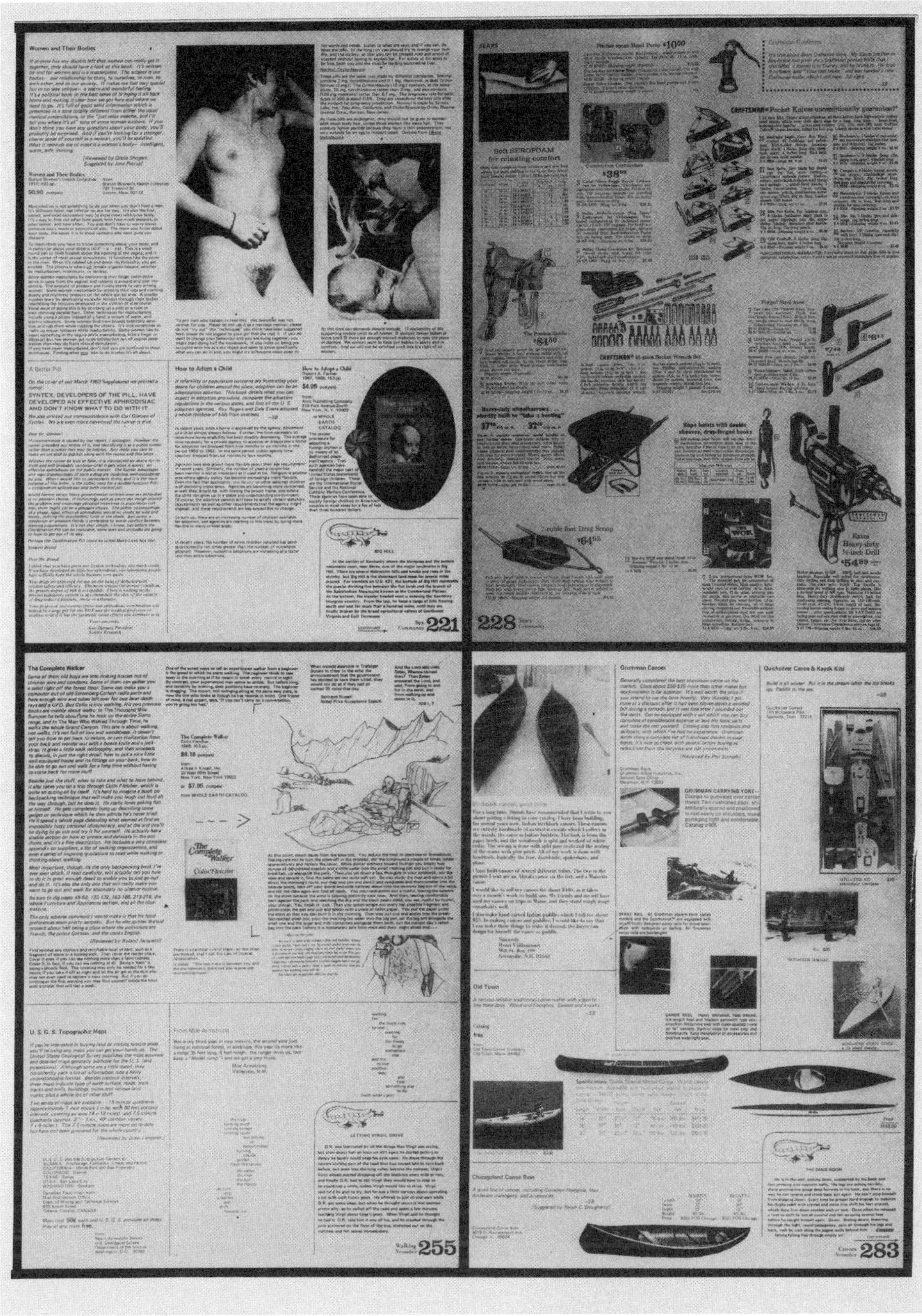
Women and Their Bodies
A Better Pill
How to Adopt a Child
Sex Community 221
SEARS
Soft SEROFOAM for relaxing comfort
CRAFTSMAN Pocket Knives unconditionally guaranteed
Heavy-duty wheelbarrows
Extra Heavy-duty ¼-inch Drill
228 Stars Community
The Complete Walker
U. S. G. S. Topographic Maps
Walking Nomadics 255
Grumman Canoes
Quicksilver Canoe & Kayak Kits
GRUMMAN CARRYING YOKE
Old Town
Chicagoland Canoe Base
Canoes Nomadics 283

APPARATUS FOR A DIFFUSE CREATIVITY

Bulletin *Global Tools*, n.1, Cover, 1974

Al di fuori del design

GLOBAL TOOLS SCUOLA DI NON-ARCHITETTURA

In un seminario svoltosi in novembre a Sambuca è stata definita l'attività della scuola per il 1975 / Global Tools, a school of non-architecture: its future activity has been discussed and defined during a seminar held in November at Sambuca near Florence

Andrea Branzi
TECNOLOGIA O EUTANASIA

Per la festa dei Morti, ma anche per quella di Tutti i Santi, grande raduno a Sambuca, vicino a Firenze, della Global Tools: al richiamo convenuto escono da libri, opuscoli, manifesti, manuali, riviste, ciclostilati diversi, gli Archizoom, i Superstudio, Ettorino e la Nanda, Buti e Signora, gli Zziggurat, i 9999, gli Ufo, Casabella, Gianni Pettena, Ugo La Pietra, i napoletani Alison e Dalisi, Franco Castelli, amici, volontari, curiosi, umanità varia e dispersa sul poggio lungo la superstrada per Siena.
Stretti dalla morsa di un freddo precoce dentro una casa colonica disabitata ma attrezzata di fuochi e cavi tapes, registratori, rotolini fotografici, castagne, salumi, legname, verdure, paste, letti, tavoli, piatti e bicchieri, alcuni cani che rincorrono bambini, presenti quasi settanta persone, parcheggi di ghiaia intasati di macchine, ruderi e cespugli, e partenza finale di una mongolfiera e suo recupero, sua nuova partenza e viaggio in alto oltre le nuvole...
Nasce ufficialmente il progetto finale della prima contro-scuola italiana di architettura, (o non architettura), (o non scuola, primo tentativo di pagine gialle della cultura, prontuario di laboratori provvisori e privati nella città, agenzie di diffusione nella società di tutte le attività creative legate all'uso di tecniche costruttive e di tutti i sistemi sotto-architettonici di identità dell'ambiente: "Una, due, cento, mille Global Tools...".
La struttura funzionante nasce dall'idea di una segreteria che mette in contatto chiunque lo desideri, con tutti i luoghi, le persone, i gruppi, che lavorano nella direzione definita come liberazione dell'uomo dalla cultura, intesa come tecnologia e codice che estranea l'individuo dal libero uso della propria creatività. In questo senso verrà preparato un piano di possibilità stagionali da offrire, perché no?, come ginnastica di recupero, come spedizione in uno strato inesplorato delle risorse umane e creative di una città (si potranno imparare sistemi volutamente imperfetti e anche sartoria, strutture instabili e anche taglio dei capelli, archeologia del futuro e anche falegnameria, viaggi come comunicazione e anche la tecnica della cartapesta...).
La sede della scuola non esiste (esiste l'indirizzo della segreteria: via Brera 9, Milano), ma esistono tante scuole quanti sono i luoghi

On All Souls' and also All Saints' there was a big gathering of Global Tools at Sambuca near Florence: on hearing the "call" there was a general desertion of books, booklets, manifestos, manuals, reviews, and sundry mimeographed sheets on the part of the Archizoom and Superstudio groups, Ettorino and Nanda, Buti and wife, the Zziggurats, the 9999s, the UFOs, Casabella, Gianni Pettena, Ugo La Pietra, the Neapolitans Alison and Dalisi, Franco Castelli, as well as friends, volunteers, people just curious... humanity, varied and dispersed along the hill running parallel to the highway to Siena. In the grip of an early cold wave, in an old house that, though abandoned, was fully equipped with fire, cables, tapes, recorders, rolls of film, chestnuts, delicatessen spreads, firewood, vegetables, pasta, beds, tables, plates and glasses, a few dogs chasing children, etc... were come, seventy people; the gravelled parkway obstructed with cars, rubble and bushes, and then the final departure of a balloon and its recovery, followed by a new departure and flight beyond the clouds...
This, then, was the official birth of the final project for the first Italian counter-school of architecture (or non-architecture; or again non-school), the first attempt at a cultural Directory or guide to provisional and private laboratories in town, an agency for the spread throughout society of all creative activities connected with the use of constructional techniques and of all the sub-architectonic systems for characterizing the environment: "One, two; a hundred, a thousand Global Tools..."
The operational structure springs from the idea of a secretariat that puts anyone who wishes in contact with all the places, persons, groups working in the direction defined as the liberation of man from culture conceived as a technology and code that inhibits the individual's free use of his own creativity. In this sense a plan of seasonal possibilities will be prepared, to be offered — why not? — as curative exercises, as expeditions in an unexplored layer of the human and creative resources of a city (deliberately imperfect systems can be learned, as well as tailoring, unstable structures and also haircutting, the archaeology of the future and also historical carpentry, travelling as communication and also the techniques of papier-mâché...). The school has no particular site (but the address of the secretarial offices is Via Brera 9, Milan), yet there are as many schools as there are places where the courses take place — Milan, Florence, Naples, but also small towns and big cities, which we will unite in a new league of free cities: Vienna, Berlin, New York, Toronto, San Francisco, Bergamo, Forlì, etc. The problem of "founding a school" coincides this time with the problem of "freeing oneself from school", of teaching to learn, of organizing in order to guarantee discontinuity, of making contacts in order to spread one's personal case, with taking one's place in history in order to remain a pure phenomenon.
We now have the discovery of

Casabella 397/1976 17

Andrea Branzi, "Technology or Euthanasia," Global Tools, in *Casabella* n. 397, 1976

dove i corsi avvengono, Milano, Firenze, Napoli, ma forse anche piccoli paesi, grandi metropoli, che riuniremo in una nuova lega di città libere: Vienna, Berlino, Toronto, San Francisco, Bergamo, Forlì ecc. Il problema di "fondare una scuola" coincide questa volta con il problema di "liberarsi della scuola", insegnare per apprendere, organizzarsi per garantire la discontinuità, collegarsi per diffondere il caso personale, storicizzarsi per restare puro fenomeno.
La scoperta delle tecniche semplici, gli elenchi di tutte le tecniche manuali che il neo-enciclopedismo americano (gli Earth Catalog del Portola Institute, i Dome Book ecc.) nato sotto la spinta di una immediata riappropriazione e gestione di tecniche che garantissero a una generazione transfuga dal benessere, con un grave complesso di colpa, il minimo di sopravvivenza e nuove qualità, ci restano in mano, queste tecniche, come le ceneri di un grande fuoco spento, come una riduzione, una miniaturizzazione della realtà assai più ampia e ricca, come un furto di informazioni sul Capitale, e su ciò di cui avremmo diritto? Oppure queste tecniche "povere" sono già un modello alternativo, di tipo cinese, di una qualità della miseria? E se così fosse, allora il nostro impegno dovrebbe essere quello di trasformare questi primi esempi di un grande sistema positivo in un più ampio modello sociale, articolato e sistematizzato, pronto per l'uso, per una società in evoluzione, che cerca altre qualità della vita oltre quelle del frusto benessere capitalistico.
Ma così facendo, ancora una volta saremmo ricaduti nel primo grande trabocchetto del Sistema, che assegna proprio alle frange più avanzate della cultura il compito di elaborare e proporre modelli sociali, come traguardi da raggiungere; progettati da specialisti, e da consigliare alle incerte masse che "non sanno mai bene da che parte dirigersi". In questo caso specifico vi sarebbero anche due vantaggi secondari non indifferenti: il primo riguarderebbe il ritrovamento di un ruolo ufficiale di progettazione per una cultura che assiste oggi impotente al proprio inesorabile consumo, priva di destino e di strumenti morali, logorata dall'inesorabile avanzata delle "classi incolte" che tutto imitano, niente progettano e tutto comprano; l'altro vantaggio consisterebbe nel proporre all'inarrestabile richiesta economica e salariale, alla sfrenata rincorsa verso il benessere, allo sfrontato desiderio di ricchezza delle masse operaie, l'alternativa di una più facile "strategia della miseria", utilizzabile subito, prima ancora della rivoluzione, come salubre terapia di rinuncia alle smanie borghesi.
Tutto quello che è stato fatto allora in questi anni non sarebbe altro che un "messaggio in codice", come un enigma da sciogliere, celato oltre l'apparenza di fenomeno puro. Ma questo non è vero e se lo fosse lo rifiuteremmo.
Che fare dunque di queste tecniche alternative, povere e semplici, eppure così affascinanti e dotate di una propria "ricchezza"?
Che fare di questa carica eversiva, distruttiva, di tanti progetti e di tante esperienze che tendono a ridurre tutte le tecnologie della cultura? Considerare il tutto una grande vacanza o il progetto in vitro

di un'altra estetica e di un'altra cultura?
Esistono alternative possibili? Forse non ne esistono, e il salto che dobbiamo fare ancora una volta è in verticale e non in avanti. Se non stiamo attenti ripercorreremo lo stesso sciagurato cammino del Bauhaus che recuperò, sistematizzò, rigenerò come energia analitica e razionale la forza distruttiva delle avanguardie, trasformando lo scardinamento della cultura i un "nuovo linguaggio" di questa.
Ciò che noi dovremmo davvero rendere permanente è la discontinuità del pensiero e della realtà, rifiutando al progetto di superare la dimensione dello spunto, dell'abbozzo, del tentativo, dell'atto imprevedibile, dirompente solo in se stesso, senza traccia duratura.
Oggi disponiamo di un brogliaccio di teorie e di pratiche; se iniziamo elaborazioni rigorosamente coscienti legando la tecnica allo sforzo teorico, chi ci garantisce dal pericolo di trasformare la furia in "nuova poetica"?
Tante volte abbiamo detto, e sempre ci ripetiamo, che ruolo dell'avanguardia è la distruzione tecnica della cultura, come operazione non terroristica ma liberatoria, come rimozione di tutte le morali, le estetiche, i codici che inibiscono la libera espressione della creatività individuale e collettiva. La nostra azione affianca, come lenta ma inesorabile corrosione degli specifici disciplinari, la grande distruzione storica della cultura, operata meccanicamente dalla crescita economica delle grandi masse lavoratrici, le quali imitano i modelli culturali borghesi, recependoli come traguardi di censo, distruggendo gli equilibri economici sui quali si basano, demolendo inesorabilmente la piattaforma morale e culturale, fatta di valori e significati universali, sulla quale la borghesia ha sempre basato il suo diritto morale alla progettazione del mondo.
Se le avanguardie, nel momento della loro presa di coscienza operano una trasformazione della propria spinta in un "sistema" di messaggi e di nuove dimensioni progettuali, recuperando al loro charlottesco operare, sempre per negativo, la dignità di un nuovo campionario formale, ancora una volta — come tanti anni fa, all'inizio degli anni '20 — daremo nuovo ossigeno e nuovo movimento a quella "cultura" che vogliamo eliminare. Allora il nostro vero dilemma è di rendere permanente il "non significato", la grande scoperta del "privo di valore", l'esasperante discontinuità della realtà che viviamo. L'aver capito e dimostrato che l'arte non è che uno sfruttamento produttivo della creatività, che l'intellettuale professionista non opera che un furto al diritto inalienabile di tutti a produrre e consumare la propria cultura privata, che la società aliena attraverso la divisione del lavoro, tutte le facoltà creative, e quindi anche politiche dell'uomo.

IL PRIMO SEMINARIO
La Global Tools — sistema di laboratori didattici per la creatività individuale — si è delineata come una scuola senza sede, un "elenco di materie" che verranno sviluppate nei luoghi loro più congeniali. Ogni stagione in qualche campagna si svolgerà un seminario di coordinamento, il cui esito sarà comunicato tramite i bollettini. Il programma del primo ciclo di attività per il 1975 verrà pubblicato nel bollettino numero 2.

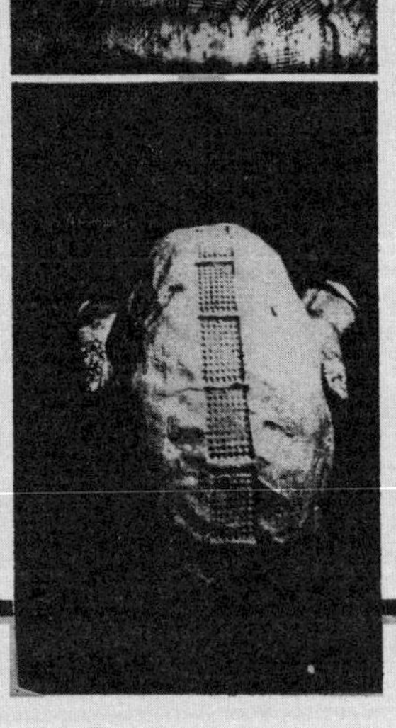

simple techniques and lists of all the manual techniques that the American neo-encyclopaedic spirit has brought out (The Earth Catalog of the Portola Institute, the Dome Books, etc.) in its drive to reappropriate and oversee techniques that will guarantee a guilt-ridden generation in flight from affluence a minimum of survival and new qualities; we are left with these techniques like the ashes of a dead bonfire, like a reduction, a miniaturization of a much broader and richer reality, like the theft of information on the Capital, and on whatever we have a right to: or are these "minimal" techniques alternatives, based on Chinese models, of a quality of poverty? And if this is so, our task would be to transform these early examples into a great positive system, into a broader social model, fully articulated and arranged, ready to be used by a society in evolution, a society seeking something else from life than the mechanisms of stale Capitalist affluence. But if we did so, we would once again fall into the first great trap of the system, which charges the more advanced sectors of the culture with the task of elaborating and proposing social models as goals to achieve, models drawn up by specialists and recommended to the uncertain masses who "never know which way to turn".
In this particular case there would also be two considerable secondary advantages: the first would be the recovery of an official planning role for a culture which is now standing by helplessly in the face of its own inexorable decline, without a future and with no moral authority, worn down by the steady advance of the "uncouth classes" that imitate everything, plan nothing, and buy everything; the other advantage would be to meet the endless requests for improvements in salaries and economic standing, the wild pursuit of affluence, and the brazen desire for riches shown by the working class with the alternative of an easier "strategy of poverty" which can be employed immediately, even before the revolution, as a healthy therapy based on an abandonment of aspirations to middle-class status.
Everything done in recent years, then, could be considered no more than a "coded message", a puzzle to be solved, lying hidden behind the appearance of a pure phenomenon. But this is not the case; and even if it were, we would reject it.
So what shall we do about these alternative techniques; minimal and plain, and yet so

fascinating and possessed of a richness all their own? What shall we do about the corrosive, destructive charge of so many projects and experiments, which tend to reduce to the same common denominator all forms of technology and culture? Consider it all one big holiday, or the germ of another aesthetic and another culture?
Are there any other solutions? Perhaps there aren't any, and the leap that we'll have to make this time will be up and not simply ahead. If we are not careful we shall find ourselves going the same way as the Bauhaus, which recuperated, ordered, and regenerated the destructive power of the avant-garde in the form of analytical and rational energy which was destined to give industry a new dynamic dimension of bourgeois culture, transforming what was really the undoing of culture into the "new idiom" in industrial design. What we should really make permanent is discontinuity of thought and reality, preventing the project from going beyond a suggestion, a sketch, an attempt, or an unpredictable act, an end in itself without anything durable or consistent to back it up.
Now we have a day-book of theories and practices; if we should work out severe and highly conscientious plans, joining technology and theory, who would guarantee that this fury would not be transformed into a "new aesthetic"?
We cannot repeat it too often that the role of the avant-garde is the technical destruction of culture, and this is seen not as an act of terrorism but as a liberation, as a removal of all the moral considerations, aesthetic creeds and codes which hamper the free expression of individual and collective expression. Our action, as a slow but inexorable corrosion of specific disciplines, goes hand in hand with the great historic destruction of culture mechanically effected by the economic growth of the working masses. These masses imitate bourgeois cultural models, assimilating them as income goals, while destroying the economic balances on which they rest and while demolishing their moral and cultural platform, a foundation of universal values and meaning on which the middle-class has always based its moral right to plan the world.
If the avant-garde, in their moment of doubt, should effect the transformation of their thrust into a "system" of messages and new scales of projects, reclaiming for their Chaplinesque behaviour the dignity of a new formal range, it would mean that once again — as we did in the early '20s — we would be giving a new lease on life to the very culture that we want to eliminate. Our real dilemma, then, is to make "non-meaning" permanent, the great discovery of "worthlessness", and the exasperating discontinuity of the reality in which we live.
For what is really important is to have understood and demonstrated that art is only the productive exploitation of creativity, that the professional intellectual only robs us of the inalienable right we all have to produce and consume our own private culture, and that society, through the division of labour, alienates all of man's creative faculties, including the political ones.

Andrea Branzi

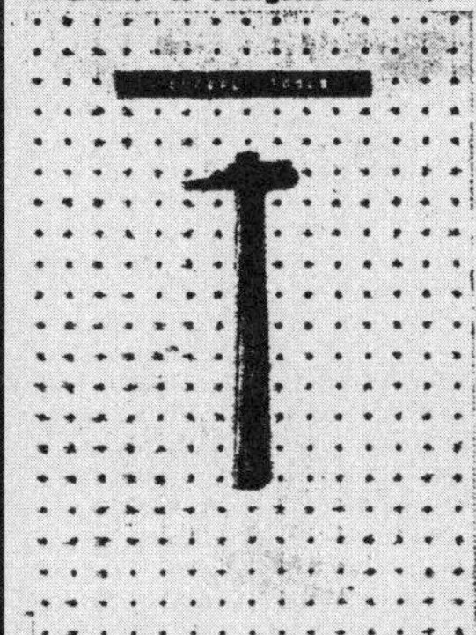

IL BOLLETTINO
Il bollettino numero zero della Global Tools si può chiedere rivolgendosi alla segreteria della scuola: via Brera 9, 20121 Milano, all'attenzione di Paola Navone. Esso contiene la prima sintesi dei significati e delle definizioni della scuola stessa.
Notizie e documenti della Global Tools sono stati pubblicati in Casabella n. 377 e 379.

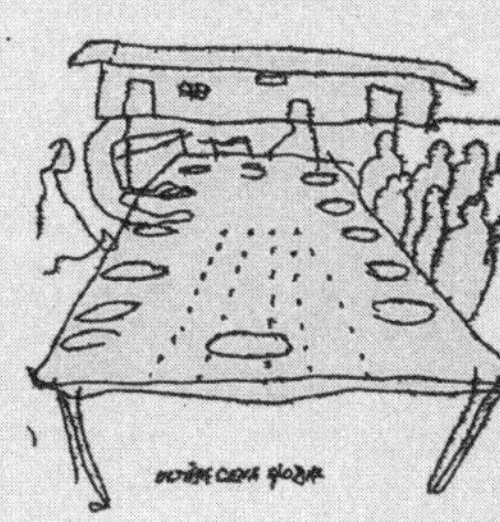

Document-o No.4 "The-Il-Program-ma"

IL PROGRAMMA PER IL PRIMO SEMINARIO, SETTEMBRE 1974.

Le esperienze che si concretizzeranno all'interno di questo mese saranno tese allo sviluppo di quattro particolari tematiche riguardanti:

— il corpo
— la costruzione
— la comunicazione
— la sopravvivenza

Attraverso l'indagine e l'approfondimento di questi settori, dell'"esperienza" individuale e collettiva, legati ad un recupero del comportamento creativo nei processi di riappropriazione dell'ambiente, si intende ricavare una serie di indicazioni e di dati indispensabili per la definizione dei programmi di lavoro da realizzarsi per tutto l'anno 1975.

PROGRAMME FOR THE FIRST SEMINAR, SEPTEMBER 1974

The activities which will be arranged during this month will have the object of developing four particular themes regarding:
- the body
- construction
- communication
- survival

By carrying out research in depth into these themes and individual and collective experiences, linked to a revival of creative activity in the process of reconquering the environment, it is the aim to obtain a series of facts and figures for the setting up of work programmes for the whole of 1975.

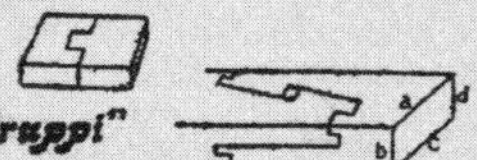

Document-o No.5 "Groups-Ae-ttivit-q-à-Dei Gruppi"

Ogni tematica sarà sviluppata da gruppi di "operatori" che definirono i programmi e le modalità operative con la partecipazione degli "iscritti".

Lo sviluppo teorico e pratico di ogni tematica avrà una durata massima di otto giorni. Le tematiche saranno svolte una successivamente all'altra. All'interno di ogni "argomento" i vari operatori si collocheranno nel seguente ordine:

— CORPO: Natalini, Pesce, Chiari, Celant, eccetera.
— COSTRUZIONE: Dalisi, Sottsass, Branzi, Alison, Fabro, eccetera.
— COMUNICAZIONE: La Pietra, Pettena, Vaccari, Mendini, eccetera.
— SOPRAVVIVENZA: Superstudio, Ufo, Raggi, 9999, eccetera.
— TEORIA: Binazzi, Celant, Sottsass, eccetera.

Each theme will be developed by groups of "workers", who will devise the programmes and the way they are going to be carried out, and this will also involve a contribution from the "students".
The theoretical and practical development of each theme will not last more than eight days. The themes will be studied one after the other. For each of the various subjects the "workers" will take the following order:

- BODY	Natalini/ Pesce/ Chiari/ Celant/ etc.
- CONSTRUCTION	Dalisi/ Sottsass/ Branzi/ Alison/ Fabro/ etc.
- COMMUNICATION	La Pietra/ Pettena/ Vaccari/ Mendini/ etc.
- SURVIVAL	Superstudio/ Ufo/ Raggi/ 9999/ etc.
- THEORY	Binazzi/ Celant/ Sottsass/ etc.

Con-versa-z-i-ion-e Tra- Binazzi Branzi Celant La Pietra Mendini Natalini Raggi Sottsass Jr.

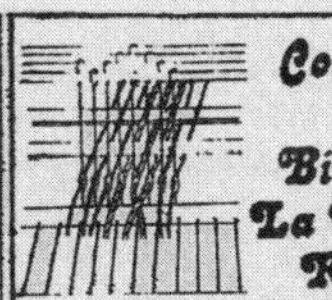

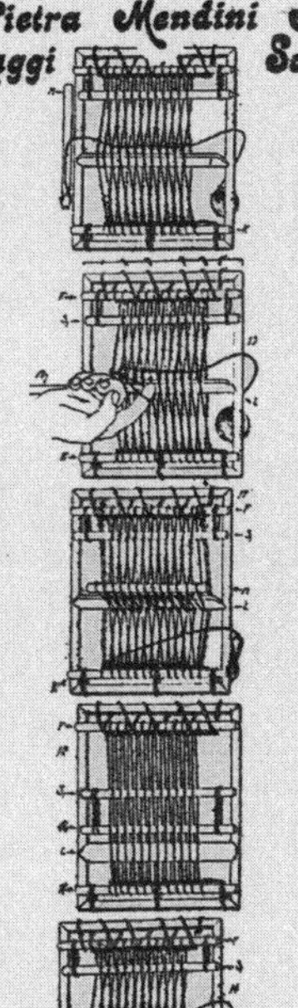

Binazzi:
...ci restano degli attrezzi rudimentali con cui possiamo fare qualcosa, un golf all'uncinetto, un ricamo, dei comportamenti rudimentali come scalare un albero, fare una nuotata, un giro in bicicletta, delle tecniche rudimentali come canalizzare l'acqua, orientarsi.

Branzi:
La Global Tools non sarà una scuola, ché nessuno ha da insegnare niente a nessuno, ma "un sistema di laboratori" dove sarà possibile recuperare, attraverso attività manuali sperimentali, quelle facoltà creative atrofizzate dalla società del lavoro.
Tale recupero non servirà a creare un nuovo sistema di modelli e di meriti, ma semplicemente a realizzare un nuovo e più avanzato equilibrio psicosomatico, e quindi un nuovo grado di libertà e di autodisponibilità.
La Global Tools non nasce per realizzare un progetto ideologico, né per cercare di elaborare un modello sociale o metodologico, ma si muove all'interno di un'area operativa priva di una programmazione formale, in cui tutti i risultati non vengono rapportati a modelli di riferimento ma acquisiti come atti di comunicazione spontanea.

Binazzi:
Gli oggetti a nostra disposizione sono scomparsi, gli accessori i soprammobili i mobili le pareti e anche la casa la città e tutto il resto, che bello!
Rimane il pianeta il cielo le stelle gli alberi... per ricominciare da capo.

Sottsass:
Se io avessi lavorato a larghi gradini la collina e se avessi scavato canali grandi e piccoli — come le vene di un braccio — perché l'acqua della pioggia fosse raccolta, curata e amministrata a coprire la terra delle terrazze, e se poi avessi piantato a spazi equidistanti le piantine di riso e guardato ogni giorno il cielo nero muscolarsi, specchiandosi, alle foglie che crescono sull'acqua, e se poi finalmente, dopo 140 giorni, avessi raccolto il riso con pazienza, questo chilo di chicchi bianchi, per me, sarebbe sacro. Lo metterei in questo vaso e il vaso lo metterei su un tavolino di lacca rossa. Poi mi metterei fisso davanti al vaso e lop-

Branzi:
...there remain for us rudimentary installations with which we can do something, a crocheted sweater, some embroidery, the rudimentary techniques for climbing a tree, going for a swim, a bike ride, some rudimentary techniques for directing the flow of water, for orienting oneself.

Branzi:
Global Tools will not be a school, since no one has anything to teach to anyone else, but a "system of laboratories" in which it will be possible, through experimental manual activities, to recuperate creative faculties atrophied in our work-directed society. Such a recuperation will not be used to create a new system of models and values, but simply to achieve a new and more advanced psychosomatic equilibrium and, consequently, a new degree of freedom and open-mindedness in design.
Global Tools was not founded with the purpose of carrying out any particular ideological scheme, or of elaborating any particular social and methodological model; in fact it moves within the limits of an operational field lacking any formal programming, a field in which the results are not compared with reference models but absorbed as acts of spontaneous communication.

Binazzi:
The objects available to us have disappeared, so have the accessories, the knick-nacks, the furniture, the walls and also the house the city and all the rest—how beautiful! There remain the planet, the sky, the stars, the trees—to start from the beginning.

Sottsass:
If I had terraced a hillside and if I had dug a system of large and small irrigation channels, like veins in an arm, to collect and carefully distribute the rain water to cover those terraces and then if I had planted young seedlings of rice at equal distances from each other and watched the sky each day, black and turbulent and reflected over the leaves growing under the water and if, in the end, after 140 days I had patiently gathered the rice, this kilogramme of little white grains would be sacred to me.
I would put them in this jar and I would-

Casabella 397/1975 19

Andrea Branzi

HOMEWORK (REMEMBERING PASOLINI)

No serious study has been made of the importance of the school in the history of culture; indeed, no history has ever been written of the school as the independent history of a social phenomenon, nor anything about its negative aspects in human development or its capacity for deforming culture.

A universal history of the school has never been written, also because such a history would of necessity have to start with an investigation of "the condition of the school" which, it is widely acknowledged, is a bio-cultural condition very hard to define. Almost by way of officially acknowledging the permanent conflict between school and society, recent decrees of the Ministry of Education have brought parents into the school; but which is more likely to be influenced by the other, the school or society? The mental deformation that a school is capable of bringing about in an individual determines his mental and social behaviour almost to the point of shaping his anthropological characteristics.

In this sense it is very difficult to defeat the school. It starts out with the premise that history and culture have already been written down, and the writing is made up of names and dates. Those who remember them are cultured, the others are uncultured. This sort of Limbo often lasts far beyond the limits of the school age. In intellectuals

Casabella 409/1976

Non è mai stata seriamente studiata l'importanza della scuola nella storia della cultura, anzi non è mai stata scritta una storia della scuola come storia autonoma di un fenomeno sociale, dei suoi risvolti negativi nella formazione umana e della sua capacità di deformazione della cultura stessa. Lo stesso termine "scolastico" indica più intuitivamente il sospetto di tutto questo, che non una coscienza esatta del fenomeno.

Non è mai stata scritta una storia universale della scuola anche perché tale storia dovrebbe necessariamente muovere dalla indagine della "condizione scolastica" che notoriamente è una condizione bio-culturale difficilmente definibile. A quanto mi risulta solo W. Gombrowicz in « Ferdidurke » ha tentato una analisi del genere.

Il fenomeno scolastico, come luogo separato dalla storia civile, ha movimenti non geometrici ma più simili ai liquidi, senza una direzione identificabile e senza un destino chiaro. Il fatto stesso che persone separate da funzioni diverse sono proprio per questo costrette a vivere insieme per decine d'anni (maestri, professori, allievi, supplenti, bidelli ecc.) determina interrelazioni talmente violente che la stessa funzione scolastica ne risulta devastata: pazzi, maniaci, malati, buffoni, deformi, ridicoli, mostri costituiscono alla fine il normale panorama scolastico del giovane, già di per se stesso in preda a crisi di crescenza, con turbe sessuali e rimpinzato di pane e burro.

L'insegnamento, come atto di trasmissione dal docente al discente di informazioni culturali, è nella realtà scolastica uno psicodramma autonomo da qualsiasi contenuto didattico.

Ivan Illich nel suo libro « La descolarizzazione della società » rilevava molto chiaramente come la funzione scolastica non sia in rapporto all'insegnamento ma piuttosto alla funzione di intrattenere, impegnandola scolasticamente, l'umanità dai sei a ventiquattro anni, deformandola definitivamente con modelli di comportamento.

I decreti delegati quasi a voler ufficialmente riconoscere il conflitto permanente tra scuola e società hanno oggi introdotto nella scuola i genitori: ma sarà la scuola che somiglierà alla società o sarà la società che finirà con l'assomigliare alla scuola?

La deformazione mentale che la scuola è in grado di lasciare in un individuo ne determina il comportamento mentale e sociale fino quasi a figurarne le caratteristiche antropologiche. In questo senso è molto difficile sconfiggere la scuola. Essa parte dalla premessa che la storia e la cultura sono già state scritte: questa scrittura è costituita da date e nomi. Chi ricorda queste date e questi nomi è una persona col-

I COMPITI A CASA (ricordando Pasolini)

it becomes a permanent condition which allows one to name reality and to discuss it in lessons and writings as an area of literary and scientific competence, or as an object with a form and logic of its own.

It was while considering these intellectuals who have never really graduated from secondary school that I recalled Pasolini who, in a moment of happy intuition, perceived that there was another reality that cannot be defined by the critical yardstick, because it is a cultural non-condition, rather than a counter-culture or popular culture. All those who had never really graduated from secondary school were waiting for Pasolini's coffin to pass, and when it finally came they found in it a confirmation that life (one's external life) is indeed mortal. It is no accident that they are called "the immortals"...

We have had a school, and still more a society of highly trained town-planners who talk about things that they do not really know, of politicians who do not know whom they represent, and of sociologists who only know the man that they meet on the way to school. And these people, on hearing how Pasolini was murdered and how his body was mistaken for a bag of rubbish, immediately cry that it was a crime against culture. They do not know what ignorance is. And it is ignorance that sooner or later will change the world.

Andrea Branzi, "Homework. Remembering Pasolini," in *Casabella* n. 409, 1976

ta, gli altri non sono colti.

La scuola è una alternativa completa alla vita e alla realtà, una loro totale sostituzione, in cui la « terapia della parola », di cui parla Moravia, si attua compiutamente.

Non a caso la contestazione studentesca è nata e morta all'interno di questo pianeta allo stato gassoso, in cui la simulazione della realtà esterna, politica e sociale, si realizza nei compagni, nei professori e Nixon nel preside.

Questa condizione di limbo si protrae spesso fin oltre i confini dell'età scolastica; essa diviene, negli intellettuali, una condizione permanente che permette di nominare la realtà e di parlarne, in lezioni o in scritti, come di un'area di competenza letteraria o scientifica, in ogni caso un oggetto dotato di forma e di logica autonoma, disinnescato e riprodotto in cera.

E' pensando a questi intellettuali, che non sono mai usciti dal liceo, che mi viene in mente Pasolini, il quale in un felice momento ha intuito che esiste anche una realtà che non è definibile con metri critici perché è una non-condizione culturale (più che una contro-cultura o una cultura popolare). Questa non-condizione è costituita da un largo strato sociale il quale, per il fatto stesso che non organizza in termini culturali (scolastici) la propria esperienza, vive in termini informi la propria vita. Informi prima ancora che drammatici. I suoi romanzi erano un pacco di parolacce, e la "storia" non si svolgeva in alcun modo, non aveva né andamento prospettico né morale, ma mortale, cioè andava verso la morte e basta. Come Accattone che morendo dice « ... va male, va male ». Ma tutta la sua esperienza e la sua morte è già un paragrafo di un libro di testo in cui si dice: « Perché leggendo Le Ceneri di Gramsci noi ci sentiamo riempire di commozione? Perché Pasolini era un grande poeta ». Tutti quelli che non sono mai usciti dal liceo aspettavano la sua salma, e quando è arrivata ne hanno tratto la conferma che la vita (esterna) è davvero sempre mortale. Non a caso si chiamano gli immortali... Abbiamo avuto una scuola, e più ancora una società di urbanisti preparatissimi a parlare di cose che non conoscono, di politici che non sanno chi rappresentano, di sociologi che conoscono solo la gente che incontrano andando a scuola. E dell'uccisione di Pasolini scambiato per un sacco di spazzatura dicono subito che è un delitto contro la cultura.

E non sanno che cosa è l'ignoranza e che sarà questa che alla fine cambierà il mondo.

A. Branzi

Casabella 409/1976 9

1.3

PROTOTYPES OF DISSOLUTION

THE NEGATIVE THOUGHT

Following page:
Archizoom Associati, "Urban Photomontages: Housing Unit on the Red Square," 1969
Archizoom Associati, "Urban Photomontages: Water Games in the Messina Strait," 1969

A
THE DISSOLUTION OF ARCHITECTURE

Urban Photomontages and Speeches by Images

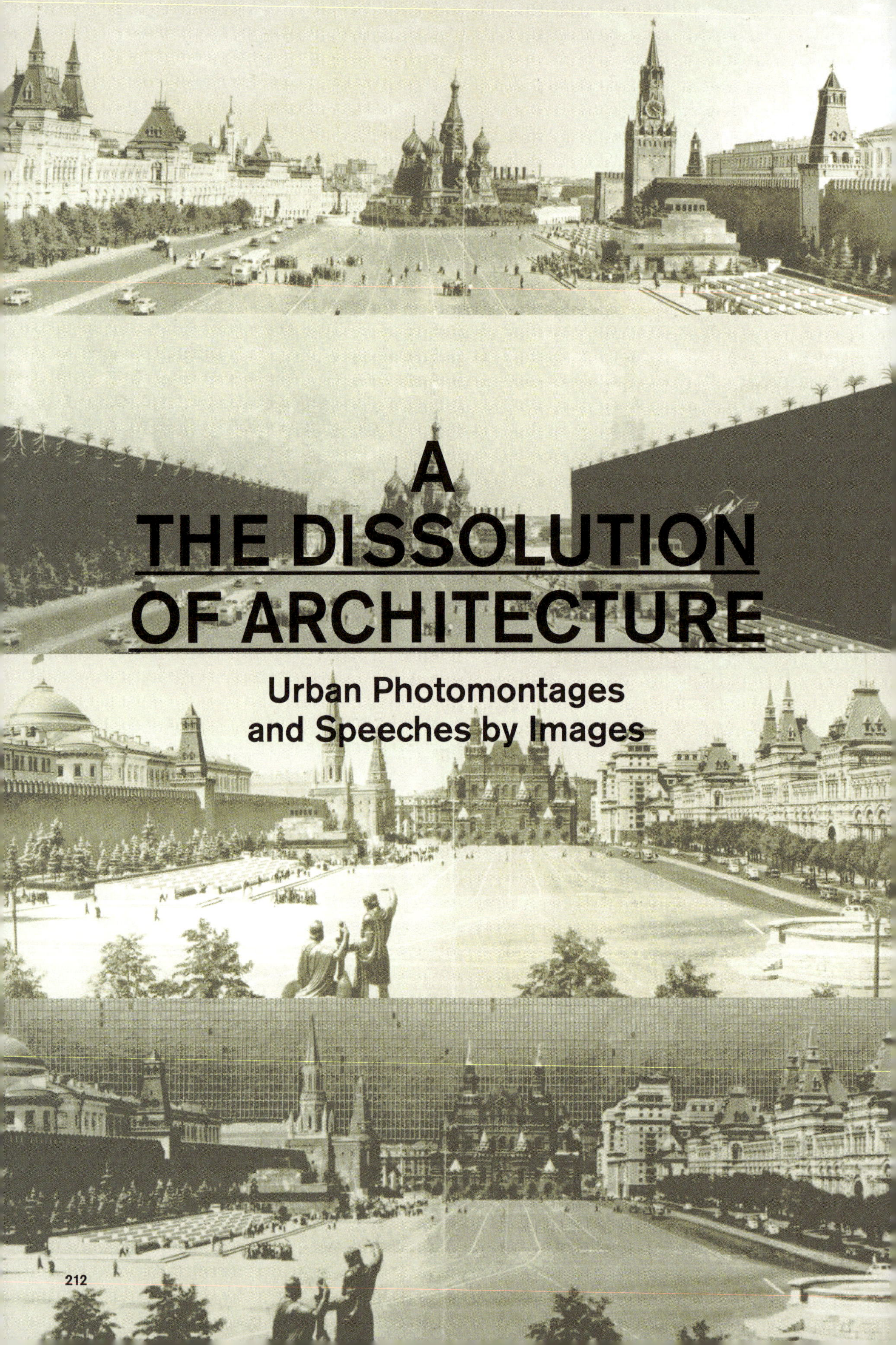

Archizoom Associati, "Urban Photomontages : Skyscraper with Ficus Leaves in New York," 1969

« Aerodynamic City », 1969

ARCHIZOOM: DISCORSI PER IMMAGINI

« Archizoom »: Andrea Branzi, Gilberto Corretti, Paolo Deganello, Massimo Morozzi, Dario Bartolini, Lucia Morozzi

« edificio residenziale per centro storico »

Archizoom Associati, "Discorsi per immagini - Speeches by Images," in *Domus* n. 481, 1969

« belvedere »

« roof garden »

« sventramento a Bologna »

«Sono ormai cinque o sei anni che si è cominciato a rendersi conto della impossibilità manuale e mentale a rappresentare il Sistema dentro il quale viviamo (cioè a ricondurlo ad un'unica immagine simbolica), non tanto a causa della sua dimensione mondiale, ma piuttosto per uno strano capovolgimento delle reciproche posizioni tra Lui e la Cultura.
Se all'inizio del secolo infatti l'Intellettuale si batteva per un'arte tutta logica metodologia, contro la continua tendenza alla cultura della forma e dell'apparenza da parte del Mondo, adesso le posizioni si sono invertite ed il Sistema è diventato solo e soltanto impalpabile razionalità funzionale di metodo, di igiene e di efficienza, mentre la cultura si spinge disperata ad afferrarlo, in una forma e in un'immagine, prendendolo in giro con ritratti-barattolo di conserva, facendoci una magra figura, tra l'altro, con i business-men molto più corinzi ed apollinei di Rosenquist.
C'è da aggiungere inoltre questo, che dopo tanti anni di cocenti delusioni, del cuore e della mente, dopo le violente iniezioni di adrenalina causate dal quotidiano tradimento, l'Intellettuale oggi è finalmente troppo triste e stanco per poter credere ancora in tutte quelle cose che dieci anni fa permettevano a Le Corbusier e a tutti gli altri di fare dell'architettura, e si rifiuta di correre incontro ai bambini che sorridono.
Non crede più nel sole, nel verde, nella fruizione strutturale, nel radicalismo didattico, cioè in pratica non crede più nella FELICITÀ DELL'UOMO. Del resto noi viviamo in una società che si fonda sulla ferrea certezza che la FELICITÀ DELL'UOMO sia raggiungibile solo nel binomio concertato « più soldi-meno lavoro », sulla cui forza universale di convinzione si appoggia qualsiasi seria ipotesi rivoluzionaria; non ci sembra sinceramente il caso di andare a scovarne un'altra, escluso che ne esista una più travolgente.
In una simile situazione ci sembra oltremodo doveroso mette-

« colline di riporto su città di pianura »

« quartieri paralleli per Berlino »

re in guardia contro assunzioni di impegni sociali, che il Sistema sarebbe ben felice di incoraggiare, per sistemare certe ultime sbavature alla sua perfetta adesione all'intera Società, non necessitandogli più il persuasore occulto, subdolo ma lento e incerto, quando con il Piano il Consorzio Umano può divenire tout-court un sistema di produzione.
In questa prospettiva, certamente, è facile cadere nella esagerazione: se anche l'intellettuale non produce beni non ha diritto all'esistenza sociale. Ma è anche vero che oggi l'unica attività cerebrale che abbia un senso è quella politica, (da non confondersi con il vecchio engagement) e quindi produttiva. Così vanno scomparendo naturalmente, per la sottile ironia della inutilità, moltissime delle tradizionali attività dello Spirito.
Ciò nonostante l'architettura continua ad esistere, forse solo come problema fisico, probabilmente in virtù del proprio infimo (almeno in Italia) livello di integrazione su tutti i piani, da quello industriale a quello di servizio.
Ma è anche vero che a ben guardare proprio nel mondo delle cose architettoniche la posizione del Sistema non è così solida come sembrerebbe. È certo infatti che le città e tutti i sistemi connettivi territoriali, magari giganteschi per estensione e altezza, sono dotati di un equilibrio che si basa su certi standard elementari, tipo la profondità degli edifici e le tipologie, elementi questi che sono rimasti stranamente ancorati a equilibri spontanei: illuminazione e aereazione naturale, e superficie pro-capite, che sono il risultato di una immagine di vita equilibrata con gli elementi naturali e con le condizioni generali dell'economia.
Viene spontaneo chiedersi con quale faccia tosta si richieda all'individuo il rispetto di queste due condizioni così remote e quotidianamente smentite! Proviamo sfacciatamente a rifiutarle, ed il Cervello del Sistema comincerà ad impazzire. Infatti, invece di continuare ad immaginare una società migliore e più giusta, in cui le case siano più belle, proviamo ad interessarci al fatto che queste case siano sempre più grandi. Cioè in pratica proviamo a battere il Sistema sul suo terreno, senza coinvolgerlo nella Crociata contro il Male, ma piuttosto sul piano della Utopia Quantitativa. Per la Cultura probabilmente questa sarebbe l'ultima occasione di continuare ad operare « dentro le cose », cercando di evitare la continua spinta alla sua estromissione.
Bisognerebbe davvero imparare ad essere meno educati (a parte nei riguardi di questa insopportabile igiene, che poi non è altro se non razzismo ideologico) ma anche nei riguardi di questo implacabile e continuo auto-collocamento critico e storico dei prodotti culturali e provare a seminarli dove e quando capita, al di fuori di sistemazioni metodologiche.
Fare dell'autobiografismo senza riguardi e una scalciante e charlottesca serie di invenzioni come liberazione psico-motoria.
Per noi infatti che siamo i figli traditi del « razionalismo esaltato » occorrono continuamente idee guida, cioè immagini formali alle quali riportare il nostro agire architettonico.
Queste immagini, che possono essere invenzioni architettoniche o altro, servono a dare il contenuto narrativo al nostro progettare, come contenuti esterni al metodo compositivo stesso.
In un Sistema che ha realizzato se stesso, e, come direbbe il filosofo, ha raggiunto il proprio dover essere, o meglio ancora, in una realtà dove il noumeno e il fenomeno si sono identificati, potremmo anche, con tutta legittimità nei riguardi della storia, tornare a pensare l'azione estetica non implicata direttamente nella prassi di progettazione, ma semplicemente indaffarata a sistemare simmetricamente le cose o a disporle in ordine decrescente.
Proviamo, in questo mondo delle funzioni, ad andare in giro collocando su ciò che gia esiste le foglie di palma, e si scoprirà come la « decorazione » crei bellissimi ordini su di una realtà così compromessa».

ARCHIZOOM

Speeches by Images

Archizoom Associati, 1969

///

It has been five or six years that we have begun to recognize the manual and mental inability of representing the System in which we live (that is of returning it to a single symbolic image), not because of its global dimension, but rather due to a strange reversal of the reciprocal positions between the System and Culture.

If, in fact, at the beginning of the century the Intellectual fought for an art that was all logic and methodology, against the persistent trend towards the culture of form and appearance on the part of the World, now the positions have been reversed and the System has become the only and solely intangible functional rationality of method, of hygiene and efficiency, while culture goes desperately to grab it, in a form and in an image, mocking him with portrait-jars of preserves, making a poor impression with the more Corinthian and Apollonian businessmen of Rosenquist, among others.

It should also be added that, after so many years of bitter disappointments of the heart and mind, after violent injections of adrenaline caused by the daily betrayal, the Intellectual today is finally too tired and sad to still believe in all those things that ten years ago allowed Le Corbusier and everyone else to do architecture, and he refuses to run towards the smiling children.

He no longer believes in the sun, in greenery, in structural fruition, in radical teaching, which means practically that he no longer believes in the HAPPINESS OF MAN.

After all we live in a society that is based on the ironclad certainty that the HAPPINESS OF MAN is accessible only in the concerted binomial of "more money-less

work," upon which universal force of conviction any serious revolutionary hypothesis rests; it genuinely does not seem to us to be the case to unearth another one, except if there would be a more overwhelming one.

In a such situation, it seems to be our great duty to warn against assumptions of social commitments, that the system would be only too happy to encourage, to fix some last smudges on its perfect adhesion to the whole of society, no longer needing the hidden persuader, sneaky but slow and uncertain, when with the Consortium Plan the Human can become a production system tout-court.

In this perspective, it is certainly easy to fall into an exaggeration: even if the intellectual does not produce goods, he is not entitled to a social existence.

But it is also true that today the only brain activity that makes sense is the political kind, (not to be confused with the old engagement), and therefore productive. Thus, due to the subtle irony of futility, many of the traditional activities of the Spirit are naturally disappearing. Nevertheless, architecture continues to exist, perhaps only as a physical problem, probably because of its consistently lowest (at least in Italy) level of integration on all levels, from the industrial to service facilities.

But it is also true that if we look more closely into in the world of architectural things, the position of the System is not as solid as it seems. It is certain in fact that the city, and all connective territorial systems, perhaps gigantic by extension and height, are equipped with an equilibrium that is based on certain elementary standards, such as the depth of buildings and typologies, all elements that are strangely anchored to spontaneous equilibriums: lighting and ventilation, and per capita surface, which is the result of a picture of life in equilibrium with natural elements and general economic conditions.

We wonder with what nerve they require from the individual the respect for these two conditions that are so remote and denied daily!

When we try to blatantly refuse them, the Brain of the System begins to go crazy. In fact, instead of continuing to imagine a better and fairer society, where houses are more beautiful, let's focus on the fact that these houses are getting bigger. In practice, we try to beat the System on its own terrain, without involving it in the crusade against Evil, but rather in terms of a Quantitative Utopia. For Culture this would probably be the last chance to continue to operate "inside of things," trying to avoid the continued push toward its inspirational mission.

We should really learn to be less educated (except with regard to this unbearable hygiene, which after all is nothing if not ideological racism), but also concerning this relentless and continuous critical and historical self-employment of cultural products, and we should try to leave them behind where and when it happens, outside of methodological arrangements.

We should create a merciless autobiography and a kicking and Chaplinesque series of inventions as psycho-motor liberation. For us, in fact, we who are the betrayed children of "exalted rationalism," require continuous guiding ideas, or formal images that bring our architectural act.

These images, which can be architectural inventions or something else, serve to give the narrative content to our design as external contents for the compositional method.

In a system that has realized itself, and - as the philosopher would say - has reached its having to be, or better, in a world where the noumenon and the phenomenon are coincident, we could, with all the legitimacy with regard to history, come to think of aesthetic action as not directly involved in design practices, but simply busily symmetrically arranging things or arranging them in a descending order.

Let us try, in this world of functions, to go around placing palm leaves on what already exists, and you'll discover how to create beautiful decorative orders on a reality that has been so compromised.

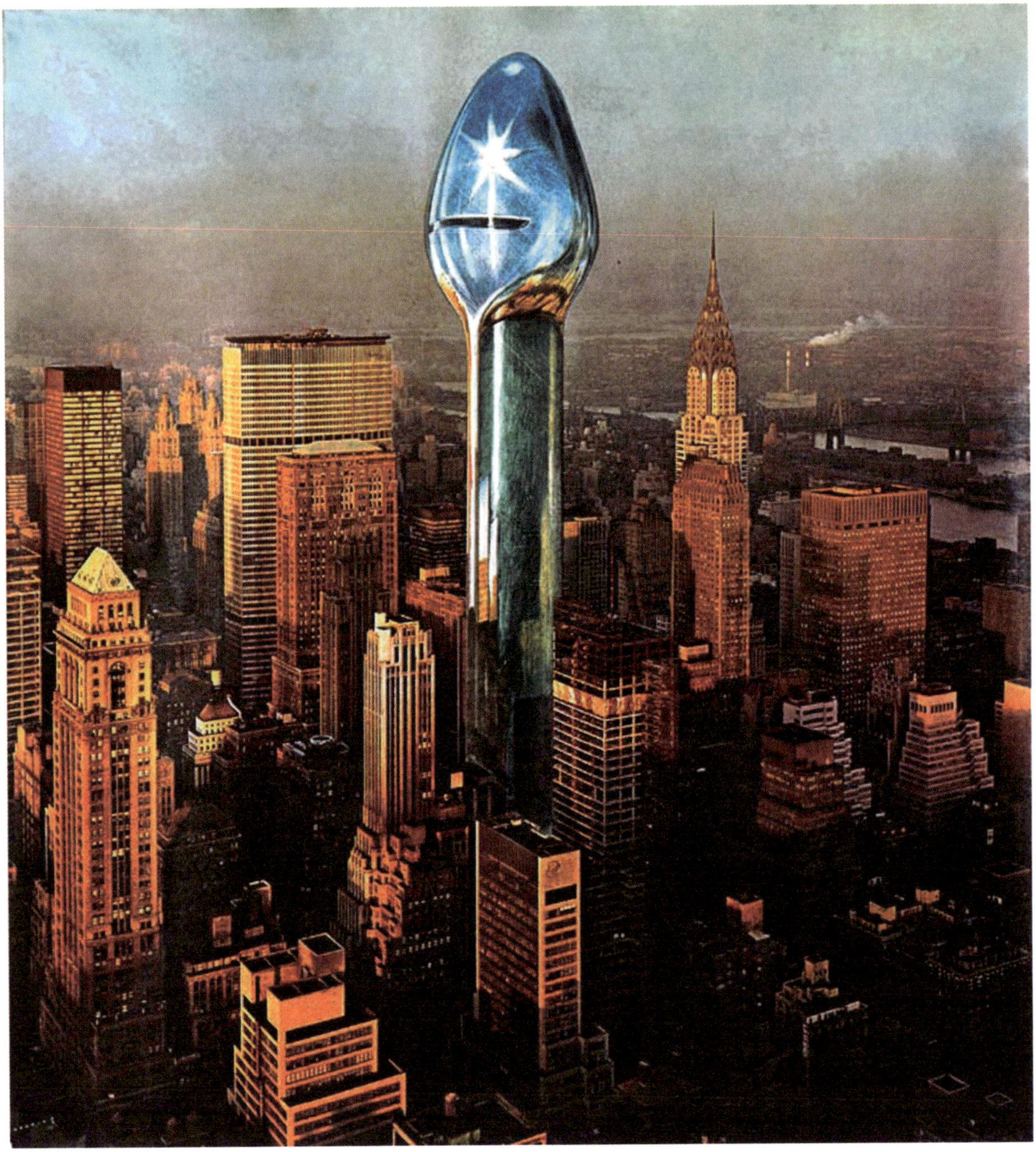

Archizoom Associati, "Urban Photomontages
Skycraper in Manhattan," 1969

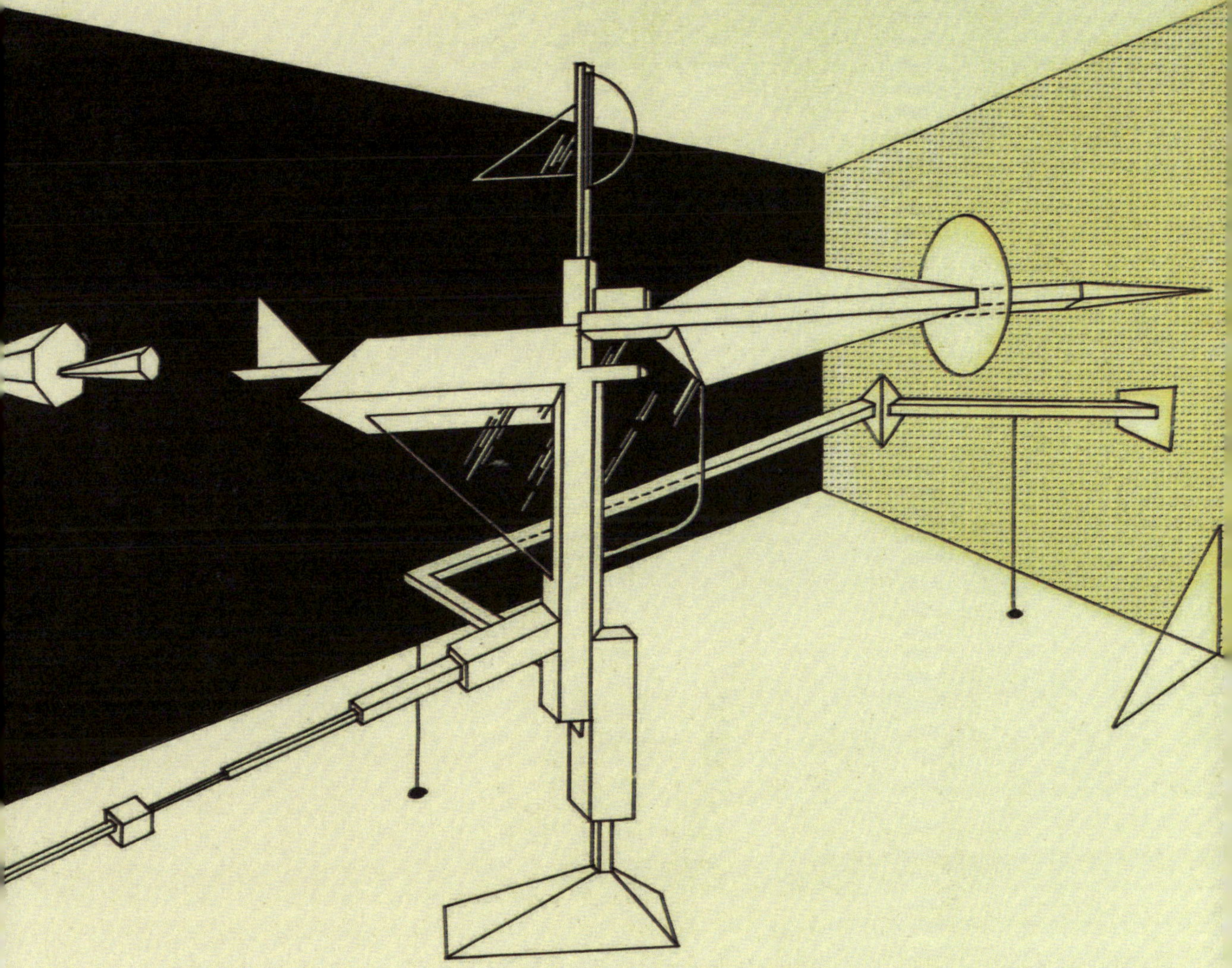

B
THE LIQUEFACTION OF THE OBJECT
Situationist Components

Archizoom Associati, *Drawing of Geometric Object*, 1971

4

Archizoom associati
La distruzione degli oggetti

L'apprendista stregone:
la trecentocinquantamillesima ninfa

Il capitale saluta il nuovo secolo con una delle sue più importanti scoperte: egli capisce di non essere soltanto un sistema di produzione industriale, impegnato a produrre a macchina ciò che fino ad allora veniva prodotto manualmente, ma sotto forma di "vocazione sociale" scopre la propria possibilità di modificare attraverso la produzione industriale quel mondo che fino ad allora aveva soltanto riprodotto.
Infatti realizzando il processo di trasformazione dell'artigianato in forza lavoro, toglie all'uomo la gestione delle proprie facoltà produttive, costringendolo a venderle come unico bene in grado di garantirgli il diritto alla sussistenza. Assoggettando così ogni capacità direttamente produttiva alla logica del profitto, tramite l'imposizione del salario, il Capitale allarga progressivamente il suo dominio a tutta la società, organizzandola in termini produttivi.
Fino a quel momento l'artista e l'intellettuale avevano avuto un ruolo di collaboratori liberi al progresso industriale: la dimostrazione di una coincidenza tra le capacità riproduttive della macchina ed i caratteri estetici dell'oggetto riprodotto non veniva ricercata. Al contrario la producibilità in serie degli ordini classici confortava la tradizionale gerarchia di valori, discendenti dello spirito alla materia inerte.
Tale gerarchia rimase intatta fino a quando non vennero operate le prime verifiche generali del processo produttivo, che furono le grandi Esposizioni Universali.
Allora per la prima volta, mettendo in fila tutta la produzione industriale (chilometri di anfore in ghisa, tonnellate di drappeggi, centinaia di migliaia di fauni, ecc.) si scopre che la realtà esistente, una volta riprodotta un milione di volte, diventa complessivamente una realtà diversa da quella iniziale.
Si constata cioè che proprio la materia inerte, una volta assoggettata nel vuoto degli stampi ai voleri dello spirito, ribalta il rapporto in una fuga prospettica priva di senso, nella quale i "contenuti" perdono di qualsiasi significato.
La trecentocinquantamillesima ninfa prodotta industrialmente, non solo non comunica più le stesse cose del suo prototipo, ma benché identica alla prima delle copie, è diventata una realtà autonoma difficilmente giudicabile.

Il modello di fabbrica

A quel punto viene constatato un fallimento, ma anche un trionfo: la produzione industriale si rivela come uno strumento di scardinamento di un vecchio mondo e dei suoi valori.
È in tale mondo che essa è nata, ma è proprio in questo che essa ha sperimentato la propria realtà autonoma.
Da quel momento tale realtà diviene

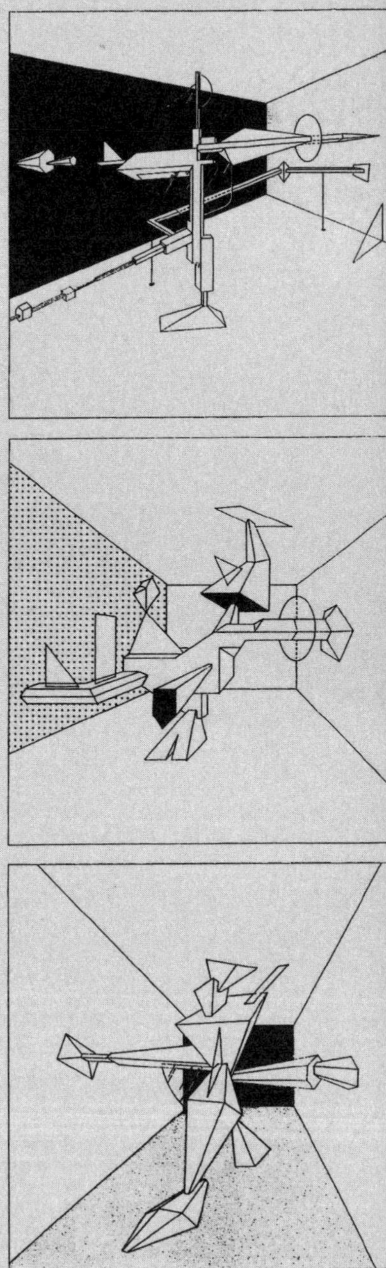

Archizoom associati 1

Archizoom Associati, "The Distruction of the Objects," in *IN* n. 2-3, 1971

'unico riferimento.
.'intera società impegnata a produrre
ndustrialmente deve trovare i propri
nodelli e la propria realtà
on esternamente al mondo del proprio
avoro, ma anzi nella logica profonda
he lo determina.
.a "fabbrica" diventa l'unico modello
lella società, proprio perché il capitale,
coprendo la realtà del
'progresso" come proprio unico fine,
ende ad investire l'intera società
on la capacità razionale di
rganizzazione e suddivisione
lel lavoro.
.'estensione del "modello di fabbrica"
ella società significa però anche.
soprattutto, assumere la logica della
roduzione come unica legge formativa
on solo della società, ma dell'immagine
lobale del sistema stesso.
.'immagine globale, cioè l'insieme
nitario della produzione, deve
arantire la verifica della
aturalità dell'intero sistema,
deve costituire il quadro di
iferimento di una morale intima della
roduzione, che garantisca l'assoluzione
ei meccanismi di sfruttamento
ome pegni fatali al superiore destino
el progresso.
.a morale del sistema deve essere
uindi tutta interna alla produzione
tessa, e non più modello
ovrastante che la produzione
ndustriale ripropone in maniera
nitativa.

La morte della cultura": Design

: in questa prospettiva che il rapporto
ra produzione e cultura
nuta radicalmente:
intellettuale viene assunto
on più come elaboratore esterno
i utopie, ma come operatore
tto dentro il ciclo, anzi mediatore
iretto tra la produzione
ome fatto tecnologico e il fine sociale
ella produzione stessa.
.a morte della cultura come
"bene improduttivo", non
avviene quindi solo come momento
del processo di integrazione di
tutta intera la società nei cicli
produttivi, ma come scoperta di una
"moralità intrinseca alla natura dei
processi produttivi stessi".
La "giustizia" del capitale è la
distribuzione omogenea
dei Consumi, in una società resa
omogenea dalla Produzione.
L'integrazione globale simula il
livellamento delle classi.
Il consumo mistifica la giusta
distribuzione dei beni.
È qui che nasce il designer:
egli acquista il ruolo duplice di
trasformatore
delle necessità produttive in valori
razionali, svelando la culturalità
spontanea della produzione,
e contemporaneamente opera
da riduttore a zero della cultura
come momento libero di elaborazione
di ideologie e valori, esterno
ai processi industriali.
La contraddizione, nel duplice ruolo
di culturizzatore e di liquidatore
della cultura è solo apparente:
identificando preliminarmente
il razionale con il producibile
il designer tenta
di demandare all'industria il suo stesso
compito. Il suo sforzo è quello
di rivelarla a se stessa, fino
al punto di renderla autonoma:
far raggiungere al prodotto
il livello ottimale di identificazione
tra qualità tecniche e comunicative,
significa porre le premesse affinché la
produzione possa lanciarsi nella
Serie Definitiva, al di là del tempo
e dello spazio, in una società resa
omogenea dai consumi.
La cultura tende così in maniera
profonda all'industria:
l'universalità della serie assolve
e giustifica l'universalità dell'arte.
L'assolve ed insieme la liquida. Il
prodotto definitivo diviene la sua
utopia e insieme il suo destino.

archizoom associati 2

6

Consumi e Sviluppo
Ma questo processo è il fallimento funzionale del proto-design: fallimento tutto interno alla logica del sistema.
Ponendosi infatti come filtro tra le necessità produttive e le realtà fisica della merce, egli opera la trasformazione della realtà in dati elementari, in figure geometriche semplici, al fine di facilitarne la produzione.
La lettura strutturale dell'oggetto e la sua riduzione a elementi primari ne permette l'introduzione nel processo produttivo, non come unità formale (verificata solo a processo terminato), ma come insieme astratto di componenti tecnologiche diverse.
Lo smontaggio dell'oggetto facilita così l'organizzazione del lavoro; a questo punto però l'identificazione tra logica interna della forma e necessità produttive diviene totale, e la soluzione progettuale obbligata.
Il processo è allora quello di individuare un'estetica unica e definitiva, frutto di un processo razionale e scientifico della formatività stessa dell'oggetto, coincidente con i propri processi produttivi.
Il prodotto diviene "oggettivamente" valido per tutti.
Ma questo significa individuare il producibile come campo limitato, come cioè un campionario finito di prodotti definitivi.
E questo è contro gli interessi stessi del Capitale.
Radicalizzando il problema il designer ha infatti portato al livello generale una tendenza concretamente verificabile in ogni singolo processo imprenditoriale: eliminare la concorrenza con un prodotto insostituibile.
Tale ipotesi significherebbe la fine del dinamismo stesso di crescita del Capitale: il monopolio non può essere accettato neppure per eliminare il pericolo della deflagrazione

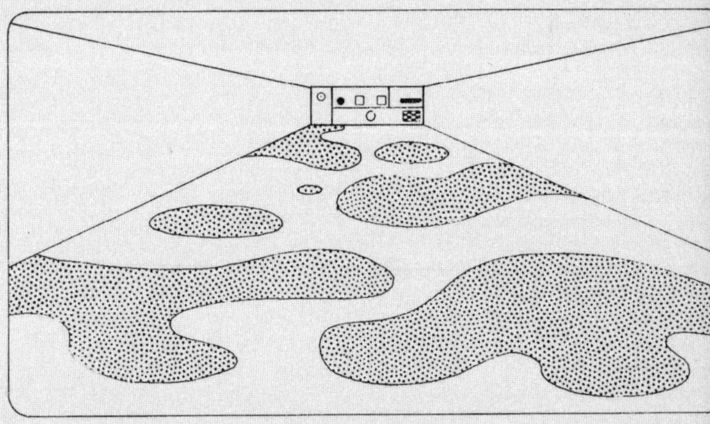

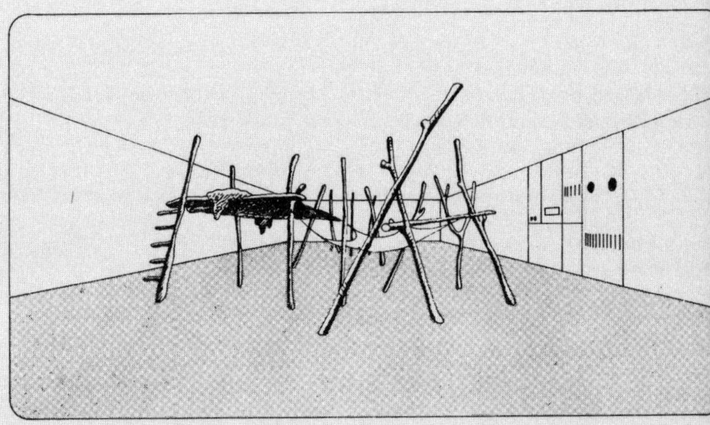

Archizoom associati 3

nterna per libera concorrenza.
Il Capitale è continuo divenire,
cioè continuo integrare e continuo
equilibrare le contraddizioni interne.
Tale processo dinamico non può
essere inteso come percorso ad uno
stato finale privo di storia:
al contrario la relatività è l'unica
verità di una sua realtà,
sempre perfettibile.
Intendere quindi l'estetica razionale
come operazione di individuazione
di modelli definitivi, significa
nsieme intendere la produzione
come operazione a termine.
Capire cioè i consumi come
semplice riempimento di un vuoto
che una volta colmato non richiede
se non normale manutenzione.

L'existenz-minimum

Su questo punto avviene anche
'errore culturale.
Trasformare l'intera società
nel modello di fabbrica significa
trasformare l'intera società in forza
avoro organizzata,
ma significa assumere anche la logica
della produzione come evento
non esterno alla natura
dell'individuo,
ma anzi proiezione diretta
di questa.
L'uomo nuovo della "civilisation
machiniste" è l'uomo che adotta
le leggi produttive come propria
intima natura. Prima tra tutte le leggi
quella della catena di montaggio,
nella quale riconosce non solo lo
strumento scientifico
di conoscenza della realtà (design),
ma anche soprattutto la propria
più profonda formatività
(cubismo). Solo così il rapporto
tra fabbrica e società diviene
legge naturale.
La macchina diviene apparentemente
lo strumento di demistificazione proprio
di quei processi di mercificazione,
indotti dalla produzione industriale
stessa. Il design, pura logica
di produzione, sembra coincidere
con il più rigoroso processo di
distruzione dei feticci borghesi della
merce. Ma in realtà solo
apparentemente.
L'oggetto infatti viene ridotto
alla sua essenza geometrica
elementare, ma il processo razionale
di progettazione che lo ha generato,
diviene una sorta di allegoria che
prefigura e simula
il "comportamento razionale"
dell'utente. Il comportamento razionale
significa prima di tutto adozione
profonda delle logiche di fabbrica,
non più come necessità esterne,
ma come diretta realizzazione della
natura intima della società.
In questa adesione soltanto può esservi
infatti la garanzia di successo per
il processo di organizzazione nel
lavoro dell'intera società:
tale processo non deve apparire
indotto ma autogeno.
Tale prefigurazione intima della realtà
produttiva nella società non può però
contrastare l'altra premessa
indispensabile allo sviluppo, che è
quella della generalizzazione
dei consumi attraverso la libera
creatività della società.
L'uomo nuovo della "civilisation
machiniste" non può essere solo logica
di produzione, ma deve essere anche
dinamica di consumo.
Il suo "comportamento razionale"
non può coincidere con il
"consumo razionale".
L'uomo "tutta-produzione" infatti
sacrifica a questa tutto:
egli sublima le proprie ambizioni
borghesi in un "existenz-minimum",
circondato da oggetti-utensili
di povertà francescana.
Ogni sua energia si riversa
sublimata nella propria
potenzialità produttiva.
In questo senso profondo l'operazione
del design risulta repressiva.
Non solo: nell'integrazione
totale viene simulata la liberazione
dell'operaio dalla condizione borghese.
Il recupero da parte del Capitale
delle utopie socialiste diventa
strumento di ricatto.
Nel suo processo di analisi razionale
dell'oggetto il design giunge infatti al
punto di smontarne totalmente
le superfetazioni ideologiche, non tanto
per fornire una maggiore autonomia
dai miti, quanto piuttosto per indurre
alla rinuncia agli oggetti stessi.
Affiora qui per la prima volta
la contraddizione apparente tra
logica di produzione e logica di
consumo, che solo la crisi degli anni
trenta permetterà di superare
organicamente nella riorganizzazione
generale del Capitale.

Sviluppo equilibrato e salario

La riorganizzazione del Capitale dopo
la grande crisi degli anni trenta parte
alla scoperta dei meccanismi del
conflitto di classe
come la dinamica del suo stesso
sviluppo. È a questo punto infatti
che il processo di integrazione
"del" fenomeno sociale del Piano,
può essere mistificato globalmente
come integrazione del Piano
"nel" sociale.
L'ideologia keynesiana conferma come
bene l'aumentata ricchezza sociale,
che sviluppa il mercato, e la parte
imprenditoriale è pronta al sacrificio
temporaneo di un aumento del costo
della forza lavoro.
Ma fino a un certo punto.
La rivoluzione permanente dei redditi
all'interno dello sviluppo equilibrato
del sistema rimane il limite estremo,
il quadro dei riferimenti di fondo che
non è possibile valicare. A questo
equilibrio si attribuisce il valore di un
dato oggettivo, scientifico, che
conferma la natura sociale del
Capitale come bene collettivo.
Aumenti dunque sì, ma senza crisi.
A questo punto il salario diventa
la categoria politica più propria
della classe operaia:

lo slogan "più soldi-meno lavoro"
diviene così il programma
rivoluzionario massimo, al livello di
integrazione massima.
L'assenza infatti di "contenuti umani"
in un programma rivoluzionario
mette in crisi la capacità
di contenimento del sistema:
egli è pronto a fare propria qualsiasi
componente del problema
sociale ma non può mettere
in crisi la scientificità dei suoi
equilibri economici.
Il rifiuto di presentare "modelli
alternativi" come quadri di riferimento
a cui rinviare il significato
di ogni atto rivendicativo,
l'assenza di un possibile
controllo formale
dell'insieme delle tensioni,
l'impossibilità di verificare i
limiti reali di queste tensioni
all'interno di un programma,
fanno sì che ogni atto divenga
una struttura aperta,
dal significato generale
incontrollabile.
E questo è il Male, per il Sistema,
poiché sposta il dibattito politico
dai "contenuti" al potere.
Lo scontro non è più tra Capitale
e non-Capitale.
Quando infatti non si pongono
più una contro l'altra l'ideologia
della miseria,
che è l'ideologia di uno stato
sociale transitorio, e l'ideologia della
ricchezza, che è l'ideologia di uno stato
sociale definitivo, si pone invece
brutalmente il problema unico
che è quello della "gestione operaia"
del Capitale stesso.
E qui la demifisticazione
della miseria significa non riconoscere
alla miseria un valore positivo,
ma solo uno stato di assenza
di ricchezza. Cioè la condizione
operaia come uno stato di neutralità
creativa, che non genera
valori o cultura.
L'assenza di modelli unitari di

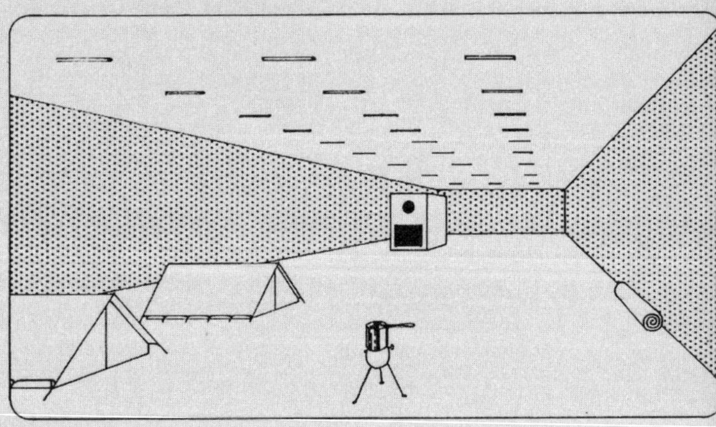

iferimento significa accettare
a prassi rivoluzionaria
come unico strumento di elaborazione,
utilizzare il comportamento come
"struttura aperta", non allegorica,
priva di contenuti in codice,
che si verifica continuamente
sul piano della realtà oggettiva.

La fine dell'utopia

E qui l'equilibrio tra l'ideologia del lavoro e l'ideologia del consumo può essere ricomposto in maniera unitaria. La cultura infatti, e soprattutto il design come operazione più direttamente legata al Capitale permanente, serve a capovolgere i dati reali del processo di integrazione: non è la società che somiglia alla fabbrica, ma la fabbrica che somiglia alla società. Cioè il processo di proletarizzazione generale all'interno del piano non trasforma il cittadino in operaio, ma al contrario l'operaio in cittadino.
La produzione non richiede la riduzione dei consumi, ma anzi il suo progressivo incremento.
Un uomo soddisfatto è un operaio migliore.
La cultura deve così valorizzare i consumi creando modelli transitori di comportamento.
Il problema infatti non è più quello di elaborare delle utopie ottimali, che minacciano di radicalizzare le contraddizioni dello sviluppo, ma quello di creare un sistema dinamico di modelli, che si contestino reciprocamente e dinamicamente si sovrappongano.
La cultura perde la sua connotazione unitaria, e al posto di una nascono mille e mille utopie. Non più la scientificità del Bauhaus, ma lo sperimentalismo di un Picasso.
L'unità della forma viene liquidata, nel momento in cui si realizza di fatto l'identificazione tra società e Piano. Se infatti tale identificazione è reale, al limite i contenuti del Piano coincidono con i contenuti spontanei della società stessa.
Non è più funzionale l'ideologia generale:
la sua morte deve essere anzi la dimostrazione della scientificità oggettiva del Piano stesso come puro coordinamento tecnico. A questo punto sono proprio i consumi che forniscono il campo di azione a questa spontaneità:
essi non forniscono un modello unico, ma al limite tanti quanti sono le individualità in azione.
È chiaro quindi di quale genere di spontaneità e libertà si tratta:
il Campo dei consumi simula la contestazione al sistema e garantisce un falso recupero della propria individualità, alienata dalla realtà del lavoro.
Il problema allora per il Capitale non è più quello di elaborare l'oggetto che induca ad un comportamento razionale:
tale rapporto statico di comunicazione tutta contemplativa, tutta allegoria, deve cedere il posto ad un rapporto più dinamico, all'interno di un sistema che preveda l'azione dell'utente come unica forma di fruizione.
Il sistema fornisce così una "libertà modulare", che è la più grande delle mistificazioni della libertà. Lo stimolo all'azione, lo stimolo all'intervento da parte del soggetto, viene simulato all'interno di un environment del quale già esiste un controllo globale.
La libertà modulare garantisce una verifica continua del processo creativo, essendo il paesaggio interno già globalmente messo a punto.
Il problema della casa diviene così quello della "casa del futuro" in quanto prefigurazione di un divenire che solo apparentemente il soggetto contribuisce a individuare.

Il rifiuto del lavoro

"Più soldi meno lavoro" è il programma rivoluzionario massimo, al livello massimo di integrazione; è l'adozione strategica del meccanismo del benessere, al fine di fare metodicamente impazzire il Cervello del Piano.
Risolvere il conflitto sociale in termini quantitativi significa infatti adottare la logica stessa del sistema come unico piano di scontro, e contestare punto per punto gli equilibri raggiunti.
Alla radice dello slogan "più soldi meno lavoro" cresce inarrestabile la demistificazione dello scontro, e l'affermazione sempre più generale del rifiuto del lavoro.
Tale rifiuto rappresenta la componente oggettiva, la legge di fondo, della nuova dinamica sociale:
significa concretamente assicurarsi una solida base per spingere ad una crescita vertiginosa il prezzo della stessa forza lavoro.
Rifiutare il lavoro come condizione umana "naturale", vuol dire rimuovere nella lotta le strutture morali e ideologiche che accompagnano il lavoro e lo rendono accettabile. La libertà come fine diventa strumento immediato di lotta.
Non si tratta della prima formulazione di una "dottrina dell'uomo" latente nella classe:
non è l'affioramento di un umanesimo operaista spontaneo.
Al contrario esso rappresenta il ribaltamento in termini quantitativi e scientifici di qualsiasi dibattito sull'uomo.
La contestazione del lavoro non costituisce il quadro di fondo a cui allegoricamente tendono tutti gli atti rivendicativi, ma costituisce la base unitaria che permette la spinta spontanea del rifiuto operaio.
Oggi qualsiasi discorso sul design e

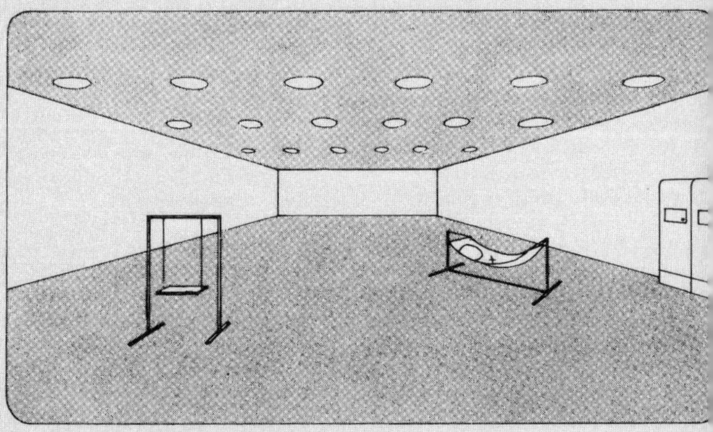

sulla casa non può non partire dalla presa di coscienza di questa tendenza generale in atto.
Se il problema rimane quello di fornire una casa nella quale recuperare rapidamente l'equilibrio psico-fisico per lavorare meglio, qualsiasi discorso diventa inutile.
L'abolizione del lavoro significa il recupero di tutte quelle facoltà creative ed intellettuali atrofizzate da secoli di lavoro sfruttato: è in tale prospettiva che è possibile superare la distinzione borghese tra produttore e consumatore di cultura.
Ognuno infatti autoproduce, non solo i propri modelli culturali di comportamento, ma recupera il diritto a realizzare il proprio habitat come immediata e incontrollabile manifestazione della personalità individuale.
L'atto di progettazione, come prefigurazione del futuro, viene a cadere; l'unica forza agente diviene la produzione intellettuale di massa.
Se l'eliminazione del lavoro vuol dire che l'unica produzione umana diventa quella intellettuale, per garantirsi che tale condizione non diventi il grado supremo della alienazione, o la "libertà nei consumi", è necessario garantire la gestione collettiva dell'automazione.

La distruzione dell'oggetto
Il designer è ancora legato al "proprio" prodotto come allo strumento che gli permette la circolazione più vasta del proprio messaggio e dei propri contenuti.
L'utente rimane semplice destinatario di una operazione a lui estranea della quale deve però subire il contraccolpo in termini di comportamento e di adesione.
Questo genere di rapporto corrisponde esattamente alla divisione borghese del lavoro e ne perpetua i circuiti

li frustrazione:
a distinzione tra produttore e
'ruitore della cultura
)ermane come premessa alla cultura
stessa. Il designer, come qualsiasi
'produttore di merce", resta
estraniato dall'uso che del bene
stesso viene fatto, non solo
commercialmente,
na culturalmente. Tale estraniazione
sembra anzi confermare
'artisticità della sua operazione,
nentre in realtà lo pone nella esatta
condizione del produttore che non
conosce mai totalmente
a compiutezza del ciclo.
L'ignoranza critica della serie di
nduzioni che la sua opera è in grado di
nettere in moto
embra confermargli il proprio ruolo
"produttivo" all'interno della catena.
l rapporto tra produttore (designer)
utente si capovolge se affrontiamo
l problema del design
non come strumento di prefigurazione
del futuro, ma solo come
disciplina terapeutica.
Quando il problema di disegnare
un oggetto non è più quello di
omunicare un messaggio, ma semmai
quello di mettere in moto
di cedere spazio ad un processo
reativo realmente liberatorio
incontrollato da parte dell'utente.
n questa direzione acquista
ignificato la "distruzione degli oggetti",
ntendendo *con questo indicare*
na operazione tendente a ridurre a
ero tutte le comunicazioni simboliche
he attraverso gli oggetti
engono fatte.
Distruggere gli oggetti significa dunque
berare l'uomo dalle
trutture formali "significanti"
he agiscono con le loro interrelazioni
ome media figurali alla sua azione,
ondizionandola e reprimendola
ome tutte le strutture morali,
ulturali e di comportamento.
Ridurre a zero la "comunicazione
ttraverso gli oggetti" significa anche
non intendere il design come struttura portante della figurazione della casa, ma solo come parte neutra, funzionalmente esatta, che ha il solo scopo di sgombrare la casa stessa assolvendo al maggior numero possibile di servizi.
Il problema non deve essere più quello se produrre a macchina la casa o se trasformare la casa in una macchina. Il problema è semmai quello di garantire le condizioni ottimali sul piano del comfort, permettendo alla casa di funzionare come "spazio-vuoto-attrezzato", cioè come un parcheggio neutro dentro il quale sia possibile operare liberamente al difuori di una figurazione architettonica e spaziale preesistente. Il diritto ad elaborare privatamente il proprio habitat significa non riconoscere nessuna "cultura ufficiale" e insieme riconoscere nella libertà l'unica cultura possibile.
Solo così è possibile evitare l'ennesima elaborazione di un modello ottimale della casa: il vuoto che noi qui descriviamo è una semplice ipotesi strategica.

Il design come terapia

Se gli uomini sono tutti uguali, come è vero, non esiste che una differenza provvisoria tra artista e utente.
La liberazione dal lavoro e la morte della cultura "gestita" significano proprio questo: la chiusura di una divaricazione nell'uso delle capacità intellettuali individuali, creatasi e radicalizzatasi all'interno del sistema borghese di suddivisione del lavoro.
Unico compito possibile oggi per un intellettuale è proprio quello di agire in questa direzione.
L'operazione complessiva diventa molto simile a quella che parallelamente sta compiendo la psicologia moderna: essa ha capito che la nevrosi ha origine nei rapporti sociali e nelle contraddizioni reali del sistema, e che quindi qualsiasi terapia può apparire come semplice palliativo, complice se non connivente, della mistificazione delle motivazioni reali della patologia.
Tale grado di conoscenza non può però risolversi in una strategia della non-azione: fare crescere a dismisura la nevrosi collettiva fino a una deflagrazione dell'intera società.
Tale ipotesi è soltanto apocalittico nihilismo.
Il problema risulta invece ben posto quando la terapia della nevrosi significa la rimozione delle strutture caratteriali che impediscono proprio la libera disponibilità individuale all'azione politica.
Qualsiasi individuo oggi avverte infatti la propria proletarizzazione chiaramente: ciò nonostante non riesce a collocarsi di fronte a tale problema in maniera diretta proprio perché bloccato dai meccanismi inibitori che la società ha tessuto dentro di lui.
La salute psichica non deve quindi simulare una libertà di fatto inesistente, ma piuttosto deve significare il collocamento dell'individuo, totalmente disponibile del proprio equilibrio, davanti alla storia.
Per fare questo bisogna contestare metodicamente le strutture repressive, morali ma anche formali, che restituiscono all'individuo l'ambiente che lo circonda come condizione consacrata da "valori e significati" naturali e razionali, proiezione diretta della "sua" stessa natura.
Il problema allora è quello di fornire all'uomo una condizione in più per procurarsi la libertà da solo, e non di cercare di capire che genere di libertà va cercando.

The Distruction of the Objects

Archizoom Associati, 1971

//

After the Industrial Revolution, capital had a way of extending its dominion over the whole of society. But the progressive growth of production, with the consequent infinite reproducibility of the same object, has served as instrument the unhinging of the old world and its values which capitalists, want to keep intact. The factory becomes the only model of society, production logic becomes the new moral of the newborn system. It is clear that the relationship between culture and the intellectual then changes radically: the intellectual enters completely into the productive cycle, becoming himself an "operator," while culture dies as an "unproductive good." Consumption for everybody is the new justice offered, consistently, by the system dominated by the capital, in a society rendered homogeneous by production. It is here that the designer is born, both the culturized and the liquidator of culture, who aims, such being the situation, only at industry and to its universality offers his own universality.

Unfortunately, however, the requirements of production are such that the objects created must be technologically "possible and easy to make": consequently any aesthetics become relative at the initial stages, and that "rational" sense, (where rational means consistent with the technology expressed by capital).

Taking it then for granted, that the modern natural law is the connection between factory and society, the first productive low, and hence socio-cultural, is that of the assembly line (design-cubism).

New man of the mechanic civilization is, at the same time, logic production and dynamic consumption. But capital and production have found themselves faced with serious discrepancies, the greatest of all coming out in the 1929 crisis. Since capital is a continuous becoming that is to say, continuous integration and continuous balancing of the internal discrepancies, the fatal crisis has, however, been gotten over with the creation of a dynamic system of models, which dynamically. So consumer goods are broken up and a false individuality, alienated from the reality of work, is salvaged. The system offers thus a "modular freedom," the greatest falsification of freedom (the house of the future). The maximum revolutionary program is "more money, less work," but what happens is that which no plan or brain could foresee, the refusal of work itself by the workers, whose progressive cultural and human alienation, has reached pollution levels. So it would seem that the system brings about its own opposite.

Until work shall be abolished, suppressing, together with exploitation, the bourgeois distinction between producer and consumer of culture. To reach this, one must, without a doubt, contest the present structure methodically. In this direction "the destruction of objects" acquires meaning, an operation aiming at reducing to zero all the symbolic communication which are made up through objects: all this is to free man from the structures, the media of repressive culture.

Design then must think about "empty" for the house, rendering it a fitted-up empty space, a neutral "parking lot" where is possible to operate freely outside a pre-existing architectonic and special figuration. There is no official culture any longer, and the only culture is freedom.

Design is a therapeutic discipline.

C

THE REMOVAL OF THE CITY

Liberation of the Habitat

Destruction and Re-appropriation of the City

Archizoom Associati, 1969

//

A Cartesian system of reference on an urban fabric made by captive balloons reporting the coordinates of the anchor point.

To split a traditional urban fabric in accordance with a criterion of rational recognition that allows bringing any episode of the urban scene to a background framework. It is a way of numbering and cataloging the episodes—among them always different—of the bourgeois city, removing them from their natural location of being exceptions to include them in a spatial catalogue where all points are equal to each other and all phenomena are mutually homogeneous.

It is a way to render the city continuous and no longer the sum of spaces and different uses, but a neutral plane in which the events cease to be themselves in order to become the numbers of their own coordinates. The experience of a city, in fact, (with all its streets, its buildings, its boulevards, its churches, its squares, its rivers), can be traced to a single cognitive fact. But what we propose is not an operation of synthesis, on the contrary.

What we propose is an analytical criterion of construction of the city itself, and then to destroy the city, since we remove its episodes from the context in which they are to add them to another one. The construction in fact should never be interpretation or dream, but firm reason that brings a reality to knowledge. A rational instrument of transmission of data from one place to another and from one user to another.

The staging is a way of measuring reality, freeing objects from a viscous logic or ordering them in a neutral field, according to a grid of homogeneity able to defuse any last cultural signification of a material intended for scientific memory.

The popular chain reaction of Petuzzo, in which the cat eats the mouse, the mouse eats the rope, the rope saws the horse, the horse drinks water, water extinguishes fire, fire burns the bat and the bat beats Petuzzo, no longer exists from the moment that he, numbering the world, has made it homogeneous, guarding against the prospective availability of reality.

To dispute methodically formal structures, such as repressive structures, which, like the moral, religious, and cultural ones, remove the individual's personal freedom of judgment in the face of history, returning to such structures the surrounding environment as a natural condition consecrated by "values and meanings." This is our task.

"Today there is no doubt in recognizing the urban phenomenon as the weakest point of the entire industrial system." The metropolis, the traditional "big stage of Progress," is today the more undeveloped and confused sector of reality in the Capital; and all this at such a level that one wonders if the modern city, more than an unresolved problem, is not an objectively surpassed historical phenomenon.

We need to understand if the Capital stands today, as it did a century ago, as the problem of the management of its own image and of its functioning at the level of urban form, or whether if the past and ongoing transformations have not transferred its reality onto another scale, transforming the concept itself of the city.

At this time, therefore, the problem is no longer to imagine a more human and more orderly metropolis, but rather to deeply understand the objective laws that govern the urban and architectural phenomena, demystifying the complex ideology that accompanies the debate and that conditions its shape.

The naturalistic myth of the free market established the city of trade and commerce in order to ensure the ideal conditions for the market, creating a natural balance between the competing interests, within the general framework of the achievement of harmony between technology and nature.

Today the use of electronic media replaces direct urban practice: the artificial

induction to consumption allows a much deeper infiltration into social reality than the fragile information channels of the city.

The metropolis ceases to be a "place" to become a "condition": it is precisely this condition in fact which is circulated homogeneously in social phenomena through consumption.

The future dimension of the metropolis coincides with that of the market itself.

The metropolis as intensive concentration corresponds to the outdated phase of the spontaneous accumulation of Capital. In a programmed society, in fact, the management of interests doesn't need to organize itself in the same place as the trades. The total availability of the territory and its total penetration eliminates the city-terminal and allows for the organization of a mesh of progressive organisms of control over it.

In bourgeois ideology, ecological balance and social justice become part of the same battle: the city provides, through its image, the formal verification of that balance.

In Urban Planning therefore the impossible harmony between the General and the Particular interest is sought: but those categories are always acquired as antithetical, contrasting, and soluble phenomena.

As the most general medium possible, traffic becomes then the objective and figural scheme of urban functioning. The street not only serves the compact tissue of the private, but it also "sections" and "shapes" it, identifying outcrop planes of architectural language.

The skyline becomes the diagram of the transpired and natural accumulation of the Capital itself.

The bourgeois metropolis remains primarily a visual place, and the experience of it is linked to this type of communication. The realization of the social organization of work through the Plan removes the "white space" in which the capital was expanding in its growth process. There no longer exists in fact a reality external to the system itself: the whole visual relationship with reality is undermined, the distances between the subject and the phenomenon cease to exist.

The city no longer "represents" the system, but "becomes" the system itself, programmed and isotropic, in which the different functions are contained in a homogeneous manner and without contradictions.

Production and Consumption have an identical ideology, which is that of Programming. Both presuppose in fact a social and physical society that is absolutely continuous and undifferentiated. There are not *autres* realities.

Manufacturing and the Supermarket effectively become the true typological models of the future city: optimal urban structures, potentially infinite, where functions are distributed spontaneously on a free plane, homogenized by a system of micro-air conditioning and optimal information.

The "natural and spontaneous" equilibria of the light and air are in fact overcome: the building becomes an equipped parking lot. Inside there are no hierarchies or spatially conditioning representations.

The typology, as a functional representation of society, torn between the detection of a social reality as a matter of course, and the aspirations of this reality as probable data, gets caught in the allegorical return of this conflict, which becomes an extra-functional cultural factor.

Trying to provide as many degrees of freedom to the user, in the most stringent possible "figure," architecture has to recognize within the urban phenomenon its true destiny, and within the private its true nature.

So, in a contradictory way, it prefigures on each occasion a general order of things, and at the same time it comes to defend the partiality of individual experience with respect to collective experiences.

Thus it mediates, in a figurative manner, the contradiction between public and private.

Today, however, the conflict is no longer left to the speculative level of pure existential consciousness. The Plan, by organizing productively throughout society, eliminates the conflict, recognizes such contradiction as apparent, and assumes as experimental any data on a strictly individual scale.

To date, the great bulk of people have remained excluded from the architectural phenomenon: a temporary supplementary Existenz-Minimum of a much more real workday, people have used the house to eat and to sleep. In it everything was already identified by a comforting architecture: there remained only the hanging of pictures on the walls. The house was the first and most important step of the adoption of the total model of bourgeois life.

But now, thanks to a new and ever-increasing capacity for self-determination attained in the workplace, people should take possession of the house, freeing it from any previously established cultural and social model, dismissing the subtle intellectual links and the hysterical language knots that characterize architecture as figuration of space.

Freed from its "character armor," architecture must become an open structure, available for a mass intellectual production that communicates the collective landscape thought strong figures. The problem then becomes to free man from architecture as a formal structure. Today the only utopia is the quantitative one.

Social conflict in fact no longer passes through the juxtaposition of alternative models, but through the contractual dialectic between a balanced development of the system and a rising cost of labor.

The fight is no longer on an ideological level, but in terms of quantity: it is through this parameter that the aggregation of different phenomena apparently unrelated to each other is made possible. Quantitative language replaces that of quality, becoming the only medium for a scientific approach to the undifferentiated stratification of production, and therefore of reality.

Eliminating the general framework of reference, behavior becomes a structure without moral allegories. Freedom, as an outcome, immediately becomes an instrument of struggle.

ARCHIZOOM ASSOCIATI

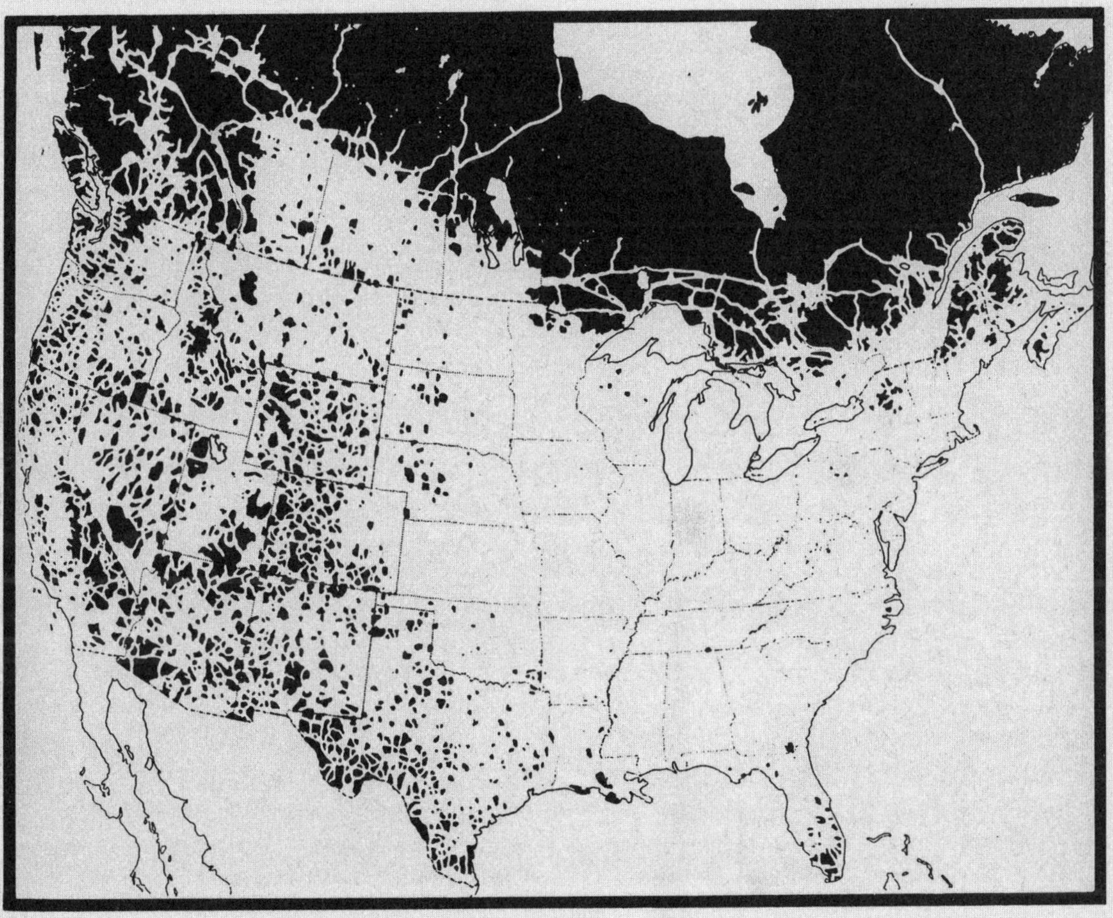

In nero le zone «selvagge» dell'America, distanti 5 miglia da strade, ferrovie, canali navigabili

15

Archizoom Associati, "Destruction and Re-Appropriation of the City," in *IN* n. 5, 1972

Paesaggio urbano

Un sistema cartesiano di riferimento sopra un tessuto urbano realizzato con palloni frenati riportanti le coordinate del punto di ancoraggio.
Suddividere un tessuto urbano tradizionale secondo un criterio di riconoscimento razionale che permetta di ricondurre qualsiasi episodio della scena urbana ad un quadro di fondo. È una maniera di numerare e catalogare gli episodi, tra loro sempre diversi, della città borghese, rimuovendoli dalla loro naturale localizzazione di eccezioni per inserirli in un catalogo spaziale dove tutti i punti sono tra loro uguali e tutti i fenomeni sono tra loro omogenei.
È una maniera di rendere la città continua e non più sommatoria di spazi e di usi diversi, ma piano neutro in cui gli avvenimenti cessano di essere tali per divenire i numeri delle proprie coordinate. L'esperienza di una città infatti, (con tutte le sue strade, i suoi palazzi, i suoi boulevards, le sue chiese, le sue piazze, i suoi fiumi), può essere ricondotta ad un fatto conoscitivo unico. Ma ciò che noi proponiamo non è una operazione di sintesi, al contrario.
Ciò che noi proponiamo è un criterio analitico di allestimento della città stessa, e quindi di distruggere la città, dal momento che rimuoviamo i suoi episodi dal contesto in cui si trovano per inserirlo in un altro. L'*allestimento* infatti non deve essere mai interpretazione o sogno, ma ferma ragione che introduce una realtà alla conoscenza. Strumento razionale di trasmissione di dati da un luogo ad un altro e da un utente all'altro.
L'allestimento è una maniera di *numerare* la realtà, liberando gli oggetti dalla vischiosa logicità e ordinandoli all'interno di un campo neutro, secondo una griglia omogenea in grado di disinnescare qualsiasi ultima significazione culturale di un materiale destinato alla memoria scientifica.
La famosa reazione a catena di Petuzzo, per cui il gatto mangia il topo, il topo rode la fune, la fune sega i buoi, i buoi bevono l'acqua, l'acqua spegne il fuoco, il fuoco brucia la mazza e la mazza picchia Petuzzo, non esiste più dal momento che egli numerando il mondo lo ha reso omogeneo, premunendosi contro la disponibilità prospettica della realtà.
Contestare metodicamente le strutture formali, come strutture repressive, che al pari di quelle morali, religiose, culturali, tolgono all'individuo la propria libertà di giudizio davanti alla storia, restituendogli, tali strutture, l'ambiente che lo circonda come una condizione naturale consacrata da « valori e significati ». *Questo è il nostro compito.*
« Non esiste oggi alcun dubbio nel riconoscere nel fenomeno urbano il punto più debole dell'intero sistema industriale ».
La metropoli, tradizionale « scena madre del Progresso », è oggi di fatto il settore più arretrato e confuso della realtà del Capitale; e tutto questo ad un tale livello che viene da domandarsi se la città moderna, più che un problema non risolto, non sia un fenomeno storico oggettivamente superato.
Bisogna cioè capire se il Capitale si pone ancora oggi, come un secolo fa, il problema della gestione della propria immagine e del proprio funzionamento al livello della forma urbana, o se piuttosto le trasformazioni avvenute ed in atto non hanno trasferito la sua realtà su di un'altra scala, trasformando il concetto stesso di città.
In questo momento dunque il problema non è più quello di immaginare una metropoli più umana e più ordinata, ma piuttosto quello di capire profondamente le leggi oggettive che presiedono al configurarsi del fenomeno urbano-architettonico, demistificando la complessa ideologia che ne accompagna il dibattito e ne condiziona la forma.
Il mito naturalistico della libera concorrenza poneva la città degli scambi e del commercio a garantire le condizioni ideali del mercato, realizzando l'equilibrio naturale tra gli opposti interessi, nel quadro generale della raggiunta armonia tra tecnica e natura.
Oggi l'uso dei medium elettronici sostitui-

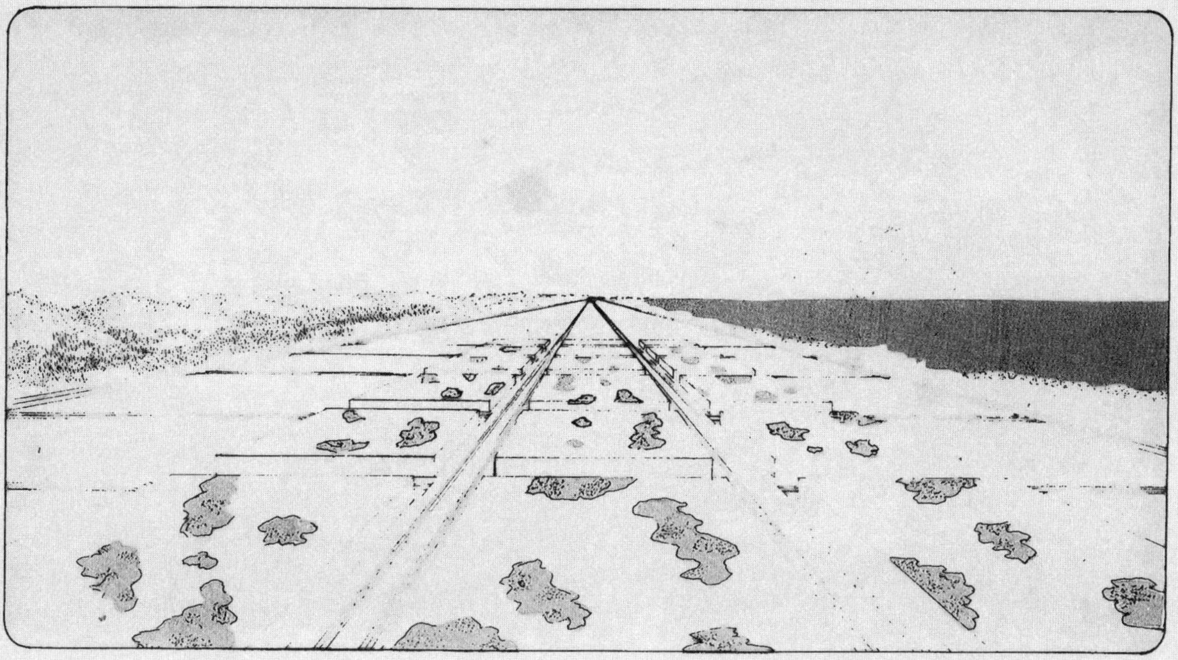

Paesaggio urbano

Paesaggio urbano

W
Z
X
Y

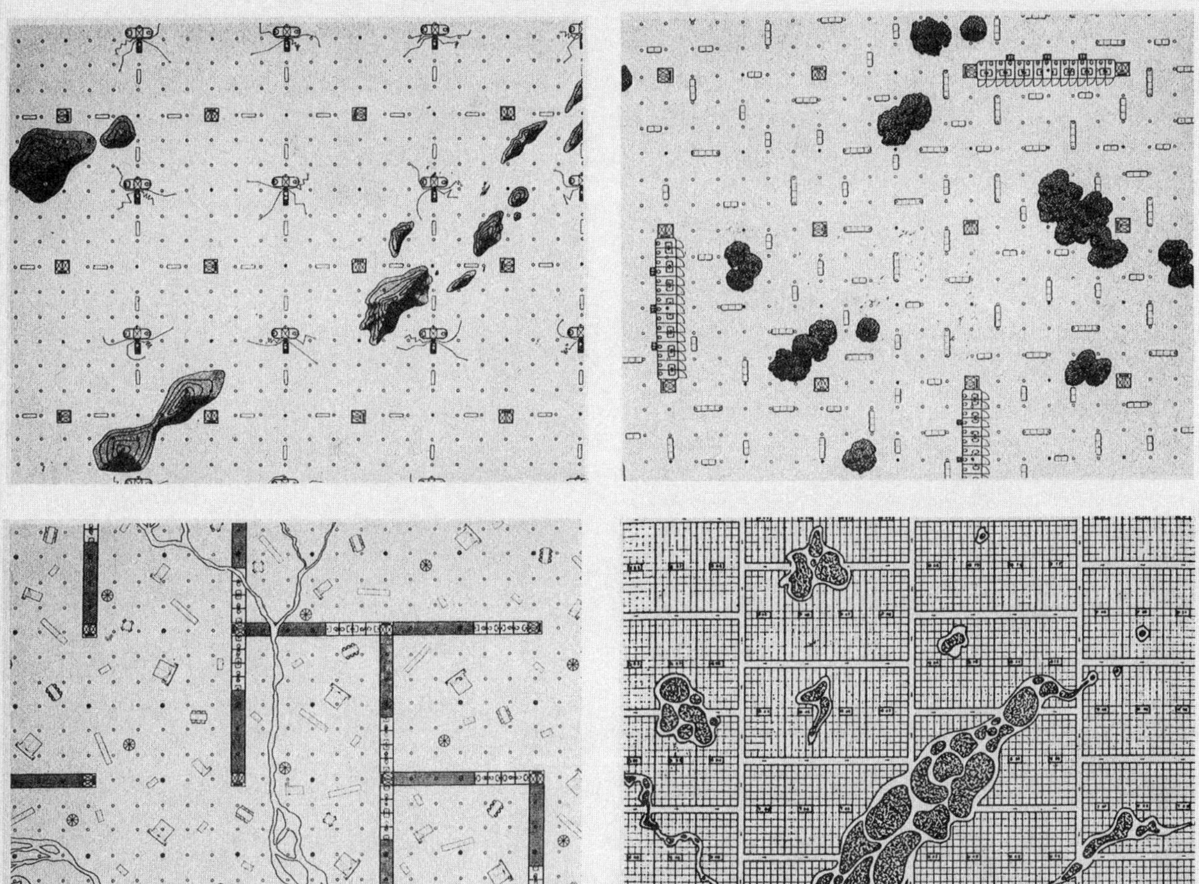

C
A

D
B

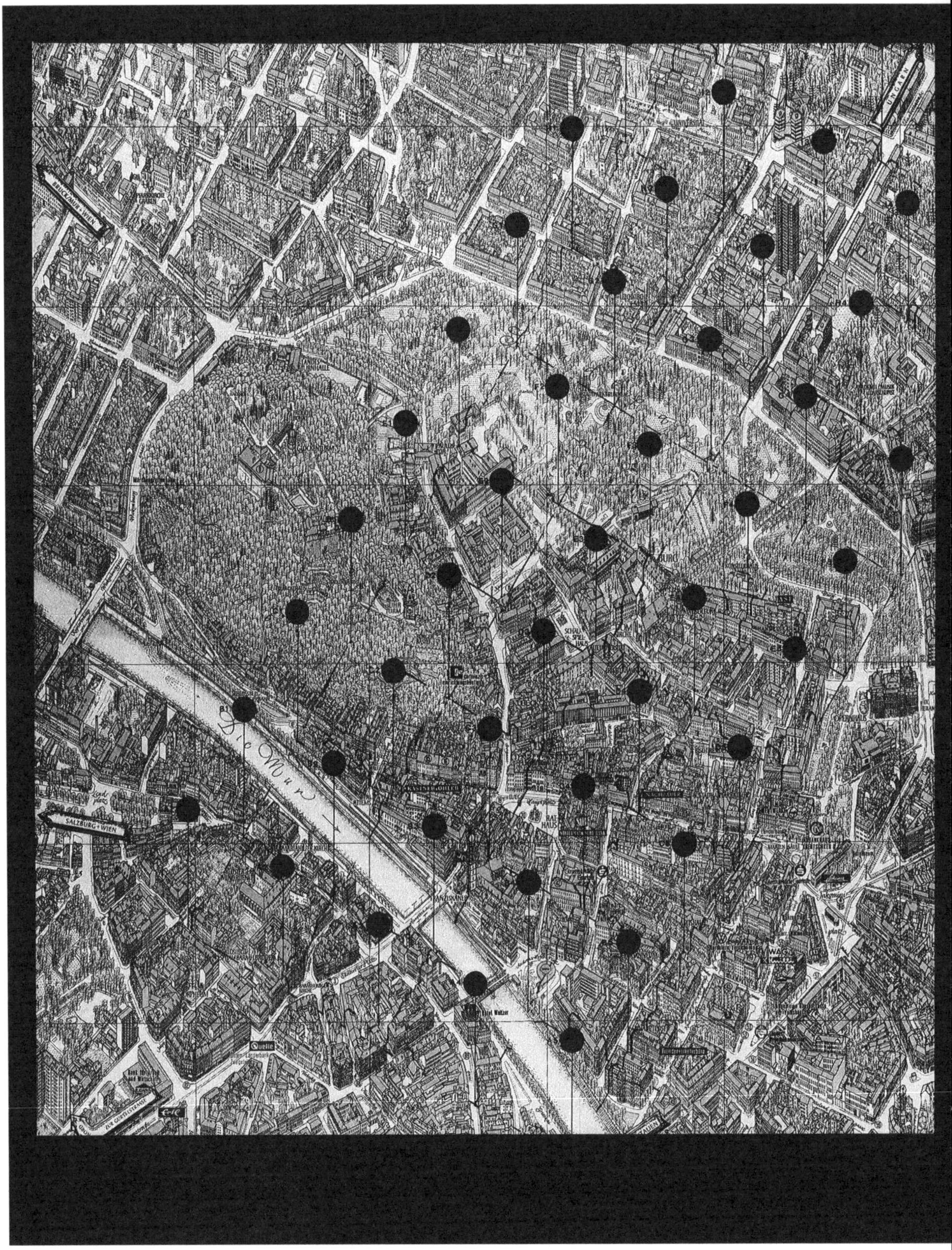
UNGARN
SALZBURG • WIEN
Quelle

sce la prassi urbana diretta: l'induzione artificiale al consumo permette una ben più profonda infiltrazione nella realtà sociale che non i fragili canali di informazione della città.
La metropoli cessa di essere un « luogo » per divenire una « condizione »; è proprio tale condizione infatti che viene fatta circolare in maniera omogenea nel fenomeno sociale attraverso i Consumi.
La dimensione futura della Metropoli coincide con quella del Mercato stesso.
La metropoli come concentrazione intensiva corrisponde alla fase ormai superata della accumulazione spontanea del Capitale. In una società programmata infatti la gestione degli interessi non ha più necessità di organizzarsi sul luogo stesso degli scambi. La totale disponibilità del territorio e la sua totale penetrazione elimina la città-capolinea e permette l'organizzazione di una maglia progressiva di organismi di controllo su di esso.
Nella ideologia borghese equilibrio ecologico e giustizia sociale diventano parti di una stessa battaglia: la città fornisce con la propria immagine la verifica formale di tale equilibrio.
Nel Piano Urbanistico dunque viene ricercata la non impossibile armonia tra l'interesse Generale e quello Particolare: tali categorie però vengono sempre acquisite come fenomeni antitetici, contrastanti e solubili.
Come tramite il più generale possibile, il traffico diventa allora lo schema oggettivo e figurale del funzionamento urbano. La strada infatti non solo serve il tessuto compatto del privato, ma lo « seziona » e lo « figura » anche, individuando i piani di affioramento del linguaggio architettonico. Lo skyline diventa il diagramma della avvenuta accumulazione naturale del Capitale stesso.
La metropoli borghese resta quindi soprattutto un luogo visuale, e la sua esperienza rimane legata a tale tipo di comunicazione. L'attuazione della organizzazione sociale del lavoro attraverso il Piano, elimina quello « spazio » vuoto nel quale il Capitale si espandeva nel proprio processo di crescita. Non esiste più infatti una realtà esterna al sistema stesso: l'intero rapporto visuale con la realtà viene meno, cessando di esistere la distanza tra il soggetto e il fenomeno.
La città non « rappresenta » più il sistema, ma « diviene » il sistema stesso, programmato ed isotropo, in cui le diverse funzioni sono contenute in maniera omogenea e senza contraddizioni.
La Produzione e i Consumi possiedono una identica ideologia, che è quella della Programmazione. Ambedue ipotizzano infatti una realtà sociale e fisica assolutamente continua e indifferenziata. Non esistono realtà *autres*.
La Fabbrica e il Supermarket diventano di fatto i veri modelli campione della città futura: strutture urbane ottimali, potenzialmente infinite, dove le funzioni si dispongono spontaneamente su di un piano libero, reso omogeneo da un sistema di microclimatizzazione e informazione ottimale.
Gli equilibri « naturali e spontanei » della luce e dell'aria sono superati di fatto: la casa diviene un'area di parcheggio attrezzato. Nel suo interno non esistono gerarchie o figurazioni spaziali condizionanti.
La tipologia, come figurazione funzionale della società, incerta tra il rilevamento di una realtà sociale come dato certo, e l'assunzione delle aspirazioni di tale realtà come dato probabile, resta impigliata nella restituzione allegorica di tale conflitto, che diviene un coefficiente culturale extra-funzionale.
Cercando di fornire il maggior numero di gradi di libertà all'utente, all'interno di una « figurazione » la più rigida possibile, l'architettura si trova a riconoscere nel fenomeno urbano il suo vero destino, e nel privato la sua vera natura.
Così in maniera contraddittoria essa prefigura in ogni singola occasione un ordine generale delle cose, e contemporaneamente si pone a difesa della parzialità della esperienza individuale nei riguardi delle esperienze collettive.
Essa media così in maniera figurale, la contraddizione tra pubblico e privato; oggi però tale conflitto non viene più lasciato al livello speculativo della pura coscienza esistenziale. Il Piano, organizzando produttivamente tutta la società, elimina tale conflitto, riconosce come apparente tale contraddizione e assume come sperimentale qualsiasi dato su scala strettamente individuale.
Fino ad oggi la grande massa della gente è rimasta esclusa dal fenomeno architettonico: ospite temporanea di un existenz-minimum integrativo di una giornata lavorativa ben più reale, la gente ha usato la casa per mangiare e dormire.
In essa tutto era già individuato da un'architettura consolatoria; restava solo da attaccare i quadretti alle pareti. La casa era il primo e più importante gradino della adozione totale del modello di vita borghese.
Ma oggi, forte di una nuova e sempre crescente capacità autodecisionale conquistata sui luoghi di lavoro, la gente si deve impossessare della casa, liberandola da qualsiasi modello culturale e sociale precostituito, liquidando i sottili legami intellettuali e gli isterici nodi linguistici che caratterizzano l'architettura come figurazione dello spazio.
Liberata dalle proprie « armature caratteriali », l'architettura deve diventare una struttura aperta, disponibile alla produzione intellettuale di massa come unica forza figurante il paesaggio collettivo. Il problema diventa dunque quello di liberare l'uomo dalla architettura, come struttura formale. Oggi l'unica utopia possibile è quella quantitativa.
Il conflitto sociale infatti non passa più attraverso la contrapposizione di modelli alternativi, ma attraverso la dialettica contrattuale tra uno sviluppo equilibrato del sistema e un crescente costo della forza lavoro.
Lo scontro non avviene più su di un piano ideologico ma in termini quantitativi: è attraverso tale parametro che si rende possibile la sommatoria di fenomeni diversi apparentemente tra loro non collegati.
Il linguaggio quantitativo sostituisce quello della qualità, divenendo l'unico medium scientifico per l'approccio alla stratificazione indifferenziata della produzione, e quindi della realtà.
Scomparendo i quadri generali di riferimento, il comportamento diventa una struttura priva di allegorie morali.
La libertà, come fine, diventa subito strumento di lotta.

ARCHIZOOM ASSOCIATI

LA CITTA' AMORALE

«L'utopia era la parte integrante della sua costituzione originaria e la città, proprio perché nata inizialmente come proiezione di un ideale, poté dar vita a realtà che sarebbero forse rimaste latenti per un tempo indefinito per piccole comunità governate con maggior prudenza, tese a fini più limitati e restii a compiere sforzi che trascendessero le loro abitudini quotidiane e le loro speranze terrene».
Condividiamo la «proiezione ideale» che ha generato i primi nuclei urbani; ne fa testimonianza l'origine mitica di ogni nucleo urbano antico che vela intenzionalmente ogni interpretazione funzionale per porre in primo piano la rappresentazione del sociale attraverso l'allegoria urbana.
Questa è però una interpretazione preindustriale ed è difficile sostenerla in una società mercantile dove l'«umano» diventa foza lavoro e i rapporti sociali sono regolati da quantità fisiche misurabili come lo sfruttamento e l'accumulazione del capitale. Ma se ci guardiamo intorno vediamo che la città è ancora quella della definizione del Mumford, almeno nella sua parte ufficiale perché nessuno riconosce dignità urbana ai margini post industriali sorti con l'introduzione del lavoro salariato e non a caso per queste «frange urbane» si parla di «recupero» per riscattare la loro fastidiosa vocazione terrena.
Questa sorta di occultamento di un figlio illegittimo anche se travestita da lucida autocritica del sistema appare almeno strana e comparabile ad uno strato nevrotico del comportamento in quanto si rifiuta di riconoscere un ambiente fisico come la naturale proliferazione dell'organizzazione del sociale.
In realtà questa figlia mentale ha origini lontane tanto da richiedere un attimo di riflessione.
La cattiva coscienza e la schizofrenia è all'origine della borghesia prima mercantile e poi industriale; è in fondo la psicologia del parvenu che rinnega le origini materiali del suo censo e cerca di offuscare la realtà dei nuovi rapporti umani dietro la cortina fumogena della spiritualità dell'arte levitante al di sopra dei quotidiani rapporti d'uso.
E da allora come i corpulenti commercianti del cinquecento amavano farsi ritrarre come principi dell'artigianato pittore che veniva promosso al nuovo ruolo di artista per alienare il rapporto fisico del denaro, unica garanzia sostanziale della borghesia nascente, così i lati più reconditi della psicologia del sistema preferiscono negare allo spazio urbano da esso partorito la sua oggettività di spazio d'uso orientandosi verso la più confortante interpretazione di spazio figurativo e allegorico. Mentre nell'ambiente del lavoro, la fabbrica, il sistema raggiunge la sua immagine più fedele, nello spazio urbano fugge nauseato di fronte al riversarsi in esso delle inevitabili frange dell'ambiente del lavoro e di fronte ad esse i metri di giudizio e di critica improvvisamente subiscono un'amnesia storica arretrando di parecchi secoli.
Così mentre la storia non ha senso nel mondo del lavoro (quale industria sacrificherebbe nuovi e più efficienti processi produttivi nel nome della testimonianza storica?) appare invece valida e sensata nell'ambiente urbano.
Non crediamo sia semplicistico ricondurre a questa dialettica tra misticismo e logica, qua-questa dialettica tra misticismo e logica, qualità e quantità i confini di campo e la linfa nutritiva delle battaglie culturali degli ultimi decenni. In questo intorno si muovono i filoni fondamentali della cultura sulla città, lo storicismo monumentale e l'utopia tecnologica. Entrambi, anche se con metodi diversi, perseguono il fine del superamento del sistema da sinistra: l'uno attraverso il 9consolidamento ostinato di posizioni apparentemente conservatrici ma destinate a sconvolgere la logica dei consumi con la lucidità incontestabile e stratosferica del monumento; l'altro accettando palesamente questa logica per portarla trionfalmente alla sua sublimazione.

In realtà il preteso superamento da sinistra attraverso una fuga irraggiungibile finisce per diventare un giro vizioso a destra dell'ideologia borghese in quanto viene ancora una volta ribadita l'autonomia del «fare artistico» rispetto all'oggettività dei rapporti di produzione coltivando in serre sempre più inaccessibili i privilegi dei nati sotto Saturno.
La realtà è che riconoscendo valore d'uso all'ambiente urbano si finisce per demolire l'ultima torre d'avorio dell'intellettualismo e con essa il sancta santorum della morale borghese perché si rischia di introdurre nel mondo della Cultura la logica e l'amoralità dei rapporti produttivi di fronte alla quale non pochi sarebbero imbarazzati nell'accertare la propria creatività misurabile in quantità e non più in qualità e in definitiva uguale a quella di tutti gli uomini.
A questo punto è molto difficile sostenere la funzionalità della divisione del lavoro e soprattutto la morale stessa del lavoro.

Archizoom Associati, "The Amoral City," in *IN* n. 7, 1972

The Amoral City
Archizoom Associati, 1972

//

"Utopia was the integrant part of the original constitution, and the city, for the reason that it was initially conceived as the projection of an ideal, was able to give life to a reality that would perhaps have remained latent for an indefinite period of time for small communities governed with greater prudence, having more limited aims, and reluctant to make exertions which would transcend their normal everyday habits and their earthly hopes."

We agree with the "projection of an ideal" which gave rise to the first urban nuclei; testimony to it is the mythic origin of every ancient urban nucleus which intentionally conceals any functional interpretation in order to focus on the representation of social factors by means of urban allegory. This is, however, a pre-industrial interpretation, and one difficult to sustain in a mercantile society in which "human" has the meaning of labour force and social relationships are regulated by measurable physical quantities such as the exploitation and accumulation of capital.

But if we look arounds, we can see that the city is still that defined by Mumford, at least as regards its official side, because no-one acknowledges urban dignity on the post-industrial fringes which sprang up with the introduction of fixed wages and it is no accident that one speaks of "reclaiming" these "urban fringes" in order to redeem their troublesome earthly vocation.

This kind of concealment of an illegitimate child, even if it is disguised as a shining self-criticism of the system, appears strange, to say the least, and comparable to a neurotic type of behavior inasmuch as it refuses to recognize a physical environment as the natural proliferation of the organization of social factors.

In reality, this mental film has origins so old as to require a moment of reflection.

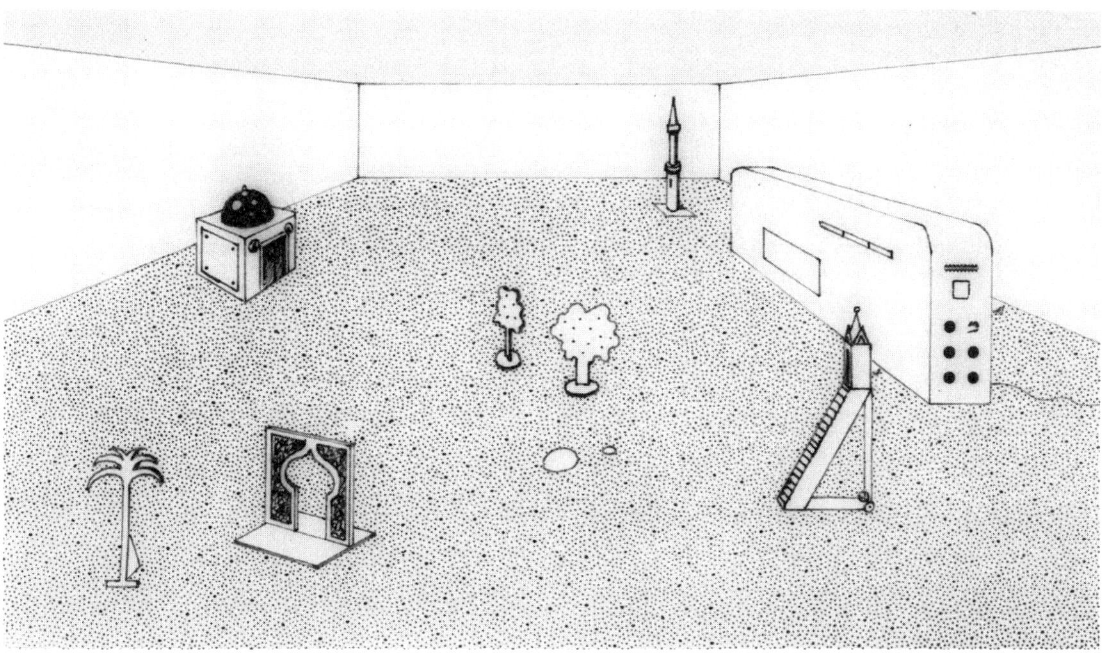

Archizoom Associati, "The Distruction of the Objects," 1971

A guilty conscience and schizophrenia are at the base of the middle-class, which was first mercantile, then industrial; it is basically the psychology of the parvenu who disowns the material origins of his wealth and tries to blur the reality of a new human relationships behind the smokescreen of the spirituality of levitating art suspended above everyday use relationships.

And as once the corpulent merchants of the sixteenth century loved to be depicted as princes by the artisan painter, who was promoted to the new role of artist in order to avoid physical intercourse with money, the only substantial guarantee the rising middle-class had, so the most recondite faces of the psychology of the system prefer to deny the urban space form which it arose its objectivity of usable space, directing itself towards the more comforting interpretation of figurative and allegorical space. Whilst in the working environment of the factory the system achieves its truest image, in urban space it runs away, nauseated, from the invading of this with the inevitable fringes of the working environment, and faced with these the parameters of judgement and criticism suddenly suffer a historical amnesia, retreating several centuries.

Thus, while history does not make sense in the working world (what industry would sacrifice new and more efficient production methods in the name of historical testimony?), it appears valid and meaningful in the urban environment.

Do not believe it is simple to bring back into this dialectic between mysticism and logic, quality and quantity, the disciplinary boundaries and the nutritious lymph of the cultural battles of the last ten years. In this sphere flow the fundamental currents of urban culture, monumental historicism and the technological utopia. Both of these, although using different methods, pursue the goal of overcoming the system from the left; one by the firm consolidation of positions apparently conservative but destined to upset the logic of the consumer society with incontestable and stratospheric lucidity of the monument; the other openly accepting this logic in order to bring it triumphantly to its sublimation.

In reality, the alleged overcoming from the left by means of an unattainable flight ends up by becoming a corrupt swing to the right of middle-class ideology, inasmuch as yet again the autonomy of "artistic behavior" becomes fixed in the respect to the objectivity of production terms, cultivating in ever more inaccessible hot-houses the privileges of those born under Saturn.

The truth is that by recognizing the use values of the urban environment one ends by demolishing the last ivory tower of intellectualism, and with this the sancta sanctorum of middle-class morality, because one risks introducing into the world of Culture the logic and the amorality of productive terms faced with which not a few would be embarrassed at the verification of their creativity, measurable in quantity and no longer in quality and, in the end, the same as that of all men.

At this point it is very difficult to sustain the functionality of the division of labour and, above all, the morality of labour.

D
NEUTRAL FIELD NEUTRAL SURFACE

Reactive Surfaces and Artificial Landscape

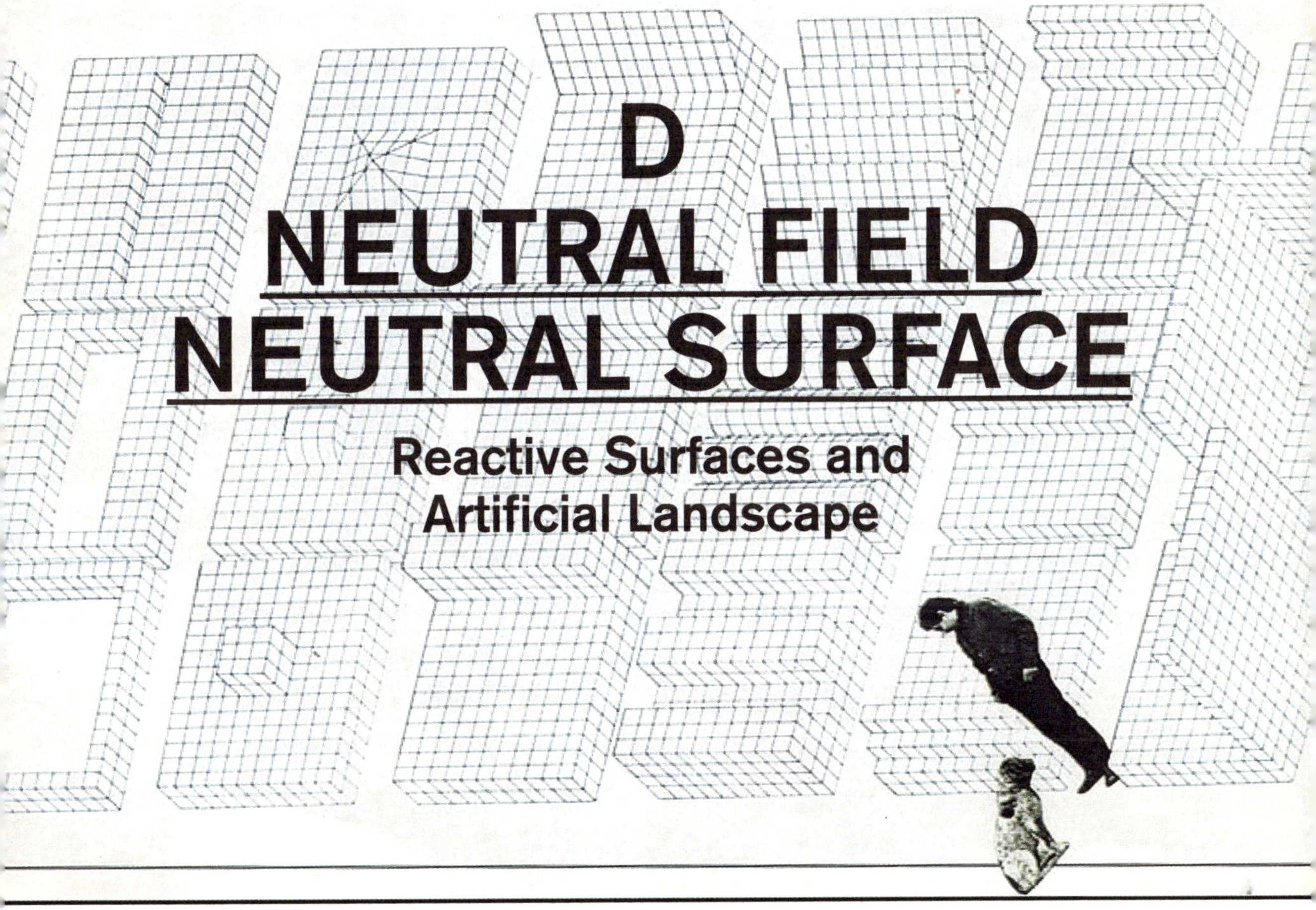

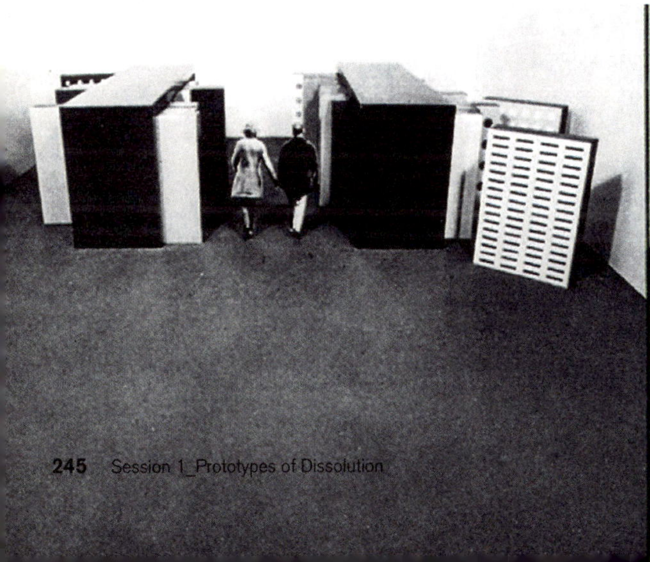

The Invention of the Neutral Surface
Archizoom Associati, 1973

//

What we are trying to hypothesize is not a different home, but a different "use" of the home.

Much has been invented, but for users - by now - any design product they get in the home runs the risk of increasing their degree of alienation to increasingly frustrate their human potential. Why?

Because in a society like the present one, based on work and on its division, all those individual energies that are not destined for productivity are fatally destined to remain atrophied.

Only a minimal percentage of people are destined, or conditioned, to develop their creative faculties, becoming intellectuals or artists, committed to producing in the form of consumer goods a culture that always has an exact circuit: from the producer to the consumer, who suffers the repercussions in terms of behavior and cohesion.

But if people are all equal, as is true, there is only a temporary difference between artist and user.

It is here that the distinction of work exceeds the limit of the simple functional organization of production, for which you build the hammer and I build the nails, and it becomes the alienation of a sacrosanct right, which is that of self-producing and self-consuming your own culture.

Archizoom Associati: "The Invention of the Neutral Surface"
in *Elementi: quaderni di studi, notizie, ricerche*, Abet Laminati, 1973

ARCHIZOOM ASSOCIATI

Quello che noi cerchiamo di ipotizzare non è più una casa diversa, ma un « uso » diverso della casa.
Molto è stato inventato, ma per l'utente ormai qualsiasi prodotto di design si metta in casa, corre il rischio di accrescere il suo grado di alienazione e frustrare sempre più profondamente la propria potenzialità umana. Questo perché?
Perché in una società come quella attuale, basata sul lavoro e sulla divisione di questo, tutte quelle energie individuali che non siano destinate alla produttività sono destinate fatalmente a restare atrofizzate.
Solo una percentuale minima di uomini è destinata, o condizionata, a sviluppare le proprie facoltà creative divenendo intellettuali o artisti, impegnati a produrre sotto forma di bene di consumo, una cultura che ha sempre un esatto circuito dal produttore al consumatore, che ne subisce il contraccolpo in termini di comportamento e di adesione.
Ma se gli uomini sono tutti uguali, come è vero, non esiste che una differenza provvisoria tra artista e utente.
È qui che la distinzione del lavoro supera il limite della semplice organizzazione funzionale della produzione, per cui tu costruisci il martello e io i chiodi, e diviene l'alienazione di un diritto sacrosanto, che è quello di autoprodurre e autoconsumare la propria cultura.
È il diritto a recuperare tutte le proprie facoltà creative, atrofizzate e inutilizzate da secoli di impegno produttivo, e insieme a questo il diritto ad autogestire la propria comunicazione e la propria disponibilità sulla realtà circostante, fisica e storica.
Gestendo le proprie facoltà creative si rimuove la gestione centralizzata della cultura la quale è sempre impegnata a restituire all'individuo un ambiente consacrato da « valori e significati », che agiscono come strutture repressive e punitive sul suo diritto ad esistere liberamente, al di fuori da qualsiasi allegoria morale precostituita.
Anche la casa, fino ad oggi, è stata organizzata come un breve confine inserito tra le ore di lavoro, nella quale recuperare le energie perdute per un nuovo giorno produttivo; una casa che faciliti un riposo di morte, il silenzio, un fragile equilibrio psichico, e attraverso un po' di sole che entra dalle finestre, l'illusione di una integrazione con la natura, e attraverso la natura, con la società.
All'interno della casa la famiglia si è

suddivisa i compiti, come una piccola società di produzione.
L'arredo stesso simula all'utente una cultura che non possiede e una scelta che non ha fatto, ma che altri hanno fatto per lui e per lui prodotto.
Il diritto quindi ad autogestire la propria casa è una lotta per liberare la propria vita dal lavoro.
Rimuovendo il lavoro dalla propria esistenza la casa diviene un laboratorio disponibile alla sperimentazione continua delle proprie facoltà creative, continuamente superate e continuamente rivissute senza che necessariamente esse si congelino in una verifica formale che costituisca l'« arredamento ».
La casa può divenire allora una sorte di « parcheggio attrezzato », nel senso che da essa scompaiono tutte le prefigurazioni tipologiche e tutte le permanenze spaziali della casa attuale, per lasciare il posto libero alla figurazione spontanea e incontrollata dell'ambiente.

Ce que nous cherchons d'envisager n'est plus une maison différente, mais un « emploi » différent de la maison.
Beaucoup de choses ont été inventées, mais désormais pour l'usager quel que soit le produit de « design » qu'il place dans sa maison, il court le risque d'accroître son degré d'aliénation et de frustrer toujours plus profondément sa potentialité humaine.
Pourquoi cela?
Parce que dans une société comme la nôtre, basée sur le travail et sur la division du travail, toutes les énergies individuelles, qui ne sont pas destinées à la productivité, sont destinées fatalement à rester atrophiées.

6 ARCHIZOOM ASSOCIATI

Seul un pourcentage réduit d'hommes est destiné, ou conditionné, à développer leurs facultés créatrices pour devenir des intellectuels ou des artistes, engagés à produire sous forme de biens de consommation, une culture qui suit toujours un circuit exact allant du producteur au consommateur, qui en subit le contrecoup en termes de comportement et d'adhésion.
Mais si les hommes sont tous égaux, comme c'est le cas, il n'existe qu'une différence provisoire entre artiste et usager.
Et c'est ici que la distinction du travail dépasse la limite de la simple organisation fonctionnelle de la production, selon laquelle toi tu fabriques le marteau et moi les clous, et devient l'aliénation d'un droit sacré, qui est celui de produire et de consommer soi-même sa propre culture.
C'est le droit de récupérer toutes ses facultés créatrices, atrophiées et inutilisées par des siècles d'effort productif, et en même temps que ces dernières le droit de gérer soi-même sa communication et sa disponibilité sur la réalité environnante, physique et historique.
En gérant ses propres facultés créatrices, l'on enlève la gestion centralisée de la culture, qui est toujours engagée à restituer à l'individu un milieu consacré par « des valeurs et des significations », qui agissent comme des structures répressives et punitives sur son droit à exister librement, en dehors de toute allégorie morale pré-établie.
Jusqu'à aujourd'hui, la maison a été organisée elle aussi comme une courte marge intercalée entre les heures de travail, où récupérer les énergies perdues pour un autre jour de production; une maison qui facilite un repos de mort, le silence, un équilibre psychique fragile, et, grâce à un peu de soleil qui entre par les fenêtres, l'illusion de s'intégrer à la nature, et, à travers la nature, à la société.
A l'intérieur de la maison, la famille s'est réparti les tâches, comme une petite société de production.
L'ameublement lui-même simule à l'usager une culture qu'il ne possède pas et un choix qu'il n'a pas fait, mais que d'autres ont fait et produit pour lui.
Par conséquent le droit à gérer soi-même sa maison est une lutte pour libérer sa propre vie de travail.
En enlevant le travail de son existence, la maison devient un laboratoire disponible à l'expérimentation permanente de ses facultés créatrices, constamment dépassées et constamment revécues, sans qu'elles se congèlent nécessairement en une vérification formelle qui constitue « l'ameublement ».
La maison peut devenir alors une sorte de « parking équipé », dans le sens que disparaissent toutes les préfigurations typologiques et toutes les permanences spatiales de la maison actuelle, pour laisser la place à la figuration spontanée et incontrôlée du milieu.

E GREY ENVIRONMENTS MoMA

Italy: The New Domestic Landscape

Andrea Branzi, Ettore Sottsass Jr., XV Triennale of Milan, 1974. Triennal Archive. Photo: Ettore Sottsass Jr.

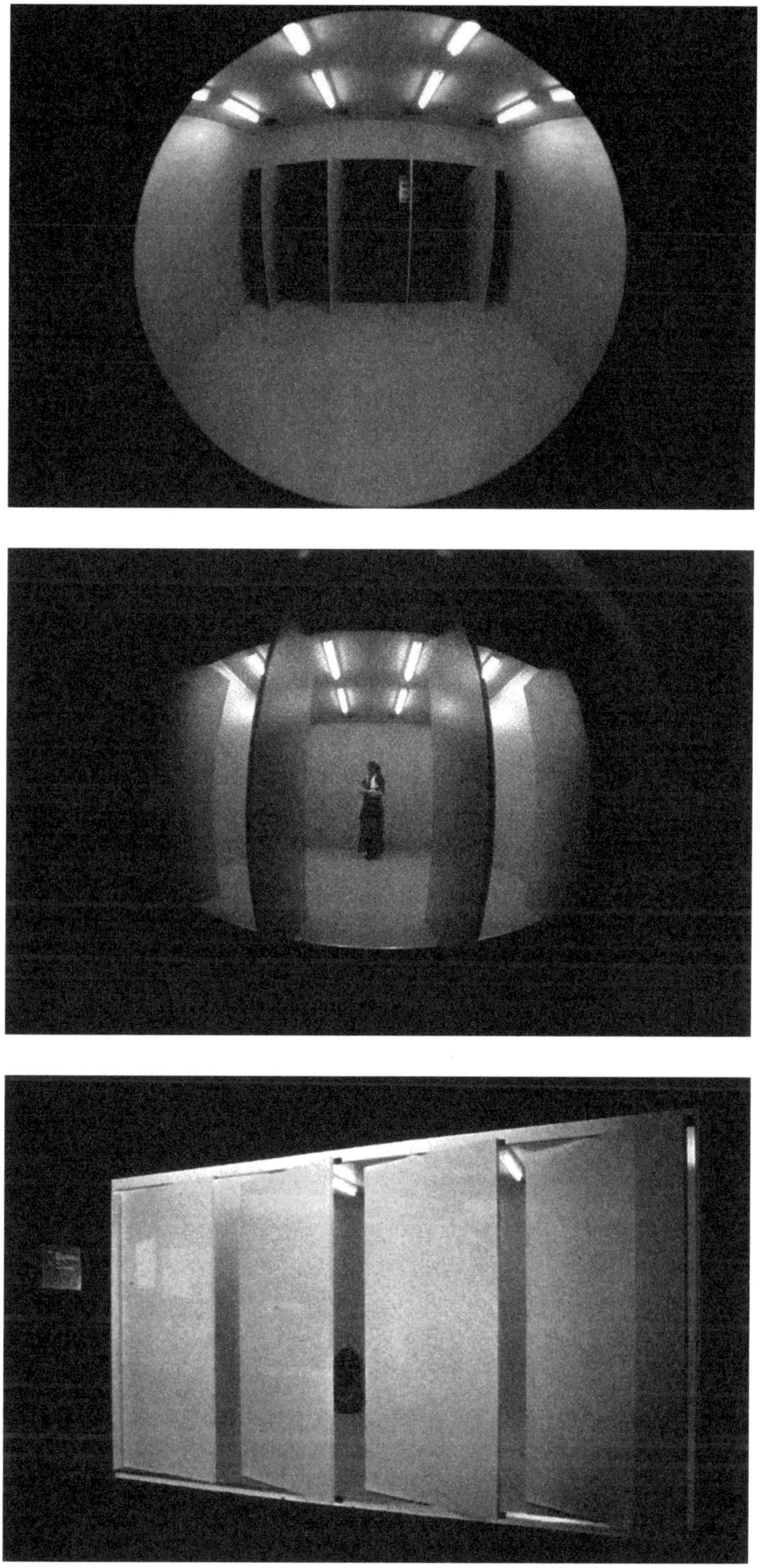

Archizoom Associati, *Gray Environments*, in *Italy: The New Domestic Landscape: Achievements and Problems of Italian Design*, 1972
Photos: Cristiano Toraldo di Francia

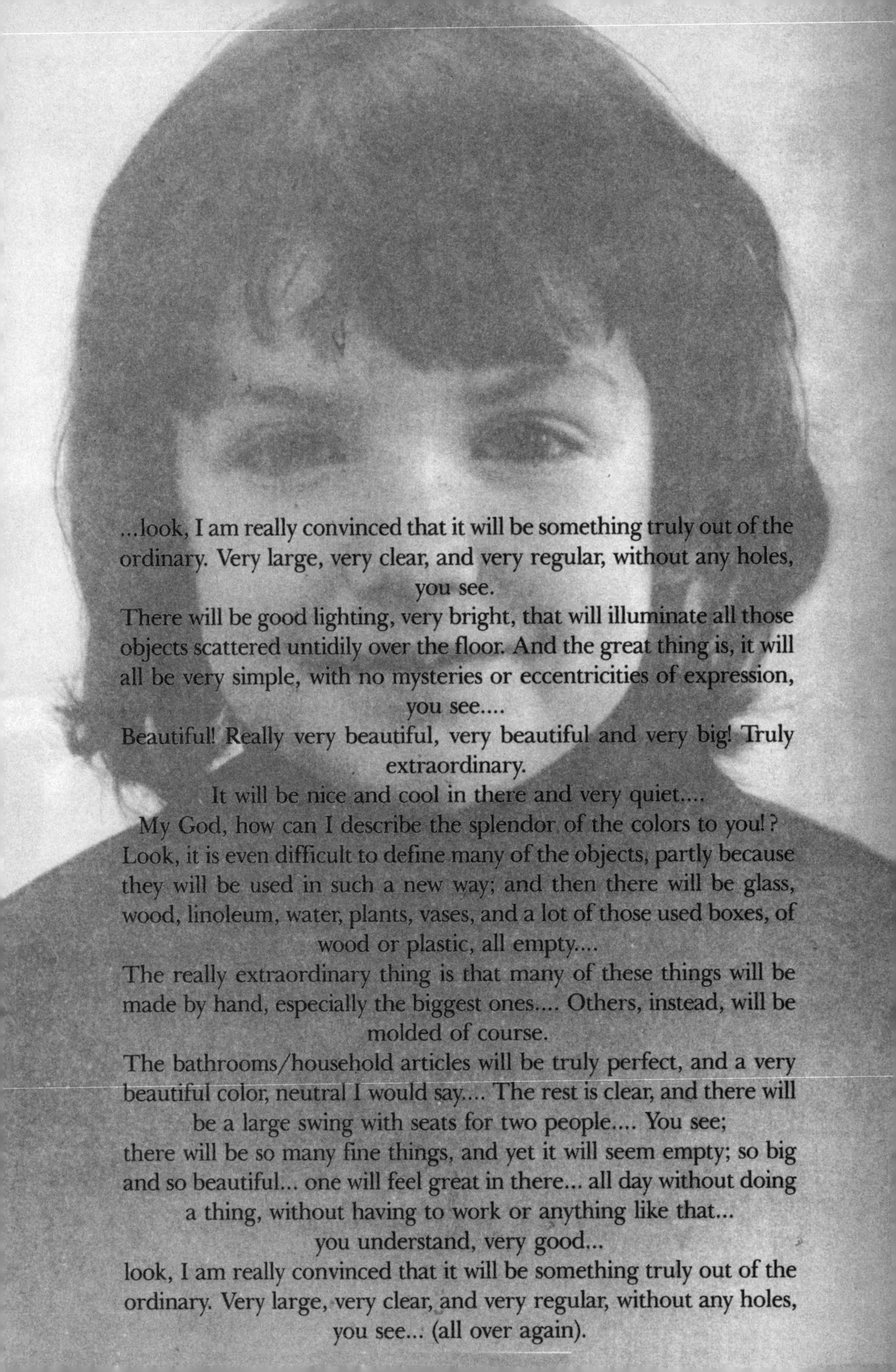

...look, I am really convinced that it will be something truly out of the ordinary. Very large, very clear, and very regular, without any holes, you see.

There will be good lighting, very bright, that will illuminate all those objects scattered untidily over the floor. And the great thing is, it will all be very simple, with no mysteries or eccentricities of expression, you see....

Beautiful! Really very beautiful, very beautiful and very big! Truly extraordinary.

It will be nice and cool in there and very quiet....

My God, how can I describe the splendor of the colors to you!?

Look, it is even difficult to define many of the objects, partly because they will be used in such a new way; and then there will be glass, wood, linoleum, water, plants, vases, and a lot of those used boxes, of wood or plastic, all empty....

The really extraordinary thing is that many of these things will be made by hand, especially the biggest ones.... Others, instead, will be molded of course.

The bathrooms/household articles will be truly perfect, and a very beautiful color, neutral I would say.... The rest is clear, and there will be a large swing with seats for two people.... You see;

there will be so many fine things, and yet it will seem empty; so big and so beautiful... one will feel great in there... all day without doing a thing, without having to work or anything like that...

you understand, very good...

look, I am really convinced that it will be something truly out of the ordinary. Very large, very clear, and very regular, without any holes, you see... (all over again).

The Museum of Modern Art

11 West 53 Street, New York, N.Y. 10019 Tel. 956-6100 Cable: Modernart

NO. 26
FOR RELEASE:
MAY 26, 1972

ITALY: THE NEW DOMESTIC LANDSCAPE, one of the most ambitious design exhibitions undertaken by The Museum of Modern Art, will be on view in the galleries and gar- from May 26 through September 11. Directed and installed by Emilio Ambasz, Curator Design in the Museum's Department of Architecture and Design, the exhibition reports current design developments in Italy with 180 objects for household use and 11 en-ronments commissioned by the Museum.

The exhibition is presented under the sponsorship of the Ministry of Foreign Trade of Italy and the Italian Institute of Foreign Trade (I.C.E.) and the Gruppo ENI, with contributions from ANIC and Lanerossi (companies of Gruppo ENI), Fiat, Olivetti, Anonima Castelli, Alitalia, and Abet Print, and with the collaboration of a large number of Italian industries.

Italy, Mr. Ambasz says, is not only the dominant product design force in the world today but also illustrates some of the concerns of all industrial societies. Italy has assumed the characteristics of a micro-model where a wide range of possibilities, limitations and critical problems of contemporary designers throughout the world are represented by diverse and sometimes opposite approaches. These include a wide range of conflicting theories about the present state of design activity, its relation to the building industry and to urban development, as well as a growing distrust of objects of consumption.

The exhibition will be organized into two parts: Environments and Objects. The objects were selected and the environments were commissioned because of their relevance to particular current attitudes toward "the task of design." The exhibition therefore devotes major areas to audio-visual presentations explaining the purpose of the exhibits, and a concluding audio-visual section in which the director of the show, Mr. Ambasz, gives an analysis and critique of the problems raised. In addition, most of the environments contain a TV screen on which is shown a three- to four-minute film made by

(more)

Emilio Ambasz, Press Release, *Italy: The New Domestic Landscape*, The Museum of Modern Art, NY, 1972 the designer to explain his environment.

Made in Italy and shipped to New York, the environments are intended for two modes of contemporary living -- the permanent home and the mobile unit. Four illustrate the counter-design approach of designers who believe no more objects should be added to our cluttered consumer-dominated culture and that social and political changes are needed before we can change the physical aspects of our society. Seven pro-design environments were made by designers who believe it is possible to improve the quality of life by improving our physical environment.

The pro-design environments pay special attention to new forms emerging as a result of changing patterns of life style: more informal social and family relationships and evolving notions of privacy and territoriality, as well as the exploration of new materials and production techniques. Each environment occupies a 16 x 16 foot area in the galleries. Among them are Ettore Sottsass' micro-environments in plastic, each on casters so occupants can easily re-arrange them to fit their needs; Joe Colombo's fixed plastic units for bath, kitchen, sleeping, and storage that can be put into any existing space; Gae Aulenti's molded plastic elements which can be combined to form architectural multi-purpose environments; Rosselli's aluminum mobile house which expands from 7 x 14 feet to 20 x 29 feet; Zanuso-Sapper's house, an aluminum container from which two plastic molded shells housing bedroom and bathroom/kitchen units telescope; and Mario Bellini's glass-walled "exploration" car can also expand when stationary. La Pietra's environment suggests a bridge between the pro-design and counter-design proposals; he believes we can liberate ourselves from present conditions by better use of the communications network.

As a prologue to the environments section, and functioning as an ironic commentary on the present, there is Gaetano Pesce's "underground room." It represents the remains of a habitat of the year 2000 as found in the year 3000. The counter-

(more)

design environments consist of Superstudio's 6 x 6 foot box of polarized mirror glass with a grid in the floor through which tubes project bringing air, food, water and communications to the occupants, who can also watch a film on TV that describes the designers' vision of the world and see pictures of clouds projected on the ceiling; and Archizoom group's empty room containing only a microphone over which come harsh words about the destruction of objects and institutions, followed by a pleasant voice describing a utopian world. Derossi, Ceretti, and Rosso, a group of young designers from Turin who believe there is no point in designing any objects or environments until the entire urban policy is redirected, wrote three pamphlets which are given to visitors, describing the present and the future.

Complementing the environments, there will be a display of 180 objects produced it Italy during the last decade by more than 100 designers. These examples of product design (furniture, lighting fixtures, flatware and china) were selected for their design quality and to illustrate the various intellectual design positions which have evolved in Italy in the last 10 years.

The objects section illustrates three prevalent attitudes toward design in Italy today: "conformist," "reformist," and "contestatory," Mr. Ambasz says.

Most are by conformist designers who are concerned with exploring the aesthetic quality of single objects such as chairs, tables, bookcases, which answer the needs of traditional domestic life. Bold use of color, imaginative utilization of the possibilities offered in new hard and soft synthetic materials, and advanced moulding techniques characterize this work. About 60% of the objects on view are in this category, including Joe Colombo's "Poker" table (1968) in laminated wood and steel; the "Soriana" lounge chair (1970) by Tobia and Afra Scarpa, in polyurethane and dacron covered with fabric; the "Arco" floor lamp by Achille and Piergiacomo Castiglioni (1962) in steel

(more)

with a marble base; and the "Giunone" floor lamp (1969) in lacquered metal, and the "Selene" stacking chair (1965) in reinforced polyester, both by Vico Magistretti.

Describing the reformist designers, Mr. Ambasz observes that they do not invent substantially new designs but rather re-design known objects with new, ironic and sometimes self-deprecatory socio-cultural and aesthetic references. Examples are the "Donna" armchair with footstool (1969) shaped liked a woman, by Caetano Pesce in polyurethane; the "Sassi" stones, different size seats by Piero Gilardi, in polyurethane; and the "Joe" sofa (1970), designed to look like a baseball glove in polyurethane and leather by De Pas, D'Urbino and Lomazzi.

While the "contestatory" designers believe that an object can no longer be designed as a single isolated entity, their reaction is to conceive of their designs in terms of environments and to propose objects that are flexible in function and permit multiple modes of use and arrangement. The results of this mode of Italian design do in fact seem to correspond to the preoccupations of a changing society, Mr. Ambasz observes. Among the examples on view are "Tavoletto," (1967) a low table on casters with folding bed inside, by Alberto Salvati and Ambrogio Tresoldi in lacquered wood; "il Serpentone" (the jumbo snake), a settee of unlimited length that can be bent into concave or convex curves of any radius to suit the user's needs, designed by Ms. Cini Boeri (1971) in polyurethane; the "Sacco" or bean bag chair (1969) by Gatti, Teodoro and Paolini in polyurethane filled with little balls; and the "Ghiro" mattress-lounge chair (1967) in polyurethane and fabric by Umberto Catalano and Gianfranco Masi.

The objects will be exhibited in the upper and lower terraces of the Museum's Garden in containers especially designed by Mr. Ambasz.

An accompanying publication,* edited by Mr. Ambasz, and published by The Museum of Modern Art, illustrates the environments and objects shown in the exhibition, and

*ITALY: THE NEW DOMESTIC LANDSCAPE edited by Emilio Ambasz. 432 pages; 380 illustrations (110 in color); clothbound $15.00; paperbound $7.95. Published by The Museum of Modern Art, New York. Clothbound edition distributed to the trade by New York Graphic Society Ltd. in the United States and Canada.

(more)

SONO PARTITI PER NEW YORK

Il 26 maggio si aprirà al pubblico, al Museum of Modern Art di New York, la mostra « Italy: the New Domestic Landscape ».
La mostra, una « major exhibition » per il Museum of Modern Art, avrà tre inaugurazioni speciali: il 23 maggio una « special preview evening » (black tie) in onore degli italiani, il 24 un « gala » di beneficenza con musica e danze, il 25 una «preview» di dodici ore per i 40.000 membri del Museo.
La mostra è diretta da Emilio Ambasz che ha anche disegnato l'allestimento (collaboratori: Thomas Czarnowski per la coordinazione e Anna Tucci per la documentazione e la raccolta degli oggetti), ed è stata completamente realizzata in Italia, con il contributo di industrie italiane — fra cui l'Anic, la Fiat, l'Olivetti, l'Alitalia, l'Abet Print, l'Anonima Castelli.
Due sono le parti in cui la mostra si articola. La prima parte presenterà una serie di ambienti studiati e disegnati appositamente per la mostra da architetti e designers italiani (« Scopo di questi ambienti sarà quello di esaminare il "paesaggio domestico" tenendo presenti i suoi *luoghi*: gli spazi e gli artefatti che danno loro forma, le cerimonie e i modi di agire che danno loro un significato »). Per fornire alla prima parte un contesto storico, e per dare una identità alle diverse posizioni del design in evoluzione in Italia, la seconda parte della mostra presenterà una selezione dei più interessanti esempi di disegno industriale realizzati in Italia negli ultimi dieci anni.
Qui, come primo annuncio, diamo le prime immagini delle « proposte » di ambienti — ambienti realizzati in Italia e da poco partiti per New York — ed anche qualche immagine dei progetti che hanno vinto il concorso per « micro-ambienti » e « micro-eventi » bandito in Italia dal Museum of Modern Art in occasione della mostra.
Daremo più avanti il resoconto di « Italy: the New Domestic Landscape » (la mostra resterà al Museum of Modern Art fino all'11 settembre).

First announcement of « Italy: the New Domestic Landscape », an exhibition presented by the Museum of Modern Art of New York (May 25 to September 11) and directed by Emilio Ambasz. Here, images of the eleven « environments for living » especially designed for the exhibition by Italian architects. Built in Italy, the environments have been shipped to New York.

Germano Celant, "They left for New York," in *Domus* n. 510, 1972

ARCHIZOOM

Archizoom Associati have been active as a group since 1966, maintaining a studio in Florence for product design, architecture, interior design, and the installation of exhibitions. In 1966, they organized the first exhibition of 'Superarchitecture' at Pistoia, followed by a second one in Modena in 1967, and by the 'Center for Eclectic Conspiracy' stand which they presented at the XIV Triennale, Milan, 1968. Since then, they have carried on their polemical activities through such exhibitions as 'No-stop City (Residential Parking),' 1970; participation in the VII Biennale, Paris, 1971; and conferences and publications, including the preparation of a special issue of the periodical *IN* (June 1971) devoted to 'the destruction of the object.' In 1970, in collaboration with Superstudio, they undertook a research project in airport design under the auspices of the Cesare Cassina Center of Studies, Meda (Milan) and in the same year entered two national competitions, at Catanzaro and Genoa, for the designing of airports.

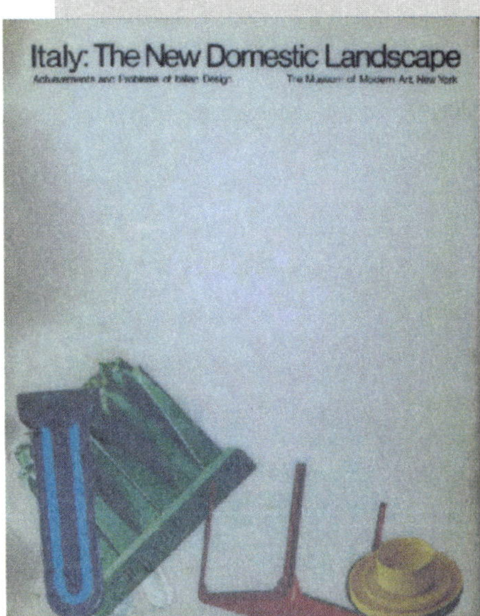

Designers: Archizoom (Andrea Branzi, Gilberto Corretti, Paolo Deganello, Dario Bartolini, Lucia Bartolini, Massimo Morozzi)
Patron: ABET-Print
Audio-score: Giuseppe Chiari

232

Archizoom Associati, "Italy: The New Domestic Landscape", in E. Ambasz, *Italy: The New Domestic Landscape: Achievements and Problems of Italian Design*, The Museum of Modern Art, NY, with Centro Di, Florence, Moma Press, 1972

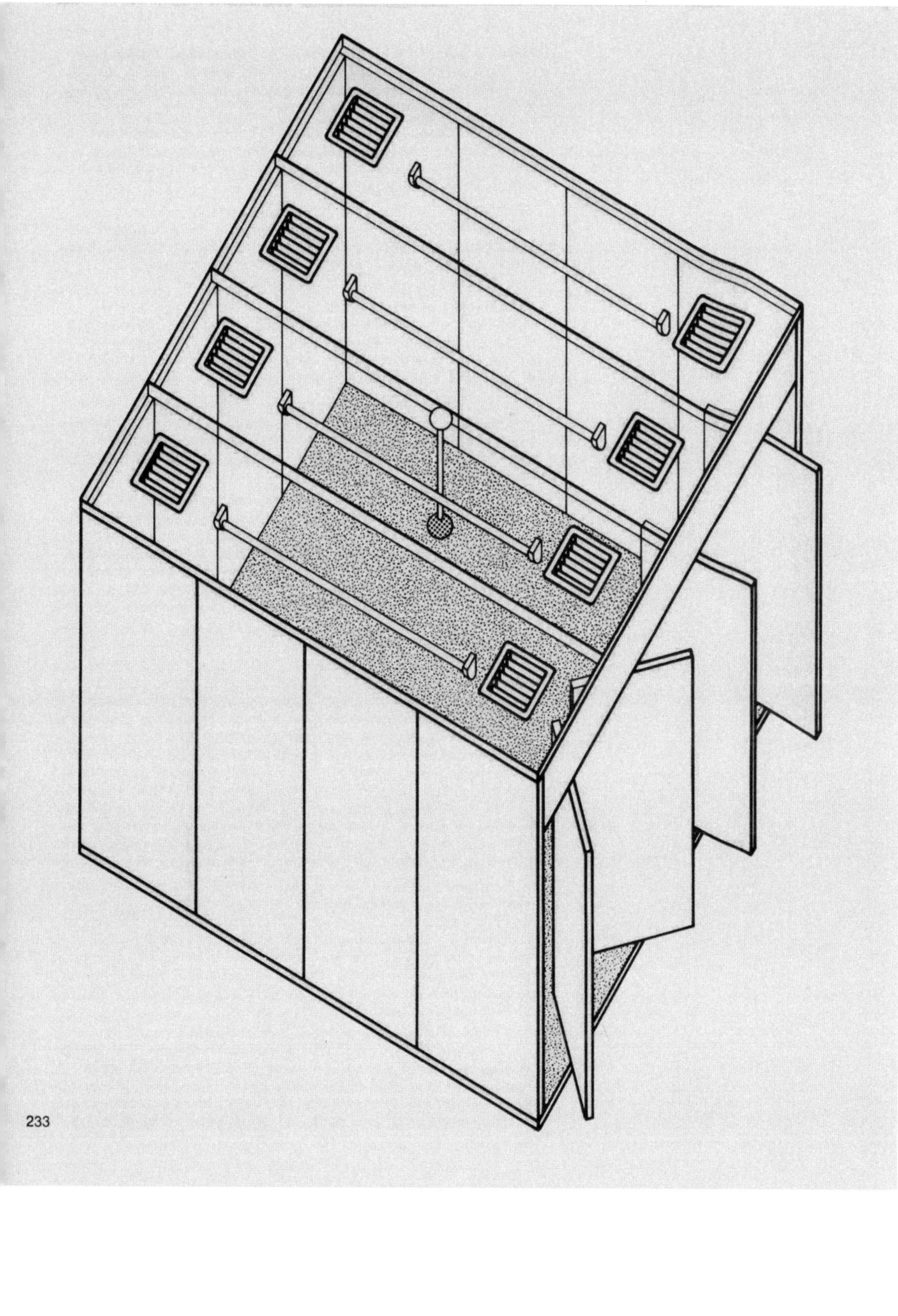

233

'Listen, I really think it's going to be something quite extraordinary. Very spacious, bright, really well arranged, with no hidden corners, you know. There will be fine lighting, really brilliant, that will clearly show up all those disordered objects.

'The fact is, everything will be simple, with no mysteries and nothing soul-disturbing, you know. Wonderful! Really very beautiful — very beautiful, and very large. Quite extraordinary! It will be cool there too, with an immense silence.

'My God, how can I describe to you the wonderful colors! You see, many things are really quite hard to describe, especially because they'll be used in such a new way. And then, there'll be glass, wood, linoleum, water, plants, vases, and many of those boxes they used to use, in wood or plastic, and all empty....

'What's really extraordinary about all this is that many of these things will be handmade, especially the largest ones. Of course, others will obviously be machinemade. The household equipment will be just perfect, in wonderful colors, neutral colors, I should say... All the rest will be bright, and there'll be a big swing with room for two.

' You see, there'll be a lot of marvelous things, and yet it will look almost empty, it will be so big and so beautiful... How fine it will be... just spending the whole day doing nothing, without working or anything... You know, just great...' (And so on, starting all over again at the beginning.)

What we use, then, in creating our environment is the least physical thing in the world, namely, words. Of course, that doesn't at all mean that in postponing the physical realization of this environment, we have avoided picturing it. On the contrary, we have refused to complete a *single* image, our own, preferring instead that as many should be created as there are people listening to this tale, who will imagine this environment for themselves, quite beyond our control.

Not a single utopia, then, but an infinity of utopias, as many as there are listeners. Not just a single culture, but one for each individual. We have given up making an environmental model, partly because, in general, we think it's time to begin learning how to do without models; and partly because, if we were to present just a single model — the one we think the best — we should have to eliminate an infinite number of others, and that would be quite a waste. Creating culture today is no longer — at least, it shouldn't be — the privilege of a few intellectuals, who provide users with the critical apparatus with which to explain the world and organize the form of their environment, too. The right to go against a reality that lacks 'meaning' (because it is a reality produced by a system that is 'meaningless' in itself) is the right to act, modify, form, and destroy the surrounding environment. This is an inalienable right, and a capability each one of us possesses.

Culture, and the making of culture, the formal act of doing so, doesn't mean expressing oneself through allegory or metaphor. It is a political right, not a subject for linguistic criticism. It is the task of rediscovering and asserting those physiological capacities that are linked to the body's material substance and the electrical energy of the nervous system. Thanks to these, the making of art or the making of culture take on a meaning quite complete in themselves, like a kind of liberating psycho-physiotherapy.

The self-production and self-consumption of culture imply the ability to free oneself from all those repressive systems that 'official culture' has woven around us, by attributing an infinite variety of 'values' and 'meanings' to the reality around us and thus, in fact, taking away our freedom to modify that very environment at will. Our task, then, is to reduce to zero the moral weight of things, methodically questioning all the patterns of religious, aesthetic, cultural, and even environmental behavior.

In putting aside for a moment the formulation of our ideas as designers, we also interrupt that one-way circuit by which things become a means of communication, with the users remaining passive and unconscious recipients. We can't let anyone else plan our private models of behavior, nor limit ourselves to hanging up inside some reproductions of French Impressionists.

It isn't much use to go on planning 'different' houses, if the way in which they are used is always the same — that is, the relationship that society imposes with respect to everything not directly connected with work: a limbo in which to regain that minimum of energy and minimum of balance needed to let us produce again the next day. And so our home becomes primarily the place in which we try to conserve ourselves most, where we try to establish all our contacts with a motionless landscape that doesn't stimulate us, but instead soothes us with its immobility, while we contemplate our own 'status.' It is clear, then, that the form of the house is not a political problem; as Engels once said, the problem is rather that of commandeering the houses already built. And the only effective way to do this is to take possession of them.

To become their masters, that's the problem; since first of all, we must be able to become 'masters' of our own existence, our own time, our own health, and our own actions.

To become the master of one's own life, one must first of all *free oneself from work*. This is the only way in which to recover all the untapped creative faculty that man has available within himself. which has become atrophied throughout the centuries because of frustrating work.

The home — that small, functional organization at the service of the tiny production company that is the family — imitates in its forms and furnishings that culture and those choices no user has ever made, nor has ever had time enough to test.

Only by rejecting work as an extraneous presence in one's life can one picture a new use for the home: a perpetual laboratory for one's own creative faculties, which are continually being tried out and continually being surpassed.

So, then, it's no longer of any importance to imagine the form of this home, because the only thing that matters is the use made of it. Its image is manifold, never final, and has no codified meaning nor spatial hierarchy. A kind of 'furnished parking lot,' from which all antecedent types have vanished, giving way to a spontaneous shaping of the environment; a completely accessible enclosure within which to exercise one's regained freedom of action and judgment.

For us, the problem is no longer that of trying to understand what kind of freedom man is seeking, or perhaps even trying to foresee it in terms of current reality. The problem, instead, is to give man the kind of freedom that will enable him to obtain it for himself.

What we have been trying to do since 1969 is to make a scientific study of the problem of the house and of the city. Through this scientific work, we seek at least to remove all the usual qualitative criteria for present concepts of architecture and city planning.

The streets, squares, boulevards, monuments, theaters, churches, public buildings, and façades of a traditional city are the stage setting for the great spectacle of itself that the city offers, using architecture as medium for presenting thousands upon thousands of different episodes. Every corner of the city, street, or square, every square foot of asphalt, is thus very different from all others, because it occupies a different position in relation to the city's landmarks. The history of individual cities, and their geographical location, make each urban fact seem 'unique' of its kind, not comparable to other urban phenomena but isolated in its own singularity. Each city appears to have its own intrinsic 'quality,' a synthetic expression of its virtues and defects. Up to now, the study of the city has been limited to surveying these separate histories, without any general laws that could be applied to them all, and that could be useful because based on previous experience.

Even modern town planning, despite the profound changes that have taken place in modes of life and in technology, continues to make the same proposals, which are like series of scenic episodes, brought up to date in their forms, but still based on a kind of memory that the city retains within itself — the memory of the 'village.'

The 'village,' in fact, is that experience which, although he has never lived through it, still accompanies the man who dwells in a metropolis, helping him to encounter phenomena of gigantic proportions by means of a lens adjusted to small things and to small scale. The metropolis continues to be a 'village,' to the extent that it presents itself, and develops through, traditional scenic events — the actual streets, squares, buildings, churches, fountains, trees, etc. Thus, the metropolis seems to be the logical successor of some ancient former existence that survives directly, greatly enlarged and confused, but nevertheless retaining those structural characteristics that constitute its deepest nature. When we confront the problem of the modern city, its nonfunctioning, etc., we often continue to accept tacitly the backward model that the city has taken as its point of departure, seeking to introduce technical standards that regularly continue to fail, and just as regularly are reproposed for each new urban experiment.

The ideology of the middle-class city derives from the seventeenth-century discovery of the city as a 'natural object,' that is, a reality homogeneous with the surrounding countryside, in that it has been created in accordance with the same rational laws that regulate the entire world of nature; these give the city a universal significance as a 'naturally' existing reality, rather than as an artificial creation with an autonomous logic of its own. Moreover, since the city is the common product of man's labor, it represents in middle-class ideology the civilized bridge between man and nature, and between man and society. Social balance and ecological balance must be achieved simultaneously. Thus, in the City Plan, what is sought is a not-impossible harmony between the Public, the Private, Nature, and Buildings; these diverse entities are regarded as mutually incompatible elements. The end result, in fact, need not be a 'unity,' but rather a 'harmonious succession' of different and contrasting logics. Having become a 'citizen,' man enjoys an equilibrium achieved through forms, celebrating his 'natural' integration into society. The city always seems to him something far more complex and more spiritual than any practical use that he can make of it in his daily life; to be a citizen means to adopt a mode of behavior that is fully conscious of the existence of that cultural 'unity' upon which society is based. Thus, the middle-class city becomes an ideological superstructure, a screen between the individual and the hierarchical systems of society.

The middle-class city is that spontaneous mechanism in which goods circulate freely and acquire 'value.' Production is hidden away in the remote outskirts, without ever attaining the urban dignity of a recognized function. In this way, the city — completely organized as a means of realizing the ideology of Consumption — inverts the reality of its systems by emphasizing the act of exchange, while concealing the far more real one of production.

Violent conflicts, uncontrolled disorder, and the spontaneous growth of means of communication, are the shock tactics that the city adopts to compel the citizen to integrate himself within consumer society. Urban chaos is the most common mechanism for accomplishing this process of integration and induction, but it is also the least easy to control; it is still the outcome of a system of free competition. Nowadays, the use of programmed electronic media has replaced direct urban procedures; they ensure a far deeper penetration of patterns of consumption into social reality than the fragile channels of information that the city affords.

By arranging city events as if they were different theatrical scenes, the metropolis maintains a visual relationship with its own inhabitants. For the individual, this visual relationship becomes the fundamental system whereby he organizes his own experiences and his own memory of the city. The stratum of the city that he uses has a depth of two meters of ground; as Kevin Lynch has said, he builds memory-tunnels, which are completely personal, and which allow him to arrange his own system of images, composed of illuminated advertising signs and other isolated elements of the town's furnishings. In practice, the city as a unified entity of images and culture is no longer conceivable.

Architecture is no longer a means for representing a system, because the city no longer offers an enjoyable image. The attempt to make the *maquiniste* logic of industrial civilization coincide with a *maquiniste* architecture is an historical blunder, the result of a simple linguistic updating. Actually, the logic of a single factory, or a single machine, cannot be brought, like the part to the whole, into relation with the reality of Planning. The rules of montage permit combining different parts of an object or a building, but the ideology of Planning permits combining different parts of the whole of society, making it a homogeneous production without any functional contradictions or any 'other' kinds of reality.

The modern city, as an intensive concentration, has its origins in the territorial distinction between town and country. Capitalism, born of the city, was identified at the outset with urban management of the land; but as a result of Planning, it now extends its own rational power throughout the whole country, which it organizes for the sake of productivity. The 'urban condition' — being a citizen — does not imply being more integrated than a non-citizen, since there are no longer any territorial regions not organized within the system. The city, therefore, has ceased to be a 'place' and has become a 'condition'; and Consumption disseminates this condition homogeneously throughout the country and throughout society. The town, therefore, corresponds to the size of the market, and not to the size of any particular locale.

Avant-garde architecture no longer seeks to design a 'better' city in opposition to the present one. It performs another function: it challenges the ideology of the middle-class city, denouncing its fraudulent role, and establishes city planning anew as a system to be put to a different use, other than an instrument for social manifestation and induced values. Besides, as Engels said, the problem of a different city does not arise for the worker; his problem is, rather, to take possession of the city that already exists. The new town, in fact, will be born from an inversion of the town as it is at present.

It is to this end that our efforts are directed: to see and understand the city, no longer as a cultural unit, but rather as a structure to be used;

a homogeneous ensemble of services, upon which is superimposed a mesh of scenic happenings, of spatial episodes, that give this ensemble of functions a unified cultural meaning. The street, which divides and serves this compact mass of facilities, becomes a dynamic sequence, in which the flat surfaces of the façades of individual buildings allow the growth of an architectural language, whose forms serve to verify the various functional organisms.

Within this make-believe unity, the citizen must achieve his own civic integration, to the extent that he adopts the patterns of social behavior that the city, as a cultural unit, demands. We are trying, therefore, to overthrow this relationship by defining the city as 'a latrine every hundred square meters,' rejecting the problem of its 'form,' and defining its space, not as an ensemble of architectural volumes, but rather as a 'hollow space.'

A workers' city doesn't exist — because there exists no workers' culture. The belief that the worker, in the course of his struggle to work less and earn more, develops a culture of his own, replete with new meanings and values, is typical middle-class humbug. As a matter of fact, not only does the working class fail to produce a new culture, but it even uses the cultural patterns of the middle class as a strategy to mark the stages of its own economic advance. As it uses them, it also destroys them, precisely because in attaining these stages it destroys the economic balance on which the patterns were based.

The places in which the industrial system has completely realized its own ideology of Planning are the Factory and the Supermarket. Consumption and Production are not, in fact, contrasting logics, for both predicate a social and material reality that is entirely continuous and undifferentiated; both the Factory and the Supermarket are optimal urban systems, potentially unlimited, in which the functions of production and of merchandising information are freely organized according to a continuous plan and are made homogeneous by a system of artificial ventilation and lighting, without any interferences.

An outer image of these organisms 'does not exist,' since the plane of their façades does not indicate the linguistic structure of the organism but is simply the surface where two situations in different degrees of integration encounter one another.

If we were to apply the technological level and functional organization that has already been attained in these sections of the city to housing as well, we should see a complete transformation of the city. In fact, the metropolis today, like the traditional city, still adheres to certain standards of natural lighting and ventilation; no factory may exceed an established depth, in order that light and air may permeate its interior. This has resulted in a continuous 'formation' of architectural blocks made up of inner courtyards, façades, and interruptions. Il we were to introduce on an urban scale the principle of artificial lighting and ventilation, we should see that it is no longer necessary to follow the procedure of a continual breaking-up into apartments, in the typical fashion of a traditional city; the city would become a continuous residential structure, without empty spaces, and hence without architectural images. Traffic would no longer divide the city into sections but would be arranged in an autonomous, optimal fashion, uniformly distributed throughout the land.

The city as a technical artifact and the territory that it occupies would no longer coincide. Nature and the city would run on two parallel tracks, without interfering with one another; while in the middle-class city, nature seems to the citizen to be the perfect reconciliation of the industrial system with natural laws, something to be used as a means of consolation, in our hypothetical 'homogeneous city,' nature is no

238

longer an urban episode, but recovers its own complete autonomy. No longer would the individual have his contacts with nature contaminated by architectural elements that tend to attribute to it some cultural significance. Nature would, instead, remain a neutral area, lacking any meaning and therefore entirely open to physical awareness, without any intermediary.

These large microclimatized plans make it possible to overcome the limitations of present-day residential typology and the prevailing concept of architecture. Actually, architecture today, seeking to provide the greatest possible number of various kinds of freedom to the user, is bound to recognize in the urban phenomenon its true destiny, and, in the private phenomenon, its true nature. And so, in a contradictory fashion, on every occasion it sets forth the general state of affairs, while simultaneously coming to the defense of the partial, individual experience as against the collective experience. It thus serves symbolically as mediator in the conflict between public and private life.

The limitations of this mediating role cannot be overcome by the processes of design, but only by a change in the use made of architecture itself. It must be regarded as a neutral system, available for undifferentiated use, and not as an instrumentality for the organization of society; as a free, equipped area in which it may be possible to perform spontaneous actions of experimentation in individual or collective dwelling.

Arduino Cantafora, *La città analoga*, 1973
Aldo Rossi, *Omaggio a Rogers* (Tribute to Rogers), 1974, Triennale Archive

1.4

MICRO ENVIRONMENTS AND *NEW DESIGN*

Archizoom Associati, "The Empty Rooms and the Gazebos," in *Pianeta Fresco* n. 1, 1967

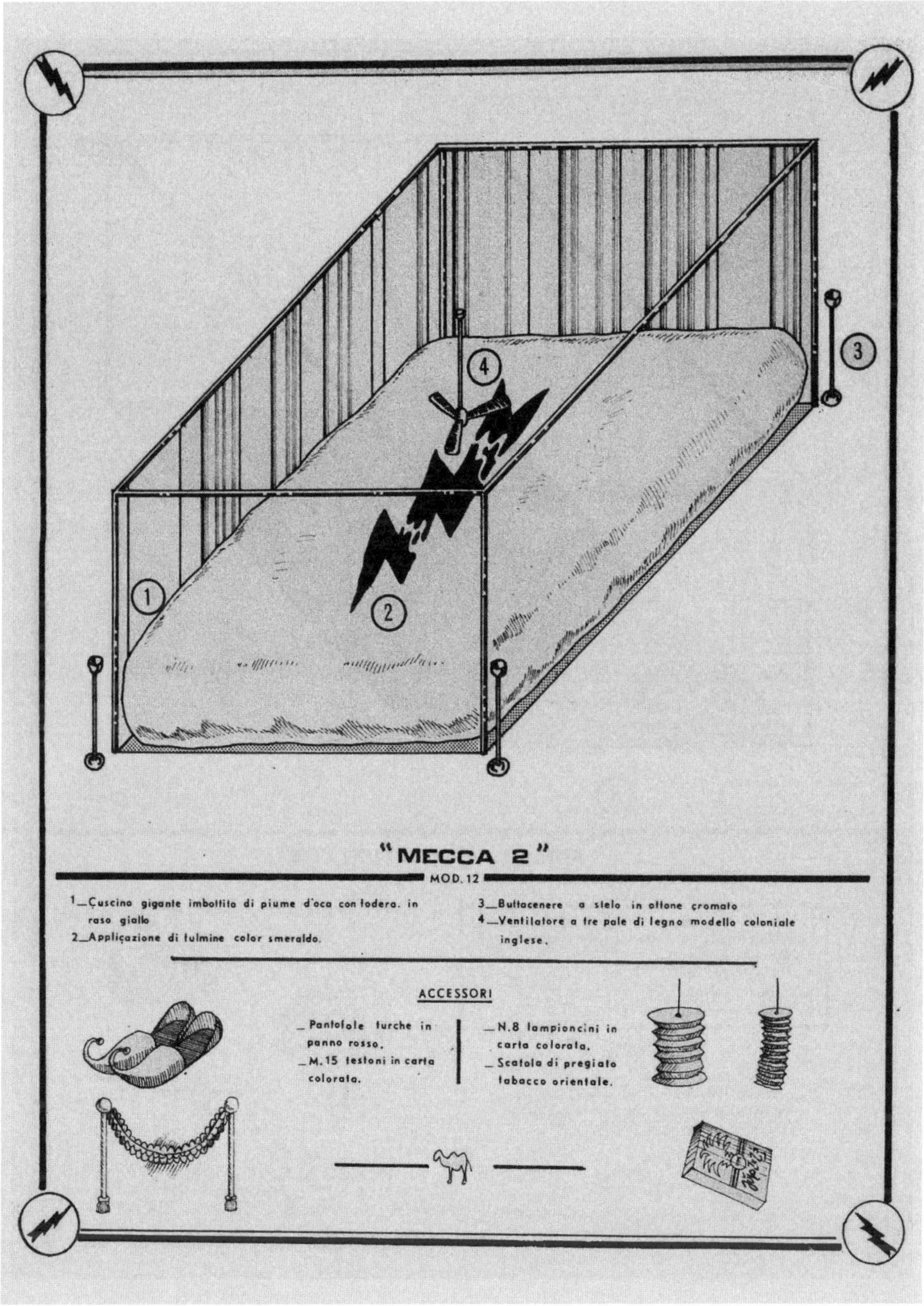
4
1
2
3
"MECCA 2"
MOD. 12
1_Çuscino gigante imbottito di piume d'oca con fodera. in raso giallo
2_Applicazione di fulmine color smeraldo.
3_Buttacenere a stelo in ottone cromato
4_Ventilatore a tre pale di legno modello coloniale inglese.
ACCESSORI
_Pantofole turche in panno rosso.
_M. 15 testoni in carta colorata.
_N.8 lampioncini in carta colorata.
_Scatola di pregiato tabacco orientale.

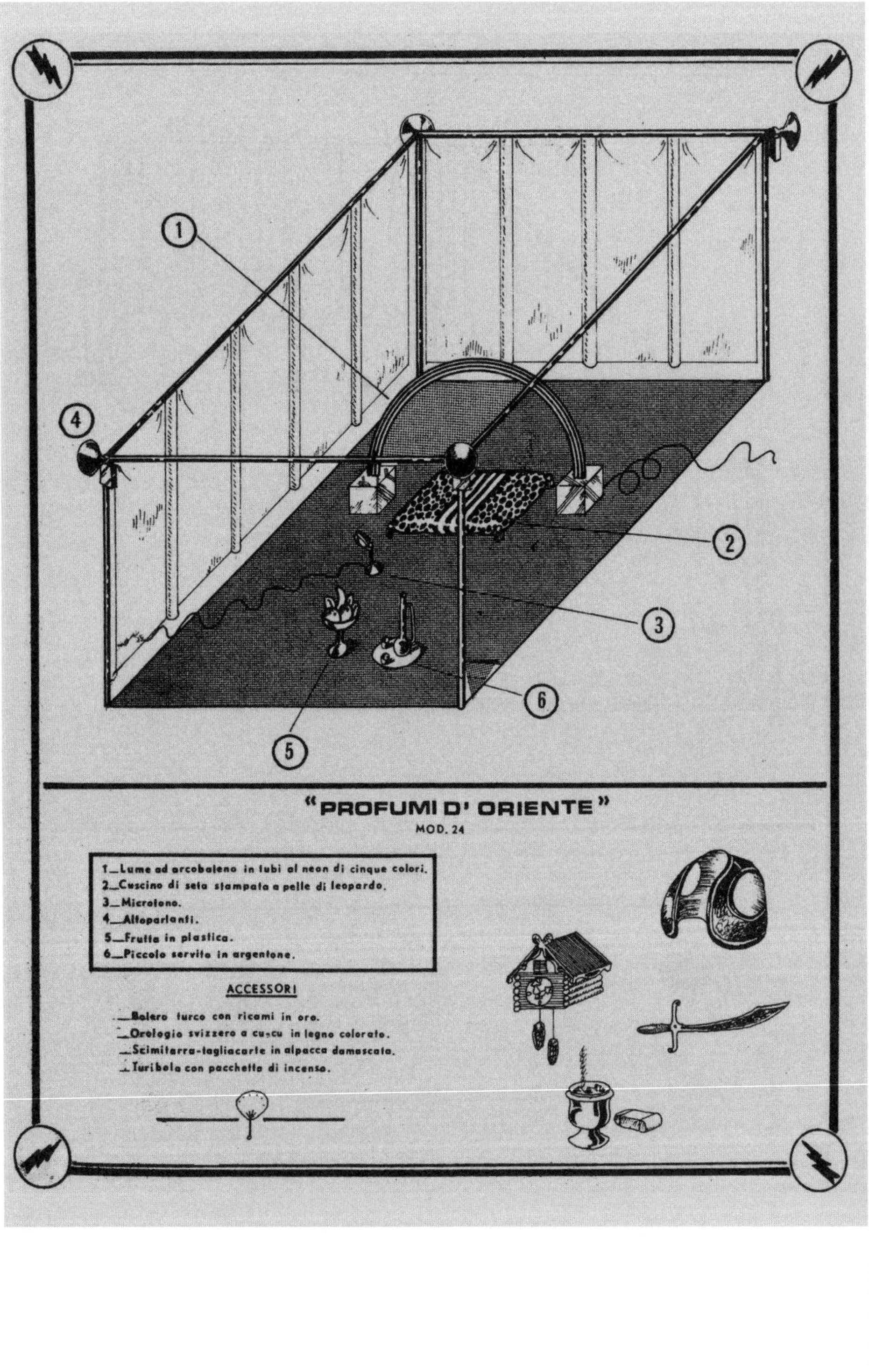

1
2
3
4
5
6
"PROFUMI D' ORIENTE"
MOD. 24
1_Lume ad arcobaleno in tubi al neon di cinque colori.
2_Cuscino di seta stampata a pelle di leopardo.
3_Microfono.
4_Altoparlanti.
5_Frutta in plastica.
6_Piccolo servito in argentone.
ACCESSORI
_Bolero turco con ricami in oro.
_Orologio svizzero a cu-cu in legno colorato.
_Scimitarra-tagliacarte in alpacca damascata.
_Turibolo con pacchetto di incenso.

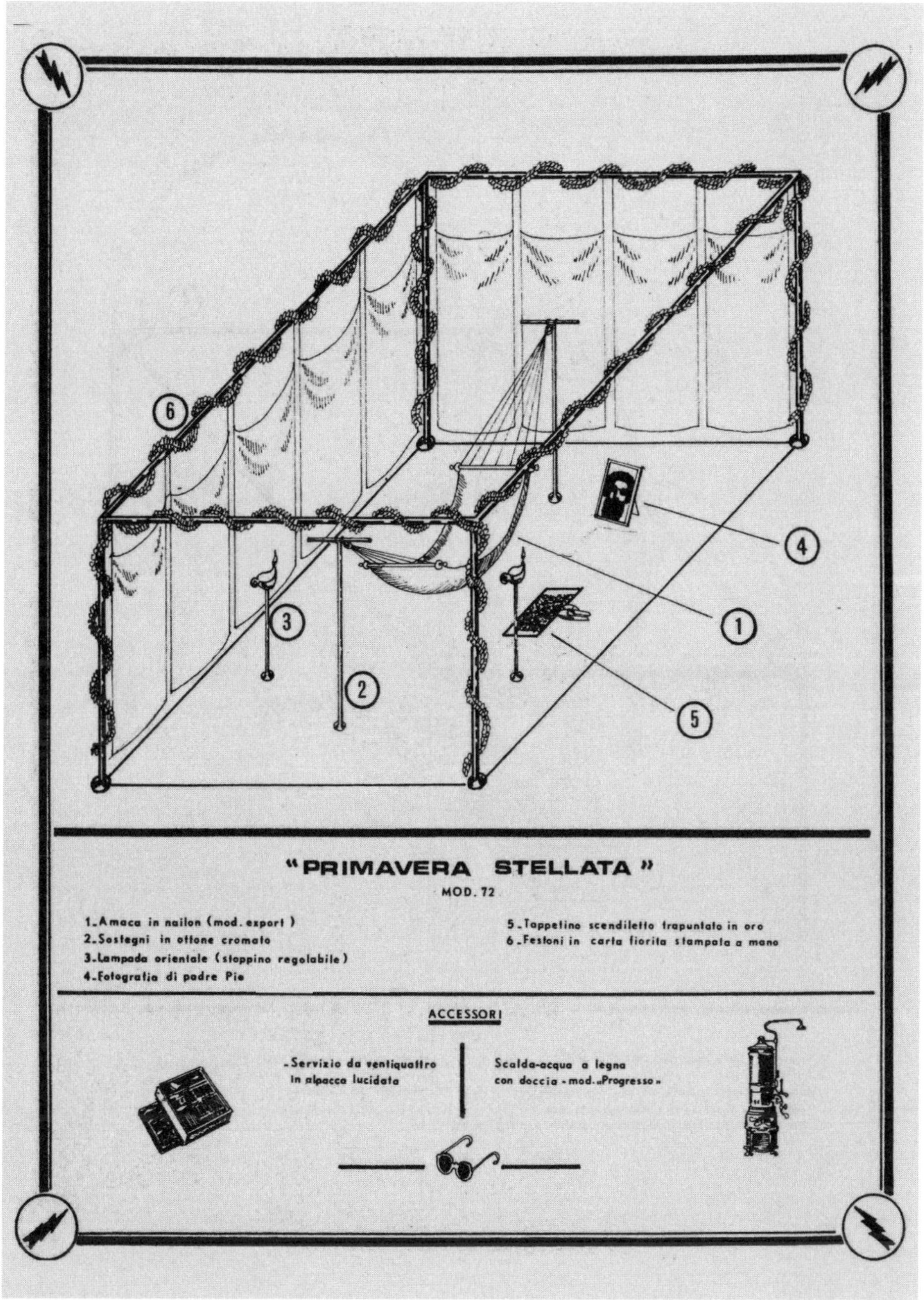
6
4
1
3
2
5
"PRIMAVERA STELLATA"
MOD. 72
1. Amaca in nailon (mod. export)
2. Sostegni in ottone cromato
3. Lampada orientale (stoppino regolabile)
4. Fotogratia di padre Pie
5. Tappetino scendiletto trapuntato in oro
6. Festoni in carta fiorita stampata a mano
ACCESSORI
- Servizio da ventiquattro in alpacca lucidata
Scalda-acqua a legna con doccia - mod. «Progresso»

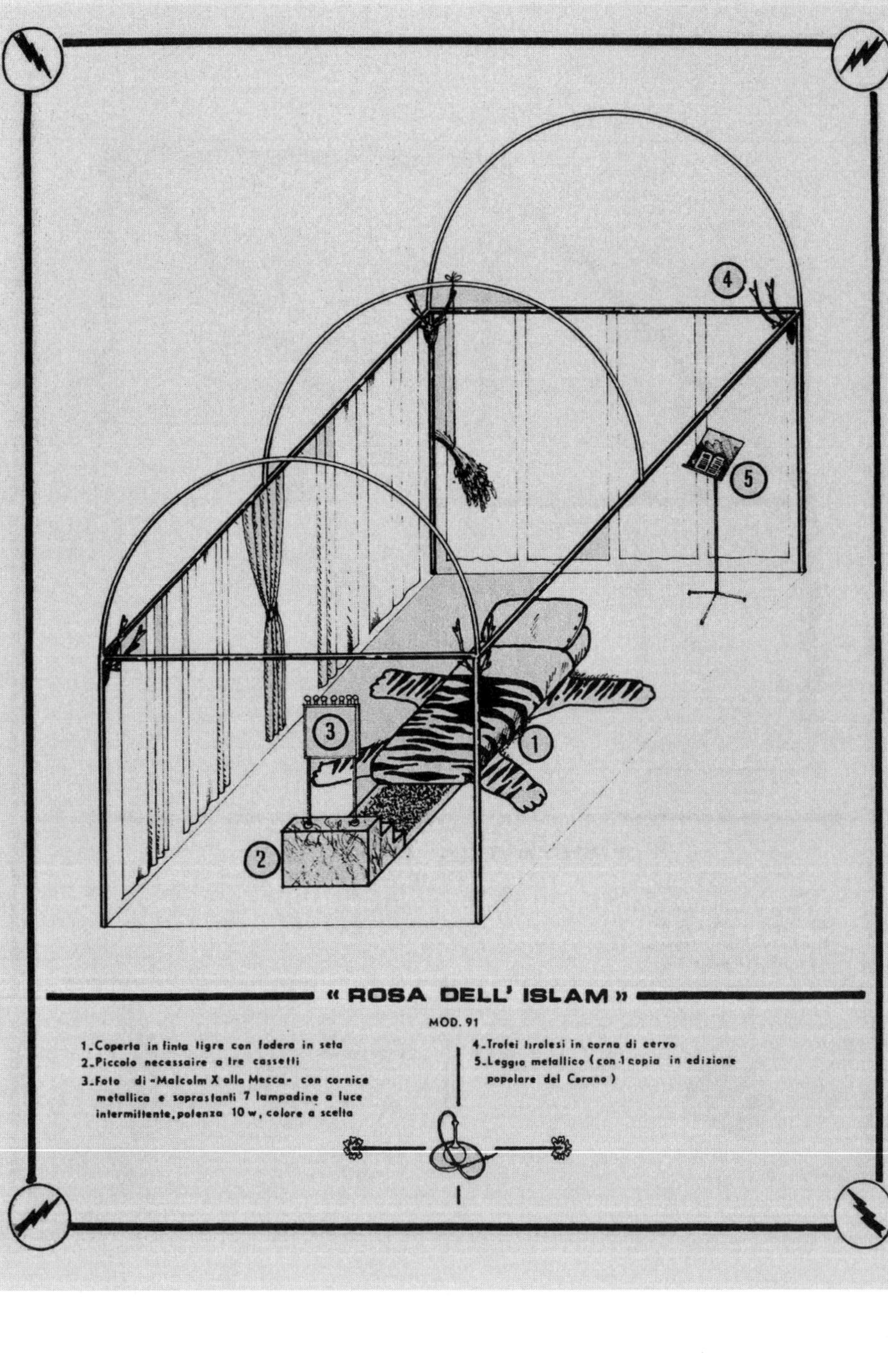

4
5
3
1
2
« ROSA DELL' ISLAM »
MOD. 91
1.Coperta in finta tigre con fodera in seta
2.Piccolo necessaire a tre cassetti
3.Foto di «Malcolm X alla Mecca» con cornice metallica e soprastanti 7 lampadine a luce intermittente, potenza 10 w, colore a scelta
4.Trofei tirolesi in corna di cervo
5.Leggio metallico (con 1 copia in edizione popolare del Corano)

Queste sono le immagini ipotetiche di un teatro impossibile. Le immagini o le illustrazioni di una idea diversa della cultura, o meglio di una diversa maniera di porsi di questa, in qualsiasi luogo ed occasione. Sono le illustrazioni di una teoria, (accettata come tale, cioè come ipotesi impossibile ma significativa), per cui la cultura accetta improvvisamente di essere tale e si trincera duramente in cerca di capire il proprio destino politico. Esse non sono l'anticipazione di un teatro futuro o migliore, ma l'uso che noi facciamo di lui nella nostra mente e nella situazione attuale. Innanzi tutto esse sono un teatro portato al suo stesso limite, cioè da una parte alla presentazione di un fatto culturalmente e formalmente concluso, di una tecnica ortodossa di restituzione, presentata come tale al pubblico in una stanza; dall'altra alla scomparsa del limite, difficilmente rintracciabile, tra teatro e vita, sia essa sociale che segretamente intima. Potremmo anche dire che esse sono il teatro in cui uno dei suoi termini costituzionali, pubblico e azione scenica, sono scomparsi e non possono più fondersi e dialogare, essendo ormai scaduto il tempo sereno per queste cose, ma possono solo sopraffarsi, violentarsi e sbranarsi a vicenda.

In ognuna di queste scomparse esiste la testimonianza fisica dell'impossibilità da parte di una cultura in elaborazione di accettare il dialogo e lo scambievole confronto con il proprio utente. Sarebbe come dire che per un attimo, anche per uno solo, cessa di esistere il vaglio ed il controllo, cioè la verifica democratica, da parte di una società su di una cultura nata e sviluppatasi nel suo stesso seno. Questo perché al concetto corrente di cultura come libero dibattito di idee noi sostituiamo quello di cultura come momento formativo di una teoria o ideologia in elaborazione che tende a conquistare il potere. In questo senso essa acquista un valore strategico interno, cioè segretamente privato, non rivelabile se non a coloro che partecipano della stessa situazione e della stessa intenzione. Il rifiuto chiaro e dichiarato di non voler partecipare fattivamente "alla soluzione dei problemi del Progresso" che la Società Ufficiale offre, significa elaborare un concetto diverso del progresso stesso, e non trarre le proprie premesse da un condizionamento di cause fortuite, ma anzi liberarsene il più possibile non dichiarandosi esplicitamente sui principi, prevaricando e tradendo le occasioni stesse.

Una cultura quindi dei teatri muti, dei libri incollati, dei quadri incartati, delle case murate, della musica non scritta, dei vicoli ciechi, delle città vuote, della vita finta: una cultura dura e clandestina, chiara quindi e visibile perché dichiarata come tale. Inutile a tutti se non a coloro che la producono e a coloro che rispecchiandovisi vi si riconoscono, una cultura cioè da tenere nascosta nei soppalchi e nelle cantine come le armi o la farina buona per il Giorno della Grande Festa.

ARCHIZOOM

Firenze, 16 marzo 1968

TEATRO IMPOSSIBILE

pianeta fresco 2-3

Archizoom Associati, "The Impossible Theatre," in *Pianeta Fresco* n. 2-3, 1968

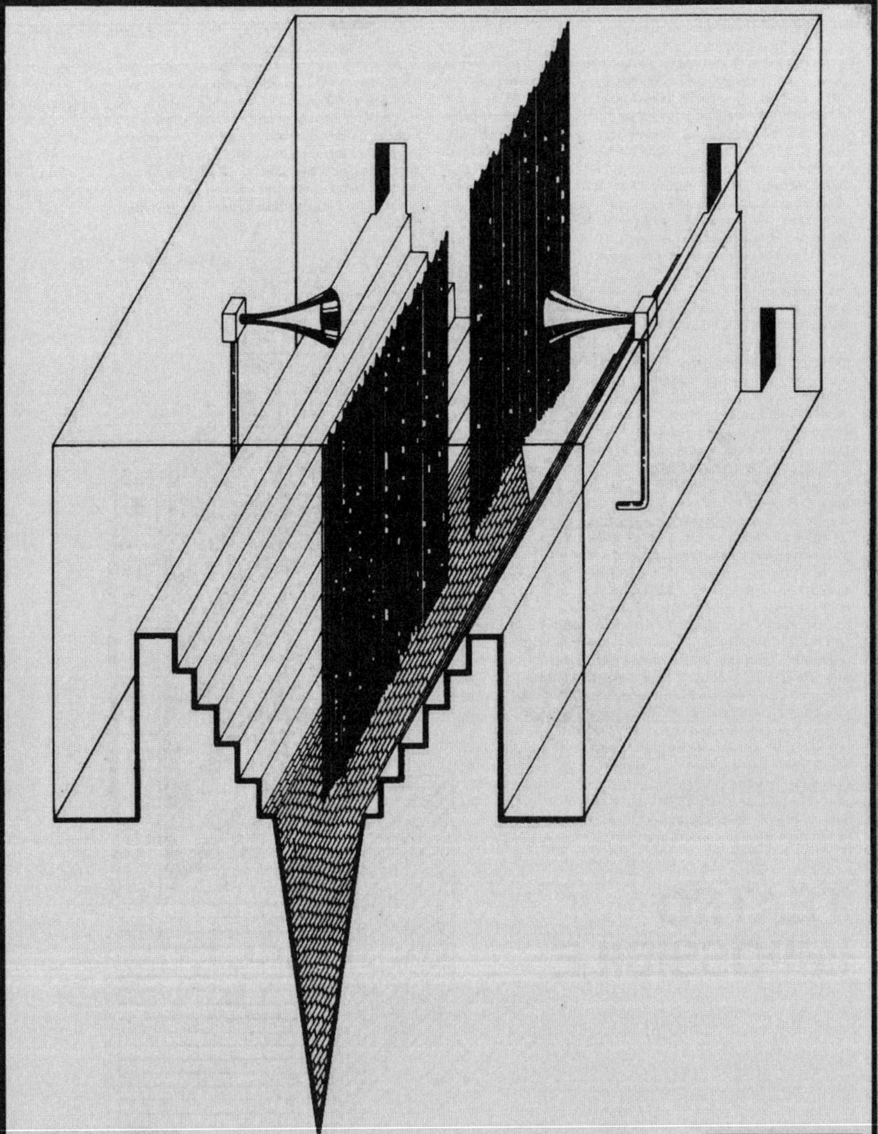

TEATRO D'INCONTRO IDEOLOGICO

CON BARATRO MURATO

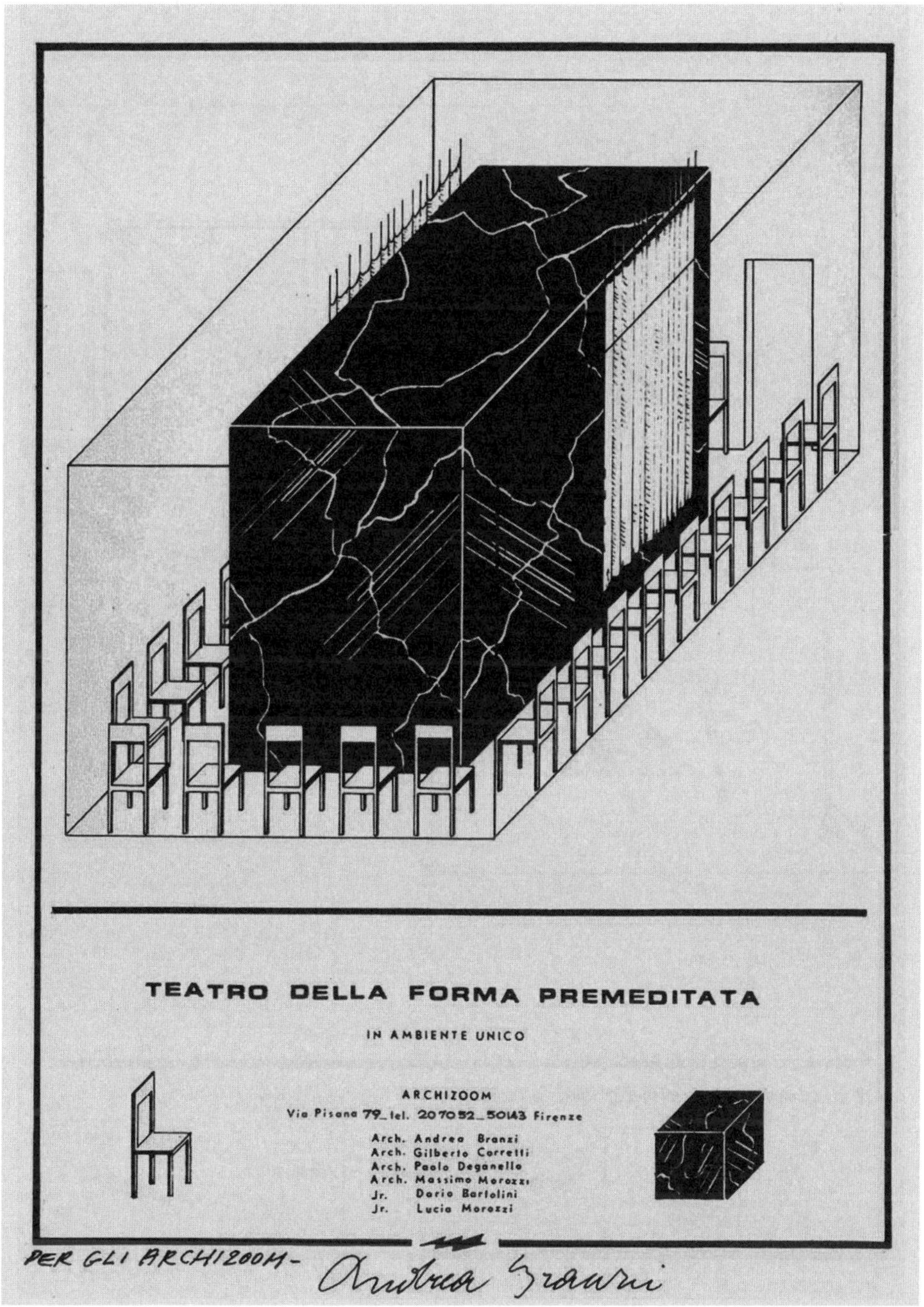
TEATRO DELLA FORMA PREMEDITATA
IN AMBIENTE UNICO
ARCHIZOOM
Via Pisana 79_tel. 207052_50143 Firenze
Arch. Andrea Branzi
Arch. Gilberto Corretti
Arch. Paolo Deganello
Arch. Massimo Morozzi
Jr. Dario Bartolini
Jr. Lucia Morozzi
PER GLI ARCHIZOOM-

TEATRO SEGRETO IN AMBIENTE DOMESTICO
CON GAZEBO METALLICO
accessori.
pianeta fresco 2-3

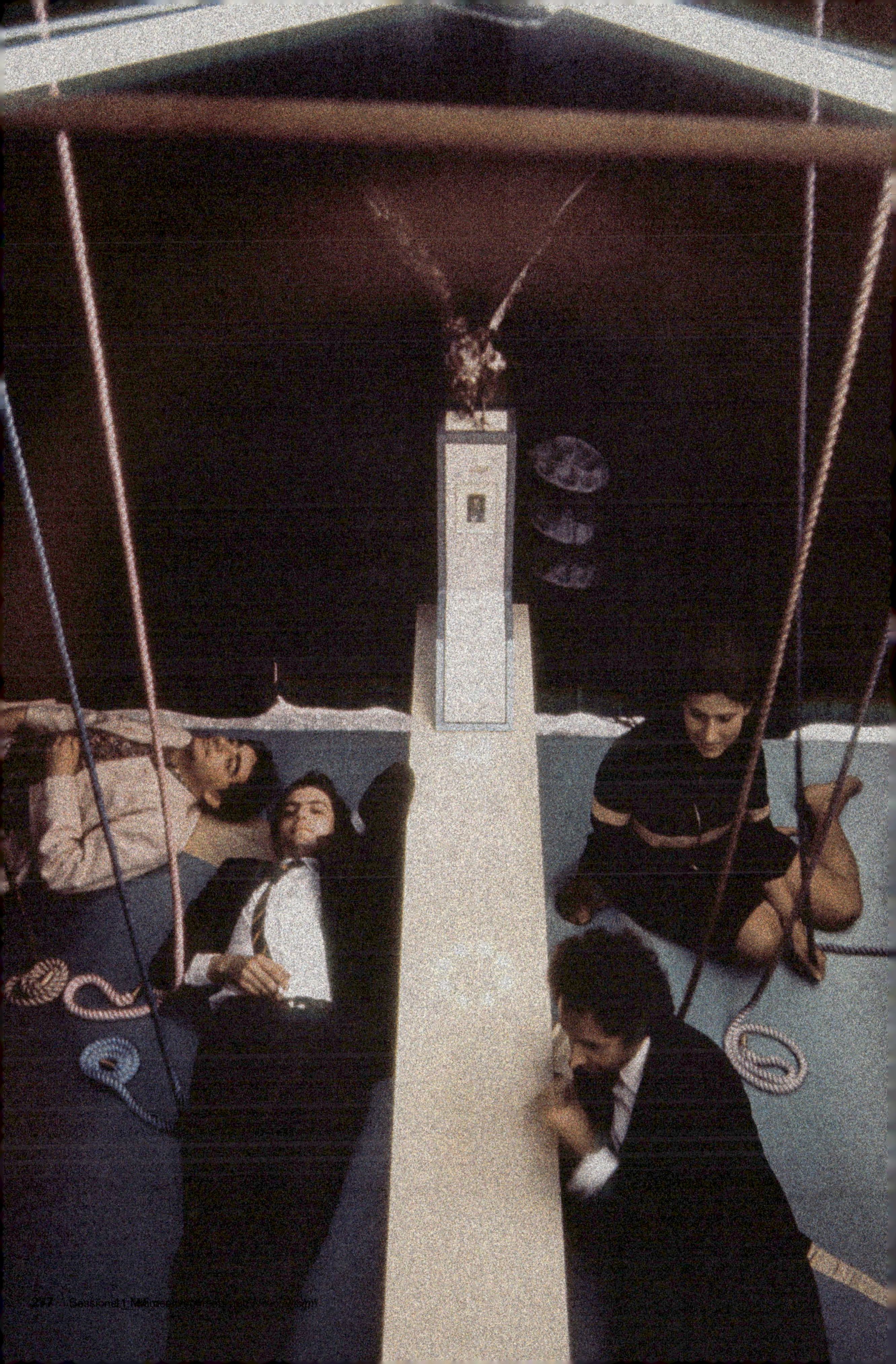

Il «centro di cospirazione eclettica» del gruppo **Archizoom** *di Firenze:*

« Esistono dei momenti in cui la cultura si trova impegnata a scoprire il significato della propria presenza all'interno di fenomeni più generali, e a stabilire o variare i legami logici e intuitivi che la pongono in contatto con il mondo dei suoi possibili utenti.
Nel caso specifico della cultura architettonica tali rapporti sono di natura formale (o dimensionale) e di uso: la capacità di un oggetto di porsi all'interno dell'ambiente preesistente, naturale o manufatto, e di stabilire con questo un rapporto di continuità o di crisi; il grado di tolleranza con cui un oggetto si offre all'uso, ed esaurisce o meno in esso le ragioni della propria esistenza.
Se noi portiamo tali tipi di rapporto al limite, eliminando da una parte qualsiasi tipo di correlazione am-

bientale (sia di omogeneità che frattura) e dall'altra sospendendo individuazione di un uso specific in pratica non facciamo altro c interrompere intenzionalmente scambio delle idee fra noi e l'uten creando nel flusso della cultura bacino chiuso dove cessano i co trolli critici e linguistici abituali, verifiche democratiche.
Al concetto di spazio, come stru tura dello scambio reciproco, contatto, si sostituisce quello di « luogo » appartato e ben recinta possibilmente fresco, dove più ag vole risulta coltivare gli atti dell' telletto, tramare le cospirazioni: sedimentano e prendono forma componenti eclettiche della nost cultura, le grandi stratificazioni d l'Impero, la natura si trasforma in concetto immobile, si insinua crudeltà.
Garanzie, per ora, non ne vogliar dare (semmai ne chiediamo).
Si salvi pure, chi vuole, sui cusc della psicologia e del comportame to, si faccia pure, chi può, compli dei costumi, nella segreta speran che il rapido consumo renda giust. cazione della mediocrità dei meriti

domus 466, *settembre 1968*

Archizoom Associati, "Center of Eclectic Conspiracy," in *Domus* n. 466, 1968

ARCHIZOOM ASSOCIATI - VIA DI RICORBOLI 7 - 50126 FIRENZE - TEL. 671.885

"Il pollo di marmo"
"Siamo i simboli delle tue passioni- gli risponde un enorme leopardo- esse, come noi, ti assalirono, ti impedirono di scorgere il fine della tua missione: dato che non ti riusci di vincerle, come potrai trionfare su di noi?".
Marchese de Sade: "Rodrigo o la torre incantata".

...In realtà il fenomeno a cui in questi anni assistiamo, anche se esso è la naturale causa di una civiltà mercantile (e non scientifica), dimostra una verità molto più importanteee per certi aspetti nuova: essa è il capovolgimento e la scomparsa di una concezione di una legge generale di sviluppo...
Noi oggi constatiamo come il sistema tende a svilupparsi per "salti", cioè per assorbimento più o meno violento di modelli sociali, politici, economici e culturali che volta a volta gli si pongono davanti, e che esso ingloba come momenti di violento balzo in avanti nel processo del suo sviluppo...

La dimostrazione forse più chiara è lo sfruttamento che il sistema oggi compie delle ideologie di sinistra, non solo come classe politica, ma in generale come atteggiamento protestario utilizzato come area specializzata dei costumi: dalla moda alla canzone. L'ideologia è divenuta quindi anch'essa bene di consumo, divenendo ideologia artificiale, e non più sistema alternativo di affrontare i problemi . Se noi accettiamo l'esistenza di questo meccanismo di sviluppo che avanza per grosse "scosse", senza quel continuum naturale di sviluppo organico, vengono a porsi anche per le dottrine estetiche e per la cultura architettonica, una serie di conseguenze importanti, sia dal punto di vista strategico che strutturale...

Anche la cultura cioè tende ad uno sviluppo per "salti", cioè per inglobamenti di realtà nate e cresciute al di fuori di lei e che necessariamente deve, in determinati periodi storici che corrispondono a forti rivoluzioni culturali, scontrare e scontare se vuole progredire e continuare a svolgere il suo compito conoscitivo e di giudizio...

Quella di oggi è una civiltà imperiale, è la civiltà dei grandi trust internazionali, delle grandi imprese finanziarie e fondiarie, del petrolio, dei grandi giacimenti. E' una civiltà fondamentalmente non labile, ma estesa e cosmopolita, che va dall' America ai paesi arabi, composita, eclettica, sincretica, ma lucida e luminosa, senza dubbi e problemi.
Essa ha l'architettura di un grande impero...

Essa non pone mai il problema di nuovi organismi, ma risolve quelli esistenti con un metodo da industrial design, al quale si chiede di disegnare una cosa che già esiste.
Non ha nessuna "concezione dello spazio", ma problemi nuovi di rappresentanza. Se ne infischia dei problemi architettonici come noi possiamo infischiarcene di quelli di chi ci taglia un abito.

Essa non è la civiltà della tecnica o della scienza, ma dei traffici e del commercio: il turbine del consumismo e la rapidità di fagocitazione del "grande numero" non devono trarci in inganno, perchè dietro di esso vi è un pollo di marmo che non

Archizoom Associati, "The Marble Chicken," 1968, Original document, published in *Casabella* 325, 1968 si mangia e non si sposta...

Le rivoluzioni sociali si svolgono adesso in maniera diversa: non morire perchè difendi un ideale, ma combatti per realizzarlo; non avere armi tue, usa quelle del nemico; non combattere apertamente, ma di notte ed in terreno favorevole; e soprattutto non perdere mai una battaglia...

Un'altra cosa importante è oggi capire e cogliere. Lo stesso "grande numero", proprio per la capacità di portare al parossismo i termini del problema, pur sembrando gettare un ombra di relatività su tutte le possibili decisioni, in realtà permette di entrare in rapporto con i problemi di fondo della cultura stessa. Non a caso in questi anni siamo tornati a parlare della città, della antropologia, dei grandi sistemi di produzione, eccetera.

Nella concezione architettonica da un certo momento in poi si comincia a parlare di "concezione dello spazio", arrivando cioè a materializzare un dato che non esiste o se esiste è solo un elemento della fruizione del fatto architettonico molto più complesso e dotato di leggi compositive non fruibili spazialmente...

Se noi vogliamo riguadagnare le dimensioni dei grandi sistemi culturali, noi che viviamo in un grande sistema sociale, dobbiamo superare l'eccessiva culturalizzazione tipica dei paesi sottosviluppati: in certo senso potremmo dire che noi vogliamo fare dell'architettura dello spirito e non della psicologia. Dobbiamo ritrovare la serenità propria del fare architettonico.

Il padiglione da noi proposto ha un motivo fondamentale di rappresentazione di una situazione ormai esistente: dai quattro altoparlanti laterali una voce legge in continuazione uno dei tanti testi critici oggi esistenti sul problema del "grande numero" (ad esempio il testo stesso del bando), al cospetto di sette obelischi cromati, immobili e lucidi sui quali si accampano sette fregi colorati rappresentanti stemmi alati. Tali obelischi non sono né scultura né macchine, ma piuttosto automobili, cioè oggetti di design che hanno raggiunto un livello supremo di simbolizzazione imperiale e trionfale.

Perchè questa secondo noi può essere la risposta italiana al problema del "grande numero"? Essa secondo noi rappresenta, in una qualche misura, una condizione tipicamente italiana: in parte perchè esiste una profonda tradizione architettonica nostra, abbastanza classica, di rappresentare e non giudicare un sistema, rifiutando di strumentalizzare la cultura, ma credendo nella sua capacità di restituzione ad un livello conoscitivo maggiore. In parte perchè l'Italia conserva, proprio per la sua situazione di nazione per metà industriale e per metà contadina, la capacità di avvertire i problemi e di controllarli anche ironicamente...

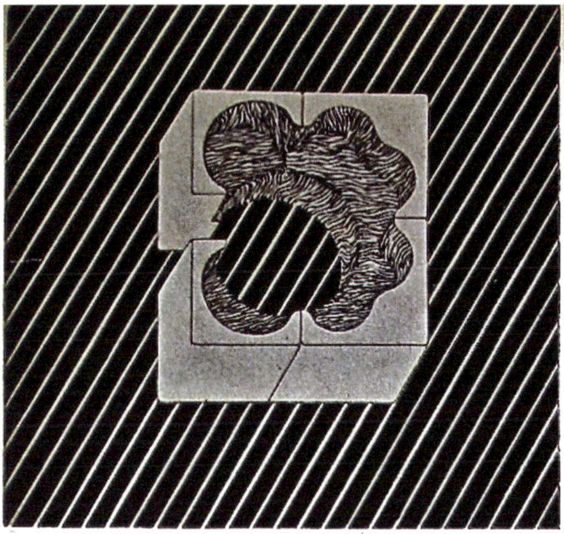

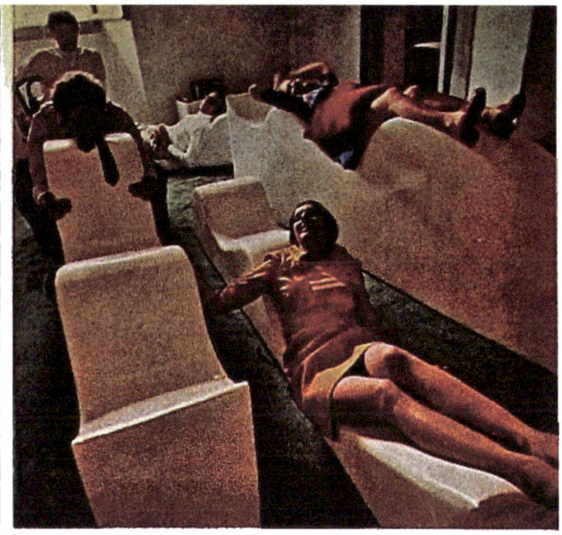

GLI ARCHIZOOM

Sono molto contento che tocchi a me di fare il discorso per questi Signori Archizoom e per i loro prodotti dato che i loro prodotti mi sembrano molto efficaci nel gettare il panico tra gli interessati, in questo paese di cose della cultura e delle ideologie, ben organizzate, stratificate, sedimentate e stereotipate. Qualcuno deve sempre gettare il panico se si vuole che il senso delle cose sia continuamente rivelato, se si vuole che le ore trascorrano in presa diretta con noi stessi o con quello che ci circonda, e anche se si vogliono rompere e rimescolare un po' gli organismi del potere, quelli che si sistemano pian piano, velenosamente, nei momenti di calma, come il grasso si infiltra in mezzo ai muscoli e intorno al cuore quando uno sta seduto troppo tempo e prende la macchina anche per andare dal tabaccaio, ecc., ecc.

Questa volta il panico lo getteranno gli Archizoom che sono dei bravi ragazzi abbastanza cattivi per non lasciarsi inibire dai vecchi discorsi, dagli affari complicati, dalle sistemazioni, dagli applausi che potrebbero anche accoglierli con facilità: cattivi al punto da cercare altri applausi e altro pubblico e da sopportare le inevitabili risate, le scrollate di spalle, gli occhi perplessi, i « non ci capisco niente » oppure i « sono degli esibizionisti » e questo genere di cose.

Quanto poi alla spiegazione didascalico-esoterica delle immagini che andiamo ad osservare, non c'è tempo per farla e forse è anche meglio non farla per lasciare che queste immagini scottanti e imbarazzanti continuino ad esserlo (scottanti ed imbarazzanti) e possano far sentire fino in fondo la carica che è stata loro assegnata. E così *adesso vediamo che cosa succede;* che è poi la stessa frase che dicevamo dopo aver mangiato un'immensa quantità di cibo fatto di pane, cipolle, aglio, pepe, aceto (e altre cose che non sono riuscito a definire) e preparato dagli Archizoom, i quali insistevano nel dire che era un cibo popolare toscano.

Ettore Sottsass

Ettore Sottsass, "Archizoom", in *Domus* n. 455, 1967

GLI ARCHIZOOM

Nella prima pagina di questo servizio: in alto a sinistra, divano componibile « Safari » (in quattro pezzi in p.v.c. con illuminazione interna; produzione Poltronova); in alto, a destra, divano « Superonda » in resina espansa, con rivestimento in tessuto plastificato bianco lucido (produzione Poltronova); in basso, a sinistra: « La farfalla di Battista », coperta; in basso a destra: tappeto componibile « Milano-Laghi » imbottito in poliuretano espanso, cm 60 x 60 (serie « Grandi viaggi »). Nella pagina a fianco: divano « Superonda » in resina espansa con rivestimento in tessuto plastificato bianco lucido (prod. Poltronova).
In questa pagina, a destra: coperta « Ubi maior », e, sotto, letto in lamiera stampata « Rosa d'Arabia » (serie « Rosa Imperiale ») con lume « Grande A » (serie « Grandi luci »).

GLI ARCHIZOOM

« Il problema potrebbe essere quello di sapere se i gelati esistono perché l'uomo nell'universo ne ha bisogno, se esistono perché costano, se esistono perché la crema gelata mantiene la forma. Ma forse il problema è un altro: avere una strada molto molto calda ed una gelateria molto molto fresca . . . E allora si mette sopra la coppa la panna, il biscotto, lo spicchio di ananas, la ciliegia, la cannuccia, il cucchiaino, la bandiera e la coca-cola su tutto in modo che uno si serva del gelato in una maniera tale che quando se ne va rimane servito.
Per noi il problema è invece quello di imbandirgli un gelato che gli faccia passare la voglia di mangiarne per tutta la vita. Oppure un gelato che una volta comprato diventi una cosa più grande di lui e lo umilii. Oppure che diventi una fetta del mondo che lo circonda e lo spaventi . . . Insomma un gelato senza alternative: o lo mangi te o ti mangia lui. O meglio: comincia a mangiarti appena l'hai finito.
E allora pensiamo: bombemela, caramelle velenose, bugie quotidiane, false informazioni, insomma coperte, letti o cavalli di Troia che messi in casa distruggano tutto quel che c'è. Vogliamo introdurvi tutto ciò che rimane fuor dall'uscio: la banalità costruita, la volgarità intenzionale, arredi urbani, cani mordaci. Al progresso scientifico, frutto dell'intelligenza che spiega tutto e dell'eleganza che salva tutto (disinnescando le micce ed apparecchiando sorridente il futuro), preferiamo un cartaceo orizzonte radioso solcato dall'arcobaleno. Come i finti pacifisti ci togliamo la sera barbe e baffi meditando il tradimento più violento. Vorremmo anche dire: non siamo dove ci cercano, non fidatevi troppo di come vi salutiamo.
E poi c'è in giro questo profumo di rose morte che non ci piace troppo . . . ».

Archizoom

THE ARCHIZOOM

letto « Elettro rosa » (serie « Rosa imperiale »), in lamiera stampata, con lume « Atlante » (serie « Luci medie »); fotografie di D. Bartolini

I am very pleased to have been picked to present these « Archizoom » gentlemen and their products to you because I find these products of theirs most conducive to the spreading of panic among those with vested interests in a country like ours, where things cultural and ideological are so highly organized, stratified, stereotyped and sedimentary. You always need someone to spread panic if, that is, you want things constantly shown up for what they are, and prefer to spend your time tuned in to yourselves and the things around you, and also if you wouldn't mind seeing the power cliques shaken up and mixed around a bit. I refer to the cliques that get themselves surreptitiously and insalubriously organized just when things seem nicely settled, like the fat that seeps between your muscles and clogs your heart when you lead too sedentary a life and take the car even to pop round the corner for cigarettes and so on. This time it is these « Archizoom » gents who are spreading all the panic, they're nice chaps, you know, but naughty enough not to get taken in by all the old chat about how complicated things are, by the need to settle down and by the easy approval: so naughty, in fact, that they are after other kinds of approval, a different audience, and are quite prepared to put up with the inevitable laughter, shrugging of shoulders, quizzical looks, « I fail to understand » or « makik a show of themselves » and all that sort of thing. Now, as for the esoteric-didactical explanation of what you are here seeing, you'll just have to do without it, and it may perhaps be just as well because, that way, these shocking and embarrassing exhibits can continue to be (shocking and embarrassing) thus giving us the full benefit of the voltage they've been charged with. So, now let's just wait and see — which, incidentally, is the identical phrase we used after eating immense portions of some dish of bread, onions, garlic, pepper, vinegar (and other unidentified ingredients) served up by the same « Archizoom » gents as good wholesome Tuscan home-cooking. E.S.

Impossible Theater

Archizoom Associati, 1968

//

These are the hypothetical images of an impossible theater. Images or illustrations of a different idea of culture, or rather of a different way of presenting it, in any place and occasion. They are the illustrations of a theory (accepted as such, as an impossible but significant hypothesis), for which culture suddenly accepts to be such and firmly entrenches itself in order to understand its own political destiny.

They are not the anticipation of a better or future theater, but the images of the use we make of it in our minds or in the current situation.

First of all, they are a theater brought to its own limit, that is, on the one hand to the presentation of a culturally and formally concluded fact, of an orthodox technique of restitution, presented as such to the public in a room; on the other hand, the disappearance of the limit, hardly traceable, between theater and life, both social and secretly intimate. We could also say that they represent the theater in which its constitutional terms, the audience and the action on stage, have disappeared and can no longer merge and have a dialogue – the clear weather having now passed for these things – but can only overwhelm, violate, and tear at each other.

In each of these disappearances there exists the physical testimony of the impossibility of a culture in process of ascertaining the dialogue and the exchange with its user.

It would be like saying that for a moment, even for a single one, the screening and the control, i.e. democratic oversight, of a society over a culture born and developed in its own bosom ceases to exist. This is because for the current concept of culture as a free debate of ideas we substitute that of culture as a formative moment of a theory or ideology in elaboration that tends to conquer power. In this sense, it acquires an internal strategic value, that is, secretly private, not detectable except to those who participate in the same situation and the same intention. The clear and declared refusal of not wanting to actively participate "in solving the problems of Progress" that the Official Society offers, means elaborating a different concept of progress itself and not deriving its premises from a conditioning by fortuitous causes, but rather getting rid of them as much as possible, by not declaring itself explicitly on principles, by prevaricating and drawing on the opportunities themselves.

Thus, a culture of silent theaters, glued books, wrapped canvases, walled houses, unwritten music, blind alleys, empty cities, and fake life: a hard and clandestine culture, therefore clear and visible because declared as such.

Useless to all if not to those who produce it and to those who - by recognizing themselves in it - recognize it. A culture that is to be kept hidden in the mezzanines and cellars as weapons or good flour for the Day of the Great Party.

Florence, March 16, 1968

Eclectic Conspiracy Center

Archizoom Associati, 1968

//

There are times when culture is committed to discovering the meaning of its presence within more general phenomena, and to establish or change the logical and intuitive links that put it in contact with its possible users in the world.

In the specific case of architectural culture, these relationships are of a formal (or dimensioned) nature and use: the object's ability to place itself within the pre-existing environment - natural or manufactured - and to establish a continuity or a crisis with this environment; the degree of tolerance with which an object offers

itself to use, and whether or not it depletes the reasons for its existence.

If we carry these types of relationship to their extreme, eliminating on the one hand any type of environmental correlation (both homogeneous and fractured ones) and on the other suspending the identification of a specific use, in practice we do nothing, but intentionally we stop the exchange of ideas between us and the user, creating in the flow of culture the closed basin where the usual critical and linguistic checks cease, as do the democratic verifications.

The concept of space, as a structure of mutual exchange, replaces that of a secluded and well-enclosed "place," possibly fresh where it is easier to cultivate the acts of the intellect and plot conspiracies: where the eclectic components of our culture, the great stratifications of Empire sediment and take shape, Nature is transformed into an immobile concept, and cruelty insinuates itself.

We do not want to give guarantees for now (if anything, we ask for guarantees).

Let us also be saved, whomever wants to, on the pillows of psychology and behavior. Let us be made, whomever can, an accomplice of customs, in the secret hope that rapid consumption will justify the mediocrity of the merits.

The Marble Chicken
Archizoom Associati, 1968

//

"We are the symbols of your passions - answered a big leopard - they, like us, attacked you, prevented you from seeing the end of your mission: since you cannot beat them, how will you triumph over us?"

Marquis de Sade: "Rodrigo or the Enchanted Tower".

...In fact, the phenomenon that we have seen in recent years, although it is the natural result of a mercantile (and unscientific) civilization, demonstrates a more important and in some aspects newer truth: it is the reversal and the disappearance of a conception of a general law of development...

We see today how the system tends to develop itself through "jumps," to absorb more or less violent patterns of social, political, economic, and cultural factors that from time to time lie ahead, and that it encompasses moments of a violent leap forward in the process of its development...

Perhaps the clearest demonstration is the exploitation by the system today of the Left's ideologies, not only as a political class, but in general as an attitude of protest used as a specialized area of customs: from fashion to song. Thus, ideology has also become a consumer good, becoming an artificial ideology, rather than an alternative system to fight against the problems. If we accept the existence of this development mechanism that advances by large "shocks," without that natural continuum of organic development, we have, for aesthetic doctrines and for architectural culture as well, a number of important consequences, both from the strategic and structural point of view...

Which is to say that culture also tends to develop itself through "jumps," i.e. by incorporation outside of itself and which necessarily must, in certain historical periods that correspond to major cultural revolutions, collide and reduce if it wants to progress and to continue to fulfill its cognitive and judgmental role...

The civilization of today is an imperial one; it is the civilization of the great international trusts, of the large financial and landed companies, of oil, of large resource. It is a civilization that is not fundamentally weak, but extended and cosmopolitan, ranging from America to the Arab nations, composite, eclectic, syncretic, but lucid and luminous, without doubts or problems. It has the architecture of a great empire...

It never raises the issue of new organisms, but instead resolves the existing ones with a method of industrial design, which is asked to draw something that already exists.

It has no "concept of space," only new problems of representation. It does not care about architectural problems, in the way we can care little about who cuts a dress for us.

It is not the civilization of technology and science, but of traffic and commerce: the whirlwind of consumerism and the rapid engulfment of the "large number," should not deceive us, because behind it there is a marble chicken that you can't eat and that doesn't move...

Social revolutions take place now in a different way: not because you defend a dying ideal, but because you fight to achieve it; not by having your own weapons, but by using those of your enemy; not by fighting openly, but fighting at night and in favorable conditions; and above all never losing a battle...

Another important thing today is to understand and to overtake. The same "large number," precisely because of the ability to bring the terminal phases of the problem to a climax, even though it seems to cast a shadow of relativity over all possible decisions, can actually get in touch with the underlying problems of culture itself. It is not fortuitous that in recent years we have returned to speaking about the city, anthropology, the great systems of production, etc...

In architectural design, from a certain point of view, one begins to speak of a "concept of space," i.e. coming to materialize a fact that does not exist or, if it exists, it is only one element of a much more complex fruition of the architectural fact, and with no spatially usable laws of composition...

If we want to relate to the size of the great cultural systems, we who live in a large social system, we must overcome the excessive culturalization typical of underdeveloped countries: in a sense we could say that we want to create the architecture of the spirit and not of psychology. We have to find the serenity of architectural practice itself.

The pavilion we have proposed has a fundamental motive: to represent an actual situation through four lateral speakers, over which a voice continuously reads one of the many critical texts that exist today on the issue of the "large number" (for example, the wording of the bid itself), in the presence of seven chromatic obelisks, motionless and shiny, on which seven colorful friezes are pitched, representing winged arms. These obelisks are neither sculptures nor machines, but rather cars, i.e. design objects that have reached a level of supreme imperial and triumphant symbolization.

Why do we believe this may be the Italian answer to the problem of the "great number?" This, in our view, represents a typically Italian condition: in part because we have our own profound architectural tradition, quite classical, of representing and not judging a system, of refusing to exploit culture, but believing in its ability to return to a higher level of knowledge. In part because Italy preserves, precisely through its situation of being a half-industrial and half-peasant nation, the ability to detect problems and to control them also ironically...

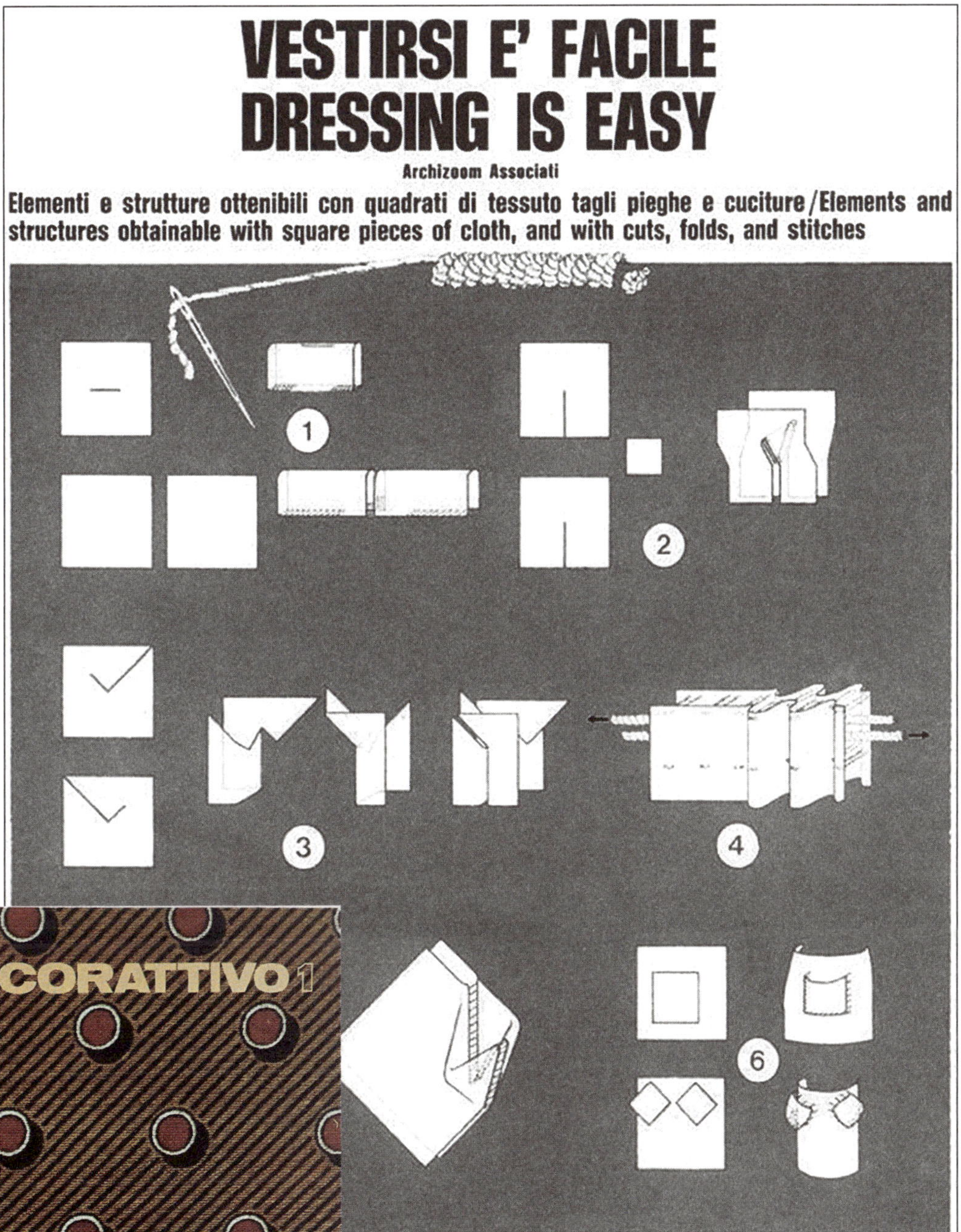

Archizoom Associati, "Dressing is Easy", in *Casabella* n. 384, 1973
Decorattivo, Cover, 1976

mantello / A small wrap

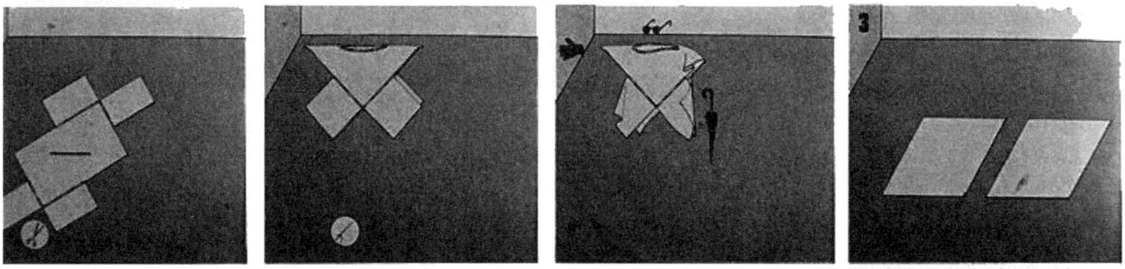

Grembiale con tasche ricavate nel

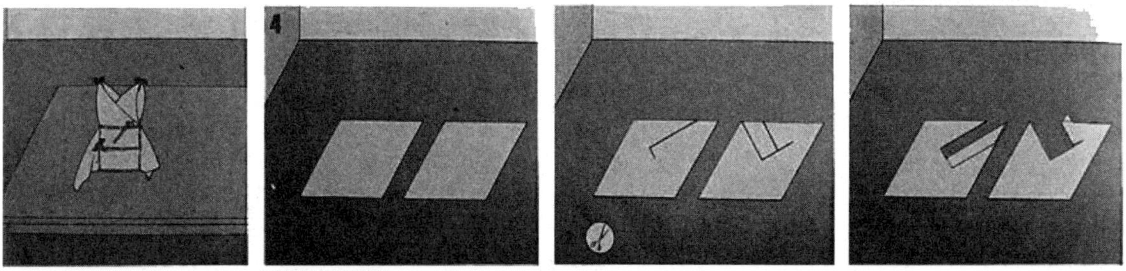

Pantaloni / Trousers

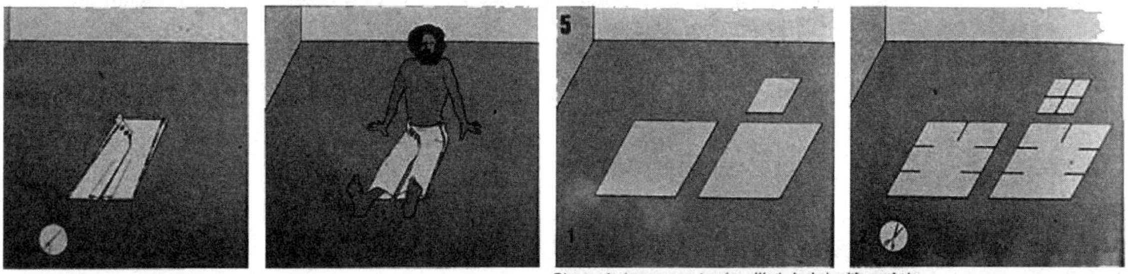

Giacca da lavoro con tasche / Work jacket with pockets

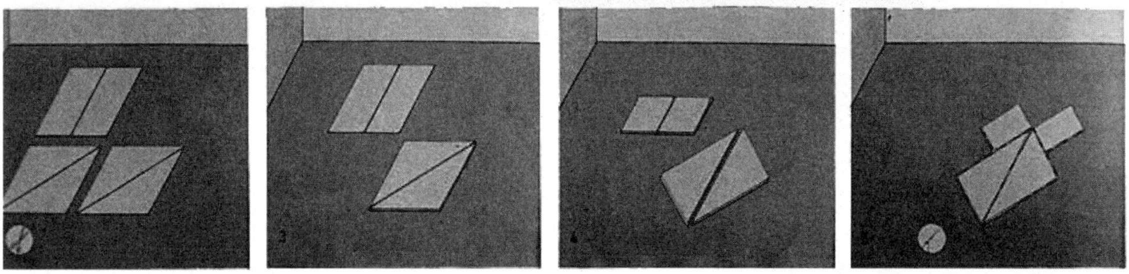

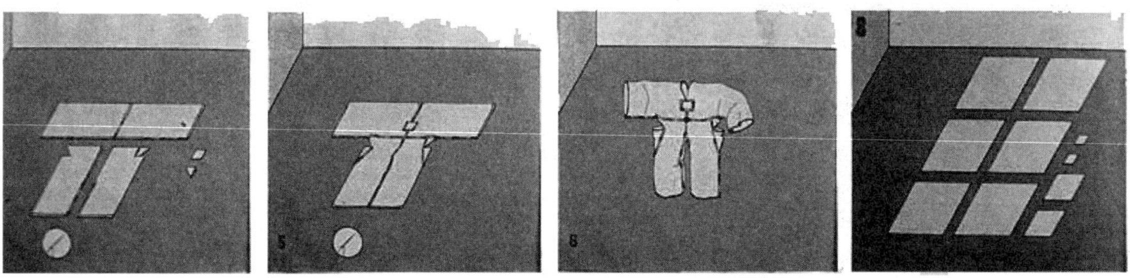

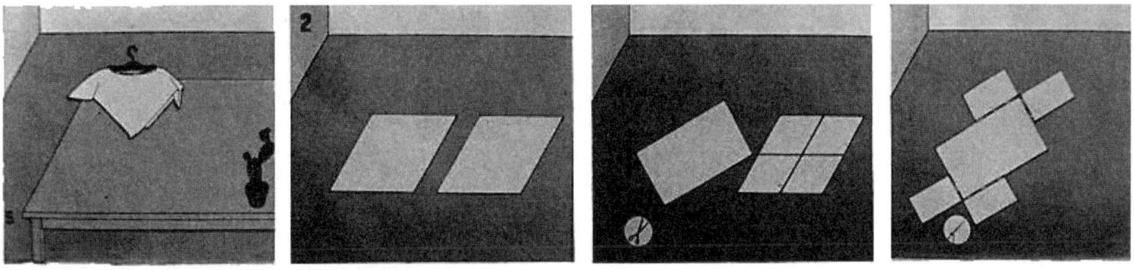

Mantello / A cloak

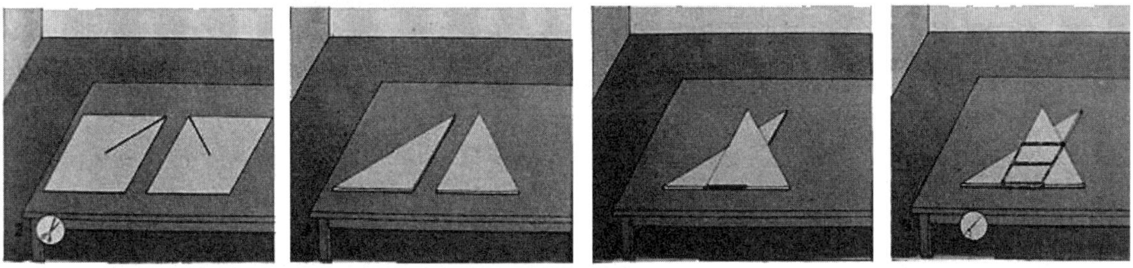

oppio spessore della stoffa / Smock with pockets made out of double layer of material

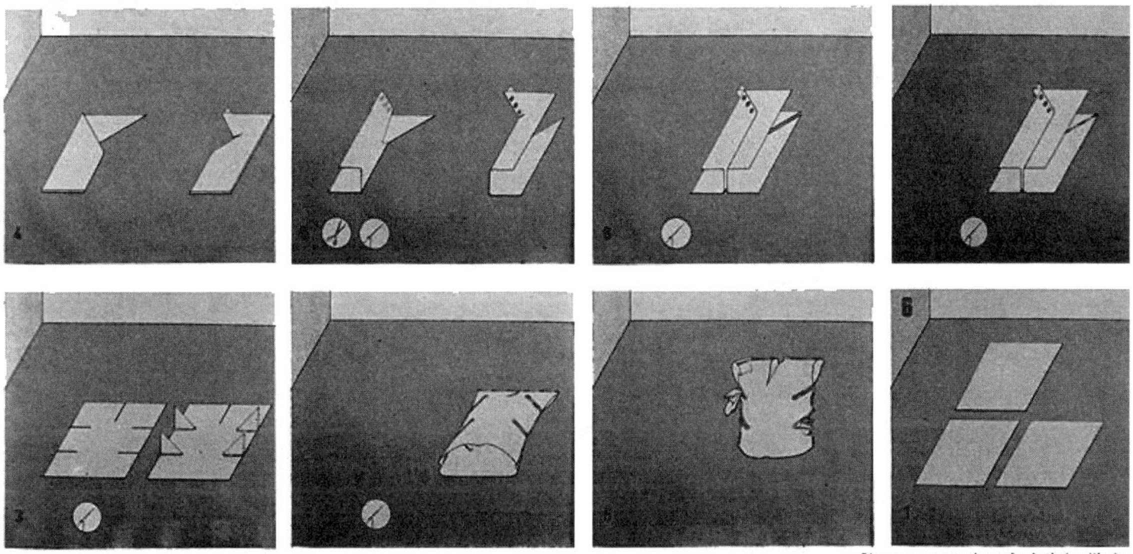

Giacca con poggiamani / Jacket with ha

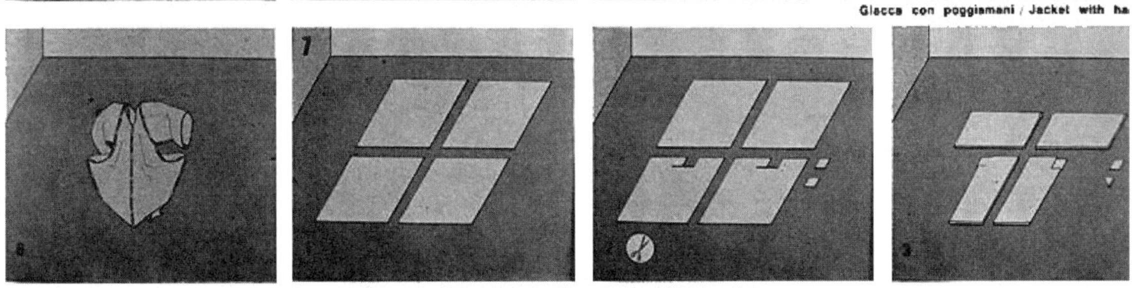

Tuta con tasche e taschino / Overalls with pockets and breast pocket

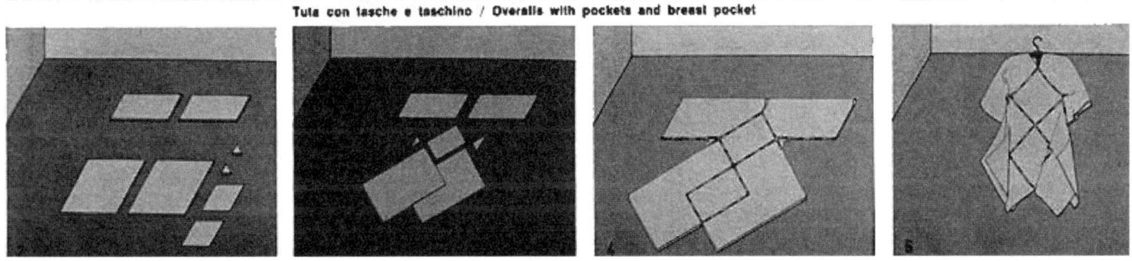

Session 2

NO-STOP CITY

THE INFINITIVE METROPOLIS AND THE HYPOTHESIS OF A NON FIGURATIVE LANGUAGE

In Archizoom Associated's *No-Stop City*, the city is described as a dematerialized reality, as unlimited territory and melting pot of information, products, and services, where architecture becomes an accessory, expressionless, a catatonic reality.

In the project *No-Stop City*, shaped from 1967 to 1972, many anti-compositional and anti-typological components came together, as a synthesis of a society that, due to its state of alienation, realized a new configuration of itself and of its organization on a territory.

Freeing itself from the rhetorical forms of Humanitarian Socialism and of Social Democratic progressivism, the project looked fearlessly to the logic of an atheistic, played down, gray industrialization, where serial production realized urban settings without those character structures mentioned by Wilhelm Reich as the inhibitory constraints for a liberation of the orgonic energy of man...

The colorful visions of pop architecture are now replacing the ruthless urban images of Ludwig Hilberseimer, a "city without quality" for a "man without qualities," a homogeneous and inexpressive metropolis which denied society the hope for a new modernity bearing positive values.

The homogenization of mass society as a counterpart of democratic egalitarianism; alienation as liberation from every bourgeois tradition was the new existential condition that Richard Hamilton and pop culture had overturned as the mature fruit of a radical materialism.

This attitude of extreme realism highlighted the self-destructive process of modernity: "The ultimate goal is the elimination of modern architecture itself." The overcoming of the theological limits of modern politics began to appear, its schematic operating with a view of history as an eternal struggle between good and evil, between rich and poor. A tireless history producing tragedies, fed by an unquenchable rhetoric, marked by continuous definitive clashes...

No-Stop City was instead the dramatic result of a totally played-down vision of history, returned to its secular dimension, devoid of tragedy because without metaphysics.

An extreme view of industrial civilization as producer of a repetitive, horizontal, no cathedrals system; a diffuse and fluid system, in which the difference between architecture and nature was dissolved and disappeared into the amniotic space of the metropolis, homogenized by the common belonging to a single production system, a single economic logic, which was that of global capitalism...

This monological attitude was very close to the range of ambient sounds of Brian Eno and especially to the music of Philip Glass, who in those years was beginning his work on the horizontal and non-compositional sound (as defined by Pierre Boulez), for a diffuse and molecular music, more closely related to artificial microclimates than to symphonies.

Then, unlike those who thought that the architecture of the machine society had to resemble a machine (Archigram) and who found in the exhibitionism of its constructive components (girders, bolts, braces) the social justification for its own existence, Archizoom thought that the best technology was made by the invisible technology (electronics). This attitude refused the figurative parameters of modern architecture, creating an urban realm of silent style and of the dispersion of borders. The city as a territory defined by a lift every $50m^2$...

The name *No-Stop City* itself originated from the idea of a continuous metropolis, without external and internal borders: a metropolis corresponding directly to the market, without a distinction of places and functions; a living forest where you can live and work in any non-place; a metropolis made up of an all-functions incubator, available for indeterminate activities, gyms available for individual creativity, residential parking for metropolitan nomads.

The Civilization of Commodities was realized in an infinite landscape where the only protagonists were industrial products.

Industrial design was interpreted as the total commodification of the world and of life; the city as a shapeless plankton of goods, services, information, people.

In the early diagrams of *No-Stop City* in 1967, done via a typewriter (because computers did not exist), the search for a "non-figurative architecture" is explicitly declared, i.e. one devoid of expressive qualities and ideological testimonies...

The metropolis was seen as a big interior space, air-conditioned and artificially illuminated. Like a large factory or a shopping center, the organisms adhering more closely to the homologous logic of capitalism (production and consumption), containers deprived of an outside, within which everything is transient.

This "introvert space," or this generic and immoral metropolis, constituted a sort of second nature; a high-tech Amazonia, within which all functional zoning piled up and melted and the standards related to natural lighting and air-conditioning disappeared; true armor that through their presence prevented the city from overcoming its laborious function of harmonization between technology and nature, history and society, internal and external, public and private...

Andrea Branzi, 2014

ARCHIZOOM ASSOCIATI
DIAGRAMMA ABITATIVO
OMOGENEO

IPOTESI DI LINGUAGGIO
ARCHITETTONICO NON FIGURATIVO

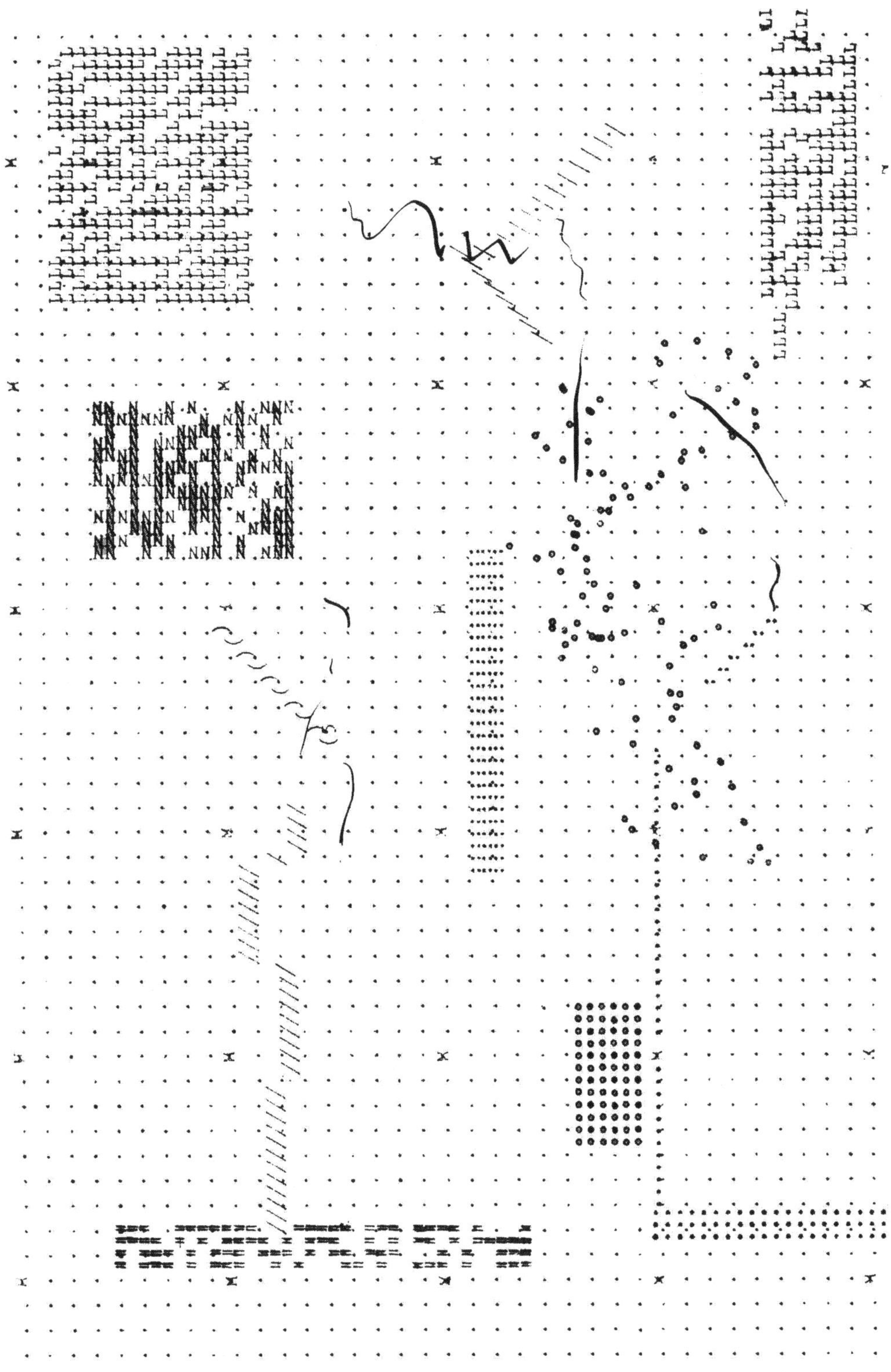

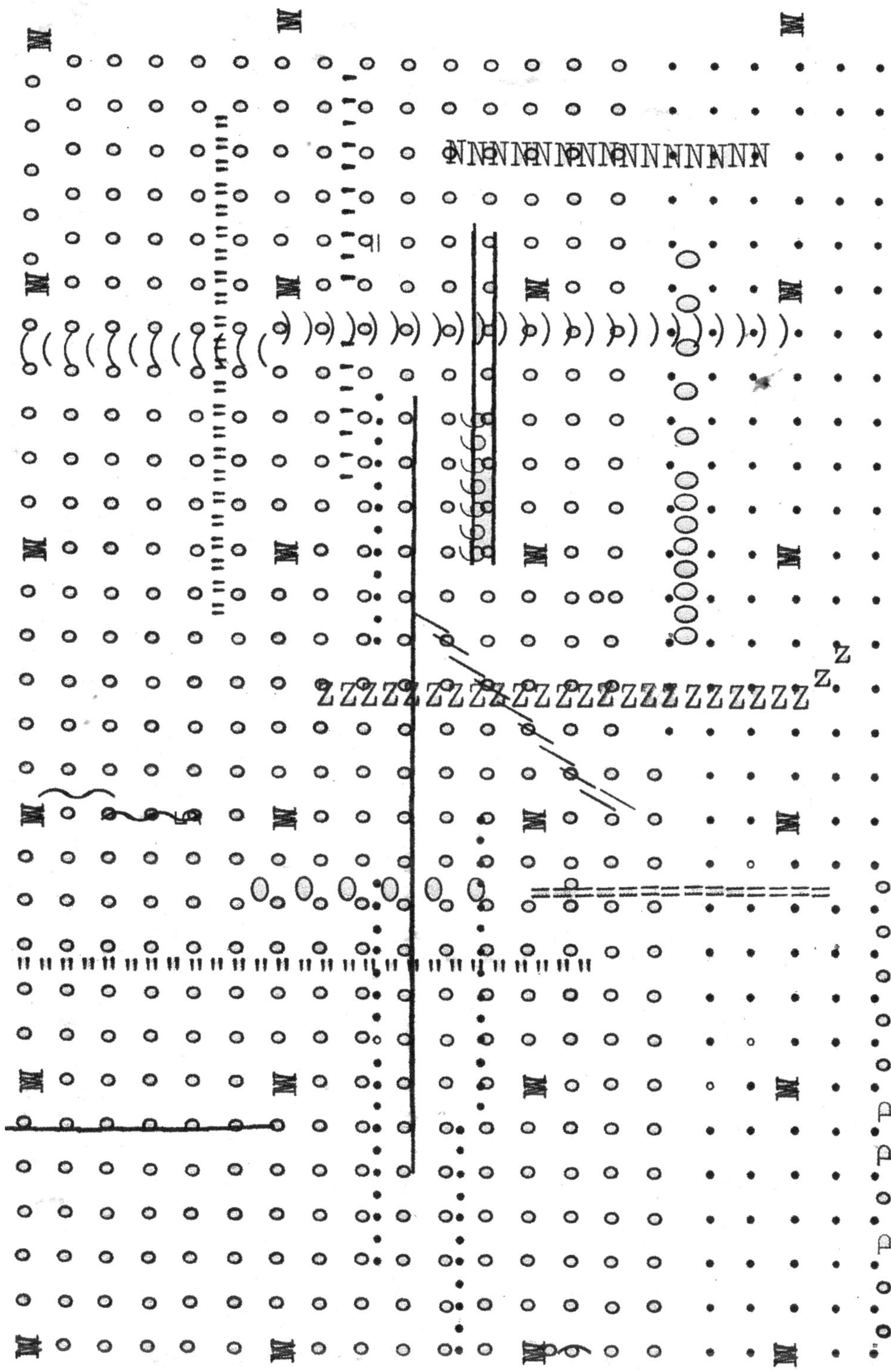

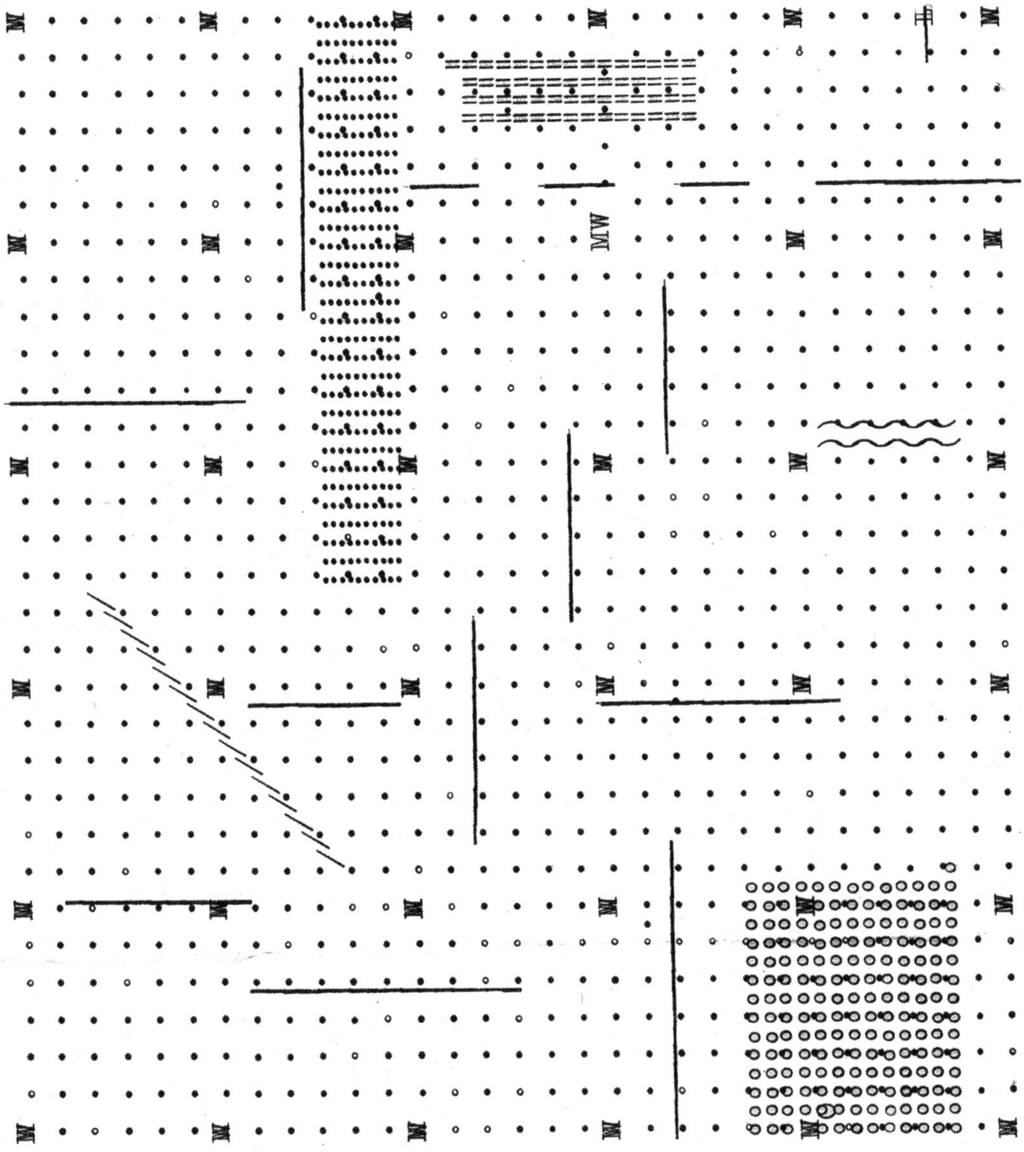

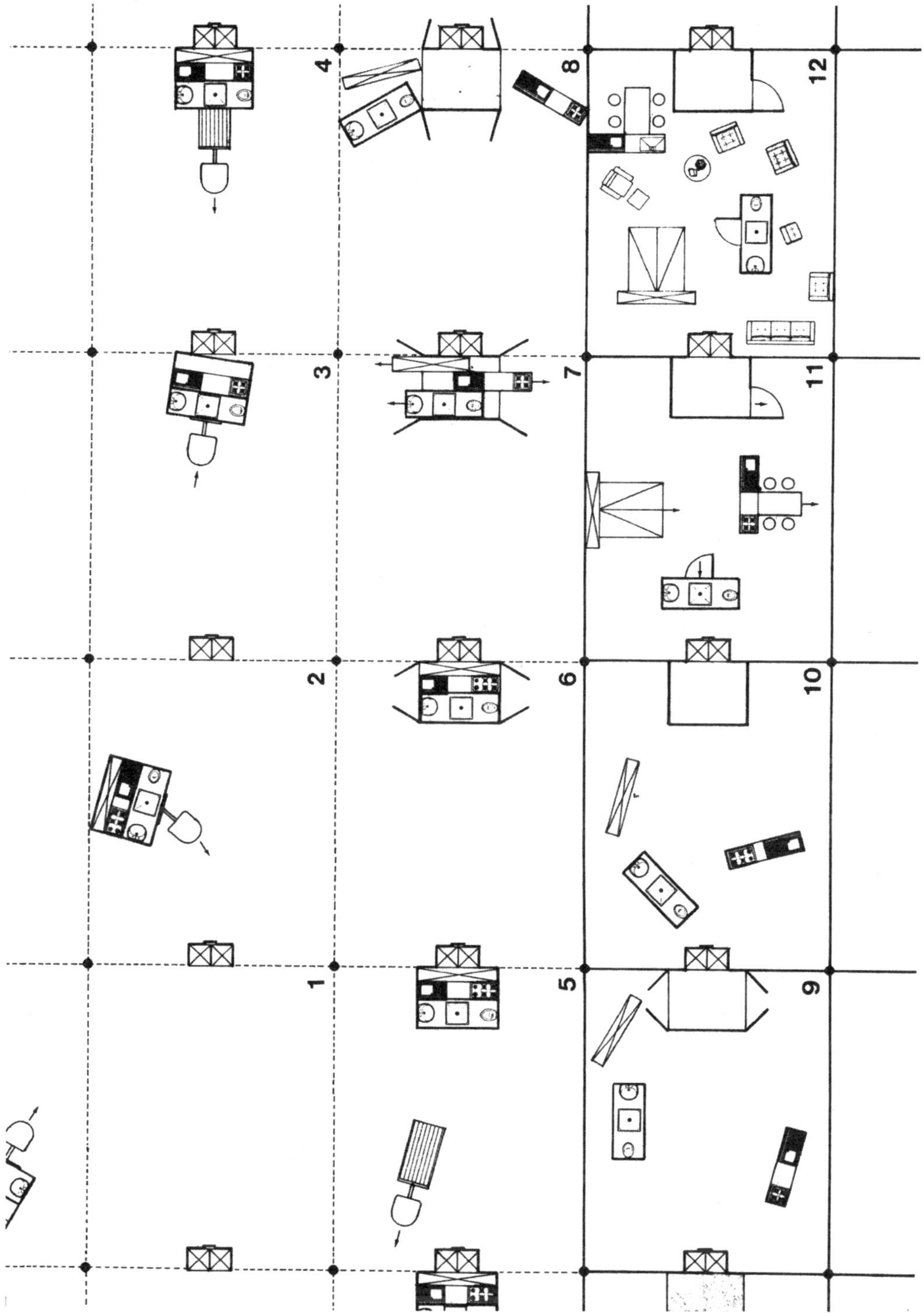

Archizoom Associati, *No Stop City*, *System of Temporary Houses*, 1971

Archizoom Associati, *No Stop City, Continuous and Homogeneous City-System or Future City*, 1970

Archizoom Associati, *No-Stop City*, Model, 1969

MANIFESTA

Città, catena di montaggio del sociale

ideologia e teoria della metropoli • Archizoom associati

As a physical and social phenomenon the metropolis derives from the Capital and develops in line with its logic. The capital imposes its own general ideology on the metropolis, and this ideology conditions it. This general ideology consists of the Policy of Equilibrium among Opposites: it is also the Policy of Equilibrium among the Internal Contradictions of the Capital itself: indeed, as a natural extension of the Factory Model within Society, the Metropolis of the Capital insists on its autonomous right to assume the shape of a brutal functional system, and at the same time, the Metropolis is called on necessarily to represent Nature and Technology as operating on the same plane of experiences, achieving a spontaneous anthropological balance of Opposites and becoming a kind of "Great Village". However, it is indispensable to make one point clear: that there is no such thing as a Workers' Metropolis. In fact, just as there is no Class Political Economy, there is no Urbanistic Theory of Class, but only a Class Critique of Urbanistic Theory. The Utopia that we utilize, then, is only a more General Critical Language, which makes more immediate and direct Communication possible: such a Utopia, in fact, is not posed on the plane of a Qualitative clash of Values but on that of a Quantitative challenge. For all its high degree of technological development, the Modern Metropolis is compelled to accept a number of Natural Equilibria such as the depth of buildings in relation to ventilation and natural light. Despite this, we see that at the points where the system directly realizes its functional rationality on the urban plane, it actually goes beyond the "spontaneous" limit of light and air, realizing unified artificial systems which rise to the level of true General Urban Models. Samples of this may be seen in the Factory and the Supermarket. The first as a Productive Structure which is still partial with respect to the whole of society, foreshadows the whole urban organization as a homogeneous system of services and of space, superseding the 19th century clustering of the various urban functions still extant in the Metropolis. The second, as the Structure of Consumption, foreshadows the complete circulation of goods in the urban area, as the direct realization of a rational system of organizing consumption.

In both cases we see an identical ideology with respect to ground and space: the Metropolis, which is the meeting point of Production and Consumption, is thus subject to this law and not to others, and as a social phenomenon it is from this point of view that it must be studied.

Consequently, within the framework of a single objective law of ground and space, as necessarily homogeneous and not discontinuous realities in the logic of Production and Consumption, the Model of the City will be realized which is harmonious and not discontinuous within the homogeneity and discontinuity of the Country, and this to the extent that the two realities run along two different planes. On the one hand Architecture ceases to be Natural, on the other Nature ceases to be Culture. Such an Urban Model, however, does not represent the alternative to present reality, but present reality at a new level of Critical Awareness.

1

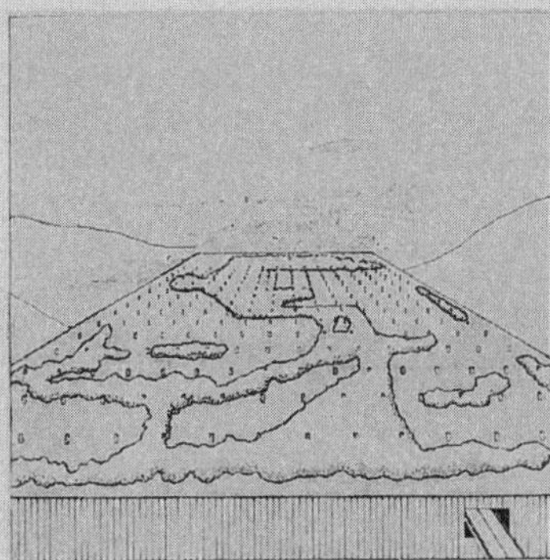
2

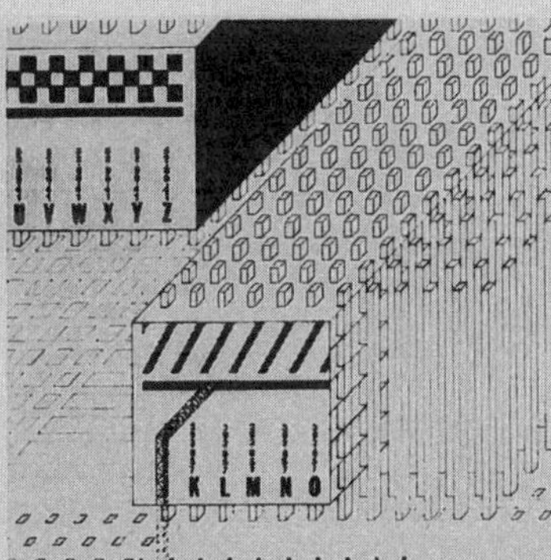

3

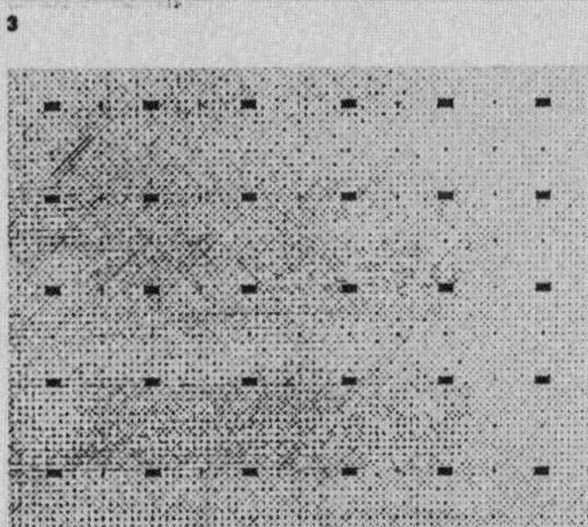
4

1
Archizoom associati: struttura urbana monomorfa.
2
Diagramma abitativo omogeneo.
3
Assonometria schematica.
4
Griglia strutturale.

Quale dovrebbe essere il rapporto fra la linea ideologica di chi ha la responsabilità culturale di una rivista e quella degli autori che essa pubblica?
Difficile stabilirlo rigidamente, se non si vuole essere una mafia e nemmeno una delle tante parrocchie chiuse della cultura italiana. Se « Casabella » pubblica un articolo, quindi, ciò non significa necessariamente che tutta la redazione lo debba condividere.
Personalmente, dissento in gran parte dal saggio così apodittico che segue, anche perché il mio modo di pensare alla comunicazione mediante la carta stampata è totalmente diverso da quello dei suoi autori. E' difficile per me persino esprimere delle critiche, perché questo modo di scrivere mi fa girare la testa, soprattutto per l'uso smisurato e un po' snobistico delle maiuscole: non trattandosi né di Hegel, né tampoco di Arbasino, mi si inceppa continuamente la lettura, come se camminassi sopra un mucchio di sassi.
Debbo però informare i lettori che la mia opinione è strettamente personale, e che il Modo Di Condurre Il Discorso Ideologico degli « Archizoom » ha se non altro il pregio della novità, ed un indubbio seguito fra i giovani.
«Casabella» ospita questo scritto, a cui una maggiore concisione avrebbe certo giovato, pensando alla giovane generazione di architetti, più preparata della mia alle riflessioni sulle teorizzazioni ideologiche, nella speranza di suscitare una utile discussione.

G. K. K.

43

Archizoom Associati, "City, Assembly Line of the Social," in *Casabella* n. 350-51, 1970

« A mezzogiorno, in un giorno di una stagione qualsiasi. Non piove, eppure il cielo è uniformemente grigiastro, comune, senza festosità; nella strada è una luce opaca che esclude ogni mistero, ogni stranezza dell'anima ».
T. Mann: *« Altezza Reale »*

La città moderna « nasce nel Capitale » e si sviluppa all'interno della sua Logica: il Capitale impone ad essa una propria Ideologia Generale, che ne condiziona lo sviluppo ed il configurarsi.
Tale Ideologia Generale è costituita dalla Politica degli « Equilibri » tra i Contrari, perseguita sul piano delle rivendicazioni economiche e « realizzata di fatto » sul piano del funzionamento urbano.
Politica dell'Equilibrio tra i Contrari, ma anche Politica dell'Equilibrio delle Contraddizioni Interne al Capitale stesso: infatti come naturale estensione del Modello di Fabbrica nella Società, la Città del Capitale rivendica una propria autonoma libertà a configurarsi come brutale sistema funzionale secondo la Logica della Produzione; come Equilibrio Realizzato tra Interesse Individuale e Interesse Generale, la città è costretta ad equilibrare forzosamente Natura e Tecnica su di un unico piano di scorrimento delle Esperienze. (Il "Grande villaggio" di cui parla M. Mc Luhan)
Ciò che d'altra parte è indispensabile premettere è che: « non esiste la Metropoli Operaia ».
La nascita Capitalistica della Città Moderna, non le permette infatti una crescita politica autonoma (cosa possibile alla Classe Operaia), ma solo la possibilità di guadagnare i termini che, superata la Mistificazione Ideologica dell'argomento, permettano uno svolgimento scientifico del dibattito.
Di una Teoria dunque, si tratta, e non di una proposta « alternativa ».
Come « non » esiste una Economia Politica di Classe, ma solo una Critica di Classe all'Economia Politica, così non esiste una Teoria Urbanistica di Classe, ma solo una Critica di Classe alla Teoria Urbanistica. Per compiere tale operazione noi utilizziamo un linguaggio classico scritto, ed uno grafico, più strettamente disciplinare.
Il primo ci fornisce strumenti di analisi ampiamente collaudati; il secondo ci permette una elaborazione creativa dei risultati del processo stesso.
Ma la creatività in questo caso è rappresentata solo dall'uso del linguaggio architettonico ad un livello esplicativo diretto, altrimenti impossibile.
Infatti dal momento che il problema del linguaggio è quello della « Comunicazione Ottimale » (cioè della comunicazione più esplicita e generale possibile), « esso diviene necessariamente UTOPIA ».
L'Utopia però che noi utilizziamo è solo strumentale: essa rappresenta se stessa, ma non come prefigurazione di un Modello Diverso del Sistema (che non esiste Metropoli Operaia), ma Ipotesi critica sul Sistema stesso.
Non esiste quindi lo scontro sul Piano Qualitativo dei Valori, ma soltanto la sfida « Quantitativa », che senza presupporre logiche " autre ", accetta la Logica stessa della Produzione come piano di scontro tra le due contraddizioni del Sistema: « Quantità Massima » ed « Equilibrio Massimo ».
Solo così si può interrompere la continuità dei processi e dei legami, facendo impazzire il Cervello del Sistema.
44 A questo punto è necessario premettere chiaramente un'altra constatazione: la « morte » della Cultura funzionale e dell'Arte.
La prima come Ideologia della Unità della Forma, e come tensione civilizzante della Parte al Tutto, cessa di esistere nel momento in cui il Parziale si attua nel Generale attraverso il Piano.
La seconda, come elaboratrice di modelli di comportamento, in quanto capacità spontanea di trasformare i dati "razionali" in "valori naturali", cessa il suo scopo al contatto di una Società che rifiuta i Modelli di Riferimento ed accetta il Comportamento come "struttura aperta".
Il « Progetto » allora, come modello di azione, come elemento limitato e parziale prefigurante una Realtà Universale, vede capovolgere di fatto il proprio « ruolo », divenendo "riduttore" di un Insieme ormai Attuato ad una realtà parziale.
La « tecnica dello "choc" » che la Cultura, sempre e soltanto Borghese, ha adottato come sistema di comunicazioni traumatizzante, ai fini dell'integrazione, cessa il proprio ruolo.
Prefigurando infatti l'attuazione di una "Civilisation Machiniste" come legge "naturale e necessaria" del divenire delle cose, o consacrando le nuove forme "inculturalizzate" di linguaggio come strutture "spontanee" della comunicazione, l'Arte ha adottato ormai lo "choc" come sistema stabile di restituzione nel Particolare di una Potenzialità Generale deflagrante. (M. Tafuri)
Dopo quaranta anni Duchamp per primo conclude il ciclo togliendo i baffi alla sua Gioconda.
L'arte dunque, come tecnica di integrazione attraverso lo "choc" estetico, ha sempre teso ad una realtà più generale, alla « città » cioè, che rappresenta il manufatto dove la tecnica dello "choc" è nata dalla spontanea sommatoria dei Contrari, e come strumento più generale possibile di integrazione del Sociale.
È la città dunque che trasforma le leggi "naturali" della Pittura in « realtà »: essa è il Fine dell'Arte, continuamente sottinteso dall'Arte stessa, poiché la "prefigurazione" che essa Arte compie deve pur sempre restare "azione", probabilità e speranza, tensione cioè ad un Divenire che realizza Valori Universali.
Ma sarà proprio la Città allora, al momento in cui assurge al ruolo di protagonista del proprio dibattito, a dare all'Arte il suo colpo di grazia.
Questo nel senso che nel momento in cui la città, come manufatto, passa dalla sua fase Ideologica alla conquista di una propria « Teoria », si interrompe il legame tra la città e le azioni culturali che stanno a monte della sua « forma », e che demandano a questa la verifica oggettiva dei Valori individuati.
Liberando il dibattito sulla città dalle sue sovrastrutture, è possibile superare il circolo vizioso che sposta continuamente la « verifica » urbana dal piano "funzionale oggettivo", a quello "formale" e viceversa. È possibile superare cioè la Mitologia dell'Equilibrio per guadagnare l'impatto con la Stratificazione e l'Accumulazione Omogenea della Realtà, come unica legge della realtà che ci circonda.

La Società a cui l'ideologia della città attuale fa riferimento è ancora un sistema nel quale la « distinzione » perimetrale tra Processo Produttivo e Processo di Circolazione delle Merci (Centro e Periferia) garantisce di fatto il capovolgimento costante dei valori reali.

La «Produzione» è limitata ed accessoria nei riguardi di una Società impegnata a "creare naturalmente" i Valori economici.
Pur essendo la Fabbrica il Centro dell'Intero Ciclo Produttivo, essa resta nascosta come "fenomeno vergognoso" nella Periferia del Sistema.
Quando però il Capitale raggiunge l'Organizzazione Produttiva dell'Intera Società attraverso il Piano, quando cioè il Modello di Fabbrica coincide con il Modello del Sociale, la Società riconosce drammaticamente se stessa come quadro nel quale il Sistema « ha realizzato il proprio dover-essere, ed insieme la sua contraddizione massima ».
Nella realizzazione della "organizzazione sociale del lavoro", cioè nella estensione la più generale possibile della struttura produttiva nella società, per la prima volta si zazione" dell'intero Sistema Sociale.
Si realizza così il paradosso estremo: l'Ordine coincide al limite nel Caos. L'Unità si realizza nella Contraddizione.
Il Capitale assiste al rischioso capovolgimento dei propri "Valori" premessi: il Bene, il Progresso si realizzano, ma nel Male, cioè nella "proletarizzazione" della Società Capitalistica. Il che è "vergognoso" per una società classista.
Da qui l' "angoscia" crescente del Capitale e della "sua" Società che assistono alla realizzazione nel proprio negativo.
Risulta necessario allora per il Sistema « mistificare » il processo di "proletarizzazione" organizzando la Politica del Consenso. Come capovolgimenti dei dati reali, lo Stato gestisce "la partecipazione al Potere dei lavoratori", giun-

realizza l' "intima eticità" del Capitale, cioè la sua tensione ad un dover-essere. (Licciardello)
Il « Dolore » del Capitale è sempre stato quello di avvertirsi come settore limitato di un Tutto a lui esterno ed estraneo: la propria concentrazione come settore razionale all'interno di un Mondo Sconosciuto, gli forniva la forza di una potenzialità Universale, il carisma di una propria fatalità naturale. L'Immagine del « Progresso » diviene così quella stessa dell'« Integrazione ».

Adesso però che tale Integrazione si realizza nel Piano, il Capitale scopre l'attuazione della sua Contraddizione massima: la trasformazione della Società tutta intera in forza lavoro organizzata, significa di fatto la "proletarizgendo a negare la differenza tra Cittadino e Operaio: non è la Società che somiglia alla Fabbrica, ma la Fabbrica che somiglia alla Società.
La Cultura si impossessa del riflesso sovrastrutturale di tale processo: essa analizza l'Angoscia, « introspettandone le cause », cioè esternandole al soggetto come realtà naturali.
Essa acquisisce infatti come materiale "vitale" i dati stessi del problema; l'Angoscia diventa una "ricchezza", un modo di essere complesso ma culturale, fino a divenire valore Universale, in quanto Generale.
Lo sforzo della Cultura è quello di restituire come realtà autonoma la controforma del Capitale stesso, l' "impronta" cioè che esso lascia sulla società.

45

L'Architettura come CULTURA DELLO SPAZIO, nel suo sforzo di figurare autonomamente la fruizione, giunge a materializzare un dato che non esiste.

Il Capitale nella marcia verso la "sua" Società, cioè verso la propria identificazione con « tutto » il fenomeno sociale attraverso il Piano, transita attraverso necessarie fasi di inglobamento di realtà "selvagge", prive ancora dell'etica universale, che investe invece la sua intima natura di Fenomeno Civile.
Tali realtà "selvagge" costituiscono dunque ogni volta uno scatto in avanti ed insieme l'oscuro inserimento di un corpo estraneo all'interno di un meccanismo razionale.
La più grande di tutte queste realtà "selvagge", anzi la loro somma, è quindi la Classe Operaia, che nasce nel Capitale in quanto Forza Lavoro, ma che rappresenta di fatto la sua Alternativa.
Ma questo non ha eccessiva importanza, perché nella Contraddizione il Capitale sperimenta la propria vocazione all'Unità.
È dal conflitto sociale da lui indotto infatti che esso sperimenta la propria spontanea "vocazione sociale".
Nello inglobamento dei Modelli Sociali progressivi, elaborati da Parte Operaia, esso attua il proprio destino nell' "umano" generale così come la Cultura sperimenta nella "realtà inculturalizzata" la propria dimensione di Valore Civilizzante.
L'adozione brutale della tecnologia e della morfologia industriale, il recupero dei linguaggi spontanei e realizzati di fatto, in pratica l'utilizzo dell'intero fenomeno industriale come di un gigantesco " ready made ", garantisce a questo un valore "naturale e necessario", ed alla sua logica il valore di un sistema "oggettivo" di progresso e di salvamento.
La Cultura garantisce così al Capitale la gestione della propria realtà, evitando il più possibile le implicazioni estroverse e l'utilizzo unidirezionale dei processi razionalizzanti da esso stesso messi in moto.
Ma quando la Classe Operaia viene a « coincidere » con la Società stessa attraverso il Piano, quando cioè il Capitale vede « confermata » la sua Vocazione all'Unità, in quanto non esiste più una realtà "autre" sulla quale proiettarsi, la tensione etica della Cultura come potenzialità al dover-essere, si attenua.
All'interno di una Società organizzata dentro un Piano produttivo, in un sistema dunque ove agisce solo la distinzione di "funzioni" diverse, complementari ma omogenee, la Cultura deve compiere il passo che le permetta di integrarsi alla nuova realtà di fatto.
Essa deve cioè divenire una "funzione" produttiva, una CATEGORIA IMPEGNATA A PRODURRE QUANTITATIVAMENTE. Liquidata l'UNITÀ DELLA FORMA, come tensione del Particolare al Generale, nella realizzazione dell'Identico, il « medium visuale » non risulta più funzionale alla individuazione di un Oggetto che non si estranea dal Soggetto.
L'intero processo di Visualizzazione, come rapporto di razionale identificazione dei contrasti, « viene meno ».

Quando il Capitale scopre il Meccanismo dei Rapporti di Classe da lui indotto, come la dinamica della sua stessa integrazione « del » Sociale, capovolge i termini del problema, al fine di confermare la sua integrazione « nel » Sociale.

L'Ideologia keynesiana conferma del resto come "bene" l'aumentata ricchezza sociale, che apporta una maggiore richiesta del mercato, e quindi la Parte Imprenditoriale accetta come fatale, ma positivo, l'aumento del "costo" della Forza Lavoro. Ma fino a un certo punto.
La RIVOLUZIONE PERMANENTE DEI REDDITI all'interno dello SVILUPPO EQUILIBRATO DEL SISTEMA, rimane il limite estremo, il quadro dei riferimenti di fondo che non è "possibile" valicare. La gestione di questo equilibrio può anche essere spartita; a questo Equilibrio infatti si attribuisce il Valore di un dato Oggettivo, Scientifico, che conferma la natura Politica del Capitale, ponendosi al di sopra di questo come Dogma Naturale che presiede le singole decisioni e le singole richieste.
Aumenti sì, dunque, ma senza « Crisi ».
In questo senso il "salario" diventa la categoria "politica" più propria: lo strumento unitario capace di provocare una crisi generale, e insieme la cartina di tornasole delle "possibilità" della richiesta operaia.
Lo slogan "più soldi-meno lavoro" diviene così il programma rivoluzionario massimo, al livello di integrazione massima. (M. Tronti)
L'assenza infatti di "Contenuti" sociali in un programma rivoluzionario mette in crisi la capacità di contenimento del Sistema: egli è pronto a fare propria qualsiasi componente del Problema Sociale, ma non può mettere in crisi la "scientificità degli equilibri economici", sulla quale si basa.
Il rifiuto di presentare "modelli alternativi" come quadri di riferimento a cui rinviare il significato di ogni atto rivendicativo, l'assenza di un possibile controllo formale dell'insieme delle tensioni, l'impossibilità a verificare i limiti reali di queste tensioni all'interno di un programma, fanno sì che ogni atto divenga una Struttura Aperta, dal significato generale incontrollabile. E questo è il MALE.
La Classe Operaia così, integrata attraverso il Piano alla intera Società, trasforma tutta intera questa in una "realtà selvaggia".
Il Capitale stesso diviene allora, nella sua identificazione col sociale, una realtà "selvaggia" priva di "contenuti". Ciò costringe fatalmente a spostare il dibattito dai "Valori Sociali" al problema del "Potere".
Quando cioè il conflitto Sociale si costituisce nei termini di una richiesta di Gestione Operaia del Capitale, e non più come conflitto tra Capitale e non-Capitale, si smascherano automaticamente le sovrastrutture dello scontro.
Quando infatti non si pongono più una contro l'altra, anzi una alternativa all'altra, l'Ideologia della Miseria, che è l'ideologia di uno stato sociale "transitorio", e l'Ideologia della Ricchezza, che è l'ideologia di uno stato sociale "definitivo", ma si pone invece come problema unico quello di una "integrazione" sempre più sfrenata nel "meccanismo del Benessere", adottando tout-court i termini stessi della realtà senza ipotizzarne una diversa, il Capitale si trova a dover denunciare l' "artificialità" delle proprie mosse, come « strumento » di Sfruttamento e di Potere.
Gettando nella lotta il proprio grado estremo di Alienazione per battere il Capitale sul suo stesso terreno, la Classe Operaia testimonia della « assenza » di una Cultura Operaia di Opposizione, spontanea e stimolante, nata dalla prassi di una lotta naturale per la sopravvivenza, e denuncia la realtà del Capitale come struttura priva di induzione di Valori e quindi di un Destino.

Demistificare l'Ideologia della Miseria infatti significa non riconoscere alla Miseria un valore positivo, ma solo uno stato di « assenza » di Ricchezza.
Non a caso il Capitale non ha mai negato alla Parte Operaia la spontaneità di un umanesimo contadino che esso conserverebbe intatto dentro di sé, e che costituirebbe anzi lo stesso fermento rivoluzionario, tendente ad instaurare una Società depositaria di Valori Umani. La Classe Operaia, quale Puro Agnello, non ancora macchiato dal Benessere, si immolerebbe per la salvezza generale.
Ma la Classe Operaia nasce invece nel Capitale, come Forza Lavoro Organizzata, e ne rappresenta la Contraddizione Massima. Qualsiasi ulteriore ruolo Vitale ad essa attribuito come produttrice spontanea di Cultura "autre", non è altro che Ideologia tendente ad Oggettivare lo Sfruttamento come realtà possibile, come fenomeno astraibile dal processo politico, per riferirlo quindi ad un dato naturale e positivo di equilibrio.
Impostare dunque la Lotta Politica sulla sola Categoria del "salario", significa ottenere in partenza le migliori condizioni di scontro: lottare al massimo delle forze con il massimo della concentrazione. Nessun dato del Problema viene posto al di fuori.
Accettare come Unico Obiettivo il Potere, significa la possibilità reale di affrontare una Lotta Finale senza l'ausilio di Modelli Unitari di Riferimento, Alternativi Qualitativamente al Sistema.
Ouesta è stata l'importante conquista teorica della Opposizione di Massa al Capitale.
L'accettazione della Prassi Rivoluzionaria come unico strumento di elaborazione, significa individuare il comportamento, cioè le azioni, come una « struttura aperta », non allegorica ma priva di "contenuti in codice", che si verifica continuamente sul piano della realtà oggettiva, accettata come unico quadro omogeneo di valori.
In questo senso, ove occorresse, viene prefigurata nella prassi una diversa Società, che rifiuta inizialmente l'introspezione dell'Angoscia e la demistifica come "male" indotto da una realtà a lei estranea e che rifiuta.

L'« ideologia » della metropoli attuale nasce dalla scoperta settecentesca della "città come oggetto naturale", non struttura di accumulazione e trasformazione delle rendite, ma fenomeno necessario e fatale, teso a realizzare il delicato equilibrio tra l'uomo e il suo ambiente naturale: il mondo delle cose e la collettività.
La città diviene dunque il tramite principe tra l'uomo e la propria « naturalità sociale » compromessa, tra l'uomo e la selva dei rapporti con il reale: l'ARTE diviene il valore radicale che trasforma la « ragione » in « natura », cioè un bene collettivo universalmente fruibile, oggettivo quindi e a-storico.
Nella "città come oggetto naturale" si riproducono le due antitesi dell'eterna dialettica della Natura: il « Caos » e l'« Ordine », che non tendono qui a deflagrare, ma a conquistare un equilibrio dinamico e stimolante, all'interno del campus deputato del sociale.
Facendo coincidere il Caos e l'Ordine con le Categorie Sociali del PRIVATO e del PUBBLICO, l'ideologia della metropoli tende a porre il fatto urbano come prova campione della realizzazione storica di un valore metastorico: l'equilibrio tra la Parte e il Tutto, tra l'Individuo e la Collettività, tra la Tecnica e i Valori, tra l'Uomo e la Natura.

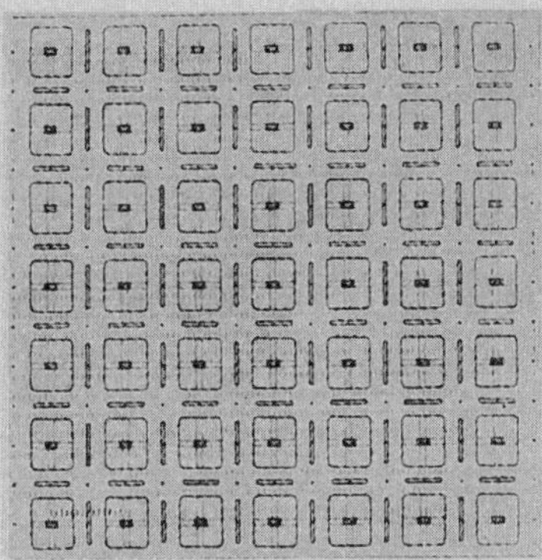
5

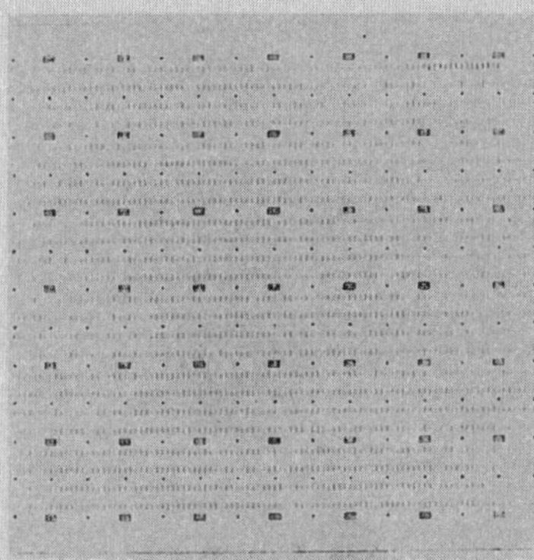
6

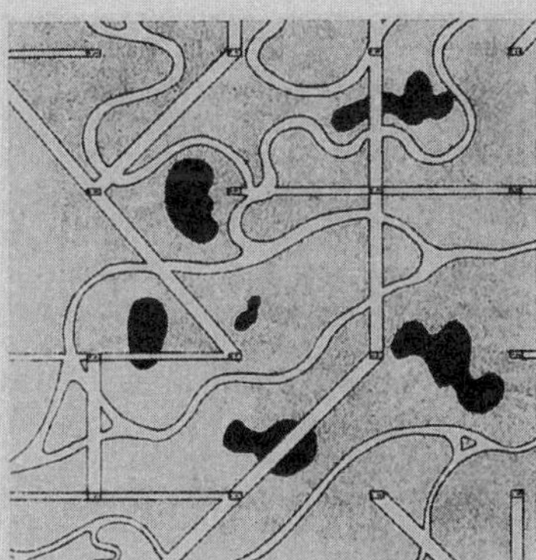
7

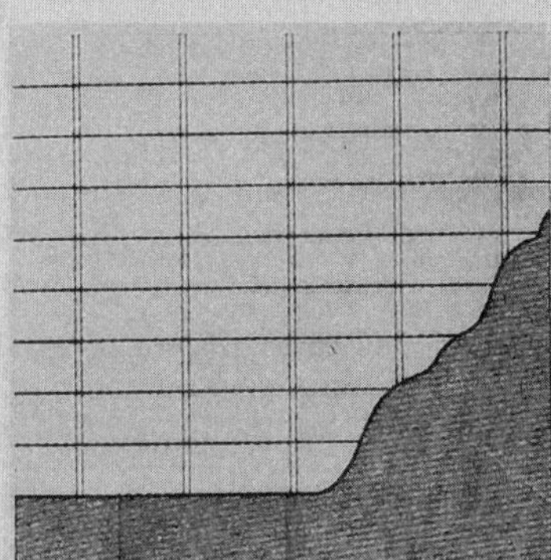
8

5
Schema viario omogeneo.
6
Griglia di impianti di microclimatizzazione e di comunicazioni verticali.
7
Piano superiore di « affioramento ».
8
Sezione trasversale.

« Equilibrio ecologico » e « Giustizia sociale » divengono parti di una stessa battaglia cui la metropoli sembra garantire spontaneamente la verifica formale.

Operando con continuità all'interno della identificazione tra « Urbano » e « Civile », la metropoli attuale tenta la realizzazione della Unità nell'Equilibrio.
Nel Piano viene riversata la verifica formale di una «non» impossibile Armonia, funzionale e quindi civile, tra Interesse Generale e Particolare.
Si cerca di individuare una maglia bidimensionale in cui tutte le componenti si equilibrano con eguali gradi di libertà e servizi, che il Collettivo sembra chiamato a organizzare e distribuire omogeneamente.
Come tramite il più generale possibile, il « Traffico » diviene lo « schema "oggettivo" » del funzionamento generale, struttura urbana non di servizio, ma schema « figurale » e razionale del formarsi del fenomeno urbano ordinato.
Secondo un naturale procedere dal generale al particolare, per poi risalire con una verifica inversa, il traffico individua spontaneamente, per negativo, le Zone del Privato, aree libere e neutre, nelle quali si realizza, attraverso il delicato equilibrio dei "quanti", il giusto e scientifico rapporto tra componenti naturali e privacy.
La raggiunta omogeneità sul piano degli interessi, e quindi dei servizi, viene rappresentata nello skyline del Centro Direzionale, o Cuore della Città, « luogo visuale » dove l'attività terziaria testimonia nella sua accumulazione della avvenuta "naturalità" del potere, fornendo l'immagine campione del Progettato: frutto dell'Armonia tra Individuale, Collettivo, Naturale e Funzionale.
La città come struttura degli « Scambi » e del « Commercio » (e quindi basata sulla funzione fondamentale del Traffico), trae la propria conferma « intensiva » e « concentrica » dalla Civilità Ferroviaria del secolo scorso.
Sui « nodi » di una rete di collegamenti territoriali si collocano le Città Capolinea, intervallate dalla sequenza continua del "Paesaggio", che per la prima volta viene scoperto come un sistema connettivo generale, bene dell'intera comunità nazionale e non più patrimonio dei singoli fenomeni urbani e abitativi.
La città degli Scambi e del Commercio, in quanto Realizzato Equilibrio tra Particolare e Generale, e Libertà massima del singolo nell'insieme, configura le condizioni ideali per la Libera Circolazione delle Merci, struttura utopica della Libera Creazione dei Valori, attraverso tessuti omogenei, limitati ma generalizzanti, intorno ai « segmenti Produttivi », sacrificati e parziali rispetto al Tutto.

La città diviene così all'untempo strumento di « Integrazione » e di « Giudizio ».
Come libera circolazione dei « modelli di comportamento », e come campus all'interno del quale l'« interclassismo » raggiunge "l'oggettività di un ambiente naturale", la città pur contraddittoria e choccante, stimola alla adozione « totale » del fenomeno sociale.
L'Ideologia di Classe, recepita sui luoghi di lavoro come esatta percezione della struttura produttiva e dei suoi meccanismi di sfruttamento, ottiene la sua conferma generale a contatto del "quadro visivo" e quindi "razionale" della città come strumento di trasformazione economica.
48 Il Caos e l'Ordine, il Pubblico e il Privato, il Centro e la Periferia, la Residenza e il Lavoro divengono termini oggettuali di una tensione politica alla quale la città sembra costituire l'« inalienabile premessa ».
L'esperienza visiva, diretta quindi, rimane la premessa per l'utilizzazione della città come momento di « Conoscenza attraverso la Prassi » per una nascente Volontà Rivoluzionaria.
La sua Concentrazione ne garantisce la Fatalità Strategica, sia come accumulazione di Funzioni Vitali al Sistema, sia però come inevitabile verifica, come trabocchetto di un inevitabile campo di battaglia.
« Metropoli » come realtà formale di un Equilibrio tra Interessi Generali e Particolari, tra Tecnica e Natura, e la Rivoluzione Permanente dei « Redditi » all'interno dello Sviluppo Equilibrato del Sistema, divengono adesso chiaramente due facce dello stesso identico problema Ideologico del Capitale.

Il rifiuto del dato "naturale" come coefficiente di fatalità nella Ideologia della Metropoli: questo è il primo atto da compiere sul percorso della sua « demistificazione ».
La Città degli Scambi e del Commercio, naturale equilibrio tra Particolare e Generale, Libertà Massima del Singolo nell'Insieme (cioè la Città come Garanzia al completamento "spontaneo" del Ciclo Produttivo), al momento in cui nel Piano si realizza l'« identità » tra Produzione e Consumi, vede crollare proprio quel mito naturistico della Libera Concorrenza sul quale si basava.
Le condizioni Ideali di un mercato, sviluppato ed equilibrato dalla dinamica dialettica della Domanda e dell'Offerta, vengono sostituite di fatto da un massiccio ed omogeneo sviluppo di un sistema in grado di creare e sostenere "artificialmente" i consumi attraverso l'induzione della domanda come Bisogno Apparente, in ogni momento e in ogni luogo.
La manipolazione dei media « elettronici » e delle telecomunicazioni, permette di fare circolare i "modelli di consumo" come "modelli artificiali di comportamento"; lo "choc" viene utilizzato come tecnica traumatica in grado di creare artificialmente un salto di tensione nella massa dei consumatori.
Così il caricamento di "contenuti" nella merce, cioè la feticizzazione del prodotto, permette di creare fenomeni di « ideologia artificiale » come copertura culturale del Consumo.

Tale processo avviene solo in minima parte attraverso la "prassi urbana" diretta: la circolazione elettronica dei modelli permette una infiltrazione "profonda", omogenea e totale, nella realtà non discontinua del fenomeno sociale.
L'Induzione dei Modelli di Consumo diviene lo strumento di integrazione più mistificante: il Capitale propone nel Consumo un suo proprio Modello Sociale che supera la realtà di Classe, in quanto presuppone al suo sviluppo una realtà sociale omogenea.
Un meccanismo del genere non ha più bisogno dei presupposti dell'Equilibrio Naturale che la Città gli fornisce: egli stesso è pronto adesso a divenire Natura, grazie alla sua "azione profonda", che gli garantisce una modificazione permanente anche se duttile del reale.
La metropoli che perde, nello sviluppo del Sistema, il proprio ruolo di "rappresentazione sociale", è una metropoli che perde l' "immagine di se stessa"!
Essa cessa di essere un "luogo" per divenire una "con-

dizione"; è tale "condizione" che viene fatta circolare in maniera omogenea nel reale attraverso i Consumi.
La dimensione della Megalopoli allora non è più quella di un mostruoso gigantismo della vecchia città, legata ai suoi equilibri come modelli formali, ma è la dimensione del Mercato stesso che supera la distinzione tra urbano ed agricolo all'interno della propria capacità di razionalizzare (produttivamente) l'intero fenomeno geografico.
La "capacità di rappresentare il Sistema" quindi, come una realtà esterna, in sviluppo sul territorio, cade: il sistema diviene una condizione isotropa di essere che « si rappresenta benissimo da sola ».
Tutti gli attuali sforzi di attribuire ancora alla città questa capacità di rappresentazione, come "macchina gigante" o come "struttura degli scambi", non servono altro che a attribuire significato ad una struttura che « significa soltanto se stessa ».
Il "ready made" torna così al suo posto esatto, dentro la propria catena di montaggio, ad assolvere la propria "specifica funzione meccanica".
Il Capitale trova ormai in se stesso la conferma al proprio dover-essere: esso tutto insieme compie il salto che lo porta sulla Luna. Così si realizza sulla Terra l'Unità che è per il Capitale Unità nell'Economia.

L'Identificazione del Capitale con il Mondo attraverso la "necessità" naturale del Benessere, permette di fare assurgere la « logica » della Produzione Industriale al valore di Legge Universale.
La Logica della Produzione Industriale è rappresentata compiutamente dalla legge della « Catena di Montaggio ».
La « Serie » infatti è la Matrice di tutti i Modelli Sociali del Capitale: l'Oggetto Prodotto Industrialmente è un oggetto che contiene in se stesso il proprio "smontaggio", contenendo « implicitamente » la logica meccanica che lo ha prodotto. Ogni singola "parte" della Serie è assolutamente omogenea all'insieme: non esistono, e non devono esistere, gerarchie di valore nella realtà, causa la frattura della Catena stessa.
La "legge del montaggio" diviene anche la legge della « socialità della merce », in quanto nella serie i singoli oggetti perdono significato, e lo acquista la relazione intercorrente nella « catena », alla quale è l'« utente » stesso che dà significato, divenendo parte fondamentale del processo.

La Città allora, come "catena di montaggio del sociale", è in grado di restituire il maggior numero possibile di interrelazioni della catena stessa: essa diviene la « struttura stabile » delle comunicazioni sociali, l'insieme dei punti di distribuzione delle informazioni elettroniche e dei Consumi.
L'identificazione tra Capitale Industriale e Civilità Urbana ha questo significato: il Capitale, che nasce nella città, vi identifica il proprio modello di comportamento, come verifica di integrazione e come negazione alla propria « alternativa » preliminare che è la Campagna.
Ma allora, se Capitale e non-Capitale, scompaiono nel Piano, scompare la contraddizione che stava a monte della città stessa e che presiedeva la sua "formazione": l'Urbano e l'Agricolo.
È la città stessa allora che tende a scomparire: l'unità della Metropoli nel paesaggio si realizza infatti nella unificazione degli interessi economici.

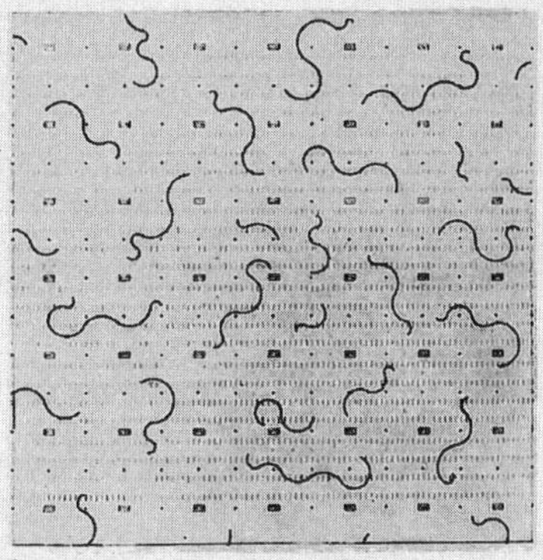
9

10

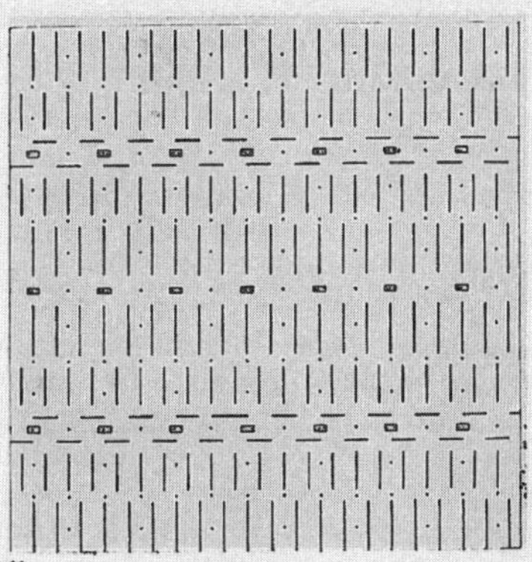
11

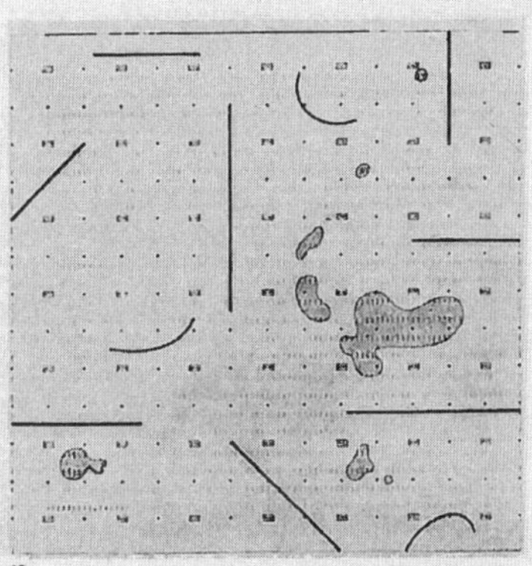
12

9-10-11-12 Diagrammi abitativi omogenei.

Il « terreno », nella logica del Piano, equivale al Sociale nella logica dei Consumi: assoluta omogeneità e continuità causa l'interferenza di un coefficiente " autre " non programmato.
La Metropoli come « concentrazione » dunque non è altro che l'interferenza di interessi particolari all'interno dell'intero sistema: maggiore concentrazione = maggiori rendite fondiarie. A questa logica parziale il Capitale Programmato risponde: maggiore estensione = maggiore controllo. Estensione Totale = Controllo della Realtà.
Le due posizioni risultano antitetiche solo apparentemente: la rendita fondiaria concentrata, come la concentrazione industriale, sono residui dell'accumularsi « spontaneo » del Capitale. Adesso che egli acquista nel Piano coscienza del proprio essere come "bene sociale", realizza la propria "giusta distribuzione".
L'Eterna tensione dunque tra interesse particolare e interesse Generale si ricompone nella Programmazione come Equilibrio nell'Ordine.
La concentrazione della Metropoli dipende inoltre dalla prevalenza della attività « terziaria » su qualsiasi altro genere di attività: essa concentra le funzioni ed intensifica il tessuto. Questo perché la fase Spontanea del Capitale costringe la gestione degli interessi ad organizzarsi sul luogo degli scambi.
All'interno del Piano, in cui le responsabilità sono demandate a strutture politiche scalate progressivamente sul territorio, tale prevalenza può essere capovolta. La Città del Capitale può presentarsi allora come "habitat", struttura funzionale al seguito di scelte civili preliminari, tese a risolvere il "bene urbano primo", il suo stesso destino, cioè appunto l' "abitare".
La Città del Capitale, come soluzione di una "funzione primaria", diviene dunque un "habitat" di servizi complementari, struttura antropologica, "grande villaggio", ritrovando così una possibile gerarchia delle scelte ed un possibile Ordine Naturale al suo interno. La struttura urbana conferma il suo ruolo di "mistificazione" della realtà del "lavoro". La "Proletarizzazione" torna lontana, ricacciata sul piano delle coscienze turbate.
Nell'Habitat si riproduce il « doppio » destino della Metropoli del Capitale: da una parte come struttura produttiva di "plus-valore", come estensione nel sociale della fabbrica, la città tende ad acquistare una propria brutale realtà funzionale, indipendente e atuonoma da interferenze sovrastrutturali; dall'altra come "mistificazione" della realtà del "lavoro" tende a far raggiungere alle proprie sovrastrutture la purezza di una "realtà oggettiva", divenendo addirittura la "Città del Tempo Libero".
Si riproduce così artificialmente nella Città il conflitto tra l'Ideologia del Lavoro e l'Ideologia del Tempo Libero. La prima come Struttura Stabile prefigura l'Establishment, mentre la seconda come struttura più labile, e quindi più tecnica, prefigura Valori "Autre". Si ricrea quindi artificialmente lo "choc" di una tensione, ma questa volta con segno inverso, cioè come valore di "contestazione".
La Contestazione SIMULATA dentro la città, tra due ordini diversi di strutture, garantisce la mistificazione della Protesta come Attività Creativa, difficile ma alfine positiva ai fini di un Generalizzarsi e di un Vivificarsi del Sistema.

Il fine ultimo dell'Architettura Moderna, è l'« elimina-
50 zione » dell'architettura stessa.
Questo avviene secondo la traiettoria di due forze contrarie, una centripeta e l'altra centrifuga.
Come struttura razionale tendente a risolvere il maggior numero possibile di problemi funzionali ad un livello tecnico « ottimale », l'architettura tende a conquistare soluzioni « definitive », a intendere cioè la soluzione dei problemi come progressione all'Assoluto.
In questo senso profondo l'Architettura "tende" all'Industria: identificando preliminarmente il "razionale" con il "producibile", essa tenta eroicamente di demandare all'Industria il suo stesso destino. Lo sforzo del Design infatti è proprio quello di far raggiungere al prodotto il livello ottimale di identificazione tra qualità tecnica e artistica, ponendo le premesse affinché la Produzione possa lanciarsi nella "Serie Definitiva", al di là del tempo e dello spazio, in una Società resa omogenea dai Consumi. L'Universalità della Serie assolve e giustifica l'Universalità dell'Arte. L'assolve e insieme la liquida. Il Prodotto Definitivo diviene la sua Utopia e Insieme il suo Destino.
Contemporaneamente l'Architettura, Moderna, come struttura che cerca di garantire il maggior numero possibile di gradi di libertà all'utente, all'interno di una "figurazione" la più rigida possibile, riconosce nel fenomeno urbano il suo vero « destino », ed insieme nel "privato" la sua vera « natura ».
Allora essa da una parte ammicca continuamente ad un Ordine Generale a lei identico, di cui lei anzi rappresenta la prefigurazione potenziale nel particolare, e dall'altra si pone come "difesa" di una parzialità umana su scala minore, alla quale il Generale deve far continuamente riferimento se vuole guadagnare il proprio diritto di Equilibrio Realizzato.
Tale mediazione si esaurisce nel momento in cui i rapporti tra il Particolare ed il Generale cessano di essere oggetto delle "ipotesi" reciproche e divengono realtà di fatto all'interno del Piano. La tensione etica al dover-essere si estingue al contatto dell'Essere Realizzato.

Tale chiarissima vocazione all'auto-eliminazione, della Architettura Moderna, come logica estensione nel Reale della Logica della Produzione, è sempre stata mistificata dal Capitale come valore Culturale "superiore", positivo e razionale, conferma indiretta della "naturalità" dei rapporti tra Arte e Industria.
Così, ciò che la Ragione distrugge, si ricompone più avanti come Cultura Razionale, e rientra nel Ciclo Produttivo. Ma per quale motivo il processo di Auto da Fè dell'Architettura, come intimo destino e vocazione, non ha mai raggiunto un « livello di coscienza » chiaro neppure per la Critica stessa del Movimento Moderno? Per quale motivo l'auto-distruzione non è mai divenuta un programma esplicito della Cultura Architettonica?
Le implicazioni Ideologiche della Città come equilibrio realizzato tra Tecnica e Natura, tra Individuo e Collettività, hanno costretto di fatto a limitare il processo di auto-disintegrazione della architettura, entro limiti perimetrali precisi.
Tale processo cioè si è venuto a verificare, non sulla scala dimensionale che gli era propria, e cioè quella della città, ma nei limiti tradizionali del singolo intervento, acquistando il valore di rivoluzione-disciplinare, tecnica e linguistica, ma pur sempre "architettonica".
Tali « limiti » sono quelli che "spontaneamente" certi equilibri naturali individuano: la « profondità » degli

edifici in rapporto alla « areazione » e alla « illuminazione naturale ».
Tale coefficiente, superato dunque dalla « tecnologia » delle condizioni ottimali di « lavoro » della Fabbrica, è divenuto una sorta di "sacro fossato" che non è possibile superare nella città.
Il Capitale ha rinunciato ad avere una vera città "sua", per adottare il modello settecentesco.
L'illuminazione e l'areazione naturali sono diventati così una sorta di limite spontaneo indiscutibile, capace di simulare nel Totale i limiti consentiti al Privato, e per testimoniare che ciò che si realizza nella Fabbrica non è che un fenomeno aberrante, che non può e non deve essere generalizzato alla Società.
Così i Processi Produttivi diventano di fatto Logica Generale, ma la "condizione di Fabbrica" non deve divenire "condizione generale".
Ancora una volta la proletarizzazione non deve esistere come realtà politica ma come frustrazione psicologica, frutto di una "uguaglianza" nei Consumi ma non nella Produzione!
Il Sistema che diventa "natura profonda", rifiuta di diventare "natura formale", di uniformare assolutamente alla propria logica la realtà urbana.
Come logica del "Montaggio" e dei Consumi la realtà del Capitale si presenta come realtà omogenea ed indifferenziata, sempre meno legata a processi formali e sempre più dilagante; come logica degli Equilibri Naturali tale realtà è continuamente costretta a "figurarsi", ad interrompere cioè il proprio slancio potenziale nella forma.
Poco importa se nella realtà della Metropoli attuale i termini « aria » e « luce » non esistono di fatto: il Capitale si impegna a ripristinarli, fino a solo sottintenderli.

La « tipologia » come progettazione della società, come riduzione della sua realtà a "quanti funzionali" e dimensionali, rimane una operazione ambigua. Da una parte infatti sembra accettare come "definitivo" lo stato attuale della distribuzione economica, dall'altro sembra poter prefigurare e favorire un Modello di Società diversa.
Così facendo opera su due campi diversi, quello della "realtà assoluta", e quello dell' "utopia": in questo rapporto tra "certo" e "probabile" ciò che ne risulta è il così detto coefficiente di "flessibilità", conquista dell'Architettura Moderna, come equilibrio di una « Approvazione nel Dissenso ».
Ma questo dilemma ha una origine più profonda: come "strumento conoscitivo" l'Architettura non rinuncia a considerarsi il miglior strumento di rappresentazione dell'intero Sistema, come strumento sociale essa non rinuncia al suo ruolo di Prefigurazione.
Così operando essa compie due errori uguali e distinti; crede possibile ancora un rapporto visivo col Sistema, e crede ancora funzionale alla lotta il Modello Alternativo.

L'unico punto in cui il Modello di Fabbrica e il Modello dei Consumi si identificano, è costituito dal Supermarket. Esso è il vero modello campione della Città Futura, e quindi dell'intera realtà: struttura utopica omogenea, intima funzionalità, sublimazione razionale dei Consumi. Massimo risultato con il minimo sforzo.
Il Supermarket prefigura una struttura priva di immagine, ma sistema ottimale di informazione merceologica, all'interno della quale si realizza direttamente l'omogeneità del

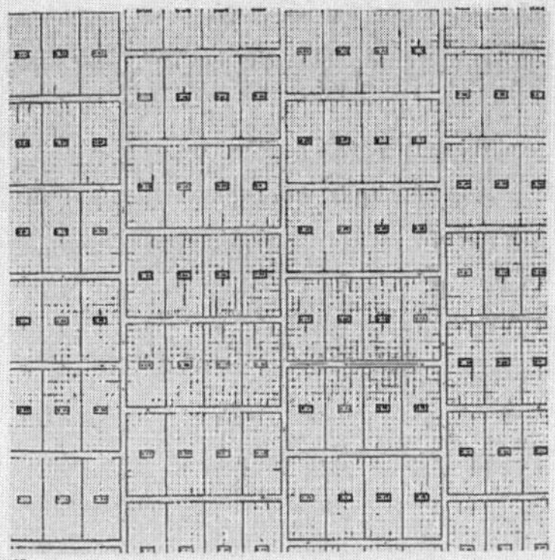
13

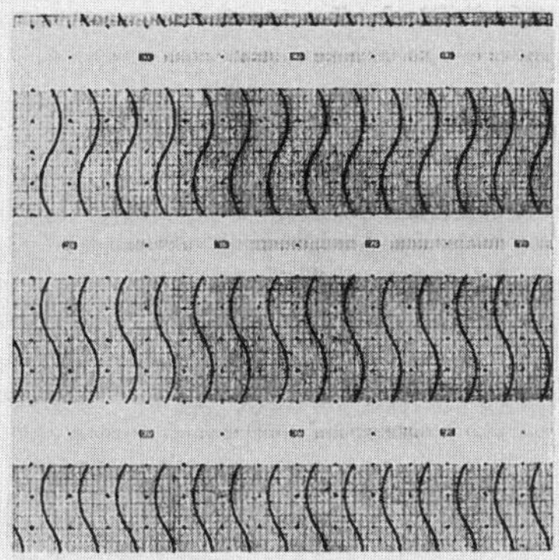
14

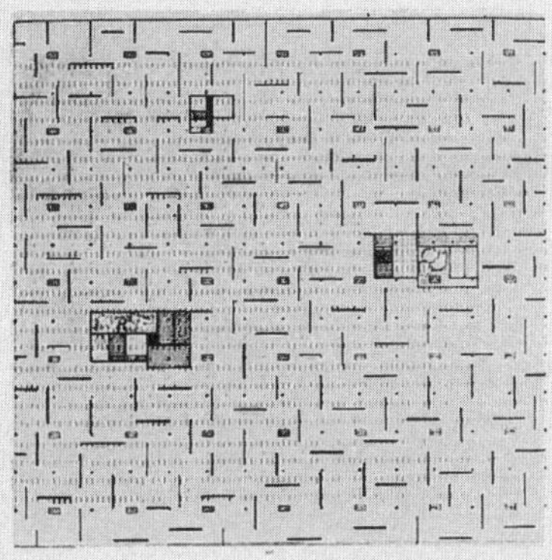
15

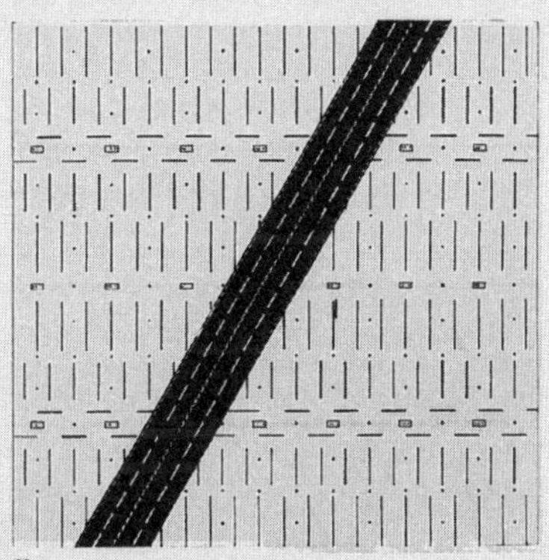
16

13-14-15-16 Diagrammi abitativi omogenei.

51

prodotto, come omogeneità di tutti i dati reali: non esistono più "zoning".
Esso diviene il campo sperimentale dove si verifica di fatto il superamento di due culture diverse del « suolo », quella urbana e quella agricola.
Come in agricoltura infatti, anche nel Market, gli "alzati" sono costituiti dalla pura accumulazione funzionale della realtà: il « paesaggio » non esiste più come fenomeno esterno, poiché la "natura profonda" del Capitale diviene libertà formale ad esprimere liberamente tutta la propria potenzialità razionale.
Nel Market il Settore Terziario, il Controllo degli Interessi, tende a divenire un diaframma verticale bidimensionale, una sezione neutra omogenea e trasparente di scambio tra Interessi diversi, priva di una propria struttura.

Affinché dunque le singole funzioni non siano costrette ad incastrarsi secondo la logica settecentesca degli Equilibri Naturali, la città deve organizzarsi su livelli di scorrimento diversi, su una stratificazione di "piani liberi" omogenei.
La struttura delle Comunicazioni deve giuocare il proprio ruolo di "servizio"; il « traffico » non rappresenta una logica propria, con leggi « esterne » al fenomeno urbano. La rete delle Comunicazioni deve infatti fornire un circuito « continuo », non interrotto dal "privato", in maniera tale da servire ad un livello ottimale il piano « continuo delle informazioni », che diviene la struttura bidimensionale portante, il piano di scorrimento generale.
Tale piano individua una griglia razionale e regolare di comunicazioni verticali. I piani superiori risultano serviti in maniera uniforme da tale griglia: essi sono costituiti da un tessuto di impianti tecnici che forniscono le condizioni di illuminazione e areazione ottimali. I perimetri di tali strutture continue orizzontali, cadono secondo « caso » o secondo « criterio »: in ogni modo essi non rappresentano che una sezione verticale del fenomeno, senza mai costituire l'insieme dei punti in cui si realizza la migliore condizione di contatto tra struttura e natura.
È all'interno di tale sistema artificiale infatti che si organizza bidimensionalmente l' "abitare", come libera ed infinita combinazione di possibilità diverse, in espansione all'interno di un piano continuo.
Dentro tale tessuto, senza soluzione di continuità, si collocano i servizi sociali ed i consumi, come piccole piastre fisse all'interno di un campo magnetico in continua rivoluzione.
Il piano di « affioramento » di tale sistema, cioè il suo livello massimo, è costituito dalla "natura", cioè dalla superficie di contatto diretto con il sole e con la luce.
Tale piano allora non è più la superficie di incastro tra figurazione naturale e figurazione urbana: la politica delle "immagini" reciproche e complementari è superata di fatto dalla « non discontinuità » sia della « città » che della « natura ».
L'organizzazione su livelli diversi delle funzioni urbane garantisce di fatto il superamento della città come equilibrio: la Metropoli diviene oggettivamente una Categoria Quantitativa, priva di immagine, cioè di « ideologia propria », sistema razionale che nasce nel Capitale ed acquista in questo la coscienza di una propria Teoria.

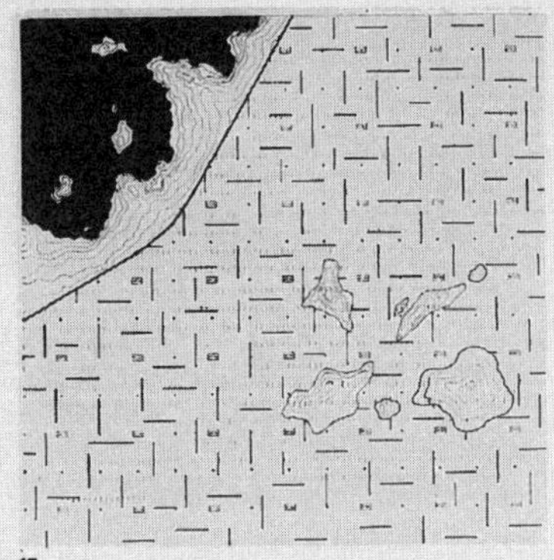
17

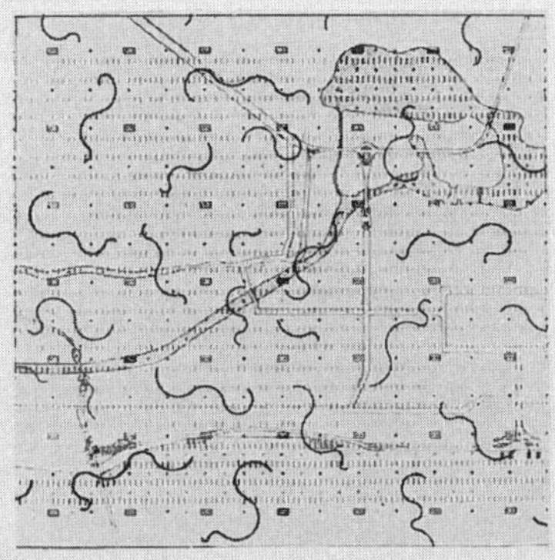
18

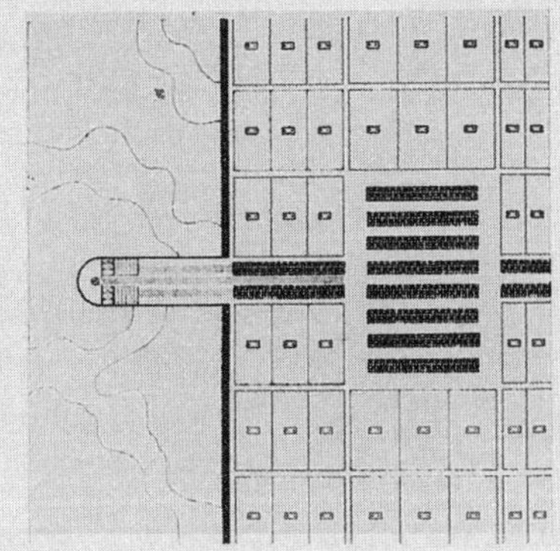
19

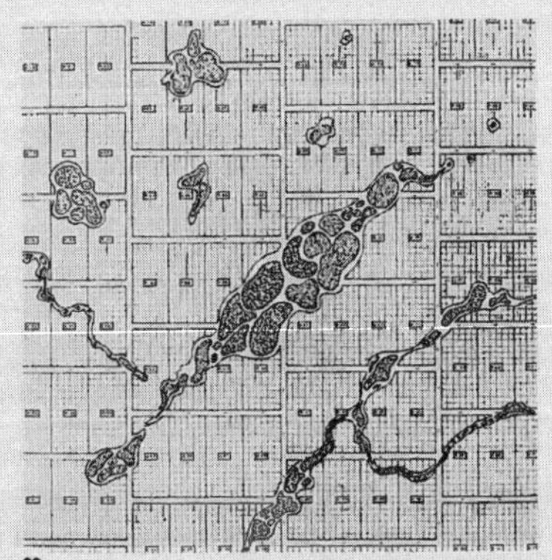
20

17-18-19-20 Diagrammi abitativi omogenei.

Utopia of Quality, Utopia of quantity
Archizoom Associati, 1971

//

The Metropolis, as a physical and social phenomenon, comes into being in the Capital and develops within its own Logic; the Capital imposes its own general Ideology on it, which conditions its development and its configuration. This general Ideology is made up of the *Policy of Balances between Opposites*. The Revolution of Revenues in the economic Balance (where trade union claims are concerned) is made *de facto* at the level of urban functioning.

The Metropolis achieves *identity* and *harmony* between private interest and collective interest. *The Policy of Balance between Opposites* is also the Policy of Balance between the internal *Contradictions* of the Capital itself: as a natural extension of the Factory Model in Society, the Metropolis of the Capital actually claims the autonomous freedom of being configured as a brutal functional system, an immediate projection of the Logic of Production; at the same time, as a balance made between individual Interest and general Interest, the Metropolis is called upon to configure by force both Nature and Technology on a single level of all experiences, start to finish, spontaneously achieving the anthropological balance of opposites, and becoming a kind of "Big Village."

It is, however, crucial to point out right away that: *the working-class Metropolis does not exist*. In fact, just as there is no such thing as political Class Economy, but merely a Class Critique of political Economy, so there is no such thing as any urbanistic Class Theory, but just a Class Critique of Urbanistic Theory.

The Utopia that we use is thus solely language. A more general Critique, which permits more immediate and more direct Communication: this Utopia does not actually position itself on the level of the *Quantitative* battle of Values, but on the level of the *Quantitative* challenge. Without coming up with global alternatives in the guise of preliminaries, it accepts the very Logic of Production, like a confrontational plan between the two contradictions of the System: *maximum Quantity and maximum Balance*.

The Modern Metropolis, even at its advanced degree of technologization, has no option but to accept certain Natural Balances as the internal law of its own configuration, like the depth of buildings in relation to ventilation and *natural lighting*. This notwithstanding, we can see that, at the points where the system directly achieves its own functional rationality at the urban level, in actually goes beyond the "spontaneous" limit of *light* and *air*; creating unitary artificial systems which are raised to the rank of general urban Models, no less.

These model or standard points are represented by the *Factory* and the *Supermarket*. As a Productive Structure, which is still partial in relation to society taken as a whole, the former in fact foreshadows the whole of urban organization, as a homogeneous system of services and space, going beyond the association, bequeathed by the 19th century, of the different urban functions still in effect in the metropolis.

As a *Structure of Consumption*, the latter fore shadows an absolute circulation of goods on the urban ground, like the direct creation of a traditional system of Consumer organization.

In both cases we can see an identical ideology of ground and space: the Metropolis, as a meeting point of Production and Consumption, is thus subject to *this law*, and to no other; and as a social phenomenon it is subordinate to it; this is a viewpoint requiring examination. So it is within a single objective law of ground and space, conceived as perforce *homogeneous* and *not discontinuous* realities in the Logic of Production and Consumption, that the Model of the non discontinuous and homogeneous City is created, in the homogeneity and the non discontinuity of the Countryside, in so far as both realities act on two planes which unfold differently.

On the one hand, Architecture stops being Natural, and on the other hand, Nature stops being Culture. This Urban Model does not, however, represent the alternative to present day reality; rather, it represents present day reality at a new level of Critical Consciousness.

Fortezza da Basso
Archizoom Associati, 1968

///

Radical architecture began in 1968, when different groups were formed and consolidated, each acquiring a clearer identity.

That year a competition for the new headquarters of the Craft Fair inside the Fortezza da Basso was announced in Florence. It was the occasion of a sort of derby among the Radicals: Superstudio participated with a Kahanian pop pyramidal model, symmetrical and full of pipes; Archizoom with a germinal project, a single large industrial covering, inexpressive, which occupied the entire area of the Fair incorporating the historical pre-existences.

None of us won the project, which was realized much later by the studio of Pier Luigi Spadolini.

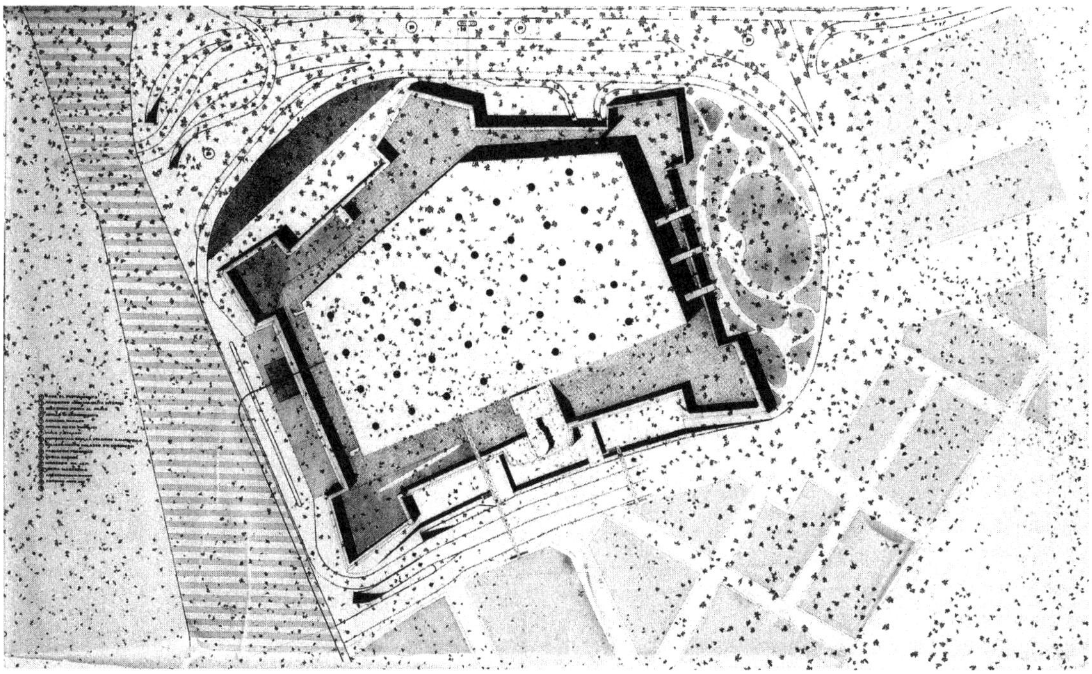

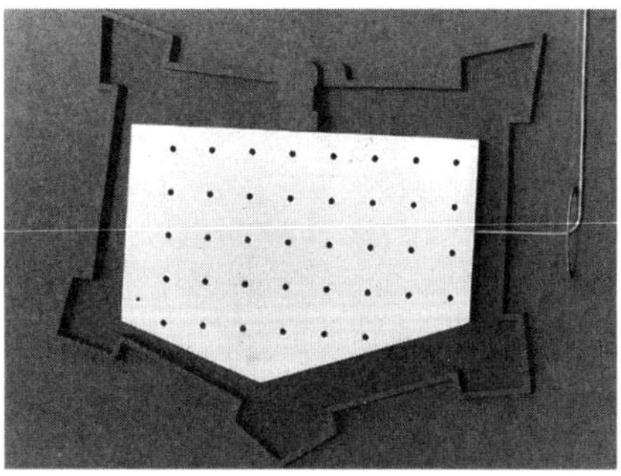

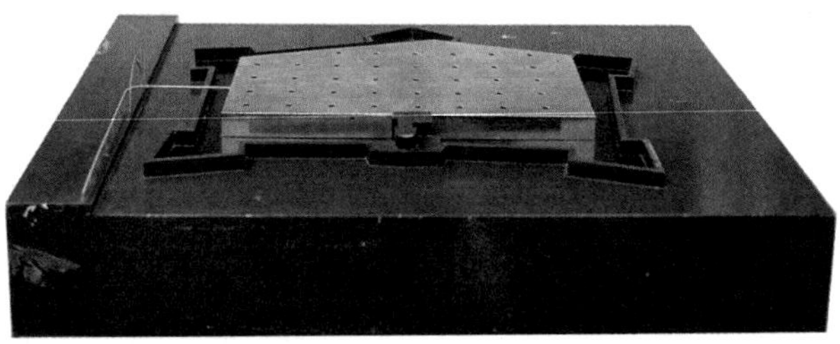

Archizoom Associati, Competition, *Fortezza da Basso*, 1968

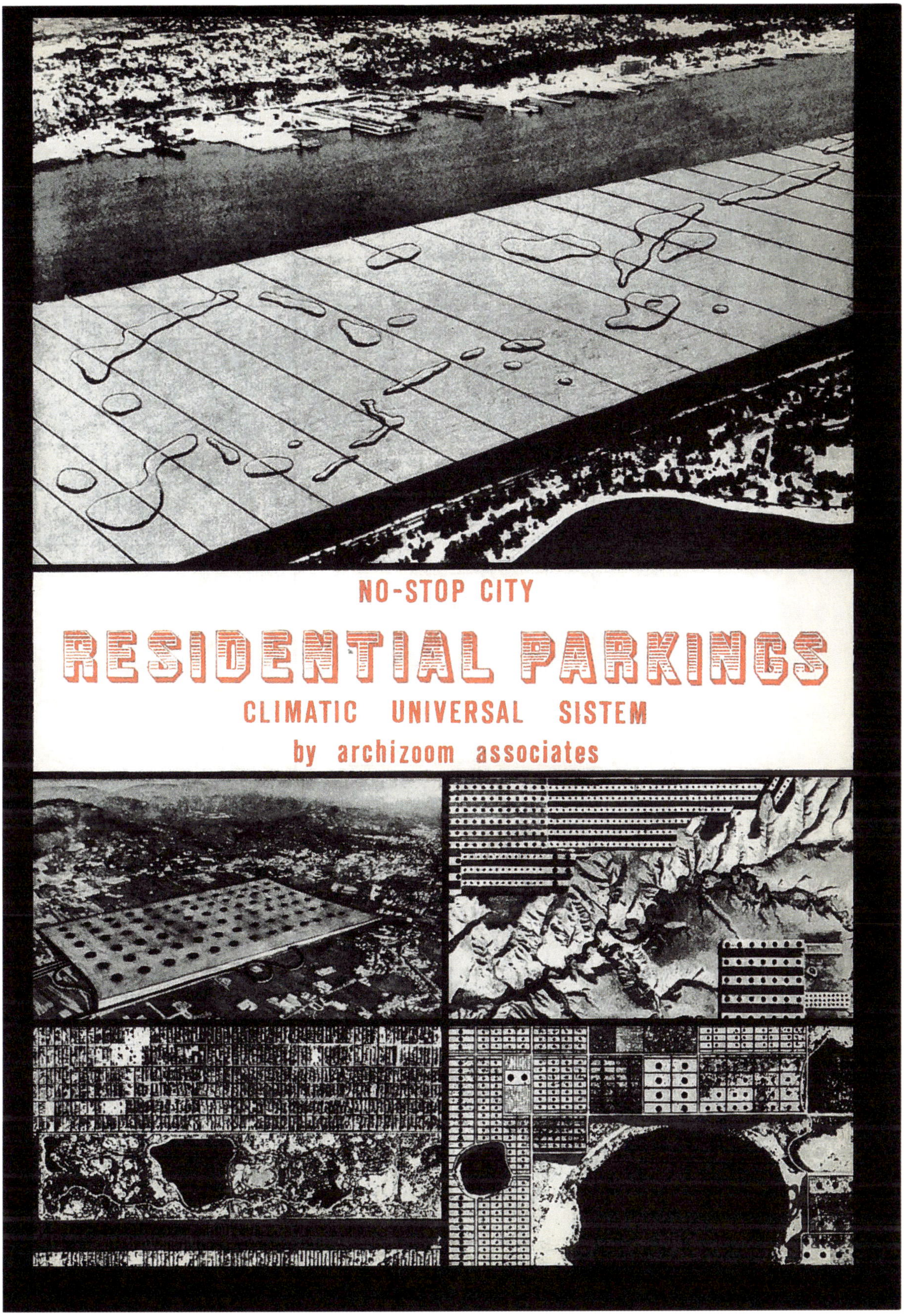

Archizoom Associati, "No-Stop City Residential Parkings Climatic Universal Sistem," in *Domus* n. 496, 1971

...ei esempi di piano abitativo continuo

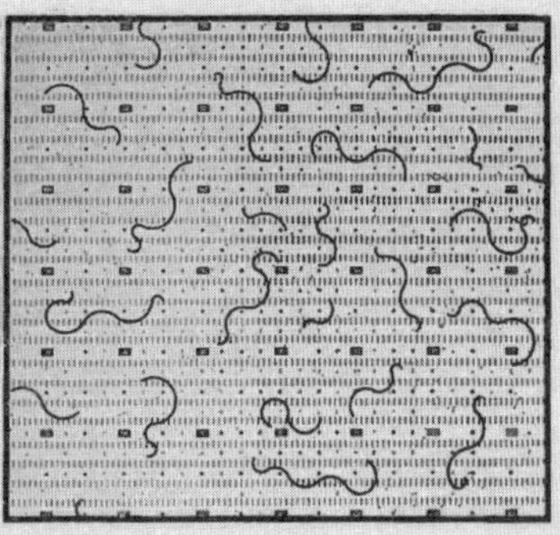

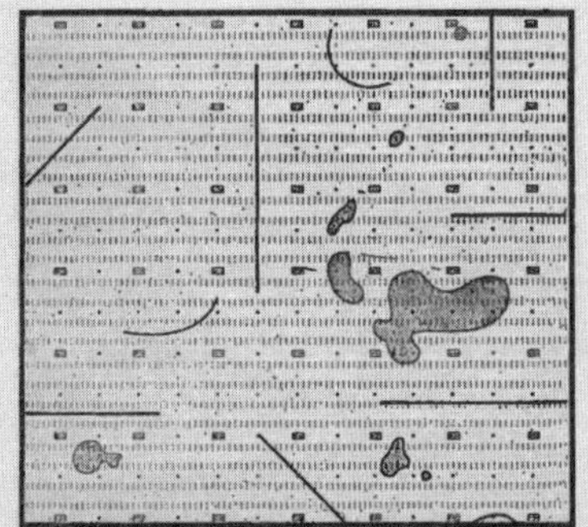

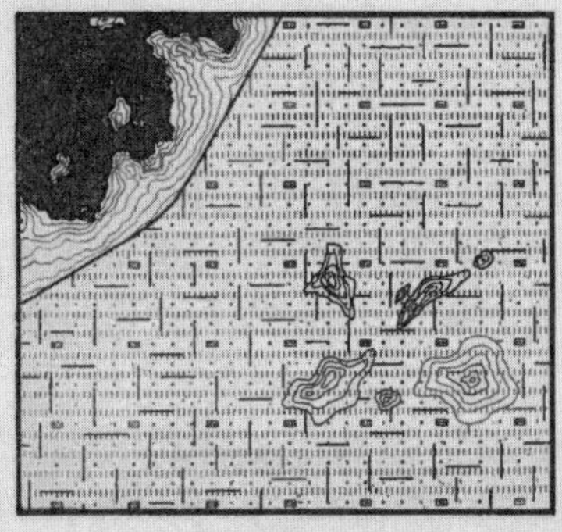

« Non esiste oggi alcun dubbio nel riconoscere nel fenomeno urbano il punto più debole dell'intero sistema industriale.
La metropoli, tradizionale « scena madre del Progresso », è oggi di fatto il settore più arretrato e confuso della realtà del Capitale; e tutto questo ad un tale livello che viene da domandarsi se la città moderna, più che un problema non risolto, non sia un fenomeno storico oggettivamente superato.
Bisogna cioè capire se il Capitale si pone ancora oggi, come un secolo fa, il problema della gestione della propria immagine e del proprio funzionamento al livello della forma urbana, o se piuttosto le trasformazioni avvenute ed in atto non hanno trasferito la sua realtà su di un'altra scala, trasformando il concetto stesso di città.
In questo momento dunque il problema non è più quello di immaginare una metropoli più umana e più ordinata, ma piuttosto quello di capire profondamente le leggi oggettive che presiedono al configurarsi del fenomeno urbano-architettonico, demistificando la complessa ideologia che ne accompagna il dibattito e ne condiziona la forma.

Il mito naturalistico della libera concorrenza poneva la città degli scambi e del commercio a garantire le condizioni ideali del mercato, realizzando l'equilibrio naturale tra gli opposti interessi, nel quadro generale della raggiunta armonia tra tecnica e natura.
Oggi l'uso dei medium elettronici sostituisce la prassi urbana diretta: l'induzione artificiale al consumo permette una ben più profonda infiltrazione nella realtà sociale che non i fragili canali di informazione della città.
La metropoli cessa di essere un « luogo » per divenire una « condizione »; è proprio tale condizione infatti che viene fatta circolare in maniera omogenea nel fenomeno sociale attraverso i Consumi.
La dimensione futura della Metropoli coincide con quella del Mercato stesso.

La metropoli come concentrazione intensiva corrisponde alla fase ormai superata della accumulazione spontanea del Capitale.
In una società programmata infatti la gestione degli interessi non ha più necessità di organizzarsi sul luogo stesso degli scambi.
La totale disponibilità del territorio e la sua totale penetrabilità elimina la città-capolinea e permette l'organizzazione di una maglia progressiva di organismi di controllo su di esso.

Nella ideologia borghese equilibrio ecologico e giustizia sociale diventano parti di una stessa battaglia: la città fornisce con la propria immagine la verifica formale di tale equilibrio.
Nel Piano Urbanistico dunque viene ricercata la non impossibile armonia tra l'Interesse Generale e quello Particolare: tali categorie però vengono

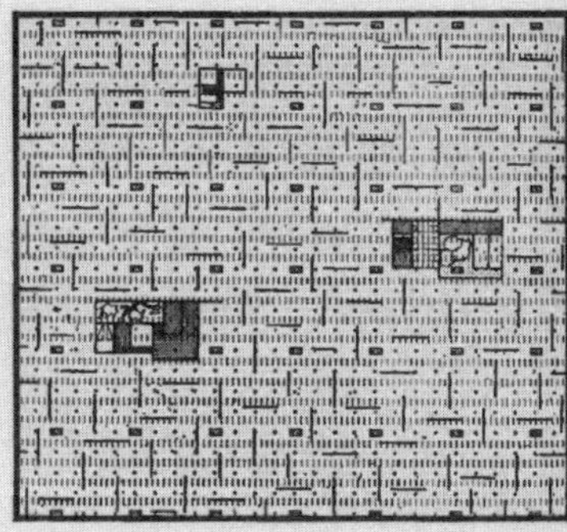

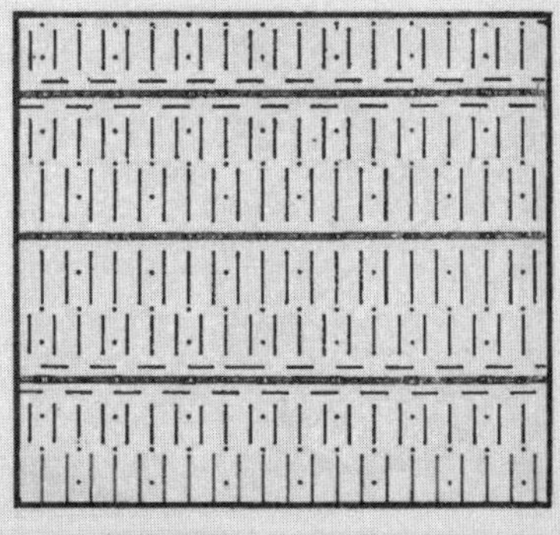

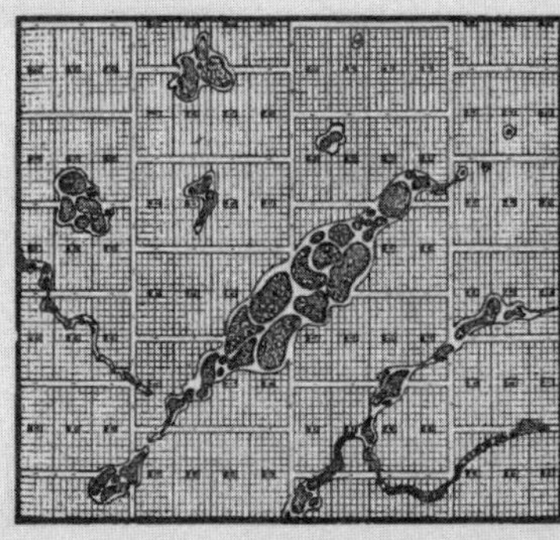

▶ paesaggio interno — interior landscape

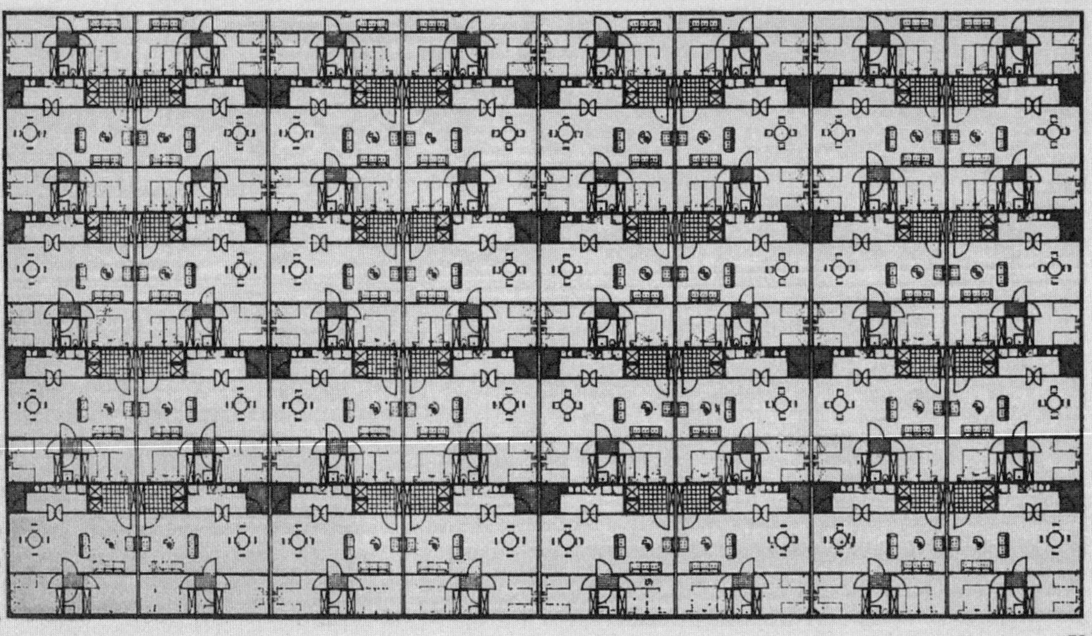

piano tipologico continuo

PATATE CHIPS
RITZ

struttura teatrale continua — non-stop theatre

sempre acquisite come fenomeni antitetici, contrastanti e non mediabili.
Il problema diventa allora quello di trovare una maglia bidimensionale che garantisca l'incastro di tali componenti non solubili.
Come tramite il più generale possibile, il traffico diventa allora lo schema oggettivo e figurale del funzionamento urbano. La strada infatti non solo serve il tessuto compatto del privato, ma lo « seziona » e lo « figura » anche, individuando i piani di affioramento del linguaggio architettonico.
Lo skyline diventa il diagramma della avvenuta accumulazione naturale del Capitale stesso.
La metropoli borghese resta quindi soprattutto un luogo visuale, e la sua esperienza rimane legata a tale tipo di comunicazione.

L'attuazione della organizzazione sociale del lavoro attraverso il Piano, elimina quello « spazio » vuoto nel quale il Capitale si espandeva nel proprio processo di crescita.
Non esiste più infatti una realtà esterna al sistema stesso: l'intero rapporto visuale con la realtà viene meno, cessando di esistere la distanza tra il soggetto e il fenomeno. La città non « rappresenta » più il sistema, ma « diviene » il sistema stesso, programmato ed isotropo, in cui le diverse funzioni sono contenute in maniera omogenea e senza contraddizioni.

La Produzione e i Consumi possiedono una identica ideologia, che è quella della Programmazione. Ambedue ipotizzano infatti una realtà sociale e fisica assolutamente continua e indifferenziata. Non esistono realtà autres.
La Fabbrica e il Supermarket diventano di fatto i veri modelli campione della città futura: strutture urbane ottimali, potenzialmente infinite, dove le funzioni si dispongono spontaneamente su di un piano libero, reso omogeneo da un sistema di microclimatizzazione e informazione ottimale.
Gli equilibri « naturali e spontanei » della luce e dell'aria sono superati di fatto: la casa diviene un'area di parcheggio attrezzato. Nel suo interno non esistono gerarchie o figurazioni spaziali condizionanti.

La tipologia, come figurazione funzionale della società, incerta tra il rilevamento di una realtà sociale come dato certo, e l'assunzione delle aspirazioni di tale realtà come dato probabile, resta impigliata nella restituzione allegorica di tale conflitto, che diviene un coefficiente culturale extra-funzionale.
Cercando di fornire il maggior numero di gradi di libertà all'utente, all'interno di una « figurazione » la più rigida possibile, l'architettura si trova a riconoscere nel fenomeno urbano il suo vero destino, e nel privato la sua vera natura.
Così in maniera contradditoria essa prefigura in ogni singola occasione un ordine generale delle cose, e contemporaneamente si pone a difesa della parzialità della esperienza individuale nei riguardi delle esperienze collettive.
Essa media così in maniera figurale, la contraddizione tra pubblico e privato; oggi però tale conflitto non viene più lasciato al livello speculativo della pura coscienza esistenziale. Il Piano, organizzando produttivamente tutta la società, elimina tale conflitto, riconosce come apparente tale contraddizione e assume come sperimentale qualsiasi dato su scala strettamente individuale.

Fino ad oggi la grande massa della gente è rimasta esclusa dal fenomeno architettonico: ospite temporanea di un existenz-minimum integrativo di una giornata lavorativa ben più reale, la gente ha usato la casa per mangiare e dormire.
In essa tutto era già individuato da un'architettura consolatoria; restava solo da attaccare i quadretti alle pareti. La casa era il primo e più importante gradino della adozione totale del modello di vita borghese.
Ma oggi, forte di una nuova e sempre crescente capacità autodecisionale conquistata sui luoghi di lavoro, la gente si deve impossessare della casa, liberandola da qualsiasi modello culturale e sociale precostituito, liquidando i sottili legami intellettuali e gli isterici nodi linguistici che caratterizzano l'architettura come figurazione dello spazio.
Liberata dalle proprie « armature caratteriali », la architettura deve diventare una struttura aperta, disponibile alla produzione intellettuale di massa come unica forza figurante il paesaggio collettivo.
Il problema diventa dunque quello di liberare l'uomo dalla architettura, come struttura formale.

Oggi l'unica utopia possibile è quella quantitativa.
Il conflitto sociale infatti non passa più attraverso la contrapposizione di modelli alternativi, ma

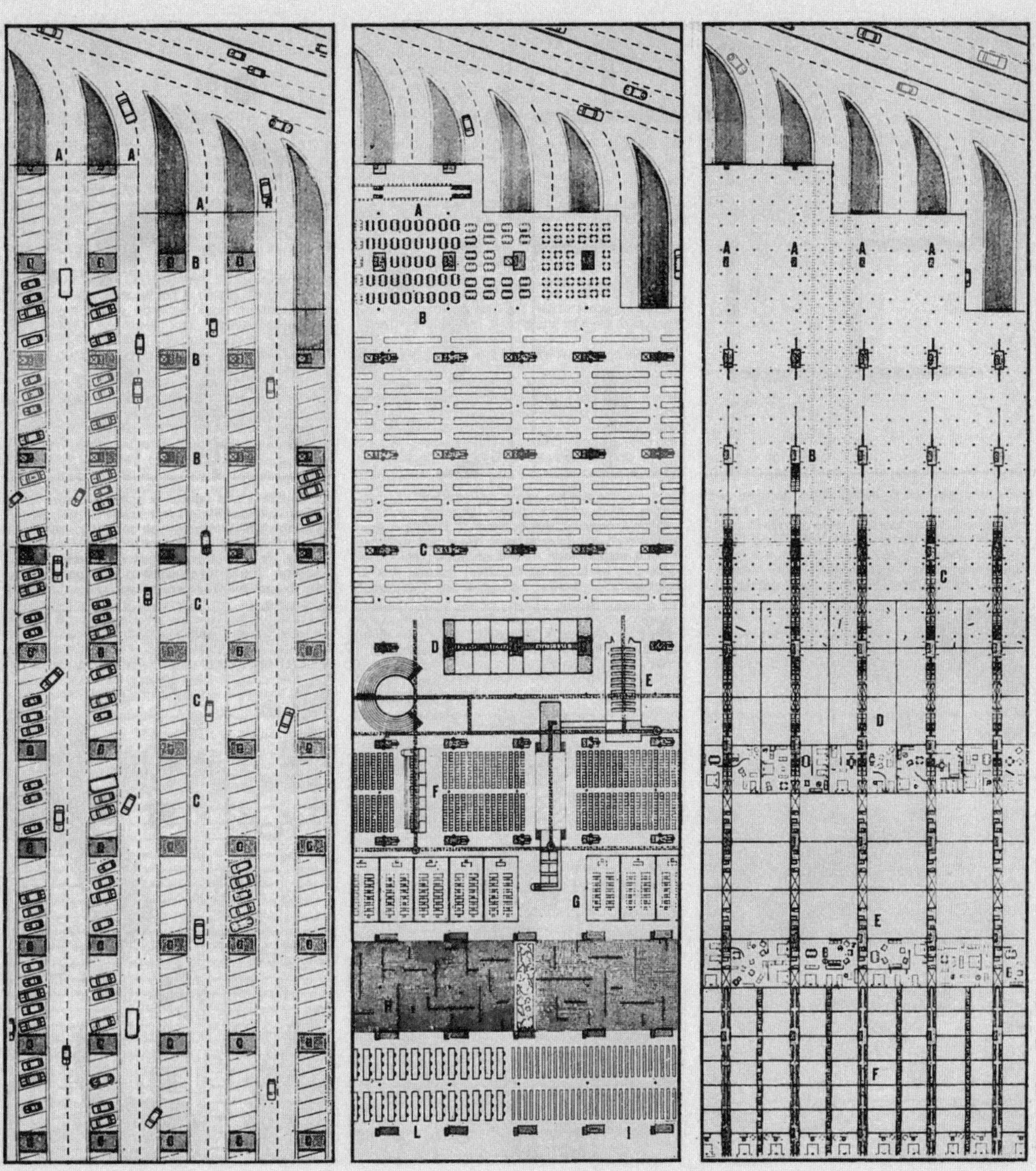

piano continuo di penetrazione del traffico: A corsie di penetrazione; B sistema regolare di comunicazioni verticali; C parcheggi

piano continuo di servizi: A tavola calda; B ristorante; C supermarket; D uffici; E cinema; F teatro; G scuola; H esposizioni; I archivi; L biblioteca

piano continuo di parcheggi residenziali: A sistema regolare di comunicazioni verticali; B accessi; C assi attrezzati; D appartamenti per coppie; E appartamenti familiari; F camere singole

attraverso la dialettica contrattazione tra uno sviluppo equilibrato del sistema e un crescente costo della forza lavoro.
Lo scontro non avviene più su di un piano ideologico ma in termini quantitativi: è attraverso tale parametro che si rende possibile la sommatoria di fenomeni diversi apparentemente tra loro non collegati.
Il linguaggio quantitativo sostituisce quello della qualità, divenendo l'unico medium scientifico per l'approccio alla stratificazione indifferenziata della produzione, e quindi della realtà.
Scomparendo i quadri generali di riferimento, il comportamento diventa una struttura priva di allegorie morali.
La libertà, come fine, diventa subito strumento di lotta ».

Nowadays there can be no hesitation in admitting that the urban phenomenon is the weakest point in the whole industrial system. The metropolis, once the traditional « birthplace of progress », is today, in fact, the most backward and confused sector of Capital in its actual state: and this is true to such an extent, that one is led to wonder if the modern city is nothing more than a problem which has not been solved, or if, in reality, it is not a historical phenomenon which has been objectively superseded. That is, we must determine whether Capital still confronts the task of managing its own organisation and image on an urban level, as it did a hundred years ago, or whether the changes which have taken and are taking place have not altered its actual sphere of action, thus transforming the concept of the city. The problem then, is no longer that of creating a metropolis which is more humane and better organized, but rather that of understanding the objective laws which control the shaping of the urban-architectural phenomenon, demistifying the complex ideology which surrounds the discussion and conditions the form it takes.

According to the naturalistic myth of free competition, it was the city, as a centre for trade and commerce, that guaranteed ideal market conditions, making for a natural equilibrium between opposite interests, in the generale background of the harmony reached between technology and nature. But now the use of electronic media takes the place of the direct urban praxis: artificial inducements to consumption allow a much deeper infiltration into the social structure than did the city's weak channels of information. The metropolis ceases to be a « place », to become a « condition »: in fact, it is just this condition which is made to circulate uniformly, through Consumer Products, in the social phenomenon. The future dimension of the metropolis coincides with that of the market itself.

The intensitively concentrated metropolis corresponds to the now superseded phase of spontaneous accumulation of Capital. In a programmized society, the management of interests no longer needs to be organized on the spot where trade is to take place. The complete penetrability and accessibility of the territory does away with the terminus city and permits the organization of a progressive network of organisms of control over the area.

tre esempi di « residential-wood »

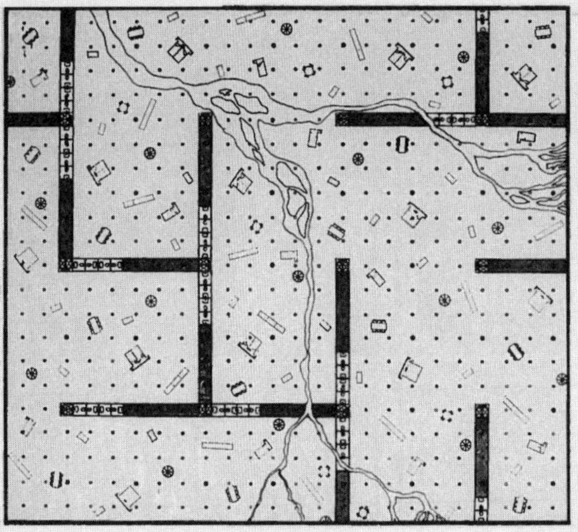

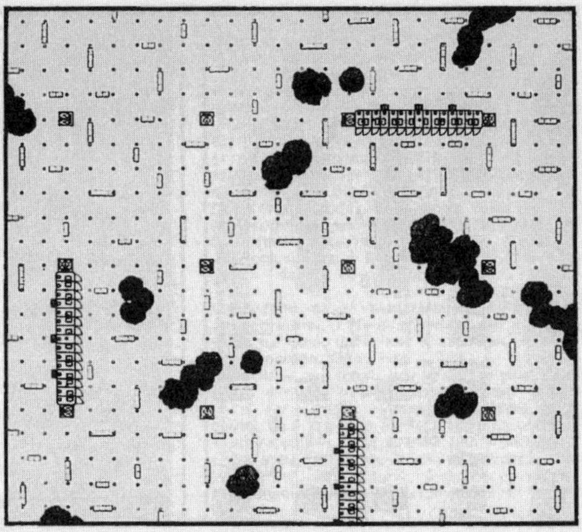

In the bourgeois ideology ecological balance and social justice become part of the same battle: the appearance of the city gives a formal verification of this equilibrium. In Town Planning, therefore, an attempt is made to achieve a not impossible harmony between the Public Interest and the Private Interest: these two categories, however, are always taken as antithetical, contrasting, and unreconcilable phenomena. The problem therefore becomes that of finding a two-dimensional net, to guarantee the fitting together of such components as are unreconcilable. The traffic can be taken as the most general link of communication between the two, as it becomes the objective and figurative schema of the functioning of urban life. In fact roads do not merely serve the compact fabric of what is private, but they also dissect it and make it communicating, making place for the emergence of architectonic language. The skyline becomes a diagram of the natural accumulation which has taken place of

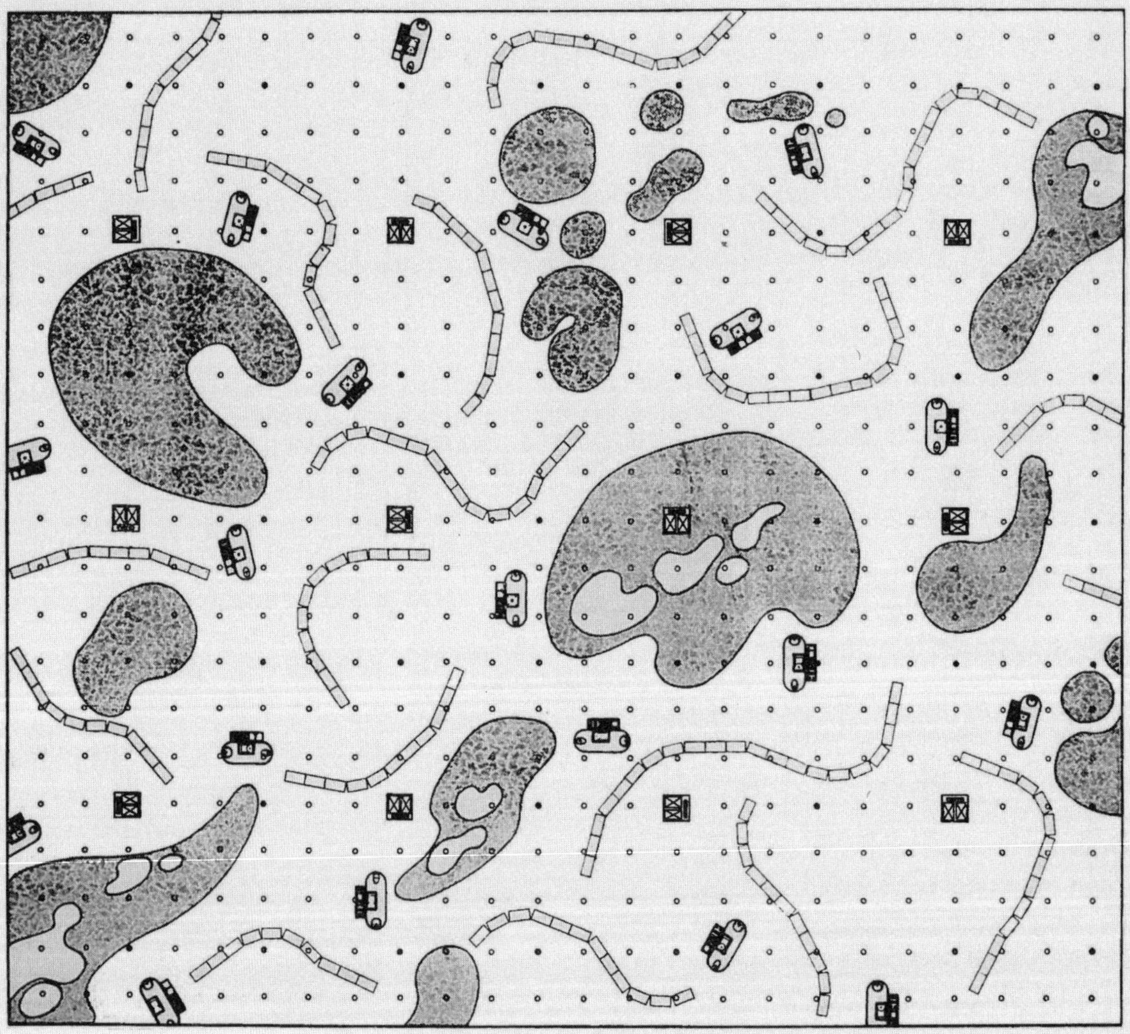

Capital itself. So the bourgeois metropolis remains mainly a visual place, and its experience remains tied to that type of communication.

The carrying out of a social organisation of labour by means of Planning eliminates the empty space in which Capital expanded during its growth period. In fact, no reality exists any longer outside the system itself: the whole visual relationship with reality loses importance as there ceases to be any distance between the subject and the phenomenon. The city no longer « represents » the system, but becomes the system itself, programmed and isotropic, and within it the various functions are contained homogenously, without contradictions.

Production and Consumption possess one and the same ideology, which is that of Programming. Both hypothesize a social and physical reality completely continuous and undifferentiated. No other realities exist. The factory and the supermarket become the specimen models of the future city: optimal urban structures, potentially limitless, where human functions are arranged spontaneously in a free field, made uniform by a system of micro-acclimatisation and optimal circulation of information. The « natural and spontaneous » balance of light and air is superseded: the house becomes a well equipped parking lot. Inside it there exist no gerarchies nor spacial figurations of a conditioning nature.

Typology, as a functional figuration of society, undecided between the certain datum of a survey of a social structure and the almost certain datum of an assumption of the aspirations of that society, rests entangled in the allegorical representation of such a conflict that it becomes an extra functional cultural coefficient. In an attempt to supply the user with the highest degree of liberty within the most rigid possible « figuration », architecture comes to recognize its real destiny in the urban phenomenon, and its real nature in the private. Thus, in contradictory fashion, on each single occasion it will prefigure a general lay-out of things and at the same time set itself up to defend the partiality of the individual experience with respect to collective experiences. Thus it mediates between the contradicting forces of public and private: now, however this conflict is no longer left on the speculative level of existential consciousness. Economic Planning, by organizing the whole of society productively, eliminates the conflict, considers the contradiction fictitious and takes any strictly individual datum as experimental.

Up till now, the mass of the general public has been excluded from the architectonic phenomenon: being temporary guests of the integrative « existenz-minimum » of a much more real day's work, people have used home only to eat and sleep in. Inside the house everything had been thought out by an architecture whose aim was to console: nothing was left but to hang a few pictures on the walls. The house was the first, most important step in the total adoption of the bourgeois way of life. But now people, being strengthened by the new and ever increasing capacity to decide for themselves which they have won at work, must take housing into their own hands, freeing it from all preconstituted cultural and social models, breaking the subtle intellectual links and hysterical linguistic knots which characterize architecture as the figuration of space. Freed from the armour of its own character, architecture must become an open structure, accessible to intellectual mass production as the only force symbolizing the collective landscape. Therefore, the problem becomes that of freeing mankind from architecture insomuch as it is a formal structure.

Nowadays the only possible utopia is quantative. Social conflict is no longer going through the phase of the confrontation of alternative models, but is in that of dialectical negotiation between a balanced development of the system and the growing cost of the labour force. The clash no longer takes place in the field of ideology but in quantitative terms: it is via this parametre that

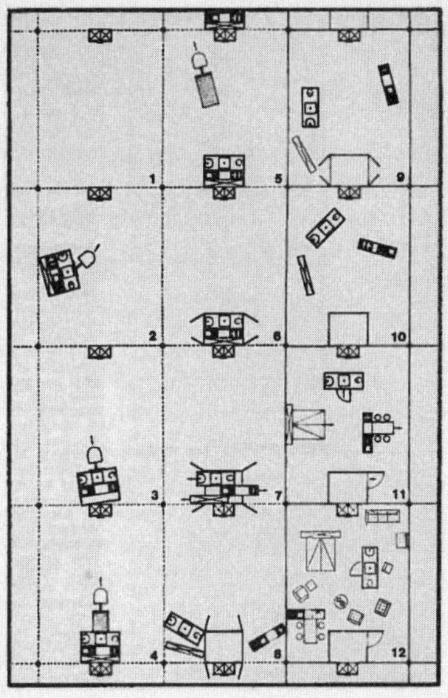

schema di montaggio di abitazioni temporanee

the summing together is made possible of different phenomena which apparently have no link with one another. Quantitative language replaces qualitative, thus becoming the only scientific means of approach to the undifferentiated stratification of production and hence of reality. As general terms of reference disappear, behaviour becomes a structure free from moral allegories. Freedom, as an end, becomes an instrument of struggle.

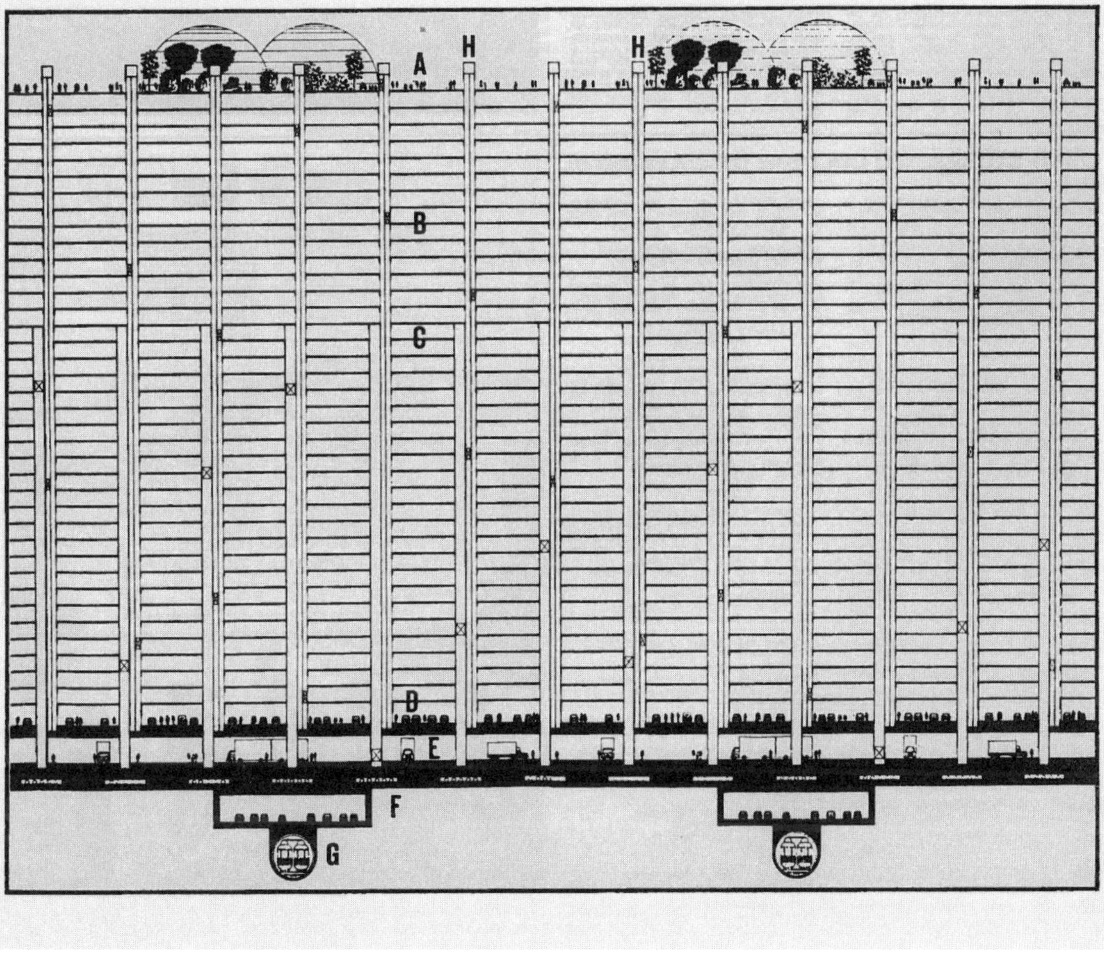

sezioni: A piano naturale; B piani abitativi; C piani di servizi; D piano di penetrazione del traffico; E arrivo merci-magazzini; F autostrada; G metropolitana

No-Stop City
Andrea Branzi, 2006

//

The "radical" movement has hither to been regarded as a unifying phenomenon made up of many different groups, but forming a single front, in terms of both criticism and projects. In 1966, they managed to jolt the certainties and optimism of classical modernity, and ushered in a lengthy period of crisis, which is still running its course.

In order to take an in-depth look at this phenomenon, I think it would be a good idea to make a closer analysis of the various theoretical factors which have informed its inner trends. So let us regard he "radical" movement not as some monolith, but rather as a reality made up of different tendencies which, over time, have given rise to completely different results.

Most of the present-day representatives of modern architecture readily acknowledge their indebtedness to the Movement, as clearly illustrated by their very manner of seeing the relations between city and architecture, project and discipline: Frank Gehry, Hans Hollein, Daniel Libeskind, Arata Isozaki, Toyo Ito, Rem Koolhaas, Bernard Tschumi and so many others have all been directly involved activists in the "Radical" Movement or, at the very least, recognize it as the springboard for a new way of producing architecture. The Postmodern Movement of the 1980s would not have existed itself without those remote forerunners, who were the first to detect the changes at work in the physical and urban condition of the West, and see in them a positive opportunity to experiment with all the breaks and fractures within the culture of the project.

This essay has come about from the idea that the moment is finally at hand, after so many years, to offer a finer analysis of the inner workings of the factors behind the "radical" movement, by overviewing some of the generic projects hallmarking it. My own testimony will focus specifically on the Archizoom group's *No-Stop City* (I was once a group member) a generational project; as Catherine David defined it at the 1997 *Documenta*. I shall thus attempt to describe its genesis and understand its goals and purposes.

This project got under way in 1968, and was published for the first time the following year in *Casabella* (n. 350-351). We worked on it until 1972. It did not come about in an off-the-cuff way, like some polemical gesture. Rather, it was the outcome of a lengthy period of incubation, and it dealt in a disciplinary form with certain complex political themes typical of that period. When we discuss *No-Stop City*, we can thus also talk about many other things, behind the scene, within it, and out in front of it.

A re-creation of the debate from which *No-Stop City* originates involves the beginnings of the crisis in modern politics, and its proposal to contain not only social but also urban growth within the framework of reformism. Modern architecture was one of the quintessential instruments of those policies.

European rationalism describes progress as a long path leading towards a society of order and development: a path to be travelled along within industrialization, as the only way capable of offering positive responses to all the delays, contradictions and boundaries in society. These contradictions and boundaries had, in any event, to be attributed to the delays and distortions that were produced within industrialization processes. This positive, collective and democratic vision of a path to be travelled along together towards progress was what lent modern architecture its function as an instrument (in the figurative sense as well) of social reconstruction. From Lewis Mumford to Siegfried Giedion and Nikolaus Pevsner, from Carlo Giulio Argan to Ernesto N. Rogers, and from Leonardo Benevolo to Gillo Dorfles, all theoreticians of architecture, along with actual architects, proposed a democratic and positive confrontation between authors of projects and political powers-that-be.

It was to the "powers-that-be" that Le Corbusier dedicated his book *Vers une Architecture*, while Walter Gropius talked in terms of an "integrated architecture," conceived as an instrument of a democratic social order. The architecture, therefore, capable of taking into account social authorities and political differences, and coming

up with positive solutions to them by encouraging an upsurge in technological advances, as well as in the field of aesthetics.

Many books have been devoted to the reasons why this ideal project collapsed, as from 1964, in all western countries. I do not wish to develop this historical theme in any depth, by analyzing the reasons for this abrupt reversal and this quest for a revolution; nor do I wish to develop the reasons why this revolution never happened. I would simply say that I have found indirect - but more comprehensive - answers by reading those French historians who have analyzed not this failed revolution, but the one which was so successful two centuries earlier: the French Revolution. From the great Alexis de Tocqueville to Gavotte and François Furet, they have all tried to unravel the inextricable tangle of contradictions, acts of genius, acts of folly, as well as the suicidal thrusts to be found behind those great historical traumas.

The old Marxist theories which interpreted history as the arena for the conflict between rich and poor, bosses and workers, whites and blacks have bequeathed a theorem associating theology and politics theorems that are too simple and altogether unsuitable to analyze revolutions, which are, precisely because of their very nature, more complex and more simple at the same time (hence different), than such theoretical plans. It seems to me that Francois Furet came up with an interesting response when he talked about the French Revolution (but possibly about the failed revolution as well) not as a conflict between a society eager for renewal and a power standing in its way, but rather as a conflict between a society which has already undergone a thorough renewal and a power that is slow to digest this change. Personally, it is my view that something similar occurred in 1969.

The innovative and libertarian cultures of the young generation, which were already being applied and disseminated, came up against working-class institutions defending their old theological plan for a politics based on the conflict between the middle class and the proletariat, between the good and the bad. The failed revolution was actually (in Italy at least) a conflict within the Left, thus altogether outside institutions, altogether extra-parliamentary, and altogether media-related, a verbal, not to say armed conflict, occurring within means of communication (cf. Aldo Moro affair), and incapable of constructing a new democratic organization. Otherwise put, the difference between the French Revolution and the failed revolution resides in the fact that the latter had no such figure as a Louis XVI summoning the Estates General. This is to say it lacked the theatre of revolution: the *Jeu de paume* and the Winter Palace. People sought it in every manner of demonstration, in every assembly and at every funeral, in evocations of the Resistance, and the Spanish Civil War but it was never to be found.

It was a failed revolution because the political avant-gardes were pitched against the cultural avant-gardes. The former lost their revolution; the latter (perhaps) won theirs. So it was an incomplete revolution, but maybe the only one possible.

We should bear in mind this extremely specific political climate in order to understand the thinking that the most politically evolved fringe of the "Radical" Movement was embarked upon, and which, as it happens, focused on the issue of the project.

The old text by Friedrich Engels on *The Question of Dwellings*, had been doing the rounds for a long time in the architecture faculty at Florence, and people produced a painstaking, sarcastic reading of it directed against social-democrat reformism. In that famous book, Karl Marx's colleague explained that there was no such thing as a "working-class metropolis," but only a "working-class critique" of the existing metropolis. This meant that the problem did not involve conceiving a better city but rather taking possession of the present-day city. The role of the project did not reside in innovation, but in the ability to demystify the systems of logic on which the bourgeois city was based. The real political problem was not to guarantee that the city would function, but to prevent the present-day city from functioning (with barricades).

This pre-revolutionary climate was altogether theoretical, and based on the paradox

consisting in imagining a new socialist revolution just when the real socialist revolution was in the process of foundering. Yet the real objectives of this paradox were not political but cultural, because this type of radical, rigid and sarcastic attitude challenged the capacity of the modern culture to come up with appropriate responses to the political conflict, and rejected its role of social go-between.

Nowadays, it is quite possible that the political component of the modern culture is (precisely) a matter of no importance. In 1964, however, the real basis of the role of modernity was entirely political; in the immediate postwar years, in a ravaged Europe, terrified by the monstrousness of its dictatorships, the only hope was to reconstruct democracy and modernity altogether.

Two concepts around which architects laboured with a great deal of application, from Alvar Aalto to Le Corbusier, and from Walter Gropius to Mies van der Rohe (also covering over one or two age-old and inadmissible situation). By rejecting this civil go-between, modern architecture was stripped of its historical mandate, and light was shed on the limits of its rationalist theorems, which were incapable of interpreting and managing the serious social and cultural conflicts which forced industrialization was in the process of creating. So the Modern accordingly foundered before the complexity if its world. But behind this failure, there was nothing of the culture of the Post-Modern which, 15 years later, would fill magazines with so many inanities. What emerged, with the fall of the Modern, was a hard inexpressive, pagan world, produced by the conflict between two clashing giants: the capital and the working class. Two realities devoid of values, immoral, pitiless, capable of grand endeavours and great dictatorships. This is the "Marble Chicken" referred to by Archizoom members: the imperialist bloc emerging from benehat the humanist issues of a superficial modernity. Capitalism and the working class were two enemy giants, but alike and often allied as in the world war against Hitler and in the USSR of 1922, in Lenin's NEP program concerning "the working-class use of capitalism." Two giants which clashed by refusing go-betweens, and even less if the go-between were offered by modern architecture, because both were foes of mediocrity. The present world was made up of these two parties: reappraising one involved reappraising the other.

The originality of the Archizoom group lay precisely in the fact that it connected socialist realism and Pop Art, because both issued from a realist, radical and extreme stance, wherein in the contents of the political avant-gardes overlapped with those of the artistic avant-gardes. Working-classism and consumerism, Mario Tronti and Andy Warhol: opposite worlds but not so remote from one another, because both obeyed the materialistic logic of "more money and less work." The third way did not exist, and just as readers for Frantz Fanon thought that negritude did not exist because "Black wants to become White," the worker wanted to become the boss, and the colonized wanted to become the colonizer. But the opposite way is not true.

The critique of Modernity thus became the critique of architecture as disciplinary institution, and a qualitative category in a pagan world devoid of quality. Its role was not to offer a mediation between the extreme forms of logic of the system, but to represent them as clearly as possible. That is, by creating the urban arena of history and its contradictions to which we referred earlier: a clear, limpid arena, where things spoke for themselves. Just as in Paul Nizan's *Aden Arabie*, which describes a city where, in the end of the day, all the mechanisms of French colonialism are clear to see.

In Florence the student movement had been pondering these questions for a while. In 1962, the large exhibition of Le Corbusier's work held in the Palazzo Strozzi, had helped people to question certain of the Swiss architect's specific projects. The Chandigarh project, among others, whose plan reproduced the caste divisions of Indian society, without any suggestion of going beyond it. The plan of Algiers, likewise, contrasted the old Arab kasbah with the new European city, without proposing any halfway measures.

This line thinking revolved around the hypothesis of a new role to be given to architecture; it was not the role of modern reformism, but consisted in a kind of direct representation of power mechanisms, social divisions, and castes. A civil architecture, therefore, clearly rooted in 18th century enlightenment (Boullée and Ledoux were especially admired), capable of stimulating a critical effect by its very presence within a confused and compromised city.

In 1964, we started to prepare for a fourth year involving architectural composition, and we came up with a megastructure of production and consumption along the Florence-Prato axis, introducing it as the *décor* of the capitalism system (the didactic and political purpose is quite obvious in the illustrated report).

It was in the same spirit that, in 1965, Claudio Greppi, a left-wing student leader, presented his thesis, in which the plan to reorganize the Florence-Prato textile system was presented as a readable diagram of the assembly line and the accumulation of financial capital. Against this political backdrop, Pop Art themes took on a special significance: a sarcastic denunciation of the realities of the world of commodities and consumerism, such as the Modern Movement, which was purist and abstract, was incapable of coming up with.

In 1966, for my own thesis, I presented the project for a permanent amusement-park in Prato, and one of the earliest works by Archizoom was the *Dream Beds*, kitsch furniture capable of destroying the good taste of middle-class homes, like new Trojan horses. The optimism of modernity was replaced by an enthusiastic desire for its flop.

In 1969, at the Milan Triennale, the Archizoom group presented an "Eclectic Conspiracy Centre," Afro-Tyrolean in style, dedicated to Malcolm X; and the pages of Ettore Sottsass's *Pianeta Fresco* sported a postal catalogue of Arab-Style garden follies. The pacifist Hinduism of flower children was answered by ironical mention of the Islamic holy war. A tragic and surprising prophecy.

But the period of early Pop Art and "super architecture" (with the Superstudio group) appeared before very long as a period of transition preceding more radical themes, and following a very specific theoretical thread. It is from this theoretical thread that *No-Stop City* came into being, doing away with every trace of Pop representation. It was based on the following established fact: behind the façade of popular assemblies, and behind a collectivism trumpeted in too ostentatious a way, the political debate that was gathering momentum within the student movement and in the street disguised itself as a refusal of culture, an of the radical dimension of the Modern, sees as a way of freeing people from culture and not as an opportunity to formulate a different culture. The various forms of an absolute secularism, and the downfall of all manner of qualitative utopia, thus making way for the only possible utopia of quantity, represented a liberating aspect which was not to be hidden by the political conflict.

The idea of an inexpressive, catatonic architecture, outcome of the expansive forms of logic of the system and its class antagonists, was the only modern architecture interest to us: a liberating architecture, corresponding to mass democracy, devoid of *demos* and devoid of *cratos* (people and power), and both centreless and imageless. A society freed from its own alienation, emancipated from the rhetorical forms of humanitarian socialism and rhetorical progressivism: an architecture which took a fearless look at the logic of grey, atheistic and de-dramatized industrialism, where mass production produced infinite urban *décors*, stripped of those temperamental structures which Wilhelm Reich described as inhibiting restrictions, hampering the liberation of men's organic energy. The colorful vision of Pop architecture were replaced by Ludwig Hilberseimer's pitiless urban images, those of a city without qualities designed for people without preordained qualities. Free, therefore, to express in an autonomous way its own creative, political and behavioral energies. The greatest possible freedom occurred where integration was strongest; the limits of the system lay in the new conditions related to knowledge and project, the zero project form which everything was possible (and unpredictable). Alienation was a new artistic condition, which Richard Hamilton had been the first to pinpoint, crossing the uncrossable boundary of human tragedy, the same one that Francis Bacon had posited at the same time and in the same city (London).

What was beginning to be glimpsed, in this attitude of extreme realism and uncompromising rejection, was the transcendence of the theological boundaries of modern politics, and their diagrammatic method of action within a vision of history conceived as the everlasting confrontation between the good and the bad, the rich and the poor. A productive politics, never wearied by tragedy, fuelled by an inextinguishable rhetoric, and marked by continual and definitive clashes.

On the other hand, *No-Stop City* proposed a totally de-dramatized vision of history, restored to its lay dimension, and completely devoid of tragedy, because it was devoid of metaphysics. An extreme vision of industrial civilization as the producer of a decorative-repetitive, and horizontal system, and one thus devoid of cathedrals. A system based on the repetition of sign, at once diffuse and fluid, within architecture and nature, like so many exceptions and incidents, dissolved and disappeared into the amniotic space of metropolises.

The simplistic, innocent attitude is very akin to Andy Warhol's series and the environmental music of Philip Glass who, in that period, was starting to work on horizontal tones (which is how Pierre Boulez defined them), an anti-composition for a music close to continuums, without any exterior and without interior boundaries: a metropolis corresponding directly to the market, where any distinction of places and different functions no longer existed. A real residential wood, where people can live inside a shopping center, where houses are already empty incubators, available for undefined creativity, and residential parking lots or metropolitan nomads.

The industrial design concept was interpreted as a total commodification of products and life, affording a gain in freedom and independence. The house was an inhabitable cupboard, an equipped zone, without order or meaning, where each occupant exercised his right to imagine the form of his own space on his own behalf.

In 1972, at New York's MoMA, as part of the exhibition *Italy: The New Domestic Landscape*, the Archizoom group presented a grey and empty room where a young girl's voice described a well-lit and colorful house, which onlookers could imagine for themselves in different ways. Our slogan back then was: "Inhabiting is easy."

As in the large monochromatic works of Mark Rothko, mass society was seen as an endless ocean, free and mellow, with neither a centre and nor frontiers. The pictures of Cy Twombly also spring to mind, where swarms of tadpoles move about in the amniotic fluid of the global market. In *No-Stop City*, this social dimension became a spacial dimension: the mirrors inside the models reflected images by multiplying them *ad infinitum*, going beyond the limits of architecture and interior space.

The metropolis was seen as one large interior, a single space, air-conditioned and artificially it.

As in a large factory or warehouse, organism overlapped directly with the certifying logic of the market: they where blank, expressionless containers, within which everything was possible. This introverted space, this hybrid but generic and immoral metropolis formed a sort of second nature, a high-tech Amazonia, within which all functional zonings accumulated and dissolved, and the standards associated with lighting and artificial ventilation vanished; all temperamental frameworks preventing the city from going beyond its historic form of an organism, harmonizing technology and nature. Our *No-Stop City* idea involved a city freed of architecture, where technology and nature were not harmonized, but merged together. A city without architecture, because it was freed of the go-between function linking interior and exterior, and technology and nature a function that architecture had always assumed. The whole "radical" Florentine movement worked, in different forms, on the theme of the end of the relation between city and architecture, and between architecture and objects.

In the 1960s, the real theoretical nucleus of the "radical" Florentine Movement was that of the crisis, or end, of the link between these dimensional and project-oriented categories. Small, medium, large and extra-large, which Rem Koolhaas today regards as completely homogeneous and interchangeable, were on the contrary seen by the Movement as conflicting, incompatible categories, because each one laid claim to its absolute centrality. Theorists started with the assertion of opposite priorities which were antagonistic and irreconcilable.

The hunch about the end of the unity of the project, and of the latent conflict between city and architecture, and between architecture and the world of objects, came about from the radical verification of the ungovernable dimensions of the contemporary metropolis, which, with *No-Stop City*, had become an original reality for the Archizoom group a reality no longer had any link of continuity with the historic city; an artificial world within which architecture dissolved like an ingredient of a primordial broth.

A city without architecture therefore, where the urban landscape (cityscape) was formed by large anonymous containers, merchandise, industrial products, the plankton of data, and the market. So the nub of our research was a new urban typology.

For Superstudio, it was architecture that managed its conflict with the city: by way of the *Continuous Monument*, it asserted its entitlement to monumentality, today denied, in order to put itself forward as a macro-structure within which cities like New York ran aground. An architecture capable of reconstructing narratives and grand metaphors, as in the *Twelve Ideal Cities*, and thus capable of restoring an order and a cosmic sense to an expressionless metropolis.

An architecture without city, therefore, distributing its passwords to the world of objects (*Quaderna*), and to the world of great walls. The centre of their research was accordingly a new extra-historical architecture.

For the UFO group, the hub of the urban revolution was formed by the centrality and absolute autonomy of the world of objects, and interior space. A world evolving over conceptual make-believe. A world of objects grappling with architecture and with the city, in order to assert the right to imagine the humdrum, the pun, and the literary as the world's sole driving force. This was the basis of the clash between its categories, made up of inhabitable architectures (the *ANAS Houses*), crossable placed (the *Tour of Italy*), and the new object-related archetypes. Objects without architecture and without city, therefore, affirming a world of disorder and discontinuity. This sights of their research were trained towards objects seen as new centers of the world, at once mysterious and conceptual.

For each one of these groups, and for the "Radical" Florentine movement in general, the crisis in the discipline and the end of the unity of the project offered an extraordinary opportunity to experiment at long last with a city which was no longer a city, an architecture which were no longer objects (but concepts).

Here, there was a chance, as a result of the crisis of rationalist modernity, to go beyond the boundaries of Modernity and its fear of moving forward towards the unthought-of and the uninhabitable, categories still defined on the basis of a thoroughly traditional idea of the organic link between the different parts of the project: programming, constructing, and furnishing. Otherwise put, offering a hospitable world to a society which, on the contrary, was busy looking for new kinds of inhospitality, and disorganization, so as to go beyond the temperamental limits of its own development.

Archizoom Associati, "No-Stop City Viewfinders," 1971

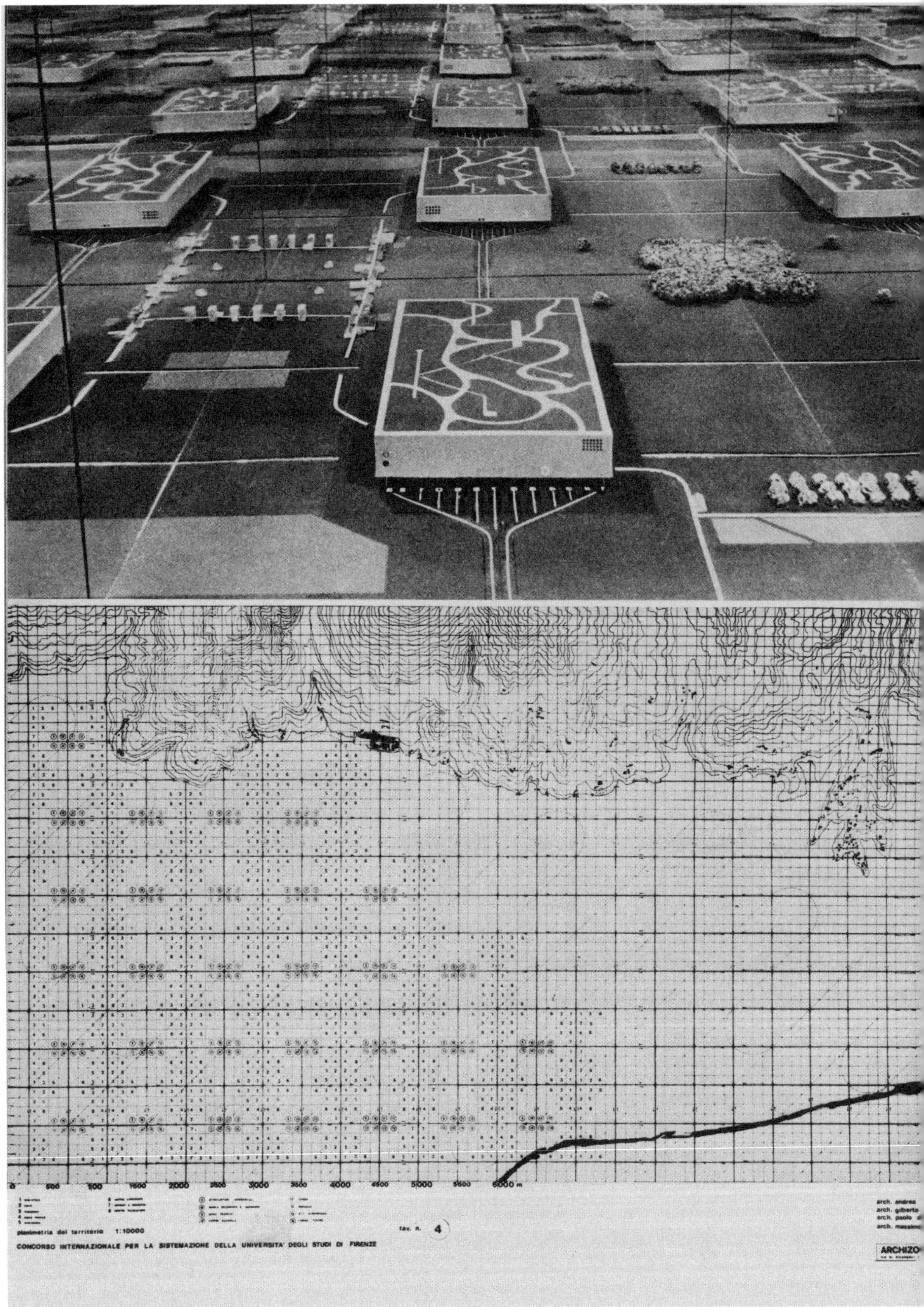

Archizoom Associati, University of Florence Competition, in *Domus* n. 509, 1972

Competition for the University of Florence
Archizoom Associati, 1972

//

We took part in the International Competition for the New University of Florence, presenting some drawings with our name, surname, and address under the theme "The projects are not signed," and therefore being automatically eliminated from the competition itself. This gesture sought to be a way to direct the jury, and to those who are involved in modern architecture, toward a message on a number of problems that more and more concretely affect those who practice, teach, learn, or judge architectural design.

The specific case of Florence interests us only because it offers the opportunity to underline a number of further general misunderstandings that, in a certain measure, are also fueled under the theme of a competition.

In the meantime, we could marginally note how the themed competition, to be defined as such, should presuppose a mechanism of absolutely hermetic anonymity. Apart from the political improbability of this hypothesis (on which we are not interested in polemicizing at the moment), it is the case that this mechanism of judgment proves, for the competitor, the incentive to personalize the project as much as possible, in order to make it immediately legible and recognizable to the jury, so that few projects are actually "signed" as those under the theme.

The originality of the project becomes an indispensable, bureaucratic condition.

Moreover, it will not be difficult, after the long years spent in the university, to elaborate the famous "projects on roofs," intended for edible models in walnut and metal, more gluttonous and stimulating for intoxicated teachers.

The result is the so-called "roof architecture," in the sense that it hypothesizes sculptural effects that can only be verified from 10,000 meters high.

The "roof design" thus stimulates architecture destined to itself, to its own bureaucracy, never verifiable in reality, but easily distinguishable in an exam or in a contest, from the tide of the other personal examples presented within the deadlines.

Therefore, to carry out the bureaucratic unfairness that we carried out is also a way of temporarily self-positioning ourselves out of play. Out of play with respect to the rules of the specific case and to the general planning conditions. In the specific case, the competition required a large project of distributive characteristics, in order to redeem an uncertain urban destination, by blackmailing the designer into "making culture," into finding the appropriate territorial location, according to absolutely private criteria.

As general planning conditions, at the level of language and organism, they are those that a misunderstood modern tradition gives us, for which language stands as a formal verification of social and spiritual equilibria, and the organism as a verification between functional problems and old Freudian allegories.

Now in our specific case, in which we believe, coincidentally, in none of these things, but we believe in others, in the sense that we have understood other things, there was no other way but to really design "out of competition." And not so much, as many believe, on the level of cheerful utopias, but on that of a rigorous experimentation of rigorous premises. But then it is no longer even very important to know what one believes or does not believe in, since the world does not go further on the basis of individual cultural or moral opinions, or love for this or that thing, but having abolished the abstract concept of Good and Evil, grinds full steam ahead on the basis of the More and the Less.

The great limitation of Le Corbusier - when he was an old man - was precisely that of loving, or of causing to love, that particular architecture which in his youth he so tenaciously sought to liquidate, releasing it into the limbo of things that are or are not, but on which it is not the case of splitting hairs. His youthful effort to see architecture as the result - not necessarily controlled - of deeper and more objective operations and reasons than design, was not the vice of self-flagellation of a repressed architect, nor the effort to anchor himself to objective reasons in order to justify a formal language, but arose from the intuitive conviction - and today for us firmly demonstrable - that the link that binds man to reality, both formal and historical, cannot still be visual, as in past centuries: the distance that once existed between man and society, between man and phenomena, has now totally disappeared.

Indeed, the degree of entanglement existing today between man and his cultural and physical habitat is infinitely more intense than in the past, when history, politics, moral society, etc., always stood outside human reality. Today, we know that external to man there are only other men, and since all men are equal this reality that surrounds us is the same, homogeneous and continuous. Outside our body there is only a system of media designed to put us in communication with the bodies of others. And all this cannot be represented, and it makes no sense to try to do it.

The task, let's say historical, of our generation can no longer be a battle for a "better" architecture, one that is more human or more beautiful, but it must be that of "liquidating" the problem of architecture, not so much by finding an aesthetic or a meta-historical methodology, but rejecting architecture as a problem of formal and historical verification.

Architecture does not "represent" the system anymore, but it "is" the system itself; the city is no longer a "place," but a "condition" of the market.

The only architectural form that we would have liked to produce was therefore a wandering fog over the plain between Florence and Pistoia. Not so much as inspiration or poetic invention, but in the sense that we refuse to design an object, preferring instead to design its use.

The proposed structure is therefore a system of continuous, artificially illuminated and aerated floors, within which the various functions can be rationally organized: any correspondence between the shape of the building, the structure, and the functions contained therein, is not absolutely verifiable.

The external perimeter of the whole is not identified or represented: we are not interested in its shape since it will be the result of certain quantitative relationships that determine it.

The resulting building is a first elementary application of the current technological level of facts such as the elevator and the air conditioner and electric lighting, applied on the urban level.

In this sense, there is no formal difference between a productive structure, a supermarket, a residence, a university, or an industrialized agriculture area. The location of these organisms on the territory is not important (and ecologists, do not attack us) because if the conditions of equilibrium between the natural environment and the artificial environment must be equal and optimal in any point of the territory (and not only in national parks), it means that it must be possible to have tools that work, from an environmental point of view, wherever they are, since the territory is a neutral, continuous and homogeneous material. So it is for production, and so it is therefore for everything.

APPARATUS:

RADICAL NOTES

CASABELLA 1972-1976

- n. 1, "A Long-Term Strategy," in *Casabella* n. 370, 1972
- n. 2, "The Dream of the Village," in *Casabella* n. 371, 1972
- n. 3, "Publications on the Avant-Garde," in *Casabella* n. 372, 1972
- n. 4, "The Abolition of School," in *Casabella* n. 373, 1973
- n. 5, "Rock and Revolution," in *Casabella* n. 374, 1973
- n. 6, "The Street at Eindhoven," in *Casabella* n. 376, 1973
- n. 7, "Global Tools," in *Casabella* n. 377, 1973
- n. 8, "The Elite and Mass Creativity," in *Casabella* n. 378, 1973
- n. 9, "Small, Medium and Large," in *Casabella* n. 379, 1973
- n. 10, "Except for Pure Wasteland," in *Casabella* n. 380-381, 1973
- n. 11, "Dirty and Clean," in *Casabella* n. 382, 1973
- n. 12, "Unsealing the Shrine," in *Casabella* n. 383, 1973
- n. 13, "Minimal Technology," in *Casabella* n. 385, 1974
- n. 14, "Mountain Climbing and Existenz Minimum," in *Casabella* n. 388, 1974
- n. 15, "Fascism and the Avant-Garde," in *Casabella* n. 389, 1974
- n. 16, "A Golden Model," in *Casabella* n. 390, 1974
- n. 17, "Louis Kahn Superstar," in *Casabella* n. 391, 1974
- n. 18, "The Role of the Rear-Guarde," in *Casabella* n. 392-393, 1974
- n. 19, "Apollo e Dioniso in Gallarate," in *Casabella* n. 395, 1974
- n. 20, "Architecture and Modesty," in *Casabella* n. 396, 1974
- n. 21, "Architecture and Freedom," in *Casabella* n. 399, 1975
- n. 22, "Design and Minority Culture," in *Casabella* n. 401, 1975
- n. 23, "Town Planning (Law) and Order," in *Casabella* n. 402, 1975
- n. 24, "The Great Slow-Down," in *Casabella* n. 403, 1975
- n. 25, "Architecture and Sex," in *Casabella* n. 407, 1975
- n. 26, "Suspicion," in *Casabella* n. 411, 1976
- n. 27, "Modern Movement?," in *Casabella* n. 412, 1976

As a term, "radical architecture" includes all the experiments of the last few years — experiments often difficult to interpret — which have the common characteristic of lying outside the strictly professional line and of launching, often in opposite directions, as a kind of radical (of course) revision of the whole architectonic field; they are: counter-design, conceptual architecture, Utopia, neo-monumentalism, minimal technology, eclecticism, iconoclasm, neodadaism, nomadism, etc.
The programmatic statements of these groups and even their most outrageous insults have met with silent smiles (not to be confused with tolerance).
The positions of the professionals remain untouched by this wave of publicity-hunting and, of course, as we all know, sooner or later these youthful excesses peter out for everyone...
Into this breach created partly by the often neutral availability of the specialized reviews and partly by the strategic retreat of the Old Masters, diverse forces charge, carefully avoiding clashes among themselves. And this makes for strange meeting: this year at the London Summer Session, for example, even Italia Nostra (sic) took part!
And indeed the outlook is hardly bright: on the one hand we are threatened by a repressive ecology, that great tool in the cultural renewal of the whole bourgeois ethos (the concept of "nature" moves directly from liberal economics to urban planning); on the other hand by an avant-garde glad to exist but incapable of clearly defining itself or presenting a programme. And by this I do not mean uniform programmes (everyone has a right to make and to consume his own culture), but the ability to find outside oneself analogous phenomena and structural laws as reference points.
The whole matter would be of no importance if this experimental production were homogeneous, and though varied, constant: actually there is pround ambiguity in much of the avant-garde work, ambiguity which becomes troublesome as soon as the tide turns back and one's destructive drives begin to fail one, leaving in their wake an expanse of "beautiful" works of architecture and cultural arrogance.
The symptoms are familiar enough: a cultural-anthropological hodgepodge, refined elegance, salvoes against the consumer ethos, etc.
Coming into their own again are the élite of knowledgeable fools, of sham-drugged puppets, ready to lecture the whole of society through architecture. At such moments the Establishment culture has always wisely let them blow off their initial steam and then has moved in, when things had calmed down, to recuperate them on the plane of linguistic renewal.
It is no mere chance that the destructive drive of the Modern Movement has come back into circulation as a positive drive towards the formal renewal of architectonic culture. And indeed the "destruction of architecture" as a slogan created to underscore the negative constant present in the experimental work of the last few years, has no future if it is not accompanied by a "long-term strategy".
By "long-term strategy" I mean at least an awareness of the whole cycle of cultural production — that is, an awareness of the real relationships existing between the planning-operations man and the client in terms of creative alienation, the technological barrier in the arts, and the social disintegration inherent in current aesthetic and cultural programmes in general.
The "destruction of culture" remains no more than a simple apocalyptic statement if one's work has not been related to the structural laws governing social development and one has failed to outgrow the limits of a temporary though inevitably decadent anarchic nihilism.
Establishing a rapport with social laws, however, does not mean political integration, but only the utilization of science in any plan, no matter how advanced: if Utopia is simply used to substitute present-day society in futuristic terms, it won't get us anywhere; but it is valuable if it is utilized as an artificial accelerator of the process on which one intends to operate.
As we all know, the "destruction of culture" is not effected through an alternative culture, but through a different social use of the same culture; a long-term strategy is of use for the very reason that it singles out this passage from one to the other, and gives a positive meaning to the closing down of the one-way channels of communication constituted by aesthetic work.
One thing we should all be committed to is a confrontation over theses of vital importance which enable us to draw up the premises for more incisive work, work which addresses itself directly to reality and does not avoid it. Which is no call to order but a preparation for the final attack.
This column, written not by a critic but by an "operator", could be of use in that preparation.

A long-term strategy
Strategia dei tempi lunghi

✶✶ ANDREA BRANZI ✶✶

RADICAL NOTES

Il termine "radical architecture" raccoglie tutte le esperienze di questi ultimi anni, esperienze spesso di difficile lettura, che possiedono la caratteristica comune di collocarsi al di fuori della linea retta professionale e di rilanciare, spesso in direzioni contrastanti, una sorta di rifondazione radicale (appunto) di tutta la disciplina architettonica: contro-design, architettura concettuale, utopia, neo-monumentalismo, tecnologia povera, eclettismo, iconoclastia, neo-dadaismo, nomadismo, ecc. ecc.
Le dichiarazioni programmatiche dei gruppi e anche le offese più sanguinose, sono passate sotto un sorridente silenzio (erroneamente valutabile come tolleranza).
Le posizioni professionali restano al sicuro da questa ondata di foto-montaggi e, si sa, gli eccessi giovanili prima o poi passano per tutti.... In questo varco creato da una parte da una disponibilità spesso neutra delle riviste specializzate e dall'altra da una ritirata strategica dei grandi padri, forze diverse irrompono, guardandosi bene dal misurarsi tra di loro. E si fanno degli strani incontri: quest'anno alla Summer Session londinese ha preso parte anche Italia Nostra (sic)!
Ed in effetti non c'è da stare allegri: da una parte incalza repressiva l'ecologia, grande strumento di rifondazione culturale di tutta la morale borghese (il concetto di "natura" passa direttamente dall'economia liberale all'urbanistica), e dall'altra un'avanguardia felice di esistere ma incapace di dare le proprie generalità o di dimostrare i propri programmi. E qui non intendo programmi unitari (a ciascuno il diritto di farsi e consumarsi la propria cultura), ma la capacità di reperire al proprio esterno fenomeni analoghi e leggi strutturali alle quali fare riferimento.
La cosa non sarebbe di nessuna importanza se la produzione sperimentale si presentasse come un corpo omogeneo, variato ma costante: in realtà esiste una ambiguità anche profonda in molti fenomeni della avanguardia, ambiguità che preoccupa al momento in cui inizierà l'inevitabile riflusso e certa spinta distruttiva comincerà a venire meno, lasciando scoperta una spiaggia fatta di "belle" architetture e di protervia culturale. I sintomi sono poi i soliti: minestroni cultural-antropologici, eleganza raffinata, bordate repressive contro i consumi ecc.
Si ricostruisce l'élite dei somari sapienti, dei bambolotti finti drogati, pronti a fare scuola con l'architettura a tutta intera la società. La cultura ufficiale in simili momenti è sempre stata molto saggia, lasciando sfogare la carica iniziale, e recuperando poi ad acque più calme sul piano del rinnovamento linguistico.
Non a caso tutta la carica distruttiva del Movimento Moderno è rientrata in circolazione come spinta positiva ad un rinnovamento formale della cultura. In effetti la "distruzione dell'architettura" come slogan creato per sottolineare una costante di segno negativo all'interno dei fenomeni sperimentali di questi ultimi anni, non ha alcun destino storico se non è accompagnata da una "strategia dei tempi lunghi".
Per "strategia dei tempi lunghi" intendo almeno la coscienza dell'intero ciclo della produzione culturale, cioè dei rapporti reali esistenti tra operatore progettuale e utente, in termini di alienazione creativa, di barriera tecnologica delle arti, di corrosione sociale della piattaforma dei valori estetici e culturali in genere
La "distruzione della cultura" resta una semplice affermazione apocalittica se non viene realizzato il collegamento con leggi strutturali di sviluppo sociale, superando limiti di un temporaneo nihilismo anarchico, sempre decadente. Il rapporto con le leggi sociali non significa integrazione politica, ma piuttosto un riscontro scientifico ad una elaborazione quanto si vuole avanzata: l'utopia, se sostituisce semplicemente in termini avveniristici la società attuale non serve a niente, ha valore quando viene utilizzata come acceleratore artificiale dei processi attuali sui quali si intende operare.
Come ben si sa la "distruzione della cultura" non avviene attraverso una cultura alternativa, ma attraverso un diverso uso sociale della cultura stessa; una "strategia dei tempi lunghi" serve appunto a individuare questo passaggio di mano, fornendo un senso positivo alla riduzione a zero dei canali di comunicazione unidirezionali costituiti dal lavoro estetico.
Un impegno che dovremmo assumerci tutti è quello di un confronto su tesi, riconosciute come portanti, che permettano di costituire le premesse per un lavoro più incisivo che scontri frontalmente la realtà, e non la eluda. Non un richiamo all'ordine, ma la preparazione dell'attacco finale.
Questa rubrica, tenuta non da un critico, ma da un addetto ai lavori, potrebbe servire a questo.

L'equivoco forse più caratteristico che accompagna qualsiasi dibattito di urbanistica consiste nella tacita certezza che la città rappresenta il momento più alto e completo della cultura sociale.
L'idea della città come opera collettiva, come specchio formale e spontaneo di una civiltà, è talmente radicata che sembra impossibile scindere il termine città da quello di cultura sociale.
Se tale unità si è verificata in qualche momento storico (le polis? i comuni?) ciò è sempre dovuto al fatto che ha funzionato la copertura ideologico-culturale alla unità tra il sistema economico e l'organizzazione territoriale.
Il sogno del villaggio, della piccola comunità unita ed equilibrata nella vallata, accompagna come il sogno di una perduta infanzia (mai vissuta) tutte le esperienze urbane, dai nuovi quartieri alle megalopoli.
Tale sogno sempre tradito è diventato lo strumento di verifica delle condizioni attuali di vita urbana, la unità di misura delle disfunzioni e delle tragedie di questa.
Utilizzando questo parametro, la collettività assume il problema urbano non in termini funzionali a cui rispondere sul piano tecnico, ma come problema civile alla cui soluzione tutta intera la società deve concorrere. Tale unità civile però non è ricercata mai sul piano dell'uso collettivo della città, ma su quello della unità formale, che è l'unica possibile verifica che, stando così le cose, può essere fatta di quel miscuglio di contraddizioni che è la città, sia moderna che antica (pubblico, privato, verde, costruzioni ecc. ecc.).

Le singole componenti del problema urbano (le abitazioni, il traffico, il verde, i servizi ecc.) non ricevono mai una soluzione scientifica, ma quella che riesce ad inserirsi nell'insieme di tutte le altre senza metterle in crisi.

Ed in effetti quando parliamo di città moderne commettiamo un grosso errore perché di città moderne non ne esiste nemmeno una:

1) le grandi megalopoli, New York, Londra, Tokyo, Parigi ecc., in realtà non sono città moderne ma città molto antiche, con tracciati e con una storia molto antica, che progressivamente sono state adattate, bene o male, alle esigenze attuali, e le soluzioni che presentano sono sempre frutto dell'emergenza e del "caso per caso";

2) le città nuove, cioè le città sorte in questo secolo sulla base di un progetto unitario (le New Towns inglesi, Chandigarh, Brasilia ecc.), più che la ricerca di soluzioni nuove, si sono poste il problema di somigliare il più possibile alle città vecchie, proprio accettando quella verifica formale che l'architettura garantisce alle soluzioni urbane tradizionali;

3) le città avveniristiche proposte dalle avanguardie, nel 99% dei casi consistono in un rinnovamento linguistico dei temi tradizionali, con invenzioni machinistes, ma confermando in pieno il rapporto visuale tra cittadino e città.

Stando così le cose è chiaro che le città sono oggi il punto meno funzionante di tutto il sistema produttivo e commerciale: tale disfunzione urbana è così permanente e diffusa da ingenerare l'equivoco che il malessere da essa prodotto faccia parte di una sorta di angoscia esistenziale dell'uomo moderno. Il disservizio urbano cessa di essere un problema tecnico per diventare una lotta dell'uomo contro se stesso, una condizione di crisi culturale.

Il sistema oggettivizza l'angoscia facendola diventare cultura, e soprattutto lascia in gestione alla società tutte le proprie disfunzioni e contraddizioni, alla cui soluzione viene così attribuito un valore collettivo.

La società trova così già determinato e condizionato il proprio dibattito politico e culturale da scelte che essa non ha fatto e che può contribuire solo a perfezionare.

Si ripete al livello urbano ciò che accade nella fabbrica, in cui la classe operaia è costretta spesso a gestire in proprio le carenze produttive e tecnologiche come traguardi politici, anche dove tali carenze sono dannose agli interessi stessi della produzione.

Il problema di affrancarsi da tale genere di ricatto impostando una problematica basata non sulle deficienze del sistema ma sul possesso di questo (riconoscendo nelle contraddizioni funzionali un problema strettamente padronale), viene affrontato oggi dalle avanguardie politiche, le quali rifiutano le battaglie culturali per svolgere lo scontro in termini strettamente quantitativi.

(Come diceva Engels infatti, da parte operaia il problema di una città diversa non si pone, si pone semmai il problema del possesso della città attuale.)

Da parte imprenditoriale ugualmente il problema urbano va estratto dai vincoli del dibattito culturale, dalle verifiche formali e dagli equilibri storici e geografici, che rischiano di trasformare la città in uno specchio permanente delle contraddizioni strutturali del sistema.

La rifondazione scientifica del problema urbano diventa la nuova frontiera: la radicalità della ricerca deve garantire, non il livello utopistico, ma la trasferibilità delle soluzioni; la neutralità formale deve garantire, non lo squallore, ma il superamento della componente estetica come elemento prevaricante l'uso libero e aperto delle strutture.

Il sogno del villaggio
The dream of the village

✱✱ ANDREA BRANZI ✱✱

RADICAL NOTES

Debates on town-planning are invariably bedevilled by the tacit belief that the city represents the highest and fullest expression of social culture. The idea of the city as a collective work, as the formal and spontaneous mirror of a civilization is so deeply rooted that it is almost impossible to divorce the term "city" from "social culture".
If such unity was ever achieved in the past (the city-states? the communes?), it was always due to the fact that an ideological-cultural factor was operating as the element unifying the economic system and the territorial organization.
The dream of the village, of a small united and well-balanced community in a valley, lingers on like the dream of an inexistent lost childhood and haunts all urban experiments, from new quarters to big cities.
Though repeatedly betrayed this dream has become an instrument for testing the conditions of contemporary urban life and for measuring its malfunctions and tragedies.
Applying this parameter the social group addresses urban problems not in functional terms to be dealt with on a technical level, but as civil problems calling for the participation of society as a whole. This civil unity, however, is never sought in the collective use of the city but only on a formal level, which is the only possible verifiable unity — things being what they are — in that mass of contradictions called the city, whether modern or ancient, being made up, as it is, of both public and private elements, of both green areas and constructions, etc.
The single component of the urban problem (dwellings, traffic, green areas, services, etc.) is never given a scientific solution but one which enables it to be fitted in among all the other components without seriously disrupting them.
And indeed, when we talk about modern cities we are using a misnomer because there is no such thing as a truly modern city: 1) the great metropolises such as New York, London, Tokyo, Paris, and so on, are not really modern cities but ancient ones, with very old patterns and histories which were gradually adapted, successfully and unsuccessfully, to current requirements, and the solutions they offer are always the product of an emergency and a "case by case" policy; 2) the new cities, that is to say the cities which arose during this century on the basis of a unified project (the English "New Towns", Chandigarh, Brasilia, etc.), have not really sought new solutions but have tried to resemble as much as possible the old cities, by accepting the very same formal test that architecture applies to traditional urban solutions; 3) in 99% of the cases the futuristic cities proposed by the avant-garde are only the result of a linguistic renewal of traditional themes, with maquiniste inventions which only confirm the usual visual relationship between the town-dweller and his town.
This being the case, it is clear that cities are the least efficient element in the whole productive and commercial system; indeed, this disfunction of the city is so permanent and widespread as to create the delusion that the malaise it produces is part of a kind of existential anxiety afflicting modern man. Urban disservice thus ceases to be a technical problem and becomes the struggle of man against himself, a matter of cultural crisis.
The system objectifies this anxiety and transforms in into culture, leaving society itself responsible for its own disfunctions and contradictions and attributing a collective value to their solution. Consequently, society finds that even its political and cultural debates are determined and conditioned by choices that it did not make and that it can only help to improve.
There is a repetition on the urban level, then, of what occurs in the factory, where the working class is often called on to accept productional and technological failings as political goals, even when these failings are damaging to the interests of production itself.
The problem of how to get rid of this kind of blackmail, by formulating the question not on the basis of the system's deficiencies but on the ownership of the same (in which the functional contradictions of the system are seen to be a strictly managerial problem), is now being addressed by the political avant-garde, which rejects the cultural battle and plans its attacks in strictly quantitative terms. (As Engels says, the problem of a different city just doesn't exist for the ownership of the actual city).
In the case of the entrepreneurs as well, the urban problem should be disentangled from the mesh of the cultural debate, from formal tests and from matters of historical and geographical equilibrium — all of which could transform the city into a permanent mirror of the structural contradictions of the system.
The new frontier, then, is the reformulation of the problem of the city in scientific terms: this radically new approach should guarantee not utopian but transferable solutions; neutrality of form should guarantee not squalor but an advance beyond the aesthetic solution, the element now blocking the free and open use of structures.

La non grande bibliografia sulle avanguardie d'architettura degli anni '70 inizia con quel numero unico di Design Quarterly 78-79, edito a Minneapolis nell'ottobre del 1970 e gestito interamente da John S. Margolies, sulla "conceptual architecture"; il primo grande catalogo generale, ragionato, è costituito da « JAM: Projecte der Arthropoden zur Gestaltung der Zukunft », edito nel 1971 a Colonia e preparato da James Burns.
Tra le altre pubblicazioni importanti, oltre alla istituzione di questo filone sui recenti numeri di Casabella e alla rubrica "Cosmorama" di A.D., ci sono i due articoli di Charles Jencks nel numero di giugno 1971 e su quello di gennaio 1972, sempre su Architectural Design, dedicati all'avanguardia italiana.
Meno noto anche perché totalmente intraducibile, il ponderoso saggio sulle avanguarrdie fiorentine pubblicato da Arata Isozaki su Monthly Art Magazine a Tokyo, nell'ottobre del 1971.
Un caso a parte, per univocità di contenuto, è costituito dalla serie di numeri che IN, a partire dal giugno del 1971, dedica all'avanguardia internazionale d'architettura.
Le tesi proposte sono: "La distruzione dell'oggetto" (IN 2-3), "Distruzione e riappropriazione della città" (IN 5, 6 e 7), e quale riferimento il più generale possibile "La abolizione del lavoro".
Già nella scelta di questi temi può essere notato il particolare taglio dato alla ricerca editoriale, la quale vuole sottolineare la componente tecnico-distruttiva del ruolo storico delle avanguardie, all'interno però non di un nichilismo decadente o di un terrorismo repressivo, ma piuttosto nel quadro di un processo di auto-liberazione dell'individuo dalle armature comportamentali costituite dalle estetiche e dalle morali correnti.
Il dato positivo, progettuale, viene rifiutato proprio in ragione di questa radicale rifondazione della cultura, intesa non più come settore produttivo di modelli e valori universali (settore che trae la propria ragione dalla totale alienazione culturale della società che lavora), ma come forma spontanea di comunicazione e di vita.
L'unica prospettiva all'interno della quale tale ipotesi può porsi è appunto quella dell'abolizione del lavoro, intesa come legge di tendenza di tutti i fenomeni sociali attuali e come unica utopia generale delle estetiche liberatorie dell'avanguardia.
Non tutti gli interventi presentano una direzione parallela alle tesi proposte; ecco infatti alcune tipologie più particolari di comportamento:
1) molti gruppi sviluppano una componente anarchica (i Salz der Erde, la Coop. Himmelblau, ecc.) accentuata dall'uso degli happenings, la cui forza dissacrante corre sovente il rischio di riproporre il gruppo "provocatore" come casta di sacerdoti dionisiaci, che agiscono in preda al proprio raptus sacro, mentre gli "altri" stanno a guardare e a aumentare la propria alienazione.
2) i gruppi "ecologici" (gli Street Farm, gli Ant-Farm ecc.) che identificando natura con libertà propongono una sorta di terrorismo verde, moraleggiando su una arcadia preindustriale come ipotesi di uno stato pre-urbano. L'assedio della campagna alla città viene letto in termini di conflitto ideologico.
3) i gruppi "concettuali" (gli U.F.O. Gianni Pettena, ecc.) si liberano dei linguaggi e degli strumenti disciplinari per inviare messaggi in codice, ironici in maniera didattica, ma spesso di difficile circolazione. La loro operazione sembra spesso tendere a una morte dall'interno delle discipline stesse, consunte e esauste dalla propria estrema auto-coscienza.

✶✶ ANDREA BRANZI ✶✶

RADICAL NOTES

Pubblicazioni sulle avanguardie

Publications on the avant-garde

The rather limited bibliography on the architectural avant-garde in the seventies begins with the single edition of the « Design Quarterly » 78-79 published in Minneapolis in October 1970, an edition which John S. Margolies devotes entirely to "conceptual architecture".
The first big systematic general catalogue consist of « Jam: Projekte der Arthropoden zur Gestaltung der Zukunft » edited by James Burns and published in Cologne in 1971.
Among the other important publications, besides the series on this theme in recent issues of « Casabella » and in the "Cosmorama" column of « Architectural Design », there are two articles by Charles Jencks in the June 1971 and January 1972 issues of « Architectural Design » dedicated to the Italian avant-garde.
Less well-known, also because it is completely untranslatable, is the ponderous article on the Florentine avant-garde published by Arata Isozaki in « Monthly Art Magazine » of Tokyo, in October 1971.
For singleness of purpose, a special case will be found in the series of issues which « IN » has been dedicating to the international avant-garde in architecture since June 1971. The subjects proposed are: "The destruction of the object" (IN 2-3), "The destruction and reappropriation of the city" (IN 5, 6 and 7), and as the most general reference "The abolition of work". The very choice of these themes reveals the direction taken by the editorial research, which tends to underscore the technical-destructive component of the historical role played by the avant-garde, not inspired by any decadent nihilism or repressive terrorism, but seen rather in the context of a process of self-liberation of the individual from the rigid behavioural patterns found in current aesthetics and morals.
The given positive element, design, is rejected on the grounds of this radical refoundation of culture — culture no longer in the sense of a sector producing universal models and values (a sector rooted in the total cultural alienation of working men and women), but in the sense of a spontaneous form of communication and life. The only prospect in which such a hypothesis can be postulated is that based on the abolition of work, which is seen as the law underlying all current social phenomena and as the unique general Utopia of the liberating aesthetics propounded by the avant-garde.
Not all contributions run parallel to the theses advanced here; here, for instance, are a few of the more detailed behavioural typologies: 1) many groups develop an anarchic component (Salz der Erde, Coop. Himmelblau, etc.) accompanied by the use of happenings whose desecrative virulence often seems to cast the "provocatory" group in the role of Dionysian priests seized by a fit of sacred frenzy, while the "others" look on and become increasingly alienated; 2) the "ecological" groups (the Street Farm and Ant Farm groups, etc.) who, by identifying nature with liberty, propound a kind of green terrorism, moralizing on a preindustrial Arcadia as a hypothesis for a pre-urban state. The siege waged by the country against the town is interpreted in terms of ideological conflict; 3) the "conceptual" groups (the UFO, Gianni Pettena, etc.) have divested themselves of the usual disciplinary idioms and implements in order to send out didactically ironic messages in code — messages, however, not so easily circulated. Their operation often seems to tend towards a death within the disciplines themselves, which are now worn out and exhausted by their own extreme self-consciousness.

In the attempt to trace technical contributions to the process of clarifying ends and themes of radical architecture, Ivan Illich's book on the « Descholarisation of society, for an alternative to the scholastic institution » (ed. Bompiani) takes its place along the road of the progressive demystification of culture and its social role, and therefore of all its normal and physical structures.
Illich's criticism deals with a strictly disciplinary field such as the school, but as he himself initially declares, the choice of such a field is only an instrumental matter, not so much because an ideological criticism is made of it — and therefore a general criticism —, and much less so because the school represents the most symbolic branch of the contradictions of the system, but rather for the fact that this sort of analysis could be applied indifferently to other branches and to other forms with identical results: the army, the family, work etc. And, we wish to add, the town.
Ivan Illich makes a very precise initial observation: in our present-day society everything that used to be instrumental to achieving an end has ended up by gaining the upper hand over the end itself, substituting it with a bureaucratic structure. In the case of the school it is clear how it has come to substitute the "end of culture" by becoming "culture" itself, denying all right to everything that does not officially pass through it. It is possible to note the same transforming tendency in the case of the town, so that if the town is born as a necessity of "civilization" it has ended up by becoming "the civilization" putting forward its own image as an end in itself that society must try to reach.
Ivan Illich does not fall into the all too frequent fault of envisaging a "better" school — that is to say, trying to single out alternative subject matter to the present one; his analysis is always moving along a strictly technical plane. In fact he reveals how it is at the very level of the aims it sets itself that the school does not function. It does not educate, inasmuch as the formation of young people never takes place within the school walls but elsewhere, in times and places that are not controlled scholastically. It does not provide a technical preparation with the capital used and the time it utilizes. All the programmes aimed at improving its functioning have promptly failed, owing not so much to weakness or mistakes but because the school is not an organism capable of being improved beyond a certain point. Moreover the hypothesis of an open school for all young people irrespective of their social class is a technical, and not a political, utopia that is quite inaccessible. A demostration of this assertion has come from the efforts carried out in the United States in recent years.
All these observations could be applied directly to the town when underlining the technical, not political, impossibility of exceeding a functional limit which cannot be objectively improved beyond a certain minimum level. The battle to improve towns as they are at present is limited by having to operate on a body that is full of structural rather than social contradictions which no new equilibrium will ever manage to regenerate, a body that is too old to absorb a newly-conceived vision of existing and living.
Ivan Illich's conclusion is that the present-day school only functions in relation to the productive structure of consumption models in society, and its real aim is to "guard" boys for a certain number of years. As this is the school's function it is therefore always and only negative in whatever society it operates independent of the values and aims it has set itself.
You will never obtain anything useful from school, as is the case with prisons.
All those who believe that one day it will be possible to have schools that teach how to carry out a revolution do not realize this truth. So too the town, which formalizes society in a moment of its social transformation in a functional manner, posing immediately as an autonomous cultural and figurative patrimony that cannot be transformed: the town will never be a revolutionary weapon unless it is through its own failure (barricades).
Ivan Illich does not hypothesize so much in terms of a flow-back towards general ignorance, just as we do not hypothesize a return to cave-life, but a different system of spontaneous, creative, individual culturalization within society itself and not in the school, something more functional which we must now define, as Ivan Illich says, in terms of « those individual objectives that can favour the advent of an Age of free time (scholé) in opposition to an economy dominated by service industries ». In effect the basic aim of a radical critic of institutions, whether scholastic or urban, is not to make them instruments of revolution but instruments in the hand of man, thereby enabling him to take a decisive step towards liberation from work.

The Abolition of School

✱✱ ANDREA BRANZI ✱✱

RADICAL NOTES

L'abolizione della scuola

Nel tentativo di reperire contributi tecnici al processo di chiarimento dei fini e dei temi della radical architecture, il libro di Ivan Illich sulla « Descolarizzazione della società, per una alternativa all'istituzione scolastica » (ed. Bompiani) si colloca sulla strada della progressiva demistificazione della cultura e del suo ruolo sociale, e quindi di tutte le sue strutture formali e fisiche.
La critica dell'Illich si muove in un campo strettamente disciplinare, come quello della scuola, ma come egli stesso dichiara inizialmente, la scelta di tale campo è solo strumentale, non tanto perché ne viene fatta una critica ideologica (e quindi generale), né tanto meno perché la scuola rappresenti il settore più emblematico delle contraddizioni del sistema, ma piuttosto per il fatto che tale genere di analisi potrebbe essere indifferentemente applicata ad altri settori e ad altre strutture con identici risultati: l'esercito, la famiglia, il lavoro, ecc.
E la città, aggiungiamo noi.
Ivan Illich fa un rilevamento iniziale molto preciso: nella società attuale, tutto ciò che un tempo era strumentale al conseguimento di un fine ha finito per prendere il sopravvento sul fine stesso, sostituendolo sotto forma di struttura burocratica. Nel caso della scuola, è chiaro come essa ha sostituito il "fine della cultura" divenendo essa stessa "la cultura" e negando tutto quanto non transita ufficialmente attraverso di lei. Nel caso della città, è possibile riscontrare lo stesso processo involutivo, per cui se la città nasce come necessità di "civiltà", essa ha finito per diventare "la civiltà", ponendosi come fine chiuso in se stesso che la società deve cercare di raggiungere.
Ivan Illich non cade nell'errore, fin troppo frequente, di ipotizzare una scuola "migliore", cercando cioè di individuare contenuti alternativi a quelli attuali, ma muove la sua analisi sempre su di un piano strettamente tecnico. Egli rileva infatti come la scuola non funzioni proprio sul piano degli scopi che si prefigge: non educa nel senso che la formazione del giovane non avviene mai nell'ambito scolastico ma altrove, in tempi e in luoghi non scolasticamente controllati; non fornisce una preparazione tecnica ai capitali impiegati e ai tempi utilizzati: tutti i programmi tesi a migliorare il suo funzionamento sono puntualmente falliti, non tanto per debolezza o per errori, ma perché la scuola non è un organismo in grado di essere migliorato più di tanto. Non solo, ma l'ipotesi di una scuola aperta a tutti i giovani di tutte le classi sociali è un'utopia tecnica, e non politica, assolutamente irraggiungibile. Lo sforzo compiuto negli Stati Uniti in questi ultimi anni ne è una dimostrazione.
Tutte queste osservazioni potrebbero essere applicate direttamente alla città, nel sottolineare la sua impossibilità tecnica, e non politica, a superare un limite funzionale che oltre un certo livello non può essere oggettivamente migliorato. La battaglia per "migliorare" le attuali città ha il limite di operare su di un corpo pieno di contraddizioni strutturali più che sociali, che nessun nuovo equilibrio riuscirà mai a rigenerare, un corpo troppo vecchio per contenere una visione appena nuova del vivere e dell'abitare.
La conclusione di Ivan Illich è che oggi la scuola assolve solo alla funzione di struttura portante di modelli di consumo nella società, e il suo scopo reale è quello di "custodire" i ragazzi per un certo periodo di anni. La funzione della scuola in quanto tale è quindi sempre e soltanto "negativa", in qualsiasi società agisca e indipendentemente dai valori e dagli scopi che si prefigge.
Dalla scuola, come dalla prigione, non si otterrà mai niente di buono: non si rendono conto di questa verità tutti coloro che credono che un giorno potrà esistere una scuola che insegna a fare la rivoluzione. Così la città che formalizza funzionalmente la società in un momento della sua trasformazione sociale, ponendosi immediatamente come patrimonio culturale e figurativo autonomo non trasformabile: la città non potrà mai essere strumento rivoluzionario se non attraverso il proprio fallimento (le barricate).
Ciò che Ivan Illich ipotizza non è un riflusso nell'ignoranza generale, come noi non ipotizziamo un ritorno alle caverne, ma un diverso sistema di culturalizzazione individuale spontaneo, creativo dentro la società stessa e non dentro la scuola, più funzionale già oggi a precisare, come dice Ivan Illich, « quegli obbiettivi individuali che possono favorire l'avvento di una Età del tempo libero (scholé) in opposizione a una economia dominata dalle industrie dei servizi ».
Il fine ultimo infatti di una critica radicale alle istituzioni, scolastiche e urbane, non è quello di farne strumenti di rivoluzione, ma strumenti in mano all'uomo, facendolo decisamente incamminare verso la liberazione dal lavoro.

All such modification in customs as were introduced in the '60s, most studies agree, may be traced to a spark which set off a chain of consequences still with us. This presage of future storms was the rock and roll of the King of Memphis, the great Elvis Presley.
Elvis, and all the phenomena that followed him — from the Beatles to Bob Dylan, from pop art to underground art — are generally gathered by historians of the period into a kind of "parallel history" evolving side by side with other phenomena considered autonomous and of a strictly social nature, such as the youth protest movement, the French May "revolution", the extra-parliamentary political movements, the great strikes, etc.
The latter, for the very reason that they spring from the "structural contradictions" of the social system, seem to have a logic of their own not subject to influences of a cultural kind, and least of all to musical influences. But this is true only up to a certain point.
It is quite true that the political struggle has nothing to do with culture, and it is also true that it is not the intellectuals but economic considerations that determine the great events of history; nevertheless, it is still true that there is a nexus between such phenomena as Elvis Presley and the May "revolution" in France, a nexus of a peculiar kind which is not so much casual as psycho-physical. In fact, the contradictions of the system are always with us, there are thousands of reasons for rebelling, and we all know what they are, for they are part of our lives; yet years and years pass without any mass protest or social action. No one is strong enough to move, to break up the patterns of his own behaviour moulded by moral and aesthetic considerations conducive to passivity.
This sets the stage for such mass phenomena as rock and roll or Mary Quant's thighs-to-the-breeze miniskirts: the unleashing of such psychomotor activities as pop dancing or sex as the basis of spontaneous communication creates a new freedom which becomes freedom of judgement and of movement and, consequently, new political thrust aimed at the destruction of a fictitious equilibrium based on inhibition. These mass-consumption phenomena that so deeply influence the customs of a society and its evolution towards self-determination do not offer the consumer a cultural model to follow nor any codified ideological message, but simply make him perform a number of activities which are in themselves therapeutic.
And this is precisely the direction taken by the avant-garde as well: it radicalizes the primary component of cultural phenomena, which is always spontaneous, and tends to level down to zero all technologies and codes of a formal nature.
Moreover music, being a homogenous international medium, becomes a common denominator for many other phenomena of a different kind. The direct connections between pop music and avant-garde movements have always remained within this framework. The only exception, I would say, is the 9999 group of Florence (Fiumi, Galli, Caldini and Birelli) which for the last four years has been running the Space Electronic, a big dancing hall which has engaged the services of some stars of international pop-music. Their connection with this pop world has been fundamentally sound, because they do not pose as whining missionaries engaged in a crusade in favour of modern music, for they know that this music transmits no codified messages but is important only for those who play it and dance it. In fact, the only cultural vocation that the group have coherently espoused on a theoretical level is quitting work so as to dedicate themselves entirely to living. A vocation of great importance and great maturity, this, which the intellectuals have lacked the courage to admit, preferring to conceal their "do-nothing" attitudes behind a kind of middle-class affluence, and not to brandish them as a radical revolt against work carried out at great personal risk. The choice made by the 9999 group is clear-cut: to run their own culture privately, without handing it over to institutional structures. This is why they have to get into the thick of things and often do the job by hand, with unpretentious craftsmanship unburdened by aspiration to a managerial role. An example of this is a book on their work which they put out in 500 copies, the cover in hand-embossed copper. A job that took six months.

Rock and Revolution

✱✱ ANDREA BRANZI ✱✱

RADICAL NOTES

Rock e rivoluzione

Tutte le analisi sulla storia delle modificazioni del costume negli anni '60, risalgono concordemente ad un fenomeno nel quale riconoscono la scintilla che ha scatenato un processo a catena, che ancora non ha cessato di crescere. Tale segno premonitore delle future tempeste è stato il r'n'r' del Re di Memphis, il grande Elvis Presley.
Lui e tutti quei fenomeni che lo hanno seguito, dai Beatles a Bob Dylan, dalla pop art all'underground, vengono generalmente raccolti dagli storiografi in una sorta di "storia parallela" ad altri fenomeni, considerati autonomi e dotati di una natura strettamente sociale, come la contestazione giovanile, il maggio francese, i movimenti extra-parlamentari, i grandi scioperi, ecc.
Questi ultimi fenomeni, proprio perché generati dalle "contraddizioni strutturali" del sistema sociale, sembrano possedere una logica autonoma libera da gestazioni culturali e tanto meno musicali.
Il che però è relativamente vero.
E' vero che la lotta politica non è un fatto culturale, ed è vero altrettanto che non sono gli intellettuali a guidare i grandi fenomeni storici ma è l'economia, però è altrettanto vero che esiste tra questi fenomeni (Elvis Presley-maggio francese) un legame di natura particolare, non di causa-effetto, ma piuttosto direi di natura psico-fisica. Mi spiego.
Le contraddizioni del sistema esistono in permanenza, motivi per ribellarsi ce ne sono sempre stati a migliaia, tutti li conoscono e li vivono continuamente, eppure passano lunghi periodi di anni senza una voce o un moto di protesta sociale: nessuno possiede la forza di muoversi, di rompere quelle strutture del proprio comportamento che le morali e le estetiche ci costruiscono intorno, disponendoci alla passività.
E' questo il piano sul quale agiscono fenomeni di massa come il r'n'r' o le cosce all'aria di Mary Quant: lo scatenamento di una attività psicomotoria come il ballo pop, o il sesso come base di comunicazione spontanea, creano nella società o in una parte di essa una nuova libertà che diventa di giudizio e di movimento, e quindi carica politica nuova che muove alla distruzione di un equilibrio fittizio basato sull'inibizione.
Questi fenomeni di "largo consumo" che così profondamente possono agire sul suo sviluppo verso l'auto-determinazione, non propongono al consumatore un modello culturale da raggiungere, non possiedono un messaggio ideologico in codice, ma gli fanno compiere alcune azioni, alcuni movimenti, e alcune attività che sono di per se stesse terapeutiche.
E' esattamente questa la direzione verso la quale muove anche l'avanguardia: radicalizza nei fenomeni culturali la componente primaria, che è sempre spontanea, e tende a ridurre a zero tutte le tecnologie e i codici di lettura formale.
Non solo, ma la musica rappresentando un medium internazionale omogeneo, costituisce un riferimento di fondo a tanti altri fenomeni di natura diversa. I legami diretti tra musica pop e movimenti di avanguardia sono sempre rimasti su questo piano di riferimento; l'unico caso diverso credo sia quello del gruppo fiorentino dei 9999 (Fiumi Galli Caldini Birelli) che da quattro anni gestisce lo Space Electronic, un grande locale da ballo nel quale si sono esibite le maggiori stars della pop-music internazionale, alle quali spesso il gruppo funge da impresario. Il loro rapporto con tale mondo è dei più sani: non si presentano come missionari lamentosi di una crociata per la musica moderna, perché hanno capito che tale musica non possiede messaggi in codice ma è importante solo per chi la suona e chi la balla. La vocazione culturale che infatti il gruppo coerentemente teorizza è quella di riuscire a smettere di lavorare per potersi dedicare esclusivamente a vivere: vocazione di grande importanza e di grande maturità, che spesso gli intellettuali non hanno avuto il coraggio di confessare, preferendo camuffare il loro "non far niente" dietro a una sorta di benessere borghese e non come rivolta radicale, condotta rischiosamente in prima persona, contro il lavoro.
La scelta fatta dal gruppo dei 9999 è precisa: gestire in privato la propria cultura, senza demandarla a strutture istituzionali. Per questo devono entrare "dentro" alle cose per compierle manualmente, con modestia artigiana priva di ambizioni manageriali; hanno fatto per esempio un libro dei propri lavori, in 500 copie, con copertina in rame sbalzato a mano. Una fatica durata sei mesi.

The Van Abbemuseum of Eindhoven has dedicated an exhibition and a beautiful catalogue to the roads of the world, from those of pre-industrial Europe to those of China, etc. The exhibit offers a mass of complex documentary material on urban traffic circulation, which is treated as one of the fundamental structures underpinning the complex functional and ideological balance of the city — whether modern or historical — as a structure of commercial and cultural exchange, and as a public patrimony. As an urban phenomenon the street is inextricably bound up with that of the city itself, but it has an autonomous cultural identity of its own and belongs to a particular phenomenological category, so that it is possible to concentrate on the street (and perhaps also on its crisis and decline) independently of other urban factors.

The myth of free trade as a natural fact has charged the city with guaranteeing ideal conditions in the market, just as organic tissue guarantees vital exchanges between various cells. This state of optimum functionality theoretically consists in the mediation between private and public interests which the city, by definition, is supposed to guarantee in the much broader context of an equilibrium of technology and nature. In the bourgeois ethos, in fact, ecological equilibrium and social justice are only parts of a single problem (hence, among other things, their radical resistance to solution), so in theory the city becomes the place where this equilibrium is formally achieved in physical and linguistic structures (!). This being the case, the Town Plan becomes an instrument of mediation between general and particular interests — between Culture and Technics, Nature and Engineering, Man and Society — all this to be found inside a rigid functional system, which should have a scientific pattern of its own, albeit retaining a certain linguistic grace preferably within the context of a responsible civic awareness. (The fact, however, that it is now absolutely impossible to carry this out creates an added complication, because it leads to a misunderstanding as to the political meaning of such a mechanism). It is clear that inside all this highly complicated balance of forces and of different logical schemes the street network becomes the objective and "figurative" plan of the city's functional life, for the very reason that it is that part of the city that we can all use (besides our flats and offices) and it is moreover the place from which we can "see" the city. In fact the street not only serves the compact private tissue (homes), but by sectioning it singles out the floors on which the architectonic language will appear (the façades).

The street, and more generally the bourgeois metropolis, remains a visual structure in spite of all, and as an experience it is confined to that type of communication. The commercial information traditionally provided by the street added to all the contradictions of its messages and idioms, has remained what it was a century ago except for neon lighting. That is, while electronic information is working on the social body in depth, in the sense that it has gone beyond the limits of purely "visual" information (as Marshall Mc Luhan tells us), the city and its commercial structures are still largely based on the 19th century shop in their use and optical message.

As a social structure, the street has generated some complex phenomena of cultural misunderstanding, so that not infrequently one happens upon town-planners who complain about the steady impoverishment in the "qualification" of urban spaces, which is like a theatre critic complaining about the historical crisis in the theatre and citing the boredom of intervals as proof.

As a problem of distribution and of the homogeneous penetration in the territory, the street has been seriously obstructed in historical cities, and in modern ones has been assigned the unsuitable role of a kinetic tracing of urban phenomena.

The organization of sales within a planned society cannot accept as permanent the concept of "exploration" which the distribution of sales points along the city streets represents (a system inherited from ancient practice and habit), and in fact the supermarkets, which have addressed the problem of sales in a radical manner, have completely discarded the street formula and substituted another one which is artificial, regular and millimetric in the total penetration of its merchandise, without the mediation of architecture. It is in such contexts that the concept of the street is seriously challenged as I said, because if consumption joins production in organizing itself independently of the city (that is, of the urban pattern and its symbolic structures) the whole functional organism of the city will undergo a crisis, its system of balances will be upset, and the city itself will have to be completely redesigned.

The street at Eindhoven

** ANDREA BRANZI **

RADICAL NOTES

La strada a Eindhoven

Il Van Abbemuseum di Eindhoven ha dedicato una mostra e un bel catalogo alle strade del mondo, da quelle europee pre-industriali a quelle cinesi ecc. Il materiale documenta una complessa casistica viaria urbana, intesa come una delle strutture fondamentali sulle quali si basa il complesso equilibrio funzionale e ideologico della città, sia moderna che storica, come struttura di scambi commerciali e culturali, come patrimonio "pubblico". La strada come fenomeno urbano è connaturata a quello stesso di città, ma possiede una propria connotazione culturale autonoma e una propria categoria fenomenologica, per cui è possibile meditare sulla strada (e forse della sua crisi o del suo tramonto) indipendentemente dagli altri fattori urbani.

Il mito naturalistico della libera concorrenza ha posto la città dei commerci a garantire le condizioni ideali del mercato, come un tessuto organico garantisce gli scambi vitali tra le diverse cellule. Tale condizione di ottimalità funzionale è costituita in ipotesi dalla mediazione tra gli interessi privati e quelli comunitari che la città dovrebbe per definizione garantire, nel quadro più ampio dell'equilibrio fra tecnica e natura.

Nella ideologia borghese infatti equilibrio ecologico e giustizia sociale sono parti di un unico problema (da qui tra l'altro la radicale irresolvibilità di entrambi) e la città diventa teoricamente il luogo dove tale equilibrio si realizza formalmente in struttura fisica e linguistica (!). Stando così le cose il Piano Urbanistico diventa uno strumento di mediazione tra Interessi Generali e Particolari, tra Cultura e Tecnica, tra Natura e Ingegneria, tra Uomo e Società, e chi più ne ha più ne metta, il tutto all'interno di un sistema funzionale rigido, che dovrebbe possedere una propria scientificità non disgiunta da una certa grazia linguistica, possibilmente all'interno di una cosciente testimonianza civile. (Il fatto poi che tutto questo ormai non possa assolutamente realizzarsi costituisce una complicazione a parte perché determina un malinteso sul significato politico di tale meccanismo.) E' chiaro che all'interno di tutto questo complicatissimo equilibrio di forze e di logiche diverse la struttura viaria diventa lo schema oggettivo e "figurale" del funzionamento urbano, proprio perché è quella parte di città che tutti possiamo usare (oltre al proprio appartamento e ufficio) ed è inoltre il luogo dal quale possiamo "vedere" la città. La strada infatti non solo serve il compatto tessuto privato (le abitazioni) ma sezionandolo individua i piani di affioramento del linguaggio architettonico (le facciate).

La strada, e più in generale la metropoli borghese, resta infatti, nonostante tutto, una struttura visuale e la sua esperienza rimane legata a tale tipo di comunicazione. L'informazione merceologica che tradizionalmente la strada fornisce, incentivata da tutte le contraddizioni dei messaggi e dei linguaggi, è restata quella di un secolo fa con in più il solo neon. Cioè, mentre le informazioni elettroniche stanno operando nella profondità del corpo sociale, nel senso che hanno superato il limite dell'informazione puramente "visuale" (come Marshall McLuhan insegna), la città e le sue strutture commerciali sono rimaste legate ad un uso e ad un messaggio ottico di natura ottocentesca e bottegaia.

La strada come struttura comunitaria ha generato fenomeni complessi di equivoci culturali, per cui non è difficile imbattersi in urbanisti che lamentano il progressivo depauperamento della "qualificazione degli spazi urbani" come se critici teatrali lamentassero la crisi storica del teatro prendendo in considerazione la noia degli intervalli.

Il traffico come problema di distribuzione e di penetrazione omogenea sul territorio, dalle città storiche ha avuto solo gravi impedimenti, e da quelle moderne il ruolo improprio di lettura cinetica dei fenomeni urbani. L'organizzazione delle vendite, all'interno di una società pianificata, non può accettare come permanente il concetto di "esplorazione" che la distribuzione dei punti di vendita sulla strada cittadina rappresenta (eredità di antiche realtà e abitanti) ed infatti i supermarkets, che affrontano il problema delle vendite in maniera radicale, si astraggono totalmente dal sistema viario e lo sostituiscono con un altro artificiale, regolare e millimetrico, di compenetrazione totale nella merce senza la mediazione della architettura. E' in questi contesti che il concetto di strada entra in crisi, come dicevo, perché se oltre alla produzione anche i consumi cominciano ad organizzarsi indipendentemente dalla città (cioè dalla forma urbana, dalle sue strutture simboliche) tutto l'organismo funzionale di questa entra in crisi, gli equilibri si rompono, e la città diventa un problema di totale rifondazione.

In this issue of Casabella (page 4) it is announced that GLOBAL TOOLS has been founded by all those groups and individuals in Italy that make up the spearhead of radical architecture. The act was an important one in consideration of both the homogeneous composition of the committee and the particular moment chosen for its founding.
When I began this column I emphasized the immediate need for all the avant-garde forces in architecture to go beyond their occasional forays in the reviews and to develop a much broader "long-term" strategy in which they might cope with more general themes and hypotheses and thereby acquire a much more precise role and purpose.
It was on this understanding that Global Tools was founded, and founded not so much for the purpose of measuring heterogeneous forces in an abstract verification of their "contents", as for bringing to bear on simple and direct themes all the energy gathering strength from the crises in situations external to them. Such energy could be quickly brushed aside in the absence of any deep roots or deep motivation, but it could also form the nucleus of a radical transformation of architecture. The manual work and handicraft (or "minimal") techniques promoted by Global Tools are by no means to be understood as alternatives to industrial production, for this would only revive the useless controversies of sixty years ago, but rather as ways of redefining the field of production itself, which would no longer be regarded as a mechanism for reproducing the whole range of objects and functions around us, but as a specific and limited sector which serves and stimulates a non-provisional area dedicated to individual creativity and spontaneous communication. As part of our efforts to achieve the goals that we have set for ourselves, we should all join in producing programmatic documents for a common cultural pool, which would be of inestimable value in our research and experimental work.
Such documents would spring from a few initial observations, such as the fact that in the context of the ideology and methodology now current in industrial design, it is practically impossible to move ahead without the danger of complete suffocation within a very short period of time: it will be necessary to move on to external and original experiments which make full use of the cultural experiments, critical frontiers, and new social awareness of creativity that have come to the fore in recent years and become the common patrimony of the avant-garde. It is virtually impossible that such a patrimony could be introduced into the world of industrial design as it now stands, for that world is based on a culture which sprang up in 1920 and has never been radically renewed since then. Again, it is virtually impossible that such a patrimony should be developed inside the present-day university system, not so much because of the political debate now sweeping through it as because the whole debate has been monopolized by the generation of teachers which sprang up during the war; it is this generation which has sought to take full advantage of the student protest movement and to use it to prove its own historical validity, while carefully concealing the fact that it is this older generation alone that is responsible for the social failure of the university.
And indeed the links which are forming between the present generation of students and the survivors of the ex "Action Party" constitute one of those tragic errors that cannot fail to block the whole thrust of the protest movement for renewal and to transform it into the haughty intellectual creation of a few who, with all the bourgeois insolence that we know so well, will claim for themselves a charismatic social and cultural mandate. This enlightened culture, then, will continue to offer itself as the sole legitimate heir to the throne, in place of an effectual social renewal. Within the university today the culture-power equation is still the most important. When we consider the groups who hold such views of culture and, on the other hand, the groups spearheading the radical movements, who have attacked the social blackmail and alienating role of culture and would assign it a much more spontaneous and liberating function, it is not difficult to understand why a dialogue between the two groups is not only very difficult but practically impossible.
In this sense Global Tools will not be a school, since no one has anything to teach to anyone else, but a "system of laboratories" in which it will be possible, through experimental manual activities, to recuperate creative faculties atrophied in our work-directed society. Such a recuperation will not be used to create a new system of models and values, but simply to achieve a new and more advanced psychosomatic equilibrium and, consequently, a new degree of freedom and open-mindedness in design.
Global Tools was not founded with the purpose of carrying out any particular ideological scheme, or of elaborating any particular social and methodological model; in fact it moves within the limits of an operational field lacking any formal programming, a field in which the results are not compared with reference models but absorbed as acts of spontaneous communication.

Global Tools

★★ ANDREA BRANZI ★★

RADICAL NOTES

In questo numero di Casabella viene dato l'annuncio della fondazione della GLOBAL TOOLS da parte di tutti i gruppi e di tutte quelle persone che in Italia coprono l'area più avanzata della radical architecture. L'iniziativa che nasce è di grande importanza, sia per l'omogeneità dei componenti il "comitato", sia per il momento particolare in cui tale iniziativa nasce.
Quando cominciai questa rubrica sottolineai la necessità immediata che tutte le forze dell'avanguardia d'architettura si dessero, al di là dell'effimera vita dei colpi di mano sulle riviste, una più ampia "strategia dei tempi lunghi", misurandosi su temi e ipotesi generali e acquistando un ruolo e un destino precisi.
È da tale ipotesi che la Global Tools nasce, e nasce non tanto per misurare forze eterogenee su di un piano di astratta verifica di "contenuti", ma per far convergere su temi semplici e diretti tutte quelle energie che oggi traggono forza dalla crisi di situazioni a loro esterne. Tali energie domani potrebbero essere spazzate via a causa dell'assenza di profonde radici e di profonde motivazioni, oppure potrebbero essere il primo nucleo di una radicale rifondazione dell'architettura.
La lavorazione manuale e le tecnologie artigiane (o povere) che la Global Tools promuove non si pongono assolutamente come alternativa alla produzione industriale, ché sarebbe ripiombare nelle inutili polemiche di sessanta anni fa, ma semmai servono a definire diversamente l'area della produzione stessa, non più intesa come meccanismo di riproduzione dell'intera fenomenologia degli oggetti e delle funzioni che ci circondano, ma come settore specifico e limitato che serve e stimola un'area non provvisoria destinata alla creatività individuale e alla comunicazione spontanea.
Nello sforzo di portare a compimento lo scopo che ci siamo prefissi, dovremo tutti insieme produrre documenti programmatici che costituiranno un patrimonio comune, prezioso per il prosieguo della ricerca e della sperimentazione.
Tali documenti nascono da alcuni rilievi iniziali, come quello che all'interno dell'attuale ideologia e metodologia dell'industrial design è praticamente impossibile procedere oltre senza rischiare entro breve tempo l'asfissia completa: occorre procedere a esperienze esterne e originali che tengano conto, in maniera vitale, di esperienze culturali, di frontiere critiche e di una nuova coscienza sociale della creatività, che in questi anni sono state portate avanti e sono diventate patrimonio comune delle avanguardie. Tale patrimonio è impensabile possa essere introdotto nell'attuale mondo dell'industrial design, che trae origine da una cultura iniziata nel 1920 e mai radicalmente rinnovatasi; così come è impensabile che tale patrimonio possa essere sviluppato all'interno delle attuali strutture universitarie.
Questa impossibilità è generata non tanto dal fatto che il dibattito politico di cui le università sono teatro non permette lo svolgimento di sperimentazioni d'avanguardia, ma piuttosto dal fatto che tutto il dibattito culturale che vi si svolge è monopolio della generazione professorale formatasi durante la guerra, la quale oggi dalla contestazione studentesca cerca di trarre il massimo vantaggio e la conferma dei propri meriti storici, evitando accuratamente di mettere in evidenza il fatto che è proprio imputabile a lei il fallimento sociale delle università.
E in effetti il collegamento che sta avvenendo tra la attuale generazione studentesca e i superstiti dell'ex partito d'Azione, è uno di quei tragici errori che riusciranno a bloccare tutta la spinta rinnovatrice della contestazione in altezzoso merito intellettuale di pochi, appropriandosi con la protervia borghese che ben conosciamo un carismatico mandato sociale e culturale. La cultura illuminata continuerà così a proporsi come unica e legittima pretendente al potere, in sostituzione di un effettivo rinnovamento sociale. Il sinonimo cultura-potere, dentro l'università è ancora la struttura portante.
È quindi comprensibile il fatto che un colloquio tra tale concezione della cultura e le avanguardie dei movimenti radicali, che della cultura denunciano il ricatto sociale e il ruolo alienante, ipotizzandone una funzione spontanea e liberatoria, è molto difficile se non impossibile.
La Global Tools in questo senso non sarà una scuola, ché nessuno ha da insegnare niente a nessuno, ma "un sistema di laboratori" dove sarà possibile recuperare, attraverso attività manuali sperimentali, quelle facoltà creative atrofizzate dalla società del lavoro.
Tale recupero non servirà a creare un nuovo sistema di modelli e di meriti, ma semplicemente a realizzare un nuovo e più avanzato equilibrio psicosomatico, e quindi un nuovo grado di libertà e di autodisponibilità.
La Global Tools non nasce per realizzare un progetto ideologico, né per cercare di elaborare un modello sociale o metodologico, ma si muove all'interno di un'area operativa priva di una programmazione formale, in cui tutti i risultati non vengono rapportati a modelli di riferimento ma acquisiti come atti di comunicazione spontanea.

The rôle of avant-garde culture consists in reducing all the technologies and value systems of contemporary culture and aesthetics to zero. Its activities run parallel to those of the radical movements whose purpose is also the reduction of all the structures of middle-class morality to zero. This process of "reduction" has replaced the post-war efforts of committed culture which aimed at alternative models: it ousts and replaces these efforts in the name of an awareness acquired in recent years through private tragedy and social crisis — an awareness that there is no such thing as a "proletarian" culture.

There is no such thing in the sense that the mass of social claims put forward by the working class do not constitute a single cultural entity on which to build new values: that these claims are of a "quantitative" and not "qualitative" nature; that the cultural models that the working class looks to are not at all autonomous but only bourgeois models used in a different way — that is, no longer as cultural values but as economic goals. The cultural revolution coincides with the social revolution because once cultural models have been acquired as steps in an economic escalation, the system of economic balances on which these models are based is eventually destroyed. And the destruction of these cultural models is precisely the end-purpose of all avant-garde activities. Such a destruction is not brought about by cultural terrorism alone, but its use is meant to eliminate all the inhibitory structures which prevent man from being free before himself and before history. Avant-garde culture today no longer proposes, as it did in the post-war years, a cultural model to realize or to have society realize; it rather proposes to avoid establishing any model to imitate, and claims that the only possible reference is to be found in the free creativity of the individual extended to society as a whole, and no longer the social appanage of a class of professional intellectuals. Hence the tendency is no longer to consider culture an aggregation of technical and linguistic norms without which it is impossible to achieve "the universal value of an aesthetic message", but to try to make that culture coincide with the very nature of man — that is, with his spontaneous creativity (all men are equal and the artist is only an example of what everyone is), with his neuro-electrical circuits, and with his bio-chemical make-up.

With this tendency, the action undertaken by the avant-garde becomes an élite culture (and this is no play on words). The technical destruction of culture, in fact, means to carry forward an experiment far from normal cultural circuits and normal consumer expectations. The whole thing seems to be creating a tragic contradiction between the libertarian aims professed by the avant-garde and the reality of recondite experimentation; between the generalization of creativity proposed and the reality of an often incomprehensible refinement. But this contradiction has to be accepted and lived with, not as an error but as an historical condition. For if the proposed aim (mass production of intellectual material) is not an impossible Utopia, but the result (however distant in time) of social and historical forces, there is no need to be troubled by the lack of any immediate verification, since the avant-garde is not concerned with elaborating present-day models of behaviour but with a long-term process of liberation.

Luigi Nono's flurry of plans for avant-garde concerts in factories are of no interest; much more interesting are the experiments of John Cage which, though unusable ideologically, have been wreaking perhaps irreparable damage upon so-called modern music. Nono, realizing that society does not work, would have art modify it; conversely, Cage, realizing that art does not work, would have society modify it. In any case, it is impossible to define creativity differently without presupposing a different society; without presupposing, that is, a non-productive end for creativity itself. And that hypothesis postulates The Abolition of Work.

It is within such a referential pattern that we can consider the hypothesis of creativity — in terms of individual energy not dedicated to nourishing the aesthetic and cultural structures of society. The conditions for meta-historical creative activity lie in the possibility of generalizing as much as possible the use of such energy, which is liberating and self-fulfilling, therapeutic and non-allegorical.

The Elite and Mass Creativity

8

✶✶ ANDREA BRANZI ✶✶

RADICAL NOTES

Elite e creatività di massa

Il ruolo della cultura d'avanguardia consiste nella riduzione a zero di tutte le tecnologie e di tutti i sistemi di valori della cultura e dell'estetica attuale. La sua azione si affianca a quella dei movimenti radicali che tendono a ridurre a zero tutte le strutture della morale borghese. Questo processo "riduttivo" viene a sostituire il grande sforzo della cultura impegnata del dopoguerra che si proponeva di elaborare modelli alternativi: lo sostituisce e lo scavalca in nome di un dato di fatto in questi anni acquisito attraverso tragedie private e crisi sociali, e cioè questo, che non esiste cultura "proletaria". Non esiste nel senso che l'insieme delle rivendicazioni sociali della classe operaia non costituiscono un corpo culturale unitario sul quale e dal quale partire per una elaborazione di nuovi valori, che tali rivendicazioni sono di natura "quantitativa" e non "qualitativa", che i modelli culturali a cui il proletariato fa riferimento non sono autonomi, ma al contrario sono gli stessi modelli borghesi usati in maniera diversa, cioè non più come valori culturali ma come traguardi economici. La rivoluzione culturale coincide con quella sociale proprio perché acquisendo i modelli culturali come tappe di una escalation economica si distruggono alla fine gli stessi equilibri economici sui quali tali modelli si basano. E la distruzione dei modelli culturali è appunto il fine ultimo dell'azione svolta dalla cultura d'avanguardia. Tale distruzione non è generata da puro terrorismo culturale, ma si prefigge invece di eliminare con questi tutte le strutture inibitorie che impediscono all'uomo di agire liberamente davanti a se stesso e davanti alla storia. La cultura d'avanguardia oggi non si propone più, come negli anni del dopoguerra, un modello culturale da realizzare o da far realizzare alla società, ma si propone di non stabilire nessun modello da imitare, affermando che l'unico riferimento possibile consiste nella libera creatività individuale estesa a tutta intera la società, e non più dono sacro della classe degli intellettuali professionisti.

Da qui lo sforzo di far coincidere la cultura non più con un insieme di norme tecniche o linguistiche, solo attraverso le quali è possibile oggi raggiungere il "valore universale del messaggio estetico", ma cercando di far coincidere la cultura con la natura stessa dell'uomo, cioè con la sua creatività spontanea (gli uomini sono tutti uguali e l'artista è solo l'esempio di ciò che tutti sono), con i suoi circuiti elettrico-nervosi e con la sua sostanza bio-chimica. In questo sforzo l'azione dell'avanguardia diventa (e non è un gioco di parole) una cultura d'élite. La distruzione tecnica della cultura infatti vuol dire portare avanti una sperimentazione lontana dai normali circuiti culturali e dai normali consumatori. La cosa sembra creare una contraddizione tragica tra i fini libertari proposti e la realtà di una sperimentazione ermetica. Tra la generalizzazione della creatività proposta e la realtà di una raffinatezza spesso inafferrabile. Ma tale contraddizione va accettata e va vissuta non come un errore, ma come una condizione storica. Se infatti il fine proposto (la produzione intellettuale di massa) non è una utopia impossibile, ma il risultato, lontano quanto si voglia, di forze sociali e storiche, non deve preoccupare l'impossibilità di una verifica immediata dal momento che essa avanguardia non elabora modelli attuali di comportamento, ma un processo di liberazione a lungo termine.

L'affanno di un Luigi Nono che vuole tenere concerti d'avanguardia nelle fabbriche non interessa; interessano invece esperienze al limite come quelle di Cage, inutilizzabili dal punto di vista ideologico ma che stanno arrecando alla così detta musica dei danni forse irreparabili. Il primo, vedendo che la società non funziona vorrebbe che fosse l'arte a modificarla, il secondo vedendo che l'arte non funziona vorrebbe che fosse la società a modificarla.

Del resto non è possibile dare una diversa definizione della creatività senza presupporre una realtà sociale diversa: senza presupporre cioè un fine non-produttivo della creatività stessa. Tale ipotesi è quella dell'ABOLIZIONE DEL LAVORO.

È su tale "quadro di riferimento" che possiamo ipotizzare una creatività quale energia individuale non destinata ad alimentare le strutture estetiche e culturali della società. Le condizioni per una attività meta-storica della creatività risiedono appunto nella possibilità di generalizzare il più possibile l'uso di tale energia la quale è una energia liberatoria compiuta in se stessa, terapeutica e priva di allegorie.

Even today different parameters of judgement are hardly ever applied in comparing urban phenomena of such differing scales as the metropolis, the town, and the village.
The instruments of study applied to such urban agglomerates are differentiated only as far as the volumes of traffic or the markets of the area are concerned, but substantially the specialists in this field are still convinced that between such phenomena (metropolis, town, and village) there is no more than a difference in scale.
Indeed, qualitative judgement tends to be inversely proportional to their size, so that the village represents the best model of urbanization owing to the balance which has been struck between the individual, urban spaces, and the "overall form" of the village; and the metropolis is judged by the same yardstick — that is, according to whether or not certain "values" typical of the village have been preserved.
This "continuity" within differences of size is supposed to guarantee the permanence of a human scale (to judge from what one commonly hears) even in big agglomerates, and juvenile delinquency becomes the symptom of the disappearance of such qualities.
There has been no progress at all in the elaboration of differentiated models of behaviour: the sun, green areas, the square, the fountain, the municipal park with its benches — have all remained the immovable symbols of a dream, and are still the only typically urbanistic-architectonic tools for mediating between the individual and the megalopolis.
The visual relationship which bound the villager to his village is still the same which accompanies the town-dweller to the metropolis: urban phenomena are seen as being no more than visual structures.
To this day the town-planner is still unable to comprehend an urban structure which does not correspond to a certain system of representation. Mediating architectonically between the individual and his city, or between the individual and nature, has become the outer limit beyond which town-planning will not venture.
Differentiated figurative episodes within the city limits should constitute a kind of qualitative and narrative succession of use in orientation (and for the markets of the area), and more generally, taken as a whole, they do make up the so-called "FORM OF THE CITY".
The "form of the city" is a hierarchical structure capable of qualifying every single square metre of town, and of organizing single buildings and single sequences in relation to one another and in relation to the whole.
In cities and villages such an overall figurative structure is made up of the traffic lanes (which originated in the history of the birth and formation of the said city) and the location of significant episodes of a monumental or natural character.
In the metropolis such systems of reference and figuration no longer exist, and even if they exist they no longer play the structural role described above. The Manhattanite walking along the regularly patterned streets of his town will always be in the same figurative point in the sense that he never encounters scenically differentiated episodes but always the same elementary perspective structure created by the perpendicular crossing of two streets.
His urban experience goes no further than the reading of street signs: above this level (of 5 to 6 metres) the city is no longer a phenomenon that he perceives. The skyscraper is no longer the super-monument that it was in the thirties: it is the undifferentiated accumulation of cubic metres which may rise to dizzy heights but can hardly be felt as a figurative presence. Such an accumulation rises from an elementary and extremely low distributive base (wich is what the town-dweller figuratively utilizes) and develops in proportion to the cost of the area.
In its time the Empire State Building was proposed as a kind of mega-cathedral for an improbable mega-village: today nothing differentiates it from the cluster of other Manhattan skyscrapers, unless perhaps the error in foresight it reveals.

Small Medium and Large
9
Piccolo medio grande

✶✶ ANDREA BRANZI ✶✶

RADICAL NOTES

Ancora oggi non vengono usati parametri di giudizio differenziati per accostare, conoscitivamente, fenomeni urbani di scala diversa, come METROPOLI, CITTÀ e VILLAGGI.
Gli strumenti di studio di tali agglomerati urbani vengono differenziati solo per quanto riguarda il volume del traffico o i mercati delle aree, ma sostanzialmente resta ferma negli specialisti del settore la convinzione che tra questi fenomeni (metropoli, città e villaggi) non esista che una diversità di scala.
Anzi il giudizio di qualità è inversamente proporzionale alla loro dimensione, per cui il villaggio rappresenta l'optimum tra i modelli di urbanizzazione, per il raggiunto equilibrio tra individuo, spazi urbani e "forma complessiva", e la metropoli viene giudicata in rapporto allo stesso parametro, cioè alla misura in cui essa riesce a conservare alcuni "valori" propri del villaggio.
Questa "continuità" all'interno della diversità dimensionale dovrebbe garantire la permanenza di una dimensione umana (come normalmente si sente dire) anche nei grandi agglomerati, e la delinquenza giovanile diventa il sintomo della scomparsa di tale qualità.
Non è stato fatto un passo avanti nella identificazione di tipologie di comportamento differenziate: il sole, il verde, la piazza, la fontana, il giardino pubblico, la panchina restano ancora i simboli inamovibili di un sogno, e restano gli unici strumenti tipicamente urbanistico-architettonici (oltre alle attrezzature pubbliche, come scuole, teatri, biblioteche ecc. che hanno però origine politica) per mediare l'individuo ai grandi fenomeni mega-urbani.
Il rapporto visuale che legava il paesano al suo villaggio (il campanile, la chiesa, il monumento, la panchina e il giardino) resta lo stesso che accompagna il cittadino nella metropoli (la facciata, i parchi, le piazze, la panchina): i fenomeni urbani restano limitati a strutture visuali. Queste strutture figurative sono costituite appunto da sequenze sceniche e linguistiche, da episodi spaziali differenziati.
Per l'urbanista non è ancora oggi comprensibile una struttura urbana che non coincida con un certo sistema di rappresentazione di se stessa.
La "mediazione architettonica" tra l'individuo e la sua città, o tra l'individuo e la natura, resta la soglia limite al di là della quale l'urbanistica non riesce a verificarsi.
Gli episodi figurativi differenziati all'interno della città dovrebbero costituire una sorta di successione qualitativa e narrativa che facilita l'orientamento (e il mercato delle aree) e più in generale, nel loro insieme, costituiscono la così detta "FORMA DELLA CITTÀ".
La "forma della città" è una struttura gerarchica in grado di qualificare ogni singolo metro quadrato del suolo urbano, e di organizzare i singoli edifici o le singole sequenze in rapporto tra di loro e in rapporto all'insieme.
Tale struttura figurativa complessiva è in generale, nelle città e nei villaggi, costituita dalle arterie del traffico (originate dalla storia della nascita e della formazione della stessa città) e dalla dislocazione di episodi preminenti di natura monumentale o naturale (le cattedrali o il fiume o la collina).
Nelle metropoli tali sistemi di riferimento e di figurazione non esistono più, o se anche esistono non svolgono più il ruolo strutturale sopra descritto. Il cittadino che percorre la maglia regolare di strade di Manhattan si trova sempre nello stesso punto figurativo, nel senso che egli non attraversa episodi scenici differenziati, ma ha sempre davanti a sé una struttura prospettica elementare costituita dall'incrociarsi perpendicolare di due strade.
La sua esperienza urbana giunge fino alla lettura delle scritte stradali: al di sopra di questa quota (5-6 metri), la città non è più un fenomeno che egli percepisce. Il grattacielo non è più il super-monumento degli anni trenta: è l'accumulazione indifferenziata di metri cubi che può raggiungere quote vertiginose ma che non interviene come presenza figurativa. Tale accumulazione parte da una base distributiva elementare, molto bassa, che è quella che il cittadino fruisce figurativamente, e si sviluppa proporzionalmente al costo delle aree.
Traversando Manhattan possiamo verificare la variazione di un diagramma qualitativo costituito dai materiali dei rivestimenti dei basamenti degli edifici. Ciò che avviene al di sopra di quella quota non ha importanza, e sul piano dell'esperienza urbana di fatto non esiste.
L'Empire State Building si propose a suo tempo come mega-cattedrale di un improbabile mega-villaggio: oggi niente lo differenzia dal mazzo dei grattacieli di Manhattan, se non l'errore previsionale in esso fatto.

12

In 1881 William Morris wrote his famous definition of architecture: « My concept of architecture envisages a union and collaboration of the arts in which everything is subordinated to everything else and kept in harmony with it. It is a broad conception, because it embraces human environment as a whole. We cannot escape architecture as long as we are part of civilization, because architecture represents the whole of all the modifications and alterations effected on the surface of the earth, in answer to human requirements, except for pure wasteland ».

This famous definition has been widely accepted and will be found at the base of all didactic treatments of modern architecture.

With this theory, in fact, architecture ventures beyond its narrow disciplinary limits and becomes an attempt to give a significant structural sense to the physical space which man inhabits on the earth, not only in the typological sense of the home and building, but also to his very "existence in this world".

A great dream of architecture is thus born — an architecture seen as a whole of formal, constructive, and vital arts which concur in "representing" the destiny and rôle of man in the world; an architecture which becomes a thorough verification of history and progress.

The presence of architecture is inevitable, because, as Morris sees it, man is an architectonic animal: the complex phenomenology of objects and structures surrounding us ends by becoming the only medium of our "being".

The pinpointing of this way of life carried on within a physical structure which is always "significant" (space) in its technical and linguistic implications, transforms Morris's dream into a nightmare and discloses the alienating limits of individual action, which is forever conditioned not by the results of a conscious choice but by the "exterior" reality that one is subjected to.

Our relationship with the physical-architectonic environment which has come down to us from remote historical periods and from constructional procedures, is dark and grey. The past surrounds us, and beyond this the fact of living (inhabiting) itself seems to lose all meaning.

Our relationship with the form of objects and with nature — that is, with their "raison d'être" — eventually becomes an exclusively visual relationship, owing to our continual quest for a qualitative meaning. The mediation of architecture (total mediation) becomes the grounds for an alienation caused by our increasing difficulty in identifying ourselves with the planned world around us, because the plan offers us more a model to accept than a structure to use. For Morris architecture is still "quality": not monumental quality, but civilized quality, linguistic quality, historical and political quality; and if these preliminary objectives have not been achieved we cannot hope to have an architecture worthy of the name.

Which is all very well if we formulate the problem as Morris does, but it is no longer true if the right to have architecture is not presented as a problem of quality but as a right to a service comparable to the service which provides us with a refrigerator or a computer.

For Morris the wasteland consists of a neutral reality without meaning and without characteristics of its own, but simply a negative counter to the kind of civilization that advances and, as it advances, organizes and creates order by means of its own choices.

This concept of the wasteland implies the concept of progress, and in this case progress is a matter for contractors.

The much-celebrated collaboration between the arts that Morris called for implies the acknowledgement that architecture is the noblest and most complete of all the arts; it is in its interior that harmony is achieved, and man is identified with the highest level. Morris is sure that in any case man achieves his identity through "works" which immediately become his heritage and the common patrimony of all.

There is no other way out: our only hope lies in that wasteland... And it is our attempt to seek it not outside but within civilization, meaning by wasteland not the absence of communications, but a total lack of heritage of any kind.

Eccettuato il puro deserto

10

Except for Pure Wasteland

✶✶ ANDREA BRANZI ✶✶

RADICAL NOTES

William Morris scriveva nel 1881 la sua famosa definizione dell'architettura: « Il mio concetto di architettura è nell'unione e nella collaborazione delle arti, in modo che ogni cosa sia subordinata alle altre e con esse in armonia. È una concezione ampia perché abbraccia l'intero ambiente della vita umana; non possiamo sottrarci all'architettura finché facciamo parte della civiltà, poiché essa rappresenta l'insieme delle modifiche e delle alterazioni operate sulla superficie terrestre, in vista delle necessità umane, eccettuato il puro deserto ».

Tale celebre definizione è stata largamente accettata e posta alla radice di ogni discorso didattico dell'architettura moderna.

Con questa teoria infatti l'architettura ha superato il suo stretto ambito disciplinare per diventare una operazione che comporta il tentativo di strutturare in senso "significativo" lo spazio fisico che l'uomo abita sulla terra, non solo in senso tipologicamente riferito alla casa e all'edilizia, ma al suo stesso "essere nel mondo".

Nasce il grande sogno di un'architettura come insieme di atti formali, costruttivi e vitali, che tutti insieme concorrono a "rappresentare" il destino e il ruolo dell'uomo nel mondo; l'architettura diventa la verifica più completa della storia e del progresso.

La sua presenza è inevitabile, poiché, secondo Morris, è l'uomo che è un animale architettonico: la complessa fenomenologia di oggetti e di strutture che ci circonda finisce per divenire l'unico medium al nostro stesso "esistere".

Il rilevamento di questa condizione di vita all'interno di una struttura fisica, sempre "significativa" (spazio) per le sue implicazioni tecniche e linguistiche, trasforma il sogno di Morris in un incubo, denunciando il limite alienante dell'azione individuale, sempre perimetrata non dai risultati di una scelta cosciente, ma da una realtà "esterna" subita.

Il rapporto con l'ambiente fisico-architettonico che ci giunge da strati storici remoti e da prassi costruttive, è un rapporto grigio e buio. Il passato ci circonda, e al di là di esso il fatto stesso di vivere (abitare) sembra perdere qualsiasi significato.

Il rapporto che ci lega alla forma degli oggetti e alla natura, cioè alla loro "ragione d'essere", finisce per diventare un rapporto esclusivamente visivo, proprio per la ricerca continua di un significato qualitativo. La mediazione architettonica (mediazione totale) diventa la condizione di una alienazione generata dalla impossibilità crescente di identificare noi con il mondo progettato che ci circonda, perché tale progetto ci propone un modello da accettare, prima che una struttura da usare. Per Morris l'architettura è ancora "qualità", non qualità monumentale, ma qualità civile, qualità linguistica, qualità storica e politica; senza aver raggiunto questi obiettivi preliminari non possiamo sperare di avere un'architettura degna di questo nome.

Il che è vero se il problema lo impostiamo come Morris lo imposta, ma non è più vero se il diritto ad avere l'architettura non lo si pone come problema di qualità, ma come diritto ad un servizio paragonabile a quello che ci fornisce un frigorifero o un calcolatore elettronico.

Il deserto per Morris è costituito da una realtà neutra, priva di significato, non dotata di connotazioni proprie, ma semplice negativo, controforma alla civiltà che progredisce, e progredendo organizza e ordina attraverso le proprie scelte.

Questo concetto di deserto implica il concetto di progresso, e il progresso in questo caso è imprenditoriale.

La famosa collaborazione tra le arti auspicata da Morris implica il riconoscimento dell'architettura come la più nobile e completa di tutte le arti; è al suo interno che l'armonia si realizza, e l'uomo si identifica al livello più alto. La sicurezza di Morris è che l'uomo si identifica in ogni caso attraverso "opere", che diventano subito eredità, patrimonio comune.

Non esistono vie d'uscita: l'unica salvezza diventa proprio quel deserto... Il tentativo nostro è di non cercarlo fuori ma dentro la civiltà, intendo per deserto non l'assenza di comunicazioni, ma il vuoto di eredità di qualsiasi genere.

8

È noto che dopo la grave crisi economica degli anni '30 il Capitalismo ha formulato e messo a punto la propria ideologia generale all'interno dello slogan: « Rivoluzione permanente dei redditi all'interno dello sviluppo equilibrato del sistema ».
È la scoperta della politica socio-economica degli equilibri.
Tale politica ha avuto, dopo gli anni della contestazione più violenta (1968), un grande rilancio sub specie ecologica.
L'ecologia nel suo uso popolar-giornalistico è passata da scienza dei micro ambienti biologici, a strumento di verifica "formale" della crescita delle diverse parti della società sul territorio e del loro rapporto con un non meglio identificato "equilibrio naturale" delle cose, equilibrio che non deve essere turbato se non a rischio di più gravi malanni.
Ancora una volta il concetto di Natura è diventato lo strumento ideologico più generale e più mistificante: dall'economia liberale il concetto di Natura transita direttamente all'urbanistica territoriale, e come al solito viene proposto quale strumento "scientifico".
L'allarme ecologico sfrutta abilmente la mobilitazione nata negli anni '60 dalla crisi del rapporto Società-Produzione, si appropria di tale mobilitazione e la dirotta sul piano (molto più metafisico) di una crisi del rapporto Società-Natura.
Utilizza certa protervia verbale propria della contestazione, e la mette a disposizione di classi che dalla contestazione erano rimaste escluse. Simula un attacco al Capitalismo, non sul piano dei rapporti di potere, ma sul piano della pulizia del suo sviluppo, permettendo a tutti di sentirsi rivoluzionari senza grandi sforzi e pericoli.

I danni fatti al pianeta dallo sviluppo del Capitalismo sono indubbiamente ingenti, ma non deve meravigliare il fatto che a gestire la battaglia ecologica siano proprio gli autori ravveduti di tale scempio; e non potrebbe essere altrimenti, dal momento che il disinquinamento si sta prospettando come un affare commerciale di dimensioni macroscopiche.

Le componenti che spingono a livello individuale gli invasati della conservazione totale sono di duplice natura, storica e psicologica. È la crisi viscerale che colpisce per prime proprio quelle persone, illuminate e di censo agiato, che hanno sempre caldeggiato una giusta crescita economica delle classi più povere e che oggi sono colpite duramente dagli effetti secondari di tale crescita (spiagge invase, rumori, cattivo gusto, traffico, spazzatura ecc.), e subiscono la crisi di rigetto, il rifiuto della presenza degli "altri" cioè di "loro," di questi sudicioni che non sanno vivere e che lasciano merde e carta dappertutto.

E istintivamente (quanto istericamente) li associano in un'unica condanna agli speculatori edili.

Attraverso la gestione scandalistica della battaglia ecologica la classe borghese ottiene due risultati pratici non indifferenti: rilancia il processo di valorizzazione del mercato edilizio introducendo parametri più raffinati della semplice accumulazione di metri cubi (la Natura diventa un prodotto di grande qualità, il vuoto vale molto più del pieno); rifonda una nuova morale basata sugli equilibri naturali dopo il crollo di tutti gli schemi morali precedenti (sesso, religione, integrazione produttiva ecc.).

Il vecchio sogno piccolo borghese della città-giardino ottiene un rilancio insperato come alternativa alla metropoli: il dibattito urbanistico si arena sul problema del verde.

Lungi dal rifondare un possibile rapporto tra UOMO e NATURA, l'ecologia crea una nuova e più sottile barriera tra i due. Se prima il rapporto si esauriva in un frustrante tentativo di possesso reso vano dalla mediazione edilizia (per possedere un bosco devo costruirci un condominio dentro), adesso la natura viene consacrata come un bene culturale che non può essere toccato, un quadro di fondo impenetrabile se non attraverso un codice di comportamento. Questo codice è costituito dall'emancipazione sociale. La natura è una struttura didattica e un premio lontano dal quotidiano; un prodotto grande e generale che deve essere confezionato per divenire prima di tutto l'immagine di se stesso, e non una struttura neutra e libera.

Sporco e pulito 11
Dirty and clean

✱✱ ANDREA BRANZI ✱✱

RADICAL NOTES

It is well known that after the serious economic crisis of the '30s Capitalism formulated and perfected its general ideology within the terms of the slogan: « A permanent revolution of incomes within the balanced development of the system ».

This was the discovery of the socio-economic policy of balances. During the years of the most violent form of protest (1968) this policy was launched again in ecological terms.

As used by the popular press, the term ecology has passed from the science of biological micro-environments to an instrument for the "formal" verification of growth in the various parts of society inhabiting the territory, and of their relation with "a natural balance" (whatever that may be) of things, a balance which must not be disturbed on pain of the direst consequences.

Once more the concept of Nature has become the most general and mystifying of ideological instruments: from the liberal economy the concept of Nature crosses directly over to town-planning on a regional scale, and as usual is proposed as a "scientific" instrument. The alarm over ecology has cleverly exploited the mobilization of the '60s over the crisis in the relation of Society to Production, and has appropriated that mobilization and steered it in the much more metaphysical direction of a crisis in the relation of Society to Nature. It uses some of the verbal arrogance proper to the protest movement and puts it at the disposal of classes which had been excluded from the movement. It simulates an attack on Capitalism, not on the grounds of its power relations, but on the grounds of the cleanliness of its development, allowing everyone to feel like a revolutionary without too much effort or danger. The damage done to this planet by the development of Capitalism is unquestionably immense, but no one should be surprised that those directing the ecological battle are the very perpetrators of that enormous damage: it was inevitable as soon as it became clear that the anti-pollution drive promises to be a profitable business on a macroscopic scale.

The components driving, on an individual level, those obsessed with total conservation are essentially two: historical and psychological. It is the gut crisis which hits first of all those enlightened persons with a comfortable income who all along have cried out for a fair economic growth of the poorer classes, and have now been badly hit by the secondary effects of that growth (overcrowded beaches, noise, bad taste, traffic, litter, etc.) and are now going through the "reject" phase — that is, the rejection of the presence of "others", specifically "them", the scum that do not know how to live, who litter the place with shit and paper wherever they go. And instinctively (and hysterically) the poor are lumped together and condemned with the housing speculators.

By conducting this ecological battle by means of a series of scandals the middle-classes obtain two practical results of considerable importance: they re-launch the process of exploiting the housing business by introducing parameters much more refined than the simple accumulation of cubic metres (Nature becomes a high quality product and empty space becomes more valuable than occupied space); they set up a new moral system based on balances in nature, after the collapse of all the preceding moral schemes (sex, religion, the integration of production, etc.).

The old petty-bourgeois dream of the garden-city thereby obtains an unhoped for revival as an alternative to the great metropolis: the debate on urban-planning comes to a standstill over the question of green areas.

Far from putting the relation of Man to Nature on a new basis, ecology has created a new and more subtle barrier between the two. While at first the relationship ended in a frustrating attempt at possession blocked by the intervention of the building industry (to claim possession of a wood one need only raise a building in it), now nature has been consacrated as a cultural good not to be tampered with, an area not to be trodden on without a code of conduct in hand. This code consists of social emancipation. Nature is a didactic structure and a reward far from the workaday world; a great and general product which must first of all be wrapped up to look like a perfect image of itself, and not simply a neutral and free structure.

Fin dal primo numero di questa rubrica ho lamentato il fatto che intorno alle ricerche dei gruppi di avanguardia italiani si fosse stabilito una sorta di congiura del silenzio, un silenzio sorridente e benevolo di chi o non afferra i pro blemi o tende a minimizzarli; questi silenzi e questi sorrisi da una parte celavano un processo di riassestamento all'interno del mondo accademico, e dall'altra creavano un vuoto di tensione all'interno del quale molti gruppi si sono sbandati o hanno iniziato un lento processo di involuzione.
Ma una volta ristabilitisi alcuni schieramenti e presentatasi l'occasione propizia, dalla parte da cui era più logico attenderselo l'attacco contro i gruppi dell'architettura radicale è stato sferrato con estrema decisione.
La Sezione Internazionale d'Architettura alla 15a Triennale di Milano, curata da Aldo Rossi, si è trasformata in un Summit della restaurazione disciplinare.
La condanna dei gruppi dissidenti è stata importante, cieca e intransigente.
Il Suslov della situazione è stato in questo caso Massimo Scolari, che sul catalogo della Sezione di Aldo Rossi (« Architettura Razionale », ed. Franco Angeli) ha tenuto la requisitoria ufficiale contro i non ortodossi, in un articolo intitolato: « Avanguardia e Nuova Architettura ».
Come tutte le requisitorie, anche quella di Scolari segue solo apparentemente un andamento logico e tecnicamente corretto: in realtà egli solleva la polemica ma evita accuratamente di entrare nel merito specifico del problema (tra le tante citazioni, da Camillo Boito a Quatremère De Quincy, neppure una degli imputati). Più attento alla sentenza da dare che alla sostanza della colpa, il Nostro prende possesso della Cultura Architettonica e spazza via dal campo qualsiasi presenza non allineata, sacrificando alla Realpolitik gli ingenui, i sognatori, i visionari infantili, gli anarchici.
Gl errori che commette sono molteplici e di duplice natura, tecnica e sostanziale.
Commette un errore tecnico quando con noncurante semplificazione nomina a ricorrente esempio il Superstudio, i 9999 e gli Archizoom, come un unico fenomeno.
Ma i primi, guarda caso, si muovono di fatto dentro alla « scuola di Aldo Rossi » al punto che espongono nella sua Sezione alla Triennale (ed il loro testo, del 1969, che accompagna il progetto di due villette e un condomino è forse il più reazionario dell'intero catalogo: « Per chi come noi sia convinto che l'architettura è uno dei pochi mezzi per rendere visibile in terra l'ordine cosmico, per porre ordine tra le cose ecc.... Crediamo in un futuro di architettura ritrovata, in un futuro in cui l'architettura riprenda i suoi pieni poteri ecc... »)
I 9999, gruppo di giovani architetti-artigiani fiorentini, hanno abbandonato da tempo qualsiasi discorso disciplinare dedicandosi alla gestione di un locale da ballo e alla costruzione di una nave di legno, testimoniando di una scelta assolutamente privata, e quindi è almeno scorretto travolgerli in una condanna per cose che non hanno mai fatto.
Gli ultimi, gli Archizoom Associati, sono gli autori di quella più volte citata No-Stop City la quale rappresenta a tutt'oggi la più radicale applicazione proprio del concetto di architettura razionale.
Quindi Scolari non distingue che un confuso schieramento e lo bombarda in blocco. Ma se non entra lui nel merito sostanziale della questione, vi entrerò io dicendo quali sono le differenze tra i due schieramenti, poiché le differenze esistono e sono importanti. Diciamo preliminarmente questo: che l'architettura radicale si colloca allo interno del più generale movimento di liberazione dell'uomo dalla cultura, intendendo per liberazione individuale dalla cultura la rimozione di tutti i parametri formali e morali che agendo come strutture inibitorie impediscono all'individuo di realizzarsi compiutamente.
L'architettura radicale tende a ridurre a zero tutti i processi di progettazione rifiutando il ruolo di settore disciplinare impegnato a prefigurare attraverso le strutture ambientali un improbabile futuro.
Essa stabilisce con la città un rapporto scientifico, nel senso che rimuove dal dibattito urbano qualsiasi concetto di qualità tipico dell'architettura borghese, riportando il fenomeno ai soli parametri quantitativi.
Piazze, palazzi, boulevards, strade, case, chiese, uffici, teatri ecc., sono momenti di un vecchio concetto teatrale di città, città con la quale è possibile stabilire solo un rapporto di natura visuale. Dicendo che il nostro tentativo è quello di rimuovere i parametri qualitativi e estetici delle strutture abitative, intendiamo affermare che una nuova

Si scopron le tombe 12
Unsealing the shrine

★★ ANDREA BRANZI ★★

RADICAL NOTES

Ever since this column first appeared, I have complained in it of that sort of conspiracy of silence that has been established around Italian avant-garde groups, the smiling and benevolent silence of those who either do not grasp the problems or tend to minimize them. On one hand this silence and these smiles concealed a process of readjustment within the academic world. On the other, they created a vacuum of tension within which many groups dispersed or undertook a slow process of involution. But once a few groups reassembled and the propitious occasion arose, the attack against radical architecture was launched with extreme decisiveness by those from whom it could logically be most expected.
The International Section of the 15th Triennale of Milan, organized by Aldo Rossi, has turned into a Summit of disciplinary restoration. The sentence against the dissident groups has been noteworthy, blind and intransigent. The Suslov of the situation in this case has been Massimo Scolari. In the catalogue for Aldo Rossi's section (« Architettura razionale », Franco Angeli Editore), he delivered the official reproof of the unorthodox with an article entitled "Avant-garde and New Architecture".
Like all accusations, Scolari's only apparently follows a logical and technically correct progression. In reality, he contests, but carefully avoids dealing with the specific substance of the problem (among the many authors quoted, from Camillo Boito to Quatremère De Quincy, not even one of the accused). More concerned with the sentence to deliver than with the substance of the crime, the author claims possession of Architectonic Culture and brushes aside any unaligned presence, sacrificing to his Realpolitik, the naive, the dreamers, the infantile visionaires, the anarchists.
The errors he commits are multiple and of two kinds, technical and substantial. He commits a technical error when he repeatedly cites the Superstudio, the 9999 and the Archizoom in careless oversimplification as examples of the same phenomenon. But the former, what a coincidence, actually move within the "Aldo Rossi school": they even exhibit in his section at the Triennale (and the text accompanying their project of two houses and a condominium is perhaps the most reactionary and punitive of the entire catalogue: « For those who are convinced, as we are, that architecture is one of the few means to render cosmic order visible on earth, to make order out of things... We believe in a future of rediscovered architecture, in a future in which the architect shall again take up his full powers... »).
The 9999, a group of young Florentine architect-artisans, has long given up any talk of discipline, dedicating itself to the management of a dance hall and the construction of a wooden ship, testifying to an absolutely private choice. It is then at least incorrect to bowl them over with a sentence for things they have never done.
The last, the Archizoom Associati, are the authors of that often cited No-Stop-City which stands at this date as the most radical application of the very concept of rational architecture.
Scolari, then, only distinguishes a confused grouping which he attacks as a whole. But if he refuses to discuss the substance of the matter, I shall not. Since differences between the two groups do exist and are important, I intend to point them out.
First, let me say this: radical architecture lies within the more general movement for the liberation of man from culture, meaning for individual liberation from culture, the removal of all formal and moral parameters which, acting as inhibitive structures, prevent the individual from realizing himself completely. Radical architecture tends to reduce all the processes of design to zero; it rejects the rôle of a discipline engaged in prefiguring an improbable future by means of environmental structures.
It establishes a scientific relation with the city in the sense that it deletes from urban debate any concept of quality, typical of bourgeois architecture, restating the phenomenon in solely quantitative parameters.
Squares, buildings, boulevards, streets, houses, churches, offices, theatres, etc. are moments of an old theatrical concept of the city, city as a place with which it is possible to establish a relation of a visual nature only. When we say that we attempt to remove qualitative and aesthetic parameters from structures for habitation, we mean

2

architettura non può nascere da un semplice atto di progettazione, ma dalla modificazione dell'uso che l'uomo può fare del proprio ambiente.
Più questo ambiente possiede connotazioni culturali e linguistiche proprie, più il suo libero uso ne resta impedito; più l'individuo è costretto a muoversi all'interno di un medium culturale già codificato e più egli rinuncerà all'uso delle proprie facoltà creative, già profondamente atrofizzate dal proprio destino di produttore (e non di creatore).
La casa tradizionale (perfettamente funzionale all'interno dell'attuale e non libera e spontanea forma di società dove la produzione di cultura significa « valori universali » e non libera e spontanea forma di comunicazione individuale) agisce come comunicazione sociale codificata; tali codici non sono posseduti dall'utente ma dal progettista, il quale opera scelte culturali in sua vece.
Uscire fuori da questo circuito di rapporti produttore-utente significa lasciar cadere le connotazioni spaziali dell'ambiente per puntare all'individuazione di un vuoto vivibile: la casa come tipologia sociale non ci interessa, ci interessa la casa come palestra disponibile, come parcheggio attrezzato, come laboratorio.
Non la sua forma interessa appunto, ma il suo uso.
L'utopia che l'architettura radicale utilizza non rappresenta un modello migliore di società da proporre al mondo, ma costituisce piuttosto uno strumento di accelerazione della realtà attuale al fine di ottenerne una lettura migliore e l'individuazione delle sue leggi di sviluppo; essa utopia dichiara che fine ultimo della lotta sociale è la liberazione dell'uomo dal lavoro, e che fine ultimo dell'eliminazione della cultura è la produzione intellettuale di massa.
Dice Scolari: « [L'utopia dell'avanguardia] si configura con l'elaborazione di un pensiero negativo che proietta nel futuro tutto il potenziale figurativo scaturito dal rifiuto del passato. Nella sua volontà di ricominciare da zero essa nega la storia per ritrovare un nuovo, quanto illusorio, punto di partenza; e così facendo raggiunge facilmente l'utopia e il suo isolamento dalla realtà. In definitiva gioca un ruolo sostanzialmente reazionario poiché, con la sua autoesclusione, contribuisce al rafforzamento della condizione che voleva distruggere. »
In tutta sincerità non vedo come si possa ricevere l'accusa di rifiuto della storia (è una colpa?) da parte di chi considera la storia solo come un campionario di forme architettoniche variamente utilizzabili, e ignora le grandi modificazioni che la storia realizza anche nel campo dei meccanismi di produzione della cultura.
Non vedo come si possa ricevere l'accusa di utopisti (è una colpa?) da parte di chi si propone un mondo architettonico tautologico, astratto dal presente, inutile alla società perché arretrato rispetto al grado di sviluppo di qualsiasi suo settore.
Non vedo come si possa ricevere l'accusa di reazionari da chi si propone una restaurazione disciplinare ferrea, attestata sulla difesa del valore e della qualità della cultura.
Non vedo come si possa parlare di Tendenza (come Scolari fa in contrapposizione al termine Avanguardia) quando di fatto si organizza una mostra che invece di proporci una architettura di Tendenza ci propone un architettura di Qualità, usando come unico criterio di selezione una sorta di generico monumentalismo, per cui partendo da Rogers si arriva a Dezzi.
Sarei felice se qualcuno riuscisse a farmi convinto che l'azione che Aldo Rossi porta avanti può essere paragonata a quella di De Chirico nel campo della distruzione della pittura: rifiutare l'evoluzione e il progresso per fermare la cultura stessa, attraverso un micidiale processo di cortocircuito.
Ne sarei felice e riconoscerei in lui un fratello e un maestro geniale.
Temo invece un'altra realtà; temo che Aldo Rossi creda che la rivoluzione proletaria sia utilizzabile solo come dittatura del proletariato cioè strumento non di liberazione ma mezzo per la conferma e l'assunzione della cultura di stato.
E temo anche di peggio: temo che dietro alla rifondazione disciplinare si nasconda la restaurazione didattica, le facoltà restaurate, lo slogan « Meno discorsi, mano alla matita: la qualità dell'architettura è già un fatto rivoluzionario! ».
Massimo Scolari cita una frase di Le Corbusier che diceva che tra un buono e un cattivo architetto passano pochi centimetri di differenza. Vorrei sapere chi crede di avere in mano il metro per cominciare le misurazioni...

1. Terry Roze: progetto di quartiere residenziale, elaborato nel corso di progettazione di Aldo Rossi al Politecnico Federale di Zurigo, 1973. 2. Raffaele Conti, Domenico Di Claudio, Loredana Scatolati: progetto nel corso di composizione di Umberto Siola alla Facoltà di Architettura di Pescara, 1973. 3. Laura Thermes: proposta di ristrutturazione del quartiere San Lorenzo a Roma. Progetto di laurea alla Facoltà di Architettura di Roma, relatore Ludovico Quaroni, 1971.

(Da: « Architettura Razionale », Sezione Internazionale di Architettura, XV Triennale di Milano.)

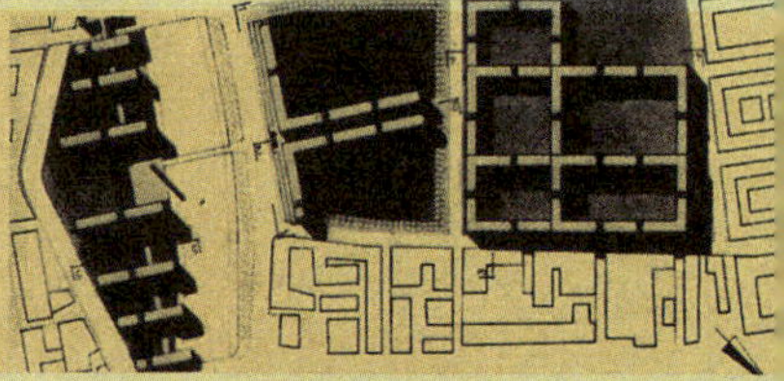
1

to affirm that a new architecture cannot be born of the simple act of design, but from the modification of the use that man can make of his environment.
The more this environment possesses cultural and linguistic connotations of its own, the more his free use of it is impeded; the more the individual is forced to move within a cultural medium that is already codified, the more he gives up the use of his own creative faculties, already profoundly atrophied by his fate of producer (and not creator).
The traditional house (perfectly functional within present society where the production of culture means "universal values" and not a free and spontaneous form of individual communication) acts as a codified social communication. Such codes are not owned by the consumer, but by the designer who makes cultural choices in his stead.
To leave this circuit of producer-consumer relation means to let the spatial connotations of the ambient lapse in order to concentrate upon the individualization of a livable vacuum: the house as social typology does not interest us, for we are interested in the house as a free court, an equipped parking lot, a laboratory. We are not interested in its form, but in its use. The utopia radical architecture utilizes is not a better model of society to propose to the world; it constitutes rather an instrument for the acceleration of present reality to obtain a better reading of it and the individualization of its laws of development. This utopia declares that the final aim of social struggle is the liberation of man from work and that the final aim of the elimination of culture is the intellectual production of the masses.
Scolari says: « [The avant-garde utopia] is shaped from the elaboration of a negative thought, projecting on the future all the figurative potential released by rejection of the past. In its determination to begin from scratch, it denies history, to renew a new as well as imaginary point of departure. In so doing, it easily reaches utopia and its isolation from reality. All in all, it plays a rôle that is substantially reactionary, since with its autoexclusion, it adds to the reinforcing of the conditions it set out to destroy ».
In all sincerity, I do not see how an accusation of rejection of history (is that a crime?) can be brought by one who considers history only a series of samples of architectonic forms to be used in various ways, neglecting the great modifications that history brings about in the field of mechanism of cultural production as well. I do not see how an accusation of utopianism (is that a crime?) can be brought by those who propose a tautological architectonic world, abstracted from the present, useless to society since it is behind with respect to the degree of development of any of its sectors.
I do not see how the accusation of reactionary can be brought by those who propose a rigid disciplinary restoration, sworn to the defense of the "value and quality" of culture.
I do not see how one can speak of Tendency (as Scolari does in contrast to the term Avant-garde) when in fact the exhibit organized, instead of proposing an architecture of Tendency, offers us an architecture of Quality, employing as its only criterion of selection a kind of generical monumentalism that starting from Rogers ends up at Dezzi.
I should be happy to have someone convince me that the action Aldo Rossi is undertaking can be compared to that of De Chirico in the field of the destruction of painting: the rejection of evolution and progress to make culture immovable through a lethal process of short circuiting.
I should be happy to see in him a brother and a brilliant teacher.
fear, instead, another reality: I fear that Aldo Rossi believes that the proletarian revolution can be used only as a dictatorship of the proletariat, that is, not an instrument of liberation, but as a means for the confirmation and the rise of state culture.
And I fear something worse: I fear that behind the return of discipline a didactic restoration lies in hiding with the faculty restored and the slogan « Less talk, more pencil work the quality of architecture is already a revolutionary fact ».
Massimo Scolari quotes a phrase of Le Corbusier which says that there are only a few centimeters of difference between a good and a bad architect. I should like to know who thinks he has the measuring rod in hand to begin to measure them...

3

Rimuovendo anche temporaneamente dalla tecnologia il codice logico dei suoi rapporti, si spalanca il baratro dello sperpero delle energie costruttive: giunti traballanti, chiodi sconnessi, obliquità, approssimazione, schegge, fragilità, iperdimensionamento, fratture, povertà...
I "limiti di sicurezza" si possono scavalcare a monte e a valle e di fatto non rappresentano che un alibi morale. I "limiti di insicurezza" invece permettono il libero accesso ai processi costruttivi (e creativi) a interi strati di popolazione esclusa finora dall'ars aedificatoria.
La scoperta preliminare della tecnologia povera consiste nel fatto che le strutture stanno sempre in piedi, e che non importa farsi tredici anni di scuola inferiore e cinque di università per far star su un palo.
L'identità tra struttura costruttiva e logica mentale ha sempre confortato la cultura architettonica dal settecento in poi, costituendo una sorta di sicurezza inattaccabile, un dogma naturale da proporre come quadro di fondo a ogni possibile evoluzione culturale.
Correttezza o non-correttezza strutturale è l'ideologia civile che separa in due il mondo delle cose costruite: l'unica energia costruttiva finora riconosciuta è la Scienza, mentre l'Ignoranza non è mai stata individuata come energia potenziale di segno inverso. Come l'Inferno e il Paradiso che però si sottintendono reciprocamente, e hanno senso solo reciprocamente.
Riccardo Dalisi guida con abbiezione mistica la scoperta dell'energia creativa (o costruttiva) dell'Ignoranza (o dello stato Selvaggio). Operando esperimenti di didattica-spontanea di gruppo, e anche di provocazione attraverso prototipi offerti alla manipolazione, Dalisi agisce finalmente senza alcun metodo tra i bambini del Rione Traiano a Napoli. Senza alcun metodo e senza alcun destino. Mi spiego: il suo esperimento non è la ennesima ricerca di un metodo didattico basato sullo spontaneismo, ma un sondaggio all'interno di uno spessore inesplorato di energia. Senza destino, proprio perché questi esperimenti non sono destinati né a migliorare i bambini (ché le loro condizioni di vita sono talmente disperate), né a creare i reperti di una nuova arte negra in Italia. L'assenza di destino qui coincide con l'assenza, a mio avviso, di qualsiasi sviluppo, sistematizzazione e prosieguo possibili.
L'esperimento infatti, una volta reso permanente il metodo, confluirebbe fatalmente in un neo boyscoutismo, o in una più grave forma di sfruttamento della miseria, intesa come categoria culturale possibile. L'esperimento di Dalisi infatti non è un esperimento sociale né didattico ma un esperimento scientifico.
E' un esperimento scientifico perché si propone di verificare di fatto la liberazione della creatività collettiva, senza indirizzarla alla formulazione di principi generali, ma come puro e semplice stato di energia naturale.
L'utilizzo dei bambini poveri e semiselvaggi del Rione Traiano a Napoli è da capire come tentativo di reperire campioni il meno inquinati possibile dalla cultura, in maniera tale che la loro reazione creativa sia la più vicina ad uno stato di spontaneismo totale. E' possibile utilizzare lo stato di totale arretratezza del quartiere come condizione di habitat non strutturato.
I rapporti immediati tra avanguardia e sottoproletariato si fermano qui: non bisogna cedere alla tentazione di intravedere in questo importante esperimento di Dalisi una coincidenza più profonda, una identità ideologica fra tecnica povera e guerriglia urbana. I meccanismi non sono gli stessi.
I reperti di tecnologia povera sono modelli di comprensione di un possibile recupero pubblico dei processi produttivi della cultura: scaricamento completo di significati e di modelli terminali, sperimentazione di una comunicazione decodificata e spontanea.
Il lavoro di Dalisi, ricco di pericoli e di stimoli, può riuscire di grave danno a qualsiasi ulteriore metodologia formale di progettazione, o può al contrario costituire una prima formalizzazione delle ipotesi radicali con tutte le contraddizioni che la cosa comporta.

Tecnica povera 13 Minimal technology

✶✶ ANDREA BRANZI ✶✶

RADICAL NOTES

If, even temporarily, we deny technology the logical code of its relationships, we are opening the door wide on an enormous waste of constructional energy: wobbly joints, broken nails, non-linearity, approximation work, splinters, fragility, oversized structures, cracks, drabness...
"Safety limits" can be disregarded before and after, and in fact are no more than a moral alibi.
"Danger limits", however, give free access to the constructive (and creative) processes to entire population levels that have so far been excluded from "the art of construction".
The identity between a constructive structure and mental logic has always supported architectonic culture since the eighteenth century, constituting a kind of unassailable safety point, a natural dogma to be offered as a basic background for any possible kind of cultural evolution.
Structural correctness or non-correctness is the civil ideology which divides the world of constructed things: the only constructional energy acknowledged so far has been Science, while Ignorance has never been singled out as a potential energy with an inverse sign. Like Heaven and Hell, however, they imply one another and neither of them makes sense without the other.
Riccardo Dalisi, with mystic abasement, moves on to the discovery of the creative (or constructional) energy of Ignorance (or of the Savage state). Carrying out spontaneous and stimulated didactic group experiments through prototypes offered for manipulation, Dalisi finally acts without any method among the children of the Traiano quarter in Naples. Without any method or any specific purpose. I hasten to add, however, that his experiment is not to be taken for just another experiment in didactic method based on spontaneity, but an exploration in an as yet unexplored field of energy. Without any specific purpose because these experiments are aimed neither at improving the lot of these children (their living conditions are practically hopeless) nor at creating the basis for a new negro art in Italy. The absence of a purpose coincides here with the absence, as I see it, of any possible development, systematization, or follow-up.
In fact, once the method was made permanent, the experiment could fatally lead to a new kind of boy-scout attitude, to an even more serious form of exploitation of poverty in the sense of a possible cultural category. Dalisi's experiment, in fact, is neither a social nor a didactic experiment but a scientific one. It is a scientific experiment because it aims to verify experimentally the liberation of collective creativity, without directing it towards the formulation of general principles, but as a pure and simple state of natural energy.
The employment of poor and semi-savage children of the Traiano quarter in Naples is to be understood as an attempt to discover the purest possible samples of culture, in such a way that their creative reaction will be the nearest to a state of total spontaneity.
It is possible to utilize the state of total backwardness of the quarter as a condition of non-structured habitation.
The immediate relationship between the avant-garde and the lumpenproletariat stops here: one must resist the temptation to see in Dalisi's important experiment a much deeper coincidence, an ideological identity between minimal technique and urban guerrilla warfare.
The mechanisms are not the same.
The discoveries of minimal technology are models of comprehension aimed at the possible public recuperation of the productive processes of culture: complete abandonment of meanings and terminal models, and experiments in a decodified and spontaneous communication.
Dalisi's work, which is bristling with dangers and stimuli, could turn out to be a grave threat to any further formal methodology in planning; on the other hand, it could constitute the first formal exposition of radical hypotheses, with all the contradictions that it entails.

6

An as yet unexplored field of study is the influence that mountain-climbing has exerted on Italian culture and on individual behaviour throughout history.
There are, of course, various kinds of mountain-climbing of different political shading, ranging from Catholic to Socialist, and in America there is even Zen mountain-climbing, which Kerouac discusses in his « Dharma Bums » as the origin of the beat movement. But while Catholic mountain-climbing tends towards introversion, Socialist mountain-climbing, which is much more extrovert and programmatic, has become a component of a certain limited but significant stratum of the Italian cultural class.
By Socialist mountain-climbing we mean the whole complex ideological phenomenology which has chosen the mountaineer as a model of private and political behaviour.
Grafted onto the proto-working class myth of "thick boots but fine intelligence" is the Great War myth of the "Good old Alpine troops". Socialist mountain-climbing springs from an imitative middle-class deformation of socialism and working-class solidarity, and breaks the ideology down into behavioural statistics. It all adds up to a rather dangerous and widespread involution which might be labelled "Mountain-climbing as a childhood sickness of Socialism". These parliamentary behavioural patterns have been taken from a kind of "Plain Man's Guide" to behaviour, which the Socialist mountain-climber regularly consults. So we find him tieless with pipe or Italian cigar and a glass of wine to hand, engaged in a game of bowls or cards, or discoursing on regional cookery... University professors or professional intellectuals commonly conform to this pattern. It is not simply a set of habits, of a kind that few really have, but a ritual leading to an ideological exemplification of one's personal role and of fundamental problems.
In this sense it was through mountain-climbing that a certain part of the post-war lay Establishment became aware of itself; in out-of-the-way chalets or on gentle slopes progressive entrepreneurs, former anti-Fascist exiles, intellectuals, professors, newspapermen, "old boy" deputies, and government under-secretaries passed one another like salmon fighting their way upstream.
But Socialist mountain-climbing is also practised down in the plains, of course: in the Comacchio valley, the Langhe hills, the Po valley, the Lodi countryside, and Emilia-Romagna, which have all become so many ideological parks.
The energy crisis only underscores the intimately punitive nature of mountain-climbing: in a round-about way the Arabs have paid their respects to the Matterhorn. So it's back to hiking and fresh air!
Those great bores Galbraith and Sicco Mansholt were among the first to interpret this world crisis as the revenge of the masses, even though it is the workers who will suffer most from it. Socialist mountain-climbers regard it as validating a whole way of life. Matters like the disappearance of sliding scale salary increases and the re-structuring of industry by means of mass lay-offs are presented as the triumph of the bus over the private motor-car, of the Aosta valley over Milan, or Lodi sausages over tinned meat.
In this climate of opinion, the (programmed?) recession is seen as some kind of misdeed to be atoned for, a punishment that we all deserve, but one that will send us back to the elementary values of life.
The "Dream of the Village" (see "Radical Notes" in Casabella 371), ever encouraged by the more conservative part of Italian planning in the 60s, threatens to become the basic choice for future city development programmes.
Those fostering the myth of a city "made to the measure of man", which is nothing but a combination of a model middle-class residence and a system of social services, have again launched the Swedish quarter as the only possible example to follow. But there are also those who are dreaming of chalets and tapering steeples...
Consequently (and paradoxically) the only obstacles in the way of this advance today are the "Tendency groups" (in Italy gathered around Aldo Rossi) which propose urban models uncompromisingly rationalist and monumental in character. The paradox is that while the Democratic-Socialists offer us an old model, the pseudo-Stalinists have offered an even older one. While the former are like mountain-climbers, the latter are like the "carabinieri". The clash is between two possible revivals. Within the limits of this debate it has become almost impossible to come by the objective data needed for making a correct choice, as the conflict lies between two different concepts of quality in town-planning, of cultural strategies, etc.
Can anything be done to shift the debate towards more realistic and concrete data and away from the mountain-climbing ethos? Probably, the only operation possible today, and the most correct one, is to brutally force the debate away from urban patterning towards purely quantitative requirements. In other words, instead of "the house beautiful" or the house of the future, we should begin to think about the house only in terms of square metres and services, driving demand towards unbridled quantity. We would propose a kind of "Tenants' Charter" in virtue of which every member of whatever family has a right (and it already exists today) to two rooms, a drawing-room, a work-room, a bathroom, a sauna, a dressing-room, a kitchen, a room for medicine and domestic medical appliances, a library, etc. We would suggest, that is, definitely discarding the "Existenz Minimum" formula in favour of an avalanche of requests for more rooms and services.
This kind of demand, and the simplest for that matter, is the only one that the traditional city could never meet without undergoing a fatal crisis.

14 Alpinismo e Existenz Maximum

Mountain climbing and Existenz Maximum

★★ ANDREA BRANZI ★★

RADICAL NOTES

L'influenza storica dell'alpinismo nella cultura italiana e nel comportamento privato, è ancora tutta da studiare.
Esistono alpinismi di vario genere e di varia coloritura politica, da quello cattolico a quello socialista. (Esiste in America anche un alpinismo Zen di cui parla J. Kerouac ne « I vagabondi del Darma », come origine della beat generation..). Mentre l'alpinismo cattolico tende all'introversione, il socialismo alpestre, estroverso e programmatico, è diventato una componente di un certo strato limitato ma significativo della classe culturale italiana.
Si intende per socialismo alpestre tutta quella complessa fenomenologia ideologica che riconosce nel montanaro un proprio modello di comportamento privato e politico.
Sul mito proto-operaista (« scarpe grosse cervello fino »), si innesta il mito dei « Bravi Alpini! » contratto durante la prima Guerra Mondiale.
Il socialismo alpestre nasce in una deformazione borghese (di natura imitativa) del socialismo e dell'operaismo, risolvendo in cifre di comportamento l'ideologia. Alla resa dei conti, si rivela una pericolosa ma diffusa involuzione. (Potremmo dire: « Alpinismo come malattia infantile del socialismo ».) Queste formule di comportamento parlamentare sono tratte da un "codice dei semplici" che il socialista alpestre mima: la pipa, il giuoco delle bocce, lo scopone scientifico, il sigarino, la cucina regionale, il bicchiere di vino, la camicia senza cravatta... Professori universitari o intellettuali professionisti lo praticano diffusamente. Non è un semplice supporto di abitudini, che nessuno possiede, ma è una ritualistica che introduce a una esemplificazione del proprio ruolo e dei problemi primari.
In questo senso nel dopoguerra parte della classe dirigente laica si è riconosciuta attraverso l'alpinismo; in baite sperdute o su dolci declivi imprenditori progressisti, ex esuli antifascisti, intellettuali, professori, giornalisti, ex liceali, onorevoli, sottosegretari, si sono incrociati come salmoni che risalgono alle sorgenti.
(Il socialismo alpestre viene praticato anche in pianura: Comacchio, le Langhe, la valle del Po, il Lodigiano, l'Emilia-Romagna, sono parchi ideologici.)
La crisi energetica conferma l'anima intimamente punitiva dell'alpino: i paesi arabi rendono un indiretto omaggio al Cimon della Pala. Tutti a piedi, aria fresca! Menagrami come Galbraith o Sicco Mansholt guidano la lettura di questa crisi mondiale in chiave di rivincita popolare, anche se questa crisi passerà tutta sulla pelle operaia. Il socialismo alpestre la attende come conferma di tutta una vita. La scomparsa dei margini di sviluppo dei salari, ristrutturazioni industriali basate sui licenziamenti vengono presentati come trionfo dell' autobus sull'auto privata, della Val d'Aosta su Milano, della salama Lodigiana sulla Simmenthal.
In questo clima, la recessione (programmata?) passa come colpa da scontare da parte di tutti, giusta punizione che ci riaccosterà ai valori più semplici della vita.
Il "Sogno del Villaggio" (vedi Radical Notes, Casabella 371), sempre cullato dalla parte più immobile della cultura urbanistica negli anni '60, rischia di diventare la scelta di fondo dei futuri programmi urbani.
Il mito della città a "misura d'uomo", che altro non è se non il montaggio tra il modello di residenza borghese e un sistema di servizi sociali, rilancia il quartiere svedese come unico possibile campione da imitare. Ma c'è già chi sogna baite e campanili azzurri...
Così paradossalmente, oggi, l'unica barriera a tale avanzata è costituita dai gruppi di Tendenza (asserragliati in Italia intorno a Aldo Rossi) che propugnano modelli urbani di dura impostazione razionalista e monumentale. Il paradosso consiste nel fatto che se i socialdemocratici ci propongono un modello vecchio, i finti stalinisti ce ne propongono uno più vecchio ancora. Se gli uni sono alpini, gli altri sono carabinieri. Il conflitto diventa tra due possibili revivals.
All'interno di questo dibattito diventa quasi impossibile rintracciare dati oggettivi che facilitino una scelta corretta, essendo il conflitto tra due diversi concetti di qualità urbanistica, di ipotesi di strategia culturale, ecc.
Che fare per spostare il dibattito verso dati meno inesistenti e imponderabili e per uscire dall'alpinismo? Probabilmente l'unica operazione oggi possibile, e la più corretta, è quella di scavalcare brutalmente il dibattito dalla composizione urbanistica alla rivendicazione puramente quantitativa. Cioè, invece di pensare case più belle, o alla casa del futuro, cominciamo a pensare alla casa solo in termini di metri quadri e di servizi, spingendo la domanda in termini di una irrefrenabile ascesa quantitativa. Proponiamo una sorta di "Carta dell'inquilino" in cui si chiede per ogni membro di qualsiasi famiglia il diritto (già oggi reale), ad avere due camere, un salotto, un laboratorio, un bagno, una sauna, uno spogliatoio, una cucina, un ambulatorio, una biblioteca ecc. Proponiamo cioè il definitivo scavalcamento dell' "Existenz Minimum" e puntiamo su una crescita indiscriminata della richiesta di spazio e di servizi.
Questo genere di domanda, la più semplice del resto, è l'unica che la città tradizionale non potrà mai accogliere senza entrare in una crisi definitiva.

We have been told that Fascism coincides with the negation of culture: the picture of Nazis burning books in public squares serves as a kind of dust jacket on the black book of horrors that culminate in the gas chamber. The mechanics of this identity has never been clearly demonstrated (Fascism = non-culture); indeed, all too often, Fascism appears to be an excess of culturalization and serves as a substitute for unrealized social programmes. Armando Plebe, for example, and by no mere chance, offers quite the contrary analysis, viz., communism = non-culture. The idea that culture is an anti-fascist constant is based on tautological middle-class thinking in which aesthetic quality is seen as solely and unfailingly revolutionary. The facts of the case will not suffrage this thesis: Ezra Pound is a typical case to the contrary, and history itself confirms that all the great intellectuals of this century (not to mention the past) belong to the moderate, and often eccentric right wing of social thought.
All of which is of perhaps small interest, considering the decreasing influence of the cultural component in our society today, the crumbling of ideologies and their transformation into pure behaviour. It is however much more interesting to observe that certain processes of involution on the right spring from avant-garde cultural movements, and that this danger will always be found in all attempts at a radical restructuralization of culture, when these movements act not so much on the contents as on the social mechanisms producing that culture.
In this regard, I think that Italian neo-monumentalism should be closely examined, both for the highly complex and contradictory motivations it contains and for the influence that it might exert, in time, in the Italian universities. Those who have read Aldo Rossi's books know that there is little similarity between his motivations and the empty maximalist postures of his followers, who seem to be engaged in a competition to see who can be holier than the Pope. Let us just say that there is an initial point of departure which came to a head in the early sixties, a point where all Italian avant-garde groups began, and it consists in the rejection of immediate compromise (the social-democrat moderatism of the schools of architecture), and in the thrust towards radical exploration, both theoretical and Utopian, but already in keeping with the reality of an overall commitment.
With restructuralization as a base, the danger of a leap towards the « rediscovery of the fundamental values of culture », of long-lost archetypes, is always present, with all its implications of an involution to the right: the culture extracted from the compromise of day-to-day mediocrity, acquires the value of an autonomous stand and bears witness to moral intransigence.
In doing this, one is not liberating the individual form « culture » as a pattern, but rather offering him a dimensional and symbolic representation of reality. When it first sprang up, neo-monumentalism was a tragic way of « shocking the bourgeoisie », of beating the middle-class at its own game, and closing it up in its own contradictions, by rejecting its dreams of progress and reproposing the academic manner. It was an underhanded way of depriving the bourgeois of its most deceptive weapon, culture, and of turning it into a rigid, useless, and backward side-show. But time has shown that this strategy is only schematic and ambiguous, for the middle-class no longer rejects fascism but looks to it as a strong-arm solution to cope with a tragic chain of mistakes. The young people behind the monumentalist movement have been driven to it by the rejection of social-democratic teachings, and indeed they are only little reactionaries frightened by the disciplinary vacuum. Time, that is, has transformed this ironic-reactionary game into an appetizing reality: in founding a « school » Aldo Rossi has lost the terrorist diaphragm that separated him from the reality of his work, a diaphragm which allowed him a perceptible margin of ambiguity and, therefore, of salvation.
And this is the really tragic thing, that today he should be standing with those who defend the values of culture; he who in speaking at the beginning of the sixties of « the logical foundation of architecture » tried to save it from the cultural battles of those years and to transfer it inside a scientific and autonomous system.
Consequently, the only revolutionary guarantee that neo-monumentalism offers today is the « aesthetic quality » of the project: the middle-class myth of beauty as the primary revolutionary value is thereby confirmed. And the process of involution is complete.
What is excluded from their system is precisely the awareness of the irreversible crisis in all aesthetic and cultural values, which have been undermined by the destruction of all the socio-economic balances on which they were based. The formal qualities of architecture and its enlightened teachings are no longer parameters capable of playing a role inside urban life. Monumental hierarchies are now in disuse, having been burnt up in the frenetic use to which architectonic structures have been put at all levels.
Indeed, today « architecture » no longer exists: in the qualification of an enclosed space much greater importance is attributed to air-conditioning, and to the quality of the light and colours, than to the secret logical harmony governing the growth of the whole organism. The city is nothing more than a usable structure inside which any systems of representation (architecture) constitute a theatrical impediment, an old and neurotic system of control.

15 Fascism and the Avant-garde

Avanguardie e fascismo

★★ ANDREA BRANZI ★★

RADICAL NOTES

Ci hanno insegnato che il fascismo coincide con la negazione della cultura: l'immagine dei nazisti che bruciano i libri sulle piazze fa da copertina al libro nero degli orrori che conducono alle camere a gas. La meccanica di questa identità in realtà non è mai stata chiaramente verificata (fascismo = non cultura), anzi al contrario spesse volte il fascismo si presenta come eccesso di culturizzazione, che funge da surrogato a programmi sociali mancanti. Armando Plebe per esempio, e non a caso, fa una analisi contraria (comunismo = non cultura). L'idea della cultura come costante anti-fascista si basa sulla tautologia borghese della qualità estetica come valore sempre e unicamente rivoluzionario. La verifica degli eventi non conforta questa sicurezza: Ezra Pound valga per tutti, e semmai la storia ci conferma che tutti i grandi intellettuali di questo secolo (tacendo per pietà dei secoli passati), appartengono ad un'ala moderata, spesso eccentrica a destra, del pensiero sociale.
La qual cosa oggi poco forse ci interessa, a causa della progressiva emarginazione della componente culturale nella società odierna, la caduta delle ideologie e la loro trasformazione in puro comportamento.
Ci può invece interessare, e molto, come certi processi di involuzione a destra possano nascere da movimenti di avanguardia culturale, e come questo pericolo sia permanente in tutti i tentativi di rifondazione radicale della cultura, se si tenta di agire non sui contenuti ma sui meccanismi sociali di produzione della cultura stessa.
A questo proposito credo che l'attuale fenomeno italiano del neo-monumentalismo sia da analizzare in profondità, per il grado complesso di motivazioni contraddittorie che contiene e per il peso che potrebbe assumere, con il passare del tempo, nelle università italiane.
Chi ha letto i libri di Aldo Rossi sa bene che non è possibile confondere le sue motivazioni con le scelte vuotamente massimaliste dei suoi seguaci, impegnati in gara ad essere "più realisti del re". Diciamo che esiste un dato iniziale, maturato già al principio degli anni '60, dal quale si sono mossi tutti i gruppi di avanguardia italiani, e che consiste nel rifiuto del compromesso immediato, del moderatismo socialdemocratico delle università di architettura, e nello stimolo ad una ricerca radicale, teorica e utopica, ma di fatto già in scala con la realtà di un impegno globale.
Da questa base di rifondazione il pericolo di un balzo verso la "riscoperta dei valori fondamentali della cultura", degli archetipi smarriti, è però già presente con tutte le sue implicazioni di involuzione a destra: la cultura estratta dalla compromissione della mediocrità quotidiana acquista il valore di fondazione autonoma, testimonianza di una intransigenza morale. Così facendo non si libera l'individuo dalla "cultura" come modello progettato, ma al contrario gli si propone un riferimento dimensionale, simbolico, della realtà. Al suo nascere il neo-monumentalismo è stato una maniera tragica di "épater le bourgeois", di battere la borghesia sul suo stesso terreno, di chiuderla nelle sue contraddizioni rifiutandosi al suo sogno progressista, e riproponendole l'Accademia. E' stata una maniera equivoca di togliergli l'arma più mistificante della cultura, trasformando questa in un rigido baraccone inutilizzabile e arretrato.
Ma il tempo ha dimostrato questa strategia schematica e equivoca: la borghesia oggi non rifiuta più il fascismo, ma anzi lo ambisce come soluzione di forza a una tragica catena di errori. I giovani che aderiscono al monumentalismo, spintivi dal rifiuto della didattica socialdemocratica, sono di fatto piccoli reazionari spaventati dal vuoto disciplinare.
Il tempo ha cioè trasformato il giuoco ironico-reazionario in realtà appetibile: Aldo Rossi fondando una "scuola" ha perduto quel diaframma terroristico che lo separava dalla realtà della sua opera, diaframma che gli consentiva un margine leggibile di ambiguità e quindi di salvezza.
E la cosa tragica è proprio questa, che egli si trova oggi schierato di fatto con chi difende i valori della cultura, lui che parlando all'inizio degli anni '60 di « fondazione logica dell'architettura» tentava di sottrarla alle battaglie culturali per trasferirla all'interno di un sistema scientifico e autonomo.
Così l'unica garanzia rivoluzionaria che il neo-monumentalismo oggi ha è proprio la "qualità estetica" del progetto: il mito borghese della bellezza come primo valore rivoluzionario ne esce confermato. Il processo di involuzione è concluso.
Ciò che resta escluso dal loro sistema è proprio la coscienza della crisi irreversibile di tutti i valori estetici e culturali, travolti dalla distruzione di tutti gli equilibri economici e sociali sui quali si basavano. La qualità formale dell'architettura e la sua funzione illuministica non sono più parametri in grado di giuocare un ruolo all'interno della vita urbana; le gerarchie monumentali sono media ormai deserti, bruciati dalla frenesia d'uso a cui le strutture architettoniche sono soggette a tutti i livelli.
Già oggi l'"architettura" non esiste più: nella qualificazione dell'ambiente è molto più importante il condizionamento dell'aria, la qualità della luce e del colore, che non la segreta logica armonia che presiede alla formazione dell'intero organismo. La città non è altro che una struttura d'uso, all'interno della quale i sistemi di rappresentazione (architettura) costituiscono un impedimento teatrale, un vecchio e nevrotico sistema di controllo.

Poche persone ancora, e architetti pochissimi, possiedono la coscienza di quanto arretrata e involuta sia l'architettura attuale.
Intendo per architettura tutti gli strumenti formali, strutturali, funzionali e progettuali che di fatto costituiscono ancora l'atto terminale della professione dell'architetto, dell'urbanista e del designer. Fin tanto che tale professione si è spostata verso tutti gli atti tecnici e politici che stanno a monte della progettazione, è riuscita a recuperare un nuovo spazio e un ruolo originale, ma al momento di rientrare nell'ambito degli strumenti istituzionali, per completare il proprio ruolo coerentemente, vive una contraddizione generata non tanto dal passaggio tra competenze così diverse, quanto dalla reale arretratezza dell'architettura stessa.
Basti pensare a tutti i modelli urbanistici in questi anni sperimentati in tutto il mondo: Chandigar, Brasilia, le New Towns inglesi, le Unità di Abitazione, i quartieri Svedesi, i quartieri Razionalisti ecc. Non esiste modello, forma urbana o quartiere campione che non abbia fallito o sia sulla strada del fallimento. Le riserve di modelli oggi disponibili per un urbanista si stanno paurosamente assottigliando o sono già scomparse del tutto, al punto di tentare spedizioni all'indietro nel tempo.
Il puntuale fallimento di tutti i possibili modelli operativi comincia a far pensare più in generale sulla impossibilità (storica) di reperirne di nuovi funzionanti. Ormai l'urbanistica si fa con le leggi e forse tra non molto la si farà con i mitra.
Tra l'altro le difficoltà che in Italia si incontrano alla realizzazione di qualsiasi politica urbanistica e le battaglie conseguenti generano un malinteso politico-culturale.
La crisi di tutti i modelli urbani ha origini complesse che sono i limiti oggettivi di tutti gli strumenti architettonici e la crisi di rapporto tra architettura e società.
Esiste sempre all'origine del disastro dell'urbanistica moderna una crisi tra i criteri di giudizio “quantitativi” che formano il pre-progetto urbano (numero degli abitanti, servizi collettivi, tipologie, collegamenti, standards urbanistici ecc.) e lo strumento “qualitativo” che ne presiede la realizzazione (architettura). Se quest'ultimo fallisce, come in generale fallisce, non esiste ipotesi urbanistica, corretta sul piano sociologico, che si possa dire riuscita. La “qualità” architettonica infatti è ancora sottintesa in qualsiasi forma urbana, però essa non fa ancora parte dei criteri scientifici di cui la ricerca urbanistica già largamente dispone. Del resto quest'ultima si realizza sì attraverso una corretta politica territoriale, ma deve di fatto passare la mano, nella fase finale, a strumenti che non sono politici.
Così da una parte si assiste a una disciplina che lavora all'individuazione di una struttura non territoriale formale, nel senso che può verificare a tavolino tutti i suoi presupposti, e poi vi introduce un sistema di verifica improprio al metodo di lavoro usato fin lì, chiedendo all'architettura una sorta di verifica visuale del valore civile delle sue operazioni. Dall'altra vediamo un'architettura che pur utilizzando strumenti compositivi tradizionali cerca attraverso il corretto rapporto strutturale di restituire (allegoricamente) al cittadino la fase finale di un processo e di un metodo politico che attraverso la “qualità” architettonica può essere valutato. Non solo, ma di fatto si cerca di rendere unitaria tale “qualità” formale alla “qualità” sociale dell'intera operazione politica, attribuendo alla prima un valore sociale e alla seconda quindi un valore estetico.
Nell'ideologia borghese infatti la città è l'organismo supremo dove avviene la mediazione generale tra gli interessi privati e gli interessi comunitari. Stando così le cose il Piano Urbanistico diventa lo strumento di mediazione tra Cultura e Tecnica, Natura e Ingegneria, Uomo e Società, all'interno di un sistema funzionale rigido, dotato di una propria scientificità non disgiunta da una certa grazia linguistica, all'interno di una cosciente testimonianza civile.
Tale miracoloso equilibrio non è mai esistito, e se anche un giorno soltanto nella storia si è realizzato, tale giorno è tramontato da secoli. In realtà l'urbanistica e l'architettura moderna agiscono su di un piano di totale utopia: il che è un dato di fatto permanente alla natura del progettare, ma che oggi pesa duramente e ne limita l'applicazione, perché si tratta di una utopia inconscia e non strategica.
Il risultato di questa crisi storica dell'architettura moderna viene vissuto nella stragrande maggioranza dei casi come una semplice rivalsa professionale contro la speculazione incontrollata o contro l'ignoranza dei politici; ma basta vedere i progetti presentati a qualsiasi concorso di architettura o urbanistica per verificare come la soluzione sia ricercata sulla riduzione dimensionale della progettazione.
Il plastico sostituisce tutti i processi di verifica: macro-soprammobili territoriali, allegorie tecnologiche, citazioni da oggetti d'uso . . .
Il plastico, come strumento il più sintetico per comunicare il “progetto”, è divenuto esso stesso il “p getto”: nella sua assurda perfezio placa la nevrosi e esorcizza il sicu fallimento.
Gli effetti plastici che esso rapp senta saranno percepibili solo 10.000 metri d'altezza: l'andamen formale delle coperture (del tut invisibili nella realtà) sono nel p stico la dimensione principale hanno assunto il ruolo che un te po svolgeva la “facciata”...
Gli strumenti di rappresentazione un progetto di architettura sono a cora legati alla simulazione, alla n niaturizzazione della realtà, e con zionano i parametri della proget zione stessa.
Questo gravissimo limite fa sì c l'architettura tenda a rinnovarsi s lo sul piano linguistico: anche mo gruppi d'avanguardia hanno comp to questo errore (Archigram, Me bolism) accettando la tautologia c l'architettura di una civiltà tecno gica deve essere una architettu tecnologica, o che l'architettura una società organica deve essere c ganica essa stessa.
Permane il vecchio rapporto alleg rico tra architettura e società, p cui la città, prima che una struttu d'uso, è una grande sistema figu tivo di rappresentazione della s cietà.

Un plastico d'oro

16

A golden model

★★ ANDREA BRANZI ★★

RADICAL NOTES

Few people, and even fewer architects, realize how backward and inward-looking contemporary architecture truly is. By architecture I mean all the formal, structural, functional, and planning instruments that in practice constitute the terminal act in the work of the architect, town-planner, and designer. As long as the work of these men moved towards all the technical and political acts preliminary to the act of planning, it managed to claim new space and an original role, but on returning to the world of institutional instruments in order to complete its role coherently, it runs into a contradiction caused not so much by passing through such different fields as by the backwardness of architecture itself. One need only consider the models of city development tried throughout the world in recent years: Chandigarh, Brasilia, the English New Towns, the various Unités d'habitation, the Swedish quarters, the Rationalist quarters, etc.
There is hardly a model, urban form or model quarter which has not failed or is not on the way to failure. The number of models available today for a town-planner has dwindled to a terribly low level and many have disappeared altogether, so that there is always a temptation to exploit the past. The persistent failure of all possible operational models leads to the more general thought that perhaps it is historically impossible to find any new operational models. Nowadays town-plans are made by laws; tomorrow they may be made by the law of the machine-gun.
Moreover, the difficulties met with in Italy in trying to carry out any policy in town-planning, and the consequent battles, create great political and cultural confusion. The critical state of all models of city-development has very complex causes which ultimately are the objective limits of all architectonic instruments and the crisis in the relationship between architecture and society. Fundamentally, the disaster which has hit modern town-planning may be traced to a crisis between the "quantitative" yardstick applied in drawing up the preliminary town plan (the number of inhabitants, collective services, typologies, connexions, development standards, etc.) and the "qualitative" instrument governing its realization (architecture). If the latter fails, as in general it does, practically no sociologically "correct" urban plan can be said to be successful. For architectonic "quality" is still implicit in any urban form, but it no longer figures among the scientific criteria now so widely available to research in this field. Moreover, quality can be achieved through a correct territorial policy, but in the final phase it must give place to non-political instruments. Thus, on the one hand we have a discipline which seeks to work out a non-formal territorial structure in the sense that all its presuppositions can be verified at the drawing board, and then a control system is introduced which is inappropriate to the method of work employed until then, expecting architecture to provide a kind of visual verification of the civic value of its operations.
On the other hand we see an architecture which indeed employs traditional compositional techniques, but depends on correct structural relationships for restoring (allegorically) to the townsman the final phase of a process and a political method which can be evaluated on the basis of architectonic "quality". What is more, in practice there is always an attempt to make this formal "quality" overlap with the social "quality" of the whole political operation, attributing a social value to the former and, therefore, an aesthetic value to the latter.
In the ideology of the middle-class, in fact, the city is the supreme organism mediating between private and community interests. This being so, the Development Plan becomes the instrument of mediation between Culture and Technology, Nature and Engineering, Man and Society inside a rigid functional system provided with its own scientific organization, which is not lacking in a certain linguistic elegance, in the context of a conscious civil stand.
Such a miraculous equilibrium has never existed, and if ever in history it had been achieved, even for a day, that day is forever gone. Actually, town-planning and architecture nowadays operate on a plane of total utopia; this is one of the permanent facts in the nature of planning, but today it is a particularly heavy burden to bear and it limits the range of application, because this utopia is unconscious and not strategical.
In most cases this historical crisis in modern architecture is seen as simply professional revenge on unbridled speculation or on the ignorance of men in public office. One need only glance at the projects submitted to any competion in architecture or town-planning to realize that solutions are sought in the reduced dimensions of a project. Plastic models have now replaced all controlling operations: large territorial reliefs as knick-knacks, technological allegories, quotations from use objects... As the most synthetic instrument for communicating, the relief model has itself beco a project: however absurd, it soothes the neurotic and exorc almost certain failure. The plas effects which it represents woul be preceptible only at a height of 10,000 metres: the formal progress of the covering (completely invisible in reality) constitutes the main dimension in the relief model and plays role which was once taken by the façade...
The instruments representing a project are still bound up with simulation and the miniturization of reality, and condition the parameters o the project itself.
This very serious limitation means that architecture tends to renew itself only the lingui plane: even many avant-garde groups have made this mistake (Archigram, Metabolism) by accepting the tautology that th architecture of a technological civilization should be a technological architecture, or tha the architecture of an organic society must be organic itself. Still present is the old allegoric relation between architecture an society, in which the city is not simply a usable structure a great figurative system representing society.

★★ ANDREA BRANZI ★★

RADICAL NOTES

17 Louis Kahn Superstar

Era uno di quei personaggi che oltre a esistere nel tempo reale sono anche un revival di se stessi, un segno che ricorda un periodo della nostra vita, un particolare significativo di un quadro d'insieme molto più ampio; in una edizione integrale di « American Graffiti », tra yogurts e turbe puberali, non dovrebbe mancare, sullo sfondo, una partita a tennis tra Louis Kahn e Herbert Marcuse...
Ci ha fatto correre gravi pericoli, ma oggi possiamo, con un sorriso rivolgerci alla sua immagine per ricordare "come eravamo", senza correre il rischio di diventare di pietra.
Quando la sua stella apparve agli inizi degli anni '60, eravamo tutti fermi a discutere sulla perfezione socialdemocratica dei quartieri scandinavi, e le vacanze si passavano in autostop sperando nelle svedesi...
Circondati da mediocri insegnanti che discutevano della prefabbricazione delle scuole, Louis Kahn rappresentò allora la dimensione biblica dei Campus Universitari Americani, il mito ancora possibile del Maestro, ultimo esemplare della gerontocrazia che in quegli anni dominava il mondo dell'architettura (tenue legame con i Grandi Padri, ai quali era impensabile ribellarsi).
Il suo richiamo alle origini classiche e più precisamente romane, fu la risposta accademica alla situazione di stallo dell'architettura moderna, che continuava a citarsi come "ordine" razionale, di cui villa Savoye rappresentava il Partenone, e Siemensstadt la Polis.
A questo immobile rimirarsi, greco e euclideo, Louis Kahn contrapponeva uno spostamento latino, una sperimentazione mossa dal destino, un richiamo a una maniera romana di intendere l'architettura, in cui volume e struttura, funzioni e monumentalità concidevano. Fu allora che cominciarono a circolare le prime riproduzioni del Piranesi e le prime visite a Villa Adriana. Purtroppo, come al solito, qualcuno non si è più ripreso...
In fondo le novità compositive di Louis Kahn erano molto piccole, e in questo senso servivano a rivelare come le origini classiche fossero ancora latenti, appena sotto la pelle dell'architettura moderna. Fu il primo sintomo visibile della crisi di credibilità del Movimento Moderno, crisi da lui vissuta tutta a destra.
Fu anche l'ultima occasione per uno stanco dibattito sull'architettura e sulle sue leggi compositive; poi fu il diluvio.
Fu il diluvio perché improvvisamente tutti capirono che Carnaby Street, gli Animals, i Birds, Bob Dylan, i Beatles e i Mamans and Papas erano molto più importanti, significativi e completi di qualsiasi profezia destinata ai muratori.
Il nostro stacco è avvenuto allora, su quei personaggi e su quei canali, e da qel momento la nostra formazione è avvenuta in altri luoghi e non più nelle facoltà d'architettura.
La sconfitta di Louis Kahn non consisté tanto nella confutazione delle sue teorie, ma nello scontro con un salto generale della cultura giovanile, nella irruzione di nuovi potentissimi media, nell'ingresso in scena della creatività pubblica.
La sua sconfitta fu soprattutto sugli strumenti: il sound di un LP, l'abbigliamento, la droga erano strumenti di formazione più potenti di qualsiasi architettura. Il grande salto consisteva nella capacità di questi "media profondi" di toccare masse imponenti in tutte le parti del mondo; inziava una rivoluzione culturale che superava il conflitto sui contenuti, per investire il numero incredibile dei suoi consumatori.
L'architettura, come comunicazione culturale, non ha possibilità di raggiungere i traguardi "quantitativi" dei moderni media elettronici o dei modelli di comportamento. L'architettura, in un mondo in cui il messaggio circola simultaneamente in ogni dove, resta un oggetto immobile che bisogna raggiungere in pellegrinaggio, un oggetto per metà strumento d'uso e per metà allegoria, chiuso nella sua dimensione disciplinare, che solo una ridicola vocazione monumentale riesce a imporre a un ristretto campo d'influenza urbana.
La città stessa non coincide più con un "luogo architettonico" ma con un modello di consumo. La qualità di tale modello è importante quanto una struttura di servizi urbani; qualsiasi luogo raggiunto dalla televisione, dal telefono, dalla moda, è parte integrante del sistema culturale urbano. La metropoli non è più un luogo ma una condizione...
Lasciamo dunque che i morti seppelliscano i morti.
Con Louis Kahn è morta l'architettura, non una semplice concezione di essa, perché lui la intendeva così come tutti l'hanno sempre intesa: un problema di qualità.

**He was one of those personages who besides existing in real time are also a revival of themselves, a sign recalling some period of our lives, a significant detail in a much larger picture; in the background of an uncut version of "American Graffiti" teeming with teen-agers and their yogurts, one should see a game of tennis going on between Louis Kahn and Marcuse...
He made us run terrible risks, but today we can smile at the thought of him and remember "the way we were" without any danger of our turning to stone. When his star rose in the early sixties we were all firmly settled in our admiration for the socialdemocratic perfection of the Scandinavian quarters, and our hitchhiking holidays were spent discussing our hopes to meet Swedish girls...
Surrounded by mediocre teachers who talked of prefabricated schools, Louis Kahn then represented the almost biblical symbol of the campuses of American universities, a myth still possible of the great Master, the last specimen of the gerontocracy that dominated the world of architecture in those years (a tenuous link with the Founding Fathers, against whom rebellion was unthinkable). His allusions to the classical origins of architecture — Roman, to be exact — was the academic answer to the stalemate to which modern architecture had been reduced, an architecture which continued to point to itself as a rational "order", with the Villa Savoye as its Parthenon and Siemensstadt as its Polis.
As a counterbalance to this motionless Greek and Euclidean self-admiration, Louis Kahn proposed the Latin example, an experimentation brought on by destiny, an allusion to a Roman way of looking at architecture, in which volume and structure, function and monumental purpose coincided. It was then that the first reproductions of Piranesi began to be passed around, and the first visits to Villa Adriana took place. There are still some who haven't recovered from it all...
At bottom Louis Kahn's original compositional contributions were very few, and were useful in revealing that after all classical architecture was still latent under the skin of modern architecture. It was the first sign of a credibility crisis in the Modern Movement, and this crisis he lived from positions on the right. It was also the last weary debate on architecture and its laws of composition; then came the deluge. It was a deluge because suddenly everyone realized that Carnaby Street, the Animals, the Birds, Bob Dylan, the Beatles and the Mamas and Papas were much more important, significant and complete than any prophecy meant for the masons.
It was then that we broke off, because of those personages and along those lines; from that moment on our education went on elsewhere, and no longer in schools of architecture.
Louis Kahn's defeat was not due so much to the confutation of his theories as to the general leap forward taken by the youth culture, to the appearance of new and powerful media, and to the entrance of public creativity on the public scene. It was the instruments, especially, that brought about his defeat: the sound of an LP record, clothing, and drugs were educational instruments more powerful than any form of architecture. The great leap consisted in the capacity of these "depth media" to appeal to the masses everywhere in the world. A cultural revolution had begun which went far beyond the conflict over its content and swept over unbelievable numbers of consumers.
Architecture, as cultural communication, has no way of achieving the same "quantitative" following as modern electronic media or models of behaviour. In a world in which a message spreads simultaneously everywhere, architecture remains an immovable object which one must travel to reach, as on a pilgrimage; an object which is half a usable instrument and half allegory, closed within its disciplinary limits and successfully imposed in a narrow field of urban influence only because of a ridiculous aspiration to the monumental. The city itself no longer coincides with an "architectural area" but only with a consumer model. The quality of that model is as important as that of any municipal structure; any place reached by the television, telephone, fashions, is an integral part of the urban cultural system. Indeed, the metropolis is no longer a place but a condition...
Let the dead look after their dead, then. With Louis Kahn architecture died and not simply a particular concept of it: he, like everyone else before him, saw it as a problem of quality.**

**Il Nuristan è uno dei luoghi più isolati dell'Afganistan, un territorio prevalentemente montagnoso abitato da una popolazione per tradizione indipendente, proprio grazie alla ubicazione dei villaggi alti e fortificati.
Gli insediamenti presentano un particolare interesse come campioni di economie chiuse basate ancora sul baratto, le tradizioni sono così profonde e gli scambi col mondo esterno così ridotti che ogni villaggio ha una sua lingua, una certa sua tradizione.
Le soluzioni spaziali e la forma delle abitazioni di ogni villaggio rispondono a complesse esigenze. La difesa, l'uso di spazi pubblici per il lavoro delle donne che, diversamente che in altri villaggi sotto l'influsso islamico, ricoprono un ruolo di autonomia nella produzione e gestione della casa e sono abbastanza parificate all'uomo.
Grandi terrazze, scale a pioli ricavate da tronchi di albero, che tolte costituiscono un sistema di isolamento e difesa, grandi loggiati esterni ai piani superiori dimostrano una profonda rispondenza tra bisogni e soluzioni. Molto ricchi appaiono i modi di utilizzazione dell'abitazione e riportano la nostra attenzione verso civiltà che il colonialismo ci ha abituato a considerare inferiori per proposte e soluzioni e che oggi in verità ci si presentano con l'evidenza e la provocazione di una qualità di vita e soluzioni perdute dalla sofisticata produzione industriale. Le norme, le soluzioni tipologiche, la tradizione sono una vera garanzia comune. L'economia del baratto (una mucca vale una casa, una capra una stanza), fa sì che le misure della qualità non mediate attraverso il metro astratto della moneta appaiano molto più evidenti. Particolarmente ingegnoso l'approvvigionamento dell'acqua con canalizzazioni sospese scavate in tronchi di legno. La casa ha un patio esterno dove per lo più si vive e si produce e si hanno contatti con la popolazione, all'interno due stanze, una con al centro il caminetto. Mobili bassi e un tavolo uso letto costituiscono l'arredo fantastico e funzionale.
Stanley Hallet, professore di architettura all'Università dello Utah, ha insegnato nel 71-72 all'Università di Kabul. Da questo soggiorno in Afganistan nascerà un libro sulle tipologie abitative tradizionali del paese. La rivista « Architecture plus » ne ha pubblicato un saggio campione nel numero di dicembre 1973, dal quale sono tratte le immagini qui riprodotte.**

La storia, ci vien detto, non è caos incomprensibile; ogni evento rivela un significato se riferito alle leggi motrici della società. Anche la scienza possiede una propria conoscibile "intenzionalità", e la sua storia non è una collana di singole "invenzioni" individuali; anche la storia dei disastri meccanici, all'apparenza totalmente al di fuori della storia sociale, ha con questa un rapporto di simbolo, di sintomo ideologico...
Esistono infatti avvenimenti di cronaca che sono chiaramente "allegorie" di eventi più generali, modelli di mutazioni storiche, coincidenze non fortuite di altre coincidenze sociali: l'affondamento del Titanic, per esempio, con la folla che continua a ballare in prima classe, non fu chiaramente che l'"allegoria" di un'altra e più ampia cecità borghese dinanzi alla propria tragedia storica.
Un altro recente avvenimento si ripropone per la sua meccanica (che sarebbe follia credere accidentale) come chiave simbolica, letteraria, della storia. Intendo parlare di quel gruppo di giovani uruguayani precipitati sulle Ande con un aereo, e sopravvissuti mangiando i cadaveri dei propri compagni vittime dell'incidente. Una sorta di Zattera della Medusa (Delacroix).
L'antropofagia, il consumo totale dell'individuo, è già di per se stessa un concetto attuale, ma nel caso specifico degli uruguayani essa diviene un simbolo ancora più specifico, in quanto risultato finale di una banale storia borghese, imperniata su una partita di rugby e su un volo aereo; storia che si rivela appunto meccanismo di involuzione totale che trascende i limiti nei quali era stata progettata per divenire tragedia letteraria, simbolo generale appunto.
La ricerca di questa chiave simbolica non è difficile.
Sappiamo che il Capitale ha raggiunto, attraverso la Programmazione Economica, l'integrazione di tutta intera la società nei suoi meccanismi, organizzandola in maniera funzionale nel lavoro. Il Capitale ha raggiunto così la sua "intima eticità", cioè la sua tensione ad un dover essere. Ma il Piano Economico, la Programmazione, rappresenta contemporaneamente l'integrazione massima e la contraddizione massima. Trasformare l'intera società in forza lavoro significa di fatto "proletarizzare" l'intero sistema sociale. Si realizza così, alla fine di un processo di progresso, il paradosso estremo: l'unità si realizza nella contraddizione, l'ordine nel caos. La società assiste al mostruoso capovolgimento di tutti i valori premessi; il bene, il progresso, si realizzano, ma nel male, cioè nella proletarizzazione della società e non nella sua evoluzione civile! Il che per una società classista come quella borghese, è "vergognoso". Da qui l'angoscia crescente della società, che assiste alla realizzazione del proprio negativo, e vede la fine del progresso, chiuso da uno specchio che riflette il cammino già percorso.
La "fine del progresso" (o i limiti dello sviluppo) hanno una origine profonda nella cultura della società borghese, nella sua contraddittoria ideologia storica: è il rifiuto mentale del futuro, scuro e sordo, che significa morte e forse rivoluzione, è l'impossibilità reale di progettare un futuro non possedendo più i parametri morali o culturali a cui riferire il progetto. Questa crisi, questa sosta sul ciglio di un baratro, questa angoscia terribile per il proprio futuro, diventano, di nuovo, cultura.
Occorre infatti mistificare sempre i processi avvenuti, capovolgere i dati stessi della realtà: il caos, la contraddizione è libertà di scelta; l'angoscia è una energia vitale, una ricchezza; la nevrosi è un modo di essere complesso ma culturale. Non è la società che somiglia alla fabbrica, ma la fabbrica alla società. Non è il cittadino che è diventato operaio, ma l'operaio cittadino. Il passato non è il nostro cadavere, ma è il nostro futuro. I morti servono a vivere. Sciolto lo enigma delle Ande, il simbolo ci aiuta a comprendere molte cose.
La storia recente viene continuamente rivisitata dai revivals, ripercorsa, in cerca di briciole, di odori, frugando senza un metodo, imitando, riproponendo. Percorriamo segmenti della storia del costume, come file di prodotti disponibili all'uso, che possiamo estrarre liberamente fuori della loro "storia", delle loro passioni. Sappiamo infatti che i prodotti non seguono una "nessità", ma una logica autonoma: la storia allora diventa un pozzo senza fine di cose utilizzabili indipendentemente dalla loro ideologia; anzi la loro ideologia "artificiale" può essere rispolverata e ancora indossata per giuoco.
La Retro-guardia crea un confine continuamente scavato tra noi e i momenti del nostro presente immediato, è il "revival" di noi stessi: prima gli anni '20, poi '30, poi '40, poi '50, adesso i '60, e poi vediamo la realtà stessa che viviamo nascere già confezionata per essere rivissuta. La crisi dell'energia (creativa) ci spinge a riciclare la storia. La Retro-guardia ha questo ruolo importante: mistificare il passato come futuro. Il ruolo è reazionario, per definizione, ma la sua gestione strategica potrebbe anche rivelarsi genialmente rivoluzionaria. Biba a Londra, il Teatro del Gruppo Tse a Parigi, l'edizione dei "Nostalgia", sono strumenti del passato che servono a spiegare il presente. Se il passato infatti è finto (e questo lo si vede chiaramente) anche il presente allora è finto; tutto è progettato, i valori naturali o spontanei non esistono, l'ecologia e tutto il presente è una macchina micidiale, come i miti che l'hanno preceduta.
Tra i tanti passati e presenti ognuno può scegliere il proprio, la propria area culturale, può fingere radici, vestire le donne come la propria istitutrice e, finalmente, scoparla...

18 Il ruolo della Retro-guardia
The Role of the Rear-Guard

★★ ANDREA BRANZI ★★
RADICAL NOTES

History, we are told, is not « just one damned thing after another »; any event will yield a meaning if it is examined in the light of the laws of social dynamics. Even science has a knowable « purposefulness » of its own and the history of science is hardly a string of single « inventions »; even the history of mechanical disasters, which would seem to lie entirely outside social history, relates to that history as a symbol as an ideological symptom...
Indeed, there are certain everyday occurences that are clearly « allegories » of more general events or patterns of historical mutations, non-fortuitous coincidences resulting from other social coincidences: the sinking of the Titanic, for example, while the first class passengers went on dancing, was clearly the « allegory » of another and much more general middle-class blindness to the reality of their historical tragedy. Another, more recent event reveals in its mechanics (which it would be folly to consider accidental) a symbolic, literary key to history. I am referring to the group of young Uruguayans whose plane crashed in the Andes and who managed to survive by eating the bodies of their dead companions. A sort of Medusa raft (Delacroix). Cannibalism, or the total consumption of an individual, is in itself a concept of current interest, but in this specific case it is a more specific symbol in the sense that it is the final result of a rather commonplace « bourgeois » story; a story, indeed, which reveals a mechanism of total involution that goes beyond its appointed limits to become a tragedy in a literary sense and a general symbol. The search for this symbolic key is not really difficult.
We know that Capital, through economic planning, has managed to fully integrate society in its mechanisms and to organize it functionally in work. Capital has thus achieved its « close ethical cohesion » — that is, its tendency to become a « must ». But the Economic Plan, Programming, etc., represent at once maximum integration and maximum contradiction. For transforming a complete society into a work force also means proletarianizing the whole social system. Thus, at the end of a process creating progress one finds an extreme paradox: unity is achieved in contradiction, and order in chaos. Society witnesses the monstrous reversal of all the values it had taken for granted; Good and progress in society are achieved, but by way of evil — that is, by way of the proletarianization of society, and not its development of civilized values! All of which, for a class' system like the bourgeois one, is « shameful ». Hence the growing anxiety of a society which is witnessing the realization of its negative and sees the end of progress, now closed off by a mirror, reflecting a road already travelled.
The « end of progress » (or the limits of development) dates far back in the culture of bourgeois society, in its contradictory historical ideology: it is the mental rejection of a dark and impenetrable future which spells death and perhaps revolution, and the real impossibility of planning a future which no longer possesses the moral and cultural parameters to which a plan might be related. This crisis, this pause on the edge of the abyss, this terrible anxiety about one's future, again become culture.
In fact things that have already taken place have to be continually misinterpreted, and the very facts of reality turned upside down chaos and contradiction become freedom of choice; anxiety becomes vital energy and rich personal resources; and neurosis becomes a way of being complex but cultural. It is not society that resembles the factory but the reverse. It is not the citizen who has become a worker, but the worker who has become a citizen. The past is not our dead bodies but our future. The dead are of use to the living.
Recent history is being continually revisited and retraced in search of crumbs and fragrances, but it is an aimless rummaging, with imitations and revivals. We pass through segments of the history of manners as if they were lines of products at our disposal which we could use at pleasure and freely extract from their historical context and all their passions. For basically they have taught us that products don't follow a logical connection but follow a logic of their own. On this way history becomes a bottomless well of things that can be utilized without regard for their ideological nature; indeed, their « artificial » ideology can be brushed up and donned in play. The Rear-Guard is continually digging a trench between us and our immediate present, between us and our own « revival »: first the twenties, then the thirties, then the forties, then the fifties, and now the sixties; and then we see the very reality that we are now living already packaged and ready to be relived. The (creative) energy crisis makes us recycle history. The Rear-Guard has this important task: to palm off the past as the future. It is by definition reactionary, but its strategic application might prove to be brilliantly revolutionary. Biba in London, the Tse Group Theatre in Paris, and the editions of « Nostalgia » are instruments of the past which are useful in explaining the present. For if the past is a fiction, so is the present; everything is a fabrication, natural and spontaneous values are inexistent, ecology and all of the present are a murderous machine, like the myths that preceded it. From all these pasts and presents everyone can take his pick, his own cultural area; he can pretend to be rooted in this area, dress women like his own governess an at last fuck her.

no Zevi nel rispondere a Aldo
si sul n. 226 di « L'Architettura
ache e storia », mi coinvolge
ttamente nella polemica.
'ultimo numero di « ContrTospa-
» Aldo Rossi aveva respinto con
celata sufficienza le accuse mos-
i da più parti definendo di
da" le riviste e da "strapaese"
ccuse (cosa del resto ovvia da
e di chi possiede una cultura
concetto di città quasi austro-
arico, giudicare "moda" e "stra-
se" tutto il resto dei mortali e
mondo) e scusandosi con il Mo-
nto Studentesco di aver accet-
tato l'incarico della Triennale definendosi un ingenuo accademico, estraneo a simili valutazioni. Ma non così ingenuo da non mettere insieme una mostra che oltre alla Tendenza allinea tutti i progetti dei più importanti professori universitari, rilancia la grande architettura staliniana come anti-borghese, ma si guarda bene dal rivalutare con pari coerenza l'opera di Albert Speer (questa è una sfida precisa). Bruno Zevi contesta a suo modo le tesi e le risposte di Aldo Rossi, e in chiusura dell'editoriale, quasi a conferma esterna delle sue tesi, cita quasi per intero il mio "radical notes" nel quale analizzavo il processo di involuzione della scuola rossiana, nata come reazione alla situazione tardo-funzionalista e socialdemocratica della didattica e finita a riscoprire le fonti eterne dell'architettura, accompagnando il mio scritto con un suo titolo « Socialdemocratici? Meglio che fascisti! ».

★ ANDREA BRANZI ★★

RADICAL NOTES

Su questa frase, che politicamente condivido, possono però nascere equivoci d'altro genere, dal momento che vengo interpretato: « Visto cosa succede ad allontanarsi dalla retta via del socialismo riformista e del Movimento Moderno? Ci si perde, si diventa fatalmente fascisti! Non vi è salvezza fuori dell'ortodossia moderna... »: il che, oltre ad essere lontano dalle mie intenzioni, risulterebbe come un mea-culpa, come un pentimento, quasi a riconoscere un mio oltre che altrui errore, essendo anch'io un transfuga, anche se in un altro emisfero. E' necessario quindi fare alcuni doverosi distinguo.

A tale proposito, nella mia rubrica sul n. 388 di Casabella, analizzando il fenomeno del così detto socialismo-alpestre, avevo sottolineato come trovandoci oggi a dover scegliere fra la tradizione ortodossa del Movimento Moderno e il fenomeno involutivo del neo-monumentalismo, facciamo in ogni caso una scelta solo culturale, in quanto la crisi dell'architettura non si risolve scegliendo tra due diverse qualità formali, ma esplorando fino in fondo questa crisi, fino a scoprirne le radici nei mutati meccanismi di produzione della cultura e nella fine del ruolo culturale della città, divenuta struttura di servizi e non più struttura di "rappresentazione" della società, e il trasferimento dell' "identità urbana" su nuovi media. Alla fine, appunto, concludevo scegliendo, tra queste due diverse ma in fondo analoghe qualità, il paradosso della "quantità", dell'Existenz Maximum, della rivendicazione planimetrica; paradosso del resto fino a un certo punto, dal momento che i più grandi salti qualitativi della cultura architettonica e urbana hanno sempre coinciso con grandi rivoluzioni di ordine quantitativo, con lo scardinamento di quegli standard naturali sui quali la cultura borghese sempre si arrocca: valgano per tutti il grattacielo e l'Unità d'Abitazione. E' tanto vero che il conflitto tra modernisti e neo-monumentalisti mette a confronto due tesi accademiche, che la prova ce la fornisce lo stesso Zevi, quando nello stesso editoriale con grande chiarezza dice « ...il compito e la sfida consistono nel codificare un linguaggio alternativo a quello Beaux-Arts, un linguaggio moderno basato sull'elenco funzionale, sulle dissonanze, sulla tridimensionalità antiprospettica, sulla scomposizione quadridimensionale, sul coinvolgimento strutturale di ogni elemento architettonico, sulla temporalizzazione dello spazio e sulla reintegrazione edificio-città-territorio, insomma su quanto è scientificamente deducibile dall'esperienza del passato, remoto e recente ». Cioè: dal momento che i Grandi Padri sono morti organizziamo la loro eredità, rendendo sistematiche le loro scoperte compositive, elencandole, usandole ogni qualvolta se ne presenti l'occasione, e garantendoci così la sopravvivenza in questo periodo incerto... Veramente mi sembra che tra questa posizione e quella di Aldo Rossi, che invece di quella moderna recupera una tradizione più remota e più simmetrica, le differenze siano più apparenti che reali.

Ambedue vedono il "fare architettonico" come l'uso di una qualche tradizione formale e linguistica, ed il conflitto si esaurisce in un confronto tra una posizione progressista e una intollerante. All'attuale vuoto disciplinare ognuno di loro propone una protesi culturale diversa.

Ambedue parlano di "rifondazione", ma nei fatti si muovono nell'ambito di un neo-eclettismo, che per definizione rifiuta qualsiasi reale rifondazione della cultura, preferendo ruotare linguaggi e citazioni, come una sorta di respirazione artificiale. Una riprova di quanto dico lo fornisce il recente quartiere Gallaratese a Milano (vedi Casabella numero 391), dove esemplarmente vediamo affrontate due opere di scuola diversa: Aldo Rossi e Carlo Aymonino. Nessun confronto potrebbe risultare più accademico: « Il rigido controllo compositivo di Rossi fa risaltare le componenti eclettiche di Aymonino ».

In realtà il confronto è tutto fatto sulla base della simulazione: l'uno porta avanti Terragni e Muzio, l'altro risponde facendo suonare il suo Le Corbusier giapponesizzato. Nessuna delle reali qualità dei Grandi Padri citati è rispettata, tutto un "patrimonio" viene dilapidato in pura semplice cultura. L'uno fa voti a Apollo, dio della bellezza immobile, autofondata, l'altro fa offerte allo spirito di Dioniso, dio dell'ebrezza e del divenire.

(E qui risparmierò il sarcasmo sull'episodio dell'occupazione del quartiere Gallaratese che quasi in maniera allegorica ha riproposto il tema di Hengels sull'interesse operaio alla proprietà e non alla forma della città borghese, dal momento che ambedue gli immobili sono stati occupati senza scelte culturali. Ma sarebbe troppo facile rimettersi a questo giudizio della storia, dal momento che della storia poco mi fido.)

E il mondo dell'architettura continua a ruotare, riproponendoci dopo dieci anni di silenzio una polemica fittizia, a cui non credono neppure gli stessi protagonisti (dal momento che Rossi ha presentato Aymonino nella sua mostra di Tendenza alla Triennale).

Riemerge da un lungo e buio tunnel lo stesso mondo astratto che pensavamo di aver lasciato alle nostre spalle, per riproporci in termini ideologici che ben conosciamo, la solita disputa compositiva.

19 Apollo e Dioniso a Gallarate

is reply to Aldo Rossi in
226 of « L'Architettura cronache
oria » Bruno Zevi directly
lves me in the controversy.
he latest number of
ntrospazio » Aldo Rossi had
cted with thinly-veiled
gance all the accusations
had been levelled against
from various quarters, calling
reviews "trendy" and the
sations "jingoistic".
n, offering
apologies to the Student
ement for having accepted the
ctorship at the Triennale, he
d himself a naïve academic
in no way deserving
accusations. But
so naïve as to be
pable of setting up an
bit which, besides the Trend,
up all the designs of the
important university
essors and reproposes massive
inist architecture as an
bourgeois gesture, while
fully avoiding any equally
rent revaluation of Albert
er's work (this is a
ct challenge).
is own way Bruno Zevi
ests Aldo Rossi's viewpoints
replies, and on closing his
orial, almost as an external
oboration of his position, he
es my "radical notes"
ost "in estenso". In them I had
ined the involutionary
process that Rossi's school has been undergoing as the result of a reaction against the late-functionalist and social-democratic state of teaching today and as a result of its persuasion that it has rediscovered the eternal sources of architecture; I had headed my "notes" with one of Rossi's own titles: "Social-democrats? Better than Fascists!".

However, this phrase, which expresses a political view I share, could give rise to considerable confusion of another kind as soon as it is interpreted: "See what happens when you stray from the righteous way of reform socialism and the Modern Movement? One gets lost, one inevitably becomes Fascist! There is no salvation outside modern orthodoxy...". Which, besides being far from my intention, would appear to be a "mea-culpa", a repentance, almost an acknowledgement of my own as well as others' mistakes, since I am myself something of a renegade albeit in another hemisphere. It is therefore important to make a few distinctions. In this connexion, in analyzing the so-called Alpine socialism in my column for Casabella No. 388, I emphasized the fact that in being obliged to choose between the orthodox tradition of the Modern Movement and the involutional phenomenon of neo-monumentalism, we are only making a cultural choice, because the crisis in architecture cannot be resolved by choosing between two formal qualities, but by getting to the bottom of this crisis until we discover its roots in new mechanisms of production and in the end of the cultural role of the city, which has become a "service" and no longer a "representative" structure, "urban indentity" having been transferred to other media. In the end I concluded by choosing, in these two different but essentially analogous qualities, the paradox of "quantity", of Existenz Maximum, of planimetric vindication; a paradox, however, only up to a certain point, since the greatest qualitative leaps in architectonic and urban culture have always coincided with great revolutions of a quantitative order, with the undoing of those natural standards on which middle-class culture has always made its stand; the skyscraper and Unité d'habitation are examples of it. The proof that the conflict between modernists and neo-monumentalists is merely a confrontation between two academic theses will be found in Zevi's editorial, when he states with great clarity « ...the task and the challenge consist in the codification of an alternative to the idiom of the Beaux-Arts, a modern idiom based on functional values, dissonances, antiperspective tridimensional views, quadridimensional break-down of composition, the structural involvement of every architectonic element, the temporalization of space, and the reintegration of building, city, and territory — in other words, on whatever can be scientifically deduced from the experiences of the past whether remote or recent ». Which is to say: now that the Great Fathers of Architecture are dead, let us organize their heritage and make their compositional discoveries systematic; let us list them and utilize them whenever we have occasion to, thereby ensuring survival during this uncertain period... It seems to me that between this position and Aldo Rossi's, which rather than the modern tradition would recuperate a more remote and symmetrical one, the differences are more apparent than real. Each of them sees the making of architecture as the use of some kind of formal and idiomatic tradition, and the conflict boils down to a confrontation between a progressive position and an intolerant one. Each proposes to fill the present disciplinary vacuum with an artificial cultural solution of his own. Both talk of "re-foundation", but actually they are both moving in a field of neo-eclecticism, which by definition rejects any truly real re-foundation for culture and prefers to cling to idioms and quotations like some sort of artificial respiration. The proof of this is provided by the recent Gallaratese quarter of Milan (see Casabella No. 391), where we see an exemplary comparison between two works of different schools: Aldo Rossi and Carlo Aymonino. No comparison could be more academic: « Rossi's rigid compositional control throws Aymonino's eclectic components into relief ».

Actually, the comparison is carried out on the basis of simulation: one comes forward with Terragni and Muzio, the other replies with a kind of Japanese Le Corbusier. None of the great fathers' real qualities are respected, a whole patrimony is squandered in pure and simple culture. One makes his vows to Apollo, the god of motionless and self-generated beauty; the other makes his votive offerings to the spirit of Dionysus, the god of drunkenness and the future.

At this point I'll refrain from any sarcasm regarding the occupation of the Gallaratese quarter by squatters, an episode which almost allegorically represents Engels's assertion that the worker is more interested in the ownership than the form of the bourgeois city; I refrain because both the places were occupied without any cultural choices having been made.

And the world of architecture turns round and round, and after ten years of silence offers us a fictitious controversy which even the participants do not believe in (Rossi, for example, presented Aymonino in his Trends exhibition at the Triennale).

And out of a long and dark tunnel emerges the abstract world that we thought we had left behind, raising again in ideological terms that we know only too well, the same old controversy over composition.

L'architettura, con lo sviluppo dei media elettronici e della cultura di massa, è divenuta un'arte minore. Se si intendono infatti con questo termine riduttivo tutte quelle attività culturali applicate a strutture e sistemi di comunicazione minori, questa distinzione, anche se del tutto accademica, può servire schematicamente a rilevare la modificazione dei pesi specifici tra diverse tecniche culturali nella società.
L'architettura, un tempo considerata la più nobile e completa delle arti, ha perduto il suo primato non solo per tutte le difficoltà esterne, di ordine politico ed economico che tradizionalmente il suo ruolo incontra, ma per una profonda crisi interna che oggi la travaglia al contatto di modifiche dei meccanismi di produzione della cultura e della stessa funzione urbana.
La città è oggi sempre di più una struttura di servizi e di pure funzioni abitative, e non è più una struttura culturale della società; la comunicazione che l'architettura compie, tutta basata sull'allegoria degli equilibri tra l'uomo e la tecnica e tra l'uomo e l'ambiente naturale, è immobile nello spazio ed esclusa dalla dimensione "profonda" che tutti i media elettronici hanno raggiunto; la città non è più oggi un "luogo" culturale ma una "condizione".
La cultura urbana cioè è un fenomeno indipendente dal luogo urbano e coincide con la cultura dei consumi.
Essere oggi cittadino non vuol dire abitare in una città, ma vuol dire adottare un determinato modello di comportamento, costituito dal linguaggio, dall'informazione stampata e televisiva, dall'abbigliamento, dalla musica che si ascolta: fin dove arrivano questi media arriva la città.
Non esiste più una cultura esterna al fenomeno urbano dal momento che non esiste più una campagna legata ad una reale logica alternativa, non esiste un luogo che in qualche modo e in qualche misura non sia in "comunicazione" con la città e con i suoi modelli.
La "condizione urbana" coincide con la circolazione sociale della merce, esportabile all'esterno di qualsiasi area metropolitana. Ogni giorno vengono prodotti milioni di metri cubi di questo nuovo tipo di città, e ogni giorno milioni di metri cubi di città diventano spazzatura, secondo le leggi di un metabolismo ignoto agli immobili equilibri urbani.
Il concetto di cultura sta mutando; fino a ieri prodotta da un gruppo ristretto di intellettuali professionisti e consumata da una sterminata schiera di lettori, visitatori, abbonati, appassionati e voyeurs, che niente altro dovevano fare se non comprare il libro, il disco, il biglietto, istituzionalmente esclusi da qualsiasi diritto a produrre e consumare in proprio una cultura privata come un diritto naturale (in quanto la cultura è un bene superiore, "universale", alla cui produzione si accede attraverso uno stressante iter di esercizi, prove, studi, esami, consultazioni, a cui dedicare una intera vita), la cultura dicevo è oggi vissuta come un bene immediato, spontaneo, prodotto diretto di un comportamento sociale, di un modello di consumo, come stimolo economico. Ecco allora che assistiamo al primo capovolgimento delle gerarchie tradizionali; è più importante il vetrinista, l'arredatore, il creatore di moda, l'esperto in colori, il decoratore, l'opinion leader, l'emarginato radicale, l'assaggiatore, il truccatore ecc. che non l'"artista" impegnato a inviare al mondo messaggi allegorici. La qualità architettonica è assai meno importante della qualità del microclima che vi si respira dentro, il regime acustico più delle leggi compositive...
L'architettura diventa "arte minore", impegnata a risolvere armonicamente problemi funzionali e strutturali, collocandosi fuori dei circuiti reali che determinano la "qualità della vita" e della cultura.
Il "capolavoro architettonico" è finito nel momento in cui non solo la cultura è divenuta un bene di consumo, ma da quando la professione ha preso definitivamente il posto dell'arte: fin tanto che le scuole d'architettura erano club per pochi appassionati la metodologia di progettazione permetteva di recuperare larghi spazi a varianti "creative", oggi che è necessario insegnare la progettazione architettonica a centinaia di migliaia di persone, non è possibile pensare di introdurre nel discorso incognite di alcun genere.
Le incognite che oggi la progettazione architettonica deve effettivamente affrontare sono quasi ridotte a zero; la variante progettuale consiste in un semplice schema compositivo di natura spesso aleatoria, non corrispondente più a aree culturali diverse, ma all'uso di elementi differenziati solo sul piano della produzione industriale.
Pasolini dice che non esiste più una differenza somatica tra i giovani di destra e di sinistra; è vero ugualmente che non esistono ideologie che al livello del linguaggio architettonico siano in grado di fornire risultati differenziati. L'annosa battaglia italiana contro i geometri, rei di un basso livello culturale nella scena urbana, è frutto di un equivoco che affonda le sue radici nella sicurezza che il Movimento Moderno ha a lungo cullato sulla identità inscindibile tra qualità urbana e civiltà.
La qualità che oggi chiediamo alle città non è né formale né compositiva, ma è la qualità dei servizi sociali e del mercato. Per gli architetti è venuto il momento della modestia...

Architettura e modestia
20
Architecture and Modesty

** ANDREA BRANZI **

RADICAL NOTES

With the development of the electronic media and mass-culture, architecture has become something of a minor art.
Even if by this reductive term one means all those cultural activities applied to minor structures and systems of communication, this distinction, however academic, may be of some schematic use in revealing the modifications in specific weight to which the various cultural techniques have been subjected in our society.
Architecture, once considered the most complete and noble of the arts, has lost its pre-eminence not only because of the external difficulties of a political and economic nature that it has always encountered, but also because of a deep internal crisis now afflicting it as a result of modifications in the mechanisms of cultural production and of the urban function itself.
Today the city is becoming more and more a structure offering services, a place merely to live in; it is no longer one of society's cultural structures. The communication carried out by architecture, based on the allegory of balances between man and his natural environment, is motionless in space and lacking in the depth of psychic penetration that the electronic media have achieved. Today the city is no longer a cultural "place" but a "condition". Urban culture, in other words, is independent of the city as a place and it coincides with the culture of consumption.
To be an urbanite today does not mean to live in a city but to adopt a specific model of behaviour made up of a certain way of speaking, of printed and televised information, of a particular kind of clothing, of the music one listens to: wherever these media arrive, the city arrives.
There is no longer any culture external to the urban phenomenon inasmuch as there is no longer any countryside representing a real and logical alternative; there is no place which does not to some extent communicate with the city and its models.
The "urban condition" coincides with the social circulation of goods, which can be exported from any metropolitan area. Every day millions of cubic metres of this new type of city are produced, and every day millions of cubic metres of city become rubbish, in keeping with the laws of a metabolism unknown to the immoveable equilibria of the city.
The concept of culture itself is changing. Until quite recently produced by a small group of intellectual professionals and consumed by a numberless mass of readers, visitors, subscribers, enthusiasts and voyeurs who had only to buy the book, disc or ticket, and were institutionally excluded from any right to produce or consume a private culture as a natural right (since culture is a higher and "universal" good, to produce which one must undergo a stressful series of exercises, tests, studies, examinations, consultation, and dedicate his life to it), culture, as I was saying, is now experienced as an immediate, spontaneous good, the direct product of a certain social behaviour and a model of consumption, an economic stimulus. What we are witnessing here is the reversal of the traditional hierarchies; more importance is attributed to the window dresser decorator, fashion designer, expert in colours, upholsterer, opinion leader, taster, make-up expert, etc. than to the "artist" intent on sending out allegorical messages to the world.
Architectonic quality is much less important than the quality of the microclimate one experiences inside, and good acoustics are preferred to observance of the laws of composition...
Architecture now becomes a "minor art" applied to the harmonious resolution of functional and structural problems and kept outside the real circuits determining the "quality of life" and culture.
The masterwork of architecture ended not only when culture became an article of consumption but when the profession definitely took the place of the art; as long as the schools of architecture were clubs for a few enthusiasts, methodological planning opened large areas of "creative" variations; but now that architectonic planning has to be taught to thousands of people, it is idle to think of introducing unknown quantities of any kind. The number of unknown factors that architectonic planning is called on to resolve today has been reduced almost to zero. Variation in design consists of a simple compositional scheme often chosen at random without regard for different cultural areas, but only for the availability of elements differentiated on the industrial plane alone. Pasolini claims that there are no longer any somatic differences between youths of the left and the right. It is also true that there are no ideologies capable of producing different results in the architectonic idiom. The long Italian battle fought against construction surveyors, responsible for the low cultural level of much urban architecture, is the result of a mistake rooted in the certainty long cultivated by the Modern Movement that there is an indivisible identity between urban quality and civilization.
The quality that we ask of the city today has nothing to do with form or composition, but only with the quality of social services and the market.
For architects the time has come for a bit of modesty...

Fine ultimo dell'architettura moderna è l'"eliminazione" dell'architettura stessa.
Come "struttura razionale" tendente a risolvere il maggior numero di problemi funzionali, ad un livello tecnico ottimale, l'architettura moderna tende a raggiungere soluzioni e tipologie definitive, a intendere cioè la soluzione dei problemi come una progressione verso la eliminazione di tutti i problemi aperti, attraverso la loro successiva soluzione.
Essa tende cioè a collocarsi come processo progettuale che raggiunge soluzioni, non culturali ma scientifiche, dei problemi abitativi.
Il grado di "inesorabilità" di molte soluzioni architettoniche e di una diffusa metodologia didattica, cerca di far transitare oltre la storia, e quindi oltre la cultura, gran parte dell'architettura moderna per spingerla verso una soglia di sicurezza inamovibile, che la preservi da giudizi storici e da ulteriori evoluzioni linguistiche e formali.
In questo senso il processo riduttivo di tutte le sovrastrutture estetiche e di tutti gli orpelli formali diviene il progetto di eliminazione dell'architettura come struttura culturale: essa non rappresenta più lo status symbol della classe sociale, e più in generale non "rappresenta" più niente, che non sia la pura disponibilità delle strutture ad un uso indifferenziato e culturalmente neutro.
Contemporaneamente, ed in senso diametralmente opposto, l'architettura si propone come esperienza strettamente ed esclusivamente privata, come estensione diretta del corpo e delle sue disponibilità espressive, come spazio creativo legato all'individualità psico-fisica, non più spazio progettato, ma esperienza comunicativa infinitamente variabile.
In questo senso l'architettura si definisce come esperienza non codificabile (e quindi non progettabile) se non attraverso una prassi sperimentale, di fatto estranea a qualsiasi metodologia culturale e disciplinare.
All'interno di questa contraddizione l'architettura storica si è proposta come struttura "culturale" che cerca di garantire il maggior numero di gradi di libertà all'utente, nel fenomeno urbano il suo vero destino, e nel privato la sua vera natura.
Il conflitto è dunque tra individuo e architettura, tra pura fenomenicità e ordine universale, tra non-significato e messaggio artistico. Conflitto e non dialettica, perché è in termini di scontro che oggi si pone tale rapporto, dal momento che tutti gli atti di auto-liberazione che l'individuo compie sono destinati a collocarlo fuori dei vincoli inibitori della morale, dell'estetica e della cultura codificabili.
Il movimento di liberazione dell'uomo da questi "codici di comportamento" tende a fargli recuperare la cultura come pura energia creativa, come definizione spontanea della propria identità.
La coscienza di questo diritto si scontra con l'organizzazione di tutta la società attuale, basata sul lavoro produttivo e sulla divisione sociale di questo. Si determina così da una parte l'attuale professionismo intellettuale, per cui una ristrettissima parte della società "produce cultura", e dall'altra la grande massa di persone che di questa cultura riceve solo il consumo, sotto forma di prodotti, strutture, modelli di comportamento, che simulano nell'utente l'uso delle proprie facoltà creative di fatto atrofizzate.
Il problema di fondo dell'architettura, e della cultura, è dunque quello della "libertà". Le Corbusier propose la pianta "libera", la facciata "libera", il terreno "libero" dall'edificio attraverso i pilotis, uso "libero" delle coperture ecc., ponendo il problema della "libertà" al centro della qualità architettonica. Però le Corbusier imposta tale problema ancora in termini "architettonici", cioè compositivi, confermando il ruolo di figurazione e di mediazione sociale proprio della tradizione storica dell'architettura. Tale mediazione è svolta dall'architettura in termini di allegoria, ma tale mediazione si esaurisce quando i rapporti tra realtà particolare e generale cessano di essere effetto di "ipotesi" reciproche e stabiliscono tra di loro un confronto direttamente ed esclusivamente politico.
Il progresso stesso quindi, sociale e culturale, a cui l'architettura partecipa, rimuove lentamente le sue stesse premesse di struttura culturale, cioè ideologica.
L'architettura si trova quindi per sua natura al centro di un incrocio dove confluiscono le contraddizioni di fondo di tutte le attività progettuali, le quali tendono oggi (sotto la spinta della scienza) a raggiungere "soluzioni definitive" e dall'altra a garantire (sotto la spinta della crescita sociale) la "assoluta relatività" di ogni processo privato come difesa dell'uomo contro gli ordini universali che lo condizionano e lo limitano. Da una parte cioè si tende a saltare la soglia superiore del significato, collocandosi sopra la storia, e dall'altra si tende a varcare la soglia inferiore del significato collocandosi dentro le parti infinitesimali della storia stessa. Complessivamente oggi l'architettura tende a risolvere il suo problema esistenziale eliminando se stessa.

21 Architettura e libertà
Architecture and Freedom

✱✱ ANDREA BRANZI ✱✱
RADICAL NOTES

The end-purpose of modern architecture is the « elimination » of architecture itself.
As a « rational structure » tending to resolve the greatest number of functional problems at an optimum technological level, modern architecture tends to work out definitive solutions and typologies, to regard, that is, the solution of problems as a progression towards the elimination of all unsolved problems through their gradual solution.
It tends, that is, to present itself as a planning process which finds solutions, not of a cultural but of a scientific nature, to housing problems.
The « inevitable » quality of many architectonic solutions and of widerspread didactic methodology suggests an attempt to lead a large part of modern architecture beyond history and therefore beyond culture and to drive it towards a threshold of unshakeable security where it will be safe from historical judgement and from future evolutions in idiom and form.
In this sense the process of stripping away all aesthetic superstructural material and formal decorative elements becomes a plan for the elimination of architecture as a cultural structure: it no longer represents the status symbol of a social class, and more generally, it no longer « represents » anything at all, unless it be the mere availability of the structure for indiscriminate and culturally neutral use.
At the same time, and in a diametrically opposite sense, architecture is offered as a strictly and exclusively private matter, as a direct extension of the body and of its expressive possibilities, as creative space related to one's psycho-physical individuality, and no more as planned space but as an infinitely variable communicative experience.
In this sense, architecture is defined as an experience that cannot be codified (and therefore cannot be planned), unless it be through some kind of experimental procedure which is in fact extraneous to any kind of cultural or disciplinary methodology.
Within the limits of this contradiction, historical architecture is presented as a « cultural » structure that seeks to guarantee the highest number of freedoms for the houseowner in the urban context (which is his real future) and in private (where he unfolds his real nature).
The conflict, then, is between the individual and architecture, between pure phenomenon and universal order, between meaninglessness and artistic message. But it is conflict and not dialectics, because it is in terms of a clash that this relationship is couched today, since all the acts of self-liberation that the individual carries out are destined to put him beyond the moral, aesthetic, and cultural inhibitions of the current Establishment.
The movement for the liberation of man from these « behavioural codes » helps him to regain culture as pure creative energy and as the spontaneous definition of his own identity.
Any awareness of this right immediately clashes with the whole organization of contemporary society, which is based on productive labour and on the division of the same. This determines, on the one hand, the intellectual profession, whereby a highly restricted part of society « produces culture », and on the other, the great mass of people who are expected only to consume it in the form of products, structures, and models of behaviour, which simulate the use of creative faculties that, in point of fact, have atrophied.
The fundamental problem of architecture and of culture, then, is that of « freedom ». Le Corbusier proposed a « free » plan, a « free » façade, grounds « free » from the building, thanks to his pilotis, the « free » use of roofing, etc.; thereby putting the problem of « freedom » at the very centre of architectonic quality. However, Le Corbusier still formulates this problem in « architectonic » (i.e. compositional) terms, thereby confirming the figurative and mediatory social role played by the historical tradition in architecture. This mediation is carried out in terms of allegory, but it breaks down when the relationships between specific and general reality cease to be the effect of reciprocal « hypotheses » and establish with each other a confrontation which is directly and exclusively political.
Social and cultural progress itself, then, to which architecture contributes, slowly removes its own premises or cultural structure — that is, its ideology.
By its very nature, then, architecture lies at the centre of a crossroads into which the basic contradictions of all planning activities flow and, driven by the science, these activities strive to achieve « definitive solutions », while at the same time guaranteeing (driven by social growth) the « absolute relativity » of every private process as a defence of man against the universal orders that condition and limit him.
On the one hand — that is — there is a tendency to go beyond the upper limits of meaning and to place onself above history; on the other hand, there is the tendency to cross the lower threshold of meaning and to place oneself within the infinitesimal folds of history itself.
All in all, today architecture tends to solve its existential problem by eliminating itself.

Design and minority culture

The conflict between systems of international culture (design, functional architecture, etc.) on the one hand, and local, minor, or traditional cultures on the other, has been increasing, along with a feeling of insecurity, and undermining all our cultural and technological certainties, gradually becoming the basic theme of a generation. The death of architecture, its disappearance as one of the elements contributing to gracious living, its liquidation as the cultural structure of society, has become the premise for a reappraisal of all cultural instruments and for a confrontation with all the minor systems. As the great ideologies spring from spontaneous, philosophic and sentimental premises, and with these premises immediately come into conflict in the name of an historical dimension larger than life, so modern culture (in design and architecture) springs from the revelation of all the simple, and even naïve, methodologies, distills them and extracts a universal method of doing things, of building, and of using things.

This method, however, immediately replaces all previous minor heritages and becomes an alternative and evolved form, fighting everything that cannot be controlled by its method of selection and analysis. This substitution represents a political, as well as cultural conflict, and creates attrition between two incompatible dimensions, each of which claims to be a universal system of organizing experience and the only true way of appraising reality. The outcome of this debate might lead to either the risk of serious cultural involution or the possibility of a brilliant affirmation of the freedom of culture and its instruments.

It should be pointed out that there are two different and contrasting conceptions of the term "minor culture": one which regards it as a sampling of objects to be revived, as a complex of backward techniques to be reproposed and, in general, as a quantity of "historical values" to be defended. This definition is largely accepted by a middle-class culture now in the midst of a crisis, as the only way to throw together a viable cultural context. In Italy the conservation of culture has always been substantially Fascist, both in the way in which tradition has been reproposed (as a quest for identity and destiny) and in the way in which it has been administered — that is, in purely authoritarian and repressive terms.

All the talk one hears today in the salons and the headquarters of civic committees (assemblies of politicians, landowners, and architects) is dangerous, because it never sufficiently clarifies the relationship between cultural conservation and social conservation. Without this clarification, misunderstandings become infinite and the whole matter is automatically instrumentalized by reactionary forces.

Let us take country culture as an example. It is born and develops within the context of social co-operatives based on poverty, sickness, and exploitation. The archaic and simple techniques of the peasants spring from the theft of technical information methodically carried out by the landowning class, as a technical premise for social exploitation. Peasant culture develops within an historical dearth of human, cultural, and commercial contacts, within a backward and repressive social system: the country. It is impossible to save peasant culture, in the sense of an operational cultural system, without conserving the overall historical conditions it was born in and carries on, unless we are satisfied with putting some order in the remains of so many country houses abandoned long ago. When peasant culture is reappraised as "the peasant condition", when poverty is called simplicity and ignorance is called alternative culture, reaction has won the day.
It is behind this attitude, in fact, that one finds the biggest social swindles, the ecological fraud, the plans for the management of society as a superior cultural operation (Fascism).
But there is still another conception of minor culture, consisting in the search for a different relationship between man and technology and between culture and spontaneous creativeness. The minor cultures, in fact, propose the replacement of official aesthetic codes and technological taboos with experimentation in a pure and direct "functional and private" use of artistic endeavours, not in the sense of a universal experience, but as a constructional act directly related to the group's or the individual's creative drive.
This kind of experimentation and tradition is a precious document on a different way of producing culture, in which culture is regarded as being produced and consumed by the whole community and not by some specialized sector; as being directly related to biological and economic life and not as a separate channel for alternative experiences. This is what interests us in past and present-day minor cultures, and it is this that interests us for the future and not for an already dead past.

Design, I should say, will have to cope with this heritage and with this prospect, for it is in this direction that the world is moving. The automation of productional technology and the rejection of labour will transform the whole organization of culture and develop all the creative energies of society through the unlimited extension of leisure.

This "extreme" prospect has in effect already transformed the concept of design itself, which is now no longer committed to the production of individual machine-domiciles or status symbols, inasmuch as the gradual transformation of residential time proportionally modifies the codifying of cultural symbols in the direction of a state of continual and ineffable experimentation with one's own creativity in places of residence. Which adds up to fully furnished space designed for total use; the house no longer as a system of representing one's identity, but a place where that identity can be realized directly.

22 Design e culture minoritarie

Il conflitto tra i sistemi di cultura internazionale (design, architettura razionalista ecc.) e le culture locali, minoritarie o tradizionali, cresce insieme all'incertezza su tutte le sicurezze culturali e tecnologiche, e diviene mano a mano tema di fondo di una generazione. La morte dell'architettura, la sua scomparsa come qualità stessa del vivere, la sua liquidazione come struttura culturale della società, diventa premessa a una verifica di tutti gli strumenti culturali e ad un loro confronto con tutti i sistemi minori.
Come le grandi ideologie nascono da premesse spontanee, filosofiche e sentimentali, e con queste premesse entrano subito in conflitto in nome di una dimensione storica più globale della vita, così la cultura moderna (del design e dell'architettura) nasce dal rilevamento di tutte le metodologie semplici, anche naïf, le distilla e ne estrae un metodo universale di fare, costruire, usare; tale metodo però si sostituisce subito ad ogni precedente eredità minoritaria divenendone l'alternativa e la evoluzione, combattendo anzi tutto ciò che sfugge al controllo del suo metodo di selezione e analisi.
Questa sostituzione rappresenta un conflitto politico, oltre che culturale, divenendo l'attrito tra due dimensioni non integrabili, proponendosi ciascuna di queste dimensioni come sistema universale di organizzazione dell'esperienza, e come esclusiva verifica della realtà.
Intorno a questo dibattito si giuoca il rischio di una grave involuzione culturale o la possibilità di una uscita luminosa delle libertà e degli strumenti culturali.
Esistono (ed è bene chiarirlo) due concezioni diverse e opposte del termine ''cultura minoritaria''.
Esiste una concezione che intende la cultura minoritaria come campionario di oggetti da reperire, come complesso di tecnologie arretrate da riproporre, e in generale come insieme di ''valori storici'' da difendere. Questa definizione è oggi largamente accettata dalla cultura borghese in crisi, come unica possibile ricucitura di un contesto culturale gestibile.
La ''conservazione culturale'' è sempre stata in Italia, e lo è adesso, sostanzialmente fascista, sia per come la tradizione viene riproposta (ricerca di identità e di destino), sia per come viene gestita in termini puramente autoritari e repressivi.
Tutti i discorsi che si sentono oggi fare nei salotti e nelle sedi dei comitati civici (combinati tra politici, proprietari terrieri e architetti) sono pericolosi perché tralasciano sempre di chiarire bene i rapporti esistenti tra conservazione culturale e conservazione sociale. Non chiarendo questo rapporto le possibili ambiguità diventano infinite e la strumentalizzazione reazionaria del discorso quasi automatica.
Prendiamo l'esempio della cultura contadina: essa nasce e si sviluppa all'interno di consorzi sociali basati sulla miseria, la malattia e lo sfruttamento; le tecnologie contadine, arcaiche e semplici, nascono dal furto di informazioni tecniche perpetrato con metodicità dalla classe dei proprietari terrieri, come premessa tecnica allo sfruttamento sociale; la cultura contadina si sviluppa dentro a una carenza di contatti umani, culturali e commerciali, dentro a un sistema sociale regredito e repressivo come la campagna.

E' impossibile salvare la cultura contadina, intesa come sistema culturale operante, senza conservare le condizioni storiche complessive in cui essa è nata e funziona; a meno di accontentarsi di ordinarne i reperti tra le tante testimonianze di cose scomparse.

Quando con la cultura contadina si rivaluta la ''condizione contadina'', quando la miseria passa per semplicità, l'ignoranza per cultura alternativa, il gioco della reazione è già fatto.

E' dietro a questo atteggiamento infatti che passano le più grosse truffe sociali, gli inganni ecologici, il disegno di gestione della società come operazione superiore e culturale (fascismo).

Esiste invece un'altra concezione della cultura minoritaria; questa concezione consiste nella ricerca di un diverso rapporto tra l'uomo e le tecniche e tra la cultura e la creatività spontanea. Le culture minoritarie propongono infatti un superamento dei codici estetici e dei tabù tecnologici ufficiali, per sperimentare spesso un uso puramente e direttamente ''funzionale e privato'' del fare artistico, non inteso come esperienza universale, ma come atto costruttivo direttamente legato alla spinta creativa del gruppo o dell'individuo.
Questo genere di esperienze e di tradizione è prezioso documento di un modo diverso di produrre la cultura, intesa come bene prodotto e consumato dalla intera comunità e non da un settore specializzato di questa; la cultura intesa come bene direttamente collegato alla vita biologica e economica e non come canale separato di esperienze alternative.
Questo è ciò che a noi interessa delle culture minoritarie di ieri e di oggi, ed è questo che ci interessa per il futuro e non per il passato già morto.
Il design, io credo, deve misurarsi su questa eredità e su questa prospettiva, perché è in questa direzione che il mondo sta andando.
L'automazione delle tecniche produttive e il rifiuto del lavoro trasformeranno tutta l'organizzazione produttiva della cultura, facendo sviluppare l'energia creativa della società attraverso l'estensione indeterminata del tempo libero.
Questa prospettiva ''al limite'' trasforma già di fatto la concezione stessa del design, non più impegnato a individuare macchine abitative o status symbols, dal momento che la trasformazione progressiva dei tempi di residenza modifica proporzionalmente la codificazione dei simboli culturali verso uno stato di continua e indefinibile sperimentazione della propria creatività nei luoghi abitativi.
Il vuoto attrezzato disponibile ad un uso totale. La casa non più come sistema di rappresentazione della propria identità, ma luogo ove questa identità si realizza direttamente.

La tradizione culturale e politica italiana non è mai riuscita ad avere nessun reale collegamento con la cultura del Movimento Moderno. Mentre il Movimento Moderno cresceva e si sviluppava, gli architetti italiani erano impegnati a progettare per il fascismo o si cimentavano nei littoriali; trenta anni di dopoguerra e di permanente malgoverno democristiano prima, e democristiano e socialista poi, hanno definitivamente bruciato l'entroterra nel quale la disciplina di una moderna architettura e urbanistica passano in una società. Questo entroterra è costituito da una complessa rete di situazioni sociali e produttive, che vanno per esempio dalle abitudini di vita familiare alla programmazione industriale, dalla diffusione dell'assistenza sociale a tradizioni radicate nelle tipologie abitative ecc. Quando queste situazioni esistono, quando cioè esiste un così detto ordine sociale, la presenza di una architettura e di una urbanistica moderne non rappresenta che l'atto terminale di un processo già tutto esistente nella realtà, di cui non resta che la formalizzazione nelle strutture abitative in totale omogeneità con la società.

In Italia non esistono queste premesse, storiche e culturali, per cui l'architettura moderna è apparsa ai suoi inizi come personale ricerca di professionisti isolati, e successivamente, dopo l'ultima guerra, come tema didattico sul quale poggiare la vita delle facoltà di architettura. Si è dovuto attendere gli anni '60 e la maturazione del capitalismo fondiario privato per vedere nei quartieri di gran lusso, esterni alle città ormai invivibili, i primi modelli urbani con servizi e verde invece del tradizionale brutale accumulo di metri cubi. L'assenza di questo contesto storico e sociale ha fatto sì che la cultura architettonica italiana soffrisse di alcune deformazioni patologiche. La principale di queste deformazioni consiste nell'elevatissimo grado di ideologicizzazione, per cui progettare non vuol dire operare all'interno di una certa realtà omogenea, ma anzi dichiararsi politicamente contro la realtà esistente per metterla in crisi.

Da questa situazione derivano due fenomeni: il primo consiste nel fatto che la storia dell'architettura italiana sia costituita da opere isolate, di natura polemica, in quanto generalmente tendono a contrapporsi polemicamente al contesto esistente e al suo elevato grado di compromissione. Il disastro territoriale è oggi ormai presupposto nell'atto stesso del progettare, ed è parte fondamentale di questo in quanto quadro di riferimento rispetto al quale collocarsi. Il linguaggio architettonico diventa così dichiarazione programmatica e ideologica: basti pensare al fenomeno del neo-monumentalismo come malinteso rigore morale, e all'architettura organica come pura allegoria della democrazia. Progettare in Italia vuol dire puntare sulla discontinuità, sulla esaltazione dei contrasti, sulla esasperazione linguistica.

Il secondo fenomeno indotto dall'elevato grado di ideologicizzazione consiste nella certezza che alla qualità architettonica corrisponde la qualità politica. Confondendo causa con effetto l'architettura viene intesa come operazione in grado di "creare" una situazione politica, e non viceversa.

Da sinistra si ricerca una gestione urbanistica dal basso come strumento rivoluzionario generale, e da destra si propone l'urbanistica come strumento d'ordine "tout court", come possibile surrogato autoritario a un ordine sociale che non c'è. Vedi situazione di Roma.

Quest'ultimo atteggiamento è il punto di arrivo, tutto italiano, di un processo di tragica involuzione verso forme autoritarie di una politica illuminata. Si abbattono i palazzi e le baracche abusive, non importa abitate da chi, mettendo migliaia di persone sul lastrico, dopo che sono state truffate, dopo che per anni si è finto di non vedere niente. E' sufficiente la vicinanza alle elezioni per dare inizio a una tragica simulazione autoritaria, la quale essendo applicata all'urbanistica non potrà essere criticata in alcun modo. Gli immigrati tornino a casa, l'assenza di quartieri popolari non riguarda i pretori, impegnati a simulare una sanatoria impossibile ma "sempre coraggiosa...".

Fa meraviglia come simili fenomeni passino sotto il silenzio della cultura urbanistica ufficiale: tempo fa avevo detto nella introduzione al libro « Architettura radicale » (di Paola Navone e Bruno Orlandoni): « Ormai l'urbanistica si fa solo con le leggi, e tra non molto la si farà con i mitra... ».

23 Urbanistica e ordine (pubblico)

Town-planning, (law) and order

✶✶ ANDREA BRANZI ✶✶

RADICAL NOTES

The Italian cultural and political tradition has never managed to establish any real rapport with the culture of the Modern Movement. While the Modern Movement was growing and developing, Italian architects were engaged in planning for Fascism and in trying their mettle in contending for the regime's architectural contracts. Thirty years of post-war misgovernment under the Christian-Democrats first and then under a Socialist and Christian-Democrat coalition have definitely burnt up the hinterland where modern architecture and town-planning develop in a society. This hinterland consists in a complex network of social and production patterns which range, for example, from the habits of family life to industrial programming, from the spread of social security to traditions rooted in certain types of homes, etc. When these conditions exist, when — that is — there is what we call a social order, the presence of modern architecture or development plans only represent the last act of a process already existing in reality, so that all there remains to be done is to formalize this condition in the structures of new homes in complete harmony with society.

These historical and cultural premises not being present in Italy, modern architecture seemed only the personal experimentation of a few isolated professionals in the beginning, and after the war only a didactic theme to provide a basis for the curricula of architectural schools. It was not until the '60s and the full ripening of private real-estate capitalism that one saw, in the de-luxe quarters outside the city (the city now being uninhabitable), the first urban models with services and some green in the surroundings, instead of the usual brutal heaping up of cubic metres. The absence of this historical and social context has led to a number of pathological symptoms in Italian architectonic culture. The main symptom is the great extent to which everything has been subjected to ideology, so that designing is not a matter of operating within a certain homogeneous reality, but of declaring oneself to be politically against existing reality in order to undermine it. This has produced two results: firstly, that the history of Italian architecture now consists of isolated works of a polemical nature, in that they tend to clash polemically with the existing context and its high degree of compression.

A disaster at the territorial level is now taken for granted in the very act of designing and is a fundamental part of it as a reference system within which to fit one's work. Architectonic idiom thus becomes a programmatic and ideological statement; witness neo-monumentalism with its misplaced moral severity, or organic architecture, seen as a pure allegory of democracy. Designing in Italy means aiming for discontinuity, for the heightening of contrasts, and for idiom carried to extremes.

The second result of the pervasive presence of ideology in architecture is the certainty that architectonic quality is tantamount to political quality. Mistaking cause for effect, some see architecture as an operation capable of "creating" a political situation (and not viceversa).

On the left there is a quest for the management of town-development "from below" as a general instrument of revolution, and on the right town-development is seen as an instrument for achieving "order" as a possible authoritarian surrogate for a "law and order" that is inexistent. Rome is a case in point. The latter attitude is the last (and completely Italian) stop in a process of tragic involution towards the authoritarian forms of an enlightened policy. Illegally built blocks of flats and huts are demolished, no matter who lives in them, and thousands of people end up on the street, after they have been swindled or after years of the authorities pretending not to see anything. The mere proximity of the elections is enough to set off a tragic simulation of authority which, being applied to city-development, can hardly be criticized. The immigrant squatters are sent home, for the absence of low-cost living accomodations is not the concern of the magistrates, engaged in simulating an impossible but "still courageous" clean-up compaign.

It is surprising how such things are quietly ignored by the official line on town-planning: some time ago, in the introduction to « Architettura radicale » by Paola Navone and Bruno Orlandoni, I predicted that « Town planning is by now only being carried out by laws; before long it will be carried out with machine guns... ».

Si sta ricomponendo nel mondo un nuovo equilibrio culturale. Anche in Italia, nonostante la maggiore presenza di conflitti sociali, si ricompone un quadro costituito da un insieme abbastanza organico di "contenuti" ufficiali, non più contestabili, sufficientemente ampi e generali da garantire un quadro di fondo ai singoli prodotti. La generatrice strutturale di questo insieme è "conservativa": la cultura degli anni '70 ha infatti recuperato ufficialmente il tema della conservazione culturale e quindi, anche se non esplicitamente, conservazione sociale.

Bisogna conservare perché la recente crisi energetica ha insegnato che niente deve essere sciupato, bisogna conservare perché il futuro non offre sufficienti garanzie, bisogna conservare perché sprecare vuol dire governare male. Ma soprattutto bisogna conservare perché, secondo la tautologia borghese, conservare vuol dire essere rivoluzionari.

Conservare vuol dire intanto fermare il progresso tecnico (crescita zero), conservare vuol dire salvare i valori dell'uomo, perché l'uomo è la storia e chi distrugge la storia distrugge anche la dimensione umana dell'uomo. Salvare che cosa? Tutto, perché oggi abbiamo riscoperto che tutto ha significato, che anzi troppi significati sono stati sacrificati fino ad oggi in nome della novità! Salviamo la natura, salviamo la cultura popolare e non popolare, salviamo il buon senso, salviamo la semplicità, salviamo i capolavori, salviamo la lingua, salviamo il mare, salviamo le tradizioni gastronomiche, salviamo i Colli Euganei, salviamo l'Italia, salviamo gli Italiani che non sanno di essere un popolo e si sono sperduti su spiagge straniere... Chi lo compie questo salvataggio? Tutti insieme, tutta la società recuperando la propria coscienza sociale e riscoprendo il proprio innato amore per le cose belle e vere. Cioè riconoscendo un quadro di valori naturali che non devono e non possono essere manomessi.

L'unità culturale si ripropone come unità naturale della società, e dove esiste una unità naturale nessuna frattura può avvenire se non in maniera "innaturale", esterna, abnorme, cattiva. La conservazione diventa così auto-conservazione della società.

La conservazione culturale richiede implicitamente garanzie da quella che è la più micidiale macchina distruttiva dei valori culturali, che è costituita dalla crescita economica delle classi incolte. Bisogna creare una intercapedine, una camera di sicurezza in cui incanalare la crescita operaia e ovviare la distruzione imitativa dei modelli culturali. Questo vallo deve garantire le spalle alla borghesia salvaguardando i contenuti fondamentali della classe preservandoli dalle rivendicazioni sociali. Da una parte infatti si devono produrre "capolavori", e dall'altra bisogna crescere economicamente dentro a modelli permissivi dinamici, ma non in grado di modificare i meccanismi attuali di produzione della cultura.

La classe illuminata si è proposta come amministratrice di questa operazione sui due fronti, conservazione e produzione di cultura.

Erano molti anni che in Italia non si producevano tanti capolavori; sembra un miracolo ma negli ultimi tempi ne sbucano fuori con grande facilità: romanzi, opere liriche, architetture ecc. Gente che ha passato quindici anni in un armadio a preparare nuove lingue, romanzi anarchici, addirittura opere liriche sugli scioperi generali. Chi credeva che la consacrazione di "capolavoro" fosse definitivamente relegata al secolo passato non ha che da ricredersi. E la crisi culturale? Niente altro che naturale incertezza di un momento, che prepara un presente di ricuperata certezza creativa.

La grande frenata è cominciata: legarsi le cinture di sicurezza...

Stralci da un documento inviato c
da Enzo Mari:
Un gruppo di studenti della Uni
versità Bocconi di Milano ha chie
sto agli artisti milanesi di studiar
la possibilità di produrre un'oper
monumentale che celebri la me
moria e il significato della mort
del compagno Roberto Francesch
colpito dalla polizia il 23 gennai
1973, durante una manifestazion
per il rinnovamento della scuola
l'avvenire democratico del paese.
Numerosi artisti hanno accolt
l'appello e hanno deciso di costi
tuirsi in Comitato Promotore (l
cui segreteria è composta da A
Cavaliere, M. Ceretti, G. Pardi, M
Staccioli, T. Valieri) per la proge
tazione di un'opera che esprima i
significato e l'emblematicità del sa
crificio di Franceschi e di tutti co
loro che hanno perso la vita i
questi anni per affermare la demo
crazia nel nostro paese.
La madre del compagno Francesch
ha scritto agli artisti riuniti i
Assemblea la lettera che qui ripo
tiamo:
« Il 23 gennaio di quest'anno h
detto alla Camera del lavoro ch
i morti per una società verament

PER I CADUTI

24 La grande frenata
The great slow-down

ANDREA BRANZI

RADICAL NOTES

A new cultural balance is beginning to take shape throughout the world. In Italy, too, despite the increased pressure of social conflicts, a unified picture of cultural production is coming into focus: it consists of a fairly organic whole of official and no longer challengeable "contents" that are sufficiently wide and general to provide a solid background for individual products.

Structurally, this generating force may be called "conservative": the culture of the '70s, in fact, has officially recuperated the theme of cultural conservation and therefore, though not explicitly, social conservatism.

Conservation is the word today, because the recent energy crisis has shown that nothing must be wasted, conservation because the future is unsure, because waste means bad government. But above all, conservation (i.e. conservatism) because, according to middle-class tautological thinking, to be "conservative" means to be revolutionary.

Again, to be conservative means to bring technological progress to a standstill with zero growth; to be conservative means to save the values of mankind, because man is history and to destroy history means to destroy man's human dimension. But to save what? Everything, because today we have discovered once again that everything has meaning, and that indeed far too many meanings have been sacrificed to this day in the name of novelty! Let us save nature, popular and non-popular culture, common sense, simplicity, masterpieces, our language, the sea, our traditions in cookery, the Euganeian hills, Italy and the Italians, who don't realize that they are a people and are scattered about in foreign climes... And who is to do all this salvaging? All of us together, society as a whole, thereby recuperating its own social awareness and rekindling its inherent love for the true and the beautiful. That is, by acknowledging a set of natural values which must not and cannot be tampered with.

Cultural unity is presented as the natural unity of a society, and where a natural unity exists, there can be no fracture, unless it be "unnatural", external, abnormal, and wicked.

Conservation, thus becomes the self-conservation of society.

Cultural conservation implicitly calls for guarantees against the greatest engine of destruction of cultural values, which is to be found in the economic growth of the uncultivated classes. A cavity wall will have to be built, a safety chamber in which to canalize the pressure of labour and avert the imitative destruction of cultural models. This wall should cover the middle-class at the rear, safeguarding the fundamental contents of the class and protecting it from social demands. In fact , on the one hand masterpieces must be produced; on the other, there must be economic growth within dynamic permissive moulds, but not so permissive as to modify current systems of cultural production.

The enlightened class has offered to direct this operation on two fronts: the conservation and production of culture.

It has been quite a number of years since Italy produced such a spate of masterpieces. It may be a miracle, but in the last few years they have been budding forth in great profusion: novels, operas, works of architecture, etc. Works produced by people who have spent the last fifteen years holed up in their dens in the preparation of new languages, anarchic novels and even grand operas singing of general strikes. Those who thought that the consecration of a "masterpiece" was something definitely relegated to the last century are now changing their minds. But what about the cultural crisis? Nothing more than the natural uncertainty of the moment, which is giving way to a present of renewed creative certainty.

« We are coming down now, ladies and gentlemen. Please fasten your seatbelts ».

NELLE LOTTE POPOLARI DAL '45 A OGGI

democratica, per il socialismo no
sono dei morti, essi sono vivi, ess
sono più vivi di coloro che no
si accorgono che la resistenza co
tinua e come negli anni eroici d
'43 - 44 - 45 bisogna coalizzare tut
le forze democratiche in una vig
lanza attiva, che non permetta ch
i campi di sterminio, delimitati
no da filo spinato, funzionino a
cora. E' per questo che io vi dic
che Roberto questa sera è present
in questa sala,vivo nella continui
delle vostre lotte, lotte che voi, a
che attraverso l'arte, portate avan
Vi ringrazio perché voi oggi n
permettete di ricordare il 12 d
cembre 1972.
Il 12 dicembre 1972 in occasion
dello sciopero generale per i fat
di piazza Fontana rispose ad u
mia frase apprensiva guardandon
con quei suoi occhi meravigliosi -
mamma se mi dovesse capita
qualcosa tu devi continuare nel

E' sempre esistito un rapporto tra l'architettura e il corpo umano. Sarebbe interessante analizzare questo rapporto all'interno della storia, e il suo variare in relazione al variare della morale corrente, o almeno in relazione al peso della sessualità nella società e nella vita comune. W. Reich ha scoperto che più della metà del nostro tempo, almeno fino all'età matura (cioè circa cinquant'anni), lo passiamo a pensare al sesso, nostro e altrui, ipotizzando combinazioni e accoppiate, e che l'attività sessuale non solo è un tipo di libera comunicazione sociale, ma più in generale è una forma di energia fisica che condiziona tutte le nostre esperienze. Tra queste, ritengo, in maniera preminente il sesso condiziona la nostra "esperienza spaziale", cioè la nostra capacità di concepire quello spazio vuoto esistente tra noi e gli altri, e che è normalmente inteso come spazio architettonico, come medium sessuale, come luogo di libero scambio di messaggi e di ipotesi di relazioni o esperienze sessuali.
Questo tipo di ipotesi, del resto sufficientemente elementare per essere vera, è ufficialmente assente nella storia dell'architettura. Esistono casi isolati di intuizioni in tal senso, ma quasi sempre limitatamente a fenomeni di architettura antropomorfica o fallica, e mai come ipotesi disciplinare ufficialmente adottata.
In una società come la nostra che vive le avvisaglie di una rivoluzione sessuale, credo che questa ipotesi, di architettura come luogo preminentemente del sesso, avrà un futuro. In quale maniera è difficile dirlo, ma è certo che un legame così potente nei rapporti inter-familiari e urbani non potrà più a lungo essere sottaciuto, dal momento che la sua scoperta è un fenomeno scientifico prima ancora che morale. Non dimentichiamoci che la scoperta della socialità dell'architettura e della città solo da poco è stata adottata ufficialmente, dopo una lunga ripulsa, come volgare interferenza in una disciplina fondata su se stessa.
Per il sesso potrebbe essere ugualmente: la stessa storia dell'architettura potrebbe essere riletta alla luce di questa ipotesi, scoprendo l'itinerario di una lunga battaglia dell'umanità contro il sesso.
Lo stesso rapporto esistente tra concetti architettonici e esperienza sensoriale dello spazio, potrebbe essere una prima chiave di indagine. Nel medioevo, quando il sesso era ufficialmente negato dalla morale, la percezione dello spazio architettonico esaltava tutti i dati fisici, così come l'eremita respingeva i richiami della carne soffocando lo stimolo sotto sensazioni più forti, come quelle del dolore fisico. Basta pensare alle cattedrali gotiche o romaniche, dove la percezione dell'organismo monumentale era strettamente legata a esperienze fisiche come la differenza di temperatura tra l'interno e l'esterno, l'odore di quei luoghi non areabili, un certo tipo di acustica, la luce filtrata dalle vetrate ecc. La comunicazione sessuale in quei luoghi di comunità, già totalmente pieni di dati sensoriali oltre che religiosi, risultava impossibile.
Nel Rinascimento, con l'avvento di un'autorifondazione dell'architettura, il rapporto con l'esperienza fisica dello spazio cessa, affermandosi un tipo di rapporto ideologico, filosofico con l'ordine classico; i rapporti con il corpo umano passano dall'esperienza diretta ai rapporti proporzionali. L'architettura diventa un tipo di esperienza del tutto concettuale, priva di odori, suoni, immersa in un universo luminoso privo ufficialmente di turbe sessuali.
Questo tipo di impostazione è giunto fino a noi senza grandi varianti, che non fossero di origine freudiana, cioè sul diffondersi anche presso gli architetti della coscienza che l'organizzazione dell'esperienza è più relativa di quel che si credeva.
Ma il ruolo dell'architettura come grande strumento di repressione sessuale resta confermato.
Eppure le battaglie per la libertà compositiva, per il superamento del funzionalismo come repressione del libero comportamento, sono ormai giunte al collegio dei geometri; ma il passaggio dall'architettura organica all'architettura orgonica sembra molto lontano.

Architettura e sesso

25

✶✶ ANDREA BRANZI ✶✶

RADICAL NOTES

Architecture and sex

**There has always been a relationship between architecture and the human body. It would be interesting to examine this relationship from inside history and to study its variations in relation to variations in current moral standards, or at least in relation to the importance given to sexuality in society and in daily life.
W. Reich discovered that more than half of our time, at least until we reach middle-age (about fifty), is spent thinking about sex, about our own and other people's sex lives, imagining combinations and couplings, for sexual activities are not only a free kind of social communication but a form of physical energy that conditions all our experiences. Of these, I should say, sex most deeply influences our "experience of space" — that is, our capacity to conceive the empty space lying between us and others (which is normally taken to be architectonic space) as a sexual medium, as a place for the free exchange of messages and for possible or actual sexual experiences.
This kind of theory, which is moreover elementary enough to be true, is officially absent in the history of architecture.
There are some isolated cases of intuition in this regard, but they are almost always limited to cases of anthropomorphic or phallic architecture and never concern any officially adopted architectonic guidelines.
In a society like ours now experiencing the first symptoms of a sexual revolution, I think there is a future for this idea of architecture as a predominantly sexual place. Just how, it is hard to say, but it is quite certain that such a powerful link in inter-family and urban relationships can hardly be silenced much longer, all the more so because its discovery is more a scientific than a moral matter.
Let us not forget that the discovery of the sociality of architecture and of the city has only recently been officially acknowledged, after long being rejected as a vulgar interference in a discipline based on itself.
The same thing might happen with sex in architecture: the whole history of architecture could be reinterpreted in the light of this hypothesis, and trace the course of humanity's long battle against sex.
The relationship between architectonic concepts and the sensorial experience of space might constitute the first step in our inquiry. In the Middle Ages, when sex was officially condemned by moral opinion, all the physical data of architectonic space were heightened, just as the hermit would resist the call of the flesh by suffocating the stimulus under more powerful sensations such as physical pain. One need only think of Gothic and Romanesque cathedrals, in which one's perception of the monumental organism was closely related to such physical experiences as differences in temperature between the interior and the exterior, the odour of such unventilated places, a certain kind of acoustics, light filtering in through the windows, etc. Sexual communication in such places of communal gathering (which were already completely full of both sensorial and religious stimuli) became impossible.
With the Renaissance came a restructuralization of architecture from within. In it the relationship with the physical experience of space is replaced by a kind of ideological-philosophical relationship with the classical order, while relationships with the human body shift from direct experience to proportional relationships. Architecture became a completely conceptual kind of experience, soundless and odourless, immersed in an illuminated universe officially undisturbed by sexual vibrations.
This kind of approach has been handed down to us without any appreciable variants, apart from those of Freudian inspiration resulting from the growing feeling among architects and many others that the organization of experience is much more relevant than it was once thought.
But the role of architecture as the great instrument of sexual repression has been reconfirmed. The struggles for compositional freedom, for the discarding of functionalism as a repression of free behaviour have now reached the surveyors' college; but the road from organic architecture to orgonic architecture, it seems, will be long and hard.**

Mi sembra che uno dei fenomeni piú interessanti di questi ultimi anni sia la progressiva separazione in atto tra avanguardie politiche e avanguardie culturali.
Non si tratta, mi sembra, soltanto di una divisione tra due diversi specifici di competenza, ma piuttosto di una polemica sugli strumenti tattici che nasconde una piú profonda separazione sui contenuti.
Gli appunti sempre piú acidi che l'avanguardia politica lancia ai compagni delle sperimentazioni culturali, non riguardano piú le scale di priorità, ma una insofferenza profonda verso tutto quello che esula, genericamente, da un'immediata e semplice applicabilità politica, e tra breve, prevedo, si giungerà ad un esplicito anatema contro i poeti "compagni di strada".
Si tratta, per molti versi, di una "querelle" tradizionale alla storia della sinistra, quasi un tema classico sul quale sono già stati versati fiumi di inchiostro: pure, sembra ieri, è esistita una straordinaria unità di lotta, nata nella comune matrice storica e nella maturazione simultanea (1968), nella quale si collocava ogni atto, creativo o politico, come un momento miracolosamente unitario, legato ad un piú travolgente destino rivoluzionario di una generazione.
Adesso si comincia ad invecchiare, e male; i litigi crescono con il crescere stesso della involuzione parallela dei due movimenti, quello politico e quello culturale.
Adesso che la cometa è scomparsa, al suo posto è subentrata una complessa e difficile osservazione astronomica, piena di calcoli e misure.
Che di involuzione si tratti, penso non esistano dubbi.
Da una parte, paradossalmente, si soffre il 15 giugno come una sorta di sconfitta, proprio nel momento in cui il paese si è svegliato "quasi comunista", ha dimostrato l'isolamento e la fine della crescita delle avanguardie politiche, rimaste dimensionate al 1968, e che vedono chiudersi i tradizionali pascoli giovanili, che hanno dimostrato, con il voto, di aver scelto l'ordine e il buon governo. La disubbidienza civile, la fantasia al potere, tutto e subito, sembrano vecchie parolacce senza sapore.
E cosí essi sentono crescere l'angoscia di sentirsi esclusi da un grande avvenimento storico del paese, avvenimento che pure è stato preparato da tanti San Giovanni che gridavano nel deserto; cresce la perplessità di svolgere un ruolo "anti-comunista" in un momento in cui gli anti-comunisti veri si presentano alle casse dell'America e si preparano a vendere l'anima e il paese pur di non perdere il potere.
Allora spesso la reazione è quella di un indurimento nervoso verso tutto ciò che non è immediatamente ortodosso, il rifiuto dei tempi lunghi, o l'adozione mistica di tempi lunghissimi. Cresce la paura e il sospetto, e torna ad affacciarsi la tesi che l'unica attività creativa è la rivoluzione, e che quindi ogni ulteriore interferenza non significa che pericolosi sviamenti dall'impegno totale della politica. Tesi questa arcinota e puntualmente smentita dalla storia, dove ogni momento rivoluzionario è stato preceduto da una vorticosa crescita delle avanguardie culturali, che spesso hanno preceduto e partorito (1968) quelle politiche. Il timore verso il non-ortodosso finisce per nascondere una generica intolleranza.
Si torna di fatto a riproporre una sorta di realismo socialista utile per i vari festivals popolari come puro e semplice momento di illustrazione di contenuti politici.
Dall'altra parte vediamo una avanguardia culturale perdere il proprio mordente e il riferimento ad una crescita della creatività collettiva come momento di liberazione politica; si vede riproporre la scatola di montaggio come ipotesi di partecipazione culturale; si sente valutare l'ignoranza come cultura alternativa; si ritrova la goliardia come possibile attività sperimentale; si ritrova l'ecologia come ideologia giovanile...
Soprattutto, nel campo dell'avanguardia di architettura, si assiste ad un altro fenomeno: l'adozione di quella che viene chiamata contro-architettura (o architettura radicale) come una categoria definitiva, come un atteggiamento confermato ufficialmente, cioè come una "maniera" di progettare. Una maniera per fare concorsi, mostre, tesi di laurea, esami, pubblicazioni, discorsi: una sorta di canale parallelo che non interferisce con la professione, un nuovo linguaggio liberamente utilizzabile da chiunque.
Cosí vediamo fior di professionisti abbandonare per un attimo riga e squadra e dedicarsi a fantasiosi fotomontaggi, scherzi radicali, utopie fumose. Le università, ci, aprono le porte a questa sorta di gi[...] che intrattiene finalmente gli studenti za danni per loro stesse e per l'arc[...]tura, che da questa vacanza ne uscirà forzata come seria testimonianza di i[...]gno civile (« In un paese in cui mancar[...] case, non ci si può permettere... »). I[...] dell'architettura radicale, come la sco[...] scientifica della creatività pubblica [...] energia spaziale, la fine dell'architettura [...]rica come possibile categoria culturale [...] la società, l'utopia come strumento di [...]dio sulla crisi definitiva del concetto [...]centesco degli equilibri urbani, le tecr[...] povere come testimonianza della crisi [...] meccanismi tradizionali di produzione [...] cultura, tutto questo e altro ancora [...] sfiora il neo-radicale, che anzi ne [...] la conferma della sua disponibilità as[...]ta a correre tutte le avventure senza ris[...] alcuno.
Cosí l'avanguardia, che invece di an[...] deserta diventa stranamente superaffo[...] e si vede confermata come uno "stile [...]ciale dell'architettura moderna", anzi il [...]vimento Moderno tout-court (Zevi), si t[...] nella impossibilità di creare shock a de[...] (università, professione, ecologia ecc.) e [...]pre la tentazione di creare shock a sini[...] tentazione oggettivamente pericolosa, [...] non fa altro che alimentare il "sosp[...] delle avanguardie politiche. Sospetto [...]proco, del resto, dal momento che la s[...] d'Italia ci ha effettivamente insegnato [...] il pericolo fascista nasce nella sinistra.

26 Il sospetto Suspicion

ANDREA BRANZI

RADICAL NOTES

It seems to me that one of the most interesting phenomena in the last few years has been the gradual separation taking place between the political and cultural avant-gardes.
In my view this is not simply a division between two different spheres of competence, but a contrast regarding tactical instruments which conceals a much wider separation over matters of content.
The increasingly corrosive comments made by the political avant-garde against their comrades engaged in cultural experimentation no longer regard matters of priority but reveal an attitude of extreme intolerance towards anything of no immediate and simple political utility.
I expect that before long they will solemnly excommunicate these poetic fellow-travellers.
Actually, in many respects, this sort of "squabble" will be found quite frequently in the history of the Left; it is almost a classical theme, one about which far too much has already been written.
And yet, it seems like yesterday, there was once an extraordinary identity of purpose in the struggle, an identity born of a common historical matrix and simultaneous maturation (1968), in which every creative or political act fitted as a miracle of unity bound to the overwhelming revolutionary destiny of a generation.
But now everything is ageing, and badly: quarrels break out along with the rapid deterioration being suffered by both the political and cultural movements.
Now that the comet has disappeared, its place has been taken by a complex and difficult astronomical observation bristling with calculations and measurements.
That it is indeed deterioration, there can be little doubt. Paradoxically, in one sense, the Italian June elections were felt to be a kind of defeat, just when the country woke up "almost Communist". This demonstrated the isolation and arrested growth of the political avant-garde movements still thinking in terms of 1968, for they now see their traditional grazing grounds being closed, as they have demonstrated with their votes that they preferred order and good government. Civil disobedience and dreams of complete and immediate power now have lost their bite.
Accordingly, they are now suffering the anguish of feeling excluded from a great event in the country's history, an event however that has been prepared by a great many John the Baptists crying in the desert.
There is a feeling of anxiety about playing an "anti-Communist" role at a time when the real anti-Communists are turning up at American cash-desks ready to sell their souls and their country to boot in order to hold on to their power. Consequently, the reaction tends to be nervous and hard towards anything not immediately seen as orthodox, towards long-term thinking or the mystical adoption of the very long view.
There has been a growth of fear and suspicion, and a reappearance of the argument that the only truly creative activity is the revolution and that therefore any deviation can only mean a dangerous defection from one's total commitment to political struggle.
This well-known argument has been duly refuted by the facts of history, for every revolutionary event has always been preceded by the whirlwind growth of cultural avant-garde movements, which often preceded and gave birth to political ones (see 1968). The fear of the non-orthodox ends by concealing a generalized intolerance.
Indeed, it has now been proposed that we should return to a kind of socialist realism of some use for the various people's festivals as pure and simple illustrations of political contents.
On the other hand, we are witnessing a cultural avant-garde that is beginning to lose its thrust; references made to the growth of collective creativity speak of it as political liberation, the construction kit is now being proposed as an instance of cultural participation; ignorance is now valued as a cultural alternative; student life is seen as a possible area of experimental activity; and ecology has been rediscovered as a youthful ideology...
Especially in the field of avant-garde architecture we are witnessing another phenomenon: the adoption of what is called counter-architecture (or radical architecture) as a definite category, as an officially confirmed attitude — that is, as a "way" of designing. Indeed, as a way of doing competitions, exhibits, graduation theses, examinations, publications, speeches: a sort of parallel channel that does not interfere with one's profession, a new language that anyone can use at will.
And thus we see the cream of the profession set aside ruler and square to dedicate themselves to fantasy photo-montages, radical jokes, and cloudy Utopias. The universities happily open their gates to this sort of game which, without any harm to themselves or to architecture, finally manages to entertain the students. And out of this vacation architecture will emerge strengthened as a witness to civic commitment (« In a country with a housir[...] problem we cannot allow... »).
Such subjects as radical architecture, the scientific discovery of public creativity as spatial energy, the end of historical architecture as a possible cultural catego[...] of society, Utopia as an instrument for the study of the definitive crisis of the 19th century concept of urban equilibrium[...] minimal techniques as witnesses to the crisis in the conventional mechanisms for the production of culture — all this and more hardly touches the neo-radical, who rather sees in it the confirmation of h[...] eternal readiness to undertake any kind of[...] adventure, without the slightest risk.
Thus, far from being abandoned, avant-ga[...] movements are curiously overcrowded and confirmed as the "official style of mod[...] architecture". Indeed, the Modern Movement itself (Zevi), finding it impossib[...] to create shock on the right (University, profession, ecology, etc.), is tempted to create it on the left. This temptation, objectively, is quite dangerous, for it only serves to increase the suspicion of the political avant-garde. And the suspicion is mutual, for as the history of Italy has taug[...] us, the Fascist threat is born in the left.

Resta da capire fino in fondo se la definizione di Movimento Moderno che sta alla base di tutta la storiografia d'architettura, corrisponde ad un dato storico realmente accaduto, cioè oggettivamente riscontrabile nei fatti, o se piuttosto questo concetto non è esso stesso un "progetto", cioè una ipotesi operativa costruita su una intuizione critica e non sui fatti. A leggere i moderni critici (Benevolo, Zevi, ecc.) sembra non esservi ombra di dubbio sulla esistenza di un contesto di idee, programmi, ideologie e progetti che, salvo alcune sbavature perimetrali, è chiaramente identificabile in un "movimento" nato all'inizio del XX secolo e sviluppatosi fino ai nostri giorni. Pure già nella lettura di quelli che dovrebbero essere i dati inoppugnabili di partenza risultano grosse diversità e tesi anche contrastanti apertamente, e questo non tanto perché, come si potrebbe dire, la storia specie se recente è sempre un quadro illuminato dall'ideologia di chi la esplora, ma perché questi nudi dati cronologici sono chiaramente, troppo chiaramente, ambigui.

Diciamo che sembra dato per certo che almeno tra le due guerre il Movimento Moderno viene presentato come un fenomeno chiaramente "unitario", dotato di una ideologia, una metodologia e uno stile, con scelte politiche chiare e con un destino preciso. Questo fenomeno storico sarebbe stato l'unico a realizzarsi, dal momento che le sue coetanee (pittura, musica, letteratura) tutto possono essere definite all'infuori che ricerche unitarie, cioè dirette nella stessa direzione e operanti nello stesso contesto ideologico.

Nessuno storico si sottrae a questa ipotesi unitaria, sia che come il Benevolo ce ne presenti i contenuti con miracolosi passaggi volanti, sia come il Tafuri che al buio ricostruisce una perversa trama di connessioni con il capitale avanzato.

Di questa unità sembrano esistere le prove tangibili in simultaneità, coincidenze, passaggi precisi di informazioni, unità di stile e punti di saldatura costituiti dai Ciam. Pure, se leggiamo i testi scritti dei protagonisti, le lettere o i diari, non troviamo mai traccia di una chiara intenzione programmatica comune. Né questa gente viveva in un unico contesto storico in grado di fornire di fatto una unità: paesi diversi, culture diverse, intenzioni diverse.

La risposta a questo dubbio naturalmente non è che "la storia non esiste", ma piuttosto che effettivamente di questi fatti avvenuti (perché dei fatti sono avvenuti) è stata data una "interpretazione" operativa sul presente, cioè si sono letti a sostegno di teorie attuali, puntello di ipotesi critiche posteriori. E questo è notoriamente un problema che riguarda tutta la storiografia. Ma in questo caso specifico potrebbe anche trattarsi di un falso storico, che forse, invece che chiarire una situazione attuale la nasconde, la maschera dietro a "dati storici oggettivi" che magari non sussistono.

Facciamo una prova: invece di considerare il Movimento Moderno un fenomeno unitario lo considero una sparsa fenomenologia di azioni non programmate e non confrontabili, una pura e semplice successione di progetti. Voglio dire: se invece di vedere il Movimento Moderno come nascita di una nuova cultura dentro una società industrializzata, come atto vitale dopo la morte dell'architettura storica, si vede questo come ultimo atto di quella stessa cultura storica che muore a contatto dello sviluppo industriale; se invece di "nuovi valori" cioè di nuovi contenuti prodotti dalla cultura moderna, leggiamo questa come progressiva scomparsa della cultura stessa; se invece di capolavori rivoluzionari vediamo testimonianze della fine di antichi sistemi di pensiero e di cultura, allora del Movimento Moderno e della sua fenomenologia risulta una immagine diversa dalla precedente. Cambiando l'ottica, il segno o la direzione, non avremmo semplicemente un paesaggio storico "negativo", che non serve a nessuno, ma otterremmo due risultati interessanti.

Per prima cosa riusciremmo a dare un senso piú preciso alla lunga serie dei fallimenti che il Movimento Moderno ha realizzato; non starò qui ad elencarli uno ad uno, ma basti per tutti quello della città moderna, che tutti gli altri comprende. Lo scollamento tra Movimento Moderno e la realtà (sia sociale che industriale) acquista in questa chiave di lettura una giustificazione credibile e un senso positivo. La sua evidente continuità con l'ar-

27 Movimento Moderno? Modern Movement?

ANDREA BRANZI

RADICAL NOTES

We still have to get to the bottom of the question of whether the definition of the Modern Movement that underpins all modern histories of architecture corresponds to an historical event that actually took place, that objectively fits the facts; or whether this concept is not itself a "project" — that is, a working hypothesis elaborated out of critical intuition, and not out of facts. If we read the modern critics (Benevolo, Zevi, etc.), there seems to be hardly any doubt as to the existence of a context of ideas, programmes, ideologies, and plans which, except for a few marginal digressions, can be clearly identified as a movement which started at the turn of this century and has continued to this day. Even a perusal of what should be the irrefutable basic data reveals considerable diversity of opinion and even positions in open conflict. And this is not so much because, as one might imagine, history (especially recent history) is always suffused with the ideology of whoever happens to be exploring it, but because these stark chronological data are all too clearly ambiguous.

At all events, it seems to be accepted that at least during the inter-war years the Modern Movement was presented as a clearly "unitary" movement endowed with its own ideology, methodology and style, and unambiguous in its political orientation and ultimate purposes.

And this historical phenomenon was supposed to be the only one to be fully realized, since the other contemporaneous arts (painting, music, and literature) can be called anything but unitary explorations — that is, moving in the same direction and operating within the same ideological context.

Hardly any critic escapes the influence of this unitary theory. Certainly not Benevolo, who presents his material with miraculous flights of fancy, nor Tafuri, working in the dark on the idea of some perverse plot of connexions with advanced capitalism.

Tangible proofs of this unity can apparently be found in the simultaneity, coincidences, precise passages of information, unity of style and junction points that made up the CIAM. And yet if we read the texts, letters or diaries of the leading figures, we find hardly a trace of any clear intention to form a common programme.

Nor were these people living in the same historical context, which might have given them "de facto" unity: their countries, cultures, and intentions were different.

The way to deal with these doubts, of course, is not to claim that "there is no such thing as history", but rather to acknowledge that an interpretation has been given with an eye on the present — that is, things have been interpreted to support current theories, as a prop to "a posteriori" appraisals. And this, as we all know, is a problem that concerns all historiography. But in this particular case we might even be dealing with an historical forgery which, instead of clarifying a current situation, has hidden or disguised it with a mass of "objective historical data" which may have no validity whatsoever.

Let us make a test; instead of considering the Modern Movement a unitary phenomenon, let us consider it a scattering of actions with no programmes and no common denominator, and thereby eliminate all connexions between the various stages in its progress, so that we come down to a pure and simple succession of projects.

What I mean is: if instead of seeing the Modern Movement as the birth of a new culture within an industrialized society, as a gesture towards life after the demise of historical architecture, one saw it as the last act of that same historical culture which died on coming into contact with industrial development; if instead of its "new values" — that is, of the new contents produced by modern culture, one interpreted it as the gradually disappearing culture itself; if instead of revolutionary masterpieces one should see only evidence of the passing of ancient systems of thought and culture — then, evidently, the Modern Movement and everything connected with it would project a quite different image. By changing viewpoint, sign, and direction we obtain something more than a "negative" historical view, which is of no use to anyone: we obtain two interesting results.

To begin with, we can now make much more sense out of the long series of failures suffered by the Modern Movement. There is no point in spelling them all out here: one need only mention the modern city, which includes them all.

The alienation of the Modern Movement from reality (both social and industrial) acquires in this light both a credible justification and a positive sense. Its evident continuity with historical architecture

SESSION 3

WEAK AND DIFFUSE METROPOLIS OF THE SECOND MODERNITY

For a Non Figurative Architecture

This section proposes two goals: to analyze the innovations that the twenty-first century is introducing to the world of design, to the passage from the strong and concentrated modernity of the twentieth century to the weak and diffuse current one, and to investigate whether there is, in this passage, the possibility of imagining a future for non-figurative architecture.

An architecture that becomes an urban semiosphere, surpassing its constructing limits and becoming a producer of immaterial qualities that change over time.

It is a question, therefore, of setting oneself outside of the architectural tradition seen as a formal metaphor of history, which limits to solely figurative and symbolic codes its function with respect to the major questions of the contemporary urban condition.

This urban condition is made up of services, information technologies networks, product systems, environmental componential practice, microclimates, commercial information, and above all perceptive structures that produce systems of sensorial and intelligent tunnels that are contained within architecture, but can not be represented by architecture's figurative codes.

Contemporary architecture still suffers from a delay in respect to the previous century's culture, which derives from the fact that this culture attributes its fundamental urban and civil role to a figurative function.

This culture is unable to imagine itself as an abstract, immaterial reality, which does not have a direct relation to the form of structures, but to the contemporary metropolitan condition, which cannot be related to formal questions, but in stead to physiological, internal questions of the urban organism.

Contemporary architecture still attributes its own foundation to the acts of building, constructing visible spaces; metaphors limited to a single building and single typologies, and does not take the opportunity to represent a dispersed, inverted, and immaterial urban condition.

Today, it is a question of imagining an architecture focused not on creating definitive projects typical of classic modernity, but focused rather on creating imperfect and incomplete subsystems typical of the new modernity of the twenty first century, following the logic of relational economy, diffuse work, and mass entrepreneurship.

The constructed world today seems to derive evident advantages from the ever weaker connections that unify the city, architecture, and the world of objects. The strong programs that used to unify all dimensions of modern design have melted, allowing each of these three spheres to acquire autonomy and efficiency.

The functioning of the contemporary city is deeply influenced by the world of objects and electronic instruments: the processes of urban "refunctionalization" caused by lay-offs and new forms of entrepreneurship are spontaneously actuated through the sole interior transformations of the buildings. The urban landscape's whole image no longer corresponds to the activities carried out within it.

The close relationship between form and function has dissolved: the computer has no function, but has functions as numerous as the operator's needs. We have gone from the age of functionalism to the age of functionoids, instruments that do not possess a single function, but as many functions as the operator's needs.

This search is therefore aimed at:

- designing models of weak urbanization, in other words, reversible, evolving, provisory models that correspond directly to the changing necessities of a reformist society that is continually elaborating its own social and territorial organization, dismissing and re-functionalizing the city;

– an architecture that is less composite and more enzymatic, meaning an architecture capable of inserting itself in the processes of the territory's transformation without using external figurative codes, but internal environmental qualities, dispersed throughout the land, not closed within the building's perimeter;

– an architecture aimed at surpassing the limits of building as a structural and typological concentration, to activate methods and services diffuse throughout the environment, beyond the traditional confines of the single construction, becoming an open system of environmental componential work;

– a traversable architecture that guarantees the penetration of territory and space, no longer marked by closed confines, but by open filters like a three-dimensional agriculture;

– an evolving architecture where the variable of time is a structural, dynamic element, integrated in and symbiotic with nature;

– an architecture that corresponds to a fluid society and an elastic democracy free of ideologies that produces programs as a result of a diffuse genetic energy utterly without metaphysics.

It's not the first time that architecture attempts to go beyond architecture, but in the twenty-first century this utopia seems to be for the most part realized within the contemporary city, where the environmental evolutionary processes and immaterial reality of computer networks have already created a *de facto*, dynamic, invisible, and abstract metropolis that is progressively substituting (or moving to the background) the physical and figurative metropolis.

It is a matter, therefore, of moving on to an adaptation (non-violent) also in designers' way of thinking; too often they deny or ref use this extraordinary opportunity to try out new logics and new operative dimensions, taking refuge in the myth of architecture as a producer of only certainties.

Andrea Branzi, 2006

From the *No-Stop City* to the Cocept on Infinity: City without Architecture

The *No-Stop City* arises from the observation that our society has passed from the Architectural Civilization to the Commodities one. A society fully integrated into the world-market logic, interested only in the quantitative utopia.

The Radical Movement, in its various components, worked on strategies that emerged from the de-territorialisation of the city, which is no longer a set of architectural boxes, but an uninterrupted system of goods, information, services and relationships. A territory defined by the presence of a personal computer every 20 sq.m.; a molecular system made of billions of different images, but without an overall image; a blind and catatonic landscape, where there isn't an external environment to contemplate, but experiences to consume, plankton of objects to look at so much that a 'non-iconic' effect is obtained.

The contemporary urban decay fully invests architecture, whose difficult survival is precisely witnessed by the archi-star phenomenon creating super-icons which contrast (as mere visual exceptions) with the loss of sense of the overall urban landscape.

Instead, as Amazon Indians, we live in an integrated space shaped by nature, magic, animals, dreams and sacredness, but we are unable to have an outside view of such a space, like the fishes that live in the sea but never see it.

Chaos is not the fall of an order, but the law governing the universe. Tragedy and normality identify themselves.

The models of weak urbanization arise from the observation that the border – that once existed between the town and the countryside and between rural and urban civilization – has disappeared. Both civilizations are nothing else than different outcomes of the same law of economic profit.

So we live in a system that apparently has no outside any more; an infinite but imperfect system, monologic but conflictual, where everything is tainted, fluidifies, becomes dull.

Of these historical mutations, as well as of the tragedies that spanned the entire twentieth century, no trace is found in the line of continuity of modern design, which is always self-referential, elegant, intelligent, technologically updated.

Unlike all other creative activities, it did not plunge into the suffering of history and was not renovated by it. Indifferent to the real history in favor of its disciplinary history, modern design set itself as the guarantor of the happy ending of the Industrial Civilization.

Andrea Branzi, 2016

3.1

SCENARIOS

The Second Modernity

A Strong Century
Andrea Branzi, 2006

//

Europe came out of the twentieth century proving the deterioration of its principal cultural and political theorems. On the one hand is the failure of right – and left – wing political programs born of its generous revolutionary hopes and exported with negative effects to many countries of the world. Fascism, Communism and Nazism – in various forms and with various rewards – lie buried along the ruins of the brief century that has just ended. The ethical supremacy of the Old World, cradle of Christianity and moral philosophy, has been discredited by the atrocities of the second-half of the century.

Add to this ethical-political debacle the crisis of European Rationalist Modernism, whose hopes have failed under the uncontrollable complexity of its own creation: a progress made up of an industrial and social growth completely different from (if not opposite) the universe of order and logic upon which this modernity had founded its purist prophecy.

The code of classic modernity presents itself today as a rigid concept, overwhelmed by the fluidity of commerce, the invasion of innovations, the ungovernable nature of the world economy, and a climate facing a constant pollution crisis. Neo-capitalism, which has trumped throughout the world since 1989, seems to survive itself solely on the condition that it knows how to reform, modify, and in practice deny its own doings on a daily basis.

Seen from the viewpoint of an ever-growing distance, the period of time from the French Revolution to the end of the twentieth century was, in the West, a long season of *grand* ideologies that were incessantly fed by the energies of extreme and irreversible transformations. These transformations were the fruit of archetypal thoughts and expressions of a society that tried to combine secularism and theology, leaving the search for design and definitive solutions to politics and culture – as though these were the instruments of a human science, aimed at solving once and for all the unresolved problems of the selfsame human sciences. In this sense, the key physical and metaphysical technology of the last two centuries has certainly been mechanics; this strong technology, based on the transmission of movement through the friction of bodies and the stress of gears, has been interiorized by modern man and his machines, which were seen as instruments of work and as perfect motors for the transformation of history and of the world.

The end of this epoch of forced modernization, marked by strong logic and the search for irreversible and definitive solutions, therefore coincides, as François Fouret claims, with the end of the historic epoch begun by the French Revolution and ended in 1989 with the fall of the Berlin Wall. Revolutions and the vanguards of future (artistic) revolutions have been the studios where creative minorities worked, driven to a quest for the new. This was always understood as a discovery of the true, of the authentic hidden under the over structures and hypocrisy of history. This was a search, therefore, aimed at broadening the available repertory of certainties, always looking for a truth that already existed, but was previously unseen.

Very few among the heroes of that distant season, particularly among the architects, had the doubt that their work was not aimed at seeking the deep foundations of a new secular, rational civilization capable of confronting the long time periods of an eternal modernity – finally and definitively eternal because they were founded on inviolable principles.

That long period of violent and genial structural transformations is followed today by a different, more experimental epoch. This is an epoch more attuned to the values of normalcy, even if composed entirely of exceptions, in a context where spread out laboratories of permanent vanguards work, intent on producing daily their due measure of innovation and research, without making reference to global models, and above all without having any sort of stable certainty at their disposal. The current epoch is open to obstructing the weak and diffuse energies of new politics, like the weak and diffuse energies of nature and of informational networks. This is an epoch in search of energetic systems capable of producing, without trauma and earthquakes, vast social and physical upheaval.

No more, then, will there be the strong, concentrated cathedrals of the old modernity; in their place will come articulated cognitive processes, reversible climactic transformations, invisible and penetrating network systems. This will be a modernity capable of using weak and diffuse energies that do not produce the din of mechanics, but create forces similar to those created by stars, the moon, and the planets, capable of moving each night and all the oceans of the world without producing a single sound.

The twenty-first century has begun without the stimulus of mega-design for the future; the new times are signaled by an ability to work in a world constructed according to a logic that we will call weak and diffuse, and that we will try to illustrate as the theme of many designs and research programs.

The concept of weakness that we speak of does not imply, however, any negative value of inefficiency or inability; this indicates rather a particular process of modification and cognition that follows natural logic, not geometric logic – diffuse, diluted processes, reversible and self-stabilizing strategies. Gianni Vattimo was the first to talk about a weak thought, that is, a type of hermeneutics that develops without looking to the great syntheses of the twentieth century, or to the unifying systems of politics and projects that were typical of classic modernism. Instead, this hermeneutics proceeds following more incomplete, imperfect, disarticulated types of cognizance and transformation, which are more ductile and therefore able to absorb the new and confront the surprises and complexities that this produces. The same weak word is now used in relation to new information technologies, fed by the low energies (i.e. ten volt, etc.) of electronics; from this derives its performative ability that follows logical and productive processes very close to those of physiology and the human brain. Electronic technology is, therefore, less traumatic than the old mechanics in its relationships to man, and is certainly able to deeply modify the logic of work, the economy, culture, and the relationships among people.

Such a silent mutation has not yet truly entered the world of design, doing so thus far only in the most superficial manner, often associated with the possibility of simulation offered by graphic computers.

In 1995 for the first time the theme of a weak modernity emerges, like a new statute under which architecture sees itself as a threshold presence among major metropolitan mutations (and endings) and the universe of informational networks. This is a non-compositional, anti-typological architecture, like an enzyme capable of transforming vast terrain according to criteria of reversibility and navigability, completely new with respect to the typological, physical, and reinforced limits of classic modernity.

Fuzzy Thinking
Andrea Branzi, 2006

//

This terms was firstly used in the sixties by logician Lofti Asker Zadeh, ad more recently by Bart Kosko; it belongs to a specific tradition in modern science that propelled the field towards a previously unexplored boundary, going beyond the rigid dual logic upon which science itself is based.

Bart Kosko affirms: "One day I realized that science isn't true," in the sense that is not part of the real world, but is a parallel abstract thought, and as such is not capable of giving certain answers. As Albert Einstein said in Geometry and Existence: "When the laws of mathematics refer to reality, they are not certain. And when they are certain, they do not refer to reality."

The inquiry regarding the limits of science belongs to the thinking of many twentieth-century scientists and philosophers, from Mach to Heisenberg, Thomas Kuhn to Paul Feyerabend, all the way to Karl Popper. They took scientific thought to its most extreme consequences to reveal its contradictions and limits as well as to enlarge its cognitive capacity.

This sort of skepticism regarding the scientific method has now become the only scientific position possible, because it is the only one that permits the development of an integration of science and nature – two realities that as of yesterday were irreconcilable. On the one hand are science's great mathematical geometries, its universal laws, and its perfect speculations, which are accepted only when reproducible in the laboratory. On the other hand are nature's great complexity, chance, and accident, produced by phenomena everlastingly different from one another, builders of reality that are utterly irreproducible in a laboratory setting.

A universe where time changes reality, producing fluid systems of experience in continually evolving contexts.

**The possibilities of electronic calculation of large numbers, and the ability to enter a very high number of variables into these calculations, now permits us to recognize and reproduce in fractals the logical vortices of nature's elementary phenomena.
We could say that if Galileo Galilei had removed air's friction for the sake of demonstration of the law of gravity, today we are looking to give back to science the real world's high level of friction and viscosity.**

The refusal of the scientific method, which Bart Kosko claims to promote, is therefore the sign of a structural passage of science, which now – pushed by the influence of Eastern cultures, by Shintoism and the vision of great Asian nuances, but also by the new instrumental possibilities and new logical methodologies – disputes its old, rigid statutes. This evolves as so-called fuzzy thinking, which no longer represents the purity of geometry and the precision of mathematical paths, and instead represents very well the fuzzy reality of the universe, of its evolutionary stage – a nebulous, milky intermediate between mass and energy. This way of thinking is the figurative metaphor of a new, expansive period of science, as a positive end to its methodological crisis, leading towards a new naturalism.

This scientific and technological naturalism, which no longer considers nature a primitive phase in need of change, bur rather an evolved model to imitate in the process of building the new, belongs wholly to this regime of a different modernity, intent on elaborating richer, less rigid design instruments in order to realize diffuse transformations that take advantage of previously unknown ambient and social energies.

A Liquid Modernity
Andrea Branzi, 2006

//

In 2000, the sociologist Zygmunt Bauman published with Polity Press "Liquid Modernity," an essay in which he outlines a long analysis of the transformational processes of the concept of modernism at the beginning of the twenty-first century.

For Bauman, the term "liquid" positively indicates the idea of a state of material that does not possess its own form (rather, that of its container) and tends to follow a temporal flow of transformations. These conditions converge to describe "the nature of the current, and in many respects new, phase of the history of modernism."

The concept of liquefaction belongs to the primitive processes of modernity, as a movement of liberation from the structural nodes of history, the melting of the academic disciplinary blockades, dispersion of the aggressive structures of repression (William Reich). The same authors of the Communist Manifesto proposed to "merge the solid bodies" as a preliminary act in a process of political and creative liberation. One must remember, though, that the "liquefaction of solid bodies" that the first modernity proposed did not in the least presuppose the formation of a permanent liquid state. On the contrary, it represented a transitory phase, a necessary premise for the reconstruction of new, more resistant solid bodies. This search for new, more solid foundations in the twentieth century happened without success for culture and politics, but for Bauman it was at the formative base of modern capitalism's entrepreneurial spirit and its capabilities to construct large, stable economic empires.

Let's not forget that the great political dictatorships of the twentieth century were born also as an attempt to confront the devastating reality of the economic and methodological apparatus of national and international capital, based on the naked laws of profit. To confront this major historical collision twentieth-century politics looked to construct new (and disastrous) societies – Fascist, Communist, Nazi. This happened even contradicting, at times, those libertarian premises from which the dictatorships originated.

These containers, these solid bodies, have become – in the current, high complexity societies of extremely rigid organisms, and because of the extreme normative force that they must exert in order to organize reality's multiplicity – obsolete, fragile structures, utterly unusable and distant from any efficient praxis. The resulting operative void is, for Bauman, now filled by the spontaneity of individual behaviors, local initiatives, constant reform, and the destruction of all chains, up to the point where the system's flexibility "is the product and the sediment of freedom expressed by human agents."

Deregulation, the freeing of enterprise, flexibility, the fluidity of unions, and free access to financial markets all together represent the inverse process of all that solid modernity had created as a container of the liquid state of all that was modern. In this sense, the end of the epoch of Revolutions, as producers of normative mega-containers, derives from the definitive (and apparent) identification between entrepreneurship and society, economy and its over overlying structures, spontaneity and politics – between the fluidity of institutions and that of the market.

The fusion of solid bodies carried out by current modernity has been directed towards the liquefaction of political process, understood as instruments for transmitting aggregating design and the radical transformation of the existent; already in the seventies individual freedom tended to identify itself with consumption, seen as an indispensable act of constructing one's own identity. The political clout of society, after the failed revolution of 1968, has been greatly lightened, and no longer tends to elaborate designs and global statutes for substituting the system. Modernity becomes the sole judge of modernity itself; it folds over on itself and proceeds on to its own modernization. The powers of coercion have gone from the system to life, descending from a macro to micro scale.

Bauman concludes that "ours is a type of individualized, privatized modernity, in which the onus of connecting the dots and the responsibility of failure fall mainly on the shoulders of the individual." Individual freedom therefore presents itself now in apparent coincidence with the freedom of the system's liquefaction from the moment when, in the era o mass entrepreneurship, there is no longer any apparent distance between the whole and a small part of it, between private interests and collective interest. The free creativity of the market drags along the free creativity of enterprise.

The Men without Quantities
Andrea Branzi, 2006

//

The Man without Quantities is a man who lacks information on the quantitative dimension of certain phenomena occurring around him; in lieu of having such information, he continues to refer to superseded criteria of evaluation that lead him to make often grave errors. He still believes that looking at the world is enough to understand it; instead, there are many invisible new levels of reality, on which one must be prepared with organized packets of information.

The twenty-first century is characterized by progressive, deep, often barely evident changes that grow within an outline until they suddenly determine general, very visible transformation that only a few observes had suspected. The Man without Quantities is therefore a characteristic figure of our time because he hasn't any consciousness of the existence of phenomena in slow and progressive growth that are silently changing our overall picture. After the end of the great ideologies the state of intellectual awareness fell; we lack the condition of social pre-alarm, people are more distracted, and therefore there is a greatly diffuse absence of sensitive point of observation that is able to keep these slow mutations – typical of an era of tremors (not of earthquakes) in an age of weak and diffuse modernity – under control.

Among the many underestimated novelties of the twenty-first century we can list: all the processes of "refunctionalization" of the contemporary city carried out directly through the universe of objects; the advent of mass entrepreneurship and the relational economy derived from it (based on virtual, as opposed to real, exchanges); and many other things that are silently and irreversibly changing our way of designing (both interior and exterior) architecture.

But there exists a natural, purely human phenomenon that our designer colleagues seem not yet to have understood in all of its innovative dimensions. The phenomenon consists the fact that, for the first time in the history of the human consortium, the number of the living has reached the record point of 6.5 billion people. Fifty years ago there were just over half that number, and fifty years from now we'll number far above 10 billion.

This is a rapturous number of people who move freely through the constructed world and determine an absolutely new landscape phenomenon.

Beyond the political, social, and economic questions this phenomenon brings with it, 6.5 billion people (a temporary and growing number) represent a physical and corporeal reality expressive of completely unusual dimensions; it is this very original aspect that now calls for reflection.

In our cities, a sort of active filter has formed, a dynamic curtain composed of the bodies of hundreds of thousands of people, which form *a bona fide* mobile landscape made up of expressive presences that invade every space and every place, substituting the traditional architectural backdrop and inducing new qualities and new devices for the elaboration of the real quality of the environment. (...)

That which differentiates one city, street, and territory from the next is no longer architecture and its formal, rigid immobile, and distant symbols rather, it is the invasive, lively, varied human presences; unique cells that bring true diversities, exceptions, and deep cultural information; terminals of living memories of various stories. It is the quality of the people, their gestures, their dress, their (inevitably no-global) physiognomy that marks the evident differences between Delhi and Milan, Paris and Naples, and there are increasingly fewer local architectural repertories that create the recognizable elements of metropolitan environment. Human presences interrupt the perspective and create unrepeatable flows of not only anthropological, but also corporeal, scenes.

Six-and-half billion people make up a sort of horizontal, developing plankton that invades space and creates, by extension and density, a specific visual experience. The city's space, once empty, where architecture was the sole protagonist, is now made up of a whole full objects, products, messes, and, above all, people. Thus the true result of the electronic revolution consists not in the presence of information technologies within the environment, but rather the human presence, which invades the scene and imposes, with its uncontainable formal anarchy, a serious revision of all the traditional strategies that govern the quality of the environment.

Factories have emptied and millions of workers, who were once gray, monotonous laborers within the industrial cycle, have been liberated within the environment, and built it like a colored and changing surface within which human physiognomies, qualities of dress, relational gestures, and urban ceremonies and rites act together.

For those who design the environment and for those who are bent on governing it, all this is paramount to a verification that the unique and concentrated act of designing is now substituted by a sort of diffuse crowd of design vibrations that each subject present in space produces in order to signal itself, its creative presence, its economic search, and its genetic energy.

Thus design and architecture begin the twenty-first century comparing themselves with this unexpected invasion on the part of all that is human, and what all that is human brings with it.

The direct relationships between people, the ability to manage interpersonal contracts with the necessary social gallantry, the good manners of the accounts and sales-people, and the efficacy to operative rituals and ceremonies have become a fundamental element in the qualities of places within contemporary city. The human metropolis is therefore a reality that cannot be taken on in unified operative terms; and perhaps, as an overall result, it also cannot be designed.

But if the environmental effects of the presence of 6.5 billion people can be difficult to imagine, there exist other urban phenomena whose dimension hasn't been intercepted by the man without quantities.

For example, in all the large industrial cities of the world, the phenomenon of factories falling into disuse is noted and very evident: our suburbs are spangled with former industrial areas that are no longer in use, which present themselves as a grouping of decaying structures, obsolete machines, and rusted looms.

But there also exist less evident dismissals, which have reached large proportions: the abandonment of tertiary spaces is rapidly growing. Globalization, the surpassing of old office typologies, and the reduction of spaces (and workers) has created a large void within buildings and skyscrapers that seem to be in full use, but have actually become dead structures where the lights are no longer turned on each evening.

There exist, then, realities submerged within dimensions that make up an important resource for national and local economies. The national and local economies need, in order to consolidate and expand, adequate spaces and resources. The adequate resources now consist not only of the availability of technicians and entrepreneurs, but also of an elevated number of creative people – not necessarily designers and artists, but subjects able to operate like a (weak and diffuse) innovative energy; in other words, elements able to activate dynamic strategies for setting offer in motion, renew the domestic market, and confront international competition.

In this picture, the demand for professional education corresponds to the exponential growth of universities and design schools that aim to educate not only traditional designers, but also experts in innovative strategy. (...)

This is, therefore, not a superficial phenomenon, but a stabilized trend that has roots in the typical processes of out time, such as globalization, mass entrepreneurship,the relational economy, and demand for innovation within various industrial systems.

All these phenomena began in the final years of the last century and have rapidly grown (silently and in the penumbra) to the point of producing completely new general situations that signal the true beginning of the twenty century.

Time and Network
Andrea Branzi, 2006

//

Western architecture originated from the classical tradition, a tradition deeply rooted in the pagan myth of Kronos (Time), father of all the gods who hate his own children, continually destroying his progeny.
To save architecture from this fatal destiny it was necessary to define a space outside of time. Graeco-Roman architecture rested on this foundation, produced by the separation of time and space. The monument was the best testimony of history, but did not belong to history.

Classical architecture did not, in fact, evolve; it repeated itself outside time. History, natural cyclical time was human time, the scenario of a repeating destiny, where everything was false and deteriorated as if in a theatrical scene. Classical time was therefore twofold: the eternal time of myth, and the circular, human time, in which development did not exist, merely an eternal return. Only with the fall of pagan culture and the advent of Christianity was time divided into a before and after: beginning with the creation of the world up until the Incarnation, and after this up until the end of the world and the Resurrection of the dead. Time thus became a linear concept, with beginning and end, and was no more an elliptical succession of scenes, but rather a continual process of evolution.

Even taking part in this evolution through its various styles, Western architecture still maintained its classical statute of eternity, of a presence that challenges time, perforating seasons and history while remaining intact (...). The problem and stimulus towards the future pushed modern architecture to accentuate its contradiction of eternal testimony, but was also destined to guide us towards a different future. The refusal to demolish modern monuments proves this.

Modernization has happened, and progress no longer corresponds to a linear process, but rather to a dispersed galaxy. The future is no longer one, but manifold, diffuse, and its force of attraction is becoming weak.

From the age of great hopes we have moved into an age of permanent uncertainty and sable transition. This is an age of crises that is not an intermission between two seasons of certainty – that of the past and that of the future – but an age subject to a process of certainties – that of the past and that of the future – an age subject to a continual process of updating, change, and innovation without end and without a goal.

The future is no longer a destination, but a reality that works for the present.

In a certain sense, time once again becomes elliptical, reversible, seasonal, and space becomes unlimited, natural, and traversable in all directions. Boundaries and limits belong to history and geography; they no longer belong to our culture, virtual spaces, and the real time of web-based culture.

Web culture develops, abolishing history and geography; the Internet allows the retrieval of information in real time, accessing a state of availability that nullifies distance. From any point on the Net another point on the Net can be immediately accessed; the Net rests not on the ground, but in virtual space. Because of this history and geography are not structural parts of information, but rather elements of appreciation, accessories. The Net is traversable in the sense that internal perimeters do not exist, only distributing portals of organized information.

The perception of time and space are therefore destined to change according to the original methods, involving the modes of designing as well.

3.2

THEORIES OF WEAK URBANIZATION

The Crisis of Complexity, the Crisis of Quality and the Relational Space

Andrea Branzi, 1996

//

Eight years after the collapse of the Berlin Wall, no systematical analysis of the epistemological effects on wester culture, and especially on design, has yet been undertaken.

Perhaps this is not the place to get involved in such an analysis and maybe I am not the right person to undertake it, nevertheless, as a *militant designer* I do feel I can contribute in some way to a phenomenon which has so affected our work.

The historical period which came to an end with the collapse of the wall and the socialist countries behind the Iron Curtain cannot be compared to other normal political changes such as the end of Francoism in Spain or the fall of Salazar in Portugal. The demise of such socialism has far more significant historical overtones.

It should be remembered that the collapse of the wall goes back to 1968 Europe and to the creative period which preceded it. The sixties were not at all a happy epos of the *power of creativity*, of imaginative youth and spontaneous revolution against out-of-date moral and political conventions. Taken as a whole, it was a dramatic decade which gave birth to the first, irreversible crisis of modernity: the end of a system of certainties from which the history of the twentieth century developed, and the beginning of an era – still being played out – based on the advent of a system of permanent *uncertainties and doubts* as the sole means of knowledge and work.

The *public creativity* of new fashions, music and radical avant-garde of those years was nothing less then a reaction to the collapse of stability which up until then rationalism had offered to a west ready to believe in it. The vital, intuitive response of youth creativity was fired by a pressing need to replace the Establishment with an experimental permanent creativity. Here was a generation revolt with two opposing fronts: on the one hand defending the values of political orthodoxy based on the Brechtian dichotomy of a master/worker society, and on the other, introducing complex, anarchic elements against that very orthodoxy. Pop art was seen as an attempt to spread consumerism throughout Europe, and it tried to defend the last shreds of individualism against the greyness of mass culture.

The overall result proved the exact opposite of what the youth groups had intended, for while lifestyles, social attitudes and means of expression changed, political institutions in Europe remained utterly impervious to extraparliamentary assembly and all forms of radical democracy.

The beginning of the next decade saw the germ of an ever more complex and fractured society giving way to the planning of a new more flexible and open model of the system which has come to be known as *post-industrial civilization*.

This was the start of a large-scale productive restructuring based on the introduction of electronics onto the assembly line and to warehouse management. It led to a *differentiated series* as a reaction to increasing fractured and inconstant market demands. In ten years things had gone from a utopian programmed society to a utopian controlled complexity and from citizen power to consumer power.

The success of new development strategies of electronic neocapitalism created the basis for the collapse of those socialist states still struggling with out-of-date technology, inadequate social services and a market totally incapable of satisfying single consumer demands.

All of us, from freelancers whiling away the time in London to radical designers contributed – and quite rightly so – towards the failure and breakdown of this political period which rapidly became police-orientated, backward and indefensible. As we now know, the collapse can be traced back to the failure of 1968 and to the consequent political uncertainties in the face of the massive industrial and social rebuilding produced by post-industrial capitalism and mechanized updating of the factories.

The theatrical, rhetorical response to such a failure was the wave of 70s European terrorism which simulated a non-existent civil war and shifted the fight well and truly into the communication field. Politics was now a case of *what to say rather than what to do.*

Other non strictly political considerations stem from the fall of the Berlin wall; from that moment on for example and for the first time since the postwar period, western culture was operating as it were, from within a complex, contradictory and discontinuous system based exclusively on market laws.

As a result of this new creeping homologation, *complexity* which constituted the great discovery of the seventies and eighties, not only lost credibility but took on an entirely new aspect. In a universal monological system, *complexity* did not mean real difference but a unit of possible variants, a catalogue of possible exceptions. These formed a sort of greyness or monotonous undertone where their mixture was no longer an explosive event but a kind of *cold fusion* producing an energy totally devoid of deflagration.

Although the discrepancies (as they would once have been referred to) of the system still persist, they no longer provoke any kind of cultural or public debate. On the contrary, they cause meaningless violence, localized revolts and ethnic unrest in a society based on intolerance, neuroses and fear.

The failure of the Socialist Revolution marks the end of an era begun two centuries earlier with the French Revolution in which it was believed problems caused by industrial progress could be solved by inventing power structures, by setting up new mechanisms of economic, artistic and – by implication historical – formulation. Both this and the era of Historical Avant-garde are now behind us, and revolutionary gestures have given way to perhaps more complex ones of a permanent and profound reformism within a free market system which moves inexorably forward and lacks any alternative. And if this market is not to bring about a definitive social and environmental crisis, its laws and patterns have to be continually revised.

The project becomes a means to this permanent reformism, to the need for self-revision that mature industrial societies must address. With the absence of any sort of alternative pattern everything has now changed and become more complex.

The era of Historical Avant-garde is over but another which we shall call Permanent Avant-garde is beginning. Here, reformist patterns of development can be offered to saturated markets and to technologically advanced industries brought to a creative standstill by the plethora of new electronic equipment in a market demanding everything and nothing at the same time while demands from the poorer countries only get the answer the rich countries have already experimented in mass consumerism.

As a category able to embrace a multiplicity of patterns of development, behavior and identification, the *complexity* crisis forms an integral part of this difficult stage of western culture. Many forces however work *against complexity*. Every ecologically designed project has shown that in order to reduce the environmental impact of industry, both technology and materials have to be simplified. The final recovery of the product means that diversification of its constructive components must be drastically reduced. Recycling conjures up a world of single-material products in a metropolitan society where a mere four categories of solid waste – *damp matter, paper, glass, and plastic* – can already be collected.

Yet another significant enemy of complexity is the advancement of integralism which can be traced back to Arab religiousness and which is now found in western society where ideological, religious and moral crimes are increasing at an alarming rate. In Asia too, powerful religious sects are approaching the market ready to offer products of absolute spiritual value.

The force of religious and secular *integralism* has its roots in the refusal of complexity and in the search in life for far-reaching cultural simplification and objective certainties. Western environmental extremism already represents the melting pot for this type of secular extremism which tends to reduce options. Integral products can become part of an *integral project* which holds that the qualities and values we can recognize are to be found in the natural substance of thing. So instead of learning about and handling complexity, we try to demolish it.

The geopolitical turning point at the end of the eighties was also responsible for bringing the crisis of our concept of *quality* to the fore: a concept which lacks any form whatsoever of transferable to recognizable elements. The lengthy debate of the eights when it was thought possible to substitute a *quantitative development* model of the system with vaguely identifiable *qualitative development*, turned out to be mere verbal hypothesis. Nobody was able to define *quality* in practical terms except by recognizing it as a general recovery of spiritual, religious or environmental values which were then demonstrated to be totally impracticable in a secular society.

Our crisis of the concept of *quality* has ancient origins although western culture – particularly European culture – has no historical definition of socially practicable quality. (...)

The only qualitative category existing in the west is derived from the appropriation of a way of life of the nobility by the emerging industrial bourgeoise in the aftermath of the French Revolution of 1789. But these were qualities obtained by force, not offered and received as in Japan.

Although these customs, or qualitative standards, were subjected to severe criticism and protest and judged vulgar and useless for two centuries, they were never replaced with any new qualitative system. The Soviets did try during the emerging of socialist society but Lenin's NEP (1922) put an immediate end to that by defining *socialism as proletarian use of capitalism* and not as the laboratory of a new society with different concepts of quality. So perhaps it shouldn't surprised us today that while the west criticizes the welfare state, it is unable to pin down or define a new development model acceptable to everyone.

I believe the mistake lies in the use and misuse of the term qualitative to indicate what is new or desirable, because the term itself lacks a precise definition. The western model of quality still has an aristocratic nature which two hundred years of secularism and democracy have tended to criticize rather than replace.

The *complexity* crisis is bound up with the crisis of our concept of *quality* which, with its aristocratic origins, does not take willing to being taken over by mass culture or constructing an ethical and cultural aristocracy by means of the project.

So here we are suspended between the crisis of the aristocratic concept of mass quality and our capacity to find any alternative lay-democratic models. The proud refusal of Marie Antoinette's cake led us to the discovery of Marcel Proust's equally aristocratic madeleines, while Rodchenko's stale bread was (quite rightly) refused by everyone.

The crisis of our concept of *quality* is pertinent to the culture of the European project both as regards architecture and design for the very reason that it appears to discourage innovation at the moment reformist demand makes alternative proposals to unstable development models so urgent.

Architecture based on the formation of expressive organisms is in trouble, and the futile search for new forms of expression when quality has lost its meaning, gives way to a different concept of the project where territory and structure (large and small-scale) come together in what we shall call the *relational* space concept.

In relational space the important things are the relationship it permits and the information and filters which can be activated.

When we speak of relational space, we mean a whole space in which the dimensional categories of the urban, architectural and design project are superceded by processes in which the small and the large-scale meet without any form of disciplinary distinction. Rather than coming from a unitary project and from the knowledge of the definitive collapse of figurative (and narrative) systems of architectural as such.

The characteristics of this space then are not aesthetic, compositional or narrative, but to do with performance, which is not to say *functional* as the pragmatists (making a clear distinction between functional and aesthetic) used to define it.

The distinction has no meaning with regards to relational space; aesthetics are the functional part of the project in the same way the functional issues is part of the aesthetics of the same.

The widespread advent of electronics has overturned the last utopia of Radical Avant-garde which believed robotics would bring about a society of Leisure Time, and put an end to work; where the individual would become protagonist of intellectual mass production. But computers have brought about a society of Widespread Work in which Leisure Time has all but disappeared and the individual has become protagonist of mass consumerism as the only possible means of creativity.

Relational space is not a functional zoning but the result of the fluidization of this zoning produced by electronic instrumentation and its relational multiplicity. Everywhere is like everywhere else because stylistic codes linked to the specialist functions of living, working, producing, traveling, buying and selling are starting to mix in what Marc Augé calls a *Non Place* system with a low-level identity and considerable functional flexibility. Relational space can be seen as a widespread system of *incubators* where new productive and relational activities can be developed; a space where the public and the private blends with production and leisure time in a sort of flexible territory where the figurative is unrecognizable but where there is considerable potentiality of service. Within this area the project may have no strategies or global visibility but the capable of moving within the design of services, interface, micro-climates and macro programming and politics. It consists in the creation of new links within wide spread relational networks.

So relational space comes from the *overcoming* of the *complexity* concept in a disconnected but monological system set up at the end of the eighties. It is a space where the difference between project and non-project tends to disappear and where post-industrial society faces in grave problem of what the future holds for the masses. It is where there is the likelihood of uncontrolled and violent minorities staging ecological revolts, of widespread voluntarism and dangerous fundamentalist temptations. The strongest definition of the term post-industrial can be applied when industry becomes more highly automated and breaks away from *its society* to become a separate channel and specific economy no longer filling the role of running society (which work is forced to re-invent every day), the market or the metropolis. The role of reform is again in the hands of a new metropolitan form of politics, in problematic experimenting and Permanent Avant-garde which are the only ones willing to take over the relativity of values as an element of the project.

The *polis* lies at the heart of the political issue inasmuch as it cannot be the uncontrolled result of economic and social relations. The *polis* is the main project contained by those economic and social relations to which it gives sense. The risks of a possible ecological disaster of democratic and affluent societies prove that the project must be the Polis, not politics.

One might have said that the issue was wholly political rather than aesthetic and as such, demanding a political response.

Today, suffice to say it is a political issue demanding an aesthetical answer. While it was one thought that the *aesthetical issue* was a small, unimportant part of the far larger political category, today it can be said that the political issue is a small part of the large *aesthetic issue*. And if politics cannot build an aesthetically better world, then they have failed.

The metropolis is once again at the heart of the culture of the project; after twenty years, research and experiment now provide a means of considering and interpreting recent events while avoiding (the very dangerous) question of saving architecture.

Territories of the Imagination
Andrea Branzi, 1988

//

If I had to point to the most significant inventions in the field of design during the first half of this century, I would have no hesitation in choosing the skyscraper and Le Corbusier's *Unitè d'habitation*. Not because these works are the finest or the most important, but because they are perfect representatives of the fundamental concept of Utopia that held sway during the first half of the century, the idea of a quantitative utopia: "the greatest quantity, in the shortest possible time."

But if I were to indicate the crucial inventions in design in the second half of the century, I would have no less hesitation in picking out the system of industrial objects, as a perfect response to the second great utopia, that of quality: "the greatest quality, in the shortest possible time." So the only real constant in this century of forced industrialization has been the acceleration of pace. The true protagonist of current planning culture is design, and not architecture.

That design has taken over the leading role during the last forty years is due to the progressive maturation of a number of "environmental" conditions triggered by the Industrial Revolution. Until the end of the eighteenth century architecture was the sole representative of the world of construction. The only non-natural objects in man's environment were architectural buildings, houses, palaces, monuments, and roads. Other objects were rare and absolutely secondary. Chairs, tables other items of furnishing and implements used for work represented a minor adjunct. The number of them found in people's homes was small.

Architecture produced and controlled the whole set of signs used for territorial and environmental reference, and it was within this easy-to-perceive-and-understand code that the city dweller's life unfolded, from birth to death.

Among the many and radical upheavals resulting from the Industrial Revolution, there was also a change in the nature of objects. There was a progressive evolution of commodities, items of furniture, tools, appliances, systems of products, and services. Over the span of roughly 200 years these commodities invaded the whole field of existence, until they formed a continual and close-packed presence in people's daily life. At the beginning of the last century, the home of a reasonably well-off family of four contained a set of objects comprising no more than 150-200 items including crockery and clothing. The home of a comparable family today might contain 2500 to 3000 objects, including electric appliances and items used in the pursuance of hobbles but not such items as books, records, and tapes. What occurred, through a slow but relentless process, was a true revolution, one in which the environmental presence once represented by architecture was replaced by industrial and nonindustrial objects. The number of these objects has continued to increase, and their uses and modes of function have actually created an almost unbridgeable gap in the metropolitan experience of man. He lives and works within a universe of objects that renews itself, grows more specialized and in fact constitutes his true interface with the world outside.

Today we can use old works of architecture and parts of ancient cities, or even primitive ones, as long as the available set of objects and services is functionally and culturally adapted to the activities that we wish to carry out there. We can live in houses built five hundred or a thousand years ago, if they contain the furnishings, facilities and sources of information that we need. All that we use of these works of architecture is a number of symbolic codes.

This change has not just shifted the center of gravity from architecture to design but has, in fact, created a new metropolitan theorem. This theorem recognizes that changes in the metropolis take place not only through the construction of architectural structures, road systems or urban services, but also thought the renewal of the system of objects and of individual commodities that improve and transform the cultural and technical fitness of places for habitation, creating the city of the present inside that of the past and that of the future inside the present one.

This explains the great difficulty, indeed impossibility, of planning the present day metropolis and its growth. It is made up of a swarm of microstructures, objects, and services that eludes any logic of planning and control. A swarm that invades the scene, fills the environment and provides a support for the use of the city, rendering it flexible and capable of coping with a wide variety of different requirements. We live in a megasystem of furnishing and fittings, within a gigantic "light-scape," in a wired-up territory in which an infinity of terminals are linked together, like an all-embracing interface, artificially ventilated and riddled with tunnels of information and signs that have nothing in common with architecture. Design is the only discipline that gets its hands dirty in this hybrid, compromised, but terribly real universe. It works with objects and commodities, and therefore at the heart of the true problems of this age.

I cannot imagine what European cities might be like in twenty or thirty years. Not so much in terms of size, which will probably not increase greatly, or even number, since there are no new cities under construction in the West.

Rather I am thinking of the exponential growth in the number of industrial products that affect the quality of urban life. Their influence is predominant today, to an extent that may never have been matched in the history of man and his cities.

Where industrial products are concerned, investments are made in technological research and market surveys. We know everything there is to know about an object's criteria of acceptability. The languages of commodities and the market are analyzed in an almost scientific manner. Information is available on the colors of products and on chromatic trends in society. Centers of scientific research work on the development of new materials and new technology for the manufacture of commodities. There are even industrial research centers investigating the quality of external finishes. Design, at this moment, stands at a crossroads on which an enormous mass of energies, interests, and research is converging.

All these efforts, all this concentration of energies, have given prominence to man's relationship with the system of objects that surrounds him, intensifying (and perhaps aggravating) it to the point where we are often compelled to resort to a paradox in order to refer to this new but real hierarchy of values, by saying that if the cultural, functional, and psychological relationship between a man and his glass does not work, then neither will bis relationship with the city be lives in. Since the city, in the end, is made up of glasses.

A metropolis of objects with no exterior is taking shape. It invades the whole field of existence, the whole of human territory. No longer is there any experience that can claim to lie outside the metropolitan condition. The city is coextensive with the dimension of the market, and the term city dweller can be used for anyone who uses industrial products, gets his information from the television and other electronic devices and eats industrially distributed produce. French philosophers have even spoken of a metropolis that has no real connection with its own history. Today it is a totally original reality, lacking a past and even lacking a future. Within the existing metropolis, it is not one but many futures that are realized: simultaneous, diffuse, temporary or permanent futures. The concept of unitary transformation of the urban phenomenon belonged to the era of engineering and architectural design. Today instead we can speak of a simultaneity of futures within a global system that has no external model of reference, in which everything clashes and is hybridized.

We are beading toward a "full-up" situation. Space becomes solid, an amniotic fluid of information. With such total saturation, what space is left for growth of the system? What sites are left for further development or planning? I believe that the answer can only be found in metaphorical terms.

Today the industrial system of production, whether of information or of objects, lies wholly within the territories of the imagination, of pure narration. Even asking for "more money and less work" only means countering the present state of affairs with another possible model; the outcome of necessity it is true, but a model that only puts in an appearance because the present one is inadequate to cope with the collective or private imagery that society is capable of expressing at that moment in time.

New patterns of consumption and behavior are created as soon as anyone is cap able of imagining them. New languages and new products come into circulation thanks to the inventiveness of whoever produces them. In this way they permit those who use them to enter a territory, or to come into contact with an object that had no prior existence.

It has been said on more than one occasion that this is the *Society of Spectacle* and of services. In point of fact, the production of visual narratives (cinema and television) has created a system so extensive and sophisticated that it has become profoundly mixed up with reality, to the point where they have become homologous. Thus postindustrial society develops by enhancing the human being's great potential for creativity and the production of images. A human being freed from repetitive labor is often the prisoner of his role as a professional consumer. Hence people move within many fictional territories, imagined and experienced, which are the only virgin lands of our society, the only spaces left for the evolution of identity and social reactions. Hence the architectural or design project today is no longer an act intended to alter reality, pushing it in the direction of order and logic. Instead the project is an act of invention that creates something to be added on to existing reality, increasing its depth and multiplying the number of choices available. Thereby, the consumer is caught up in a new environmental narrative. The project is like the set of a film or television program. A new scene is created (temporarily or permanently, the difference is insignificant), an environment that did not previously exist and that therefore greatly extends the field of reality. The style, materials, colors, and odors of a place have been designed to create a scene within which it is possible to move. But this place has meaning and is identifiable only if it is different from or represents an alternative to surrounding places and to the setting. Hence the designer must succeed in imparting a strong measure of identity to the place or the product, using the instruments of style (rigorous or fantastic) in order to obtain the "fiction," that is, an effect that draws one away from the setting. The more effective and sophisticated this fiction, the greater its ability to transport the user to a different world from the existing one. The existing world, in turn, is made up of many territories that have been imagined in the past.

The project becomes a constructive, real, and physical act, but at the same time a metaphor of itself. It represents itself, displays its own peculiar logic and occupies a location through a screenplay that refers to the narration of a new and original code of expression. All the functions contained in it, all the services and technologies, must in some way be redeemed and regenerated to find a new identity in that place.

What is triggered is perpetual, digressive, and rigorous invention, in accordance with the intentions and state of mind of the designer or planner. But two contrasting ways of thinking come into collision in this spiral that extends into the unforeseen. The first is the need for possession of a strong but above all stable language. The other (and apposite one) is the need for continual regeneration of one's own code of expression in order to create new and unexpected solutions. In other words, there is uncertainty over whether to permanently occupy a linguistic box (in that stylistic matrix we have spoken of) or to ride the tiger of perpetual renewal by creating new imaginary territories. In practice we have to choose between freedom of speech and a new and permanent vocabulary, between noise and sound.

There is probably no general solution to the problem; everyone is free to make his own choice. As there are no external models of development for the system, it is difficult to make a comparison between attitudes and cultures. Each can be measured in relation to itself, to its own efficacy and true incisiveness. In this absolute sense of realism, design today also operates within a number of processes of change that lie completely outside the traditional activity of the formal and physical design of objects, in order to move forward into the world of services, to the interchange of information.

During the seventies there was a great deal of talk about primary design, that is, about the design of the soft structures of the environment, no longer regarded as technical data but as cultural qualities of space. The microclimate, the quality of light, and the soundproofing are structures for real use of the environment and coincide with a sophisticated physical consumption of the latter. The same holds for the color, odor, and surface finish of objects. Today we can say that even their weight is an element of design, since electronics have miniaturized the internal mechanisms of many objects, turning them into empty boxes that people find it difficult to adjust to.

Some machines talk and their voices are an important element of an interface between man and their mode of function. Male voices or female ones? A cool voice or an alluring one? It is a matter of choosing an element of form that can be fundamental to the success or failure of a service. Moreover, electronic services are gradually replacing many elements of physical information, and who is to say that design will not be affected by this change in information processing?

These two approaches provided a metaphorical gauge of the two souls of present-day design. One approach pushes it toward the threshold of information processing, within the interstices of reality, to vanish within a strategy of minute growth of the real, and the other sees design as a strong charge of energy and symbolism imparted to objects and places, reconstructing man kind's archetypal links with his home and his tools.

These two strategies, comparable to the difference between a bradyseism and an earthquake, are not necessarily mutually exclusive alternatives. Personally, I feel that all instruments are useful. It is sufficient to know how to use them and to have an extensive design capacity, able to produce purposeful synergies.

It is not yet possible for us to choose between micro — and macro effects: eighty years of radical modernism have compelled us to make a choice between all and everything, black and white, beautiful and ugly.

I believe that it is time to accept a strategy full of compromises, of hybridation and of imitations, so long as they are effective. We have been shit off from the whole, boundless continent of intermediate values. Might not we be better off with half-light, dampness, coolness, and mediocrity than with darkness, aridity, burning heat, and perfection?

A Classic Elasticity

Andrea Branzi, 2006

//

In our critical tradition, classical architecture is represented as the greatest producer of movements, triumphal arches, amphitheaters, and imperial palaces. But the cities of Ancient Rome and the Latin world had nothing of the formal unity of the Greek *polis*, above all that of the Athenian model, unified around the hill of the Acropolis, upon which the Parthenon rested. Rome was a polycentric urban system distributed over seven hills, capital of an endless empire that extended from Latium to Africa and the distant East.

That territory urbanized through a very simple architectural system, based solely on post and lintel construction where stylistic elements totally coincided with the static elements. With that system it was possible to build an imperial palace or a shepherd's hut, supports for a vineyard or a temple of Minerva; it was sufficient just to change the construction material, be it wood, stone, or marble, to change the sense of architecture. The city, its forum, and its agricultural land were constructed from a vast system of columns, pillars, and posts, all placed in a orderly fashion at a distance that corresponded to the length of the lintels. Atop this regular fabric the wall segments were connected, until they composed the city's warp and weft, and around this were the fields where crops were equally ordered according to the same rule.

The classical nature of agriculture (and the agricultural nature of architecture) originates from this process of the land's transformation, where single constructions are joined as a visible intensification of a theoretical mesh. This type of traversable, indifferent, extensive continuation, which contained cities, buildings, cultivated fields and streets, corresponded to the Latin concept of a civilization founded not on single cities, but, as Cicero explains, on the principles of the Right and on civil institutions, summarized by the abstract formula *Senatus Populusque Romanus*. The classical city therefore had its foundation in an immaterial judicial system that the troops defended and expanded, and that architecture rendered visible. Thus the Roman Empire presented itself as a great symbolic system where style and politics coincided — an expandable framework within which it was possible to hold all the most contradictory cultures, crops, logics, and religions.

The Italian Renaissance of the fifteenth century returned to this elastic nature of classical architecture when the end of the medieval unity opened an incurable crisis in the rapport between faith, science, and politics.

The Renaissance's aesthetic apotheosis originated from the role assigned to (classical) art as symbolic paradigm, able to hold together a polycentric system of weak and irreconcilable truths. Each was imperfect, incomplete, but with a totalizing vocation: a Christianity that lives together with pagan culture, science that signs along with Galileo its own abjuration, politics that refund themselves with Machiavelli on the ashes of their own failure. Since its birth the classical code of the Renaissance was made up of an elastic material, able to make those opposites live together: from the oval in Brunelleschi's cupola up to the eighteenth-century revivals, that code demonstrates its ability to stitch together incompatible spaces and philosophies.

Modernity inherited that same role as a great cosmic system, of a stylistic, civil nature capable of continually changing in order to remain always itself. It kept together the most incurable contradictions: opulence and minimalism, liberalism and planning, local realities and globalization, mechanism and electronics, monuments and virtual webs, technology and spontaneity, innovation and tradition. For the next two or three centuries modernity will construct the (evolving yet stable) landscape of Western culture, providing the highest levels of freedom within those stylistic and intellectual confines determined at the beginning of the twentieth century and continually revisited with new sensitivity and methods.

The weak and diffuse modernity that marks the beginning of the twenty-first century is the result of a diffuse and extensive refinement of a culture that now spread beyond design disciplines to collide with the enzymatic transformation of land and environment. This is an expansive phase in the porosities of a world, still in large part divided into heterogeneous jurisdictions and velocities. Elastic classicism is the model to which our elastic modernity refers as a deformable system, within which social, technological, and productive transformation of society find space, thus avoiding trauma and fracture and continuing to finely construct the best conditions for freedom and knowledge.

Architectural Link

Andrea Branzi, 2006

///

We see today that contemporary architecture, after a long period of silence, is opening new studios of design research in order to finally develop a positive reflection on its own crisis. This reflection is capable of developing an investigation of design that is not exclusively bound to building opportunities, but parallel and autonomous from these; not bent, therefore, on resolving short-term problems, but rather focused on opening new ones for the future to better understand the often obscure and misunderstood present.

Just as theoretical physics precedes and feeds applied physics, providing the later with the necessary information and base theorems, design research must be an open studio for reflection as manifestation of a designing thought that does not lose itself in the pure practice of building.

In an epoch like the present one, continually traversed by the new, incurable conflicts, a permanent reformism, and by an absence of general models, design has chosen the route of incessant research, following the fluctuating dynamic of the matter and history. In other words, the whole culture of design has entered a state of permanent crisis, which is in a condition of permanent difficulty, corresponding to the slow pace of a stably experimental epoch. This is an epoch in which conditions of social, cultural, and economic crisis, as Kevin Kelly asserts, are the premise for any short of social, cultural and economic growth. The crisis, therefore, functions as a positive developmental concept, as a premise for the elaboration of a dynamic adjustment to the new.

The crisis of contemporary architecture is one that feeds on a double difficulty.

The first difficulty consists of the end of design's unity: city, architecture, and products are no longer synergetic universes, but conflicting and alternating systems that follow diverging logics.

The city no longer foresees architecture; architecture presents itself as alternative to the city. The world of industrial objects affirms its centrality with respect to the city and architecture. Design itself often comes forward as pure creative energy – one that cannot be reduced to the act of construction, but rather to the definitions behaviors, already complete in themselves, which therefore do not refer to successive processes of realization.

This state of things no longer has to be lived as a negative condition, as the disappearance of the epistemological foundations of architecture, inasmuch as a discipline bringing order and unity. On the contrary, the schizophrenic state of the designed world opens the possibility of finally deepening the by-laws of architecture so that it is no longer seen merely as an art of construction, but as a complex and mutable cognitive thought process that no longer refers to the (impossible) unity of technology and idioms, but to the weak and diffuse energies of transformation of terrain and space. This is architecture, therefore that is no longer architecture, for a city that is no longer a city.

To this completely new, historically unprecedented operative condition is added a more specific difficulty, born of the confrontation between the virtual world and *the solid side* – the constructed side of reality.

This solid side is one component of the (positive) crisis in the transformation of urban space into a virtual system of information, services, telecommunication products, and relational networks independent from architecture as constructed presence. It seems almost as thought the reign of that which we call architecture has now been transformed into a thin, traversable diaphragm, in a sort of transparent screen placed between two continents – that of the networks and virtual urban series, and that of internal spaces, of operative systems, of ambient component ware, flexible and ductile, capable of following the continuous mutation of productive and social functions.

The term "architectural link" indicates precisely this perimeter – oriented nature of architecture in the contemporary city, of its being an interface between two formative processes of urban dynamics, a filter that must be thought of as a fluid, traversable, reversible reality. No longer a carrier of metaphors and definitive solutions, architecture is an active presence in a context that foresees the theoretical and practical nuance of future layouts.

Hence it's a question of a mental and technical search that aims to go beyond the impassable disciplinary limits that have held twentieth century architecture back from a courageous and radical confrontation with the crisis of its historical foundations. Because of these disciplinary limits contemporary architecture significantly lags behind other modern cultures such as painting, music, writing, and logic.

Cities Without Architecture

Andrea Branzi, 2006

//

The new alliance between objects and territories, between communication and the urban scene, seems to have begun by bypassing architecture and its complex composite system. A disconnect has come between city and architecture, and between architecture and the system of objects.

These categories, no longer define a structural continuity, and no longer do they belong to the unity of design; rather they indicate conflicting logics that do not find their re-composition in the Plan. Interior design, architecture, and urban planning follow autonomous logics that cannot be reassembled; these belong to autonomous layers, each of which vindicates its own centrality.

Beginning with each of these categories it is indeed possible to develop designs that differ from one another, not because they are based on different instruments, but because they aim to affirm absolute, different, irreconcilable priorities.

This crisis of the discipline's unity is a great cultural chance because it opens up new spaces for design. Design is no longer set within a logical chain that from small brings it without contradictions up to extra-large, from micro to macro; instead it causes design to intercept all the contradictions of the constructive processes, bringing to light all the potentialities that each dimensional category can offer with respect to the whole.

In other words, with the fall of the rapport that positively joined the city to architecture the unifying path that always entrusted metaphysics with the verification of physics's efficacy has been interrupted. This gave the greater good the right to pass judgment on the lesser good, the large over the small, the general over the particular. This system of evaluation as always produced rigidity, and in the world of architecture made it practically impossible to reform the typologies, go beyond the concept of building and the processes of territorial integration. In other words, it rendered the foundations of the discipline indestructible, transforming them into an obligatory route of connected responsibilities often foreign to the transformations of society and technology.

The city without architecture is the city whose functions no longer occur through the devices of architecture, but now occur through systems of electronic instruments, products, information, and above all through the componential approach to interior design, which permits the refunctionalization of its interior spaces in real time. This is, therefore, a city whose external image no longer corresponds to the activities carried out in its internal spaces; such activities are now done in an independent fashion, separated from the architectural backdrop.

3.3

DEFINITIONS: THE THEORETICAL METROPOLIS

The Latin Genesis of the Theoretical Metropolis
Andrea Branzi, 1999

//

In our analysis, the metropolis plays a dual role. As a general system of construction of the designed universe (and as a territory for the intensive circulation of merchandise), it contains in its vast belly all of the specific designs, whether they be homogeneous, unconnected, or dissociated from one another or from the metropolis. The metropolis, however, also plays a more symbolic role, a general metaphorical function that facilitates all of the various design approaches and all of the building strategies. The metropolis is a reality, but it is also a concept that varies over time, in history; it corresponds to a general theoretical model of the world, which is modified from time to time in order to pursue new configurations. The role of such a theoretical model is that of defining in a clear way certain ideologies and meta-design strategies, which serve as contexts of reference.

These theoretical models do not necessarily correspond to reality, but they serve rather to explain it, that is, to contain it within a single framework. A bit like certain theoretical models of the atom, which describe within a unified hypothesis the way in which matter functions; these models are often a full-fledged moral, cultural, and mental metaphor, typical of a certain historical period. They perform the task of stabilizing and reducing the possible variants, the errors, and they also make it possible to measure newness.

In this century, many architectural and design projects have made reference more often to a theoretical metropolis than to any real metropolis; in our era, design is generated in the face of so complex and articulated a reality as to be practically unknowable. And so we see that the design becomes in part a proposal for the modification of this reality, but it also become a system for the portrayal of said reality, by making reference to a reduced simulation of it, that is, to a theoretical model of the metropolis.

When we talk about a design discipline that takes its starting point from the places and objects of everyday life, it is important to investigate the direct or indirect connection that these places and objects have with the broader setting of the city and architecture.

Such a connection can be of a formal and functional continuity, but it can also be of an alternative and desired discontinuity. We will see that in the case of Italian design, the relationship between an everyday object and the city exists and is a strong one, while its relationship with architecture is often weak or even conflictual. A kind of design that therefore presupposes a direct engagement with the city (both real and theoretical), yet not mediated through architecture.

A kind of design that claims its own cultural autonomy with respect to architecture, and which affirms the centrality of the system of objects and of small spaces within the great urban backdrops, in order to establish that the private, intimate dimension of everyday life is a non-alienable part of material history, and the domestic object represents its verification and the most profound foundation.

In fact, it could be pointed out that, throughout history, if there existed civilizations without architecture and even without cities, civilizations never existed without domestic objects, without bowls, vases, or furnishings.

Beginning already in the earliest classical age, history and the city have not always corresponded to real concepts and physical realities, but often to more distant speculative levels, which posited themselves as noble and abstract referents of the experience of places and of the functions of daily life, conferring upon them a particular cultural value.

Unlike the Greeks, the ancient Romans never had a unitary model of a *polis*. The latter did not correspond to the profile of Athens, of its acropolis, and of the Parthenon, posited as a formal and aesthetic verification of democracy. Rome, the city of seven hills, full of forums, basilicas, temples, triumphal arches, and thermal baths, could not be modernized: it was too complex and contradictory to become, in everyday experience, a concrete model of reference. Its glory, its monuments, constituted the elements of an identity more ideal than physical. Thus, in the construction of furnishings, works of architecture, and monuments, the reference was not so much the real city, everyday Rome, but rather its mythical identity, its history, its political glory.

We can thus say that the classical culture of design was born without referring to a real urban model. The city was already, in ancient Rome, an abstract concept, theoretical, not practicable as a whole, but knowable only in parts, in individual segments, and in symbolic citations.

The foundation of new cities was of military origin and took place around the *castrum*, always the same and functionally essential. The Romans intervened in the occupied cities, introducing into them first of all the *forum*, which was a self-referential structure with monumental wings, almost an internal space that excluded the surrounding urban landscape, and which unified civic life.

If in ancient Greece buildings were a sort of existenz-minimum, and much of daily life took place in the city, in its markets, and in the baths, for the Romans, the *domus* was instead a rich and articulated enclave, a place of lust, secret or on display, as seen in Pompeii and in Herculaneum. If the polis was for Greek philosophers the theater of their speculation and their experience, where the philosopher Theophrastus listed the curious "characters" of the people he met, as proof of the overly abstract ideas of his teacher Aristotle, the city was for Roman philosophers a reality in which to defend themselves, a relational chaos from which to save oneself. The Epicureans, the skeptical followers of Pyrrho, the Stoic philosophers, they all proposed different techniques to defend themselves from urban chaos, and to create a gap between themselves and the events of daily city life that would make the looming horizon abstract and empty it of its intrusiveness. The *ataraxia* of the Epicureans, as indifference to institutional and parental bonds, in favor of those built by free choice, and cultivated in the Epicurean Garden, is a good example of how they saw the city as a place of conventional and useless relations to avoid; the apathy of the Stoics against worldly passions and unnecessary urban relations; the *epochē* of the skeptics of Pyrrho as a bracket in which to place reality in order to temper it as an immaterial and defused presence.

That particular Rome that continuously grew out of its natural boundaries, to reach those of the Empire, ended up becoming an abstract, conceptual reality, a theoretical metropolis with which it was no longer possible to establish relations if they were not mediated through philosophical techniques. Nowhere in Latin literature are there any toponymic references to real places in Rome, if not only to the Senate, the forums, or the circus, as separate parts in a context of anonymous districts of the Suburra.

The *Consecutio Spatiorum*

I believe that a good example of what is meant by a theoretical metropolis in Roman culture can be found in the Roman and Pompeian wall paintings from the 3rd century b.C. to the 1st century a.D., for it clearly provides us with two distinct levels of the concept of architecture: on the one hand, we see a work of architecture represented in the frescoes as an element of the landscape, like a backdrop made up of volumes, palaces, circuses, temples, and columns, as they appeared in the city; then there is another level of representation of architecture, consisting of a system of frames painted onto the walls of the rooms. These do not correspond to a constructed landscape seen from the outside, but to a more abstract linguistic category that arises from within, from the void, from the darkness.

This specific room thus becomes also a place of a conceptual experience, projected into a vast immaterial space, in which the stylistic, mythological, or narrative elements float as if inside a virtual *aquarium*. In the decorations of the Villa Imperiale of Boscotrecase, in the Villa di Fannius Sinistro in Boscoreale, or in the Villa dei Misteri in Pompeii, the space of the room is emptied of its walls, and placed within a limitless diagram of abstract styles that represent a theoretical city, a dimension of architecture that no longer coincides with the categories of Vitruvius, but instead with their linguistic and conceptual essence.

If Greek political thought sees in the *polis* a community of men, Cicero sees it founded on law: not a simple aggregate of individuals, but a group united by a legal and political consensus, one that is summed up in the abstract institutional formula "Senatus Populusque Romanus." Even urban space is thus a philosophical experience that transcends architectural and typological dimensions, in order to a become pure design thought moving within a theoretical space that transcends and empties the interior space. The *consecutio temporum* of Latin syntax seems here to thus be accompanied by a sort of *consecutio spatiorum*, capable of putting the experience of the internal environment into relation with the more general and theoretical dimension of the external space.

The perspective of the Italian Renaissance perhaps has its deep roots here, as a capacity to translate the hierarchies of an individual's spatial experience into a single system of reference.

Gottfried Semper, in his book *Der Stil in den technischen und tektonischen Künsten, oder Praktische Aesthetik* (*Style in the Technical and Tectonic Arts; or, Practical Aesthetics*) of 1863, describes the *circumlitio* present in several rooms in the house of Sallustio in Pompeii: it is a decorative technique on the walls that created a dual identity of the place: the natural building materials were left exposed, but veiled by a decorative patina that changed its identity without replacing it completely. In such a way, the *circumlitio* made it possible to simultaneously incorporate the two different levels of belonging to the wall: that of the real building, built and present, and that of the larger category of the theoretical metropolis. The *consecutio spatiorum* therefore placed these two different levels of experience into relation: the individual and local one with the mythical, theoretical one. Like how today we know how to connect flowers placed in a vase with the idea of the nature of which flowers are part, in the same way classical culture placed into relation every single domestic environment not so much with the architectural envelope that contained it, but with the artificial nature of which it was a part, which we can call the theoretical metropolis.

The theoretical metropolis was thus a general category of the construction of the designed universe, and as a territory of the circulation of relations it contained in its great depths all the particular places, houses, monuments, and political settings, and associated them with each other and with itself. We will see that over time the theoretical metropolis has also had a more symbolic role, a more general metaphorical function, as a concept that corresponds to a formal model of the world, which changes to adapt to new configurations.

The role of such a theoretical model, which transcends and contains that of the city, of architecture, and of domestic objects, consists in defining in a perceptible way the belonging of the single spatial experience to global formal and political scenarios of reference.

These theoretical models thus do not correspond to reality, but rather serve to explain it, that is, to contain it in a unitary model of reference. A bit like certain theoretical models of the atom that describe the functioning of matter in a unitary way and that are often a truly philosophical metaphor, typical of a certain historical period, and not the scientific description of the structure of matter. Or how the idea of nature changes throughout history, according to the literary and philosophical seasons, becoming of a Romantic, classical, or scientific nature and, although always identical to itself, the model of reading, the key to interpretation changes over time; in the same way, artificial nature, that built by man, has since the classical age been the object of a feeling, of a symbolic icon that collects it all, describes it, without losing itself in an infinite list of variants.

Even today, many architectural and design projects refer more to theoretical metropolises than to real ones: design comes into being in the face of a reality so complex and articulated to the point of being unknowable. Here, then design becomes a proposal for modifying this reality, but also a system of representation, referring to its reduced and practicable simulation.

Thus, speaking of design and the culture of design, we will often use this reference to theoretical metropolises, placing different dimensional scales in communication with one another, and linking them to a unitary concept that changes over time.

Classical culture therefore consisted not only of a repertoire of forms, but also of knowing how to mentally (rather than practically) connect domestic spaces, the micro-systems of the environment, with the larger dimension of artificial landscapes and metropolitan macro-systems, and this capacity provided the domestic places and internal spaces of Latin domesticity with an extremely specific cultural originality, which did not derive only from the formal elements of space (pilasters, frames, trabeations), but rather from the capacity of this space to relate with categories that were larger dimensionally and higher culturally.

A Weak Metaphysics

In ancient Roman times, metaphysics was a widespread but weak system.

Roman culture never produced the tragedies of Aeschylus, the result of being confronted with a strong metaphysical system and of a destiny overwhelmed in myth. Roman comedy instead created a more equal exchange between daily life and the presence of a polytheistic system that commingled with it.

In pagan mythology, the father of the gods was Kronos, or time, who ate his children, continually destroying his offspring: so to save the vestiges of man from this fatal destiny, it was necessary to construct a space that was placed outside of time.

Greco-Roman architecture was based on this foundation, produced by the separation of space from time: the monument was the greatest witness of history, but it did not belong to history.

This ancient theorem remained fundamental for all of Western antiquity, constructing a space that was born of history, but which came into being as a reality destined for extra-historical times and producing a design capable of transferring the occasion of building into a region of definitive values.

In ancient Rome, this rigid separation between space and time was mediated by the less abstract identity of places, which were marked out in valleys, rivers, and woods, each one endowed with unique narrative values, from *genius loci*, which made visiting them more mediatable to human experience. Therefore, each place with its own mystery, its minor divinity; to each home a domestic sacred Lar protected the hearth; each man his Penates who mediated the relationship with great and lofty history.

In Roman culture, nature was therefore inhabited and made inhabitable by a vast generation of minor divinities, and each space was identified by an invisible network of relationships with the great theorems of myth and religion. Already in the most ancient Italy, the Etruscan Haruspices were lay people capable of interpreting objects, animals, and nature, finding in these useful indications for tackling political decisions. Outside the major dominant theologies, our Etruscan forefathers looked lower down at the more casual day-to-day to grasp the sense of a guide for more complex strategies.

The home furnishings of the Roman home were "inhabited" by domestic spirits, for whom they signaled their presence with small legs and heads, which confirmed their expressive independence relative to their function: objects as friendly presences, and not simply bare tools – almost domestic animals that protected the home, keeping away evil influences and misfortune.

The animist and mythical structure of space, this *consecutio spatiorum* of which we have spoken, was related to a time already designated in history, and which repeated itself as if it were a decorative ring. A circular time, without development, of which the Stoic philosophers spoke, in which history returned and where everything had already been described by logos, which regulated everything according to an irremovable law that could not be evaded; and where everyone had to do their best to play their part, like an actor on a stage.

It is interesting to note that almost all of the characters on the frescoes of the walls of Rome and Pompeii are wearing theatrical masks that exult, with the monstrosity of their presence, an irrepressible tendency toward delirium. Against these backgrounds of landscape fragments or abstract spatial frames, these disquieting figures appear, draped in colorful fabrics rich in folds. In these paintings, man appears as a mystery of the universe, as a dark point of reality: a man close to the subterranean wonders of the Sybil Cumana, but also to the lucid research of Pliny the Elder; a man, therefore, who tried to explain the world to himself, but was unable to explain himself. A hero but also a puppet of a story already written.

And this sense of dual belonging to both a literary and an institutional setting was present in classical furnishings: lanterns, summoned by the handful by the Palatine Anthology as living witnesses of their secret love, or Pompeian beds and stools, as stylistically perfect as small works of architecture, almost as if their function were not private but public, suitable for an imperial scenography.

Such an ambiguous Roman object (part domestic tool, part animist presence, part theatrical simulation of itself), belongs to the minor scale of classicism, but in some ways it clearly bears witness to the scission between fiction and destiny, between private life and myth, which then fueled the great theoretical dimension. A culture to which the West has referred for almost two millennia, not to find unlikely certainties of golden seasons, but to feed a restless search without answers, and precisely for this reason continuously renewable.

The Civilization of Vision

Roman time was therefore a circular time, where there was no evolution, design, innovation, creation, but only the Eternal Return, of which Nietzsche also spoke – of masks that were smiling and those distorted by anguish.

Design, creation, and innovation are terms that we use today as synonyms for art and culture, but they were introduced only at the advent of Christianity, when the concept of time changed profoundly. With the coming of Christ, time was divided into a before and an after: starting from the creation of the world, up to the Incarnation, and after this up to the Apocalypse, the Last Judgment, and the Resurrection of the Dead (which in each case was then considered imminent).

Time thus became a linear concept, moved by history, no longer an elliptical succession of events, but a process of evolution and transformation towards a goal, where design also contributed to changing the world, and art continually created new languages, making the previous ones age.

If today we open a manual of classical art, it is difficult for us to know (if we are not experts in the field) which century it is. Likewise, if we open a book of oriental art, it will be difficult to understand to which century or millennium the images belong. That is because in both cases time is not linear, and therefore the new is not necessarily different from the old, and perhaps it is a confirmation or only a refinement. If instead we open a book of art history after the 3rd century, we see the continuous change of languages and iconography. It was indeed Jewish-Christian ethics that disseminated the idea of the creation of art, according to a vision that repeats, as in Genesis, the creation of the world, thus its continuous renewal, towards progress, towards the expectation of the end of time with the coming of the Kingdom of Heaven.

With the passage from polytheism to monotheism, the many stories merged into a single story; the many animist places, into the spiritual centrality of Rome, the new Jerusalem.

With Christianity, aesthetics and art became an instrument of religion, indeed, they became religion; in the sense that starting from St. Augustine, after the collapse of pagan culture, the whole West reorganized its theological theorems, putting together Greek philosophy and Catholic religion. Two cultures for which there was no longer direct access to the sources: Greek culture had collapsed, and the holy places (Jerusalem and Palestine) were remote and inaccessible. Thus, all European religious and civic thought was organized by taking its starting point from a representation of these sources, through their image produced by art, by painting, by aesthetics, which in fact became the very landscape of Western religion, its synonym. We can say that since then, the West, and Italy in particular, has become a civilization of vision.(...)

Thus, art and aesthetics have become, especially in Italy, sacred elements, instrumental parts of a moral exegesis that transcended them. The sacred used beauty, saved it, disseminated it, but it transcended it: it emptied it of its design contents, in order to transform it into a setting of salvation in the Celestial Kingdom, not into an operative tool within the things of the world. New Jerusalem became the new theoretical metropolis, the place of the final recomposition of a provisional historical condition, to which the coming of the Resurrection of the Dead would finally end.

The Church saw this world as a temporary reality, and art as a narrative simulation that produced removable, hanging, narrative cult objects. In 1323, St. Francis invented the Nativity scene at Greccio, as a provisional simulation of a no longer accessible sacred site. In 1320, in the Chapel of the Santo Capitolo in Padua, Giotto di Bondone arrived at the point of representing the angels unfolding and supporting the frescoed surface, to testify to its being a sheet, a two-dimensional support for a sacred representation.

The Early Christian Dismantling

The early Middle Ages in Europe was a long period of archetypes of a Spartan domesticity, deliberately and intentionally poor, in contrast with the imposing icons of faith that art produced.

Domestic objects exhibited their essential ignorance, their formal minimalism, and their obscure technological complexity: experimentalism had taken the place of classical systems, but mental technology produced masterpieces of scholastic philosophy, Patristics, and a global reflection on the fate of the world, of men, and of history; of the physical world like that of the souls that belonged to it.

It is interesting to note that already in early Christian architecture, there was no effort to found a new language: its building elements were physically removed from the monuments of the most ancient architecture, from pagan temples and from the friezes of forums and circuses.

The casual relaxation of that particular pagan universe testified to the early Christian decision to use that collapsed world in a different way, within a new, open, and almost inexpressive structure, where the poor symbols of a new system of values prevailed: an early Christian basilica like Santa Sabina was built on the model of a large agricultural barn, with its floor at street level. A transitory universe that had its center in a reality that was not visible, a universal one, and one that did not require the creation of a new stylistic code, but the realization of a new code of ethical values.

The catacombs, underground cemeteries awaiting the coming resurrection of the bodies, were dug into the tufa and constituted a sort of refounding of the architecture starting from its bowels, from its underground matter; they were environments devoid of any monumental sense, unlike the great classical and pre-classical funerary tradition.

It therefore emerges that the quality of early Christian space was not only of a formal or linguistic nature, but above all a relational one, based on the ability to construct, from within, relationships and connections with higher levels of knowledge and morality, within the community and with God.

Romanesque Sensoriality

A monotheistic religion like that of Catholicism presupposed not only the oneness of history, but also the existence of a single direction to which history led.

Linear time, determined by the coming of Christ, gave form and meaning to history and through this also to the economy, the city, and society. The great Gothic cathedrals that rose throughout Europe beginning in the tenth century, before being architectural monuments were great programs that presupposed the imposition of a vertical direction to the development of labor and to the agricultural and commercial economy of the city community, activities that until then had been only horizontal realities, that is, based on a network of exchanges between people and markets.

The symbolic importance of the Gothic cathedrals went far beyond their architectural content: they belonged to the religious endeavor to give an ethical and symbolic foundation to the great abstract mass of the exchanges that traversed society and that conditioned interpersonal relations and politics.

We could say that Europe came into being with its cathedrals, as a formalization of its economy, and therefore as a constitutive element of its nations. It is no coincidence that in Italy these great cathedrals were rare, and that the Gothic style was short-lived: the formation of the nation took place very late, penultimate in Europe before Germany, both heirs of a strong idea of Empire and a weak one of Nation.

The centrality of Rome, the presence of the papacy, the division of the country, emptied of meaning the planning of similar mega-projects. The Italian national identity remained a weak one, based on an economy of master craftsmen, and not of great constructive political platforms; a religion of saints, mystics, thinkers, and churches, whose founding dimension was only municipal or regional – many buildings for the families of the new merchants, churches, convents, Carthusian monasteries, Romanesque abbeys, but not national collective works as the Gothic technique required. (...)

With the turning point of the year 1000, even the Italian Romanesque style matured as a technique and as a role, acquiring its rather original theorem, which remained unique in the history of Western architecture. In the Romanesque church, the quality of the space could not in fact be defined through the lightness, height, and transparency of the structures, as in the Gothic cathedral: the Romanesque basilica, technically simpler, constituted a patchwork of intense sensorial experiences.

The large thickness of the walls established a major thermal difference between the interior and the exterior; the penumbra filtering through just a few polychrome windows; the intense scent of that unrivalled space full of incense and candles; the soft acoustics of a construction of great thermal inertia, constituted as a whole a sensorial reality that transformed, in physical and corporeal terms, the religious practices and the cults that took place there.

The Romanesque basilica was therefore not related to a simple constructive and spatial diagram, but referred back to an integrated religious sensory experience, which modified the traditional distance between architectural space, faith, and corporeal experience.

In Giotto di Bondone's paintings, there is no difference between objects of furniture and architecture, which are positioned in equal fashion in the always human stories. In his frescoes, the human bodies completely fill the pieces of architecture that surround them, and their limbs become structures, filling the space. Architectural pieces are in fact for Giotto, and for the painting of the fourteenth century, corporeal spaces, placed within a landscape deconstructed into single figurative elements.

The use of the human body as a calculator of cultural and religious experiences was an important innovation compared to the tradition of the early Middle Ages, because it valued the most earthly and fragile component with respect to the soul, introducing a chapter that the Renaissance will develop in depth, with studies on the relationship between architecture and the human body.

Those new cities of the Municipalities, inhabited by already totally secular and liberated merchants, whom Giovanni Boccaccio describes in *The Decameron*, were lively and organized around the *Duomo*, full of earthly sensations, scents, sounds, penumbras, humidity, full of Saints and enthroned Madonnas. Without either an apparent or secret contradiction, they prepared the Renaissance revolution as the first true birth of contemporary modernity, Italian rather than European.

The poets of the *Dolce Stil Novo*, as Dante called them in the *Convivio*, referring to the gentle love of French troubadour origin, marked the end of the Middle Ages, testifying to the advent of a generation of poets and friends who brought a new sensibility, the first sign of an anti-historical revolt that the Renaissance was. Guido Cavalcanti, Guido Guinizzelli, Lapo Gianni, Cino da Pistoia, and Dante Alighieri met, inside their real, walled cities, in the market and in the streets of Florence, their earthly Madonnas, claiming the ability to exalt through the woman the sense of a new spiritual greatness through earthly love.

The end of the European Middle Ages was therefore a phenomenon prepared for in Italy through a series of very specific cultural and economic mutations. These mutations came to maturity in a country like ours, where the seemingly most difficult conditions for such a change existed.

The existence of the papacy, the division of the country, its long imperial decadence, and the invasions by foreign armies certainly did not constitute favorable elements for such a profound cultural revolution.

The very absence of a Gothic culture demonstrates how municipal economies were struggling to acquire a national dimension, and the organization of labor had not yet reached the form of large guilds capable of building cathedrals for which work would continue for many generations, managing huge economic resources; ours remained the artisanry of the *bottega*, with the organization of projects on a city scale, and a capitalism made up of private bankers who lent money to kings all over Europe.

The Romanesque technique, backward compared to Gothic engineering, testified to a deficiency when it came to the development of major building programs. But it can be noted that this absence of advanced and extensive state organizations left the field open to an aesthetic production of extraordinary quality by painters, sculptors, and artisans, who worked by producing from within the autonomous guilds that represented them from the bottom, and selling the fruit of their art directly to clients. This type of basic liberal micro-system found its civic equivalent in the nascent mercantile, pagan, and even devout, society. The Church's commitment to building in this world, and ever less so in New Jerusalem, its own survival contributed to establishing a climate of great realism, under the overarching umbrella of the monarchical and imperial superstructures.

It was the weak Italian system that favored the breaking up of the medieval fort system.

In the religious painting of the thirteenth and fourteenth centuries, there was a considerable use of altars and thrones: in place of cathedrals and palaces, the altarpieces and triptychs on a gold background display Madonnas sitting on high-backed seats, as if in small architectural pieces totally filled by their large bodies.

The Italian capacity to attribute to the object a dignity even higher than that of the monument can be seen in these paintings on wood panel. For Giotto, architecture and domestic objects are completely equal, perfectly described as homologous parts of an urban landscape made up of object-focused actions, into which the great bodies of the protagonists of the narrated story are placed. The chairs in which sit the *Maestà* of Giotto and Taddeo Gaddi are elements of a rhetorical architecture that comes from pagan times: the Madonnas seem to be the heirs of the goddesses of fertility, the Italian mothers of the sacred camp of Nola. They sit not on the throne as a symbol of power, but on a domestic object that becomes sacred through the motherhood it holds. The chair becomes for Giotto a niche, a baptistery, the protagonist of a vision that bypasses architecture.

The Christian deities sit on domestic objects, turning them into a reality that replaces hierarchies, and places them directly on gold backgrounds.

It seats them in Paradise, therefore, in the absence of a complete and impossible New Jerusalem.

The Mechanical Metropolis
Andrea Branzi, 1990

//

Over the course of this century, several theoretical models of the metropolis can be singled out.

The first is one which corresponds to the birth and growth of the historical avant-garde movements, and we can refer to it as "Mechanical Metropolis." It dates back to the Twenties and the Thirties, and for the first time it offered a complete integration of society in the logic of the Industrial Revolution.

The Mechanical Metropolis was in fact made up of separate parts of reality, of bodies that were in counterpoint both socially and culturally. However, these different parts clash dramatically, producing a single energy of transformation. It is the metropolis of the period from the beginning of the century up to the twenties, perfectly portrayed in Fritz Lang's film *Metropolis*. (Incidentally, it is interesting to note that in this century it has not been architecture but the cinema, painting, and literature that have succeeded in describing the metropolitan condition effectively.)

This tension was produced by a world dense with contradictions that sought to adapt itself to a new order of logic, a new and highly contracted code of expression, without renouncing the complexity of the language. Neoplasticism was born out of this moral quandary: how to speak universally to everyone, using an elementary code of symbols, without losing the depth and complexity of the information conveyed. I am reminded of Moholy-Nagy's films in which the cinematographic technique of montage could be seen as an attempt to combine, in what amounted to a virtual obsession with integration, chunks of social reality and everyday life with the primary figures of the neoplastic code.

The historical avant-garde movement took on the task of marking the most profound and dramatic genetic mutations. The Futurists saw man as immersed in a metropolitan existence continually overwhelmed by the evolution of technology. Man's space lost all reference to perspective and became a "rising vortex," abstractly moving upward, without any real development or destiny. The abstract nature of the Futurists' work developed precisely out of this dramatic derivation of "abstraction" from man's experiences within the industrial metropolis.

And it was in the Mechanical Metropolis that the first true industrial design was created, as a way of accommodating the extant to the logic of a factory. From the formal and substantial point of view: objects as tools, houses as offices, men as laborers, the metropolis as huge workshops in a society that was just one huge mechanical factory. Every design was a cog in the wheel, each site was the wheel of a mechanism that transmitted its tension by traction. Each part was different from the whole – but only from the whole could it attain sense and destiny, that is, function, aim, significance, and form. Thus the Cubists, who took up the law of the industrial object at the base of the depiction of reality: assembled, devoid of a formal and ethical unity, multiple, empty, opaque.

The Homogeneous Metropolis

Andrea Branzi, 1990

///

The theoretical model of the Mechanical Metropolis was succeeded between the wars and up until the Fifties by another reference model. This hypothesized a metropolis that had overcome its major internal contradictions of a formal nature to become a great, homogeneous system of construction, almost a territorial diagram of the assembly line. This type of Homogeneous Metropolis corresponds to a moment of dramatic realism in the culture of design: it now saw and accepted the multiplicative logic of the industrial system.

The homogeneous metropolis corresponds to the urban visions of Hilberseimer and Rationalism, to the obsessive repetition of gray and scientific modules right up to the distant horizon. It is the metropolis of Musil's *Man Without Qualities* in which the design project implemented its dream of total surrender, to the point of self-sacrifice, to the rational logic of the system. The very definition of design was radically altered: its description as a process of industrialization of the world was accepted. The individual project was defined as a segment of the global process of industrialization. This was the period in which the mass-individual developed within the context of mass markets.

The egalitarianism of the postwar period laid the philosophical and cultural foundations for the establishment of a para-scientific basis of design.

The School of Ulm theorized this new vision of endless manufacturing for a theoretically infinite market. It took the reality of the cosmic dimension of industrial manufacturing as a surrealistic theorem of the impossible eternal perfection of serially produced objects. This became a sort of Moebius strip that constantly led to the rediscovery of its own tautological foundations.

The world became washable, stackable, modular, and flexible; true mass modernity was born, the international style, annihilation of exceptions.

In the Homogeneous Metropolis, chaos, contradictions, and the discontinuity of the real world were only a provisional condition, a toll that had to be paid to make up for the delays in industrialization. Than industrialization, in its development, was to produce a homogeneous and logical universe, a territory ordered by rational technologies.

It was not until the great crisis of the sixties that "complexity" was given a value and also profoundly different philosophical meaning. Post-industrial society, in fact, was created at the moment when discontinuity, chaos, and complexity were no longer seen as provisional conditions destined to disappear in the great industrial order, but – to the contrary – as the most complete and mature result of industrialism itself. Industrialism produced discontinuity as it developed, and perceived complexity as an indispensable environmental and market condition.

The great crisis of growth at the end of the Sixties took place in the tectonic overthrow of the value of "complexity," which from that moment onward became a positive element of diversification and growth.

The premonitory signs of this traumatic taking possession can all be seen in the hyper-realist theorems of Pop Art, and in its exalted acceptance of the devastated reality of the System. An acceptance that was neither painless nor a form of renunciation, but, on the contrary, the opening of a political and moral revolt, which failed but which was indispensable to the growth of society. It was from this refoundation that *New Design* developed, and later accepted the metropolitan reality as an historical and existential condition.

The Hybrid Metropolis

Andrea Branzi, 1988

//

The third theoretical metropolis, after the Mechanical Metropolis and the Homogenous Metropolis, is the one we are living in now: it corresponds to the birth of the postindustrial society and can be defined as the Hybrid Metropolis.

In the Hybrid Metropolis the project is no longer something aimed at modifying the world. Rather it is an act that creates a new reality to be added to the existing one, making it richer and more complex and increasing the number of possible options. The project has become one of the imaginary territories of narration and communication; territories in which the postindustrial system is expanding, such as the cinema, television, and information.

Within the hybrid metropolis the project of design (or architecture) no longer constitutes a general critical category. On the contrary it becomes a fragmentary, discontinuous system, which accentuates differences and exceptions instead of the great ideological unities.

We can say that in the hybrid metropolis the approach to thinking about design is a "way of thinking in strong segments." That is to say, a way of thinking (and a sign and a project) that is "weak" on the level of general connections and of its participation in global theorems and unifying ideological programs but "strong" within separate segments, in limited portions. In this sense it does not suffer from a weakness of design. On the contrary it possesses an expressive energy that is discharged through the creation of objects of high expressivity and in places with a strong identity.

Within this seething and feverish reality the nature of our visual perception is profoundly altered. Claude Nicolas Ledoux represented his theater in Besanon reflected in the eye of the beholder, where the natural laws of vision coincided with those of architecture itself. Since his time, much of modern culture has professed a cold, analytical, detached, and rational visual culture. Paul Klee and Piet Mondrian saw the human gaze as a device that probes reality in order to grasp its structural, fundamental laws: a vibrant gaze that penetrates the world of appearances to reveal the basic choices that lie before it.

In the Hybrid Metropolis the human eye blazes, as in the opening sequence of *Blade Runner*, sharing in an urban emotionality. All critical distance is scorched away in a total adherence to reality, a reality of which the human eye forms an integral part.

Let us look at how and when the Hybrid Metropolis has modified the very epistemology of design.

In the treatises of the Modern Movement the relations between industrial design and city planning were all set within the framework of a single ideology for transformation of the real: in the modern view the three great disciplines of the project (design, architecture, and city planning) appeared to be three different phases in a single great and all-embracing design that stretched "from the spoon to the city." For the postwar rationalist movement the object of design (bearing in mind the factors of size and mass production) had an orderly place within the global transformation of the metropolis, a transformation that was the product of the great reformist strategies with their objective of a rapid but balanced industrialization.

From this perspective the relation of design to the modern metropolis was that of the gears to a large machine in movement: it transmitted the motion, shared in a common destiny, and produced quality on a small scale.

Up until the end of the Sixties, therefore, designers saw the metropolis as the "general plan" to which they could contribute their energies by working modestly but with passion on mass-produced objects. Harmony between the "three sisters of the project" was the premise on which each of the three acquired meaning and strategic direction. The overall strategic direction was that of the construction of an orderly, efficient, and industrialized domain, with the secular and reformist modern city located at its center. Order and quality were in fact synonymous.

For this reason the confused and multifaceted real city has always been regarded by the Modern Movement and Rationalism as a phenomenon not yet under the complete control of the project. Hence they have seen it as a transitory phenomenon, one destined for profound change over the course of time. In fact the idea has always been there that the confusion and contradictions of the city would eventually disappear and that orderly and efficient metropolitan settings and modes of behavior would gradually be attained in the Homogeneous Metropolis. So it seemed that the logic of industrial production and of modern planning would reorganize this urban confusion, still seen as an accident to be eliminated.

Out of this optimistic hypothesis of development a different analysis of urban chaos began to emerge in the years that gave birth to postindustrial society. The chaos was no longer seen as the temporary effect of a transient situation but as the most mature result of the entire industrial system.

Overall, the industrial system of production is rational (for it utilizes technologies, machines, and manufacturing systems that have a rational logic), but each sector of production operates according to an autonomous, partial, and compartmentalized logic, moving in totally opposite directions. In those years the awareness grew that the industrial system was not evolving in a single direction, but moving simultaneously in many different directions. Within the metropolis, which is the place where merchandise enters into circulation, this produces a great linguistic chaos, a mix of many different cultures. Technological culture itself, in spite of its rational, rigid, and scientific basis, determines a setting that is eclectic on the whole, simply because the cultures of production to which it gives rise are separate cultures that are not engaged in a search for unity but in the pursuit of differentiation, competition, and alternative solutions.

In a sense the ideal theoretical model for the Hybrid Metropolis is no longer Oslo, the pearl of the far north, but other far more contradictory and fragmented cities – hybrid ones, in fact – like New York and even Hong Kong, or the system of Canadian cities in which each provincial capital represents an internal frontier within the country, a reservoir of memories and identities belonging to other places or European homelands. But even the great Latin American conurbations, such as Mexico City or Brazil's Sao Paolo, serve as models, metropolitan universes that contain within themselves everything and its opposite, every contradiction and every unity. Perhaps the city that best defines the concept of Hybrid Metropolis is Beirut, a city that is the theater for a civil war whose deflagrating mechanisms look totally incomprehensible from the outside – incomprehensible because our own culture interprets politics according to mechanical criteria: a right, a left, progressive forces, and conservative forces. Whereas in Beirut there is a series of formations that confront one another, forming alliances and giving battle according to criteria that are completely extraneous to our culture. For these are armed clashes based on family, religion, and tribe, traditional conflicts inherited from past centuries that have created a cockpit of violence only understandable from within the metropolis itself.

In the Hybrid Metropolis a number of traditional hierarchies have been altered, and the perspective within which we operate has to be revised, together with the means we adopt for intervention. Both general and particular choices are more cultural than logical in nature, more intuitive than rational.

In one part of the United States an investigation has been carried out into the criteria for administration of such complex and contradictory metropolitan organisms. It has been shown that the traditional instruments at the disposal of a rational planner are wholly inadequate. Better results can be achieved by an artist or a housekeeper, through the application of creative logic or simple common sense.

Set against this dynamic background, in which so many different patterns of behavior and territories of the imagination are blended, the industrial product must succeed in getting across its own identity, system of relationships, and modes of consumption in a very short space of time. It finds itself today in the situation of a flower or an animal in a forest, having to emit its own genetic codes, made up of signs, colors, and odors, so as to capture the right partner.

The days of the old products that "suit everyone" are over. One survives today by producing diversity and a range of choice.

Lots of identical human beings, all with different characters, shoes, and signs of the Zodiac.

The Cold Metropolis
Andrea Branzi, 1990

//

The Cold Metropolis is produced by mature post-industrial society. A society in which all of devastating experimental tensions, typical of the years of change, have been reconciled.

The change of those years is now complete, and the languages and modes of behavior produced by twenty years of experimentalism have become permanent categories, and as such no longer produce experimentation but fine-tuning. A new "majority" has been consolidated; it is no longer grey and depressing like in the Sixties, and it is now variegated, multiple, differentiated, and it has adopted the qualities and behaviors generated over twenty years by the "minorities" transforming them into stable categories. A society, therefore, in the form of a checkerboard (or matrix), in which every square holds a style or a transformational trend.

All of the differences, the contradictions, and the explosive oppositions that seemed to bring the system to the brink of destruction during the Seventies, have remained intact; but the energy has cooled, and the violence has become abstract, cold. An internal and deforming violence, no longer explosive (and therefore, liberating). For twenty years, the chaos produced by the change seemed to be a new liberated universe, in which the system attained so elevated a level of complexity that it became impossible to know the entire system. Within that system, the individual broke all residual character armor, imposing his or her own explosive personality in total anarchy. But there is more. The enormous mass of differences that the metropolis produces, and of which it is made, are more apparent than real. The formal differences that it contains are the tangible sign of the human and spiritual diversity of the men that live in it, but such diversity in its overall reach produces a sort of annihilation of the foundations of the differences themselves: every part of the system is different from the rest, and it draws its own reason for existing from its differences. Every place, every product, every sign exists because it is different or an alternative to the context. This specific difference, which it bears, is nothing more than a metaphor for a difference of being, and for its inalienable right to exist.

And so we see that differences are only so many different metaphors for the same reality. They are nothing but the formal sign (produced by diversified series, by compositional combinations, and variations on the sign) of a substantial unity of the system. A unity made up of infinite variations on itself. And so we see that in the Cold Metropolis, the contradictions are no longer competitive and explosive; they are the fruit of a new balance of energy, which the "cold fusion" accurately hypothesized: an energy that does not produce the explosion of the system, but which is generated by its profound natural equilibrium.

The Cold Metropolis removes the apparent contradictions and no longer calls for the liberation of the individual in the destruction of the contradictions of the system. And the energy and the violence all remain trapped within, as the unexploded internal force for the transformation of things.

In the Cold Metropolis, therefore, design is no longer a generator of pure and simple local and object identities (Hybrid Metropolis), nor the old transformer of the world into industrial standards (Homogeneous Metropolis), nor is the violent producer of social and functional conflicts (Mechanical Metropolis). In the Cold Metropolis, design has two paths open to it – either to become the source of a new normality, deformed and icy, made up of many official minorities, an abnormal and multiple normality, substantially a world of neo-homologues. Or else, to become the producer of "profound qualities," that are ethical, poetic, and anthropological; the only qualities that cannot be dispersed in the great standardization of the differences, within the Cold Metropolis.

The post-industrial manufacturing system attains its greatest level of complexity in the Cold Metropolis, and it is here that all possible behaviors and methods of production coexist, within an enormous semiosphere of marketing categories and information that are only apparently contradictory – Mass-production and hand-made production, programming and anarchy, new standards and infinite diversification, improvisation and historical codes, archetypes and pure ephemera, international languages and dialects, culture and consumerism, mass languages and private codes. Design must therefore operate without losing any of this wealth; it will not longer be a partisan of mass production as against all other forms of building (Rationalism), nor will it be proponent of conflictual experimentation (New Design).

In the Cold Metropolis, all forms of production – in the norm and in the variation – in the short-term and over long-term – have acquired equal dignity. Design need not find improbable overall, definitive solutions, it must rather produce local equilibriums, a new ecology of the artificial world, which can transform – into an environmental asset, into a positive value – the great depth of the interface between man and this system of *artefacta* that surrounds man.

In the Cold Metropolis, places begin to take on a new status. This status is no longer typological or functional, but determined by a progressive, invisible, but inexorable tendency toward standardization.

In this sense, the domestic site (the home) tends to disappear as a specialization, and it becomes interchangeable with other functional structures that are close and complementary to it; in the Homogeneous Metropolis, the house was supposed to resemble the office, and today it is the office tends to resemble the house. Tomorrow, the two will simply resemble each other, without trauma, unified in a single flow and a single plankton of services and shadows.

The Cold Metropolis becomes (in this progressive disappearance of typological distinction) the generic "metropolis," no longer dramatic but still violent, where the setting of living and working alternate, sliding on the climatized and well-equipped platform of the artificial universe.

The Cold Metropolis is this, too – a new frontier in which formal distinctions no longer constitute the fundamental experience of man, but rather his possible ethical choices. The only ones that profoundly mark his experiences and actions in the constructed world.

3.4

PROTOTYPES OF WEAK URBANIZATION

Models of Weak Urbanization

Andrea Branzi, 2006

//

Models of weak urbanization refer to a concept of reversibility and a traversable quality typical of agriculture, and they indicate a way of understanding structures as a temporary, light, elastic reality set within a constructed territory but mixed in with agricultural production as well. Traversable and free of insurmountable borders just like agricultural production, weak urbanization is where architecture becomes a free availability of components and no longer coincides with the concept of buildings and stable typologies.

Models of weak urbanization are for a relational architecture not defined by precise functions, yet like a computer available for many different activities; a functionoid therefore that responds positively to the changing of necessities, even seasonal ones. This is an architecture in which the component of time returns as a variable in an imperfect and incomplete equation that adapts itself to change.

We are not speaking about the city of the future here, but of a new type of integrated agricultural park situated beside historic or modern cities; a sort of high-tech favela, and like the favelas mixed in with nature this is constructed using light, manageable materials that create a multimedia campus. It is a ductile, open structure that represents a compromise between current agricultural facilities and an urban sub-system.

Western architecture in the twentieth century experimented with very few new typologies: during the age of strong and concentrated modernity skyscrapers and Le Corbusier's Unité d'Habitation were born. In the age of weak and diffuse modernity, there is a need to seek out new typologies, diligently analyzing those few that have been spontaneously born.

The favelas are among these; produced by a state of necessity and grave social discomfort, they objectively constitute one of the few novelties in the urban setting. These must be evaluated independently of the social groups that constructed them in the peripheries of the large cities in order to understand their innovative potential.

Many master of all is modern had intuited a dispersed architecture open to nature (Mies van der Rohe, Le Corbusier, Niemeyer), but it was always in terms of a new construction finally definitive and immobile in time, an irreversible typology that perfectly corresponded to the given functions. It is a question, then, of trying, through new models of weak urbanization, the possibility of adapting the design to the bypassing of these historical binds, rendering it more adequate for time that changes and a society that renews itself.

A
THE GENETIC METROPOLIS

Amniotic Liquid and Subjective Heritage

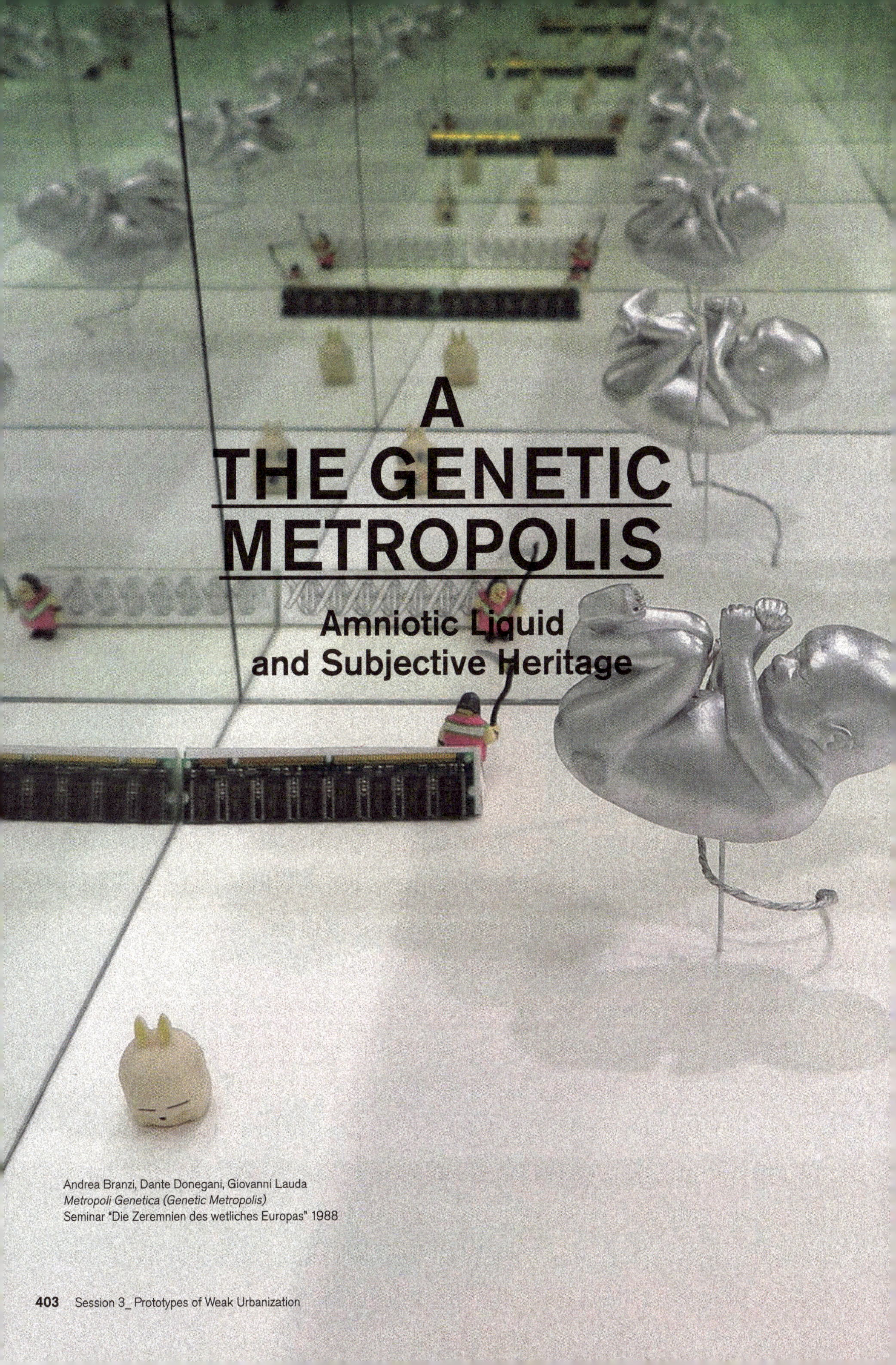

Andrea Branzi, Dante Donegani, Giovanni Lauda
Metropoli Genetica (Genetic Metropolis)
Seminar "Die Zeremnien des wetliches Europas" 1988

The Genetic Metropolis
Andrea Branzi, 2006

//

This vision of a conclusive coincidence between subject and system, individual and entrepreneurial market, introduces a new definition of the metropolis as a great genetic bed - a layer in the ancient sense that we can imagine in Imperial Rome, in current Mumbai, or in the great African capitals like Lagos: an urban reality where architecture is nothing but a weak system connecting a heap of human presences, relations, interests, and exchanges that completely fill the space. Kevin Kelly, in *Out of Control*, writes: "There's only one epoch in the history of the planet, when each single individual and each single thing become connected, and we are alive in that exact moment. This enormous interconnection, permitting us to exchange ideas, information, intermediations, and money everywhere, anytime, and with whomever, is our promised land."

The metropolis of the information age is not, then, the capital of technology; it is rather the land of the humane, in all its ability to connect its own DNA with that of business, disseminating its own genes in a tight network of parental and entrepreneurial relations.

The genetic metropolis is one where the biological energies of society free themselves and reach their maximal level of liquefaction, fully invading every infrastructure and overflowing every possible designed form of containment. This promised land that Kelly speaks of consists in a vast bio-technological system, moved by weak and diffuse energies aimed at the expansion and defense of the system's genes and the search for better conditions to protect and reinforce them in order to improve living conditions.

It is therefore a large vital system where the interests of a single being intertwine with the analogous, primordial interest of others and outside distinctions of class, religion, and culture; in other words, a class, religion, and culture that have not disappeared, but which change the statutes governing solid bodies in order to become instrumental values and a means by which to legitimately defend the amniotic liquid in which the metropolitan gene moves.

In this evolving logic, any paradigm or organized model is always to be considered transitory, traversable ground in the search for better environmental and social systems for the defense and consolidation of its own lineage.

This defense no longer occurs in its aggressive form, which sought the elimination of the weak or the different, but rather anticipates a reinforcement of the defenses of its own DNA through the mingling with that which is different, creating preventive systems that protect the weak component of society.

The ethic of information networks has taught us of the existence of great ad vantages that social interconnection offers. Or – as Hinduism, a religion that greatly influenced twenty-first-century electronic thought, teaches us – these advantages exist in an interconnectedness of all that is vital, in a unique system that extends itself from the human world to the plant world.

It's strange that precisely the two great twenty-first-century technologies – information technology and genetics – have not yet adequately been joined in order to be understood as weak and diffuse technologies that work within all the processes of liquefaction now underway. The genetic metropolis is, in fact, the vision of a territory within which architecture no longer defines a permanent segmentation of space, but becomes the theater of a vast elastic (in other words, reversible) modification of infrastructures, services, and metropolitan underpinnings from the bottom up.

There is a great fear of speaking about genetic energy as a positive factor because the affirmation of race, genetic manipulations, and the uncontrollable egoism that this concept brings to mind suggest an extreme prudence. Nevertheless, there is a need to create a less limited, less fearful vision of this great vital patrimony, this anthropological layer that moves history; the great creativity expressed by genetic systems, in their unstoppable tendency to free themselves from the limits and chains that genes manifest in their growth, cannot be the object of misunderstandings.

In a great book entitled *In Praise of Imperfection*, Rita Levi Montalcini described man's ability to design as a positive result of his biological imperfection, of his never being completely and definitively homogenous with the physical and historical environment. This imperfection, with respect to the surroundings and history, pushes the human genetic system to design, experiment, and search for the best survival conditions for itself and its lineage. The absence of a final model and pre-established path within this search represents in the most complete manner the condition of contemporary man: freed of many impediments and false models, he seeks out his path starting from within his own nature.

The Genetic Metropolis represents this level of evolved aggregation as the best market of opportunities and parental mingling. Its constructed form is not significant because current society can no longer be represented by a succession of forms and places. Current society more and more resembles the great textile-based civilizations of the past (or present) like that of the Indians-societies which represent themselves in a continuous network, a flexible and transparent fabric able to resist the knocks and tears of the internal transitions and collision with the new. Indian civilization is based on textiles, and is therefore an anti-architectural, anti-mechanical, anti-logical, and anti-constructive one capable of understanding in terweaving processes as a cosmic philosophy wherein each person's life continues beyond death, within the warp and weft of other lives. Mahatma Gandhi began his revolution by returning to the primordial act of spinning cotton as the base of a radical re-foundation of society. Thus, by skipping all the processes of modernization connected to the strong energies of mechanics, India landed autonomously in the world of the web via a religious path, becoming in a very short time the world's third largest producer of software, behind only the United States and Japan. The backdrop of Indian society, with its codes of metropolitan identity still linked with the presence of textile colors and patterns, coincides, much more than does architecture, with the mobile system of bodies in a bio-technological environment.

Speaking, then, of a genetic metropolis, we mean a theoretical model of a land where the vital and entrepreneurial energies coincide with the form of the city itself, through a constructive, reversible, and traversable apparatus. A model that corresponds to an asset that is not necessarily chaotic, but rather to an elastic system that changes with time and the needs of relations. This type of bio-technological environment is closer to the management of agricultural systems, linked to seasonal cycles, weather, and the reversibility of crops more than to the paradigms of the urban government, which act through traditional architecture.

The Genetic Metropolis therefore resembles a high-tech favela more than the great American cities. It is more similar to ancient Dharavi in the center (not the periphery) of Mumbai – where for three centuries 500,000 people have lived in a unified, fluid system of thatched huts – than to the historical European city centers, which are rigid, fragile, and untouchable.

The architectural links we have spoken of correspond to the idea of a constructive, reversible, and traversable system, perennially incomplete and imperfect, but adapted to contain a space made up of networks, services, and relations, thus always open to transformation over time.

Genetic Tales
Andrea Branzi, 1998

//

This Catalog contains (almost) every type of human creature present on the earth at the end of the millennium.
If you notice that someone is missing, you can insert him or her yourself.
The catalog is an illustrated atlas of genetics; starting from the couple, it explains how crowds take shape.
It is divided into the following chapters:
Couples: wherein the immediate effects of the procreative activities of two subjects can be seen;
Families: consisting in an extension of the original couple;
Family Trees: useful to clarify the lines of succession of a given family;
Groups: composed of numerous individuals who come together for different reasons;
Crowds: masses of individuals making up humanity;
General Catalog, of different human types:
according to their similarity, affinity and closeness.
The catalog can be used to classify strangers or to identify friends.
Keep it handy.

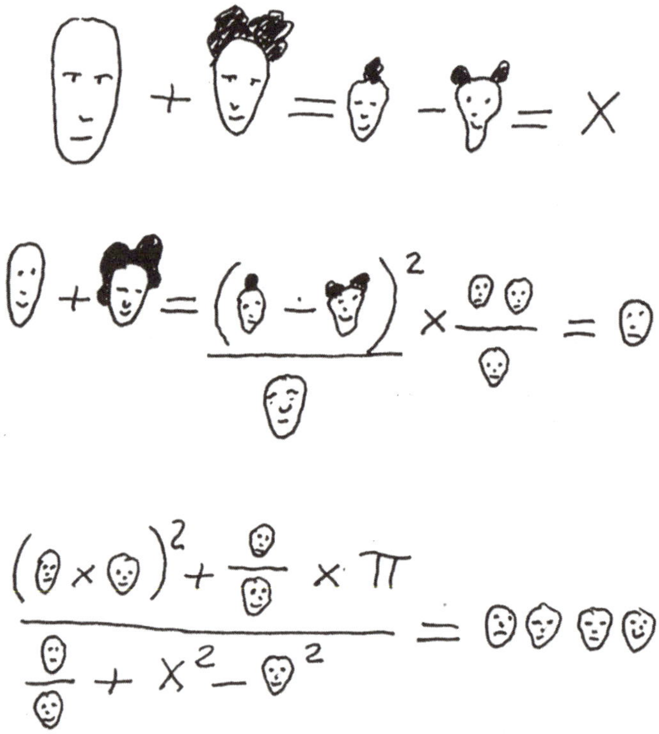

B
THE METROPOLIS AS SECOND NATURE

The Solid Side: Agronica
Andrea Branzi, 1995

//

**Project: Andrea Branzi, Dante Donegani, Antonio Petrillo, Claudia Raimondo with Tamar Ben David, Agronica, 1995
Domus Academy**

Agronica. An Incomplete Utopia

Agronica is a theoretical and design reflection within the framework of the end of the project's unity.

So, if there were positive utopias (*Ville Radieuse*) and critical utopias (*No-Stop City*), there are also incomplete utopias (*Agronica*). Incomplete utopias because they are destined not to produce global models of cities, but only (conflicting) parts of these.

The city is a set of conflicting logics, and as such, it cannot be resolved, but is only manageable within a stratification of planes in contrast with each other and, therefore, in an unstable equilibrium.

When we talk about the fall of the project, we mean that urban planning is divided according to an opposite logic: projects of the metropolis, cities, small towns, villages. These realities are not destined to disappear in the process of the fatal transformation of the village into metropolis: the village will remain village, and so will the cities or small towns. Thus, different projects for different urban places.

But it is not enough; if there is still unity between technology and urban image in the village, this unity no longer exists within the metropolis. Within the metropolis, buildings, urban signs, and interior design correspond to projects, technologies, and separate logics that cannot be traced back to any unity.

Agronica is a partial utopia because it is placed as "part" of the existing, next to it and not in place of it. It designs a part of the territory next to the metropolis, the city, and the existing village alongside the traditional road system and the existing goods market.

Agronica elaborates a further model of urbanization never explored, which consists of a weak system that guarantees the survival of the agricultural and natural landscape, in the presence of evolved but no longer all-encompassing urban services.

It, therefore, tends to overcome the old conflict between city and countryside through innovative mediation, in the certainty that these two realities correspond to sclerotic concepts that are not able to divide the world.

Agronica, as an incomplete utopia, is not based on the advent of new technologies (which also exist), but on the will to go beyond the boredom generated by the old question of the uniqueness of the place identity and the unity of the project.

A Model of Weak Urbanization

In the previous phase of the Industrial Revolution, a strong correlation between the constructive solutions, the territorial morphology, and the organization of activities was maintained: the factory, the office, and the networks had their own expressive form determined by the constraints of technical and functional organization.

This correspondence is no longer necessary. The different settlement realities reproduce codes that are only citations of self-referential morphologies that no longer have any real relationship with the activities that take place in them.
All the functions and works that take place in an office building, university, or industrial laboratory could be carried out in a group of farmhouses or in a disused thermoelectric power plant.

Therefore, seven statements are enunciated:

1. Separation between technology and form

There is no longer a correspondence between construction technologies and the form of the artifacts (urban and of use).

If there was once a close relationship between mechanics and objects, today there is no longer a direct relationship between electronics and the form of products derived from it.

2. Separation between function and form

The electronic instrumentation allows us to perform the same functions in every place.

The places lose their functional identity altogether.

The function of the places no longer corresponds to a visible stylistic code (home, office, factory), but to a software that changes the use of places, a program on the net that specializes the activities in real time.

3. Weak urban planning

Urban planning still pursues the objective of matching physical and functional models. The very word "plan" is the illusion of being able to create a system of analogies transferring the multiplicity of structural metropolitan dimensions onto a single level.

On the contrary, today's territory is a sum of physical and virtual places independent of each other and responding to different organizational logics, constantly interpenetrating and re-adapting. All this makes the metropolis an environment full of functions, but without syntax and structure.

The terms and grammars that are still used to describe the metropolis (center/periphery, residence/work, houses/infrastructures, living spaces/links) are remnants of previous realities (the military city, the industrial city, etc.). What we consider the physical form of cities are thickenings, sutures, and concretions of antecedent tissues that have been lacerated and dissolved.

In a new building, without historical pre-existences to refer to, the current functional density would not correspond to any physical image, any reference model. This is the design diagram of the informal metropolis of the Third World.

A trace of this new structure of the city can be found in the traditional conception of the Japanese city, where the distinction between city and countryside does not have a precise definition.

In the ideogram of the city (*machi*), both the rice field (*ta*) and the agglomerate of houses (*cho*) are represented, and similarly in the closest term to our concept of countryside, *inaka*, the rice paddy and the house (*sha*) appear again, in this case divided into two ideograms.

Also in the ideogram that defines the village walls, trees (*ki*) and an ancient measurement (*sun*) are represented, focusing on the village intended not as a grouping of buildings, but as a controlled territorial system. It could, therefore, be said that Edo, the ancient Tokyo, was an example of weak urbanization, with the rice paddies that extended up to the walls of the castle of the shogun, interspersed with houses, markets, centers of handicraft production, and districts of pleasure.

4. Living is a shopper

The dissolution between form and organization must be considered positively.

The urbanized territory is no longer a geometric landscape made up of valleys or constructive orders, a recognizable physiognomy like those that appear in the backgrounds of Renaissance paintings. The entire metropolitan reality has become an immense supermarket of existential offerings, in which everyone goes shopping and fills their needs with different product choices.

The morphological order of the territory no longer represents its structure, the framework on which the different organizational processes of metropolitan life find a place, but is one of the physical levels of what is offered, a system of perceptual stimulation such as advertising, the faces and bodies of people, the pulsations of telephone and television transmissions via the ether.

5. Virtual metropolis and natural metropolis

With the evolution of the metropolis, the end of mass society has been consumed. Television broadcasting is the last of the frames: an information system that still guarantees universality of news and coincidence of phenomena.

With interactive television, we will definitely be dispersed in hypertexts in which the meetings will be random. Living in these virtual spaces opens up, however, the possibility of pacifying the physical economy of relations with nature.

The form of settlement should no longer be the expression of a social design, a level in which the strategies of identity and regulation of cultural life models are manifested (the form of work, the structure of the family, etc.). Its definition can be a function of the interaction of the human species with the environment, in which the constructive models that emerge will have a relationship not so much with the social choices as with the technical and ecological balances that the natural and artificial circuits can to establish from time to time.

6. Weak urbanization

In this global re-articulation, the same historical utterances of a city or country lose their meaning.

The settlement technologies are now part of territorial metabolic systems, in which the functions disintegrate and re-articulate according to previously unimaginable combinations (coincidence of production and consumption of food products, residential spaces interspersed with agricultural or research activities, technique at the service of transport and residence, etc.).

The metropolis no longer corresponds to the concentration of goods, technologies, and information. It corresponds to a weak urbanization model, which also coincides with the highest level of available technologies, which is the "symbiotic" one.

7. The vineyard does not represent wine

The horizon of aesthetic quality changes.

Agronica coincides with the end of domestic composition as the exaltation of a place, a microcosm in which to realize and reproduce all the qualities offered by a production system. Living becomes a dispersed pleasure, joining the surface of the territory.

Until today, the project culture has worked on the relationship between architecture and industry (modernity), in the certainty of a symbolic value of the latter; in the relationship between architecture and communication (post-modernity), in the certainty of a symbolic value also of the latter.

Agronica proposes working in the relationship between architecture and agriculture, in the certainty of the absence of a symbolic value of the latter.

The vineyard does not represent wine.

Andrea Branzi, Dante Donegani, Antonio Petrillo, Claudia Raimondo
with Tamar Ben David
Agronica, the Symbiotic Metropolis, Domus Academy, 1995

Three Theorems for an Ecology of the Artificial World
Andrea Branzi, 1990

//

Project: Andrea Branzi, Italo Rota, Ronan and Erwan Bouroullec, *Virgilian Park*, 2004

When we speak of ecology, of a new relationship between man and artificial and natural environments, we are doing nothing more than indicating in improper terms a vast cultural and political problem of historical dimensions. This problem is presented nowadays in the form of a search for a "balanced" model of development; but tomorrow it will take on the unexpected dimensions of an industrial and social mega-system that has lost not only its own internal model of development, but also its external model of alternatives.

By the collapse of the external alternative model, I am indicating the collapse of the myth and the hope that could be proposed and achieved in a social and technological world that is radically different from the existing world.

For the first time, we find ourselves operating within the context of a system that possesses physical boundaries – beyond which lies environmental catastrophe – as well as political boundaries, beyond which lie social failure and dictatorship.

This condition does not console us, nor does is strengthen us, because the contradictions of the system remain, along with the system's injustice; and they are no longer destined to be transformed into ideological energy, and into political struggle, but more likely into pure, cold violence, into devastating energy, which will demolish from within the shapes and modes of Western society.

The choice that we must make is still the same as always: does the system have a destination? If not, how can it make any basic choices? Is the only possible criterion respect for nature?

In fact, in the absence of a reform-oriented design of broad sweep, that is new and is based on cultural and ecological fundamentals, there is the risk of transforming design as well into a discipline that is devoted to producing unprecedented, strange, or useless objects, devoid of a long-term strategy with broad horizons and great utopias, and which will therefore be useless to manufactures as well, just like what we see happening to a great portion of European architecture, which is devoted to saving the "specific aspects of the discipline," its own historical continuity, good composition – while remaining incapable of analyzing the transformations of the post-industrial metropolis, and therefore of understanding in what world it lives and in what direction it should move.

The ability to imagine a different and better world is not merely a useless fantasy; this creative capacity also accounts for the system's capacity to grow, to develop, and to produce new qualities.

In a highly industrialized system such as our own, in which it seems that everything has already been designed, already manufactured, already offered, where the basic necessities of man and the most sophisticated requirements have already received an exhaustive and well-articulated response, the spaces that can accommodate new products and new design exist only in the territories of imagination, in the ability to dream of a better world than the one that exists.

And this is the role that design is to play – therefore, a role that is central to the imagination of society, as well as that of industry. The great architects were not the great composers, but those who were capable of developing a more vast cultural project than architecture alone, to which architecture was summoned to bear witness, to serve as a tool of prefiguring.

But no one can dream of replacing the rich and complex ethical cathedral that was erected by reform-oriented culture with a design that works upon a model typical of a service-industry company, ready to solve in the most straightforward manner all of the industrial problems that are set before it.

The role of design, rather, is to open new problems for industry; to push it to propose new profound qualities, to create a more advanced ecological equilibrium between man and the artificial environment.

And if the century of the avant-garde movements and of revolutions is coming to a close, a century of true, in-depth transformations is about to begin, and these are the most difficult and perhaps the most dangerous.

When we speak, therefore, of an ecology of the artificial world, we are not speaking only about the possibility of producing ecologic products – we are indicating, rather, the possibility of detecting new settings and new horizons of meaning for the activity of design.

No intellectual could have imagined that, at the end of the century and of the millennium, the industrial landscape would have attained this level of complexity.

The rationalists of the Modern Movement believed that all of the processes of industrialization would have produced a physical and socially ordered world, based upon a single logic and a unification of a languages and technologies. The effort they made was to attain, through industry, this order.

In the post-industrial Metropolis, everything is hybrid, every object and every site makes sense in that it is different and an alternative to all that which surrounds it.

But it is from this multiform and complex reality that the problems emerge which we are discussing today – the numerous voices produce an indecipherable sound, the many colors produce grey, just as the many alternatives are summed up in a "generic" supply.

This is the Cold Metropolis which we are facing - a highly complex and differentiated system that, *de facto*, as we have said, produces its own substantial standardization; everything, in order to be different from everything else, produces a homogeneous reality, made up of the sum of apparent diversities, whose total is zero.

The only true differences, in the Cold Metropolis, are ethical differences, the only ones that give us new perceptive and selective capacities. Ethical qualities this become the only compasses that can help us to find our bearing in the context of the hyper-supply of such complex industrial system.

The search for a secular and progressive ecology of the artificial world is set within the context of this debate. The ecology, therefore, problematic and dynamic as it is, is based upon three great humanistic theorems.

1. We will call the first theorem "ecology of complexity." It derives from the observation that, like in nature, the artificial environment that surrounds us is made up of a polycentric and extremely differentiated logic.

In the metropolitan environment manufacturing and technological systems which are apparently in contrast one with another coexist and balance each other out.

This diversity constitutes a positive value; this complexity is an anthropological condition to be managed, not to be eliminated. Design must cease waging war in favor of a designable standardization of the world – the environment cannot be encapsulated and contained in a design. It is, rather, a set of different designs and different destinies. This is a positive factor; this is the richness of the home of man.

We must therefore work to find the correct provisional and experimental environmental equilibrium, amidst these different technological and manufacturing principles,in accordance with a rich and exciting vision of the artificial environment.

2. We will call the second theorem that of "design ecology." It sets out from the observation that, like with nature, man establishes with artificial objects a relationship does not ever consist exclusively of technical and ergonomic functionality; rather, it is enriched with fundamental symbolic, literary, emotional, and psychological components. This complexity of relations is a positive value, a wealth to be developed and not to be battled against.

The culture of design, therefore, is faced with the challenge of creating a rich interface between man and the artificial world; an interface that is not only functional and technical, but also capable of producing emotions, narrations, and profound qualities.

In order to achieve this result, it is necessary for design to renew its sensibilities, its methods of planning, its languages. The important thing is the result that we wish to achieve, not the methodologies that should be respected.

Andrea Branzi, Italo Rota, Ronan and Erwan Boroullec, *Virgilian Park*, 2004

3. The third and final theorem can be dubbed the "ecology of relations." It derives from the observation that, just like toward nature, man today must reconstruct a balanced relationship with the human environment, that is, with his neighbors. The processes of industrial automation are producing an enormous emigration of the working population from large and small factories to the service industry, trade, within the heart of the post-industrial metropolis. This historical human emigration, which remains to be analyzed, produces the effect of an extremely dense environment of human interfaces.

The basis of our Western education, always aimed at the substance of things and relationship, and never at their form (always considered secondary and false), become dangerous in a society in which the environment will increasingly be characterized by the quality of the person that work in it, and by their capacity to relate with others, without transmitting neuroses and violence. And so we see that the ecology of human relations, that is, the capacity to determinate new codes of interpersonal behavior, will become one of the major themes in the culture of design.

The old ergonomics, entirely devoted to solving dimensional problems, and proxemics, which works to describe the territorial spaces that pertain to an individual, must grow into a new area of research, devoted to defining the modes and forms of a new behavioral science that will allow us to deal with the metropolitan future, without the risk of a collapse due to an uncontrolled excess of human contacts.

The rapid deterioration of our Western environment certainly is a result of the crisis of values and ethical traditions, but also of culture's failure to establish a gentle ecology of human relations.

And so we see today that the ecologists themselves propose new natural qualities, but in fact they operate in an antisocial funk, and social work extends as an opposition culture. What I am chiefly interested in, on the other hand, is using the art of design to create objects that speak to a different, non-aggressive code of values that respect man and his delicate nature. A design that is committed to a Dolce Stil Novo, capable of building a livable house, once again.

Architecture and Agriculture

Andrea Branzi, 2006

//

Project: Andrea Branzi, *Architecture and Agriculture*, 2005

The architecture of the twentieth century stabilized a preferential axis with the world of industry, adopting its morphologies and construction technologies. (...) This alliance also included the idea of the factory as a concentrated, closed place with respect to the city, as a strong presence of modernization, a place in which definitive choices based on productive reason were made. So the factory, as Zygmunt Bauman would say, is viewed as a place of reconstruction of the solid bodies of modernity.

Virtual products, "informationized" markets, and global construction processes have all transformed the market into a multimedia system where the physicality of the product is a little part of a vast system of relations and services. In this more fluid, more articulated world the factory no longer expresses the centrality of organized work, but is instead an accessory presence, a backstage of the market that is usually best hidden and sometimes best shipped abroad to distant countries. (...)

A large part of mass entrepreneurship and the diffuse research we have spoken of was developed in districts, or produced new districts. The self-branding of the new economy is a typical phenomenon in a regime organized by district, where each subject produces business and wealth, beginning with its own ability to create innovation.

In this context, it is the territory that becomes the privileged protagonist of the post-industrial economy, acting as a place for working out the weak and diffuse emerges of a powder fine productivity, which perfectly matches the powder fine and ever-changing reality of the market.

The concentrated city and locked-down factory, in the end, become a difficult-to-manage reality because they are both too rigid; only when placed in a context of districts that provide an articulated support and different specialties can the city and factory successfully become a reality adequate and appropriate for the global markets. (...)

These new productive orders have many similarities with the territorial systems of modern agriculture: both are diffuse systems, which correspond to a constructive energy fed by the weak energies of nature, the climate, and genetics. This agriculture is no longer tied to traditional techniques, and is able to use symbiotic technology to intervene in large territories, transforming them into flexible systems of food production. The agricultural enterprise is now, according to management theorist, a self-balancing productive organism, regulated by seasonal cycles, fed by natural energies, and able to spontaneously produce diversified series of edible and biodegradable products.

The diversified series actually originated in nature: a grouping of one million apples is always made up of single apples, one different from the next.

In nature, the same form, same leaf, or same apple is never repeated twice. Natural technology is therefore becoming the most sophisticated construction model to which industrial technology looks while seeking to imitate its cycles and services. The artificial world, born in order to substitute an inadequate natural world, is rediscovering nature as an unparalleled realm of technology, as having an extraordinary ability to produce materials, products, eco-compatible services, feeding on the weak and diffuse technologies of nature in whole regions.

Agricultural industrial civilization creates a horizontal landscape, without cathedrals traversable and reversible: the turnover of crops allows the management of the agricultural landscape following a transitory logic, which adjusts to the productive equilibrium of the terrain, the passage of seasons, and the market. Because of these combined motives contemporary architecture should begin to look at modern agriculture as a reality with which new strategic relations can be made.

This is an architecture that completely renews its model of reference, confronting the challenge of a liquid modernity. New relations can be established with a culture such as the agricultural one, which is not a constructive culture in the traditional sense, but is productive in enzymatic terms, and which follows bio-compatible logic and uses highly evolved supporting technologies.

This design hypothesis is set within a less rigid, absolute way of understanding the transformational forces o the city.

An Ecology of the Artificial

Andrea Branzi, 1988

//

Project: Andrea Branzi, *Residential Agriculture*, 2005

What is required of design today is the creation of a new ecology of the artificial universe. The form of industrial objects, the ergonomic way in which they function, the interface with electronic technology, and the identity of new materials are no more than different aspects of a great theorem concerning the relationship of humanity with the artificial world that surrounds it. All the functional aspects of the objects coexist with their cultural dimension.

We are moving in the direction of an impassioned an d vigorous kind of design which, applied to segments of reality and to individual objects, is capable of stirring up lively emotional reactions in the consumer. This wealth of sensations and feelings has to fit into a gamut of natural and almost spontaneous patterns of behavior in human beings (assuming that spontaneity and naturalness actually exist). This is why we speak of techno-ecology.

The new electronic technology and the structure of postindustrial culture have given a slight twist to the project. This twist, which may not yet have been clearly grasped or given a theoretical underpinning, has gradually and gently (in conformity with the new style) brought to a close the era of the Avante-garde movements and their powerful and all-embracing grip on design.

The age of technological trauma is over. This age, which was actually controlled by the avant-garde, sought to turn those traumas into potential values and new cultural frontiers.(...) A new alliance is being formed between industry and culture (involving design as well), in which the designer is no longer just required to collaborate with industrial culture in matters of form but also has to devise a natural interface between man and the new technology. Culture is creating new areas of production – theoretical, fictional, and literary areas, the only ones in which there is still room for industry to grow. Such areas exist in natural continuity with man and his imagery. Electronics does not require a new anthropology. It is a technology of service that does not produce an invasion of human space in the way that mechanics does. It produces information in real time, synthesizes logical processes and cuts down on the mechanisms of productive labor in accordance with a logic that appears strikingly similar to that of human physiology.

Hence the nature of man is no longer an impediment to technological development but almost its indispensable premise. The way in which electronics works is undermining the classic instruments of rationality and strengthening those of the senses and intuition. If we look at the internal mechanism of a mechanical clock we can understand, through attentive use of the eye, the dynamics of its function. It is sufficient for there to be light (in the sense of enlightenment) and a great deal of attention, and everything is comprehensible and objective. If we look at the works of an electronic clock, the eye and enlightenment are no longer of any use to us. The clock has the appearance of a set of microorganisms wired together, producing information in an incomprehensible fashion. The underlying dynamics and energy of the electronic system remain a mystery to us, similar in nature to the animal or plant but profoundly different from the artificial world of mechanics. This similarity in modes of functioning results in a sort of mimesis. The human being experiences the electronic instrument, with its silent operation and prompt response, as an extension of is own organism. It is a reality with which he can hold an almost spontaneous dialogue, putting questions and receiving answers (this is very important) in the same language.

The physical and spiritual trauma brought about by man's contact with the great technologies of change is diminishing. In its place is developing a sort of logical union between man and his computers. At times this union is so profound as to be embarrassing. No longer does he need to interiorize the mixer, or adjust to these new and artificial situations by changing his own internal way of thinking. The machine adapts to him. We know this impression is not entirely accurate. The man who moves his fingers over the keyboard of the computer is the late twentieth-century man, who has already undergone profound changes on the behavioral and psychological level. Thus the concept of naturalness mentioned in connection with electronic technology is a relative one. In spite of this, the strategy underlying the rapport between man and machine has shifted, in the direction described, and in any case the reality of the exchange is far less traumatic in its effects.

Wood of Architecture
Andrea Branzi, 2016

///

Project: Andrea Branzi, *Wood of Architecture*, 2016

This design is part of a research project that, over time, has had several titles, from weak urbanization to "abstract" architecture, in the sense that it is aimed at identifying "functionoids," i.e. the organisms that do not have a specific function or a determined perimeter, more similar to a territory than to a building, and which offer a discontinuous kind of protection.

This type of anti-compositional and anti-typological architecture, of a low level of identity and specialization, corresponds to a time when the difference between internal and external spaces disappeared; where the functions change over time, and the city is no longer just a set of architectural boxes but rather an experiential territory, where the quality of the space no longer depends on the form of the buildings, but on intangible experiences, on the goods that are purchased, on the relationships that can be established, and on the information that circulates.

This type of research is not intended to be realized immediately, but rather it develops theorems that, like in theoretical physics, are intended for the long term and for renewing the iconographic repertoire on which architecture is based. Abstract architecture is not an abstract project but a gesture of realism with respect to a world that already today is abstract, that is to say, devoid of a recognizable form and a representable function.

Andrea Branzi, *Bosco di Architettura, Wood of Architecture*, 2007

Andrea Branzi, *Architettura e agricoltura*, *Architecture and Agriculture*, 2005

Andrea Branzi, *Agricoltura residenziale, Residential Agriculture*, 2007

C
THE REVERSIBLE METROPOLIS

Andrea Branzi with Ernesto Bartolini and Lapo Lani
Favela High Tech
Masterplan Eindhoven, Philips Design, 2000

Reversible Urbanism
Andrea Branzi, 2016

//

In history, everything changes; great empires become scattered ruins, unrecognizable fragments. In the present everything changes, without any given direction. We continue to live, immersed in semi-darkness with no sign of the horizon, in a neo-prehistory where we are uncertain of the significance or the direction in which we are going.

Yet in this world where everything is temporary, the tracks of ancient chariots have continued to mark our land for thousands of years: Via Flaminia, Aurelia, Cassia, Ardeatina, Appia, Via Emilia, Clodia, Salaria, Tiburtina, Nomentana, Collatina, Prenestina – they are like indelible scars that sink into the fields, the woods, the Apennines. Around these streets made of rocks and stones, the tracks of herds, the impressions of both animals and humans having brushed through the grass like a net through sand, remain eternal.

Therefore, the streets, the paths, or the trails are the only pieces of evidence to traverse time; at one time they connected towns and villages, which no longer exist. These ancient paths, whose wayfarers are all dead, represent the only possibility of eternal memory. This system of roads on which the paths of our cities and our countryside are drawn - so indelible and widespread - is somewhat discordant with regard to our current standard of living and designing; like an ultimate foundation that draws eternal perimeters, it seems like the legacy of an alien civilization that is no longer our own.

Yet today the technology exists to build roads, bridges, and reversible infrastructure, which is easily put up and taken down. It is this type of infrastructure that was implemented during the Second World War as a strategy for invasion or temporary repositioning. Bridges, airports, canals, depots, etc., all transportable and dismantlable without leaving a trace behind. It is so similar to our way of life, the way in which we act as protagonists in a story where everything is provisional, uncertain, and reversible.

Current technology also makes it possible to separate the urban tracks from the large rings of bypasses via suspension bridges that hang above the congestion of the territories. Like gliders that trace suspended paths through the sky, from which to descend towards drawbridges that open and close without welding themselves to the ground.

The era of reversible urbanization is within our reach, saving the land from the eternal system of road layouts. However, environmentalists ignore this type of reversible infrastructure that is already produced industrially, because they unconsciously reject all that represents progressive construction, preferring a verbal, exhortative preaching in order to achieve a cleaner world, but that is attainable through punitive processes. They do not want to reduce energy consumption by 10%, but to reduce global energy consumption to 10%; a goal that is unachievable without pushing our civilization backwards to a primordial level, towards a sort of genocide that would reduce the seven billion people alive today to just 10% of that.

Reversible urbanism and its realization remains hidden in the acidic folds of a social moralism that actually freezes all possible solutions.

Andrea Branzi, *Strade leggere*, Light Streets, 2010

Andrea Branzi, *Cielo e Terra, Sky and Earth*, 2010

Andrea Branzi with Ernesto Bartolini and Lapo Lani
Favela High Tech, Masterplan, Eindhoven for Philips Design, 2000

D

THE SENSORIAL METROPOLIS

The Sensorial Revolution

Andrea Branzi, 2006

//

In the future there will be a large growth in human ability to produce and consume imaginative and immaterial goods. The result of this growth cannot be reached through social, technological, or cultural change; rather it will be reached through sensorial change.

For some time a silent but radical Sensorial Revolution has been occurring. When we speak of Sensorial Revolution, we mean sort of genetic mutation that the advent of new media has produced (or is producing) in society.

For the rationalist culture of the Modern Movement, "understanding" reality was more important than "perceiving" it, analyzing it through its elementary components, discovering its dynamic mechanisms, and never stopping at the surface. Those who did not know how to lead these in the right direction were "fooled by the senses"; they were inferior, untrustworthy, and substantially obscure perceptive instruments. They provided accessory, intuitive, superficial, and therefore substantially misleading information.

At the end of the Sixties an immense haste for information and stimuli to determine that which we call Sensorial Revolution developed, and consisted in an unchecked growth of sensorial information and consequent development of all the perceptive sensitivities of man. This great informational, musical, and behavioral sensitivity is based on a new perceptive hierarchy: the senses are no longer a simple instrument that transmits inert information to reason, which only reason can then transform into organized conscience. The senses have become a refined, vibrating, cognitive instrument reality and an element of he individual's political formation.

The reality produced by music, fashion, and social behaviors, but also by electronics and new materials, is a reality of surfaces, which imposes a knowledge of surfaces. If modern man's sensitivity was analytical and mechanics, that of contemporary man is synthetic, electronica, and resonant.

The Sensorial Revolution displaces some of the old codes in order to introduce new ones; it does not produce a new vanguard. It is rather a mater of a series of filters, additional lenses, and sonorous amplifiers that tend to revisit a world of absolute immediacy. This is not a spontaneous, simple world; quite the contrary, it is an extremely sophisticated universe, where, however, there no longer exist a critical and ideological distance between man and the phenomena that surround him.

The perceptive ability capable of instinctively choosing useful elements of the complex stratification of informational fabric that reaches the individual through space is growing. This new "auditory ability" that the metropolitan inhabitant is developing consists in the integrated use of all the perceptive abilities of the body: we could paradoxically say that he sees through touch, listens with the eyes, and smells with the ears. In the sense that all messages, real or virtual, that he receives imply a whole, sensorial deciphering. A film on television is not only a question of seeing and hearing; it moves an appreciation and secret connections of other senses, like touch, smell and taste. On this mechanism all advertisements produce sensorial short circuits: a color smells, a brand scratches, a sign makes sound.

The eye was the illuminist symbol in the mechanical age, when a glance allowed a deep inquiry into the logic of reality's movement, similar to that of a large clock.

The hand was Le Corbusier's symbol that, through Le Modulor, gave the modern world a chance to recover a human dimension in the act of making.

The symbol of man in the post-industrial world now is the ear, that strange, enigmatic organ perennially open to the outside, and within which simultaneously millions of complex information bits are input, allowing us to perceive within the great soundtrack of the metropolis the light hum of the computer, a bird's song, or the sound of a jingle.

The ear represents quite will the Sensorial Revolution, where "understanding" the internal mechanism phenomena no longer counts, rather "perceiving" the effects of these mechanisms, choosing the sounds and information, transforming into culture the grey mass of sounds present in space.

We are in contact with these sounds; we are not in contact with who and what produced them. Only war, the voice of human tragedy, the important music of our culture reaches us, but it is the ear that chooses and finds them mixed amid all the slag and useless choruses floating around space, transforming them into political sensations, emotions, and anguish.

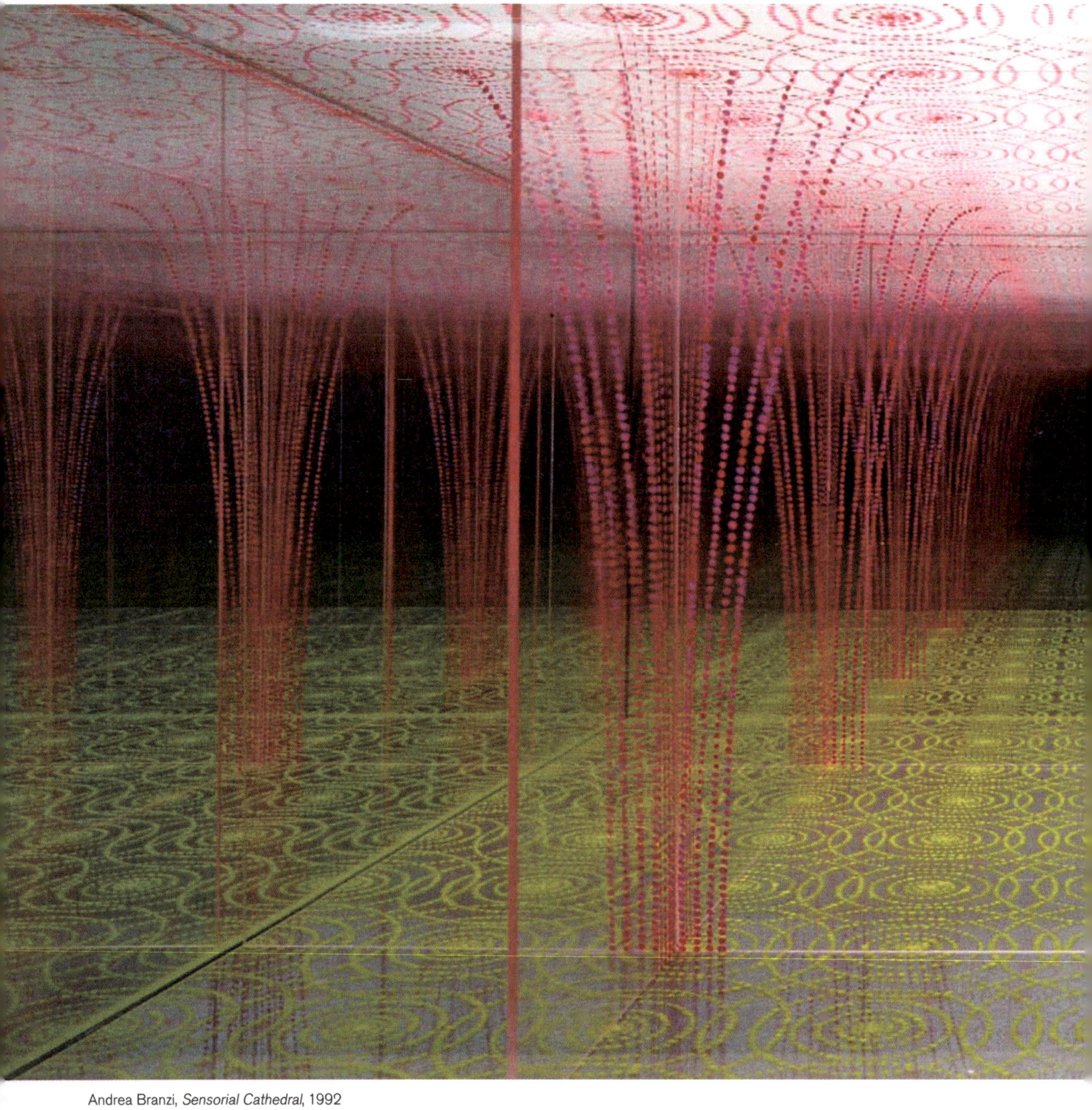

Andrea Branzi, *Sensorial Cathedral*, 1992

One single view of the world is no longer enough if there is not any sound information to act as its key: do those imagines come from a film, or are they real sense from the Gulf War? Is the chase of those traffickers function or a scene from Bolivia?

We listen, and we will understand.

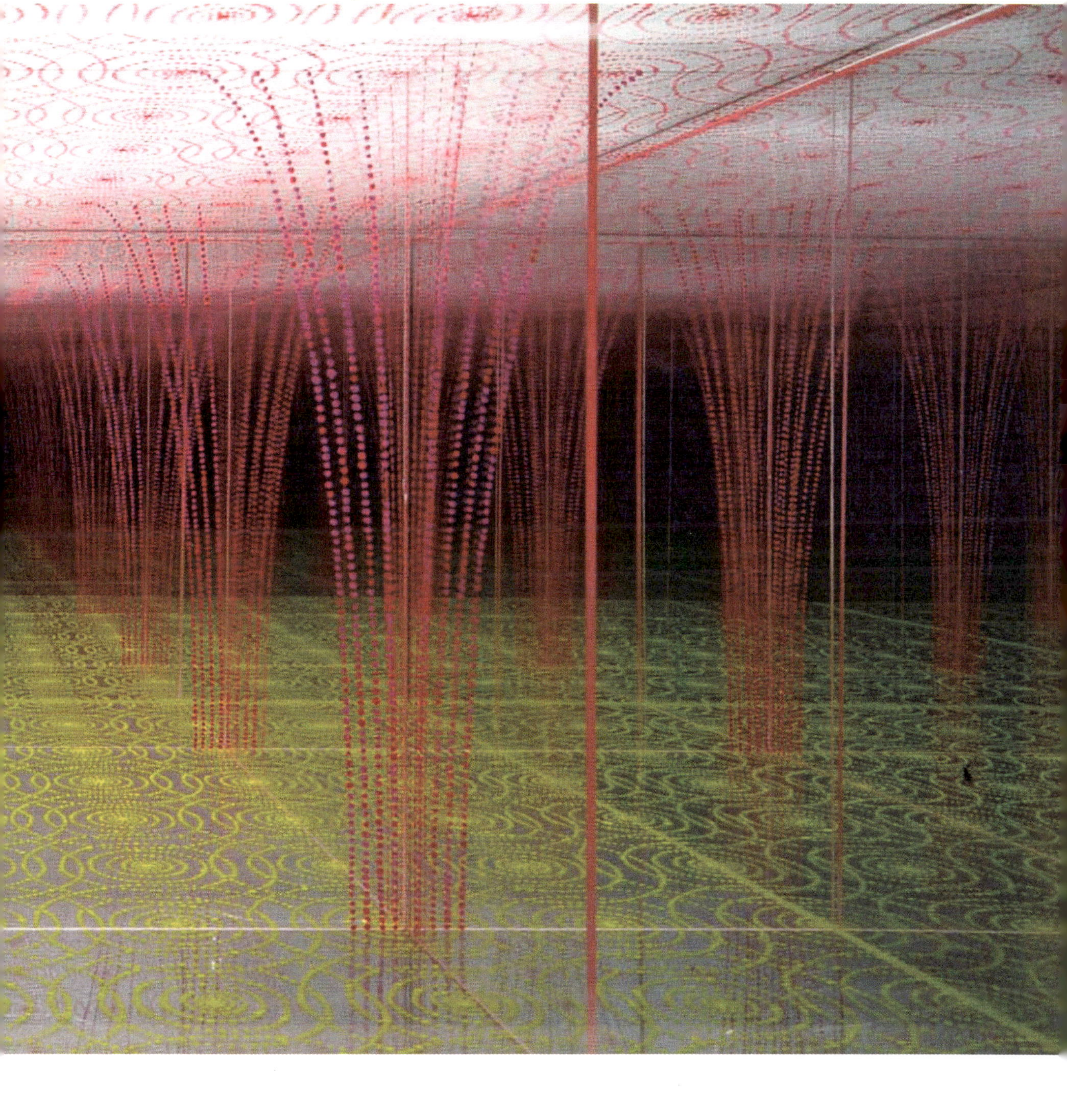

Andrea Branzi, *Enzymatic Territory*, 2006

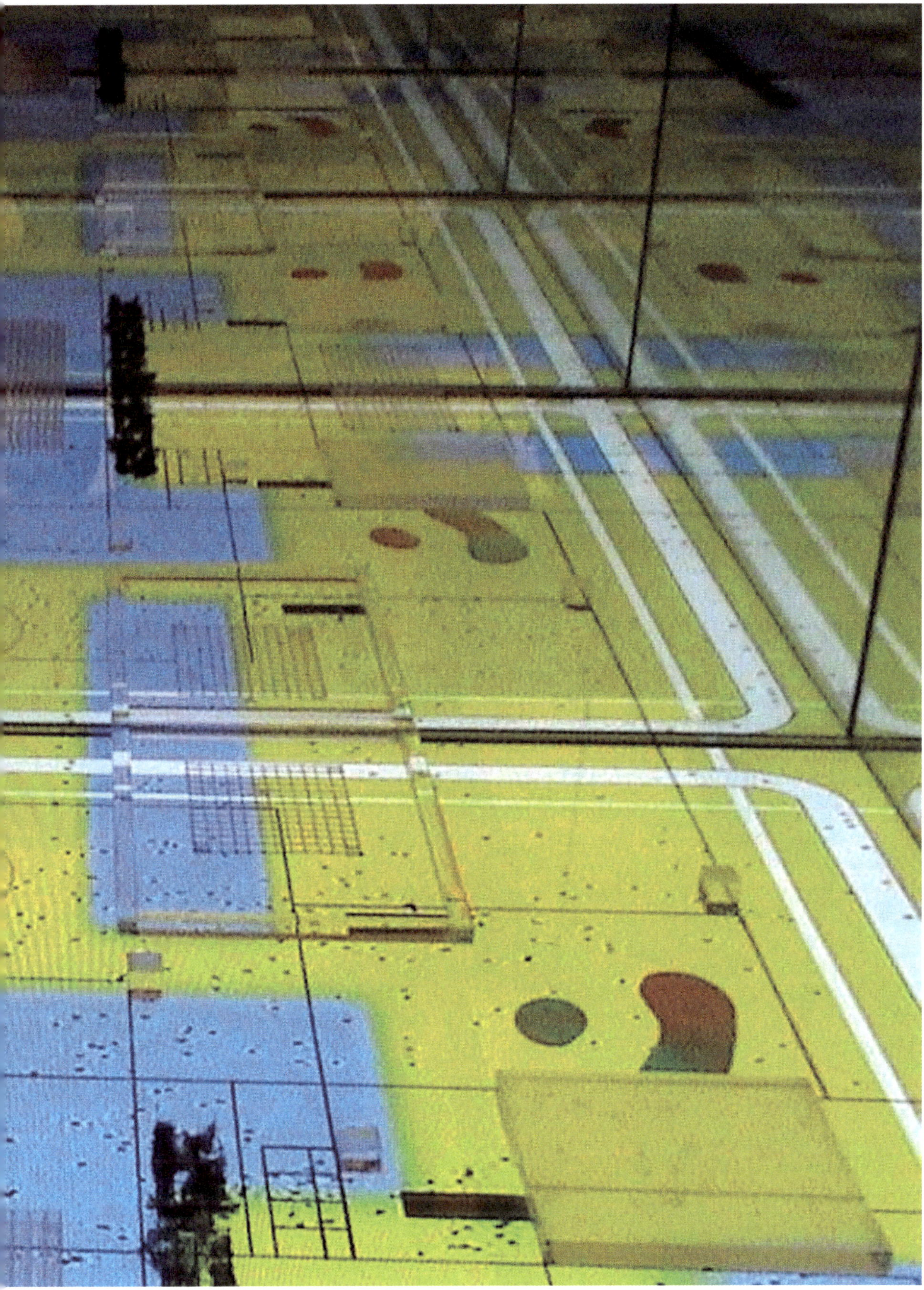

Andrea Branzi, *Models of Wet Urbanization*, Expo Saragoza, 2008

E
THE METROPOLIS OF COMMODITIES

The Object as New Urban Subject

Andrea Branzi
The Metropolis of Commodities (or *The Real City*), 2010

Houses and other Things
Andrea Branzi, 1988

//

Today the gap that separates architecture and design no longer consists of mere professional differences - that architects design houses and the others design objects or that the objects have become so important and intrusive that they have pushed the whole architectural scene onto the sidelines.
There is a profound difference in method and in strategy between the two disciplines.

At present European architecture is in a state of deep crisis, arising out of an erroneous attitude toward the process of design. When confronted with the external difficulties architecture encounters in the postindustrial world, it has been unable to refrain from taking a defensive, reactionary position to project "what is specific to architecture," without making any move toward an acceptance of the real situation. Its failure to grasp the change in historical circumstances has meant that it has been unable to draw on the extraordinary source of positive energy that has been opened up for design.

Architectural culture in Europe has been concerned primarily with defending architecture as such, thereby rendering it impervious to innovation. This is due to the mistaken belief that architecture represents an institutional asset that must not be brought into question. The results have been redundant and useless thoughts and constructions that have been poured, without any figurative force, into the meat grinder of reality.

At this moment, European architecture has nothing of real interest to offer, whether in technical, urban, or human terms. It has faced the crisis in classic modernity some ten years later than design, and it has done so in the wrong way.

The Postmodern movement, in fact, thought that it could be able to handle the crisis is faced by modifying its formal languages, by forcing the physical presence of architecture onto the city, and by seeking to define this discipline as the most mature product of history, without apprehending the necessity and the opportunity for a more sweeping process of self examination.

European culture has failed to understand that the increasingly superfluous character of architecture in the metropolis was not the consequence of a momentary crisis but the outcome of a complex shift in the lines along which reality takes shape. It has not grasped that the deterioration of its linguistic heritage could not be halted by drawing indiscriminately on historical codes but that it had to deal with the new codes of current social structure, codes that are perhaps less lofty but certainly more vital.

Equally it has not understood that its appeal to history placed it outside the framework of history itself and in conflict with the technology, symbols, patterns of behavior, and dreams of the present day. Refusing to look at the world, it has shut itself up within the universities, turning into an academic discipline based entirely on the power of education; that is to say, on self-reproduction.

Judging by the exhibitions of the last few years, European architecture also seems to have renounced its final, extreme moment of nobility, represented by the architecture of the drawing-board, to accept even professional ugliness, as if it were an act of extreme realism. By doing so, it made a show of adapting to the existing situation. In reality, learned architecture found itself in an extremely frustrating situation. It was aware of being extraneous to any real process of change in the metropolis. But this situation, common to the whole of modern art (and which also constituted its grandeur and bore witness to its indispensability in anthropological terms), was perceived by European architecture as something disgraceful and shameful, a sin to be concealed by donning the mask of tragic drama or of the most trite and reactionary professionalism, opposed to innovation and change.

It has severely criticized the experiments of Nuovo Design, regarding them as abstraction, without comprehending the element of courage contained in the attempt to lay new foundations. It now finds itself carrying out far more abstract operations, without the seeds of its renascence at hand.

It has lost touch with the inner and behavioral needs of its consumer and with the physical quality of his domestic space, and strives to survive on the level of pure composition. It has given up any attempt to confront new forms of technology, and continues to put itself forward as its own material, as pure construction of a historical mode of thought.

Equally (and with justification), architects have criticized city planning and the policy of the development scheme, but by transforming the crisis in the planning of territory into an opportunity to take revenge on the planners. Today it finds itself having to operate within the urban revolution of postindustrial society without any kind of overall picture of the changes under way or any valid means of interpreting the situation.

Thus European architectural culture has experienced the brief period of senile happiness represented by the postmodern dreaming the impossible dream of Europe regaining its central position in the world (and architecture with it). It is now left alone and dismayed, stretched out on one of Portoghesi's couches, unable to decide which window to jump out. The heart of the matter is this unlike design, contemporary architecture has refused to carry out a serious and redeeming analysis of its own epistemological crisis, and has therefore failed to join forces with currents more vital than its own. It has ignored movements in design that are taking new, powerful social and cultural needs into account, movements that might have involved architecture in more forceful and less theoretical constructive mechanisms. In practice, European architecture has wasted twenty years in a reorganization of its power base. At the end of the eighties it is in a much graver situation than when the crisis in modernity actually began, possessing an authority that is merely academic and therefore extremely fragile, vulnerable to any attack from the outside and to any renewal, unequal to the demands made on it.

On the other hand the generation that has begun the long process of laying new foundations, taking design as its filed, has also chosen another strategy. They are starting over from the minimum threshold of the real, from the set of object and implements that surrounds man and that forms his most intimate and almost corporeal habitat. It is a habitat, as we have seen, that is almost beyond the scope of design, compromised by the processes of industrialization and by the habits of the consumer society, traversed by constant flows of information and violated by alien cultures. And yet it is from that nucleus of objects that a new relationship is emerging between man and the artificial world. Design has not been afraid getting its hands dirty with minor tasks; for twenty years it has been prepared to carry out complex linguistic and technological experimentation, managing in the end to get directly in touch with new environmental qualities, new materials, and new patterns of everyday behavior.

Design now finds itself in possession of an extraordinary wealth of perceptions, of new directions in design, and of a great range of expression; and just at the moment when the structural mutation of postindustrial society has been established, this great store of energy can start to pour back into the architectural project.

The generation of Nuovo Design must take possession of the great themes of architecture and the metropolis, for it is the only one that has the right tools for the design of reality, having accepted and plugged into it a long time ago.

The return to architecture does not mean adjusting to a game whose rules are already fixed, but it does signify prescribing new techniques of working first. It means constructing autonomous, imaginary territories, as we once did, delimiting and defending free areas of work that were often regarded as outright utopias by others, but which were in reality important laboratories fora general revision and re-foundation of the project: Global Tools in 1970, Primary Design in 1975, Alchymia in 1978, Memphis in 1980, Domus Academy in 1983, and Zabro in 1985. We shall do the same in architecture, working in total freedom and outside the straitjacket of university authority, grasping every opportunity, whether genuine or false, to repaint the scenery - discontinuous but feasible - of a new domestic and urban civilization.

Be careful though. It is not just a matter of changing scale, of replacing the object by the house. It is a matter of going on designing objects until the house and the city have been refashioned, for it is of objects that they are made. It is a question of designing the soft structures of metropolitan domesticity, the shells that contain them, the sensitive surfaces that divide up space, the odors and colors of the environment, and its territorial signals. New links of meaning have to be established, new areas of sensitivity introduced into the project and into the organization of human relationships. The new architecture is not born out of "architectural composition," but out of a new cultural, civil and artistic attitude.

When one speaks of redesigning a possible domestic scenery, this does not in fact mean new uniformity of places, technologies and languages. In point of fact I do not suggest that the new generations or the protagonists of Nuovo Design should bring their efforts to bear within an enclosed space, inside the building, as Walter Gropius did sixty years ago with the Bauhaus, when he proposed that the historical avant-garde movements be recycled in the industrial design of household articles. Rather we must face up to the discontinuity of the real and its violence, accepting the need to define a "nest" that will still be private, a sacred place to pass the night, a bordered carpet on which to reflect. In 1920 the aim of the Bauhaus was the acceptance of industrialism as a blessing and not a tragedy. Today the aim of a new architecture is the perpetual violation of space, to be transformed into blessing and not tragedy.

Today's men and women suffer from a continual onslaught of information and sensations, a constant violation of their sense of identity. They react to this with violence as the sole act by which they are able to affirm their uniqueness and unity. This problem cannot be solved with traditional architectural composition, by constructing architecture as mega-objects containing generic functions, remote from any sort of ordinary, immediate, and real relationship with the culture of use. By culture of use, I mean complex, literary, emotional, and symbolic relationship between man and his system of objects and structures. This result is obtained by turning the traditional process of composition on its head, arriving at the architecture by starting out from the infinitely small, from the air conditioning, or from the surface of materials.

On this assumption the traditional distinction between design and architecture breaks down. The distinction breaks down because in today's world everything is industrial design. If it is not industrial, it is plain design. Design operates to day by linking together apposite extremes. On the one hand there are the elements of the environment, from objects to walls, from colors to perfumes. On the other hand, there are the great mental and symbolic movements that we design, the imaginary territories that define a place, that give it a recognizable identity as an alternative to its surroundings. Along this route there are no interruptions, no passing from hand to hand between different areas of professionalism, as the human home is created out of an accumulation of stimuli, a summation of languages, and not out of attempts at synthesis from the outside, as "architectural composition" tends to do.

The feeling of a place, its identity, is a wholly internal matter. The urban significance of a building, on the other hand, is obtained through the use of different techniques of communication from the codes of architectural composition. Grand gestures, symbols, colors, and textures are the pure and simple scenic representation of architecture, but not the actual architecture itself. This is what many architects do not understand, and I am convinced that their effort to shift around the masses and parts of a building (for that is all that it amounts to by now) is still an activity connected in some way with the noble tradition of architecture, a tradition that extends as far as Palladio or Vitruvius. They do not realize that they are carrying out a completely new operation, outside the "vetustas" and the "aura" of the project but involving the *mise-en-scene* of a "sham" architecture, the portrayal of something that is cited in the conventional representation on which the metropolis is based. It is a representation that has nothing to do with history but which fictionally portrays history (and therefore architecture) for the simple reason that it provides an effective narrative and scenic language. In this game architecture is only a character that has no real existence. It is an element of scenery, a presence reconstructed in the studio in accordance with the script.

Architecture today finds itself in the position of having to fulfill two needs that are dramatically different from one another. One is an affective domesticity, made up wholly of warmth and information, filters and openings. The other is having to stand up to comparison with the great simulations of the society of communication and entertainment. So far European architecture has been unable to respond to either of these two requirements. In fact, it frequently shows that it has failed to grasp the problem thoroughly.

To be caught between indispensable reality in the private sphere and pure scenic make-believe in the public one is not a comfortable situation. Yet there is no choice but to frankly accept this schizophrenic split, tackle the problems separately, and carefully avoid any kind of synthesis of composition. In practice, this means architecture has to cope with its epistemological crisis without creating mental alibies. It must look the collapse of the unity of the discipline in the face, as one of the possibilities looming on the horizon. Indeed it has to accept the disappearance of architecture as a process that is well advanced, as a given from which to work.

A classic reaction to this situation is a refusal to believe that all this has happened or that it could ever happen. After all man is an architectural animal and, to paraphrase William Morris, everything is architecture, "except for the open desert."

People who hold this view are confusing project with architecture, and it is fairly easy to do. The misunderstanding is an amusing one since they are mistaking effect for cause and the part for the whole. In fact they say that everything is architecture, but then they make haste to distinguish between architecture and building or engineering. They are accepting that in reality architecture is not the construction itself but a very small part of it and that its realm is a fragile and shifting one.

Many architects do not realize that, just when they think they are really making architecture, they are in fact playing a game of chess with themselves. That is, they are inventing problems and then solving them brilliantly. Since the game of chess is a difficult one that requires intelligence, they feel their efforts have significance away from the chessboard as well. Marcel Duchamp, who for a long time gave up art in order to devote himself to chess, demonstrated the unity of the two procedures by a *reductio ad absurdum*. Yet he never believed that this meant that art could stand by itself, but rather that it had been turn ed into "something else." And from this "something else" it derived great freedom and stimulation.

Another recurrent attitude is voiced by people who understand how things stand, but who believe this represents a great tragedy for mankind. They are convinced that the internal split that has opened up within the discipline is an omen that the human race is going to come to a sticky end. Curiously, these people do not have the same reaction to modern painting, which went through exactly the same drama at the beginning of the century and dealt with it brilliantly by accepting its own abstraction. Indeed, it became "abstractionism," which was an opportunity for the regeneration of painting as free creative activity, gesture, and energy of communication.

In point of fact architecture today has become a pure, gratuitous art, which should be left in the hands of great artists and not professors. It is no longer concerned with the solution of problems of construction but emits pure energy of urban communication, pure domestic imagination. It is not clear why this should be regarded as a tragedy.

The third and last group, of which I am member, considers this situation to be a unique opportunity, not to be missed. It allows architecture, for the first time this century, to be included among the great liberal arts, the ones concerned not with objective problems but with free, creative activities. We can let go of the belief that it is possible to solve problems of construction in an artistic manner and apply this artistic bent instead to the invention of new problems of construction. This freedom at last makes the architect face up to his responsibilities as an artist and not a builder. Construction is no more than a remote premise, as all materials are in the realm of art. His job will exist only for as long as he is capable of inventing it, otherwise it will vanish. Masons who speak Latin are no longer needed, as Adolf Loos put it. Building is no problem today and knowing Latin may be of no help in the creation either of effective mass languages or of warm and snug homes. Knowing Japanese or how to sing might be more useful less noble perhaps, but more fun.

European architecture, unlike American architecture, has not yet accepted this situation. As a result it has become a minor art, a not very up-to-date activity. And for the opposite reason Italian and European design, in spite of their fragility and unsettled state, are vital. As are fashion, painting, poetry, music, and entertainment, which have to contend every day with success, with the effectiveness of their own languages. They are continually having to provide confirmation of their specific qualities, whereas European architecture relies on its historical definition, which serves to cover up its inadequacy.

While talking to me about a house that he was building in Arizona, Ettore Sottsass once said: "Actually for me the problem is not making a house, but giving a house. Which is something quite different."

The designer, unlike the university-trained architect, is inclined to see the work of architecture as the end result of a process of accumulation of elements that collect around a new hierarchy of functions until a whole is created. This whole is the outcome of different schemes of logic, of different plans and materials, held together by a powerful domestic tension.

The public languages of architecture, its apparent complexity, are part of the fiction that I have referred to. Today there is no possibility of applying the same method to the interior and to the exterior, except in very rare cases, where a unity of narrative can be produced, a complete scenario. Usually the problems are different. The interior produces emotional and sensory qualities while the exterior creates public metaphors.

It is on the basis of these premises of method and knowledge that design has operated over the last twenty years, investigating many new fields, from the soft structures of space (light, sound, odors, colors) to new archetypal languages, the figurative filtration of new materials, the domestic scenario and the interface needed to hold a dialogue with intelligent objects. These are all aspects that profoundly affect man's new habitat, and that have led to major changes in it over the last few decades, as compared with the age of mechanical technology. This may well be the main reason for impatience with current European architecture and its insistence on themes of composition. It shows that it is still trapped in the methods and themes of the mechanical age, in which communication took place by movement of masses, or by rotation and horizontal translation of bodies. Today we are already living in an age in which communication, owing to the advent of electronics, takes place in a planar way, through the pulsation of a liquid crystal, through the flow of low voltage currents, performing highly sophisticated functions similar to those of human physiology.

The transition from one technological era to the other involves profound changes in attitude and the application of different processes of logic and cognition. It also greatly alters the techniques of cultural communication. This change is taking place at different speeds in different areas of society. Some people are in the vanguard, others are being left behind. There are some who are aware of how much the times and the nature of art have already changed, and there are those who will be informed of it in ten years' time, through reading books.

Andrea Branzi
The Metropolis of Commodities (or The Real City), 2010

BVLGARI
Lustucru
RIZ COMPLET
BVLGARI

FLAN
ENTREMETS
kiri

スエヒロ
Kellogg's
山でん

F
THE METROPOLIS OF LIQUID WORK

De-Specialization and Versatility

Places of the Continuous Work

Andrea Branzi, 1994

//

I increasingly find myself taking a long, hard (and fresh) look at the projects we did in the late Sixties, comparing and contrasting them with the way we think and work today.

It's no coincidence, I think, that I should be doing this now, at a time when many people are trying to draw initial conclusions and build a framework to accommodate all the difficult and far-reaching design changes that our recent political, cultural, social and industrial crisis has brought in its wake.

In the Sixties we believed that the advent of electronic tools in production processes would usher in a Leisure Society in which the concept of work would disappear altogether. This would lead to Intellectual Mass Production and free, self-determination of living spaces, with the home as unregulated personal territory that would be both highly complex and ultimately uncontrollable.

Comparing this optimistic, radical utopia of the Sixties with the way things are now things can help us to see what the underlying features of the present age really are. What we have created today is virtually the antithesis of what was envisaged then: the advent of electronic tools has made possible a Continuous Work Society in which the concept of leisure has disappeared altogether.

Instead of Intellectual Mass Production we have Electronic Mass Production: you work in the office, at home, in the street, on the road, at the airport and even on holiday. The places in cities where this diffuse, unspecific, unclassifiable, indefinable work is carried out have become so indistinguishable from one another as to be virtually interchangeable, with no real functional specialization. The home is as goods as an airport or an office, and vice-versa. The code of spatial identification seems to be disappearing in an extended, neutral metropolitan circuit with a "low identity level" in which living means very much the same as working, traveling or shopping.

So the people who design these spaces are asking whether all this a good or a bad thing. Is loss of spatial identity and diversification an anthropological catastrophe or an unprecedented form of liberation? A process of metropolitan recomposition gaining momentum as the white heat of diversity begins to cool, or the final frontier, the point of no return in a process of human alienation in an artificial universe that is becoming more and more like itself as each day passes, to the point where all traces of memory and feeling are lost? Personally, I see these as political problems, not just matters of design, and like all political problems they need a poetic response.

For some time my poetic response has been directed towards small sites where everyday objects are incorporated in architectural microspaces, i.e. the embryonic nuclei of a new architectural space. In fact, objects as such are gradually disappearing as they become pure vibrations, or parts of a larger, more indefinable whole. So I often use the arch as a traversable structure at the centre of a more extensive itinerary, as a ring into which objects can be fitted.

I'm no longer interested in the composition of objects and volumes, but in assembling these things in a random, almost inexpressive way. My new working categories are things on top of each another and things inside each another, which is already an attempt to dismantle and reassemble the world from scratch using existing materials. The approach may not radical in itself, but it derives directly from radical principles; and not as a style but as a concept of living at a time when radical questions are being asked again, new basic choices can be made and new opportunities can be seized.

Andrea Branzi. *Models of Corporate Identity*
Exhibition *Citizen Office*, Vitra Design Museum, Weil am Rhein, 1994

New Forms of Enterprise

Andrea Branzi, 2006

//

Zygmunt Bauman's *Liquid Modernity* describes an age in which the political forms of both right and left are liquefying and often fluctuate among themselves. In the absence of the great consolidated values systems, the forms of politics once again become an object of creative research, like the invention of new logics, no longer based on great schemes of mechanical contraposition between workers and managers, or rich and poor, but between much more nuanced social subjects that contain less evident conditions of diversity – ignorant and informed, nomads and fixed populations, monotheists and polytheists.

The same form of enterprise (productive or commercial) is the object of new critical reflection. It is no longer considered a given form, a monad from whose aggregations the general economic system is composed.

It seems more a form projected over time, a completely artificial structure, which has always corresponded to a theoretic/formal model of human and productive relations.

Imagining new models of productive organization is an integral part of any design culture: a new modernity is born only from a new model of enterprise. The form of manufactured objects cannot be separated from the form of the industrial nuclei that produce them, just as it cannot be separated from the consequential environmental structures.

In liberalism, just as in socialism, enterprise has always been the result of a theoretical model of the world, the formalization of productive energy and of the present exchanges in society. Enterprise is the result of a philosophy of human relations and the production of value. Therefore any design that does not presuppose a reflection on the organisms of production is always an inadequate design.

The concept of Modernity in the twentieth century belongs to the ideology of the transformation of technologies, idioms, and behaviors used by industry; the "form of enterprise" has been one of the most adequate instruments for creating this transformation. The mechanical age produced a model of enterprise like a motor, a (strong and concentrated) machine of an economy made up of correlated but different, separate, antagonistic parts.

The classic enterprise is organized according to specialized, sector-based knowledge, capable of creating "definitive products and above all permanent wealth" that are situated in history as pillars of a new time-honored societal foundation – new permanent values, and new definitive riches.

With the net-economy and e-commerce, mass entrepreneurship, and the inclination towards diffuse innovation, the mechanical-military model has fallen into crisis: it no longer corresponds to the society of access and above all no longer corresponds to the ebb and flow of a global economy developed with no model of reference, without stable orders and fixed rules, with transitory virtual wealth and circumstantial economies. This is, then, a "buzz economy" that follows discontinuous flows of an energy that is more relational than productive. This is an economy constantly in expansion because it is constantly in crisis, and vice versa; it is inadequate for governing its lively impulses, always on the brink of failure, as an indispensable premise for its leaps ahead.

From this tumultuous phase of maturation it becomes clear that the classic industrial economy, where wealth was produced by enterprise (a rigid form within a fluid society), is a rapidly setting sun. Enterprise and society coincide; the entrepreneurial disposition coincides with the same vital energy of society and individuals.

In this sense, the social economy, like an evolving energy, coincides with the natural form of generic systems – with the Genetic Metropolis. They are a conglomeration of weak and diffuse energies that traverse history and produce its unstable state. They are the symptom of a continuous evolution, produced by the

individual's necessity to increase the conditions of environmental and social safety of its own genes.

**It is a question, therefore, of rethinking the forms of economy and enterprise as specific parts of a new vision of history (and politics), one that makes reference to a fluid universe, a dynamic system in continuous evolution and renewal.
The concept of new modernity must make reference to these new genetic, dynamic concepts, rethinking the present enterprise like an inadequate, rigid, fragile organism. This means moving from a closed, stable, specialized form to an open, provisory, liquid form.**

It is therefore necessary to introduce new key words: traversable enterprise, reversible enterprise, that assume in their own organized form a state of permanent crisis, the instability of the market, the uncertainty of values, producing organization charts capable of liberating expansive energies beginning with its own dissolution. This means moving from enterprise to agency, from the armadas of Julius Caesar to the disposable army of Genghis Khan.

The design energy of the modern enterprise, its coincidence with the capacity to produce innovation, aims to surpass brand understood as a tribe of belonging, as a micro-society motivated by competition, to become instead a molecular system that traverses fluid plankton, continually liberating its form, and creating ever-new aggregations and new working alliances. No more, then, permanent forms, but fluid energies that coagulate and move only following terminal strategies and with working methods that are irreproducible in any classic form. In the essay *Treatise on Efficiency* by French sinologist François Jullien, there is mention of a surpassing of the Western concept of efficiency, based on Clausewitz's military model, in favor of ju-jitsu techniques, the Chinese martial art that uses adverse force to reach one's goal.

The growth of enterprise is no longer, then, a dimensional growth, but coincides rather with its dynamic capacity, the continuous reduction of apparatuses, the dismissal of workers, and thereby the continuous betterment of its working capacities.

Today, the great operations can happen through the organization of provisory apparatuses, programmatically destined for dismissal; temporary apparatuses of a gene that grows only as a specialization, intelligence, experience, and not as a complex structure.

This complexity, as a qualitative category for organisms bent on surpassing environmental difficulties through the multiplication of their own components, leaves room for inverse processes of simplification of working modules, for the liberation of enterprise's energetic nuclei, freeing them from all formal over-structures.

Andrea Branzi, *Continuous Work*, 1994

Andrea Branzi, *Continuous Garden*, 2010

HUMAN ACCESSORIAL
HUMAN ACCESSORIAL
MEETING ext.
MEETING int.

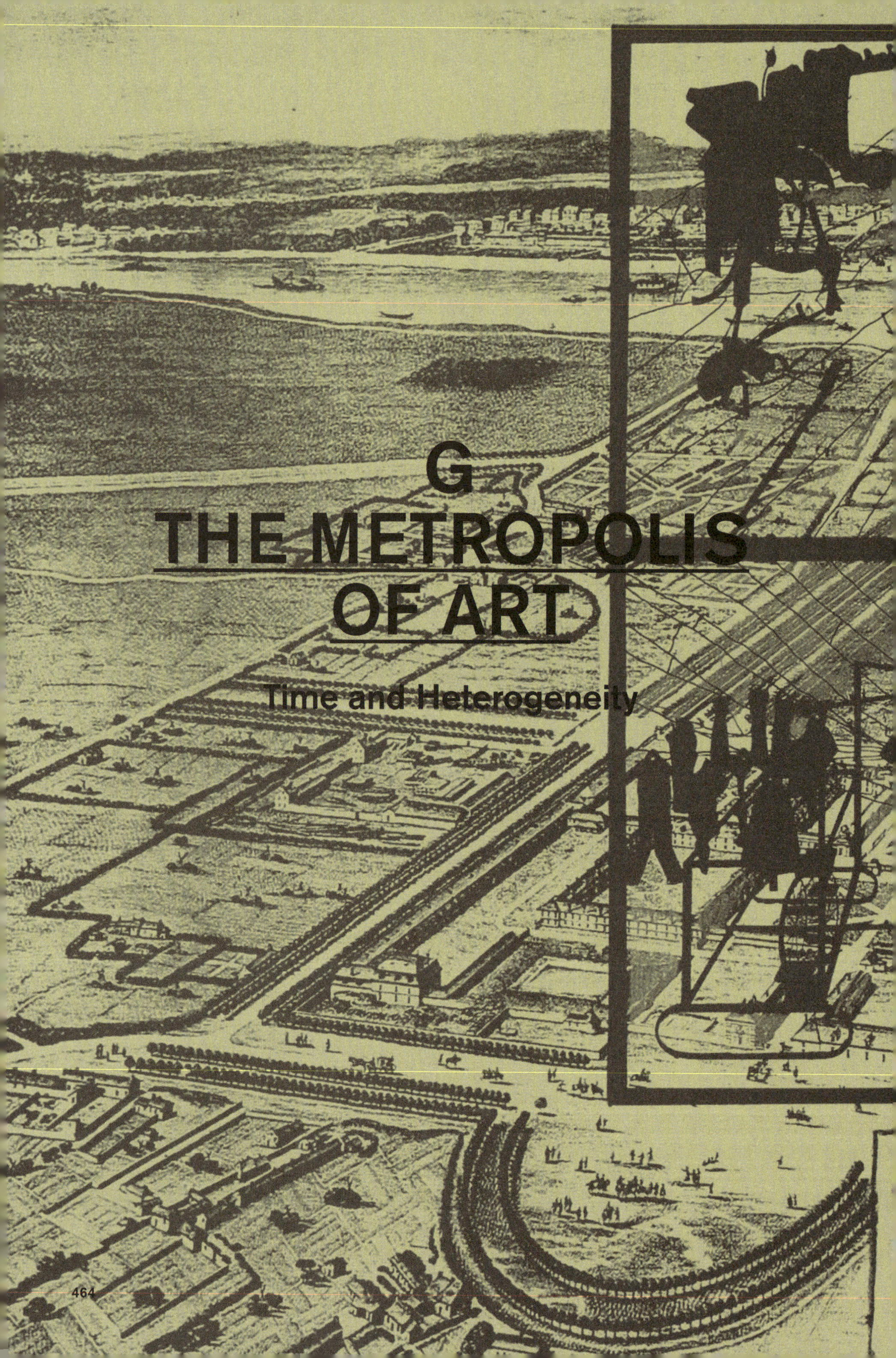

G
THE METROPOLIS OF ART

Time and Heterogeneity

The Metropolis of Art
Andrea Branzi, 2016

//

Modern thought and culture begins with the French Revolution (1789-99); liberated from the hierarchical constraints of monarchies and ecclesiastical prohibitions, art begins the long journey that will carry it toward modernity and postmodernity. Anti-monumental art becomes a monument to the secularism of the unexpected, like a revealed religion occupies the stage of history without providing an explanation. It breaks definitively its connection with the urban context, it upsets the balance: a wonderful monster goes beyond the known horizon, as powerful as the large urban artifacts that it confronts without fear.

The Metropolis of Art is similar to the metropolis of the archi-star, continually interrupted by visual, formal, and technological exceptions. Without the French Revolution, the world would never have known about the existence of a counter-history, that a different social hierarchy was possible: that art could have become an anti-aesthetic mystery.

FAUSTO MELOTTI'S "SEVEN WISE MEN" AROUND THE "ARC

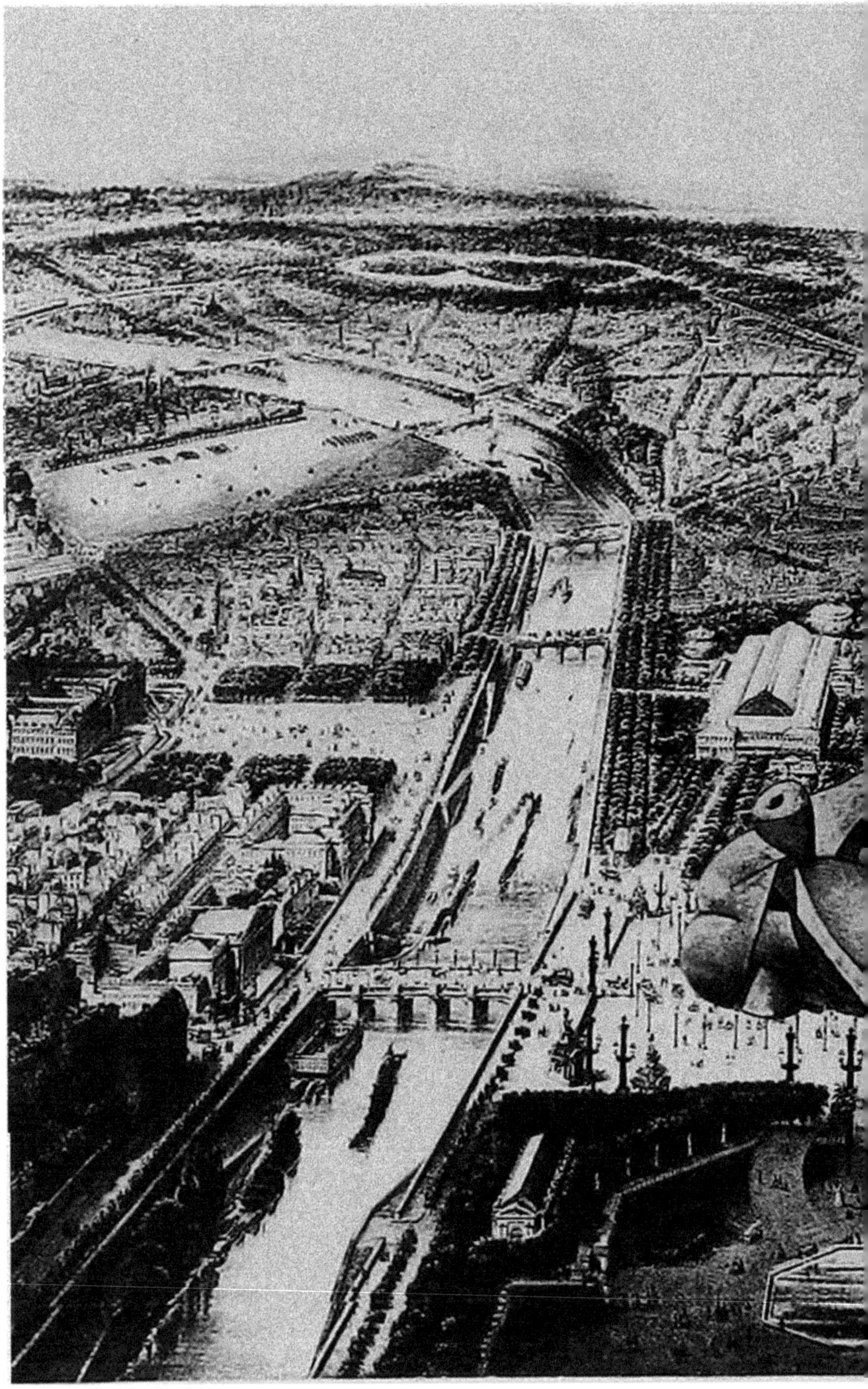

PICASSO'S "SEASCAPE" AT THE "CHAMPS ELISE

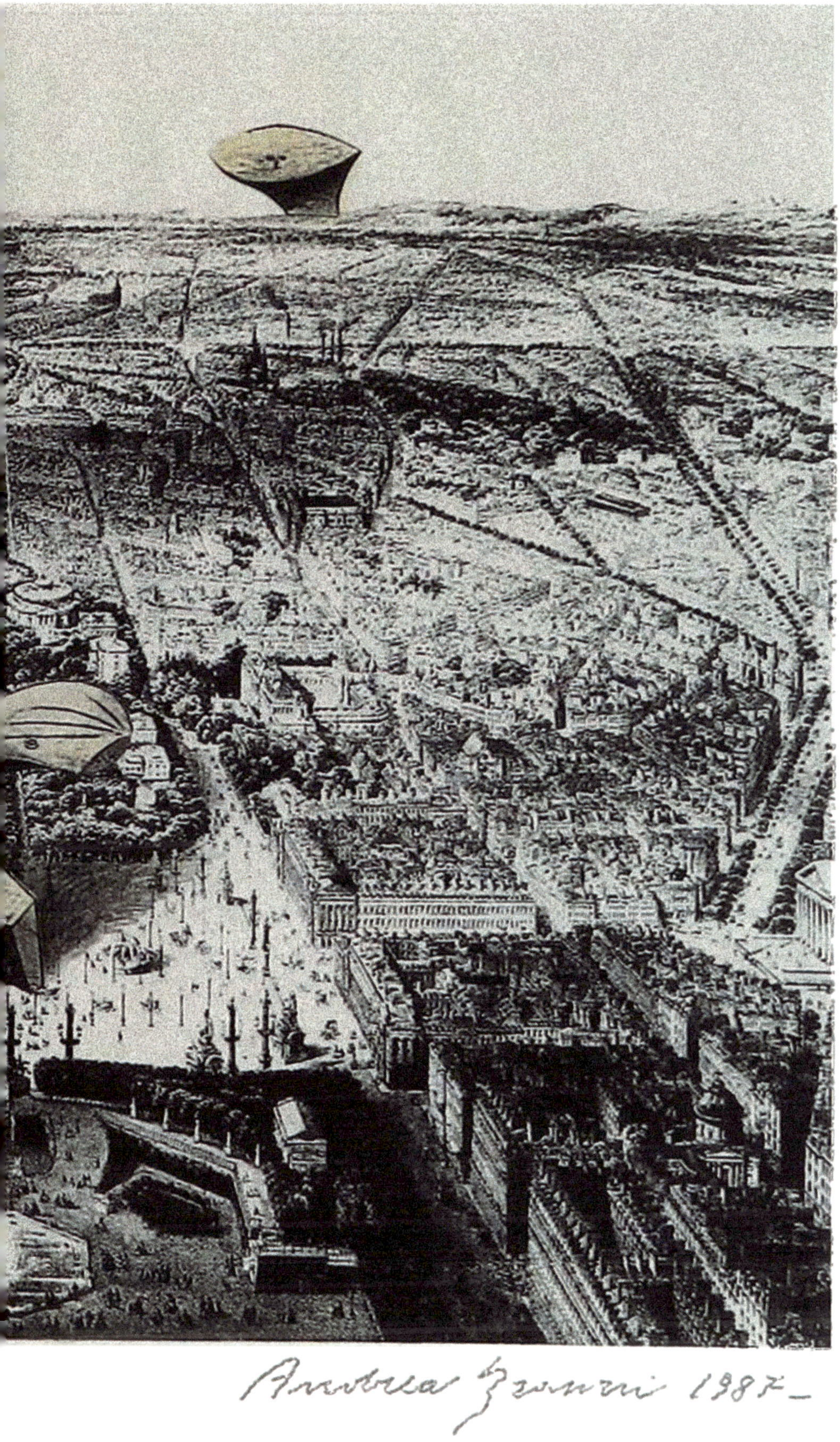
Andrea Branzi 1987

- PICASSO' WOMAN'S HEAD IN THE MIDLE OF THE

"FENCE"_ Andrea Branzi 1987_

-MARCEL DUCHAMP'S "LA SPOSA MESSA A NUDO"

FRONT OF THE "ECOLE MILITAIRE"_

Andrea Branzi 1987

-FERNAND LEGER ET PIET MONDRIAN AT THE "PLACE ROYAL"-

- TWO GREAT KANDISKIES ON THE "SACRE COEUR" HILL -

Andrea Branzi 1982

- GREAT CALDER'S "BALANCE" OVER THE "TOUR EIFFEL" -

SESSION 4

TERRITORIES FOR A NEW URBAN DRAMATURGY

Andrea Branzi. *Parietal Rock Interior*, 2015

The XXI Century and the New Urban Dramaturgy

The previous noble and icy indifference no longer corresponds to the realities of the new century. A century discovering that globalization had already failed before it was born; that the world is divided into the West and Islam and, despite the rational certainty of the end of all religions, is already immersed in an undeclared religious Third World War, featured by a constellation of local irresolvable conflicts.

A West that after the failure of Socialism has to realise the failure of Capitalism.

Contemporary design assists the penetration of civilisations, cultures and religions - coming from other ancient and noble civilisations, economies, logics of production, of trade and behaviour - that from the Far East and the deep South of the world attain and desecrate the sacred fences of our modernity.

The anthropocentric culture is in decline and anthropology no more provides the deep certainties that we have always credited to it, as demonstrated by the failure of Minimalism and of its hope that there could be primary, shared and permanent shapes in which the society, devastated by the environmental complexity, could finally find peace. Anthropology, as the science of man, of his nature and his primordial roots, is nothing else than one of our noble inventions.

As the artist-philosopher Paul McCarthy says, ketchup not blood is now flowing in the veins of man. We can add that his memory is contained in a computer hard disk, his route is guided by a navigation system and his knowledge of the world occurs through the internet.

Only his free animal nature connects man to the universe of all living creatures. His creative amnesia is not more dangerous than that of wise men.

The urgency of a New Design Dramaturgy arises from the evident contrast between tragedy and normality, between consumerism and death, between theology and technology, between the silence of reason and the voice of an irrational reality.

This opens a fascinating season of search for a new narrative, figurative, dramaturgic mode capable of snatching design from the grasp of solitude through its contamination with the real world. A search aiming at the renewal of our aesthetics of perfection through the catharsis generated by the new history.

Andrea Branzi, 2014

4.1

THE PRIMITIVE METROPOLIS

Andrea Branzi. *Pietre e Sassi, Rocks and Stones*, 2008

The Primitive Metropolis
Andrea Branzi, 2014

//

Heretical Design is twenty-first century design: heretical, not because it's opposed to orthodoxy, but because no true orthodoxy exists anymore.

The legacy of the twentieth century, its dogmas and its principles of ethics, are obsolete and useless; the twenty-first century presents itself with totally original and contradictory features, which need to be reflected upon in an exploratory way, without attempting to recreate a new orthodoxy, but rather a rarefied system of anarchic hypotheses and experimentation, more akin to an era like ours – experimental and anarchic.

Therefore, this does not mean looking for refoundation, but perhaps acknowledging a definitive disintegration of the project (maybe already in an advanced stage). This hypothesis is not the outcome of pessimism. Quite the contrary, it aims to open up new levels of harsh realism and therefore of freedom.

Project culture is not a secondary part of vaster historical scenarios underway and therefore subject to profound cultural and strategic mutations. In other words, if project culture does not pertain to the culture of men, it's a discipline I'm not interested in…

Covered by the consolidated myths of the Modern Movement, industrial societies did not realize that as early as the 1960s, the West went from being an Architecture Civilization to a Commodity Civilization; from the certainties of the high civil value of building sound, permanent works based on indestructible foundations and armored perimeters, unchallenged protagonists on the urban scene, we passed on to a molecular system of exportable, negotiable, groundless, stackable products, which freely circulate in the vast territory of a market that from China has reached all the way to Australia and which are able to penetrate any domestic gap.

This dynamic reality de-territorializes the very notion of the city, which can no longer be defined as a whole of architectural boxes, of boundaries and barriers, but rather the fragment of a world market that can be crossed, that is fluid, boundless, without an exterior. An unlimited land of exchange, services, information; an immaterial space that can be defined as a personal computer every 20 sq m.

At the center of the twenty-first century there is the crisis of the city, both as a historical institution and as a visible point where operations are concentrated.

An unstable fragment of a world market in permanent crisis, it contradicts the hypothesis that globalization would have created a mono-logic universe, based upon free competition, rendered uniform by shared laws of profit. But none of this came true: globalization, understood as *Pax Romana*, proved to be a conflicting reality, which heightened local diversities, accentuating commercial strife: a widespread system of crisis – each different from the other, without a common model of use. Therefore, an unstable, experimental world society, which each day must elaborate new laws and new statutes to positively manage its own permanent state of crisis.

Globalized neo-capitalism is therefore revealing its financial nature, based upon accumulating and speculating enormous immaterial legacies, which give rise to the world crisis currently underway. A crisis that is not the result of unpredictable circumstances, but the riper result of a system that expands only in the presence of imbalances that need to be rebalanced, of unanswered questions, of gaps that must be filled.

After the failure of Socialism, can we predict the failure of Capitalism as well?

These two ideologies opposed one another over the course of the twentieth century in a long Cold War, mutually supporting each other as global alternatives, but separated they are gradually collapsing. Once there saw no true alternative, Capitalism found great difficulty in self-creation, thus becoming a rigid system hard to manage...

Amidst the fall of the Berlin Wall and the Twin Towers attacks, it seemed that the effect of the free market in former Socialist countries only encouraged illegally

and local crime; but this phenomenon corresponded to the initial level of Capitalism itself, as what took place in America in the 1920s and subsequently in the world.

But on September 11, 2001 we had to come to terms with the fact that this sort of consumer pacification was not unfolding but instead had sparked and undeclared Holy War; on the one side the industrialized societies and on the other, Islam. A Holy War very hard to face for the West, which during the twentieth century had (incorrectly) sustained that religion and theological issues were destined to disappear, overwhelmed by the power of industrial logic. Today, West and Islam measure themselves on political, territorial and economic issues, but overall they remain, like during the Crusades, within the solid armor of a religious conflict.

Therefore, among the unpredictable novelties of the twenty-first century there emerges a theological issue able to split the world in two, an issue that also revolves around the project theme: on the one hand the design society of the West, involved in defining its own uncertain future, and on the other, Islam, which refuses innovation because it is involved in searching for certainties in its own past. It is no coincidence that Mohamed Atta, who organized the Twin Tower attacks, was an architect who graduated in Cairo with a Master in Munich…

We're not dealing, therefore, with a traditional territorial war but instead a widespread, spontaneous, often individual conflict, which crosses Arab deserts, Afghani mountains, and world megalopolises, inhabited by seven billion people: seven billion destined to grow exponentially, driven by the energy of eros, by an exchange of genomes up to filling the environment with an energy of expression able to replace traditional urban scenarios with a motley, creative, individual swarm of bodies in motion. Bodies that affirm their identity, their diversity, their uniqueness; a multitude that creates new economies, new poverty, and new rarefied conflicts. An energy of life and expression that places itself and fills the emptiness left by the crisis of the real city, replacing it in a large and creative genetic laboratory.

The city of humans therefore substitutes the cities of stone with the flow of their own colors, of decorations, of fabrics.

The globalization crisis has intertwined with this uncontrollable, unpredictable phenomenon, which does not follow market laws but rather it overturns them, replaces them.

In this unforeseeable context what resist are only the orthodox minorities that oppose the surrounding environmental heresy.

If the Modern Movement guaranteed throughout the twentieth century a sort of general happy ending, advancing a future in the order of the reason of science and social justice, the twenty-first century shows that the true spin-off of Industrial Civilization creates a present made up of exceptions, improvisations, injustice. The general happy ending is no longer guaranteed for anyone.

If in the past we could imagine progress as the spontaneous result of system qualitative growth, today the notion of progress is no longer a shared hypothesis, because the system we live in follows the sole logic of quantitative expansion. The myth of the Future has been replaced by the reality of a Present continuous. It seems that linear time has been substituted by a neutral pause, where past, present and future are interchangeable…

That distance of real history which distinguished the project culture throughout the past century is today leading us down a dead end: elegance, practicality, technology are now no longer enough to establish an acceptable contact with the times we live in.

Unlike all the other creative cultures such as art, music, literature that plunged into and were reborn in the tragedies of the twentieth century, we must acknowledge that the project culture crossed two world wars, an atomic conflict, racial extermination, great right and left dictatorships, without provoking any sort of turbulence along the horizontal line of language.

We could say that its disciplinary history has replaced real history … A self-referential discipline, which cannot be unruffled, based upon solid foundations able to resolve the problem, once and for all.

The twenty-first century, therefore, placed in the limelight the crisis of cities and, as a consequence, the crisis of the project as a tool of order, progress, and beauty. This new historical context has given rise to that minority trend which crossed against the tide project optimism in the past century.

A radical trend that stemmed from the sacred roots of the first avant-gardes and has traversed like a karstic river – disappearing and later reappearing – the long course of that tragic history industrial design totally ignored.

The counter-trend we are speaking about is the one that, in searching for deeper archetypes, goes back to man's "animal condition," interpreting Darwin's law as a reversible process: if man descends from apes, man may reclaim this legacy by returning to his primordial state as an animal, interpreted not as "regression" but as extreme freedom and modernity.

Along this strategic line we find some great innovators, like Kurt Schwitters who in the late 1930s started building his Merzbau, caves of rubble and fragments in constant evolution; Jackson Pollock who in the 1950s stated "I am nature;" Francis Bacon where in his paintings, man-ape is the prisoner of a modernity closed upon itself.

In the 1960s Pierre Restany, after having walked across the Amazon rainforest upon request of the Brazilian government, wrote his "Manifesto of the Rio Blanco," where he compares the condition of contemporary man to that of the Indios; both live in a totally saturated environment (the city and the forest), where dreams, nature, magic, technique, the cult of the dead constitute a single reality. Like fish in the sea, both never have an "outside" view of their own habitat, plankton that possess neither boundaries nor horizons.

These extreme themes are resurfacing today, at a time when Western culture, after the failure of Socialism, is experiencing the failure of Capitalism. In a system that "does not develop but expands," that projects is only in front of itself and can trace back its deepest anthropological roots; to that primordial condition from which the human environment began its long course.

These unsettling and magical signs are appearing spontaneously in our unrecognizable metropolises which like virgin forests host the *hikikomori*, young hermits from the nerd culture, who live naked in their micro-habitats, invaded like dumps for commercial products; surrounded by their telematic tools that replace any direct connection with the outside world.

Like the plumbing who search for their natural roots by putting their heads in toilet bowls, indifferent to the world surrounding them like ancient stylites. Like the Owling who are similar to owls on rooftops and fences, looking – motionless – upon a senseless universe. Or like the parkours who by following their founder, David Belle who flew as if from one tree to the next, cross our cities like sacred monkeys, jumping into nothing, hurling themselves into the abyss as if inside a forest, possessed by unbridled animal energy.

The spread of tattoos or piercing is irreversible, everlasting signs that accompany young people until they die; signs of belonging not to a tribe but rather to oneself as a unique, niche, unrepeatable, independent.

This behavior, which answers to the resurfacing of a quite ancient primordial root, does not acknowledge urban order and spatial hierarchies, but interprets them as a wild free territory.

These avant-gardes, which are not composed of intellectuals or artist, which theorize nothing, directly and successfully bear witness to the failure as well as the human reinvention of our urban civilization, without contesting the foundation but accepting and reinventing them starting with the "monkey inside us."

Andrea Branzi.
Sacred Field, 2012-2013

We are primitives
Andrea Branzi, 1985

///

We are the primitives in two ways at least: analogically and linguistically.

We are analogically primitive because our condition is that of those who, having fallen from an airplane into the middle of the Amazon territory, find themselves operating with technologically advanced elements still on board, as well as with natural materials of the forest. The ideological parachute no longer works, and the transformations we accomplish in that jungle are meant to realize an accelerated renewal circuit rather than a design for global progress. Culture and design no longer are forces that slowly but heroically move the world toward salvation through logical and ethical radicalism. They are mechanisms of emotions and adaptations of changes that fail to drag the world toward a horizon; they only transform it into many diffuse diversities. Progress no longer seems to be valued; instead, the unexpected is valued.

The grand unitarian theorems no loner exists, nor do the leading models of the rational theologies. What exists is a modernity without illuminism. We are witnessing a definitive and extreme secularization of design, within which design represents itself and no longer is a metaphor for a possible unity of technologies and languages. Human nature and the artificial nature of mechanisms, information, and the metropolis cohabit in sensorial identification, just as the Indian who identifies with the forest.

That neoprimitive condition is not a design in the sense that it does not wish to be the latest trend of avant-garde fashions; but it is precisely a condition into which various languages and already diffuse attitudes fuse. To perceive that condition helps move postmodernism out of reactionary equivocations and, probably, gives greater freedom and awareness to our mode of designing. The communication of the primitive, indeed, achieves its maximum efficiency inside a closed system: it operates by archetypes and myths, working inside a circuit of users capable of perceiving its metaphorical keys and subject to its specific energy. Outside those conditions, the culture of the primitive is nothing but a formal repertory that currently is heeded and used by a large number of operators, artists, and designers. A password has not yet become effective, and already we detect the symptoms of a great attention paid to neoprimitive languages, to the extent that we have had to make a selection among the many possible examples of that latent condition.

There also exists, therefore, a so-called neoprimitive linguistic fashion that pays great attention to languages, to anatomical aspects and artifacts of primitive men, to technological animism, and to primitive ethic. This fact coincides with a need of both users and designers. The first sees stable signs, powerful but liberating, in the neoprimitive style. Designers are seeking the original key to their own identities, the building code of their own languages, setting themselves up as possible tribal heads.

The design panorama that awaits us in that extreme secularization of design consists of an ensemble of linguistic families grouped around ever more numerous family heads who will assemble around their own expressive minor archetypes and aggressive followers. That tribalization of cultural society is at once a result of the neoprimitive condition and awaiting the fall of the old cultural tinsels in front of a new different civilization. Similar to the good savage, we are naked while awaiting the worse or the better.

HouseMother
Integral Model of Co-housing
Andrea Branzi, 2016

//

In the era of globalization, we must begin to experiment with the fusion of our enlightened concept of neutral hospitality and the broader sense of belonging to the realm of the living that comes from the East, within an environment whose quality is not only related to the absence of pollution, but also in a deep anthropological and aesthetic sense.

An environment in which the reduction of energy consumption is not only a technological matter but one that coincides with a broader design of a cultural, spiritual, and metaphysical nature.

Thus, less anthropocentric metropolises and ones that are more open to the concept of universal hospitality, moving towards biodiversity and the kingdom of the dead.

Housemother does not aim to be realized but is part of a research project to compare our design culture (too static and real estate-oriented) with the complexity of the social and cultural transformations that are underway, experimenting with new structures and new dimensions of thought of design, and looking at the long time of history rather than just the short time periods of the professional market.

Fundamentalism
Andrea Branzi, 2016

//

This neologism today indicates a form of “extremism,” both religious and political. Ours is often called the Age of Extremism, where terrorism constitutes the most devastating manifestation of an unpredictable and conflictual energy with which it is impossible to have a dialogue.

The Holy War that characterizes the 21st century broke out, unexpectedly, on September 11, 2001, with the attack on the Twin Towers; since then, the intransigence and rigidity of the conflicting parties, the West and Islam, have become two extreme ways of seeing the world, and "Fundamentalism" is not only a strategy of war, but a much broader cultural category, which was generated at the moment when, after the failure of Socialism, the failure of Capitalism has also been envisaged. Capitalism and Socialism were two opposing forms of Fundamentalisms, which via the Cold War ensured the ideological/military balance in the second half of the twentieth century.

In this sense, it is not necessarily that because of their radicality extremisms produce not just a kind of "undeclared war," but ensure an "unsigned peace."

If last century's political ideologies characterized all human behavior, Fundamentalism must be understood as a syndrome that affects our whole culture, that deprives the long-standing references between modernity and reaction, between past and future, it tends to go back to "Primordial Fundamentals," not only of religion, but of thought and global action.

Fundamentalism is the manifestation of a desire for purity, for the rediscovery of ancient primordial sources. The discovery of a modernity where the present, the past, and the future find an original ground of coexistence.

Megalithic culture, the dolmens and menhirs from which architecture originated, are extreme forms of a search for the historical foundations of design, today deprived of those utopian myths on which they were nourished for a long time.

Fundamentalism is nothing more than an extreme form of a crisis of design that is seeking new nourishment from outside the professional discipline. Contaminating stones, pebbles, and rocks with fragments of a modernity that survives itself and finds in the power of nature the capacity to create new and unimaginable powerful images, according to a entirely typical mode of our way of existing, outside and within the past, to contemporaneity, in a continuous present, indifferent to historical chronology, but where everything is again possible, where the "unexpected" is the only legitimate research.

If this is Fundamentalism, it is no longer a danger, but the West's last chance to address the violence of the sacred, introducing the sacred into design, initiating the search for a new dramaturgy capable of engaging with those anthropological platforms that modernity has always ignored, such as life, death, eros, destiny, and mystery.

The West and Islam confront each other precisely in terms of the question of the project: on one side, our planning-oriented society, always looking for a better future, and on the other, an Islam that rejects all forms of future, in search of certainties from their own past.

Andrea Branzi, Collection *Grandi Legni*, 2009

Andrea Branzi, *Dolmen Collections*, 2013-2014

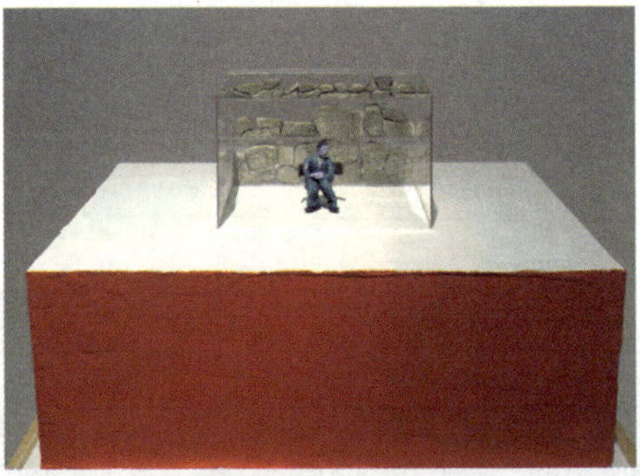

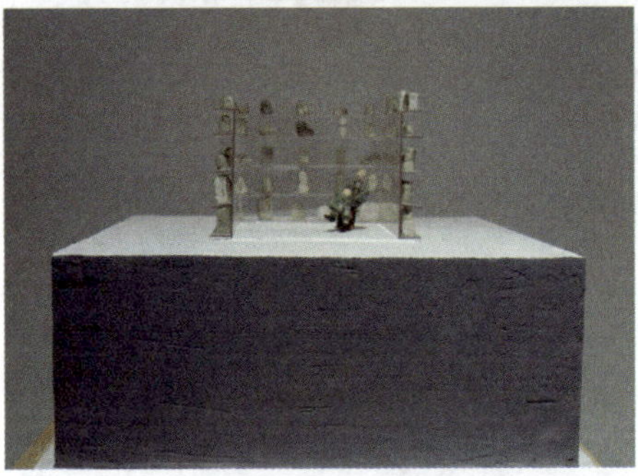

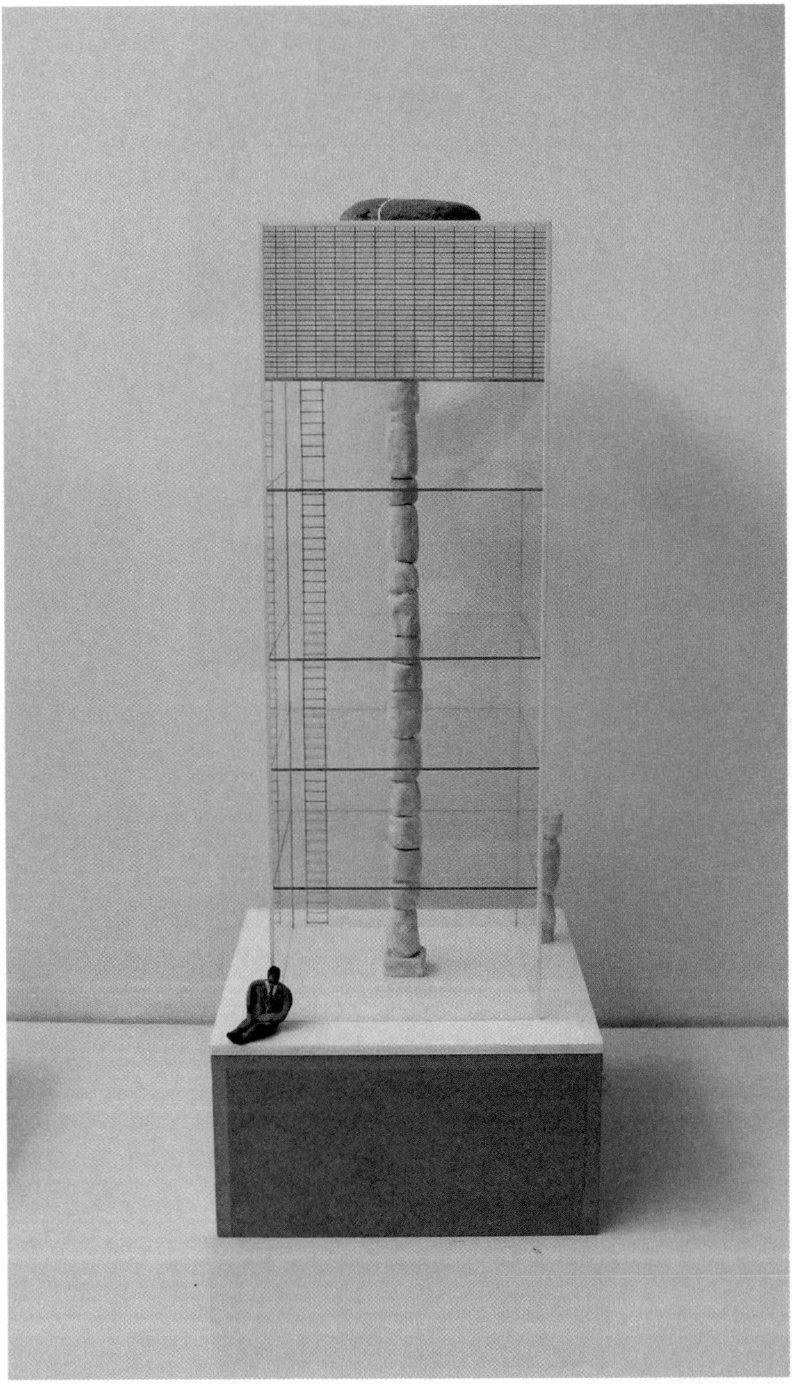

Andrea Branzi, *Casa Madre, Modello di co-housing integrale*
HouseMother, Model of integral co-housing, 2008

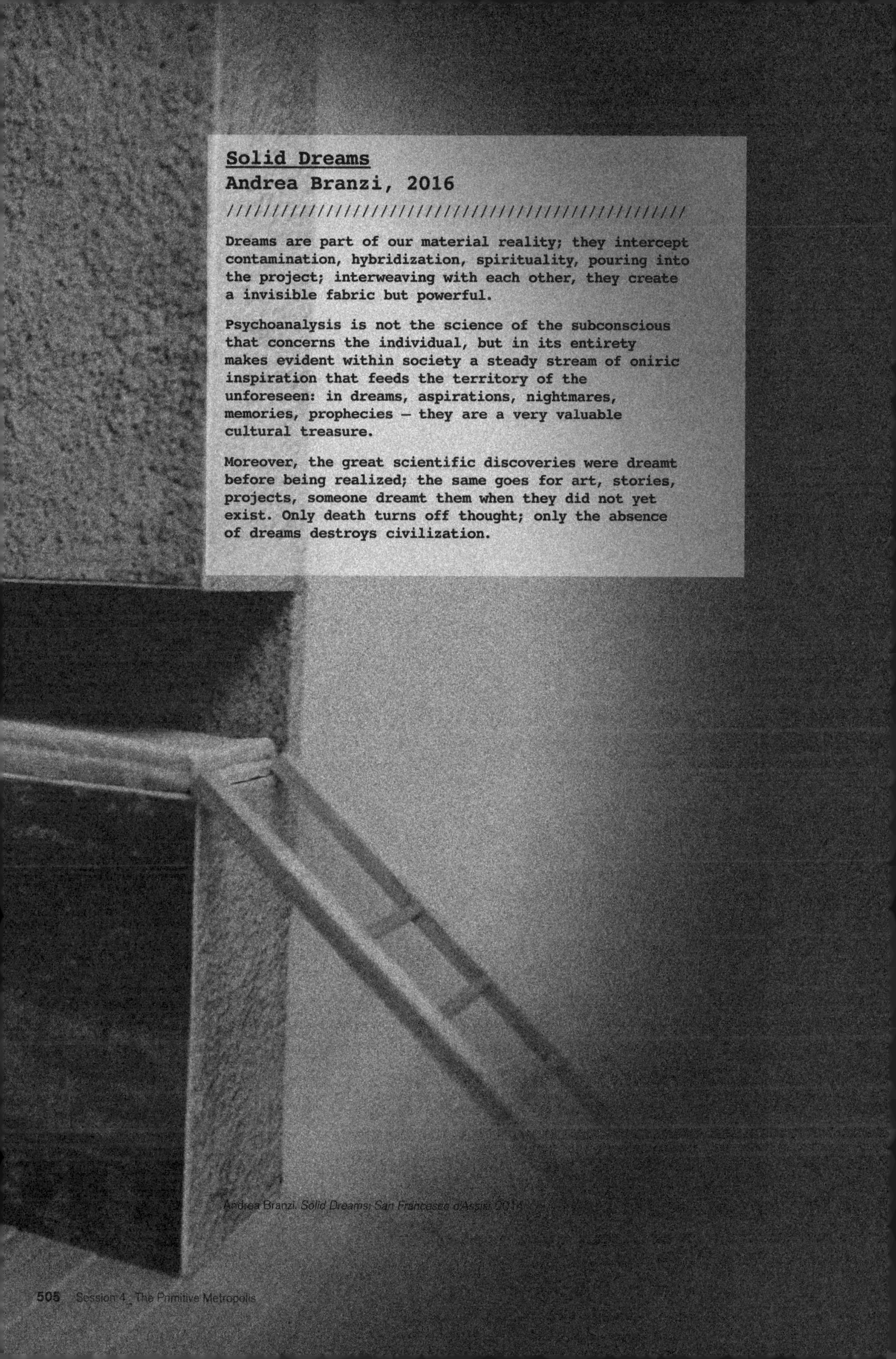

Andrea Branzi. *Solid Dreams: San Francesco d'Assisi* 2016

Andrea Branzi, *Solid Dreams, Recinto,* 2014

Andrea Branzi, *Solid Dreams, Pontormo*, 2014

Andrea Branzi, *Solid Dreams*, *Pavone*, 2014

Andrea Branzi, *Solid Dreams*, *Croce*, 2014

Andrea Branzi, *Solid Dreams, Giotto*, 2014

Art as Revealed Religion
Andrea Branzi, 2008

//

There is a long tradition of religions founded by intellectuals, philosophers, mystics or individuals who declare themselves prophets inspired by God (or the gods) to spread rules of behavior designed to guarantee Heaven after death or the benevolence of the divinities during life.

Among these religions the most famous are those founded by Buddha, Zarathustra, Confucius, Lao-Tze, Janus; all these faiths were contemporaries of our occidental philosophy, founded by Plato in the 5th century b.C., a century that marks the true of birth of the history of human culture. In general, these were polytheist creeds, with very detailed theological systems, that also included divide laws impossible to implement by men (like the total pacifism of Jainism), or tactical atheism (like Confucianism) that theorizes the inexistence of the gods, but also the need to regulate human existence with ceremonies and rituals, to ward off social and cosmic catastrophe. Other beliefs, like Taoism, sought immortality on earth through virtuous living, rather than focusing on life after death.

Then there were the great revealed religions (said to come directly from God), like Judaism, Christianity and Islam, all heirs to Abraham, all monotheist, concentrating on life after death and on relatively similar standards of moral behavior.

Unlike Christianity, the other two faiths are rigorously aniconic, forbidding the representation of the figure of God and his name. As we know, Christianity instead assigned art the task of representing the episodes of the Sacred Scriptures, and of offering images of the physical sites of the Revelation and the Passion. If we read the book of Carlo Ginzburg *Indagine su Piero* (della Francesca), published by Einaudi in 1981, we can understand how theological issues formed an internal structure of all the great art of the Christian Occident, for which devotional practices, rituals and prayer must always take place in the presence of a sacred "image."

This tradition has encouraged the great development of art in the entire Occident, as a favored vehicle of the sacred, thus itself becoming the focus of worship, to the point that in certain historical periods - like the Renaissance - aesthetics replaced ethics, and its contents were examined with great severity for signs of heresy.

Starting in the 18th century this alliance between art and religion broke down: like all other religions, Christianity took a critical stance with respect to modernity, while art set off on its long path in pursuit of total autonomy.

In recent times, however, we have seen an original trend: art seems to be re-establishing ties with the theme of the sacred, but through an inverse perspective, no longer as a tool of devotional illustration, but interpreting itself as a new revealed religion. A religion revealed not from the heights of the heavens, but from the below, from human nature, form the guts, the fear of death, perversions, violence. Like a new Taoism, art investigates the possibility of an artificial immortality" (maybe worse than death) offered but genetic engineering, chemistry, surgery, transplants. This is a merciless art that sees the human body as a living tomb, pain as an intrinsic part of its nature, perversion as an expression of its creativity. So this is a religion revealed by man himself, a bearer of sacrality without symbols, without metaphysical hopes, where the biological ethic replaced aesthetics, and the sacred comes from the progression of death.

Andrea Branzi, *Solid Dreams, Chiesa Nera, Black Church*, 2014

The End of Eurocentrism

Andrea Branzi, 2013

//

With the start of globalization, Europe has lost its centrality and begun to backtrack, under the pressure of the cultures and economies of the emerging Brics nations (Brazil, Russia, India, China and South Africa); the philosophies of these distant empires are modernizing our old, weary modernity. Eurocentrism is slowly declining.

Immigration, industrial pressure, the influence of new religions all seem to violate the antique hearth of our hypothetical Judeo-Christian supremacy. The hybridization we are talking about, in fact, does not consist only of a new stylistic eclecticism, but in the advent of logics and philosophies that are totally distant from the rationalism of the 20th century and its evidently fragile certainties; events, that is, capable of ushering in a new period of design culture all over the world.

If Europe is subjected to the influx of the Far East and Deep South, it also true that these territories now import fragments and segments of our culture. This is perhaps the only positive aspect of globalization, which has failed as a conveyor of a mono-logical order: it has not produced a standardization of brains but, instead, it has opened up a new space of knowledge between men and about men.

This sort of hybridization of the human race does not iron out differences, but produces a new definition of anthropological certainties, no longer guaranteeing objective parameters, but a state of opacity regarding our very roots, blocking access to what seemed like ancient birthrights. Roots that over time have given us the illusion that outside the Occident there was just a desert, where - as we used to say - hic sunt leones...

I cannot forget that way back in 1969 we participated, as the radical group, at the Milan Triennale with an installation in Islamic style: many decades later, that intuition seems prophetic: another side of the moon really does exist.

These are some of the aspects that characterize the 21st century, so different from its predecessors: hybrids, contaminations, syncretism and, at the same time, a reawakening of diversities, local specificities, religious absolutes. Our design culture, then, operates with great difficulty in the midst of this complexity and these new opportunities: it is substantially self-absorbed and Calvinist, continuing to contemplate itself, while somehow realizing that its path is about to reach an epochal turning point.

The end of Eurocentrism is a challenge that impacts our whole society: this challenge opens up a difficult period of transition, and the results have yet to be understood.

Andrea Branzi. *Unitè tempoestosa, Stormy Unitè*, 2014

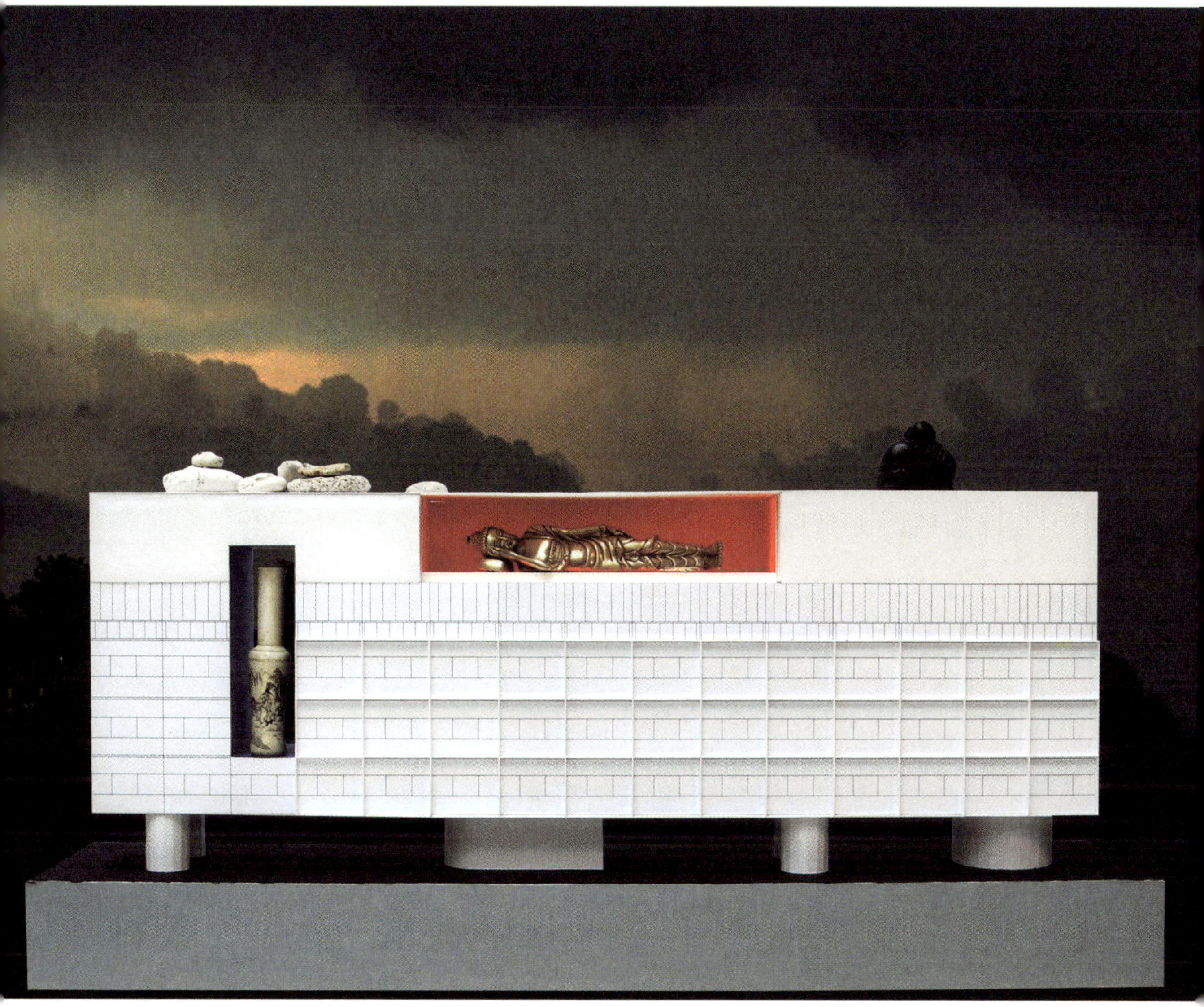

020
Sound
To make noises to arouse people's attention by hitting, blowing or playing things that emit sounds.
Suonare
Fare un rumore che desta l'attenzione di altri uomini, soffiando o percuotendo un oggetto in grado di generare un suono.
鳴らす
021
Condole
Tumulare
弔う

Neo-Prehistory: 100 verbs
Andrea Branzi, 2016

//

The Neo-Prehistory illustrates the eternal uncertainty of our work, which takes place step by step, without a precise awareness of what our future will be. It is therefore "Design After Design" – in other words, a form of design that has lost the "design of itself."
(...)

A hundred verbs, a hundred vital forces guide the viewer from primeval flints to the silicon of micro-technologies.

Through a dark and boundless space, where one comes across dolmens and highly sophisticated tools, we find a human history that expands in all directions, partly the result of technical handbooks and partly of an artificial intelligence. At times a technical advance shines a light through the darkness, the violence, the mysteries and legends that have always accompanied human existence on this planet.

The twenty-first century is profoundly different from the previous one, with its optimistic rationalism in which Modernity guaranteed a Future of order and Infinite Progress. The design of the twentieth century, so self-referential, elegant, intelligent, and forever new, simply ignored two world wars, racial extermination and atomic conflicts, without any of this upsetting its code.

It chose Disciplinary History in place of Real History.

This new century – so different, so contradictory – must take a bold look at the Present rather than at the Future, because it is now that the hardest game is being played out. It is being played out in an increasingly complex and contradictory world, where politics and design appear unable to act as instruments of order, of planning, or even of justice.

"Design After Design" is a reference to this lack of continuity in the practices and processes of design, accepting Chaos not just a lack of order but also as participation in the laws that govern the world of people and things.

In this sense, "Neo-Prehistory" means living with a New Anthropology, with a New Dramatic art that retraces the dark paths of a world unable to find peace, but only brilliant, generous, enlightened inspiration, in a land whose borders we cannot know. A land that constantly brings into play the idea of Infinite Progress but without showing how it is to be interpreted, while violence co-exists (and at time coincides) with the miracles of Science.

So it is not a matter of painting a "pessimistic" picture of the Present, but rather a "realistic" one, far from utopian ideas and from the old optimism of a Modernity that proved incapable of controlling what it induced.

The uncertainties, fears, and vital energy of Prehistory are coming back to guide our progress towards a provisional Future, in a multi-ethnic society of seven billion people, where each individual is an exception and a potential but also a riddle that cannot be solved.

Andrea Branzi, *Neo Prehistory*, XXI Triennal of Milan
Photos: Gianluca di Iola

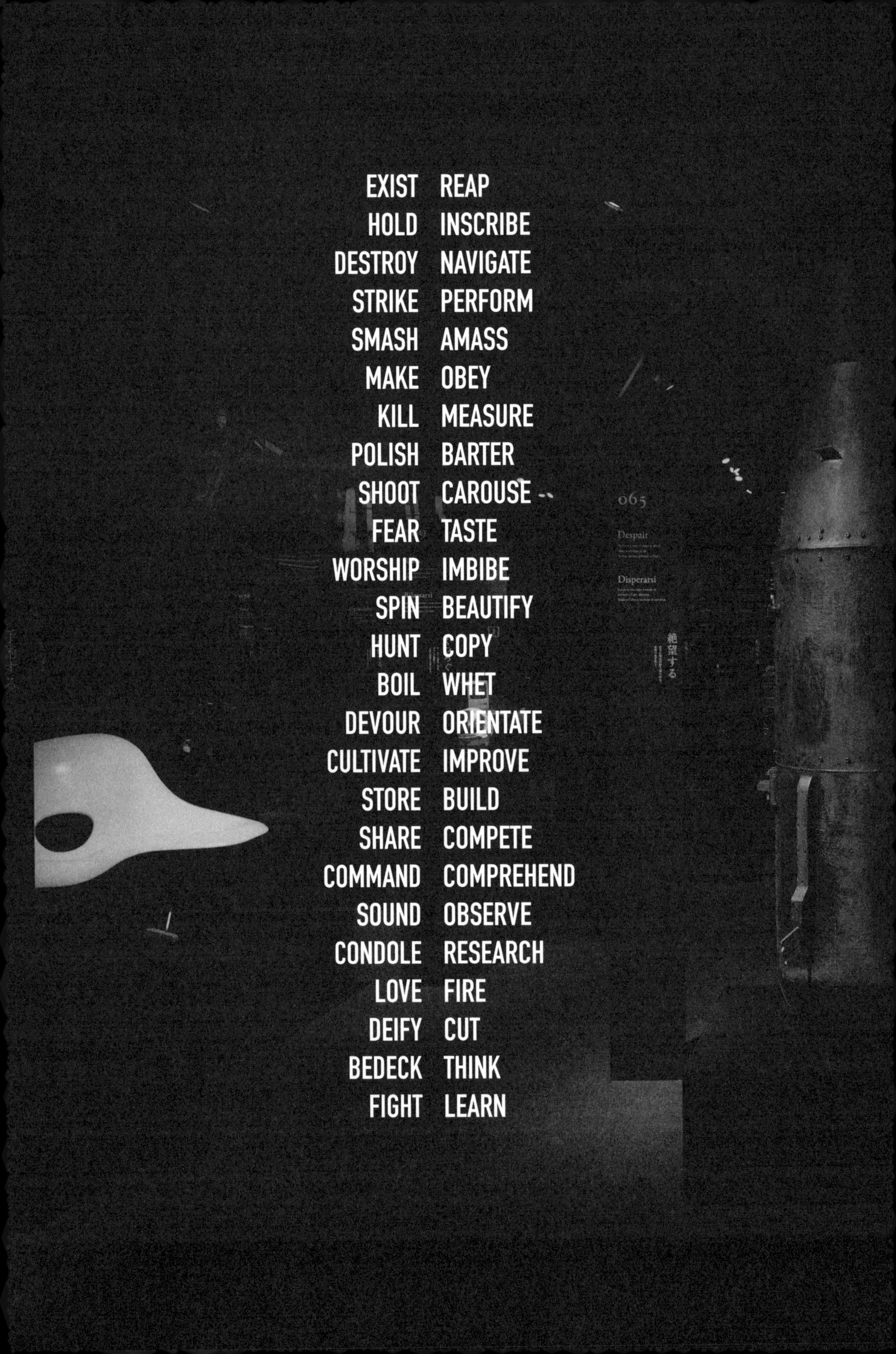

EXIST	REAP
HOLD	INSCRIBE
DESTROY	NAVIGATE
STRIKE	PERFORM
SMASH	AMASS
MAKE	OBEY
KILL	MEASURE
POLISH	BARTER
SHOOT	CAROUSE
FEAR	TASTE
WORSHIP	IMBIBE
SPIN	BEAUTIFY
HUNT	COPY
BOIL	WHET
DEVOUR	ORIENTATE
CULTIVATE	IMPROVE
STORE	BUILD
SHARE	COMPETE
COMMAND	COMPREHEND
SOUND	OBSERVE
CONDOLE	RESEARCH
LOVE	FIRE
DEIFY	CUT
BEDECK	THINK
FIGHT	LEARN

PLAY CONSOLIDATE
MOVE EMBELLISH
CHERISH TRAVEL
WORK COMMEMORATE
EARN CELEBRATE
GAMBLE OVERINDULGE
ACCELERATE RECYCLE
POLLUTE COMMUNICATE
INVENT CONDENSE
MANUFACTURE SHOP
PILOT AUTOMATE
ANNIHILATE IMITATE
SLAUGHTER FLY
ATTACK SURVIVE
DESPAIR PRETEND
SURRENDER DELIVER
OPERATE OUTPUT
FASCINATE RESTORE
RELAX REMOTE-OPERATE
COOK SCRUTINIZE
PLAN RELY
TRANSMIT MINIMIZE
EXPAND SELF-ORGANIZE
TREND VISUALIZE
INTIMIDATE REGENERATE

Andrea Branzi, *Neo Prehistory*, XXI Triennal of Milan
Photos: Gianluca di Iola

002
Hold
Afferrare
持つ

4.2

TEN MODEST ADVICES FOR A NEW ATHEN'S CHART

Andrea Branzi with Angela Rui, *Ten Modest Advices for a New Athen's Chart*, 2014

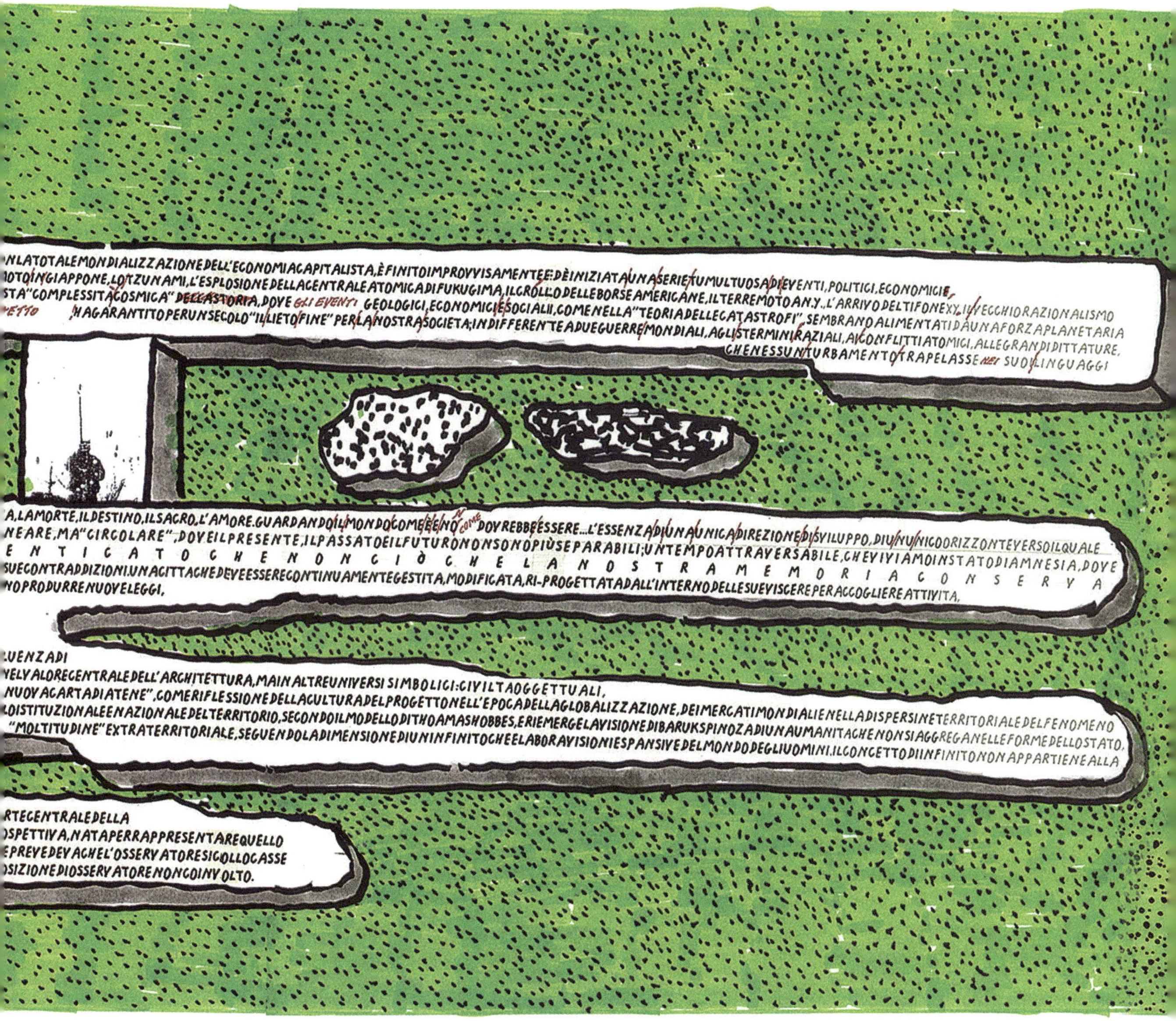
NLATOTALEMONDIALIZZAZIONEDELL'ECONOMIACAPITALISTA,ÈFINITOIMPROVVISAMENTEE:ÈINIZIATAUNASERIETUMULTUOSADIEVENTI,POLITICI,ECONOMICIE,
MOTOINGIAPPONE,LOTZUNAMI,L'ESPLOSIONEDELLACENTRALEATOMICADIFUKUGIMA,ILCROLLODELLEBORSEAMERICANE,ILTERREMOTOAN.Y.,L'ARRIVODELTIFONEXY,ILVECCHIORAZIONALISMO
STA"COMPLESSITÀCOSMICA"DELLASTORIA,DOVE GLI EVENTI GEOLOGICI,ECONOMICIESOCIALII,COMENELLA"TEORIADELLECATASTROFI",SEMBRANOALIMENTATIDAUNAFORZAPLANETARIA
ETTO ,HAGARANTITOPERUNSECOLO"ILLIETOFINE"PERLANOSTRASOCIETA;INDIFFERENTEADUEGUERREMONDIALI,AGLISTERMINIRAZIALI,AICONFLITTIATOMICI,ALLEGRANDIDITTATURE,
CHENESSUNTURBAMENTOTRAPELASSE NEI SUOILINGUAGGI
A,LAMORTE,ILDESTINO,ILSACRO,L'AMORE.GUARDANDOILMONDOCOMEÈENO COME DOVREBBEESSERE...L'ESSENZADIUNAUNICADIREZIONEDISVILUPPO,DIUNUNICOORIZZONTEVERSOILQUALE
NEARE,MA"CIRCOLARE",DOVEILPRESENTE,ILPASSATOEILFUTURONONSONOPIÙSEPARABILI;UNTEMPOATTRAVERSABILE,CHEVIVIAMOINSTATODIAMNESIA,DOVE
E N T I C A T O C H E N O N C I Ò C H E L A N O S T R A M E M O R I A C O N S E R V A
SUECONTRADDIZIONI.UNACITTACHEDEVEESSERECONTINUAMENTEGESTITA,MODIFICATA,RI-PROGETTATADALL'INTERNODELLESUEVISCEREPERACCOGLIEREATTIVITA,
NOPRODURRENUOVELEGGI,
LUENZADI
VELVALORECENTRALEDELL'ARCHITETTURA,MAINALTREUNIVERSI SIMBOLICI:CIVILTAOGGETTUALI,
NUOVACARTADIATENE",COMERIFLESSIONEDELLACULTURADELPROGETTONELL'EPOCADELLAGLOBALIZZAZIONE,DEIMERCATIMONDIALIENELLADISPERSINETERRITORIALEDELFENOMENO
LOISTITUZIONALEENAZIONALEDELTERRITORIO,SECONDOILMODELLODITHOAMASHOBBES,ERIEMERGELAVISIONEDIBARUKSPINOZADIUNAUMANITACHENONSIAGGREGANELLEFORMEDELLOSTATO.
"MOLTITUDINE"EXTRATERRITORIALE,SEGUENDOLADIMENSIONEDIUNINFINITOCHEELABORAVISIONIESPANSIVEDELMONDODEGLIUOMINI.ILCONCETTODIINFINITONONAPPARTIENEALLA
RTECENTRALEDELLA
OSPETTIVA,NATAPERRAPPRESENTAREQUELLO
EPREVEDEVACHEL'OSSERVATORESICOLLOCASSE
OSIZIONEDIOSSERVATORENONCOINVOLTO.

Ten Modest Advices for a New Athen's Chart

Andrea Branzi, 2009

//

In recent years my work has been mainly concentrated on the search for new "weak models of urbanization," theoretical models that try to interpret the social and functional conditions of the Twenty-first century.

These conditions are profoundly different from those of the previous century, but have not yet been properly and globally interpreted.

It is not my intention to produce a unitary model of the modern "goods civilization" city, but rather to make a contribution to its different interpretation, still too bound to the centrality of architecture.

Le Corbusier's Map of Athens of 1933 was never implemented, but was a useful mental model for interpreting the "industrial city" – a city consisting of specialized zoning (residential, leisure, production, traffic, old city centers) serving a single specialized function, separated like the teeth of a gear, though each maintaining its own autonomy.

The Twentieth-century city always assumed the presence of a "perimeter," a "boundary," a "threshold" that separated it from a politically different world, from the agricultural world, or from ore-industrial culture. These limits have now gone and, as the philosophers say, we live in a world "that no longer has an exterior"; a globalized world where states are ever weaker and society has become a "multitude"; a world where architecture and agriculture merge, where capitalism and socialism co-exist, where technology and the sacred are a single thing.

So it is a world where the category of the "infinite" (as Erwin Panofsky wrote) is the only possible symbolic form of an "opaque, ambiguous form, free of any external image"; an "infinite" that must exist in our mind, in our psyche, before existing in reality: mind and psyche are the only possible territories for a refounding of architecture.

So the aim of a *New Chart of Athens* is not the city of the future, but rather the city of the Present, with all its limits and contradictions. A city that must be constantly "rethought, readapted, and replanned," in search of temporary balances. A city that corresponds to our "reformist society," free of any unitary reference model, that must every day produce new laws, new statutes, and new rules to positively manage its own permanent state of crisis.

First recommendation:
Consider the city as a "high-tech favelas"; avoid rigid and definitive solutions and favor reversible, incomplete, imperfect systems that allow the urban space to be constantly adapted to new unexpected and unplanned activities.

Second recommendation:
Consider the city as a "personal computer every twenty square meters": avoid the identification of form and function, specialist types, rigid systems, armored perimeters; create areas similar to "functionoids" that can host every activity in every place, changing function in real time.

Third recommendation:
Consider the city as a place of "cosmic hospitality": encourage "planetary coexistence" between man and animals, technology and divinities, living and dead, as in the Indian metropolis; cities that are less anthropocentric and more open to biodiversity, the sacred, and human beauty.

Fourth recommendation:
Consider new models of "weak urbanization": imagine permeable districts between city and country, hybrid semi-urban and semi-agricultural places; productive and hospitable areas that follow the changing of the seasons and seasons and climate, creating conditions of widespread and reversible livability.

Fifth recommendation:
Consider blurred and accessible confines and foundations; create organisms with an uncertain perimeter, within an urban fabric where the difference between interior and exterior, public and private disappears, creating an integrated district without functional specializations.

Sixth recommendation:
Design "light, temporary, reversible infrastructure"; build roads, bridges, connections with non rigid, non definitive, removable logistical systems that leave no trace on the ground and adapt to the change of local needs over time.

Seventh recommendation:
Consider the city as being "micro-conditioned all-full"; interpret the city as a place where architecture is not a "visual" presence, but a "sensorial, experiential, immaterial" reality; a place of computer relations and virtual economies; an anthropological area in constant renewal, movement, replacement.

Eighth recommendation:
Consider the big transformations as the "result of micro operations;" interpret urban quality as the result of the semiosphere made up of domestic objects, tools, services. goods, people; like Mohamed Yunus's microcredit, you have to go into the domestic economies and interstices of everyday life.

Ninth recommendation:
Consider the city as a "genetic laboratory": interpret the city as a "factory of life;" place of genome exchanges, sexual experiences, development of one's own gene; cities of humans, bodies, flows of sperm, births, and deaths.

Tenth recommendation:
Consider the city as "living plankton": interpret the city as a "bio-technological" system, in constant transformation, that produces economy and culture as a spontaneous effect of its own expansive energy.

A Society without a Project

In his masterpiece *The Tropic of Cancer*, Henry Miller wrote that he had carefully scrutinized inside a vagina and assured us that, "There is nothing inside."

The discovery of the "emptiness" within a human organ at the center of much interest and the desire of half of humanity, is similar to the description that Nikolai Gogol makes of the "trading of nothing" in the novel *Dead Souls* that describes not only the paradox of the law on Gleba's Slaves but of the whole of Tsarist Russia.

Paradoxical prophecies of the imminent "jump into the void" that at certain moments society must perform to discover – with vertigo – that the old apparatuses of values must disappear because other social or cultural frameworks are pressing; paintings not yet defined, but which certainly need the "void" to manifest.

Making a "clean sweep" is an act of refounding similar to the *Black Square* on *White Background* of Malevich, as a new primordial alphabet for a completely new society.

Ever since Cézanne left large spaces of unpainted canvas, a race began among artists to empty the painting, like Pollock, Hartung, or Fontana, who replaced representation with signs or cuts, and like Cage who definitively interrupted the music... Silence, emptiness; there is nothing to say or to show.

We also dance on the abyss of a liberated "void," whose destiny is not defined, but for which we need to prepare a "space" that is not encumbered with old pre-existences.

After all, what indispensable thing should we preserve? Ideologies have disappeared; the parties have dissolved; religion concerns a minority in a crisis of identity; social relations are a strictly private matter; art has become (rightly) incomprehensible; literature is silent; poetry is boring, pop music repetitive, fashion self-referential, the family superfluous, women equal to men; only transsexuals seem to be the bearers of new times...

The world is inhabited by seven billion people who overwhelmed by Eros continue to multiply exponentially and uncontrollably; most of them are dissatisfied with where they are and want (rightfully) to emigrate; you have to make space...

After all, the Third World War has already broken out, but it is called Asymmetrical or Virtual, and it seems to concern television more than armies.

In conclusion: the world must urgently be emptied, freed from old hierarchies and any design interference.

We must recreate the "Void," that is, a space where there is nothing inside; there is us, and that's it. Without violence and without spreading terror or death, instead favoring everyone's dreams.

In 1972, with Archizoom we did something similar, a sort of general test of the possibility of "removing everything" from an environmental project; in the great exhibition *Italy: The New Domestic Landscape* at the MoMA in New York dedicated to Italian design, we created a large, empty, gray, inexpressive room, in which only the voice of a child could be heard, vaguely describing a colorful, bright, welcoming house; each visitor could imagine it as they wanted [...] It was a way to opt out of the festival of new technologies, of the machines for living of which the exhibition was full, and to simply state that "Living Is Easy."

"Emptying" space has never been easy, because "emptiness" is not produced through "nihilism" but through a radical, positive, velvety creative act, capable of producing mysterious fragrances, distant sounds, transparent shadows, within which the voice of Amy Winehouse and the music of Chet Baker and Charlie Parker rise like a wisp of smoke. An "emptiness" full of elusive beauty; a Nirvana similar to the Buddhist renunciation of the possessions and temptations of this world? The perfect "misery" of St. Francis? The perennial fasting of the Indian gurus? To each the choice of their own bed and their own silence.

This is what we need today, and this can be achieved: a micro-air-conditioned space, opaque like a wall of fog, inside which you can move as if in an aquarium made of vibrating molecules.

Too many physical and immaterial presences crowd around us: a society "without a project" and "without perspective" is what we are looking for, as an extreme act of classical modernity, which drains and reflects on its dogmas and useless legacies.

Among these, there is the "law of perspective" that concerns a discovery (of a more philosophical and optical nature) through which Filippo Brunelleschi affirmed the principle according to which in order to "represent" an event, an image, or a landscape, the observer had to place himself "outside" the scene, occupying that "point of view" that from then on will define our position with respect to the scenario of History.

Now, that distance is no longer sustainable, and the "observer" has to physically enter the "theater of the world," inside that sublime "void" of existence, and as Henry Miller discovered that inside "there is nothing," but only the shadows of our sacred dead, from Janis Joplin, to Jimi Hendrix, to Jim Morrison, to Freddie Mercury, and to all those young people who drugged themselves to survive a world that was killing them. Like the Indians of the Andes holding a coca leaf under their tongue, not to "escape from the world" but to "survive in the world."

Is it worth it "to judge" the world and history again, or is it better to be silent, not to look, not to plan? Or rather how the "stylites" place themselves up high and internalize the world as if it were an "empty sphere"? The uselessness of "judging" to save our souls is a practice that no longer works because it does not interest anyone. Better silence, the "emptiness," without a project and without uselessly occupying the territory of one's own existence and of others.

A "void" as big as a canvas by Pollock, Hartung, Rothko, Bacon, on which to dance like men who through the reversibility of Darwin's law have returned to the "animal" state, as the freest and most modern one.

Around me, I see a "cold generation" growing, plaintive and silent, atheist and "politically correct," devoid of motivations and emotions, attracted by the "emptiness" but unable to create it. Zygmunt Bauman told us at the beginning of the 21st century about "Generation X" being the "first generation without God," as the effect of a "Liquid Modernity" devoid of its own form; but now it is the "First Generation Without A Project," both liquid and solid.

A generation that wants to start again from zero, to free oneself of the Past, of the Future, but also of the Present; a "neo-primitive" generation that lives in the penumbra of an unlimited space, with no horizon, where every event is an "end in itself," and is not part of a destiny but of chaos, which is not the result of the lack of an order, but of the laws that govern the Universe.

A generation that, thanks to the "emptiness" that surrounds it, can "return to seeing the stars again"...

Andrea Branzi, 2017

CRITICAL CONTRIBUTIONS

Probable Autobiography
Andrea Branzi, 2017

//

I believe that the possibility of inventing a part of one's life is a great privilege.

That is why this document, written by me in the third person, contains true information and false news.

This is not a chronology, but instead a "theoretical document" like many others characteristic of my work: it is not objective information, but an organic part of my way of working.

I made this decision because the true story of my life has no direct relationship with what I did and with what I think.

This account is divided into separate parts, because life never has a linear development but traverses seasons that between them are never even.

The very important moments are very few, and often very brief and not easily traceable.

In general, architects' biographies are boring because they are made up of one philological list of dates and completed works: a list like that has no meaning.

Those who believe that the history of architecture is only made up of completed works are mistaken.

Often more important were those projects that were conceived, failed, or were interrupted, which originated by chance, via the market, or from theory. Events like these, which apparently have nothing to do with the "noble history of architecture," but they have to do with the private life of the architect.

For me, the life (true or false) of a poet, an artist, or an architect has always been more important than the list of his or her works. In this biography, I have therefore tried to force some episodes, invent others, and recount some as they actually happened.

I did not undertake a self-analysis or an examination of conscience but instead a literary narrative to explain to myself and to others how things happened confusedly, or how it might have been better to have happened...

Amid the mysteries of life with which we are overwhelmed, it is useless to look for a logical thread that does not exist; existence is always an expression of chaos, and chaos is the general law of the universe.

Everyone can interpret it, describe it, or change it at will. The truth is not an absolute category, and it will never be traceable.

Many people get attached to a mistaken image of themselves: invented, that is, by themselves.

Therefore, I did not try to clear up the misunderstandings that concern me, but I tried to make them more interesting and complex.

After all, I believe that this is the role of the architect: to modify, alter, transgress parts of reality, without ever transforming it completely.

It is no coincidence that there are no two identical works of architecture in the world, the variant being the architect himself, his ambitions, or his weaknesses.

Probable Autobiography

Andrea Branzi was born on November 30, 1938 in Florence, at Via Giovan Battista Amici No. 10, in the parish of San Gervasio, on the outskirts of the city.

Andrea is the youngest of seven siblings (four brothers and three sisters); the family, of Jewish origin but fervently Catholic, had recently moved to the city from the province.

Renato, the father, originally from Montelupo, had worked on the railways from where he had been removed for political reasons.

The paternal grandfather had been a prison guard, and his two children (Renato and Lina) had grown up among lifers and criminals. Retired, the grandfather had managed an itinerant cart selling shoes in Signa.

Lorenza Corsi, the mother, was the daughter of a small mechanical entrepreneur (early motorcycles, early bicycles) with a workshop in Lastra a Signa, on the banks of the Bisenzio River.

The two were married in 1922.

When they arrived in Florence, they opened the "Libreria Scolastica Fiorentina" (Florentine Scholastic Bookstore) on Via del Corso, in the historic center of the city. The mother, despite the seven children, ran the store while the father was increasingly involved in clandestine political work.

Even though he was an accountant, he continued studying French and had one of the first editions of Italo Svevo's *La Coscienza di Zeno* (*Zeno's Conscience*) on his bedside table.

Little Andrea was baptized at Ospedalino Mayer where he was born. It was very cold in the chapel (it was the first days of December), and the infant came down with a serious case of pneumonia that took him to the brink of death. While the family was already mourning him, a hot "poultice" of semolina arrived from the kitchen (that is how pneumonia was treated back then) that was applied to the dying infant, who showed weak signs of life.

The baby grew up slim, with delicate health, with alternating long periods at the hospital and with bronchitis, tonsillitis, and pulmonary problems, taken care of at home with long bed rests of endless convalescence.

From this period, he has always preserved confused memories and the feeling of being different from his siblings and from other children.

In 1940, Italy entered the War. Andrea's first clear memory dates back to 1943 when the first Allied bombing of Florence took place.

The family rushed to the cellar, and when the alarm ceased, strange news arrived about bombs that had produced deaths through "blasts of air," a phenomenon that no one had ever heard of.

After the first bombing, the San Gervasio district was no longer safe because the Allies hit the infrastructure of the suburbs. Over the course of the incursions, two schools of thought formed: those who said that when a bombing began, it was necessary to stay in place (because those who had fled had died) and those who, on the other hand, stated that it was necessary to flee (because who had stayed had died).

So, the family fled to Vaglia, a small agricultural town north of Florence, where Andrea spent three happy years. The contact with the countryside, the streams, and the animals did everyone some good. The older brothers got engaged to female evacuees whom they later married.

During that time, in addition to the paternal and maternal grandparents, a cousin named "Franchino di Genova," and a Jewish girl named Branca Radich, called Mady, who had fled from Yugoslavia were added to the family.

In 1945, the family returned to Florence housed by a relative living on the Lungarno Torrigiani, from where the child curiously scrutinized the first air battles and from where he saw a large herd of oxen, pushed by the retreating Germans, pass through the deserted city, crossing under the monumental arcades of the Uffizi in silence like a sacred, sacrilegious procession.

In that torrid and luminous summer, life had become dangerous for everyone.

The father Renato, wanted by the Fascist police, had to go underground in order not to be shot along with other political prisoners.

The two older brothers had to choose whether to enter the Partisan formations or to enlist in the army of the Republic of Salò.

Franco, the second-born, was supposed to join the barracks, but having been picked to shoot deserters, he managed to escape, but sustained the syndrome for life of being a predestined victim of misfortune, which would lead him many years later to die due to severe psychosomatic disturbances.

Meanwhile, the "Libreria Scolastica Fiorentina" had become one of the centers of the Catholic Resistance, and Lorenza the mother, strict and elegant, acted as a relay and held (by memory) the "Freedom Chest."

The eldest of the brothers, Giancarlo, a student of medicine, was supposed to join the Catholic Partisans, but at the last moment the Commando preferred to have him work inside the university, and in his place Franco Sbrilli was chosen, and was shot by the Germans in the Apennines.

But in July 1945, as the Allies (as agreed) were about to transfer outside of Florence, "the open city," the Germans were surprised by the frontal attack of the Partisans, who wanted to enter the city and institute a provisional government. The Germans re-entered the city and mined the bridges over the Arno and in the neighborhoods around the Ponte Vecchio. The population was displaced, and the Branzi family fortunately moved to a small four-room apartment on Via XXVII April, where a total of 24 people were hiding: relatives, friends, Partisans, Jews, deserters.

Of the first night in that apartment, Andrea has always preserved a particular memory: without lights, without water, with the danger of traitors, in a city that was preparing for the final battle, on the hot summer night lit by the moon, the small community gathered in prayer.

A profound happiness was present in everyone. A world was about to end, and the bombs were falling, breaking apart the old small villas of Umberto I and with it the ugly humanity that inhabited them: evil, reactionary, violent, villainous families, leaving their place to a new generation.

The nights spent in the cellar, the real and false alarms, would follow one after the other, while in the city a violent civil war developed between the Partisans and the Fascist snipers positioned on the roofs. After two weeks, the emergency ended, and members of this community came outside because the war seemed over. They had only eaten a hundred kilos of sweet onions, the flavor of which remained in the family's DNA for a long time... The American soldiers gave out chocolate in the streets, but the sight of the rubble troubled the little Andrea, who asked an old man what all that gray stuff was. "It's the rubble," he replied, "but to me, it makes me want to cry," he said instinctively; "And yes, son, this is what they've reduced our beautiful Florence to," said the man.

After the war, the Branzi family moved to Borgo Ognissanti No. 9, in the Palazzo Gerini, in a labyrinthine 24-room apartment, packed together but not very airy or bright, like many other noble family palazzos divided up by the heirs.

Andrea lived in that apartment until his wedding day in 1969.

The 1950s in Florence and in Italy were marked by a devastating mediocrity: after the war, everyone tried to imagine a different, modern, industrial life, destroying their origins without having different quality models of life. One ate badly, drank badly, dressed badly, wished for everything, but was afraid of everything. The Italy of the "economic miracle" emptied itself out by transforming into a confused, provincial, modest, politically apathetic, poor, but ambitious country totally devoid of identity.

Instead of sending Andrea to school, the decision was made to have him do elementary school at home: this decision had serious consequences. When the child was enrolled in 1950 in the middle school of the Padri Scolopi of Via Cavour, he did not know how to study, and he was afraid of the teachers and the other children. Quickly, the severe disorder of dyslexia manifested itself, with difficulties in writing and reading, accompanied by "ontological crises," consisting of an anguished feeling of "not existing." Childhood disorders that can lead to schizophrenia. Being treated as in inpatient in specialized clinics managed to stabilize these pathologies.

At the age of ten, he began to instinctively look after himself by devoting himself obsessively to drawing, becoming a kind of child prodigy. Nonetheless, he had a disastrous start to his education, which lasted through high school, during which he had to repeat four classes. At the Liceo Dante in Piazza Indipendenza and the Congregazione Mariana of Viale Don Minzoni run by Jesuit priests, Andrea made many friends, beginning the socialization he had never had. With some of these friends, he established relationships that endure to today.

When he entered university, despite some perplexity on the part of the family that he would enroll in the Faculty of Architecture, he brilliantly passed the 37 exams graduating in 1966 with the highest marks. His graduate project has been preserved in the historical Archive, of the Centre Pompidou.

In the early 1960s, he had begun to frequent the early circles of political philosophy of the *Quaderni Piacentini, Quaderni Rossi,* and *Classe Operaia,* which had a great influence on his intellectual development.

The most difficult period of his life was ending; the sense of difference that had always accompanied him was becoming a cultural advantage with respect to a generation that was witnessing the crisis of the Modern Movement, of old politics, of old bourgeois customs, but also the birth of new music, youth fashion, and Pop Art.

More than from the professors, he learned from what went on outside the university and from other students who were much more mature and cultured than him, with which the Archizoom group initiated the movement that Andrea baptized with the name of Radical.

The most important moment of his education, which will always accompany him in the future, occurred when he interpreted the significance of all the processes of social liberation as a new spatial dimension (*No-Stop City*). A dimension that surpassed the fragmentation of traditional urbanism and regained the dimension of the "infinite." A dimension that adhered to the void produced by the bourgeois crisis and the quantitative utopia of neo-capitalism; the highest level of alienation coincided with the highest level of freedom.

In 1968, when he went skiing in Switzerland, he suffered a serious injury, for which he still lives with the consequences; it forced him into a lengthy hospital stay in Interlaken in front of the glaciers of the Jungfrau, giving him time to reflect and to make important decisions about his future: Andrea has always considered that period of solitude as one of the happiest of his life.

Among the decisions he made was that of marrying, after many engagements, of which one with two different sisters, and after a long relationship with a young Jewish writer, in 1969 Andrea Branzi married Nicoletta Morozzi, much younger than him, sister of Massimo, a member of the Archizoom group. Their marriage took place together with Lucia Morozzi and Dario Bartolini, all from the Archizoom group.

In 1969, the first daughter Orsola was born, and the following year, the second, Lorenza.

In the meantime, Andrea abandons, without any issue, the religious faith and the very closed family environment: his three sisters married, in succession, three brothers. His new environment was among the friends of the Radical movement and pop music.

For a long time, Andrea identified with the image of Bob Dylan.

Yet, the early years of life with the Archizoom Associati group (Gilberto Corretti, Paolo Deganello, Massimo Morozzi, and later Dario and Lucia Bartolini), notwithstanding the rapid local and international growth of the Radical movement, were very difficult. The growing opposition of local professionals, the freemasons, and the university led to a criminal charge for defacement of monuments. The four-year-long trial, with convictions and acquittals, ended with the end of the terms of custody.

In 1974, the group made the mutual decision to disband, and part of the group moved to Milan. Together, Andrea Branzi and Massimo Morozzi became consultants in charge of the Design Center of Montefibre, a chemical fibers manufacturing industry. The Center produced the first experiences that Andrea baptized with the term of "Design Primario" (color, ambient decor, trend guides, sensory structures, bodily perceptions).

In 1978, the Center ended its activity and was awarded the Compasso d'Oro for the first collaboration of design with an industry of raw materials and the operation of the first Design of Services.

Milan in the 1970s was marked by the beginning of terrorism and of violence in the streets. In the early days, going underground was still a worldly game.

One evening, going to dinner with Ettore Sottsass and Fernanda Pivano at the Hotel Continental, we met Gian Giacomo Feltrinelli, whom no one was looking for, disguised and in drag.

But soon the climate degenerated: Ettore was attacked in the Galleria Vittorio Emanuele, unwitting friends massacred by blows, Alessandro Mendini's wife was wounded in the attack in front of the Questura, our studio at the Ponte delle Gabelle searched. You could not pass by Piazza San Babila without the danger of being beaten up.

During that period, the relationship of friendship with Ettore Sottsass continued to grow, right up until his death in 2007. Milan was considered the world's capital of design, but the Masters were all trained in the 1950s during the reconstruction period of the Cold War and of Rationalism. The new Radical generation, increasingly numerous, changed the cultural milieu of Milan, through a spontaneous and widespread movement that Andrea baptized with the name of Nuovo Design Italiano (New Italian Design).

Then a conflict began to build between the protagonists of this new trend and the followers of Aldo Rossi, and in 1973 at the XV Triennale di Milano there was a violent theoretical and physical confrontation.

While Aldo Rossi's followers retreated to the ivory tower of the university, New Italian Design continued its independent research from which, at the end of the 1970s, the first independent experimental laboratories were founded, first Alchymia and later Memphis.

The backdrop for these experiments was the end of the great Mass Markets and the emergence of niche markets (which the industries had not yet understood) that required a new expressiveness of the products, capable of selecting their users, using artisanal materials and production in small series.

This new market structure, ten years later, became known as Post-Industrial Society.

The initiatives of New Italian Design quickly enjoyed great international success. But soon both Alchymia and Memphis became stylistic academies, which imitated themselves. Faced with this setback, Andrea Branzi took on the '80s with a very ambitious new initiative – the foundation of a small school able to tackle new technologies, new ways of using objects, new social needs.

In 1982, Domus Academy was born, for which Andrea was the cultural director for ten years.

Behind Domus Academy, there was the long history of cultural reflection that began in the 1960s with the Radical Movement, but Andrea even convinced some of the Masters to collaborate on this initiative, challenging them to tackle the new issues. In addition to Ettore Sottsass, Vico Magistretti, Mario Bellini, Pierre Restany, and Gianfranco Ferrè committed themselves to the unknown adventure of teaching. New Technologists and New Sociologists formed within this tiny organism (thirty students).

The teaching methodology was very simple: it focused on the "designer" and not on the "design"; towards a future of complexity and not of order. The international anticipation for this initiative was enormous.

From the first year, students came from Canada, USA, Australia, China, Japan, India, and European countries. In 1984, there were 34 pupils from 29 different countries.

During these ten years, Andrea held conferences in France, Belgium, the Netherlands, Germany, England, Austria, Spain, Portugal, the United States, Brazil, Argentina, Japan, Taiwan, Korea, China, Singapore, Thailand.

For two years, he moved to Japan to head the Domus Design Agency, promoted by Mitsubishi for design development in small innovative industries.

For these activities, he received the career "Compasso d'Oro" in 1987.

At the same time, from 1982 to 1984, Andrea was also director of the magazine Modo, founded a few years earlier by Alessandro Mendini.

In those same years, a small orphan nephew was adopted by his family.

The stress of so many commitments and responsibilities led him to a severe nervous breakdown.

But the international experiences convinced him that design was becoming a "mass profession" all over the world, which provided international markets with the particular energy of innovation that is indispensable for taking on international competition.

At the end of the 1990s, Andrea thus decided to abandon the dimension of the small schools to enter the Faculty of Design of the Politecnico di Milano, where he became a tenured professor and President of the Interior Design Program.

In 2007, Andrea underwent serious heart surgery, and in the same year received the Laurea Honoris Causa from the Università della Sapienza of Rome and was appointed Honorary Member of London's Royal Design for Industry.

Andrea formed a school of thought at the Politecnico that interpreted interior design not as a simple decor, but as a fundamental activity in the processes of re-functionalizing the city. The decline of architecture, rigid and specialized, was no longer able to follow the continuous renewal of functions and services in the urban territory.

This transition from our Architectural Civilization in a Commodity Civilization had now been achieved, intuited by the Radical Movement, where the planetary circulation of goods was creating the political and social globalization of the planet.

This new unlimited dimension of the market and the territory corresponded to that idea of the "infinite" to which Andrea always referred: a dimension where everything becomes fluid, renews, transforms, where the perimeters become traversable and design no longer seeks definitive solutions.

In this new historical dimension, Andrea began the first research on "Weak Urbanization models," such as *Agronica*, where agriculture and architecture coexisted by merging together. Fluid models corresponding to the new self-reformist society, forced to continually modify their structure in order to deal with the cyclical crises that globalized neo-capitalism produces as the only possibility of development.

In 2010, he presented his proposal for a *New Athen's Charter* at the Venice Architecture Biennale, which referred to this new historical reality.

The new century was thus originating in a completely different way than the Classical Modernity of the twentieth century. Globalization was rapidly entering into crisis.

"Pax Capitalistica" did not exist, and a serious financial and industrial crisis was going through the markets.

After the failure of Socialism, the failure of Capitalism loomed as well.

During the previous century, the culture of design, indifferent to two World Wars, to the Cold War, to racial extremes, to the Great Dictatorships of the Right and the Left, had guaranteed a "happy ending" for industrial society, in a future of order and rationality.

Now the "Happy Ending" is no longer guaranteed, and design must overcome its aspect of Intelligent Profession (which responds to Intelligent Tomorrows) to become a "Culture" capable of addressing the great existential themes that Modernity always ignored, like death, life, destiny, the sacred, animals.

Andrea interpreted the emergence from the fractures internal to globalization as large, profound, remote, primordial "anthropological platforms" in which all human beings are recognized.

The frontier of a New Dramaturgy therefore marks the culture of the design in the 21st century: a vital but conscious dramaturgy of the profound and mysterious relationship that binds humankind to the natural and artificial environment.

Pier Vittorio Aureli

A Designer in the Age of Late Capital

Notes on the Work of Andrea Branzi

In 1970, the Italian design studio Archizoom Associati (formed by Andrea Branzi, Gilberto Corretti, Paolo Deganello, and Massimo Morozzi) drew up a series of typewriter-generated city plans. Comprised of a grid of periods and other punctuation marks, the plans simulate what the group referred to as a *No-Stop City*.[1] One such drawing, *Diagramma abitativo omogeneo* (*Homogeneous Housing Diagram*) (1970–71), is posited as an "ipotesi di linguaggio architettonico non figurativo" ("hypothesis for a non-figurative architectural language"). It consists of a repetitive grid of periods punctuated by X's (each of which represents a load-bearing structure), and describes the city as a continuous, inhabitable expanse, with no divisions between interior and exterior spaces. In this vision of the city, there are no more rooms, houses, blocks, streets, piazzas, parks, or monuments. This is an urban landscape broken down into its most rudimentary parts: a column every 5 meters, a bathroom every 10 meters, a lift every 50 meters.

Diagramma abitativo omogeneo is the synthesis of an idea of the city that Andrea Branzi has pursued over 50 years of research. The *No-Stop City* is devoid of the forms and figures that, for centuries, have organized the city as a field of differentiated spaces. Archizoom's use of "non-figurative language" defines the city as a vast urban interior, representing a stage in the urban condition in which all things are determined by the mastery of capital: within the interior, everything is a commodity.

According to Marx, the capitalist mode of production can be interpreted as an accumulation of commodities.[2] For Marx, commodities are multi-faceted: among their various attributes, they have a purpose (their use-value), and an exchange-value (or monetary value).[3] Within the system of exchange-value, anything that exists can be thought of in terms of its monetary counterpart, which works as the ultimate "universal equivalent." Within the capitalist mode of production, the logic of monetary value is ubiquitous and governs all human relationships. This logic can be imagined as an ever-expanding "interior" that turns everything within its borders into a potential commodity.

During the 19th century, one of the most spectacular symbols of the expanding world of commodities was the *Crystal Palace*, designed by the English gardener Joseph Paxton in 1851 for The Great Exhibition in London's Hyde Park. Here, products from all over the world were gathered within the vast, basilica-like space. The material elements of the structure were reduced to a bare minimum—steel and glass—minimizing the distinction between the interior space and the world outside. In the *Crystal Palace*, capital's *modus operandi*—the universal equivalence of all things—was translated into space by the gigantic, unobstructed interior, in which visitors could contemplate industrial production as an elevated, almost mystical spectacle. Branzi's body of work can be considered both a radical acceptance and a radical critique of this spectacle.

The ambivalence of Branzi's position towards the capitalist city is exemplified by the conflict between his model for the *No-Stop City* and the objects he has designed over the span of his career. While the *No-Stop City* represents a sea of unlimited urbanization, Branzi's objects resist easy accommodation within this condition. The objects are Trojan horses: while they overtly manifest their status as commodities, they simultaneously demystify the role of design within the capitalist value system. Contradictions of this kind play a vital role within Branzi's oeuvre.

2.

Branzi's practice begins with Archizoom's formation in the early 1960s at the School of Architecture in Florence. The school was one of the most politicized within the Italian university system, with many students involved in far-left politics.[4] In 1963, students staged a protest against the school's academic tradition of encouraging its pupils to develop studio projects individually rather than in groups.[5] This prompted several of the future members of Archizoom (as well as Superstudio) to work together on projects that challenged the conservatism of studio briefs. Among these projects, *Città Estrusa* (*Extruded City*) (1963–64) anticipated what would later become the hypothesis for *No-Stop City*. Developed by Branzi and his fellow students (including the future member of Superstudio, Cristiano Toraldo di Francia), the project responded to a brief asking students to re-imagine the site of the school as part of a new masterplan of the Piana di Sesto Fiorentino. The *piana* was a wide, flat territory outside Florence, densely urbanized and filled with small-scale factories. The area was a clear example of how the rapid economic development of the 1950s affected the Italian countryside, forming what at that time was labeled a *città-territorio*.[6] Rather than simply designing a group of buildings, Branzi and his collaborators proposed an integrated structure that included the university, as well as factories, offices, housing, and leisure space. The goal of the *Città Estrusa* was to integrate all the components of a city into a single apparatus: an all-inclusive, industrial space for production, as well as consumption.

A year before the students' proposal for *Città Estrusa*, the philosopher and political militant Mario Tronti published an essay in the journal *Quaderni Rossi* entitled "La fabbrica e la società" (The Factory and Society).[7] In the text—which would have a seminal influence on the *Operaismo* (workerism) movement—Tronti argued that, under capitalist development, the cycle of production-distribution-exchange would eventually become a unified and coherent process. Even social reproduction (housing, education, healthcare, and so on) would be woven into this system, becoming yet another mode of production. Tronti argued that within the capitalist city, the entire spectrum of social relationships would become defined by the logic of the factory.[8] It was Tronti's thesis that inspired the Florentine students to conceive of the city as a large-scale assembly line. Instead of designing a city for an alternative political or economic system, the future members of Archizoom chose to depict the existing reality of the capitalist city with unrelenting realism. It was this approach that pushed Archizoom to embrace pop-art sensibility in their early projects.

Think of Archizoom's early furniture piece, the *Safari* sofa (1966–7). With its leopard print upholstery and flamboyant shape, the ostentatious design of the sofa slyly condemns the fashionable decor of the *petit-bourgeois* apartment (which in mid-1960s Italy was becoming the domestic reality for the majority of industrial workers). Describing their approach to the design, Archizoom stated that their goal was "to re-evaluate stupidity and vulgarity as a proper artistic language freed from the intelligence and elegance of capitalism."[9] For Archizoom, the "intelligence and elegance" of capitalism was represented by Scandinavian design (what would later define the world of IKEA) whose smooth functionality represented the ideal of bourgeois society, the tacit goal pursued by the Welfare State.

Archizoom's lack of interest in political correctness in their designs is best represented by what is arguably their most confrontational project, the *Dream Beds* (1967). For this series, Archizoom re-imagined the most canonical domestic space: the bedroom. Traditionally a temple of privacy and marital love, Archizoom's "dream bed" is an altar of lust, a platform that defies its role as the locus of rest and reproduction and becomes, instead, a temple of dissipation. Like the *Safari* sofa, the *Dream Beds* were conceived as gestures of domestic terrorism against the smooth politeness of postwar design culture, in which everything was elegant, affordable, and functional.

Archizoom's name itself was a parody of the then-famous London-based architectural group, Archigram. While Archigram enthusiastically embraced technology and pop culture as an innocent means of liberation—think of Peter Cook's *Plug-In City* (1964)—Archizoom embraced the same ideals but with politically minded sarcasm. While for Archigram, pop culture was a celebration of mass culture, for Archizoom, pop emphasized the working class's increasingly consumerist ethos. For Archizoom, the hedonism of consumer culture was the embodiment of what the workerists defined as the working class's refusal of the well-tempered austerity implicit in the wage system. If, within capitalism, the wage earner is a dependent variable of profit, the workerists saw in the workers' demands for less work and more money their will to escape the logic of capital, which pushes workers to work more for less. Archizoom mobilized the crass vulgarity of pop culture as an expression of proletarian hedonism against the moralizing austerity invoked even by left-leaning organizations such as unions and the Italian Communist Party. This attitude was further defined in *Superarchitettura* (1966), Archizoom's first joint exhibition with Superstudio. "Super-architecture" was a working-class architecture freed from the moralism of bourgeois culture (notably, the exhibition was held in a fishmonger's shop). "Super-architecture" could freely express its class antagonism, even via the reified forms of commodity culture.

3.

Towards the end of the 1960s, Archizoom abandoned the use of pop references in their design work. The collective felt that pop culture's representation of the capitalist city was too simplistic. Instead, they became increasingly interested in understanding the functioning of the city as an abstract system defined by technologies such as air-conditioning and artificial lighting. In 1969, the members of Archizoom read Manfredo Tafuri's famous essay "For a Critique of Architectural Ideology,"[10] in which the Roman architectural historian makes a sweeping critique of progressive architecture's utopian aspirations. Inspired by Tafuri's argument, Archizoom created *No-Stop City*,[11] an exaggeration *per absurdum* of the capitalist city. Composed in a similar way to Ludwig Mies van der Rohe's sparse universal spaces, *No-Stop City* consists of a series of hypostyle spaces populated by free-standing walls, topographical elements, and furniture. The limitless interior of *No-Stop City* represents the three dominant typologies of the capitalist city at the time: the factory, the supermarket, and the parking lot.[12] Indeed, *No-Stop City* follows the simplest architectural system possible: the typical plan.[13] For Archizoom, the typical plan represented not only the fundamental spatial datum of the capitalist city but was also an exaggeration of the two most important inventions of modern architecture: Mies's universal space and Le Corbusier's *Dom-Ino House* (1914–1915). In both cases, architecture was reduced to a minimal load-bearing structure, creating an indeterminate interior space that was open to different uses.[14]

Archizoom understood the factory as a kind of architecture that neither gave form to nor represented that which it contained: the machine. Unlike Claude Nicolas Ledoux's *architecture parlante* ("speaking architecture") in his project for the salt works in Chaux, where every element of the production process is symbolized by a specific building, or Archigram's high-tech architecture, which is a literal translation of the techno-futurist ethos of consumer society, in Archizoom's *No-Stop City*, architecture is reduced to a grammar of elementary forms: columns, walls, and elevators. In *No-Stop City*, Archizoom suggest that a city's functionality has little to do with its architectural form, but is instead wedded to elements that lie outside the traditional vocabulary of architectural design, such as the bathroom, the elevator, or the air conditioning system. Archizoom pushed the Miesian "almost nothing" into an absolute "nothing"—what Branzi would later define as a "city without architecture."

Following Tronti, Archizoom understood that capital provides the foundation for the entire spectrum of social relationships. Unlike traditional Marxism, the workerists considered the alienation of the working class to be the most effective leverage in their revolt against capital. Archizoom imagined *No-Stop City* as a space in which workers would be confronted by such a stark and radical version of the capitalist city that they would be mobilized to take power over it.[15]

No-Stop City was a conceptual template within which to rethink the role of design. If, in their early work, Archizoom utilized vulgarity as a means of critiquing the "elegance" of capitalistic design, the abstraction of *No-Stop City* inspired Branzi and his collaborators to create objects that were devoid of any formal qualities. An example of this is the *Armadio abitabile* (*Habitable Wardrobe*) (1972), an interlocking arrangement of furniture that, like a Swiss Army knife, contained all the tools and accessories necessary for living. Abstract pieces of furniture like this led Archizoom to work on what would be their last major (and often overlooked) work: *Vestirsi è facile* (*Dressing is Easy*) (1973), a collection of clothing designed for Elio Fiorucci (for whom Branzi would later design a showroom in New York). In *Vestirsi è facile*, Archizoom applied their "non-figurative" language to what is arguably the ultimate architecture: clothing. Branzi and Archizoom understood that there is a direct link between clothing and the formation of subjectivity. The term "habit" which describes routine (and therefore an ingrained way of thinking) comes from the Latin *habitus*, which means a specific way of dressing. Far from being a superficial form of expression, clothing is one of the most effective means by which subjects are individuated. Within the history of capitalism, we see two seemingly contradictory forces in the realm of clothing: on the one hand, due to the rise of industrial labor, clothing has become increasingly generic and unisex (think of jeans or T-shirts), on the other hand, in order to tame the deterritorializing force of wage-labor and its tendency to abstract traditional gender distinctions, cliché female and male signifiers are reimposed via various trends within fashion. With *Dressing is Easy*, Archizoom's goal was to destroy any gender attribute by proposing a unisex collection of clothes which could be worn inter-seasonally (as the inhabitants of *No-Stop City* would live in a climate-controlled environment, seasonal dressing would no longer be necessary). *Dressing is Easy* demonstrates Branzi's unconventional approach to design, in which architecture, fashion, environment, and the city are approached as essentially one and the same thing.

With the dissolution of Archizoom in the mid-1970s, Branzi began to develop his interest in non-figurative architecture by addressing the role of interior decoration. Branzi considered decoration to be a powerful yet nebulous form of architecture, existing, as it does, in the background. While traditionally, architecture has been conceived as a composition of figures and objects, Branzi thinks of architecture as an immersive environment comprised of texture, color, and acoustic effects. He defines this approach to architecture as "primary design," because it focuses on the elements of an environment that cannot be formally composed.[16] For Branzi, color charts such as the Pantone or Munsell color systems are among the most successful design apparatuses, as they have become the codes of reference for the production of any industrially manufactured product.[17] In 1975, working in close collaboration with the Centro Design Montefibre (a company focused on the production of raw materials made of synthetic fibers), Branzi and his collaborators worked on a series of manuals that mapped trends in environmental decoration. In these manuals, Branzi visualized the infinite range of patterns through which the most ubiquitous industrial products were organized. Following the spatial logic of *No-Stop City*, Branzi created a design based on the repetition of generic visual components such as grids, lines, and other basic patterns. For Branzi, these forms were the ideal way of describing the urban environment, allowing the city to be portrayed—rather than as a static figurative image—as an atmosphere comprised of color, sound, odors, and surface finishes.

For Branzi, patterns are the ultimate form of non-figurative architectural language. As they are without scale, a pattern can be the template for a textile or a city. Their repetitiveness produces an environmental experience in which there is no beginning and no end. If, for Christopher Alexander, patterns were the organic template of traditional design forms, for Branzi, the dominance of patterns in the organization of space reflects the pervasive abstraction of the world under the rule of capital.[18] Branzi has continually refined his non-figurative language by going beyond architectural models—such as the factory or the supermarket—and towards a de-materialized landscape. Patterns suggest a method of design that is radically anti-compositional and thus transcends fundamental distinctions such as figure vs. ground or natural vs. artificial.

Branzi's interest in patterns incidentally led him to develop a fascination with agriculture, compelled by the industry's consistent, "horizontal" landscape and cyclical, transitory condition. In the early 1990s, Branzi began work on *Agronica* (1993–94),[19] his second major "model" for urbanization after *No-Stop City*. Rather than suggesting a return to a pre-industrial society, or proposing an "ecologically correct" approach to city-making, *Agronica* is a space that simply dissolves the barriers between the form of the city and new forms of production. If the image of the industrial city is rooted in the mechanical logic of the factory, the image of the post-industrial city is based on the intangible domain of electronics. *Agronica* represents a city in which the most rudimentary forms of architecture—columns, platforms, and canopies—provide the basic means for habitation. *Agronica* is a city-as-factory in which workers produce services and information, the main constituents of post-Fordist modes of production. *Agronica* gave form to Maurizio Lazzarato's notion of "immaterial labor." With the increasing importance of computers and cybernetics in production processes, cognitive labor—which produces the informational and cultural content of a commodity[20]—is the new subjectivity of work. With immaterial labor, the production of culture, taste, fashion, and art become legitimate forms of work (unthought of during the industrial age), and life and labor become one and the same.

This condition has profound consequences for the city, as it undermines the separation between home and labor formerly maintained by the industrial environment. Within the paradigm of immaterial production, art and creativity are no longer the domain of the bourgeoisie, but the subjectivity of a newly emerging working class (the "cognitarians" or "precariat"). By removing the traditional ideological representations of the city (streets, piazzas, monuments, offices, houses, factories), Branzi reveals the hegemony of immaterial production. In this sense, *Agronica* can be understood as a polemic against architecture and its tendency to "mask" the generic quality of the urban condition. *Agronica* portrays the city as an expanded, borderless factory that puts everyone and everything to work.

It is from within the framework of hypothetical urban models such as *Agronica* that we might reflect on Branzi's earlier design work. Just as *No-Stop City* was the conceptual template for Branzi's work in the 1970s, *Agronica* formed the theoretical background for Branzi's later work from the 1980s to the present. However, the relationship between *Agronica* and Branzi's later work is one of contrasts rather than congruence. While *Agronica* represents the capitalistic reification of the city, Branzi's later work counters this condition by prefiguring micro-scenarios that conflict with the totalizing forces of urbanization.

4.

In his book *Introduzione al Design Italiano* (1999), Branzi argues that a common thread of 20th-century Italian design was the rejection of the reformist ethos of modernist industrial design.[21] Italian designers such as Gio Ponti or the Castiglioni brothers produced idiosyncratic furniture designs that were at odds with the normalized domain of the modern home. While modernist design (from the Bauhaus to the Ulm School of Design) was obsessed with functionality and the use-value of domestic objects, the formal eccentricity of Italian modernist design meant that objects were often completely devoid of use-value.[22]

In the modern metropolis of the 19th century, confronted with the rise of the commodity as spectacle, Charles Baudelaire wrote poetry that read like a form of commodity fetishism. As noted by Giorgio Agamben, it was Baudelaire's acceptance of the commodified status of things that allowed the poet to oppose any utilitarian interpretation of the work of art and to claim art for art's sake.[23] In this way, Baudelaire pushed the commodified condition of art to its extreme. His poetry was an "absolute commodity"—it existed in defiance of its use- or exchange-value.[24]

Something similar seems to be at work in the tradition of Italian design seen through Branzi's lens. Castiglioni's chest of drawers, *Rampa* (which Archizoom appropriated and reinvented as a flamboyant pop object in the mid-1960s), is so blatantly monumental and iconic that its lack of any explicit functional purpose is made outstandingly clear. If, in the 1970s, Branzi's objects postulated the negation of design as a formal problem—think of his work on patterns—in the 1980s, Branzi pursued the opposite strategy, by designing a disconcerting series of objects whose use was entirely unclear. Consider *Archi, fusi e forcelle* (1980) a series of domestic sculptures that relate to the most archetypical figure in architecture: the arch. Or think of *Cariatidi* (1980), a series of portable, decorative statues. Rather than trying to elevate these objects to the status of fine art, Branzi mimicked the aesthetic of domestic knickknacks that filled the typical bourgeois interior at the time. Like Baudelaire with his poetry, Branzi reclaimed the autonomy of design from its commercial reification, not by resistance, but by making design objects that looked unapologetically like commodities.

Branzi's objects function as architecture; small and self-sufficient buildings that stoically ignore the space around them. Notably, in publications or catalogs, Branzi's objects are often starkly photographed in a bare room (unlike most designers, Branzi never shows his objects in use). This approach was made explicit in a series of "aggressive and extravagant" wardrobe designs published in the magazine *IN* in 1970.[25] A clear reference to El Lissitzky's *Proun*, these structures were conceived as abstract, almost obstructive designs. Here, we can see Branzi's objects' disruptive role within the house, emphasizing it as a space of domestic labor. As Hannah Arendt wrote in her seminal book *The Human Condition*, labor is the sheer unending business of our species' reproduction: eating, sleeping, and cleaning, giving birth and raising children, taking care of the household.[26] What characterizes labor activities is that they do not leave anything material behind: the product of labor is destined for immediate consumption. The traditional place of labor is thus the home, whose purpose is reproduction. Following Aristotle's distinction between the household (*oikos*) and the city (*polis*), Hannah Arendt noted how in the realm of the home, relationships are not political, as they are unregulated by norms or laws.[27] In the home, relationships are despotic (master/slave), paternal (father/son), or marital (husband/wife), and therefore seen as "natural," unchangeable.

Industrial design has contributed enormously to the "naturalness" of domestic labor by transforming the home into a micro-factory, or, in Le Corbusier's words, a "machine for living."[28] Think of progressive pieces of design such as Margarete Schütte-Lihotzky's *Frankfurt Kitchen*, which, by easing reproductive labor, justified the presence of the kitchen (and its labor) within the home. Or think of the recent wave of "smart" technological apparatuses that have turned the home into an endless source of data to be extracted from the inhabitant's life for the sake of corporate profit. Against the constant individuation of domestic functions within the house, objects such as Branzi's *Vertical Home* (a shelf that simultaneously functions as a desk, wardrobe, and alcove) confuse and thus negate the functional spatialization of the home. As it neglects to cater to any domestic function in particular, *Vertical Home* rejects the organization of the home into specific reproductive zones such as the kitchen, the bedroom, and the living room.

Rather than proposing furniture that complements the architecture of an interior, Branzi designs objects that often don't fit easily within the traditional spaces of the home. In this way, furniture is no longer a movable object, but an architectural form in itself, with a monumental presence inside the home. If Branzi's urban models—from *No-Stop City* to *Agronica* to his most recent models for *Residential Agriculture*—propose a non-figurative architecture, his objects seem to deliberately recuperate the power of figuration. This is evident in one of Branzi's most recent series, which offers an eloquent synthesis of his approach to design: the *Grandi legni* (*Large Timberworks*) (2008).[29] The *Grandi legni* are large-scale shelves that can act as supports for a multitude of objects. Unlike the shelves of a library whose function is to be filled with books, these timber works are essentially sculptures devoid of any specific use. Unlike Branzi's earlier design pieces, the *Grandi legni* use old materials and archaic symbolism. Yet, in the commissioned photographs documenting them, beside reproductions of Roman mosaics or details from Giotto's frescoes, the *Grandi legni* support disposable objects such as plastic bottles and cardboard boxes. As Branzi explains, the *Grandi legni* address the difficulty of distinguishing the past from the present, claiming the "past" not as something irremediably lost but as a living part of our contemporary condition. In doing so, Branzi removes the authoritative aura often given to the past as something "to preserve." Moreover, by reclaiming the past not as "history" but as something that belongs to the present, Branzi challenges "newness" as the only horizon of contemporary design. In a way, the *Grandi legni* are archetypical structures, vaguely reminiscent of the Western archetype par excellence: the Christian cross. Yet, to directly refer to such an archetype would be too strong a gesture, which is why Branzi attenuated the figurative power of the cross through the pieces'tabstract compositions.

With the *Grandi legni*, Branzi returns to the monumentality of his early collaborations with Archizoom—but, this time, without the reference to pop culture. Branzi defines this renewed approach to design as a "new dramaturgy," asserting that the contemporary culture of design has to include pain, death, and the sense of hopelessness that characterize our time. Above all, Branzi's new dramaturgy knowingly represents the failure of design to do something, to justify its presence with arguments about its "social" value.

Branzi's *Recinti* (*Enclosures*) (2010) follow a similar approach to the *Grandi legni* by appropriating another archaic archetype: the perimeter often used by farmers to enclose a pasture. The *Recinti* are enclosures made of simple materials such as wood, metal wire, and glass. Their form refers to the most essential element of architecture, which is to separate and protect. The *Recinti* seem to suggest an inhabitable place, although they hold no objects or give any other sign of habitation, and their fragility infers that they are temporary structures. Branzi neutralizes the potential "biopolitical" condition of this architecture by ensuring this archetype isn't identified as a form of domestic enclosure (the *Recinti* do not have a roof, they are not "shelters"). In this way, the *Recinti* are not inhabitable forms whose relevance need be justified in terms of "necessity." The *Recinti* speak about the desire to construct a place in order to give orientation to our lives; they evoke the condition of human beings as animals who never feel at home and therefore must construct an environment in order to exist. Within the smooth space of *No-Stop City* and *Agronica*, the *Recinti* seem to open up a space of friction, a stoppage, a moment of halt.

Here, Branzi finally discloses what was inside his Trojan horse objects all along: the possibility of disturbing the vast interior of our urban condition. And yet in Branzi's work, the gesture of disturbance is not aimed at introducing an alternative order to the existing condition. For Branzi, disturbance is a way of keeping the contents of the urban interior open to contingency. Seen from the vantage point of the new dramaturgy, Branzi's work appears as a radical deterritorialization of architecture and design where the managerial logic of both disciplines is forcefully interrogated and used as a way to question the world we inhabit.

1 See: Archizoom Associati, "Città, catena di montaggio del sociale. Ideologia teoria della metropoli," in *Casabella* XXXIV, 350–351, July–August 1970, 45–52; Archizoom Associates, *No-Stop City. Residential Parkings, Climatic Universal System* in *Domus* n. 496, March 1971, 49–55. For a complete presentation of the project see: Andrea Branzi, *No-Stop City: Archizoom Associati* (Orleans: XY, 2007); see also Roberto Gargiani, *Dall'onda pop alla superficie neutra. Archizoom Associati, 1966-1974* (Milan, Electa, 2007), pp. 169–225;

2 Karl Marx, *Capital*, Volume I. Ben Fowkes, trans. Penguin: London, 1992, p. 125;

3 p. 3. Ibid. pp. 157–163;

4 See: Roberto Gargiani, *Dall'onda pop alla superficie neutra. Archizoom Associati, 1966–1974*, pp. 7–45;

5 Ibid. 7;

6 On the concept of "città-territorio," see: Manfredo Tafuri, "Main Lines of the Great Theoretical Debate over Architecture and Urban Planning 1960–1977", *A+U 100* (January 1979), p. 140;

7 See: Mario Tronti, "La fabbrica e la società" in *Quaderni Rossi* n. 2, 1962, 1–31; Republished in: Mario Tronti, *Operai e Capitale*, Einaudi, Turin, 1966, pp. 39–59;

8 Ibid. 42;

9 Quoted in Roberto Gargiani, *Dall'onda pop alla superficie neutra. Archizoom Associati, 1966–1974*, p. 47;

10 Manfredo Tafuri, "Per una Critica dell'ideologia architettonica" in *Contropiano* n. 1, 1969, pp. 31-79; See also, Manfredo Tafuri, *Progetto e Utopia*, Laterza, Bari, 1973;

11 An earlier version of this was published with the title *City as Assembly Line of the Social.* See: Archizoom Associati, "Città catena di montaggio del sociale. Ideologia teoria della metropoli", in *Casabella* XXXIV, 350–351, July–August 1970, pp. 45–52;

12 Ibid;

13 On the typical plan see: Francesco Marullo, *Architecture and Revolution*, and "The Typical Plan as Index of Generic" in *The City as a Project*, edited by Pier Vittorio Aureli, Ruby Press, Berlin 2014, pp. 216–260;

14 See: Pier Vittorio Aureli, "The Dom-ino Problem: Questioning the Architecture of Domestic Space," in *Log* No. 30 (Winter 2014), pp. 153–168;

15 We should remember that *No-Stop City* was conceived in the aftermath of 1969 *Autunno caldo*, the intense season of workers' strikes that took place in the industrial centers of northern Italy;

16 See: Andrea Branzi, "Design Primario," in *Luoghi : The Complete Works*, Ernst & Sohn, Berlin, 1992, pp. 80–81;

17 Ibid. 80;

18 Christopher Alexander, Sara Ishikawa, Murray Silverstein, Max Jacobson, Ingrid Fiksdahl-King, Shlomo Angel, *A Pattern Language: Towns, Buildings, Construction*, Oxford University Press, New York, 1977;

19 On the urban model *Agronica* see: Andrea Branzi, Dante Donegani, Andrea Petrillo, and Carlo Raimondo, "Symbiotic Metropolis: Agronica," in *The Solid Side*, ed. Ezio Manzini and Marco Susani, Amsterdam: V+K Publishing / Philips, 1995, pp. 101–120; Andrea Branzi, *Weak and Diffuse Metropolis, The World of Projects at the Beginning of the 21st Century*, Milan: Skira, 2007, pp. 135–146;

20 Maurizio Lazzarato, "Immaterial Labor," Paolo Virno, Michael Hardt (ed.), *Radical Thought in Italy: A Potential Politics*, Minneapolis, Minnesota University Press, 1996, pp. 133–150;

21 Andrea Branzi, *Introduzione al Design Italiano*, Milan, Baldini & Castoldi, 1999, p. 6;

22 See: Paolo Virno, *Esercizi di Esodo. Linguaggio e azione politica*, Ombre Corte: Milan, 2002, p. 65;

23 Giorgio Agamben, *Stanze. La parola e il fantasma nella cultura occidentale*, Turin: Einaudi, 1977, p. 51;

24 Ibid. 52;

25 Archizoom Associati, "La distruzione degli oggetti," in *IN: Argomenti e Immagini di Design*, n. 2-3, March–June 1971, pp. 9–13;

26 Hannah Arendt, *The Human Condition*, Chicago, University of Chicago Press, 1999 [1958], pp. 79–135;

27 Ibid. 78;

28 Le Corbusier, *Toward an Architecture*, trans. John Goodman, Los Angeles: Getty Research Institute, 2007, p. 35;

29 On the Large Timberworks see: Andrea Branzi, *Grandi Legni*, Milan: Design Gallery, 2009; on the Enclosures see: Patrick Gries, *Open Enclosures*, Paris: Fondation Cartier, 2008.

Rahul Mehrotra, Felipe Vera

Ephemeral Urbanism and Branzi's Weak Territories

Today, urban environments face ever-increasing flows of human movement as well as an accelerated frequency of natural disasters and iterative economic crises that dictate the allocation of capital toward the physical components of cities. As a consequence, urban settings are required to be more flexible in order to be better prepared to respond to, organize, and resist external and internal pressures. At a time in which uncertainty is the new norm, urban attributes like reversibility and openness appear to be critical to a more sustainable form of urban development. Therefore, in contemporary urbanism around the world, it is clear that in order for cities to be sustainable, they need to resemble and facilitate active fluxes in motion, rather than be limited by static, material configurations.

Temporary cities have a lot to offer in the study and application of contemporary urbanism. However, given their heterogeneous nature, it is difficult to organize a cohesive terrain of scholarship from which to springboard into mainstream application. For this reason, Andrea Branzi's prototypes form the first alternative and taxonomic hypotheses oriented to these new configurations, as alternative to the stable cities, and a crucial scientific platform on which to incorporate theoretical work into the rethinking of the urban structure. In this parallelism between theory and phenomena lies the conjunction of our research areas.

As the contemporary temporary cities, Branzi's weak urbanization models, and his new principle of universal and reversible urbanism, unlike more permanent ones that have a range of elements that simultaneously support their continuity, are usually structured around one main purpose. This *modus operandi* is not only the central force that defines an ephemeral city's dimensions and complexity, but also the life cycle of the settlement, its material composition, and its place in the cultural memory of its society. Following this line of thought, it is possible to categorize ephemeral cities in clusters of cases configured in diverse taxonomies, as Branzi's definition of a new glossary for urbanization, taxonomies fused by their common characteristics of ephemerality and temporariness.

In their concrete phenomenology, these varied taxonomies could be a useful way to organize cases that are differentiated through variables such as length, size, metabolism, generated levels of risk, patterns of spatial use, grid morphology and complexity, technology, logistical implementation, et cetera. They respond to particular conditions and contexts while sharing the certainty—or at least the expectation—of a date of expiration. Thus, they challenge us to develop tools for intervening and thinking about impermanent configurations as a legitimate and productive category within the discourse on urbanism. In fact, they represent an entire surrogate urban ecology that grows and disappears on an often extremely tight temporal scale. When temporary urban landscapes are seen as the expression of a distinctive form of urbanism, then a potentially productive dialogue is established between ephemeral settlements. These settlements span a diverse range, from refugee camps to weekend-long festivals, along with other temporary urbanizations meant for celebration.

Andrea Branzi's ten recommendations for the construction of a *New Athens Charter* offered critical provocations for the radical rethinking of the urban as a more inclusive and less Eurocentric project. Of his ten recommendations, the third seems to point directly to the construction of a new concept of time in a city that should be thought of as a place for "cosmic hospitality" in which designers could encourage "planetary coexistence" between "man and animals, technology and divinities, living and dead." In doing so, a model for the city could be found that is "less anthropocentric and more open to biodiversity, to the sacred, and to human beauty."[1]

Religion as a taxonomy of ephemeral urbanism—as Branzi's expresses it in his texts and project on new Fundamentalisms—seems to advance this line of thinking, reactivating the contents forgotten by the Modern Movement, and proposing temporary reconfigurations of the urban that are, in a way, short glimpses of this very city model. In this sense, ephemeral landscapes of religion are constituted by cases in which the urban space is modified, totally transformed, or even created in order to facilitate the practice of faith. These cases present thoughtful strategies for ephemeral configurations deployed to celebrate religious beliefs. Some of the cases, such as the Qoyllur Rit'i in Peru, go so far as to generate temporary megacities from almost nothing. Others convert streets into open temples, such as the light constructions made annually to host the Durga Puja in Kolkata, while others transform massive regional infrastructures into a procession path, as in Lo Vásquez, Chile, to demonstrate an alternative urbe of the stable stateof the city.

As deeply expressed in his *Models of Weak Urbanization* and in his most recent research, the ephemeral city is often constructed out of light materials, which allows it to adapt to a range of contexts, to be transported, and to colonize all sorts of spatial conditions. In many cases, an ephemeral city is constructed outside urban centers, as in the case of *Burning Man*, which is assembled in the middle of the Nevada desert. In the Qoyllur Rit'i (translated as the "Snow Star Festival") in Peru, an ephemeral settlement is deployed in the once vacant valley near Mahuayani. For this religious celebration, devotees travel the steep cliffs and long trails of the Andes. People come from all over the region to gather once a year at the shrine of Qoyllur Rit'i to sing, dance, and wear traditional costumes. What makes the Qoyllur Rit'i unique is that it is one of the most physically enduring religious events in the region. It requires participants to carry tents, material for stages, instruments, and other festival gear with them during their journey up the mountain to pay respect to the shrine perched precariously at a great altitude. Given the walking nature of the pilgrimage, all the goods used to assemble the ephemeral city are extremely light. Plastic, fabric, and light, portable structures are used in the construction of the city. The lightweight image of the settlement is juxtaposed with the aggressive and heavy presence of the rock-faced mountains.

In the same way that religious ephemeral settlements are a means for what a society perceives as valuable and memorable, other ephemeral forms play similar but secular roles. Temporal celebratory landscapes are also ways to provide space and place for the conservation of social traditions, enhancing the values of cohesion and allowing for interactions in the form of cathartic gatherings. In this way, in addition to ephemeral settlements fostering the encounter with the sacred, many other impermanent landscapes appear for the support of the celebration of the mundane, inside and outside the city. Sacred ephemeral landscapes open opportunities for inverting hierarchies and making horizontal social relationships in the city. They also transform thresholds, softening them. Both things are achieved by the implantation of a major common purpose that unifies differences.

Celebratory ephemeral manifestations achieve the same effect, as they provide heterotopic spaces in which one can usually see the dissolution of social predetermination and a diversity that is not normally achieved in the everyday city. Nonreligious cultural celebrations have historically been places of social intensity and cultural expression. Many settlements regularly pop up around the globe, creating "contact zones" for groups of people that would otherwise not interact with or even find each other. These structures are well expressed in the softer, secondary layers that penetrate the permanent city, as in the case of Latin American carnivals and street parties or the massive artistic performances that activate urban spaces, or even in the form of discrete settlements outside or adjacent to urban centers all around the world. The increasing scale and frequency of subtle settlements is causing the expansion of more and more erected structures within and outside of urban areas. Music festivals, such as Exit in Serbia, Coachella in California, and Sziget in Budapest, motivate the construction of extended ephemeral settlements that for short periods of time congregate large groups of people. They range from relatively small gatherings, like Burning Man in Nevada or Fuji Rock in Japan, which attract around 40,000 people, to events like Glastonbury in England, the Roskilde Festival in Denmark, and Rock Werchter in Belgium, which draw in around 350,000 people.

As we have seen, temporary celebratory landscapes are disruptions to the "business as usual" condition of the city. They open the way for very intense, short-term interactions that physically transform the urban space, allowing for cultural expression in perhaps its most radical condition. In these contexts, the individual and the community are placed at the center through great strategies for social and spatial bonding. The permanent city becomes secondary to the idea of a shared cultural connectivity.

There are other forms of the temporal in which architecture and urban design work in completely opposite ways to that of ephemeral cities of celebration. This is a neutralizing urbanism that disposes of grids and units, as well as any expression of identity, reducing life to its more basic and "bare" condition.

The refugee camp[2] would offer an exact exemplification, as the new emergent city following natural calamities. As Agamben said: "Today, it is not the city but rather the camp" that is "the fundamental bio-political paradigm of the West."[3]

Often representing the overturning of ephemeral cities, since they are transformed from temporary encampments to real consolidated cities, camps connect directly to another prototype, one that is linked to military needs, through the construction of removable and temporary infrastructures.

As Branzi pointed out through the idea of reversible urbanism and weak infrastructures, military settlements seem to offer an exact example, closer to the dynamics and structures of the cities destroyed because of natural disasters.

Also the global problems provide an expression of the ephemeral city on the rise. Changes in climatic conditions are increasingly making evident the importance of temporary shelters as holding strategies or short-term solutions. In the Philippines, Haiti, Chile, and several other afflicted nations, temporary cities are built in the context of disaster.

Today, the planet is facing unprecedented uncertainty, as climate change is rendering once stable areas of the planet vulnerable. The ecological uncertainty and the growing challenges tied to climate change bring notions of space, occupation, and public health to the forefront. Moreover, social inequality unveils urban and rural settlements as we are pushed to seek alternative methods for dealing with the current conditions. These landscapes of disaster create camps all over the globe.

Or, mentioning another term of our glossary, the ephemeral city is shaped where there are some natural resources.

In these cases, the life cycle of temporary cities aligns with the duration of the extractive activity and the presence of the resource. Therefore, most of these settlements are developed knowing that they have a predictable expiration date.

In the ephemeral landscapes of extraction, the structure of the camp, rather than a biopolitical management artifact, often becomes a productive engine for the profitable management of the territory, subjugating every aspect of life to that purpose. This is a form of urbanism at the service of global economic flows, which determine the patterns of growth in relation to the demand for commodities based on access to natural resources. In this sense, ephemeral landscapes of extraction are a by-product of the extractive activity that, being local in its operation, is determined by global needs and aspirations. They emerge as highly efficient systems that maximize productivity, optimize processes, and produce automated and standardized results. It is the perfect embodiment of the paradigm behind every extraction activity: efficiency. Indeed, it is efficiency that drives the layout of the site, the organization of logistics, the spatial configuration, and the processing of the resources once they are extracted. It is the same efficiency that constructs the conditions for bare life to be predominant, for "action" to retreat as secondary human activity.

David Harvey's continuation of C. Wright Mills's notions of sociological imagination coalesce with Louis Wirth's ideas of urbanism as a way of life in order to provide contexts of extraction that act in the service of efficiency. They are therefore "deprived" of their "cityness" in order to fulfill their main purpose of accommodating people for a limited period of time, providing minimum levels of comfort and human interaction.

Conceptually speaking, in ephemeral landscapes of extraction the structure of the camp is recognizable not only in those that are set up explicitly as encampments but also in other layers of the urban—as the camp is the thinnest expression of a settlement. Such thinness is not only material, but it also impacts the social and political aspects of the camp, creating a constant tension between both paradigms of space production. On the one hand, referring to its material conditions, the camp operates in a similarly fluid way to that of the city. Despite its seemingly fragile appearance, it incorporates systems embedded with a great degree of elasticity and flexibility, which are able to adapt to transformations within the environment.

Like other ephemeral settlements, the extractive camp has the capacity to be constructed within a short period of time. It can also be deconstructed at the same speed, simply by inverting the construction process.

As well expressed with great power of anticipation, Branzi's prototypes of weak urbanization, the mentioned cases make us think about urbanism is a nuanced way. The city clearly needs to find alternative ways to give space to a more pluralistic economy, allowing flexible functional occupations to generate micro-operations that activate the urban landscape. Referring to this, Martha Chen advocates, "What is needed, most fundamentally, is a new economic paradigm: a model of a hybrid economy that embraces the traditional and the modern, the small scale and the big scale, the informal and the formal. What is needed is an economic model that allows the smallest units and the least powerful workers to operate alongside the largest units and most powerful economic players."[4] In this way, acknowledging the contributions made by the range of different cases included in this book might help us to find the agency of urban design and planning in the design of such conditions.

1 F. Vera, J. Sordi, ed., *Andrea Branzi: From Radical Design to Post-Environmentalism*, Ediciones arq, Santiago, 2015;

2 Michel Agier, *Managing the Undesirables*, Polity, Malden, MA, Cambridge, 2011, and "World at War", *unhcr Global Trends: Forced Displacement 2014*, http://unhcr.org/556725e69.pdf, July 2017;

3 Giorgio Agamben, "The Camp as Nomos," in *Homo Sacer: Sovereign Power and Bare Life*, trans. Daniel Heller-Roazen, Stanford University Press, Stanford, 1998;

4 Marta Alter Chen, "The Informal Economy: Definitions, Theories and Policies", in *WIEGO Working Papers 1* August 2012, p. 20, http://wiego.org/sites/wiego.org/files/publications/files/Chen_WIEGO_WP1.pdf.

Patrizia Ranzo

Design as a staging of life
Theories and works of Andrea Branzi

Branzi himself has always spoken of his works and thoughts in the first person; for his theoretical and physical geographies, he has always provided the coordinates; he has also provided it to his generation of designers and to all the young people he has formed directly or through his works. Ettore Sottsass, his great interlocutor, regularly said that if there were no Branzi, few designers would have understood the meaning of their project. So Branzi is not only the best critic of himself, but also the one who has built the path of a "new Italian design," highlighting its interactions with the phenomena of contemporary society.

It is unusual for a designer to affirm that design is not the center of his interests, a sentence I have often heard him say and that contains the meaning of his intellectual and design work – a disconcerting but very clear statement in relation to his training as a great Italian "critical" designer. In fact, design for the European generation of intellectuals, but even more for the Italian generation, is the theoretical place that has been able to accommodate and understand the great changes in human life in relation to the evolution of contemporary capitalism and trajectories of technology.

Branzi's interest is aimed at the extremely dialoguing nature of design with production and merchandising systems, which constitute the reality in which we are immersed: design is the medium between man and the complex socio-techno-economic system of our planet. Architecture is no longer the primary scene of life; it is indifferent to it, often the surplus. It is in "industrial" design that man re-establishes the ability to project himself into the world, to enter the point of tangency with the continuous evolution of technology as the fabric of everyday life. The changed nature of technology, which has moved from the dermis of the world deeper into its constitutive mechanisms, has radically transformed design dynamics and the sense of the project itself: Andrea Branzi has understood the conditions in which the project is nowadays to act; devoid of a perspective view, it is realized here and now, in a sort of "extemporaneous" action.

Branzi's thinking and the whole of his work are always characterized by extreme realism (utopia is often an act of realism, a reading that starts from the present) and an impressive logical continuity. After many years, his visions of the reality of living have found correspondence in the evolution of the metropolitan plankton, in the completely immersive human existential condition, between fragments of nature, technologies, and artifacts. A civilization (especially that of the new generations) that is living through "the primitive re-founding of our urban civilization, without challenging its foundations, but accepting and reinventing them in the happiness of their animal condition; outside the limits of anthropocentrism."[1]

The ecological interpretation of some of Branzi's projects often does not identify his real intentions: once again the prefiguration of a fabric made of fields, residences, fragments of civilizations, technologies, and workplaces is nothing but the vision of a world without discontinuity, of a possibility that "is" already as such. The reality of many suburbs of the world that are incorporated into the metropolitan fabric, revitalized by new and continuous tertiary, productive, and residential initiatives. A real world, life as it is: fragmented, simultaneous, and chaotic with islands of peace within it. Primitive and technological at the same time; ready to seize the opportunities of their time.

Branzi's sensibility in presenting the complexity of everyday life through the project assimilates his work to a composition by Cage: contemporary civilization expressed through a compositional realism, open to listening to the world, to its polyphony where there is not a before and an after, but endless interpenetration.

It is life in our complex society that is the fulcrum of Branzi's work; a careful reading and a continuous forward-looking interpretation of the phenomena of late capitalism accompany his projects and his overall visions. A great trust in man as the creator of worlds starting from small things and objects is the energy that moves his activity.

Man as an autobiographical animal

Recently Branzi wrote a short autobiography; his intention was to make the latter a theoretical document and then to add to real facts of his life elements that were not true but even more useful to deeply understand his background; a project of the past, therefore, not a chronological list of events that happened. A literary story truer than life itself: "I made this decision – Branzi says – because the true story of my life has no direct relationship with what I have done and with what I think."

In the essay "The Animal That Therefore I Am," Jacques Derrida[2] states that man is an autobiographical animal, that is, man is an animal that writes his life; the affirmation of one's own humanity and of being in life resides in this difference with respect to other living beings, but also in the consciousness of the "missing" being. "Man – says Derrida – is an animal missing from himself" – compared to other animals, he is naked and knows he is. This particular access to humanity is a distinctive privilege more than the word itself; self-consciousness as a lack is the engine of the world, the engine that continuously accesses the new, the designing imagination. Human nudity corresponds to the possibility of projecting ourselves onto the world to complete ourselves through it. It is possible, Branzi suggests, to plan one's own past to make it correspond to our truth. Branzi's nudity with respect to the world allowed him to engage in continuous research through the project, anthropologically focused on the intertwining of his rich human affairs and post-twentieth-century mankind. A humanity more than ever welded to a hybrid ecosystem, made of things strictly and technologically related to man, nature, artifice. A "dense," viscous humanity in which the subject's identity is plural.

In his "literary" autobiography, Branzi sets his youth in Florence, the city where he really was born and was formed, where he met the most important people in his emotional life and work. In the same way, he stages the second part of his life in Milan, as it really happened and not by chance, as they are the central places for the development of his autobiography, which also corresponds to his life project. Both cities are an important part of his intellectual journey: Florence as fulcrum of humanistic culture and cultural debate during the turbulent years of the Italian post-war period, Milan as a city in dialogue with the rest of the world, a physical yet abstract city, the heart designing new qualities of the late industrial world.

Florence represents for Andrea Branzi necessary baggage, but also a place to get away from, in order to enter an environmental and social dimension that can offer to his work effective degrees of cultural freedom. In the dialectic between these two realities is Branzi's Italian project: the influence of the great culture of the Italian city par excellence, of its beauty as the maximum expression of human ability to express quality as a project of the original '"lack of self" and the metropolitan nature of Milan, in the apparent form of a city, of a harsh and concrete beauty. This dichotomy has produced the beauty (a beauty expressed as a capacity for profound realism) of his work, his adherence to the world through a design vision capable of making the complex temporal and spatial dimensions contemporary and therefore syncretically realistic.

Radical realism

The years in Florence, years of early youth education and then of intellectual commitment, constitute the political and humanistic observatory from which his reflections depart; the militant aspect of his commitment is certainly determined by his family environment, by the paternal figure and by his importance in Florentine and Italian history for democratic values and freedom of expression. This value matures in Branzi during the university years and through the comparison with the generation of his peer architects. These are the years when the words of youthful unease in the face of post-war capitalist models resonate in Bob Dylan's songs and especially in the life of people like Jim Morrison: words, music, and life are confused in a sort of dramaturgy of words and action and of militant criticism.

Art fully acknowledges the reality of a world made of goods, of popular icons and new urban myths. This representation of the life of those years is perfectly reflected in the emerging culture of the architects formed around the radical Florentine movement that came into being, Branzi reminds us, starting with an exhibition called Superarchitecture, held in Pistoia in 1966. It has been said that the Radical Movement was born above all as a critique of the mature capitalist system: among the various individuals of the movement, there was certainly this component, but in Branzi's and Archizoom's vision there is certainly the acceptance of the inescapable reality of a civilization that has already passed from an industrial nature - inserted into a prospective and temporal reality - to a commodity-based and diffuse reality, without a destiny outside of a continuous feeding of its reproductive mechanisms. This planning conscience will be the reflective and logical seed of all Branzi's work to come: the condition of whoever finds himself working on a project is determined by an action without perspective, if not that of the "here and now," and of the possible qualities in that determined context: "I can almost say that I am an architect who has always worked around one big project. The hypothesis of a non-figurative architecture, made of immaterial qualities, information, microclimate, objects [...] An architect who no longer recognizes his fundamental values in architecture."[3]

The genetic characteristic of all of Branzi's architectural projects lies in this vision, which is also accentuated by his representative modes, such as the use of mirrors to blend the image in an endless perspective and without focal points. The certain non-iconic nature of his architectural landscapes is indifferent to the nature of the places, as well as the diffuse metropolises of the world, which include pieces of agricultural land, industrial archeology, pieces of orography and nature. Exactly like the virtual metropolis that we experience in the daily life of our computers, the networks of our relationships. Everything without hierarchies, without a sense of temporal belonging or identity: a techno-natural whole in which we have had to invent new systems of orientation and communication and in which we live our life experiences.

Radical realism leads to the definition of new qualities, which are more closely related to the life of man, qualities that architecture is no longer able to express: "Urban quality is an experiential quality, not of a formal nature and even less of a compositional nature." [4]

Hence, the rigorous decision to identify in product design culture the territory in which to experiment and to propose new possible qualities. The loss of adherence to the world by architecture, which can only be proposed as a monument of itself, pushes Andrea Branzi to invest theoretically and by design in the new context of product design, the new productive interlocutors, and the contaminating noise of the commodity society.

"You can change the world through roses ..."

The decision to move to Milan marks a period of intense theoretical and project work under the banner of the matured awareness of wanting to explore the territory of opportunities of a "modernity without Enlightenment," but one rich in new qualities and degrees of freedom. These are years of great enthusiasm and possibilities, of human and professional associations that produced unique experiences in the panorama of the industrial design project.

Branzi participates in Milan's intellectual life immediately, coagulating energy and providing meaningful scenarios for the international environment that gravitates around the south European metropolitan reality of Milan. The apparently small urban dimension of its urban context (everything takes place within a few canonical streets and places) brings together everything and everyone in a continuous relaunching of ideas and initiatives. Alchimia and Memphis are moments of great synergy and inclusion, a set of anarchist and independent projects expressive of their historical moment without certainties, but of pure energy. Branzi is one of the engines of this energy, but always, in some way, with a borderline view, to be able to interpret, as well as experience, the codes of the world around him.

The strength of his projects lies in the ability to precipitate these codes, revealing their concreteness and beauty, opening them to the universe. A concept of beauty deriving from the complete acceptance of life as it is staged through its continuous transformations. A capacity for expression typical of the younger generations, but which in Andrea Branzi is a continuous vibration.

Written works and object theories follow one another with great consistency, testifying to his vision which is the vision of New Italian Design. A system of object-thought and qualities that bear witness, as a whole, to a new humanity that is no longer anthropocentric but certainly more contradictory, with no certainties but that understands and accepts the richness of the new condition: "The project no longer possesses a future vision of itself, and it dates back to its deepest mystery roots, to that primordial condition from which the human environment began its long journey."[5]

The belief that "we can change the world through roses" is the origin of many projects within the sphere of everyday aesthetic and sensory enjoyment: objects, those of Branzi, which dialogue with cultures, without differences between past and present, recovering the archetypal animism that supports the system of Mediterranean everyday objects. The vase with flowers of Roman glass that gently looks at us from a Pompeian painting is the same one that Branzi has imagined in acrylic: "Objects look at us," Baudrillard would say, and this look gives us back the sense of a possible humanity.

Archetypes of the future

The new millennium expresses itself, in the work of Andrea Branzi, always with the same coherence, but with a deeper exploration of the theme of the dense humanism that characterizes our time. Everything has changed, and nothing has changed.

Paradoxically, our condition of men and women closely connected in a colloidal and technological system brings us, according to Branzi, to an almost natural condition of new primitives in our urban environment. Objects actively participate in our lives, facilitating human contacts and at the same time accelerating them. Everything happens simultaneously, flattening the temporal axis, stacking cultures on top of each other, eliminating our ability to look into the distance. The iconic nature of contemporary culture puts the past and present together, in an indistinct way, and this happens in all fields: in music, in art, in fashion, in our metropolises. Faced with such a characteristic present, we do not need the future, which is already with us, in this "coexistence" of various physical and temporal dimensions. The design gaze turns inwards: the *Nature Morte* (Still Life) and *Grandi Legni* collections are a new feature in the Milanese and international design scene, as well as the independent design exhibition at the Milan Triennale. The great themes of life and death and of the sacred conflict with the crisp images of international Nordic design. The staging of a new humanism that looks at itself without the myths of industry and without God breaks the classical schemes of the idea of design, in some way a scandal, which is precisely the mechanism of dramaturgy. After "the end of the grand narratives," we return to recount, to look at the world with a gaze that is the same as the angel of Benjamin: "We live in a polluted world, devoid of boundaries, certainties, thickness. Maybe it's time to change the tone of our voice, our music, and our dramaturgy. Objects are not silent instruments of furniture, but speaking witnesses of our time; lanterns in the darkness of history, they exorcise our fears and accompany our destiny. In this circular and opaque time, Nature Morte looks at what has always remained outside our projects, technology, and marketing. They try to approach the lofty themes of life, but also mediocrity. Through death, they represent life and its eternal renewal."[6]

Bringing images of death into design, where everything must be "polished and perfect surfaces," Branzi intends to break the silence on our conditions, summoning us to an aesthetic deeply connected to the meaning of life and to our nature as human beings.

Faced with the greatest phenomenon of our time, the disappearance of history, Andrea Branzi stages life: "We can assume that the acceleration of modernity, technical, event-based, mediatic, the acceleration of all exchange, economic, political, sexual, has led us to a speed of liberation that allows us to get out of the referential sphere of reality and history: we are freed in all senses of the term, so liberated that we have emerged from a certain space-time, from a certain horizon in which the real is possible because the gravitation is still strong enough to make it such that things can be reflected, and therefore have some duration and some consequences."[7]

A world without history: the end of linear time, of the before and after, of the perspectival view. A world where everything is present simultaneously, a flat world that needs continuous reference points in order to orientate its activities and give directions that can return reality to its phenomenology.

The background of Branzi's most recent works seems to me to be this: in the face of a constantly expanding space, its involution or evolution depends on the critical mass of humanity. To be able to express this critical mass syncretically with respect to the kinetic energy that pushes us outside of reality is the only possible condition.

Mass slows down time, requires thought and action, "creates" time. The solid thoughts of Andrea Branzi are both time and mass, reflective space, the ability to impress upon the apparent freedom of which we enjoy a real choice of directions. "*The Grandi Legni* originate from the impossibility of distinguishing the past from the present; from the discontinuity of memories and from the new dimension of our mental geography,"[8] says Branzi; a happy idea to represent our human condition as a possibility in the project.

The New Dramaturgy of the project therefore derives from the desire to explore the still free space of the mind, to welcome the deepest meaning of human culture and its absolute dimension, which is made up of myths and archetypes, but also of so much daily necessity.

1 A. Branzi, *Una generazione esagerata*, Baldini & Castoldi, Milan, 2014, p. 197;
2 J. Derrida, *The Animal That Therefore I Am*, Jaca Book, Milan, 2006;
3 A. Branzi, *Andrea Branzi. Museo Alessi Design*, Interview by Maurizio Corraini, Mantova, 2007, p. 19;
4 A. Branzi, *Andrea Branzi. Oggetti e territori*, Silvana Editoriale, Milan, 2008, p. 16;
5 A. Branzi, *Una generazione esagerata*, Baldini & Castoldi, Milan, 2014, p. 195;
6 A. Branzi, *Nature Morte*, Introduction, Galleria Clio Carvi Rudy Volpi, Milan, 2011;
7 J. Baudrillard, *The Illusion of the End*, 1992;
8 A. Branzi, *Andrea Branzi. Grandi Legni*, Nilufar, Design Gallery, Milan, 2009.

ANDREA BRANZI'S MAIN WORKS

ANDREA BRANZI'S MAIN WORKS

WITH ARCHIZOOM ASSOCIATI (1966-1974)
(Andrea Branzi, Gilberto Corretti, Paolo Deganello, Massimo Morozzi, Dario Bartolini and Lucia Morozzi):

1966: Sofa *Superonda*, Poltronova, Agliana;
1967: - First exhibition *Superarchitettura*, Jolly Gallery, Pistoia;
- Second exhibition *Superarchitettura*, Municipal Gallery, Modena;
- *Safari*, sofa, Poltronova, Agliana;
- *Dream Beds*, Poltronova, Agliana;
1968: - Exhibition/Installation *Centro di Cospirazione Eclettica*, XIV Triennal of Milan;
- New Italian Pavillon, National Competition, Osaka Expo;
- Exhibition/Installation *Stanze vuote e Gazebo*, Mana Art Market Gallery, Rome;
- *Villa Bernini*, Porto Santo Stefano, Grosseto;
- Church project, Zingonia, Bergamo;
- Interior design, Libreria Editrice Fiorentina, Florence;
- Houses Le Caldinem, Florence;
- *San Remo*, lamp, Potronova, Agliana;
1969: - Exhibition/Installation RAI, Electronics Trade Fair, EUR, Rome;
- Video clip *Vestirsi è facile (Dressing is Easy)*;
- Internationl Competition *Yamagiwa*, Tokyo, second prize;
- *Mies*, Armchair, Poltronova, Agliana;
- Entrance, project, archeological site S. Reparata, Florence;
- House restoration, via San Gallo, Florence;
- *Fotomontaggi Urbani*; Theoretical project;
1970: - New Airport, National Competition, Genoa;
- New Airport, National Competition, Catanzaro;
- Design Research, New light devices, Flos;
1971: - New University, International competition, Florence;
- House project, Les Champs de Mars, Paris;
1972: - *Armchair*, Centro Ricerche B&B, Milan;
- Façade restoration, Palazzo Guadagni, Florence;
- House, project, Le Piagge, Florence;
- House, project, Soffiano, Florence;
- Day-Hospital project, Florence;
- Standa Point, Florence;
- *AeO*, chair, Cassina, Milan;
- *Come è fatto il cappoto di Gogol*, video clip, XIV Triennal of Milan;
- *Ambienti Grigi*, Museum of Modern Art, New York, in *Italy, the new Domestic Landscape*;
- *No-Stop City*, Theoretical project of a diffuse metropolitan sistem;
1974: Traditional Dress competition, Tripoli, Libya.

WITH CDM (1974-1982):

1975/1982: Founder of *CDM* (Milan Design Consultants), with Massimo Morozzi, Clino Trini Castelli, Ettore Sottsass jr., Alessandro Mendini and Gianni Cutolo;
1975: Coordinated image and landscape design, Airport Leonardo da Vinci (Fiumicino, Rome), Airport Society of Rome (Italstat group);
1978: - Colours system design, Piaggio, Torino;
- New experimental materials, Louis Vuitton, Paris;
- New information systems project, Italian Ministry of communications;
1979: Landscape design and corporate image, Sonatrac, Algeria.

INDIVIDUAL PROFESSIONAL ACTIVITY

1975-1979: Global image, art director, Fiorucci, Milan;
1975: Interior design, Fiorucci store, New York, with Ettore Sottsass jr.;
1981: Project, Focus showroom, Munich;
1982: Founder of Domus Academy, First post lauream international school of design;
1983: Interior design, Santini e Dominici store, Naples;
1984: Interior design, Italimpianti & co. restaurant, Genoa;
1986: - Montedison colonies, project, Marina di Massa, with Studio Zini;
1987: Project, New Modern Art Gallery and General project for the S. Francesco's block, Arezzo;
1988: Project, New Cemetery, Carpi, with Tullio Zini;
1990: - *Tokyo City X*, meta-project for Mitsubishi Co., with Isao Hosoe, Clino Castelli and Tullio Zini, Tokyo's Bay;
- *Folly10 Pavillon*, Landscape Expo, Osaka;
- *Il grande grigio*, Theoretical environment;
- *Diaphos*, Abet Laminati, Milan;
- Restoration, Casa Fontanella, Biella;
1991/1995: - Coordinator consultant, PRG, Arezzo;
- Project, New residential areas: Quinto Basso, Sesto Fiorentino, with Di Benedetto, Banchini and Meli Office;
1992: - Strategic consultant, Biennal of Interior Design, Kortrjik, Belgio;
- Restoration, Villa Sant'Ignazio, Fiesole, with Gaetano Di Benedetto and Francesco Gurrieri;
1993: *Citizen Office*, Vitra Group, with Ettore Sottsass jr. and Michele De Lucchi;
1994: - Interior design, restoration, Villa Boulez, Sint Truiden, Belgium;
- Project, Villa *La Quiete*, Gignese, Novara;
1995: - *Agronica*, Theoretical project, with Centro Ricerche Domus Academy, for Philips Corporation;
- Research project, New light qualities, Artemide, Milan;
1996: Restoration, Argentarium Gallery, Antwerp, Belgium;
1997: - Research design, Hospital spaces, for Anshen+Allen Architects San Francisco, in collaboration with Domus Academy;
- Research design, Hospital waiting rooms, for Anshen+Allen Architects, San Francisco, in collaboration with Domus Academy;
1998: Interior design, Lawrence Steel's house, Milan;
1999: Residential houses, project, Zotteghem, with Eddy François;

2000: Master-plan for abandoned areas, Philips, Eindhoven;
2002: - Gallery of Modern Art, Arezzo;
- Interior design, De Smet's House, Belgium, with Eddy François;
2007: Preliminary project, Martiri della libertà Square, Pontedera, with Atelier Arturo Carmassi e And Studio;
2009: Restoration, Casa Bruschi, Arezzo.

OBJECTS DESIGN

1978: - *Relitech*, three-dimensional laminate, Abet, Milan;
- *Vallechiara*, sistem of lamps, Croff Casa, Milan;
- New car, experimental project, Alfa Romeo, with Ettore Sottsass Jr.;
1979: - *Bauhaus1*, Experimental furnitures, Alchimia, MIlan;
1980: - *Bauhaus2*, Experimental furnitures, Alchimia, MIlan;
- *Giorno e notte*, Lombarda Cuscini, Milan;
1981: - *Gritti*, bookcase and *Beach*, chaise longue, Memphis, Milan;
- *Utopia*, bookcase, *Stadio*, bookcase, *Lume amaro*, lamp, Studio Alchimia, Milan;
1982: *Labrador*, sauce boat and *Century*, sofa, Memphis, Milan;
1983: *Derby*, chair, Memphis, Milan;
1984: *Magnolia*, bookcase, Memphis, Milan;
1985: *Animali Domestici Collection*, objects and furnitures, Zabro-Zanotta, Milan;
1986: - *Berlino*, sofa, Zanotta, Milan;
- *Tatzine and Tatzone*, Tendenze, Milan;
- Adam&Eve, clocks, Seibu, Milan;
1987: - *Andrea*, sofa, Memphis, MIlan;
- *Aida e Armida*, chairs, Zanotta, MIlan;
- Vases and boxes, Ceramiche Ronzan, Treviso;
1988: - *Mama-ò*, kettle, Alessi, Verbania;
- *Foglia*, lamp, Memphis, Milan;
1989: - *Martina*, fountain and *Quadrio*, table, UP&UP, Massa;
- *Axale*, sofa, *Eucidi*, tables, *Barione*, bookcase, Cassina, Milan;
- *Neolia*, bed and *Judolia*, bench, Zanotta, Milan;
1990: - *Tibet*, bookcase, Max International, Milan;
- *Metropolis*, credenza, Lapis;
1991: - *Toothstick Holder*, pepper mill, salt mill and corkscrew, Twergi Collection, Alessi, Omegna;
- *Amnesie Collection*, Design Gallery, Milan;
- *Grande York* and *Piccolo York*, bookcases, Acerbis, Bergamo;
- *Bolgheri*, credenza, Unitalia;
1992: - *Lubekka*, chair, Cassina, Milan;
- *Luoghi Collection*, Design Gallery Milan;
- *Altera*, chair and *Catai*, table, Zanotta, Milan;
1993: - *Revers*, chair, and *Gerrit*, table, Cassina, Milan;
- *Niccola*, armchair, and *Potto*, magazine rack, Zanotta, Milan;
- Car stereo, Pioneer, Tokyo;
- Glasses, Murai, Tokyo;
1994: - *Bond*, handle, Olivari, Novara, with Francesco Messori;
- *Vertical Home*, experimental project for a vertical furniture, Cappellini, Milan;
- Moquette, Vorwerk, Wuppertal;
1995: Handles, Valli&Valli, Milan;
1996: - *Wireless*, lamps collection, Design Gallery Milan;
- *Polidoro*, lamps, Artemide, Milan;
1997: - *Wood&Stones Collection*: wood lamps, stone boxes, sound vase; *Arco*, chaise longue and table with a central seat, Argentaurum Gallery, Gent;
- Bijoux Collection, Argentaurum Gallery, Gent;
- *Fuzzy Design Collection*, Design Gallery Milan;
1998: - *Quirino*, lamp, Artemide, Milan;
- *Passaggi*, lamps collection, Design Gallery Milan;
- *Tano* e *Nina*, jewellery boxes, Marutomi, Tokyo;
- Bathroom accessories, Octupus, Munich;
2000: - *Solferino*, steel box, Alessi, Verbania;
- *Età del bronzo Collection*, Design Gallery, Milan;
- *Genetic Tales Collection*, Alessi, Omegna;
- New products research, MontBlanc, Hamburg;
2002: - Bed, OAK, Como;
- *Tano*, tables, Danese, Milan;
- *Newton*, lamp, Omikron Design, Milan;
- Glass Vases, Alessi, Omegna;
- *Newton*, lamp, Omikron Design, Milan;
- Fountain pen, ACME Studio, Maui;
2003: *Goccia*, lamp, Rotaliana, Trento;
2004: - *Blister Collection*, Design Gallery, Milan;
- *Giardini Consolle Collection*, Galleria Clio Calvi Rudy Volpi, Milan;
2005: - *Simbiosi Collection*, Galleria Clio Calvi Rudy Volpi, Milan;
- *Enzimi Collection*, plexiglass vases, Metea and Galleria Scacchi, Milan;
- Urban furnitures, Pyeongchon Chungang Park, Anyang;
- *Trattore*, oil vase, Alessi, Omegna;
2006: - *Tartan Collection*, plexiglass vases, Metea, Galleria Scacchi, Milan;
- *Canneti Collection*, Galleria Clio Calvi Rudy Volpi, Milan;
- *Uomini e Fiori Collection*, vases, Design Gallery, Milan;
- *Agricoltura – Architettura (Agriculture-Architecture)*, territorial simulator with mirrored viewfinder;
- Clocks *Out_Time Collection*, Alessi, Omegna;
- *Drill*, glass vases, C.I.R.V.A. Marseilles;
2007: - *Sugheri Collection*, glass vases, for C.I.R.V.A., Marseilles and Galleria Clio Calvi and Rudy Volpi, Milan;
- *Sciami Collection*, plexiglass vases, Metea, for Galleria Scacchi, Milan;
- *Platone*, lamp, Design Gallery Milan;
- *Portali*, vases collection, SuperegoDesign, Asti;
- *Tsukimi*, fruit bowl, Fiorichiari, Milan;
2008: - *Incubator*, kitchen, Veneta Cucine, Biancade;
- *Hansel e Grethel*, consolle, Galleria Clio Calvi, Milan;
- *Canarie Basket Collection*, Design Gallery Milan;
- *Medusa*, vase, Massimo Lunardon & C., Vicenza;
2009: - *Picassincoccio Collection*, vases, Biennal of Ceramics, Albisola;
- *Campanula*, lamp, Rotaliana, Trento;
- *Les Treilles Collection*, Ceramiche Bernardaud;
- *Grandi Legni Collection*, Design Gallery MIlan and Nilufar, Milan;
2010: *Epigrammi Collection*, Galleria Clio Calvi Rudy Volpi, Milan;
2011: - *Nature Morte Collection*, Galleria Clio Calvi Rudy Volpi, Milan;
- *Vasi Erbe Collection*, Nilufar, Milan;
- *Scoiattolo*, nutcracker, Alessi, Omegna;
2012: - *Anticonfort*, armchair, Riva, Como;
- *Bosco Collection*, Superego Design, Asti;
2013: - *Pergamo Collection*, composed by *Vasi* e *Gabbie con Uccelli*, Galerie Isabella Bortolozzi, Berlin;
- *Ticino*, chaise longue, Superego Design, Asti;
- *Uomini e Bestie Collection*, Galleria Clio Calvi Rudy Volpi, Milan;
- *Eros Collection*, Galleria Clio Calvi Rudy Volpi, Milan;
2014: - *Wall Collection*, Galleria Friedman Benda, New York;
- *Solid Dreams Collection*, Galleria Clio Calvi Rudy Volpi, Milan;
- *Santambrogio Collection*, De Vecchi MIlan 1935, Milan;
2015 : *Dolmen Collection*, Galleria Antonia Jannone, Milan;
- *Corpi Collection*, Galleria Clio Calvi Rudy Volpi, Milan;
- *Papier Collection*, Great Design Gallery, Paris;
- *Ofelia Collection*, Metea, Galleria Luisa delle Piane, Milan;
- *Luoghi Collection*, Galleria Antonia Jannone, Milan;
2016: - *Oro, Gesso e Pesci Collection*, Galleria Clio Calvi and Rudy Volpi, Milan;
- *Gabbie Collection*, Galleria Luisa Delle Piane, Milan;
- *Plank Collection*, Galleria Friedman Benda, New York;
2017: - *Altri Luoghi Collection*, Galleria Antonia Jannone, Milan;
- *Madri Collection*, Galleria Clio Calvi and Rudy Volpi, Milan;
- *Maschere* e *Figuranti Collections*, Galleria Luisa Delle Piane, Milan.

SCENOGRAPHIES

1978: *Molly cara*, director: Ida Bassignano, with Piera Degli Esposti;
1985: *Per mangiare le nuvole*, director: Giancarlo Gialli, Teatro Regio, Turin;
1998: *Pinocchio*, coreography: Karole Armitage, Teatro della Pergola, Maggio Musicale Fiorentino;
2000: *Casanova*, by Karole Armitage, Hellenic Festival, Taormina;
2002: *Barbebleu*, coreography: Karole Armitage, Teatro dell'Opera, Nancy.

URBAN INSTALLATIONS

1997: *Grandi Vasi*, Segur;
1999: *Grande Vaso*, Museum of Applied Arts, Gent;
2002 : New Roppongi Hill, Tokyo;
2005: *Giardino Interno*, Palazzo Tursi, Genoa European Capital of Culture, 2005;
2013: *Recinto Sacro*, Chaumont-sur-loire.

COMPETITIONS

1983: - New Railstation, Bologna, with Tullio Zini;
- Urban Park *Manifattura Tabacchi*, Bologna, with Tullio Zini;
- Ponte dell'Accademia, Biennal of Venice, with Tullio Zini;
1988: - *Over the Wall*, Berlin, First prize;
- *Urban Design of Historical City Center*, Castel di Sangro, L' Aquila, First prize;
- Manhattan West Waterfront, New York, New York Art Society, Second prize, with Tullio Zini, Rhea Alexander, Dante Donegani, Giorgio Ferrando, Corrado Gianferrari, Giovanni Levanti, Ernesto Spicciolato;
1989: Tokyo International Forum, with Franco Lani and Tullio Zini;
1991: Thematic Park *Fiabilandia*, Rimini;
- Fitness Center *Tennozu Club*, Tokyo;
1993: School Campus, Trento, with Tullio Zini;
1995: - Minamata Memorial Competition;
- Hopping centers MCC World (Swatch e Mercedes) competition, Invited candidates;
1997: - Urban valorization of central area, San Donato milanese, with Tullio Zini, Michele Zini, Claudia Zoboli, Mattia Parmigiani, Grazia Franzoni, Stefano Maffei, Lapo Lani;
2000: Restoration, ex-Ansaldo in Milan, with Arata Isozaki and Alessandro Mendini, Finalist;
2001: New Gent Forum, with Toyo Ito and Eddy François, Finalist;
2003: Landscape design, Garibaldi Porta Nuova, Milan, with Italo Rota, Ronan and Erwan Bouroullec, Finalist;
2010: Museum Maribor Art Gallery, Slovenian, Maribor European Capital of Culture 2012, with 2A+P Studio;
2012: Itinerant Pavillon, Expo 2015, Invited candidate.

PERSONAL EXHIBITIONS

1978: - *Interno urbanistico*, Palazzo dei Diamanti, Ferrara;
- *Assenza-Presenza nell'architettura moderna*, Museum of Modern Art, Modena;
1982: Installation *Mussolini's Bathroom*, Centro Domus, Milan;
1985: Memphis' objects, Seibu Department Store, Tokyo;
1986: - Installation *Il grande tappeto ibrido*, Musée Saint Pierre, Lion;
- *Case a Pianta Centrale*, Documenta, Kassel;
- *Centro Cayc*, Buenos Aires;
1991: *Amnesie*, Design Gallery Milan;
1992: *Luoghi*, Design Gallery, Milan;
1994: *Archivi militanti*, Colombari Gallery, Milan;
1996: - *Wireless*, Design Gallery Milan;
- *Wood&Stones*, Argentaurum Gallery, Knokke Zoute;
1997: - *Fuzzy design*, Design Gallery Milan;
- *Wood&Stones*, Argentaurum Gallery and Seno Gallery, Milan;
1998: - *Passaggi*, Design Gallery Milan;
- *Silver and Gold*, Museum of Design, Gent;
2000: - *Oggetti e territori*, Cultural Center Scharpoord, Knokke and Society of Architecture, Bruxelles;
- *Età del Bronzo*, Design Gallery, Milan;
2003: *Blossoming the gap*, Studio Rendl and Spitz, Colonia, with Ronan and Erwan Bouroullec;
2005: - *Simbiosi*, Clio Calvi and Rudy Volpi Gallery, Milan;
- *Enzimi*, Scacchi Gallery, Milan;
- *Modernità Debole*, Le Bain Gallery, with Shigeru Uchida, Tokyo;
2006: - *Sciami*, Scacchi Gallery, Milan;
- *Canneti*, Clio Calvi and Rudy Volpi Gallery, Milan;
- *Uomini e fiori*, Design Gallery, Milan;
- *Des hommes et des fleures*, Mouvemet Modern Gallery, Paris;
2007: - *Sugheri*, Clio Calvi and Rudy Volpi Gallery, Milan;
- *Portali*, Superego Gallery, Milan;
2008: - *Open Enclosures*, Fondation Cartier Pour L'art contemporain, Paris;
- *Grand-Hornu Images*, Hornu, Belgio;
- *Wood & Stones*, Argentaurum, Belgio;
- *Uomini e Fiori* e *Canarie*, The Gallery, Bruxelles;
-*Oggetti e Territori*, Milly Pozzi Contemporary Art and Pinacoteca Comunale, Como;
- *Hansel e Grethel*, Clio Calvi Gallery, Milan;
2009: - *Flower*, Daniele Gallery, Padoa;
- *Grandi Legni*, Azzedine Alaïa Gallery, Paris;
- *Les Treilles*, Terzo Millennio Gallery, Milan;
2010: - *Tutti i nodi vengono al pettine*, Plart Foundation, Naples;
- *Epigrammi*, Clio Calvi and Rudy Volpi Gallery, Milan;
- *Things, Thoughts & Territories*, Seno Gallery, Milan;
2010: *Louis XXI Porcelaine Humaine*, boutique Van Cleef & Arpels, Milan;
2011: *Nature Morte*, Clio Calvi and Rudy Volpi Gallery, Milan;
2012: - *Monoliti*, Clio Calvi and Rudy Volpi Gallery, Milan;
- *Trees*, Carpenters Gallery, London;
2013 : - *Eros*, Clio Calvi e Rudy Volpi Gallery, Milan;
- *Uomini, Gabbie e Canarini*, Bertolozzi Gallery, Berlin;
- *Uomini e Animali*, Clio Calvi and Rudy Volpi Gallery, Milan;
2014: *Filastrocche*, Antonia Jannone Gallery, Milan;
- *Solid Dreams*, Clio Calvi and Rudy Volpi Gallery, Milan:
- *Andrea Branzi, pleased to meet you – 50 ans de création*, MADD Musée des Arts décoratifs et du Design, Chiesa Saint-Rémí, Architecture Center Arc en Rêve, Bordeaux;
- *Heretical Design*, MARCA Museum, Catanzaro;
2015: - *Dolmen*, Antonia Jannone Gallery, Milan;
- *Papier*, Great Design Gallery, Paris;
- *Corpi*, Clio Calvi and Rudy Volpi Gallery, Milan;
- *Transparency*, Luisa Delle Piane Gallery, Milan;
- *Flat – Domus – Luoghi*, Antonia Jannone Gallery, Artissima 2015, Turin;
2016: - *Opere Recenti*, Blu di Prussia Gallery, Naples;
- *Anime*, VOLUME! Gallery, Rome;
- *Oro, Gesso e Pesci*, Clio Calvi and Rudy Volpi Gallery, Milan;
- *Gabbie*, Luisa Delle Piane Gallery, Milan;
- *Interiors*, Friedman Benda Gallery, New York;
- *La metropoli primitiva*, Nivola Museum, Orani;
- *La metropoli multietnica*, XXI International Exposition *Design after Design*, Triennal of Milan.

VIDEO (selection)

2010: - *Epigrammi*, Clio Calvi and Rudy Volpi Gallery, Milan;
- *Grandi Legni*;
- *Infinities*, Biennal of Architettura, Venice, 2010;

2011: - *Trees and Stones*;
- *Il Mondo Salvato dai Vegetali*, Clio Calvi and Rudy Volpi Gallery, Milan;
- *Immersions*;
- *Figure e Figurine*;

2012: - *Monoliti*, Clio Calvi and Rudy Volpi, Milan;
- *Dolmen*;

2013: - *Eros*, Clio Calvi and Rudy Volpi Gallery, Milan;
- *The Primitive Metropolis*;
- *Skin*;
- *Uomini e Bestie*;

2014: - *Solid Dreams*;

2015: *Papier*;

2016: - *Mozart*;
- *Anime*;

2017: - *Palchi*;
- *Teatro*;
- *Corpi*.

EXHIBITION AS CURATOR

1973: General Coordination, Product Design Session, XV Triennal of Milan, with Ettore Sottsass jr.;

1976: Coordination, *First Italian Exhibition of furnishing fabrics*, Institute for the Foreign Trade, Imperial Hotel, Tokyo;

1977: Coordination, *The Italian Design since the Fifties*, Centrokappa, Noviglio, Milan;

1990: Chief, *Les Capitales Europèennes du Nouveau Design: Barcelone, Düsseldorf, Milan, Paris,* Centre Georges Pompidou, Paris and Kunstmuseum, Düsseldorf, with François Burckhardt;

1991: - Organization, ideation, *Il Dolce Stil Novo (della Casa)*, Pitti Immagine, Palazzo Strozzi, Florence;
- Organization, *Il design Italiano*, Domus Design Agency, Tokyo;

1992: - Curator, *La lunga tovaglia del XX secolo*, Pitti Immagine Casa, Fortezza da Basso, Florence;
- Strategic consultant, Biennale Interieur, Kortrijk, Bruxelles;
- Curator, *Il Giardino delle Cose*, XVIII Triennal of Milan;

1993: - Curator, *Tessuti Notturni*, Pitti Immagine Casa, Fortezza da Basso, Florence;
- Curator, *Citizen Office*, Vitra Museum, Weil am Rhein, with Michele De Lucchi and Ettore Sottsass jr.;

1994: Curator, *Stanze Segrete*, Pitti Immagine Casa, Fortezza da Basso, Florence.;

1995: - Curator, Design Session, *Italian Methamorphosis*, Guggenheim Museum, New York;
- Ideation, *European Qualities*, Biennal of Interieur, Belgium;

1997: *No-Stop City*, Documenta X, Kassel;

2000: Curator, Architectural Session, *Continuità. L'arte in Toscana*, Florence, Pistoia, Prato;

2001: Curator, *Italia Giappone: Design come stile di vita*, within *2001 Italia in Giappone*, Yokohama and Kobe;

2007: - Curator, *New Italian Design, Il paesaggio mobile del nuovo design italiano*, Triennal of Milan;
- Scientific curator, *Le sette ossessioni del design italiano*, Triennale Design Museum, Milan;

2008: - Curator, *Opening soon. ..*, Benetton – Polidesign, Triennal of Milan, with Luisa Collina;
- Curator, *Terrazzo 1986-1996. Ettore Sottsass*, Triennale Design Museum, Milan;
- Curator, *Les jardins de Sèvres*, showroom Sèvres, Paris;

2012: - Scientific curator, *The New Italian design 2.0*, second edition, Triennale Design Museum, Beijing, Nantou, Alhondiga, San Francisco, Santiago del Cile, Triennal of Milan;

2014: - Scientific curator, *The New Italian design 2.0*, The Waterfront Lookout, Cape Town;

2015: - Scientific curator, *The New Italian design 2.0*, Gwangju Design Biennale, South Korea;

2016: - Curator, *Neo Prehistory – 100 Verbs*, XXI International Exposition *Design after Design*, Triennal of Milan, with Kenya Hara;

2017: Curator, *Serie Fuori Serie*, National Museum of China, Pechino, with TDM.

THEORETICAL ACTIVITY
MAIN PUBLICATION

1980: *Moderno, Post-moderno, Millenario*, Studio Forma/Alchymia publisher, Milan;

1981: *Il Design italiano degli anni '50*, Editor and Introduction, IGIS edition, Milan;

1983: *Merce e Metropoli - esperienze del Nuovo Design italiano*, Epos publisher, Palermo;

1984: *La Casa Calda: Esperienze del Nuovo Design Italiano*, Idea Books, Milan; English edition: *The hot house: Italian new wave design*, M.I.T. Press, Cambridge, and Thames and Hudson, London; French edition: *La casa calda: le design italien*, L'Equerre publisher, Bruxelles;

1986: *Animali Domestici*, Idea Books, Milan; English edition: *Domestic Animals: The Neoprimitive Style*, M.I.T. Press, Cambridge;

1988: *Learning from Milan*, M.I.T. Press, Cambridge, English translation of the original book *Pomeriggi alla media-industria*
- *Design e Seconda Modernità*, Idea Books, Milan;

1990: *La Quarta Metropoli*, Domus Academy Edition, Milan;

1991: - *Formes des Métropoles - Nouveaux Designs en Europe*, Centre Georges Pompidou publisher, Paris;
- Exhibition catalog *Capitales Europennes du Nouveau Design*, Centre Georges Pompidou publisher, Paris; German edition *Neues Europaische Design*, Ernst und Sohn, Berlin;
- Exhibition catalog, *Il Dolce Stil Novo* (della Casa), Palazzo Strozzi for Pitti Immagine Casa, Alessi publisher, Milan;

1992: - *Nouvelles de la Metropole Froide*, Centre Georges Pompidou publisher, Paris;
- *Luoghi, Andrea Branzi's main works from 1966 to1991*, Rizzoli International Publisher, New York; Italian edition published by Idea Books, Milan; English edition: Thames and Hudson, London; German edition Ernst & Sohn publisher, Berlin;
- *Arezzo, verso un inurbamento maturo*, Comune di Arezzo publisher;
- *La civiltà dell'ascolto - e altre note sul Giappone moderno*, with Nicoletta Branzi, Cronopio publisher, Naples;

1994: *Villa S. Ignazio a Fiesole*, with Francesco Gurrieri, Alinea publisher, Florence;

1996: *Il design italiano 1963-1990*, Electa publisher, Milan;

1997: *La crisi della qualità*, Edizioni della Battaglia, Palermo;

1998: *Genetic Tales*, Alessi publisher, Omegna;

1999: *Introduzione al design italiano*, Baldini & Castoldi publisher, Milan;

2001: *Italia e Giappone: Design come stile di vita*, Nihon Keizai Shimbun (Nikkei) publisher, Tokyo;

2003: *Verso una Modernità Debole e Diffusa*, Polidesign publisher, Milan;

2006: - *No-Stop City - Archizoom Associati*, 2006, HYX publisher, Orlean;
- *Modernità debole e diffusa - Il mondo del progetto all'inizio del XXI secolo*, Skira publisher, Milan; English edition: *Weak and Diffuse Modernity, the World of Projects at the beginning of the 21st Century*, Skira publisher, Milan;
- *Il libro degli omini*, with Lorenza Branzi, Corraini publisher, Mantua;

2007: - *Capire il design*, Giunti – Scala publisher, Florence;
- *Spazi per la cultura e cultura degli spazi - Nuovi luoghi di produzione e consumo della cultura contemporanea*, with Alessandra Chalmers, Francoangeli publisher, Milan;

2008: - *Introduzione al design italiano - una modernità incompleta*, Balidini e Castoldi publisher, Milan;
- *Il design italiano 1964-2000*, Triennale Electa publisher, Milan;
- *Che cosa è il disegno italiano - le sette ossessioni*, with

Silvana Annicchiarico, Triennale - Electa publisher, Milan;
2009: *Serie Fuori Serie*, with Silvana Annicchiarico, Triennale - Electa publisher, Milan;
2010: *Ritratti e autoritratti di design*, Marsilio publisher, Venice;
2013: *Gli strumenti non esistono, la dimensione antropologica del design*, with Armin Linke, Alessandro Rabottini, Johan&Levi, Monza;
2014; - *Una generazione esagerata*, Baldini & Castoldi publisher, Milan;
- *The Primitive Metropolis*, Fortino Editions, Miami.

ESSAYS

Casabella:

1970: Archizoom Associati, "Città Catena di Montaggio del sociale, ideologia e teoria della metropoli," in *Casabella* n. 350-51;
1972 : - "La Gioconda sbarbata. Il ruolo dell'avanguardia," n. 364;
- "L'Africa è vicina. Il ruolo dell'avanguardia," n. 364;
- "Abitare è facile. Il ruolo dell'avanguardia," n. 365;
- "Radical Notes," nn. 370, 371, 372;
1973: - "Radical Notes," nn. 373, 374, 376, 377, 378, 379, 380-81, 382, 383;
1974: - "Radical Notes," nn. 385, 388, 389, 390, 391, 392-93, 395, 396;
1975: - "Radical Notes," nn. 399, 401, 402, 403, 407;
1976: - "Radical Notes," numeri 411, 412.

MODO (main essays):

1977: - "Bruno Zevi con Andrea Branzi," n. 1;
- "Nanni Balestrini con Andrea Branzi," n. 3;
- "Paolo Portoghesi con Andrea Branzi," n. 4;
1983: - "Dal cucchiaio alla città trent'anni dopo," n. 63;
1984: - "Senza mistero l'uomo è numero," n. 66-67;
- "Nella crisi della cultura industriale," n. 72;
- "Design sul pentagramma," speech with Rodolfo Bonetto, n. 70;
- "Il gioco del fare," speech with Bruno Munari, n. 71-72;
1985: - "Il dialetto e la lingua," Riccardo Dalisi and Enzo Mari in conversation;
- "La bellezza," Mario Bellini and Michele De Lucchi in conversation, n. 81;
1986: - "Verso una casa... a pianta centrale," n. 86;
- "Il Sud come modello del mondo?," n. 94;
- "Un pensiero a segmenti forti," n. 94;
- "Verso una normalità anormale," n. 95;
1987: - "Luci sula citta; il piacere del tramonto," with Cristina Morozzi, n. 99;
- "Il veleno nelle radici," vol.10 n. 101;
1990: "Teoremi per un'ecologia del mondo artificiale," n. 127.

Terrazzo (main essays):

1988: - "The Second Modernity," n. 1;
- "Architecture in Shadow," n. 2;
1989: "Purple Shadows," n. 3;
1990: "Dolce Stil Novo," n. 5;
1991: "Humanism versus Environmentalism," n. 6;
1995: "Development and Reduction," n. 10;

Domus (main essays):

1968: - Archizoom Associati, "Le stanze vuote e i gazebo," n. 462;
- Archizoom Associati, "Il Centro di Cospirazione Eclettica," n. 466;
1969: Archizoom Associati, "Per Osaka," n. 471;
1971: Archizoom Associati, "Residential Parkings," n. 496;
1980: "Triennale anno zero," n. 604;
1980: "Dentro la città," n. 612;
1982: "Domus Academy," n. 633;
1988: - "Progetto Manhattan waterfront," n. 696;
- "Cose e Case," n. 699;
1990: "Ecologia metropolitana," n. 712;
1996: "Dalle avanguardie storiche alle avanguardie permanenti," n. 783;
1997: - "Un macro-oggetto fuori scala," n. 792;
- "Oggetti post-tecnologici," n. 797;
1998: "Il sopravvento della logica fuzzy," n. 800;
2002: "Italia e Giappone: nuovi paesaggi del design," n. 846;
2005: - "Per una architettura enzimatica," n. 878;
- "La rivoluzione poetica di Constant," n. 880;
- "Sponge Forum," n. 887;
2006: - "Rivoluzione viscerale," n. 897;
- "Insegnare il design," n. 891;
2008: "Casa Madre," n. 917.

Interni (main essays):

1988: "Sette tesi per il design," n. 383;
1994: - "Native: il nuovo livello della sensibilità nell'uso delle tecnologie," n. 443;
- "Corporate qualities," n. 445;
1995: - "Gli italiani a New York: crolla il muro della Pop Art," n. 447;
- "Sopra e sotto," n. 499;
- "Dalla società post-tecnologica alla società post-industriale," n. 453;
2002: - "Italia e Giappone: nuovi paesaggi del design," n. 518;
- "Il Giappone salvato dai divani," n. 524;
- "Un parco tematico per il design italiano," n. 525;
- "Architettura a metà della crisi," n. 526;
2005: - "Arti e architettura," n. 548;
- "Avanguardie Musulmane?," n. 550;
- "La metropoli degli umani," n. 551;
- "Modernità invisibile," n. 554;
- "Uomini e donne nell'ambiente," n. 555;
- "Il mistero dei gioielli," n. 556;
- "Un riformismo colorato," n. 557;
2006: - "Industrial Design (o no?)," n. 558;
- "Architettura per una città che cambia," n. 559;
- "Made in Italy in bilico?," n. 560;
- "La città dopo Atene," n. 561;
- "Tafuri e i maestri cattivi," n. 565;
- "Interni e/o prodotti," n. 566;
2007: - "The New Italian Design," n. 570;
- "La scrittura d'architettura," n. 571;
- "È arrivato Godot?," n. 573;
- "Per un postambientalismo," n. 573;
- "Un museo diverso," n. 576;
2008: - "I colori instabili, dell'incertezza," n. 578;
- "L'arte come religione rivelata," n. 579;
- "Ettore Sottsass o la libertà del pensiero creativo," n. 580;
- "Grazie, Napoli," n. 581;
- "Contro un mondo governato dagli scienziati," n. 583;
- "Contro l'architettura," n. 584;
- "Due strade," n. 585;
- "Vacanze veneziane," n. 586;
- "Michele (o la felicità del fare)," n. 587;
2009: - "Università: tempi nuovi, tempi duri," n. 588;
- "È senza pensiero il design?," n. 589;
- "Il mondo (era) piatto," n. 590;
- "Una generazione di pre-socratici," n. 591;
- "Design senza pensiero?," n. 592;
- "I progettisti," n. 594;
- "L'innovazione nella società globalizzata," n. 595;
- "Per chi suona la campana?," n. 560;
2010: - "Grandi Legni," n. 598;
- "Scuole a vendere," n. 599;
- "Senza orizzonti," n. 600;
- "Una società oggettuale," n. 601;
- "L'epoca della moltitudine," n. 603;
- "La responsabilità politica del design," n. 604;
- "Indipendent Design," n. 605;
- "Patty Smith the dark lady," n. 607;
2011: - "Il cimitero diffuso," n. 609;

- "Nemo propheta in patria," n. 610;
- "Il nuovo secolo all'improvviso," n. 613;
- "Il design nell'epoca post-fordista," n. 614;
- "Design ostile," n. 615;
- "Addio telefoni bianchi," n. 616;
- "Il Brasile come modello del mondo," n. 617;

2012: - "Quella Francia che vede il mare," n. 618;
- "Un silenzio assordante," n. 619;
- "Elogio dell'autodidatta," n. 620;
- "Oltre il design," n. 621;
- "Progetto e antiprogetto," n. 623;
- "Architettura italiana," n. 625;
- "Addormentati nel bosco," n. 626;

2013: - "Wild metropolis," n. 628, International english issue;
- "Italy calling the world," n. 628, International english issue;
- "Design proibito," n. 629;
- "La fine dell'eurocentrismo," n. 630;
- "Across the ocean," n. 631;
- "Pauperismo e ingenuità," n. 634;
- "La memoria che nasconde la memoria," n. 636;
- "Tante righe," n. 637;

2014: - "Portable cosmology," n. 638;
- "L'anti grafica," n. 639;
- "Impariamo dalla moda," n. 640;
- "Solid Dreams," n. 641;
- "Religione e laicismo," n. 643;
- "Una generazione esagerata," n. 644;
- "Biennale ma non biennale," n. 645;
- "Luoghi e mostre," n. 646;
- "Le grand malade," n. 647;
- "Rolling seventies," in *Interni 60 Anni*;

2015: - "1+1=3," n. 648, International English Issue;
- "Lost in translation," n. 649;
- "La Scuola di Piazza Bausan," n. 651;
- "Le Corbusier alla gogna," n. 654;
- "Design after Design," n. 655;
- "La Metropoli Merceologica," n. 656;
- "Il ritardo italiano," n. 657;

2016: - "Holy Wars," n. 658;
- "Radici Animiste," n. 659;
- "Un problema irrisolvibile," n. 660;
- "After fifty years," n. 661;
- "Giappone Segreto," n. 663;
- "Neo-preistoria, neo-modernità," n. 664;
- "La potenza dell'impensato," n. 666;
- "L'arte dentro alla storia," n. 667;

2017: - "Quella generazione esagerata," n. 668;
- "Altri luoghi," n. 669;
- "Eremiti Urbani," n. 670;
- "The animist object," n. 671.

Interni Annual (main essays):

1991: "La cultura dell'abitare," *Annual Home*;
1991-92: "Dalla qualità ambientale alla qualità totale," *Annual Office*;
1992-93: "Oltre la scrivania," *Annual Office*;
1993: "Un sistema in trasformazione," *Annual Home.*

L'Unità (main essays):

1993: "Il design in crisi cerca il modello del Duemila," Tuesday 20 November;

1994: - "Gio Ponti, il paradiso dell'architetto," Tuesday 22 February;
- "Tafuri, l'architettura come forma sovrana," Thursday 24 February;
- "La fabbrica del Rinascimento," Thursday 31 March;
- "La città moderna dopo il progetto? È il teatro del caos," Sunday 17 April;
- "Architetti, torna dall'America il grande progetto," Thursday 19 May;
- "Arriva l'Alberti. Teoria e arte dell'uomo moderno," Sunday 4 September;
- "L'America dice addio alla pop-art," Tuesday 18 October;

1995: "L'utopia fallita di una città ben ordinata," Saturday 21 January;
1996: "E Terragni creò il National Style," Friday 26 July;

Other articles:

1975: "Tecnologia sotto accusa," in *Rassegna*, n. 38-39;
1978: "Design Searches," in *Japan Interior Design*;
1988: "La metropoli ibrida," in *Alfabeta*, n. 106;
1989: - "Scenografie del prossimo millennio," in *Gap Casa*, n. 54;
1991: - "Quale Piano?," with Franco Lani, in *Edilizia Popolare*, n. 215;
1994: "I luoghi del lavoro continuo," in *Abitare*, n. 333;

1995: - "Il futuro delle avanguardie," in *Stileindustria*, n. 1;
- "MIlan. Metropoli post-industriale," in *Il Mondo Nuovo*, n. 14;
- "La Ville: sei interviste," in *Lotus International*, n. 84;

1997: - "Il progetto lanuginoso," in *Pluriverso*, n. 2;
- "Considerazioni generali," in *Domus extra*, n. 789;
- "Visionen und Formlosigkeit," in *Design Report*;

1999: "Lavoro e creatività diffusa," in *Panorama Interni*, n. 1;
2000: "L'urbanistica dell'indeterminatezza," in *Lotus International*, n. 107;

2001: - "Dalle avanguardie storiche alle avanguardie permanenti," in *In Form+Action*, n. 2;
- "Lo specchio dell'anima," in *Lotus Navigator*, n. 3;

2003: - "La città debole," in *Opere*, n. 2; anno I;
- "Bellezza urbana/metropolitana di Firenze," in *Opere*, n. 3, anno I;
- "Luoghi sfumati," in *Opere*, n. 7, anno II;

2004: "Architectural link," in *GUD*, n. 4;

2005: - "Dal cucchiaio al cucchiaio," in *DIID. Disegno Industriale Industrial Design*, n. 13;
- "Design, un'altra definizione," in *DIID. Disegno Industriale Industrial Design*, n. 16;
- "Quelle macchine inutili," in *Abitare*, n. 451;
- "Mutazioni in superficie," in *Ottagono*, n. 184;
- "Il declino dell'oggetto," in *Opere*, n. 10, anno III;

2006: - "La placenta mediterranea," in *DIID. Disegno Industriale Industrial Design*, volume 18;
- "La decorazione non è soltanto decorazione," in *DIID. Disegno Industriale Industrial Design*, volume 23;
- "Il naturalismo del dopo-Kobe," in *Area*, volume 84;
- "Andrea Branzi," in *Area*, volume 85;

2007: - "Pineta di Architettura," in *Abitare*, n. 477;
- "Un museo diverso," in *Opere*, n. 576;
- "Il miglior design della nostra vita" e "Il secolo ha perso tutti i suoi confini," in *L'Europeo*, n. 6;
- "Architetture per i fiori," in *Gardenia*, n. 282;

2008: - "Futuristes pessimistes?," in *Archistorm*, n. 34;
- "Quaranta anni di storia del design - Marco Casamonti incontra Andrea Branzi e Michele de Lucchi," in *Area*, n. 76;
- "Conversazione con Andrea Branzi," in *Made in Cassina*, ed: Giampiero Bosoni, Skira publisher, Milan;
- "Andrea Branzi Oggetti e Territori," speech with Manolo De Giorgi, Silvana editoriale, Milan;
- "Fratelli e progetti," in *DIID. Disegno Industriale Industrial Design*, n. 31;

2009: - "La metropoli genetica," in *A fior di pelle / Skin deep*, Centro di Medicina Rigenerativa di Modena, ZPZ Partners, Electa, publisher, Milan;
- "Il retail nell'era della globalizzazione," in *Opening soon*, ed: Luisa Collina and Laura Pollini, Poli.design/Fabrica publisher, Milan;
- "Neuf conseils pour une Nouvelle Charte d'Athènes," in *L'enjeu capital(es). Le métropole de la grande échelle*, Centre Pompidou publisher, Paris;

2010: "Per una nuova Carta di Atene – for a new Charter of Athens," in "*The Innov(e)tion valley magazine*, n. 4;
2011: "Dieci modesti consigli per una nuova Carta di Atene," in Enrica Bistagnino, *Sguardi mediterranei, 10 rappresentazioni di paesaggi italiani*, Franco Angeli publisher, Milan;
2012: *The contemporary interior landscape*, ed.: Giampiero Bosoni, Agnese Rebaglio, Francesco Scullica, Abitare publisher, Milan;

2013: - "La sostanza opaca della metropoli," in Franco Guerzoni, *La parete dimenticata*, Exhibition catalog, Skira publisher, Milan;
- "La scimmia che è in noi," in *Abitare*, n. 531;
- "Verso uno spazio integrato," in Luciano Crespi, *Da spazio nasce spazio*, Postmedia, Milan;
- "Art Forest, Contemporary Art Museum," in *DD, Alternative Destinies, design Document series*, n. 38, ed.: 2A+P e DAMDI;
- "Dante Donegani e Giovanni Lauda," in *La Casa Fredda*, ed.: Carlo Vannicola, Forma publisher, Florence;
- "La metropoli selvaggia," in *Monograph Research*, n. 5, List Lab publisher, Trento;
- "The monkey in us," in Lidewij Edelkoort, *Fetishism in Fashion*, ed.: Philip Firmano, Forme publisher, Amsterdam;
- "La chaise comme modèle idéologique" and "Une grâce perdue," in *Design: l'Antologie*, ed.: Alexandra Midal, EPCC Cité du design - ESADSE et HEAD publisher, Geneva;
- "Radical Notes," in *The Italian Avant-Garde 1968-1976*, ed.: Catharine Rossi e Alex Coles, Sternberg Press, Berlin.

ESSAYS

1974: *Introduction*, in Paola Navone e Bruno Orlandoni, *Architettura Radicale*, *Casabella* publisher, Milan;

1986: *Preface*, in Aldo Tanchis, *Bruno Munari*, Idea Books publisher, Milan;

1987: "L'ambiente," in *I cento linguaggi dei bambini*, A.A.V.V., Regione e Comune di Reggio Emilia publisher;

1990: - "L'oggetto della metropoli: Domus Academy come strumento di ricerca," in *Design Italiano: quale scuola?*, ed.: Nicola Sinopoli, Franco Angeli publisher, Milan;
- "Kopien und Nicht-Kopien," in *Ispirazione Italiana - Italienische Design-Klassiker und was daraus wurde*, Exhibition catalog, Kunstmuseum, Düsseldorf;

1991: - "La pietra calda," in A.A.V.V., *Neolite*, Domus Academy publisher, Milan;
- *Introduction*, in Volker Albus and Wolfgang Schepers, *Rude ma sincero*, Idea Books publisher, Milan;
- "Folly 10," in *Osaka Follies*, Architectural Association publisher, London;

1993: "La qualità formale del mondo," Introduction on Ettore Sottsass jr., Exhibition catalog, Centre Georges Pompidou publisher, Paris;

1994: - "Italian Design and the Complexity of Modernity," in *The Italian Metamorphosis 1943-1968*, Exhibition catalog, Guggenheim Museum, New York;
- "La metropoli accidentale," in *La metropoli accidentale*, ed.: Patrizia Ranzo, Cronopio publisher, Naples;
- Interview, in *La Ville*, Le Moniteur, Paris;
- "Padri e figli," in *Ritratto di Sottsass*, ed.: Silvio Sanpietro, L'archivolto publisher, Milan;
- "La Belgique secrète" and "European Qualities," in *Design Made in Belgium, Interieur '94* Catalog;
- "Andrea Branzi, workshop," in *Television at the Crossroad*, ed.: Stefano Marzano, V+K Publishing, Amsterdam;

1995 : "Symbiotic Metropolis, Agronica," and "Aesthetics, Freed Space," in *The solid side*, eds.: Ezio Manzini and Marco Susani, V+K Publishing, Amsterdam;

1996: - "Shiro Kuramata, Purple Shadows," in *Kuramata*, catalog of the Hara Museum of Contemporary Art, Tokyo;
- "Architecture Radicale," in *Dictionnaire de l'Architecture du XX Siècle*, Hazan, Institut Français d'Architecture, Paris;
- "Testo per CD ROM," in *Gae Aulenti*, ed.: Margherita Petranzan, Rizzoli publisher, Milan;

1998: "Educational and relational space," in Giulio Ceppi and Michele Zini, *Children, spaces, relations-metaproject for an environment for young children*, Reggio Children publisher, Reggio Emilia;

2001: - "Progetti politici," in *Shadows*, ed.: Lapo Lani, Catalog of the Furniture Collection for Neglia, Arezzo;
- "Memorie Relazionali" in *Memoria quotidiana, Comunità e comunicazione nell'era delle reti*, ed.: Federico Casalegno, Le Vespe publisher, Pescara-Milan;
- "Un concorso difficile" in *Idee per Piazza Mercatale*, ed.: Comune di Prato;
- "Per Ettore Sottsass," in *Ad honorem*, ed.: Graziella Buccellati and Benedetta Manetti, Politecnico di Milano publisher;

2002: - "L'oggetto fotografato," in *Photo e Design, L'immagine Alessi*, ed.: Claudia Zanfi, Silvana publisher, Cinisello Balsamo;
- "L'ossessione della storia," in *Continuità, Arte in Toscana 1945-2000*, ed.: SMAC, Maschietto publisher, Pistoia;
- "Preface," in Marek Nester Piotrowski, *Progettare in fiera, progettare la Fiera*, Lybra Immagine publisher, Milan;
- "A Homeless Country," in *Italy Contemporary Domestic Landscape 1945-2000*, ed.: Giampiero Bosoni, Skira publisher, Milan;
- "Architettura e Design," in *Arte in toscana 1945/2000 Continuità*, ed.:SMAC, Maschietto publisher, Pistoia;
- "La arquitectura soy yo – L'architecture c'est moi," in A.A.V.V., *Architecture Radicale*, Exhibition catalog, Institut d'art contemporain – IAC publisher, Villeurbanne;

2003: - "Le mouvement radical," in A.A.V.V., *Architectures Experimentales 1950-2000*, HYX Editons, Orlean;
- "Modernizing modernity," in *The Berlage Institute Report* n. 6/7, Rotterdam;

2004: "L'oriente dell'Occidente," in Shigeru Uchida with Ikuyo Mitshushashi, *Interiors, fornitures and architecture*, Rikuyo-Sha publisher, Tokyo;

2005: - "Notes on No-Stop-City: Archizoom Associates 1969-72," in *Exit Utopia - Architectural Provocations 1956-1976*, ed.: Martin Van Schaik, Otakar Macel, Prestel publisher, New York;
- "Architettura, un'altra storia," in Germano Celant, *Arti e Architettura* Volume 2, Skira publisher, Milan;
- "Una strega innocente," in Sonzogni Annalisa, *Teorema: Praga, Torino, Lyon*, Edizioni Nepente;
- "La progettazione degli interni," in *Architettura degli Interni*, ed.: Adriano Cornoldi, Il Poligrafo publisher, Padua;
- "Premessa remota," in *Opdipo*, ed.: Marco Maiocchi, Ettore Lariani, Youngju Oh, Franco Angeli publisher, Milan;

2006: - "O Brasil como modelo do mundo," in Dijon De Moraes, *Análise do design brasileiro*, Editora Edgard Blucher ltda, San Paolo;
- "L'autonomia del design degli interni," "Il design primario," "Un paese senza casa," "Allestimento come metafora di nuova modernità," in *Design degli interni. Contributi al progetto per l'abitare contemporaneo*, ed.: Luca Guerrini, FrancoAngeli publisher, Milan;
- "Blue Bovisa," in A.A.V.V., *Progetto Bovisa*, Polipress - La Triennale di Milano publisher, Milan;
- "No-Stop city. Progetto di una città come grande contenitore," in *Milano Malpensa, la regione urbana nello spazio dei flussi*, ed.: Ernesto d'Alfonso, Alinea publisher, Florence;
- "Il declino degli oggetti," in Francesca La Rocca, *Il tempo opaco degli oggetti. Forme evolutive del design contemporaneo*, FrancoAngeli publisher, Milan;
- "La placenta mediterranea," in Massimo Giovannini, *Spazi e culture del Mediterraneo*, Edizioni Kappa, Rome;
- "Enzo Mari," in A.A.V.V., *Questo non è uno scolapasta*, Compositori publisher, Bologna;

2007: - "Onde parallele," in *L'artiste, l'atelier, le verre*, ed.: CIRVA, Editions Xavier Barral, Paris;
- "Sette gradi di separazione," in Andrea Branzi, Silvana Annicchiarico, *The New Italian Design*, La Triennale di Milano publisher, Milan;
- "Spazi per la cultura e la cultura degli spazi," in *Gli interni nel progetto sull'esistente*, ed.: Adriano Cornoldi, Il Poligrafo publisher, Padoa;
- "Radical Design," in A.A.V.V., *Anni Settanta - il decennio lungo del secolo breve*, Skira - La Triennale di Milano publisher, Milan;
- "Un'idea di Reggio Emila," in *Reggio Emilia, scenari di qualità urbana*, ed.: Luca Molinari, Skira publisher, Milano;
- "La progettazione degli interni nella città contemporanea," in *Architettura degli Interni*, ed.: Adriano Cornoldi, Il Poligrafo publisher, Padoa;
- "La città, un computer ogni venti metri quadrati," in *Vertigo - Il secolo di arte off-media dal futurismo al web*, ed.: Germano

Celant, Gianfranco Maraniello, Skira-MAMbo publisher, Milan;
- "Modernità debole e diffusa," in *Florence Exit. Segnali e fermenti di una nuova generazione di architetti*, ed.: Alberto Breschi, Maschietto, Florence;

2008: - "Retailing in the globalization era" in *Place and Themes of interiors Contemporary Research Worldwide*, ed.: Luca Basso Peressut, Imma Forino, Gennaro Postiglione, Francesco Scullica, Interior studies Franco Angeli publisher, Milan;
- "La radice del terrazzo," in A.A.V.V., *Terrazzo 1988-1996*, Electa-Triennale di Milano publisher, Milan;
- "Per una nuova visione strategica del furniture design," in *Made in Cassina*, ed.: Giampiero Bosoni, Skira publisher, Milan;
- "Il retailing nell'epoca dellla globalizzazione," in *Opening soon*, Polidesign publisher, Milan;
- "Il design oggi," in Treccani *Il libro dell'anno 2008*, Istituto dell'Enciclopedia Italiana publisher, Rome;
- "La prophetie de Pierre Paulin," in *Pierre Paulin*, ed.: Catherine Geel, Archibooks publisher, Paris;

2009: - "Gli incubi ironici di Fornasetti, in *Fornasetti: l'artista alchimista e la bottega fantastica*, Vol. 2, ed.: Barnaba Fornasetti and Mariuccia Casadio, Mondodori Electa publisher, Milan;

2010: "Per una nuova Carta di Atene – for a new Charter of Athens," in *The Innov(e)tion valley magazine*, n. 4;

2012: - "Le projet à l'époque de la crise de la globalisation: vers une "nouvelle charte d' Athènes," in *Le visiteur, revue critique d'architecture*," n. 18, Paris;

2013: - "Le Mouvement Radical," in *Architecture Experimentales 1 950-2012*, Collection du FRAC Centre, HYX editeur, Orlean;

2014: - "Architettura e design a Florence nel '900," Catalog of the New Museum of '900 of Florence;

2015: - "Per una nuova drammaturgia del progetto," in Luca Basso Peressut, Giampiero Bosoni, Pierluigi Salvadeo, *Mettere in scena, mettere in mostra*, Letteraventidue publisher, Siracusa;
- "Urbana Bellezza," in *Cultura Commestibile* n. 140;
- "Tra le rane e le canne," in *Poltronova Backstage, Archizoom Sottsass e Superstudio*, ed.: Francesca Balena Arista, Fortino Edition, Miami;

2016: *Sull'autostrada per Carnac. Riflessioni sulla metropoli Primitiva*, ed.: Richard Ingersoll, Postmedia Books publisher, Milan;

2017: "Andata e ritorno," in La Pina, Federico Giunta, *I Tokyo*, Vallardi publisher, Milan;

COLLABORATION AND DIRECTION OF MAGAZINES

1972/1976: "Radical Notes," in *Casabella*;
1983/1987: Director of the Industrial design magazine *Modo*;
1991/1995: Editorial Consultant, *Interni*;
1984/1990: Editorial Consultant, *Idea Books Publisher*, Milan;
2000/present: Editorial Consultant, *Interni*;

ESSAYS ON ANDREA BRANZI'S WORK

1969: "Archizoom," in *L'Architecture d'Aujourd'hui*, n. 145;
1970: Archizoom Associati, "Archizoom," in *A.D.*, July;
1971: Germano Celant, "Senza titolo," in *Domus*, n. 496;
1972 : - Charles Jencks, "Supersensualist," in *AD*, n. 1;
- Emilio Ambasz, *Italy, the New Domestic Landscape: Achievements and problems of Italian Design*, MoMA press, New York;

1973: - Charles Jencks, *Modern Movements in Architecture*, Penguin Books publisher, London;
- Franco Raggi, "Radical Story," in *Casabella*, n. 382;
- Almerico De Angelis, "L'antidesign," in *Op. Cit.*, n. 26;

1974: - Charles Jenks, "The Supersensualists II: Death," in *Late Modern Arhitecture*, Academy Edition, London;

1977: A.A.V.V., *Il dibattito architettonico in Italia dal 1945 al 1975*, Bulzoni publisher, Rome;

1978: - Bruno Zevi, "Una mostra di buone intenzioni," in *L'Espresso*, n. 29, 23 July;

1981: - Benedetto Gravagnuolo, "I linguaggi ereditati," in *Domus*, n. 619;
- Charles Jenks, "The New International Style e altre etichette," in *Domus*, n. 623;

1982: - Lea Vergine, "Progettare con il coltello," in *Modo*, n. 47;
- Gabriella D'Amato, "Il design tra radicale e commerciale," in *Op. Cit.*, n. 53;

1984: Alessandro Mendini "Intervista Andrea Branzi," in *Domus*, n. 648;
1985: Ettore Sottsass jr., "La Casa Calda," in *Domus*, n. 658;
1987: Gilberto Corretti, "Industriale, post-industriale o provinciale?," in *P.A. Professione Architetto*, n. 5-6;

1988: - Brigitte Fitoussi, "Entretien: Andrea Branzi," in *L'Architecture d'Aujourd'hui*, n. 257;
- Sophie Tasma-Anargyros, "Portrait Andrea Branzi," in *Intramuros*, n. 18;
- T. de Beaumont, "Les metteurs en scene du design: Andrea Branzi," in *L'Atelier*, n. 126;
- Giacinto Di Petrantonio, "Andrea Branzi," in *Flash Art* n. 143;
- Silvia Giacomoni, Attilio Marcolli, *Designer italiani*, Idea Libri publisher, Milan;

1989: Benedetto Gravagnuolo, "La seconda modernità," in *Modo* n. 113;

1996: - Giampiero Mughini, "Saranno profeti in patria?," in *Panorama*, 25 April;
- Marco Belpoliti, "Artefatti: l'Italia degli oggetti," in *Il Manifesto*, Friday 3 May;
- "Andrea Branzi" and "Archizoom Associati," in *Dictionnaire de l'Architecture du XXe siecle*, Hazan publisher, Paris;
- Giovanna Franco Repellini, "Dal saccoso al bolidoso," in *Il Sole 24 Ore*, Sunday 7 July;

1997: Cristina Rattazzi, *Andrea Branzi. Militanza tra teoria e prassi*, Franco Angeli publisher, Milan;

1998: - Cristina Morozzi, François Burkhardt, *Andrea Branzi*, Dis Voir publisher, Paris;
- Paola Bartolini, "Andrea Branzi: l'uomo, il burattino, la modernità," in *Domus* n. 808;

1999: "Andrea Branzi," in *Enciclopedia Europea* Vol. XIII, Garzanti publisher, Milan;

2004: - Andrea Branzi and Toyo Ito, "*Forum for Music, Dance and Visual Culture, Ghent*," in *Lotus International* n. 123;
- "Urban housing: discussion between Andrea Branzi, Pierluigi Nicolin and Cino Zucchi," in *Lotus International* n. 120;
- Dominique Rouillard, *Superarchitetture, le future de l'architecture 1950-1970*, Villette publisher, Paris;
- Franco Raggi, interview "La città è un grande interno enzimatico," in *FLARE*, Architectural Lighting Magazine n. 36;

2005: - Antonio Scarponi, "Andrea Branzi: la ville continue," in *Moniteur Architecture AMC* n. 150;
- Matteo Vercelloni, "Urban ready-made," in *Interni* n. 548;
- Enrica Bistagnino, "Per una architettura evolutiva, reversibile, attraversabile," in *Progetto*, n. 23;

2006: - Patrick Tuttofuoco, interview, in "Revolving," Sandretto Rebaudengo Foundation, Skira publisher, Milan;
- Catherine Geel, "La cité du design: Andrea Branzi," Editions de l'Amateur et France Culture;

- A.A. V.V., Exhibition catalog, "Visioni A-Moderne, cultura del design in Campania," Triennale Aversa;
- Giampiero Bosoni, "Il modo italiano – design et avantgarde en Italie du XX siècle," Skira e Musée des Beaux Arts de Montréal publisher, Milan;
- Alessandra Burigana, Mario Ciampi, "Italian Designers – storie e stili di vita dei protagonisti del design italiano," Verba Volant publisher, London;
- Lucio Altarelli, "Live Design," Molteni and Università la Sapienza publisher, Rome;

2007: - Interview "Un colloquio con Andrea Branzi," in *Domus* n. 906;
- Roberto Gargiani, *De la vague pop à la surface neutre - Archizoom Associati 1966-1974*, Electa and Politecnico di Losanna publisher, Milan;
- Roberto Gargiani, *Dall'onda pop alla superficie neutra - Archizoom Associati 1966-1974*, Electa and Politecnico di Losanna publisher, Milan;

2008: - Pier Vittorio Aureli, "The project of autonomy," in *Politics and Architecture within and against capitalism*, Buel Center/ Forum, Princeton Architectural Press, New York;
- Germano Celant, "Andrea Branzi, un progetto ellissoidale," in *Interni* n. 582;
- Kazys Varnelis, "Programming after program: Archizoom's No-Stop City," in *Praxis*, Issue_8 - RE: Programming, Boston;
- Pier Vittorio Aureli, "Architecture as framework: the project of the city and the crisis of neoliberism," in *New Geographies* n. 1, Harvard Graduate School of Design publisher, Cambridge;
- Christian Simenc "One or two things about our lucky generation," in *Azimuts*, n. 30;
- Christian Simenc, Intervew: "Je travaille à l'idée d'une ville sans architecture," in *Le journal des Arts*, n. 278, 28 March -10 April;
- Anne-Marie Fèvre, Intervew: "Dés petites choses qui choses qui changent la vie" in *Liberation* n. 5;

2009: - Stefano Follesa, Interview: *"Pane e progetto, il mestiere di designer,"* Franco Angeli publisher, Milan;
- Elisabetta Pasini and Franco Natili, Interview: *"Carisma, il segreto del leader,"* Garzanti publisher, Milan;
- Giulio Bandini, "Progetti senza cantiere," in *Terzocchio* n. 10;
- "Breve conversazione con Andrea Branzi," in *2Over design over, materia, tempo e natura nel design contemporaneo*, ed.: Marco Rainò and Andrea Margaritelli, Silvana Editoriale, Milan;

2010: - Mohsen Mostafavi, "Why Ecological Urbanism? Why now?," in *Ecological Urbanism*, Lars Muller Publishers, Baden;
- Charles Waldheim, "Weak Work: Andrea Branzi's 'Weak Metropolis' and the Projective Potential of an "Ecological Urbanism," in *Ecological Urbanism*, Lars Muller Publishers, Baden;

2011: - Stefano Caggiano "Oggetti di confine," in *Interni* n. 612;
- A.A.V.V., "Weak Urbanisation," in *San Rocco Magazine*, "Island" n. 1;
- Tahl Kaminer, *Architecture, Crisis and Resuscitation, the reproduction of post-Fordism in late-twentieth-century architecture*, Routledge, London;
- A.A.V.V., *Monolithes, ou l'architecture en suspens* (1950-2010), Exhibition Catalog, FRAC Centre, Orlean;
- "Archizoom Associati, progetto di concorso per la Fiera dell'artigianato a Florence," in *Recycle, strategie per l'architettura, la città e il pianeta*, ed.: Pippo Ciorra, Sara Marini, *I libri del MAXXI*, Museo Nazionale per le Arti del XXI secolo, Electa publisher, Rome-Milan;

2012: - Francesca Balena Arista, "L'Aquila LAB," in *Abitare* n. 522;
- "La tentation du verre, un choix d'oevres la collection du centre international de recherche sur le verre et les art plastique," ed.: Zia Mirabdolaghi, Vence chateau de villeneuve, fondation Emilie Hugues, Vence;

2013: - Rosa Tessa, "Eros e design," in *Interni* n. 612;
- Roberto Gargiani, "Per una critica marxista della metropoli: la No-stop city," in *La Città Nuova, oltre Sant'Elia, 1913-2013 cento anni di visioni urbane*, Exhibition catalog, Como Villa Olmo Pinacoteca Civica, Silvana Editoriale, Milan;
- Pier Vittorio Aureli "More money /less work: Archizoom," in *The Italian Avant-Garde 1968-1976*, ed.: Catharine Rossi and Alex Coles, Sternberg Press, Berlin-New York;
- Gianni Pettena, "Archizoom Associati," in *Architecture Experimentales 1950-2012*, Collection du FRAC Centre, HYX, Orlean;
- Nadine Labedade, "Andrea Branzi," in *Architecture Experimentales 1950-2012*, Collection du FRAC Centre, HYX, Orlean;
- Julien Donada, Interview, in *Les Visionnaires, une autre histoire de l'architecture*, Petit à Petit Production, FRAC Centre Les Turbulences, Orlean;

2014: - *Andrea Branzi. Objets et Territoires/Objects and Territories*, ed.: Constance Rubini, Gallimard publisher, Paris;
- *Andrea Branzi – Para una nueva carta de Atenas*, ed.: Jeannette Sordi and Felipe Vera, ARQ publisher, Santiago de Chile;
- *Andrea Branzi. Design Antropologico e drammaturgia degli oggetti*, in *Lezioni di Architettura e Design*, ed.: Alessandra Coppa, Abitare-Corriere della Sera, Milan;

2015: Elisa C. Cattaneo, *Weakcity. Notes on Landscape Urbanism*, ListLab publisher, Trento;

2016: - Daniel Daou and Pablo Pérez-Ramos, *New Geographies After Zero / Departement of Urban planning and Design* n. 8, Harvard University publisher, Graduate school of Design, Cambridge,
- Charles Waldheim, *Landscape as Urbanism: A General Theory*, Princeton Univ Press.

AWARDS

1969: Silver Medal, Yamagiwa (Tokyo) competition, with Archizoom Associati;

1979: Golden Compass, with Clino Castelli and Massimo Morozzi;

1983: - International Award, First Design Biennal of Buenos Aires, with Domus Academy;
- Merit Mention, Golden Compass;

1987: Golden Compass, Lifetime Achievement Award;

1989: Certificate of Commendation, Robert Maxwell Prize, Royal College of Art, London for the essay "Seven Theses on Design";

1991: Baden Wüttemberg for the stone table *Quadrio*, Up&UP;

1994: Special Mention, Europea *eur*;

1995: Golden Compass, for the activity at Domus Academy;

1996: - First Prize, Hannover Fair, Video: *I protagonisti del design i taliano. Lo scenario, le storie, i prodotti, le utopie*, edited by Dialogo Multimedia / Editoriale Domus;

1997: First Prize, "Pirelli Energy" competition;

2008: - Laurea Honoris Causa, Università La Sapienza, Rome;
- Honorary Memeber, *Royal Society for the encouragement of Arts, Manufactures and Commerce* (RSA), London;

2009: Member of CID: Design Committee, Italian Ministry of Culture.

IMAGES: SOURCES, COPYRIGHT AND CREDITS

Cover: Archizoom Associati, "Bosco Residenziale," *No Stop City*, 1969; MoMA, NY;

E. C. Cattaneo, *Urban Theories since 1956*, 2013; Elisa C. Cattaneo;

Manifesta, *Utopia e/o Rivoluzione*, Turin, 1969;

Classe Operaia n. 1, 1964, Cover; *Classe Operaia*, Archive;

Archizoom Associati, "Dichiarazione al XVII Convegno Internazionale Artisti Critici Studiosi d'arte," Rimini, 1968; Paolo Deganello Archive;

Quaderni Rossi n. 2, 1962, Cover; *Quaderni Rossi*, Archive;

Contropiano n. 1, 1969, Cover; *Contropiano*, Archive;

Manifesto, Le Corbusier, exhibition, Palazzo Strozzi, Florence, 1963; Archive;

"Arno Flood," 1964; Locchi Archive, Florence; copyright Locchi, Archive, Florence;

Andrea Branzi, Gilberto Corretti, Massimo Morozzi, Cristiano Toraldo di Francia, Ali Navai, with Sergio Pastorini and Pietro Spagna, *Città Estrusa. Produzione, Accumulazione, Meccanica*, Faculty of Architecture, Florence, 1964; Centre Pompidou, Archive;

Andrea Branzi, Gilberto Corretti, Massimo Morozzi, Cristiano Toraldo di Francia, Ali Navai, with Sergio Pastorini and Pietro Spagna, *Città Estrusa. Allegoria morale della città estrusa*, Faculty of Architecture, Florence, 1964; Centre Pompidou, Archive;

Andrea Branzi, Gilberto Corretti, Massimo Morozzi, Cristiano Toraldo di Francia, Ali Navai, with Sergio Pastorini and Pietro Spagna, *Città Estrusa. Il nastro della produzione industriale*, Faculty of Architecture, Florence, 1964; Centre Pompidou, Archive;

Andrea Branzi, Gilberto Corretti, Massimo Morozzi, Cristiano Toraldo di Francia, Ali Navai, with Sergio Pastorini and Pietro Spagna, *Città Estrusa, Machina Proiectionis*, Faculty of Architecture, Florence, 1964; Centre Pompidou;

Paolo Deganello, Carlo Chiappi Marliani, *Struttura urbana per 70.000 abitanti a Brozzi*, Faculty of Architecture, Florence, 1963-64; Archive, Deganello;

Andrea Branzi, *Master Thesis Free-time Facilities, Prato*, 1966; CSAC, Archive, Parma; Photos: Cristiano Toraldo di Francia;

Andrea Branzi, *Relazione Tesi di Laurea*, 1966, Original document; Andrea Branzi Archive;

Andrea Branzi, "Luna Park permanente a Prato," in *Casabella* n. 366, 1972; *Casabella*, Archive;

Archizoom Associati, Logo Archizoom; Andrea Branzi Archive;

Archigram, Cover *Archigram* n. 4, 1964; Archigram Archive;

Archizoom Associati and Superstudio, *Superarchitettura*, 1966, Pistoia Exhibition- recto; Gilberto Corretti Archive;

Archizoom Associati and Superstudio, *Superarchitettura*, 1966, Modena Exhibition - recto; Gilberto Corretti Archive;

Archizoom Associati and Superstudio, *Manifesto Superarchitettura*, 1967, Modena Exhibition - recto; Andrea Branzi Archive;

Archizoom Associati and Superstudio, *Manifesto Superarchitettura*, 1967, Modena Exhibition - verso; Andrea Branzi Archive;

Archizoom Associati and Superstudio, *Superarchitettura*, 1964; Photos (n. 3): Cristiano Toraldo di Francia; Poltronova, Archive;

Archizoom Associati, *Superonda*, 1967; Photo: Dario Bartolini; Dario Bartolini Archive;

Archizoom Associati, 1967; Andrea Branzi Archive;

Germano Celant, "Untitled," in *Domus* n. 496, 1971; *Domus*, Archive;

Cover *Casabella* n. 367, 1972; *Casabella*, Archive;

Alessandro Mendini, "Radical Design," in *Casabella* n. 367, 1972; *Casabella*, Archive;

Charles Jencks, "Supersensualist," in *AD* n. 1, 1972; *AD*, Archive;

"Archizoom," in *L'Architecture d'aujourd'hui* n. 145, 1969; *L'Architecture d'aujourd'hui*, Archive;

Archizoom Associati, 1967; Photo: Dario Bartolini; Andrea Branzi Archive;

Elisa C. Cattaneo, *Movimento Radical - Diagram*; Elisa C. Cattaneo;

Archizoom Associati, "Architettonicamente," in *Casabella* n. 334, 1969; *Casabella*, Archive;

Andrea Branzi, "L'Africa è vicina. Il ruolo dell'avanguardia," in *Casabella* n. 362, 1972; *Casabella*, Archive;

Andrea Branzi, "La Gioconda Sbarbata. Il ruolo dell'avanguardia," in *Casabella* n. 364, 1972; *Casabella*, Archive;

Andrea Branzi, "Abitare è facile. Il ruolo dell'avanguardia," in *Casabella* n. 365, 1972; *Casabella*, Archive;

Andrea Branzi, "Crisi e protesi culturali," in *Casabella* n. 385, 1984; *Casabella*, Archive;

Andrea Branzi, "Radical Architecture. Il rifiuto del ruolo disciplinare," in *Casabella* n. 386, 1974; *Casabella*, Archive;

Cover, *Global Tools* n. 1, 1969;

Andrea Branzi, "Tecnologia o Eutanasia," Global Tools, in *Casabella* n. 397, 1976; *Casabella*, Archive;

Andrea Branzi, "Compiti a Casa. Ricordando Pasolini," in *Casabella* n. 409, 1976; *Casabella*, Archive;

Archizoom Associati, *Fotomontaggi urbani: Unità di Abitazione sulla Piazza Rossa*, 1969; n. 4 images; Andrea Branzi, Archive;

Archizoom Associati, *Fotomontaggi Urbani: Grattacielo a Manhattan*, 1969; Andrea Branzi Archive;

Archizoom Associati, *Fotomontaggi urbani: Giochi d'acqua nello stretto di Messina*, 1969; Andrea Branzi, Archive;

Archizoom Associati, "Discorso per immagini," in *Domus* n. 481, 1969; *Domus*, Archive;

Archizoom Associati, *Sequenza della dissoluzione di oggetti geometrici*, 1971; FRAC, Archive;

Archizoom Associati, "La distruzione degli oggetti," in *IN* 2-3, 1971; Ugo La Pietra Archive;

Cover *IN* n. 5, 1972, Ugo La Pietra, Archive;

Cover *IN* n. 7, 1972, Ugo La Pietra, Archive;

Archizoom Associati, "La città amorale," in *IN* n. 7, 1972; Ugo La Pietra, Archive;

Archizoom Associati, "Distruzione e riappropriazione della città," in *IN* n. 5, 1971; Ugo La Pietra, Archive;

Abet Laminati, Cover *Elementi: quaderni di studi, notizie, ricerche*, 1973;

Abet Laminati, Poster *Elementi: quaderni di studi, notizie, ricerche*, 1973;

Archizoom Associati and Superstudio, Poster *Elementi: quaderni di studi, notizie, ricerche*, Abet Laminati, 1973;

Archizoom Associati, "L'invenzione della Superficie neutra," in *Elementi: quaderni di studi, notizie, ricerche*, Abet Laminati, 1973;

Emilio Ambaz, Press release, *Italy: The New Domestic Landscape*, 1972; MoMA, Archive;

Archizoom Associati, "Ambienti Grigi," Exhibition *Italy: The New Domestic Landscape: Achievements and Problems of Italian Design*, 1972; photos (n. 3) Cristiano Toraldo di Francia;

Germano Celant, "Sono partiti per New York," in *Domus* n. 510, 1972; *Domus*, Archive;

Archizoom Associati, "Italy: The New Domestic Landscape," E. Ambasz, *Italy: The New Domestic Landscape: Achievements and Problems of Italian Design*, The Museum of Modern Art, NY, with Centro Di Florence, Florence, 1972; MoMA Press; MoMA, Archive;

Arduino Cantafora, *La città Analoga*, 1973; Triennale of Milan, Archive;

Aldo Rossi, *Omaggio a Rogers*, 1974; Triennale of Milan, Archive;

Elisa. C. Cattaneo, "Microenvironments," 2016; Elisa C. Cattaneo;

Archizoom Associati, "Le stanze vuote e i gazebo," in *Pianeta Fresco* n. 1, 1967;

Archizoom Associati, "Teatro Impossibile," in *Pianeta Fresco* n. 2-3, 1968;

Archizoom Associati, "Il Centro di Cospirazione Eclettica," in *Domus* n. 466, 1968; *Domus*, Archive;

Archizoom Associati, *Il Centro di Cospirazione Eclettica*; Andrea Branzi, Archive;

Andrea Branzi, "Il Pollo di Marmo," Original document; Andrea Branzi, Archive;

Ettore Sottsass jr., "Gli Archizoom," in *Domus* n. 455, 1967; *Domus*, Archive;

Archizoom Associati, "Vestirsi è facile," in *Casabella* n. 384, 1973; Casabella, Archive;

Andrea Branzi, Cover *Decorattivo* n. 1, 1976;

Archizoom Associati, *No-Stop City, Diagramma abitativo omogeneo*, 1967; Author: Andrea Branzi; Centre Pompidou, Archive;

Archizoom Associati, *No-Stop City, Diagramma abitativo omogeneo*, 1967; Author: Andrea Branzi; Centre Pompidou, Archive;

Archizoom Associati, *No-Stop City, Diagramma abitativo omogeneo*, 1967; Author: Andrea Branzi; Centre Pompidou, Archive;

Archizoom Associati, *No-Stop City, Diagramma abitativo omogeneo*, 1967; Author: Andrea Branzi; Centre Pompidou, Archive;

Archizoom Associati, *No-Stop City: Schema di montaggio di abitazioni temporanee*, 1971; Andrea Branzi, Archive ;

Archizoom Associati, *No-Stop City: Città non discontinua e non omogenea o città futura*, 1970; Andrea Branzi, Archive;

Archizoom Associati, *No-Stop City: model*, 1969; CSAC, Archive; Photo: Gilberto Corretti;

Archizoom Associati, *No-Stop City: Città Catena di Montaggio del sociale, ideologia e teoria della metropoli*, in *Casabella* 350-51, 1970; *Casabella*, Archive;

Archizoom Associati, *La Fortezza da Basso*, Competition, masterplan, models, 1967-68; CSAC, Parma, Archive;

Archizoom Associati, *No-Stop City Residential Parkings Climatic Universal Sistem*, in *Domus* n. 496, 1971; *Domus*, Archive;

Archizoom Associati, *No-Stop City: Visori*, 1971; Andrea Branzi Archive;

Archizoom Associati, "Bosco Residenziale," 1969; MoMA, Archive;

Archizoom Associati, "Progetto di Concorso per l'Università di Firenze," in *Domus* n. 509, 1972; *Domus*, Archive;

Andrea Branzi, Radical Notes n. 1, "Strategia dei tempi lunghi," in *Casabella* n. 370, 1972; *Casabella*, Archive;

Andrea Branzi, Radical Notes n. 2, "Il sogno del villaggio," in *Casabella* n. 371, 1972; *Casabella*, Archive;

Andrea Branzi, Radical Notes n. 3, "Pubblicazioni sulle avanguardie," in *Casabella* n. 372, 1972; *Casabella*, Archive;

Andrea Branzi, Radical Notes n. 4, "L'abolizione della Scuola," in *Casabella* n. 373, 1973; *Casabella*, Archive;

Andrea Branzi, Radical Notes n. 5, "Rock and Revolution," in *Casabella* n. 374, 1973; *Casabella*, Archive;

Andrea Branzi, Radical Notes n. 6, "La strada di Eindhoven," in *Casabella* n. 376, 1973; *Casabella*, Archive;

Andrea Branzi, Radical Notes n. 7, "Global Tools," in *Casabella* n. 377, 1973; *Casabella*, Archive;

Andrea Branzi, Radical Notes n. 8, "Elite e creatività di massa," in *Casabella* n. 378, 1973; *Casabella*, Archive;

Andrea Branzi, Radical Notes n. 9, "Piccolo, medio, grande," in *Casabella* n. 379, 1973; *Casabella*, Archive;

Andrea Branzi, Radical Notes n. 10, "Eccetto il puro deserto," in *Casabella* n. 380-381, 1973; *Casabella*, Archive;

Andrea Branzi, Radical Notes n. 11, "Sporco e Pulito," in *Casabella* n. 382, 1973; *Casabella*, Archive;

Andrea Branzi, Radical Notes n. 12, "Si scoprono le tombe," in *Casabella* n. 383, 1973; *Casabella*, Archive;

Andrea Branzi, Radical Notes n. 13, "Tecnica povera," in *Casabella* n. 385, 1974; *Casabella*, Archive;

Andrea Branzi, Radical Notes n. 14, "Alpinismo e Existenz Maximum," in *Casabella* n. 388, 1974; *Casabella*, Archive;

Andrea Branzi, Radical Notes n. 15, "Avanguardie e Fascismo," in *Casabella* n. 389, 1974; *Casabella*, Archive;

Andrea Branzi, Radical Notes n. 16, "Un plastico d'oro," in *Casabella* n. 390, 1974; *Casabella*, Archive;

Andrea Branzi, Radical Notes n. 17, "Louis Kahn Superstar," in *Casabella* n. 391, 1974; *Casabella*, Archive;

Andrea Branzi, Radical Notes n. 18, "Il ruolo della retroguardia," in *Casabella* n. 392-393, 1974; *Casabella*, Archive;

Andrea Branzi, Radical Notes n. 19, "Apollo e Dioniso a Gallarate," in *Casabella* n. 395, 1974; *Casabella*, Archive;

Andrea Branzi, Radical Notes n. 20, "Architettura e modestia," in *Casabella* n. 396, 1974; *Casabella*, Archive;

Andrea Branzi, Radical Notes n. 21, "Architettura e libertà," in *Casabella* n. 399, 1975; *Casabella*, Archive;

Andrea Branzi, Radical Notes n. 22, "Design e culture minoritarie," in *Casabella* n. 401, 1975; *Casabella*, Archive;

Andrea Branzi, Radical Notes n. 23, "Urbanistica e Ordine (pubblico)," in *Casabella* n. 402, 1975; *Casabella*, Archive;

Andrea Branzi, Radical Notes n. 24, "La grande frenata," in *Casabella* n. 403, 1975; *Casabella*, Archive;

Andrea Branzi, Radical Notes n. 25, "Architettura e sesso," in *Casabella* n. 407, 1975; *Casabella*, Archive;

Andrea Branzi, Radical Notes n. 26, "Il sospetto," in *Casabella* n. 411, 1976; *Casabella*, Archive;

Andrea Branzi, Radical Notes n. 27, "Movimento Moderno?," in *Casabella* n. 412, 1976; *Casabella*, Archive;

"Andrea Branzi, *Giardino Interno*, 2004; Photo: Studio Branzi; Andrea Branzi archive";

Andrea Branzi, Dante Donegani, Giovanni Lauda, *Metropoli Genetica*, Model, Seminar "Die Zeremonien des wetliches Europas," 1988; Friedman-Benda Collection, NY; Photo: Andrea Branzi Archive;

Andrea Branzi, *Genetic Tales*, 1998; Museo Alessi;

Andrea Branzi, *Genetic Tales*, 1998; Museo Alessi;

Andrea Branzi, *Architettura e agricoltura*, 2005; Friedman-Benda Collection, NY; Photo: Daniele Macchi - Studio Branzi; Andrea Branzi Archive;

Andrea Branzi, Dante Donegani, Antonio Petrillo, Claudia Raimondo with Tamar Ben David, *Agronica*,1995 (Domus Academy); Archive Pompidou; Photo: Studio Branzi; Andrea Branzi Archive;

Andrea Branzi, Dante Donegani, Antonio Petrillo, Claudia Raimondo with Tamar Ben David, *Agronica*,1995 (Domus Academy); Archive Pompidou; Photo: Studio Branzi; Andrea Branzi Archive;

Andrea Branzi, Dante Donegani, Antonio Petrillo, Claudia Raimondo with Tamar Ben David, *Agronica*,1995 (Domus Academy); Archive Pompidou; Photo: Studio Branzi; Andrea Branzi Archive;

Andrea Branzi, Italo Rota, Ronan and Erwan Bouroullec, *Parco Virgiliano a Milano*, 2004; Italo Rota Archive;

Andrea Branzi, Italo Rota, Ronan and Erwan Bouroullec, *Parco Virgiliano a Milano*, 2004; Italo Rota Archive;

Andrea Branzi, *Bosco di Architettura*, 2007; Friedman-Benda Collection, NY; Photo: Daniele Macchi - Studio Branzi; Andrea Branzi Archive;

Andrea Branzi, *Bosco di Architettura*, 2007; Friedman-Benda Collection, NY; Photo: Daniele Macchi - Studio Branzi; Andrea Branzi Archive;

Andrea Branzi, *Architettura e agricoltura*, 2005; Friedman-Benda Collection, NY; Photo: Daniele Macchi - Studio Branzi; Andrea Branzi Archive;

Andrea Branzi, *Agricoltura residenziale*, 2007; Friedman-Benda Collection, NY; Photo: Daniele Macchi - Studio Branzi; Andrea Branzi Archive;

Andrea Branzi with Ernesto Bartolini and Lapo Lani, *Favela High Tech, Masterplan per Eindhoven per Philips Design*, 2000; Frac, Archive; Photo: Daniele Macchi - Studio Branzi; Andrea Branzi Archive;

Andrea Branzi, *Strade leggere*, 2010; Friedman-Benda Collection, NY; Photo: Daniele Macchi - Studio Branzi; Andrea Branzi Archive;

Andrea Branzi, *Cielo Terra*, 2010; Friedman-Benda Collection, NY; Photo: Daniele Macchi - Studio Branzi; Andrea Branzi Archive;

Andrea Branzi with Ernesto Bartolini and Lapo Lani, *Favela High Tech, Masterplan per Eindhoven per Philips Design*, 2000; Frac, Archive; Photo: Daniele Macchi - Studio Branzi; Andrea Branzi Archive;

Andrea Branzi, *Modelli di Urbanizzazione Umida*, 2008; Expo Saragoza; Photo: Daniele Macchi - Studio Branzi; Andrea Branzi Archive;

Andrea Branzi, *Cattedrale Sensoriale*, 1992; Friedman-Benda Collection, NY; Photo: Daniele Macchi - Studio Branzi; Andrea Branzi Archive;

Andrea Branzi, *Territorio Enzimatico*, 2006; Friedman-Benda Collection, NY; Photo: Daniele Macchi - Studio Branzi, Atelier Pixel; Andrea Branzi Archive;

Andrea Branzi, *Modelli di Urbanizzazione Umida*, 2008; Expo Saragoza; Photo: Daniele Macchi - Studio Branzi; Andrea Branzi Archive;

Andrea Branzi, *La metropoli Merceologica (Città reale)*, 2010; Friedman-Benda Collection, NY; Photo: Sean Dean Martin; Andrea Branzi Archive;

Andrea Branzi, *La metropoli Merceologica (Città reale)*, 2010; Friedman-Benda Collection, NY; Photo: Sean Dean Martin; Andrea Branzi Archive;

Andrea Branzi, *La metropoli Merceologica (Città reale)*, 2010; Friedman-Benda Collection, NY; Photo: Sean Dean Martin; Andrea Branzi Archive;

Andrea Branzi, *Lavoro Continuo*, 1994; Friedman-Benda Collection, NY; Photo: Daniele Macchi - Studio Branzi; Andrea Branzi Archive;

Andrea Branzi, *Modelli di Corporate Identity*, Citizen Office exhibition, Vitra Design Museum, Weil am Rhein, 1994; Andrea Branzi Archive;

Andrea Branzi, *Interno Continuo*, 2010; Friedman-Benda Collection, NY; Photo: Daniele Macchi - Studio Branzi; Andrea Branzi Archive;

Andrea Branzi, *I Territori Dell'arte/4, Marcel Duchamp's La Sposa messa a nudo in front of the École militaire,* 1989; Andrea Branzi Archive;

Andrea Branzi, *I Territori Dell'arte/1, Fausto Melotti's Seven Wise Men around the Arc de Triomphe,* 1989; Andrea Branzi Archive;

Andrea Branzi, *I Territori Dell'arte/2, Picasso's Seascape at the Champs-Élysées,* 1989; Andrea Branzi Archive;

Andrea Branzi, *I Territori Dell'arte/3, Picasso's Woman Head in the Middle of the La Défense,* 1989; Andrea Branzi Archive;

Andrea Branzi, *I Territori Dell'arte/4, Marcel Duchamp's La Sposa messa a nudo in front of the École militaire,* 1989; Andrea Branzi Archive;

Andrea Branzi, *I Territori Dell'arte/5, Fernand Léger and Piet Mondrian at the La Place Royale,* 1989; Andrea Branzi Archive;

Andrea Branzi, *I Territori Dell'arte/6, Great Kandinskies on the Sacré-Cœur Hill,* 1989; Andrea Branzi Archive;

Andrea Branzi, *I Territori Dell'arte/7, Great Calder's Balance over the Tour Eiffel,* 1989; Andrea Branzi Archive;

Andrea Branzi, *Interno Rupestre,* Andrea Branzi Archive;

Andrea Branzi, *Pietre e sassi*; Photo: Daniele Macchi - Studio Branzi; Andrea Branzi Archive;

Andrea Branzi, *Campo Sacro. Carnac*, 2012-2013; Photo: Daniele Macchi - Studio Branzi; Andrea Branzi Archive;

Andrea Branzi, Grandi Legni; Photo: Daniele Macchi - Studio Branzi; Andrea Branzi Archive;

Andrea Branzi, *Dolmen Collections*, n. 15 images, 2013-2014; Centre Pompidou, Paris; Photo: Daniele Macchi - Studio Branzi; Andrea Branzi Archive;

Andrea Branzi, *Casamadre*; Photo: Daniele Macchi - Studio Branzi; Andrea Branzi Archive;

Andrea Branzi, *Solid Dreams. San Francesco,* Clio Calvi Rudy Volpi; Photo: Daniele Macchi - Studio Branzi; Andrea Branzi Archive;

Andrea Branzi, *Solid Dreams: Recinto*, Clio Calvi Rudy Volpi; Photo: Daniele Macchi - Studio Branzi; Andrea Branzi Archive;

Andrea Branzi, *Solid Dreams. Pontormo/Immersion,* Clio Calvi Rudy Volpi; Photo: Daniele Macchi - Studio Branzi; Andrea Branzi Archive;

Andrea Branzi, *Solid Dreams. Animals/Pavone,* Clio Calvi Rudy Volpi; Photo: Daniele Macchi - Studio Branzi; Andrea Branzi Archive;

Andrea Branzi, *Solid Dreams. Croce,* Clio Calvi Rudy Volpi; Photo: Daniele Macchi - Studio Branzi; Andrea Branzi Archive;

Andrea Branzi, *Solid Dreams. Giotto,* Clio Calvi Rudy Volpi; Photo: Daniele Macchi - Studio Branzi; Andrea Branzi Archive;

Andrea Branzi, *Solid Dreams. Chiesa nera*, Clio Calvi Rudy Volpi; Photo: Daniele Macchi - Studio Branzi; Andrea Branzi Archive;

Andrea Branzi, *Solid Dreams. Unité tempestosa 1*, Clio Calvi Rudy Volpi; Photo: Daniele Macchi - Studio Branzi; Andrea Branzi Archive;

Andrea Branzi, *Solid Dreams. Unité tempestosa 2*, Clio Calvi Rudy Volpi; Photo: Daniele Macchi - Studio Branzi; Andrea Branzi Archive;

Andrea Branzi, *100 verbi,* XXI Triennal ; 2016; Photo: Gianluca di Iola;

Andrea Branzi, *100 verbi,* XXI Triennal; 2016; Photo: Gianluca di Iola;

Andrea Branzi, *100 verbi,* XXI Triennal; 2016; Photo: Gianluca di Iola;

Andrea Branzi, *100 verbi,* XXI Triennal; 2016; Photo: Gianluca di Iola;

Andrea Branzi, *Angela Rui, La nuova Carta d'Atene*, 2014; Andrea Branzi Archive;

Andrea Branzi, Photo, 1945; Andrea Branzi Archive;

Andrea Branzi, Photo, 1940; Andrea Branzi Archive;

TEXTS: CREDITS AND SOURCES

ESSAYS BY ANDREA BRANZI:

$E=mc^2$ The Project in the Age of the Relativity, unpublished, 2015;

The Commodity Civilization, unpublished, 2014;

"The Sunset of Gods: The Fracture with the Modern Movement," in A. Branzi, *Una Generazione Esagerata*, Baldini&Castoldi Publisher, Milan, 2014;

"The Negative Thought and the Annunced Death," in A. Branzi, *Una Generazione Esagerata*, Baldini&Castoldi Publisher, Milan, 2014;

"The Existential Verism: Micro-catastrophes and Operaismo," in A. Branzi, *Una Generazione Esagerata*, Baldini&Castoldi Publisher, Milan, 2014;

"Florence," in A. Branzi, *Una Generazione Esagerata*, Baldini&Castoldi Publisher, Milan, 2014;

"The Florentine School," in A. Branzi, *Una Generazione Esagerata*, Baldini&Castoldi Publisher, Milan, 2014;

"Free-Time Facilities," unpublished, 2016;

Report, Master Thesis, Original document, 1966, Andrea Branzi Archive;

"Tempo morto," in *Casabella* n. 366, 1972; *Casabella,* Archive, Milan;

"Superarchitecture," in A. Branzi, *Una Generazione Esagerata*, Baldini&Castoldi Publisher, Milan, 2014;

"An Exaggerated Generation," in A. Branzi, *Una Generazione Esagerata*, Baldini&Castoldi Publisher, Milan, 2014;

"Architettura radicale," Introduction, *Architettura Radicale*, ed.: Paola Navone and Bruno Orlandoni, *Casabella*, Milan, 1974;

"L'Africa è vicina," in *Casabella* n. 362, 1972;

"La Gioconda Sbarbata," in *Casabella* n. 364, 1972;

"Abitare è facile," in *Casabella* n. 365, 1972;

"Crisi e protesi culturali," in *Casabella* n. 385, 1984;

"Radical Architecture," in *Casabella* n. 386, 1974;

"Tecnologia o Eutanasia," Global Tools, in *Casabella* n. 397, 1976;

"Compiti a Casa. Ricordando Pasolini," in *Casabella* n. 409, 1976;

"No-Stop City," unpublished, 2014;

"No-Stop City," in *No-Stop City*, Hyx publisher, 2006;

"Fortezza da Basso Competition," unpublished, 2016;

Radical Notes n. 1, "Strategia dei tempi lunghi," in *Casabella* n. 370, 1972;

Radical Notes n. 2, "Il sogno del villaggio," in *Casabella* n. 371, 1972;

Radical Notes n. 3, "Pubblicazioni sulle avanguardie," in *Casabella* n. 372, 1972;

Radical Notes n. 4, "L'abolizione della Scuola," in *Casabella* n. 373, 1973;

Radical Notes n. 5, "Rock and Revolution," in *Casabella* n. 374, 1973;

Radical Notes n. 6, "La strada di Eindhoven," in *Casabella* n. 376, 1973;

Radical Notes n. 7, "Global Tools," in *Casabella* n. 377, 1973;

Radical Notes n. 8, "Elite e creatività di massa," in *Casabella* n. 378, 1973;

Radical Notes n. 9, "Piccolo, medio, grande," in *Casabella* n. 379, 1973;

Radical Notes n. 10, "Eccetto il puro deserto," in *Casabella* n. 380-381, 1973;

Radical Notes n. 11, "Sporco e Pulito," in *Casabella* n. 382, 1973;

Radical Notes n. 12, "Si scopron le tombe," in *Casabella* n. 383, 1973;

Radical Notes n. 13, "Tecnica povera," in *Casabella* n. 385, 1974;

Radical Notes n. 14, "Alpinismo e Existenz Maximum," in *Casabella* n. 388, 1974;

Radical Notes n. 15, "Avanguardie e Fascismo," in *Casabella* n. 389, 1974;

Radical Notes n. 16, "Un plastico d'oro," in *Casabella* n. 390, 1974;

Radical Notes n. 17, "Louis Kahn Superstar," in *Casabella* n. 391, 1974;

Radical Notes n. 18, "Il ruolo della retroguardia," in *Casabella* n. 392-393, 1974;

Radical Notes n. 19, "Apollo e Dioniso a Gallarate," in *Casabella* n. 395, 1974;

Radical Notes n. 20, "Architettura e modestia," in *Casabella* n. 396, 1974;

Radical Notes n. 21, "Architettura e libertà," in *Casabella* n. 399, 1975;

Radical Notes n. 22, "Design e culture minoritarie," in *Casabella* n. 401, 1975;

Radical Notes n. 23, "Urbanistica e Ordine (pubblico)," in *Casabella* n. 402, 1975;

Radical Notes n. 24, "La grande frenata," in *Casabella* n. 403, 1975;

Radical Notes n. 25, "Architettura e sesso," in *Casabella* n. 407, 1975;

Radical Notes n. 26, "Il sospetto," in *Casabella* n. 411, 1976;

Radical Notes n. 27, "Movimento Moderno?," in *Casabella* n. 412, 1976;

"For a non Figurative Architecture," Introduction, in *Weak and Diffuse Modernity. The World of Projects at the beginning of the 21st Century*, Skira, Milan, 2006;

"From the No-Stop City to the Concept of Infinity: The City without Architecture," unpublished, 2015;

"A Strong Century," in *Weak and Diffuse Modernity. The World of Projects at the beginning of the 21st Century*, Skira, Milan, 2006;

"Fuzzy Thinking," in *Weak and Diffuse Modernity. The World of Projects at the beginning of the 21st Century*, Skira, Milan, 2006;

"A Liquid Modernity," in *Weak and Diffuse Modernity. The World of Projects at the beginning of the 21st Century*, Skira, Milan, 2006;

"Men Without Quantity," in *Weak and Diffuse Modernity. The World of Projects at the beginning of the 21st Century*, Skira, Milan, 2006;

"Time and Network," in *Weak and Diffuse Modernity. The World of Projects at the beginning of the 21st Century*, Skira, Milan, 2006;

"Crisi della qualità, crisi della complessità e spazio relazionale," in A. Branzi, *La Crisi della qualità*, Edizioni Della Battaglia, Florence,, 1996;

"I territori dell'immaginario," in A. Branzi, *Pomeriggi alla Media Industria. Design e seconda modernità*, Idea Books Edition, Milan, 1988;

"A Classic Elasticity," in A. Branzi, *Weak and Diffuse Modernity. The World of Projects at the beginning of the 21st Century*, Skira, Milan, 2006;

"Architectural link," in A. Branzi, *Weak and Diffuse Modernity. The World of Projects at the beginning of the 21st Century*, Skira, Milan, 2006;

"City Without Architecture," in A. Branzi, *Weak and Diffuse Modernity. The World of Projects at the beginning of the 21st Century*, Skira, Milan, 2006;

"The Latin Genesys of the Theoretical Metropolis," Original title: "Le metropoli teoriche," in A. Branzi, *Design Italiano*, 1999;

"La metropoli meccanica," in A. Branzi, *La quarta metropoli. Design e cultura ambientale*, Domus Academy Edizioni, Milan, 1990;

"La metropoli omogenea," in A. Branzi, *La quarta metropoli. Design e cultura ambientale*, Domus Academy Edizioni, Milan, 1990;

"La metropoli ibrida," in A. Branzi, *Pomeriggi alla media industria. Design e seconda modernità*, Idea Books, Milan, 1988;

"La metropoli fredda," in A. Branzi, *La quarta metropoli, Design e cultura ambientale*, Domus Academy Edizioni, Milan,1990;

"Models of Weak Urbanization," in A. Branzi, *Weak and Diffuse Modernity. The World of Projects at the beginning of the 21st Century*, Skira, Milan, 2006;

"The Genetic Metropolis," in A. Branzi, *Weak and Diffuse Modernity. The World of Projects at the beginning of the 21st Century*, Skira, Milan, 2006;

Introduction, in A. Branzi, *Genetic Tales*, Alessi spa, Print: Arti Grafiche Meroni, Verbania, 1998;

"The Solid Side. Agronica," in *The Solid Side*, ed.:E. Manzini e M. Susani, ed. V+K Publishing, Blaricum, 1995;

"Tre teoremi per un'ecologia del mondo artificiale," in A. Branzi, *La quarta metropoli. Design e cultura ambientale*, Domus Academy Edizioni, Milan, 1990;

"Architecture and Agriculture," in A. Branzi, *Weak and Diffuse Modernity. The World of Projects at the beginning of the 21st Century*, Skira, Milan, 2006;

"Un'ecologia dell'artificiale," in A. Branzi, *Pomeriggi alla media industria*, Idea Books, Florence, 1988;

"Wood of Architecture," unpublished, 2016;

"Reversible Urbanism," unpublished, 2016;

"A Sensorial Revolution," in A. Branzi, *Weak and Diffuse Modernity. The World of Projects at the beginning of the 21st Century*, Skira, Milan, 2006;

"Cose e Case," in *Domus* n. 699, 1988;

"I luoghi del Lavoro Continuo," in *Abitare* n. 333, 1994;

"New Form of Enterprise," in A. Branzi, *Weak and Diffuse Modernity. The World of Projects at the beginning of the 21st Century*, Skira, Milan, 2006;

"The Metropolis of the Art," unpublished, 2016;

"The XXI Century and the New Dramaturgy," unpublished, 2014;

The Primitive Metropolis, Fortino Editions, Miami, 2014;

"I primitivi siamo noi," in *Modo* n. 80, 1985;

"HouseMother," unpublished, 2016;

"Fundamentalism," unpublished, 2016;

"Solid Dreams," unpublished, 2016;

"L'arte come Religione rivelata," in *Interni* n. 579, 2008;

"La fine dell'eurocentrismo," in *Interni* n.4, 2013;

"The Neo-Prehistory," Introduction, *Neo-prehisotry. 100 verbs*, ed.: Andrea Branzi and Kenya Hara, Triennale di Milano Servizi, Milan, 2016;

"Ten Modest Advices for a New Athen's Chart," 2009;

"A Society without Project," unpublished, 2017;

"Probable Autobiography," unpublished, 2015;

ESSAYS BY ARCHIZOOM ASSOCIATI:

"Dichiarazione al XVII Convegno Internazionale Artisti Critici Studiosi d'arte," 1968; Paolo Deganello Archive;

Archizoom Associati and Superstudio, Text: Manifesto *Superarchitettura*, 1966, Pistoia exhibition- recto; Gilberto Corretti Archive;

Archizoom Associati and Superstudio, Text: Manifesto *Manifesto Superarchitettura*, 1967, Modena exhibition, recto; Andrea Branzi Archive;

Archizoom Associati and Superstudio, Text: Manifesto *Manifesto Superarchitettura*, 1967, Modena Exhibition, verso; Andrea Branzi Archive;

"Architettonicamente," in *Casabella* n. 334, 1969; *Casabella*, Archive; "Discorsi per Immagini," in *Domus* n. 481, 1969;

"La distruzione degli oggetti," in *IN* n. 2-3, 1971;

"Distruzione e riappropriazione della città," in *IN* n. 5, 1971;

"La Città Amorale," in *IN* n. 7, 1972;

"L'invenzione della Superficie neutra," in *Elementi: quaderni di studi, notizie, ricerche*, Abet Laminati, 1973;

Andrea Branzi, Ettore Sottsass jr., *Exhibition, XV Triennale*,1974; Photos: Ettore Sottsass jr.; Triennale of Milan, Archive;

"Italy: New Domestic Landscape," in E. Ambasz, *Italy: The New Domestic Landscape: Achievements and Problems of Italian Design*, The Museum of Modern Art, NY, with Centro Di Florence, 1972; MoMA Archive;

"Le stanze vuote e i gazebo," in *Pianeta Fresco* n. 1, 1967;

"Teatro Impossibile," in *Pianeta Fresco* n. 2-3, 1968;

"Il Centro di Cospirazione Eclettica," in *Domus* n. 466, 1968; *Domus*, Archive;

"Il pollo di marmo," Original document, 1968;

"Vestirsi è facile," in *Casabella* n. 384, 1973;

"Città Catena di Montaggio del sociale, ideologia e teoria della metropoli," in *Casabella* 350-51, 1970;

"Utopia della qualità, utopia della quantità," in *IN* n.1, 1971;

"No-Stop City Residential Parkings Climatic Universal Sistem," in *Domus* n. 496, 1971;

"Progetto di Concorso per l'Università di Firenze," in *Domus* n. 509, 1972;

OTHER TEXTS:

Charles Waldheim, *Preface*, unpublished, 2017;

Elisa C. Cattaneo, *"The Grin without a Cat,"* unpublished, 2016;

Elisa C. Cattaneo, *"Architecture as Theoretical Physics,"* unpublished, 2016;

Germano Celant, "Untitled," in *Domus* n. 496, 1971; *Domus*, Archive;

Alessandro Mendini, "Radical Design," in *Casabella* n. 367, 1972; *Casabella*, Archive;

Charles Jencks, "Supersensualist," in *AD* n. 1, 1972; *AD*, Archive;

Arata Isozaky, Introduction, *The Hot House. Italian New Wave Design*, MIT Press, Cambridge, 1984;

Giuseppe Chiari, in *Italy: New Domestic Landscape*, 1972; Text and image: Giuseppe Chiari; Andrea Branzi Archive;

Emilio Ambaz, Press release *Italy: The New Domestic Landscape*, 1972; MoMA Archive;

Archizoom Associati, Exhibition *Italy: New Domestic Landscape*, 1972; Text and image: Giuseppe Chiari; Andrea Branzi Archive;

Germano Celant, "Sono partiti per New York," in *Domus* n. 510, 1972; *Domus*, Archive;

Ettore Sottsass, "Gli Archizoom," in *Domus* n. 455, 1967; *Domus* Archive;

Pier Vittorio Aureli, *"A Designer in the Age of Late Capitalism. Notes on the Work of Andrea Branzi,"* unpublished, 2016;

Rahul Merotra, Felipe Vera, *"Ephemeral Urbanism and Andrea Branzi's Weak Works,"* unpublished, 2016;

Patrizia Ranzo, *"Design as a Staging of Life. Theories and Works of Andrea Branzi,"* unpublished, 2016.

Andrea Branzi
E=mc². The Project in the Age of Relativity

Published by
Actar Publishers, New York, Barcelona
www.actar.com

Authors
Andrea Branzi, Elisa C. Cattaneo

Edited by
Elisa C. Cattaneo

Graphic Design
Ramon Prat, Marga Gibert

With contributions by
P. Vittorio Aureli, Rahul Mehrotra,
Patrizia Ranzo, Felipe Vera, Charles Waldheim.

Copy editing and proofreading
Elisa C. Cattaneo

Printing and binding
Arlequin

Distribution
Actar D, Inc. New York, Barcelona.

New York
440 Park Avenue South, 17th Floor
New York, NY 10016, USA
salesnewyork@actar-d.com

Barcelona
Roca i Batlle 2-4
08023 Barcelona, Spain
eurosales@actar-d.com

Indexing
English ISBN: 978-1-945150-73-9
PCN: Library of Congress Control Number: 2017955981

Printed in Spain
Publication date: 2020